Ethics, Left and Right

Ethics, Left and Right

The Moral Issues that Divide Us

BOB FISCHER

Texas State University

New York   Oxford

OXFORD UNIVERSITY PRESS

Oxford University Press is a department of the University of Oxford.
It furthers the University's objective of excellence in research, scholarship,
and education by publishing worldwide. Oxford is a registered trade mark of
Oxford University Press in the UK and certain other countries.

Published in the United States of America by Oxford University Press
198 Madison Avenue, New York, NY 10016, United States of America.

For titles covered by Section 112 of the US Higher Education
Opportunity Act, please visit www.oup.com/us/he for the
latest information about pricing and alternate formats.

Library of Congress Cataloging-in-Publication Data

Names: Fischer, Bob (Robert William), editor.
Title: Ethics, left and right : the moral issues that divide US / [edited by] Bob Fischer.
Description: New York, NY : Oxford University Press, 2020. | Includes
  bibliographical references and index. | Summary: "The only contemporary
  moral problems text to focus directly on the ethics of current, divisive
  political issues, Ethics: Left and Right features newly commissioned
  essays on twenty contentious debates, written expressly with
  undergraduate students in mind. It offers two position pieces on each
  issue-one left-leaning, one right-followed by a reply from each author,
  giving you and your students the opportunity to engage in in-depth
  discussions of serious issues. Case studies at the end of every main
  contribution encourage students to examine related problems and/or delve
  deeper into the current issue. Ideal for courses in contemporary moral
  problems, introduction to ethics, and political philosophy, Ethics: Left
  and Right allows you and your students to debate a wide range of
  conservative and libertarian arguments that are rarely represented in
  the philosophical literature"—Provided by publisher.
Identifiers: LCCN 2019031349 (print) | LCCN 2019031350 (ebook) | ISBN
  9780190882785 (paperback) | ISBN 9780190882792 (ebook)
Subjects: LCSH: Ethical problems—United States. | Political ethics—United
  States. | Right and left (Political science)—United States. | Political
  culture—United States.
Classification: LCC BJ1031 .E784 2020 (print) | LCC BJ1031 (ebook) | DDC
  172—dc23
LC record available at https://lccn.loc.gov/2019031349
LC ebook record available at https://lccn.loc.gov/2019031350

Printing number: 9 8 7 6 5 4 3 2 1
Printed by LSC Communications, Inc., United States of America

TABLE OF CONTENTS

CONTRIBUTORS

Ryan T. Anderson is William E. Simon Senior Research Fellow in American Principles & Public Policy at the Heritage Foundation.

Vaughn Baltzly is Assistant Professor of Philosophy at Texas State University.

Daniel Bonevac is Professor of Philosophy at the University of Texas at Austin.

Tully Borland is Assistant Professor of Philosophy at Ouachita Baptist University.

Jason Brennan is Robert J. and Elizabeth Flanagan Family Term Professor of Strategy, Economics, Ethics, and Public Policy at McDonough School of Business at Georgetown University.

Gillian Brock is Professor of Philosophy at the University of Auckland, New Zealand.

Loren Cannon is Lecturer of Philosophy at Humboldt State University.

Spencer Case is an International Research Fellow at Wuhan University in China.

John Corvino is Dean of the Irvin D. Reid Honors College and Professor of Philosophy at Wayne State University.

Dustin Crummett is Postdoctoral Researcher at the Ludwig Maximilian University of Munich.

Dan Demetriou is Associate Professor of Philosophy and Philosophy Discipline Coordinator at the University of Minnesota, Morris.

Saba Fatima is Associate Professor of Philosophy at Southern Illinois University Edwardsville.

Sam Fleischacker is Professor of Philosophy at University of Illinois at Chicago.

Christopher Freiman is Associate Professor of Philosophy at the College of William & Mary.

John F. Gaski is Associate Professor of Marketing at the Mendoza College of Business at the University of Notre Dame.

Sherif Girgis is a PhD candidate in philosophy at Princeton University.

Sherry Glied is Dean and Professor of Public Service at the Robert F. Wagner Graduate School of Public Service at New York University.

Nicole Hassoun is Professor of Philosophy at Binghamton University.

Allan Hillman is Associate Professor of Philosophy at the University of South Alabama.

Tim Hsiao is Instructor of Philosophy at Grantham University.

Michael Huemer is Professor of Philosophy at the University of Colorado, Boulder.

Megan Hyska is Assistant Professor of Philosophy at Northwestern University.

Peter Jaworski is Assistant Teaching Professor of Business Ethics at the McDonough School of Business at Georgetown University.

Hrishikesh Joshi is Assistant Professor of Philosophy at Bowling Green State University.

Stephen Kershnar is Distinguished Teaching Professor of Philosophy at the State University of New York at Fredonia.

Jennifer Kling is Assistant Professor of Philosophy at the University of Colorado, Colorado Springs.

Michael LaBossiere is Professor of Philosophy at Florida Agricultural and Mechanical University.

Philippe Lemoine is a PhD candidate in philosophy at Cornell University.

Annabelle Lever is University Professor at the Paris Institute of Political Studies (SciencesPo, Paris), Associate at the Center of Political Researches of SciencesPo, and Co-Editor of the *Critical Review of Social and Political Philosophy*.

Dan Lowe is Lecturer of Philosophy at the University of Michigan, Ann Arbor.

Luke Maring is Assistant Professor of Philosophy at Northern Arizona University.

Seth Mayer is Assistant Professor of Philosophy at Manchester University.

C. A. McIntosh is a PhD candidate in philosophy at Cornell University.

Kristina Meshelski is Associate Professor of Philosophy at California State University, Northridge.

Nathan Nobis is Associate Professor of Philosophy at Morehouse College.

Mark R. Reiff is a Visiting Professor of Philosophy at the Frankfurt School of Finance and Management and an Affiliated Researcher in Philosophy at the University of California, Davis.

Dan C. Shahar is Assistant Professor of Philosophy at the University of New Orleans.

Patrick Taylor Smith is Assistant Professor of Political Science at the National University of Singapore.

Travis Timmerman is Assistant Professor of Philosophy at Seton Hall University.

Chris Tollefsen is College of Arts and Sciences Distinguished Professor and Department Chair of Philosophy at the University of South Carolina.

Rebecca Tuvel is Assistant Professor of Philosophy at Rhodes College.

Bruno Verbeek is University Lecturer at the Institute for Philosophy at Leiden University.

Mark Zelcer is Assistant Professor of Philosophy at Oswego State University of New York.

A NOTE TO TEACHERS

I teach at a large public university in Texas. I want to explore the social and political issues that matter to my students, many of whom are conservative. However, this isn't easy given current textbook options. Some of those books don't include many conservative views, and students object to such books as biased. Others do better in terms of representation, but the material is pitched too high. The rest are out of date: They aren't addressing the current conversation. My goal was to create a book that avoids these pitfalls. With some luck, it will help me talk with students about the issues that divide the country.

When selecting topics and commenting on drafts, I tried to balance several considerations. Among them:

1. Was this being discussed in 2016? Is it likely to be with us in 2020? Is there a decent chance that it will be with us for a bit thereafter?
2. Do people say things like this in popular discussions of the issue? Do people actually *believe* things like this, even if they don't usually advertise those beliefs?
3. Is this as rigorous as it can be in the space available (a hard cap of 4,000 words for main contributions and 1,000 words for the replies)?
4. Is this creative? Is it an angle that people haven't seen?
5. Is this topic already covered extensively elsewhere? (Can I get away *without* covering it, as shorter books are cheaper?)
6. Are students going to want to talk about this? (Do *I* want to talk about it?)
7. Would I be willing to teach this text, regardless of who's in the room?
8. Can I actually find people to have this debate?

I never compromised on #7: That one's nonnegotiable. Obviously, I couldn't compromise on #8. But the rest were hard to weigh. And given what contributors wanted to do, and my own objectives for the volume, I prioritized different considerations in different cases. In saying this, I am not criticizing what anyone contributed. Instead, I'm trying to encourage you, as an instructor, to think about this as a book that was written to make important conversations possible. These aren't journal articles that I cut down for length; they are teaching tools. The contributors are, therefore, all too aware of the limitations of what they've written, and I'm to blame in every case: I simply didn't give them room to say more. So please use these essays as intended. None of them is the last word, much less the only word, from one of the many camps with a stake these debates. Instead, they are in all offered to prompt more thoughtful, more honest, and more focused discussions about the ethics behind our politics. I hope your discussions go well.

DON'T SKIP THIS: A NOTE TO STUDENTS

I put this book together for my students. I want to help them think through the controversies in the news. I want them to understand why people believe things that they don't. And where they have no views, I want them to form views carefully, having considered a range of arguments, rather than simply saying whatever their team says.

But let's be honest. It's easy—and, frankly, kind of fun—to write people off as evil or crazy, racist or ridiculous. And it's very tempting to read this book for talking points, looking for ways to shut down your parents or some protesters. If my students do these things, they won't be thinking through the controversies in the news. They won't understand their political opponents (who, of course, they'll see as opponents). They won't ask whether their team is ever wrong.

I hope it doesn't go this way. (I don't think it will; I have faith in them.) But whatever my students do, *you* can make thoughtful choices as a reader, as a learner, and as a conversation partner. You can resist the temptation to demonize. You can recognize that you are fallible, that you make mistakes. You can commit to giving people the benefit of the doubt, assuming that they—like you—are just doing their best to find the truth. (If you want to see all this in action, just consider many of the contributions to this book. Some of them are just fantastic in this regard.)

And speaking of giving people the benefit of the doubt, let's talk about labels. These days, everything is "left" or "right," "liberal" or "conservative," "Democrat" or "Republican." And I wanted to get this book into your hands. So, I used that left/right split to make a catchy title (anyway, *I* think it's catchy). When you look a bit closer, though, neither people nor ideas split into such tidy little categories. "Left" and "right" are actually big umbrella terms, including wildly diverse political groups. Folks on the left include social democrats, democratic socialists, Christians, Marxists, libertarians, communists, Greens, and many others. Folks on the right include Reagan Republicans, neoliberals, Christians, capitalists, libertarians, alt-righters, and lots more. And, of course, there are plenty of people who don't fit neatly into any of these groups. What's the right way to classify gay libertarians who are worried about immigration from socially conservative countries? How about Christians who think that gay sex is against God's will, but who vote for progressive candidates because of their convictions about helping the poor? Do you know how to categorize socially liberal, pro-business Muslims? Labels only take us so far.

If the categories of left and right are useful at all, it's because they help you get the view from 30,000 feet, the roughest picture of what's going on in contemporary American politics. But once you go past that—as we will here—it's obvious that we need to think in more fine-grained ways. In the pages that follow, you're going to find pairs of essays where one person is the "conservative" while the other is the "liberal." But as you'll see, sometimes the "conservative" isn't that conservative or the "liberal" that liberal. Sometimes it isn't clear that they even *count* as conservatives or liberals, at least as those terms are often used. Sometimes there's a lot of agreement between the two conversation partners; other times there's barely any. There are cases where the author makes just the moves you would expect; there are cases where you'll have no idea what's coming next.

In every case, though, don't just slap a label on an author. Think about the arguments; do your best to assess them patiently and carefully. Politics is hard enough when we're *willing* to hear to one another, when we're really, genuinely, and honestly open to someone else's ideas. Let's not make it any harder.

ACKNOWLEDGMENTS

I'm grateful to all the contributors, for their fine work and patience; to Robert Miller, for believing both in the project and in me; to the production team at Oxford University Press; and to the reviewers whose feedback helped shape this volume, including Brian Barnett at St. John Fischer College and the State University of New York at Geneseo, Steve Dickerson at South Puget Sound Community College, Mitchell R. Haney at the University of North Florida, Mattias Iser at the State University of New York at Binghamton, W. Glenn Kirkconnell at Santa Fe College, Timothy J. Madigan at St. John Fisher College, and Alistair Moles at Sierra College. I owe a special thanks to my research assistants—Brooke Robb, Amanda Standlee, and Alyse Spiehler—without whom everything would have taken far longer. And as always, I'm indebted to Jennifer, who's relieved that I got tenure well before this book appeared.

This book is for my parents, from whom I acquired my love for questions and conversation.

Introduction

WHAT ARE WE DOING HERE?

Newsflash: People disagree about politics.

Sometimes those disagreements are just about empirical issues. *My* expert says that if we raise the minimum wage, prices on consumer goods will rise too; *your* expert says that if we raise the minimum wage, prices on consumer goods will basically stay constant. Who's right? By and large, that's a question for economists rather than philosophers. If you want the answer, you'll need to sort through *their* research.

However, lots of political disagreements aren't—or aren't just—about empirical issues. They're about *ethical* or *moral* issues (I'll use those words interchangeably). Maybe I think the current minimum wage is *fair*, and you think it isn't. If that's where we don't see eye to eye, then we can't turn to economists to settle the debate. In fact, we can't turn to *anyone* to settle the debate, because no one has the power to declare what the answer is. That isn't how morality works. Presidents, Congresspeople, imams and pastors, your great-aunt Sally, your professor, Hollywood celebrities, and YouTube sensations: They can all make mistakes.

This is a book about those ethical issues. It's a book about what's right and wrong. But it isn't a book that tries to teach you *what's* right and wrong. The goal isn't to make you believe the things I believe—or that any of the contributors believe—about all the issues you're going to explore.

Sometimes people *do* have that aim. At my university, the faculty and staff have to go through "ethics training." Among other things, we learn that we aren't supposed to use the university's money to buy drugs, that we aren't allowed to hit or hit on students, and that you can't hire someone to cater your luncheon just because he happens to be your husband. In these training sessions, *the rules aren't up for debate*. You don't get to say, "But what if . . . ?" There is no "what if." You just learn the rules and follow them, whether or not they're good rules. (To be clear: No objections to these particular examples!)

Not so when doing philosophy: Here, the rules *are* up for debate. There are two reasons for this. The first is that when we do ethics training, someone gets to say what the rules are—the members of the board, or the director of the company's human resources department, or the founders of a professional organization. But in philosophy, no one gets to say. Instead, philosophy involves understanding, evaluating, and constructing *arguments*—that is, reasoning that supports a conclusion. So, you always get to ask, "What's the argument for that?" And if you don't find the argument convincing, then—after articulating your objection—your conversation partner has to reply to what you've said. She could do that by revising her argument, offering an entirely new argument, or abandoning her position. And you get to reply to her reply, and so on. There is no one with the authority to settle the dispute; we just have to wait and see what the best argument says. And how do we find the best argument? Through honest and careful debate.

I'm not going to lie: It's hard work. It's harder still because philosophers like to discuss controversial *topics*, like abortion and affirmative action, where it's especially difficult to get people to see eye to eye. Additionally, we philosophers don't just care *that* something's true; we care at least as much about *why* it's true. So even if the claim itself isn't controversial (e.g., you shouldn't cheat), the explanation for its truth might be. (At bottom, should you avoid cheating because things will go better *for you* if you don't, at least in the long run? Or because it's disrespectful to others to cheat? Or because it's dishonest? Something else entirely?) Finally, you should know that philosophers tend to think that some of the "obvious" isn't. The odds are good that you don't think that there's anything wrong with buying a new outfit, even if you've got plenty of others already in your closet. However, some philosophers say that it *is* wrong to do that—instead, you should give the money to help people in the developing world who are dying of treatable diseases. (That escalated quickly!)

The upshot of all this is that, unlike ethics training, we should expect disagreement about whether we should have open borders, or a smaller military budget, or a progressive income tax—all topics you'll find in the pages to follow. But our disagreements should be informed ones, reached through serious study of the arguments on all sides. Of course, agreeing would be great, at least if we agree because we're all convinced that the same arguments are the best ones. The point is just that we aren't after agreement per se. This book is designed to teach you how to approach moral questions, not what you're required to offer as answers to them.

So how *do* we figure out whether something's fair—or just, or good, or morally required, or anything else? The details are tricky, and you'll have a chance to think about them as you work through this book. But very roughly, most philosophers say this: We figure things out by *making and evaluating arguments*. In other words, I tell you some things that I take to support a conclusion, and then we talk about (1) whether those things I said are true and (2) whether, even if they are true, they support the conclusion that I say they support. And then you take your turn, and we go back and forth in hopes of agreeing that one position—maybe yours, maybe mine, maybe some third or fourth or fifth option—is most likely to be correct.

The process is slow: Don't expect any quick results. Moreover, it takes intellectual honesty: Everybody has to be committed to *determining* what's true, rather than simply defending whatever they *want* to be true. Finally, it can be disappointing: We can do our best without getting an answer; sometimes we'll leave the conversation more confused than when we started.[1]

Unfortunately, though, there isn't a better option *if we care about the truth.* There are plenty of better options if we don't. If you want to advance your own ideas, you can simply shout down your opponents. Or you can mock them. Or you can manipulate people's emotions, playing on their fears and tugging at their heartstrings. Or you can gain political power, and then make laws that shape the culture—and so many people's beliefs—to your liking. Or you can lie, cheat, and resort to violence. True: Long, focused, and respectful conversations are our best shot at figuring out what we have most reason to believe. But they are *not* our best shot at "winning"—or if they are, it's only in the very long term. So why bother?

Here are a few reasons:

1. We should care about the truth *simply because it's the truth.*[2] That's the goal of inquiry; it's what we're after as rational beings.
2. Bad laws and policies can harm people in all sorts of ways. If a particular law is unfair, or unjustified, or extraordinarily morally important, then it matters that we know, since we shouldn't harm people unnecessarily.
3. Again, bad laws and policies can harm people in all sorts of ways. If we don't have good *reasons* to believe that we're passing the right laws and policies, then it seems like we're being negligent, and that seems disrespectful to the people who will be affected.
4. The central idea behind democracy is that *we the people* are governing. We aren't doing it directly, of course; we have representatives. But indirect governance is still a kind of governance. And if we are governing, then surely we have a responsibility to figure out what we ought to do.

Of course, there's a lot more to say here, and if this were an essay on the value of truth seeking in politics, I'd say it. But it isn't that essay, and we've got other ground to cover. So I'll leave it there, while readily admitting that I've only made the first move in a conversation: I've offered some arguments, and they still need to be evaluated. That's philosophy. That's ethics.

PREVIEW

Before going any further, let me give you a preview of coming attractions. In the next section, I'm going to try to say a bit more about what ethics is and isn't. Then, I'm going to talk a bit about what it means to think critically. After that, I say a lot more about the idea of making and evaluating arguments. By that point, you'll have a decent scaffolding built up, and we can start being more precise about the sorts of premises that those arguments can involve. This brings us to moral theory, and I'll walk you through—and provide you with some classic readings on—some of the major approaches to ethics. We'll close by thinking through some of the barriers to having good conversations about ethics and politics—including the worry that it's all relative. At the end of all this, I hope you'll be ready to start working through the fascinating debates that make up the rest of the book.

"ETHICS," YOU SAY?

Getting Our Bearings

Let's step back for a minute. I've been throwing around words like "ethics" and "morality." What am I talking about?

Ethics is about what's right and wrong, good and bad, worthwhile and worthless. It's about how we should live our lives, about who we ought to become. It's about whether there are lines that we should never cross. It's about what we should hope to achieve in our daily lives, on our campuses, in our country, and in the world.

That all sounds nice. However, those statements don't constitute a nice, neat definition. I wish that I had one of those to offer you, but I don't. (Frankly, I'm a bit suspicious of people who think they do.) What I can do, however, is supplement the above with some ideas about what ethics *isn't*, and we can see how far that gets us.

Ethics and the Law

First, it's a mistake to think of ethics as just another way of talking about the law. On this sort of view, what's legal is what's moral, what's illegal is what isn't.

This definitely isn't right. First, there are plenty of things that are legal and immoral. The law, for example, allows you to be a pretty terrible person. It's totally legal to tell your spouse that you are going out of town for a business trip while you are actually having a weekend getaway with your spring fling. Lying in this way is perfectly legal (even in jurisdictions where adultery is a crime), but it's obviously wrong. Second, there are plenty of things that are illegal and perfectly moral. Consider, for instance, Division 6, Part 1, Chapter 7, Article 2 of the California Fish and Game Code:

> Any person may possess any number of live frogs to use in frog-jumping contests, but if such a frog dies or is killed, it must be destroyed as soon as possible, and may not be eaten or otherwise used for any purpose.

Now suppose that you own a live frog that you intend to use in a frog-jumping contest, and—quite tragically—it dies. Do you really think that it's *immoral* not to destroy its body as soon as possible? Still, it's illegal.

Moreover, there are cases in which it might not just be *permissible*—morally OK—to break the law. Instead, something stronger might be true: Perhaps the law *ought* to be broken. For example, some cities, like San Antonio, Texas, have banned feeding the homeless. But many people think that they've got a moral obligation to feed the hungry. If they're right, then perhaps they ought to do exactly what the law prohibits. (*Perhaps*. After all, if everyone stopped following the laws that they believe to be unjust, there would be chaos. There has to be some strong presumption in favor of following laws that got on the books through the democratic process. Still, if civil disobedience is ever justified, then there will be some cases where that presumption can be overridden.)

Ethics and Your Behavior

Second, ethics isn't just about *the choices you would make* in various situations. It's important to remember that while your choices might be *relevant* to what's right—in the sense of being evidence for it, at least insofar as you're a decent person—your choices might be wrong. It's easy to have overly rosy views of ourselves; we tend to think we're good people, whether or not we are. So, we're strongly inclined to think that what we'd do is what we ought to do, or at least what it's OK to do. But if we're honest with ourselves, we'll admit that we don't always do what we think is right. (Let's be more honest: Sometimes the gap between our ideals and our behavior is *huge*.) So before jumping from "I'd do that" to "That's OK," we need to be very careful to consider whether we're simply trying to protect our respective self-images.

Ethics and What You've Got Good Reason to Do

Third, ethics isn't just what it makes sense for you to do, or what you've got good reason to do. After all, you've got reasons to do all sorts of things: have lunch, get a college education, watch reruns of *Law & Order* (the original is the best), and so on. Sometimes it makes sense to do one of these things. But there are plenty of cases in which the sensible choice is just plain wrong.

It's 11 p.m. on a Sunday. You've got a paper due at midnight. You've been working hard on things for your other classes, so you haven't had time to write. Moreover, you've got two big exams during the week, so you can't afford to turn this in late; it's got to be done so that you can study for bio-chem, which is going to be a beast. What should you do?

Well, your professor has a strict no-late-papers policy, so you can't just take a hit on the grade. But she's got a lot of students, so you think that she might only skim the papers to see whether people have made a good-faith attempt. She probably wouldn't detect a little copying and pasting, especially if you switch a few words around. Moreover, everybody games the system once in a while, and it's not like you've just been sitting around playing video games for the last three weeks. Should you cheat?

Of course, it's *wrong* to steal someone else's work and then lie about it being yours—which is what plagiarism involves. But there are plenty of times when it makes a lot of sense—maybe even the *most* sense—to do what's wrong. So whatever ethics is, it isn't about making an "understandable" choice, at least if we cash out that idea in terms of what would be sensible (or even best) for *you*. Ethics is about other people's interests too. (In this case, for example, it requires thinking about your professor's interest in getting what she asked for—namely, your work—and other students' interest in competing on a level playing field.)

Ethics and What's Realistic

Finally, ethics isn't always about what's realistic or achievable. For example, it seems plain that slavery has always been wrong, even when it was legal. However, when it *was* legal, I'm sure there were people who said things like this:

> We're never going to be rid of slavery. The economic argument for slavery is just too strong: We just couldn't run our plantations without them. Of course, we should try to make the lives of slaves better. For example, people shouldn't be allowed to whip their slaves for trivial offenses. But there's no point criticizing owning humans in and of itself.

The claim here is that *it doesn't make sense to criticize the institution of slavery*; there's no way to change such a deeply entrenched aspect of the culture. And at the time, it may not have been unreasonable to say this. Surely there were periods in American history when slavery seemed like it would be with us forever. Moreover, it would have been good for someone to be opposed to whipping slaves for trivial offenses. However, even if there was a time when it would have been useless to advocate publicly for the end of slavery—even if criticizing people for owning slaves wouldn't have made any difference at all—it doesn't follow that there was no point in criticizing the idea that it's OK to own humans. Maybe people will never change (thankfully, of course, they have!), but it's still worth asking how things *ought* to be, even if it seems impossible to make them that way. In part, this is because we can be completely wrong (as our imaginary speaker was) about what sorts of changes are possible. But it's also because it's worth knowing what we should strive for, even if those goals are unattainable. Knowing what we should hope to achieve helps us think more clearly about what is, and isn't, true progress.

Some of the essays in this book argue for claims that might sound pretty idealistic. I've mentioned one of them already—namely, the claim that we should have open borders. It's a big and important claim, and if it's true (which it may not be—we'll have to inspect the arguments!), it has big implications for the way society is organized. And given that it has such big implications, it would be easy to dismiss it as a pie-in-the-sky fantasy. But we should be wary of that response. Again, it's worth knowing what we should strive for.

So . . . ?

I've now said a tiny bit about what ethics is, and a fair amount about what ethics isn't. The takeaway is that there really are big moral questions out there for us to examine, and we should be mindful about how we try to answer them. First, the law matters, but it answers to ethics—not the other way around. Second, you might be someone who makes good choices, but you might not be. (Sorry!) So, what you'd do isn't always the best guide to what should be done. Third, don't confuse what's *reasonable* for you to do with what you *ought* to do. Lots of reasonable things are wrong; some unreasonable things may be morally mandatory. Fourth, don't confuse what's realistic with what's right. Sometimes a campus, or a country, gets things entirely wrong. When that happens, even *hoping* to make progress can seem crazy. That doesn't mean, however, that it wouldn't be progress—that change wouldn't be for the better.

THINKING, FAST AND CRITICALLY

With those preliminaries behind us, let's turn to some of the resources you'll need to think more clearly about moral matters. Later on, we'll talk about some moral theories, which help you ask better questions about ethically complex situations. First, though, we're going to focus on the process of thinking itself—how to think about your own moral judgments, as well as how to make moral arguments.

Intuition

There are some real hurdles to thinking clearly. Perhaps the biggest one is that *things just seem true to us*. In other words, it's incredibly hard to get some critical distance from your own moral judgments—your own ideas about what should and shouldn't be done. Instead, we all experience our own ideas as the right ones (if we didn't, we'd have different ideas!), so it's hard to imagine being mistaken.

In lots of contexts, that's fine. I don't want my students wondering whether it's OK to cheat on a test, and I don't want my doctor wondering whether he's *really* got an obligation not to do any harm. But when we're trying to engage in serious debate about moral matters, this psychological tendency usually leads us into shouting matches rather than productive exchanges.

In part, this is because *our intuitions often drive our ethical judgments.* Translation: In everyday life, we tend to trust our gut. If it feels right, we think it *is* right, and vice versa for things being wrong. But is our gut that reliable?

Well, there are plenty of non-moral cases in which our intuitions can't be *that* far off—if they were, we wouldn't survive for long. (Driving, for example, would go pretty poorly; it's kind of important that we be good at knowing when to brake.) However, there are lots of other cases in which our intuitions lead us astray—consistently, systematically, and without any hint of what's happening.

That, in essence, is the lesson of Daniel Kahneman's *Thinking, Fast and Slow*. It's a great book, and I want to share just two examples from it.

The first is quite famous: "the Linda problem." In that study, Kahneman and his partner, Amos Tversky, told participants about Linda:

> Linda is thirty-one years old, single, outspoken, and very bright. She majored in philosophy. As a student, she was deeply concerned with issues of discrimination and social justice, and also participated in antinuclear demonstrations.[3]

The participants were then asked whether it was more probable that Linda is a bank teller, or that she's a bank teller and active in the feminist movement. Overwhelmingly, participants said that the second option was more probable. But this can't be right: The probability of p (e.g., her being a bank teller) is bound to be *higher* than the probability of p and q (e.g., her being a bank teller who's active in the feminist movement). Why? Because probabilities always range from

0 to 1, and you get the probability of *p* and *q* by multiplying the two together. That's why the probability of *p and q* is always lower than both the probability of *p* on its own and the probability of *q* on its own.[4]

You might think that people are hearing more in "Linda is a bank teller" than is actually being said. As a result, they take the options to be: (a) Linda is a bank teller *who isn't active in the feminist movement* and (b) Linda is a bank teller who *is* active in that movement. But if that's what's happening, then they're making a different mistake. The world is chock full of bank tellers, and there are a great many people who *were* socially engaged in college but let go of their idealism right around graduation. There aren't very many people, however, who are currently active in the feminist movement (on the assumption that Facebook slacktivism doesn't count). So even given her description, it's still more likely that Linda isn't active in the feminist movement. (This error has a name. Ignoring the relative numbers of bank tellers, once-activists, and current activists is called "the base rate fallacy.")

What's going on? Plainly, people aren't assessing the probabilities of these statements in the way that statisticians do. Instead, they're using their *stereotype* about people who are active in the feminist movement, and they're matching that stereotype to the description of Linda. There are, of course, cases where a stereotype gives you the right answer. In this one, however, it leads people astray. And I'll bet you can imagine plenty of more serious cases—think, for example, of scenarios in which young black men are accused of crimes—where relying on stereotypes might lead people to assess probabilities in much more disastrous ways. Your gut might say one thing, but the evidence says another.

In other cases, intuition—our fast, effortless judgment about a case—doesn't exactly lead us to believe the wrong thing. However, even when it doesn't lead us into error per se, it still might not be as consistent as we think it is. Consider, for example, the "Asian Disease Problem." First, Kahneman and Tversky had people read this prompt:

> Imagine that the U.S. is preparing for the outbreak of an unusual Asian disease, which is expected to kill 600 people. One possible program to combat the disease has been proposed.[5]

Then, they had to choose between two options. However, not everyone was given the same options. Some people were given Options A and B:

A. If this program is adopted, 200 people will be saved.
B. If this program is adopted, there is a one-third probability that 600 people will be saved and a two-thirds probability that no people will be saved.

Other people were given Options C and D:

C. If this program is adopted, 400 people will die.
D. If this program is adopted, there is a one-third probability that nobody will die and a two-thirds probability that 600 people will die.

Take a second and do the math: Option A is equivalent to Option C, and Option B is equivalent to Option D. So, people should choose Options A and C at equal rates and Options B and D at equal rates.

But they don't. What Kahneman and Tversky found was that people tended to prefer the sure thing when faced with Options A and B, but they tended to prefer the gamble when they were faced with Options C and D. What does this mean? In short, it suggests that people are skittish about taking risks when it sounds like they might lose something they've already got, and open to taking risks when they see themselves as being in a situation where loss is unavoidable. This is a *framing effect*—the way the options are framed affects how people respond, even though the options are identical. This phenomenon can make a big difference when we're considering arguments about different military strategies, or affirmative action, or health care policies. (For example, people are much more open to "aid in dying" than they are to "physician-assisted suicide," even though the terms are synonymous. What's different is the frame, not the reality.) We have to pay attention to how information comes to us, and think about alternative ways of representing it.

These aren't the only examples of intuition being misleading or inconsistent. There are lots of others. For example, we like to infer causes when there aren't any—we can't accept that some things just happen. We tend to think that personality-based explanations of behavior—"He did it because he's a jerk!"—are much better than situational explanations—"He did it because he was under a lot of pressure at work." We're inclined to think that past events—such as a terrorist attack—were predictable, even though no one could have known that they were going to happen. And familiar ideas seem more true to us than unfamiliar ones, regardless of whether we have any evidence for or against them. We jump to the wrong conclusions all the time.

Fallacies
What's more, we often go wrong even when we aren't relying on our intuitions. We take the time to form an argument, but not one that supports its intended conclusion. It's an easy thing to do. After all, plenty of arguments *sound* good, but are really pretty poor.

When a bunch of poor arguments are poor for the same reason, we call them instances of an *informal fallacy*, and we give those sorts of arguments specific names. If you become familiar with some informal fallacies, they become easier to spot, and so you can avoid being taken in by bad reasoning (whether yours or someone else's).

There are lots of informal fallacies, but I'll just mention a few of them here. The first to know is the *ad hominem* fallacy—that is, arguing "against the man." The idea here is that it's a mistake to criticize the *source* of the argument, rather than the argument's premises or logic. So, for example, you shouldn't reject a pro-choice person's pro-choice argument—or a pro-life person's pro-life argument—simply because a pro-choice or pro-life person made it. Instead, you should think about the merits of arguments on their own terms.

We often don't do this. Instead, we often think: "Well, of *course* she'd say that—she's pro-[fill in the blank]!" But this is really a defense mechanism. Instead of having to engage seriously with someone's ideas, we can use his or her identity to write them off. That's both intellectually lazy and unkind. We owe our conversation partners more respect than that.[6]

You can find some of the same vices behind the *strawman* fallacy. Imagine a student who comes to a professor at the end of the semester and says, "I know that I haven't earned a B in this course, but it's been a really hard semester for me, and I'll lose my scholarship if I don't maintain my GPA. Please, Professor, let me do some extra credit to bump up my grade!" The professor says, "I'd love to help you, but there isn't anything I can do for you that wouldn't be unfair to other students. If I don't give them the same opportunity, then I can't give it to you. I'm sorry." The student replies, "So you don't care if I lose my scholarship!" That reply is an example of the strawman fallacy. First, the professor didn't say that she doesn't care about the student's scholarship; she just said that she can't help the student because she has to act on a policy that's fair to all the students who are taking her course. So the student *misrepresented* the professor. Second, the student is putting a much weaker argument in the professor's mouth than the one she actually gave. If the professor were denying the student an opportunity to do extra credit based on not caring about the student's fate, she would be acting insensitively. But that wasn't the story!

A different way of going wrong is to set up a *false dilemma*. A dilemma is when you're forced to choose between two options; a *false* dilemma is when someone presents only two options, but there are really others. Let's suppose that someone says, "Look, we just have to close the borders entirely. If we don't, we're going to have drugs and guns pouring into the country." This is a false dilemma: It presents two options (closing the borders entirely/having drugs and guns pouring into the country) when there are others, such as improving border security without preventing any and all traffic.

False dilemmas are common because we like simplicity so much. It's just *easier* to think that there are only two options, whatever the issue at hand. Recognizing all the options, and then holding them all in your head, takes significant mental energy. False dilemmas are also common because they're really effective as a strategy in a debate. In the example I just gave, imagine having someone give the "close the borders or face an influx of drugs and guns" line to you in the middle of a heated exchange. It would take a minute to realize that you're being set up, to recognize and reject the assumption behind the choice that's being offered to you. And because of that, false dilemmas can be good ways of winning points—albeit by obscuring the truth. But again: We owe our conversation partners better. We're not here to win points; we're here to think clearly together. With some effort, we can hope to figure out what's true.

I'll mention just two more informal fallacies. The first is called the *red herring* fallacy. The basic idea is that a statement is a red herring when it changes the subject or otherwise dodges the issue at hand. Consider, for example, a debate about whether fraternity culture fosters sexist attitudes. In response to an argument that they do foster such attitudes, someone might say, "But they do so much good in the community! The guys of SAE participate in the Adopt-a-Highway program, and they also volunteer at the elementary school as tutors." All of this might be true, but none of it's relevant to whether fraternity culture in general—or even the culture of that particular fraternity—encourages sexist attitudes.

Of course, the good deeds of fraternity brothers might be relevant to a *different* question—namely, whether we should have fraternities on campus at all. They just aren't relevant to the issue that's actually being discussed. Unfortunately, red herrings—irrelevant statements—get in the way of careful conversations. They distract us from the very thing on which we were trying to focus.

Finally, let's talk about the *slippery slope* fallacy. This is an especially common one, and I think it's one of the most important. Suppose that someone says, "We shouldn't legalize marijuana. If we do, then we'll soon be legalizing heroin, and that would be disastrous." In other words, if we get on this slippery slope—if we legalize marijuana—we'll soon slide down to the bottom, where much harder drugs are legal.

Even though this is a fallacy, *the prediction might be true.* The problem is *not* that the prediction is necessarily mistaken. Rather, the problem is that the prediction is baseless; we aren't given any reason to think that the prediction will come true. Maybe it's the case that once you legalize some drugs, the public will think that it's arbitrary to ban others, and so marijuana legalization will lead to the end of drug prohibition generally. Alternately, maybe the public is very sensitive to the severe effects of some drugs, so they'd never support complete legalization. To make a reasonable judgment one way or the other, we'd need some evidence. And that's precisely what we didn't get in the example I just gave. In short, then, the problem with slippery slope reasoning is that it involves making a big claim about the consequences of a course of action, but without explaining why we should expect those consequences.[7]

You see slippery slope reasoning all the time. "If we allow gay marriage, soon we'll have to let people marry their pets." "If we let people carry firearms in public, then we'll eventually have to let them have firearms in elementary schools." And so on. As before, I think this is partly a function of laziness. It takes a lot of work to build the case for a prediction, and we'd rather just say something that sounds reasonable and wins us points in a debate. But it's also because we often don't realize that there are other possibilities—that, for example, we might legalize marijuana *without* there being certain negative consequences. It just seems so obvious to us that two things are linked, we don't even see that we need to argue for the link. Nevertheless, we do.

I've discussed five fallacies: *ad hominem*, strawman, false dilemma, red herring, and slippery slope. I've discussed these because I think they're the ones you'll find most often in conversation.[8] Knowing about these reasoning errors isn't going to make you a perfect reasoner, nor will it help you win every argument. (Nothing will do that!) However, knowing about them can make it easier to have more focused and productive conversations. When you know what to avoid, and can call out the errors of others, you can avoid some unnecessary distractions.

Doing Better

So there are plenty of cases in which what seems true—our intuitive reaction—is just wildly wrong. Likewise, there are plenty of cases in which what feels like a good argument isn't. This may not sound like good news, but it is. We can learn more about how our minds work; we can become better at noticing when we're likely to go wrong; we can foster the discipline of slowing down, thinking hard, and double-checking whether the reasons in front of us support what they're supposed to support. Of course, these things take a lot of effort, and we're not going to achieve perfection. Still, we can make progress. We can do better.

In *The Righteous Mind*, Jonathan Haidt has some good advice about where to start:

> . . . each individual reasoner is really good at one thing: finding evidence to support the position he or she already holds, usually for intuitive reasons. We should not expect individuals to produce good, open-minded, truth-seeking reasoning, particularly when self-interest or reputational concerns are in play. But if you put individuals together in the right way, such that some individuals can use their reasoning powers to disconfirm the claims of others, and all individuals feel some common bond or shared fate that allows them to interact civilly, you can create a group that ends up producing good reasoning as an emergent property of the social system. This is why it's so important to have intellectual and ideological diversity within any group or institution whose goal is to find truth (such as an intelligence agency or a community of scientists) or to produce good public policy (such as a legislature or advisory board).[9]

Clearly, Haidt thinks that we can make some progress as reasoners: We just need to reason *together*, in *diverse groups*, rather than working on these issues independently or in homogeneous groups. If we do, then we can go beyond the wisdom of any one particular individual or culture, finding new and better ways to think about the problems we face.

In any case, what I've said in this section barely scratches the surface of the literature on intuitions, reasoning, and how to move forward. I don't share this sketch with you because it's adequate, but because it should be the starting point for further investigation on your part. At this stage, all I'm trying to do is cultivate a healthy degree of caution. We need to go beyond trusting our gut, and we need to take a harder look at our reasons.

MAKING ARGUMENTS

With all that behind us, let's think a bit more carefully about how to make and evaluate arguments. Granted, you aren't going to operate this way all time. Usually, we go with the flow. When we read an article on Facebook, we don't think much about the author's argument—we just skim. We certainly don't check the sources. And we absolutely don't look for *another* article that defends the opposite view, just to see what can be said for the alternative.

Sometimes, that's fine. We don't always have to have our guard up. But we should be *able* to slow down and evaluate things carefully. We should have the capacity for critical, careful thought. In practice, this means:

1. *Slowing down*, taking the time to really process what you're reading, hearing, watching, etc.
2. *Asking the right questions*, the most important ones being:
   a. What am I being asked to believe? In other words, what's the main claim that the author (or whoever) wants me to accept?
   b. Why am I supposed to believe it? That is, what's the argument for this claim?
   c. How good is the argument for this claim? This breaks down into two questions. First, is this the kind of argument that's worth taking seriously? Second, how plausible are the premises of this particular argument?

I'm going to focus here on (2b) and (2c). In particular, I want to explain what philosophers mean when they talk about arguments.

From Reasons to Arguments

When philosophers try to convince one another that different things are true, they offer arguments. Here, arguments aren't loud disagreements. Instead, an argument is composed of some *premises* (statements) that are supposed to support a *conclusion* (another statement). The crucial thing here is to learn how to interpret ordinary reason-giving (i.e., someone saying "We ought to do this *because*" or "Such and such, *so*") as a way of making arguments. If you get a handle on that, you'll be able to see the link between what you normally do and what philosophers do.

Here's an example. When you ask someone why it's wrong to steal, his first response is often something like "Because it's illegal." Philosophers rewrite this claim as follows:

1. If an act is illegal, then it's always morally wrong.
2. Stealing is illegal.
3. So, stealing is always morally wrong.

Again, the last line in an argument is its *conclusion*; the other lines are its *premises*. The advantage of expressing a reason this way is that we can see its complexity. Here, what looked like one idea ("stealing is wrong because it's an illegal act"), is really two (Premise 1 and Premise 2) plus an inference (the move from Premise 1 and Premise 2 to the conclusion).

How did I get from the original claim ("stealing is wrong because it's illegal") to the argument above? Essentially, I worked backward. In this case, someone—let's call him Bill—is trying to defend why he thinks that stealing is wrong. That's his conclusion; that's what he wants to justify. The task now is to figure out the premises that are supposed to support it. Bill said that stealing is wrong "because it's illegal." He seems to think that stealing's being illegal is *enough* to make it wrong, since he didn't mention anything else. He could have added that stealing *violates the original owner's right to her property,* or *causes financial hardship for the original owner of the property.* But he didn't say either of these things. Hence, Bill didn't give us any reason to think that he sees something special about the act of stealing; the problem is simply that it's illegal. So, I came up with Premise 1 as a way to express the idea that being illegal is sufficient—in and of itself—to make an action wrong.

Premise 1 amounts to a link between two things: an action's being illegal and an action's being wrong. But that's all it is; you can't get the conclusion from Premise 1 alone. After all, someone might believe Premise 1 while insisting that *stealing* isn't illegal—it's only stealing *in certain circumstances* that's problematic. After all, police can take your vehicle in an emergency, regardless of whether you want to give it to them. That seems to be stealing, but it isn't illegal.

Now, you might deny that this is *really* stealing, precisely because it's legal. The cops are *allowed* to commandeer your car in special situations. But unless it's totally settled that a kind of action is wrong, it's a mistake to define that act so that it includes illegality or immorality. When we do that, we can't ask whether the action *should* be illegal, or really is immoral. It's better to define the action in a neutral way—stealing, for example, we might define as *taking someone's property against his or her will*—so that we don't beg any questions in the debate.

By the way, many people now use the phrase "begs the question" to mean something like "invites the question" or "leads us to ask the question." But this isn't how philosophers use this phrase. We use it to mean something like "assume what you set out to prove." So, for example, by defining stealing so that stealing is the *wrongful* taking of someone else's property, you beg the question against someone who thinks that stealing is sometimes permissible. And since that seems like a reasonable view—I'd think that it's permissible to steal food to feed your starving children—you shouldn't beg the question against that person. Instead, you should define it neutrally, and then *argue* that stealing is always wrong (if that's your view).

In any case, if a person thinks that stealing isn't *always* illegal, then Premise 1 wouldn't give her cause to believe that it's always morally wrong. Premise 2 is there to show that Bill *does* think stealing is an illegal act. So when we unpack Bill's claim, we discover that it's got three parts:

> *first*, there's the idea that an action's being illegal is sufficient for its being wrong;
> *second*, there's the idea about stealing's being illegal;
> *third*, there's the conclusion—the claim that stealing is wrong—which is supported by the first and second parts.

The form of this little argument is called "modus ponens." The name doesn't matter much, but the form itself is worth remembering:

1. If X, then Y.
2. X.
3. So, Y.

Modus ponens is a *valid* form of inference—which is to say that if the premises are true, then the conclusion *must* be true. The nice thing about valid inference forms is that you can be sure that the conclusion is true if the premises are. (Not every argument form is like this.[10]) The practical upshot is that if an argument uses a valid (or truth-preserving) inference form, then you can't deny the conclusion without denying at least one of the premises. So, if you can represent a line of reasoning this way, then you won't have to worry about whether the logic is squirrely. Instead, you can focus on deciding what you think about the premises.[11]

Granted, it takes some work to put things this way. Is the hassle worth it? In lots of contexts, probably not. But when we're talking about important issues (like ethics!), it can be.

In part, this is because the formal way of presenting Bill's idea helps us see different ways of engaging with him. When you first thought about Bill saying that stealing is wrong because it's illegal, you probably had one of two reactions:

- you found yourself agreeing or
- you felt the urge to throw out a different reason entirely.

You probably didn't think to say:

- "Maybe you're right: Stealing is illegal. So what?"

The "I agree" reaction is probably explicable in terms of confirmation bias: You tend to think that stealing is wrong; someone gave a reason that doesn't sound crazy; so, you went with it. The "Here's a different reason" reaction just disregards what Bill said, and we've got to resist this temptation. Some ideas deserve to be ignored, but Bill's isn't one of them. True, it's not the most sophisticated reply in the world, but it's a good start. And if we don't slow down and *evaluate* Bill's response, then we can't learn from it.

The interesting reaction is the "So what?" reaction, which targets Premise 1. We might not be sure whether stealing is inherently illegal, or whether there are more complicated conditions involved. However, we can be pretty confident that it's not always wrong to do things that are illegal. One of the most inspiring examples of civil disobedience—Martin Luther King Jr.'s program of non-violent resistance—was certainly against the law. It was illegal, but certainly not immoral. So, we've got a *counterexample* to Premise 1—which is just to say that we have a case demonstrating that there can be illegal actions that *aren't* morally wrong. That means that Premise 1 is false. Bill's argument, while valid, isn't *sound*—that is, at least one of the premises is false. It follows that he hasn't given us a good reason to believe its conclusion.

Our gut doesn't tell us to think about Bill's first premise; we default to the second, or we jump to a new theory of the wrongness of stealing. And maybe there's some wisdom to that. But if we never formulate reasons as arguments, then we can miss pretty serious problems with those reasons—and that makes progress harder than it needs to be.[12]

Progress, Such as It Is

Here, in short, is the method I just summarized: We come up with a reason; we try to reformulate it as an argument; and then we think about whether there are any counterexamples to the premises. Let's call this "the Counterexample Method." This method primes us to look for flaws, and there are usually flaws to find.

In a sense, the progress here is *negative*. In the example above, what we discovered was that *Bill's reason wasn't a good one*. We didn't actually figure out *whether there is anything wrong with stealing*; we just figured out that we shouldn't criticize it on the basis Bill gave.

Making that sort of progress is better than making none at all, but it probably isn't the forward movement you wanted. What you'd probably like—what I'm sure *I'd* like—is a set of answers to the hard questions we face. Is there anything wrong with abortion? Should I be giving more of my money to the poor? Is it OK to lie to a friend if it makes everyone's life a bit easier? Should we be executing certain violent criminals? And while we're wishing, it would be nice to know *why* the correct answers are correct.

The Counterexample Method can help us get there, but only in a roundabout way. Why? Well, this method amounts to a process of elimination, throwing out all the bad reasons in hopes of being left with a good one. It's a sort of "trial by fire" approach to finding the truth. Of course, when almost any interesting argument is on the table, you can come up with cases that seem to make trouble for one or more of its premises. So, it's unlikely that when the stakes are high—as they are in the issues just mentioned—we're going to find arguments where it's uncontroversial that each premise is true. Still, if you come across a valid argument and you can't find anything wrong with any of the premises, then that's a pretty good reason to take the argument seriously. That's progress.

Much of the hard work of critical thinking is figuring out what, exactly, you're being asked to believe, and then why, exactly, you're supposed to believe it. The rest of the work is evaluating the argument that you've uncovered. And what you'll find is that thinking critically in ethics tends to have a negative payoff: It rules things out instead of ruling things in. That said, the last argument standing might just be the one to believe.

DEALING WITH DATA

Now that you've got a better handle on how philosophers think about arguments, let's spend a little time on the premises. Where do we get them?

This book is focused on moral questions, so we'll spend a long time thinking about specifically moral premises. However, there are lots of cases where we *agree* about the moral claim, but we disagree about some empirical issue. That is, we might agree that we should do whatever produces the best consequences, but we disagree about the course of action that's going to have the best results. "We should do whatever's best for our economy!" OK: So does that mean more immigration, roughly the same amount, or less? "We should do whatever save the most lives!" Fair enough, but does that mean restricting firearm access, keeping things as they are, or relaxing gun laws? To answer these questions, we need to know what the research says.

Here's a thing that happens all the time. You get into a debate with someone about a policy issue—the merits of affirmative action, or whether military spending is excessive, or what the minimum wage should be. So you go on Google, skim the first page of results, find a website that supports your view, and glance through it for talking points. You know you're right; you just need the stats that show it. After finding them, you toss them at your conversation partner like a grenade, expecting his mind to be blown.

This is a bad strategy for silencing a stranger on the internet, but more importantly, it's also a bad strategy for trying to get at the truth. It takes a lot more to know what the science says on a particular topic. What are some better fact-finding habits?

We need to be honest with ourselves here. It takes work to figure out what's true, and we don't always want to put in the work that's required. Suppose, for instance, that you want to know whether unemployment increases when the minimum wage goes up. What should you do? Well, if you really want to know, then you should dig into the scholarly literature on this question. This might mean going on Google Scholar (rather than regular ol' Google) and searching for studies that address this specific question. That is, you would limit yourself to work that's been published in peer-reviewed journals and books by credentialed experts. So instead of just getting an answer from a stranger on reddit, you are getting the informed judgments of people who have trained extensively at reputable institutions. And instead of having upvotes as the metric of quality, you have peer review, where other credentialed experts vet the research for quality.

Moreover, you wouldn't look at *one* study; you'd look at as much recent work as possible. You'd try to get a good sense of the conversation *as a whole*, not just what one person found. One way to do this is to look for *meta-analyses*, which aggregate the results of a bunch of individual studies. After all, a single study might tell you what happened in one city in Oregon in 2012. And no matter how well that study is designed, it may not be able to control for every possible confounder. (In other words, a single study might say "No, unemployment is unaffected," but it's saying it for the wrong reason. Maybe the minimum wage *would* have affected unemployment if it weren't for some other factor: for example, some savvy laws that were put in place around the same time.) Meta-analyses increase the odds that the reported effects are real effects, or the reported absence of an effect is a real absence.

But you could go further still! Again, you dig through a bunch of peer-reviewed research and you find the most recent meta-analyses available. *Then* you do a bit of research about the authors to check whether they have some obvious ax to grind. After all, maybe they were funded by a political action committee that advocates for high minimum wages, and you'd want to know that before trusting them. Bias is real, and even if it doesn't totally corrupt research, it can skew it in significant ways. (That said, be sure to separate *being biased* and *having a view*. Researchers are going to have views about the topics they research: They often do the research because they want to know what to think. You can't hold that against them, and you can't discount their work simply because they actually believe things based on the evidence. After all, what else should they do? However, you can indeed be wary of people with a strong financial or political incentives to reach certain conclusions.)

Finally, you would think about the *quality* of the evidence you've got, only then making a claim about the impact of minimum wages on unemployment. That is, you wouldn't just say, outright, that the truth of the matter is XYZ. Instead, you would think about the degree of confidence that the research seems to warrant, and you would adjust your confidence accordingly. So, if it looks like there is *some* evidence for high minimum wages increasing unemployment, but there's a lot of variability based on circumstances, then you probably shouldn't make this your hill to die on. Instead, you should admit that the evidence seems to point in one direction, but it's far from definitive.[13]

That, in a nutshell, is basically what it takes to form a responsible belief about an important empirical question. Unfortunately, we often aren't willing to do this much work. Sure, on a certain Thursday in November, I care about the impact of the minimum wage because I'm in the middle of a heated debate with my uncle that is, ultimately, about which team's better: Red or Blue. But after the pumpkin pie has been served and the game is on, I no longer find myself fascinated by the nuances of labor markets.

There's a lesson here, of course. If my interest in a topic basically ends when dessert is served, then what are the odds that I understand it thoroughly? And if the answer to that question is "Not super high," then I may not be entitled to an opinion about the issue. Maybe I should sit this one out.

But suppose you think you *should* form an opinion—maybe it's going to determine how you vote—and yet you find yourself unable to sort through the research yourself. You plan to rely on journalists or other intermediaries, hoping that they'll give you a good sense of what's up. Not ideal, but often the way things go. If that's your situation, then here are some good questions to ask as you're browsing the web:

1. *What do you know about the source?* This is actually a bunch of different questions all packed into one. Among them: What do you know about the *website* that you're visiting? Does it generally publish high-quality, well-researched stuff? Says who? What do you know about the *author* whose work you're reading? Does she generally write high-quality, well-researched stuff? Says who? What do you know about *the author's sources?* For instance, does the author link to news articles from reputable outlets, such as Reuters and the Associated Press? Or does the author link to news articles from places with an obvious and significant political slant? Does the author provide links to peer-reviewed research when making controversial claims about how the world works? Or are there are lots of unsupported assertions?

2. *What's the argument?* On what *basis* does the author want you to believe whatever the article says? Are you supposed to believe it on the basis of someone's personal experiences? Why think that those experiences are representative—that is, not just an isolated case, but part of a much larger

trend? Has the author based her case on *other people's* experiences? Why think that she's interpreting them correctly? Is the author relying on *empirical* evidence for her conclusion? As before, what's the source? Is the author making a *moral* argument? What's the moral principle on which it relies? Would most people accept that principle, even people who aren't sympathetic to the author's conclusion? And even if so, why should we think that most people are right?

3. *What's missing?* This is probably the hardest question, but in a sense, it might be the most important. The idea is simple: Learn to ask about what *isn't* being said. This matters because it's very easy to feel like you're getting the whole story from a single source. But as you well know, it's rarely the case that one article is going to give you a complete picture of what's at stake. Think for a minute about how much research you do for ordinary consumer purchases. The last time I bought headphones, I read six different reviews. I didn't trust anyone to give me the whole story about fit, sound quality, water resistance, and long-term durability: I figured that different people would test the product in different ways, and different costs and benefits would be emphasized in each review. And, of course, there *were* different costs and benefits emphasized in each review. I'm not saying that anyone was trying to mislead me. I'm just pointing out that had I only read one review, I would have missed information that was relevant to my purchase. But if I understand that perspective matters when it comes to headphones, I should certainly appreciate it when it comes to economics, or foreign policy, or health care. Different authors are going to include and emphasize different things, based on their own experiences and expertise. For any complex issue, those differences in what's mentioned and emphasized are probably important. So ask yourself: What isn't showing up in this analysis?

If you ask these questions, you'll be in a much better position to separate good resources from bad ones. None of this is foolproof, of course, but it helps.

MORAL THEORY

So those are some tips for getting better answers to empirical questions. What about moral ones? As I said before, no one gets to decide what's right and wrong. We have to work together to figure it out. If you want some places to start, though, then we should learn a little *moral theory*. The goal of moral theory is to explain why some actions are morally right and others are morally wrong. In other words, we try to find the features that are shared by right actions that *make* them right, and hence the features that *aren't* had by wrong actions. Along the way, it would be nice to be able to give an account of some other moral concepts: goodness and badness, praiseworthiness and blameworthiness, and so forth. The hope is that we can find the One True Moral Theory. If we can, then we'll put it to use as a premise in moral arguments.

In what follows, I'm going to give you quick overviews of several influential moral theories. They include utilitarianism, Kantianism, care ethics, virtue ethics, and social contract theory. After each introduction, I'll give you taste of a classic text that represents this moral tradition.

Utilitarianism

Utilitarianism is a form a consequentialism, and consequentialism is a deceptively simple moral theory. Very roughly, the idea is that you're morally obligated to do the most good you can. When you say it like that, it might seem totally trivial: *Of course* we ought to do the most good we can. When we think this through, though, we quickly discover some surprising implications.

But let's not get ahead of ourselves. We should begin with a more precise statement of consequentialism, which we can then unpack. The core claim is this:

An action is morally obligatory if and only if it maximizes the good.

What does this mean?

In short, the idea is that an action is morally obligatory—you ought to do it, and it would be wrong not to—if the consequences of that action make the world better than it would be if you did anything else. On this view, morality asks a lot of us. After all, lots of the things you do almost certainly don't make the world better than it would've been if you did anything else. For instance, I recently bought some running shoes. (I love buying running shoes.) But the truth is that I already have some good running shoes, and I didn't need to spend $64 on new gear. You might think, "Well, maybe not the smartest purchase, but $64 isn't that much for shoes, and in any case, we all have our thing; buying running shoes is a way better use of money than, say, buying meth." But if consequentialism is correct, then you are letting me off way too easy. Just think about what I could've done with $64 that I did not do: I could have donated it to the Against Malaria Foundation, which provides nets to poor people to spare them from getting malaria via mosquito bites. (Google it. It's an organization worth knowing about.) Those nets cost about $2 apiece, so instead of making exactly one person happy—namely, myself—I could've made at least thirty-two people happy. And surely it's better to have thirty-two happy people than one. So, if consequentialism is true, then it's very likely that it was morally wrong for me to buy those running shoes. Moreover, unless you can think of a way of significantly benefiting more than thirty-two people with $64, then it may well have been morally wrong for me to do *anything* with that money other than donate it to the Against Malaria Foundation. That's what I ought to have done.

This might seem a bit wild to you: "But it's your money! You can spend it how you want!" And, of course, there's a sense in which that's true: Morality isn't like physics, where you can't violate the laws. There is nothing that's going to *force* you to do the right thing (if donating is, in fact, the right thing). So what, though? We already knew that. You know plenty of people who do things that you judge to be morally wrong; nothing stops them from doing those things either. Morality can't make you do stuff.

"That's not what I meant," you might say. "I meant that you have a right to spend your money how you want." Granted, there's also a sense in which *that's* true. I do indeed have a *legal* right to spend my money on running shoes; the government can't tell me that if I don't give that money to the Against Malaria Foundation, I'll go to jail. However, as we discussed earlier, we aren't focused on what the law says: We are trying to figure out what morality says. And if consequentialism is true, then morality is decidedly egalitarian. My interests don't count more than your interests, or more than those of the many people who would be benefited by my donating money to purchase mosquito nets. Consequentialism tells us that we should evaluate the various things we can do *impartially*. We are asking what makes the *world* best overall, not what makes *me* best overall. So when we look at all the options that I had available to me, and think about which would make the world better than all the others, the consequences *for me* certainly count. But they don't count more than the consequences for anyone else. After all, from an impartial point of view, there's nothing special about me: I'm just one among many; there's no reason to give me preferential treatment. And since I could do much more good for others that I could for myself, I'm supposed to donate.

The way we just approached my shoe-buying is the way consequentialism says we should approach all moral matters:

1. Answer the question "What can you do?" In the example I just gave, I can do lots of things with $64: I can buy running shoes, I can buy ice cream, I can leave the money in the bank, I can hand it out dollar by dollar to people who happen to pass me on the street, I can donate it to the Against Malaria Foundation, and countless other options.
2. Determine which of those options makes the world better than all the others. Whatever that is, that's what you ought to do.

Of course, as soon as we state that second idea—about determining which option makes the world better than all the others—we realize that we need to say something about what makes the world better and worse. Sure, it seems plausible that it's better to have thirty-two people not get malaria than it is to have one person enjoy some new running shoes. But there are going to be cases where things aren't so clear, and we need some guidance.

Consequentialism, then, is really a family of moral theories, where different theories are distinguished by what they say about what makes the world better and worse. There are lots of possibilities. You could think that what we should do is maximize how *just* the world is. Or how *virtuous* people are. Or the *number of rights* that are respected. Or what have you. Here, I'm just going to focus on the most influential form of consequentialism—namely, utilitarianism.

Utilitarianism says:

An action is morally obligatory if and only if it maximizes *utility*.

Let's unpack this claim.

The term "utility" is an old one, and it's stuck around because of the influence that utilitarianism has had. But for our purposes, you can think about "utility" as roughly equivalent to "well-being" or "welfare" (in the "how some-one's doing overall" sense, not the social program sense). So the claim is that you ought to maximize well-being—remembering that no one's well-being counts for any more than anyone else's. In other words, the goal is to produce as much well-being as possible with each action, regardless of whose well-being it is. It seems pretty clear that utilitarianism is going to deliver the same verdict about my running shoes that we got from our intuitive form of consequentialism: Yes, the shoes improve my well-being, but not nearly as much as mosquito nets improve the well-being of those thirty-two people, especially when we consider the amount that their well-being is *collectively* improved.

Why would we focus on well-being as the thing to maximize, as opposed to justice or whatever else? The answer, according to the utilitarian, is that well-being is a very plausible candidate for being the one thing that's *intrinsically valuable.*

To see what I mean, think about the value of a $20 bill. A $20 bill is *instrumentally* valuable: It's valuable because of what you can do with it, and not because it's valuable in itself. You care about having $20 because it means you can buy some groceries, or pay part of your electric bill, or go see a movie. It isn't that your $20 bill is precious in itself: It's just a piece of paper. It isn't particularly beautiful, or good to eat; it will not rub your feet or do your laundry for you. If it weren't for the fact that you can trade it for things that you care about, it would be worthless. That's what it is to be instrumentally valuable: The value comes from its usefulness, not from what it is on its own.

Utilitarians say that if we think hard about all the things that matter to us, we'll soon discover that nearly all of them are like money: They are good because of what they can do, and not because of what they are in themselves. And what is it that all these instrumentally good things can do? They can improve our well-being. New running shoes are good, but only because it feels good to run in them. A nice car is good, but that's because we enjoy driving it, and we're safer in it, and so on. Meaningful work is good, but that's because meaningless work makes us unsatisfied. Being in a relationship is good, but only because we're often happier in relationships than we are without them. If you're miserable in your relationship, then it isn't good anymore. And so on. Utilitarians look around and see only one thing that really matters—well-being—and then they make the plausible observation that your well-being isn't any more important, at least from the point of view of the universe, than anyone else's. So what we should do is act in ways that produce as much well-being as possible, regardless of whose well-being it is.

There are, of course, objections to every theory, and utilitarianism is no exception. I'd guess that one of them has already occurred to you—namely, that this moral theory is too demanding; it asks too much of us. The thought is just this. If utilitarianism is true, then many ordinary actions—like getting clothes you don't need, or a fancy iPhone when you could get by just as well with a budget Android device—are arguably morally wrong. And it isn't just luxury shopping that's subject to criticism here: There are any number of situations where you could do more good by sacrificing your own interests, and yet it doesn't always seem like you're morally obligated to make that kind of sacrifice.

There are several things that utilitarians might say, but let's just consider two. First, they might just say that we should *bite the bullet*—which is an expression that philosophers use to mean something like "accept that the theory really does imply that counterintuitive thing, and yet insist that we should believe the theory anyway." On this view, morality is indeed demanding, and the real problem is our not wanting to live up to that standard.

The second thing they might say is that although *this version* of utilitarianism demands a lot of us, the theory can be modified so that it's a bit less extreme. Utilitarians could say, for instance, that we should trade this:

An action is morally obligatory if and only if it maximizes utility.

. . . for this:

An action is morally obligatory if and only if it's required by a rule such that, if most people followed it, utility would be maximized.

This is *rule* utilitarianism—in contrast with *act* utilitarianism, which is the view that we've been considering until now. Rule utilitarianism recognizes that when people mostly follow the rules of conventional morality—don't steal, don't murder, respect the law, etc.—there is much more well-being than there would be if people didn't follow those rules. And rule utilitarianism also recognizes that most of us are willing to sacrifice roughly as much as the people around us will sacrifice; we're conformists, not leaders. (Moreover, the people around us aren't willing to do all that much: If we're honest with ourselves, we generally shoot for a B in ethics, not an A.) Finally, rule utilitarianism gets that the world is complicated, we're often motivated reasoners, and there is only so much time in the day for moral deliberation. This means that we need pretty simple rules to keep us on track. So, rule utilitarianism might say that we should mostly follow the rules of conventional morality, with the notable exception that we should give away at least 10% of our income to good causes. If that's the story, then morality is more demanding than we ordinarily take it to be—the average American gives away about 2% of her income, not 10%—but it doesn't take everything from us.

A different objection to utilitarianism—both to the act and rule versions—is that there are going to be cases where producing the most good involves some injustice. Imagine a situation where exploiting some very small group of people produces huge benefits for a very large group of people. Maybe it's the case that if the very large group enslaves the very small one, then the overall amount of well-being will be very high—even though the members of the very small group will all suffer in extraordinary ways. If we ought to do what maximizes well-being, then we ought to enslave the very small group. But that seems terribly wrong.

This is a tricky problem for utilitarians to navigate. Again, some of them might just bite the bullet: They might insist that there is no *realistic* case where this would be true, and so utilitarianism would never *actually* tell us that we ought to enslave anyone. And, in the merely hypothetical cases where it would, we should just accept that enslaving people would indeed be morally correct. Not exactly inspiring.

It might be better to argue that we need to keep the very far future in mind when we assess the consequences of a particular course of action. In the short run, it may look like you maximize well-being by enslaving people. But we need to think about the long-term implications, including creating a culture that's willing to run roughshod over people's rights, the kinds of violent practices that would be required to keep slaves in their place, and so on. When we engage in a more systematic evaluation of the consequences, it may turn out that it will be very, very rare that you should do what's unjust, since while it might produce benefits in the immediate future, things almost never pan out down the line.

I'll leave it to you to consider how promising this reply is. Let's now consider a different moral theory, one that doesn't face this kind of problem at all.

Kantianism

Recall: Because utilitarianism says that we ought to maximize well-being, and maximizing well-being sometimes involves acting unjustly, utilitarianism sometimes implies that we ought to act unjustly. That's bad. Maybe we need to get back to basics to avoid this kind of problem, leaning on a very familiar moral principle—namely, the Golden Rule. According to the Golden Rule, you should do unto others as you would have them do unto you. In other words, you should treat people as you would like to be treated. Presumably, you don't want to be enslaved by others, so you shouldn't enslave them. Presumably, you don't want to be lied to by others, so you shouldn't lie to them. Problem solved!

Unfortunately, the Golden Rule faces its own troubles. For instance, I would really like others to give me piles and piles of money; that would make my life much better. But I take it that no one is morally obligated to give me piles and piles of money—much to my chagrin. And here's an even more serious issue. Imagine the Genocidal White Supremacist. The Genocidal White Supremacist thinks that all non-white people should die, with no exceptions whatever. Imagine that, in a twist of fate, the Genocidal White Supremacist discovers that he isn't actually white. (Perhaps he discovers that his parents are Argentinian, and though he passes as white, he's actually Latino.) The Genocidal White Supremacist now thinks that he should die too: He's that much of a believer. If his only moral guidance is to do unto others as you would have them do unto you, then he is morally permitted—or maybe even morally required—to kill non-white people. After all, it's how he would like them to treat him, now that he knows that he's non-white as well!

There may be ways to fix the Golden Rule. But these sorts of problems suggest that it's worth looking for a different way of blocking the problem of permitting injustice. Immanuel Kant (1724–1804) had a theory about this, and it remains highly influential. He proposed that the *categorical imperative* is the test for whether we are acting permissibly:

> An action is morally wrong if and only if its maxim isn't universalizable.

It might sound complicated, but it isn't really. Let's start with the notion of a maxim. Very roughly, you can think of a maxim for an action as your intention regarding that action. Let's consider Shawn the Shoplifter. When Shawn goes into the store, his plan is to take some headphones without paying for them. That's his maxim.

The next step is to figure out what it means for a maxim to universalizable. The basic question is this: Is your maxim one that everyone could get behind and live by? So we can now ask: Could everyone be willing to take headphones without paying for them, as Shawn does? Absolutely not. If they did, the store wouldn't stock them. Stores can make products available precisely because people are willing to exchange money for them. If people won't do that, stores can't make the products available. Of course, it might turn out that no one is hurt by Shawn's shoplifting, and he's made very happy by having free headphones. On balance, the world could be better with his theft than without it. Yet that seems irrelevant to the assessment of his behavior. Shawn is doing something wrong, and any good consequences don't matter. And why is he doing something wrong? According to Kant, it's because Shawn is trying to make an exception of himself; he's trying to act such that, if everyone else tried to act as he wants to act, his plan would be undermined. That's what it means to say that his maxim isn't universalizable.

This sounds pretty good, and it seems to rule out a lot of things that we want to rule out. Do you think it's OK to enslave people when it would be convenient for you? Not so fast: It's impossible for everyone to act on that maxim, since slaves can't enslave their masters. Think it's OK not to report your tips on your taxes, despite enjoying the things that taxes pay for? Wrong again: If everyone failed to report income, then there would be no tax base, and so none of those benefits would be there to enjoy. Think it's OK to plagiarize an assignment? I don't think so: If everyone does it, then professors can't trust that anyone's work is their own, and so can't assess anyone.

However, trouble's around the corner. Here's a case that should be a slow pitch: It had better turn out that it's wrong for me to kill my colleague, Eric Gilbertson, on Tuesday, October 23, 2018, for the purpose of acquiring his very cool single-speed bike. But think about that maxim. Is it universalizable? It certainly seems to be: Everyone could act as I'm proposing to act; there is nothing self-undermining about the plan. This case isn't at all like Shawn the Shoplifter, where it's only possible to shoplift because there's an expectation that people won't do that, but will instead pay for what's for sale. Eric would be there, as a very killable human being, quite independently of whether I plan to kill him. (Or, if my plan *is* self-undermining, it's self-undermining in a way that leads to other bizarre results. Consider a similarly detailed maxim: My plan is to drink a particular cup of coffee—the one sitting on my desk right now—at 9:21 a.m. on Tuesday, October 23, 2018. Not everyone could have that plan, since not everyone could drink my coffee; there simply isn't enough. But surely that doesn't make my plan to drink coffee wrong, and so it can't be the thing that makes it wrong to kill Eric—whom, I should emphasize, I actually like very much.) It seems like a very bad result that it's permissible to kill Eric, and so we have reason to worry about Kant's ethics.

What Kant should say here is that maxims should be *general*—they shouldn't be so specific. So Shawn's maxim isn't something like "I will take headphones without paying for them when it's convenient for me," and my maxim isn't something like "I will kill my colleague, Eric Gilbertson, on Tuesday, October 23, 2018, for the purpose of acquiring his very cool single-speed bike." Instead, Shawn's is something like "I will take products without paying for them whenever I want," and my maxim is something like "I will kill people whenever that allows me to acquire their belongings." Neither of these maxims appears to be universalizable, and so Kant seems to be in the clear.

Of course, Kant has to explain why we should attribute these more general maxims to people. He might say that Shawn and I aren't really being honest with ourselves: Shawn isn't really just willing to take headphones, and I'm not only willing to harm one particular person to get what I want. I'm not so sure that this is true, but even if it is, the move won't work in every case. Consider crimes of passion, where people kill their cheating partners. It may well be the case that they would never harm anyone else; it's only *this* person, in *these* circumstances, that they would ever even consider hurting.

However, Kant had a very different way of thinking about our obligations, and it can help us avoid the weird results that we just got from the categorical imperative. We haven't yet said very much about why somebody would think that the categorical imperative is so important in ethics. Part of the story is that Kant takes our rationality—our capacity to deliberate about and act for reasons—as fundamental to who we are as moral beings. It's a characteristic we share that deserves deep respect. And if we ought to respect our own rationality (by adopting maxims that are coherent and contradiction-free), then we also ought to respect the rationality of others. We ought to treat them in ways that reflect an appreciation for their rationality, for their ability to act based on reasons of their choosing. Kant describes this as treating people as *ends in themselves*, rather than as *mere means*.

Plainly, I wouldn't be treating Eric as an end in himself if I were to kill him for his bike. That wouldn't be at all respectful of his plans. And so that course of action would be wrong. This way of thinking also seems to rule out all the other behaviors that the categorical imperative is designed to prohibit. Shawn the Shoplifter isn't treating the store owner and her employees as ends in themselves. You wouldn't be treating a person as an end in himself if you were to enslave him. And so on.

Does the "treat people as ends in themselves" idea lead to bizarre results? Am I failing to treat an Uber driver as an end in himself when I use him to get from one point to another? No. This is where we need to distinguish between treating someone as a *means* and treating him as a *mere* means. I can use people to get what I want *as long as they consent to be used in those ways*. The Uber driver wants to exchange his time and energy for my money, and I'm glad to make the exchange. So each of us is using the other as a means. But neither of us is using the other as a mere means: We are both on board with the deal. By contrast, imagine if I took a ride with him, and then, at the very end, forced him at gunpoint to cancel the charge. That would definitely be wrong, and that's because I would be treating him as a mere means; I would simply be using him to get what I want without his consent.

This seems like real progress over the categorical imperative. And in some sense, it is: It leads to more intuitive results. However, we might wonder whether "it gets the right results" because of what we *assume* about respectful treatment, and not because we are actually getting much guidance from the principle. Let's grant that we should always treat people as ends in themselves. Does this mean that there is no need for a minimum wage, because as long as people consent to work for a given wage—no matter how low that wage is—they aren't being exploited? Or consider an ambiguity in the claim that we should always treat people as ends in themselves. Is the claim that we should treat everyone as an end in himself—where that implies that we have obligations to everyone in the world—or is the claim that *when we interact with someone*, we ought to treat that person as an end in himself? The former interpretation may end up making the view very demanding, much like utilitarianism. And the latter view might make the view much too permissive, allowing us to neglect all sorts of people simply by avoiding them.

I'm not saying that these problems aren't solvable. The point is just that it's an attractive feature of utilitarianism that it gives fairly clear advice about what we should do. By contrast, the claim that we should always treat people as ends in themselves is a bit ambiguous. It isn't obvious how to interpret it, or what, exactly, it requires of us.

Care Ethics

Here's a thought: Maybe a bit of messiness is a feature, not a bug. In other words, maybe it's a mistake to want too much precision from our ethical theory; maybe we should want a theory that reflects the complexities of life. If so, though, it seems likely that we need something a bit different than a principle like "treat others as ends in themselves." That principle is probably too narrow to cover the full range of situations where we need moral guidance. After all, the hard moral questions aren't about whether to steal or pay your taxes or threaten Uber drivers. They are about the difficult questions that come up when we try to be good parents and partners and friends. What sort of principle, if any, could tell us how to proceed in all these relationships and roles?

Maybe none. Isn't being ethical about more basic things? Raising your children well? Mowing your elderly neighbor's lawn? Volunteering for the undesirable tasks at work? Some philosophers have thought so. They have argued that it's a mistake to focus on abstract principles, which makes it seem as though rationality is central to the moral life. They insist, to the contrary, that morality is fundamentally about recognizing and attending to the needs of others, which requires appreciating the details of their lives and your place in it. Morality is about caring.

We can distinguish three important aspects of care ethics. We can call the first *particularism*. Care ethics began as a feminist critique of traditional moral theories, like utilitarianism and Kantianism. Both of those theories say that if you have all the facts about a situation, then you can simply apply their preferred principle to find out what people should and shouldn't do in that situation. Carol

Gilligan and Nel Noddings were some of the first to argue that this amounts to privileging overly rational, "male" ways of thinking. On their view, there isn't any one principle that explains why all right actions are morally right and all wrong ones are morally wrong. Actions are still right and wrong—they aren't denying that. They are saying, however, that you can't just feed the details of a situation into some "tell me the morally correct thing to do" machine, turn the crank, and get an answer.

We might worry that this makes it difficult to know what we should do. But care ethicists think that these worries are overblown. This is because they offer us two different tools for assessing our obligations, which brings us to the second aspect of care ethics—namely, the importance of care itself.

Here's one way of thinking about it. Caring about someone has many dimensions. It involves feeling certain emotions: being happy when they're happy; being sad when they're sad. It involves being attentive to them: You notice how they are, and you think about the various things that might be affecting them (work, school, relationships, etc.). It involves wanting what's good for them. It involves being willing to do things for them—sometimes at considerable cost to yourself. Actions are good, on this view, if they are motivated by care; they are bad if they are motivated by the opposite of care, which is either neglect (the passive form) or hostility (the active form).

Of course, there are plenty of cases where it's difficult to know exactly what caring requires of you. Am I enabling this person or simply being supportive? Am I caring for someone the appropriate amount, or am I caring too much and so letting others down? But regardless of our moral outlook, these kinds of cases are often tricky, so maybe it's no fault of care ethics that it doesn't give precise guidance on them.

This brings us to the third aspect of care ethics, which concerns the importance of relationships. Care isn't some abstract idea: It's a way of feeling and relating to another person. And the nature of that care, and the responsibilities it generates, are affected by the kind of relationship in which it occurs. My care for my parents is different than my care for my wife, which is different from my care for my children, which is different from my care for my colleagues at work. We can't separate a discussion of care from a discussion of the really complicated details of individual relationships, and the special obligations that we have as parents, partners, and so on. The claim isn't just that we need to act out of care, but that we need to care in ways that reflect those special responsibilities.

There is something very attractive about this picture. It's hard to find a single principle that sums up our ethical obligations. Plainly, caring is very important to being a good person, and to acting well in so many situations. And it obviously matters that we are sisters and children and parents and employees; any ethic that overlooks these relationships is missing something important. However, we might worry that care just isn't enough to address all the moral questions we face. It seems right to pay closer attention to our emotions and relationships, but a mistake to limit ourselves to caring. What about the various character traits that can help us rein in our tendency to care too much, such as honesty and civic responsibility and a sense of justice? Think about the mother who is convinced that she ought to lie to cover up her son's crime. She might be caring excellently and yet still acting wrongly. The care ethicist might agree, and say that the problem here is that she doesn't care enough about victims, or that she cares for her son in the wrong way. But how are we going to explain why she isn't caring enough about the victims, or the sense in which this is the wrong way to care? What explains why she's striking the wrong balance? It would be helpful to have other values to which to appeal—something else to tip the scales in favor of truth-telling and explain why it's the right choice in this case.

Virtue Ethics

If you find this sort of criticism compelling, but you are otherwise sympathetic to the emphasis on your character and relationships, then virtue ethics may be attractive. The thought is that, ultimately, the goal is to cultivate and act out of the virtues—namely, character traits like being courageous and honest and merciful and fair.

Which traits are on the list? Virtue theorists disagree here, but here's one way the story can go. Things can go well and badly for human beings: We can live rich, meaningful, flourishing lives, and we can live shallow, petty, or impoverished lives. The virtues are those character traits that lead to the better kind of life, the flourishing life, whereas the vices—the negative character traits—are the ones that lead to living poorly.

Which traits are the ones that lead to the better kind of life? Well, once we know what that better kind of life is, then we are left with an empirical question—one that's going to be answered by social scientists, not philosophers. They would look at those best lives and then determine what those lives have in common, at least in terms of the character traits that make them possible. Let's suppose that the best lives are lived by people with deep relationships, a strong sense of purpose, a willingness to sacrifice for others, and so on. The virtues are those traits that make such lives possible. Presumably, you need to be honest, faithful, and kind to sustain deep relationships over time. (Dishonest, unfaithful, and cruel people don't have those kinds of rich connections with others.) You need to be someone with discernment to find your role in the world. (People without judgment, or those who aren't sensitive to the nuances of what's happening around them, probably aren't going to recognize where they can do the most good.) You need to be humble and compassionate to be willing to sacrifice for others. (The proud and selfish probably won't.)

This might all sound pretty good. And there is something very attractive about virtue ethics. But there are drawbacks as well. First, I made it seem like it's pretty clear which lives are best. And depending on your views about lots of other things, you might feel like you have a pretty good handle on that issue. For instance, if you have a certain religious outlook, then you may think that lives lived in God's service are best; if you have another one, then you may think that the best lives are those spent helping others break free of the cycle of rebirth. But if we don't have those kinds of religious convictions, then there is bound to be much more disagreement about who is and isn't flourishing. And if there is disagreement about that, there are going to be disagreements about the virtues and the vices.

Virtue theorists say different things about this objection. Some of them simply agree that virtue ethics makes most sense when it's developed in a framework where people have a purpose, where there is something that people are *for*. Others think that it's easy to overstate how much disagreement there is. Positive psychology now provides a fairly clear picture of the factors that contribute to human happiness. Maybe we already know enough to determine what the virtues are. I'll let you sort this one out.

Here's a second worry about virtue ethics. There are some cases where it's fairly clear what the virtuous would do. For instance, they probably wouldn't kill my good friend Eric for his supercool bike. However, what would the virtuous do when it comes to abortion, or capital punishment, or immigration policy, or other hot-button issues? There is a risk here that we will simply twist our interpretation of the virtues so that they support whatever we wanted them to say. If, for instance, you think that abortion is deeply wrong, then you probably think that virtuous people wouldn't get abortions, and that they would discourage others from getting them. If you don't think that abortion is deeply wrong, then you probably think that virtuous people would get abortions in certain circumstances. The goal, though, was to get guidance from moral theory, not simply to use it to express the answers that we'd already reached on independent grounds.

The risk here is real. But perhaps it's tolerable. Remember: Part of what motivates virtue ethics is the idea that life is messy, and our ethical theory should reflect that complexity. The easy issues should be easy to resolve, and the hard ones should be hard to resolve. Moreover, the virtue ethicist might argue that when trying to figure out what we ought to do morally, we will need to display some *intellectual* virtues as well. This might mean cultivating intellectual humility, where we don't assume that our views are right simply because they're ours. It also might require some patience, accepting that it will take time to work out answers to thorny moral problems. And so on. We shouldn't expect ethics to be easy!

Social Contract Theory

Whatever the problems and prospects for virtue ethics, we might think that this is all pretty far from the kinds of conversations that dominate the contemporary political landscape. Sure, being virtuous is important. But we might think that in many policy debates, the central question is not whether we would be virtuous in enacting it, but whether we would violate anyone's rights in enacting it. Obviously, rights talk is pretty common: We debate whether people have a right to health care, whether fetuses have a right to life, whether there's a right to be forgotten, and much else besides. But where do rights come from? How do we argue that someone has a particular right, or make clear what it requires of others?

Here's one view: We have *natural* rights. These are rights that aren't granted by any human person or government; they are pre-political, in the sense that there doesn't need to be any sort of political order for us to have them. Instead, governments are supposed to protect our natural rights, and bad governments are the ones that fail to do this.

This view should be somewhat familiar, since it's baked into the Declaration of Independence:

> We hold these truths to be self-evident, that all men are created equal, that they are endowed by their Creator with certain unalienable Rights, that among these are Life, Liberty and the pursuit of Happiness.—That to secure these rights, Governments are instituted among Men, deriving their just powers from the consent of the governed,—That whenever any Form of Government becomes destructive of these ends, it is the Right of the People to alter or to abolish it, and to institute new Government, laying its foundation on such principles and organizing its powers in such form, as to them shall seem most likely to effect their Safety and Happiness.

If the authors of the Declaration of Independence are correct, then these natural rights have an origin: They aren't given by governments, but by God. Of course, many people no longer regard it as self-evident that God gave us unalienable rights, since they don't regard it as self-evident that God exists at all. Moreover, even if you do think that God exists, there remains the task of explaining how we know that God gave us any particular right. It's easy to say that it's self-evident that God gave us a right to liberty, but how, exactly, might we argue for that if someone doesn't find it so obvious?

These sorts of problems, among others, have led many philosophers to think differently about our rights. Social contract theory is one such way.

The basic idea is that your rights are the result of a deal. Of course, you probably don't remember making a deal with anyone, and that's probably because you never did. So this deal is hypothetical: It's the deal we *would* make if we were to think things through. It's the arrangement that we would accept in the right circumstances.

Imagine this. You're living in the state of nature—an imaginary place where there are no rules at all, which means that anyone can do anything to get whatever they want. In the state of nature, there is no such thing as ethics; we are all acting out of pure self-interest, trying to do what's best for ourselves. Moreover, it's a place where there is scarcity; not everyone can have everything they want. In such circumstances, you are constantly at great risk. Suppose that you and I really like pineapple, and we're both after the last one. There's no rule preventing you from stabbing me in the back to stop me from getting it. Likewise, there's no rule preventing me from clubbing you in the knees to prevent *you* from getting it. We are both able to use violence to achieve our ends. That's bad, because no matter how good pineapples are—and they are indeed delicious—they aren't worth the risk of knives in the back and broken kneecaps.

So what do we do? We make a deal. I promise that I won't break your kneecaps, and you promise that you won't stab me in the back. We will still compete for the pineapple, and one of us will walk away disappointed. But that's it: One of us will *only* be disappointed, rather than both disappointed and injured. In such circumstances, it's worth trading the power to use violence for the benefit of knowing that violence won't be used against you.

Social contract theory says that this is how all our rights are grounded. Consider the right to control property. Again, imagine if there weren't such a rule. At any time, you would be able to go and take things from others. All on its own, that would be pretty great. Remember my friend Eric, with the awesome single-speed bike? No killing would be required: I would just have to take advantage of some moment when he forgot to lock it up. But of course, I would be vulnerable to the same threat. He could take the bike back, and anything else of mine he happened to want. And so we might well conclude: This is a terrible arrangement; we should make a deal to get out of it. And what would that deal be? Again, we would trade a power for a benefit. We would give up the power to take things from others for the benefit of knowing that others won't take our things.

Here's the problem, though. Let's suppose that you are really strong and I'm weak and vulnerable. Why bother striking a deal with me? Why not just take what you want—including my life—since I pose no threat to you? On the face of it, this seems like a totally reasonable thing to do, at least if I only care about myself and there really are no rules that tell me not to act this way.

One way out of this problem is to accept that the state of nature will lead to all sorts of crooked deals, or no deal at all, where the powerful continue to exploit the weak. But maybe we don't really need to start in the state of nature. Instead, we can start with some of our deepest convictions, just as we do everywhere else in ethics. And one of those convictions, which is also clear in the Declaration of Independence, is a commitment to equality. Suppose that we really care about treating people equally: Which deals would we make in those circumstances? Perhaps the answer to that question will help us get a better sense of our rights.

The trick here is to figure out how equality should factor into our deal-making. One idea—often attributed to John Rawls, but the core of it goes back to a Hungarian economist named John Harsanyi—is that there was nothing wrong with letting self-interest guide our deal-making, and not even anything wrong with having self-interest be the *only* thing that guides our deal-making. The problem comes from knowing our situations too well. The reason why you don't want to make a deal with me when you are powerful and I am weak is because you *know* that you are powerful and I am weak. It's clear to you that you have no incentive to compromise for my sake. So, if we want to dodge this problem, we need to deprive you of some information.

Think about it like this. I have two kids, and like many such creatures, they want to consume as much sugar as possible. If I let my older one cut slices of pie, and then let him choose what slice of pie he gets, he will cut a very large slice for himself, leaving much less for his younger brother. I could deal with this by doing the cutting and distributing myself. But I don't. Instead, I let the older one cut, and then I let the younger one choose the slice he wants. And guess what? My older son becomes remarkably interested in cutting slices of pie that are of equal size. Self-interest with full information? Big brother gets lots, little brother gets a sliver. Self-interest in the context of ignorance? Perfect equality.

Here, then, is one contract-based story about our rights. Our rights are the rights we would agree to give one another if we didn't know who we were going to be in our society. That is, suppose that you don't know whether you're going to be black or white, male or female, gay or straight, rich or poor, religious or secular, able-bodied or disabled. If you were self-interested, what set of rights would you agree to give people? You could be a wealthy Latino banker, a homeless Vietnam vet, a gay black middle school teacher, or any combination of other identities, histories, and socioeconomic situations. Again, you would be thinking about trading power for benefits. But now you wouldn't be so focused on preserving the particular powers you currently enjoy, which may well come from having a relatively privileged position in society. Instead, you would be thinking about the risk of winding up in one of those disadvantaged positions, and you would want to make sure that you have some basic protections. Sure, you would want the right not to have violence used against you, as well as the right to control property. But you would also want a bunch of other protections: freedom to vote, the promise of a fair trial, the ability to marry whomever you want, the ability to say unpopular things without harassment, and so on.

There are problems with the simple version of this story. For instance, why should we think that our rights come from this hypothetical deal-making, rather than the actual deals we make? What's more, why should we care about this hypothetical deal-making when we might agree to rights that make the society worse off than it would be otherwise? In other words, maybe it's the case that if you didn't know who you were going to be in a society, you would be really concerned about protecting private property. But maybe it's the case that our concern for private property makes it really hard to redistribute resources. So instead of being able to maximize well-being, we end up with a situation where some people have a lot, lots of others have a little, and there is nothing we can do about it. Finally, we might be suspicious of any approach to our rights that strips us of our identities. We might think that our identities are essential to determining which rights we've got, and that it's a mistake to abstract away from the details of people's lives.

We won't explore all these issues here. Instead, I simply want to point out that even if we can address all these problems, we shouldn't think that we will have then said everything there is to say about ethics. There are lots of ethical questions that don't have anything to do with rights, even in the political realm. For instance, suppose we spend some time thinking about what we would agree to if we didn't know who we were going to be in our society. We decide that everyone should have a right to vote, and we decide that we should codify that in law in the following way: We make it illegal for anyone to prevent you from voting. But that leaves lots of room for debate about how much we should do to *help* people vote, and even room for debate about how much the government should help people vote—by, for instance, declaring a national holiday on any election day, or by making public transportation free on those days, or by expanding the number of people who can vote by mail (which, in some states, is basically restricted to the elderly and the disabled). I'm not saying that we *should* help people in these ways.

Instead, I'm just saying that we *might* think we should, and not because anyone has a *right* to a day off, or to vote by mail, but for other sorts of reasons entirely. These could be utilitarian or Kantian or virtue ethical reasons, or they could be of some other type. The point is just that although rights matter, let's not think that rights are the *only* thing that matter.

Getting Perspective

As we wrap up this quick tour through moral theory, it's worth reflecting on the uses and abuses of these moral theories. Perhaps the most common *abuse* of these moral theories is to use them to say whatever you already wanted to say. So, for example, if you want torture to be OK, you suddenly argue like a utilitarian; if you're critical of sex work, you're now a Kantian; if you're in favor of helping the homeless, virtue ethics becomes your thing. This is to use the theories to *avoid* thinking about considerations that run counter to what we want to be true.

In my view, a better use of these theories is to use them as ways to focus our attention. When we want to defend a moral claim, we should look at it from several angles. What would the consequences be? Will we have to take advantage of anyone—or otherwise be unfair—in the process? What kind of people will we become by acting this way? And so on. These questions help us get a more complete picture of the moral situation. Once we've got that picture, we can begin thinking about why, in some particular context, one of these questions is the most important one.

RELATIVISM

I want to conclude this introduction by addressing a certain kind of skepticism about ethics.

A lot of people seem to be convinced that there are facts and there are opinions, and ethical claims are definitely in the "opinions" camp. Ethical claims might be important insofar as they help us to regulate our communities, but they aren't binding across cultures. There are just American values and Afghani values, and there's no choosing between them.

I find this hard to swallow. Every year, thousands and thousands of girls—usually between the ages of four and twelve—have their genitals mutilated by women in their communities. Those who maintain this practice do so for a number of reasons. An important one is promoting chastity: They think that "uncut" girls are too interested in sex. Uncut girls can't be trusted to remain pure for their future husbands, nor can they be trusted to remain faithful to those husbands once they're married. Cutting solves this problem by making sex painful: You won't stray if there's no pleasure in it.

This practice seriously injures its victims. They face many medical complications as a result, as do their children. (The risk of neonatal mortality is higher among cut women.) It is, moreover, a way of maintaining a social system in which women are systematically disenfranchised. Women don't benefit from having their genitals mutilated—men do.

In cultures that practice female circumcision, the practitioners are not horrified by it.[14] Indeed, they think that it would be wrong *not* to damage young girls in this way. What I take to be unjust, they regard as an important good. This is a disturbing example of *cultural variation*—the thesis that people in different cultures have different beliefs about what's right and wrong.

Cultural variation is a well-established fact. *Cultural relativism* is a further thesis: It says that each culture has the *correct* moral views, even though those views conflict with the ones in other cultures. More precisely, it says that actions are right and wrong *because* of the norms of the culture. So, if my culture says that it's wrong to cut young girls, it's wrong in my culture to do so; if your culture says that it isn't, then—in yours—it isn't. Cultural relativism is *not* the claim that cultures don't see eye to eye on moral issues; rather, it's the (much stronger) claim that all their respective views are true—or, at least, true-within-their-respective-cultures.

Should we be cultural relativists? Should we think that culture determines not just what we *believe* to be right and wrong, but what's *actually* right and wrong?

It's a tempting view. However, this isn't the sort of thing you want to be mistaken about, so we'd better not jump to conclusions. If cultural relativism is true, then we might need to rethink (for example) the way we intervene to prevent human rights violations. After all, if cultural relativism is true, then the things that *our* culture regards as human rights violations *aren't* human rights violations in the cultures that tolerate those practices. However, if cultural relativism is false, then perhaps we should be more concerned to disrupt traditions like female genital mutilation. Given the huge costs to the victims, why shouldn't we stop it from happening insofar as we can?

So let's just consider one of the main factors that seems to push people toward relativism—namely, *persistent disagreement*.

The idea is as follows. If I like vanilla, and you like chocolate, it doesn't seem to matter how much we rave about our respective favorites: I'll still think that vanilla is the best, and you'll still believe that chocolate deserves that accolade. In the face of this disagreement, the natural conclusion is that there's no fact of the matter about which is better. I like vanilla more, and so it's true—for me—that it's the best. You like chocolate best, and so it's true—for you—that chocolate is the best. But there's no "absolute" truth here; there is just truth relative to people's preferences.

Cultural relativism approaches ethics the same way. People continue to disagree about moral matters, and there doesn't seem to be much we can say—if anything—to change people's minds. So, the natural conclusion is that there's no fact of the matter about what's right and wrong. Ethics is just the name we give to the preferences of particular groups.

This argument may carry the day. But it's worth noting that we've got *another* way to explain disagreement. We are, after all, beings who rely heavily on our intuitive responses to situations; we tend not to reason deeply about moral matters. Moreover, people are often ignorant of the empirical facts that are relevant in moral disputes, though they aren't willing to admit as much. (Would policy X really have consequence Y? Well, we're not sure. But we'll certainly make up something that sounds good.) And, of course, we often have a horse in the race, which makes us unwilling to think things through in a dispassionate way. (If I'm a wealthy white male, I might want to preserve laws that benefit wealthy white males—even if I can see that they're horrendously bad for other people.)

So now we have two competing explanations of persistent disagreement: On the one hand, there's the claim that there's no fact of the matter; on the other, there's the claim that there *is* a fact of the matter, but there are a thousand hurdles to our determining what it is. With respect to the example mentioned earlier, there are two options. On the one hand, there's the claim that there's no trans-cultural fact of the matter as to whether female genital mutilation is morally wrong; whether it's right or wrong just depends on the culture that you're in. That's cultural relativism. On the other, there is the claim that there *is* a fact of the matter, and it's just really hard for some people to see that. That position is called *objectivism*.

Which should you believe? The choice isn't simple or straightforward. Let me just make a few observations.

First, it's easy to overstate how much disagreement there is. Sure, we disagree about all sorts of things. But again, that's often because we disagree about empirical questions, because we are motivated reasoners, and because we are stuck in traditional ways of thinking that we can't—or don't want to—escape. Moreover, the vast majority of people in the vast majority of cultures share a lot of moral views. There are general prohibitions against murder and theft and lying and rape and plenty of other things. It isn't just disagreement that requires explanation, but agreement too. Cultural relativists have something to say here: They can argue that different cultures have chosen to solve various social problems by adopting similar moral principles, but it's still the culture that gives those principles their authority. And maybe that's a satisfying story. But the convergence is quite striking, and objectivism provides a natural way of thinking about it: Just as agreement in science is some evidence that we're on the right track, agreement in ethics is some evidence we're on the right track.

Second, cultural relativism isn't necessarily the *tolerant* answer. The idea that we should be tolerant is a moral idea: It's the thought that it's morally good to be respectful of the views of others, allowing them to pursue what seems best to them. If cultural relativism is true, though, then the claim that we ought to be tolerant is just one more commitment of our culture. It's true here, but it's no fault of any other culture if they refuse to be tolerant. So, if you think that the intolerant people are making a mistake—that they can't simply defend their intolerance by saying that it's their culture—then you sound like an objectivist.

Third, objectivism doesn't mean that your views are the correct views. It isn't the (truly arrogant) claim that you've got everything figured out. As I mentioned, the objectivist thinks that *there are a thousand hurdles to determining what the truth is*. That's why the objectivist thinks we have to work really hard to figure out what's right, engaging in careful argumentation. Cultural relativists don't think we need to do that. They think we just need to do some sociology. On their view, if you want to know what morality requires in the United States, do some surveys. Of course, the objectivist agrees that if we want to know what people *believe* about morality, then surveys are a great idea. But the objectivist doesn't think that surveys can tell you whether those people are correct. And if you think that the majority can get things very seriously wrong—if you think that most people in a culture can believe one thing, and yet the opposite can be true—then yet again, you sound like an objectivist.

Fourth, let me just put my cards on the table. I'm inclined to say that there is a fact of the matter about whether female genital mutilation is wrong. But let's suppose you aren't. Instead, you think that everything is up to your culture. Even if that's right, *we still have to talk to people who support female genital mutilation.* Or, at the very least, we're going to have to talk to people who disagree with us about abortion, or the scope of the right to bear arms, or how we should change to mitigate the threat of climate change. In this messy, interconnected, highly globalized world, we're going to have conversations with people who deeply disagree with us about moral matters. Sometimes we'll have to make decisions that affect them, or we'll have to make decisions together. When that happens, we'll need to think about how to dialogue well. We'll have to figure out how to talk about our values, and theirs, and how to reason together toward conclusions that everyone can accept—or at least live with. We can't avoid moral debate, even as skeptics about morality.

The upshot is this. You can think that there are facts of the matter in ethics— that we can get it wrong, sometimes do, and need to discover the truth. Or you can be a pragmatist about ethics. You can think that there aren't any facts, and yet our values still help us coordinate our lives, and as the world becomes more connected, it becomes harder and harder to avoid negotiations about how, exactly, the coordination should go. Healthy skepticism takes seriously the possibility that we're making things up as we go along. *Unhealthy* skepticism says that if we're making things up as we go along, then ethics doesn't matter. Don't believe it.

GOING FORWARD

That should be enough to get you started. As you go forward, here are a few things to keep in mind:

1. Ethics isn't about the law, or about what you'd do, or what's sensible. It's about what you *should* do, even if the law isn't on your side, or you'd normally never act that way, or that course of action seems a bit radical.
2. Your gut response can be wrong. Obviously, you aren't going to completely bracket what seems true to you. At the same time, you don't need to believe everything you think. (Protip: Talk with people who don't share your beliefs. No one is better at noticing your mistakes than someone who disagrees with you.)

3. You're about to spend a lot of time reading and thinking about arguments. Figure out their structure. Then, figure out whether they're any good.

4. When people disagree very deeply, it's easy for conversations to devolve into mudslinging. You've got to work pretty hard to avoid this. It's challenging to engage in serious, informed, and humble dialogue. It's often frustrating to listen carefully and charitably to a view that you regard as very seriously wrong. But it isn't clear that we have any better options. Sure, it would be nice if things were easier. But since they aren't, let's not pretend otherwise.

5. Remember: This is not ethics training. I'm not here to teach you what to think. If you ever feel like this book is pointless, ask yourself whether you've been waiting for a sound bite—for some "gotcha" line that will silence your roommate. If that's what you want, check out memes on reddit. Here, we're after arguments. And let me tell you: They're pretty fascinating.

"WHAT UTILITARIANISM IS"
JOHN STUART MILL

John Stuart Mill (1806–1873) was a British philosopher and politician. Although he didn't invent utilitarianism—that was Jeremy Bentham's (1748–1832) claim to fame—Mill developed and defended it systematically. In this short excerpt from his book, Mill explains what it is to say that the principle of utility—the "Greatest Happiness Principle"—is "the foundations of morals." There are lots of questions to answer. What is happiness? What's really valuable? What's the relationship between the Greatest Happiness Principle and the Golden Rule? Does the Greatest Happiness Principle ask too much of us? Can religious people get on board with it? As you work through this text, do your best to figure out Mill's answers.

The creed which accepts as the foundation of morals, Utility, or the Greatest Happiness Principle, holds that actions are right in proportion as they tend to promote happiness, wrong as they tend to produce the reverse of happiness. By happiness is intended pleasure, and the absence of pain; by unhappiness, pain, and the privation of pleasure. To give a clear view of the moral standard set up by the theory, much more requires to be said; in particular, what things it includes in the ideas of pain and pleasure; and to what extent this is left an open question. But these supplementary explanations do not affect the theory of life on which this theory of morality is grounded—namely, that pleasure, and freedom from pain, are the only things desirable as ends; and that all desirable things (which are as numerous in the utilitarian as in any other scheme) are desirable either for the pleasure inherent in themselves, or as means to the promotion of pleasure and the prevention of pain . . .

Now, such a theory of life excites in many minds . . . inveterate dislike. To suppose that life has (as they express it) no higher end than pleasure—no better and nobler object of desire and pursuit—they designate as utterly mean and grovelling; as a doctrine worthy only of swine, to whom the followers of Epicurus were, at a very early period, contemptuously likened . . .

When thus attacked, the Epicureans have always answered, that it is not they, but their accusers, who represent human nature in a degrading light; since the accusation supposes human beings to be capable of no pleasures except those of which swine are capable . . . Human beings have faculties more elevated than the animal appetites, and when once made conscious of them, do not regard anything as happiness which does not include their gratification . . . [T]here is no known Epicurean theory of life which does not assign to the pleasures of the intellect, of the feelings and imagination, and of the moral sentiments, a much higher value as pleasures than to those of mere sensation . . . It is quite compatible with the principle of utility to recognise the fact, that some kinds of pleasure are more desirable and more valuable than others. It would be absurd that while, in

An excerpt from Chapter 2 of *Utilitarianism* (1863)

estimating all other things, quality is considered as well as quantity, the estimation of pleasures should be supposed to depend on quantity alone.

If I am asked, what I mean by difference of quality in pleasures, or what makes one pleasure more valuable than another, merely as a pleasure, except its being greater in amount, there is but one possible answer. Of two pleasures, if there be one to which all or almost all who have experience of both give a decided preference, irrespective of any feeling of moral obligation to prefer it, that is the more desirable pleasure. If one of the two is, by those who are competently acquainted with both, placed so far above the other that they prefer it, even though knowing it to be attended with a greater amount of discontent, and would not resign it for any quantity of the other pleasure which their nature is capable of, we are justified in ascribing to the preferred enjoyment a superiority in quality, so far outweighing quantity as to render it, in comparison, of small account . . .

From this verdict of the only competent judges, I apprehend there can be no appeal. On a question which is the best worth having of two pleasures, or which of two modes of existence is the most grateful to the feelings, apart from its moral attributes and from its consequences, the judgment of those who are qualified by knowledge of both, or, if they differ, that of the majority among them, must be admitted as final . . .

According to the Greatest Happiness Principle, as above explained, the ultimate end, with reference to and for the sake of which all other things are desirable (whether we are considering our own good or that of other people), is an existence exempt as far as possible from pain, and as rich as possible in enjoyments, both in point of quantity and quality; the test of quality, and the rule for measuring it against quantity, being the preference felt by those who in their opportunities of experience, to which must be added their habits of self-consciousness and self-observation, are best furnished with the means of comparison. This, being, according to the utilitarian opinion, the end of human action, is necessarily also the standard of morality; which may accordingly be defined, the rules and precepts for human conduct, by the observance of which an existence such as has been described might be, to the greatest extent possible, secured to all mankind; and not to them only, but, so far as the nature of things admits, to the whole sentient creation . . .

[T]he happiness which forms the utilitarian standard of what is right in conduct, is not the agent's own happiness, but that of all concerned. As between his own happiness and that of others, utilitarianism requires him to be as strictly impartial as a disinterested and benevolent spectator. In the golden rule of Jesus of Nazareth, we read the complete spirit of the ethics of utility. To do as you would be done by, and to love your neighbour as yourself, constitute the ideal perfection of utilitarian morality. As the means of making the nearest approach to this ideal, utility would enjoin, first, that laws and social arrangements should place the happiness, or (as speaking practically it may be called) the interest, of every individual, as nearly as possible in harmony with the interest of the whole; and secondly, that education and opinion, which have so vast a power over human character, should so use that power as to establish in the mind of every individual an indissoluble association between his own happiness and the good of the whole; especially between his own happiness and the practice of such modes of conduct, negative and positive, as regard for the universal happiness prescribes; so that not only he may be unable to conceive the possibility of happiness to himself, consistently with conduct opposed to the general good, but also that a direct impulse to promote the general good may be in every individual one of the habitual motives of action, and the sentiments connected therewith may fill a large and prominent place in every human being's sentient existence. If the impugners of the utilitarian morality represented it to their own minds in this, its true character, I know not what recommendation possessed by any other morality they could possibly affirm to be wanting to it; what more beautiful or more exalted developments of human nature any other ethical system can be supposed to foster, or what springs of action, not accessible to the utilitarian, such systems rely on for giving effect to their mandates.

The objectors to utilitarianism cannot always be charged with representing it in a discreditable light. On the contrary, those among them who entertain anything like a just idea of its disinterested character, sometimes find fault with its standard as being too high for humanity. They say it is exacting too much to require that people shall always act from the inducement of promoting the general interests of society. But this is to mistake the very meaning of a standard of morals, and confound the rule of action with the motive of it. It is the business of ethics to tell us what are our duties, or by what test we may know them; but no system of ethics requires that the sole motive of all we do shall be a feeling of duty; on the contrary, ninety-nine hundredths of all our actions are done from other motives, and rightly so done, if the rule of duty does not condemn them. It is the more unjust to utilitarianism that this particular misapprehension should be made a ground of objection to it, inasmuch as utilitarian moralists have gone beyond almost all others in affirming that the motive has nothing to do with the morality of the action, though much with the worth of the agent. He who saves a fellow creature from drowning does what is morally right, whether his motive be duty, or the hope of being paid for his trouble; he who betrays the friend that trusts him, is guilty of a crime, even if his object be to serve another friend to whom he is under greater obligations.

But to speak only of actions done from the motive of duty, and in direct obedience to principle: it is a misapprehension of the utilitarian mode of thought, to conceive it as implying that people should fix their minds upon so wide a generality as the world, or society at large. The great majority of good actions are intended not for the benefit of the world, but for that of individuals, of which the good of the world is made up; and the thoughts of the most virtuous man need not on these occasions travel beyond the particular persons concerned, except so far as is necessary to assure himself that in benefiting them he is not violating the rights, that is, the legitimate and authorised expectations, of any one else. The multiplication of happiness is, according to the utilitarian ethics, the object of virtue: the occasions on which any person (except one in a thousand) has it in his power to do this on an extended scale, in other words to be a public benefactor, are but exceptional; and on these occasions alone is he called on to consider public utility; in every other case, private utility, the interest or happiness of some few persons, is all he has to attend to. Those alone the influence of whose actions extends to society in general, need concern themselves habitually about so large an object. In the case of abstinences indeed—of things which people forbear to do from moral considerations, though the consequences in the particular case might be beneficial—it would be unworthy of an intelligent agent not to be consciously aware that the action is of a class which, if practised generally, would be generally injurious, and that this is the ground of the obligation to abstain from it. The amount of regard for the public interest implied in this recognition, is no greater than is demanded by every system of morals, for they all enjoin to abstain from whatever is manifestly pernicious to society.

The same considerations dispose of another reproach against the doctrine of utility, founded on a still grosser misconception of the purpose of a standard of morality, and of the very meaning of the words right and wrong. It is often affirmed that utilitarianism renders men cold and unsympathising; that it chills their moral feelings towards individuals; that it makes them regard only the dry and hard consideration of the consequences of actions, not taking into their moral estimate the qualities from which those actions emanate. If the assertion means that they do not allow their judgment respecting the rightness or wrongness of an action to be influenced by their opinion of the qualities of the person who does it, this is a complaint not against utilitarianism, but against having any standard of morality at all; for certainly no known ethical standard decides an action to be good or bad because it is done by a good or a bad man, still less because done by an amiable, a brave, or a benevolent man, or the contrary. These considerations are relevant, not to the estimation of actions, but of persons; and there is nothing in the utilitarian theory inconsistent with the fact that there are other things which interest us in persons besides the rightness and wrongness of their actions. The Stoics, indeed, with the paradoxical misuse of language which was part of their system, and by which they strove to raise themselves above all concern about anything but virtue, were fond of saying that he who has that has everything; that he, and only he, is rich, is beautiful, is a king. But no claim of this description is made for the virtuous man by the utilitarian doctrine. Utilitarians are quite aware that there are other desirable possessions and qualities besides virtue, and are perfectly willing to allow to all of them their full worth. They are also aware that a right action does not necessarily indicate a virtuous character, and that actions which are blamable, often proceed from qualities entitled to praise. When this is apparent in any particular case, it modifies their estimation, not certainly of the act, but of the agent. I grant that they are, notwithstanding, of opinion, that in the long run the best proof of a good character is good actions; and resolutely refuse to consider any mental disposition as good, of which the predominant tendency is to produce bad conduct. This makes them unpopular with many people; but it is an unpopularity which they must share with every one who regards the distinction between right and wrong in a serious light; and the reproach is not one which a conscientious utilitarian need be anxious to repel.

If no more be meant by the objection than that many utilitarians look on the morality of actions, as measured by the utilitarian standard, with too exclusive a regard, and do not lay sufficient stress upon the other beauties of character which go towards making a human being lovable or admirable, this may be admitted. Utilitarians who have cultivated their moral feelings, but not their sympathies nor their artistic perceptions, do fall into this mistake; and so do all other moralists under the same conditions. What can be said in excuse for other moralists is equally available for them, namely, that, if there is to be any error, it is better that it should be on that side. As a matter of fact, we may affirm that among utilitarians as among adherents of other systems, there is every imaginable degree of rigidity and of laxity in the application of their standard: some are even puritanically rigorous, while others are as indulgent as can possibly be desired by sinner or by sentimentalist. But on the whole, a doctrine which brings prominently forward the interest that mankind have in the repression and prevention of conduct which violates the moral law, is likely to be inferior to no other in turning the sanctions of opinion against such violations. It is true, the question, What does violate the moral law? is one on which those who recognise different standards of morality are likely now and then to differ. But difference of opinion on moral questions was not first introduced into the world by utilitarianism, while that doctrine does supply, if not always an easy, at all events a tangible and intelligible mode of deciding such differences.

It may not be superfluous to notice a few more of the common misapprehensions of utilitarian ethics . . . We not uncommonly hear the doctrine of utility inveighed against as a godless doctrine. If it be necessary to say anything at all against so mere an assumption, we may say that the question depends upon what idea we have formed of the moral character of the Deity. If it be a true belief that God desires, above all things, the happiness of his creatures, and that this was his purpose in their creation, utility is not only not a godless doctrine, but more profoundly religious than any other. If it be meant that utilitarianism does not recognise the revealed will of God as the supreme law of morals, I answer, that a utilitarian who believes in the perfect goodness and wisdom of God, necessarily believes that whatever God has thought fit to reveal on the subject of morals, must fulfil the requirements of utility in a supreme degree. But others besides utilitarians have been of opinion that the Christian revelation was intended, and is fitted, to inform the hearts and minds of mankind with a spirit which should enable them to find for themselves what is right, and incline them to do it when found, rather than to tell them, except in a very general way, what it is; and that we need a doctrine of ethics, carefully followed out, to interpret to us the will God. Whether this opinion is correct or not, it is superfluous here to discuss; since whatever aid religion, either natural or revealed, can afford to ethical investigation, is as open to the utilitarian moralist as to any other. He can use it as the testimony of God to the usefulness or hurt-fulness of any given course of action, by as good a right as others can use it for the indication of a transcendental law, having no connection with usefulness or with happiness.

Again, Utility is often summarily stigmatised as an immoral doctrine by giving it the name of Expediency, and taking advantage of the popular use of that term to contrast it with Principle. But the Expedient, in the sense in which it is opposed to the Right, generally means that which is expedient for the particular interest of the agent himself; as when a minister sacrifices the interests of his country to keep himself in place. When it means anything better than this, it means that which is expedient for some immediate object, some temporary pur-pose, but which violates a rule whose observance is expedient in a much higher degree. The Expedient, in this sense, instead of being the same thing with the useful, is a branch of the hurtful . . .

Again, defenders of utility often find themselves called upon to reply to such objections as this—that there is not time, previous to action, for calculat-ing and weighing the effects of any line of conduct on the general happiness . . . The answer to the objection is, that there has been ample time, namely, the whole past duration of the human species. During all that time, mankind have been learning by experience the tendencies of actions; on which experience all the prudence, as well as all the morality of life, are dependent. People talk as if the commencement of this course of experience had hitherto been put off, and as if, at the moment when some man feels tempted to meddle with the property or life of another, he had to begin considering for the first time whether murder and theft are injurious to human happiness. Even then I do not think that he would find the question very puzzling; but, at all events, the matter is now done to his hand.

It is truly a whimsical supposition that, if mankind were agreed in consider-ing utility to be the test of morality, they would remain without any agreement as to what is useful, and would take no measures for having their notions on the subject taught to the young, and enforced by law and opinion. There is no diffi-culty in proving any ethical standard whatever to work ill, if we suppose univer-sal idiocy to be conjoined with it; but on any hypothesis short of that, mankind must by this time have acquired positive beliefs as to the effects of some actions on their happiness; and the beliefs which have thus come down are the rules of morality for the multitude, and for the philosopher until he has succeeded in finding better . . .

But to consider the rules of morality as improvable, is one thing; to pass over the intermediate generalisations entirely, and endeavour to test each individual action directly by the first principle, is another. It is a strange notion that the acknowledgment of a first principle is inconsistent with the admission of second-ary ones. To inform a traveller respecting the place of his ultimate destination, is not to forbid the use of landmarks and direction-posts on the way. The proposi-tion that happiness is the end and aim of morality, does not mean that no road ought to be laid down to that goal, or that persons going thither should not be advised to take one direction rather than another. Men really ought to leave off talking a kind of nonsense on this subject, which they would neither talk nor listen to on other matters of practical concernment. Nobody argues that the art of navigation is not founded on astronomy, because sailors cannot wait to calculate the Nautical Almanack. Being rational creatures, they go to sea with it ready calculated; and all rational creatures go out upon the sea of life with their minds made up on the common questions of right and wrong, as well as on many of the far more difficult questions of wise and foolish. And this, as long as foresight is a human quality, it is to be presumed they will continue to do. Whatever we adopt as the fundamental principle of morality, we require subordinate principles to apply it by; the impossibility of doing without them, being common to all systems, can afford no argument against any one in particular; but gravely to argue as if no such secondary principles could be had, and as if mankind had remained till now, and always must remain, without drawing any general conclusions from the experience of human life, is as high a pitch, I think, as absurdity has ever reached in philosophical controversy.

The remainder of the stock arguments against utilitarianism mostly consist in laying to its charge the common infirmities of human nature, and the general difficulties which embarrass conscientious persons in shaping their course through life. We are told that a utilitarian will be apt to make his own particular case an exception to moral rules, and, when under temptation, will see a utility in the breach of a rule, greater than he will see in its observance. But is utility the only creed which is able to furnish us with excuses for evil doing, and means of cheating our own conscience? They are afforded in abundance by all doctrines which recognise as a fact in morals the existence of conflicting considerations; which all doctrines do, that have been believed by sane persons. It is not the fault of any creed, but of the complicated nature of human affairs, that rules of conduct cannot be so framed as to require no exceptions, and that hardly any kind of action can safely be laid down as either always obligatory or always condemnable. There is no ethical creed which does not temper the rigidity of its laws, by giving a certain latitude, under the moral responsibility of the agent, for accommodation to peculiarities of circumstances; and under every creed, at the opening thus made, self-deception and dishonest casuistry get in. There exists no moral system under which there do not arise unequivocal cases of conflicting obligation. These are the real difficulties, the knotty points both in the theory of ethics, and in the conscientious guidance of personal conduct. They are overcome practically, with greater or with less success, according to the intellect and virtue of the individual; but it can hardly be pretended that any one will be the less qualified for dealing with them, from possessing an ultimate standard to which conflicting rights and duties can be referred. If utility is the ultimate source of moral obligations, utility may be invoked to decide between them when their demands are incompatible. Though the application of the standard may be difficult, it is better than none at all: while in other systems, the moral laws all claiming independent authority, there is no common umpire entitled to interfere between them; their claims to precedence one over another rest on little better than sophistry, and unless determined, as they generally are, by the unacknowledged influence of considerations of utility, afford a free scope for the action of personal desires and partialities. We must remember that only in these cases of conflict between secondary principles is it requisite that first principles should be appealed to. There is no case of moral obligation in which some secondary principle is not involved; and if only one, there can seldom be any real doubt which one it is, in the mind of any person by whom the principle itself is recognised.

COMPREHENSION QUESTIONS

1. On Mill's view, what is the foundation of morals?
2. Mill distinguishes between the "rule of action" and the motive of action. What's the point of drawing this distinction?
3. Mill thinks that religious people can be utilitarians; he doesn't see any tension there. Why might someone think that there is a tension, and why doesn't Mill agree?
4. What's the point of the Expediency/Principle distinction?
5. Mill says that "[t]here is no difficulty in proving any ethical standard whatever to work ill, if we suppose universal idiocy to be conjoined with it." What's the objection to which he's responding, and what point is he making?

FUNDAMENTAL PRINCIPLES OF THE
METAPHYSICS OF MORALS
IMMANUEL KANT

Immanuel Kant (1724–1804) is a towering figure in the philosophical world, and certainly the most important German philosopher. His work on ethics is particularly famous, and what follows is a short excerpt from his *Fundamental Principles of the Metaphysics of Morals*. Kant thinks that our wills are what matter, not the consequences of our actions. In other words, what matters is that you act for the right reasons, not that you produce the best results. According to Kant, there are two ways to test whether you're acting for the right reasons. First, you can check to see whether everyone could act based on the principle that guides your action. Second, you can check to see whether you're treating people as ends in themselves, rather than as things at your disposal.

The Good Will

Nothing can possibly be conceived in the world, or even out of it, which can be called good, without qualification, except a good will. Intelligence, wit, judgement, and the other talents of the mind, however they may be named, or courage, resolution, perseverance, as qualities of temperament, are undoubtedly good and desirable in many respects; but these gifts of nature may also become extremely bad and mischievous if the will which is to make use of them, and which, therefore, constitutes what is called character, is not good. It is the same with the gifts of fortune. Power, riches, honour, even health, and the general well-being and contentment with one's condition which is called happiness, inspire pride, and often presumption, if there is not a good will to correct the influence of these on the mind, and with this also to rectify the whole principle of acting and adapt it to its end. The sight of a being who is not adorned with a single feature of a pure and good will, enjoying unbroken prosperity, can never give pleasure to an impartial rational spectator. Thus a good will appears to constitute the indispensable condition even of being worthy of happiness.

There are even some qualities which are of service to this good will itself and may facilitate its action, yet which have no intrinsic unconditional value, but always presuppose a good will, and this qualifies the esteem that we justly have for them and does not permit us to regard them as absolutely good. Moderation in the affections and passions, self-control, and calm deliberation are not only good in many respects, but even seem to constitute part of the intrinsic worth of the person; but they are far from deserving to be called good without qualification, although they have been so unconditionally praised by the ancients. For without the principles of a good will, they may become extremely bad, and the coolness of a villain not only makes him far more dangerous, but also directly makes him more abominable in our eyes than he would have been without it.

1785; translated by Thomas Kingsmill Abbott (http://www.gutenberg.org/files/5682/5682-h/5682-h.htm)

A good will is good not because of what it performs or effects, not by its aptness for the attainment of some proposed end, but simply by virtue of the volition; that is, it is good in itself, and considered by itself is to be esteemed much higher than all that can be brought about by it in favour of any inclination, nay even of the sum total of all inclinations. Even if it should happen that, owing to special disfavour of fortune, or the niggardly provision of a step-motherly nature, this will should wholly lack power to accomplish its purpose, if with its greatest efforts it should yet achieve nothing, and there should remain only the good will (not, to be sure, a mere wish, but the summoning of all means in our power), then, like a jewel, it would still shine by its own light, as a thing which has its whole value in itself. Its usefulness or fruitlessness can neither add nor take away anything from this value. It would be, as it were, only the setting to enable us to handle it the more conveniently in common commerce, or to attract to it the attention of those who are not yet connoisseurs, but not to recommend it to true connoisseurs, or to determine its value . . .

We have then to develop the notion of a will which deserves to be highly esteemed for itself and is good without a view to anything further, a notion which exists already in the sound natural understanding, requiring rather to be cleared up than to be taught, and which in estimating the value of our actions always takes the first place and constitutes the condition of all the rest. In order to do this, we will take the notion of duty, which includes that of a good will, although implying certain subjective restrictions and hindrances. These, however, far from concealing it, or rendering it unrecognizable, rather bring it out by contrast and make it shine forth so much the brighter.

I omit here all actions which are already recognized as inconsistent with duty, although they may be useful for this or that purpose, for with these the question whether they are done from duty cannot arise at all, since they even conflict with it. I also set aside those actions which really conform to duty, but to which men have no direct inclination, performing them because they are impelled thereto by some other inclination. For in this case we can readily distinguish whether the action which agrees with duty is done from duty, or from a selfish view. It is much harder to make this distinction when the action accords with duty and the subject has besides a direct inclination to it. For example, it is always a matter of duty that a dealer should not overcharge an inexperienced purchaser; and wherever there is much commerce the prudent tradesman does not overcharge, but keeps a fixed price for everyone, so that a child buys of him as well as any other. Men are thus honestly served; but this is not enough to make us believe that the tradesman has so acted from duty and from principles of honesty: his own advantage required it; it is out of the question in this case to suppose that he might besides have a direct inclination in favour of the buyers, so that, as it were, from love he should give no advantage to one over another. Accordingly the action was done neither from duty nor from direct inclination, but merely with a selfish view.

On the other hand, it is a duty to maintain one's life; and, in addition, everyone has also a direct inclination to do so. But on this account the often anxious care which most men take for it has no intrinsic worth, and their maxim has no moral import. They preserve their life as duty requires, no doubt, but not because duty requires. On the other hand, if adversity and hopeless sorrow have completely taken away the relish for life; if the unfortunate one, strong in mind, indignant at his fate rather than desponding or dejected, wishes for death, and yet preserves his life without loving it—not from inclination or fear, but from duty—then his maxim has a moral worth.

To be beneficent when we can is a duty; and besides this, there are many minds so sympathetically constituted that, without any other motive of vanity or self-interest, they find a pleasure in spreading joy around them and can take delight in the satisfaction of others so far as it is their own work. But I maintain that in such a case an action of this kind, however proper, however amiable it may be, has nevertheless no true moral worth, but is on a level with other inclinations, e.g., the inclination to honour, which, if it is happily directed to that which is in fact of public utility and accordant with duty and consequently honourable, deserves praise and encouragement, but not esteem. For the maxim lacks the moral import, namely, that such actions be done from duty, not from inclination. Put the case that the mind of that philanthropist were clouded by sorrow of his own, extinguishing all sympathy with the lot of others, and that, while he still has the power to benefit others in distress, he is not touched by their trouble because he is absorbed with his own; and now suppose that he tears himself out of this dead insensibility, and performs the action without any inclination to it, but simply from duty, then first has his action its genuine moral worth. Further still; if nature has put little sympathy in the heart of this or that man; if he, supposed to be an upright man, is by temperament cold and indifferent to the sufferings of others, perhaps because in respect of his own he is provided with the special gift of patience and fortitude and supposes, or even requires, that others should have the same—and such a man would certainly not be the meanest product of nature—but if nature had not specially framed him for a philanthropist, would he not still find in himself a source from whence to give himself a far higher worth than that of a good-natured temperament could be? Unquestionably. It is just in this that the moral worth of the character is brought out which is incomparably the highest of all, namely, that he is beneficent, not from inclination, but from duty . . .

Thus the moral worth of an action does not lie in the effect expected from it, nor in any principle of action which requires to borrow its motive from this expected effect. For all these effects—agreeableness of one's condition and even the promotion of the happiness of others—could have been also brought about by other causes, so that for this there would have been no need of the will of a rational being; whereas it is in this alone that the supreme and unconditional good can be found. The pre-eminent good which we call moral can therefore consist in nothing else than the conception of law in itself, which certainly is only possible in a rational being, in so far as this conception, and not the expected effect, determines the will. This is a good which is already present in the person who acts accordingly, and we have not to wait for it to appear first in the result.

But what sort of law can that be, the conception of which must determine the will, even without paying any regard to the effect expected from it, in order that this will may be called good absolutely and without qualification? As I have deprived the will of every impulse which could arise to it from obedience to any law, there remains nothing but the universal conformity of its actions to law in general, which alone is to serve the will as a principle, i.e., I am never to act otherwise than so that I could also will that my maxim should become a universal law. Here, now, it is the simple conformity to law in general, without assuming any particular law applicable to certain actions, that serves the will as its principle and must so serve it, if duty is not to be a vain delusion and a chimerical notion. The common reason of men in its practical judgements perfectly coincides with this and always has in view the principle here suggested. Let the question be, for example: May I when in distress make a promise with the intention not to keep it? I readily distinguish here between the two significations which the question may have: Whether it is prudent, or whether it is right, to make a false promise? The former may undoubtedly often be the case. I see clearly indeed that it is not enough to extricate myself from a present difficulty by means of this subterfuge, but it must be well considered whether there may not hereafter spring from this lie much greater inconvenience than that from which I now free myself, and as, with all my supposed cunning, the consequences cannot be so easily foreseen but that credit once lost may be much more injurious to me than any mischief which I seek to avoid at present, it should be considered whether it would not be more prudent to act herein according to a universal maxim and to make it a habit to promise nothing except with the intention of keeping it. But it is soon clear to me that such a maxim will still only be based on the fear of consequences. Now it is a wholly different thing to be truthful from duty and to be so from apprehension of injurious consequences. In the first case, the very notion of the action already implies a law for me; in the second case, I must first look about elsewhere to see what results may be combined with it which would affect myself. For to deviate from the principle of duty is beyond all doubt wicked; but to be unfaithful to my maxim of prudence may often be very advantageous to me, although to abide by it is certainly safer. The shortest way, however, and an unerring one, to discover the answer to this question whether a lying promise is consistent with duty, is to ask myself, "Should I be content that my maxim (to extricate myself from difficulty by a false promise) should hold good as a universal law, for myself as well as for others?" and should I be able to say to myself, "Every one may make a deceitful promise when he finds himself in a difficulty from which he cannot otherwise extricate himself?" Then I presently become aware that while I can will the lie, I can by no means will that lying should be a universal law. For with such a law there would be no promises at all, since it would be in vain to allege my intention in regard to my future actions to those who would not believe this allegation, or if they over hastily did so would pay me back in my own coin. Hence my maxim, as soon as it should be made a universal law, would necessarily destroy itself.

I do not, therefore, need any far-reaching penetration to discern what I have to do in order that my will may be morally good. Inexperienced in the course of the world, incapable of being prepared for all its contingencies, I only ask myself: Canst thou also will that thy maxim should be a universal law? If not, then it must be rejected, and that not because of a disadvantage accruing from it to myself or even to others, but because it cannot enter as a principle into a possible universal legislation, and reason extorts from me immediate respect for such legislation. I do not indeed as yet discern on what this respect is based (this the philosopher may inquire), but at least I understand this, that it is an estimation of the worth which far outweighs all worth of what is recommended by inclination, and that the necessity of acting from pure respect for the practical law is what constitutes duty, to which every other motive must give place, because it is the condition of a will being good in itself, and the worth of such a will is above everything . . .

The Categorical Imperative

Now all imperatives command either hypothetically or categorically. The former represent the practical necessity of a possible action as means to something else that is willed (or at least which one might possibly will). The categorical imperative would be that which represented an action as necessary of itself without reference to another end, i.e., as objectively necessary.

Since every practical law represents a possible action as good and, on this account, for a subject who is practically determinable by reason, necessary, all imperatives are formulae determining an action which is necessary according to the principle of a will good in some respects. If now the action is good only as a means to something else, then the imperative is hypothetical; if it is conceived as good in itself and consequently as being necessarily the principle of a will which of itself conforms to reason, then it is categorical . . .

[T]here is an imperative which commands a certain conduct immediately, without having as its condition any other purpose to be attained by it. This imperative is categorical. It concerns not the matter of the action, or its intended result, but its form and the principle of which it is itself a result; and what is essentially good in it consists in the mental disposition, let the consequence be what it may. This imperative may be called that of morality . . .

When I conceive a hypothetical imperative, in general I do not know beforehand what it will contain until I am given the condition. But when I conceive a categorical imperative, I know at once what it contains. For as the imperative contains besides the law only the necessity that the maxims shall conform to this law, while the law contains no conditions restricting it, there remains nothing but the general statement that the maxim of the action should conform to a universal law, and it is this conformity alone that the imperative properly represents as necessary.

There is therefore but one categorical imperative, namely, this:

Act only on that maxim whereby thou canst at the same time will that it should become a universal law.

Now if all imperatives of duty can be deduced from this one imperative as from their principle, then, although it should remain undecided what is called duty is not merely a vain notion, yet at least we shall be able to show what we understand by it and what this notion means.

Since the universality of the law according to which effects are produced constitutes what is properly called nature in the most general sense (as to form), that is, the existence of things so far as it is determined by general laws, the imperative of duty may be expressed thus: Act as if the maxim of thy action were to become by thy will a universal law of nature.

We will now enumerate a few duties, adopting the usual division of them into duties to ourselves and to others, and into perfect and imperfect duties.

1. A man reduced to despair by a series of misfortunes feels wearied of life, but is still so far in possession of his reason that he can ask himself whether it would not be contrary to his duty to himself to take his own life. Now he inquires whether the maxim of his action could become a universal law of nature. His maxim is: "From self-love I adopt it as a principle to shorten my life when its longer duration is likely to bring more evil than satisfaction." It is asked then simply whether this principle founded on self-love can become a universal law of nature. Now we see at once that a system of nature of which it should be a law to destroy life by means of the very feeling whose special nature it is to impel to the improvement of life would contradict itself and, therefore, could not exist as a system of nature; hence that maxim cannot possibly exist as a universal law of nature and, consequently, would be wholly inconsistent with the supreme principle of all duty.

2. Another finds himself forced by necessity to borrow money. He knows that he will not be able to repay it, but sees also that nothing will be lent to him unless he promises stoutly to repay it in a definite time. He desires to make this promise, but he has still so much conscience as to ask himself: "Is it not unlawful and inconsistent with duty to get out of a difficulty in this way?" Suppose however that he resolves to do so: then the maxim of his action would be expressed thus: "When I think myself in want of money, I will borrow money and promise to repay it, although I know that I never can do so." Now this principle of self-love or of one's own advantage may perhaps be consistent with my whole future welfare; but the question now is, "Is it right?" I change then the suggestion of self-love into a universal law, and state the question thus: "How would it be if my maxim were a universal law?" Then I see at once that it could never hold as a universal law of nature, but would necessarily contradict itself. For supposing it to be a universal law that everyone when he thinks himself in a difficulty should be able to promise whatever he pleases, with the purpose of not keeping his promise, the promise itself would become impossible, as well as the end that one might have in view in it, since no one would consider that

anything was promised to him, but would ridicule all such statements as vain pretences.

3. A third finds in himself a talent which with the help of some culture might make him a useful man in many respects. But he finds himself in comfortable circumstances and prefers to indulge in pleasure rather than to take pains in enlarging and improving his happy natural capacities. He asks, however, whether his maxim of neglect of his natural gifts, besides agreeing with his inclination to indulgence, agrees also with what is called duty. He sees then that a system of nature could indeed subsist with such a universal law although men (like the South Sea islanders) should let their talents rest and resolve to devote their lives merely to idleness, amusement, and propagation of their species—in a word, to enjoyment; but he cannot possibly will that this should be a universal law of nature, or be implanted in us as such by a natural instinct. For, as a rational being, he necessarily wills that his faculties be developed, since they serve him and have been given him, for all sorts of possible purposes.

4. A fourth, who is in prosperity, while he sees that others have to contend with great wretchedness and that he could help them, thinks: "What concern is it of mine? Let everyone be as happy as Heaven pleases, or as he can make himself; I will take nothing from him nor even envy him, only I do not wish to contribute anything to his welfare or to his assistance in distress!" Now no doubt if such a mode of thinking were a universal law, the human race might very well subsist and doubtless even better than in a state in which everyone talks of sympathy and good-will, or even takes care occasionally to put it into practice, but, on the other side, also cheats when he can, betrays the rights of men, or otherwise violates them. But although it is possible that a universal law of nature might exist in accordance with that maxim, it is impossible to will that such a principle should have the universal validity of a law of nature. For a will which resolved this would contradict itself, inasmuch as many cases might occur in which one would have need of the love and sympathy of others, and in which, by such a law of nature, sprung from his own will, he would deprive himself of all hope of the aid he desires . . .

If now we attend to ourselves on occasion of any transgression of duty, we shall find that we in fact do not will that our maxim should be a universal law, for that is impossible for us; on the contrary, we will that the opposite should remain a universal law, only we assume the liberty of making an exception in our own favour or (just for this time only) in favour of our inclination. Consequently if we considered all cases from one and the same point of view, namely, that of reason, we should find a contradiction in our own will, namely, that a certain principle should be objectively necessary as a universal law, and yet subjectively should not be universal, but admit of exceptions . . .

Supposing, however, that there were something whose existence has in itself an absolute worth, something which, being an end in itself, could be a source of definite laws; then in this and this alone would lie the source of a possible categorical imperative, i.e., a practical law.

Now I say: man and generally any rational being exists as an end in himself, not merely as a means to be arbitrarily used by this or that will, but in all his actions, whether they concern himself or other rational beings, must be always regarded at the same time as an end. All objects of the inclinations have only a conditional worth, for if the inclinations and the wants founded on them did not exist, then their object would be without value. But the inclinations, themselves being sources of want, are so far from having an absolute worth for which they should be desired that on the contrary it must be the universal wish of every rational being to be wholly free from them. Thus the worth of any object which is to be acquired by our action is always conditional. Beings whose existence depends not on our will but on nature's, have nevertheless, if they are irrational beings, only a relative value as means, and are therefore called things; rational beings, on the contrary, are called persons, because their very nature points them out as ends in themselves, that is as something which must not be used merely as means, and so far therefore restricts freedom of action (and is an object of respect). These, therefore, are not merely subjective ends whose existence has a worth for us as an effect of our action, but objective ends, that is, things whose existence is an end in itself; an end moreover for which no other can be substituted, which they should subserve merely as means, for otherwise nothing whatever would possess absolute worth; but if all worth were conditioned and therefore contingent, then there would be no supreme practical principle of reason whatever.

If then there is a supreme practical principle or, in respect of the human will, a categorical imperative, it must be one which, being drawn from the conception of that which is necessarily an end for everyone because it is an end in itself, constitutes an objective principle of will, and can therefore serve as a universal practical law. The foundation of this principle is: rational nature exists as an end in itself. Man necessarily conceives his own existence as being so; so far then this is a subjective principle of human actions. But every other rational being regards its existence similarly, just on the same rational principle that holds for me: so that it is at the same time an objective principle, from which as a supreme practical law all laws of the will must be capable of being deduced. Accordingly the practical imperative will be as follows:

> So act as to treat humanity, whether in thine own person or in that of any other, in every case as an end withal, never as means only.

We will now inquire whether this can be practically carried out.

To abide by the previous examples:

Firstly, under the head of necessary duty to oneself: He who contemplates suicide should ask himself whether his action can be consistent with the idea of humanity as an end in itself. If he destroys himself in order to escape from painful circumstances, he uses a person merely as a means to maintain a tolerable condition up to the end of life. But a man is not a thing, that is to say, something which can be used merely as means, but must in all his actions be always considered as an end in himself. I cannot, therefore, dispose in any way of a man in my own person so as to mutilate him, to damage or kill him. (It belongs to ethics proper to define this principle more precisely, so as to avoid all misunderstanding, e.g., as to the amputation of the limbs in order to preserve myself, as to exposing my life to danger with a view to preserve it, etc. This question is therefore omitted here.)

Secondly, as regards necessary duties, or those of strict obligation, towards others: He who is thinking of making a lying promise to others will see at once that he would be using another man merely as a means, without the latter containing at the same time the end in himself. For he whom I propose by such a promise to use for my own purposes cannot possibly assent to my mode of acting towards him and, therefore, cannot himself contain the end of this action. This violation of the principle of humanity in other men is more obvious if we take in examples of attacks on the freedom and property of others. For then it is clear that he who transgresses the rights of men intends to use the person of others merely as a means, without considering that as rational beings they ought always to be esteemed also as ends, that is, as beings who must be capable of containing in themselves the end of the very same action.

Thirdly, as regards contingent (meritorious) duties to oneself: It is not enough that the action does not violate humanity in our own person as an end in itself, it must also harmonize with it. Now there are in humanity capacities of greater perfection, which belong to the end that nature has in view in regard to humanity in ourselves as the subject: to neglect these might perhaps be consistent with the maintenance of humanity as an end in itself, but not with the advancement of this end.

Fourthly, as regards meritorious duties towards others: The natural end which all men have is their own happiness. Now humanity might indeed subsist, although no one should contribute anything to the happiness of others, provided he did not intentionally withdraw anything from it; but after all this would only harmonize negatively not positively with humanity as an end in itself, if every one does not also endeavour, as far as in him lies, to forward the ends of others. For the ends of any subject which is an end in himself ought as far as possible to be my ends also, if that conception is to have its full effect with me.

COMPREHENSION QUESTIONS

1. What does Kant mean when he says that nothing is good except a good will?
2. Kant says that kindness to others has no moral value if you do it because it brings you joy to be kind. Why does he think this?
3. What, on Kant's view, is wrong with telling a lying promise?
4. What's the difference between hypothetical and categorical imperatives? Why does this distinction matter in Kant's ethics?
5. Kant states the categorical imperative in two ways: the universal law formulation and the humanity formulation. What's the difference? Are they saying the same thing?

THE ETHICS OF CARE
VIRGINIA HELD

Virginia Held (b. 1929) taught at Hunter College and the CUNY Graduate Center for many years. She's one of the most prominent defenders of the ethics of care, and in this excerpt from her book on that topic, she outlines the view. Held says that the ethics of care (1) starts with the relationships that tend to occupy us, (2) values our emotions, (3) rejects abstraction as the model for moral reasoning, (4) argues that the "private" sphere is actually political, and (5) understands people as relational rather than independent individuals. She also argues that care isn't simply an add-on to more fundamental concerns about justice and that care encourages us to transform society.

The Ethics of Care as Moral Theory

The ethics of care is only a few decades old. Some theorists do not like the term "care" to designate this approach to moral issues and have tried substituting "the ethic of love," or "relational ethics," but the discourse keeps returning to "care" as the so far more satisfactory of the terms considered, though dissatisfactions with it remain. The concept of care has the advantage of not losing sight of the work involved in caring for people and of not lending itself to the interpretation of morality as ideal but impractical to which advocates of the ethics of care often object. Care is both value and practice . . .

I think one can discern among various versions of the ethics of care a number of major features.

First, the central focus of the ethics of care is on the compelling moral salience of attending to and meeting the needs of the particular others for whom we take responsibility. Caring for one's child, for instance, may well and defensibly be at the forefront of a person's moral concerns. The ethics of care recognizes that human beings are dependent for many years of their lives, that the moral claim of those dependent on us for the care they need is pressing, and that there are highly important moral aspects in developing the relations of caring that enable human beings to live and progress. All persons need care for at least their early years. Prospects for human progress and flourishing hinge fundamentally on the care that those needing it receive, and the ethics of care stresses the moral force of the responsibility to respond to the needs of the dependent. Many persons will become ill and dependent for some periods of their later lives, including in frail old age, and some who are permanently disabled will need care the whole of their lives. Moralities built on the image of the independent, autonomous, rational individual largely overlook the reality of human dependence and the morality for which it calls. The ethics of care attends to this central concern of human life and delineates the moral values involved. It refuses to relegate care to a realm "outside morality." How caring for particular others should be

From Virginia Held, *The Ethics of Care: Personal, Political, and Global* (New York: Oxford University Press, 2006), 9–19.

reconciled with the claims of, for instance, universal justice is an issue that needs to be addressed. But the ethics of care starts with the moral claims of particular others, for instance, of one's child, whose claims can be compelling regardless of universal principles.

Second, in the epistemological process of trying to understand what morality would recommend and what it would be morally best for us to do and to be, the ethics of care values emotion rather than rejects it. Not all emotion is valued, of course, but in contrast with the dominant rationalist approaches, such emotions as sympathy, empathy, sensitivity, and responsiveness are seen as the kind of moral emotions that need to be cultivated not only to help in the implementation of the dictates of reason but to better ascertain what morality recommends. Even anger may be a component of the moral indignation that should be felt when people are treated unjustly or inhumanely, and it may contribute to (rather than interfere with) an appropriate interpretation of the moral wrong. This is not to say that raw emotion can be a guide to morality; feelings need to be reflected on and educated. But from the care perspective, moral inquiries that rely entirely on reason and rationalistic deductions or calculations are seen as deficient . . .

Third, the ethics of care rejects the view of the dominant moral theories that the more abstract the reasoning about a moral problem the better because the more likely to avoid bias and arbitrariness, the more nearly to achieve impartiality. The ethics of care respects rather than removes itself from the claims of particular others with whom we share actual relationships. It calls into question the universalistic and abstract rules of the dominant theories. When the latter consider such actual relations as between a parent and child, if they say anything about them at all, they may see them as permitted and cultivating them a preference that a person may have. Or they may recognize a universal obligation for all parents to care for their children. But they do not permit actual relations ever to take priority over the requirements of impartiality. As Brian Barry expresses this view, there can be universal rules permitting people to favor their friends in certain contexts, such as deciding to whom to give holiday gifts, but the latter partiality is morally acceptable only because universal rules have already so judged it. The ethics of care, in contrast, is skeptical of such abstraction and reliance on universal rules and questions the priority given to them. To most advocates of the ethics of care, the compelling moral claim of the particular other may be valid even when it conflicts with the requirement usually made by moral theories that moral judgments be universalizable, and this is of fundamental moral importance. Hence the potential conflict between care and justice, friendship and impartiality, loyalty and universality. To others, however, there need be no conflict if universal judgments come to incorporate appropriately the norms of care previously disregarded . . .

In trying to overcome the attitudes and problems of tribalism and religious intolerance, dominant moralities have tended to assimilate the domains of family and friendship to the tribal, or to a source of the unfair favoring of one's own. Or they have seen the attachments people have in these areas as among the nonmoral private preferences people are permitted to pursue if restrained by impartial moral norms. The ethics of care recognizes the moral value and importance of relations of family and friendship and the need for moral guidance in these domains to understand how existing relations should often be changed and new ones developed. Having grasped the value of caring relations in such contexts as these more personal ones, the ethics of care then often examines social and political arrangements in the light of these values. In its more developed forms, the ethics of care as a feminist ethic offers suggestions for the radical transformation of society. It demands not just equality for women in existing structures of society but equal consideration for the experience that reveals the values, importance, and moral significance, of caring.

A fourth characteristic of the ethics of care is that like much feminist thought in many areas, it reconceptualizes traditional notions about the public and the private. The traditional view, built into the dominant moral theories, is that the household is a private sphere beyond politics into which government, based on consent, should not intrude. Feminists have shown how the greater social, political, economic, and cultural power of men has structured this "private" sphere to the disadvantage of women and children, rendering them vulnerable to domestic violence without outside interference, often leaving women economically dependent on men and subject to a highly inequitable division of labor in the family. The law has not hesitated to intervene into women's private decisions concerning reproduction but has been highly reluctant to intrude on men's exercise of coercive power within the "castles" of their homes.

Dominant moral theories have seen "public" life as relevant to morality while missing the moral significance of the "private" domains of family and friendship. Thus the dominant theories have assumed that morality should be sought for unrelated, independent, and mutually indifferent individuals assumed to be equal. They have posited an abstract, fully rational "agent as such" from which to construct morality, while missing the moral issues that arise between interconnected persons in the contexts of family, friendship, and social groups. In the context of the family, it is typical for relations to be between persons with highly unequal power who did not choose the ties and obligations in which they find themselves enmeshed. For instance, no child can choose her parents yet she may well have obligations to care for them. Relations of this kind are standardly noncontractual, and conceptualizing them as contractual would often undermine or at least obscure the trust on which their worth depends. The ethics of care addresses rather than neglects moral issues arising in relations among the unequal and dependent, relations that are often laden with emotion and involuntary, and then notices how often these attributes apply not only in the household but in the wider society as well. For instance, persons do not choose which gender, racial, class, ethnic, religious, national, or cultural groups to be brought up in, yet these sorts of ties may be important aspects of who they are and how their experience can contribute to moral understanding.

A fifth characteristic of the ethics of care is the conception of persons with which it begins. This will be dealt with in the next section.

The Critique of Liberal Individualism

The ethics of care usually works with a conception of persons as relational, rather than as the self-sufficient independent individuals of the dominant moral theories. The dominant theories can be interpreted as importing into moral theory a concept of the person developed primarily for liberal political and economic theory, seeing the person as a rational, autonomous agent, or a self-interested individual . . . The ethics of care, in contrast, characteristically sees persons as relational and interdependent, morally and epistemologically. Every person starts out as a child dependent on those providing us care, and we remain interdependent with others in thoroughly fundamental ways throughout our lives. That we can think and act as if we were independent depends on a network of social relations making it possible for us to do so. And our relations are part of what constitute our identity. This is not to say that we cannot become autonomous; feminists have done much interesting work developing an alternative conception of autonomy in place of the liberal individualist one. Feminists have much experience rejecting or reconstituting relational ties that are oppressive. But it means that from the perspective of an ethics of care, to construct morality as if we were Robinson Crusoes, or, to use Hobbes's image, mushrooms sprung from nowhere, is misleading. As Eva Kittay writes, this conception fosters the illusion that society is composed of free, equal, and independent individuals who can choose to associate with one another or not. It obscures the very real facts of dependency for everyone when they are young, for most people at various periods in their lives when they are ill or old and infirm, for some who are disabled, and for all those engaged in unpaid "dependency work." And it obscures the innumerable ways persons and groups are interdependent in the modern world.

Not only does the liberal individualist conception of the person foster a false picture of society and the persons in it, it is, from the perspective of the ethics of care, impoverished also as an ideal. The ethics of care values the ties we have with particular other persons and the actual relationships that partly constitute our identity. Although persons often may and should reshape their relations with others—distancing themselves from some persons and groups and developing or strengthening ties with others—the autonomy sought within the ethics of care is a capacity to reshape and cultivate new relations, not to ever more closely resemble the unencumbered abstract rational self of liberal political and moral theories. Those motivated by the ethics of care would seek to become more admirable relational persons in better caring relations.

Even if the liberal ideal is meant only to instruct us on what would be rational in the terms of its ideal model, thinking of persons as the model presents them has effects that should not be welcomed. As Annette Baier writes, "Liberal morality, if unsupplemented, may unfit people to be anything other than what its justifying theories suppose them to be, ones who have no interest in each others' interests." There is strong empirical evidence of how adopting a theoretical model can lead to behavior that mirrors it. Various studies show that studying economics, with its "repeated and intensive exposure to a model whose unequivocal prediction" is that people will decide what to do on the basis of self-interest, leads economics students to be less cooperative and more inclined to free ride than other students.

The conception of the person adopted by the dominant moral theories provides moralities at best suitable for legal, political, and economic interactions between relative strangers, once adequate trust exists for them to form a political entity. The ethics of care is, instead, hospitable to the relatedness of persons. It sees many of our responsibilities as not freely entered into but presented to us by the accidents of our embeddedness in familial and social and historical contexts. It often calls on us to take responsibility, while liberal individualist morality focuses on how we should leave each other alone. The view of persons as embedded and encumbered seems fundamental to much feminist thinking about morality and especially to the ethics of care.

Justice and Care

Some conceptions of the ethics of care see it as contrasting with an ethic of justice in ways that suggest one must choose between them. Carol Gilligan's suggestion of alternative perspectives in interpreting and organizing the elements of a moral problem lent itself to this implication; she herself used the metaphor of the ambiguous figure of the vase and the faces, from psychological research on perception, to illustrate how one could see a problem as either a problem of justice or a problem of care, but not as both simultaneously.

An ethic of justice focuses on questions of fairness, equality, individual rights, abstract principles, and the consistent application of them. An ethic of care focuses on attentiveness, trust, responsiveness to need, narrative nuance, and cultivating caring relations. Whereas an ethic of justice seeks a fair solution between competing individual interests and rights, an ethic of care sees the interests of carers and cared-for as importantly intertwined rather than as simply competing. Whereas justice protects equality and freedom, care fosters social bonds and cooperation.

These are very different emphases in what morality should consider. Yet both deal with what seems of great moral importance. This has led many to explore how they might be combined in a satisfactory morality. One can persuasively argue, for instance, that justice is needed in such contexts of care as the family, to protect against violence and the unfair division of labor or treatment of children. One can also persuasively argue that care is needed in such contexts of justice as the streets and the courts, where persons should be treated humanely, and in the way education and health and welfare should be dealt with as social responsibilities. The implication may be that justice and care should not be separated into different "ethics," that, in Sara Ruddick's proposed approach, "justice is always seen in tandem with care."

Few would hold that considerations of justice have no place at all in care. One would not be caring well for two children, for instance, if one showed a persistent favoritism toward one of them that could not be justified on the basis of some such factor as greater need. The issues are rather what constellation of values have priority and which predominate in the practices of the ethics of care and the ethics of justice. It is quite possible to delineate significant differences between them. In the dominant moral theories of the ethics of justice, the values of equality, impartiality, fair distribution, and noninterference have priority; in practices of justice, individual rights are protected, impartial judgments are arrived at, punishments are deserved, and equal treatment is sought. In contrast, in the ethics of care, the values of trust, solidarity, mutual concern, and empathetic responsiveness have priority; in practices of care, relationships are cultivated, needs are responded to, and sensitivity is demonstrated.

An extended effort to integrate care and justice is offered by Diemut Bubeck. She makes clear that she "endorse[s] the ethic of care as a system of concepts, values, and ideas, arising from the practice of care as an organic part of this practice and responding to its material requirements, notably the meeting of needs." Yet her primary interest is in understanding the exploitation of women, which she sees as tied to the way women do most of the unpaid work of caring. She argues that such principles as equality in care and the minimization of harm are tacitly, if not explicitly, embedded in the practice of care, as carers whose capacities and time for engaging in caring labor are limited must decide how to respond to various others in need of being cared for. She writes that "far from being extraneous impositions . . . considerations of justice arise from within the practice of care itself and therefore are an important part of the ethic of care, properly understood." The ethics of care must thus also concern itself with the justice (or lack of it) of the ways the tasks of caring are distributed in society. Traditionally, women have been expected to do most of the caring work that needs to be done; the sexual division of labor exploits women by extracting unpaid care labor from them, making women less able than men to engage in paid work. "Femininity" constructs women as carers, contributing to the constraints by which women are pressed into accepting the sexual division of labor. An ethic of care that extols caring but that fails to be concerned with how the burdens of caring are distributed contributes to the exploitation of women, and of the minority groups whose members perform much of the paid but ill-paid work of caring in affluent households, in day care centers, hospitals, nursing homes, and the like.

The question remains, however, whether justice should be thought to be incorporated into any ethic of care that will be adequate or whether we should keep the notions of justice and care and their associated ethics conceptually distinct. There is much to be said for recognizing how the ethics of care values interrelatedness and responsiveness to the needs of particular others, how the ethics of justice values fairness and rights, and how these are different emphases. Too much integration will lose sight of these valid differences. I am more inclined to say that an adequate, comprehensive moral theory will have to include the insights of both the ethics of care and the ethics of justice, among other insights, rather than that either of these can be incorporated into the other in the sense of supposing that it can provide the grounds for the judgments characteristically found in the other. Equitable caring is not necessarily better caring, it is fairer caring. And humane justice is not necessarily better justice, it is more caring justice.

Almost no advocates of the ethics of care are willing to see it as a moral out-look less valuable than the dominant ethics of justice. To imagine that the concerns of care can merely be added on to the dominant theories, as, for instance, Stephen Darwall suggests, is seen as unsatisfactory. Confining the ethics of care to the private sphere while holding it unsuitable for public life, as Nel Noddings did at first and as many accounts of it suggest, is also to be rejected. But how care and justice are to be meshed without losing sight of their differing priorities is a task still being worked on.

My own suggestions for integrating care and justice are to keep these concepts conceptually distinct and to delineate the domains in which they should have priority. In the realm of law, for instance, justice and the assurance of rights should have priority, although the humane considerations of care should not be absent. In the realm of the family and among friends, priority should be given to expansive care, though the basic requirements of justice surely should also be met. But these are the clearest cases; others will combine moral urgencies. Universal human rights (including the social and economic ones as well as the political and civil) should certainly be respected, but promoting care across continents may be a more promising way to achieve this than mere rational recognition. When needs are desperate, justice may be a lessened requirement on shared responsibility for meeting needs, although this rarely excuses violations of rights. At the level of what constitutes a society in the first place, a domain within which rights are to be assured and care provided, appeal must be made to something like the often weak but not negligible caring relations among persons that enable them to recognize each other as members of the same society. Such recognition must eventually be global; in the meantime, the civil society without which the liberal institutions of justice cannot function presume a background of some degree of caring relations rather than of merely competing individuals. Furthermore, considerations of care provide a more fruitful basis than considerations of justice for deciding much about how society should be structured, for instance, how extensive or how restricted markets should be. And in the course of protecting the rights that ought to be recognized, such as those to basic necessities, policies that express the caring of the community for all its members will be better policies than those that grudgingly, though fairly, issue an allotment to those deemed unfit.

Care is probably the most deeply fundamental value. There can be care without justice: There has historically been little justice in the family, but care and life have gone on without it. There can be no justice without care, however, for without care no child would survive and there would be no persons to respect.

Care may thus provide the wider and deeper ethics within which justice should be sought, as when persons in caring relations may sometimes compete and in doing so should treat each other fairly, or, at the level of society, within caring relations of the thinner kind we can agree to treat each other for limited purposes as if we were the abstract individuals of liberal theory. But although care may be the more fundamental value, it may well be that the ethics of care does not itself provide adequate theoretical resources for dealing with issues of justice.

Within its appropriate sphere and for its relevant questions, the ethics of justice may be best for what we seek. What should be resisted is the traditional inclination to expand the reach of justice in such a way that it is mistakenly imagined to be able to give us a comprehensive morality suitable for all moral questions.

Implications for Society

Many advocates of the ethics of care argue for its relevance in social and political and economic life. Sara Ruddick shows its implications for efforts to achieve peace. I argue that as we see the deficiencies of the contractual model of human relations within the household, we can see them also in the world beyond and begin to think about how society should be reorganized to be hospitable to care, rather than continuing to marginalize it. We can see how not only does every domain of society need transformation in light of the values of care but so would the relations between such domains if we took care seriously, as care would move to the center of our attention and become a primary concern of society. Instead of a society dominated by conflict restrained by law and preoccupied with economic gain, we might have a society that saw as its most important task the flourishing of children and the development of caring relations, not only in personal contexts but among citizens and using governmental institutions. We would see that instead of abandoning culture to the dictates of the marketplace, we should make it possible for culture to develop in ways best able to enlighten and enrich human life.

Joan Tronto argues for the political implications of the ethics of care, seeing care as a political as well as moral ideal advocating the meeting of needs for care as "the highest social goal." She shows how unacceptable are current arrangements for providing care: "Caring activities are devalued, underpaid, and disproportionately occupied by the relatively powerless in society." Bubeck, Kittay, and many others argue forcefully that care must be seen as a public concern, not relegated to the private responsibility of women, the inadequacy and arbitrariness of private charities, or the vagaries and distortions of the market. In her recent book *Starting at Home*, Noddings explores what a caring society would be like.

When we concern ourselves with caring relations between more distant others, this care should not be thought to reduce to the mere "caring about" that has little to do with the face-to-face interactions of caring labor and can easily become paternalistic or patronizing. The same characteristics of attentiveness, responsiveness to needs, and understanding situations from the points of view of others should characterize caring when the participants are more distant. This also requires the work of understanding and of expending varieties of effort.

Given how care is a value with the widest possible social implications, it is unfortunate that many who look at the ethics of care continue to suppose it is a "family ethics," confined to the "private" sphere. Although some of its earliest formulations suggested this, and some of its related values are to be seen most clearly in personal contexts, an adequate understanding of the ethics of care should recognize that it elaborates values as fundamental and as relevant to political institutions and to how society is organized, as those of justice. Perhaps its values are even more fundamental and more relevant to life in society than those traditionally relied on. Instead of seeing the corporate sector, and military strength, and government and law as the most important segments of society deserving the highest levels of wealth and power, a caring society might see the tasks of bringing up children, educating its members, meeting the needs of all, achieving peace and treasuring the environment, and doing these in the best ways possible to be that to which the greatest social efforts of all should be devoted. One can recognize that something comparable to legal constraints and police enforcement, including at a global level, may always be necessary for special cases, but also that caring societies could greatly decrease the need for them. The social changes a focus on care would require would be as profound as can be imagined.

The ethics of care as it has developed is most certainly not limited to the sphere of family and personal relations. When its social and political implications are understood, it is a radical ethic calling for a profound restructuring of society. And it has the resources for dealing with power and violence.

COMPREHENSION QUESTIONS

1. Held says that dominant moral theories don't place enough value on our emotions. Why does she say this? And what's the alternative?
2. Held says that care ethics "works with a conception of persons as relational, rather than as the self-sufficient independent individuals of the dominant moral theories." Why would someone think that utiliarianism or Kantianism works with a conception of persons as self-sufficient independent individuals? What's the alternative?
3. Why might someone worry that there's a tension between justice and care? How does Held try to address that worry?
4. Held says that an ethics of care ought to be concerned with "how the burdens of caring are distributed." What does this mean?
5. Held says that focusing on care could lead us toward "a society that saw as its most important task the flourishing of children and the development of caring relations, not only in personal contexts but among citizens and using governmental institutions." Can you point to any evidence for thinking that our society doesn't see such things as most important? How might our society be different if those things were most important?

BOOK II OF NICOMACHEAN ETHICS
ARISTOTLE

It's difficult to overstate Aristotle's (384-322 BCE) significance in Western philosophy. His *Nicomachean Ethics* is a major part of his legacy, as it provides the foundations for two influential traditions: natural law theory (which is central to Catholic moral thought) and virtue ethics. Here, we'll focus on the latter. As you work through this excerpt, try to keep thinking about the big picture. What's distinctive about the way he approaches ethics? How is his emphasis on virtue different from what we get from utilitarianism and Kantianism? What would it look like to reason about a moral problem as a virtue ethicist?

1

Virtue, then, being of two kinds, intellectual and moral, intellectual virtue in the main owes both its birth and its growth to teaching (for which reason it requires experience and time), while moral virtue comes about as a result of habit, whence also its name (*ethike*) is one that is formed by a slight variation from the word *ethos* (habit). From this it is also plain that none of the moral virtues arises in us by nature; for nothing that exists by nature can form a habit contrary to its nature. For instance the stone which by nature moves downwards cannot be habituated to move upwards, not even if one tries to train it by throwing it up ten thousand times; nor can fire be habituated to move downwards, nor can anything else that by nature behaves in one way be trained to behave in another. Neither by nature, then, nor contrary to nature do the virtues arise in us; rather we are adapted by nature to receive them, and are made perfect by habit.

Again, of all the things that come to us by nature we first acquire the potentiality and later exhibit the activity (this is plain in the case of the senses; for it was not by often seeing or often hearing that we got these senses, but on the contrary we had them before we used them, and did not come to have them by using them); but the virtues we get by first exercising them, as also happens in the case of the arts as well. For the things we have to learn before we can do them, we learn by doing them, e.g. men become builders by building and lyre players by playing the lyre; so too we become just by doing just acts, temperate by doing temperate acts, brave by doing brave acts.

This is confirmed by what happens in states; for legislators make the citizens good by forming habits in them, and this is the wish of every legislator, and those who do not effect it miss their mark, and it is in this that a good constitution differs from a bad one.

Again, it is from the same causes and by the same means that every virtue is both produced and destroyed, and similarly every art; for it is from playing the lyre that both good and bad lyre players are produced. And the corresponding statement is true of builders and of all the rest; men will be good or bad builders as a result of building well or badly. For if this were not so, there would have been no need of a teacher, but all men would have been born good or bad at their craft.

Translated by W. D. Ross (http://classics.mit.edu/Aristotle/nicomachaen.2.ii.html)

This, then, is the case with the virtues also; by doing the acts that we do in our transactions with other men we become just or unjust, and by doing the acts that we do in the presence of danger, and being habituated to feel fear or confidence, we become brave or cowardly. The same is true of appetites and feelings of anger; some men become temperate and good-tempered, others self-indulgent and irascible, by behaving in one way or the other in the appropriate circumstances. Thus, in one word, states of character arise out of like activities. This is why the activities we exhibit must be of a certain kind; it is because the states of character correspond to the differences between these. It makes no small difference, then, whether we form habits of one kind or of another from our very youth; it makes a very great difference, or rather all the difference.

2

Since, then, the present inquiry does not aim at theoretical knowledge like the others (for we are inquiring not in order to know what virtue is, but in order to become good, since otherwise our inquiry would have been of no use), we must examine the nature of actions, namely how we ought to do them; for these determine also the nature of the states of character that are produced, as we have said. Now, that we must act according to the right rule is a common principle and must be assumed—it will be discussed later, i.e. both what the right rule is, and how it is related to the other virtues. But this must be agreed upon beforehand, that the whole account of matters of conduct must be given in outline and not precisely, as we said at the very beginning that the accounts we demand must be in accordance with the subject-matter; matters concerned with conduct and questions of what is good for us have no fixity, any more than matters of health. The general account being of this nature, the account of particular cases is yet more lacking in exactness; for they do not fall under any art or precept but the agents themselves must in each case consider what is appropriate to the occasion, as happens also in the art of medicine or of navigation.

But though our present account is of this nature we must give what help we can. First, then, let us consider this, that it is the nature of such things to be destroyed by defect and excess, as we see in the case of strength and of health (for to gain light on things imperceptible we must use the evidence of sensible things); both excessive and defective exercise destroys the strength, and similarly drink or food which is above or below a certain amount destroys the health, while that which is proportionate both produces and increases and preserves it. So too is it, then, in the case of temperance and courage and the other virtues. For the man who flies from and fears everything and does not stand his ground against anything becomes a coward, and the man who fears nothing at all but goes to meet every danger becomes rash; and similarly the man who indulges in every pleasure and abstains from none becomes self-indulgent, while the man who shuns every pleasure, as boors do, becomes in a way insensible; temperance and courage, then, are destroyed by excess and defect, and preserved by the mean.

But not only are the sources and causes of their origination and growth the same as those of their destruction, but also the sphere of their actualization will be the same; for this is also true of the things which are more evident to sense, e.g. of strength; it is produced by taking much food and undergoing much exertion, and it is the strong man that will be most able to do these things. So too is it with the virtues; by abstaining from pleasures we become temperate, and it is when we have become so that we are most able to abstain from them; and similarly too in the case of courage; for by being habituated to despise things that are terrible and to stand our ground against them we become brave, and it is when we have become so that we shall be most able to stand our ground against them.

3

We must take as a sign of states of character the pleasure or pain that ensues on acts; for the man who abstains from bodily pleasures and delights in this very fact is temperate, while the man who is annoyed at it is self-indulgent, and he who stands his ground against things that are terrible and delights in this or at least is not pained is brave, while the man who is pained is a coward. For moral excellence is concerned with pleasures and pains; it is on account of the pleasure that we do bad things, and on account of the pain that we abstain from noble ones. Hence we ought to have been brought up in a particular way from our very youth, as Plato says, so as both to delight in and to be pained by the things that we ought; for this is the right education.

Again, if the virtues are concerned with actions and passions, and every passion and every action is accompanied by pleasure and pain, for this reason also virtue will be concerned with pleasures and pains. This is indicated also by the fact that punishment is inflicted by these means; for it is a kind of cure, and it is the nature of cures to be effected by contraries.

Again, as we said but lately, every state of soul has a nature relative to and concerned with the kind of things by which it tends to be made worse or better; but it is by reason of pleasures and pains that men become bad, by pursuing and avoiding these—either the pleasures and pains they ought not or when they ought not or as they ought not, or by going wrong in one of the other similar ways that may be distinguished. Hence men even define the virtues as certain states of impassivity and rest; not well, however, because they speak absolutely, and do not say "as one ought" and "as one ought not" and "when one ought or ought not," and the other things that may be added. We assume, then, that this kind of excellence tends to do what is best with regard to pleasures and pains, and vice does the contrary.

The following facts also may show us that virtue and vice are concerned with these same things. There being three objects of choice and three of avoidance, the noble, the advantageous, the pleasant, and their contraries, the base, the injurious, the painful, about all of these the good man tends to go right and the bad man to go wrong, and especially about pleasure; for this is common to the animals, and also it accompanies all objects of choice; for even the noble and the advantageous appear pleasant.

Again, it has grown up with us all from our infancy; this is why it is difficult to rub off this passion, engrained as it is in our life. And we measure even our actions, some of us more and others less, by the rule of pleasure and pain. For this reason, then, our whole inquiry must be about these; for to feel delight and pain rightly or wrongly has no small effect on our actions.

Again, it is harder to fight with pleasure than with anger, to use Heraclitus' phrase, but both art and virtue are always concerned with what is harder; for even the good is better when it is harder. Therefore for this reason also the whole concern both of virtue and of political science is with pleasures and pains; for the man who uses these well will be good, he who uses them badly bad.

That virtue, then, is concerned with pleasures and pains, and that by the acts from which it arises it is both increased and, if they are done differently, destroyed, and that the acts from which it arose are those in which it actualizes itself—let this be taken as said.

4

The question might be asked: what we mean by saying that we must become just by doing just acts, and temperate by doing temperate acts; for if men do just and temperate acts, they are already just and temperate, exactly as, if they do what is in accordance with the laws of grammar and of music, they are grammarians and musicians.

Or is this not true even of the arts? It is possible to do something that is in accordance with the laws of grammar, either by chance or at the suggestion of another. A man will be a grammarian, then, only when he has both done something grammatical and done it grammatically; and this means doing it in accordance with the grammatical knowledge in himself.

Again, the case of the arts and that of the virtues are not similar; for the products of the arts have their goodness in themselves, so that it is enough that they should have a certain character, but if the acts that are in accordance with the virtues have themselves a certain character it does not follow that they are done justly or temperately. The agent also must be in a certain condition when he does them; in the first place he must have knowledge, secondly he must choose the acts, and choose them for their own sakes, and thirdly his action must proceed from a firm and unchangeable character. These are not reckoned in as conditions of the possession of the arts, except the bare knowledge; but as a condition of the possession of the virtues knowledge has little or no weight, while the other conditions count not for a little but for everything, i.e. the very conditions which result from often doing just and temperate acts.

Actions, then, are called just and temperate when they are such as the just or the temperate man would do; but it is not the man who does these that is just and temperate, but the man who also does them as just and temperate men do them. It is well said, then, that it is by doing just acts that the just man is produced, and by doing temperate acts the temperate man; without doing these no one would have even a prospect of becoming good.

But most people do not do these, but take refuge in theory and think they are being philosophers and will become good in this way, behaving somewhat like patients who listen attentively to their doctors, but do none of the things they are ordered to do. As the latter will not be made well in body by such a course of treatment, the former will not be made well in soul by such a course of philosophy.

5

Next we must consider what virtue is. Since things that are found in the soul are of three kinds—passions, faculties, states of character, virtue must be one of these. By passions I mean appetite, anger, fear, confidence, envy, joy, friendly feeling, hatred, longing, emulation, pity, and in general the feelings that are accompanied by plea-sure or pain; by faculties the things in virtue of which we are said to be capable of feeling these, e.g. of becoming angry or being pained or feeling pity; by states of char-acter the things in virtue of which we stand well or badly with reference to the pas-sions, e.g. with reference to anger we stand badly if we feel it violently or too weakly, and well if we feel it moderately; and similarly with reference to the other passions.

Now neither the virtues nor the vices are passions, because we are not called good or bad on the ground of our passions, but are so called on the ground of our virtues and our vices, and because we are neither praised nor blamed for our passions (for the man who feels fear or anger is not praised, nor is the man who simply feels anger blamed, but the man who feels it in a certain way), but for our virtues and our vices we are praised or blamed.

Again, we feel anger and fear without choice, but the virtues are modes of choice or involve choice. Further, in respect of the passions we are said to be moved, but in respect of the virtues and the vices we are said not to be moved but to be disposed in a particular way.

For these reasons also they are not faculties; for we are neither called good nor bad, nor praised nor blamed, for the simple capacity of feeling the passions; again, we have the faculties by nature, but we are not made good or bad by nature; we have spoken of this before. If, then, the virtues are neither passions nor facul-ties, all that remains is that they should be states of character.

Thus we have stated what virtue is in respect of its genus.

6

We must, however, not only describe virtue as a state of character, but also say what sort of state it is. We may remark, then, that every virtue or excellence both brings into good condition the thing of which it is the excellence and makes the work of that thing be done well; e.g. the excellence of the eye makes both the eye and its work good; for it is by the excellence of the eye that we see well. Similarly the excellence of the horse makes a horse both good in itself and good at running and at carrying its rider and at awaiting the attack of the enemy. Therefore, if this is true in every case, the virtue of man also will be the state of character which makes a man good and which makes him do his own work well.

How this is to happen we have stated already, but it will be made plain also by the following consideration of the specific nature of virtue. In everything that is continuous and divisible it is possible to take more, less, or an equal amount, and that either in terms of the thing itself or relatively to us; and the equal is an intermediate between excess and defect. By the intermediate in the object I mean that which is equidistant from each of the extremes, which is one and the same for all men; by the intermediate relatively to us that which is neither too much nor too little—and this is not one, nor the same for all. For instance, if ten is many and two is few, six is the intermediate, taken in terms of the object; for it exceeds and is exceeded by an equal amount; this is intermediate according to arithmetical proportion. But the intermediate relatively to us is not to be taken so; if ten pounds are too much for a particular person to eat and two too little, it does not follow that the trainer will order six pounds; for this also is perhaps too much for the person who is to take it, or too little—too little for Milo, too much for the beginner in athletic exercises. The same is true of running and wrestling. Thus a master of any art avoids excess and defect, but seeks the intermediate and chooses this—the intermediate not in the object but relatively to us.

If it is thus, then, that every art does its work well—by looking to the intermediate and judging its works by this standard (so that we often say of good works of art that it is not possible either to take away or to add anything, implying that excess and defect destroy the goodness of works of art, while the mean preserves it; and good artists, as we say, look to this in their work), and if, further, virtue is more exact and better than any art, as nature also is, then virtue must have the quality of aiming at the intermediate. I mean moral virtue; for it is this that is concerned with passions and actions, and in these there is excess, defect, and the intermediate. For instance, both fear and confidence and appetite and anger and pity and in general pleasure and pain may be felt both too much and too little, and in both cases not well; but to feel them at the right times, with reference to the right objects, towards the right people, with the right motive, and in the right way, is what is both intermediate and best, and this is characteristic of virtue. Similarly with regard to actions also there is excess, defect, and the intermediate. Now virtue is concerned with passions and actions, in which excess is a form of failure, and so is defect, while the intermediate is praised and is a form of success; and being praised and being successful are both characteristics of virtue. Therefore virtue is a kind of mean, since, as we have seen, it aims at what is intermediate.

Again, it is possible to fail in many ways (for evil belongs to the class of the unlimited, as the Pythagoreans conjectured, and good to that of the limited), while to succeed is possible only in one way (for which reason also one is easy and the other difficult—to miss the mark easy, to hit it difficult); for these reasons also, then, excess and defect are characteristic of vice, and the mean of virtue; for men are good in but one way, but bad in many.

Virtue, then, is a state of character concerned with choice, lying in a mean, i.e. the mean relative to us, this being determined by a rational principle, and by that principle by which the man of practical wisdom would determine it. Now it is a mean between two vices, that which depends on excess and that which depends on defect; and again it is a mean because the vices respectively fall short of or exceed what is right in both passions and actions, while virtue both finds and chooses that which is intermediate. Hence in respect of its substance and the definition which states its essence virtue is a mean, with regard to what is best and right an extreme.

But not every action nor every passion admits of a mean; for some have names that already imply badness, e.g. spite, shamelessness, envy, and in the case of actions adultery, theft, murder; for all of these and suchlike things imply by their names that they are themselves bad, and not the excesses or deficiencies of them.

It is not possible, then, ever to be right with regard to them; one must always be wrong. Nor does goodness or badness with regard to such things depend on committing adultery with the right woman, at the right time, and in the right way, but simply to do any of them is to go wrong. It would be equally absurd, then, to expect that in unjust, cowardly, and voluptuous action there should be a mean, an excess, and a deficiency; for at that rate there would be a mean of excess and of deficiency, an excess of excess, and a deficiency of deficiency. But as there is no excess and deficiency of temperance and courage because what is intermediate is in a sense an extreme, so too of the actions we have mentioned there is no mean nor any excess and deficiency, but however they are done they are wrong; for in general there is neither a mean of excess and deficiency, nor excess and deficiency of a mean.

7

We must, however, not only make this general statement, but also apply it to the individual facts. For among statements about conduct those which are general apply more widely, but those which are particular are more genuine, since conduct has to do with individual cases, and our statements must harmonize with the facts in these cases. We may take these cases from our table. With regard to feelings of fear and confidence courage is the mean; of the people who exceed, he who exceeds in fearlessness has no name (many of the states have no name), while the man who exceeds in confidence is rash, and he who exceeds in fear and falls short in confidence is a coward. With regard to pleasures and pains—not all of them, and not so much with regard to the pains—the mean is temperance, the excess self-indulgence. Persons deficient with regard to the pleasures are not often found; hence such persons also have received no name. But let us call them "insensible."

With regard to giving and taking of money the mean is liberality, the excess and the defect prodigality and meanness. In these actions people exceed and fall short in contrary ways; the prodigal exceeds in spending and falls short in taking, while the mean man exceeds in taking and falls short in spending. (At present we are giving a mere outline or summary, and are satisfied with this; later these states will be more exactly determined.) With regard to money there are also other dispositions—a mean, magnificence (for the magnificent man differs from the liberal man; the former deals with large sums, the latter with small ones), an excess, tastelessness and vulgarity, and a deficiency, niggardliness; these differ from the states opposed to liberality, and the mode of their difference will be stated later. With regard to honour and dishonour the mean is proper pride, the excess is known as a sort of "empty vanity," and the deficiency is undue humility; and as we said liberality was related to magnificence, differing from it by dealing with small sums, so there is a state similarly related to proper pride, being concerned with small honours while that is concerned with great. For it is possible to desire honour as one ought, and more than one ought, and less, and the man who exceeds in his desires is called ambitious, the man who falls short unambitious, while the intermediate person has no name. The dispositions also are nameless, except that that of the ambitious man is called ambition. Hence the people who are at the extremes lay claim to the middle place; and we ourselves sometimes call the intermediate person ambitious and sometimes unambitious, and sometimes praise the ambitious man and sometimes the unambitious. The reason of our doing this will be stated in what follows; but now let us speak of the remaining states according to the method which has been indicated.

With regard to anger also there is an excess, a deficiency, and a mean. Although they can scarcely be said to have names, yet since we call the intermediate person good-tempered let us call the mean good temper; of the persons at the extremes let the one who exceeds be called irascible, and his vice irascibility, and the man who falls short an inirascible sort of person, and the deficiency inirascibility.

There are also three other means, which have a certain likeness to one another, but differ from one another: for they are all concerned with intercourse in words and actions, but differ in that one is concerned with truth in this sphere, the other two with pleasantness; and of this one kind is exhibited in giving amusement, the other in all the circumstances of life. We must therefore speak of these too, that we may the better see that in all things the mean is praise-worthy, and the extremes neither praiseworthy nor right, but worthy of blame. Now most of these states also have no names, but we must try, as in the other cases, to invent names ourselves so that we may be clear and easy to follow. With regard to truth, then, the intermediate is a truthful sort of person and the mean may be called truthfulness, while the pretense which exaggerates is boastfulness and the person characterized by it a boaster, and that which understates is mock modesty and the person characterized by it mock-modest. With regard to pleasantness in the giving of amusement the intermediate person is ready-witted and the disposition ready wit, the excess is buffoonery and the person characterized by it a buffoon, while the man who falls short is a sort of boor and his state is boorishness. With regard to the remaining kind of pleasantness, that which is exhibited in life in general, the man who is pleasant in the right way is friendly and the mean is friendliness, while the man who exceeds is an obsequious person if he has no end in view, a flatterer if he is aiming at his own advantage, and the man who falls short and is unpleasant in all circumstances is a quarrelsome and surly sort of person.

There are also means in the passions and concerned with the passions; since shame is not a virtue, and yet praise is extended to the modest man. For even in these matters one man is said to be intermediate, and another to exceed, as for instance the bashful man who is ashamed of everything; while he who falls short or is not ashamed of anything at all is shameless, and the intermediate person is modest. Righteous indignation is a mean between envy and spite, and these states are concerned with the pain and pleasure that are felt at the fortunes of our neighbours; the man who is characterized by righteous indignation is pained at undeserved good fortune, the envious man, going beyond him, is pained at all good fortune, and the spiteful man falls so far short of being pained that he even rejoices. But these states there will be an opportunity of describing elsewhere; with regard to justice, since it has not one simple meaning, we shall, after describing the other states, distinguish its two kinds and say how each of them is a mean; and similarly we shall treat also of the rational virtues.

8

There are three kinds of disposition, then, two of them vices, involving excess and deficiency respectively, and one a virtue, viz. the mean, and all are in a sense opposed to all; for the extreme states are contrary both to the intermediate state and to each other, and the intermediate to the extremes; as the equal is greater relatively to the less, less relatively to the greater, so the middle states are excessive relatively to the deficiencies, deficient relatively to the excesses, both in passions and in actions. For the brave man appears rash relatively to the coward, and cowardly relatively to the rash man; and similarly the temperate man appears self-indulgent relatively to the insensible man, insensible relatively to the self-indulgent, and the liberal man prodigal relatively to the mean man, mean relatively to the prodigal. Hence also the people at the extremes push the intermediate man each over to the other, and the brave man is called rash by the coward, cowardly by the rash man, and correspondingly in the other cases.

These states being thus opposed to one another, the greatest contrariety is that of the extremes to each other, rather than to the intermediate; for these are further from each other than from the intermediate, as the great is further from the small and the small from the great than both are from the equal. Again, to the intermediate some extremes show a certain likeness, as that of rashness to courage and that of prodigality to liberality; but the extremes show the greatest unlikeness to each other; now contraries are defined as the things that are furthest from each other, so that things that are further apart are more contrary.

To the mean in some cases the deficiency, in some the excess is more opposed; e.g. it is not rashness, which is an excess, but cowardice, which is a deficiency, that is more opposed to courage, and not insensibility, which is a deficiency, but self-indulgence, which is an excess, that is more opposed to temperance. This happens from two reasons, one being drawn from the thing itself; for because one extreme is nearer and liker to the intermediate, we oppose not this but rather its contrary to the intermediate. E.g. since rashness is thought liker and nearer to courage, and cowardice more unlike, we oppose rather the latter to courage; for things that are further from the intermediate are thought more contrary to it. This, then, is one cause, drawn from the thing itself; another is drawn from ourselves; for the things to which we ourselves more naturally tend seem more contrary to the intermediate. For instance, we ourselves tend more naturally to pleasures, and hence are more easily carried away towards self-indulgence than towards propriety. We describe as contrary to the mean, then, rather the directions in which we more often go to great lengths; and therefore self-indulgence, which is an excess, is the more contrary to temperance.

9

That moral virtue is a mean, then, and in what sense it is so, and that it is a mean between two vices, the one involving excess, the other deficiency, and that it is such because its character is to aim at what is intermediate in passions and in actions, has been sufficiently stated. Hence also it is no easy task to be good. For in everything it is no easy task to find the middle, e.g. to find the middle of a circle is not for every one but for him who knows; so, too, any one can get angry—that is easy—or give or spend money; but to do this to the right person, to the right extent, at the right time, with the right motive, and in the right way, that is not for every one, nor is it easy; wherefore goodness is both rare and laudable and noble.

Hence he who aims at the intermediate must first depart from what is the more contrary to it, as Calypso advises: Hold the ship out beyond that surf and spray.

For of the extremes one is more erroneous, one less so; therefore, since to hit the mean is hard in the extreme, we must as a second best, as people say, take the least of the evils; and this will be done best in the way we describe. But we must consider the things towards which we ourselves also are easily carried away; for some of us tend to one thing, some to another; and this will be recognizable from the pleasure and the pain we feel. We must drag ourselves away to the contrary extreme; for we shall get into the intermediate state by drawing well away from error, as people do in straightening sticks that are bent.

Now in everything the pleasant or pleasure is most to be guarded against; for we do not judge it impartially. We ought, then, to feel towards pleasure as the elders of the people felt towards Helen, and in all circumstances repeat their saying; for if we dismiss pleasure thus we are less likely to go astray. It is by doing this, then, (to sum the matter up) that we shall best be able to hit the mean.

But this is no doubt difficult, and especially in individual cases; for it is not easy to determine both how and with whom and on what provocation and how long one should be angry; for we too sometimes praise those who fall short and call them good-tempered, but sometimes we praise those who get angry and call them manly. The man, however, who deviates little from goodness is not blamed, whether he do so in the direction of the more or of the less, but only the man who deviates more widely; for he does not fail to be noticed. But up to what point and to what extent a man must deviate before he becomes blameworthy it is not easy to determine by reasoning, any more than anything else that is perceived by the senses; such things depend on particular facts, and the decision rests with perception. So much, then, is plain, that the intermediate state is in all things to be praised, but that we must incline sometimes towards the excess, sometimes towards the deficiency; for so shall we most easily hit the mean and what is right.

COMPREHENSION QUESTIONS

1. What are the two kinds of virtues?
2. According to Aristotle, what's the point of learning about virtue?
3. What's the difference between (a) acting as the temperate person acts and (b) doing things just as the temperate person does them?
4. What does Aristotle mean when he says that "virtue is a kind of mean"?
5. Aristotle says that it's "no easy task to be good." What are some of the factors that make it difficult?

EXCERPT FROM LEVIATHAN
THOMAS HOBBES

Thomas Hobbes (1588–1679) was an English philosopher who was most famous for his book *Leviathan*. In it, he defends a view about what makes laws just: Namely, they are the rules to which we'd agree if we were all free, rational, and equal. Hobbes himself thought that we'd agree to be under the thumb of an absolute monarch—the Leviathan—but it's an open question whether his assumptions actually support that conclusion. In any case, in this excerpt from his book, you'll get a taste of his views. Look, in particular, for the way he defines the "state of nature," for the pressures that lead us to make contracts, and for his account of the "Laws of Nature."

Of the Natural Condition of Mankind, as Concerning Their Felicity, and Misery

Nature hath made men so equal, in the faculties of body, and mind; as that though there be found one man sometimes manifestly stronger in body, or of quicker mind then another; yet when all is reckoned together, the difference between man, and man, is not so considerable, as that one man can thereupon claim to himself any benefit, to which another may not pretend, as well as he. For as to the strength of body, the weakest has strength enough to kill the strongest, either by secret machination, or by confederacy with others, that are in the same danger with himself.

And as to the faculties of the mind, (setting aside the arts grounded upon words, and especially that skill of proceeding upon general, and infallible rules, called Science; which very few have, and but in few things; as being not a native faculty, born with us; nor attained, (as Prudence,) while we look after somewhat else,) I find yet a greater equality amongst men, than that of strength. For Prudence, is but Experience; which equal time, equally bestows on all men, in those things they equally apply themselves unto. That which may perhaps make such equality incredible, is but a vain conceit of one's own wisdom, which almost all men think they have in a greater degree, than the Vulgar; that is, than all men but themselves, and a few others, whom by Fame, or for concurring with themselves, they approve. For such is the nature of men, that howsoever they may acknowledge many others to be more witty, or more eloquent, or more learned; Yet they will hardly believe there be many so wise as themselves: For they see their own wit at hand, and other men's at a distance. But this proveth rather that men are in that point equal, than unequal. For there is not ordinarily a greater sign of the equal distribution of anything, than that every man is contented with his share.

From this equality of ability, ariseth equality of hope in the attaining of our Ends. And therefore if any two men desire the same thing, which nevertheless they cannot both enjoy, they become enemies; and in the way to their End, (which is principally their own conservation, and sometimes their delectation

http://www.gutenberg.org/files/3207/3207-h/3207-h.htm

only,) endeavor to destroy, or subdue one another. And from hence it comes to pass, that where an Invader hath no more to fear, than another man's single power; if one plant, sow, build, or possess a convenient Seat, others may probably be expected to come prepared with forces united, to dispossess, and deprive him, not only of the fruit of his labor, but also of his life, or liberty. And the Invader again is in the like danger of another.

And from this diffidence of one another, there is no way for any man to secure himself, so reasonable, as Anticipation; that is, by force, or wiles, to master the persons of all men he can, so long, till he see no other power great enough to endanger him: And this is no more than his own conservation requireth, and is generally allowed. Also because there be some, that taking pleasure in contemplating their own power in the acts of conquest, which they pursue farther than their security requires; if others, that otherwise would be glad to be at ease within modest bounds, should not by invasion increase their power, they would not be able, long time, by standing only on their defense, to subsist. And by consequence, such augmentation of dominion over men, being necessary to a man's conservation, it ought to be allowed him.

Again, men have no pleasure, (but on the contrary a great deal of grief) in keeping company, where there is no power able to over-awe them all. For every man looketh that his companion should value him, at the same rate he sets upon himself: And upon all signs of contempt, or undervaluing, naturally endeavors, as far as he dares (which amongst them that have no common power, to keep them in quiet, is far enough to make them destroy each other,) to extort a greater value from his condemners, by dommage; and from others, by the example.

So that in the nature of man, we find three principal causes of quarrel. First, Competition; Secondly, Diffidence; Thirdly, Glory.

The first, maketh men invade for Gain; the second, for Safety; and the third, for Reputation. The first use Violence, to make themselves Masters of other men's persons, wives, children, and cattle; the second, to defend them; the third, for trifles, as a word, a smile, a different opinion, and any other sign of undervalue, either direct in their Persons, or by reflection in their Kindred, their Friends, their Nation, their Profession, or their Name.

Hereby it is manifest, that during the time men live without a common Power to keep them all in awe, they are in that condition which is called War; and such a war, as is of every man, against every man. For WAR, consisteth not in Battle only, or the act of fighting; but in a tract of time, wherein the Will to contend by Battle is sufficiently known: and therefore the notion of Time, is to be considered in the nature of War; as it is in the nature of Weather. For as the nature of Foul weather, lies not in a shower or two of rain; but in an inclination thereto of many days together: So the nature of War, consisteth not in actual fighting; but in the known disposition thereto, during all the time there is no assurance to the contrary. All other time is PEACE.

Whatsoever therefore is consequent to a time of War, where every man is Enemy to every man; the same is consequent to the time, wherein men live without other security, than what their own strength, and their own invention shall furnish them withall. In such condition, there is no place for Industry; because the fruit thereof is uncertain; and consequently no Culture of the Earth; no Navigation, nor use of the commodities that may be imported by Sea; no commodious Building; no Instruments of moving, and removing such things as require much force; no Knowledge of the face of the Earth; no account of Time; no Arts; no Letters; no Society; and which is worst of all, continual fear, and danger of violent death; And the life of man, solitary, poor, nasty, brutish, and short.

It may seem strange to some man, that has not well weighed these things; that Nature should thus dissociate, and render men apt to invade, and destroy one another: and he may therefore, not trusting to this Inference, made from the Passions, desire perhaps to have the same confirmed by Experience. Let him therefore consider with himself, when taking a journey, he arms himself, and seeks to go well accompanied; when going to sleep, he locks his doors; when even in his house he locks his chests; and this when he knows there be Laws, and public Officers, armed, to revenge all injuries shall be done him; what opinion he has of his fellow subjects, when he rides armed; of his fellow Citizens, when he locks his doors; and of his children, and servants, when he locks his chests. Does he not there as much accuse mankind by his actions, as I do by my words? But neither of us accuse man's nature in it. The Desires, and other Passions of man, are in themselves no Sin. No more are the Actions, that proceed from those Passions, till they know a Law that forbids them; which till Lawes be made they cannot know: nor can any Law be made, till they have agreed upon the Person that shall make it.

It may peradventure be thought, there was never such a time, nor condition of war as this; and I believe it was never generally so, over all the world: but there are many places, where they live so now. For the savage people in many places of America, except the government of small Families, the concord whereof dependeth on natural lust, have no government at all; and live at this day in that brutish manner, as I said before. Howsoever, it may be perceived what manner of life there would be, where there were no common Power to fear; by the manner of life, which men that have formerly lived under a peaceful government, use to degenerate into, in a civil War.

But though there had never been any time, wherein particular men were in a condition of war one against another; yet in all times, Kings, and persons of Sovereign authority, because of their Independency, are in continual jealousies, and in the state and posture of Gladiators; having their weapons pointing, and their eyes fixed on one another; that is, their Forts, Garrisons, and Guns upon the Frontiers of their Kingdoms; and continual Spies upon their neighbors; which is a posture of War. But because they uphold thereby, the Industry of their Subjects; there does not follow from it, that misery, which accompanies the Liberty of particular men.

To this war of every man against every man, this also is consequent; that nothing can be Unjust. The notions of Right and Wrong, Justice and Injustice have there no place. Where there is no common Power, there is no Law: where no Law, no Injustice. Force, and Fraud, are in war the two Cardinal virtues. Justice, and Injustice are none of the Faculties neither of the Body, nor Mind. If they were, they might be in a man that were alone in the world, as well as his Senses, and Passions. They are Qualities, that relate to men in Society, not in Solitude. It is consequent also to the same condition, that there be no Propriety, no Dominion, no Mine and Thine distinct; but only that to be every man's that he can get; and for so long, as he can keep it. And thus much for the ill condition, which man by mere Nature is actually placed in; though with a possibility to come out of it, consisting partly in the Passions, partly in his Reason.

The Passions that incline men to Peace, are Fear of Death; Desire of such things as are necessary to commodious living; and a Hope by their Industry to obtain them. And Reason suggesteth convenient Articles of Peace, upon which men may be drawn to agreement. These Articles, are they, which otherwise are called the Laws of Nature . . .

The First and Second Natural Laws, and of Contracts

The RIGHT OF NATURE, which Writers commonly call Jus Naturale, is the Liberty each man hath, to use his own power, as he will himself, for the preservation of his own Nature; that is to say, of his own Life; and consequently, of doing any thing, which in his own Judgement, and Reason, he shall conceive to be the aptest means thereunto.

By LIBERTY, is understood, according to the proper signification of the word, the absence of external Impediments: which Impediments, may oft take away part of a man's power to do what he would; but cannot hinder him from using the power left him, according as his judgement, and reason shall dictate to him.

A LAW OF NATURE, (Lex Naturalis,) is a Precept, or general Rule, found out by Reason, by which a man is forbidden to do, that, which is destructive of his life, or taketh away the means of preserving the same; and to omit, that, by which he thinketh it may be best preserved. For though they that speak of this subject, use to confound Jus, and Lex, Right and Law; yet they ought to be distinguished; because RIGHT, consisteth in liberty to do, or to forbeare; Whereas LAW, determineth, and bindeth to one of them: so that Law, and Right, differ as much, as Obligation, and Liberty; which in one and the same matter are inconsistent.

And because the condition of Man . . . is a condition of War of every one against every one; in which case every one is governed by his own Reason; and there is nothing he can make use of, that may not be a help unto him, in preserving his life against his enemies; It followeth, that in such a condition, every man has a Right to every thing; even to one another's body. And therefore, as long as this natural Right of every man to everything endureth, there can be no security to any man, (how strong or wise soever he be,) of living out the time, which Nature ordinarily alloweth men to live.

And consequently it is a precept, or general rule of Reason, "That every man, ought to endeavor Peace, as far as he has hope of obtaining it; and when he cannot obtain it, that he may seek, and use, all helps, and advantages of War."

The first branch, of which Rule, containeth the first, and Fundamental Law of Nature; which is, "To seek Peace, and follow it." The Second, the sum of the Right of Nature; which is, "By all means we can, to defend ourselves."

From this Fundamental Law of Nature, by which men are commanded to endeavor Peace, is derived this second Law; "That a man be willing, when others are so too, as farre-forth, as for Peace, and defense of himself he shall think it necessary, to lay down this right to all things; and be contented with so much liberty against other men, as he would allow other men against himself." For as long as every man holdeth this Right, of doing anything he liketh; so long are all men in the condition of War. But if other men will not lay down their Right, as well as he; then there is no Reason for any one, to divest himself of his: For that were to expose himself to Prey, (which no man is bound to) rather than to dispose himself to Peace. This is that Law of the Gospel; "Whatsoever you require that others should do to you, that do ye to them" . . .

To Lay Down a man's Right to any thing, is to Divest himself of the Liberty, of hindring another of the benefit of his own Right to the same. For he that renounceth, or passeth away his Right, giveth not to any other man a Right which he had not before; because there is nothing to which every man had not Right by Nature: but only standeth out of his way, that he may enjoy his own original Right, without hindrance from him; not without hindrance from another. So that the effect which redoundeth to one man, by another man's defect of Right, is but so much diminution of impediments to the use of his own Right original.

By Simply RENOUNCING; when he cares not to whom the benefit thereof redoundeth. By TRANSFERRING; when he intendeth the benefit thereof to some certain person, or persons. And when a man hath in either manner abandoned, or granted away his Right; then is he said to be OBLIGED, or BOUND, not to hinder those, to whom such Right is granted, or abandoned, from the benefit of it: and that he Ought, and it his DUTY, not to make void that voluntary act of his own: and that such hindrance is INJUSTICE, and INJURY, as being Sine Jure; the Right being before renounced, or transferred. So that Injury, or Injustice, in the controversies of the world, is somewhat like to that, which in the disputations of Scholars is called Absurdity. For as it is there called an Absurdity, to contradict what one maintained in the Beginning: so in the world, it is called Injustice, and Injury, voluntarily to undo that, which from the beginning he had voluntarily done. The way by which a man either simply Renounceth, or Transferreth his Right, is a Declaration, or Signification, by some voluntary and sufficient sign, or signs, that he doth so Renounce, or Transfer; or hath so Renounced, or Transferred the same, to him that accepteth it. And these Signs are either Words only, or Actions only; or (as it happeneth most often) both Words and Actions. And the same are the BONDS, by which men are bound, and obliged: Bonds, that have their strength, not from their own Nature, (for nothing is more easily broken then a man's word,) but from Fear of some evil consequence upon the rupture.

Whensoever a man Transferreth his Right, or Renounceth it; it is either in consideration of some Right reciprocally transferred to himself; or for some other good he hopeth for thereby. For it is a voluntary act: and of the voluntary acts of every man, the object is some Good To Himself. And therefore there be some Rights, which no man can be understood by any words, or other signs, to have abandoned, or transferred. As first a man cannot lay down the right of resisting them, that assault him by force, to take away his life; because he cannot be understood to aim thereby, at any Good to himself. The same may be said of Wounds, and Chains, and Imprisonment; both because there is no benefit consequent to such patience; as there is to the patience of suffering another to be wounded, or imprisoned: as also because a man cannot tell, when he seeth men proceed against him by violence, whether they intend his death or not. And lastly the motive, and end for which this renouncing, and transferring or Right is introduced, is nothing else but the security of a man's person, in his life, and in the means of so preserving life, as not to be weary of it. And therefore if a man by words, or other signs, seem to despoil himself of the End, for which those signs were intended; he is not to be understood as if he meant it, or that it was his will; but that he was ignorant of how such words and actions were to be interpreted.

The mutual transferring of Right, is that which men call CONTRACT . . .

Signs of Contract, are either Expressed, or By Inference. Expressed, are words spoken with understanding of what they signify; And such words are either of the time Present, or Past; as, I Give, I Grant, I Have Given, I Have Granted, I Will That This Be Yours: Or of the future; as, I Will Give, I Will Grant; which words of the future, are called Promise.

Signs by Inference, are sometimes the consequence of Words; sometimes the consequence of Silence; sometimes the consequence of Actions; sometimes the consequence of Forbearing an Action: and generally a sign by Inference, of any Contract, is whatsoever sufficiently argues the will of the Contractor.

Words alone, if they be of the time to come, and contain a bare promise, are an insufficient sign of a Free-gift and therefore not obligatory. For if they be of the time to Come, as, Tomorrow I Will Give, they are a sign I have not given yet, and consequently that my right is not transferred, but remaineth till I transfer it by some other Act . . .

If a Covenant be made, wherein neither of the parties perform presently, but trust one another; in the condition of mere Nature, (which is a condition of War of every man against every man,) upon any reasonable suspicion, it is Void; But if there be a common Power set over them both, with right and force sufficient to compel performance; it is not Void. For he that performeth first, has no assurance the other will perform after; because the bonds of words are too weak to bridle men's ambition, avarice, anger, and other Passions, without the fear of some coerceive Power; which in the condition of mere Nature, where all men are equal, and judges of the justness of their own fears cannot possibly be supposed. And therefore he which performeth first, does but betray himself to his enemy; contrary to the Right (he can never abandon) of defending his life, and means of living.

But in a civil estate, where there is a Power set up to constrain those that would otherwise violate their faith, that fear is no more reasonable; and for that cause, he which by the Covenant is to perform first, is obliged so to do . . .

From that law of Nature, by which we are obliged to transfer to another, such Rights, as being retained, hinder the peace of Mankind, there followeth a Third; which is this, That Men Perform Their Covenants Made: without which, Covenants are in vain, and but Empty words; and the Right of all men to all things remaining, we are still in the condition of War.

And in this law of Nature, consisteth the Fountain and Original of JUSTICE. For where no Covenant hath preceded, there hath no Right been transferred, and every man has right to every thing; and consequently, no action can be Unjust. But when a Covenant is made, then to break it is Unjust: And the definition of INJUSTICE, is no other than The Not Performance Of Covenant. And whatsoever is not Unjust, is Just.

. . . But because Covenants of mutual trust, where there is a fear of not performance on either part are invalid; though the Original of Justice be the making of Covenants; yet Injustice actually there can be none, till the cause of such fear be taken away; which while men are in the natural condition of War, cannot be done. Therefore before the names of Just, and Unjust can have place, there must be some coercive Power, to compel men equally to the performance of their Covenants, by the terror of some punishment, greater than the benefit they expect by the breach of their Covenant; and to make good that Propriety, which by mutual Contract men acquire, in recompense of the universal Right they abandon: and such power there is none before the erection of a Commonwealth. And this is also to be gathered out of the ordinary definition of Justice in the Schools: For they say, that "Justice is the constant Will of giving to every man his own." And therefore where there is no Own, that is, no Propriety, there is no Injustice; and where there is no coercive Power erected, that is, where there is no Common-wealth, there is no Propriety; all men having Right to all things: Therefore where there is no Common-wealth, there nothing is Unjust. So that the nature of Justice, consisteth in keeping of valid Covenants: but the Validity of Covenants begins not but with the Constitution of a Civil Power, sufficient to compel men to keep them: And then it is also that Propriety begins.

The Fool hath said in his heart, there is no such thing as Justice; and sometimes also with his tongue; seriously alleging, that every man's conservation, and contentment, being committed to his own care, there could be no reason, why every man might not do what he thought conduced thereunto; and therefore also to make, or not make; keep, or not keep Covenants, was not against Reason, when it conduced to ones benefit. He does not therein deny, that there be Covenants; and that they are sometimes broken, sometimes kept; and that such breach of them may be called Injustice, and the observance of them Justice: but he questioneth, whether Injustice, taking away the fear of God, (for the same Fool hath said in his heart there is no God,) may not sometimes stand with that Reason, which dictateth to every man his own good; and particularly then, when it conduceth to such a benefit, as shall put a man in a condition, to neglect not only the disprraise, and revilings, but also the power of other men. The Kingdom of God is gotten by violence; but what if it could be gotten by unjust violence? were it against Reason so to get it, when it is impossible to receive hurt by it? and if it be not against Reason, it is not against Justice; or else Justice is not to be approved for good. From such reasoning as this, Successful wickedness hath obtained the Name of Virtue; and some that in all other things have disallowed the violation of Faith; yet have allowed it, when it is for the getting of a Kingdome. And the Heathen that believed, that Saturn was deposed by his son Jupiter, believed nevertheless the same Jupiter to be the avenger of Injustice: Somewhat like to a piece of Law in Cokes Commentaries on Litleton; where he says, If the right Heir of the Crown be attainted of Treason; yet the Crown shall descend to him, and *Eo Instante* the Attender be void; From which instances a man will be very prone to infer; that when the Heire apparent of a Kingdome, shall kill him that is in possession, though his father; you may call it Injustice, or by what other name you will; yet it can never be against Reason, seeing all the voluntary actions of men tend to the benefit of themselves; and those actions are most Reasonable, that conduce most to their ends. This specious reasoning is nevertheless false.

For the question is not of promises mutual, where there is no security of performance on either side; as when there is no Civil Power erected over the parties promising; for such promises are no Covenants: But either where one of the parties has performed already; or where there is a Power to make him perform; there is the question whether it be against reason, that is, against the benefit of the other to perform, or not. And I say it is not against reason. For the manifestation whereof, we are to consider; First, that when a man doth a thing, which notwithstanding anything can be foreseen, and reckoned on, tendeth to his own destruction, howsoever some accident which he could not expect, arriving may turn it to his benefit; yet such events do not make it reasonably or wisely done. Secondly, that in a condition of War, wherein every man to every man, for want of a common Power to keep them all in awe, is an Enemy, there is no man can hope by his own strength, or wit, to defend himself from destruction, without the help of Confederates; where everyone expects the same defense by the Confederation, that anyone else does: and therefore he which declares he thinks it reason to deceive those that help him, can in reason expect no other means of safety, than what can be had from his own single Power. He therefore that breaketh his Covenant, and consequently declareth that he thinks he may with reason do so, cannot be received into any Society, that unite themselves for Peace and defense, but by the error of them that receive him; nor when he is received, be retained in it, without seeing the danger of their error; which errors a man cannot reasonably reckon upon as the means of his security; and therefore if he be left, or cast out of Society, he perisheth; and if he live in Society, it is by the errors of other men, which he could not foresee, nor reckon upon; and consequently against the reason of his preservation; and so, as all men that contribute not to his destruction, forbear him only out of ignorance of what is good for themselves.

As for the Instance of gaining the secure and perpetual felicity of Heaven, by any way; it is frivolous: there being but one way imaginable; and that is not breaking, but keeping of Covenant.

And for the other Instance of attaining Sovereignty by Rebellion; it is manifest, that though the event follow, yet because it cannot reasonably be expected, but rather the contrary; and because by gaining it so, others are taught to gain the same in like manner, the attempt thereof is against reason. Justice therefore, that is to say, Keeping of Covenant, is a Rule of Reason, by which we are forbidden to do anything destructive to our life; and consequently a Law of Nature.

COMPREHENSION QUESTIONS

1. When is human life "solitary, poor, nasty, brutish, and short"? Why?
2. What are the "Laws of Nature"? In what sense are they laws?
3. Hobbes think that, in some circumstances, people will renounce or transfer their rights. Why would they ever do this?
4. Why do we need "some coercive Power"?
5. Hobbes says that "[t]he Fool hath said in his heart, there is no such thing as Justice." What, exactly, is the objection that he's considering here? What's his reply?

NOTES

1. That isn't all bad: Sometimes, success is learning that the issue is much more complicated than we thought, and so we should be much less confident in our judgments about it. In such circumstances, it's plausible that everyone should be a lot more willing to compromise, which sounds pretty good in these partisan times.
2. See Michael Lynch, *True to Life: Why Truth Matters* (Cambridge: MIT Press, 2005).
3. Tversky, A., & Kahneman, D. (1983). Extensional versus intuitive reasoning: The conjunction fallacy in probability judgment. Psychological Review, 90(4), 297.
4. . . . assuming that the probability of either p or q isn't 1 or 0.
5. Tversky, A. and Kahneman, D. 1981. The framing of decisions and the psychology of choice. Science, 211: 453.
6. Things are different when we're trying to assess whether someone's lying. If the victim's mother is on the stand, she might well say anything that increases the likelihood of a conviction. In such circumstances, we should take her testimony with a grain of salt. That's very different from having the victim's mother make an *argument* that the accused person did it, and then ignoring that argument just because the victim's mother made it.
7. Moreover, even if someone provides solid empirical evidence for the prediction, it's still up for debate whether the predicted harms of legalization outweigh the harms of criminalizing it. This invites another round of empirical investigation. For instance, does criminalization of marijuana or heroin empower organized crime, and by how much? And then there are more things to consider still. Suppose the societal harms of heroin abuse are going to be significant down the line, to the point that they will slightly outweigh the harms of not legalizing. But Andy is miserable without marijuana, and he is at virtually zero risk for heroin abuse. What gives the society the right to deny Andy release from misery so that someone in thirty years doesn't OD? We need to weigh social harms against individual rights.
8. Haidt, Jonathan. 2012. The Righteous Mind: Why Good People are Divided by Politics and Religion. New York: Vintage Books. p. 105.

9. For others, and for much more about critical thinking, I highly recommend Lewis Vaughn's *The Power of Critical Thinking: Effective Reasoning About Ordinary and Extraordinary Claims* (New York: Oxford University Press, 2015 [5th ed.]).

10. . . . which isn't to say that the others are necessarily bad. There are lots of good arguments that aren't valid, such as *strong inductive* arguments. Strong inductive arguments make their conclusions *highly probable*—which means that it's possible for the premises to be true and the conclusion false, but the conclusion is, nevertheless, very likely to be true if the premises are.

11. Modus ponens isn't the only valid form of inference; there are lots of them. Again, see Vaughn's *The Power of Critical Thinking* for more.

12. Of course, despite all this, Bill's conclusion might still be true (albeit not for the reason he gave). The show isn't over after we tackle the first consideration we encounter. The conversation continues when Bill gives us a new reason, we bang it into the shape of an argument, and we turn to the merits of *those* premises. And on we go.

13. And, of course, that should affect your confidence in the conclusions of the arguments that you might make on that basis. So, for example, if your entire argument turns on a claim about the consequences of raising the minimum wage, and the evidence doesn't settle the matter, then you shouldn't be too confident that we should endorse this or that policy.

14. It's notable, of course, that the readers of this book probably aren't horrified by the circumcision of male infants. There are some differences between these practices, but it's worth considering whether we ought to be disturbed by both.

CHAPTER 1

꘎◯

Introduction to the Left and Right

EQUALITY AS A MORAL BASIS FOR
PROGRESSIVE POLITICS
DUSTIN CRUMMETT

1. Introduction

The left contains great diversity of opinion, but a view known as *social egalitarianism* is central to much leftist thought. My goal here is to explain and draw out some of the implications of social egalitarianism, in order to help you get a better sense of what unifies the left in the United States, and why that leads to leftists supporting the policies they do.

Most people recognize *equality* as an important political value. But there are many ways in which people could be "equal," and egalitarianism is significant only if we grasp what kind of equality is important. For instance, sometimes people think "equality" is supposed to mean that people should be made equally well-off, in some all-encompassing sense. This is satirized in Kurt Vonnegut's short story "Harrison Bergeron." The people in Harrison Bergeron's dystopian society regard natural differences in ability as unjust, so they weigh strong people down with weights so they can't use their strength, make smart people listen to static so they can't concentrate, and so on. That kind of equality sounds dismal. On the other hand, people sometimes treat equality as requiring only that people be treated "the same" in some cheap sense. A few years ago, the Republican congresswoman Michele Bachmann responded to questions about gay marriage from two high school students, Jane Schmidt and Ella Newell. At this point, gay marriage was illegal in most of the United States, and Schmidt and Newell claimed this was an instance of discrimination against gay people. Bachmann responded that everyone actually had "the same civil rights," since gay couples were expected to "abide by the same law as everyone else. They can marry a man if they're a woman. Or they can marry a woman if they're a man."[1] The crowd was enthusiastic about Bachmann's response, but clearly, more or less anything could pass this test, no matter how obviously discriminatory. (Suppose someone claimed a law banning Christianity didn't discriminate against Christians, since it allowed both Christians and non-Christians equally to practice non-Christian religions, and forbade both equally from practicing Christianity.) That kind of equality sounds useless.

Social egalitarians understand equality differently. They say that what egalitarians should primarily care about is that people enjoy equal relationships with each other.[2] The modern incarnation of social egalitarianism traces back to the social movements of the 1960s (the civil rights movement, early contemporary feminism, etc.),[3] but social egalitarianism itself can be traced back, through the labor and abolition movements, to the early modern period, where it served as a critique of aristocratic societies.[4] Many of the leaders of the relevant movements then were, in turn, inspired by the ancient religious idea that we are all equal before God.[5]

It's hard to know *in detail* what a full realization of this ideal—a true world of equals—might look like. (Similarly, it would be hard for someone living under the pharaohs to imagine what our *more* equal society might look like.) But we can identify the main obstacles to making things *better*—namely, the various oppressive hierarchies that sustain unjustly unequal social relations between people. The point is not that hierarchies are *never* justifiable; an army without commanders might not last long. The point is instead that, if they are to be justifiable, those on top owe us an explanation of why the hierarchy needs to exist and why they should be at the top of it, and it must be an explanation that should be acceptable to everyone involved in light of their fundamentally equal dignity and worth.[6] (It can't, say, rest on the idea that certain types of people somehow inherently deserve to lord over others.) As Noam Chomsky notes, in practice, it turns out that real hierarchies tend to "have no justification in the interests of the person lower in the hierarchy, or in the interests of other people, or the environment, or the future, or the society, or anything else—they're just there in order to preserve certain structures of power and domination, and the people at the top."[7]

Social egalitarians generally combine this ethical ideal about the value of equality with an account of what sorts of unjust hierarchies actually exist in our society. They also suggest concrete steps that are meant to help combat oppressive hierarchies. These steps may be legal measures, or they may be, say, social movements aimed at changing individuals' attitudes. (The LGBT rights movement, for instance, has employed both of these to great effect.) Which strategies are appropriate will depend on practical considerations, but also ethical ones. For instance, when individuals' religious beliefs conflict with social equality, difficult questions arise about how best to pursue equality while also respecting religious liberty.

I don't have space to fill in every detail, so my aim here is only to *sketch an outline* of how things look to social egalitarians. I also don't have space to *defend* this picture at length, though I will try to explain it in a way that makes its appeal obvious. In the next section, in order to make social egalitarianism more concrete, I discuss some particular types of hierarchical oppression that it opposes.[8] In the third section, I explain how social egalitarians see such hierarchies functioning in our society today. In the fourth section, I explain how opposition to these oppressive hierarchies helps justify left-wing positions on a range of political issues.

2. Some Types of Oppression

It's easy to think of clear examples of unjust hierarchies from other times or places: Consider the division between the ruling class of North Korea and its citizens, between whites and blacks during slavery and the Jim Crow era, between industrialists and the workers who toiled in their factories during the Industrial Revolution, or between European imperialists and their colonial subjects. Reflecting on *why* these social arrangements are unjust might make us more sensitive to injustices around us *here and now*, which we often take for granted. I'll name four types of unequal relations between groups that help explain the obvious injustice of these situations. These may not be the only types of oppressive relations, but they are four major ones. And the four don't always go together—sometimes we find just some of them. However, for reasons that should become clear, they tend to be mutually reinforcing.[9]

An obvious type of unequal relation occurs in cases of what I'll call *domination*, where some have arbitrary, far-reaching, and unaccountable power over the actions of others. An obvious example is slavery, but there are many other ways this can happen. For instance, when whites prevented people of color from voting, or when men did the same for women, members of one group indirectly exercised power over another: The state exercises power over everyone, and one group controlled the state without input from the other. (Dictatorship, where *one* person controls the state and thereby dominates everyone else, is the limit case of this.)[10]

Notice something important here: Freedom and equality are sometimes portrayed as being in conflict, since protecting equality might require restricting free actions that work against it. Domination shows that the picture is more complicated. A certain kind of freedom (that involved in being a free *person*, rather than a servant) actually *requires* a certain kind of equality (the social equality that prevents some from exercising unaccountable power over others). Views that ignore this provide great freedom to the powerful, but no one else.

A second type of unequal relation involves what I'll call *disregard*. Here, society treats the needs and interests of some as inherently less significant than those of others, and so is less responsive to their needs. This can take the form of active *hostility* to the interests of some—think of genocides or hate crimes—but can also take the form of mere *apathy*.[11] British misrule in India led to periodic, devastating famines (famines that ceased when India gained independence).[12] During one that began in 1876, the British colonial authorities refused to provide anything but minimal famine relief, citing concerns both about the direct costs of providing food and about, essentially, making poor Indians dependent on government handouts.[13] Lord Lytton, the British viceroy of India, made clear that the colonial authorities did not regard the lives of Indians as equal to those of Britons, and were concerned only with maintaining the profitability of their colony: He derided those who would "save life at a cost that would bankrupt India" as the victims of "cheap sentiment" and "humanitarian hysterics."[14] Estimates suggest that, as a result, over six million people died.[15] Presumably, the British didn't *want* this to happen, exactly; they just didn't care enough to stop it.

A third type involves what I'll call *disrespect*. Paradigm cases occur when members of certain groups are widely subjected to demeaning stereotypes and attitudes, expressed either openly or more subtly in the form of what are called "microaggressions."[16] Alternatively, rather than receiving *negative* attention, members of certain groups may have themselves and their positive contributions simply ignored or overlooked. In the context of personal interactions, those at the bottom may be expected to grovel before their "betters" and to show respect and deference, while those at the top can humiliate or ignore them. Think here of contexts where slurs against minority groups are treated as acceptable, or of racial segregation, which was premised on, and intended to reinforce, the idea that blacks were somehow "unworthy" of living alongside whites.

A final type involves *exploitation*. Here, one person produces a benefit, usually at some cost to himself or herself, but another person unfairly seizes part or all of the benefit without providing an appropriate benefit in return.[17] Slave owners steal the fruits of the labor of their slaves; the same is true for the Victorian-era factory owner and his impoverished workers. The early twentieth-century union song "Solidarity Forever" railed against the exploitation of working people by the rich (it's the same tune as the "Battle Hymn of the Republic," if you'd like to sing along):

> It is we who ploughed the prairies, built the cities where they trade
> Dug the mines and built the workshops, endless miles of railroad laid
> Now we stand outcast and starving 'mid the wonders we have made
> But the union makes us strong!

Exploitation can also occur outside of what we normally think of as the "market." For instance, women have often been expected to do *household* labor, and, unlike "real" work, this usually goes uncompensated.[18] This complaint made it into part of a verse later added to "Solidarity Forever," sung from the perspective of women workers: "*It is we who wash the dishes, scrub the floors and clean the dirt / Feed the kids and send them off to school—and then we go to work.*" [19]

You may have noticed that the unequal relations I mentioned have benign counterparts. Parents can have power over children without dominating them, can show special concern for their children without disregarding the interests of others, and can help their children who can't repay them without being exploited. Meanwhile, those who rank sports teams judge that some people have certain good traits, and others have certain bad traits, without disrespecting them.

What separates these benign relationships from their oppressive counterparts? The overall test, again, is whether their features should be acceptable to all the relevant parties. What this means in concrete terms will be more complicated. When it comes to power relations, egalitarians generally support making them *reciprocal* where possible, so that no one has *unaccountable* power over another. For instance, political leaders have power over voters, but, in a functioning democracy, voters control the exercise of this power through the threat of replacing their leaders.[20] Employers have power over employees, but, where a strong union is present, employees have power of their own as a result of their ability to collectively bargain.[21] Where this reciprocity isn't feasible—as may be the case with, say, a sergeant and a private—egalitarians still insist that the authority possessed by the superior must be justified in terms of the general good, and must be *only* that which is necessary to promote that good. (This is why the sergeant can order the private to charge an enemy position, but can't order the private to hand over five dollars: Having the second power can't be justified by military necessity.)[22] When it comes to questions of respect and esteem, egalitarians should not, like whoever thought participation trophies were a good idea, try to pretend that everyone is equally possessed of every good quality. Instead, they should, first, emphasize the equal basic dignity we all possess; second, recognize the diversity in what people have to offer (you're better than me at some things, while I'm better than you at others); and, third, recognize that these traits can be found across demographic lines.[23] If we do this, we may still rank people as athletes, or chess players, or whatever, but won't rank them *as people* in ways that stigmatize them due to who they are, or make them feel inferior due to factors beyond their control.

Finally, the right things to say about regard and exploitation are, I think, probably pretty complicated, and not something I have space to get into here.[24] Fortunately, I think these rough remarks are sufficient for present purposes, because the unequal relationships to which I'll draw our attention clearly fall on the "unjust" side of the line, whatever the specifics of that line are.

3. Oppressive Hierarchies Today

Of course, which groups stand in which hierarchies can vary with time and place. (Irish Americans were once oppressed in the United States but no longer are.) In contemporary American society, unjust hierarchies exist between the rich and the poor, employers and many employees, men and women, whites and non-whites, straight people and gay or bisexual people, cisgender and transgender or non-binary people, and able-bodied people and disabled people, among others.[25] Internationally, they exist between citizens of powerful countries (such as Americans) and the targets of those countries' imperialism (such as Iraqis). Some examples to help clarify. Given that non-union workers without rare skills enjoy little bargaining power, have few legal protections, and are often forced by economic necessity to stay in their jobs, employers can exercise a tremendous amount of control over them, thereby dominating them.[26] The name of the "Black Lives Matter" movement serves to assert that society acts as if black lives *don't* matter—that is, that black people are disregarded. The movement focuses on the use of police violence, but there are many other examples. For instance, black women are several times more likely to die in childbirth than white women, something that one doctor tellingly describes as exposing the fact that "the system's . . . not valuing the lives of black women equally to white women."[27] When conservative politicians promote negative and baseless stereotypes about immigrants for political reasons, they disrespect them. And consider the astonishing fact that the wealthiest 1% of Americans own almost *twice* as much wealth as the bottom 90%.[28] We all contribute to the economy, but the system is set up to provide the very wealthy with far more than their fair share; this is exploitation.

I don't mean to suggest that every type of oppression mentioned is *as bad* as those mentioned in the paradigm cases in the last section. There has been real progress: Workers are better off than they were before the New Deal; gay people are better off than they were before the gay rights movement; etc. This doesn't mean that the remaining oppression is not very bad. Instead, the existence of *some* progress should make us hopeful that more can be made, and determined to fulfill the mission of those who sacrificed to get us this far.

Two more points. First, if you are wealthy, white, etc., the point is not to make you feel guilty. The way to evaluate *you*, as a moral agent, is not on the basis of your group membership, but on what you do in light of it—whether, say, you fight for equality. As Chomsky notes, "Privilege yields opportunity, and opportunity confers responsibilities. An individual then has choices."[29]

A second point is that being at the top of a hierarchy doesn't necessarily mean that one's life isn't *difficult*, for two reasons. First, social identities are complicated; one can be high in some hierarchies and low in others.[30] One routinely hears that white, working-class Trump voters who have lost their jobs and seen their communities devastated by drug abuse and economic ruin don't like being told they have white privilege. But we can recognize that, as members of the working class, they face grievous injustices, while also recognizing that, all else equal, they hold a superior social position to working-class people of color. Indeed, this is part of why one hears so much more about them than about residents of certain communities of color that have faced similar problems, or worse, for much longer.

Second, one's social position doesn't necessarily align with one's level of well-being. This is clear in certain cases: A dictator with a severe chronic illness might be *worse off* than most of his subjects, but there is nonetheless a clear sense in which he's on top. That egalitarians should worry about this would be puzzling if we thought egalitarians should be concerned with making people equally well off—after all, he isn't better off than his subjects—but makes perfect sense, given that the real concern is *social* equality. Indeed, unjust hierarchies often make *everyone* worse off, including those at the top. Again, this is clear in some cases: Our dictator might be fearful and paranoid precisely because he's a dictator, and knows others are out to get him. But consider a more mundane example: When masculinity is valorized and other ways of being are degraded, men often feel pressure to be hyper-masculine and to avoid doing anything "unmanly." Since masculinity is stereotypically associated with toughness and self-reliance, this can make men feel unable to express their emotions and unable to seek help when they need it, with dire consequences for their mental health.[31] That unjust hierarchies are often bad for everyone is just another reason to oppose them.

4. Some Applications

What we've said so far helps provide a unified justification for why leftists take the positions they do on a wide range of issues. For instance, economic inequality is a major issue among leftists. But why care about economic *inequality*? That is, it's easy to see why we should care about *poverty*—the fact that some don't have *enough*—but why care about the fact that some have *more* than others? Conservatives sometimes claim this is mere envy.[32] But the account above provides a satisfying answer. The obvious reason, already hinted at, is that vast inequalities in wealth are seldom achieved without someone exploiting someone else. They also lead to domination; since wealth can influence the political process, the rich can use it to exercise unaccountable power over the whole of society.[33] Since social standards for what it takes to appear "respectable" to others vary depending on the wealth of a society, when some people have much less than average, they are likely to face disrespectful judgments.[34] And a system that allocates to some far more than they need while others struggle to get by shows unequal regard.

Now consider an apparently unrelated issue: leftist concern for so-called political correctness, where this takes the form of opposition to, say, sexist or racist jokes, or to statues that honor Confederate generals. People sometimes think activists oppose these things just because they are *offended* by them. Conservatives note that, in principle, anyone might be offended by anything, so demanding that people never give offense is unreasonable. But the point is that these things are politically objectionable primarily because they insult some, and, in context, thereby reinforce hierarchies of disrespect. When a community honors someone with a statue because they fought to preserve a government whose sole reason for existing was to safeguard a system of horrific racial domination of blacks by whites, they clearly signal something negative about how they view blacks, even if unintentionally.

Something similar can be said about leftist support for gay marriage. Some conservatives suggested "civil unions" for gay couples, which would have provided the same tangible benefits as marriage while withholding the *symbolic* recognition of the value of gay relationships that the word "marriage" carries. Leftists rejected this, arguing that awarding a special badge of recognition to straight but not gay relationships would insult the dignity of gay couples. Justice Kennedy agreed, writing in the opinion legalizing gay marriage:

> As the State itself makes marriage all the more precious by the significance it attaches to it, exclusion . . . has the effect of teaching that gays and lesbians are unequal in important respects. It demeans gays and lesbians for the State to lock them out of a central institution of the Nation's society . . . The imposition of this disability on gays and lesbians serves to disrespect and subordinate them.[35]

Or consider yet another apparently unrelated issue: the complicated progressive attitudes regarding the relationship of the United States to the rest of the world. I've focused mostly on issues of justice *within* societies, but social egalitarians also believe that, insofar as there are relations between societies, they should also be conducted on terms of equality.[36] Proper regard for foreigners is incompatible with any narrow brand of "America First"-ism: We can't just close our borders to people in need, or otherwise refuse them help.[37] At the same time, sensible leftists are skeptical of American intentions abroad: Just like powerful people, they realize that powerful countries routinely use their power to dominate other countries, economically exploit them, and act without regard for the well-being of their people, often using humanitarian justifications as a pretext. (The most obvious recent example is our illegal invasion of Iraq, which has resulted in hundreds of thousands of deaths and, through its effects, helped plunge multiple societies into chaos. But we constantly commit crimes abroad, and many of these never even come to the attention of the American public.)[38]

These twin concerns are part of why leftists often hold out hope for international institutions, such as the United Nations (UN). Just as democracy can help prevent domination by politicians and unionization can help prevent domination by bosses, the hope is that international institutions, by giving representatives from different countries a voice and handling questions according to an established legal framework, can justly adjudicate disputes between nations, as well as appeals to the broader international community from oppressed people within nations. Unfortunately, international institutions often don't work very well themselves: Often they are totally ineffective or just rubber-stamp whatever powerful countries want anyway. Maybe someday we'll develop *better* ones: After all, the UN was only founded in 1945, which is pretty recent in the scope of history. In the meantime, we must do our best to avoid both isolationism and imperialism.

A final note about the role of government in left-wing policy proposals. Conservatives sometimes accuse progressives of having too much faith in government. I've already indicated my skepticism of those who hold power; that includes politicians. (Indeed, *Democratic* politicians routinely act in ways that are condemned by the egalitarian picture I've sketched here.)[39] The reason to sometimes rely on government action is the same reason I sometimes rely on a mechanic: There are problems only they can fix (such as, in the government's case, economic inequality). And the appropriate response to the possibility of government misconduct is the same as that to the possibility of your mechanic cheating you: Be attentive and keep them accountable. This means that justice will reliably be done only when there are movements of informed individuals who fight for it.[40] But that was true anyway. While past successes are reason for optimism, justice is not inevitable, and it cannot be achieved by theory alone. It needs flesh-and-blood people to breathe fire into its principles. It needs us.[41]

COMPREHENSION QUESTIONS

1. What is social egalitarianism, and how does it unite the political left?
2. What are the origins of social egalitarianism?
3. How is equality understood, and why is it important?
4. How do modern social egalitarians function in today's society?
5. What are some characteristics of unequal power relationships, and what examples are offered in the reading?

DISCUSSION QUESTIONS

1. How does Crummett define the following hierarchical inequalities: domination, disregard, disrespect, and exploitation? Are you satisfied by these definitions? What other examples of social inequalities exist today?
2. What is a reciprocal power relationship, and why is it important to social equality?
3. What are your thoughts on egalitarian principles? Do you think that liberals are the only ones who endorse these principles? If you disagree with these principles, what are some more suitable alternatives? Why?
4. On a global level, is there a better way to address hierarchical injustice than the United Nations?

Case 1

Racial Disparity Across Incomes

In recent years, as high rates of maternal mortality in the United States have alarmed researchers, one statistic has been especially concerning.[*] According to the CDC,[†] black mothers in the United States die at three to four times the rate of white mothers, one of the widest of all racial disparities in women's health. Put another way, a black woman is 22% more likely to die from heart disease than a white woman and 71% more likely to perish from cervical cancer, but 243% more likely to die from pregnancy- or childbirth-related causes. In a national study[‡] of five medical complications that are common causes of maternal death and injury, black women were two to three times more likely to die than white women who had the same condition.

That imbalance has persisted for decades, and in some places, it continues to grow. In New York City, for example, black mothers are 12 times more likely to die than white mothers, according to the most recent data[§]; in 2001–2005, their risk of death was seven times higher. Researchers say that widening gap reflects a dramatic improvement for white women but not for blacks.

The disproportionate toll on African Americans is the main reason the U.S. maternal mortality rate is so much higher than that of other affluent countries. Black expectant and new mothers in the United States die at about the same rate as women in countries such as Mexico and Uzbekistan, the World Health Organization estimates.[**]

Does this sort of inequity need to be corrected? If so, by whom? And, what sort of strategies might we adopt to remedy the situation?

What circumstances perpetuate this kind of social disparity? Are there other cases you can think of present today?

---

[*]https://www.npr.org/2017/12/07/568948782/black-mothers-keep-dying-after-giving-birth-shalon-irvings-story-explains-why

[†]https://www.cdc.gov/reproductivehealth/maternalinfanthealth/pmss.html

[‡]https://www.ncbi.nlm.nih.gov/pubmed/?term=Tucker+MJ%2C+Berg+CJ%2C+Callaghan+WM%2C+Hsia+J

[§]https://www.propublica.org/article/new-york-city-launches-committee-to-review-maternal-deaths

[**]https://www.centerforhealthjournalism.org/content/america%E2%80%99s-high-maternal-mortality-what-can-be-done

FOR ALL THE RIGHT REASONS
C. A. MCINTOSH

> It is very hard for a man to defend anything of which he is entirely convinced. It is comparatively easy when he is only partially convinced. He is partially convinced because he has found this or that proof of the thing, and he can expound it. But a man is not really convinced of a philosophic theory when he finds that something proves it. He is only really convinced when he finds that everything proves it. And the more converging reasons he finds pointing to this conviction, the more bewildered he is if asked suddenly to sum them up. Thus, if one asked an ordinary intelligent man, on the spur of the moment, "Why do you prefer civilization to savagery?" he would look wildly round at object after object, and would only be able to answer vaguely, "Why, there is that bookcase . . . and the coals in the coal-scuttle . . . and pianos . . . and policemen." The whole case for civilization is that the case for it is complex. It has done so many things. But that very multiplicity of proof which ought to make reply overwhelming makes reply impossible.

> —G. K. Chesterton, *Orthodoxy*[42]

Like the case for civilization, the case for an overall political philosophy is complex, not least because it must encompass so much, but also because its believer tends to be entirely convinced. Thus in this chapter, I offer not so much a case for as a *sketch* of a political philosophy shared by many on the right. If nothing else, I hope to show that there is a stable philosophy underlying popular right-wing thought today, as opposed to a mere location on a shifting political spectrum. At the highest level of abstraction, that philosophy has two essential claims: first, that the freedom of the individual and the power of government are inversely proportional; second, due respect for persons requires that the optimal relationship is some maximal degree of liberty given some minimal degree of government. Zooming in, classical liberalism, libertarianism, paleo-conservatism, and other right-wing political philosophies each argue for their own optimum. So while my own sketch below doesn't represent everyone on the right, it does represent a dominant breed: traditional American conservatives—and this for two reasons. First, I am an American who believes in traditional conservatism. But more importantly, though the roots of the right reach deep into the past, I believe it came to full bloom in the American experiment of the eighteenth century.[43]

That is not to say that America, then or ever, has perfectly embodied that philosophy. But it is precisely a commitment to that philosophy, upon which America was founded, that serves as the basis of hope for progress. Real progress is made not by destroying the imperfect and replacing it with something new and untried, but by building on the foundations of the tried and true. And that is what conservatism is all about: conserving the tried and true—*not* a blind allegiance to the past or maintaining the status quo.

I.

We begin with what may seem obvious: All human beings, regardless of contingencies of race, sex, and class, are intrinsically valuable. We have immeasurable dignity and worth just because of what we are by nature, and so ought always be treated as ends and never as mere means. But this wasn't always obvious. It was largely Christianity that bequeathed to us this idea.[44] Early Christians put into practice the doctrine that humans are created in the image of God, following Jesus's example and admonition to love thy neighbor by rescuing abandoned Roman infants; defending the unborn; caring for widows, the homeless, and the poor; befriending social outcasts; elevating the status of women; ending gladiatorial blood sport; establishing charities, hospitals, orphanages, schools; and more.[45] The West—nay, the *world*—is forever indebted to what was then a little religious movement, which sowed the seeds that eventually grew into robust declarations of universal human rights. Conservatives today carry on this tradition of cherishing and protecting human life, defensively by opposing the injustices of abortion, euthanasia, and terrorism, and offensively by advocating the justness of capital punishment and circumspect warfare.[46] Whether the belief that humans are intrinsically valuable can ultimately be justified apart from a theistic framework, I cannot argue here. Suffice it to say that were it not for the recognition that we are intrinsically valuable, I see no grounds for perhaps the most politically revolutionary claim ever made: that we have natural rights.[47]

Natural rights are like moral sanctions to perform certain actions and pursue certain activities. Chief among them, as identified by their most famous expositors, are the right to life and the means of preserving it, the exercise of liberty, private ownership of justly acquired property, the fruits of one's own labor, the pursuit of happiness, family-making and inheritance, freedom of expression, and the practice of religion. The guarantor of these rights is not a social entity like a contract or government, but the objective reality of our very nature as rational animals. A slave, for example, has the natural right to be free even if there is for him no such civil right recognized by the law of the land. His status as a slave is artificial; his status as a human being is not.

Saying these rights are objective is not to say that they cannot be restrained or trumped. Your right to liberty, for example, does not imply that you are free to murder me. That is because my right to life generates in you a moral duty not to violate it. Supposing you do, your right to life gets trumped as I defend my own. As is often said, liberty is not unrestrained license. Liberty is the freedom to flourish within boundaries prescribed by a just moral and social order. Conservatives call this "ordered liberty."

The "ordered" in "ordered liberty" is both descriptive and prescriptive. There is an objective moral order, and humans cannot flourish individually or collectively in contradiction to it. That order contains norms governing health, gender, sexual intercourse, marriage, family, non-familial relationships, and all other social arrangements. Each of these, just like anything else, is good only to the extent that it properly expresses its nature and purpose. A good knife is one that cuts well. A good heart is one that pumps blood. Likewise, there is such a thing as a good man, good woman, good sex, good marriage, good family, and so on, delimited by human nature and discovered by reason, experience, and, many believe, divine revelation. As David Oderberg puts it, "the affairs of men—governed as they are by morality—are regulated by an eternal and immutable law to which 'right reason' must conform if human agents are to be held to act morally."[48]

II.

But, it hardly needs to be said, humans don't always act morally. We lie, cheat, and steal; we fornicate, victimize, and murder—all to the destruction of others and even ourselves. Why? Answers to this question account for our political differences probably more than anything else. As the conservative sees it, external factors like rough environment, low education, poverty, joblessness, oppression, etc. cannot sufficiently explain our predilection for evil. Nor can the relatively ostensible internal reasons we give, such as selfishness, anger, or hatred. No, a deeper explanation is required.

The cold hard truth, one acknowledged by nearly every keen observer of humanity throughout history, is that the arc of man's moral nature is long, and it bends not toward justice, but evil. So while we are good to the extent that we act in accordance with our nature, the paradox of the human condition is that there seems to be something in our nature that disposes us to act contrary to it. "The heart is deceitful above all things and desperately wicked," the prophet Jeremiah said, "Who can understand it?" Evil will always beguile mankind, despite our noblest efforts. This is powerfully conveyed in Christopher Nolan's film *The Dark Knight* when Batman struggles to understand the Joker. "Criminals aren't complicated, Alfred," he says. "We just need to figure out what he's after." The much wiser Alfred replies, "Perhaps this is a man you don't fully understand. Some men aren't looking for anything logical, like money. They can't be bought, bullied, reasoned or negotiated with. Some men just want to watch the world burn."

No *just* system of government will ever be capable of eradicating or even significantly controlling human wickedness. This is the fundamental and decisive flaw inherent to all melioristic visions of humanity, such as Marxism and its kin. All attempts to implement such visions, resting on a catastrophically naïve understanding of human nature, have resulted in wild exacerbations of human suffering. "If only it were all so simple!" laments Aleksandr Solzhenitsyn in *The Gulag Archipelago*, a soul-numbingly thorough documentation of atrocities committed by the USSR. He continues:

> If only there were evil people somewhere insidiously committing evil deeds, and it were necessary only to separate them from the rest of us and destroy them. But the line dividing good and evil cuts through the heart of every human being. And who is willing to destroy a piece of his own heart? During the life of any heart this line keeps changing place; sometimes it is squeezed one way by exuberant evil and sometimes it shifts to allow enough space for good to flourish. One and the same human being is, at various stages, under various circumstances, a totally different human being. At times he is close to being a devil, at times to sainthood. But his name doesn't change, and to that name we ascribe the whole lot, good and evil.[49]

Evil can only be eradicated, not by instituting laws or expanding government, but by eradicating ourselves—as the children of all "progressive" revolutions inevitably learn.[50] Any political philosophy that doesn't acknowledge the complexity of human nature or the ineradicability of evil is a total non-starter.

Despite this, people will continue to sentimentalize utopian nonsense, as John Lennon does in his celebrated song "Imagine." Lennon recognizes that his imaginary world would have no religion, no countries, no possessions, and, most tellingly, "nothing to kill or die for." It would, in effect, be Aldous Huxley's *Brave New World*, where a paternalistic government administers a sedative to its citizens and eliminates all sources of potential suffering, such as art, music, books, and meaningful relationships—in short, humanity itself. If you would not want to live in Huxley's world, let me suggest you value autonomy and authenticity more than social serenity. We ought therefore to guard our liberty with a fierce jealousy against encroachments by the state, however seemingly beneficent or benign, as such encroachments tend to metastasize into malignancy.

III.

This is not to deny that government should have a substantive role in the body politic. Rather, it is to affirm that its role is somewhere between the "too much" of totalitarianism (order at the expense of liberty) and the "too little" of anarchy (liberty at the expense of order). Hence, the American founders aimed for the Goldilocks ideal of ordered liberty with a constitutional republic: a limited government wherein a majority rules by electing representatives to promote the common good. They were just as concerned about threats to order and liberty from a tyrannical government as from a tyrannical populace, and so, along with Aristotle, were not at all sanguine about a democracy: a government wherein a majority rules by promoting self-interest rather than the common good.

Government promotes the common good insofar as it maintains and defends the conditions necessary for us to flourish by exercising our natural rights. Or, as the opening line of the U.S. Constitution puts it, a "more perfect union" will "establish justice, insure domestic tranquility, provide for the common defense, promote the general welfare, and secure the blessings of liberty to ourselves and our posterity." It will, in other words, equally enforce laws and administer justice blindly when they're violated, provide access to civil courts that guarantee due process, maintain a military, facilitate the means of commerce by issuing currency, and so on.

Two main checks prevent the government in charge of these tasks from becoming too powerful. First, due respect is given to citizens' natural rights to life, liberty, and free expression that allows them to criticize their government and, if necessary, take up arms against it. With the power of the pen in one hand and the power of the gun in the other, a citizenry so armed, who would prefer death to the loss of liberty, is a redoubtable bulwark against a Hobbesian Leviathan.[51] Of course, with these freedoms come risks of abuse. But as ol' Ben Franklin said, "Those who would give up essential liberty, to purchase a little temporary safety, deserve neither liberty nor safety." Second, the government is structured so as to prevent centralization of power. All tasks are divided among separate branches of a central government, each with their own internal checks and balances, to which individual states (akin to little countries with their own constitutions) voluntarily submit. States themselves are in turn decentralized, being made up of separate counties, townships, cities, and so on.

This second check (federalism) is an implementation of the organizing principle of subsidiarity—deference first to the authority at the lowest level of jurisdiction—which is essential to the just ordering of society at every level, all the way down to the family.[52] Just governance occurs from the bottom up, beginning with the lowest and closest sphere of authority. Only when a problem is unmanageable at a given level is it appropriate for a higher one to get involved; otherwise, there is overreach of power. Very rarely should the state reach all the way down into the family. There is excellent reason for so ordering government and civil society: The closer someone is to a situation the more likely they are to know just what is needed, and the further one is, the less likely. This is why conservatives feel deep apprehension when the power of the federal government is called upon to address social ills. There are very few ills that cannot be more competently and effectively handled locally through private charity, volunteering, community-building efforts, and simply being a good neighbor.[53] These more personal, intimate initiatives at the ground level breed compassion, friendliness, personal responsibility, and gratitude rather than the resentment, entitlement, and potential corruption bred by impersonal aid doled from above.[54] Besides, tinkering at the top almost always results in unforeseen consequences at lower levels. Minimum wage laws, affirmative action policies, and welfare assistance are all perfect examples of well-intentioned violations of subsidiarity that have harmed more than they've helped.[55]

Notice that the lowest level of authority mentioned above is the family, not the individual. Conservatives understand that while man is no mere cog in a machine run from the top down via the ideas and desires of a powerful leader or state, neither is he an "ethical atom" free to determine himself from the bottom up via his own ideas and desires.[56] The *family* is the most basic unit in society, and so premium is placed on what is good for the family, not necessarily the individual. And what is good for the family is, first and foremost, the institution of marriage as the permanent union between one man and woman with child-begetting potential.[57] Not only as a matter of objective moral norms *ought* children be raised in stable two-parent homes, those who are fare better statistically on every measure of health and success.[58] The state, therefore, has an interest in recognizing and protecting the traditional institution of marriage, as it is the primary means of producing wholesome citizens who both preserve the state's existence and determine its moral fabric.

The chief objection to the legal recognition of same-sex marriage, therefore, isn't based on a prudish morality or religious conviction, but a conception of marriage and family essential to the state's promotion of the common good. Hence, the demand for "marriage equality" is absurd because homosexual couples are not equal with heterosexual couples in the only respect that matters to the state: their capability of producing new citizens.[59] Such incommensurability makes the notion of equality in this context not only incoherent but also unjust by treating unequals as if they were equal.

Same-sex marriage is not the only social injustice wrought in the nebulous name of "equality." There are the seemingly endless tantrums thrown by the illegitimate brainchild of Marx and Foucault: intersectional identity politics, including the modern feminist, LGBTQ+, and Black Lives Matter movements, whose child-like view of the world cannot transcend the binary categories of oppressors and oppressed, victimizers and victims. Because virtue and moral responsibility on this scheme are shifted from individuals to groups, it is necessary to vilify whole classes of people as nefariously perpetuating "systems" or "structures" of social and economic inequality. The reality is, there are only two senses in which all people are equal: in the eyes of God (in dignity and worth) and in the eyes of the law (in legal standing as citizens). And the good news is that everyone, regardless of race, sex, or class, in post–civil rights America is already equal in these two senses.[60]

Any other sense of equality is, to use Edmund Burke's apt description, a "monstrous fiction."[61] None of us are, or ever will be, equal in physical or mental ability, talents, or accomplishments. "In performance terms," quips Thomas Sowell, "the same individual is not even equal to himself on different days."[62] Nor are we equal in non-performance terms, as differences in circumstances of birth, social surroundings, inheritance, and sheer luck make clear. Equality of opportunity is just as dubious as equality of outcome. These inequalities are manifest between groups as well as individuals, the roots of which can be any combination of internal causes such as biology, culture, personality, and personal decisions; and external causes such as geography, local environment, and, yes, oppression and privilege. But we cannot simply assume, as so many do, that any instance of inequality is *ipso facto* coextensive with injustice. And even instances that are, apart from straightforward violations of the law, do not obviously justify interventions from the state. Remember, the role of government is not to eradicate all injustices, but merely to safeguard conditions in which people can exercise their natural rights. Think of it this way: As anyone who's played a sport knows, there are innumerable ways a player can be a jerk without violating established rules of the game. A referee is there to enforce the rules, not to convert assholes into honorable men, much less bias the outcome. And if the political experiments of the twentieth century have proved anything, it's that government crusades against inequalities have been a road to serfdom, paved with the bodies of untold millions.[63]

IV.

By contrast, a laissez faire approach, especially with respect to economics, has been a road to the wealth of nations. Heavy regulation is inimical to innovation, and redistributive schemes are injurious to incentive. A free market system where people can engage in voluntary transactions of goods and services for the sake of self-improvement may on a superficial level seem selfish, but on a deeper level respects man's competitive drive, the inherent dignity found in work, and the virtue of self-reliance. When left to his own devices to improve his lot in life man is generally successful, and often winds up improving the lives of others in the process. In this way (and others), economic freedom, reflecting the principles of individual freedom, isn't just pragmatically superior to competing economic systems; it is *morally* superior.[64] Free enterprise, for example, is largely responsible for the abolition of slavery in the West.[65] As Russell Kirk has pointed out, free enterprise has "emancipated the mass of men and women from involuntary labor. Until the triumph of modern industry—which went hand-in-hand with the triumph of a free economy—it was possible to obtain leisure only by living upon the labors of others. . . . But today, and especially in America, it is possible for everyone to have relatively abundant leisure: this is the fruit of industrial efficiency and a free economy."[66]

Furthermore, since many national economies and, to a large extent, the global economy has adopted free market principles since the 1970s, global abject poverty rates have fallen a staggering 80%.[67] This isn't because of government assistance programs or foreign aid. Quite the contrary. It's because a relatively uninhibited entrepreneur like Henry Ford or Steve Jobs, "though laboring for his own benefit, actually increases the common good through his private labors."[68] Thus, very little regulation is required, as the free market is guided just fine by what Adam Smith called "the invisible hand": a mysterious force that, through countless ever-changing economic realities and transactions, reliably tracks market value and creates capital out of thin air.[69] Contrary to what critics of free enterprise often assume, economics is not a zero-sum game where if one has more another has less. That myth, though easily discreditable,[70] has proven recalcitrant. The reason, I suspect, is not due merely to confusion about the nature of economics, but the nature of man. In our ignorance, we are easily roused to indignation at economic inequality, and even more easily embrace as our reason a righteous concern for the poor, as opposed to a vain sense of entitlement and envy of the rich.[71]

V.
Economic equality, then, like any other sense of equality beyond what we already enjoy before God and the law, is overrated, rivaled perhaps only by the Beatles and "diversity." In fact, diversity per se, far from being good, is bad. What's good is *unity* in diversity. "The English word 'good,'" Robert Nozick writes, "stems from a root, 'Ghedh', meaning 'to unite, join, fit, to bring together'."[72] A good painting unites a diversity of form, textures, colors, and tones into a beautiful image. A musical symphony unifies across time a diversity of sounds into a pleasing score. A good novel will tie together various themes, plots, and characters into a meaningful narrative, much like our own lives. But the goodness of these things doesn't come from their being mere collections of diverse elements, but in the diversity of their elements being united in a way that achieves harmony.

So it is with society. Conservatives believe that a diverse, multicultural, or pluralistic society is good only if there is an underlying unity that promotes social harmony. But what could possibly unite a society of people who are naturally diverse in so many ways? Not race or nationality or any other form of tribalism, but commitment to a *creed*. America, G. K. Chesterton has observed, is the only country founded on a creed, and has justly earned the reputation of being the land of opportunity for those committed to it. Relatively few who have met that commitment with thrift, entrepreneurialism, or just plain hard work have been disappointed.[73] But people with ideologies hostile or indifferent to that creed are like streaks of black paint flung across an otherwise beautifully colored canvas. Granted, that may pass as art to benighted postmodernists, but the rest of us are under no obligation to accept it as such, and for the same reason are under no obligation to accept immigration policies unlikely to contribute to social harmony.

Talk of social harmony may seem quaint these days, as the overwhelming message of academics, politicians, news media, entertainment, and culture is that there are virtuous progressives on one side and right-wing bigots on the other. In actuality, studies show that both progressives and conservatives are motivated by compassion and fairness in their political judgments. The difference is that conservatives' judgments tend to be more complex, factoring in also concerns of loyalty, respect for tradition and authority, and purity.[74] This may help explain why conservatives are stereotyped as callous; what to others boils down simply to an issue of compassion and fairness is to conservatives tempered by a range of other values. This also helps explain why the conservative tends to look more askance at popular trends and impatient calls for change in the name of "social justice." He is the ancient talking tree in *The Lord of the Rings* who needs time to consider the complexities of the issue, repeating to the young zealous Hobbits, "Don't be hasty." And like the growth of a tree, healthy social change takes a long time, as it sprouts from the ground up (one person at a time) after establishing proper roots.

This is why grassroots movements always have more purchase than the social engineering efforts of elites. They spring from practical necessity, not abstract theory. Those interested in real progress, therefore, would do well to patiently build upon the tried and true: the intrinsic value of human life, natural rights, limited government, principles of subsidiarity, the irreducibility of the nuclear family, free enterprise, and unity in diversity. It took centuries for political arrangements to be erected upon these, and such arrangements, albeit imperfect, have proven to be the most just and prosperous in human history, and so worth conserving, not destroying. Thus, a conservative, it has been said, is someone who cautions against tearing down a fence before knowing why it was built in the first place.[75] It may be there, he supposes, for all the right reasons.[76]

COMPREHENSION QUESTIONS

1. What two essential claims are important to modern right-wing philosophic thought?
2. Why did Aristotle and the American founders think a republic was superior to a democracy?
3. What is "ordered liberty"? How is it both prescriptive and descriptive?
4. What is the difference between a natural and a civil right?
5. What is the organizing principle of subsidiarity, and how does it support limited government?

DISCUSSION QUESTIONS

1. Why is the traditional family unit of central importance to conservatives? Should we accept his characterization of the family?
2. What do you make of McIntosh's skepticism about the modern ideals of "equality" and "diversity"?
3. Why does McIntosh support a laissez faire approach to economics? What are the costs and benefits of this sort of economic and political policy?
4. How does McIntosh define social harmony? Do you agree or disagree with his characterization of it? What social practices, rules, and norms do you think are necessary for achieving social harmony?

Case 2

Consider this passage from Dan Moller's *Toward a New England Libertarianism*:

Libertarianism is the widely reviled idea that we should use reason and persuasion to accomplish our distributive aims. Only reason and persuasion. According to the libertarian, it is wrong to utilize threats or violence in the form of state-sponsored coercion, however sublimated by bureaucratic routine, in order to redistribute property that we have an antecedent claim to. Aiding the worse off or promoting economic equality may be worthy aims, but these are endeavors we should persuade our fellow citizens to join, not mandates to be enforced by the state. Promoting these goals at the end of a pitchfork, whether ours or our representatives', is a moral mistake according to the libertarian.

Talk of threats and violence may seem overblown. What is at issue is generally redistribution through taxation, and what's so bad about voters democratically deciding on laws that require us to fill in certain tax forms once a year? The forms are boring but hardly violent. But threats and violence are in play whenever the state issues its demands. When the state mails us the forms requesting our money, it is not asking nicely; the demands of the state are backed by force. And when voters decide on laws that culminate in demands from the state, they are deciding to compel those around them to do their bidding, again with the implicit threat of force . . . In fact, the reason that threats and violence seem so far removed from the process of peacefully debating laws and filling in forms is in part that these threats are so successful: it is only when threats are unpersuasive that one must employ violence. Of course, many people agree with the state's demands and are happy to cooperate—I don't wish to exaggerate the coercive element. But the bureaucratic routine shouldn't blind us to the fact that the state and, by extension, democratic majorities aren't asking nicely . . .

[L]et me try to motivate what I am calling the New England approach [to libertarianism]. Imagine calling a town hall meeting and delivering the following speech:

My dear assembled citizens: I know most of us are strangers, but of late I have fallen on hard times through no fault of my own, by sheer bad luck. My savings are low, and I don't have friends or family to help. Now as you know, I've previously asked for help from you as private citizens, as a matter of charity. But unfortunately that hasn't been sufficient. Thus, I'm here now to insist that you (yes, you, Emma, and you, John) owe me assistance as a matter of justice. It is a deep violation if you don't work additional hours, take fewer vacations if

Case 2 (continued)

> need be, live in a smaller house, or send your kids to a worse school, in order to help me. Failing to do so is no less an injustice than failing to pay your debts.
>
> Moreover, calling this an injustice means that it's not enough that you comply with your obligations by working on my behalf. No, I insist that you help me to force your fellow citizens to assist me. It doesn't matter if these others say to you that they need the money for their own purposes, that they prefer worthier causes, or if they're just hard-hearted and don't care. To the extent you care about justice, you must help me to force these others to assist me whether they wish to or not, since that is what is owed me in light of my recent bad luck.
>
> Could you bring yourself to make this speech? The essence of the dispute between moral libertarians and anti-libertarians is that libertarians think that they could not in good conscience make this speech, and neither would they be persuaded by others making it. And in their view, a redistributive welfare state is simply the speech put into action and writ large through taxes and transfers.*
>
> Moller and McIntosh are both critical of the redistributive welfare state, and in that sense, we might think of them both as "conservative." But how do their conservatisms differ? What's important to McIntosh that *doesn't* show up in this passage from Moller?

———————

*Dan Moller, Governing Least: A New England Libertarianism (New York: Oxford University Press, 2019), p. 3.

REPLY TO MCINTOSH
DUSTIN CRUMMETT

McIntosh discusses many issues that seem to me only tangentially related to the left/right divide, such as the effects of Christianity, the existence of natural rights, the "complexity of human nature," and the silliness of the song "Imagine." I agree with much of what McIntosh says about these issues, and my disagreements aren't important here. I will instead focus on his views about freedom and equality, which are unsatisfactory in ways that do reflect major differences between left and right, and that help illuminate the indefensibility of his position.

McIntosh thinks the requirements of equality, properly conceived, are easier to satisfy than I do. He even rejects equality of opportunity, the view that each person should have an equal shot at succeeding in society![77] He seems to think his opponents hold something like what I called the "dismal" view of equality. He thinks they'll be disturbed by the fact that "none of us are, or ever will be, equal in physical or mental ability, talents, or accomplishments,"[78] and even mentions "Harrison Bergeron" in a footnote.[79] But I reject the dismal view (hence the name).[80] McIntosh doesn't consider the view I, and many others, actually hold: that what matters is that people stand in equal social relationships with each other, free of hierarchies of domination, disregard, disrespect, and exploitation. This has no particular relation to the claim, which I also rejected,[81] that everyone is or should be made equal in physical ability, etc. So this line of attack is irrelevant.

McIntosh also claims that views that emphasize group hierarchies, as mine does, are "child-like" and "vilify whole classes of people." But, as I noted,[82] the fact that someone is placed, *by unjust social structures*, in a privileged social position doesn't entail a negative evaluation of *their individual moral character*. I criticize no one for their group identity—only for their actions. If we say, for instance, that whites occupied an unjust position over blacks in the Jim Crow South, everyone understands that this doesn't mean every individual white person in the South was bad, and, indeed, that it is compatible with the fact that some whites played heroic roles in the struggle against racial oppression. Just apply this point to our own context.

Meanwhile, McIntosh places great importance on *freedom*. He doesn't see that, as I argued,[83] social equality is *necessary* for freedom worth having. I claim that proper respect for freedom therefore requires abandoning McIntosh's view of equality and adopting my own. Consider the stories illuminated by the #MeToo movement of women forced to tolerate sexual harassment in the workplace, knowing that speaking out might cost them their jobs and that sexist attitudes might cause them to not be believed.[84] Consider LGBT people who must hide their identity in public, or else face the risk of violent hate crime. Consider the workers in Amazon's warehouse in Allentown, Pennsylvania, who did heavy labor in a building that sometimes reached 102 degrees, were often unable to find other work due to high regional unemployment, and were punished for missing work if they passed out from heat stroke.[85] For that matter, consider any ordinary American, subject to the decrees of a government that is under the control of the wealthy rather than themselves.[86] All of these people are under someone else's thumb, and to that extent are unfree. But preventing this unfreedom requires fighting the power imbalances and demeaning attitudes that create it.

Though McIntosh overlooks threats to freedom like those just mentioned, he does worry about *government* tyranny.[87] I agreed that we should be vigilant toward government power.[88] In fact, I wish conservatives were more consistent here. McIntosh supports the death penalty.[89] The power to execute is a tremendous power, and the government wields it unjustly: Defendants are vastly more likely to be sentenced to death if they are black rather than white, or if their victim was white rather than black.[90] Another example: Though two-thirds of Americans support gay marriage,[91] McIntosh thinks the government should deny marriage rights to gay couples. The main idea is apparently that this will encourage people to form the kinds of families he thinks are best for society.[92] This seems a clear instance of "the social engineering efforts of elites"[93] that McIntosh disparages. We can see that he doesn't give the government *less* power than I do—just power in different areas.

For instance, he *does* oppose most government action *in the economic sphere*, where I think it's necessary. Astonishingly, he even opposes minimum wage laws.[94] McIntosh claims that economic inequality is unimportant, and that unregulated economies promote freedom, dignity, and prosperity. I explained earlier why we should oppose economic inequality—including because it harms freedom and dignity.[95] Meanwhile, McIntosh's claims about prosperity don't hold up. In the so-called social democracies found in places like northern Europe, the government plays a much bigger role in regulating the economy and promoting equality than in the United States, and life for ordinary people is vastly better.[96] Meanwhile, in recent decades, and especially since Reagan's presidency, the United States has moved toward an unregulated free market.[97] Adjusted for inflation, wages for ordinary workers have stagnated since the late 1970s,[98] and risky, unregulated behavior by banks helped cause the 2008 financial crisis.[99]

In closing, I'll note that I also find many of McIntosh's other empirical claims suspect. One quick example: In defense of his assertion that the children of same-sex couples fare worse, McIntosh cites the researcher Mark Regnerus.[100] Regnerus's study was funded by anti–gay marriage groups, apparently for political reasons,[101] and he made poor methodological choices that biased his research against same-sex couples, leading to its being widely rejected by other social scientists.[102] Meanwhile, the overwhelming scientific consensus is that, in the words of the American Psychological Association, "a remarkably consistent body of research" shows that "lesbian and gay parents are as likely as heterosexual parents to provide supportive and healthy environments for their children."[103] So don't uncritically assume McIntosh's citations show what he claims.

COMPREHENSION QUESTIONS

1. What is Crummett's main critique of McIntosh's essay?
2. How does Crummett's view of equality go beyond McIntosh's?
3. What are Crummett's criticisms of McIntosh's views on same-sex marriage?

DISCUSSION QUESTIONS

1. What are we trying to achieve when we work toward "freedom" and "equality"?
2. Crummett critiques McIntosh for supporting minimal government and free markets as the best path to prosperity and governance. Are his points compelling? How do their understandings of equality relate and differ? Is economic equality necessary for freedom?

REPLY TO CRUMMETT
C. A. MCINTOSH

Progressives aren't satisfied with equality before God (in dignity and worth) and equality before the law (legal standing as citizens). They also want "social equality," the moral ideal that "people should enjoy equal relationships with each other." Beyond this vague characterization, we get no positive content of that ideal.[104] So their approach is negative, attacking social *inequalities* in the form of what Dustin Crummett calls "oppressive hierarchies," which exist (in the words of Chomsky) to "preserve certain structures of power and domination." Familiar examples of allegedly oppressive hierarchies are given: amongst "the rich and the poor, employers and many employees, men and women, whites and non-whites," and so on. Space precludes discussion of specific examples.[105] I'll instead register five objections to the abstract ideal of social equality.

1. The ideal of social equality fosters undue skepticism of all hierarchies, not just oppressive ones. While acknowledging that some hierarchies are benign, such as that between a parent and child or rank in the military, Crummett says nonetheless all hierarchies must be "justified in terms of the general good, and must be *only* that which is necessary to promote that good." This gets things backwards: We should simply presume that hierarchies, ubiquitous as they are, contribute to the common good unless proven to be oppressive. These include hierarchies of competence, ability, responsibility, merit, experience, education, seniority, respect, and more. And our positions within them, bear in mind, are not static but dynamic, ever changing as we work to improve our lot in life. Hierarchies are essential to the development and maintenance of social order and have played a key role in the survival and flourishing of the human species. Evolution, it's commonly said, is conservative: It builds on what works, and what doesn't gets selected out.[106]

2. Even some unjust social inequalities may have to be permitted for the sake of the greater good of ordered liberty. For example, taxation, being akin to theft or extortion by a powerful ruling class, requires an oppressive hierarchy.[107] Yet we permit it, believing that it contributes to the common good. And beware of committing the fallacy of composition here: Just because a part of society is unjust, that doesn't mean society as a whole is unjust. An overall good society—indeed, the best of what's feasible—may well contain injustices. Just as biologists have discovered that eliminating even a tiny pest from the complex equilibrium of an ecosystem can have devastating unforeseen consequences, a substantial burden of proof is required to show that dismantling an unjust social hierarchy would not cause a ripple effect of greater injustice. Incautiously pulling threads from our social fabric in the name of "social equality" or "social justice," as utopian visions tempt us to, can lead to large-scale unraveling, just as it did in the French Revolution.[108]

3. The common presumption that social inequality is evidence of injustice is as unhealthy as it is unwarranted. The fact is, time and again we have seen careful, multivariate analyses disconfirm "oppression" as the chief cause of some instance of social inequality. Clear examples of this are the claims that the gender wage gap is due to sexism[109] and that black people are victims of systematic racism by law enforcement and/or the criminal justice system.[110] Encouraging people to believe they are mired in systems of social and legal oppression breeds learned helplessness, resentment, ingratitude, and general social unrest.[111] Thus, it's in everyone's interest to be less rash in inferring injustice from some descriptive fact of inequality.

4. The concern for social equality seems curiously selective. When is the last time we heard progressives decrying university admissions artificially penalizing Asians,[112] the barbaric treatment of women under Islamic rule, the myriad of social problems disproportionately afflicting men,[113] the massive "overrepresentation" of abortions and single parents in the black

community,[114] or the "underrepresentation" of conservatives in academia, media, and entertainment?[115] Yet concern for social equality is pushed to the extreme in other contexts, demanding, for instance, that one embrace the claim that biological males can be women. This is why many doubt that progressivism is really about social equality. Beneath the surface rhetoric, it seems more about a certain power and dominance hierarchy of its own, wherein one's rank is determined by one's group demographics (race, sex, gender, class, etc.) and conformity to popular moral-emotional sentiment.[116] It seems the true enemy of progressivism, therefore, is not unjust hierarchies, but traditional norms of individual virtue and vice, especially associated norms of personal responsibility, guilt, and shame.[117]

5. Attempting to enforce social equality with the law (i.e., by force) is unjust and self-refuting in practice. It is unjust because it requires somehow imposing handicaps on or stealing from innocents who are better off to benefit those who are worse off. That's *wrong*. It is self-refuting because it requires instituting an oppressive hierarchy to fight oppressive hierarchies, or social inequality to enforce social equality. Just imagine how much power over people is required to regulate and control their "relationships with each other"! If you need help, read Huxley and Orwell—or better, Marx and Engels. You can't have both a government powerful enough to enforce social equality *and* a free democracy devoid of the possibility of social inequalities.

In conclusion, I'm happy that Crummett says he distrusts those with institutional power, especially politicians and the government. That's why calling upon them to enforce social equality is as dubious as it is dangerous. So suppose we agree that wielding the power of government in this way is a bad idea. What's left? Crummett himself gives the answer: We are. *But this is the conservative's solution.* We already have the power to fight injustice, most poignantly by loving our neighbor as ourselves. And unlike government power, exercising this power doesn't risk causing equal or worse injustice by violating subsidiarity. We cede that power as individuals—and the responsibility that comes with it—to institutional bureaucrats and "intellectuals" not only to our detriment, but also to our shame.[118]

COMPREHENSION QUESTIONS

1. What are the five objections to social equality proposed by McIntosh?
2. Why are hierarchies important to society?

DISCUSSION QUESTIONS

1. Do you agree or disagree with McIntosh's claim that "the concern for social equality seems curiously selective"? How can you support your position?
2. Do you think the amount of government intervention needed to enforce "social equality" would significantly curtail individual liberty, as McIntosh does? Why or why not?

FURTHER READINGS

Alexander, Michelle. *The New Jim Crow: Mass Incarceration in the Age of Colorblindness.* New York: The New Press, 2010.
Anderson, Elizabeth. *Private Government: How Employers Rule Our Lives (and Why We Don't Talk About It).* Princeton, NJ: Princeton University Press, 2017.
Bloom, Alan. *The Closing of the American Mind.* New York: Simon & Schuster, 1987.
Brooks, Arthur. *The Conservative Heart.* New York: Broadside Books, 2015.
Bruenig, Matt. *Social Wealth Fund for America.* Washington, D.C.: People's Policy Project, 2019. Freely available online at https://www.peoplespolicyproject.org/projects/social -wealth-fund/.
Chomsky, Noam. *Understanding Power.* New York: The New Press, 2002.
Corvino, John. *What's Wrong with Homosexuality?* Oxford: Oxford University Press, 2013.
Current Affairs (a periodical, freely available online at currentaffairs.org)
Frank, Thomas. *Listen, Liberal: Or, Whatever Happened to the Party of the People.* New York: Metropolitan Books, 2016.
Hayek, F. A. *The Constitution of Liberty.* Chicago: University of Chicago Press, 1960.
Jacobin (a periodical, freely available online at jacobinmag.com)
Kekes, John. *A Case for Conservatism.* Ithaca, NY: Cornell University Press, 1998.
Kirk, Russell. *The American Cause.* Wilmington, DE: ISI Books, 2009.
Nisbet, Robert. *The Quest for Community.* San Francisco: ISC Press, 1990.
Postman, Neil. *Amusing Ourselves to Death.* New York: Penguin Books, 1985.
Richards, Jay W. *Money, Greed, and God.* New York: HarperOne, 2009.
Scanlon, T. M. *Why Does Inequality Matter?* Oxford: Oxford University Press, 2018.
Sowell, Thomas. *The Quest for Cosmic Justice.* New York: Touchstone, 1999.
Sowell, Thomas. *Wealth, Poverty, and Politics.* New York: Basic Books, 2015.
Stiglitz, Joseph. *The Price of Inequality: How Today's Divided Society Endangers Our Future.* New York: W. W. Norton, 2012.
Sunkara, Bhaskar. *The Socialist Manifesto: The Case for Radical Politics in an Era of Extreme Inequality.* New York: Basic Books, 2019.
Wiker, Benjamin. *Ten Books That Screwed Up the World.* Washington, DC: Regnery Publishing, Inc., 2008.
Wiker, Benjamin. *Ten Books Every Conservative Must Read.* Washington, DC: Regnery Publishing, Inc., 2010.
Zinn, Howard. *A People's History of the United States.* New York: Harper Collins, 1980.

NOTES

1. Jason Noble, "Michele Bachmann Debates Same-Sex Rights with High School Students in Waverly," *Des Moines Register*, November 30, 2011, http://caucuses .desmoinesregister.com/2011/11/30/michele-bachmann-debates-same-sex-rights -with-high-school-students-in-waverly/.
2. E.g., Elizabeth Anderson, "What is the Point of Equality?" *Ethics* 109, no. 2 (1999): 287–337.
3. See Chapter 2 of Iris Marion Young, *Justice and the Politics of Difference* (Princeton, NJ: Princeton University Press, 2011).
4. Chapter 1 in Elizabeth Anderson, *Private Government: How Employers Rule Our Lives (and Why We Don't Talk About It)*, (Princeton, NJ: Princeton University Press, 2017).
5. Anderson, *Private Government*.

6. As this remark suggests, my underlying moral theory is heavily influenced by the contrac-tualism of Rawls, Scanlon, and Darwall: John Rawls, *A Theory of Justice* (Cambridge, MA: Harvard University Press, 1971); T. M. Scanlon, *What We Owe to Each Other* (Cambridge, MA: Harvard University Press, 1998); and Stephen Darwall, *The Second-Person Standpoint: Morality, Respect, and Accountability* (Cambridge, MA: Harvard University Press, 2006). However, one need not accept contractualism to accept social egalitarianism as a socio-political ideal—one could recognize that the social oppression I discuss is wrong without having any view about the underlying explanation of why it's wrong, or could accept some other explanation. Indeed, I think the validity of the ideal itself is more certain than any particular underlying theory to which we might appeal in justifying it.

7. Noam Chomsky, *On Anarchism* (New York: The New Press, 2013), 33.

8. Specifically, I'll discuss what I call domination, disregard, disrespect, and exploita-tion. Anderson (*Private Government*, 3–4) lists hierarchies of command, standing, and esteem as the major types that have drawn the attention of egalitarians; my categories of domination, disregard, and disrespect are meant, roughly and respectively, to pick out the relevant features of the oppressive versions of these hierarchies, while I *think* that exploitation has no clear counterpart in her system. Meanwhile, Iris Marion Young (*Justice*, Chapter 2) lists as the "five faces of oppression" exploitation, marginalization, powerlessness, cultural imperialism, and systematic violence. Exploitation appears in my classification, domination corresponds roughly to what she calls powerlessness, and disregard corresponds very roughly to what she calls marginalization, though I under-stand each of these concepts somewhat differently than she does. Cultural imperialism I consider a special version of disrespect. Systematic violence I consider a special ver-sion of disregard (one where society is not only *indifferent* to, but actively *hostile* to, the interests of some). Of course, systematic violence is also a major tool for maintaining the other forms of oppression.

9. To explain this in a way that will make more sense in light of the rest of this section: When some have unaccountable power over others, they can use it to ensure that so-ciety is responsive to their own needs, but not the needs of those they dominate, to promote disrespectful stereotypes about those they dominate, and to exploit those they dominate. When society disregards the needs of certain people, it is less likely to pro-tect them from domination, disrespect, and exploitation. When demeaning stereotypes about members of certain groups are widely accepted, it's easier for people to justify dominating, disregarding, and exploiting them. And when members of one group ex-ploit another, they can use their resulting advantages to gain power over them . . . and the beat goes on. So one type of oppression often leads to another, and this, in turn, can create a positive feedback loop. But one *need* not lead to another.

10. See Philip Pettit, *On the People's Terms: A Republican Theory and Model of Democracy* (Cambridge: Cambridge University Press, 2012).

11. Cf. Jorge Garcia's account of "the heart of racism" in J. L. A. Garcia, "The Heart of Racism," *Journal of Social Philosophy* 27, no. 1 (1996): 5–46. What Garcia calls "the heart of racism" I would call "disregard on the basis of race."

12. Amartya Sen, *Poverty and Famines: An Essay on Entitlement and Deprivation* (Oxford: Oxford University Press, 1981).

13. Mike Davis, *Late Victorian Holocausts* (New York: Verso Books, 2001), 33.

14. Davis, *Late Victorian Holocausts*, 31.

15. Davis, *Late Victorian Holocausts*, 7.

16. Cf. Emily McTernan, "Microaggressions, Equality, and Social Practices," *Journal of Political Philosophy* 26, no. 3 (2018): 261–281.

17. Cf. G. A. Cohen, "The Labor Theory of Value and the Concept of Exploitation," *Philosophy & Public Affairs* 8, no. 4 (1979): 338–360, and Young, *Justice*, Chapter 2.

18. See Anderson, "What is the Point," 297 and elsewhere.

19. Lyrics for both verses are taken from "Solidarity Forever," Industrial Workers of the World, https://www.iww.org/history/icons/solidarity_forever.

20. See Pettit, *On the People's*.

21. See Anderson, *Private Government*.

22. Elizabeth Anderson, "Expanding the Egalitarian Toolbox: Equality and Bureaucracy," *Proceedings of the Aristotelian Society* 82 (2008), 139–160, 155–156.

23. Cf. Michael Walzer, *Spheres of Justice* (New York: Basic Books, 1983).

24. Anyone who really wants to know can reach me at dustin.crummett@gmail.com.

25. I think it's fairly obvious that a major form of unjust inequality in the modern world is *speciesism*—the disregard and exploitation by humans of non-human animals. So, for instance, every year, billions of animals are raised in torturous conditions in factory farms so that humans can more cheaply eat their bodies, or things that come from their bodies. If you don't know what that involves, google "factory farm pictures." But taking speciesism seriously is extremely controversial among leftists, so I won't bring it up again here. Cf. Peter Singer, "All Animals Are Equal," in Tom Regan and Peter Singer, *Animal Rights and Human Obligations* (Englewood Cliffs, NJ: Prentice-Hall, 1989), 148–162.

26. Anderson, *Private Government*.

27. Nina Martin and Renee Montagne, "Black Mothers Keep Dying After Giving Birth. Shalon Irving's Story Explains Why," *National Public Radio*, December 7, 2017, https://www.npr.org/2017/12/07/568948782/black-mothers-keep-dying-after-giving-birth-shalon-irvings-story-explains-why.

28. Matt Egan, "Record Inequality: The Top 1% Controls 38.6% of America's Wealth," *CNN*, September 27, 2017.

29. Noam Chomsky, "The Responsibility of Intellectuals, Redux," *Boston Review*, September 1, 2011, http://bostonreview.net/noam-chomsky-responsibility-of-intellectuals-redux.

30. Cf. Kimberlé Crenshaw, "Demarginalizing the Intersection of Race and Sex: A Black Feminist Critique of Antidiscrimination Doctrine, Feminist Theory and Antiracist Politics," *University of Chicago Legal Forum* 140 (1989): 139–167.

31. Y. Joel Wong et al., "Meta-Analyses of the Relationship Between Conformity to Masculine Norms and Mental Health-Related Outcomes," *Journal of Counseling Psychology* 64, no. 1 (2016): 80–93.

32. E.g., Tami Luhby, "Romney: Income Inequality Is Just 'Envy,'" *CNN*, January 12, 2016, http://money.cnn.com/2012/01/12/news/economy/romney_envy/index.htm.

33. Cf. Martin Gilens and Benjamin Page, "Testing Theories of American Politics: Elites, Interest Groups, and Average Citizens," *Perspectives on Politics* 12, no. 3 (2014): 564–581.

34. This point goes at least back to Adam Smith; see the discussion of what counts as a "necessary," as opposed to a mere luxury, good in Book V, Ch. II, Part II, Article IV of *The Wealth of Nations*. Smith argues that a linen shirt should, in his cultural context, be considered a "necessary": One doesn't need one to survive, and wouldn't have needed one in ancient Greece or Rome, but the availability of linen shirts in his society, alongside various norms around them, meant that a respectable person would be ashamed of appearing in public without one. A while ago, I got in a fender bender that damaged the front of my car. Being an austere philosopher who scorns earthly vanity, I was surprised

to find that, until I got it fixed, I was ashamed to drive it around: I thought the other drivers would look down on me. If I hadn't been able to afford fixing it, this would have been a serious cost for me. However, in a context where people routinely drove around "beat-up" cars, doing so wouldn't be embarrassing. The wealth of the United States makes possible exacting standards surrounding many things—what one's house or clothes or car or body is supposed to look like, for instance—that risk stigmatizing anyone who can't afford to "keep up appearances." (Think of derisive jokes about "rednecks" who can't afford to go to the dentist.) These are relevant to economic inequality since, if people ordinarily couldn't meet these standards, failing to meet them wouldn't be embarrassing.

35. *Obergefell v. Hodges*, 576 U.S. 14-556 (2015). The quoted material is from pp. 17 and 22 of the version of the opinion available at https://www.supremecourt.gov/opinions/14pdf/14-556_3204.pdf.
36. E.g., Philip Pettit, "A Republican Law of Peoples," *European Journal of Political Theory* 9, no. 1 (2010): 70–94.
37. Obviously, this is especially true when we are partly responsible for the fact that the refugees are refugees, or that the people in need are in need, both of which are true, for instance, in the case of the current Syrian crisis.
38. See Noam Chomsky, "Humanitarian Imperialism: The New Doctrine of Imperial Right," *Monthly Review*, September 2008, https://chomsky.info/200809__/.
39. For instance, Michelle Alexander in *The New Jim Crow: Mass Incarceration in the Age of Colorblindness* (New York: The New Press, 2010, e.g., 55–57) argues that Bill Clinton's support of mass incarceration and welfare reform helped ensure the creation of a new "racial caste system" in the United States. Both Clinton and Obama oversaw large increases in the amount of economic inequality (Chad Stone et al., "A Guide to Statistics on Historical Trends in Income Inequality," Center on Budget and Policy Priorities, February 16, 2018, https://www.cbpp.org/research/poverty-and-inequality/a-guide-to-statistics-on-historical-trends-in-income-inequality). And both made foreign policy decisions (such as those that were part of Obama's drone program) that I think are incompatible with the view sketched in this section.
40. Cf. Pettit, *On the People's*.
41. For feedback on and discussion of earlier versions of this chapter, I am grateful, among others, to Xia Allen, Joshua Blanchard, Devin Braun, Eric Brodersen, Bob Fischer, Nathan Hershberger, David Jost, Sylwia Wilczewska, and several students in my Spring 2018 Moral Problems class at the University of Notre Dame.
42. In *The Collected Works of G. K. Chesterton* Vol. I, edited by David Dooley (San Francisco: Ignatius, 1986), 287.
43. The traditional American conservatism to which I refer, as F. A. Hayek plausibly argues ("Why I Am Not a Conservative"), was largely inspired by English Whiggism, the ideals of which trace back to Montesquieu, Adam Smith, Edmund Burke, and Alexis de Tocqueville. Contemporary English conservatism, by contrast, is much too cozy with big government to be considered "right" on my spectrum. The terminology is a mess because "right" and "left" can refer to either a political philosophy or location on some political spectrum. So it is important to distinguish between political philosophies and political parties. In America, for example, the Republican Party, or GOP, while certainly farther right on the political philosophy spectrum than the Democratic Party, is not reliably conservative. Both parties have shifted philosophically leftward in recent decades. If we contrast "conservative" political philosophy with "progressive"

political philosophy, we can illustrate the relationship between party and philosophy as follows:

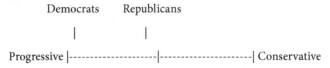

Democrats   Republicans

Progressive |--------------------|---------------------| Conservative

As you can see, because where a party is located on the spectrum is relative, it is possible to have right-wing and left-wing parties that are both left of center on the political philosophy spectrum (the space between the leftmost and rightmost parties represents the Overton Window—the range of ideas currently accepted in public discourse). It is only by equivocating the relative left/right location of party with the absolute left/right metric of philosophy that people can get away with saying that the National Socialist German Workers' Party, like the Republican Party in the United States, is "right-wing."

44. See also David Bentley Hart, "Human Dignity Was a Rarity Before Christianity," *Church Life Journal*, October 26, 2017, https://churchlifejournal.nd.edu/articles/human-dignity-was-a-rarity-before-christianity/.

45. A standard history textbook is worth quoting at length: "It is impossible to exaggerate the importance of the coming of Christianity. It brought with it, for one thing, an altogether new sense of human life. Where the Greeks had demonstrated the powers of the mind, the Christians explored the soul, and they taught that in the sight of God all souls were equal, that every human life was sacrosanct and inviolate, and that all worldly distinctions of greatness, beauty, and brilliancy were in the last analysis superficial. Where the Greeks had identified the beautiful and the good, had thought ugliness to be bad, and had shrunk from disease as an imperfection and from everything misshapen as horrible and repulsive, the Christians resolutely saw a spiritual beauty even in the plainest or most unpleasant exterior and sought out the diseased, the crippled, and the mutilated to give them help. Love, for the ancients, was never quite distinguished from Venus; for the Christians, who held that God was love, it took on deep overtones of sacrifice and compassion. Suffering itself was proclaimed by Christians to be in a way divine, since God himself had suffered on the Cross in human form. A new dignity was thus found for suffering that the world could not cure. At the same time the Christians worked to relieve suffering as none had worked before. They protested against the massacre of prisoners of war, against the mistreatment and degradation of slaves, against the sending of gladiators to kill each other in the arena for another's pleasure. In place of the Greek and pagan self-satisfaction with human accomplishments they taught humility in the face of an almighty Providence, and in place of proud distinctions between high and low, slave and free, civilized and barbarian, they held that all men were brothers because all were children of the same God." See R. R. Palmer et al., *A History of Europe in the Modern World* Vol. I (New York: McGraw-Hill Education, 2014), 17. Thanks to Elizabeth McIntosh for bringing this passage to my attention, which she recalled from her high school textbook! For more on Christianity's influence on the West, see Rodney Stark, *The Victory of Reason: How Christianity Led to Freedom, Capitalism, and Western Success* (New York: Random House, 2006) and Nick Spencer, *The Evolution of the West: How Christianity Has Shaped Our Values* (London: SPCK, 2016).

46. On all of these topics save terrorism, see David Oderberg, *Applied Ethics: A Non-Consequentialist Approach* (Oxford: Blackwell, 2000). On abortion, see Francis Beckwith, *Defending Life: A Moral and Legal Case Against Abortion Choice* (New York: Cambridge University Press, 2007); Robert George and Christopher Tollefsen, *Embryo:*

A Defense of Human Life (New York: Doubleday, 2008); Christopher Kaczor, *The Ethics of Abortion: Women's Rights, Human Life, and the Question of Justice* (New York: Routledge, 2015 [2nd ed.]). On euthanasia, see Arthur Dyck, *Life's Worth: The Case Against Assisted Suicide* (Grand Rapids, MI: Eerdmans, 2002). On capital punishment, see Edward Feser and Joseph Bessette, *By Man Shall His Blood Be Shed* (San Francisco: Ignatius, 2017). On just warfare, see Michael Walzer, *Just and Unjust Wars: A Moral Argument with Historical Illustrations* (New York: Basic Books, 2015 [5th ed.]).

47. I am persuaded that only theism has the metaphysical resources to account for the intrinsic value of human persons, and hence only theism provides a sufficient ground for natural rights. For defense, see Stuart Hackett, "The Value Dimension of the Cosmos: A Moral Argument" in *Philosophy of Religion*, edited by William Craig (New Brunswick, NJ: Rutgers University Press, 2002), 149–154; J. P. Moreland, *The Recalcitrant Imago Dei: Human Persons and the Failure of Naturalism* (London: SCM Press, 2009), 143–164; C. Stephen Evans, *Natural Signs and Knowledge of God: A New Look at Theistic Arguments* (Oxford: Oxford University Press, 2010), 142–147; Nicholas Wolterstorff, "On Secular and Theistic Groundings of Human Rights," and "Grounding the Rights We Have as Human Persons" in *Understanding Liberal Democracy: Essays in Political Philosophy*, edited by Terence Cuneo (Oxford: Oxford University Press, 2012), Chapters 7 and 8, respectively; David Baggett and Jerry Walls, *God and Cosmos: Moral Truth and Human Meaning* (New York: Oxford University Press, 2016), Chapter 4.

48. David Oderberg, "Natural Law and Rights Theory," in *The Routledge Companion to Social and Political Philosophy*, eds. Gerald Gaus and Fred D'Agostino (New York: Routledge, 2013), 376. I should say that there are conservatives who don't think natural law theory is concomitant to conservatism. I can't prove this, but I'd be willing to bet my 23.5-acre farm that the vast majority of people, but especially conservatives, embrace some form of natural law theory. And there is some evidence for this. See, e.g., Deborah Kelemen and Evelyn Rosset, "The Human Function Compunction: Teleological Explanation in Adults," *Cognition* 111, no. 1 (2009): 138–143. But for a more general, philosophical defense of natural law theory, see Robert George, *In Defense of Natural Law* (New York: Oxford University Press, 1999) and John Finnis, *Natural Law and Natural Rights* (New York: Oxford University Press, 2011 [2nd ed.]).

49. Aleksandr Solzhenitsyn, *The Gulag Archipelago* (New York: Harper & Row, 1974), 168. See also Stephane Courtois et al., *The Black Book of Communism: Crimes, Terror, Repression*, trans. Jonathan Murphy and Mark Kramer (Cambridge, MA: Harvard University Press, 1999), which puts communism's death toll between 85 million and 100 million. To get a more personal sense of how communism wrecked the lives of so many in China, see Jung Chang, *Wild Swans: Three Daughters of China* (New York: Touchstone, 2003).

50. The saying "the revolution devours its own children" became popular during the French Revolution, as many who helped initiate it were in turn destroyed by it.

51. Gun ownership also has the effect of lowering crime rates. See John Lott, *More Guns, Less Crime* (Chicago: University of Chicago Press, 2010 [3rd ed.]) and John Lott, *The War on Guns* (Washington, DC: Regnery Publishing, 2016). That said, regardless of the empirical effects of gun ownership, we have a moral right to own guns. See Michael Huemer, "Is There a Right to Own a Gun?" *Social Theory and Practice* 29, no. 4 (2003): 297–324; Timothy Hsiao et al., "The Moral Right to Keep and Bear Arms," *Public Affairs Quarterly* 29, no. 4 (2015): 345–363.

52. On the importance of robust stratifications of civil society as a buffer between the individual and the state, see Alexis De Tocqueville's classic *Democracy in America* and Robert Nisbet's modern classic *The Quest for Community*.

53. "Indeed, as Milton Friedman has pointed out, the period of greatest opposition to the role of government in the economy in the nineteenth century was also a period of unprecedented growth of private philanthropy. It was also a period of private social uplift efforts by volunteers all across America. Such efforts, incidentally, had dramatic effect in reducing crime and other social ills such as alcoholism, so these were hardly ineffectual gestures. Indeed, they were more effective than the more massive government-run programs that began in the 1960s." See Thomas Sowell, *The Quest for Cosmic Justice*, 44. Sowell doesn't provide a reference, but I believe he is referring to Milton Friedman, *Capitalism and Freedom* (Chicago: University of Chicago Press, 1962 [2002 ed.]), 190ff. One study on the efficacy of government versus private charity found that government absorbs more than two-thirds of every dollar intended for public assistance programs, whereas private charities absorb one-third or less. See James Edwards, "The Costs of Public Income Redistribution and Private Charity," *Journal of Libertarian Studies* 21, no. 2 (2007): 3–20.

54. The point applies to foreign aid as well. See Hristos Doucouliagos and Martin Paldam, "The Aid Effectiveness Literature: The Sad Results of 40 Years of Research," *Journal of Economic Surveys* 23, no. 3 (2009): 433–461. Thanks to Jason Brennan for this reference.

55. In general, see Christopher Coyne, *Doing Bad by Doing Good: Why Humanitarian Action Fails* (Stanford, CA: Stanford University Press, 2013). On minimum wage laws in particular, see David Neumark and William Wascher, *Minimum Wages* (Cambridge, MA: MIT Press, 2008) and John Gaski, "Raising the Minimum Wage Is Unethical and Immoral," *Business and Society Review* 109, no. 2 (2004): 209–224. On affirmative action policies in particular, see Thomas Sowell, *Affirmative Action Around the World: An Empirical Study* (New Haven, CT: Yale University Press, 2004) and Richard Sander and Stewart Taylor, *Mismatch: How Affirmative Action Hurts Students It's Intended to Help, and Why Universities Won't Admit It* (New York: Basic Books, 2012). On welfare programs in particular, see Michael Tanner, *The Poverty of Welfare: Helping Others in Civil Society* (Washington, DC: The Cato Institute, 2003) and Phil Harvey and Lisa Conyers, *The Human Cost of Welfare: How the System Hurts the People It's Supposed to Help* (Santa Barbara, CA: Praeger, 2016). For a more historical look at the disastrous consequences of well-intended government assistance programs in the context of America, see Amity Shlaes, *The Forgotten Man: A New History of the Great Depression* (New York: HarperCollins, 2007).

56. See Oderberg, "Natural Law and Rights Theory," 379.

57. And, of course, the two shouldn't be closely related. A sustained defense of this conception of marriage is Sherif Girgis et al., *What Is Marriage: Man and Woman: A Defense* (New York: Encounter Books, 2012). For more of a sociological than philosophical perspective justifying the traditional institution of marriage, see Linda Waite and Maggie Gallagher, *The Case for Marriage: Why Married People Are Happier, Healthier, and Better Off Financially* (New York: Broadway Books, 2000). Notice I say those with "child-begetting potential." This anticipates the common objection "What about infertile couples?" Technically, all heterosexual infertile couples still have the potential to beget children (which isn't true of homosexual couples), even though that potential is prevented from being actualized. A testament to this is that medical procedures can often overcome these obstacles. Furthermore, laws are necessarily general and so are not made to cater to particular cases, such as those where a heterosexual couple is infertile. But most importantly, it would be a gross violation of privacy for the state to inquire into the fertility status of its citizens. For a more detailed response to this objection, see Neven Sesardic, "Gay Marriage: The Victory of Bad Arguments and Political Correctness," *Prolegomena* 6, no. 1 (2007): 5–28.

58. See the empirical literature discussed in Girgis et al., *What Is Marriage*, Chapter 4, and Ryan Anderson, *Truth Overruled: The Future of Marriage and Religious Freedom* (Washington, DC: Regnery, 2015), Chapter 7.

59. Sadly, studies indicate that same-sex households are also not generally equal in their capability of rearing healthy children. See Mark Regnerus, "How Different Are the Adult Children of Parents Who Have Same-Sex Relationships? Findings from the New Family Structures Study," *Social Science Research* 41, no. 4 (2012): 752–770; Mark Regnerus, "Parental Same-Sex Relationships, Family Instability, and Subsequent Life Outcomes for Adult Children: Answering Critics of the New Family Structures Study with Additional Analyses," *Social Science Research* 41, no. 6 (2012): 1367–1377; D. Sullins, "Emotional Problems Among Children with Same-Sex Parents: Difference by Definition," *British Journal of Education, Society and Behavioural Science* 7, no. 2 (2015): 99–120. A good synopsis and commentary on Sillins is Regnerus, "New Research on Same-Sex Households Reveals Kids Do Best with Mom and Dad," *Public Discourse*, February 10, 2015, http://www.thepublicdiscourse.com/2015/02/14417/.

60. Well, almost. Alimony and abortion rights are glaring exceptions, being examples of where the legal system unjustly favors women over men and the unborn.

61. Edmund Burke, *Reflections on the Revolution in France* (New York: Oxford University Press, 2009), 37.

62. Thomas Sowell, *The Thomas Sowell Reader* (New York: Basic Books, 2011), 51. A nice synopsis of Sowell's work in this area, to which I am indebted, is his *Discrimination and Disparities* (New York: Basic Books, 2018). A powerful satire of the ideal of unbridled "equality" is Kurt Vonnegut's short story "Harrison Bergeron."

63. See Friedrich Hayek's *The Road to Serfdom* (UK: Routledge, 1944). On the devastating effects of Marxist ideology in the twentieth century, see references in endnote 49. The lesson should have been learned much sooner. An estimated 40,000 people were killed during the French Revolution waged in the name of "equality," which, of course, eventually led to the rise of an imperial dictator in Napoléon Bonaparte.

64. See Milton Friedman, *Capitalism and Freedom* (Chicago: University of Chicago Press, 1962 [2002 ed.]); Robert Sirico, *Defending the Free Market: The Moral Case for a Free Economy* (Washington, DC: Regnery, 2012); Jason Brennan, *Why Not Capitalism?* (New York: Routledge, 2014); Jason Brennan and Peter Jaworski, *Markets Without Limits: Moral Virtues and Commercial Interests* (New York: Routledge, 2015).

65. True though this statement is, it needs the proviso, mentioned above, that economic freedom reflects the principles of individual freedom as a natural right, which clearly also greatly contributed to the abolition of slavery. Here, David Horowitz is worth quoting: "In its very beginnings, America dedicated itself to the proposition that all men are created equal and were endowed by their Creator with the right to be free. Over the next two generations, America made good on that proposition, though this achievement is regularly slighted by 'progressives' because it didn't take place overnight. The historically accurate view of what happened is this: Black Africans were enslaved by other black Africans and sold at slave markets to Western slavers. America inherited this slave system from the British Empire, and once it was independent, ended the slave trade and almost all slavery in the Northern states within 20 years of its birth. America then risked its survival as a nation and sacrificed 350,000 mostly white Union lives, to end slavery in the South as well. In other words, as far as blacks are concerned, America's true legacy is not slavery, but freedom." See his "The Biggest Racial Lie" in the *Washington Times*, May 25, 2016, https://www.washingtontimes.com/news/2016/may/25/david-horowitz-america-the-worlds-most-inclusive-n/.

66. Russell Kirk, *The American Cause*, 113. This is a massively condensed and simplified version of themes in his classic *The Conservative Mind: From Burke to Santayana* (Chicago: Henry Regnery Co., 1953).

67. Measured using the $1/day living standard. See Pinkovsky and Sala-i-Martin, "Parametric Estimations of the World Distribution of Income," National Bureau of Economic Research no. 15433 (2009). See also Max Roser and Esteban Ortiz-Ospina, "Global Extreme Poverty," *Our World in Data*, March 27, 2017, https://ourworldindata.org /extreme-poverty/. Further, individuals in freer economies with fewer taxes give more to charity, as found by Charities Aid Foundation's report "International Comparisons of Charitable Giving," November 2006. See discussion in Jay Richards, *Money, Greed, and God*, 123–124.

68. Kirk, *The American Cause*, 96.

69. Adam Smith, *The Wealth of Nations* (New York: Modern Library Ed., 1994), 485.

70. See the charming illustration of the "trading game" in Richards, *Money, Greed, and God*, 60ff.

71. To paraphrase the great British statesman Margaret Thatcher, critics of free enterprise seem to prefer that everyone be poorer provided the rich be less rich.

72. Robert Nozick, *Philosophical Explanations* (Cambridge, MA: Harvard University Press, 1981), 418.

73. Take a look at Alan Elliot's *A Daily Dose of the American Dream: Stories of Success, Triumph, and Inspiration* (Nashville, TN: Rutledge Hill Press, 1998), which has an entry for each day of the year. Beyond anecdotes, the statistics bear this out. As one ages, upward economic mobility is the norm in the United States. According to one important study that tracked the income mobility of a group of Americans over a period of sixteen years, only 5% who began at the bottom quintile of income earners remained there. If these conclusions generalize, this means that only 1% (i.e., 5% of 20%) of the U.S. population who are poor remain so. See discussion in Thomas Sowell, *Wealth, Poverty and Politics* (New York: Basic Books, 2015), 326ff.

74. See Jonathan Haidt, *The Righteous Mind* (New York: Pantheon Books, 2012), especially Chapters 6–8.

75. As I began with a Chesterton quote, so I'll close: "In the matter of reforming things, as distinct from deforming them, there is one plain and simple principle; . . . There exists in such a case a certain institution or law; let us say for the sake of simplicity, a fence or gate erected across a road. The more modern type of reformer goes gaily up to it and says, 'I don't see the use of this; let us clear it away.' To which the more intelligent type of reformer will do well to answer: 'If you don't see the use of it, I certainly won't let you clear it away. Go away and think. Then, when you can come back and tell me that you do see the use of it, I may allow you to destroy it.'" From *Why I Am A Catholic* in *The Collected Works of G. K. Chesterton* Vol. III, edited by James Thompson (San Francisco: Ignatius, 1990), 157.

76. Thanks to Elizabeth McIntosh, William Vallicella, Shawn Isaacs, Steve Norman, Dan Demetriou, Dan Bonevac, Spencer Case, Tully Borland, Ben Arbour, Jannai Shields, Josh and Emily Monroe, and Bob Fischer for their helpful discussion and comments.

77. "The reality is, there are only two senses in which all people are equal: in the eyes of God (in dignity and worth) and in the eyes of the law (in legal standing as citizens). And the good news is that everyone, regardless of race, sex, or class, in post–civil rights America is already equal in these two senses. Any other sense of equality is, to use Edmund Burke's apt description, a 'monstrous fiction' . . . Equality of opportunity is just as dubious as equality of outcome." (p. 99)

78. See p. 99.
79. See endnote 62.
80. "For instance, sometimes people think 'equality' is supposed to mean that people should be made equally well-off, in some all-encompassing sense. This is satirized in Kurt Vonnegut's short story 'Harrison Bergeron.' The people in Harrison Bergeron's dystopian society regard natural differences in ability as unjust, so they weigh strong people down with weights so they can't use their strength, make smart people listen to static so they can't concentrate, and so on. That kind of equality sounds dismal . . . Social egalitarians understand equality differently." (pp. 85–86)
81. "When it comes to questions of respect and esteem, egalitarians should not, like whoever thought participation trophies were a good idea, try to pretend that everyone is equally possessed of every good quality. Instead, they should, first, emphasize the equal basic dignity which we all possess, second, recognize the diversity in what people have to offer (you're better than me at some things, while I'm better than you at others), and, third, recognize that these traits can be found across demographic lines. If we do this, we may still rank people as athletes, or chess players, or whatever, but won't rank them *as people* in ways that stigmatize them due to who they are, or make them feel inferior due to factors beyond their control." (p. 89)
82. ". . . if you are wealthy, white, etc., the point is not to make you feel guilty. The way to evaluate *you*, as a moral agent, is not on the basis of your group membership, but on what you do in light of it—whether, say, you fight for equality. As Chomsky notes, 'Privilege yields opportunity, and opportunity confers responsibilities. An individual then has choices.'" (p. 90)
83. "Notice something important here: Freedom and equality are sometimes portrayed as being in conflict, since protecting equality might require restricting free actions that work against it. Domination shows that the picture is more complicated. A certain kind of freedom (that involved in being a free *person*, rather than a servant) actually *requires* a certain kind of equality (the social equality that prevents some from exercising unaccountable power over others). Views that ignore this provide great freedom to the powerful, but no one else." (p. 87)
84. Of course, some men are also victims of workplace sexual harassment or sexual assault. These men often face special problems in coming forward, *specifically in virtue of their being men*. For instance, where it's thought that men are, or should be, sexually dominant, people may not take a man's accusations seriously, or may view being assaulted as a kind of failure of masculinity, so that it is especially humiliating. This is an extremely serious problem, and I don't have space here to say everything about it that I would like to. But note that egalitarians of my stripe will say that the problems these men face specifically in virtue of being men are largely a result of the very hierarchy that places men above women, and thereby encourages the idea that men are or should be sexually dominant. The problem is therefore an instance of the more general fact, which I discussed at the end of the third section of my chapter, that hierarchies are often bad for everyone, not just those at the bottom. Treating these men justly therefore also requires dismantling oppressive hierarchies.
85. Anderson, *Private Government*, 129.
86. Cf. endnote 33 in my earlier piece. Cf. also my discussion of the connection between democracy and freedom: "When it comes to power relations, egalitarians generally support making them *reciprocal* where possible, so that no one has *unaccountable* power over another. For instance, political leaders have power over voters, but, in a functioning democracy, voters control the exercise of this power through the threat of replacing their leaders." (pp. 88–89)

87. E.g., "the freedom of the individual and the power of government are inversely proportional." (p. 94)
88. "Conservatives sometimes accuse progressives of having too much faith in government. I've already indicated my skepticism of those who hold power; that includes politicians. (Indeed, *Democratic* politicians routinely act in ways that are condemned by the egalitarian picture I've sketched here.) The reason to sometimes rely on government action is the same reason I sometimes rely on a mechanic: There are problems only they can fix (such as, in the government's case, economic inequality). And the appropriate response to the possibility of government misconduct is the same as that to the possibility of your mechanic cheating you: Be attentive and keep them accountable." (p. 92)
89. "Conservatives today carry on this tradition of cherishing and protecting human life . . . by advocating the justness of capital punishment." (p. 95)
90. See, e.g., ACLU, "Race and the Death Penalty," https://www.aclu.org/other/race -and-death-penalty.
91. Aamer Madhani, "Poll: Approval of Same-Sex Marriage in U.S. Reaches New High," *USA Today*, May 23, 2018, https://www.usatoday.com/story/news/nation/2018/05/23 /same-sex-marriage-poll-americans/638587002/.
92. "The state, therefore, has an interest in recognizing and protecting the traditional institution of marriage, as it is the primary means of producing wholesome citizens who both preserve the state's existence and determine its moral fabric. The chief objection to the legal recognition of same-sex marriage, therefore, isn't based on a prudish morality or religious conviction, but a conception of marriage and family essential to the state's promotion of the common good." (p. 98). He also invokes the so-called "New Natural Law" view of marriage (endnote 48), which excludes same-sex couples. For a devastating criticism of this, see John Corvino, "The Case for Same-Sex Marriage," in John Corvino and Maggie Gallagher, *Debating Same-Sex Marriage* (Oxford: Oxford University Press, 2012), 33–34.
93. See p. 101.
94. "Minimum wage laws, affirmative action policies, and welfare assistance are all perfect examples of well-intentioned violations of subsidiarity that have harmed more than they've helped." (p. 98)
95. "For instance: Economic inequality is a major issue among leftists. But why care about economic *inequality*? That is, it's easy to see why we should care about *poverty*—the fact that some don't have *enough*—but why care about the fact that some have *more* than others? Conservatives sometimes claim this is mere envy. But the account above provides a satisfying answer. The obvious reason, already hinted at, is that vast inequalities in wealth are seldom achieved without someone exploiting someone else. They also lead to domination; since wealth can influence the political process, the rich can use it to exercise unaccountable power over the whole of society. Since social standards for what it takes to appear 'respectable' to others vary depending on the wealth of a society, when some people have much less than average, they are likely to face disrespectful judgments. And a system which allocates to some far more than they need while others struggle to get by shows unequal regard." (p. 91)
96. For a quick and accessible comparison of some important metrics, see Annalisa Merelli, "The US Has a Lot of Money, But It Does Not Look Like a Developed Country," *Quartz*, March 10, 2017, https://qz.com/879092/the-us-doesnt-look-like -a-developed-country/. There is a further question about whether social democracy— which maintains the basic structures of capitalism, but uses government action to constrain capitalism's downsides—goes far *enough* for leftists. Some people instead think

leftists should endorse *democratic socialism*. (Exactly how to draw the line between the two systems is not always obvious, but the difference is roughly that democratic socialism goes further in its attempts to place capital under democratic control. Cf. Michael A. McCarthy, "Democratic Socialism Isn't Social Democracy," *Jacobin*, August 7, 2018, https://jacobinmag.com/2018/08/democratic-socialism-social-democracy -nordic-countries, and Matt Bruenig, "Identifying Socialist Institutions and Socialist Countries," *People's Policy Project*, August 7, 2018, https://www.peoplespolicyproj ect.org/2018/08/07/identifying-socialist-institutions-and-socialist-countries/). I think that which of these options is better is largely an empirical question. In any event, my point here is just that social democracy is *better* than what we have in the United States, and is proven to work.

97. Cf. Joseph Stiglitz, *The Price of Inequality* (New York: W. W. Norton & Company, 2012).

98. Drew Desilver, "For Most U.S. Workers, Real Wages Have Barely Budged in Decades," Pew Research Center, August 7, 2018, http://www.pewresearch.org/fact-tank/2018 /08/07/for-most-us-workers-real-wages-have-barely-budged-for-decades/.

99. Cf. Stiglitz, *The Price*, 34: "Only if the government does a reasonably good job of correcting the most important market failures will the economy prosper. Good financial regulation helped the United States—and the world—avoid a major crisis for four decades after the Great Depression. Deregulation in the 1980s led to scores of financial crises in the succeeding three decades, of which America's crisis in 2008–09 was only the worst. But those governmental failures were no accident: the financial sector used its political muscle to make sure that the market failures were not corrected, and that the sector's private rewards remained well in excess of their social contributions—one of the factors contributing to the bloated financial sector and to the high levels of inequality at the top." This claim is defended throughout the rest of the book.

100. Endnote 18.

101. Erik Eckholm, "Opponents of Same-Sex Marriage Take Bad-for-Children Argument to Court," *New York Times*, February 22, 2014, https://www.nytimes.com/2014/02/23 /us/opponents-of-same-sex-marriage-take-bad-for-children-argument-to-court .html.

102. Here, I'll just relay one of the most important and easy-to-see problems with Regnerus's study: He compares *all* children of gay and lesbian relationships to the children of *intact* heterosexual couples. Since parental relationship stability is a major predictor of positive outcomes for children, and since he compares average outcomes for *all* children of same-sex couples to those of the *most stable* heterosexual couples, it's hardly surprising that averages for the straight couples are higher (American Sociological Association, "Brief of Amicus Curiae in Support of Respondent Kristin M. Perry and Respondent Edith Schlain Windsor," http://www.asanet.org/sites/default/files/savvy /documents/ASA/pdfs/12-144_307_Amicus_%20(C_%20Gottlieb)_ASA_Same -Sex_Marriage.pdf: 17. For further criticisms, see pp. 16–19). Suppose you compare the average swimming ability of *all* Americans to the average swimming ability of members of the Russian Olympic swim team, notice that the average is higher for the latter group, and then conclude that Russians are better swimmers than Americans. Regnerus did respond to this, and to the many other criticisms of his study ("Parental Same-Sex Relationships, Family Instability, and Subsequent Life Outcomes for Adult Children: Answering Critics of the New Family Structures Study with Additional Analyses," *Social Science Research* 41 [2012]: 1367–1377). For now, it will suffice to say that I don't find his responses at all convincing; for a more detailed discussion, see *ASA*, "Amicus," 20–22. When Regnerus's dataset is analyzed using more plausible

methodological assumptions, his conclusions no longer hold (Simon Cheng and Brian Powell, "Measurement, Methods, and Divergent Patterns: Reassessing the Effects of Same-Sex Parents," *Social Science Research* 52 [2015]: 615–626).

103. "APA Statement on Children Raised by Gay and Lesbian Parents," American Psychological Association, June 11, 2012, http://www.apa.org/news/press/response/gay-parents.aspx. For a review of this scholarly consensus and the reasons for it, see *ASA*, "Amicus," 6–14. Critics of the pro–same-sex parenting scientific consensus claim that it is driven by a political agenda (desiring not to be politically incorrect, etc.) rather than scientific evidence. They claim the same of criticisms of Regnerus and other anti–same-sex parenting researchers (such as Donald Sullins, who McIntosh also cites). I'll say that I don't think this claim is *inherently ridiculous*. Academics have biases just like other people, and this can, sometimes, lead to a sort of groupthink. So, while the scientific consensus should hold a lot of weight, I don't you to ask you to blindly trust it; feel free to look into the research on your own. My point in citing the consensus is that I don't want an inattentive reader to assume that, since McIntosh has cited some scientific research, the claim has the authority of scientific expertise behind it. The claims about same-sex parenting that McIntosh endorses are an extremely fringe view.

104. In his review of T. M. Scanlon's *Why Does Inequality Matter?* Jonathan Wolff writes, "As I read Scanlon, the philosophical weight of his project rests on his view that there is no interesting substantive analysis of equality that will advance our understanding. Inequality is what matters, and it comes in a number of forms." *Notre Dame Philosophical Reviews*, August 14, 2018. Is this not a problem? Crummett admits to being less certain of what realizing the ideal of social equality amounts to than he is of what obstacles there are to it. But if you're uncertain of where you're going, how certain can you be of what obstacles there are in the way?

105. I'll just say that the "oppressive hierarchies" narrative, popularized in part by writers like Howard Zinn, is grossly reductionistic, ignoring innumerable historical, social, and economic complexities. But the benefits that narrative offers—a sense of enlightenment and self-righteousness—are worth the price of being proven wrong in obscure scholarly literature.

106. Cf. Jessica Koski et al., "Understanding Social Hierarchies: The Neural and Psychological Foundations of Status Perception," *Social Neuroscience* 10, no. 5 (2015): 529–530: "A wealth of evidence indicates social hierarchies are endemic, innate, and most likely, evolved to support survival within a group-living context. . . . Despite some cross-species variability, there is strong evidence that hierarchies arise out of necessity and their existence is beneficial to social groups." For an engaging popular-level discussion of this point, see Jordan Peterson, *12 Rules for Life: An Antidote to Chaos* (Toronto: Random House Canada, 2018), Chapter 1.

107. See Murray Rothbard, *The Ethics of Liberty* (New York: New York University Press, 1998), 162ff for the argument that taxation is theft and Robert Nozick, *Anarchy, State and Utopia* (New York: Basic Books, 1974), 169ff for an argument that income taxation is akin to slavery. For a tidy summary and defense of both, see Edward Feser, "Taxation, Forced Labor, and Theft," *The Independent Review* 5, no. 2 (2000): 219–235. Consider a different example: age restrictions. People under the age of sixteen cannot drive, those under eighteen cannot buy a long gun, and those under twenty-one cannot buy alcohol, presumably because it is thought most people below these ages generally do not yet have the requisite competence and responsibility. But surely there are plenty of fifteen-year-olds competent and responsible enough to drive, seventeen-year-olds to

buy a long gun, and twenty-year-olds to buy alcohol. Preventing such people from enjoying these freedoms (i.e., exercising certain natural rights) is an injustice—indeed, a kind of ageism. But we permit these unjust hierarchies of age for the sake of the common good. And lest it be objected that these oppressive hierarchies are artifacts of law and not society, oppressive social hierarchies doubtlessly often spin off of oppressive legal hierarchies.

108. See Edmund Burke's *Reflections on the Revolution in France* for a brilliant and prescient analysis of the French Revolution.

109. According to research prepared for the U.S. Department of Labor in 2009: "This study leads to the unambiguous conclusion that the differences in the compensation of men and women are the result of a multitude of factors and that the raw wage gap should not be used as the basis to justify corrective action. Indeed, there may be nothing to correct. The differences in raw wages may be almost entirely the result of the individual choices being made by both male and female workers." See "An Analysis of Reasons for the Disparity in Wages Between Men and Women," CONSAD Research Corp. (2009), 2. So unambiguous is the literature debunking the gender wage gap that even mainstream progressive venues like CBS and Huffington Post have run headlines such as "The Gender Pay Gap Is a Complete Myth" and "Wage Gap Myth Exposed—By Feminists," respectively: https://www.cbsnews.com/news/the-gender-pay-gap-is-a-complete-myth/ and https://www.huffingtonpost.com/christina-hoff-sommers/wage-gap_b_2073804.html.

110. See Cody T. Ross, "A Multi-Level Bayesian Analysis of Racial Bias in Police Shootings at the County-Level in the United States, 2011–2014," *PLoS ONE* 10, no. 11 (2015). John Lott and Carlisle Moody, "Do White Police Officers Unfairly Target Black Suspects?" *Social Science Research Network* (2016). For a more general treatment of the issue, See Heather MacDonald, *The War on Cops: How the New Attack on Law and Order Makes Everyone Less Safe* (Washington, DC: Encounter Books, 2016). On mass incarceration of blacks in particular, two book-length treatments much more responsible than Michelle Alexander's celebrated *The New Jim Crow* are Michael Javen Fortner, *The Black Silent Majority: The Rockefeller Drug Laws and the Politics of Punishment* (Cambridge, MA: Harvard University Press, 2015) and John Pfaff, *Locked In: The True Causes of Mass Incarceration and How to Achieve Real Reform* (New York: Basic Books, 2017).

111. This is only recently being seriously documented and studied. See Greg Lukianoff and Jonathan Haidt, *The Coddling of the American Mind: How Good Intentions and Bad Ideas Are Setting Up a Generation for Failure* (New York: Penguin Press, 2018) and Bradley Campbell and Jason Manning, *The Rise of Victimhood Culture: Microaggressions, Safe Spaces, and the New Culture Wars* (New York: Palgrave Macmillan, 2018).

112. As I write, Harvard University is being sued for discriminating against Asian Americans in its admissions process. The lawsuit alleges that the university disproportionately rejects Asian applicants based on personality traits like "likeability." Cf. Richard Sander and Stuart Taylor, *Mismatch*, 76–77: "At most undergraduate schools for which we have data, students with marginal credentials (by the school's admissions standard) are significantly less likely to be admitted if they are Asian. When such findings are pointed out, university officials often respond that this occurs because Asian American applicants tend to have weaker 'soft' credentials than do similar whites."

113. Such as, among other things, being (i) less likely to graduate from high school, (ii) less likely to be accepted into college, (iii) less likely to graduate from college, (iv) more

likely to be arrested, (v) more likely to be the victim of a violent crime, (vi) more likely to die by an occupational hazard, (vii) more likely to commit suicide, (viii) more likely to lose custody of their children in court, (ix) more likely to die of cancer, (x) more likely have cardiovascular disease, (xi) more likely to be overlooked and stigmatized as victims of sexual assault, and (xii) more likely to be physically and psychologically abused by intimate partners. (Space restrictions prevent me from including citations for these statistics, but I can happily provide them upon request: mcintosh.chad@ gmail.com.) I would say this amounts to evidence of "the system's . . . not valuing the lives of [men] equally to [women]" in the same way Crummett thinks the mortality rate among black women in childbirth being higher than white women shows "the system's . . . not valuing the lives of black women equally to white women," but I'm generally skeptical of systematic oppression narratives as explaining inequalities. On discrimination and harmful trends against men and boys in general, see the eye-opening books David Benatar, *The Second Sexism: Discrimination Against Men and Boys* (Malden, MA: Wiley-Blackwell, 2012) and Christina Hoff Sommers, *The War on Boys: How Misguided Policies Are Harming Our Young Men* (New York: Simon & Schuster, 2015).

114. Annual rates vary, but a consistent 30% to 40% of all abortion patients in the United States are black, despite being just 12% of the U.S. population—and about half of blacks are born into single-parent homes. These tragic figures began skyrocketing in the 1960s. On the disintegration of the black family, see Thomas Sowell, *Intellectuals and Race* (New York: Basic Books, 2013), 120ff. While the epidemic of single-parenthood among blacks antedates the era of slavery by a century and predates the era of "mass incarceration" by two decades, it coincides perfectly with "a large expansion of the welfare state and its accompanying non-judgmental ideology." Sowell, *Intellectuals and Race.*

115. It is well documented that conservative academics and journalists are an extreme minority in their professions (percentages range from around 2% to 15%). But again, *pace* progressives, I agree with George Yancey that "[m]erely documenting the level of underrepresentation of some social groups does not illustrate that prejudice against those groups is rampant, and merely because a group is underrepresented does not provide us with assurances that this group experiences prejudice." See *Compromising Scholarship: Political and Religious Bias in American Higher Education* (Waco, TX: Baylor University Press, 2011), 11–12.

116. Not that this is anything new. See Sowell, *Intellectual and Race,* esp. 50–52.

117. A recent study found that expression of moral outrage reduces feelings of guilt. See Zachary K. Rothschild and Lucas Keefer, "A Cleansing Fire: Moral Outrage Alleviates Guilt and Buffers Threats to One's Moral Identity," *Motivation and Emotion* 41, no. 2 (2017): 209–229. Of course sometimes there are legitimate grievances that aren't masks for hiding guilt. It's not always easy to tell without further inquiry. The personal anecdote that Crummett relays in endnote 34 of his article presents a fascinating case that could be interpreted either way.

118. Thanks to Elizabeth McIntosh, Benjamin Arbour, Tully Borland, Michael R. Jordan, Dan Martin, and Bob Fischer for helpful discussion and comments.

CHAPTER 2

America First

AMERICA FIRST
DANIEL BONEVAC

Thomas Nagel warns of the danger of excessive impartiality:

> . . . the discovery and awakening of the objective self with its universal charac-
> ter doesn't imply that one is not also a creature with an empirical perspective
> and individual life. . . . One must arrange somehow to see the world both from
> nowhere and from here, and to live accordingly.[1]

I am a human being. I am also an American—and a Texan, a professor, a husband, and a father. My humanity gives me universal obligations to fellow human
beings, no matter who and where they are. It also gives me certain universal
human rights. To that extent, those who urge that moral status does not end
at national borders are right.[2] But my other, more particular identities, roles,
and relationships give me additional responsibilities, rights, and privileges.
I have agent-relative duties to my country, my state, my students, my colleagues,
my wife, and my children that go beyond my obligations to strangers. As W. D.
Ross observes, I have special obligations to those who "stand to me in the relation of promisee to promiser, of creditor to debtor, of wife to husband, of child
to parent, of friend to friend, of fellow countryman to fellow countryman, and
the like."[3] And I have agent-relative rights and privileges—to vote in national,
state, and city elections, for example, or to assign my students grades—that
go beyond those I possess as a human being. Relationships have normative
implications.

The common-sense idea that we have obligations to every human being and
also other, special obligations arising out of particular human identities and relationships goes back at least as far as Confucius. In this essay I argue that we
have important agent-relative obligations "fellow countryman to fellow countryman"—that those who share a nation have responsibilities to one another arising
out of that relationship.

1. Government-for-the-People Versus Cosmopolitanism

President Trump's America First doctrine admits several distinct philosophical interpretations.[4] Here are two:

(1) The President should make decisions with the goal of benefiting Americans.

(2) Americans *qua* Americans should make decisions with the goal of benefiting Americans.

President Trump intends primarily the first, referring to an obligation of his own as president: "I will fight for you with every breath in my body—and I will never, ever let you down." This doctrine is not meant to be unique to the United States. It instantiates a general principle[5]:

(3) Political leaders should make decisions with the goal of benefiting the people they lead.

Citizens owe allegiance to the political organizations of which they are citizens; their leaders are responsible for safeguarding and promoting their welfare. These responsibilities are vertical, concerning norms governing the relationship between the leaders and the led.

Thesis (2) above is horizontal, concerning norms among fellow members of a political community. It instantiates a general principle:

(4) Members of a political community, *qua* members of that community, should make collective decisions with the goal of benefiting its members.

Call theses (3) and (4) the *Government-for-the-People doctrine.*[6]

These theses appear to clash with a view popular among some contemporary political philosophers: cosmopolitanism. Gillian Brock defines it this way:

(5) "[A]ll human beings have equal moral value";

(6) "[O]ur moral responsibilities to others do not disappear once we reach the boundaries of states or nations";

(7) "No [national] categories of people have more or less moral weight."[7]

The first two are plainly compatible with the Government-for-the-People doctrine. Everyone deserves moral consideration and respect regardless of citizenship, residence, origin, background, ethnicity, etc. Nothing in the Government-for-the-People doctrine denies *that*. The existence of special obligations—of parents to children, of doctors to patients, or of leaders to those led—need not deny anyone moral value, consideration, or respect.[8]

The real issue concerns (7), the thesis that members of different political communities have the same moral weight. The key question is, *for whom?* The Government-for-the-People doctrine implies that leaders should give priority to their own people's welfare, just as parents ought to give priority to their own children's welfare. Similarly, members of a political community ought to give priority to one another's interests. The interests of Americans are no more important *sub specie aeternitatis*—when viewed from nowhere—than the interests of Italians, Russians, Nigerians, and Indonesians. To that extent, (7) is true. But they should be more important when viewed *from here*, to Americans or to the president of the United States.

Call this the *Priority Thesis*. In vertical and horizontal forms:

(8) Political leaders should give priority to the interests of their own people.

(9) Members of a political community, as such, should give priority to one another's interests.[9]

Cosmopolitans disagree, at least at the level of the nation.[10] They insist on the view from nowhere. They argue that leaders and others should promote the good for humanity in general. Generally, they take this to entail some combination of:

open borders,
international protections for human rights,
more equal distribution of power among countries,
changes in democracy to allow anyone affected by decisions to participate, regardless of national boundaries, and
massive income or wealth transfers to people in less affluent countries.[11]

They thus move from seemingly innocuous premises to radical conclusions. Even those who argue for a *rooted* cosmopolitanism that makes a place for associational norms tend to accept those prescriptions.[12]

I am arguing in favor of the Priority Thesis and against cosmopolitanism. The divide between those two positions has increasing importance, separating Republicans from Democrats and Brexit from Remain voters. It divides political parties throughout much of Europe.

2. Philosophical Arguments for the Government-for-the-People Conception

Virtue Ethics
Many virtues arise from specific human relationships.[13] A good teacher, for example, is not simply a good person and a teacher. A good president is not just a good person and a president. Social relationships and roles have distinctive virtues and vices and generate distinctive obligations.

Many of those virtues and obligations involve *valuing* people. That goes beyond judging them to be of value.[14] Good parents value their own children more than other children, even while recognizing that other children are just as valuable in the abstract, when viewed from nowhere.[15] They prioritize their own children's welfare. Just so, good leaders value their own people more than other people without denying that they are equally valuable. They prioritize their own people's welfare.

Leaders have an obligation to protect their people—not an obligation to protect any people, anywhere. They have an obligation to promote their people's interests—not merely the interests of anyone, anywhere. The Prime Minister of Romania has little or no obligation to protect me, care for me, or promote my interests. Her obligation is to the people of Romania. She should give preference to their interests. The same holds for citizens of Romania. They have little or no obligations to protect me, care for me, or promote my interests.

Virtue, as Confucius and Aristotle observe, is a mean between extremes.[16] Leaders must not give so much preference to the interests of those they lead that they attack, enslave, or oppress others. But they should not give so little preference that their people have no reason to follow them. Cosmopolitanism threatens political communities and the civic virtues that undergird them by assailing the ties people have to the communities they inhabit.

From this perspective, the Government-for-the-People doctrine is a mean between the extremes of cosmopolitanism on the one side and racism or xenophobia on the other. The cosmopolitans have too little concern for their own political communities. The racists and xenophobes have too little concern for other political communities.

Consequentialism

Consequentialism judges one action better than another if it tends to have better consequences. John Stuart Mill seems to think that this demands the view from nowhere: "As between [the agent's] own happiness and that of others, utilitarianism requires him to be as strictly impartial as a disinterested and benevolent spectator."[17] If I can't weigh my interests more heavily than others' interests, it would seem that *we* can't weigh our interests more than others' interests, and that our leaders can't either.

But that doesn't follow. As Henry Sidgwick argues, "the commonly received view of special claims and duties arising out of special relations, though prima facie opposed to the impartial universality of the Utilitarian principle, is really maintained by a well-considered application of that principle."[18] A world in which people respect, care for, promote the interests of, and love their own spouses, children, friends, neighbors, communities, and countries is better than a world in which they act with excessive impartiality. It's better for everyone if we each value and look out for our own.

Why? First, knowledge tracks proximity. People know what will have better consequences for them and those close to them to a greater extent than they know what will have better consequences for those distant from them. People can judge what will promote the interests of their own community more accurately than they can judge what will promote the interests of the world as a whole. Cosmopolitans, trying to be impartial, will mostly make mistakes.[19]

Second, concern tracks proximity. People care most about those close to them. We are situated beings; we view the world from a certain point of view, from here. Any theory that requires us to take the view from nowhere in our relationships and actions would alienate us from our natures. Even if impartiality were possible, it would not be good. Relying on distant supposed benefactors would make outcomes worse, not better.

Third, excessive impartiality is incompatible with organization. Complex tasks require organization, and organization requires hierarchy. If leaders are impartial between interests of those they lead and those of others, then the led won't feel any obligation to their leaders.

Excessive impartiality, in fact, is incompatible with any human relationships. Friends have a concern for one another beyond the concern they have for human beings in general. If they didn't, there could be no such thing as friendship. Lawyers look out for the interests of their clients. Agents look out for the interests of those they represent. If they didn't, there would be no point to hiring a lawyer or an agent. Just so, in a republic, people elect others to represent them. If representatives don't represent their constituents' interests, there's no point in electing them.

Some cosmopolitans agree that special obligations arise out of relationships, roles, and membership in families or communities. But they deny that special obligations can arise from belonging to a nation. That seems arbitrary. What makes a nation so different from a family, an organization, a town, a state, etc., that it alone is morally inert?[20] To demand the view from nowhere, no matter what, is at least consistent. To demand that our view be from nowhere, or anywhere but there, seems capricious.[21]

Kantianism

Kant seems to offer an ethical theory that promotes cosmopolitanism. We must act on maxims we could will everyone to follow, showing everyone equal respect as moral agents.[22] Kant sees this as generating an obligation to help others in need. But it does not preclude special obligations arising out of specific relationships and social roles. Kant discusses two cases undercutting a cosmopolitan interpretation of his moral theory.[23]

One concerns family relationships. The duty to care for one's family takes precedence over a duty to help others. Kant here explicitly allows obligations arising out of special relationships to take precedence over more general obligations.[24] He limits "the rights of men, as citizens of the world," to "conditions of universal hospitality"—that is, to a right of visitation, but not residence: "It is not a right to be treated as a guest to which the stranger can lay claim," and citizens "may send him away again, if this can be done without causing his death."[25]

The other relies on the distinction between perfect and imperfect obligations. The former are specific duties generated from specific relationships; the latter allow choice.[26] I have a perfect obligation to repay a debt, but an imperfect obligation to help someone in need. Kant makes it clear that perfect obligations take precedence. Someone else's need doesn't obligate me to go into debt or skip payments.[27]

Today, affluent countries are deeply in debt. They continue to run massive deficits. Kant would deny that they have obligations to borrow further to send aid to others in need. In practical political terms, the issue is not whether the United States should send its money to help impoverished countries but whether it should borrow from China—thereby putting its future taxpayers in debt—to do that.

Kant's moral theory requires respect for moral agents as ends-in-themselves. Conservatives build their philosophy on such respect—respect for the circumstances, identities, relationships, choices, and tradeoffs that real people make. Cosmopolitans inevitably treat people merely as means to some global vision. If political leaders aren't to prioritize the interests of those they serve, but instead attend to the world as a whole, they must have a conception of what the interests of the entire world are. They have no way of knowing that. So, they have no choice but to substitute their own preferred tradeoffs among competing goods for those of the people. Nominally a philosophy of universal respect, cosmopolitanism in practice is a philosophy of universal disrespect.[28]

Moral Foundations Theory

Jonathan Haidt and his associates have developed an approach to moral psychology known as Moral Foundations Theory.[29] According to that theory, people base their moral and political thinking on five foundations: care, fairness, loyalty, authority, and sanctity. Each has its opposite: harm, cheating, betrayal, subversion, and degradation. Loyalty, authority, and sanctity are *binding* foundations, foundations crucial to binding people into social groups. They support the Priority Thesis.[30]

Loyalty: Political leaders should prioritize their subject's interests. They should be loyal to their own, and their subjects should be loyal to them. People within a political community should be loyal to one another. Excessive impartiality is a form of betrayal.[31]

Authority: The leaders' positions as leaders give them obligations correlative to their authority. To take "the view from nowhere" consistently would be to reject those obligations and undermine people's reasons to follow. Members of a political community should obey legitimate authority and follow legitimately enacted laws.

Sanctity: Purity, discipline, self-control, and other virtues suggest that political leaders have an obligation to prioritize the cultural as well as material interests of those they lead. Nations are not interchangeable; they have distinctive characters. Romania is not India; India is not China; China is not Peru. The people of a country should protect its way of life, its culture— including, crucially, its political culture—and, in general, its distinctive character. Fulfilling those responsibilities requires leaders to prioritize their own people's interests.

John Rawls argues against cosmopolitanism on similar grounds. Societies have different values. They make different choices. Those choices deserve respect. But different choices of cultural, economic, and political systems and different tradeoffs within them may lead to large differences in wealth. Our obligation, Rawls insists, is to enable societies "to determine the path of their own future for themselves."[32] We have no obligation to redistribute income or wealth further. Doing so would undermine autonomy and self-determination, imposing the cosmopolitans' vision of the relative importance of economic well-being on the entire world.

Obligations to loyalty, obedience, and preservation are *pro tanto* obligations, holding in the absence of other, competing moral considerations. We have no obligation to perpetuate injustice. And, since self-improvement and beneficence are virtues, we have an obligation to try to improve and enrich our culture, not just preserve it.

3. Practical Problems of Cosmopolitanism

Moral considerations support the Priority Thesis. Political leaders should prioritize the interests of their people. People should prioritize the interests of members of their own political communities. Government should be of the people, by the people, and for the people.

Practical considerations also support the Priority Thesis. Cosmopolitan policies, like others that abstract away from real circumstances and relationships, are "great on paper, disastrous in practice."[33] Cosmopolitans' primary loyalty is to their vision of the common good for the entire world. They believe "in the easy perfectibility of man," "ready to abandon the work of centuries"—specifically, the Westphalian system of nation-states, our dominant system of political organization since 1648—"for sentimental qualms."[34]

The result? Failed states (Syria, Libya); hordes of refugees; strains on educational and medical systems; housing shortages; massive government and private debt; widespread corruption; endless military engagements; high levels of unemployment; political polarization; low levels of trust; attacks on freedom of speech and freedom of thought; rampant propaganda; disregard for truth; a focus on issues far removed from the concerns of ordinary people; the politicization of social and governmental institutions; and cultural degradation and even destruction.

That's what's happened so far. The future would be worse. In a nutshell:

Open borders would overwhelm welfare programs and social services in advanced countries, radically lowering their quality of life, destroying their cultures, and eroding social capital, turning them into low-trust societies incapable of their former levels of achievement and affluence.[35] Immigration brings benefits, but the pace matters. Rapid migrations produce social disruptions. Immigrants take jobs from natives. Increased competition from immigrants lowers wages and raises the cost of housing. Criminals cross open borders with impunity. Newcomers who don't share natives' moral and political values threaten freedoms of speech, association, and religion as well as conceptions of rights to life, liberty, and property. A right to freedom of movement across borders is, after all, a right to invade—a right to colonize. Those who cross open borders differ greatly from those who immigrate under a more restrictive system.

International protections for human rights and the idealistic foreign policy that implies tend to lead to frequent military interventions, many of whose harms outweigh their benefits. And the conception of human rights underlying these decisions might be far from our own.[36]

More equal distribution of power among countries would transfer power from those who respect human rights and the rule of law to those who don't. The example of the United Nations is not encouraging. A world in which totalitarian countries that disrespect human rights had more power wouldn't be an improvement.

Changes in democracy to allow anyone affected by decisions to participate, regardless of national boundaries, would raise serious practical and theoretical questions. Who would decide who is affected enough by a given decision to be allowed a vote? Would everyone in the world, for example, get to vote in an American presidential election? How would we conduct elections in which people all over the globe could participate? Wouldn't those outside a country have enough votes to outweigh the preferences of its citizens? Such a scheme would give an advantage to populous countries and undermine democracy itself.[37] Most of the world's people, after all, have little experience of or faith in democracy. We would each find ourselves ruled by people distant from us, who know and care little for us, who don't share our values, and who may have interests opposed to ours.

Massive income or wealth transfers to people in less affluent countries would provide incentives for corruption while helping to maintain inefficient and unjust systems, with little money going to those most in need of help. There are more than three billion people in the world living on less than $1,000 per year. Bringing them up to the world's median income could require more than $100,000 from each American, every year.[38] Problems of poverty cannot be meaningfully addressed by the equivalent of a global welfare program.

Globally, the cause of poverty is not imperialism, lack of resources, or bad luck, but a lack of economic freedom. Most poor countries suffer from political and economic systems that fail to establish the rule of law, respect property, and reward accomplishment.[39] Aid that leaves such systems in place tends to do more harm than good. In fact, aid penalizes good systems and rewards bad systems. The likely consequence: fewer good systems and more bad ones.

4. Conclusion

How might someone object to what I've said here? Many different moral and practical arguments support the Priority Thesis. So does common sense. The burden of proof surely lies on cosmopolitans to show that they all fail.

A "kinder, gentler" cosmopolitan might admit that the people of a nation should give priority to their own interests, but argue that sometimes people in other nations are so desperate that they require our aid. After all, even if I ought to prioritize my children over others, if my child is safe and another person's child is drowning nearby, I should try to save that child. Maybe international circumstances are similar. Americans are reasonably well-off, while many others are desperately poor. Perhaps their needs take precedence over the Priority Thesis.

I'll limit myself to three points in reply. First, the Priority Thesis—like all moral principles, in my view—holds in general, all other things being equal. So, there can be conditions under which we should help others whether or not it makes us worse off. We should admit political refugees in times of crisis. We should send aid to victims of natural disasters. America First does not mean America Only.

Second, cosmopolitans assume that the best way to help poor people abroad includes opening borders and redistributing wealth and political power. But, natural disasters aside, the poor need economic opportunities. They need liberty. They need the rule of law. They need stable governments that protect rights.

International trade and good government, not handouts or relocation, alleviate poverty in the long run.

Third, cosmopolitans take a lot for granted. They assume that America's success is stable—that it wouldn't be undermined by following their advice. But economies, cultures, and political institutions are fragile. It isn't inevitable that America is a good place to live, featuring individual liberty, flourishing businesses, and a strong democracy. Maintaining a thriving republic takes extensive investment and great care. Cosmopolitans risk turning successful countries into graphic demonstrations of Derek Parfit's repugnant conclusion, places overpopulated with struggling masses leading lives barely worth living.[40] Who will help them? What value will open borders have then?

In politics—though, fortunately, not in philosophical journals—cosmopolitans often call their opponents names: racists, xenophobes, supremacists, fascists, and even Nazis. As I've argued, however, this completely misrepresents their opponents' position. The Priority Thesis is a mean between the extremes of assigning everyone equal moral standing regardless of their relationship to you and assigning everyone outside a certain kind of relationship with you no moral standing or even a negative moral value. Nothing in the Government-for-the-People doctrine entails the latter. Visiting your mother on Mother's Day and buying your children gifts for their birthdays implies no negative judgment about other people's mothers or children. "Family first" implies no negative judgment about anyone outside the family. Just so, giving priority to the interests of one's own countrymen implies no negative judgment about anyone else.[41]

Cosmopolitanism is not so much wrong as one-dimensional. It captures the view from nowhere. But, as Plato, Aristotle, and Cicero all stressed, our moral and political obligations call us to maintain two seemingly contradictory views at once.[42] We are human beings *and* members of political communities. Both exert a moral pull on us, and sometimes they pull in different directions. Rabbi Hillel captured the tension between the view from here and the view from nowhere:

> If I am not for myself, who will be for me? But if I am for myself alone, what am I? And if not now, when?[43]

We should not be for ourselves alone. But if we aren't for ourselves—if we don't value and prioritize those who share our own political community—we will find ourselves outnumbered in a hostile world. Who will be for us? The cosmopolitan answer is supposed to be "Everyone." In practice, it turns out to be "No one."

Cosmopolitans offer a system that, in the name of promoting the interests of all, promotes the interests of the cosmopolitans themselves. A rootless few, they substitute their abstract vision of the common good for tradeoffs made by real people, facing real problems, in the context of real relationships. The many find themselves under assault, as "deplorables," in a culture that no longer looks like theirs, by people who despise them. Understandably, they lose trust in their political institutions and in leaders who no longer feel obliged to promote their interests. Meanwhile, those leaders justify that lack of trust by betraying their own communities and making the world a more dangerous place for everyone.

COMPREHENSION QUESTIONS

1. What does Bonevac mean by "the view from nowhere"?
2. What is the Government-for-the-People doctrine, and what general moral idea does Bonevac offer in support of it?
3. Why, according to Bonevac, does cosmopolitanism have more practical problems than his Priority Thesis?
4. How does Bonevac reply to the objection that citizens of wealthier nations might sometimes have obligations to help those who are desperately poor?

DISCUSSION QUESTIONS

1. In support of his Priority Thesis, Bonevac offers arguments grounded in four different moral theories. Which theory do you think provides the best support? Why?
2. Bonevac contends that there are special obligations that arise out of particular roles, identities, and relationships. Do you think you have duties to other people who live in your country simply because you're in the same country? What duties might you have to people who *aren't* in your country, simply because they're other human beings?
3. Bonevac notes that it seems arbitrary to allow for special obligations arising from family or community relationships but not from national citizenship. How do we know which roles, relationships, and identities—if any—create an obligation to prioritize some people's interests over others'? Do rich people have obligations to other rich people? Or white people to other white people?
4. What might Bonevac have in mind when he suggests that supporting international protections for human rights is a radical conclusion?

Case 1

According to U.S. Citizenship and Immigration Services, citizens of the United States have the following responsibilities in virtue of their citizenship:

- Support and defend the Constitution
- Stay informed of the issues affecting your community
- Participate in the democratic process
- Respect and obey federal, state, and local laws
- Respect the rights, beliefs, and opinions of others
- Participate in your local community
- Pay income and other taxes honestly, and on time, to federal, state, and local authorities
- Serve on a jury when called upon
- Defend the country if the need should arise*

Case 1 (continued)

> To what extent do these responsibilities align with the view that American citizens should make decisions with the goal of benefiting Americans? How might they conflict with responsibilities arising from lower-level relationships, roles, or identities (e.g., friend, student, parent, employer)? How might they conflict with decisions aimed at establishing and maintaining global justice?
>
> ---
>
> *https://www.uscis.gov/citizenship/learners/citizenship-rights-and-responsibilities

DEFENDING THE COSMOPOLITAN OUTLOOK
GILLIAN BROCK

1. Introduction

How should we think about our responsibilities to one another in our contemporary, globally connected world? What responsibilities, if any, do citizens of one country have to those in others? These abstract questions arise in practice in several forms. Let's consider a few illustrations.

We face many common problems in our highly interdependent world with its interlinked systems and areas of vulnerability. Examples from about the last decade include the global financial crisis and recession, rising sea levels, and multiple threats of pandemics such as Ebola and swine flu. Tackling such problems effectively requires a certain amount of global cooperation. Do we have any obligations to participate in such cooperative efforts aimed at addressing common threats?

Other large-scale problems in the international arena abound. In some places people live in conditions of dire poverty or where their most basic human rights are violated with impunity. Might those living in high-income countries with reasonably reliable provisions for basic human rights have any obligations to assist in efforts to secure the human rights of others?

Even if we are inclined toward the view that there are some obligations to others in the global sphere, how, if at all, does membership in particular states matter to responsibilities to cooperate in solving global problems and render assistance to non-compatriots? For many people, national membership can be an important part of their identity and sense of well-being. Moreover, a pro-national stance can be useful in fostering solidarity, community, social justice, and a democratic ethos. Nations might well have an important role to play in aiming for a better world. How should national membership be accommodated in an account of global justice? How should we weigh our duties to compatriots with any duties we might have to others in distant or even neighboring lands?

Fortunately, there are ways to balance concern for both local and global justice, and there are important synergies between them as well.[44] In Section 3, I sketch my cosmopolitan account of global justice, and we are then in a position to appreciate why local and global justice are often mutually reinforcing rather than in tension. First, however, I should explain what the cosmopolitan outlook essentially embodies, which I do in Section 2. There I also address two common misconceptions about cosmopolitanism and review its fundamental commitments. Once I have outlined my cosmopolitan account of global justice and illustrated it with some practical examples, we are better able to appreciate how local and global justice are far more connected than is often appreciated. We can also then see how to accommodate insights from both the cosmopolitan and nationalist traditions within one integrated model. Section 4 offers concluding reflections about the state of this debate between cosmopolitans and nationalists.[45]

2. Cosmopolitanism: Some Basic Commitments and Misconceptions Addressed

According to many contemporary cosmopolitans, every human being is entitled to equal respect and consideration no matter what her citizenship status or other affiliations happen to be.[46] Appealing to the idea of moral equality, cosmopolitans encourage us not to let local obligations crowd out responsibilities to distant others. Cosmopolitans highlight the responsibilities we have to those whom we do not know but whose lives should be of concern to us.[47] Being a cosmopolitan is often characterized in terms of being a citizen of the world. This idea succinctly captures two important aspects of cosmopolitanism as the term is often understood today, one aspect drawing attention to identity and another to responsibility. On the identity issue, being a cosmopolitan indicates that one is a person who is influenced or marked by various cultures. Being a cosmopolitan about responsibility has generated much discussion, and there is considerable debate surrounding what the cosmopolitan commitment *requires*. So, cosmopolitanism's driving ideas are sometimes best appreciated by considering what the cosmopolitan clearly rejects. For instance, cosmopolitanism rules out positions that attach no moral value to some people, or weights the moral value some people have differentially according to their race, ethnicity, or nationality. Cosmopolitanism stands firmly against ethnocentrism, racism, advantaging group members at the expense of non-members, and so forth. In Section 3, I outline what the cosmopolitan outlook plausibly includes and outline my own positive account of cosmopolitan global justice. But first, and in the spirit of clearing away misconceptions, I continue in this section with two common misunderstandings about the position.

One common assumption is that cosmopolitanism necessarily requires a world state or government. To explain how this thought involves a misunderstanding, a distinction is often drawn between moral and institutional cosmopolitanism. Moral cosmopolitans maintain that every person has global stature as the ultimate unit of moral concern and is therefore entitled to equal consideration no matter what her citizenship or nationality status. But holding this position does not necessarily commit one to a complete overhaul of the state system. While institutional cosmopolitans do argue that important institutional changes are needed to the global system in order to realize cosmopolitan commitments, such changes need not amount to a world state. Though there are some who argue for a world state, moral cosmopolitans need not support such radical institutional transformations.[48] Moral cosmopolitans typically recommend that various institutional reforms could realize cosmopolitan goals and include a prominent place for states.

A second common misconception about cosmopolitanism is that it cannot accommodate special attachments and commitments that fill most ordinary human beings' lives with much important value. It is often thought that cosmopolitans must reject attachments to those in local or particular communities in favor of an ideal of impartial justice that the individual must apply directly to all, no matter where they are situated on the globe. However, this position is not required by cosmopolitanism; in fact, this is not a position advocated by many cosmopolitans.[49] Most contemporary cosmopolitans recognize that attachments are a deep source of fulfillment in life for many people and accept that people have meaningful commitments to particular communities, be they national, ethnic, religious, or cultural. Cosmopolitans seek to articulate the legitimate scope for such partiality. They tend to do this by situating attachments in their rightful context, by offering a framework that clarifies our obligations to one another. (More on this below.) The idea is that cosmopolitan principles define that justice framework and that there is scope for partiality to operate within it.

As we also come to appreciate, cosmopolitan duties and duties to co-members of states are often mutually reinforcing. In many cases we must attend to cosmopolitan duties in order to meet our obligations to compatriots, such as when we need to establish fair international institutions that enable citizens to meet needs. And in order to discharge cosmopolitan commitments and secure global justice goals, we often must advance local institutions that can realize the means for all to enjoy prospects for a decent life. Can any cosmopolitan account deliver on all these promising ideas? In order to show how it can, I turn in the next section to sketch one such position.

3. A Cosmopolitan Account of Global Justice

I start with the insight, now well established in political philosophy, that the fundamental institutions that we collectively uphold structure and importantly influence how our lives will go. John Rawls, the preeminent political philosopher of the twentieth century, makes this a focal point of his theory. The basic structure of society—which includes all the main political, economic, legal, and social institutions—should be the core focus for an account of justice because its effects are pervasive, profound, and present from birth. Whatever we think of Rawls's particular argument, we must at least recognize some version of the central idea: The institutions that govern our lives have an important role to play in structuring our life prospects, and so it is important that we ensure these aim to approximate just ones. And this applies as much to state-level institutions as international ones.

My next key point is that we all must acknowledge the moral equality of all human beings. Call this the *Moral Equality Imperative*. It embraces the idea that no matter where people are located on the globe, simply as human beings, they deserve a certain kind of treatment that reflects their equal value and standing as human beings.

What should commitment to the Moral Equality Imperative mean for how we ought to structure the institutions we collectively uphold, at both the global and local levels? It minimally entails that as a general rule, all human beings' fundamental interests deserve equal consideration. As I develop these ideas, this means we should ensure everyone is well positioned to enjoy the prospects for a decent life. I elaborate on this via four central scaffolds.[50] First, one should be enabled to meet one's basic needs. Second, one must have adequate protection for one's basic liberties. Third, fair terms of cooperation should govern one's collective endeavors. And fourth, social and political arrangements that support these core ingredients for a decent life should be in place.

There are many ways to argue in defense of these four components as important supports for all people in trying to secure decent lives. We might start with the individual human person and reflect on what she needs to live a life of dignity, fleshing out opportunities, protections, resources, and so forth that are central to such a life. As we proceed in this way, it will clearly be important to take account of the wide variation we see around the world in human living arrangements. But taking account of diversity we can still discern core aspects of the human condition that deserve special attention. For instance, in virtue of our vulnerabilities as human beings, there are common threats that we all face; reflecting on our physical, psychological, or emotional human constitution, we can identify important areas that deserve special concern, especially if we are to have decent lives and live harmoniously with one another.[51]

Starting with individual human beings in our reflections does not mean that their associations and attachments are unimportant. On the contrary, our reflections should quickly bring us to the realization that how that person stands in relation to others is also a key part of enjoying a life of dignity. If she is subject to domination, exploitation, or other forms of extreme coercion, her life will lack important ingredients for a dignified, decent human life. If her relationships with others are characterized by extreme inequality, this may well undermine the possibility that she will be able to live a life worthy of human dignity. Even if we start with the individual in our theorizing, as I propose we do, it will be essential to include relational components in our account of what global justice requires. These relational components include the idea of standing in certain kinds of relationships with one another that recognize our moral equality. And they include the idea of fair terms of cooperation as an important way of showing recognition for our moral equality.

I have elaborated on these details of my account of global justice at length elsewhere.[52] For the purposes of this chapter, I need emphasize only a few central points. First, global justice requires that we must be concerned with everyone's prospects for a decent life in designing just institutions, at both state and international levels. Second, we all have general moral duties to lend support to such institutions, as requirements that flow out of our duties to one another. We have duties to support institutions that can secure justice (or those institutions that have credible prospects of doing so). If all persons are entitled to equal respect, then this requires assisting with measures that can ensure they are justly treated, at least when we can do so with reasonable accommodations on our part. So each of us has a limited but robust moral obligation to support institutions that can deliver on justice.

On my view, rather than having little importance, states are highly relevant in an account of global justice for several reasons.

First, many people highly value their membership in states. They have a strong sense of attachment to their fellow nationals, and they care deeply about their state's standing and achievements in the world. All of this can have an important bearing on their well-being. It is important to appreciate that such attachment has been socially constructed, typically over an extended period of time. Nations did not always exist, and when they did form, considerable nation-building effort was required (and continues to be required) to achieve the results we see in the world today. National identities can also unravel just as easily under certain circumstances. We see this for instance in secession movements such as those gathering momentum in Catalonia (Spain), Scotland (Great Britain), and Quebec (Canada). Just as impressively, a sense of attachment can grow much larger over time. Examples include the European Union and in the many nations that contain millions of citizens who have complex sub-identities, such as in the case of Indonesia, Malaysia, the United States of America, and Great Britain. Having noted that there is much scope for modifying identities over time, we also need to be cautious, since trying to change identities under the wrong conditions can be extremely destructive, for instance in provoking unhealthy backlashes. So mechanisms for modifying identities require careful treatment, such as making sure identities are not unhelpfully suppressed.[53]

While people's attachments can certainly change, there are also good reasons to make space in an account of global justice for many defensible forms of attachments, such as citizens' commitments to states. Such commitments may well fortify central elements of global justice by supporting solidarity, democracy, and social justice projects, which often require willingness on the part of some citizens to assist others, perhaps in less fortunate circumstances. In addition, on any realistic picture of what global justice should mean for here and now, states are not up for grabs. They are likely to be a core feature of our world order for many years to come. And even in an ideal world, there are good reasons to think states should remain as a robust part of the global institutional architecture. One concern that many readers will share is about how concentrated power might create too many opportunities for its abuse. Multiple centers of power provide better protection against such possibilities.

Another reason in favor of states playing an important role is that there are many state-level institutions, policies, and practices that should be of concern in ensuring the Moral Equality Imperative is implemented properly in statewide institutions. For instance, state-level institutions constitute an important site of cooperation that ought to aspire to fairness. And in the world we live in, much responsibility for ensuring core ingredients necessary for a good life is devolved to states. State agents are often the primary agents tasked with ensuring key components of justice are delivered. Effective states are enormously important to promoting citizens' well-being, and they play an immense role turning our lofty justice aspirations into reality. States, after all, are necessary to ensure key goods and services characteristic of a decent life are available. These include health care, education, water, sanitation, infrastructure, law enforcement, and security. States are also in a unique position to regulate potentially harmful activities, including economic ones. In short, states are an important vehicle through which many key ingredients of justice—both global and local—are secured.

Having explained some central elements of my cosmopolitan account of justice and the role nations can and should play in it, we can now begin to sketch some of the ways in which cosmopolitan and special duties to co-members of nations can be reconciled on many occasions. On my account, and contrary to the views of many skeptics, there are in fact important synergies between duties and they are mutually reinforcing. To state some of the general connections, with examples to follow below, we need to attend to cosmopolitan duties in order to meet our obligations to compatriots. Without a number of institutions that can ensure (say) fairness in international institutions and practices, our ability to ensure that citizens are enabled to meet needs is challenging. And in order to discharge cosmopolitan commitments and secure global justice goals, we often must advance local institutions that can realize the means for all to enjoy prospects for a decent life. For instance, to ensure people can enjoy the conditions necessary for their autonomy, to meet other core human needs, or to realize fair terms of cooperation, they need to be able to participate in local as well as global political processes that aim at self-determination. Supporting institutions that aim at securing self-determination requires international and domestic actions. My cosmopolitan position aims to support genuine self-determination and democracy at multiple levels. There are many ways in which attending to institutional fairness is a way to discharge our duties to both compatriots and non-compatriots since institutional fairness advances the interests of both.

Let's consider some examples of how this might play out in practice. Participating in various institutions that aim at solving our collective global problems and supporting fair arrangements for doing this will be very important. I provide four examples next.

Catastrophic anthropogenic climate change is proving to be a threat that could considerably undermine human beings' abilities to live decent lives. For instance, if sea levels continue to rise at current projected rates, habitable territory is likely to decrease, compromising agricultural productivity and exacerbating tensions over increasingly scarce resources. More extreme weather events are likely to make our lives much more precarious. We ought to cooperate in global initiatives that aim to avert climate disaster, and failure to do so is likely to constitute a violation of all four of my key components of justice, for both compatriots and non-compatriots. Leaders who refuse to cooperate, citing the promotion of their citizens' interests as grounds for such non-participation, not only take a highly limited view of what is in their citizens' interests, but they also fail in our duties of justice to support institutions that are able to deliver on justice for all human beings.

For another example, consider how our economies are highly interdependent. Financial and economic woes can quickly spread across the world, as was made abundantly clear during the last global recession and global financial crisis. The economic fallout of speculative investments and highly risky borrowing practices rampant in the United States and the United Kingdom quickly spread throughout the globe, rendering millions of people unemployed and unable to meet bare subsistence needs. We all have an interest in robust regulatory arrangements that can block such consequences. Our international financial and economic institutions should adopt rules capable of such protection.[54]

Another example that can be drawn from the economic sphere concerns our international tax practices. These allow multinational corporations and high-net-worth individuals to escape taxation, thereby shifting the burden of raising revenue onto others less able to take advantage of such accounting loopholes. Governments need revenue to run an effective state, and failure to collect sufficient revenue has important consequences for social justice. First, governments may fail to provide important goods and services necessary for basic domestic justice (such as law enforcement, courts, basic health care, or roads). Second, the tax burden is shifted onto disadvantaged citizens who pay the cost for the free-riding activities of those who unfairly escape the reach of tax authorities. Without global cooperation on fair tax arrangements no country can solve this problem, which is essentially one of coordinating collective action to yield effective solutions. Failure to play our part in such arrangements—failures either to be willing to work toward global rules or to enforce them adequately on our territory—again constitutes an important justice failure. We fail to secure what is needed to promote domestic justice and likewise fail to support non-compatriots in securing social justice in their countries.

The World Health Organization aims at fair and effective arrangements to deal with many health challenges, such as trying to stem the spread of contagious diseases in cases of global pandemics. States are required to comply with various rules, such as reporting disease outbreaks or supporting states that cannot manage treatment and containment when outbreaks do occur. Our commitment to fair international practice around health will sometimes require us to lend assistance by providing necessary training, skilled personnel, treatments, or equipment. Those who have great capacity to assist might be called on to help where dire need prevails. And high-income countries should be willing to assist. Protecting the interests of others is often a way to protect the interests of our fellow citizens, as might be the case with some highly contagious diseases. Even when our self-interest is not in play, cosmopolitan justice requires assistance to show our commitment to the idea that each person's health is worthy of protection, at least when such commitment requires reasonable accommodations or contributions on our part.

These examples highlight important features of a number of other examples that could be discussed.[55] Generally, we should support institutions that are effective and accountable and aim to secure justice. Sometimes there are good self-interested reasons to do so, and sometimes not. Whether or not self-interest coincides with what justice requires, we should support governance arrangements that have as their aim showing respect for all human beings' abilities to live decent lives; while the duty is limited, it is still robust. When leaders refuse to participate in international initiatives aiming at fair terms of cooperation, they fail in their basic duties on multiple grounds. They often fail to deliver on justice for citizens (for instance, citizens' needs or liberties are frequently at risk if global problems are not solved). Such failures to cooperate also constitute failures to discharge the duties we all have to support just institutions.[56]

As these examples also highlight, to promote genuine self-determination and democracy in a globally interconnected world we must attend to the global context in which states are situated. Without such concern, national ideals cannot be realized. As I have also been illustrating, there is no need to abandon states to secure the kind of global governance arrangements that might better secure justice for all. We already have a number of international bodies that have authority over particular domains, such as in health, finance, borrowing, labor, trade, or migration. These organizations include the World Health Organization, World Bank, United Nations, World Trade Organization, and International Labor Organization. What we need is reforms to such institutions so that they are better able to secure justice for all. We can make improvements given the system of global governance we have already firmly in place. Considerable constructive progress does happen, and further gains are possible.[57]

4. Concluding Reflections

Like many concepts in political philosophy, what global justice consists in is contested and the subject of much debate. I have presented one kind of cosmopolitan global justice account. Any other account of global justice with a cosmopolitan outlook will share key features. As I have also sought to emphasize, the stark contrast often drawn between cosmopolitanism and nationalism presents a false dichotomy. Most contemporary cosmopolitans recognize space for special duties to compatriots, over and above our global justice duties to all. And most credible versions of nationalism recognize that there are indeed some important obligations across borders. Characterizing the debate as a forced choice between two polar opposites is not helpful in furthering constructive dialogue. I have presented a view in which we can find adequate space for national and cosmopolitan duties to be combined in an account of global justice. I have shown how cosmopolitan and special duties to co-members of states are not only compatible but, rather often, mutually reinforcing. So the current pressing issue is not "Should we be nationalists or cosmopolitans?" Rather, there is much scope for showing creative ways to accommodate the plausible elements in both theories into one coherent, comprehensive, and compelling account.

COMPREHENSION QUESTIONS

1. What is the main moral principle that underlies Brock's cosmopolitanism?
2. According to Brock, what are some ways in which states—and people's attachment to them—could promote global justice?
3. What is the role of cooperation (among states) in promoting local and global justice?
4. Why does Brock believe cosmopolitanism and nationalism are more compatible than many take them to be?

DISCUSSION QUESTIONS

1. Brock notes that "[b]eing a cosmopolitan is often characterized in terms of being a citizen of the world." Is world citizenship an important part of your identity? If so, how? And if not, why not?
2. Do you think political leaders have responsibilities to co-operate with others internationally in attempting to solve global problems? Why or why not? And if so, what are the limits of those obligations?

Case 2

In 1978, Garrett Hardin wrote this:

> If we divide the world crudely into rich nations and poor nations, two thirds of them are desperately poor, and only one third comparatively rich, with the United States the wealthiest of all. Metaphorically each rich nation can be seen as a lifeboat full of comparatively rich people. In the ocean outside each lifeboat swim the poor of the world, who would like to get in, or at least to share some of the wealth. What should the lifeboat passengers do?
>
> First, we must recognize the limited capacity of any lifeboat. For example, a nation's land has a limited capacity to support a population and as the current energy crisis has shown us, in some ways we have already exceeded the carrying capacity of our land.
>
> So here we sit, say 50 people in our lifeboat. To be generous, let us assume it has room for 10 more, making a total capacity of 60. Suppose the 50 of us in the lifeboat see 100 others swimming in the water outside, begging for admission to our boat or for handouts. We have several options: We may be tempted to try to live by the Christian ideal of being "our brother's keeper," or by the Marxist ideal of "to each according to his needs." Since the needs of all in the water are the same, and since they can all be seen as "our brothers," we could take them all into our boat, making a total of 150 in a boat designed for 60. The boat swamps, everyone drowns. Complete justice, complete catastrophe.
>
> Since the boat has an unused excess capacity of 10 more passengers, we could admit just 10 more to it. But which 10 do we let in? How do we choose? Do we pick the best 10, "first come, first served"? And what do we say to the 90 we exclude? If we do let an extra 10 into our lifeboat, we will have lost our "safety factor," an engineering principle of critical importance. For example, if we don't leave room for excess capacity as a safety factor in our country's agriculture, a new plant disease or a bad change in the weather could have disastrous consequences.
>
> Suppose we decide to preserve our small safety factor and admit no more to the lifeboat. Our survival is then possible although we shall have to be constantly on guard against boarding parties.
>
> While this last solution clearly offers the only means of our survival, it is morally abhorrent to many people. Some say they feel guilty about their good luck. My reply is simple: "Get out and yield your place to others." This may solve the problem of the guilt-ridden person's conscience, but it does not change the ethics of the lifeboat. The needy person to whom the guilt-ridden person yields his place will not himself feel guilty about his good luck. If he did, he would not climb aboard. The net result of conscience-stricken people giving

Case 2 (continued)

> up their unjustly held seats is the elimination of that sort of conscience from
> the lifeboat.
>   This is the basic metaphor within which we must work out our solutions.*
>
> Hardin's metaphor raises lots of questions. Is he *correct* that this is "the basic
> metaphor within which we must work out our solutions"? How would you argue
> for or against his view? And if he *is* correct, does this mean that we shouldn't be
> cosmopolitans? Or should we still be cosmopolitans, but seriously adjust our ex-
> pectations for what we can accomplish?
>
> _____
>
> *https://www.garretthardinsociety.org/articles/art_lifeboat_ethics_case_against_helping
> _poor.html

REPLY TO BROCK
DANIEL BONEVAC

I agree with much of what Gillian Brock says at the start.

> The institutions we live under shape our lives.
> We should try to establish institutions that are just.
> People are equally entitled to respect and consideration.
> We should be concerned about everyone's welfare and rights.
> Human beings share many of the same problems.
> Often, cooperation makes solving those problems easier.
> Promoting the interests of our own political community and promoting
>   everyone's interests can be compatible and mutually reinforcing.

These observations, however, are only part of the story. They all take the view
from nowhere. They ignore the view from *here*. People deserve equal respect
and consideration—but not necessarily equal consideration by you, or me, or
the president of the United States. Your primary obligations are to yourself,
your family, your friends, and fellow members of your associations, including your political community. Political leaders' primary obligations are to
those they represent. As President Trump has put it, he was elected to represent Pittsburgh, not Paris. Their interests are sometimes compatible—but only
sometimes.

Brock starts with general truisms and concludes with specific policy prescriptions. Many controversial empirical assumptions are needed to get from the
truisms to the conclusions. In a short article, that's hard to avoid.

But she and other cosmopolitans do something that ought to be avoided. Her
four principles:

> First, one should be enabled to meet one's basic needs. Second, one must have ad-
> equate protection for one's basic liberties. Third, fair terms of cooperation should
> govern one's collective endeavors. And fourth, social and political arrangements
> that support these core ingredients for a decent life should be in place.[58]

Beware such general, abstract statements about cosmic justice.[59] *Who* has an obligation to do *what* to bring this about? We'd all prefer a world in which everyone's basic needs were met and their basic rights and liberties protected. The hard part is getting there. Why think it's even possible? Cosmic justice may be a snare and a delusion.[60] In any case, nothing in Brock's principles implies anything about what anyone ought to do.

Brock is surely right that countries ought to cooperate to safeguard public health and fight corruption. But other cosmopolitan proposals are dubious: climate change agreements, financial regulations, global tax authorities, carbon taxes, open immigration, and humanitarian intervention, for example.[61] The aims may be noble, but the effects could be disastrous.

The theme that links cosmopolitan proposals is cooperation. What's wrong with that?

> Cooperation is not always possible.
> Cooperation is not always good.[62]

Sometimes people (and countries) have diametrically opposed interests. They can't cooperate in striving for a common goal because they don't *have* a common goal. If I rank four possible outcomes 1, 2, 3, and 4, and you rank them 4, 3, 2, and 1, cooperation is impossible. Any gain for me means a loss for you, and vice versa.

Developing nations see economic growth as their chief priority, for example, and won't agree to abide by climate change agreements, limiting their growth for benefits that are long term and, at best, speculative. Tax havens won't surrender the wealth their status brings. Competition for territorial control is often zero sum. Such situations may allow for compromise, but not cooperation. The interests of a political community aren't always compatible with the interests of other political communities or the world at large.

Cooperation, moreover, can be bad, taking the form of cartels, collusion, even conspiracy. We have to ask,

> Who benefits from the cooperation?
> What incentives does the cooperation create?
> Does the cooperation promote the common good?

Benefits. Most cosmopolitan policy proposals transfer power from the people to a national or international elite. A carbon tax, for example, would give politicians a vast new source of revenue. A global tax authority would create a body with immense power and wealth. Financial regulations give large institutions greater power while driving small institutions out of the market. In every case, benefits go primarily to the rich and powerful.

Incentives. Those in control of cosmopolitan institutions would have incentives to manipulate them for their own advantage. Power corrupts institutions as well as individuals, so the problem would grow worse over time. Not only would power tend to corrupt those in charge; the institutions themselves would tend to attract people drawn to power, control, and wealth rather than public service. There would be strong incentives, moreover, for people and countries to defect, free-riding on others' efforts. Countries who missed emissions targets, lowered taxes, and relaxed regulations would benefit. Countries would have incentives to pretend to observe agreements while in fact violating them. It's no accident that European countries remaining in the Paris climate control agreement have missed their targets, even while the United States has lowered emissions beyond what the agreement would have required. The history of arms control and trade agreements suggests that cheating is the norm, not the exception.

The common good. The elite who would design cosmopolitan institutions would do so for their own benefit, or, at best, in accord with their conception of the common good. The rich would get richer; the powerful, even more powerful. Meanwhile, cosmopolitan policies would slow the economy, throwing people out of work, decreasing opportunities, eroding trust, discouraging innovation, and increasing inequality.

Moving power from national to international institutions would also damage the ties that bind nations together as political communities. Taking decisions about taxation, regulation, and other economic matters away from elected bodies within countries would weaken their political systems, muffling the voice people have in how they are governed.

The contrast between cosmopolitanism and the Government-for-the-People doctrine, therefore, isn't merely a matter of degree, of how we should balance the view from here and the view from nowhere. It's about who gets to decide how to balance them, and on what basis. Are we to govern ourselves? Or are we to submit to philosopher-kings and -queens whose conceptions of cosmic justice will rule our lives?[63]

COMPREHENSION QUESTIONS

1. How do Bonevac and Brock differ in their understanding of the moral obligation to treat others with equal respect and consideration?
2. What are some ways in which cooperation between nations could be harmful to citizens?

DISCUSSION QUESTIONS

1. Bonevac believes countries should cooperate to protect public health but is skeptical about cooperating to address climate change. What differences between these two concerns might he have in mind? Does it make sense to draw a line between them? Why or why not?
2. What guidelines should we use to decide which global concerns, if any, warrant cooperation between nations?

REPLY TO BONEVAC
GILLIAN BROCK

Daniel Bonevac draws attention to the need for political community leaders to promote the interests of their members. As he also notes, "leaders must not give so much preference to the interests of those they lead that they attack, enslave, or oppress others," and "America First does not mean America Only." These are important points and show that there is common ground between our positions. The debate between us revolves centrally around when obligations to others (that might appear contrary to co-nationals' interests) should have weight and what constraints there should be on leaders seeking to promote their citizens' interests. Attacking, enslaving, and oppressing others in pursuit of citizens' interests is clearly ruled out. And the cosmopolitan would supplement that list, perhaps adding other kinds of harms or human rights violations. There are some important obligations across borders that all defensible political philosophies must endorse for them to be credible. Much of the debate between nationalists and cosmopolitans is about what those obligations and constraints are, and the grounds for holding various positions.

The kind of cosmopolitanism I defend does not challenge the idea that partiality should have some important role to play in our moral and political lives. Rather, I seek to articulate the legitimate scope for such partiality. One way to do this is to situate attachments in a context that clarifies our obligations to one another. Let me sketch one way of doing so.

Today we live in states that assume they have certain rights and that agents of the state, such as its leaders, may act in certain ways that privilege the interests of their citizens. Our current arrangements may seem natural to us—the way things have always been. But they have not always been this way, and they may change. What justification can be offered for the assumed default position? Here is one argument for it:

> Premise 1: States should have the right to decide what is in their interests and to make policies and laws on the basis of their perception of those interests. States have the right to decide their policies and laws based on their own views of what is good for citizens.
>
> Premise 2: Everyone belongs to some state or other, so all persons have a government committed to advancing citizens' interests and respecting their human rights, ensuring the persons on their territory can enjoy relevant freedoms and opportunities characteristic of a good life in their home state.
>
> Conclusion: So this arrangement—our state system—is fair.

Premise 2 is patently false in our world. Sadly, not all persons live in a state governed in such a way as to respect citizens' human rights and advance their interests, assisting them to enjoy core freedoms and opportunities. Indeed, if they did, many people would not seek to migrate away from such situations. The cases of refugees seeking protection from persecution or those fleeing dire poverty are just two examples of such government failures to protect core interests and rights.

Notice what is required if we do want to pursue this argument strategy and try to make Premise 2 true. We should cooperate in a host of trans-border activities, programs, initiatives, and institutions that have as their aim securing good institutional arrangements capable of human rights protection, and sustaining freedom and opportunities in all places. So those in one state will have responsibilities to many outside of their borders to assist in projects that strengthen protection and promotion of human rights where these are being violated, to ensure people are able to enjoy freedoms and opportunities, are able to sustain institutions capable of delivering justice, and so on. A justification along these lines will require that we have many cross-border responsibilities, as a requirement of enjoying self-determination and the defensible right to privilege our compatriots' interests.

In short, if we want claims about states' rights to self-determination or compatriot favoritism to have force, then we need to work with others to make it possible that all persons no matter where they are situated can rightly enjoy the protections and opportunities that are assumed in Premise 2 in the argument above.

Partiality clearly has some important role to play in our moral lives. However, just as partiality toward (say) family members or friends may be justified in some cases and not others, partiality toward co-nationals will be similarly circumscribed. What I as a cosmopolitan seek to articulate is the global or international structures, institutions, policies, and so forth that should be in place for co-national partiality to be defensible.[64]

Note that the cosmopolitan is not committed to many of the positions Bonevac assumes she must be. I have argued at length that cosmopolitanism does not necessarily entail open borders.[65] In fact, I have argued that if we take the state as an important vehicle through which our justice aspirations can be realized, shoring up states is an important cosmopolitan obligation. Simply opening up borders without attention to the harms this would create for all affected would be folly.

There should be better provision for those who are losers under our current state system, and refugees must certainly be near the top of that list. However, it does not follow that our obligations to refugees are ones of allowing greater access to resettlement. For one thing, this does not track what many refugees actually want. Most refugees, for instance, have fled to neighboring states and many hope to be repatriated one day. The thought of starting life over in some foreign land does not appeal to all equally. Likewise, and contrary to Bonevac's assumptions, cosmopolitanism is not necessarily committed to frequent military interventions or wealth transfers that facilitate corruption.[66]

So I agree with Bonevac that the poor need economic opportunities, liberties, the rule of law, stable governments that can protect rights, fair international trade, and good government—and that strengthening states' capacities can be an effective means to secure these. The cosmopolitan hopes to achieve an international or global framework that makes all of that possible. Our current arrangements often act as an obstacle to the important goals and, when that is the case, reforms that better align with ideals that enable everyone to enjoy prospects for good lives should be made.

COMPREHENSION QUESTIONS

1. On what points do Brock and Bonevac agree?
2. Why, according to Brock, is partiality toward one's fellow nationals defensible only if certain global policies are in place?

DISCUSSION QUESTION

1. Economic globalization has been happening for a long time, and although there have been some bumps in the road (Brexit, Trump's "America First" policy), there are plenty of people who want it to continue. How does this affect your evaluation of the arguments on each side of this issue?

FURTHER READINGS

Brock, Gillian, ed. *Cosmopolitanism Versus Non-Cosmopolitanism: Critiques, Defenses, Reconceptualisations*. Oxford: Oxford University Press, 2013.

Brock, Gillian. *Global Justice: A Cosmopolitan Account*. Oxford: Oxford University Press, 2009.

Brock, Gillian and Michael Blake. *Debating Brain Drain*. Oxford: Oxford University Press, 2015.

Brock, Gillian *Justice for People on the Move: Migration in Challenging Times*. Cambridge: Cambridge University Press, 2020.

Brown, Garrett, and David Held, eds. *The Cosmopolitan Reader*. Cambridge: Polity, 2010.

Kleingeld, Pauline. "Cosmopolitanism." In *Stanford Encyclopedia of Philosophy*, edited by Edward Zalta, 2011. http://plato.stanford.edu/entries/cosmopolitanism.

Nussbaum, Martha. "Patriotism and Cosmopolitanism." In *For Love of Country? Debating the Limits of Patriotism*, edited by Joshua Cohen. Boston: Beacon Press, 2002.

NOTES

1. Thomas Nagel, *The View from Nowhere* (New York: Oxford University Press, 1986), 86.
2. See, e.g., Kwame A. Appiah, *Cosmopolitanism: Ethics in a World of Strangers* (New York: W. W. Norton, 2006).
3. W. D. Ross, *The Right and the Good* (Oxford: Oxford University Press, 1930), 19.
4. President Donald Trump, Inaugural Address, January 20, 2017.
5. Throughout, the principles I defend hold *ceteris paribus* (other things being equal). They hold in the absence of competing moral considerations, but might be undercut or overridden by such considerations.
6. The reference, of course, is to Abraham Lincoln's Gettysburg Address: "It is rather for us to be here dedicated to the great task remaining before us . . . that this nation, under God, shall have a new birth of freedom—and that government of the people, by the people, for the people, shall not perish from the earth."
7. Gillian Brock, "Liberal Nationalism Versus Cosmopolitanism: Locating the Disputes," *Public Affairs Quarterly* 16, no. 4 (2002): 307–327, 315.
8. Of course, such special obligations could deny them if pursued apart from general moral constraints. Parents who sought to benefit their child no matter what, by any means necessary, might infringe on the dignity and rights of others. Just so, a leader who sought to benefit the people by any means necessary might invade other nations,

violate treaties, or in other ways commit acts of injustice. Nothing in the Government-for-the-People doctrine implies that (3) and (4) are the only relevant principles, or that they take precedence over other moral considerations.

9. Again, we should understand these principles as holding *ceteris paribus* (other things being equal).

10. Some who call themselves cosmopolitans agree with the Priority Thesis but maintain that its role is purely instrumental. They argue that members of political communities should prioritize one another's interests as a means to benefiting people in general. They thus have no reason to object to the America First doctrine, which itself says nothing about the role of the Priority Thesis in an overall moral or political theory.

11. See, e.g., Charles Jones, *Global Justice: Defending Cosmopolitanism* (Oxford: Oxford University Press, 1999); David Held, *Cosmopolitanism: A Defence* (Cambridge: Polity Press, 2003); Seyla Benhabib, *The Rights of Others: Aliens, Residents and Citizens* (Cambridge: Cambridge University Press, 2004); Brock 2002; Gillian Brock, *Global Justice: A Cosmopolitan Account* (Oxford: Oxford University Press, 2009).

12. For discussions of the viability of a rooted cosmopolitanism—of cosmopolitanism's ability or inability to account for particular, associational obligations arising from special relationships—see Robert Goodin, "What Is So Special About Our Fellow Countrymen?" *Ethics* 98 (1988): 663–686; Samuel Scheffler, *Boundaries and Allegiances: Problems of Justice and Responsibility in Liberal Thought* (Oxford: Oxford University Press, 2001); Kok-Chor Tan, *Justice Without Borders: Cosmopolitanism, Nationalism and Patriotism* (Cambridge: Cambridge University Press, 2004); and Patti Tamara Lenard and Margaret Moore, "Cosmopolitanism and Making Room (or Not) for Special Duties," *Monist* 94 (October 2011): 615–627. I cannot discuss these issues in detail here. In brief, however, rooted cosmopolitans face a dilemma. If they posit a narrow gap between associational and universal norms, they fail to account for the strength of associational norms. If they posit a wide gap, they weaken their concept of universal norms enough that their policy prescriptions no longer follow.

13. See Alan Page Fiske, "The Four Elementary Forms of Sociality: Framework for a Unified Theory of Social Relations," *Psychological Review* 99, no. 4 (1992): 689; Tage Shakti Rai and Alan Page Fiske, "Moral Psychology Is Relationship Regulation: Moral Motives for Unity, Hierarchy, Equality, and Proportionality," *Psychological Review* 118 (2011): 57–75.

14. See, for example, Eli Hirsch, *Radical Skepticism and the Shadow of Doubt* (London: Bloomsbury, 2018), 164–165.

15. David Miller has made this point in "Cosmopolitanism; A Critique," *Critical Review of International Social and Political Philosophy* 5 (2002): 80–85, and "Against Global Egalitarianism," *Journal of Ethics* 9 (2005): 55–79.

16. See Confucius, *The Doctrine of the Mean*; Aristotle, *Nicomachean Ethics*, II, 6.

17. *Utilitarianism* (London: Parker, Son and Bourn, 1863), Chapter 2.

18. *Methods of Ethics* (London: Macmillan, 1907), 439. For a sophisticated version of the argument, see Peter Railton, "Alienation, Consequentialism, and the Demands of Morality," *Philosophy and Public Affairs* 13 (1984): 134–171.

19. As even Mill recognizes: "But the strongest of all the arguments against the interference of the public with purely personal conduct, is that when it does interfere, the odds are that it interferes wrongly, and in the wrong place" (*On Liberty* [London: John W. Parker and Son, 1859], Chapter IV).

20. More puzzling is that such cosmopolitans tend to believe that we can have special obligations arising out of transnational organizations such as the European Union or the

United Nations. Why, on the spectrum of small to large organizations, are nations alone incapable of generating obligations among their members?

21. To be sure, cosmopolitans offer some reasons. Brock, for example, argues that nationalism has led to war and oppression; that nations define themselves as being against some enemy, having "antagonism toward others as a constitutive feature" (377); and rely on myths ("The New Nationalisms," *The Monist* 82, no. 3 [1999]: 367–386). The first claim is true enough, though many other associations have also led to war and oppression, and over the past century communist internationalism—cosmopolitanism by another name?—has led to war and oppression to an even greater extent. So, it offers no reason for singling out nations as morally inert. The second and third claims, I believe, are false. Against whom, exactly, do Paraguay, Italy, Spain, Sweden, Ethiopia, Nigeria, Thailand, Indonesia, China, and New Zealand define themselves?

22. Immanuel Kant, *Groundwork of the Metaphysics of Morals*, II.

23. See "Kant on the Metaphysics of Morals: Vigilantius's Lecture Notes," in Immanuel Kant, *Lectures on Ethics* (Cambridge: Cambridge University Press, 1997). See also Jens Timmerman, "Kantian Dilemmas? Moral Conflict in Kant's Ethical Theory," *Archiv für Geschichte der Philosophie* 95, no. 1 (2013): 36–64.

24. He has other reasons, arising from social contract theory, to hold that political leaders should give priority to the interests of their own subjects. But his ethics gives him independent grounds for supporting the Priority Thesis.

25. Immanuel Kant, *Perpetual Peace* (London: George Allen and Unwin, Ltd., 1903, 1917), 137–138.

26. This distinction is ancient, tracing to Cicero's *De Officiis* (I, iii, 8), where he attributes it to the Stoic philosophers Zeno of Citium and Panaetius of Rhodes.

27. Compare Kant's fourth principle governing international affairs in *Perpetual Peace*: "No national debts shall be contracted in connection with the external affairs of the state" (111).

28. This is an analogue of Hayek's complaint about socialism. See Friedrich Hayek, *The Road to Serfdom* (Chicago: University of Chicago Press, 1944).

29. Jonathan Haidt, "The Emotional Dog and Its Rational Tail: A Social Intuitionist Approach to Moral Judgment," *Psychological Review* 108 (2001): 814–834; J. Graham, J. Haidt, and B. Nosek, "Liberals and Conservatives Rely on Different Sets of Moral Foundations," *Journal of Personality and Social Psychology* 96 (2009): 1029–1046; J. Haidt, *The Righteous Mind: Why Good People Are Divided by Politics and Religion* (New York: Pantheon, 2012).

30. Indeed, Graham, Haidt, and Nosek have used the Priority Thesis as one of the tests of a subject's reliance on loyalty as a moral foundation; their questionnaire included the item "The government should strive to improve the well-being of people in our nation, even if it sometimes happens at the expense of people in other nations."

31. Imagine a parent who tells a child applying to college, "I have the money to pay for a college education. But why should I pay for *yours*? I'm going to create a scholarship fund that will pay for the best applicant's education, and encourage everyone to apply. I'll have a committee judge applications anonymously. The winner probably won't be you." The child would rightly feel betrayed.

32. John Rawls, *The Law of Peoples* (Cambridge, MA: Harvard University Press, 1999), 118. See also David Miller, "Justice and Global Inequality," in Andrew Hurrell and Ngaire Woods, eds., *Inequality, Globalization, and World Politics* (Oxford: Oxford University Press, 1999), 187–210, and "National Self-Determination and Global Justice," in David Miller, ed., *Citizenship and National Identity* (Cambridge: Polity Press, 2000), 161–179.

33. Naseem Nicholas Taleb, *Skin in the Game* (New York: Random House, 2018), 21.

34. Evelyn Waugh, *The Essays, Articles and Reviews of Evelyn Waugh* (London: Methuen, 1983), 625.

35. Robert D. Putnam has stressed the importance of social capital, "social networks and the associated norms of reciprocity and trustworthiness" ("*E Pluribus Unum*: Diversity and Community in the Twenty-First Century: The 2006 Johan Skytte Prize Lecture," *Scandinavian Political Studies* 30, no. 2 [2007]: 137–174, 137). Putnam argues that increased diversity—by extension, cosmopolitanism—erodes social capital.

36. The membership of the United Nations Human Rights Council, for example, currently includes Afghanistan, Angola, Burundi, China, Côte d'Ivoire, Cuba, the Democratic Republic of the Congo, Egypt, Iraq, Kyrgyzstan, Mongolia, Pakistan, Qatar, Rwanda, Saudi Arabia, Senegal, South Africa, Togo, Tunisia, and Venezuela, among other countries. "A clear majority of the Human Rights Council members fail to meet even the most basic human rights standards" (Vice-President Mike Pence, speaking before the UN Security Council, "Pence: UN Human Rights Council 'Doesn't Deserve Its Name,'" CNN, September 20, 2017).

37. As of 2017, the world's ten most populous countries, in order, were China, India, the United States, Indonesia, Brazil, Pakistan, Nigeria, Bangladesh, Russia, and Mexico. More than a third of the world's people live in China or India.

38. Raising those earning under $1,000 to the median would require more than $6 trillion. It would take a similar amount to bring all the others below the median up to that level. In the United States, moreover, only about 30% of the funds spent on welfare find their way to a recipient; the rest goes to the bureaucracy. Internationally, an even smaller percentage would likely go to the poor themselves. So, that figure should, realistically, be multiplied by at least six, totaling over $36 trillion.

39. According to the 2018 Index of Economic Freedom (https://www.heritage.org/index/), six nations count as free—Hong Kong, Singapore, New Zealand, Switzerland, Australia, and Ireland—all of whom are wealthy. Twenty-one countries count as repressed—North Korea, Venezuela, Cuba, Congo, Eritrea, Equatorial Guinea, and Zimbabwe are worst—and all are poor. The United States ranks eighteenth. For graphs linking economic freedom to per capita GDP, see Terry Miller, Anthony B. Kim, and James M. Roberts, *2018 Index of Economic Freedom* (Washington, DC: Heritage Foundation, 2018), 18 (https://www.heritage.org/index/pdf/2018/book/index_2018.pdf).

40. *Reasons and Persons* (Oxford: Oxford University Press, 1984), Chapter 17.

41. Some take the slogan "America First" to allude to the anti-war America First Committee, some of whose members expressed anti-Semitic and pro-fascist opinions. The Committee formed in September 1940 to advocate adhering to the Neutrality Act of 1939, staying out of the war in Europe, so long as the United States itself was not attacked, and accelerating a defense buildup. It disbanded when Japan bombed Pearl Harbor in December 1941. Members included John F. Kennedy, Gerald Ford, Potter Stewart, and Frank Lloyd Wright. In any case, I, like the Trump administration, intend no such reference. I use the phrase simply to capture the essence of the Priority Thesis, in an American context, in just two words.

42. See Thomas Pangle and Peter J. Ahrensdorf, *Justice Among Nations: On the Moral Basis of Power and Peace* (Lawrence: University Press of Kansas, 1999), 260: "[P]olitical life is necessarily resistant to cosmopolitanism . . . there is an irreducible tension between the life of genuine human excellence—the life of philosophy—and even the most splendid political communities."

43. Rabbi Hillel, from *The Babylonian Talmud*, translated by Michael L. Rodkinson (Boston: The Talmud Society, 1918), Vol. I (IX), *Ethics of the Fathers*, 1:14, Mishna M, 51.

44. I'm certainly not going to be able to answer all these questions here, but I'll sketch a framework that suggests how we ought to start thinking about them.
45. Those identified as nationalists include quite a variety of different positions, including liberal nationalist, civic nationalist, and statist accounts. For notable examples of nationalism see, for instance, David Miller, *On Nationality* (Oxford: Oxford University Press, 1995); David Miller, *Citizenship and National Identity* (Cambridge: Polity Press, 2000); David Miller, *National Responsibility and Global Justice* (Oxford: Oxford University Press, 2007); Richard Miller, "Cosmopolitan Respect and Patriotic Concern" *Philosophy and Public Affairs* 27, no. 3 (1998): 202–224; Richard Miller, *Globalizing Justice: The Ethics of Poverty and Power* (Oxford: Oxford University Press, 2010); Yael Tamir, *Liberal Nationalism* (Princeton, NJ: Princeton University Press, 1993).
46. Locating points of difference between nationalists and cosmopolitans often requires extensive discussion of particular positions and commitments. For some of this detail see, for instance, Gillian Brock and Harry Brighouse, *The Political Philosophy of Cosmopolitanism* (Cambridge: Cambridge University Press, 2005); Gillian Brock, "Cosmopolitanism Versus Non-Cosmopolitanism: The State of Play," *The Monist* 94 (2011): 455–465; Gillian Brock, ed., *Cosmopolitanism Versus Non-Cosmopolitanism: Critiques, Defenses, Reconceptualisations* (Oxford: Oxford University Press, 2013).
47. Brock 2013.
48. Luis Cabrera, *Political Theory of Global Justice: A Cosmopolitan Case for the World State* (London: Routledge, 2004).
49. See, for instance, the essays in Brock and Brighouse 2005.
50. Brock 2009.
51. Such projects are quite common and may be best known to readers as taking the form of a human rights approach.
52. Brock 2009.
53. Gillian Brock and Quentin Atkinson, "What Can Examining the Psychology of Nationalism Tell Us About Our Prospects for Aiming at the Cosmopolitan Vision?" *Ethical Theory and Moral Practice* 11 (2008): 165–179.
54. Some might worry that the proposed regulation will reduce economic growth, but this relationship is not robust. For a discussion of a better way to measure success in the global economy see Brock 2009, Chapter 9.
55. For some further examples, see Brock 2009, Chapter 11.
56. It is worth noting also that fair arrangements are the most durable and likely to lead to stability for the right reasons, again goals we all have good reasons to support.
57. For other notable cosmopolitan justice projects see Simon Caney, *Justice Beyond Borders: A Global Political Theory* (Oxford: Oxford University Press, 2005); Darrel Moellendorf, *Cosmopolitan Justice* (Boulder, CO: Westview Press, 2002); Martha Nussbaum, *Frontiers of Justice: Disability, Nationality, Species Membership* (Cambridge, MA: Belknap Press, 2006); Kok-Chor Tan, *Justice Without Borders: Cosmopolitanism, Nationalism, and Patriotism* (Cambridge: Cambridge University Press, 2004).
58. Gillian Brock, "Defending the Cosmopolitan Outlook," this volume.
59. Cosmic justice is distinctive because it concerns the justice of circumstances—the relief of misfortune—and not of actions. Here is a typical formulation from Simon Caney: "'[O]ne's life prospects or one's access to opportunities' should not depend on 'morally arbitrary' considerations" (Caney 2005, 111–112). Statements with "to be," "to have," the passive voice, or "we" often concern cosmic justice. Andrea Sangiovanni rephrases Caney's point: "We ought to neutralize (or mitigate) differences in prospects due to

unchosen circumstances" ("On the Relation Between Moral and Distributive Equality," in Brock 2013, 57). Who, exactly, are "we"?

60. See Thomas Sowell, *The Quest for Cosmic Justice* (New York: Simon and Schuster, 1999). See also his talk, "The Quest for Cosmic Justice," summarizing the book: "Crusaders for social justice seek to correct not merely the sins of man but the oversights of God or the accidents of history. What they are really seeking is a universe tailor-made to their vision of equality. They are seeking cosmic justice" (http://tsowell.com/spquestc.html).

61. Brock's views on immigration are nuanced; she does not favor open borders (see Brock 2009, Chapter 8). But many cosmopolitans do. See, e.g., Bruce Ackerman, *Social Justice in the Liberal State* (New Haven, CT: Yale University Press, 1980) and Joseph Carens, "Aliens and Citizens: The Case for Open Borders," *Review of Politics* 49 (1987): 251–273.

62. This is obvious from the classic form of the prisoner's dilemma: Cooperation between the prisoners is good for them but bad for society at large. There are of course many other cases, including cartels, price fixing, criminal gangs, vote trading, and lobbying. See Robert Axelrod, *The Evolution of Cooperation* (New York: Basic Books, 1984).

63. For a careful exploration of cosmopolitanism's threat to self-governance and thus to autonomy and respect, see Laura Valentini, "Cosmopolitan Justice and Rightful Enforceability," in Brock 2013, 92–110.

64. For some examples, review those I discussed in Section 3 of my chapter.

65. Brock 2009; Gillian Brock and Michael Blake, *Debating Brain Drain: May Governments Restrict Emigration?* (Oxford: Oxford University Press, 2015).

66. Brock 2009; Brock and Blake 2015.

CHAPTER 3

Foreign Aid

THE CASE FOR FOREIGN AID: REFLECTIONS ON WHAT WE CAN ASK OF OTHERS AND WHAT WE ARE ENTITLED TO RECEIVE
NICOLE HASSOUN

1. Introduction

I went to graduate school in Tucson, Arizona—a few dozen miles from the border with Mexico. Had I been born on the other side of that fence, my life prospects would have been very different. I would have been lucky to get to work in a maquiladora (commonly referred to as a sweatshop) where I would likely have worked twelve-hour shifts for just a few dollars per day.[1] A great proportion of the world's population lives on less than the equivalent of what two dollars a day buys in the United States. Many cannot even secure adequate food, clean water, basic sanitation, education, health care, and so forth.[2] What can justify such great disparities in people's basic life prospects? Should not everyone be able to live at least a minimally good life?

According to international law, everyone has human rights that protect their ability to live a dignified, or minimally good, life. These rights are specified in the Universal Declaration of Human Rights and various treaties like the International Covenant on Civil and Political Rights (ICCPR) and the International Covenant on Economic, Social and Cultural Rights (ISCER). The ISCER states that everyone has a right "to the enjoyment of the highest attainable standard of physical and mental health."[3] More than 80% of states have ratified these treaties and they specify who bears the obligations correlative to human rights. Article 2(1) of the ISCER, for instance, specifies that:

> Each State Party to the present Covenant . . . [must undertake] . . . steps, individually and through international assistance and cooperation, especially

Nicole Hassoun's work could not have been completed without the support of the Templeton Foundation's Happiness & Wellbeing project.

economic and technical, to the maximum of its available resources, with a view to achieving progressively the full realization of the rights recognized in the present Covenant by all appropriate means, including particularly the adoption of legislative measures.[4]

The third General Comment states that:

The Committee notes that the phrase [in Article 2(1)] "to the maximum of its available resources" was intended by the drafters of the Covenant to refer to both the resources existing within a State and those available from the international community through international cooperation and assistance. The Committee wishes to emphasize that in accordance with Articles 55 and 56 of the Charter of the United Nations, with well-established principles of international law, and with the provisions of the Covenant itself, international cooperation for development and thus for the realization of economic, social and cultural rights is an obligation of all States. It is particularly incumbent upon those States which are in a position to assist others in this regard.[5]

That is, at least all signatory states have demanding obligations to ensure their citizens' human rights are secure. Those with the capacity to do so must also help other states that require assistance.

Although states have primary responsibility for fulfilling human rights, human rights treaties and documents also go on to explain that individuals have a role to play in ensuring that their states live up to their human rights obligations. They must at least do things like vote for leaders who support good policies and may also have to engage in activism or lobbying. So I will talk generally about "our" obligations in what follows—though I grant that what each person and organization should do will differ significantly depending on, among other things, their capacities and institutional roles.

Although not all states have signed human rights treaties (and many who have do not live up to their obligations), I believe everyone should have these rights. At least, I will argue that no one should have to suffer or die young from lack of access to the things they need to live dignified or minimally good lives (e.g., basic goods like food, water, or medicine) through no choice of their own. If so, people have a right to the foreign aid they need to secure these things.

2. Two Moral Arguments for Aid

The First Argument for Aid

Before making the case for aid, consider one way of thinking about what people need to live the kind of minimally good life human rights should protect. We might consider what, at a minimum, a person needs to reach the lowest level of flourishing. Suppose, for instance, we are reflecting on what a newborn child might need. We might conclude that she will need things like good relationships, pleasures, knowledge, appreciation, and worthwhile activities (among other things). When people have enough of these things and do not suffer from significant pain, deprivation, depression, coercion, and so forth, they often live good lives. What a particular person will need may depend on her circumstances (culture, beliefs, and so forth). Still, everyone needs at least some of the same things. People need some (internal) freedom to set goals and act on plans to achieve them, and (external) freedom from co-ercion and constraint in doing so. They require resources, capacities, and in-stitutional structures, among other things, to secure this much. They require respect from others, since it's important to human beings to be acknowledged as worthy of consideration.

The idea is not that people must have everything they want or from which they might benefit. Fortunate individuals would not trade their lives for those that are only minimally good. Still, minimally good lives are lives at the lowest levels of flourishing. A minimally good life is not simply one that's marginally better than not existing at all. It's one that a person lives well enough.[6]

I believe that everyone's life is equally valuable, and so I believe that everyone should have human rights (and rights to the aid they need) to protect their abil-ity to live a minimally good life. No one should have to suffer or die young from lack of access to the resources or opportunities they need to live minimally well. Everyone should have adequate access to things like food, water, shelter, health care, social and emotional support, and so forth. Although some of us receive a much larger share of the earth's resources to use when we are born (or manage to secure a large share through hard work), we must ensure everyone can secure enough. Increasing economic growth may eventually ensure that everyone has what they need, but countries can grow even while poverty increases. In any case, many people cannot secure what they need now without aid. Even if we do not have to help people live excellent or even simply good lives, I believe that reason-able, caring, and free people should grant that we must protect everyone's ability to live at least minimally well. Aid is an important and effective way of helping people do that.

Here's another way to get the same idea. If we are reasonable, caring, and free from coercion and constraint, we can empathize with others. And if we really understand their circumstances, history, and psychology, we can put ourselves in their shoes. Then we can ask ourselves: Could we be content (now) to live as those people? To be clear, the question is not whether any given individual would trade her current life for a minimally good one—many fortunate individuals would not. Moreover, the question is not whether the people we are deciding for will be content in their conditions, as their preferences may be adaptive and their bargaining position poor.[7] Rather, it is whether a reasonable, free, caring person could now (reflecting on, but not yet occupying, the person's life) be content to live that life fully understanding the person's circumstances, psychology, and history.[8] It is whether there are any serious reasons to doubt that the life could be well-lived. Different people will likely have different perspectives on what people need to live minimally good lives. Some may insist on maximizing the position of the least well off while others would be content with a non-comparative standard.

Still, I think most caring and appropriately impartial people will agree that everyone requires adequate food, water, shelter, education, health care, social, and emotional goods, and this is enough to establish a strong reason to aid if we can.

The Second Argument for Aid

There are also other reasons to hold that people have human rights and rights to the aid they need to secure adequate food, water, shelter, education, health care, and so forth. People need these things to protect their basic interests, freedom, autonomy, and opportunities. Moreover, in our increasingly interconnected world, we may all do better to help others reach this threshold. People who can live minimally good lives are often able to help others and engage in productive relationships. Furthermore, ensuring that everyone can live a minimally good life may help reduce global threats (e.g., the spread of terrorism and infectious disease). At least if critics can agree that everyone has justified human rights that protect their ability to secure adequate food, water, shelter, education, health care, and so forth, I think the case for aid is strong.

What Accepting the Arguments Does Not Require

People can accept the idea that we should ensure everyone can live a minimally good life and deny that they must sacrifice their lives, or even the property they need to live a minimally good life, for others. Intuitively, we do not have to imperil our own ability to live minimally well even to help others do so (though it might be very nice or kind of us to do so). So one can argue that we must provide some aid and reject the view that we have to give up everything that could do more good for others.

Moreover, if something more important is at stake, or it is just impossible to provide the needed aid, aid's advocates can maintain that we do not have to help everyone live a minimally good life. Perhaps we will have to make some terrible decisions about who to save in humanitarian emergencies, or perhaps helping people now will make development in the future too difficult. But we do need some evidence that this is the case before we deny aid to some who cannot even live minimally good lives.[9]

What can we say to those who would reject the idea that we should help everyone secure adequate food, water, shelter, education, health care, and so forth? Some believe that we should not have to sacrifice our basic entitlements for others, that we should be free to use our bodies and property as we wish. Often they think this because they believe everyone deserves what they have; that what we have is a function of the effort we are willing to put into acquiring and maintaining our property. Although what we have may well be a function of the effort we are willing to put into acquiring and maintaining our property, effort is only a small part of the equation. What property we have is also the result of our collective decisions about what we owe people, not a plausible starting point for deciding what we owe. Our ability to attain wealth depends on states enforcing the rules of the market. States must protect property rights and freedom to trade, and this protection is funded by tax money. At least there is no clear answer to the question: How much of our wealth is due to our own versus others' efforts? (Though a quick look around the world suggests that the answer is "not much," given the vastly different life prospects even the most industrious have under different institutional systems.) So it is not obvious why the entitlements we are currently granted should remain that way. And any justification that neglects individuals' ability to live even minimally good lives is one we should reject. Even Lockean libertarianism starts from the idea that we should leave enough and as good for others. Any humane version of the view would ensure that everyone can live at least a minimally good life.[10]

3. Responding to Objections: The Empirical Evidence

Aid's critics often argue that aid is ineffective or counterproductive.[11] Critics often cite studies of aid's efficacy that focus on Official Development Assistance or other measures of aid. These can include loans tied to all kinds of political and economic conditions that may not benefit poor countries, never mind those who are unable to live minimally good lives within them.[12] Many also look at aid's impact on growth or gross domestic product, which is an aggregate measure of economic welfare that is insensitive to aid's impact on poverty—never mind individuals' ability to live (minimally) good lives. After all, a country can grow because the rich get richer while poverty gets worse, or fail to grow even if the poor are getting wealthier if the rich get poorer.[13]

When we look closely at the evidence that aid can help improve individuals' ability to live good lives, it is strong.[14] There are many different kinds of aid programs. And there is extremely good evidence that many programs—focusing on everything from education to fertilizer—work.[15]

Today, scientists study aid programs just like they study new drugs and medical interventions—with randomized controlled trials. Often they randomly select some portion of a population to receive a particular kind of aid and then compare performance to similar parts of the population that do not receive aid. Randomized controlled trials do not guarantee that aid programs will work at other locations or when they are scaled up more widely. But when programs are replicated and tested widely, we can be pretty sure they will. There are also quasi-experimental studies of aid programs that control for potentially confounding factors in other ways. There is strong evidence that many programs can be scaled up widely.[16]

And even at the macro level, there are many cross-national studies of development aid that show it reduces poverty, improves health, increases life expectancy, and so forth (at least in some policy, climate, and institutional circumstances and even in sub-Saharan Africa).[17] This is so despite the fact that Official Development Assistance amounts to only about US$26 per person per year in developing countries, and many countries pay more in interest on their debts than they receive in aid.[18]

Aid's skeptics often argue that aid breeds corruption or is counterproductive for other reasons. Many point to instances where aid has had terrible consequences.[19] Others believe that real poverty-alleviating growth must be endogenous.[20] That is, they argue that local culture and institutions really explain why people fare poorly or well and maintain that no one can help build good institutions.

Although the critics have a point, it is not definitive. There are many examples of bad aid, and it can indeed be counterproductive. But the studies above demonstrate that aid often helps people and explain how we can test programs before rolling them out widely. Moreover, the evidence that foreign aid requires good institutions to be successful is mixed. At best, it makes a case for trying to improve institutional quality in giving aid[21]—and I know of no good arguments for the conclusion that aid cannot improve institutional quality. Finally, even if good institutions are a prerequisite for effective aid, one would have to conclude from the evidence above that the requisite institutions often exist.

Consider what aid's success means just for human health. In the twentieth century, smallpox killed 300 million people. Aid helped eliminate it.[22] The United States provided a great deal of funding for vaccines through the World Health Organization's Smallpox Eradication Unit, and international donors together gave US$98 million for eradication.[23] Today, we are in the final stages of an aid-funded effort to eliminate polio, which also used to cripple and kill millions every year. Moreover, the past fifteen to twenty years have seen the incredible growth of new aid organizations like the Global Fund to Fight AIDS, Tuberculosis and Malaria and the Global Alliance for Vaccines Initiative (GAVI). These health-promoting non-governmental organizations have saved millions of lives.[24] These two organizations alone estimate that they have saved 24 million lives.[25] The independent Global Health Impact organization supported by a coalition of academics and civil society members from around the world estimates that, in 2010, drugs for malaria, tuberculosis, and HIV/AIDS alleviated approximately 36% of the burden of these diseases, saving the equivalent of about 76 million lives.[26] Foreign aid supported all of these efforts.[27]

Still, there is a lot more to do. Billions lack access to clean water in their homes and access to essential health services. Millions lack access to adequate sanitation, food, and shelter.[28] Foreign aid alone will not completely solve these problems, but it can help many people live minimally good lives. We should not neglect the water for the sea.[29] Saving even one life is a good thing. A great thing.

4. Other Objections and Replies

There are many objections to obligations to aid that do not question its effectiveness. Some object that very demanding obligations to aid prevent people from caring for those close to them (parents, children, friends, etc.). Others argue that obligations to aid cannot require people to live a non-altruistically focused life.[30] Some suggest that we should give priority to helping those with whom we share citizenship or other affiliation (e.g., those of the same national or cultural background).[31] Others insist that the physical distance between those who can give and those who might receive is significant. Yet others argue that we only need to do our fair share to help others—so, if not enough others are contributing, our obligations to aid remain limited.[32]

The claim that we should provide some foreign aid is compatible with priority to compatriots, special obligations, and the moral relevance of distance, and may be sensitive to the number of others contributing.[33] One might say we should do more to help those closer to us (morally and/or physically) and yet insist that we should still do something (and potentially quite a lot) to help those beyond our borders.

It is just the view that we owe others nothing at all, no matter how desperate their straits, how low the cost, how few others are helping, how easy it is, and so forth that can undermine the claim that we should sometimes aid others. And that idea is so wildly implausible that it does not merit significant attention.

5. Conclusion

Because we know that aid works, it is hard to deny that we should at least sometimes help others, but getting clearer on *why* we should aid may let us do a better job of helping. I believe individuals' interests, autonomy, liberty, and so forth matter and that to ensure the conditions for mutual flourishing we have strong reasons to aid. Ultimately, however, I think we should help everyone live at least a minimally good life. This idea can help guide our efforts to aid. It is not enough to just protect people's autonomy or aid in an effort to prevent the spread of terrorism or infectious diseases. People do not just need "material aid . . . delivered with indifference to . . . suffering, perhaps out of expectation for reciprocity"; when misfortune befalls us, "we need our suffering to matter to others."[34] So, aid should come from a desire to help others live minimally good lives, and it should achieve this end.

COMPREHENSION QUESTIONS

1. For Hassoun, what must a human have in order to have a minimally good life? And what does this have to do with providing aid?
2. What is the point of Hassoun's "Second Argument for Aid"?
3. How is the effectiveness of foreign aid programs tested? According to Hassoun, what do the tests indicate?
4. What's a specific example of a time when foreign aid has been successful?
5. According to Hassoun, what view or stance would we need to hold in order to reject the claim that we should sometimes aid others?

DISCUSSION QUESTIONS

1. What do you, personally, think of as being necessary for a minimally good life?
2. Is rejecting the notion that we should provide foreign aid the same as rejecting the idea that we should help everyone secure adequate food, water, shelter, education, and health care when aid is an effective way of doing so? Why or why not?
3. What do you think about the idea that we should sometimes aid others at significant expense to ourselves? If there is such an obligation, what reasons can you offer in support of it?

Case 1

The Council on Foreign Relations reports that U.S. foreign aid spending in 2016 could be broken down as follows:

Long-term development aid (42%) provides ongoing funding for projects to promote broad-based economic growth and general prosperity in the world's poorest countries. More than half of this goes to bilateral health programs, including treatment of HIV/AIDS, maternal and family health, and support for government health care systems, mostly in Africa. This also includes funding to multilateral institutions such as the World Bank and the United Nations (UN) Development Program.

Military and security aid (33%) primarily goes toward helping allies purchase U.S. military equipment, training foreign military personnel, and funding peacekeeping missions. A smaller slice goes to "non-military security assistance," which includes counter-narcotics programs in Afghanistan, Colombia, Peru, and elsewhere, as well as non-proliferation and counterterrorism efforts.

Humanitarian aid (14%) is spent to alleviate short-term humanitarian crises, such as those resulting from famine, earthquakes, war, state failure, or other natural or man-made disasters. This includes State Department and Defense Department disaster relief efforts, as well as purchases of U.S. agricultural goods and funding for organizations such as the International Red Cross and the UN High Commissioner for Refugees.

Political aid (11%) is intended to support political stability, free-market economic reforms, and democratic institutions. Programs include governance and justice system reforms, backing for human rights organizations, and support for peace talks and treaty implementation.*

How does this distribution fit with Hassoun's argument? Basically, is it what it should be? Or is it off in some way or other? If it's off, how do you think she'd want it to be reconfigured?

---

*http://www.un.org/en/universal-declaration-human-rights/index.html
*https://www.cfr.org/backgrounder/how-does-us-spend-its-foreign-aid

INTERNATIONAL AID: NOT THE CURE YOU'RE HOPING FOR
JASON BRENNAN

Many people are too poor to meet their basic needs. The good news is that extreme poverty (defined as living on less than $1.90 per capita per day) is disappearing before our eyes. In 1820, about 95% of people lived in extreme poverty. By 1960, that had only dropped to about 66%. Now, less than 10% of the world lives in extreme poverty. Perhaps most remarkably, these numbers are proportions. There are many more people around, and they're living better than ever before.[35] This is a miracle, but hardly anyone notices it.

Nevertheless, many remain mired in poverty. Surely, most of us think, something must be done. Immediately, a facile solution comes to mind: Some countries—Germany or the United States—have more than enough. (Even a person at the "poverty line" in the United States is, despite the high cost of U.S. living, among the top 14% of income earners worldwide.)[36] So, it seems, curing world poverty is easy: The rich countries could just donate a bunch of money to the poor countries. Voila!

I wish it were that simple. This is a topic where normative reasoning and moral philosophy, in isolation, tend to lead us astray. If we genuinely care about solving world poverty, we need the tools of economics to help us answer two questions:

1. Why are some countries rich and others poor?
2. Does international aid, whether through private charities, government-to-government aid, or government-to-charity aid, actually succeed in lifting people out of poverty?

Philosophy might uncover what our obligations are *in light of the facts*, but it does not help us discover what the facts are. Unfortunately, philosophers of global justice are disinterested in or even hostile to learning the facts. Philosophers tend to advocate the policies economists know don't work, and tend to reject the institutions economists know work.

The overwhelming consensus in economics is that rich countries are rich because they have good institutions, while poor countries are poor because they have bad institutions. Further, the consensus is that aid generally doesn't work. Under special conditions, certain targeted forms of aid can prevent death during an immediate crisis, but that's about it. I'll explain both of these points below.

This textbook is titled *Ethics, Left and Right*, but the issue of international aid is not really a left-wing versus right-wing thing. Hassoun hopefully doesn't represent the left; I certainly don't represent the right. Our disagreement here is not about moral principles. Rather, our disagreement concerns the *relevance* of moral principles in light of what we think the facts are. Hassoun defends the minority position on development and aid; here, I recite the mainstream position.

1. False Starts

Many people believe that global justice requires wealth redistribution from rich to poor countries. Most who find redistributive views appealing do so because they also hold mistaken beliefs about empirical matters. They usually accept one or more of the following claims:

1. The reason some countries are rich and others are poor is that natural resources are unevenly distributed around the globe. The rich are rich because they have or had access to more or better resources than the poor countries did.
2. The reason some countries are rich and others are poor is that the rich countries (through conquest, colonialism, and empire) *extracted* resources from the poor countries.
3. We can easily end world poverty if rich countries simply gave some portion of their wealth to the poor.

These are *economic* claims, but they play an important role in many people's normative reasoning. People who accept these claims regard world poverty as a simple problem of misallocation: too much here, too little there. The obvious next step is to argue for redistribution in order to fix the misallocation. But the problem here is that each of these three claims is *false*.

The first two claims hold that differences in wealth result from a zero-sum process. I'll take a closer look below. But here, let's pause to note that wealth has been made, not simply moved around. We've seen an explosion of wealth and income over the past two hundred years. In 1990 U.S. dollars, GDP per capita in 1 A.D. was about $457, rising to $712 by 1820. But look what's happened since:

On a chart, as in Figure 3.1,[37] it looks like a hockey stick. In the past two hundred years, *real* (that is, adjusted for inflation and cost of living) per capita world product has increased by a factor of at least thirty.[38] The U.S. economy this year will produce *more*, in real terms, than the entire world did in 1950.

When the Great Enrichment began, Western Europe and the Western European offshoots grew faster than the rest of the world. As a result, the gap between Europe's standard of living and the rest of the world also grew. But even the poorest regions enjoyed *some* growth. It's not that Western Europe and the European offshoots grew rich while the other countries became even poorer. It's not as though Western Europe grew rich at the rate others grew poor, which would suggest a zero-sum reallocation of a fixed stock of wealth. Rather, all countries started off as poor; some got *slightly* richer over time, while the European countries and their offshoots got *much* richer over time.

Why?

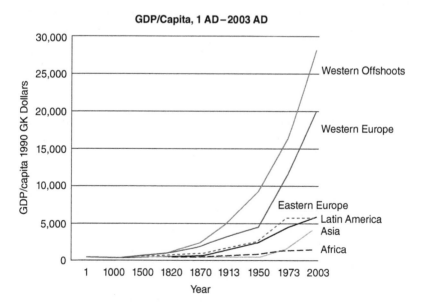

Figure 3.1
GDP per capita

Wrong Answer One: Natural Resources

Philosopher Thomas Pogge claims the world's rich have excluded the poor from their fair share of the world's natural resources. Pogge thinks this unjust. He claims people worldwide have a right to "a proportional resource share."[39]

Philosophers often assume differential natural resources explain why some countries are rich and others poor. But, as economist David Weil summarizes the empirical literature in his widely used textbook *Economic Growth*, "the effect of natural resources on income is weak at best."[40] For instance, China after the 1950s was and remains poorer (in per capita income and other standard measures) than Singapore or Hong Kong, though the latter have almost *no* natural resources to speak of. The USSR was much poorer than the United States, though the USSR had far better natural resources. In Adam Smith's time, the Netherlands and England were richer than France, though France had far better natural resources. And so on.

Indeed, while natural resources can sometimes spur growth, they more frequently *inhibit* growth. Economists refer to this problem as the "resource curse": Countries with a high concentration of easily extractable natural resources frequently suffer from economic stagnation.

Just why this is so is debated. One explanation may be that countries with abundant natural resources "do not develop the cultural attributes necessary for economic success," in part because necessity is the mother of invention.[41] Another theory is that countries that enjoy resource booms tend to consume the sudden influx of income in an unsustainable way. They don't develop capital, but eat away the extra income until it's gone (see, e.g., Venezuela). Perhaps the most popular theory (or, more precisely, the theory thought to identify the most significant set of causes) is that when a country enjoys abundant resources, this encourages governments to act in destructive ways.[42] Regardless, the idea that resources explain wealth is widely accepted by laypeople, but widely rejected by economists.

Wrong Answer Two: Imperialism

A second popular view holds that that rich countries are rich because they (or their predecessors), through policies of colonialism, imperialism, and resource extraction, stole from the so-called Third World. For instance, political theorist Seyla Benhabib complains that liberal philosopher John Rawls downplays the African slave trade and global imperialism. She says she doubts "whether early capitalist accumulation in the West could have been conceivable without colonial expansion."[43] Or, as Pogge says,

> [E]xisting radical inequality is deeply tainted by how it accumulated through one historical process that was deeply pervaded by enslavement, colonialism, even genocide. The rich are quick to point out that they cannot inherit their ancestor's sins. Indeed. But how can they then be entitled to the fruits of these sins: to their huge inherited advantage in power and wealth over the rest of the world?[44]

On this view, imperialist extraction explains (or helps to explain) why developed countries became wealthy and why undeveloped countries are poor. Our wealth is inherited stolen wealth.

European countries indeed conquered Africans, Asians, and Native Americans, murdered and enslaved them, and stole their resources for use back home. Does such theft explain why European countries and some of their off-shoots are rich? If you've never taken an economics class, you'll probably presume, as Benhabib and Pogge do, that the answer is yes.

But economists think the answer is no. Indeed, Adam Smith's 1776 *Wealth of Nations*—the book that founded modern economics—is fundamentally an economic critique of imperialism. Smith carefully surveyed the economic value of the goods Britain and other countries had extracted from the Americas and elsewhere, and then compared that to the costs these countries incurred to create and maintain those empires.[45] Smith concluded:

> The rulers of Great Britain have, for more than a century past, amused the people with the imagination that they possessed a great empire on the west side of the Atlantic. This empire, however, [is] . . . not a gold mine, but the project of a gold mine; a project which has cost, which continues to cost, and which, if pursued in the same way as it has been hitherto, is likely to cost, immense expense, without being likely to bring any profit; for the effects of the monopoly of the colony trade, it has been shown, are, to the great body of the people, mere loss instead of profit.[46]

Smith found that a minority of politically well-connected people benefited from the empire, but the majority of British subjects *lost* money. The losers lost more than the winners won. The costs of creating and maintaining the empire greatly *exceeded* the value of the raw materials obtained. (To illustrate: Imagine you paid $500 to buy a gun to rob people, but you only got $250 in earnings from all your muggings. You thereby *lost* money on your robberies.) Further, Smith showed, imperialism distorted the economy (by encouraging inefficient production methods) and so further hurt Britain and other imperial powers. Britain was getting richer despite its empire, not because of it.

The thrust of Smith's views is widely accepted. The general view among economists—who have better data today than Smith did back then—is that empires do not pay for themselves, even if we focus narrowly on the economic interests of imperial powers and ignore the harm they did to those they conquered.[47]

However, while imperialism does not explain why some countries are rich, it may partly explain why some now remain poor. When imperialist powers established colonies, they replaced existing institutions with new institutions. As economists Daron Acemoglu, Simon Johnson, and James Robinson show, the kinds of institutions imperial powers set up depended on whether Europeans could settle in the colonies. In places such as North America, where European settlers faced low mortality rates (because there were low risks of disease), imperial powers exported well-functioning, growth-creating institutions.[48] In places such as the Congo, where Europeans faced high mortality rates (because of disease), imperial powers established growth-inhibiting, extractive institutions. When the European powers abandoned or lost their colonies, these bad institutions remained behind, and generally morphed into the dysfunctional institutions those countries have today.

You might think this concession justifies redistribution: "Aha! Belgium should redistribute some of its wealth to the Congo. After all, even if the Belgians lost money in their rape, murder, and robbery of the Congo, it's still their fault that the Congo is doing badly today." In the same way, this argument goes, suppose I spent $500 to buy a gun, and then rob you, but only get $250 from doing so. Even though I lost money when I robbed you, I still owe you compensation.

But this argument treats countries as if they were people, and it obscures morally important facts. It's not that the Belgian or British people chose, as a group, to steal from Africans or Native Americans. Rather, what really happened was that, years ago, in what were non-democratic countries, the kings and queens, plus some political insiders, taxed the Belgian and British subjects to buy guns, soldiers, and warships, and then used those to steal from the Africans and Native Americans. The Belgian and British subjects were *also* victims of imperialism—their leaders exploited them (through taxes and conscription) to then exploit others (through conquest and theft). So, demanding that the Belgians pay restitution to the Congo is demanding that the descendants of some victims pay restitution to the descendants of other victims. Imagine Queen Isabella robs my grandpa to buy a gun, which she then uses to kill your grandpa. It's bizarre to hold that this would require me to compensate you.

2. Institutions Are the Answer, Unfortunately

The dominant view in mainstream development economics is that sustained economic growth results mainly from having good economic and political institutions.[49] Institutions "are the rules of the game in a society or, more formally, are the humanly devised constraints that shape human interaction."[50] As economist Dani Rodrik summarizes, when it comes to explaining economic growth and why some countries are rich and others poor, "the quality of institutions trumps everything else."[51]

Which institutions produce growth? Countries (a) with robust systems of private property and (b) open markets, (c) protected by the rule of law enforced by (d) stable and inclusive governments, offer much better prospects for significant and sustained development than those that lack such institutions.[52] The countries with institutions (a) through (d), such as Switzerland, Canada, Singapore, or Hong Kong, are nearly always rich; the countries that lack (a) through (d) are nearly always poor. The reasons why are well understood, though I can only summarize them here.

As Acemoglu and Robinson argue in *Why Nations Fail*, the main difference between good and bad institutions concerns the degree to which they foster extractive activity or instead encourage cooperation and productivity. The main difference concerns whom the institutions empower, and thus whom the institutions benefit. What they call *inclusive* institutions, such as open markets and strong protections for private property, empower people across society, and thus tend to benefit all. They give people a stake in and ability to invest long term and engage in mutually beneficial capital accumulation. By contrast, *extractive* institutions—such as dictatorships where the government owns the natural resources, or overly regulated economies where rent seekers rig the rules—empower only some, and thus tend to benefit only small groups of people at others' expense.

It's "unfortunate" that the institutional theory of wealth is correct. The reason it's unfortunate is that while we know which institutions create growth and which impede it, we don't know how to induce social change. We don't know how to get countries with bad institutions to switch to good institutions. Part of the reason institutional change is so difficult is that the leaders of countries with bad institutions nearly always have a stake in those bad institutions—they make their living by exploiting their subjects or selling favors.

3. The Aid Illusion

Though developed countries didn't get rich at the expense of poor countries, you might still hope we could solve world poverty by giving away money. It's a simple idea. We're rich. They're poor. We give them some cash. They stop being poor. As Nobel Laureate economist Angus Deaton (himself an aid skeptic) notes, if that argument were sound, then curing world poverty would require barely anything from us:

> One of the stunning facts about global poverty is how little it would take to fix it, at least if we could magically transfer money into the bank accounts of the world's poor. In 2008, there were about 800 million people in the world living on less than $1.00 a day. On average, each of these people is "short" about $0.28 a day . . . We could make up that shortfall with less than a quarter billion dollars a day . . . Taking . . . into account [differences in purchasing power in poor countries], . . . world poverty could be eliminated if every American adult donated $0.30 a day; or, if we could build a coalition of the willing from all the adults of Britain, France, Germany, and Japan, each would need to give only $0.15 a day.[53]

People may be selfish, but surely no one would balk at 15 cents a day to end extreme world poverty. It seems so easy!

But it's not easy, as Deaton then explains. In the past fifty years, hundreds of billions of dollars have been spent on government-to-government and other forms of international aid. In just the past decade, between 2000 and 2010, governments provided $128 billion in foreign aid.[54] Has it done any good? Looking at Africa over the past fifty years, Deaton finds an inverse relationship between growth and aid. He summarizes the empirics:

> Growth *decreased* steadily while aid *increased* steadily. When aid fell off, after the end of the Cold War, growth picked up; the end of the Cold War took away one of the main rationales for aid to Africa, and African growth rebounded . . . [A] more accurate punchline would be "the Cold War is over, and Africa won," because the West reduced aid.[55]

Economists left and right generally agree. (Philosophers of global justice generally ignore such economics, or cherry-pick the minority dissenting studies.) In a comprehensive review of the existing empirical literature, Hristos

Doucouliagos and Martin Paldam conclude that, overall, "after 40 years of development aid, the evidence indicates that aid has not been effective."[56] Overall, the research generally finds that aid is more likely to hurt than help. In general, economists find that aid helps a bit in countries that have pretty good institutions, but tends to hurt in countries with bad institutions.[57]

Why would it *hurt*? Acemoglu and Robinson write,

> The idea that rich Western countries should provide large amounts of "development aid" in order to solve the problem of [world] poverty . . . is based on an incorrect understanding of what causes poverty. Countries such as Afghanistan are poor because of their extractive institutions—which result in a lack of property rights, law and order, or well-functioning legal systems and the stifling domination of national and, more often, local elites over political and economic life. The same institutional problems mean that foreign aid will be ineffective, as it will be plundered and is unlikely to be delivered where it is supposed to go. In the worst-case scenario, it will prop up the regimes that are the very root of the problems of those societies.[58]

The problem is that poor countries suffer negative feedback loops. They are governed by abusive elites, people who make a living (and stay in power) by extracting resources from their countries and people. In such conditions, to pour more money into a country usually means lining the pockets of the abusers, not feeding the hungry.

When rulers make a living by extracting resources from their societies, sending more money means increasing the rewards of being in power. Foreign aid tends to make bad governments thrive without the support of their citizens, tends to encourage factions within those countries (different agencies, bureaucracies, strongmen) to compete for power in order to gain control of the incoming aid, and tends to subsidize corruption. It escalates conflicts, civil wars, and human rights violations. Rather than inducing development and growth, aid often prolongs and worsens the conditions that produce poverty and need in the first place.

No one denies that aid *can* do good sometimes. Christopher Coyne, himself another major critic of foreign aid, finds that aid seems to be most effective in increasing predetermined outputs in response to clear-cut crises.[59] If there's a sudden famine, buying and distributing food stops starvation. (Though, as Coyne documents, it can also fail at that, and sometimes even makes things worse.[60])

But there is distinction between *aid* and *development*. Development happens when a society begins to grow economically and the conditions that cause people's poverty start to disappear. There is simply no track record of aid helping to spur economic development. The reasons why are clear: To get rich, countries need good institutions, but you can't export good institutions the way you can send a sack of rice.

4. An Obligation to Help Is an Obligation to Help

Philosophers of global justice spend their time debating which normative principles would ground duties of international aid. To induce their readers to have moral intuitions that favor redistribution, they often rely on thought experiments like these:

1. If grandma gave 20 of her grandchildren 80% of the pie, and the other 166 grandkids only 20%, should the rich 20 give the poor 166 more pie?
2. Suppose my grandpa stole your grandpa's watch, which I then inherit. Should I give it "back" to you?
3. If I see a kid drowning in a puddle, shouldn't I save him, even if saving him ruins my expensive shoes?

Philosophers think the actual world is analogous to thought experiments like these. This makes foreign aid seem morally mandatory.

But economics, surprisingly, tells us that philosophers are bad at philosophy. The problem is that these three thought experiments, and all the variations on them, are *irrelevant*. The gap between rich and poor did not result from an unfair initial distribution of resources or from theft. And saving the world's poor from poverty looks almost nothing like pulling a drowning kid from a pond.

In 1799, U.S. President George Washington got a bad sore throat. His family called in doctors, who then killed him. Yes, killed him. His doctors (the best available in his day) subscribed to false and counterproductive beliefs about medicine. They bled him multiple times, extracting at least forty-eight ounces of blood. They also blistered his skin, induced vomiting, and administered an enema. The dehydrated president then died.[61] When Martha Washington sent for the doctors, despite her best intentions, she was ordering a death sentence.

An obligation to help the poor is an obligation to actually help them. Good intentions don't matter. Too often, developed countries play the part of Washington's doctors, killing instead of helping, administering a medicine worse than the disease. Philosophers of global justice today play the role of Martha Washington. They mean well, but they're calling in the bad doctors.

I'm not saying we should do nothing. I'm instead claiming we should do what works. "We" (the people in the developed world) helped Taiwan, Hong Kong, South Korea, and Japan—countries that were poor in the 1950s but are rich today—become rich not by giving them aid, but by buying their products as they liberalized their economies. If we want to help, we will open borders (see Peter Jaworski's essay in Chapter 4) to immigrants, and we'll increase international trade. We'll confine foreign aid to its rightful place and stop pretending it's the solution.

COMPREHENSION QUESTIONS

1. In Brennan's view, why are some countries rich and others poor?
2. What does Brennan mean when he states that his disagreement with Hassoun "concerns the *relevance* of moral principles in light of what we think the facts are"?
3. According to Brennan, what economic effects do imperialism and abundance of natural resources have on historically imperialist and resource-rich states?

4. What kinds of economic and political institutions support sustained economic growth?
5. Why does Brennan say it's "'unfortunate' that the institutional theory of wealth is correct"?
6. According to Brennan, what effect does foreign aid have on nations in need of economic development?
7. What does Brennan think we should do to help poor countries?

DISCUSSION QUESTIONS

1. Brennan's argument against the effectiveness of foreign aid partially rests on the assumption that the goal of foreign aid is to end global poverty. How closely does this align with Hassoun's view?
2. When arguing about the effectiveness of and moral justification for foreign aid, how important is it to consider the rationality of global wealth redistribution?
3. With regard to the issue of international aid, are political philosophers and economists the only relevant groups of experts? Who else might have important information or reasoning to contribute to the debate?

Case 2

The following is taken from a World Economic Forum article titled "How Effective Is Foreign Aid?":

> I argue that international aid affects recipient economies in extremely complex ways and through multiple and changing channels. Moreover, this is a two-way relationship—aid agencies influence policies, and the reality in the recipient country affects the actions of aid agencies. This relationship is so intricate and time-dependent that it is not amenable to being captured by cross-country or panel regressions; in fact, even sophisticated specifications with multiple breakpoints and nonlinearities are unlikely to explain the inner workings of the aid–performance connection.
>
> Bourguignon and Sundberg (2007) have pointed out that there is a need to go beyond econometrics, and to break open the "black box" of development aid. I would go even further, and argue that we need to realise that there is a multiplicity of black boxes. Or, to put it differently, that the black box is highly elastic and keeps changing through time. Breaking these boxes open and understanding why aid works some times and not others, and why some projects are successful while other are disasters, requires analysing in great detail specific country episodes. If we want to truly understand the convoluted ways in which official aid affects different economic outcomes, we need to plunge into archives, analyse data in detail, carefully look for counterfactuals, understand the temperament of the major players, and take into account historical circumstances. This is a difficult subject that requires detective-like work.[*]

On the one hand, this sounds like support for Brennan's view: *Aid is really complicated*. What should Hassoun say about it? On the other hand, this passage admits that aid sometimes works. What should Brennan say about that?

[*]https://www.weforum.org/agenda/2014/11/how-effective-is-foreign-aid/

REPLY TO BRENNAN
NICOLE HASSOUN

Jason Brennan and I agree about many things. Aid can do some good, but many other things are necessary for international development. We can also help people in other ways, for instance by increasing immigration and international trade.[62]

That is, Brennan concedes that (what he wrongly calls) my "minority" position on foreign aid is correct.[63] Aid *can* do some good. Moreover, since he does not challenge the moral arguments I provide for aid,[64] we might conclude that we *should* aid others whenever it will help. The questions that remain about aid then become ones of scope and process: How much aid can help people? How can we ensure the aid does not harm people? How can we make aid more effective?

I believe that, although the history of aid is littered with failures, aid often helps people live better lives and we have good tools for figuring out what works and what does not. Strong evidence suggests aid can do much more than Brennan thinks.[65]

Moreover, the evidence that Brennan offers does not challenge the conclusion that aid can help people live good lives. Like many economists critical of aid, Brennan seems to think that aid should *increase economic growth*; I, like most philosophical advocates of aid, think we should focus on whether it reduces poverty and helps people live good lives (even if it does not increase growth). So, the evidence he cites showing that aid does not increase growth on its own, but that the good institutions colonialists helped build in some countries (but not others) are necessary for growth, does nothing to challenge my argument. Even if the studies arguing that we should make aid conditional on institutional quality are right, they just look at aid's impact on growth and can tell us little about whether aid reduces poverty more or less well with good institutions.[66] Brennan just asserts that foreigners do not know how to build the good institutions necessary to reduce poverty with aid.[67]

On the other hand, there is strong evidence that aid can help people escape poverty even in the absence of good institutions, and I do not think anyone should deny that it can help build good institutions. What evidence exists suggests aid can work to reduce poverty (whether or not good institutions are necessary or aid can help build them).[68] Moreover, aid has helped to build many good institutions—from education to health systems.[69] In any case, Brennan cannot have it both ways: Either it is possible for foreigners to build good institutions (as he suggests when he claims colonialists who could settle helped build good institutions) or they cannot (as he suggests when criticizing aid efforts).[70]

Although Brennan does little to challenge my argument for giving aid that helps people to live minimally good lives, it is worth considering Brennan's arguments against the idea that developed countries (or their inhabitants) should aid those in developing countries because they (or their ancestors) have harmed them. He does not think developed countries (or their historical inhabitants) harmed people in developing countries.[71] Rather, he says the real causes of wealth and poverty are institutional (and foreigners do not know how to build good institutions). Moreover, even if those in developed countries have harmed those in developing countries, he says the descendants of people in developed countries have no obligation to pay restitution because many of their grandparents were coerced into harming others.

I believe that the causes of wealth and poverty are *complex* in ways Brennan fails to appreciate. No single factor can explain what causes wealth or poverty. Reflecting back on the institutional-quality literature, researchers who argue that institutions are important for development do not share a common definition of "institutional quality." While some look at "(a) robust systems of private property and (b) open markets, (c) protected by the rule of law enforced by (d) stable and inclusive governments," others are more concerned with trade, tax, or judicial policies (alone or in combination).[72] Moreover, the historical picture Brennan draws—suggesting that only local factors affect international development—is too simple. Even if colonialism was a net loss for many in colonizing countries (see below), colonialism did not only contribute to poverty when colonialists set up poor extractive institutions. Colonial divisions have played a large role in many conflicts in Africa even where colonists were able to settle. The negative consequences of these conflicts may well swamp the benefits colonies received directly from colonial powers.[73] And even though poor countries have grown a bit in recent years, they may well have fared better without the violence and division colonialism brought.[74]

If some of the things some of those in developed countries have done historically have harmed some of those in developing countries, is anyone responsible for compensating the descendants of those people? This is a difficult moral question. Let us suppose, with Brennan, that many people in colonizing countries did not benefit from colonialism. Still, their descendants may benefit significantly from the wealth colonialism created. So, some argue that they have to pay back these gains because otherwise it is like keeping stolen goods.[75] On the other hand, one might argue that there is a statute of limitations on ill-gotten gains and that the descendants of colonialists lack any obligation to compensate people today in developing countries. But the proposition that they owe compensation cannot be dismissed out of hand.

Rather than engaging in so much rhetoric—dismissing philosophers as philistines who offer only irrelevant thought experiments as reasons to provide aid and who are unfamiliar with, and uninterested in, the true science of economics—I think Brennan should engage more seriously with the empirical evidence he praises and the philosophical arguments he criticizes.[76]

COMPREHENSION QUESTIONS

1. What do Hassoun and Brennan agree on?
2. What does Hassoun think that foreign aid should achieve?
3. According to Hassoun, what effect does aid have on poverty?
4. How do Hassoun's views on the causes of wealth and poverty differ from Brennan's?

DISCUSSION QUESTION

1. Hassoun says that Brennan doesn't challenge her moral arguments in favor of providing aid. What would such a challenge look like?

REPLY TO HASSOUN
JASON BRENNAN

I strongly encourage readers to take economics classes and classes in other social sciences. Political philosophers have a lot to say about what *goals* our institutions should support and why. They have something to say about which values trump others when there's a conflict. But we need the social sciences to tell us what trade-offs we actually face and what institutions actually deliver the goods. Aid doesn't work the way philosophers want it to work—it doesn't cause development—but that doesn't stop philosophers from advocating it.

The economic consensus, from economists on the left and the right, is that focus on aid is misplaced. Places with bad institutions do not enjoy sustained development and do not escape poverty. A better bet is to move the people to the places with good institutions—that is, to open borders and change labor and housing laws to make it easy for the global poor to move where they can get rich. The average Haitian who moves to the United States sees his income go up by a factor of about fifteen, and he makes the rest of us richer by coming here.[73]

What Hassoun gets right is that some forms of aid do good, and some do a lot of good, even if aid doesn't substitute for and does not cause institutional change and development. Like Hassoun, I can list cases where "aid" did good things (e.g., polio eradication). Certain forms of private charity have strong track records of reducing some of the downsides of global poverty. Every year, GiveWell.org evaluates a number of charities and recommends four or five that give the most "bang for the buck"—that is, life-years added per dollar spent. For instance, for 50 cents per kid per year, you can cure children of parasitic worms, which has immense benefits for their health, cognitive development, and their later ability to find productive work.

Providing help like this is not merely admirable, it may be obligatory. In common-sense moral thinking, we have duties to assist others in need, though perhaps not unlimited duties to do so. The richer you are, the stronger your duties of assistance are. The reason: Helping others costs you less because you're already so well off. When LeBron James builds a school, he still lives in luxury. But for some people, giving up $200 means they can't pay rent.

It's worth noting that you, the reader, almost certainly are rich. An American at the U.S. poverty line is—adjusting for the cost of living and inflation—well among the top 20% richest people alive today, and is much richer even than middle-class Americans in 1900. You can't save the world—and neither can international aid in general—but you can save some lives, cure some blindness, and deworm hundreds of kids at little cost to yourself.

Hassoun's argument ultimately has two parts, an empirical claim and a normative claim. The normative claim is "We should help," and the empirical claim is "We can help." As I documented in my original essay, the empirical claim is largely false, unless we interpret the claim in a rather narrow way. We don't know how to make aid cause growth or development. But we do know how to make certain targeted forms of aid help certain people in certain ways. So long as

Hassoun confines her argument to these rather unobjectionable cases—so long as she isn't making the ambitious but mistaken assertion that international aid is likely to cause development and eradicate poverty, then she isn't saying anything objectionable.

To my surprise, Hassoun didn't offer much of an argument for the normative part, the "we should help." She said people should not have to suffer and that everyone's life is valuable. She suggested you might empathize with others if you consider their plight. She quickly slid from saying that people generally need X to talking about X being a human right. A full philosophical argument would try to explain not merely why needing X entitles you to X, but would explain why the duty to provide X falls upon particular people. I don't know if I agree or disagree with Hassoun's arguments because, as far as I can see, she doesn't quite provide any.[74]

At any rate, let's say for the sake of argument that every human being has a right to a decent life, and the duty to ensure everyone has a decent life falls equally on all of us. On its face, that tells us almost nothing about what to *do*. Maybe it means taxing everyone and providing trillions in government-to-government aid. Maybe it means taxing no one, but requiring the rich to fund private charitable endeavors. Maybe it means we should overthrow the leaders of countries with extractive institutions and engage in nation-building. (And it could also mean the leaders of those countries are obligated to change their extractive, illiberal institutions to economically and socially liberal, inclusive institutions.) Maybe it means breaking down borders and legal restrictions that imprison the global poor in countries with bad institutions. Philosophy—and your moral intuitions—alone can't tell us what this purported duty actually requires of us.

If you care—as I do—about ending global poverty, then you will scrupulously examine the empirical evidence about what works and why. You'll be utterly disloyal to your ideological priors—you'll be willing to throw out your beliefs and adopt new beliefs about what works when you see what the evidence actually is.

COMPREHENSION QUESTIONS

1. With regard to the issue of foreign aid, what, according to Brennan, is the role of political philosophers? What's the role of economists?
2. What is the problem with aid, according to Brennan, and what alternative does he endorse?
3. What kind of aid is most justified, according to Brennan?

DISCUSSION QUESTIONS

1. Reviewing Hassoun's essay, how do you think she might respond to the charge that she "didn't offer much of an argument" for her claim that we should help ensure that others can live a minimally good life?
2. After reading both main essays and replies, what do you think the empirical evidence about foreign aid shows?

FURTHER READINGS

Acemoglu, Daron, Simon Johnson, and James A. Robinson. "Institutions as a Fundamental Cause of Long-Run Growth." In *Handbook of Economic Growth*, Vol. 1A, edited by Philippe Aghion and Steven N. Darlauf. Amsterdam: Elsevier, 2005.

Acemoglu, Daron, and James A. Robinson. *Why Nations Fail*. New York: Crown Business, 2013.

Alkire, Sabina. *Valuing Freedoms: Sen's Capability Approach and Poverty Reduction*. Oxford Scholarship Online, 2002/2004.

Doucouliagos, Hristos, and Martin Paldam. "The Aid Effectiveness Literature: The Sad Results of 40 Years of Research." *Journal of Economic Surveys* 23 (2009): 433–461.

Easterly, William. *The White Man's Burden: Why the West's Effort to Aid the Rest Have Done So Much Ill and So Little Good*. Oxford: Oxford University Press, 2006.

Hassoun, Nicole. *Globalization and Global Justice: Shrinking Distance, Expanding Obligations*. Cambridge: Cambridge University Press, 2012.

Moyo, Dambisa. *Dead Aid*. New York: Farrar, Straus, and Giroux, 2009.

Rodrik, Dani, Arvind Subramanian, and Francisco Trebbi. "Institutions Rule: The Primacy of Institutions over Geography and Integration in Economic Development." *Journal of Economic Growth* 9 (2004): 131–165.

Sachs, Jeffrey D. *The End of Poverty*. New York: Penguin Books, 2005.

NOTES

1. Annie-Marie O'Conner et al., "Mexico: Wages, Maquiladoras, NAFTA 1998," *Migration News,* February 1998, https://migration.ucdavis.edu/mn/more.php?id=1451.
2. "World Bank and WHO: Half the World Lacks Access to Essential Health Services, 100 Million Still Pushed into Extreme Poverty Because of Health Expenses," The World Bank, accessed May 25, 2018, http://www.worldbank.org/en/news/press-release/2017/12/13/world-bank-who-half-world-lacks-access-to-essential-health-services-100-million-still-pushed-into-extreme-poverty-because-of-health-expenses.
3. UN General Assembly, "International Covenant on Economic, Social and Cultural Rights (ICESCR)," *United Nations, Treaty Series* 993, no. 3 (1966).
4. United Nations, "Universal Declaration of Human Rights (UNDHR)," International Covenant on Economic, Social and Cultural Rights, Geneva: United Nations, 1966, http://www.ohchr.org/EN/ProfessionalInterest/Pages/CESCR.aspx.
5. United Nations Committee on Economic, Social and Cultural Rights (UNCESCR), "General Comment 3: The Nature of States Parties' Obligations, Fifth Session, UN Doc. E/1991/23, annex III at 86 (1991)," Reprinted in Compilation of General Comments and General Recommendations Adopted by Human Rights Treaty Bodies, UN Doc. HRI/Gen/I/Rev. 6 at 62 (2003). Accessed April 18, 2016.
6. Nicole Hassoun, "Account of the Minimally Good Life" (working paper, Department of Philosophy, Binghamton University, New York, 2018); Nicole Hassoun, "What We Owe to Others as a Basic Minimum: The Ability to Live a Minimally Good Life" (working paper, Department of Philosophy, Binghamton University, New York, 2018).
7. For more on why we must also care for others to figure out what they need, see Martha Nussbaum, *Frontiers of Justice: Disability, Nationality, Species Membership* (Cambridge, MA: Harvard University Press, 2006).
8. Harry Frankfurt, "Equality as a Moral Ideal," *Ethics* 98, no. 1 (1987): 21–43.

9. Nicole Hassoun, *Global Health Impact: Extending Access on Essential Medicines for the Poor* (Oxford: Oxford University Press, under contract); Pablo Gilabert et al., "Political Feasibility: A Conceptual Exploration," *Political Studies* 60, no. 4 (2012): 809–825; Geoffrey Brennan, "Feasibility in Optimizing Ethics," *Social and Political Philosophy* 30, no. 2 (2013): 314–329; Pablo Gilabert, "Justice and Feasibility: A Dynamic Approach," in *Political Utopias: Contemporary Debates*, edited by K. Vallier and M. Weber (New York: Oxford University Press, 2016), 95–126.

10. John Locke, *The Second Treatise of Civil Government and a Letter Concerning Toleration* (London: Awnsham Churchill, 1689; Oxford: Basil Blackwell, 1948).

11. "Uncommon Knowledge: Dambisa Moyo," filmed July 2007, http://library.fora .tv/2009/06/05/Uncommon_Knowledge_Dambisa_Moyo; Dambisa Moyo, *Dead Aid* (New York: Farrar, Straus, and Giroux, 2009); Dambisa Moyo, "Why Foreign Aid is Hurting Africa," *Wall Street Journal*, March 21, 2009, http://www.wsj.com/articles /SB123758895999200083; Andrew Mwenda, "Aid for Africa? No Thanks," filmed June 2007 at TEDGlobal, Arusha, Tanzania, https://www.ted.com/talks/andrew_mwenda _takes_a_new_look_at_africa?language=en; Andrew Mwenda, "Foreign Aid and the Weakening of Democratic Accountability in Uganda," published July 12, 2006, in Cato Institute Foreign Policy Briefing No. 88, http://object.cato.org/sites/cato.org/files/pubs /pdf/fpb88.pdf; William Easterly, *The White Man's Burden: Why the West's Effort to Aid the Rest Have Done So Much Ill and So Little Good* (Oxford: Oxford University Press, 2006); Daron Acemoglu et al., "Why Foreign Aid Fails—and How to Really Help Africa," *The Spectator*, January 25, 2014, http://www.spectator.co.uk/2014/01/why-aid -fails/; Angus Deaton, *The Great Escape: Health, Wealth, and the Origins of Inequality* (Princeton, NJ: Princeton University Press, 2013); Ayodele Thompson et al., "African Perspectives on Aid: Foreign Assistance Will Not Pull Africa out of Poverty," published September 14, 2005, in Cato Institute, Economic Development Bulletin No. 2, http:// www.cato.org/publications/economic-development-bulletin/african-perspectives-aid -foreign-assistance-will-not-pull-africa-out-poverty; James Bovard, "The World Bank vs. the World's Poor." published September 28, 1987, in Cato Institute, Policy Analysis No. 92, http://object.cato.org/sites/cato.org/files/pubs/pdf/pa092.pdf.

12. Michael Clemens et al., "Counting Chickens when They Hatch: The Short-Term Effect of Aid on Growth," (Working Paper Number 44, Washington DC, Center for Global Development); Paul Collier et al., "Development Effectiveness: What Have We Learnt?" *Economic Journal* 114, no. 496 (2004): F244–F271; Henrik Hansel et al., "Aid and Growth Regressions," *Journal of Development Economics* 64, no. 2 (2001): 547–570; George Mavrotas, *Assessing Aid Effectiveness in Uganda: An Aid-Disaggregation Approach* (Oxford: Oxford Policy Management, 2003); Karuna Gomanee et al., "Aid and Growth in Sub-Saharan Africa: Accounting for Transmission Mechanisms," *Journal of International Development* 17, no. 8 (2005): 1055–1075; Trudy Owens et al., "Investing in Development or Investing in Relief: Quantifying the Poverty Tradeoffs Using Zimbabwe Household Panel Data" (CSAE Working Paper Series, Centre for the Study of African Economies, University of Oxford, 1999); Constantine Michalopoulos et al., "The Impact of Development Assistance: A Review of the Quantitative Evidence," in *Aid and Development*, edited by A. O. Krueger (Baltimore, MD: Johns Hopkins University Press, 1989), 111–124; Howard White, "The Macroeconomic Impact of Development Aid: A Critical Survey," *Journal of Development Studies* 28, no. 2 (1992): 163–240; Carl-Johan Dalgaard, Henrik Hansen and, Finn Tarp, "On the Empirics of Foreign Aid and Growth" [EPRU], Working Paper Series, Economic Policy Research Unit [EPRU], University of Copenhagen. Department of Economics, 2001).

13. Nicole Hassoun, "Free Trade, Poverty, and Inequality," *Journal of Moral Philosophy* 8, no. 1 (2011): 5–44.

14. Peter Boone, "Politics and the Effectiveness of Foreign Aid," *European Economic Review* 40, no. 2 (1996): 289–329; Paul Mosley et al., "Aid, Poverty Reduction and the 'New Conditionality," *Economic Journal* 114, no. 496 (2004): F217; Karuna Gomanee et al., "Aid and Growth in Sub-Saharan Africa: Accounting For Transmission Mechanisms." *Journal of International Development* 17, no. 8 (2005): 1055–1075.

15. Jonathan Isbam et al., "Does Participation Improve Performance? Establishing Causality with Subjective Data," *World Bank Economic Review* 9, no. 2 (1995): 175–200; Esther Duflo et al., "Using Randomization in Development Economics Research: A Toolkit," *Handbook of Development Economics* 4 (2007): 3895–3962; Esther Duflo et al., "Use of Randomization in the Evaluation Of Development Effectiveness," *Evaluating Development Effectiveness* 7 (2005): 205–231; Hassan Zaman, "Poverty and BRAC's Microcredit Program: Exploring Some Linkages" (Working Paper Number 18, BRAC-ICDDR,B Joint Research Project, Dhaka, Bangladesh, 1997); Sheri D. Weiser et al., "Shamba Maisha: Randomized Controlled Trial of an Agricultural and Finance Intervention to Improve HIV Health Outcomes in Kenya," *AIDS* 29, no. 14 (2005): 1889–1894; Oriana Bandiera et al., "Women's Empowerment in Action: Evidence from a Randomized Control Trial in Africa," University College London, accessed May 24, 2018, http://www.ucl.ac.uk/~uctpimr/research/ELA.pdf; Meghna R. Desai et al., "Randomized, Controlled Trial of Daily Iron Supplementation and Intermittent Sulfadoxine-Pyrimethamine for the Treatment of Mild Childhood Anemia in Western Kenya," *Journal of Infectious Diseases* 187, no. 4 (2003): 658–666; Jeff Tollefson, "Can Randomized Trials Eliminate Global Poverty?" *Nature* 524 (2015): 150–153.

16. Nicole Hassoun, "Empirical Evidence and the Case for Foreign Aid," *Public Affairs Quarterly* 24, no. 1 (2010): 1–20.

17. Humanitarian Coalition, "From Humanitarian to Development Aid," accessed May 26, 2018, http://humanitariancoalition.ca/media-resources/factsheets/from-humanitarian-to -development-aid; Paul Collier et al., "Development Effectiveness: What Have We Learnt?" *The Economic Journal* 114, no. 496 (2004): F244–F271; Paul Collier et al., "Aid Allocation and Poverty Reduction." *European Economic Review* 46 (2002): 1475–1500; Adeyemi A. Ogundipe et al., "Is Aid Really Dead? Evidence from Sub-Saharan Africa," *International Journal of Humanities and Social Science* 4, no. 10 (2014): 1–16; Kwabena Gyimah-Brempong, "Aid and Economic Growth in LDCs: Evidence from Sub-Saharan Africa," *Review of Black Political Economy* 20, no. 3 (1992): 31–52; Moussa Njoupouognigni, "Foreign Aid, Foreign Direct Investment and Economic Growth in Sub-Saharan Africa: Evidence from Pooled Mean Group Estimator (PMG)," *International Journal of Economics and Finance* 2, no. 3 (2010): 39; Didier Yélognissè Alia et al., "Foreign Aid Effectiveness in African Economies: Evidence from a Panel Threshold Framework" (WIDER Working Paper, 2014); Carl-Johan Dalgaard and Henrik Hanse, "On Aid, Growth and Good Policies," *Journal of Development Studies* 37, no. 6 (2001): 17–41.

18. Jeffery Sachs, "The Case for Aid," *Foreign Policy*, published January 21, 2014, http:// foreignpolicy.com/2014/01/21/the-case-for-aid/; Organisation for Economic Co-operation and Development, "Development Aid at a Glance: Statistics by Region: Africa," accessed May 20, 2018, https://www.oecd.org/dac/stats/documentupload/2%20Africa%20%20 Development%20Aid%20at%20a%20Glance%202015.pdf; Mark Anderson, "Aid to Africa: Donations from West Mask $60bn Looting of Continent," *The Guardian*, July 15, 2014,

http://www.theguardian.com/global-development/2014/jul/15/aid-africa-west-looting-continent.

19. Moyo, *Dead Aid*; Mwenda, "Foreign Aid"; Easterly, *White Man's Burden*; Acemoglu et al., "Why Foreign Aid Fails"; Deaton, *The Great Escape*.

20. Craig Burnside and David Dollar, "Aid, Policies, and Growth," *American Economic Review*, 90, no. 4 (2000): 847–868.

21. For discussion, see Nicole Hassoun, "Institutional Theories and International Development," *Global Justice: Theory Practice Rhetoric*, 7 (2014): 12–27, doi:http://dx.doi.org/10.21248/gjn.7.0.44 REFBACKS.

22. Sachs, "The Case for Aid."

23. Ruth Levine, *Case Studies in Global Health: Millions Saved* (Sudbury, MA: Jones and Bartlett Publishers, 2007); Colette Flight, "Smallpox: Eradicating the Scourge," *BBC*, February 17, 2011, http://www.bbc.co.uk/history/british/empire_seapower/smallpox_01.shtml.

24. Sachs, "The Case for Aid"; Jeffrey D. Sachs, *The End of Poverty* (New York: Penguin Books, 2005).

25. Global Fund, "Report Shows 17 Million Lives Saved," *The Global Fund*, September 21, 2015. http://www.theglobalfund.org/en/news/2015-09-21_Report_Shows_17_Million_Lives_Saved/.

26. Hassoun, "Empirical Evidence"; Nicole Hassoun, "The Global Health Impact Index: Promoting Global Health," *PLoS ONE* 11, no. 2 (2016): e0148946.

27. Mary Moran et al., "G-Finder 2012 Neglected Disease Research and Development: A Five-Year Review," Policy Cures, accessed May 25, 2018, http://www.policycures.org/downloads/GF2012_Report.pdf.

28. World Health Organization, "2.1 Billion People Lack Safe Drinking Water at Home, More than Twice as Many Lack Safe Sanitation," published July 12, 2017, http://www.who.int/news-room/detail/12-07-2017-2-1-billion-people-lack-safe-drinking-water-at-home-more-than-twice-as-many-lack-safe-sanitation; World Bank Group, "Indicators," accessed May 23, 2018, https://data.worldbank.org/indicator; Gustavo Capdevila, "Human Right: More Than 100 Million Homeless Worldwide," Inter Press Service News Agency, March 30, 2005, http://www.ipsnews.net/2005/03/human-rights-more-than-100-million-homeless-worldwide//.

29. World Bank Group, "Indicators."

30. Garrett Cullity, *The Moral Demands of Affluence* (Oxford: Clarendon Press, 2004).

31. Patti Tamara Lenard, *Health Inequalities and Global Justice* (Edinburgh: Edinburgh University Press, 2014); David Miller, *Principles of Social Justice* (Cambridge, MA: Harvard University Press, 2001).

32. Liam Murphy, "Institutions and the Demands of Justice," *Philosophy & Public Affairs* 27, no. 4 (1998): 251–291.

33. Miller, *Principles*; Lenard, *Health Inequalities*; Cullity, *Moral Demands*; Murphy, "Institutions."

34. John Hacker-Wright, "Is Charity a Virtue? Part 2," *The Virtue Blog*, published May 12, 2016, https://thevirtueblog.com/2016/05/12/is-charity-a-virtue-part-2/.

35. Max Roser and Esteban Ortiz-Ospina, "Global Extreme Poverty," in *Our World in Data*, accessed February 2, 2018, https://ourworldindata.org/extreme-poverty/.

36. Branko Milanovic, *The Haves and the Have Nots* (New York: Basic Books, 2012).

37. Chart made using data from Angus Maddison, *Contours of the World Economy, 1–2030 AD: Essays in Macro-Economic History* (New York: Oxford University Press, 2007), 70.

38. World per capita income as of 2014 is approximately $16,100 in 2014 U.S. dollars, up from under $500 in 1800. https://www.cia.gov/library/publications/the-world-factbook/fields/2004.html

39. Thomas Pogge, "Eradicating Systemic Poverty: Brief for a Global Resources Dividend," *Journal of Human Development* 2 (2001): 59–77, 65.

40. David Weil, *Economic Growth* (New York: Pearson, 2013 [3rd ed.]), 453.

41. Weil, *Economic Growth*, 450.

42. Weil, *Economic Growth*, 450–451.

43. Seyla Benhabib, *The Rights of Others* (New York: Cambridge University Press 2004), 100. She does not cite, mention, or engage with any of the economics literature on this subject.

44. Thomas Pogge, "Poverty and Human Rights," accessed February 2, 2018, http://www2.ohchr.org/english/issues/poverty/expert/docs/Thomas_Pogge_Summary.pdf.

45. Adam Smith, *The Wealth of Nations*, V.3.92.

46. Adam Smith, *The Wealth of Nations*, V.3.92.

47. David Landes, *The Wealth and Poverty of Nations: Why Some Are So Rich and Some Are So Poor* (New York: W. W. Norton and Co., 1999), 423; Lance Davis and Robert Huttenback, *Mammon and Empire* (New York: Cambridge University Press, 1987); Lance Davis and Robert Huttenback, "The Political Economy of British Imperialism: Measures of Benefits and Support," *Journal of Economic History* 42 (1982): 119–130; Nathan Rosenberg and L. E. Birdzell, *How the West Grew Rich* (New York: Basic Books, 1986); Mitsuhiko Kimura, "Economics of Japanese Imperialism in Korea, 1910–1939," *Economic History Review* 48 (1999): 555–574; Patrick O'Brien, "The Costs and Benefits of British Imperialism, 1846–1914," *Past and Present* 120 (1988): 163–200; Avner Offer, "The British Empire, 1870–1914: A Waste of Money?" *Economic History Review* 46 (1993): 215–238; Naill Ferguson, "British Imperialism Revisited: The Costs and Benefits of 'Angloglobalization,'" *Historically Speaking* 4 (2003): 21–27; Michael Edelstein, *Overseas Investment in the Age of High Imperialism: The United Kingdom, 1850–1914* (New York: Columbia University Press, 1982); J. Foreman-Peck, "Foreign Investment and Imperial Exploitation: Balance of Payments Reconstruction for Nineteenth-Century Britain and India," *Economic History Review* 42 (1989): 354–374; Philip R. Coelho, "The Profitability of Imperialism: The British Experience in the West Indies," *Explorations in Economic History* 10 (1973): 253–280; Paul McDonald, "Those Who Forget Historiography Are Doomed to Republish It: Empire, Imperialism, and Contemporary Debates about American Power," *Review of International Studies* 35 (2009): 45–67; D. K. Fieldhouse, "'Imperialism': A Historiographical Revision," *Economic History Review* 14 (1961): 187–209.

48. Or better, ended up being forced to set up inclusive institutions. See Daron Acemoglu, Simon Johnson, and James Robinson, "The Colonial Origins of Comparative Development: An Empirical Investigation," *American Economic Review* 91 (2001): 1369–1401; Daron Acemoglu and James Robinson, *Why Nations Fail* (New York: Crown Business, 2013).

49. Daron Acemoglu and James Robinson, "Unbundling Institutions," *Journal of Political Economy* 113 (2005): 949–995; Acemoglu and Robinson, *Why Nations Fail*; Tyler Cowen and Alex Tabarrok, *Modern Principles of Economics* (New York: Worth, 2010), 92–106; Douglas North, *Institutions, Institutional Change, and Economic Performance* (Cambridge: Cambridge University Press, 1990); Douglas North, John Joseph Wallis, and Barry Weingast, *Violence and Social Orders* (Cambridge: Cambridge University Press, 2012); Dani Rodrik, Arvind Subramanian, and Francisco Trebbi, "Institutions

Rule: The Primacy of Institutions over Geography and Integration in Economic Development," *Journal of Economic Growth* 9 (2004): 131–165; Gérard Roland, *Development Economics* (New York: Pearson, 2014), 108.

50. North, *Institutions*, 3.

51. Rodrik, Subramanian, and Trebbi, "Institutions Rule," 13; Mathias Risse, "Does the Global Order Harm the Poor?" *Philosophy and Public Affairs* 33 (2005): 349–376. Similarly, Tyler Cowen and Alex Tabarrok, *Principles of Economics*, 101, summarize, "the key to producing and organizing the factors of production [in ways that lead to prosperity] are *institutions* that create appropriate *incentives*."

52. Acemoglu and Robinson, "Unbundling Institutions"; Acemoglu and Robinson, *Why Nations Fail*; Acemoglu, Johnson, and Robinson, "Colonial Origins"; Daron Acemoglu, Simon Johnson, and James Robinson, "Reversal of Fortune: Geography and Institutions in the Making of World Income Distribution," *Quarterly Journal of Economics* 117 (2002): 1231–1294; Robert Hall and Charles Jones, "Why Do Some Countries Produce So Much More Output per Worker than Others?" *Quarterly Journal of Economics* 114 (1999): 83–116; Joshua Hall and Robert Lawson, "Economic Freedom of the World: An Accounting of the Literature," *Contemporary Economic Policy* 32 (2014): 1–19; Hernando de Soto, *The Mystery of Capital* (New York: Basic Books, 2000).

53. Angus Deaton, *The Great Escape* (Princeton, NJ: Princeton University Press, 2013), 268–269.

54. Christopher Coyne, *Doing Bad by Doing Good: Why Humanitarian Aid Fails* (Stanford, CA: Stanford University Press, 2013), 47.

55. Deaton, *Great Escape*, 285.

56. Hristos Doucouliagos and Martin Paldam, "Aid Effectiveness on Accumulation. A Meta Study," *Kyklos* 59 (2006): 227–254; Hristos Doucouliagos and Martin Paldam, "The Aid Effectiveness Literature: The Sad Results of 40 Years of Research," *Journal of Economic Surveys* 23 (2009): 433–461; I. A. Elbadawi, "External Aid: Help or Hindrance to Export Orientation in Africa," *Journal of African Economics* 8 (1999): 578–616; R. Lensink and H. White, "Are There Negative Returns to Aid?" *Journal of Development Studies* 37 (2001): 42–65.

57. Here, I draw from Coyne, *Doing Bad*, 51. See also Abhijit Banerjee and Esther Duflo, *Poor Economics* (New York: Public Affairs, 2011); Paul Collier, *The Bottom Billion: Why the Poorest Countries Are Failing and What Can Be Done About It* (New York: Oxford University Press, 2007); William Easterly, *The Elusive Quest for Growth* (Cambridge, MA: MIT Press, 2002); Easterly, *White Man's Burden*; Moyo, *Dead Aid*; R. Glenn Hubbard and William Duggan, *The Aid Trap: Hard Truths About Ending Poverty* (New York: Columbia Business School Publishing, 2009); Dean Karlan and Jacob Appel, *More than Good Intentions: Improving the Ways the Poor Borrow, Save, Learn, and Stay Healthy* (New York: Plume, 2011). Some studies claim to find that aid often has a positive effective on growth, but only on the condition that the recipient country already has good institutions, such as strong protections of private property and the rule of law (see, e.g., Craig Burnside and David Dollar, "Aid, Policies, and Growth," *American Economic Review* 90 [2000]: 847–868.) These studies corroborate the "institutions trump everything else" story: Aid is helpful only if the right institutions are in place. Other studies claim to find that aid always has *some* positive effect, even without good background institutions (e.g., see Henrik Hansen and Finn Tarp, "Aid and Growth Regressions," *Journal of Development Economics* 64 [2001]: 547–570). But most other studies claim to find *no* effect, or, even worse, that aid has a negative effect: Harold Brumm, "Aid, Policies, and Growth: Bauer Was Right," *Cato Journal* 23 (2003): 167–174; Raghuram Rajan and Arvind Subramanian, "Aid and Growth: What Does the

Cross-Country Evidence Really Show?" *Review of Economics and Statistics* 90 (2008): 643–665; Peter Bauer, *From Subsistence to Exchange* (Princeton, NJ: Princeton University Press, 2000); William Easterly, Ross Levine, and David Roodman, "Aid, Policies, and Growth: Comment," *American Economic Review* 94 (2004): 774–780; Doucouliagos and Paldam, "Aid Effectiveness"; Doucouliagos and Paldam, "Aid Effectiveness Literature"; Elbadawi, "External Aid"; Lensink and White, "Are There Negative Returns."

58. Acemoglu and Robinson, *Why Nations Fail*, 452–453.
59. Coyne, *Doing Bad*, 17.
60. Coyne, *Doing Bad*.
61. http://www.mountvernon.org/digital-encyclopedia/article/the-death-of-george
-washington/
62. Though, I do not think trade is a panacea for poverty or anything else and that we can constrain trade in ways that will make it more just. For discussion, see Hassoun, "Free Trade."
63. Mark Otter, "Domestic Public Support for Foreign Aid: Does it Matter?," *Third World Quarterly* 24 (2003): 115–125.
64. He ridicules many other arguments one might give for aid without seriously engaging with them. He simply asserts, for instance, that "philosophers are bad at philosophy" because some thought experiments others have proposed do not seem to him to be apt in light of the empirical evidence.
65. He says, "Under special conditions, certain targeted forms of aid can prevent death during an immediate crisis, but that's about it." I have already explained some of the methods researchers use to test aid programs (e.g., randomized controlled trials), and I have pointed out that testing can ensure aid does not harm people and make it more effective. So I will not belabor the point here.
66. In fact, in doing so, Brennan commits the sin he accuses other philosophers of committing: cherry-picking the evidence. Some argue that aid only promotes growth in good institutional environments and that we should make aid conditional on institutional quality. Others deny this. So, it seems further research is necessary to resolve all these debates. Moreover, the different authors use different metrics for institutional quality, and not all suppose that these institutions were instituted in colonial times. See discussion below.
67. He says, "It's 'unfortunate' that the institutional theory of wealth is correct. The reason it's unfortunate is that while we know which institutions create growth and which impede it, we don't know how to induce social change. We don't know how to get countries with bad institutions to switch to good institutions."
68. Some assume that aid will reduce poverty just in virtue of increasing growth, but different causes of growth may affect poverty differently. Moreover, the different studies use very different definitions of institutional quality. So it is difficult to draw any general conclusions from this literature. Finally, using colonial history as a proxy for good institutional quality today (as some do) seems suspect. Perhaps having better colonial rulers is what really helped some countries flourish while having worse rulers has long-lasting negative consequences. Alternatively, there may be other reasons why this difference in history matters besides the quality of the institutions the rulers left behind. For discussion and references, see Hassoun, "Institutional Theories," 20–23, and Acemoglu, Johnson, and Robinson, "Colonial Origins."
69. Consider again health aid. It seems hard to deny that some aid programs have improved health systems in developing countries while others have been successful even when health systems were lacking. Some aid aims to increase the number of hospitals and health workers available, while other aid efforts bring in foreign volunteers to

administer medicines or help people access adequate nutrition or clean water (Kramer et al., 2011; Guariso et al., 2017), But even simple drug donation programs can increase health systems' capacity. In donating ivermectin to treat and prevent river blindness in Africa, for instance, the pharmaceutical company Merck has helped train thousands of health workers, who have also gone on to distribute other drugs and interventions outside of this program. This suggests that foreign aid efforts can build good institutions, but that aid can also work in the absence of such institutions. Of course, foreign aid can also use up health system capacity and divert health workers' efforts toward aid organizations' priorities—so it is important to focus on horizontal as well as vertical programs that improve health services generally and do not just focus on specific diseases or interventions.

He, Fang, Leigh L. Linden, and Margaret MacLeod. "A Better Way to Teach Children to Read? Evidence from a Randomized Controlled Trial." Working Paper, Columbia University, May 2009. Available at: https://www.povertyactionlab.org/evaluation /searching-better-way-teach-children-read-india

Banerjee, Abhijit, Abhijit Chowdhury, Jishnu Das, and Reshmaan Hussam. "The Impact of Training Informal Healthcare Providers in India." Cambridge: Abdul Latif Jameel Poverty Action Lab (2016). Accessed 8 Oct 2018. Available at: https://www .povertyactionlab.org/evaluation/impact-training-informal-healthcare-providers-india

Guariso, Andrea, Martina Björkman Nyqvist, Jakob Svensson, and David Yanagizawa-Drott. "An Entrepreneurial Model of Community Health Delivery in Uganda." Cambridge: Abdul Latif Jameel Poverty Action Lab (2017). Accessed 8 Oct 2018. Available at: https://www.povertyactionlab.org/evaluation/entrepreneurial-model-community -health-delivery-uganda

70. Or maybe there is some reason why some colonists succeeded in building better institutions, while foreigners today cannot help build institutions with aid despite the fact that many of those who offer aid live in poor countries. But, then, Brennan must explain where the difference lies. Moreover, it strains credulity to think that the only way to help improve institutions in poor countries is to colonize them.

71. He says, "The overwhelming consensus in economics is that rich countries are rich because they have good institutions, while poor countries are poor because they have bad institutions." And: "As economist Dani Rodrik summarizes, when it comes to explaining economic growth and why some countries are rich and others poor, 'the quality of institutions trumps everything else.'"

72. Deaton, A. *Instruments of Development: Randomization in the Tropics, and the Search for the Elusive Keys to Economic Development.* Princeton University: Princeton University Press, 2009.

The World Bank Group. *Indicators of Governance and Institutional Quality.* Washington DC: World Bank, 2006. Retrieved February 26, 2018. From: http://siteresources.worldbank. org/INTLAWJUSTINST/Resources/IndicatorsGovernanceandInstitutionalQuality.pdf

Acemoglu, D., and James A. Robinson. *Why Nations Fail: The Origins of Power, Prosperity and Poverty.* New York: Crown Business Publishing, 2012.

Acemoglu, D., Johnson, S., and Robinson, J. A. "The Colonial Origins of Comparative Development: An Empirical Investigation." *American Economic Review 91*, vol. 5 (2001): 1369–1401.

73. He says, "[W]hile imperialism does not explain why some countries are rich, it may partly explain why some now remain poor. When imperialist powers established colonies, they replaced existing institutions with new institutions . . . In places such as the Congo, where Europeans faced high mortality rates (because of disease), imperial

powers established growth-inhibiting extractive institutions. When the European powers abandoned or lost their colonies, these bad institutions remained behind, and generally morphed into current dysfunctional institutions those countries have today."

74. Similarly, one can grant that African countries (and many people in them) did better when the Cold War ended, but that is not because aid stopped (it did not—in fact, official development assistance to sub-Saharan Africa has increased significantly since 1960) (World Bank, 2018). Rather, I would guess that part of the explanation for why African countries have grown in recent years is that these great powers were no longer fighting in the region—the Cold War here was a hot war in many parts of Africa (Lawrence, 2004).

   Lawrence, Mark. "Hot Wars in Cold War Africa." *Reviews in American History* 32, no. 1 (2004): 114–121.

75. Wenar, Leif. *Blood Oil: Tyrants, Violence and the Rules that Run the World.* Oxford: Oxford University Press, 2015.

76. For instance, I know of few who have argued, as does Brennan, that "the reason some countries are rich and others are poor is that natural resources are unevenly distributed around the globe. The rich are rich because they have or had access to more or better resources than the poor countries did." However, Brennan says this is one of the main reasons people "find redistributive views appealing."

73. For more on this issue, see Bas van der Vossen and Jason Brennan, *In Defense of Openness* (New York: Oxford University Press, 2018).

74. In Nicole Hassoun, *Globalization and Global Justice* (New York: Cambridge University Press, 2012), Hassoun offers more substantive arguments for why rich countries should provide high amounts of aid to poor countries. See van der Vossen and Brennan, *In Defense of Openness*, 138–142, for a critique; we think her main argument is incoherent.

CHAPTER 4

Immigration

MARKETS WITHOUT LABOR LIMITS:
CRIME, WELFARE, JOBS, AND CULTURE
PETER JAWORSKI

1. Introduction

I was a refugee. In 1984, my family decided we would never return to Poland, where I was born.

We were wealthy in Poland. That's why, in 1984, we all received permission to travel to West Germany. That was not done, typically. Typically, they might let a father and his daughter travel, while not giving passports to the mother or daughter (all passports were held at the local police station, so you had to request them to travel).

While we were on vacation in West Germany, my father got a phone call from his mother.

"There's a letter for you from the local police station," she told my father. He asked her to open it and find out what was in it.

What they wanted was to have a meeting with him.

These sorts of letters were normal in Poland at the time. Sometimes, people would just get a parking ticket, or have to pay some fine. But other times, people would disappear.

My mother had distributed anti-Communist leaflets from underneath me in downtown Wroclaw when I was a baby. My father had agreed to let his friends put a radio transmitter in our home for Radio Free Poland. My parents were worried that this letter was about their political activities. They decided they couldn't risk it, so they filed for asylum, and were granted it.

We also immediately filed paperwork to emigrate to Canada. We waited three years for the approval. Canada eventually did say yes, and so we left Germany in 1987, and became happy Canadians in 1992.

That's my personal story. There are thousands of stories just like mine. There would be millions of these stories, if it weren't for one thing: Governments around the world restrict people's movements across international borders.

They do so for many reasons. They offer reasons because they recognize that even if we begin our debate with the baseline of states having a right to enforce their borders, rather than with my preferred baseline of individuals having freedom of movement, having a right to do something doesn't mean that every exercise of that right is rightful. Your freedom of speech doesn't mean it is perfectly morally okay for you to wear a swastika on your sleeve. It's legal for you to do so, but you would be a bad person if you did. You are legally permitted to wear a shirt with Stalin's face on it, but you shouldn't. And even if states have a right to restrict freedom of movement, they shouldn't, is my view. Or, they shouldn't in the vast majority of cases. Sometimes they may be justified in acting on their right, but acting on this right requires meeting a very high justificatory burden. Canada, for example, has probably never met that burden.

As I said, restrictionists do offer attempts at justification. And there are many possible justifications. The ones I have heard most often are these: We need to restrict freedom of movement for the sake of lower crime, lower taxes (because immigrants will consume more welfare benefits), ensuring greater employment opportunities for citizens, and preserving customs and culture (including political institutions). Below, I will address each of these using a number of strategies. First, I will simply rely on the authority of economists and other social scientists to tell us what the facts are here. I'm no economist, so I turn to their literature to see what we have most reason to believe about the facts.

But not everyone accepts these facts. That's frustrating, yes, but we can try a different approach. We can just accept that restrictionists have the "true facts" and ask what follows about other policies. Here, we will look at the structure of anti–freedom-of-movement arguments and try to see if that structure generalizes in relevantly similar ways in somewhat different domains. This strategy is an attempt to show that the arguments against increasing freedom of movement are weak. They are weak because, if they were strong, those who accept them would think them weighty in these other domains as well, but they probably don't. If I'm right, we will have reductios, rather than implications.

2. Economics of Immigration

Let's begin with the easiest case in support of freedom of movement. The easiest case goes like this: World economic prosperity matters. It matters how people in Bangladesh and Poland and Ireland are doing, just as it matters how people in Canada and the United States and Mexico are doing. From a world perspective, permitting open labor markets (i.e., free movement of people) would make the world significantly richer.

Estimates suggest world gross domestic product (GDP) would double. Indeed, one article is subtitled "Trillion-Dollar Bills on the Sidewalk?"[1] The article answers that that is what we are doing—leaving a trillion dollars of value on the ground—when we restrict free movement. The title is based on an economics joke about a $20 bill on the ground:

"Look," says so-and-so to an economist, "a $20 bill on the ground!"

"Impossible," says the economist, "if there really were a $20 bill on the ground, someone would have picked it up by now."

That's basically what we've been doing—leaving plenty of $20 bills on the ground. It doesn't matter whether the estimates are precisely right, what matters is that restrictions on labor mobility make us poorer. And that's a bad thing, because that makes our lives go worse than what would otherwise be the case. This is not merely bad, but calamitous. What we are doing is condemning millions of current and future people to a life of poverty. We really should not do that.

I'm not an economist, so I rely on the expertise of economists to tell me whether or not these estimates are accurate. At the moment, the consensus among those who publish in the peer-reviewed literature is that restrictions on labor mobility slow economic growth.

Economists tell us that the data show the following: Immigration restrictions lower global GDP, and immigration restrictions in a given country generally reduce GDP for that country. Meanwhile, studies on the effect of immigration on crime show that immigrants are "much *less likely* than natives to commit crimes." Meanwhile, the "presence of large numbers of immigrants seems to lower crime rates."[2] Immigrants consume slightly more in welfare than the native-born, but their net economic effect is positive. With respect to jobs, the studies show that the effect of immigrants is not as negative as some suggest. And in terms of culture, immigrants do, in fact, integrate. So at least along those metrics, we should prefer more, rather than less, freedom of movement.

3. Flipping the Script: Where Should the Borders Be?

But let's suppose that the economists don't know what they are doing, or that they come to the wrong conclusions because they don't have access to all the relevant data, are biased, or have the wrong theory. Perhaps they do not understand that some other value—like preservation of culture, say—is worth many trillions of dollars, or is more important than avoiding misery and poverty. So, assuming all of that, here's a question: Where should our borders be?

Let's recall the reasons we have for restricting movement. They include worries about crime, taxes, and welfare; preserving jobs for insiders; and preserving the customs and culture of insiders as against outsiders.

The American journalist Colin Woodard, in his *American Nations: A History of the Eleven Rival Regional Cultures of North America*,[3] suggests that there are, as the title suggests, eleven different, and rival, cultures within North America. North America, however, consists of three countries, not eleven. The borders of these nations, in addition, do not respect national borders. What he calls "the Midlands" incorporates southern Ontario and parts of the American Northeast. "El Norte" ranges from northern Mexico, up through southwestern Texas, takes in about half of New Mexico, and continues through the southern parts of Nevada and California. "The Far West," meanwhile, begins where El Norte ends, and cuts straight up north incorporating all of those states, plus the western part of Manitoba, most of Saskatchewan and Alberta, and a slice of eastern British Columbia. One last one: "New France" takes in a great deal of Quebec and reappears as a "blip" all the way down south around and including the city of New Orleans.

Woodard might be entirely wrong about the details of his culturography, but it wouldn't matter. The precisely accurate map of cultural nations within these three countries would also demonstrate the main point, and the only relevant part of this argument: North America has many different nations within it, and those nations range across and cut within our country borders. Accepting this fact leads to this point: If culture is so important, then shouldn't borders be where the nations are, and not where our countries happen to be? Similarity of culture surely played a historical role in where our country borders were established, but so did a lot of wars, accidents, and other historical contingencies, like the sale of Alaska in 1867, or the weird Alaska boundary dispute that was settled in 1904 with the votes of five judges—two from the United States, two from Canada, and one from England—where the British, in a move that still upsets some Canadians, cast the decisive vote in favor of America.

The question is, if you think it is so important, shouldn't you want the United States, Canada, and Mexico to be carved up differently? On its face, it looks like the implication of the claim that dissimilarity of culture is a reason to keep those with different cultures out is that we should use that information to determine where borders should be. That suggests that each of the eleven nations within North America should have a country of its own. But most people who want to enforce borders don't want to change where the borders are. That suggests that however strong similarity of culture is as a reason to enforce borders, it is not really that strong. Put differently, if you think reasons of culture are very good reasons, then you, too, should be a secessionist.

4. My Dangerous Situation

To make this personal again, consider my situation for a minute.[4] I live in Arlington, Virginia. Arlington is very rich, votes Democratic, is very educated, has excellent education and health care systems, and is, in general, a wonderful place to live. Our crime rates and unemployment figures are low. Our educational attainment is very high. We are mostly a white-collar crowd, and we drink our tea with a pinky in the air.

Tangipahoa, Louisiana, is none of those things. It is very poor, is uneducated, votes Republican, has poor education and health systems, and is, in general, dramatically different from Arlington. The crime rates are higher, and job prospects are relatively a great deal poorer. Culturally, we are very different.

And yet, there is nothing stopping someone from Tangipahoa from getting in her car and driving straight up to Arlington. No one will check to make sure that she shares our culture, that she won't steal Arlingtonian jobs, that she shares our commitment to gender equality, that she practices a religion sufficiently similar to ours, that she believes in the First Amendment, and so on. No one will check her car for weapons, except if she is pulled over by the highway patrol, but this isn't guaranteed. There is no border in her path from her parish to my county. There are plenty of administrative borders, but no physical barrier where we can ensure the preservation of Arlingtonianness.

Shouldn't there be a border separating us? Whatever reasons we might offer for keeping outsiders out, they surely apply in my case. Crime? Yes. Taxes and welfare? Yes. Jobs? Yes. Culture? Yes. And so on.

But not only is there no border between us, hardly anyone is actually fighting for one. If it isn't clear, I've written the above with my tongue firmly in my cheek. I don't mean it. I don't have a problem with people from Tangipahoa getting in their car and moving to Arlington. But, then again, I don't have a problem with people from Tamaulipas, Mexico, getting in their car and driving straight up and east to Arlington. The difference between Arlingtonians and Tangipahoans is about the same as the difference between Arlingtonians and Tamaulipasians.

It's worth pointing out that there are, and have been, secessionist movements in North America. Quebec, for example, has a long history of flirting with secession from Canada. In the United States, there are sporadic movements for secession as well. The arguments of the secessionists include arguments that those who want stricter enforcement of borders sometimes make. They say, "We should preserve our culture, including our language, and so keep people with different cultures out, and have a country of our own!" The only difference is that secessionists are more honest with respect to the implication of the arguments than non-secessionist strict country border enforcers are. If they were consistent, they would think we have very good and weighty reasons to turn North America from a continent of three countries to a continent with eleven countries. They would want to put a border between Tangipahoa and Arlington.

5. Population Shock
But what if lots and lots of people were to move? People raise this as a worry. These are cases of "population shock"—cases where significant numbers of outsiders "flood" insiders. If we allowed many people to come, many people would come. And while we can integrate lots of outsiders, we cannot integrate lots and lots of them. What would happen if millions suddenly came across the border, flooding our labor market, putting strain on our institutions, and creating an enormous administrative burden in the process?

The trouble with this objection is that we have plenty of examples of population shocks without terrible consequences. The end of World War II meant the return of lots and lots of soldiers to the labor market. It took some adjustment, but our labor market managed just fine. During the Irish potato famine, millions, lots and lots, of Irish settled in the United States and Canada. Between 1820 to 1930, some estimate that about 4.5 million Irish moved to the United States alone. Now, about 32 million Americans—10% of the population!—have Irish roots. Non-Irish Americans hated the Irish, as did Canadians. All kinds of scary stories were told about the Irish; all kinds of fears were raised about them. At the time, the Irish were considered a different race from other Caucasians, so embarrassingly dumb were we back then. Protestant Americans were scared and worried about Catholics; Catholics, after all, take their marching orders from the pope in Rome, and not the president in Washington, DC, it was thought.

Sure enough, there were plenty of skirmishes between the Irish and the non-Irish, and tensions really were high. But was this a result of the Irishness of the Irish conflicting with the Americanness of the Americans? Hardly. The reason why there were skirmishes was because anti-Irish and anti-Catholic sentiment was so high, and not because the Irish were prone to skirmish. It is a bit of a self-fulfilling prophecy to predict that outsiders will cause a hullabaloo if they were permitted inside, and then immediately reach for a megaphone when they come. The stink that was raised could be traced to insiders with anti-Irish feeling, not to the Irish. Meanwhile, the economy grew.

And finally, consider the shock of permitting women into the labor force, and giving them the vote. That fits the description of a population shock. Despite all the worries about how our politics would change, and worries about the negative impact of women in the labor force, these worries did not materialize. Meanwhile, the economy also grew.

6. Two Ways to Increase Population

We can increase the population of a country in two ways. One way is through importation; the other is through procreation. People say that we should strictly enforce borders because outsiders are, in some cases, more likely to commit crimes, consume welfare more than they pay in taxes, take insider jobs, and change our culture. Of course, we don't know enough about specific individuals to make this judgment precisely, but we generalize based on socioeconomic and other characteristics. We say that people of this type shouldn't be let in. We don't need more of them.

Here, we are considering only an increase in population, and we are assuming that current insiders have a right, through their political institutions, to determine which outsiders get to come in, or whether any of them get to come in at all. Insiders get to pick and choose, based on generalizations that serve as predictive tools for how individuals will behave once inside, and what they are likely to do when they get inside.

Notice, however, that this very same method of socioeconomic generalization can be applied not just to outsiders, but to insiders as well. If these worries are really significant worries, justifying strict restrictions on who gets to increase our population by moving here, and if certain generalizations about population types are sufficient grounds for this, then these very same premises should justify restricting who can increase our population by procreating. Shouldn't we license parents?

Some people do support restricting people's right to start families. Like secessionists, these people are consistent. They consider reasons of crime, taxes and welfare, jobs, and culture to be weighty reasons. They see that those reasons, if they justify strict restrictions on freedom of movement, justify restrictions on freedom of starting a family as well. But if you, like most people, don't think those reasons are weighty enough to justify the latter, then you shouldn't think them weighty enough to justify the former either.

7. Flipping the Script Part Two: Kick 'Em Out

Recall what I said above: Some insiders are more like outsiders than they are like insiders, and vice versa. That's why there are many more than three nations within the three countries of North America.

Now consider the reasons we are looking at for keeping certain people out: crime, taxes and welfare, jobs, and culture. Every one of these reasons that we think are weighty enough to restrict people's freedom of movement is, you should notice, also a reason to kick certain people out.

The philosopher Chris Freiman pointed this out.[5] He essentially tells us the following. Look, he says, you think that the likelihood that some individual will be a criminal is reason to keep her out of Canada, or America, or Mexico, and so on. But, he continues, there are already criminals among us, and those who were born here who have a higher likelihood of committing crimes. If we suppose that, say, Brazil or Argentina or Germany offered to accept all of our deportees, then it looks like whatever reason you offer to keep someone out will be a reason to ship at least some insiders out.

So, if an outsider's being more likely to commit crimes is a reason to keep her out, then an insider's being more likely to commit crimes is a reason to kick him out. If an outsider's being more likely to be a net tax consumer rather than a contributor is reason to keep her out, then an insider's being more likely to be a net tax consumer rather than a contributor is reason to kick him out. If an outsider's being from a different culture than ours is reason to keep her out, then an insider's embracing countercultural values is reason to kick him out. And so on.

Some people do support deportation. Like secessionists and supporters of parental licensing, these people are at least consistent. They see that if crime, taxes and welfare, jobs, and culture are reasons weighty enough to justify strict enforcement of our borders, then they are weighty enough to support deportation. But if you, like most people, don't think those reasons are weighty enough to justify the latter, then you shouldn't think them weighty enough to justify the former either.

8. Conclusion

Those who want to restrict my and your freedom of movement tell us that they have very good reason to keep us from improving our lives as we see it. They tell us that crime, taxes and welfare, jobs, and culture are, each of them, very good and weighty reasons to strictly enforce international borders. But none of these reasons are very strong. If they were very strong, then they would give us reason to deport some citizens. But they don't. If they were very strong, then they would give us reason to restrict who can have children. But they don't. If they were very strong, we would all have reason to become separatists and secessionists. But they don't. Far from being very good and very strong reasons, they turn out, upon reflection, to be a pretty poor justification for illiberalism. And these are supposed to not only justify strict enforcement of borders, but be important enough for us to accept being poorer than we otherwise would be. And I would rather we all be rich.

COMPREHENSION QUESTIONS

1. What are some of the economic effects of immigration presented here?
2. If someone believes cultural preservation is a good reason to restrict movements across borders, why (according to Jaworski) should she also be a secessionist?
3. How does Jaworski respond to the objection that less restrictive immigration laws could result in "population shock"?
4. Jaworski claims that there aren't strong reasons to limit movement across borders because "those who accept [those reasons] would think them weighty in . . . other domains as well, but they probably don't." What other domains might he have in mind?

DISCUSSION QUESTIONS

1. Jaworski argues that both immigration and procreation increase population, so those who believe immigration should be restricted must also commit to the belief that procreation should be restricted. Is restricting population growth by restricting immigration morally equivalent to restricting population growth by restricting procreation? Would we need equally "strong" reasons to justify the former as we would need to justify the latter?
2. Jaworski reasons that "if an outsider's being more likely to commit crimes is a reason to keep her out, then an insider's being more likely to commit crimes is a reason to kick him out." Is keeping someone out morally equivalent to kicking someone out? Would we need equally "strong" reasons to justify the former as we would need to justify the latter? Which moral or political values might influence how someone would answer these questions?
3. Jaworski allows that states sometimes "may be justified in acting on their right [to restrict freedom of movement]." What might be an example of such a justification?

Case 1

A 2015 Gallup study found that beliefs about national and personal economic situations are strong predictors of attitudes about immigration:

> Globally, adults who believe economic conditions in their countries are "fair" or "poor" are almost twice as likely to say immigration levels should decrease (42%) as are those who say conditions are "excellent" or "good" (25%). The same pattern is evident when examining people's outlooks for their countries' economic future—those who say conditions are "getting worse" are nearly twice as likely to say immigration should decrease as those who say conditions are "getting better" (48% vs. 25%, respectively).

Case 1 (continued)

> In nearly all regions of the world, people who see their economic condi-
> tions as excellent or good are more likely to have positive outlooks on immi-
> gration. These gaps are quite large in several countries, including the United
> States (46% vs. 25%), Germany (43% vs. 25%), Canada (41% vs. 21%) and China
> (22% vs. 11%) . . .
>
> Adults who live in countries with the highest unemployment rates show
> the most negative attitudes toward immigration to their countries. Nearly half
> of adults in countries with unemployment rates higher than 15% believe im-
> migration should decrease.
>
> People's personal employment status also strongly relates to whether
> they want to see lower immigration levels. Compared with others in the work-
> force, those who are not working but are actively looking for work and able to
> begin work are considerably more likely to want immigration decreased (40%
> of the unemployed vs. 33% of those not unemployed).*

Should these kinds of factors affect how we assess Jaworski's arguments? Or
if we ourselves are facing unemployment, should we do our best to bracket that
concern?

———————

*https://news.gallup.com/poll/186341/economic-outlook-shapes-views-immigration.aspx

FOR (SOME) IMMIGRATION RESTRICTIONS
HRISHIKESH JOSHI

1. The Coercion-Based Argument

Many philosophers think that immigration restrictions involve coercion.
That is, controlling the movement of people across national borders involves
making people do what they don't want to do—namely, stay where they are
geographically—by threat of force. Where the state shares a land border with
a source of potential immigrants, it may use border guards to deter or forcibly
repel potential immigrants who lack the needed documents. When it comes to
airports, it is typically not possible to board a plane headed to a country without
the required documentation—any attempts to do so are typically met with expulsion by security guards. Furthermore, if any such attempts succeed, and a potential immigrant reaches an airport located in the said country, he will usually be
repatriated unless he can claim asylum or some other legal status.[6]

Some philosophers see this coercion as being deeply problematic: What gives
states the right to coerce foreigners in this way? The question here is not merely
about states having the right to exclusive legal power over a territory. For even if
you think that states have the right to be the sole lawmakers and enforcers on a
piece of land, it still doesn't follow that this gives them the right to exclude foreigners from entering and settling on that land. Indeed, there are many things
states may not do even if they are the sole arbiters of justice—they may not arbitrarily arrest, torture, or kill their citizens, for example. Likewise, is coercively
preventing foreigners from settling on the territory over which a state has dominion something a state may not do?

A major theme in the recent literature making such a case is that we should think of non-coercion as the moral default—and thus state coercion always stands in need of justification. In other words, the state shouldn't force people to behave in particular ways unless there are strong reasons for interfering with people's freedom. Different writers then go on to make substantive cases for why such coercion is not ultimately justified.[7]

In what follows, I consider a variety of purposes for which it's plausible that state coercion is justified. I then argue that if such state coercion is justified, then the coercion involved in certain immigration restrictions is justified as well. The reader, in the end, might of course deny that state coercion is justified in the examples I point to below—but then she is committed to a radical rethinking of much of our current policies on a host of issues. So if you think immigration restrictions are unjustified because they are coercive, you will be committed to thinking there should be drastically less state intervention in a host of other domains.

Even the most liberal modern states coerce us in many ways. The main way they do so is by stopping us from, or punishing us for, directly infringing on the (negative) rights of others. If you assault someone, the state puts you in jail, for example. But there are many other purposes for which coercion is used. For instance, whether justified or not, taxation is coercion. You don't have the option as to whether to pay your taxes. The state uses threats of force, including jail time, to make sure people pay what taxes it assigns to them.

Coercion is also often used for the purpose of protecting the interests of the domestic population with low socioeconomic status. Consider, for example, minimum wage regulations. Such regulations are coercive—if A is willing to pay B $X/hour and no more, and B desires to accept this offer, the state forbids this transaction with threat of force if X is lower than the minimum wage set by law. Furthermore, there can arise cases where high enough minimum wages are compatible with low unemployment only in the presence of trade restrictions, another form of coercion, so that cheap goods cannot be imported from elsewhere. While experts may debate the desirability of such policies, most seem to think that the state is at least within its rights to enact them.

Coercive laws are also employed to protect things we deem valuable in and of themselves. States seem to be within their rights to prohibit certain activities with respect to national parks containing valuable ecosystems—most people think it's fine for the state to forbid logging or hunting within such parks, for example.

Lastly, coercion is also legitimately used to prevent what economists call negative externalities. Consider the case of a cheap battery manufacturer. The manufacturer and consumers both benefit from his being able to use cheap toxic chemicals in the process and dumping them in the nearby river. But the state may legitimately prevent this mutually beneficial transaction, because the costs involved are not entirely internalized by the parties.

It thus seems that most people are committed to the view that states may legitimately use coercion to prevent negative externalities, promote the interests of their low-socioeconomic-status residents, and protect the existence of valuable things. If this is right, then there arises the possibility that the coercion involved in immigration restrictions is justified for these reasons, depending on what the empirical facts look like.

Let's take the case of negative externalities first. Whether or not, and to what extent, a particular immigration policy creates negative externalities on the existing population of a country is an empirical question, the answer to which cannot be determined from the armchair. It also plausibly can vary greatly based on the specifics of the immigration policy—most importantly, the characteristics and numbers of the immigrants admitted.

The recent immigration policies of Sweden and Germany, for example, which have ostensibly focused on helping large numbers of asylum seekers (though what percentage have actually been economic migrants is a topic of controversy), have arguably involved significant negative externalities, though they have no doubt benefited the asylum seekers themselves. Tino Sanandaji, an economist at the Stockholm School of Economics, has documented in detail the sorts of problems that Sweden's policy in particular has invited. Among the most striking facts is that while foreign-born people compose 17% of the Swedish population, they receive 60% of the welfare expenditures. Three-quarters of members of criminal gangs have immigrant backgrounds. A recent government-commissioned study from the Zurich University of Applied Sciences noted a surge in crime following Angela Merkel's decision in 2015 to open doors to a large number of asylum seek-ers. For example, in Lower Saxony, violent crime had decreased between 2007 and 2014, but was up by 10.4% by the end of 2016. Among the solved cases, 92.1% of the increase is attributable to newcomers. And while most of the murder victims were migrants themselves, 70% of robberies and 58.6% of sexual assault cases had German victims. In addition, several distinct sources and datasets confirm that in both Sweden and Germany, individuals with immigrant backgrounds have significantly higher violent crime rates as compared to the native population. Moreover, this appears to be the general trend over the last two decades.[8]

Given these negative economic and social externalities, it is plausible to argue that border coercion is justified. Moreover, these unpleasant facts demon-strate that immigration decisions, even if they are beneficial to parties who want to associate with potential immigrants such as family members and employers, may not always be a net positive for the welfare of the rest of a country's residents.

Consider now the second point, namely that coercion is justified in protect-ing the interests of a country's less well off. One foreseeable impact of having fully open borders is that it will drive wages down for less-skilled workers. This is just a function of supply and demand—a large influx of less-skilled workers from poor but populous countries will increase the number of people willing and able to do retail, agricultural, and fast-food jobs, for example. This will push the wages down for this type of work, thus adversely affecting the well-being of less-skilled workers already in the country.[9] For this reason, some progressive philosophers who think we have weighty special obligations to the domestic needy oppose open borders.[10] Of course, libertarians may not be convinced by this reasoning.

Hence, let me pose this as an if-then claim: If you think that we have special obligations to the domestic needy that justify coercion, then you should be wary of open borders proposals. Notice how radical denying such special obligations is, however. It would mean either that redistributive taxation is simply unjustified, or that rich countries should spend virtually nothing on their domestic needy, sending much of their tax collections abroad, since each dollar, euro, or yen goes much farther in Bangladesh or Kenya.

Lastly, as is evident in the case of national parks, coercion seems to be justified in preventing the destruction of something of value. Now, presumably liberal, high-trust societies are intrinsically valuable. Such societies embody valuable relationships among their residents, which are valuable in a way akin to the way that friendships are valuable. Liberal societies are also uniquely suited to human flourishing, for individuals there have the relatively robust ability to speak their minds, explore new ideas, create challenging writing and art, and so on.

If liberal societies are valuable in roughly these ways, and if having a regime of open borders would put the existence of such societies at risk, then there may be a further justification for border coercion. It is not unreasonable to think such a risk is substantial. Societies around the world differ not only with respect to superficial customs of dress and cuisine, but also with deeply held moral beliefs and social norms. Furthermore, some very populous countries have norms that are by any standard in tension with the norms of liberal society.

Consider the case of just one such country—Pakistan. A Pew Research survey published in 2013 found that the majority of people in the country believed that women should not have the choice as to whether to veil, that wives should always obey their husbands, that the death penalty is appropriate for apostasy, and that adulterers ought to be stoned.[11] Now, Pakistan has a population in excess of 200 million. Suppose Denmark, a broadly liberal society with a population of less than 6 million, is deciding whether to have an open borders regime or not. It seems reasonable for one to worry whether Denmark's liberal norms can survive a large enough movement of the representative citizen of Pakistan into its territory.

The issue is especially challenging given the fact that Denmark's per capita GDP is more than ten times as large as that of Pakistan, even after adjusting for purchasing power. Thus if Denmark were to announce a fully open borders policy, it's not unreasonable to expect many millions to move to the country seeking out better economic opportunities.[12] And if large enough numbers of people move, it's not unreasonable to expect that many of their social norms will remain largely intact. People don't change overnight, and they are less inclined to change if surrounded by large enough numbers of like-minded people. Of course, we don't have random controlled experiments involving such large movements between such diverse countries to make a definitive call.

But what should we reasonably expect to happen if a representative sample of 20 million people from Pakistan were to move to Denmark over the course of less than five years? Plausibly, informal social norms would move in the illiberal direction. The problem would be compounded by the eventual granting of voting rights—people will likely vote according to their antecedently held values, and it would not be unreasonable to expect newly elected politicians to enact illiberal laws. Such worries would be partially addressed by making newcomers ineligible to vote, perhaps for a long period of time. But whether this is itself consistent with liberalism is not obvious. Moreover, it's not obvious that such a policy would be feasible—disenfranchisement of large chunks of the population tends to invite social strife.

Now, I have used the case of Denmark and Pakistan to illustrate an extreme possibility. In reality there are several more roughly liberal societies besides Denmark, which are also more populous. Nonetheless, there are many societies that adopt illiberal norms on the whole as well, and several of these have rapidly growing populations.

All that is said in the preceding paragraphs applies of course to open borders policies, which by definition would not filter potential immigrants. If there is a good way for Denmark to filter immigrants from Pakistan, perhaps by using proxies like education, so that the representative immigrant from Pakistan to Denmark is not likely to continue to embrace the significantly illiberal norms accepted by the average resident of Pakistan, then the worries above will not apply for those immigrants. Furthermore, numbers will matter: If the stream of migration from broadly illiberal societies to broadly liberal ones is small enough, then some degree of assimilation is to be expected, depending on the specific context. The argument thus shouldn't be taken to suggest that Denmark is justified in admitting zero immigrants from Pakistan for this reason.

One way to resist these conclusions is to say that coercion is sometimes justified, but the bar for justification is very high—high enough that the sorts of considerations brought up earlier don't justify border coercion. The task for the defender of this position is to explain why the kinds of coercion that occur in non-immigration contexts—taxation, minimum wages, national parks—are justified. Of course, a philosopher arguing from anarcho-libertarian commitments may reject these forms of coercion as well. But if the only way to defend open borders is to adopt such a radical view of political philosophy, which in practice has very few adherents, then I consider the case for some immigration restrictions to stand on very solid ground.

2. Consequentialist Arguments

The preceding section considered open borders arguments that take deontological form—they start from the prima facie impermissibility of coercion, and argue that the prima facie case withstands scrutiny. I have claimed that the argument doesn't withstand scrutiny, given the empirical facts, and given the permissibility of state coercion in other contexts.

A separate case for open borders can be made on consequentialist grounds. In a widely cited paper, economist Michael Clemens argues that allowing for free migration would likely double world GDP. Doubling world GDP would mean lifting hundreds of millions of people out of poverty, particularly since those who would benefit most would be the global poor who would be able to move in search of better economic opportunities.[13] In light of this enormous potential good, it seems there better be very good reasons to keep immigration restrictions in place.

And perhaps, some will argue, given this enormous upside the sorts of considerations marshaled earlier are not adequate to justify immigration restrictions.

In what follows, I will tackle the consequentialist argument head-on by challenging the claim that in the long run the world would be a better place if open borders were instituted as a general rule. But before doing so, I will sketch the models and assumptions economists use when they make claims about dramatic potential increases in world GDP. I will then argue that such reasoning ignores worries about the potential long-term effects of migration.

Economists arguing for open borders start by observing that workers in different countries have vastly different productivity. Workers in the developed world are much more productive than workers in the developing world, even when controlling for the level of skill. Hence, someone moving from a poor enough country to the United States will likely experience a massive increase in productivity as well as wages. This observation is hard to dispute and is borne out by standard economic theory and available data.[14] The explanations for this change in productivity appeal to things like the infrastructure and amount of capital available in the United States, which in turn are maintained by its relatively good economic institutions.

But if this is right, then isn't allowing for free movement a way to massively increase world GDP and living standards for the global poor? How productive you are depends not only on you, but on the institutional context you find yourself in. Some countries have better economic and political institutions than others. So, instead of keeping some people stuck with bad institutions where they're less productive, shouldn't we move them to places with better institutions? Even if there are some net losers overall (for example, the poor in the developed countries), this seems to be a way to promote great good for the majority of the world population. The core proposal behind consequentialist open border thinking can be summed up thus: Let's move people from places with bad institutions to places with good institutions. In so doing, we'll be helping the global poor help themselves, as well as most of the rest of us, given increases in worldwide productivity. Hence, the average person will be much better off with open borders.

The problem with this reasoning is that it makes a crucial unfounded assumption: that the different sorts of institutions we see in different countries are fixed. But what if, as a result of large migrations, the institutions of the receiving countries themselves change? And what if they change for the worse in the long run? This possibility throws a huge wrench in the model. If we don't assume institutions are fixed, all bets are off—it may well even turn out that in the long run, open borders will result in aggregate world GDP being lower than it would otherwise been with some restrictions in place.

The worry that a country's institutions will change in the long run, depending on the numbers and average characteristics of the immigrants it accepts, is not unfounded, and there is mounting evidence to the effect. For one, new voters mean new policies, and new policies can affect long-run productivity.[15] Second, informal institutions and family relationships can travel with people as they move, and such institutions are important for economic performance.[16] In addition, trusting behavior among immigrants and its transmission to younger generations can depend significantly on the country of origin.[17] Importantly, trusting behavior affects economic growth—high-trust societies are able to grow faster and maintain higher levels of prosperity. Recent work in economics and behavioral science has also found that corruption tends to travel with people as they relocate.[18] A new paper by economist Eugen Dimant and colleagues estimates that immigration from highly corrupt countries to the Organization for Economic Co-operation and Development (OECD, a group of thirty-five fairly developed countries) dramatically raises corruption in host countries. Their models indicate a rise of almost one point out of seven, for every one hundred immigrants from highly corrupt countries per one thousand citizens. A striking result is that regardless of the econometric methodology they applied, the researchers found that movement of people from high-corruption countries boosts corruption in the host country. This is very important to keep in mind because some of the world's poorest countries, and hence those that will experience the greatest emigrations in an open borders regime, are also among the most corrupt.[19,20]

Lastly, in a paper for the prestigious *Journal of Economic Literature*, economists Enrico Spolaore and Romain Wacziarg provide strong reasons to think that prosperity has "deep roots." They write that a growing body of evidence in the economic development and history literature "suggests that economic development is affected by traits that have been transmitted across generations over the very long run."[21]

A key finding in this literature is that a country's migration-adjusted quality of institutions at 1500 A.D. strongly predicts the quality of current institutions and GDP per capita. That is, if you look at institutional quality of various places in 1500 A.D., and then take into account where people moved since then, you can predict with fairly good accuracy the institutional quality of a country today. Economist James Ang writes, "These findings suggest that a country that has more ancestors who lived in prosperous places tends to have better institutions today."[22] People, it seems, have tended to carry their institutions with them. And if they have generally done so in the past, what reason is there to think current movements will prove an exception to this centuries-long pattern?

What these emerging literatures point to is that assuming a country's institutions will remain fixed in the long run in the presence of open borders is a huge mistake. A polity's institutions don't fall down from heaven; they are a function of the residents and voters of the polity. So where does this leave us in the consequentialist calculus? Plausibly, it means we should be extremely wary of open borders. The main reason is that even if you're a utilitarian—so that you care about total well-being around the world rather than in a specific country or set of countries—you want there to be some countries with relatively good institutions. This is because these are the countries that generate much of the important scientific and technological innovations that enormously benefit the global poor. Just think of how much the global poor have benefited from antibiotics, the polio vaccine, light bulbs, fertilizers, cellphones, and so on—all of which have been invented in the developed world, thanks to its good institutions. Reducing the quality of developed-world institutions through open borders may be good, in the long run, for neither the host nations nor the global poor themselves.[23]

3. Conclusion

If you are convinced by the arguments of this essay, what kinds of immigration restrictions should you support? Would it be desirable or justifiable for developed countries to have a policy of admitting zero immigrants from poorer countries? I do not think so. Rather, what the arguments of this essay point toward is a policy of filtered restriction. Developed countries should find a way of creating filtering mechanisms when admitting citizens from countries with corrupt institutions or illiberal norms. They should find a way to admit as many immigrants as possible in a way that doesn't threaten the quality of their institutions in the long run and doesn't impose significant negative externalities on their citizens. After all, I have not denied that immigration restrictions involve coercion and that coercion should be avoided as a moral default. Moreover, freer immigration regulations with appropriate filtering mechanisms may indeed make the world a much better place.

What an adequate filtering mechanism will ultimately look like is an empirical question. Determining what the relevant and best available proxies are will require detailed social scientific research. If it turns out that highly educated immigrants are more likely to adopt liberal norms and less likely to increase the host country's corruption levels, for example, that's a reason to prefer highly educated immigrants, unless a better proxy can be found. Importantly, a just policy will involve making distinctions between different kinds of immigration, rather than treating it as an all-or-nothing issue. In the end, it will likely turn out that some kinds of immigration are to be allowed, and perhaps even encouraged, while others are not morally justified.[24]

COMPREHENSION QUESTIONS

1. What are the two claims of "defenders of open borders" that Joshi addresses in his argument?
2. What are some examples of apparently legitimate state coercion Joshi identifies?
3. How might open borders put the existence of liberal societies at risk?
4. In Joshi's imagined immigration scenario involving Pakistan and Denmark, he proposes problems related to voting that could arise. What are they?
5. What adverse long-term economic outcomes of open borders does Joshi foresee?

DISCUSSION QUESTIONS

1. What do you think it means to "be extremely wary" of open borders? What are the practical implications of such wariness?
2. Joshi identifies education status as a possible "filtering" criterion to identify potential immigrants who are more likely to adopt liberal norms (and thus should be allowed to immigrate to liberal nations). What other criteria, if any, could accomplish this task? Do you see any problems with this kind of policy approach?

Case 2

Immigration Policy in the United States

Like all other countries, the United States does not have open borders as a matter of law. It grants just over one million permanent resident spots, also known as "green cards," per year, and most people in the world are ineligible to apply.

In addition, immigration policy in the United States heavily focuses on family-based visas. In 2017, 66.4% of green cards went to family-based applications, which included spouses, parents, siblings, and children. Individuals who have a family member who is a citizen or legal permanent resident of the United States thus have an advantage over those who do not. Another 13% of green cards went to refugee and asylee applications. Just under 5% were allotted to what is known as the Diversity Lottery program where individuals from countries which have not sent more than a certain number of immigrants over the past few years can apply and are selected randomly.

Finally, 12.2% were allotted to employment-based visas, for people who had secured offers for employment in the United States with an employer willing and able to sponsor them. Employers must typically demonstrate that they are not able to find qualified workers in the United States. This category is the only one that prioritizes individuals with skills that are highly valued in the American labor market. Many applicants for such visas hold advanced degrees.[*]

American law also prevents immigration in great numbers from any specific country, regardless of its size. No more than 7% of immigrants within any category (employment, family, etc.) may be born in one particular country in any given year. As a result, individuals born in large countries like China face long waits in receiving their green cards. People born in smaller countries tend to have an advantage in this regard.[†]

What policy implications might be drawn from Joshi's arguments for the current immigration system used in the United States? What do you think should be changed, if anything?

---

[*]https://www.dhs.gov/sites/default/files/publications/Lawful_Permanent_Residents_2017.pdf
[†]https://www.uscis.gov/tools/glossary/country-limit

REPLY TO JOSHI
PETER JAWORSKI

Here's a bit more of my story: I told you I was a refugee, and that I've been an immigrant many times. For the last thirteen years, I've lived in the United States. In all that time, I haven't been able to vote. Until I became a resident two years ago, I wasn't eligible for many welfare or other tax benefits. Thirteen years without the vote; eleven without various benefits.

Joshi and I agree about a lot of things. I like his conclusion about filtering mechanisms and I share his worries about institutional quality. But while we agree about those things, I think the freedom to move is a cornerstone human freedom, and increasing wealth and well-being is especially morally weighty.

I also think that we can do a lot better for both insiders and outsiders, in terms of preserving this freedom and promoting world wealth.

So, for example, Joshi worries about what would happen to Denmark if 20 million Pakistanis were to move there. Probably, he says, it would do damage to the institutions that have resulted in Denmark being so rich. He raises this issue to forestall the argument that I, and many others, have made—namely, that we would be a lot richer if we had more immigration and emigration, based on what economists have said about the impact on world GDP from more open borders. That, he thinks, overlooks changing institutions. Why assume that Denmark would maintain the institutions that are laying the golden eggs in the face of not minor, but mass immigration? We should worry, he thinks, that many of these immigrants would come and either kill or attempt to kill the institutional geese that lay those golden eggs.

Assuming institutional quality will remain the same is, maybe, a smuggled-in assumption. But assuming that we have to hold all of the other institutions constant is also a smuggled-in assumption. Maybe there are ways to preserve the freedom of movement of Pakistanis *and* wealth-creating institutions. So, for example, we could restrict the voting rights of immigrants, in the same way that my voting rights are restricted. You can immigrate to Denmark, but you will have to wait a long time before you get to vote in our elections, the Danish might say. We could make it a ridiculously long time: thirteen years, for example.

If thirteen years is not enough, we could make them wait eighteen years. Eighteen years is how long people born in Denmark have to wait to get a say in elections. We could do the same for immigrants. I think worries about institutional quality would at least be less pronounced if we removed one of the major ways that people can change institutions: through voting.

Alternatively (or additionally), we could constitutionalize those wealth-creating, rights-protecting institutions. Whatever institutions are the ones that promote wealth and well-being, these can be incorporated into a constitutional framework that makes those institutions much more difficult to change.

As far as it goes, either or both these proposals are morally better than restrictions in at least two ways. First, people—all people, born anywhere—would preserve more of their freedom of movement. That is morally important. Second, we have every reason to believe that the world, or at least Denmark, would become richer thereby. A Denmark with 20 million additional Pakistanis would mean that about 20 million people will become richer and better off than they were before—and, most likely, the majority of 25,707,251 people will be richer and better off than before.

Rishi also worries about some of the evidence coming in from Sweden and Germany. Sixty percent of welfare expenditures are spent on immigrants, who compose only 17% of the Swedish population. And in Germany, a government-commissioned survey claims that there has been a 10.6% surge in crimes in Lower Saxony between 2014 and 2016.

If welfare expenditures on immigrants are too high, don't keep them out: Instead, let them in while limiting handouts. Make them wait, say, eleven years before they are eligible for some or any welfare benefits. Sweden has inordinately generous welfare policies; they could make them a bit more American.

If crime is a problem, don't keep them all out: Instead, exclude single, young men, fourteen to thirty years old, and let everyone else in. The study Joshi refers to shows that this group is overwhelmingly responsible for the crimes he mentions in Lower Saxony.

Although, what about all of Germany? The latest numbers show an almost 10% overall decrease in crime from 2016 to 2017 in Germany as a whole. The Federal Criminal Police reports that foreigners are less likely to commit crimes than those born in Germany in every category of crime (yes, *every*). It is also true that crimes committed by foreigners are more likely to be reported than crimes committed by Germans.

Despite Germany being one of the safest countries in the world to live, and getting safer, this is not the perception of Germans. Public opinion polls repeatedly show that Germans think crime is on the increase, and foreigners are to blame. If you ask anyone, in almost any country, they will say the same thing. In America, for example, despite reductions in crime, Americans continue to think that crime is worse now than in the past, and that foreigners are to blame.

This fact, what Bryan Caplan calls "anti-foreign bias," makes things politically difficult. Politics includes asking people what should be done, and people, despite the facts, have always said, "Close the door!" But what's best, all things considered, is to open the door.

I agree that, in principle, we have reason to enforce borders if we hold all else constant. But all those other things don't have to be held constant. Better to change welfare eligibility, voting rights, even our constitution, than to strip others of their freedom of movement, and leave all of these trillion-dollar bills lying on the ground.

COMPREHENSION QUESTIONS

1. What strategies does Jaworski offer for preserving institutions in the face of increased immigration?
2. What strategies does Jaworski offer for limiting crime and welfare expenditure increases linked with immigrant populations in Sweden and Germany?
3. Why is restricting voting "morally better" than restricting movement, according to Jaworski?

DISCUSSION QUESTIONS

1. Recall Joshi's concerns about the effects of limiting immigrants' voting rights. How could we determine whether this strategy would be effective or desirable?
2. What problems, if any, do you see with the idea of constitutionalizing institutions in order to protect them?
3. Jaworski suggests limiting eligibility for welfare benefits in order to decrease welfare expenditures on immigrants. What might be problematic about this strategy? Can you think of other strategies? What other information would it be helpful to gather in order to make an effective policy in this area?
4. How can "anti-foreign bias" be reduced?

REPLY TO JAWORSKI
HRISHIKESH JOSHI

It was a great boon to Peter Jaworski that he was able to move from Poland to Canada, and eventually the United States. I would further suggest that the receiving countries benefited as well. Jaworski teaches at a top university and trains his students to think critically about ethical issues. Overall, he likely improves U.S. institutions in the long run. It's a win–win situation.

I myself am an immigrant to the United States. I'm extremely glad to have had the chance to move here. Where I grew up, in India and St. Kitts and Nevis, the opportunities to pursue my dream of becoming a professional philosopher would have been severely limited or non-existent. For me, America has been a great source of professional, intellectual, and personal opportunities.

Given these facts, I do not and cannot advocate complete restrictionism about immigration. Immigration can be a win–win for both an immigrant and her new country. Immigrants make up about a quarter of entrepreneurs in the United States.[25] And contrary to some narratives, foreigners in STEM (Science, Technology, Engineering, and Mathematics) fields *increase* the wages of both college-educated and non–college-educated natives.[26] Immigration can have institutional benefits too. Israel's institutions have been shown to have improved as a result of large migrations from Russia.[27] Indeed, as Jaworski argues, there is much to be gained from more free movement.

But it is a mistake to conclude that *all* forms of immigration have these features. It's thus unhelpful to talk about immigration full-stop when discussing policy—it's absolutely crucial to distinguish between *different types* of immigration. Immigrants don't come from Immigrant Land. The average Iranian Ph.D. student, Somalian refugee, Nigerian doctor, Japanese tech executive, and Guatemalan migrant worker are about as different from one another as you can get.

The effects of specific immigration policies on particular outcomes also depend on the characteristics of the receiving country. For instance, Jaworski notes that immigrants commit less crime than natives, on average. This is true of the United States but certainly not true of Europe. That's because both the baseline crime rates and the immigration policy specifics differ greatly between these cases.

Jaworski's title suggests a view of open immigration policy as primarily constituting a welcome expansion of the global labor market. But as Nobel Prize–winning economist James Buchanan put it:

> The entry of an immigrant into an ongoing social-political-legal-economic order, with a defined membership, an experienced history, and a set of informal conventions, necessarily modifies the structure of "the game itself" . . . Membership involves more than a joining of the economic exchange network. Membership carries with it the power and authority, even if small, to modify the political-legal-constitutional parameters within which the economic game is played.[28]

This is admittedly abstract. Let me try to make matters concrete by way of just one example. What would happen if the United States suddenly opened its

borders—or, at least, dramatically eased immigration restrictions? One consequence, which I suspect Jaworski would agree about, is that income inequality
would spike, given that much of the population moving to the United States will
be relatively unskilled—that is, unable to perform the jobs of engineers, lawyers, and the like. Even supposing there is no downward pressure on wages of
native unskilled workers, what will result is a class of professionals and business-
people making six- and seven-figure salaries, and on the other hand, (hundreds
of) millions of workers making a handful of dollars per hour. Importantly, this
inequality might be persistent: The data show that there are strong intergenerational transmissions of educational and economic outcomes.[29] Of course, nothing nefarious needs to be going on. Workers are generally paid their marginal
product—that is, what the marginal worker contributes to the company's revenues in a competitive market.[30]

Would this be a sustainable situation in the long run? No. The massive inequality will cause people to rally for change.[31] Given that market forces will
produce such inequality when open borders are adopted, the new citizens, along
with many of their compatriots, will vote for policies that depart from market
pricing for labor—government-set wages, guaranteed work schemes, restrictions
on layoffs, and the like. But here's the rub: Lack of well-functioning markets,
coupled with bloated public sectors, is what explains much of the global disparity of income in the first place. Market-based economies, like the United States,
Japan, or Denmark, are dramatically wealthier than the more government-run
economies of Brazil or India (not to mention egregious cases like North Korea
or Venezuela). Indices of "economic freedom" correlate very strongly with GDP
per capita, as well as other indicators of development and well-being.[32] Economic
freedom also strongly predicts lower corruption.[33]

Open borders advocates might contend that all this is avoidable if the host
country denies newcomers the rights of citizenship (or, at least, delays this for a
long period). While this is the norm in countries like Qatar and the United Arab
Emirates, it is hard to think of the United States adopting such a rule. Can you
imagine living among hundreds of millions of disenfranchised people? When
open borders advocates suggest this as an option, they're idealizing too much.
Perhaps they think, from a rational perspective, such disenfranchisement would
be a good compromise. The new workers benefit after all, even if they are disenfranchised.[34] But it is difficult to imagine, given the culture and political history
of the United States, this being stable in the long run.[35]

Apart from the economic considerations, Jaworski stresses that cultural
preservation is not a good justification for restrictions. I think he is absolutely
right when it comes to things like food, language, and dress. But cultures around
the world also differ about core values and norms surrounding things like freedom of expression and the role of women in society. Here, Jaworski's point is less
obvious, especially where immigrants might not adopt equally liberal views.[36]

When thinking about immigration policy, we must look at our *non-ideal*
world and its dynamics. Good institutions are all-important but fragile. The
dilemma of immigration justice is what to do in light of this fact.

COMPREHENSION QUESTIONS

1. Why is Joshi supportive of immigration in cases like his own and Jaworski's?
2. What is one possible adverse economic outcome of eased immigration restrictions in the United States?
3. On Joshi's view, which aspects of culture in the receiving country are most important to preserve?

DISCUSSION QUESTIONS

1. Why might one believe that preserving liberal values and norms is more important than preserving other aspects of culture—like the prominence of a particular religious tradition, or some other significant aspect of how people organize their lives?
2. Joshi contends that there are important differences between immigrants and receiving countries that should be taken into account in order to implement effective policies. How might Jaworski respond to this perspective?

FURTHER READINGS

Buchanan, James. "A Two Country Parable." In *Justice in Immigration*, edited by Warren F. Schwartz. New York: Cambridge University Press, 1995.

Caplan, Bryan. "Why Should We Restrict Immigration?" *Cato Journal* 32 (2012): 5.

Carens, Joseph H. "Aliens and Citizens: The Case for Open Borders." *Review of Politics* 49, no. 2 (1987): 251–273.

Frum, David. "America's Immigration Challenge." *The Atlantic*, December 2015. https://www.theatlantic.com/politics/archive/2015/12/refugees/419976/

Huemer, Michael. "Is There a Right to Immigrate?" *Social Theory and Practice* 36, no. 3 (2010): 429–461.

Jones, Garett. "Do Immigrants Import Their Economic Destiny?" *Evonomics*, 2016. http://evonomics.com/do-immigrants-import-their-economic-destiny-garrett-jones/

National Academies of Sciences, Engineering, and Medicine. *The Economic and Fiscal Consequences of Immigration.* Washington, DC: National Academies Press, 2017.

Salam, Reihan. *Melting Pot or Civil War? A Son of Immigrants Makes the Case Against Open Borders.* New York: Sentinel, 2018.

Singer, Peter. "Insiders and Outsiders," in *Practical Ethics*, edited by Peter Singer. Cambridge: Cambridge University Press, 1993, 247–263.

Wellman, Christopher Heath. "Immigration and Freedom of Association." *Ethics* 119, no. 1 (2008): 109–141.

NOTES

1. Michael A. Clemens, "Economics and Emigration: Trillion-Dollar Bills on the Sidewalk?" *Journal of Economic Perspectives* 25, no. 3 (2011): 83–106.
2. National Academies of Sciences, Engineering, and Medicine, and Committee on Population, *The Integration of Immigrants into American Society* (Washington, DC: National Academies Press, 2016), 327.

3. Colin Woodard, *American Nations: A History of the Eleven Rival Regional Cultures of North America* (New York: Penguin, 2011).
4. I thank my colleague Jason Brennan for this thought experiment.
5. Christopher Freiman, "The Marginal Cases Argument for Open Immigration," *Public Affairs Quarterly* 29, no. 3 (2015): 257–276.
6. Notably, David Miller has argued that immigration controls are not coercive, by drawing a distinction between coercion and prevention. Here, I will grant defenders of open borders that immigration controls are coercive. If I can show that despite being granted this assumption, the case for open borders is flawed, that will make for an even stronger case for adopting some immigration restrictions. David Miller, "Why Immigration Controls Are Not Coercive: A Reply to Arash Abizadeh," *Political Theory* 38, no. 1 (2010): 111–120.
7. For varying approaches to making the case, see Michael Huemer, "Is There a Right to Immigrate?" *Social Theory and Practice* 36, no. 3 (2010): 429–461; Christopher Freiman and Javier Hidalgo, "Liberalism or Immigration Restrictions, But Not Both," *Journal of Ethics and Social Philosophy* 10, no. 2 (2016); Joseph Carens, "Aliens and Citizens: The Case for Open Borders," *Review of Politics* 49, no. 2 (1987): 251–273; Arash Abizadeh, "Democratic Theory and Border Coercion: No Right to Unilaterally Control Your Own Borders," *Political Theory* 36, no. 1 (2008): 37–65. Abizadeh argues that since immigration restrictions coerce foreigners, they must be justified to them democratically. I will not examine this issue in detail here, for considerations of space, but I do want to flag that view will commit us to having to democratically justify lots of other things (e.g., trade restrictions) to foreigners, in a way that's not feasible without one central world government.
8. See Tino Sanandaji, *Massutmaning* (self-published, 2016); Christian Pfeiffer, Dirk Baier, and Soeren Kliem, "Zur Entwicklung der Gewalt in Deutschland Schwerpunkte: Jugendliche und Flüchtlinge als Täter und Opfer" (Winterthur, Switzerland: Zurich University of Applied Sciences, 2018); German Ministry of the Interior, "Polizeiliche Kriminalstatistik (pks)," April 2017, https://www.bka.de/DE/AktuelleInformationen/StatistikenLagebilder/PolizeilicheKriminalstatistik/PKS2016/pks2016_node.html; Peter L. Martens, "Immigrants, Crime, and Criminal Justice in Sweden," *Crime and Justice* 21, (1997): 183–255; Peter Martens and Stina Holmberg, "Crime Among Persons Born in Sweden and Other Countries" (National Council for Crime Prevention, 2005); Bojan Pancevski, "An Ice-Cream Truck Slaying, Party Drugs and Real-Estate Kings: Ethnic Clans Clash in Berlin's Underworld," 2018, https://www.wsj.com/articles/ethnic-crime-families-provoke-german-crackdown-1539604801.
9. As it stands, such downward pressure is not present in the United States. See Gianmarco Ottaviano and Giovanni Peri, "Immigration and National Wages: Clarifying the Theory and the Empirics," *National Bureau of Economic Research*, 2008. However, the United States is far from a fully open borders regime.
10. See, for example, Stephen Macedo, "The Moral Dilemma of U.S. Immigration Policy: Open Borders Versus Social Justice?" in *Debating Immigration*, edited by Carol M. Swain (Cambridge: Cambridge University Press, 2007).
11. See Pew Research, "The World's Muslims: Religion, Politics and Society" (2013).
12. The most recent Gallup poll finds, unsurprisingly, that greater percentages of individuals from poorer countries want to migrate. There are some countries where the majority of residents wants to migrate. See Neli Esipova, Julie Ray, and Anita Pugliese, "Number of Potential Migrants Worldwide Tops 700 Million" (Gallup, 2017). Of course, such a

poll may not be perfectly predictive about what would actually happen if open borders were implemented, but it gives us a very rough idea.

13. See Michael Clemens, "Economics and Emigration: Trillion-Dollar Bills on the Sidewalk?" *Journal of Economic Perspectives* 25, no. 3 (2011): 83–106.

14. Bryan Caplan, "Why Should We Restrict Immigration?" *Cato Journal* 32, no. 1 (2012): 5–24.

15. A landmark paper on this examines how U.S. government changed after women's suffrage is John Lott and Lawrence Kenny, "Did Women's Suffrage Change the Size and Scope of Government?" *Journal of Political Economy* 107, no. 6 (1999): 1163–1198.

16. See, for example, Alberto Alesina and Paola Giuliano, "Family Ties," in *Handbook of Economic Growth*, edited by Philippe Aghion and Steven Durlauf (Amsterdam: Elsevier, 2014); Claudia Williamson, "Informal Institutions Rule: Institutional Arrangements and Economic Performance," *Public Choice* 139, no. 3 (2009): 371–387; Claudia Williamson and Rachel Mathers, "Economic Freedom, Culture, and Growth," *Public Choice* 148 (2011): 313–335.

17. Yann Algan and Pierre Cahuc, "Inherited Trust and Growth," *American Economic Review* 100, no. 5 (2010): 2060–2092.

18. Eugen Dimant, Tim Krieger, and Margarete Redlin, "A Crook Is a Crook . . . But Is He Still a Crook Abroad? On the Effect of Immigration on Destination-Country Corruption," *German Economic Review*, 16, no. 4 (2014): 464–489.

19. See Transparency International, "Corruption Perceptions Index 2018" (Transparency International, 2019), https://www.transparency.org/cpi2018

20. An additional factor to consider here might be the finding that people with higher IQ tend to be more cooperative in repeated games—see Omar Al-Ubaydli, Garett Jones, and Jaap Weel, "Patience, Cognitive Skill, and Coordination in the Repeated Stag Hunt," *Journal of Neuroscience, Psychology, and Economics* 6, no. 2 (2012): 71–96. Garett Jones applies this finding among others to argue that cross-nation differences in IQ can thus explain part of the variance in economic productivity of countries. See Garett Jones, *Hive Mind* (Stanford, CA: Stanford University Press, 2016).

21. Enrico Spolaore and Romain Wacziarg, "How Deep Are the Roots of Economic Development?" *Journal of Economic Literature* 51, no. 2 (2013): 325–369.

22. James Ang, "Institutions and the Long-Run Impact of Early Development," *Journal of Development Economics* 105 (2013): 1–18.

23. Economist Garett Jones argues in a yet-to-be-published manuscript that open borders may well lead to a decrease of total world GDP for roughly these reasons. The argument is that mass migration can significantly alter a country's total factor productivity (TFP). The search for a theory of what accounts for differences in TFP across countries is a neglected research area, despite having its importance been stressed by Nobel Prize–winning economist Ed Prescott. See Edward Prescott, "Needed: A Theory of Total Factor Productivity," *International Economic Review* 39, no. 3 (1998): 525–551.

24. Acknowledgments: I would like to specially thank Jonathan Anomaly, Daniel Jacobson, Garett Jones, and Kevin Vallier for detailed feedback on earlier drafts. I have also benefited from discussion with Carl Ritter, Reihan Salam, and Michael Huemer, and with audiences at the University of Michigan and the PPE Society Annual Meeting, 2018. Special thanks also to Bob Fischer for putting together this volume, and for helping make this essay better.

25. Sari Pekkala Kerr and William R. Kerr, "Immigrants Play a Disproportionate Role in American Entrepreneurship." *Harvard Business Review*, October 3, 2016, https://hbr.org/2016/10/immigrants-play-a-disproportionate-role-in-american-entrepreneurship.

26. Giovanni Peri, Kevin Shih, and Chad Sparber, "STEM Workers, H-1B Visas, and Productivity in U.S. Cities," *Journal of Labor Economics* 33, no. S1 (2015): S225–S255.

27. Benjamin Powell, Jeff R. Clark, and Alex Nowrasteh, "Does Mass Immigration Destroy Institutions? 1990s Israel as a Natural Experiment," November 17, 2016, https://ssrn .com/abstract=2871406 or http://dx.doi.org/10.2139/ssrn.2871406.

28. James Buchanan, "A Two Country Parable," in *Justice in Immigration*, edited by Warren F. Schwartz (Cambridge: Cambridge University Press, 1995).

29. Interestingly, intergenerational upward mobility of immigrants to the United States depends strongly on the country of origin. For data from Los Angeles, see Rubén G. Rumbaut et al., *Immigration and Intergenerational Mobility in Metropolitan Los Angeles (IIMMLA), 2004* (Ann Arbor, MI: Inter-university Consortium for Political and Social Research [distributor], 2008-07-01), https://doi.org/10.3886/ICPSR22627.v1. See also George J. Borjas, "Making It in America," *The Future of Children* 16, no. 2 (2006): 55–71; George J. Borjas, "The Intergenerational Mobility of Immigrants," *Journal of Labor Economics* 11, no. 1 (1993): 113–135; Julie Park and Dowell Myers, "Intergenerational Mobility in the Post-1965 Immigration Era: Estimates by an Immigration Generation Cohort Method," *Demography* 47 no. 2 (2010): 369-392.

30. Robert H. Frank, "Are Workers Paid Their Marginal Products?" *American Economic Review* 74, no. 4 (1984): 549–571; Hal. R. Varian, *Intermediate Microeconomics: A Modern Approach* (New York: W.W. Norton & Company, 2006 [7th ed.]).

31. There is a large literature on the connection between income inequality and political instability. Income inequality is also associated with lack of investment, thus putting a damper on future growth. For a landmark paper on this issue, see Alberto Alesina and Roberto Perotti, "Income Distribution, Political Instability, and Investment," *European Economic Review* 40, no. 6 (1996): 1203–1228.

32. For an index of economic freedom, see James Gwartney, Robert Lawson, Joshua Hall, and Ryan Murphy, "Economic Freedom of the World: 2018 Annual Report," Fraser Institute, 2018, https://www.fraserinstitute.org/studies/economic-freedom. For data on human development, see UN Development Programme, "Human Development Indices and Indicators: 2018 Statistical Update" United Nations Development Programme, 2018, http://hdr.undp.org/sites/default/files/2018_human_development_statistical_update. pdf.

33. Transparency International, "Corruption Perceptions Index 2018" (Transparency International, 2019), https://www.transparency.org/cpi2018; Jason Brennan, *Why Not Capitalism?* (New York: Routledge, 2014).

34. This is further legitimized from the point of view according to which a person's ability to vote doesn't make her better off, and democracy is not an intrinsic but a merely instrumental good. For a recent defense of this view, see Jason Brennan, *Against Democracy* (Princeton, NJ: Princeton University Press, 2016).

35. For further discussion of related issues, see Reihan Salam, *Melting Pot or Civil War? A Son of Immigrants Makes the Case Against Open Borders* (New York: Sentinel, 2018).

36. I discuss this point in detail in Hrishikesh Suhas Joshi, "Is Liberalism Committed to Its Own Demise?" *Journal of Ethics and Social Philosophy* 13, no. 3 (2018): 259–267. There, I also suggest a way out of Jaworski's worry that the very same reasoning given to support immigration restrictions for cultural reasons can justify deportation or limits on procreation for some citizens. My basic idea is that barriers to entry and stay stand in less need of justification than moves to deport long-term residents or to restrict procreative liberty. Not all coercive acts are created equal.

CHAPTER 5

Religious Tests

MUSLIM IMMIGRATION AND THE WEST
I. G.

In this essay, I defend at least strict restrictions—but not necessarily blanket bans—on immigration from Muslim-majority countries (hence, "Muslim countries" and "Muslim societies"). The absence of such restrictions poses a threat to Western democracies. I don't defend deportations or any other abridgment of the rights of Muslim residents or citizens in the West for such acts would set legal precedents that will harm democracy instead of protecting it. I also don't address the question of refugees from Muslim countries. I concede that the West, especially the United States, the United Kingdom, and Israel, who spearheaded recent unjust wars in the Middle East, probably have a special obligation to provide asylum to refugees from countries such as Afghanistan, Iraq, Syria, Lebanon, Libya, Palestine, and Yemen, where Western governments are partly responsible for the ongoing humanitarian crises. However, I doubt that these obligations would extend to granting those refugees immigrant status, or any other form of permanent settlement.

1. My Story

I am a former Muslim living in the United States. I was born and raised in a Sunni town in Turkey, a Muslim country, where I witnessed quite a few horrors justified by reference to Islam. On more than a few occasions, I was at the center of these horrors. For instance, from the first to the twelfth grade, I was beaten dozens of times for refusing to recite passages from the Quran in Arabic (a language I neither speak nor understand), refusing to pray on top of a teacher's desk, chewing gum and drinking water in public during the month of Ramadan, and refusing to rise to my feet for mandatory public prayer before eating at the school cafeteria. These didn't happen behind closed doors when no one was looking. They all happened in front of students, teachers, and school administrators in public schools.

Most of my batterers would describe themselves as "moderate Muslims." So would the overwhelming majority of the bystanders who watched as I was shamed, beaten, and spat at repeatedly for my childish rebellions against Islam. Admittedly, I'm one of the lucky ones. I experienced some pain; I got a few bruises. The most serious trouble, at least so far, was a skull fracture and concussion. I suffered it at the hands of a mob who decided that the best way of convincing me that Allah the Merciful exists would be to repeatedly connect my head with a steel cabinet until I was persuaded to look at the issue their way.

From age six, when I had my first doubts about God and organized religion, until the time I landed in a university community, where blasphemers weren't beaten on the spot, I experienced an almost constant and sometimes overwhelming mix of fear and desperation. On many occasions, I am ashamed to admit, fear stopped me from speaking what I knew to be the truth. Other times, my impulse to speak against superstition and lies got me into serious trouble (and let's hope the publication of this chapter isn't one such case). However, though these experiences made my youth very stressful, I would like to believe that they also gave me the wisdom to know that they can't break your spirit unless you let them. For that important lesson alone I should thank my Muslim tormentors, moderate or not.

Others weren't so lucky, however. My child eyes also had the dubious distinction of having seen a lynch mob who gleefully cheered, "Sharia will come, persecution will end!" as their victims burned to death and the police did nothing. What was the crime of the condemned unlucky, you ask? It was "insulting Islam" by simply coming out as atheists, agnostics, and heretical religious minorities.

2. Ideology and Violence
I recently saw a meme that separates the Muslims of the world into two groups. On the one hand, there are those who live in Muslim societies such as Iran, Pakistan, Iraq, Gaza, and Yemen. These Muslims, the meme said, are unhappy. On the other hand, there are those Muslims who live in non-Muslim societies such as Germany, Australia, the United Kingdom, and the United States. These Muslims, the meme claimed, are joyfully happy, the implication being that the predominance of Islam in a society makes even its Muslims miserable.

A European friend forwarded the meme to me, wondering why Turkey wasn't among the societies listed. He also thought, contrary to what the meme implied, that Islam isn't at fault in the misery of Muslims of the Muslim world. He thought that poverty, wars, and colonialism were to blame.

I am fairly certain that Turkey belongs squarely in the list of countries where a Muslim majority lives in misery. This despite the fact that Turkey isn't particularly poor,[1] Turkey hasn't been in a major war since 1922, and Turkey has never been colonized by anyone. That is, unless you count my Turkic Muslim ancestors who took it by force from its Christian inhabitants. If there are any colonists-by-progeny in Turkey today, they're the Muslims themselves.

Turkish or not, though, Muslims aren't all religious fanatics who will murder those who "insult" their religion by disagreeing with it. But this doesn't matter.

210 ETHICS, LEFT AND RIGHT

A sizable minority of Turkish Muslims will commit or at least cheer on violence for Islam,[2] and the majority will look the other way, mumbling something about it all being up to God's will. And whether they're poor, war-ridden, colonized, or not, Muslim communities somehow keep reproducing these fanatics, as well as their mumbling enablers, in every generation. That's what's wrong with Islam. The trouble with Islam isn't that it makes every Muslim a raging jihadist who will yell in Arabic as he decapitates a Japanese journalist.[3] Here lies the real problem: As Islam spreads in a society, so does flourish *a culture of fear* in which religious violence is a familiar—and even expected—part of the day-to-day social reality.

The difficulty of coming to terms with this fact and looking for an intellectually honest explanation thereof is one of the greatest challenges facing the Western left, of which I find myself an odd member nowadays. I do understand where my fellow lefties are coming from: They believe that on a fundamental level, all humanity is redeemable, or at least the unsalvageable baddies are few and distributed by Mother Nature more or less evenly between all races, ethnic groups, sexual orientations, religions, and what not. They know that "ordinary" folks are capable of doing bad things too, but they do them mostly because of environmental factors—not essentially corrupt inner selves. That's why they tend to reel back from essentialist characterizations of any group. That's why when they see our president ranting about Muslims on Twitter, they want to yell at him, "Not all Muslims are like that, you racist piece of #$%@!"

Of course they aren't. Not even *most* Muslims are like that. Most Muslims, like most non-Muslims, wouldn't hurt anyone intentionally. If anything, most Muslims are themselves victims of the culture of fear in which they're inadvertent participants or bystanders. But that's the banality of evil, the story of every community in history where atrocities were committed in the name of an ideology. Did most Communist Party members in Stalin's Soviet Union torture and kill political prisoners? Did most Nazi Party members in World War II, or even most SS men, murder civilians? Did most Chinese communists participate in ceremonial public humiliation and abuse of Mao's political rivals? Did most of Charlie Company, who were told that that there are no civilians in My Lai and no cost is too great to fight off communism, participate in the massacre of five hundred civilians? If you do believe that they did, you're wrong. They didn't. Most of them looked the other way, mumbled some excuses, and avoided getting involved.

Yet, that fact somehow fails to make me feel at ease when I think about the prospects of having more self-identifying Stalinists join my community. I don't worry that the average Stalinist would want to put a bullet in my petit-bourgeois head when I express skepticism about the Party's ability to bring about a classless utopia. Instead, I worry about what these ideologies can do to the individual and—ultimately—to the society. They tend to weaken our sympathy for the other by rationalizing his suffering. They selectively remove our respect for and recognition of universal human dignity. They desensitize us to the crimes committed in their name. That's why if there are sufficiently many people who ascribe to such ideologies in my community, inevitably there will be a few who are willing to take violent action for their beliefs. Most won't commit or even condone violence, but their weakened sympathy and diminished respect for the victims of their ideology will make them more likely to look the other way, mumble some excuses, and avoid getting involved when they see someone battering a defiant child or setting a building on fire in the name of their creed. This deadly combination is what's scary about today's Islam.

One might find the comparison to Stalinism, Nazism, and Maoism silly and repugnant. But my point isn't to suggest that there's some moral equivalency between these ideologies and Islam. Indisputably, Nazism is worse, *much* worse. Rather, my point is that it isn't necessarily bigotry to appeal to ideological factors when explaining the atrocities committed by a minority within an ideological group. Appealing to ideology as an explanation for violence isn't necessarily stereotyping all members of the group who espouse that ideology. We know how terribly powerful the bystander effect could be even without an ideological rationalization for non-intervention. My experience tells me that Islam makes it worse.

So, worrying that Islam is a religion that breeds violence isn't necessarily some essentialist overgeneralization of the violent dispositions of the few to all. Ideology—just like poverty, wars, and colonialism—is a component of the individual's environment and it should be taken into account when trying to understand violence. If war turns some into violent psychopaths, and some others into cowardly or apathetic bystanders who can't or won't lift a finger to stop those psychopaths, that's a great argument against war. I submit that if we substituted "Islam" for "war," the previous sentence would still be true.

This is why it's futile to resort to the tired retort, "Not all Muslims are like that; it's just a handful of extremists." Indeed, there are *many* "good" Muslims for every "bad" Muslim. But a good proportion of those "good" Muslims are the members of the silent majority whose cowardice or indifference give the "bad" Muslims free license to terrorize in the name of Islam. I recognize the fact that there are some heroic followers of Islam who overcome the bystander effect and try to put an end to the culture of fear. However, the record speaks for itself. As heroic as they may be, the voices of these individuals—a few of them dear friends—are drowned out by the roaring violence or the deafening silence of the rest.

If we allow Muslim immigration to shift the demographics of secular democracies of the West significantly, we will be effectively expanding that license to terrorize in the name of Islam to our own communities. The self-appointed "Sharia police" in the United Kingdom[4] and Germany,[5] the massive surge of sexual assault incidents in Cologne on New Year's Eve,[6] as well as the "homegrown" terrorist attacks in Paris[7] and Brussels,[8] are signs that a significant demographic shift is already underway in Western Europe. The United States should learn from the failed European experiment with large-scale Muslim immigration and severely restrict immigration from Muslim countries.

3. Alternative Explanations
That there's a correlation between Muslim presence and violence doesn't entail the causal link I claim, of course. However, we aren't talking about a clearly accidental correlation, such as the one between the decline of oceanic piracy and

the rise of global temperatures.[9] The perpetrators of violence themselves say that they resort to violence *because* their faith commands it. People are, of course, sometimes wrong about why they do what they do. But self-report *is defeasible evidence* of a causal link between beliefs and actions. That means, we do have evidence for a causal link between Islam and violence. Anyone who disputes the link, therefore, must produce a reasonable alternative explanation of the correlation that either rebuts or overpowers that evidence.

This is where most of my lefty friends will interject with an explanation that blames the correlation on the social and economic marginalization of Muslims in the West, and the provocations Muslims feel due to Western imperialism and military aggression. The idea is, if any other religious demographic faced the same treatment, they would react the same way.

Let's consider these alternative explanations individually. First, social marginalization: Not only is there no evidence of this, but on the contrary, most Western countries are remarkably welcoming to Muslims and their culture. In Germany, for instance, the Federal Republic mandates that every public school employs interpreters on call who can speak main immigrant languages (i.e., Arabic, Turkish, Urdu, and Kurdish). German schools also teach Islam as a major world religion.[10] Immigrant children are offered cultural integration classes and German as a second language,[11] while most of them can also continue studying their native languages throughout their education. On the streets, the situation is the same. In major German cities, for instance, virtually every other corner features a kebab restaurant or a shisha house. And Germany is happy to bring in even more Muslims, as is evident from the fact that they have already accepted over half a million Syrian, Iraqi, and Afghani asylum seekers.

Germany, however, is the norm in the Western Europe, not the exception. From the Netherlands, the very birthplace of religious freedom, to the Holy See, the home of the largest Christian church in the world, Muslims are tolerated— even celebrated—by those very Westerners who are unfairly accused of marginalizing them.

On the other side of the Atlantic, Muslim faith is protected by the Canadian and American constitutions. The rights these documents establish and guarantee, however, don't exist merely on paper. Thousands of Muslim cultural centers and mosques operate freely and openly seek converts under the protection of the law. This is in stark contrast to the intolerance for other religions in virtually all Muslim countries, where being a Christian pastor or missionary is either prohibited by law[12] or is legal in theory but extremely dangerous in practice.[13]

Of course, I am not denying the reality that some Muslims in the West might face discrimination or be targeted with violence[14] because of their religious identity. However, if we hold Western societies to the same standards as everyone else, we should conclude on the whole they're remarkably accommodating to Muslims, and much more so than Muslim societies are accommodating to non-Muslims.

As for the West's imperialism and unjust wars being provocations, I won't try to defend either, as they're indefensible. However, I will raise a question: If imperialism and unjust war are provocations that naturally result in violent retaliation against civilians, then where's the Vietnamese Al-Qaeda, Korean ISIS, or Japanese Boko Haram? In the Vietnam War, by most estimates over 1 million Vietnamese civilians were killed by the United States and its allies.[15] During the Korean War, close to 2 million Korean civilians were killed, many of them as a result of bombardment by the North Atlantic Treaty Organization (NATO).[16] But perhaps the Japanese case is the most striking of all: In World War II, the U.S. Air Force firebombed almost all major Japanese cities, in addition to dropping two atomic bombs on Hiroshima and Nagasaki, incinerating close to half a million civilians.[17] As these atrocities were taking place on the other side of the Pacific, over a hundred thousand law-abiding U.S. citizens and residents were locked up in concentration camps in the United States, for no reason other than their Japanese ancestry. The survivors of these crimes against humanity had every reason to hate the West. Yet somehow the sizeable Vietnamese, Korean, and Japanese immigrant communities in the United States or elsewhere don't seem provoked at all to wage holy wars of revenge against the Western world, and they seem perfectly happy to adapt, to integrate, to live and let live.

So, neither of these alternative explanations can account for the increased incidence of violence in societies with Muslim presence. Therefore, however unpleasant we might find it, the conclusion that Islam and violence are causally linked is the plausible one to draw from the evidence.

4. Is Fear of Islam Irrational?

At this point, someone might argue that, despite my conviction and hope to the contrary, my fear of Islam is an overreaction born out of my trauma. But this possibility doesn't justify dismissing the argument I'm making here. We wouldn't say such things casually to a survivor of other horrors, especially after they make a case that what happened to them isn't a fluke but the result of a systemic problem. The burden of proof to show that I am overreacting is on my critics, and a psychological explanation of the origin of my fear isn't a refutation of the case I am making.

I am not essentializing Islam either, for I don't think that Islam has a "true and immutable nature." Religions are social constructs consisting of diverse—and often conflicting—ideas and practices. Nor am I making any pessimistic long-term predictions about Muslim societies. Religions evolve, and so shall Islam. But that's the long run. As the famous economist Keynes rightly points out, the "long run is a misleading guide to current affairs. *In the long run we are all dead.*"[18] My primary concern is with the ways Islam manifests itself here and now, and what it can reasonably be expected to become within my lifetime. This is why it's no good to say "Christianity has been violent, too."[19] Pointing at the evidently violent history of Christianity is a good response to those who romanticize Christianity. However, I am not one of those. So, the response misses my point: Islam breeds violence today, *here and now*. And it does so more than Christianity *currently* does.[20]

Muslim countries, *relatively speaking and on average*, have significantly more religious violence per capita than those dominated by other major religions represented in the West.[21] But we aren't looking at a mere difference in degree: This is one of the occasions in which a difference in degree creates a difference in kind. The situation is a bit like traffic. If everyone obeys the rules, traffic tends to flow easily. Road networks are designed with built-in redundancy, so they tolerate the occasional driver who tailgates, speeds, changes lanes unnecessarily, or causes a collision. Things might slow down, but cars will still move. However, if more and more drivers disregard the rules, eventually traffic will undergo what physicists call a "phase transition": a sudden and qualitative change from a fluid state to a viscous state. In layman's terms, there will be a traffic jam.

Ideological violence is comparable to traffic violations. Have only a little bit of it, and things will carry on as usual. Keep adding more, and eventually there will be a sudden and dramatic transition in the political climate. That's why at some point, more ideological violence becomes *more than just more*. After some threshold, which is hard to specify because societies are much more complex than road networks, more ideological violence would inevitably have a paralyzing effect on public discourse and a terrorizing effect on the individual psyche.

However, there are two aggravating factors relevant to ideological violence that aren't represented by the traffic analogy. First, violence begets violence, not only by inviting retaliation but also by inspiring copycats, and one-uppers. There's some disturbing evidence, for instance, that some school shootings in the United States are in part caused by previous school shootings.[22] That's why ideological violence might snowball once it reaches a critical threshold.

Furthermore, there's more to the transformative effect of ideological violence than its frequency. It's a particularly horrifying phenomenon, and its psychological impact should be considered when we interpret the significance of the risk of falling victim to it. The fact that there are many fewer incidents of Islamic violence than deaths from other causes is hardly consolation. What makes Islam today an existential threat against Western democracies isn't that huge numbers are killed in its name. It's instead that the violent minority of Muslims (more than the radical factions of any other major religion today) *effectively terrorizes the dissenter*. Nothing has a more chilling effect on speech than someone being murdered because he criticized an ideology. When that happens—and it happens frequently enough where I am from[23]—democracy simply can't survive.

A further cause for worry is the difficulty of reacting calmly to increased ideological violence. Many of us, left or right, are rightly worried about the post-9/11 erosion of the Fourth Amendment protections against unreasonable searches and government intrusion. What can be reasonably expected to happen to the rest of the Bill of Rights if and when there's a religiously inspired suicide bombing or mass shooting in the United States every week? Neither the U.S. Constitution, nor any other form of liberal democracy, can continue to exist under such pressure.

5. Conclusion

Contrary to the impression I might have inadvertently made, I am not interested in demonizing Islam or Muslims. Islam manifests itself in different ways, many of which are benign or even admirable. But some of its manifestations are less than benign. People are beaten,[24] tortured,[25] executed,[26] gunned down,[27] hacked into pieces,[28] and slaughtered like animals,[29] all in the name of Islam, and at a rate that you don't see from any other major religion today. When I look at the narratives of Islamic violence from all around the world, it's hard to resist connecting the dots: Where Islam goes in significant numbers, we start seeing acts of violence committed in its name at a rate and severity that is a threat to the very possibility of liberal democracy. Given that cultural integration is tough and religions often take centuries and bloody conflicts to evolve, supporting mass or open immigration from Muslim countries would be gambling with the fate of Western civilization itself.

So from where I stand, as a former Muslim and an oddball lefty, Islam appears to be an ideology that tolerates and even encourages the few who will resort to violence in its name, and silences the vast majority of its remaining followers. I also think I understand those who aren't comfortable with the idea of large-scale Muslim immigration to the West. They aren't bigots—or, at least, most aren't. It isn't a race or some religious stereotype that they fear. What they fear, I think, is what I fear: a future in which Islam might gain a foothold in their relatively tolerant and admirably free communities, overwhelm their psychological defenses and democratic institutions, and turn them into earthly hellholes like my hometown.

Who can blame them? Not me.

COMPREHENSION QUESTIONS

1. What does I. G. advocate for as an immigration policy in Western societies?
2. I. G. claims that there is a causal link between Islam and political violence. What evidence does he provide for this claim?
3. I. G. discusses and rejects a number of alternative explanations for the apparent correlation between Islam and political violence. What are they?
4. What does it mean to "essentialize" a religion?
5. What's the point of the analogy between political violence and traffic?

DISCUSSION QUESTIONS

1. How does I. G.'s personal narrative influence your evaluation of his argument?
2. Does I. G. essentialize Islam? Provide support for your response.
3. How might immigration restrictions based on religious beliefs *hurt* Western societies?
4. I. G. warns against "supporting mass or open immigration from Muslim countries." Do you think there's a viable middle ground between this and his proposed "strict restrictions"? Would it necessarily involve religion-based exclusions?

Case 1

The Pew Research Center conducted a survey of Muslims in the United States in 2017. Two of the survey respondents are quoted here:

> "I believe Mr. Donald Trump is a very good president and he can do a lot to the economy because he spent his life as a businessman and engineer, but for politics, he did kind of strong decisions that tended to be unfair, like when he said that seven Muslim countries are not supposed to enter the United States and stuff like this. You can't treat all the people with the same guilt. Get the people who caused the trouble and prosecute them. It makes you look not that great to the whole world."—*Muslim man over 60*
>
> "I am not even sure how I feel. I wish he would just shut up. I thought he would be for the better good of the country. Is it him? Is it the media? I will say I was always Republican and never voted any other way and now I am saying, 'What is going on?' I am the first to say we should be careful who to let in the country, but there is a more diplomatic way to do it. For an educated man he is not making educated decisions. And I have family from outside this country. My husband is from Iran. So do I think we should be careful with Iran. My husband has been here since 1985. . . . I don't think it is wrong for the government to be careful, but a lot of innocent people are being hurt by this. There are family members I might not be able to see again. They would come every year and now I cannot see them. I believe in protecting our country but the way he is going about it is not the best way."—*Muslim woman in her 40s**

Which of the respondents' statements do you think are the most morally relevant, particularly in light of I. G.'s arguments? What new dimensions, if any, do they bring to the conversation published here?

---

*http://www.pewforum.org/2017/07/26/the-muslim-american-experience-in-the-trump-era/

ON THE ROAD TO LOSING OURSELVES: RELIGION-BASED IMMIGRATION TESTS
SABA FATIMA

Donald J. Trump [referring to himself in third person] is calling for a total and complete shutdown of Muslims entering the United States until our country's representatives can figure out what the hell is going on.

—DONALD TRUMP (December 2015)[30]

I'll tell you the whole history of it. So when [Trump] first announced it, he said, "Muslim ban." He called me up. He said, "Put a commission together. Show me the right way to do it legally."

—RUDY GIULIANI (January 2017)[31]

1. Introduction

Days after the December 2, 2015, San Bernardino shooting, then-presidential-nominee Donald Trump issued a statement calling for a "total and complete shutdown of Muslims entering the United States." In the fuller version of this statement, Trump expressed blanket distrust of all Muslims. Any policy that is born out of such hatred and ignorance is bound to spread more hate, as well as be vindictive and ineffective. While the statement was appreciated and cheered on by many Americans, it instilled dread in others. From the perspective of some, it was a signal that Muslims are something to be feared. Since then, President Donald Trump has switched strategies and his administration has worked through several iterations of the travel ban, such that the latest version does not explicitly discriminate on the basis of religion and has passed the test of the courts.

In this piece, however, I will not argue specifically about the current executive order in effect or about what is and what is not constitutional. This is because we have had many laws that passed the legal tests of their time, such as slavery, Jim Crow, the internment of Japanese Americans, and violations of LGBTQ rights. However, we came to realize that these violations were colossally unethical and immoral, and subsequently disavowed them. We know too well that laws of the land do not always correspond with the ethical and moral principles we ought to follow. It's also clear that the burden of our ethical misdirection is borne by the most vulnerable in our society. Here, then, I simply want to address some of the ethical and moral concerns that surround the issue of instituting a religion-based test for the purposes of immigration.

2. The Impracticality of It All

I begin by discussing a pragmatic concern: Would a religion-based immigration test serve any useful purpose?

Immigration to the United States of America is a process that is lengthy, expensive, and complicated. There are several different kinds of visas that a person can obtain to enter the United States. Many of these—for example, visitor visas, student visas, ambassador visas—cannot be transferred to immigrant status. And in order to qualify for such visas, the person must prove intent to *not* immigrate. Other visas do allow a person to transfer status from temporary visitor to permanent resident, most notably the H1B visa (given to skilled labor). However, the process is slow and cumbersome: You have to apply for such visas, wait the relevant period of time before applying for the transfer, wait for the transfer itself, and complete a great deal of documentation along the way. There are also visas given to people who are migrating to the United States with the intent to permanently settle (for example, spouses or children of American citizens), but these are increasingly difficult to get. Finally, the process of seeking asylum is perhaps the most complicated and fraught with bureaucracy. The vetting process for refugees is quite extensive: It takes an average of two years from the time a family applies for refugee status to the time that they are actually approved for it. They not only are investigated by the Federal Bureau of Investigation (FBI) for terrorism ties, but also go through a vetting process by the United Nations. This does not include the time that it might take them to get to a refugee camp from their area of conflict or the time it takes for them to become citizens.

But *all* the above processes also undergo extensive investigation on part of the U.S. Citizenship and Immigration Services (USCIS). Each step of the process requires the immigrants and the refugees to show proof of everything that they claim in their file. The application can take anywhere from two years to as long as a decade. This can be followed by several years of probation, and then another set of paperwork and fees with more documentation, until a person finally becomes a citizen. This is all to say that the current system is definitely in need of improvement, in that it needs clearer guidelines, a faster and more streamlined system, electronic modernization, a shorter path to citizenship, etc. Instead, imposing a religious test adds another cog in the already cumbersome system—a cog, as argued below, that serves absolutely no utility and is completely ineffective. The system in place is already quite thorough and exhaustive.

There are two ways such a test could be implemented. There could be an explicit test where we inquire about specific religious beliefs, or there could be an implicit one, where we might use some non-religious consideration as a proxy for religious identities and/or commitments.

If we consider the first option, it would be extremely hard to figure out exactly how we could laser focus on particular Islamic beliefs or practice. This is because religion is amorphous as it weaves in intricate and inseparable ways with people's lives, and it would be difficult to separate problematic aspects of the religious belief or practice as a distinct entity. For example, let us examine beliefs about *jihad*. *Jihad* means to strive in the way of God, and is primarily understood by most Muslims to mean that one ought to strive to better oneself against one's own flaws. It also refers to striving through one's actions (e.g., giving charity) or words (e.g., writing works that inspire peace) to make this world a more just and compassionate place because those are the sorts of actions that would help one gain nearness to God. And, of course, it also refers to striving against oppression and injustice, in some cases, by means of war. *Jihad* refers to all of these notions and much more, and for many, it is an inseparable part of what it might mean for someone to be Muslim. There is no distinct aspect of *jihad* that one can pick apart, because all these notions are interconnected and inseparable and play varying parts in how one might practice one's faith.

However, for the sake of this essay, let us imagine a world where we could figure out which theological elements of Islam we found most objectionable to our pluralistic society. Furthermore, imagine that we could formulate a set of questions that cross-examined applicants about those elements of their religion during the immigration process, perhaps something akin to the existing question on the Naturalization Form N-400: "Have you ever been a member of or in any way associated (either directly or indirectly) with the Communist Party?" Suppose further that we were to add another interview to the process that focused solely on asking applicants about their religious beliefs. Even if we were able to do all this, there is no system of enforcement that could assure us that applicants are responding with sincerity.

Faith is something that is entirely too personal to be evaluated by a bureaucracy. For the most vulnerable among the applicants, even if they did not have anything to hide, they would be likely to alter their responses to fit the narrative they think that others want to hear from them, all so that they can escape immediate and life-threatening violence. And of course, people who are intent on committing acts of terrorism in the name of Islam would lie about their malevolent intent. More importantly, interview portions of the immigration process already ask applicants questions that are pertinent to national security, and the USCIS already conducts extensive investigations into each applicant's background before and after these interviews. The process is far from perfect, often relying on the discretion of immigration officers, but the fundamental point here is that introducing a religion-based test is not going to add anything useful or constructive to the existing bureaucratic process; it simply adds more bureaucracy.

Now let us consider an implicit test, like the one that was upheld by the Supreme Court in June 2018, where nationals of seven countries, five of which are predominantly Muslim, are barred entry to the United States. In this particular case, critics would argue that the Trump administration may be using nationality to keep out Muslim terrorists. The problem is that nationality is not a good predictor of who is likely to be a terrorist. For example, as of writing this in 2019, none of the countries cited in the executive order have had any citizens that have ever committed a terrorist attack on U.S. soil. In fact, the current executive order, titled "Protecting the Nation from Foreign Terrorist Entry into the United States," would not have prevented the male shooter in San Bernardino, as he was born in Chicago. Ultimately, any implicit test would rely on creating a racialized, fictitious Muslim identity that non-Muslim Americans are made to fear. I discuss this in the next section.

For now, it is important to note that the very idea of having a religion-based immigration test, whether it'd be an explicit or an implicit one, simply does not make practical sense.

3. Fostering Islamophobia

If a religious test within the immigration process only adds to an already cumbersome bureaucratic system and cannot be effectively administered to serve the objective of identifying and keeping out terrorists, what then would be the purpose of having such a test? It would seem plausible to say that such a test is designed to foster Islamophobia. But even if one is charitable and agrees that this is not the actual intent of instituting such a test, it is still its inevitable outcome.

Historically, the United States has engaged in deterring immigration of certain religious sects. For example, in the early 1600s, the Virginia charter specifically expressed disdain for Catholics and required immigrants to swear allegiance to the Church of England. Similarly, a Massachusetts law[32] imposed fines on ships that brought Quaker immigrants to its shore. Such restrictions were based on unfounded fear of the "other" and xenophobic notions of what these religions constituted. They were the state's way of controlling who it deemed undesirable based on discriminatory standards. We should learn from our mistakes and not fall into prejudice yet again, based on our latest set of fears about the unknown.

Today, some Americans seem to fear and hate Islam and Muslims. Much of the rhetoric that surrounds Islam seems misinformed at best and intentionally malicious at worst. For example, former national security advisor Michael Flynn was reported as saying: "Islam is a political ideology masked behind a religion, using religion as an advantage against us . . . Sharia, the law of Islam, OK? Sharia is the law. Just like our Constitution is our law."[33] Rhetoric such as this appeals to our fear about the threat that Islam poses as a religion to our values and national security. Flynn here implies that Islam is not a religion in the same ways that Christianity and Judaism are, but that it is a malignant cancer bent on destroying our country.[34]

It is true that sharia refers to laws that ought to guide actions, but sharia for Muslims encompasses laws about a great number of things; for example, how to offer one's prayers, fast, or give charity. In fact, much of sharia is about how one ought to act as an individual. That is to say, sharia at its core is about day-to-day behavioral guidance. Any Muslim who observes any aspect of their faith or partakes in any ritual is following sharia. Sharia *also* guides war and has a rich tradition of reflection on just war theory. Often terrorists have little background in theology, and if they attempted to understand Islamic scholarship on war and social justice, it might make them realize that their actions cannot be rooted in the mainstream understanding of Islamic beliefs practiced by the vast majority of the global Muslim population. Prominent Islamic scholars across various sects and religious schools of thought routinely condemn terrorist tactics and underscore how such actions are antithetical to Islamic beliefs. Sharia can be an all-encompassing guide—just as encompassing and comprehensive as the rich Christian or Judaic traditions on war and social justice.

Furthermore, according to a study, Muslims who attend a mosque are less likely to radicalize. On the contrary, religious affiliation may actually be a good thing for promoting civic participation.[35] Thus, comments such as Flynn's only inflame the American tendency to fear Muslims. If we were to institute a test on all incoming immigrants to see whether they subscribe to a violent ideology, it would foster and sustain an environment of hate toward Muslims. Much like our mistakes in the past, a religion-based immigration test would rely on misconceptions and xenophobic notions of who Muslims are.

An immigration test based on religious beliefs assumes an essentialist view of Islam. As Mahmood Mamdani writes in his book *Good Muslim, Bad Muslim*, we should avoid what he terms *culture talk*. That is, we should not assume that cultures have a tangible essence that we can point to and attempt to explain politics in terms of the imaginary image of that culture. Instead, we should recognize that cultures change and adapt in various social and political contexts. It is quite easy to succumb to casting terrorism in simplistic terms of religion— person x is a Muslim, hence they hold belief y, and that is why they did z—rather than the complex historical and political conditions that contextualize our current predicament. No religion-based test can capture what is a quite complex issue. All it would do is reduce a rich and diverse population to a caricature of violence.

Once we have established an irrational fear of an entire group of people, it is easier to acquiesce to conditions that are discriminatory, cruel, and inhumane. Such a culture of fear fosters anti-Muslim racism, where the fictitious "Muslim" category is arbitrarily formed within the racist imagination. Random subjective markers, such as brown skin color, different clothing styles, beards, hijabs, accents, etc. form an illogical category in the minds of the anti-Muslim racist and ensures that we treat our Muslim citizens as perpetual outsiders. This is because if we follow the faulty logic that there is something about Islam that makes it violent, then any Muslim—and thus all Muslims—are potential terrorists. Muslims, including Muslim Americans and Muslim immigrants, would then be forced to split off parts of ourselves that might appear to others as unpatriotic.[36]

Instituting a test based on religious beliefs would not only create intolerance of those who appear Muslim within America, but would also lead to inhumane immigration policies. Currently, civilians in countries such as Syria, Yemen, Iraq, and Afghanistan are experiencing extremely dire conditions at the hands of the very terrorists that we, as Americans, want to fight. Syria is the largest humanitarian crisis of our time, with millions displaced, fleeing the brutal combination of a horrific dictator, ISIL attacks, a civil war, and a lot of foreign interference. Barring entry to people who most need to flee from such gruesome violence is beyond cruel. Again, we must remember our past when we, as Americans, turned ships of fleeing Holocaust survivors away because of the pervasive anti-Semitism of the time. We must not be complicit in history repeating itself and vehemently fight back any measure that fosters Islamophobia with the consequences of instituting cold-hearted policies.

4. Surveillance of Thought

So far, I have argued that a religion-based immigration test is impractical and fosters Islamophobia. Now I want to now look at the problematic aspects of the broader issue of government-instituted thought policing.

Suppose we live in a country where there is a mass shooting every two weeks. We don't know when and where the next one might happen, but after each one, our nation is traumatized. We grieve for our fellow country folk who died in the latest tragedy and fear for our loved ones being the next victims. After looking at the data, we figured out that most of our mass shooters are white males, born and raised in our society. We have reasoned that it is because these mass murderers ascribe to a combination of toxic masculinity and white supremacy. We recognize that in this hypothetical society, there are many good white men out there and most do not subscribe to such radical ideologies, yet the evidence appears undeniable. We then decide that the best course of action is to have all white males in our nation's high schools, universities, and workforce between the ages of sixteen and sixty-five undergo an extensive vetting process to ensure that they are not potentially our next shooter. We call each white male in at our registration sites throughout the country, register them into a database of white men, photograph and fingerprint them, and then question them at length about their beliefs regarding equality between genders, the racist and sexist norms they might subscribe to, and the role models they follow. We also screen their past to make sure it's not indicative of racial and gender bias. Men who raise concerns are then subject to greater scrutiny and surveillance from the government. If this sounds preposterous, then so should the idea of government-administered ideological tests. They are both forms of thought policing.

It's true that we have different obligations to citizens than we do to non-citizens, and the hypothetical scenario above concerns citizens. And perhaps it's true that we should be able to screen those who come into our country. However, as argued in the previous sections, an immigration test is not a practical or effective way to keep out dangerous folks. Second, given the incredible importance that Americans have attached to the principles of religious freedom and being innocent until proven guilty, we should be worried about any screening process—effective or ineffective—that conflicts with them. And surely any screening process that fosters Islamophobia, as this one would, conflicts with them. Third, we should remember that whenever the United States has instituted ideological policing in the past, it has almost always been to characterize certain populations as traitorous. An immigration test that's administered to immigrant Muslims is bound to shift the perception of Muslim American citizens in that way. In this section, I focus on the notion of thought policing itself, and the harms it can perpetuate.

There have been times in history when we have investigated people based on their beliefs, most notably during the McCarthy era in the 1950s. Senator Joseph McCarthy was convinced that communist and Soviet spies had infiltrated various American institutions and that these people needed to be investigated by a committee (with the rather unbelievable name "the House Un-American Activities Committee"). He not only accused respected high-level officials—such as General George Marshall—of being communists, but also went after artists, musicians, people in Hollywood, and writers of the time. Many of them were Jewish. He also accused people of being gay (at a time when gay sex was illegal, and homosexuality was seen as a psychological illness) and attempted to use the full force of the state's apparatus to determine which individuals were detrimental to U.S. security and moral values. Today, that period of American history is remembered as a shameful one, where folks were interrogated based on unsubstantiated and reckless allegations. It led to a nationwide witch hunt based on a supposed "Red Menace" that not only fostered a fear of communist subversion but also contributed to widespread anti-Semitism and xenophobia.

In 2011, Representative Peter T. King of New York, who was then the chairman of the House Homeland Security Committee in Congress, began an inquiry into "the radicalization" of the Muslim American community—literally placing a person's faith on trial. Many called King's hearings McCarthy-style inquisitions that would put law-abiding Muslim Americans and their religious convictions on the stand.[37] According to the Muslim Congressman Keith Ellison's testimony during the hearings, much of the FBI's intelligence over the years has come from Muslim Americans and these hearings would hold an entire community accountable for the actions of a few individuals.[38]

A government-backed inquiry into ideological beliefs is a dangerous precedent to follow, especially when it comes to communities that are already stigmatized and vulnerable within the larger society. Once a tool for surveilling
people's ideologies is put in place, its parameters can evolve to suit the needs of
the state and what it deems as threatening. The primary purpose of a state apparatus then becomes to preserve itself rather than to serve the people. There was a
time when the U.S. government considered civil rights, women's rights, and gay
rights movements as active threats to the state. The state did not see these movements for what they were, quintessentially American values in action; instead,
they viewed them as a threat to the country. The FBI had infiltrated aspects of
each of these movements, just as the FBI had recently infiltrated mosques and
Muslim student associations. This sort of micro-policing leads not just to the
suppression of free speech, but also to a hostile relationship between the state
and its people. Additionally, it makes minorities into outsiders. If a persecuted
community challenges the state to do its job better, instead of being viewed as
patriotic and politically participatory citizens, they can be considered an enemy
of the state. Opposition to war, to police brutality, etc. may then be viewed as
unpatriotic, rather than pushing America to be its best.

Furthermore, thought policing religion via the state is antithetical to
American values. There are many abhorrent beliefs that we tolerate in the name
of protecting religious liberty. We certainly know of U.S. Christian religious
communities that shun and discriminate against the LGBTQ community, or that
do not extend religious leadership roles to women, or religious communities that
refuse life-saving treatment to their minors in the name of religion, or those that
blame natural catastrophe on the moral failures of those suffering, etc. Certainly,
such stances are harmful to a large subset of our society, resulting in hate crimes,
moral judgment, death, and/or the amount of donations that the victims of a
particular disaster receive. However, the government does not employ a test to
ensure that only the "correct" or "non-harmful" interpretation of the religion is
disseminated in our society.

There is a practical reason why we do not police people's thoughts and a
philosophical reason as well. Practically speaking, we already have laws that
protect society against harms of various sorts. We even have criminal charges
for planning to commit harm. However, we do not police the thoughts of folks
who believe that gays are destined to hell, even though homophobia results in a
high number of hate crimes. The philosophical reason for not policing people
for their beliefs is that our thoughts belong to us. No one else can really have
access to them in the same way we do, nor should we be compelled to reveal our
innermost thoughts without wanting to do so on our own terms. If and when a
person begins to plan a crime, and the government has credible evidence of such
planning, it already has the laws on the books to arrest and charge that person.
Mere affiliation with the second largest practiced religion in world is not sufficient grounds for the government to destroy such a dearly held human value and
mandate access to the beliefs of some of the most vulnerable, those fleeing war
and genocide.

5. Conclusion

A religion-based immigration test would be an instance of thought policing, something that has historically been deployed by the state to further marginalize already persecuted communities. A thought policing mandate would destroy a dearly held value of having privacy of thought, and we already have laws that protect us against folks planning hateful crimes.

It is undeniable that an immigration test based on religion would be extremely hard to implement, and even if we figured out a way to execute it, it would only add more bureaucracy to an already inefficient immigration system. It would be completely ineffective in identifying terrorists; rather, it would make many Muslim immigrants ashamed and keen to hide a fundamental aspect of who they are. But it would not only impact immigrants, as non-Muslim Americans will absorb the notion that there is something inherently problematic about Muslims, creating a hostile environment toward their fellow Muslim American citizens. Most importantly, it would make us complicit in making desperate refugees, fleeing from immediate danger, even more vulnerable.

COMPREHENSION QUESTIONS

1. For Fatima, what makes religion-based immigration tests impractical?
2. What distinction does Fatima make between explicit and implicit tests? What are the problems with each type?
3. How, in Fatima's view, do immigration tests based on religious beliefs promote anti-Muslim racism?
4. How are immigration tests based on religious beliefs a form of "thought policing"?
5. Ultimately, what practical and philosophical reasons does Fatima offer in support of her view that the government shouldn't investigate people based on their beliefs?

DISCUSSION QUESTIONS

1. Fatima notes that it's plausible that religion-based immigration tests are designed to foster fear of and hatred toward the targeted religious group, but notes there could be a more charitable interpretation of such tests. What would that interpretation be?
2. Fatima suggests that using culture to explain politics can have the effect of oversimplifying people's understanding of the political situation in question and reducing religious and other cultural groups to false caricatures. Is it *ever* useful to explain political phenomena in terms of culture and/or religion? If so, when?
3. What is "preposterous" about using ideological tests to identify potential mass shooters? Do you think this is a good analogy for immigration tests based on religious beliefs?
4. Fatima asserts that people's beliefs—their thoughts—shouldn't be subject to investigation by the government. What kinds of criteria, if any, should governments use to screen people who wish to immigrate?

Case 2

> On June 26, 2018, the U.S. Supreme Court upheld the travel ban under discussion in the introduction of Fatima's essay. Justice Breyer, joined by Justice Kagan, issued a dissenting opinion in which he posited that the legality of the president's executive order turns on whether it was indeed driven by hostility toward Muslims. Arguably, the morality of the order turns on the same question. Justice Breyer wrote:
>
> > The question before us is whether Proclamation No. 9645 is lawful. If its promulgation or content was significantly affected by religious animus against Muslims, it would violate the relevant statute or the First Amendment itself. . . . If, however, its sole *ratio decidendi* was one of national security, then it would be unlikely to violate either the statute or the Constitution. Which is it? Members of the Court principally disagree about the answer to this question, i.e., about whether or the extent to which religious animus played a significant role in the Proclamation's promulgation or content.*
>
> What kind of information would you need to answer Breyer's question—that is, to determine whether Trump's executive order was primarily motivated by anti-Muslim sentiment? (Consider events leading up to and following the implementation of the order).
>
> ———————
>
> *https://www.supremecourt.gov/opinions/17pdf/17-965_h315.pdf

REPLY TO FATIMA
I. G.

Professor Fatima and I agree about several issues. First, we can't determine which aspect or version of Islam is to blame for the acts we call "Islamic terrorism." Moreover, even if we could, it would be impossible to find out who subscribes to it. That's why the only feasible religious tests are country bans and strict quotas. More importantly, Fatima and I agree about the ideals at stake: freedom of thought and religion. We are both concerned that preventing the followers of one specific religion from immigrating is in tension with the separation of church and state, constitutes government intrusion into private lives, and borders on thought surveillance.

This is where agreement ends, however: Fatima appears to think that we face an easy choice between liberty and tyranny. We don't. Thanks to radical Muslims, the West must choose between a state of terror perpetrated by self-appointed sharia police, and preemption of such terror by not letting in more potential terrorizers. I submit that the latter is the lesser of two evils.

South Park illustrates the reality of this dilemma. In one of its episodes, Jesus embarks on a violent rampage and kills several Iraqis to save Santa from captivity. In another, Mosaic Jews worship a bloodthirsty deity. Yet, the only episodes censored and pulled in its 287-episode history are the two that briefly showed the likeness of Muhammad (without any negative commentary).[39] Why? Answer: fear of violent retaliation. American entertainers can freely say that Catholic clergy are rapists who worship Spider Queen Lolth, they can call Joseph Smith a fraud and his followers dumb, and they can show the Virgin Mary's anus spraying the pope's face with blood. But if someone airs a neutral image of Muhammad for two seconds, we must start worrying about cars getting turned over, buildings burning down, and people dying.

It could have been worse. In Europe, where Muslims make up about 4% of the population, folks don't worry about retaliation; *they expect it*. Directed a film criticizing Islam? You will be pulled down from your bicycle on an Amsterdam street and slaughtered while begging for your life.[40] Printed a Muhammed cartoon? You will be gunned down with assault rifles.[41]

When such things happen often enough, "secular" authorities will happily start censoring speech in the name of "religious tolerance," as they did in the case of Olympic gymnast Louis Smith, who made a video mocking Muslims and was suspended for two months.[42] "Since when did the British start enforcing blasphemy laws?" you might ask. Answer: since Muslims moved in *en masse*.

So, the choice isn't between liberty and tyranny: It's between a society terrorized by Islam and a society shielded from it. We should close the door while we still can.

Fatima sees closing the door as futile, claiming that Trump's "Muslim ban" "would not have prevented the male shooter in San Bernardino, as he was born in Chicago." This is misleading because *the other shooter was born in Pakistan*. It's also illogical because the Chicago-born shooter's parents are Pakistani immigrants. When evaluating the effects of immigration policy we should ask what can be expected, not only from the first generation, but also from the next.

So, we should try to find a way of preventing parents such as Mr. Farook's from entering the United States, and for reasons Fatima herself eloquently articulated, the only feasible courses of action are bans or strict quotas. Which one should it be?

At first glance, quotas appear superior. Religiosity is inversely correlated with intelligence[43] and certain types of education.[44] The United States can use this to "skim the cognitive cream" of Muslim societies, letting in only those with exceptional intelligence and skills. This would greatly limit the total influx and decrease the overall religiosity of incomers. It would also benefit the United States, for the group in question tends to be hardworking, cultured, and law-abiding. Notice, this is close to what the United States is doing already. All that's new in this proposal is making high cognitive standards the exclusive criterion. Yet, a complete ban would be easier to implement. More importantly, it could also benefit Muslim societies themselves. By not stealing their best and brightest, we would let the Muslim world improve.

The life of John Snow (no, not the one in *Game of Thrones*) is an illustration of this benefit. Snow was a British physician who discovered what causes cholera. He lived before the germ theory was taken seriously. The popular belief at the time was that "bad air" caused cholera. Unlike his contemporaries, Snow suspected that the real cause was contaminated drinking water. He presented his idea to the Royal Society where he was met with ridicule, dismissal, and hostility. But Snow kept fighting. He documented hundreds of cases; interviewed countless patients and relatives; examined water wells, septic pits, and street pumps; and put together a scientific masterpiece proving that it was the water. Still, the old guard resisted and sabotaged him. Despite his hard work and genius, Snow enjoyed recognition only posthumously. But thanks to the uphill battle he fought against ignorance and superstition, London was the first city in the world to eradicate cholera.

Now the key question: "Would John Snow have stayed in his home country and fought his battle if he could have immigrated to a better, freer land, one where his work was supported rather than mocked?" I am not sure that he would have. I wouldn't have. I didn't.

I would love to believe that humanity's progress is the handiwork of the common man. In reality, however, great advances are owed almost entirely to the gifted and industrious few. Societies that lose their Avicennas, Spinozas, and Snows remain in darkness. Perhaps that's what's wrong with Muslim societies today: Those like Fatima and me, and too many others more intelligent and creative than we are, sailed beyond the sunset and the baths of all the Western stars. Perhaps we should stay home and fight for our liberty, and for yours.

COMPREHENSION QUESTIONS

1. In I. G.'s view, what sets Islam apart from the other religions he mentions?
2. According to I. G., what is at stake if the United States does not implement a religion-based immigration policy that targets Muslims? How does this differ from Fatima's view?
3. Why, according to I. G., might a complete restriction of immigration from Muslim societies be better than a strict quota?

DISCUSSION QUESTIONS

1. I. G. posits that "not letting in more potential terrorizers" is the lesser of two evil options. What is evil about this option, in his view? In yours? Or is there perhaps nothing evil about it? What do you think of this way of framing the dilemma?
2. I. G. writes, "[W]e can't determine which aspect or version of Islam is to blame for the acts we call 'Islamic terrorism.'" To what extent do you think Islam or some aspect of it is to blame? What other factors, if any, should be taken into consideration when thinking about the causes and context of violent extremism?
3. According to I. G., admitting exceptionally intelligent and skilled people from Muslim societies to the United States would be beneficial for the United States. Perhaps it would also demonstrate respect for their desires and improve their quality of life. Do you think "letting the Muslim world improve" is a more important or otherwise better goal? Why or why not?
4. Is I. G. ignoring the possible negative effects of immigration restrictions on Western countries?

REPLY TO I. G.
SABA FATIMA

I must begin by condemning the treatment that I. G. was subjected to by his tormentors. Child abuse never has any justification. I also agree with I. G. that one ought not to dismiss another's argument simply because it is rooted in personal experience or is motivated by emotions. In fact, I would go even further and say that personal experiences offer us a phenomenological account, invaluable testimony, and nuanced narrative of how oppression works, all of which cannot be garnered from an outsider report of events. So I commend and thank I. G. in having the courage to share some of his experiences to shine a light on this particular sort of trauma.

I. G.'s main argument is that Islam produces "a culture of fear," such that most practitioners of the religion remain silent, and hence become complicit in the atrocities that a minority of Muslims commit. Thus we should limit Muslim immigration into this country.

Let me start by noting that other mainstream religions have been used to incite violence. The United States has a brutal history, where Christianity was used to justify slavery and subjugation of an entire people for over a century. Slaves were forced to give up their religions, which included Islam.[45] Fast-forward into the nineteenth and twentieth century, and the Ku Klux Klan (KKK) drew its foundation from Protestant Christianity, burning crosses on the lawns of blacks and their white allies to instill fear. For Klan members, they embodied "one hundred percent American values," "but the Klan's unity was narrowly limited to those people they thought qualified as truly American—only white Protestants."[46] The amount and intensity of violence perpetrated by the KKK in the United States, up until the 1970s, cannot be understated. Even now, there has been a resurgence of white nationalist groups that draw their foundations from the KKK.[47] Does this mean that white versions of the Protestant faith are ideologically racist?

If we step outside of the United States, we observe that in China, up to a million Uighurs are being held in detention camps so that the government can cleanse the captives of Islam. The Uighurs are a Turkic Muslim minority in China. They are currently being detained for displaying any religious affiliation to Islam and are subjected to "physical and verbal abuse by guards; grinding routines of singing, lectures and self-criticism meetings; and the gnawing anxiety of not knowing when they would be released."[48] Should we screen immigrating Chinese persons on this basis?

Similarly, Buddhist-majority Myanmar has been conducting its own ethnic cleansing of Rohingya Muslims, creating the "world's fastest-growing humanitarian crisis."[49] Meanwhile, many Buddhist spiritual leaders and practitioners refuse to accept that there is even a crisis to begin with, while others look the other way. Should we have a test for Buddhists entering the country?

I give all these examples involving various religions to show that religion-based violence and oppression is neither something that is unique to Islam nor more likely than any other ideology to produce violence and a culture of fear.

In fact, the common thread in many of these acts of violence is authoritarianism. An authoritarian regime or structure is one where there is a strong central power that for the most part eclipses individual rights, limits free association of individuals, and arbitrarily exercises power without regard to accountability to constitutional law or to the subjects it governs. Modern-day China under Xi–Li, or Turkey under Islamist Erdoğan (or, for that matter, Turkey under *secularist* Atatürk[50]), or North Korea under Kim Jong-un, or the Philippines under Duterte, would all be examples of authoritarian regimes. Only one of these examples involves a Muslim-majority country, yet many folks living under these regimes would attest to the sort of violence that I. G. describes in his essay. Authoritarian structures generally rely on intimidation, repression, corruption, and, most importantly, suppression of dissent via propagandist tactics. They also instill a culture of fear in their subjects that subdues them and prevents them from speaking out. Subjects of authoritarian regimes fear that they could be the next target of the power structure.

I would claim here that violence is precipitated by various factors, such as authoritarianism, colonialism, racism, xenophobia, misogyny, etc. All these systems of oppression act upon various aspects of our identities differently, depending on where we are situated. Islam is one such aspect of identity in many people's lives. A very tiny minority of Muslims find justification for violence in Islam, while the vast majority of Muslims find Islam to be a motivation for their daily acts of kindness and living a conscientious life on this earth. Something similar is true for any major religion, despite the examples mentioned above.

These points aside, my main worry about I. G.'s argument is that it relies on a purity test to determine who can enter the United States. If we follow I. G.'s logic of keeping out someone because of where they are from and what their religion is, we end up with a mythical "pure" notion of the United States, where we keep out all those we find undesirable. But as we know through history, our conception of who we consider desirable and undesirable shifts with our racist and xenophobic biases. Furthermore, with an immigration test such as this, it is not simply that we blame people for their beliefs—which, as I argued in my main piece, is nearly impossible to do—but rather we blame them for the sins of "their" people. We indict them as a collective and ignore the atrocities being inflicted on them at the hands of the very terrorists we claim to fight against. Having an immigration test based on religion subjects individuals to gatekeeping based on our misconceptions of their group identity. Such an immigration test is bound to lead us further down the path of xenophobia and racism.

COMPREHENSION QUESTIONS

1. To what does Fatima attribute the violence that I. G. argues is produced by Islam?
2. Fatima uses the examples of detention and persecution of Muslim groups in China and Myanmar to illustrate what point?
3. What does Fatima mean when she says that I. G.'s argument relies on a "purity test to determine who can enter the United States"?

DISCUSSION QUESTIONS

1. Does Fatima identify any points of agreement between her perspective and I. G.'s? Can you identify any?
2. To what extent do you think the immigration policies I. G. supports would "lead us further down the path of xenophobia and racism"? Why?

FURTHER READINGS

Hosein, Adam. "Immigration and Freedom of Movement." *Ethics and Global Politics* 6, no. 1 (2013): 25–37.
Parekh, Serena. *Refugee Crisis: The Borders of Human Mobility*. New York: Routledge, 2018.
Sheth, Falguni. *Toward a Political Philosophy of Race*. New York: SUNY Press, 2009.

NOTES

1. http://data.worldbank.org/indicator/NY.GNP.PCAP.PP.CD?contextual=aggregate&end=2015&locations=TR&start=1967
2. http://www.hurriyetdailynews.com/polls-finding-on-islam-and-violence-should-ring-alarm-bells.aspx?pageID=449&nID=77797&NewsCatID=412
3. http://abcnews.go.com/GMA/video/isis-claims-killed-japanese-hostage-kenji-goto-28640818
4. http://observers.france24.com/en/20130122-muslim-patrols-sharia-east-london-video-tower-hamlets
5. http://www.bbc.com/news/world-europe-35059488
6. http://www.dw.com/en/string-of-new-years-eve-sexual-assaults-outrages-cologne/a-18958334; http://www.bbc.com/news/world-europe-35280386
7. http://www.ft.com/cms/s/2/a5bcc8ce-8bb1-11e5-a549-b89a1dfede9b.html#axzz47WnKkK55
8. http:// www.theguardian.com/world/2016/mar/24/brussels-attack-belgium-homegrown-jihadis-slip-net-isis
9. https://www.forbes.com/sites/erikaandersen/2012/03/23/true-fact-the-lack-of-pirates-is-causing-global-warming/#55437f403a67
10. https://www.csmonitor.com/World/Europe/2010/0120/Why-German-public-schools-now-teach-Islam
11. https://www.humanium.org/en/educating-immigrants-in-germany/
12. For instance, in Saudi Arabia proselytizing by non-Muslims is punishable by death. https://www.state.gov/j/drl/rls/irf/2008/108492.htm
13. https://www.christiantoday.com/article/turkey.christian.missionaries.horrifically.tortured.before.killings/10523.htm
14. The Christchurch massacre is a horrifying recent example of such violence.
15. G. Lewy, *America in Vietnam* (New York: Oxford University Press, 1978), 442–453.
16. R. Rhodes, "The General and World War III," *The New Yorker* (June 19, 1995), 53.
17. J. W. Dower, *War Without Mercy* (New York: Pantheon Books, 1986), 297–299.
18. J. M. Keynes, *A Tract on Monetary Reform* (Cambridge: Cambridge University Press, 2013), 65.
19. http://foreignpolicy.com/2016/06/14/if-islam-is-a-religion-of-violence-so-is-christianity/
20. http://www.timesofisrael.com/450-of-452-suicide-attacks-in-2015-were-by-muslim-extremists-study-shows/

21. A 2014 report by the non-partisan organization Pew Research Center shows that that out of twenty countries that were rated to have "very high social hostilities involving religion," eighteen are Muslim-majority. Moreover, the two exceptions (i.e., Russia and Israel) have sizeable Muslim minorities (for details, see http://www.pewforum .org/2014/01/14/religious-hostilities-reach-six-year-high/). However, the point is not limited to countries. The same pattern is visible in Muslim communities within non-Muslim countries; they also tend to produce more religious hostility and violence than the population they are embedded into.

22. https://www.newyorker.com/magazine/2015/10/19/thresholds-of-violence

23. https://en.wikipedia.org/wiki/Turan_Dursun; https://en.wikipedia.org/wiki/U%C4%9 Fur_Mumcu; https://en.wikipedia.org/wiki/Muammer_Aksoy; https://en.wikipedia .org/wiki/Bahriye_%C3%9C%C3%A7ok; https://en.wikipedia.org/wiki/Ahmet_Taner _K%C4%B1%C5%9Flal%C4%B1

24. http://www.ottawasun.com/2011/08/26/anti-muslim-author-threaten-beaten

25. http://www.theguardian.com/world/2016/feb/02/palestinian-poet-ashraf-fayadhs -death-sentence-overturned-by-saudi-court

26. http://www.iranhrdc.org/english/publications/reports/1000000512-apostasy-in-the -Islamic-Republic-of-Iran.html#326 https://www.iranrights.org/library/document/3078

27. http://www.nytimes.com/2004/11/03/world/europe/dutch-filmmaker-an-islam-critic -is-killed.html?_r=1

28. http://www.theguardian.com/world/2015/aug/07/machete-gang-kills-secular -bangladeshi-blogger-niloy-chakrabarti

29. http://www.hurriyetdailynews.com/turkey-frees-five-charged-over-2007-murders-of -christian-missionaries-------.aspx?pageID=238&nID=63345&NewsCatID=338

30. Jenna Johnson, "Trump Calls for 'Total and Complete Shutdown of Muslims Entering the United States,'" *Washington Post*, December 7, 2015, https://www.washingtonpost .com/news/post-politics/wp/2015/12/07/donald-trump-calls-for-total-and-complete -shutdown-of-muslims-entering-the-united-states/?utm_term=.33229113778c

31. Amy B. Wang, "Trump Asked for a 'Muslim Ban,' Giuliani Says—and Ordered a Commission to Do It 'Legally,'" *Washington Post*, January 29, 2017, https://www .washingtonpost.com/news/the-fix/wp/2017/01/29/trump-asked-for-a-muslim-ban -giuliani-says-and-ordered-a-commission-to-do-it-legally/?utm_term=.5a2c6624ee34

32. Rockwell and Churchill, *The Colonial Laws of Massachusetts: Reprinted from the Edition of 1660, 1889–Boston (Mass.)*, p. 155, https://books.google.com/books?id=IGJMAQAA IAAJ&pg=PA155#v=onepage&q&f=false

33. Ryan Devereaux, "An Interview with Michael T. Flynn, the Ex-Pentagon Spy Who Supports Donald Trump," *The Intercept*, July 13, 2016, https://theintercept.com/2016/07/13 /an-interview-with-lt-gen-michael-flynn/

34. RWW Blog, "RWW News: Michael Flynn: Islam Is a 'Cancer,' 'Political Ideology' that 'Hides Behind' Religion," *YouTube.com*, November 18, 2016, https://www.youtube.com /watch?v=fzh9b_vo4vs

35. See ISPU American Muslim Poll Key Findings, Institute for Social Policy and Understanding, 2016, https://www.ispu.org/wp-content/uploads/2016/08/ampkeyfindings -2.pdf: "There is no correlation between Muslim attitudes toward violence and their frequency of mosque attendance. Muslim Americans who regularly attend mosques are more likely than those who do not frequent mosques to work with their neighbors to solve community problems (49 vs. 30 percent), be registered to vote (74 vs. 49 percent), and are more likely to plan to vote (92 vs. 81 percent)." Also see Amaney Jamal, "The Political Participation and Engagement of Muslim Americans Mosque Involvement and Group Consciousness,"

American Politics Research 33, no. 4 (2005): 521–544, where the author concludes that "[f]or Arab Muslims, mosques are directly linked to political activity, civic participation, and group consciousness. For African and Arab Americans, the mosque serves as a collectivizing forum that highlights Muslim common struggles in mainstream American society."

36. Saba Fatima, "Muslim-American Scripts," *Hypatia* 28, no. 2 (2013): 353–354.

37. Dave Goldiner, "Rep. Peter King to Hold Hearings on 'Radicalization' of American Muslims, Critics Fear Witchhunt," *New York Daily News*, December 19, 2010, http://www.nydailynews.com/ny_local/2010/12/19/2010-12-19_rep_peter_king_to_hold _hearings_on_radicalization_of_american_muslims_critics_fe.html

38. Keith Ellison, "Keith Ellison's Testimony Before House Homeland Security Committee," *MinnPost.com*, March 10, 2011, https://www.minnpost.com/infodoc/2011/03 /keith-ellisons-testimony-house-homeland-security-committee/

39. https://news.avclub.com/an-uncensored-version-of-south-parks-controversial-muha -1798265835; https://en.wikipedia.org/wiki/201_(South_Park)#/media/File:Sp_1406 _Sorry.jpg

40. https://www.theguardian.com/world/2004/nov/07/terrorism.religion

41. https://www.bbc.co.uk/news/world-europe-30708237

42. https://www.theguardian.com/sport/blog/2016/nov/02/louis-smith-ban-british -gymnastics

43. M. Zuckerman et al., "The Relation Between Intelligence and Religiosity: A Meta-Analysis and Some Proposed Explanations," *Personality and Psychology Review* 17, no. 4 (2013): 325–354.

44. http://www.pewforum.org/religious-landscape-study/educational-distribution/

45. Amiri Baraka, *Blues People: Negro Music in White America* (New York: Harper Perennial, 1999), 32–33.

46. Kelly J. Baker, "The Artifacts of White Supremacy," *Religion & Culture Forum*, June 14, 2017, https://voices.uchicago.edu/religionculture/2017/06/14/813/

47. Adam Serwer, "The White Nationalists Are Winning," *The Atlantic*, August 10, 2018, https://www.theatlantic.com/ideas/archive/2018/08/the-battle-that-erupted-in -charlottesville-is-far-from-over/567167/

48. Chris Buckley, "China Is Detaining Muslims in Vast Numbers. The Goal: 'Transformation.'" *New York Times*, September 8, 2018, https://www.nytimes.com/2018/09/08/world/asia /china-uighur-muslim-detention-camp.html?module=Uisil

49. "Myanmar Rohingya, What You Need to Know About the Crisis," *BBC*, April 24, 2018, https://www.bbc.com/news/world-asia-41566561

50. Halil Karaveli, *Why Is Turkey Authoritarian? From Atatürk to Erdoğan* (London: Pluto Press, 2018).

CHAPTER 6

Taxation

TWO ARGUMENTS FOR PROGRESSIVE TAXATION
BRUNO VERBEEK

If progressive or unequal taxes are permitted, the time cannot
be distant when the majority of the voters will confiscate private
property under the cloaks or pretense of taxation, and the worst
follies and crimes of history will be repeated.

WILLIAM D. GUTHRIE,
*Lectures on the Fourteenth Article of Amendment to the
Constitution of the United States,* 1898

1. Introduction

In 2013, Warren Buffett, the multimillionaire investor, gave an interview to CNN
in which he stated that his secretary paid a larger share of her income in taxes
than he does.[1] He went on to argue that this was "clearly" unfair and unjust: How
could it be that ultra-rich people like himself—members of the 1%—pay a smaller
share of their income in taxes than average income earners?[2]

Many Americans would agree with Buffett.[3] In this chapter, I want to discuss
some reasons as to why Mr. Buffett is correct in judging this distribution of the
tax burden unfair and why a fair distribution of the tax burden requires that rich
people, like Mr. Buffett, should pay a larger share of their income in taxes than
poor people.[4]

In what follows, I will discuss two arguments in favor of progressive tax burdens. First, the argument that progressive taxation is an effective instrument for
realizing a just distribution of burdens and benefits over society. Next, I will discuss an often-heard objection to that type of argument. Answering the objection
leads me to discuss a principle that justifies a duty to pay taxes in general. In the
final sections, I will show how that principle, combined with some other considerations, leads to the conclusion that progressive tax rates are required, which
will be the second argument.

234 ETHICS, LEFT AND RIGHT

2. Progressive Tax Rates as an Instrument for Distributive Justice

For most philosophers, the question how the burdens of taxation should be distributed is part of a larger question of distributive justice.[5] Justice is not only about the distribution of the burdens; it is also a matter of the distribution of the benefits. If one focuses exclusively on the distribution of burdens, then one is guilty of what Liam Murphy and Thomas Nagel call "myopia."[6] Such an exclusive focus is myopic for two reasons. First, a tax is a burden, but "burden" is a relative notion: Something is a burden relative to some benchmark.

Many are inclined to think that taxation is a burden relative to the pretax income distribution. However, this ignores the amount of state activity that was needed to enable taxpayers to earn their pretax income in the first place. The state was instrumental for setting up a system of rights and rights protection in the form of contract law, criminal law, courts, and police. In addition, it was involved in the creation of infrastructure and other public goods and services that make economic transactions possible in the first place.

Second, it also ignores what is subsequently done with the tax revenues. For example, suppose A and B are both farmers and earn the same pretax income of $100,000. Suppose that A has to pay $5,000 in taxes while B has to pay $10,000. We could not say whether that is fair or unfair to B, unless we also look at what the state does with the tax revenue. If, for example, B receives an agricultural subsidy of $5,000 while A does not, we could not maintain that B is treated unfairly in comparison to A.

If this is correct, then it's a form of intellectual "myopia" to focus on the burdens of taxation in isolation of what made the pretax income possible and what is done with tax revenues. Furthermore, it follows that the pretax income distribution is not morally relevant for determining the just distribution of burdens and benefits. Therefore, Mr. Buffett's tax burden and that of other members of the "1%" must be assessed against the overall picture of the economic outcomes.

Rather than asking "Is it fair that Mr. Buffett faces a smaller effective rate than his secretary?" the question should be "How should Mr. Buffett and his secretary be taxed so as to realize most effectively and efficiently a just distribution of benefits and burdens?"[7] Note that on this way of thinking about taxation, there is no *special* question whether progressive taxation is fair; what matters is whether the overall outcomes of state activity are fair. Taxation on this view is just one of the instruments that states use to achieve their policy aims. For this reason, I will call this type of approach *instrumentalist*.[8]

Philosophers, like everybody else, tend to disagree about what makes a distribution just. Some argue for equality of well-being; others claim that justice requires equal opportunities for all; some accept inequality as long as it is to the benefit of the least well off; etc. Suppose that a just society is one with a moderate level of inequality where no one is below a certain level of economic circumstances ensuring that a decent life is possible. A decent life is one where you don't have to beg for food or health care, where you have a roof over your head, where you can look your fellow citizens in the eye, and where you have equal standing before the law. Full disclosure: I subscribe to that view. I believe that affluent societies, like the United States, have a duty not to let their residents fall below this threshold.

On such a view of distributive justice, there are many things that are potentially worrying about the tax burdens of Warren Buffet and other members of the "1%." For example, one could question the impact this distribution of tax burdens has on economic outcomes. If the least advantaged people are even less well off because of a lack of progression in tax burdens such that they fall below the threshold of a decent life (e.g., because certain welfare programs will be underfunded) then this would be a reason to increase the rate for individuals like Buffet. Similarly, there is (hotly disputed) statistical evidence that high rates of inequality correlate with all types of social and health problems not just for the less advantaged, but also for the middle classes and the rich.[9] In addition, there are (again, hotly disputed) worries of political equality concerning the extreme disparity in political influence the very rich have.[10] One of the remedies for all these injustices is taxation. Progressive taxation, on this view, is an instrument for the realization of a just overall distribution of economic and political outcomes.[11] This instrumentalist approach is the prevailing type of argument for progressive taxation.

3. A Violation of Property Rights?

There are challenges to this way of thinking about the fairness of progressive taxation. For starters, if this is how one would defend progressive taxation, the case for progressive taxation depends on what view of distributive justice is correct. Given that there are fierce debates within philosophy, politics, and law on this matter, chances of consensus are slim.[12] In the absence of an agreement, this does not seem a very promising strategy to pursue. However, this is not a problem unique to assessing the justice of tax burdens: Any question of fair distribution will have to confront that problem sooner or later.

There is a more fundamental objection: Such an instrumentalist approach to taxation violates people's property rights to their labor income. A good example of this view is the libertarian philosopher Robert Nozick, who argued that all taxation is a form of forced labor: "Taxation of earnings from labor is on a par with forced labor. Some persons find this claim obviously true: taking the earnings of *n* hours labor is like taking *n* hours from the person; it is like forcing the person to work *n* hours for another's purpose."[13] Nozick goes on to explain what he finds wrong with "taking the earnings of *n* hours of labor." It is a violation of the property rights that people have in their own bodies and the fruits of their efforts.[14] Since your labor income is one of these fruits, it means that you have a property right to your pretax labor income. We can extend this argument to other forms of income and wealth. For example, savings is nothing but the accumulated labor income not consumed. Inheritance is a source of income that is the result of labor and effort of previous generations, etc. Taxation, therefore, on this view, essentially is a form of theft.

To have a property right in something, Nozick continues, means that you have the right to determine what shall be done with it. Obviously, that right is restricted. As long as you do not violate the rights of others, you have absolute control over your property. If the state, or anybody else, claims part of your property, they are mistaken, and if they seize it without your consent, they are thieves. This is a powerful argument that resonates with how many people feel when they receive their tax assessments. The state is seen as forcefully taking away what rightfully belongs to citizens.[15] If one is defending taxation—especially if one is defending progressive taxation—it needs to be answered.

There are several ways in which philosophers and others have tried answering it. For instance, some argue that we *did* consent to the state taxing us and that taxation, therefore, is not a violation of our rights. They argue that, for example, by voting we appointed representatives and gave them the authority to levy taxes on us. More generally, they would argue that by participating in society, we implicitly gave our consent to the state, and that included consenting to its authority to tax us.

That is an unconvincing answer: If participating in society is to be construed as a form of freely giving consent, it must be possible not to consent. If the answer is that you can always emigrate if you do not like it, that is like saying that the Mafioso, who points a gun at your knee and offers you the choice between losing a kneecap or giving up your wallet, offers you a real choice, and that when you give up your wallet, you have freely consented to do so. In general, consent-based arguments for taxation are not very convincing.[16]

4. Absolute Property Rights?

So how can we answer Nozick's objection? Notice that Nozick can argue that taxation is theft by positing the premise that people have property rights to their income. Any claim on that income by others is illegitimate. Defenders of the instrumentalist approach to progressive taxation typically deny that premise. People do not own their pretax labor income precisely because they still owe taxes to the state. Taxation, therefore, is not a violation of property rights—because you never had a property right in your pretax income.[17] You are, as it were, the administrative placeholder where the pretax revenues of your activities are deposited. They will become yours only after all legitimate claims—including fiscal claims—on that income have been met. If this is correct, the notion that the state takes "your" money when taxing you is an illusion: It was never yours to begin with.[18]

Both the argument that taxation is theft and this reply assume that Nozick is right about what it means to have a property right to something: that you have the right to determine what shall be done with it. Such a right, it is assumed, is incompatible with claims of others on it. This is why Nozick can argue that taxation is theft and why his critics can argue that nobody owns their pretax income.

However, is this characterization of a property right as a kind of absolute right correct? Suppose I lend you $10 and you promise to pay it back to me. It now is yours to spend and do with what you want (assuming you do not use it to violate people's rights). That is, it is your property; however, you do have to repay me at some time. So it seems you can have full property in something while at the same time there are legitimate claims of others on that something. Why would this be different for the state and the tax claims on its residents? This explains why people are correct that the state is taxing their property. At the same time, it might explain why the state is not engaging in an activity that is morally on a par with theft, but only if we can show that taxpayers have a moral obligation to the state to pay their taxes.

5. Fairness and Taxation

Taxation can be regarded as a legal instrument whereby the state imposes duties on residents to achieve certain goals. The choice of instrument is not neutral. Each type of instrument comes with its own factual and normative constraints. For example, one cannot use taxation to make citizens get out of bed each day at 7 a.m. It is not a suitable instrument for that. This is a factual constraint. An example of a normative constraint is that every time the state imposes a tax, it imposes a duty on those subject to it that was not there before. This is only possible if there is a justification as to why the state has such powers. If there is not, this claim of the state is unsuccessful and the tax measure fails to meet essential normative constraints.

If we develop this thought a bit further, it means that we should start looking for a principle that explains why the state can impose new (fiscal) duties. We have already seen one such principle, consent, and rejected it. Consent is not suitable for grounding the power of the state to impose tax duties on residents.

Another, more promising principle is the principle of fairness.[19] The principle of fairness says that whenever you benefit from a cooperative enterprise, you are under an obligation to carry a share of the burdens. For example, suppose A and B dig a well. If C now uses the well to get some water, C is obliged to share in the maintenance of that well. Stated in this crude form, the principle is implausible. What if the benefits to C are purely accidental? (For example, because the well regularly spills over, thus inadvertently irrigating C's land.) What if C doesn't want the benefits bestowed on her by A and B? What if the obligation to contribute is very burdensome in comparison to the benefit enjoyed?[20]

A more plausible formulation of the principle of fairness says that the receipt of benefits from a good produced in a cooperative scheme generates an obligation to support provision if (1) the good can be presumed to benefit the recipient, (2) the good is worth the recipient's effort in supporting provision, and (3) the benefits and burdens are fairly distributed.[21] Suppose A and B dig the only well in the middle of a desert. Once it is there, there is water in abundance. If C now uses the well to get some water (so we can safely assume that the water is of benefit to C), A and B can require that C contribute to the maintenance of that well, provided the water is worth the effort for C and the effort required from C is proportionate to how much she benefits.

This formulation of the principle goes a long way in answering the questions above. The principle only applies to those who benefit from the cooperative scheme: the residents of the state. It specifies that the burdens the state imposes on residents have to be fair: They should be proportionate to the benefits received. The principle of fairness, therefore, specifies a prohibition of free riding on the efforts of others in maintaining a just and beneficial society.[22]

If this is correct—and a lot more will have to be said about this, to take away all worries that opponents still might have—we can see why there is an obligation to pay the taxes that the state levies upon us. They represent our share in the burdens in the maintenance of a just and beneficial state. It also explains why there are principled limits to how much or how little you can be taxed. Taxation that goes beyond what is proportionate is ruled out, as is taxation for purposes other than maintaining a just and beneficial state.

6. A Non-Instrumentalist Argument for Progressive Taxation

What exactly are the benefits of living in a just and beneficial state? To begin with, the state provides all kinds of goods and services that are beneficial to all: a legal system that regulates and makes possible an efficient economy, provides protection against crime, delivers safety from foreign incursions, creates infrastructure, etc. Some argue that if this is *all* that the state does, then we should not have a progressive tax rate, but a flat tax.[23] This raises an important question: What's the best way to determine a proportionate share of the burden of maintaining a just and beneficial state?[24]

Here is one proposal: Tax each individual to the extent that the marginal benefit from public spending equals the marginal benefit from private spending.[25] Since people differ in how much they benefit from the state, this means that we should have a differentiated tax rate schedule. If we further assume that Warren Buffett profits much more both in absolute and relative terms from the legal protection of property than an average wage earner, a progressive rate would be called for. For example, one could argue that Warren Buffett and other members of the "1%" benefit from the presence of a well-educated labor force to work in their companies; they benefit from a well-maintained network of roads to ship the goods their factories produce to their customers; they benefit from the protection that police and courts offer them against threats to their homes and possessions, etc. Less-well-off people benefit less, if at all, from these opportunities and protections.[26]

There is a better argument for progressive taxation based on this principle of fairness. Note that even the most ardent supporters of a flat tax defend a tax exemption or earned income allowance for part of one's income. The result is that the effective rate is progressive.[27] What is the justification for this exemption? On the instrumentalist argument, the state should exempt less advantaged people because taxing them at the same rate as rich people would lead to an unjust distribution. Such a justification does not fit well with a non-instrumentalist defense of taxation. A more appropriate justification that does not appeal to any particular conception of distributive justice is the ability-to-pay principle. This principle says, roughly, that the strongest shoulders should carry the heaviest burdens. As a consequence, if your "strength" is not enough or only barely sufficient to support yourself, you cannot be asked to shoulder an additional tax burden.[28]

Stated this crudely, the obvious question will be how to measure one's ability to pay. One answer says that one's ability should be measured in subjective terms; others argue for more objective criteria.[29] Both, however, would lead one to conclude that progressive tax rates are permissible.

At this point, it might be argued that this combination of the principle of fairness with the ability-to-pay principle would lead to quite limited progression and quite limited tax burdens for the "1%." After all, there is only a duty to pay taxes for those goods and services from which one actually benefits. However, this is too limited a view of the benefits that the state provides. We benefit in a great many ways, and these additional benefits increase our fairness obligations, constrained by the ability to pay.

Here is why. We have duties to others. Many of these duties are negative: They forbid us to do certain things to others. We should not harm others, steal their property, etc. Such duties are what Kant calls *perfect* duties: One must always do them, and there is but one way in which one can perform them.[30] In addition, we have *imperfect* duties, duties we may not disregard, but there is discretion in how we discharge these. An example of this latter kind of duty is the duty to help people in need if we can do so at reasonable cost to ourselves. Suppose that there is a natural disaster like a flood, an earthquake, or a tornado. We then have a duty to offer help and relief to the victims. This is an imperfect duty, but a duty nevertheless. It is impermissible to do nothing.

We could, of course, go to the disaster area with soup and blankets, but we will discharge this duty most effectively and efficiently if we coordinate our help efforts. The state provides such coordination services. In fact, a just and beneficial state will have invested in specialized emergency services, like the Federal Emergency Management Agency (FEMA), for this reason. Such services can only function if enough people contribute to these services. Under such circumstances, the imperfect duty to assist people in need has become a perfect duty to contribute to an institutionalized cooperative scheme that discharges that duty at reasonable cost.[31] Even though we don't directly benefit from such emergency services, we do benefit indirectly in that there is a decent, effective, and efficient scheme that discharges our duty to assist people in need at reasonable personal cost. In other words, just as we are under a fairness obligation to contribute to the state for the public goods and services it provides that benefit us directly (like a system of law, infrastructure, etc.), we are under a fairness obligation to contribute to the state for the coordinated efforts it undertakes to collectively discharge our imperfect duties to assist people in need. This holds for our duty to assist people who are victims of natural disasters, but it also holds for our duties to people who are vulnerable or fall below a decent level.

If we apply the ability-to-pay principle to these fairness obligations as well, we see that this obligation does not hold in the same degree for people who find themselves in such needy circumstances. They cannot be asked to contribute to such a scheme, whether they are victims of a natural disaster or are victims of dire economic circumstances, like welfare recipients. To do so would exceed what are reasonable costs to them. Similarly, extremely rich people can and should be asked to contribute substantially more than average wage earners to contribute to such a scheme. And that amounts to an argument for a progressive tax rate provided taxes are also used for providing emergency relief and income support for people in need.

7. Conclusion

A lot more needs to be said about this type of argument. Why is assisting others an imperfect duty? How much is a reasonable sacrifice for discharging such a duty? How effective and efficient must the state be before the imperfect duty is made perfect for ordinary taxpayers? How much more than ordinary taxpayers should extremely rich taxpayers pay? However, I hope to have shown that there are both instrumentalist and non-instrumentalist reasons why progressive income taxation with the aim of supporting the least well off in our society is not a form of institutionalized theft but is compatible with what justice and fairness require from us.

COMPREHENSION QUESTIONS

1. When people talk about "distributive justice," what are they talking about?
2. Define "myopia." Why is it important?
3. What is progressive taxation?
4. What is the principle of fairness and its function?
5. What are our duties to others on Verbeek's view?

DISCUSSION QUESTIONS

1. What are the benefits of the state, and how do citizens gain access to them? Do all people have equal access to those benefits? Equal responsibility to support their provision? Why?
2. Describe the differences between a flat and progressive tax. Which structure seems better in principle? Which seems better in practice?
3. Give examples of perfect and imperfect duties as Verbeek understands them. Do you think that there's a perfect duty to support the least well off through progressive taxation?

Case 1

Some politicians want to increase the top marginal income tax rate, say, to 70%, which means that for every dollar a person earns over $10 million, she would get $0.30. Others want to expand the estate tax.* Finally, some want to tax wealth itself:† Earnings aside, if someone already has over $50 million, that money would be taxed each year. As an article in *The Atlantic*‡ puts it:

> [Experts say] that there was nothing unusual or even that radical about [higher marginal income-tax rates]. Higher rates were common throughout the 20th century, with the top marginal rate averaging 78 percent from 1930 to 1980 and climbing up to 90 percent in the late 1950s and early '60s ... That said, if the goal is to raise more money for redistributive policies and to ensure that millionaires pay their fair share, [this] proposal isn't particularly efficient. It might not even raise that much money, instead discouraging employers from paying workers more than $10 million or workers from trying to earn more than that threshold. Imagine you were a lawyer who often earned in the high millions a year; if you hit the $9 million mark in the fall, you might work somewhat less,

Case 1 (continued)

knowing that much of what you made over $10 million would get taxed away. The tax rate would, in effect, reduce inequality in pretax incomes, as well as in posttax incomes. (It would also encourage the very rich to hide income above $10 million.)

A better way to extract money from top earners would be to get rid of the loopholes, deductions, and exemptions they use to shelter income from taxation in the first place, economists said. "Broadening the tax base is generally more efficient than changing rates," said Kyle Pomerleau of the Tax Foundation, a think tank in Washington, DC. "That would include getting at what I would call the Big Three, which is the charitable deduction, the home-mortgage-interest deduction, and the state- and local-tax deduction."

The charitable deduction allows very high earners to spend on non-profit causes that they find interesting and valuable, as opposed to turning that money over to Uncle Sam for what the broad public wants and needs . . . The home-mortgage-interest deduction prompts the rich to buy even fancier houses than they could otherwise afford. And the state and local deduction⁵ reduces the tax bills of rich families who happen to live in high-tax states. Together, the Big Three cost the government something like $100 billion a year."

How does all this relate to Verbeek's argument? What can Verbeek say about the worry that high tax rates simply create strange incentives for the wealthy—where they work less or hide their money to avoid giving it to the government? Finally, suppose that we could address our main needs, as a country, simply by adopting a flat tax and closing loopholes. Why wouldn't that satisfy Verbeek?

---

*https://www.nytimes.com/2019/01/31/us/politics/bernie-sanders-estate-tax.html

†http://gabriel-zucman.eu/files/saez-zucman-wealthtax-warren.pdf

‡https://www.theatlantic.com/ideas/archive/2019/02/here-are-progressive-tax-policies-democrats-need/581830/

§http://www.taxpolicycenter.org/sites/default/files/briefing-book/6.3.1-how_does_the_state_and_local_tax_deduction_work.pdf

**https://www.taxpolicycenter.org/briefing-book/what-are-largest-tax-expenditures

TAX BREAKS FOR THE RICH
MICHAEL HUEMER

1. Background

Let's assume for the sake of argument that government is necessary for any livable society.[32] Let us assume also that taxation is the only feasible means of financing a government. The question is: How should the tax burden be distributed? In the United States and other liberal democracies, tax rates tend to be highly *progressive*—that is, individuals with higher incomes pay a higher percentage of their income in taxes. In addition, governments commonly run social welfare programs designed to transfer wealth from high- to low-income citizens.

Nevertheless, in public political discourse, it is common to hear calls to shift more of the tax burden to the rich. A representative remark from the advocacy

Table 6.1 Income and Taxes by Income Group, United States, 2013

	LOWEST QUINTILE	SECOND QUINTILE	THIRD QUINTILE	FOURTH QUINTILE	HIGHEST QUINTILE
Market Income	15,800	31,300	53,000	88,700	253,000
Government Transfers	9,600	16,200	16,700	15,000	12,000
Federal Taxes	800	4,000	8,900	17,600	69,700
Net Tax	−8,800	−12,200	−7,800	2,600	57,700
Net Tax Rate	−55.7%	−39.0%	−14.7%	2.9%	22.8%
Net Tax Share	**−28%**	**−39%**	**−25%**	**8%**	**183%**

group Americans for Tax Fairness reads, "It's time for the wealthiest Americans and big corporations to pay their fair share of taxes."[33] At the same time, politicians and journalists on the left often attack their political opponents for offering "tax breaks for the rich."

What basis is there for declaring taxes on the rich to be unfairly low? Rarely does one hear an *argument* for this conclusion. Those calling for higher taxes on the rich often cite facts about just how wealthy the wealthy are; rarely, if ever, do they cite facts about how much those same individuals are already paying in taxes. A cynic might suspect that the implicit principle at work is something like the following: "As long as anyone remains rich, taxes on the rich are always too low."

Needless to say, we should not accept such a principle. No one is under-taxed merely in virtue of being wealthy. Whether one is undertaxed depends not only on how much money one earns, but also on how much tax one is currently paying. Therefore, we need to look at statistics on actual tax rates. Table 6.1 shows some data for tax year 2013.

These data are from a 2016 report by the non-partisan Congressional Budget Office, based on government statistics.[34] They apply to the United States only. I have added the last three rows of the table, calculated from the data in the preceding rows. "Lowest Quintile" refers to the bottom fifth (that is, the bottom 20%) of income earners, "Second Quintile" to the next 20%, and so on. The numbers in the table are *averages* for each group; for instance, the average market income for people in the top 20% was $253,000. Of course, these averages do not apply to every person. For instance, you may be in the second quintile but *not* be receiving $16,200 in government benefits; this does not show any error in the table. "Market Income" refers to an individual's income from non-government sources. "Government Transfers" refers to money and in-kind benefits individuals receive from federal, state, or local governments (Social Security, welfare, and so on). "Federal Taxes" includes individual income taxes, payroll (or social insurance) taxes, corporate income taxes, and excise taxes.

The last three rows are the most interesting. "Net Tax" refers to federal taxes paid *minus* government transfers received. "Net Tax Rate" refers to one's net

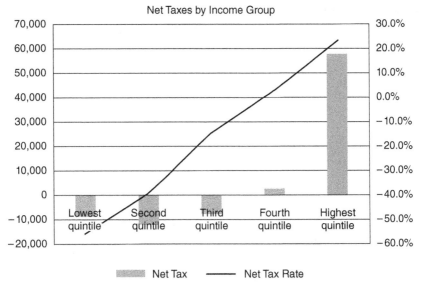

Figure 6.1
Net taxes by income group

tax expressed as a percentage of the income one earns from non-government sources. Negative numbers indicate that the government pays you more than you pay them (Figure 6.1).

What matters for assessing fairness of burdens is obviously *net* taxes (rows 4 and 5), not nominal taxes (row 3). If, for example, the government gives me $1 million but then immediately taxes all of it away, this is equivalent to no change; this would be no more or less fair than my current situation. I could not complain of injustice due to my tax rate having soared to 1,000% of my market income or 91% of my total income (assuming my market income is $100,000). Similarly, when the government gives a poor citizen $9,600 and then charges him $800 in taxes, this is equivalent to giving the citizen $8,800 with no tax.

Finally, "Net Tax Share" refers to the percentage of the total net tax burden carried by each group (that is, the group's net tax divided by the sum of net taxes for all groups, expressed as a percentage). The fourth quintile pays 8% of the net burden, while the top quintile pays *183%* of the net tax burden. The number exceeds 100% because, in addition to paying enough to give everyone else a free ride, the top group pays 83% more, in order to provide rebates to the bottom three quintiles.

2. What Is a Fair Tax?

On the face of it, it is easy to see how these facts could lead to a complaint of unfairness on behalf of the rich. But is there some conception of fairness on which the above facts add up to the rich paying unfairly *low* tax rates? Let us consider three theories about fair tax distribution.

244 ETHICS, LEFT AND RIGHT

Taxing by Ability to Pay

Perhaps individuals should be taxed in proportion to their *ability to pay*. Since one's ability to pay is determined by how much money one has, this would suggest a flat percentage *wealth* tax, rather than an income tax—that is, that individuals should pay a fixed percentage of their total accumulated wealth each year, rather than a percentage of their income over the past year. Would this be fair?

I don't think so. Note, first, that the preceding suggestion does not genuinely provide us with a *reason* for favoring high taxes for the rich. The argument simply starts from the assumption that individuals should be taxed according to their "ability to pay," which is understood in terms of their wealth: This assumption is just equivalent to the claim that people should be taxed according to how wealthy they are. This begs the question; whether people should be taxed according to how wealthy they are is what is in dispute in the first place.

Granted, it would be unjust to demand that individuals pay more than they can afford, since one cannot be obligated to do what one cannot do. Thus, the state obviously could not justly demand that poor citizens pay more than their total income in taxes. Nor could the state justly demand more than citizens can *reasonably afford* (e.g., so much that the citizens, after paying their tax bill, could no longer afford food, clothing, and shelter). But it does not follow from any of this that taxation should be *proportional to wealth*. All that follows is the much weaker claim that taxes, for any income group, should be capped at the most that individuals could reasonably afford, whatever that amount may be.

Nor does the ability-to-pay principle accord with commonsense moral judgments in other cases. Try this experiment. Go out to dinner with four friends. When the bill arrives, suggest that the person who has the most money, whoever that is, should pay for everyone else. Prediction: Your suggestion will be immediately rejected by all four others at the table. If you yourself are the person with the most money, then your offer to pay *might* be accepted since you are volunteering your own money—though even in this case, most friends with a sense of decency will protest. But if the person with the most money is someone else, someone who does not want to pay for everyone else, then everyone else at the table will categorically reject your suggestion. They will not accept the claim that it is *only fair* to expect the wealthiest person at the table to pay for everyone.

You might object to this analogy on the grounds that, in the restaurant case, it is easy to identify what portion of the total bill is attributable to each person: Just look at the prices of the items that each person ordered. But in the case of government, it is not so easy to separate out portions of the budget attributable to different individuals. This is because much of what the government provides are *public goods*: goods that, when provided, are automatically provided to everyone in the area, and whose availability for others is not diminished when one person receives them. For instance, when the government provides national defense, it automatically provides this to everyone in the country, and if you receive this good, your doing so does not diminish the amount available for anyone else. So, unlike the case of the restaurant bill, we cannot apportion military expenses according to how much of the good each individual consumed. Perhaps, then, the ability-to-pay principle applies to these sorts of public goods.

In reply, it is easy to modify my example to include public goods. Suppose that, at the restaurant, you and your friends agree to hire a mariachi band. The band provides its musical entertainment to everyone at the table, and any one person's enjoyment of the music does not diminish the amount of music available for the others to enjoy. So, just as in the case of national defense, it is impossible to apportion the expense according to how much of the entertainment each diner consumed.

The band finishes its delightful music, then hands you a bill for $500. Only then do you and your friends start to discuss what would be a fair division of the bill. Again, no normal group of friends would accept the principle of dividing up the bill according to each person's bank account balance. (Nor, of course, would they accept the idea of assigning the bill to just two of the five diners, with those two paying extra in order to give *rebates* to the three diners with the least funds.) Most likely, the friends would agree to divide the bill evenly: $100 for each person.

An added unfairness inherent in the idea of a wealth tax is that it penalizes individuals for saving. Two individuals both start out with $1,000; one saves it, and the other spends it. The one who saves must pay a tax on that money year after year, for as long as he holds the savings (if he holds it long enough, the entire amount will eventually be taxed away). By contrast, the one who spends accumulates no wealth and thus incurs no liability under a wealth tax. Intuitively, this is unfair to the saver.

Taxing by Benefits Received
Here is a more plausible principle of fair distribution: Individuals should be taxed in proportion to the value of the benefits they receive from the state. This seems to follow common sense: In the restaurant example, it would normally be considered fair to divide the tab according to what each diner ate. Similarly, why not say that each taxpayer should pay taxes proportional to the *benefits* that person receives from the government?

On the face of it, this suggestion fails to support progressive taxation, since the wealthy do not consume markedly more government services than the poor or the middle class. But one might argue that the *value* of government services to the wealthy is greater than the value of these services to the poor. The reason is that the general law and order provided by the state protects everyone's existing wealth and ability to earn income. The economic value, to a given person, of the general protection of property rights is roughly proportional to how much property that person has. If one has no property, then the general protection of property is of very little value to one; if one has vast wealth, then the protection of property rights is of great financial value to one. Similarly, the state's general provision of law and order makes it possible for most individuals to earn much greater incomes than they could in a lawless world. The economic value of this service to a given individual is roughly proportional to how much income that person in fact earns in the law-and-order world (minus whatever income they would still earn in a lawless world). Thus, one might argue that the wealthy should pay much higher taxes than the poor. This argument would seem to suggest a flat income tax and perhaps a flat wealth tax.

There are two main replies to this argument. First, note that the above rationale still does not justify anything like the current tax regime, in which the bottom three-fifths of society have net negative tax rates (it is not the case that the bottom 60% of society have received negative benefits—they are still benefiting from law and order and the general enforcement of property rights). Thus, we should still favor massive tax breaks for the rich.

Second, the idea of payment proportional to *the value to oneself* of the benefits one receives does not match our commonsense notion of fairness. Return to the restaurant example. Suppose that you happen to have a wonderful time at dinner. Everyone enjoys the dinner, and everyone wants to be there; it's just that you enjoy the whole dinner experience much *more* than the others. It does not follow from this that you owe much more for the restaurant bill than everyone else. If you tell your friends that you feel obligated to pay for almost all of the bill, because you clearly had a better time than they did, any decent friends will reject the suggestion out of hand.

Rather, what seems to be accepted in our commonsense notion of fairness is that one's fair share of the bill is determined by *the cost to the group* of the benefits one receives. Thus, one would be expected to pay according to the price, as written on the bill, of the food and drink one ordered, regardless of how much personal benefit one did or did not derive from those items. That is the commonsense interpretation of the principle of payment according to benefits received. This leads us to our third theory of fair distribution.

Taxing by Costs Incurred

Perhaps the fair tax distribution is one in proportion to how much each individual costs the state through his use of government services. This, at last, seems like an intuitively fair principle for the distribution of costs incurred in a collective enterprise. But it does not support progressive taxation. The wealthy do not cost the government markedly more than the poor. Indeed, it is most likely the poor who cost the government the most.

Some government programs are expressly limited to low-income (or at most moderate-income) citizens, so that the wealthy cannot use them even if they wish to—for example, Temporary Assistance to Needy Families ("welfare"), the Supplemental Nutrition Assistance Program ("food stamps"), and Pell Grants (need-based financial aid for college students). Even when they are permitted to do so, the wealthy sometimes decline to use government services since they prefer higher-quality private services—as in the case of private schools and private security guards.

In other cases, the wealthy and the poor seem to use about the same amount of government-provided goods; for example, people of all income levels are roughly equally dependent on roads. As noted earlier, some of the most important services provided by the government are *public goods*, such as national defense. These are "used" equally by everyone; as with the mariachi band in our earlier example, common sense suggests an equal division of the costs of these goods.

What about the goods of police protection, law and order? It is well known that the poor receive less law and order than the wealthy—that is, they suffer higher crime rates.[35] This reflects a failure of the state to adequately protect the poor from crime. But this does not mean that the wealthy are *costing the state more* for their protection. The reason the poor suffer higher crime is not that the state spends more money on protecting the wealthy; the reason is that criminals tend to be low-income individuals, who tend to victimize the other low-income individuals in their own neighborhoods. Thus, the poor as a class are almost surely costing the government more money for law enforcement than are the wealthy. There is no support for progressive taxation to be had here.

(Aside: This is all compatible with the fact that the government does a terrible job of protecting the poor and often actively harms them—for example, through police shootings and harmful laws such as drug prohibition. These government shortcomings are not the fault of the wealthy per se, and they do not at all suggest that the wealthy are paying an unfairly low share of the tax burden.)

3. What Is Best for Society?

We have just discussed what is a *fair* distribution of the tax burden. Another question is: What distribution of tax burdens is overall best for society, regardless of whether it is fair to the rich?

Diminishing Marginal Utility

There is one popular social welfare–based argument for assigning most of the tax burden to the rich: The rich need their money less than the poor do. That is, wealth has *diminishing marginal utility*: The more wealth one has, the smaller the benefit one derives from gaining an additional dollar, and the smaller the harm one suffers from losing a dollar. Thus, other things being equal, taking a dollar in taxes from a wealthy person should cause less harm than taking a dollar from a less wealthy person.

This argument is certainly correct as far as it goes. The principle of diminishing marginal utility is uncontroversial, and it clearly implies that taking from the rich does the least *immediate* harm. I emphasize "immediate," however. There are two reasons why a progressive taxation scheme might cause more harm in the *long* run than a flat tax.

Incentive Effects

The first problem is a familiar one: Taxes on income and wealth reduce *incentives for productive activity*. "Productive activity" is a broad term: It can mean working hard, or it can mean choosing to save and invest money instead of immediately spending it. It can mean taking a more productive job, or it can mean going to school to acquire the skills to do a more valuable job in the future. All of these are choices that, on average, increase one's contribution to the economy, at the same time as they result in one's acquiring a higher income. They also carry costs to the individual: Working hard is often less fun than slacking off; investing entails delayed gratification as well as the risk of loss; higher-paying jobs are often more demanding or less enjoyable than lower-paying jobs; education requires spending time and money. When we decide whether to undertake productive activities, we weigh these costs against our expected future profit. High taxes on income or wealth reduce the potential reward and thus tip the scales more in the direction of *not* choosing productive activity. Of course, this does not mean that everyone stops being productive; it means that the *marginal* productive activity stops: People who are just barely willing to undertake a productive activity (because they value the increased income slightly more than whatever they have to give up) will tip over into being barely *un*willing to undertake it, if their income tax rate increases.

Progressive taxation results in high (marginal) income tax rates for individuals at the high end of the income scale. Thus, it leaves significantly lower incentives for those individuals, who tend to be the most economically productive citizens, to undertake added productive activities. The result is that there will be slower economic growth and less total wealth in the future.[36]

The Rate of Investment

For the economy to grow, some individuals must give up immediate consumption in favor of saving and investment, where investment entails a non-trivial risk of loss. The overwhelming majority of this saving and investment is done by the wealthy; little is done by the middle class and almost none by the poor.

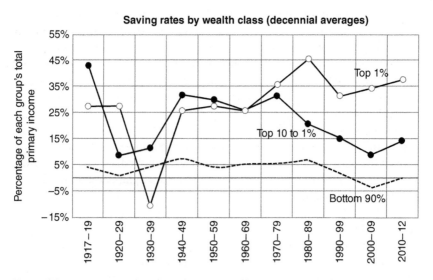

Figure 6.2
Saving rates by wealth class (decennial averages)

Importantly, the *percentage* of one's income that goes to saving and investment rises as one's income and wealth rise (Figure 6.2).[37]

Therefore, shifting the tax burden toward the wealthy lowers the overall saving and investment rates of society. For every $100 taken from a taxpayer, investment is lowered by whatever portion of that money the taxpayer would have devoted to investment. Since wealthier people invest a higher proportion of their money, taking $100 from a wealthy person reduces investment by more than taking $100 away from a poor or middle-class person.

Notice that this point is independent of the incentives argument above: Even if all wealthy people retained an absolute commitment to maximizing their productive activities, their productive activities would still decline as a result of taxation, since taxation confiscates some of the funds that they would have invested.

As a result, the policy of shifting the tax burden onto the wealthy reduces the overall economic growth rate of society. Because economic growth compounds over time, progressive taxation incurs exponentially growing costs as we move further into the future.

In the long run, the harm of reducing the rate of economic growth, per the arguments of the "Incentive Effects" and "The Rate of Investment" sections, probably outweighs the advantage cited in the "Diminishing Marginal Utility" section.

4. Conclusion

In modern liberal societies, the wealthy are a favorite scapegoat. Many people assume as a matter of course that "the rich" or "the super-rich" as a class are immoral, that they are taking advantage of the rest of us, that they are failing to do "their fair share" for society. The truth is the exact opposite: It is the rest of us who refuse to do our fair share. It is we who are exploiting the rich. Through our representatives, we impose tax laws that force the wealthy to carry the entire burden of paying for government *and then some*—we expect them not only to pay for all government services, but to pay extra money to be given to us. It is as though five friends went out to a restaurant, four of them demanded that the other one pay for everyone's food, plus some kickbacks to three of the diners, and then the four complained loudly and indignantly that the one who had paid for them wasn't "paying his fair share."

Besides its basic unfairness, progressive taxation is most likely holding back economic growth and harming future generations. A fairer and less harmful policy would be a flat tax on income over a certain amount, with a cap on the total dollar amount of tax any one person may be asked to pay. It is time for the poor and the middle class to start paying their fair share of taxes.

COMPREHENSION QUESTIONS

1. What is the difference between a wealth tax and an income tax?
2. What is the difference between a flat tax and a progressive tax?

3. What is diminishing marginal utility, and how is it relevant to debates about taxation?
4. Why does Huemer think a wealth tax would discourage long-term savings?
5. What is the ability-to-pay principle?

DISCUSSION QUESTIONS

1. Why does Huemer claim taxing the wealthy is unfair and may limit economic growth? Do you agree or disagree with his assessment? Why?
2. How does the dinner party analogy relate to taxation practices? Is this a useful thought experiment? Why or why not?
3. Why does Huemer believe the rich deserve massive tax breaks? Do you agree or disagree with his conclusions? Why or why not?

Case 2

On January 25, 2019, Noah Smith—a writer for Bloomberg—tweeted this:

> A good illustration of left-populism vs. social democracy. For left-populism, the important thing is that rich people have less. For social democracy, the important thing is that poor and middle-class people have more. It's a big difference in emphasis.

Of course, these goals aren't mutually exclusive: You can give more to poor and middle-class people by taking more from rich people. But Smith does seem to be right that it's "a big difference in emphasis," and it helps us focus on the question of whether inequality is bad in itself. Some people have thought not. Here's Harry Frankfurt, a famous philosopher:

> Economic equality is not, as such, of particular moral importance. With respect to the distribution of economic assets, what is important from the point of view of morality is not that everyone should have the same but that each should have enough. If everyone had enough, it would be of no moral consequence whether some had more than others.[*]

Here, by contrast, is someone who describes himself as "Nobody from nowhere" on Twitter:

> Part of the appeal of Left populism is that it attempts to address . . . the outsized political power that extremely wealthy people have in our system. Redistributive policies need to address the distribution of power.[‡]

What do you think of Frankfurt's view? What do you think about this worry regarding power? To what degree should we be trying to distribute resources more equally? What methods are acceptable to achieve that end?

---

[*]Harry Frankfurt, "Equality as a Moral Ideal," *Ethics* 98 (October 1987): 21.
[‡]https://twitter.com/buvox/status/1088847181581246464

REPLY TO HUEMER
BRUNO VERBEEK

Michael Huemer gives a spirited defense of a remarkable claim: that the United States (and other Western democracies that have progressive taxation) treat the rich unfairly. A just and efficient tax system would exempt the poorest citizens and would demand that everybody else pay the same percentage of their market income with an upper limit in absolute dollar amounts. He thinks, in other words, that a just and efficient tax system would be regressive rather than progressive.[38] There's much to say, but I'll have to be content with three points.

I.

Huemer argues that higher tax burdens for the rich are unfair. His main argument is an analogy with a group of friends having dinner in a restaurant. I think that analogy is misleading. For example, the reason as to why it would be wrong to make your richest friend pay for the entire meal and give some further funds to the poorer friends is not that this is unfair, but because this is not how friends treat each other. Similarly, the reason why decency demands that you pay for yourself even if your rich friend offers to pay for the meal is that accepting such an offer is demeaning. So, any lessons that you might draw about the fairness of the various ways of splitting the restaurant bill are irrelevant for figuring out the fairness of progressive taxation. Taxpayers are not friends, and the state is not a restaurant.

II.

In my contribution, I distinguished between two very different ways one can look at the fairness of the tax system. The first way, which I called instrumentalism, evaluates the tax system in relation to the overall distribution of burdens and benefits. Huemer's claim that progressive taxation is unfair and inefficient is instrumentalist because he looks at the net taxes of various groups. Notice moreover that he is only partly instrumentalist as he does not include all benefits people receive but only some.[39] For example, he includes income subsidies like Medicare and Social Security but excludes other benefits that are financed by the state. That is inconsistent: If he is going to reason in this fashion, he should include *all* benefits and burdens.[40]

However, I think Huemer's instrumentalism is the wrong way to look at taxation. Taxation is not a neutral instrument that the state can employ to realize the distribution of burdens and benefits it thinks desirable. It is a legal instrument that imposes legal duties. This sets a number of constraints on the use of taxation. One of these constraints is that the tax burden should be fair. This is not determined by only looking at the overall distribution of burdens and benefits as Huemer claims in his introduction. Doing so would imply that there is no special question about the fairness of progressive taxes in and of themselves.

III.

Huemer rejects the ability-to-pay principle, a traditional principle of taxation in virtually all states in the world.[41] Huemer claims it only determines an *upper limit* to one's tax burden. However, this is not how that principle traditionally has been conceived of by scholars and economists.[42] First, the ability-to-pay principle sets a lower limit below which one should not be taxed in the first place. Second, it says that one's fair contribution is proportionate to one's ability to pay. The reason for this has to do with the special nature of taxation. Taxes are the contribution that everybody pays for public goods the state provides. That means that once they are there, nobody can be excluded from consumption.[43] As a result, we cannot use market mechanisms to distribute such goods. Since we cannot rely on the price mechanism to determine the value of the goods and services the state provides, we need another way of determining everyone's fair share. That's where the ability-to-pay principle comes in: It says that in those situations, the fair contribution is proportionate to what one can afford.

Huemer might reject the ability-to-pay principle, thus understood. However, that raises the question how we should determine the fairness of the distribution of the costs of a public good. Huemer owes us a principle for this. He cannot claim that the current distribution is unfair without a plausible explanation as to why it is unfair.

COMPREHENSION QUESTIONS

1. What is a regressive tax?
2. What is a personal exemption, and how does it relate to the ability-to-pay principle?

DISCUSSION QUESTIONS

1. Is there a difference between (a) the state taxing you to finance the police and military and (b) a benevolent gangster coercing you to pay protection money?
2. Is the ability-to-pay principle an appropriate way to distribute the costs of public goods and benefits that cannot be distributed through normal markets? Why or why not?

REPLY TO VERBEEK
MICHAEL HUEMER

I would like to thank Professor Verbeek for his thoughtful remarks on progressive taxation. We agree on at least two points: First, one must examine the fairness of the overall distribution of burdens and benefits the state creates, not merely the nominal tax rates each individual pays; second, income below a certain amount should be exempt from taxation.

Before I get to our philosophical disagreements, I'd like to correct one misconception: Warren Buffett does not pay a lower total tax rate than his secretary; that is a mistake by Mr. Buffett. His *personal* income tax rate is lower, due to the low capital gains tax rate. But if we count *corporate* taxes, which are really paid by the owners of corporations, then Buffett pays much more than his secretary.

Now, on to the arguments for progressive taxation. Verbeek mentions three main arguments.

1. The Personal Exemption

First, Verbeek defends the *personal exemption* (the policy of exempting income up to a certain amount from taxation), on the grounds that those below a certain income level cannot afford to pay taxes, and it would be unfair and unreasonable to ask them to do so. For example, perhaps there should be no tax on the first $10,000 of income that an individual earns. Verbeek counts this policy as "progressive taxation," even if one has flat marginal tax rates on all income above the threshold.

I agree with this policy and the argument for it, but I would not count that as progressive taxation for purposes of this debate. Since virtually no one on either the left or the right disagrees with the personal exemption, we should presumably be debating some more controversial question, something that liberals and conservatives disagree about, such as whether the income tax system should be *more* or *less* progressive than it currently is, or whether there should be increasing marginal rates *for those who pay income tax.*

2. The Benefits Received by the Rich

Wealthy people receive greater benefits from the state than poorer people do; therefore, it is fair that they pay higher taxes. (Verbeek mentions this argument but then seems to reject it in an endnote.) The problem with this argument is that it does not support progressive taxation. The wealthy receive greater *absolute* benefits, so they should pay a higher *absolute* tax—that is, a larger dollar amount. It does not follow that they should pay a higher *percentage*. Plausibly, the value of the government's service of protecting property rights is proportional to the amount of property one has—so this would support a tax in proportion to wealth (that is, a fixed percentage of one's wealth). If we add that it is unfair to tax the same money over again every year merely because the citizen decided to save rather than immediately spending it, then we arrive at the idea that the tax should be a fixed percentage of one's income each year—that is, a flat tax.

That is assuming that the government's only service is the protection of one's wealth. But the state provides other benefits, most of which either benefit everyone equally or tend to benefit the poor more. A fair tax would be a fixed dollar amount for the goods and services that benefit everyone equally, plus a fixed percentage of one's income for the service of protecting property. This would amount to a *regressive* system—that is, one in which the tax *rate* decreases with one's income level. (All other goods and services have "regressive" pricing in that sense.)

It is not obvious in any case that a fair tax is one proportioned to the benefits received, rather than one proportioned to the costs the state incurs on one's behalf. On the latter view, the poor might need to pay higher absolute taxes. The

higher crime rates in poor neighborhoods mean that the state must expend more
law enforcement resources on them; hence, perhaps the poor should pay *more* for
law enforcement.

3. The Duty of Charity

Verbeek suggests that we have a duty to assist those in need. The taxation system
is a convenient tool for helping us satisfy this duty, since the state can run aid
programs for the needy and charge all of us the appropriate amount for them.
Those who are better off are obligated to give more than those who are badly off
are obligated to give. Hence, it makes sense that the wealthy pay higher taxes.

But how does this support progressive taxation? Granted, those who are very
poor should not have to give to charity—that is just the personal exemption issue
again. Among those who can afford to give to charity, it makes sense that those
with more income should be expected to give more money. But it remains unclear
why they would have to give a higher *percentage* of their income. Why shouldn't everyone who can afford to give to charity simply give, say, 10% of their income to it?

It is also extremely dubious that the government is an effective instrument
of charity. Some question whether government aid reduces poverty at all, rather
than *increasing* it (these critics argue that welfare programs create a cycle of dependency in which the poor never learn to become self-supporting).[44] Even if
government aid is beneficial, it certainly isn't optimal—that is, there are much
more effective ways of doing good. The charity review organization GiveWell regularly reviews private charities and reports on the most efficient ones, which are
vastly superior to government programs.[45] If we want to satisfy our duty to aid
those in need, we should give all our charitable dollars to the top-rated GiveWell
charities, and none to the government. Except that if we do that, the government
will send armed men to take us prisoner and forcibly extract our resources. So tell
me again how the government is efficiently helping me satisfy my duty of charity?

COMPREHENSION QUESTIONS

1. On what two points does Huemer agree with Verbeek?
2. What is the difference between a greater absolute tax for higher earners and a
   progressive tax system?

DISCUSSION QUESTIONS

1. Why does Huemer think giving to private charities would be better than spending on government aid? Do you agree? Why or why not? Do you think public
   or private giving is more effective or appropriate for addressing our duties to
   others?
2. How would you interpret a commonsense approach to taxation, according
   to which you should pay your fair share (beyond a reasonable personal exemption)? How many different ways of interpreting "your fair share" can you
   imagine?

FURTHER READINGS

Americans for Tax Fairness. "Tax Fairness Briefing Booklet." https://americansfortaxfair ness.org/files/Tax-Fairness-Briefing-Booklet.pdf, 2014.

Dworkin, R. M. *Sovereign Virtue: The Theory and Practice of Equality.* Cambridge, MA: Harvard University Press, 2000.

Murphy, Liam, and Thomas Nagel. *The Myth of Ownership: Taxes and Justice.* Oxford: Oxford University Press, 2002.

Nozick, Robert. *Anarchy, State and Utopia.* New York: Basic Books, 1974.

Rawls, John. *A Theory of Justice.* Cambridge, MA: Harvard University Press, 1971.

Reynolds, Alan. "Marginal Tax Rates." In *The Concise Encyclopedia of Economics*, edited by David R. Henderson. Carmel, IN: Liberty Fund, Inc., 2008 (2nd ed.).

U.S. Congressional Budget Office. "The Distribution of Household Income and Federal Taxes, 2013." https://www.cbo.gov/publication/51361, 2016.

Wilkinson, Richard, and Kate Pickett. *The Spirit Level: Why Greater Equality Makes Societies Stronger.* New York: Bloomsbury Press, 2011 (reprint edition).

NOTES

1. Chris Isidore, "Buffett Says He's Still Paying Lower Tax Rate than His Secretary," CNN Money, March 4, 2013, http://money.cnn.com/2013/03/04/news/economy/buffett -secretary-taxes/index.html

2. Buffet is concerned with effective rates, which is what I will focus on as well. Effective rates—the actual percentage of your income you pay in taxes—differ from statutory rates, the official rates of the income tax. For example, suppose that the official tax rate is 10% over the first $10,000 of your taxable income and 20% over the rest. Suppose, moreover, that there is an exemption of the first $8,000. A person with a pretax income of $10,000 would owe $200 in taxes, an effective rate of 2%. Somebody earning $20,000 (i.e., twice that income) would pay $2200, an effective rate of 11%.

3. "Top Frustrations with Tax System: Sense that Corporations, Wealthy Don't Pay Fair Share." (Washington, DC Pew Research Center, April 14, 2017), http://www.people -press.org/2017/04/14/top-frustrations-with-tax-system-sense-that-corporations -wealthy-dont-pay-fair-share/

4. I simplify matters considerably here. First, because besides federal income tax, there are many other forms of taxation (e.g., sales tax, dividend tax, corporate gains tax, inheritance tax, etc.). Second, because there are different kinds of taxpayers. Apart from natural persons, companies and other legal persons are taxable. I ignore all these nuances here.

5. E.g., John Rawls, *A Theory of Justice* (Cambridge, MA: Harvard University Press, 1971); R. M. Dworkin, *Sovereign Virtue: The Theory and Practice of Equality* (Cambridge, MA: Harvard University Press, 2000); Liam Murphy and Thomas Nagel, *The Myth of Ownership: Taxes and Justice* (Oxford: Oxford University Press, 2002).

6. Murphy and Nagel, *Myth of Ownership.*

7. "The real issue of political morality is the extent to which social outcomes are just, and knowledge of the distribution of real tax burdens is important only insofar as it helps us advance that aim." Murphy and Nagel, *Myth of Ownership*, 131.

8. It is in practice quite hard to determine whether a particular tax regulation is instrumentalist in this sense. See Henk Vording, "The Concept of Instrumentalism in Tax Law," *Coventry Law Journal*, May 1, 2013, 41–60.

9. Richard Wilkinson and Kate Pickett, *The Spirit Level: Why Greater Equality Makes Societies Stronger* (New York: Bloomsbury Press, 2011 [reprint edition]).

10. Martin Gilens, *Affluence and Influence: Economic Inequality and Political Power in America* (Princeton, NJ: Princeton University Press, 2012).

11. Alternatively, one could think of taxation as one's premium in a social insurance scheme that ensures people against falling below that standard of a decent life. An example of such an approach is Philipp Kanschik, "Why Sufficientarianism Is Not Indifferent to Taxation," *Kriterion* 29, no. 2 (2015): 81–102.

12. Even the rather minimal "sufficientarian" view that I suggested above is hardly uncontested.

13. Robert Nozick, *Anarchy, State and Utopia* (New York: Basic Books, 1974), 169.

14. Nozick, *Anarchy, State and Utopia*, 171.

15. Murphy and Nagel call this disapprovingly "everyday libertarianism." Murphy and Nagel, *Myth of Ownership*. They are careful to note that the straightforward inference from the quote of Nozick to the view that all taxation is theft is unwarranted and Nozick would be the first to say so. In fact, on Nozick's theory of entitlements, current pretax market outcomes are anything but just since they are the result of many grievous rights violations in the past (distant and not so distant). See Nozick, *Anarchy, State and Utopia*, 231.

16. There is much more that can be said about consent-based arguments for the authority of the state, including the authority to tax. See, e.g., A. John Simmons, *Moral Principles and Political Obligations* (Princeton, NJ: Princeton University Press, 1979), Chapters 3 and 4.

17. See, e.g., Murphy and Nagel, *Myth of Ownership*.

18. Thus, it is guilty of the kind of intellectual "myopia" mentioned above.

19. H. L. A. Hart, "Are There Any Natural Rights?" *Philosophical Review* 64, no. 2 (1955): 175; *John Rawls: Collected Papers*, edited by Samuel Freeman (Cambridge, MA: Harvard University Press, 2001), 117–129.

20. These questions reflect the criticisms of Nozick, *Anarchy, State and Utopia*, 93–95.

21. George Klosko, *The Principle of Fairness and Political Obligation*, Studies in Social & Political Philosophy (Lanham, MD: Rowman & Littlefield, 2004 [new edition]), 39.

22. For more discussion about fairness obligations to the state, see Klosko, *Principle of Fairness*, 35–36. My interlocutor in this volume rejects the existence of such obligations to the state. Michael Huemer, *The Problem of Political Authority: An Examination of the Right to Coerce and the Duty to Obey* (Basingstoke, U.K.: Palgrave Macmillan, 2013), 51.

23. A "flat tax" is a tax with the same proportionate rate for everybody. For example, if everybody is required to pay 10% of their income in taxes, this is a flat tax.

24. For a criticism of this conclusion, see Barbara H. Fried, "Proportionate Taxation as a Fair Division of the Social Surplus: The Strange Career of an Idea," *Economics and Philosophy* 2, no. 19 (January 16, 2004): 211–239.

25. This is the essentially the proposal offered by Erik Lindahl. It is endorsed even by instrumentalists like Murphy and Nagel. Erik Lindahl, "Just Taxation—a Positive Solution," in *Classics in the Theory of Public Finance*, edited by Richard Abel Musgrave and Alan T. Peacock (London: Macmillan Press in association with the International Economic Association, 1958 [5th edition]), 168–176; Liam Murphy and Thomas Nagel, "Taxes, Redistribution, and Public Provision," *Philosophy & Public Affairs* 30, no. 1 (2001): 53–71.

26. I doubt that this is convincing for either Nozick or his critics. After all, a welfare recipient benefits perhaps even more from the state than Warren Buffett and his friends, but it would be pointless to insist welfare recipients pay for the service. See also John Stuart

Mill, *Principles of Political Economy with Some of Their Applications to Social Philosophy* (London: Standard Library Co., 1848), Chapter 2.

27. Suppose that the statutory flat rate is 10% and that there is a tax exemption over the first $10,000 of one's income. Then, an income of $10,000 or less is taxed at 0%, an income of $20,000 is taxed at 5%, an income of $30,000 is taxed at 6.6%, etc., resulting in a (slowly) increasing tax rate.

28. The ability to pay has been defended by authors like Adam Smith, *An Inquiry in the Nature and Causes of the Wealth of Nations*, The Glasgow Edition of the Works and Correspondence of Adam Smith (Oxford: Oxford University Press, 1979); Mill, *Principles*. The first precise formulation of this idea can be found in the writings of Arnold Jacob Cohen Stuart, who makes the analogy with a bridge: Before a bridge can carry anything, it has to be strong enough to carry its own weight. Cohen Stuart, "On Progressive Taxation," in *Classics in the Theory of Public Finance*, edited by Musgrave and Peacock, 48–71.

29. See also Bruno Verbeek, *Philosophical Explorations of Justice and Taxation: National and Global Issues*, edited by Helmut P. Gaisbauer, Gottfried Schweiger, and Clemens Sedmak, vol. 40 (Heidelberg: Springer, 2015), 67.

30. Immanuel Kant, *Groundwork of the Metaphysics of Morals: A German-English Edition* (Cambridge: Cambridge University Press, 2011), Ak. 421.

31. Allen Buchanan, "Perfecting Imperfect Duties: Collective Action to Create Moral Obligations," *Business Ethics Quarterly* 6, no. 1 (1996): 27–42.

32. For arguments against this assumption, see my *The Problem of Political Authority* (New York: Palgrave Macmillan, 2013).

33. Americans for Tax Fairness, "Tax Fairness Briefing Booklet" (2014), p. 20, https://americansfortaxfairness.org/files/Tax-Fairness-Briefing-Booklet.pdf, accessed January 7, 2018.

34. U.S. Congressional Budget Office, "The Distribution of Household Income and Federal Taxes, 2013" (2016), p. 2, https://www.cbo.gov/publication/51361, accessed January 7, 2018.

35. U.S. Department of Justice, "Criminal Victimization in the United States, 2008: Statistical Tables" (2011), Table 14, https://www.bjs.gov/content/pub/pdf/cvus0801.pdf, accessed January 7, 2018.

36. On the evidence for this, see Alan Reynolds, "Marginal Tax Rates," in *The Concise Encyclopedia of Economics*, edited by David R. Henderson (Carmel, IN: Liberty Fund, Inc., 2008 [2nd ed.]), http://www.econlib.org/library/Enc/MarginalTaxRates.html, accessed January 10, 2018.

37. Edward N. Wolff, "Household Wealth Trends in the United States, 1962 to 2016: Has Middle Class Wealth Recovered?", National Bureau of Economic Research Working Paper 24085 (2017), Table 6, http://www.nber.org/papers/w24085, accessed January 7, 2018; Emmanuel Saez and Gabriel Zucman, "Wealth Inequality in the United States Since 1913: Evidence from Capitalized Income Tax Data," *Quarterly Journal of Economics* 131 (2016): 519–578, https://doi.org/10.1093/qje/qjw004 (Figure 6.2 in the text is copied from p. 564).

38. A regressive tax system is one where as one's income rises, one pays a smaller percentage of one's income in taxes. A flat tax rate with a lower limit and upper limit as Huemer proposes would entail that those with middle incomes face the highest effective tax burden. Now there is something to be said for the claim that currently the middle-income earners do not pay their fair share in taxes, but that does not justify reversing the situation completely.

39. What Huemer calls "net taxes" are the taxes you pay minus income subsidies, such as Social Security, Medicare, etc.
40. Also, why restrict the argument to federal taxes alone? There are many other taxes besides federal income taxes. Some of these offset the progression of the federal income tax.
41. In some countries, this principle is even enshrined in the constitution (e.g., in Germany).
42. See, e.g., Cohen Stuart, "On Progressive Taxation"; Musgrave, Richard. 1959. *The Theory of Public Finance: A Study in Public Economy*. New York: McGraw-Hill.
43. Not, as Huemer seems to suggest, that these goods are non-rival, which is that once they are there, my enjoyment of them does not diminish in any sense your enjoyment of them. The mariachi band in Huemer's example is such a good: One friend's enjoyment of the music does not take away from the enjoyment of the other friends. Not all public goods are non-rivalrous (in fact, most are not), but they are non-excludable.
44. See Charles Murray's famous study, *Losing Ground: American Social Policy, 1950–1980* (New York: Basic Books, 1984). For criticism, see Christopher Jencks, *Rethinking Social Policy: Race, Poverty and the Underclass* (Cambridge, MA: Harvard University Press, 1992), Chapter 2, and Tyler Cowen, "Does the Welfare State Help the Poor?", *Social Philosophy and Policy* 19 (2002): 36–54.
45. See www.givewell.org.

CHAPTER 7

Minimum Wage

FOR A LIVING WAGE
MARK R. REIFF

What is a living wage? Although the living wage movement has existed for more than a century, and its roots go back even farther, there is still no clear agreement on what a living wage would be.[1] People do not even agree on whether the living wage, whatever this might be, should determine where we set the minimum wage, the legal floor for what employers may pay their workers, or whether the minimum wage should be lower. In any case, the minimum wage has been largely stagnant since the late 1960s,[2] and while it has increased significantly in a growing number of localities lately and even nationally to some extent,[3] almost everyone concedes that it is in fact far below what a living wage would require in most jurisdictions.[4] But what does a living wage require? Is it merely the minimum required to keep a single full-time worker alive, with a part-time worker earning the appropriate proportionate share of this? An average family alive? An average family not merely alive, but sufficiently financially secure to actually participate meaningfully in society? In this piece, I shall defend the latter view. First, I shall argue that a living wage is a just wage, one that satisfies the moral principle of reciprocity in exchange, meaning that the wages paid should be equivalent to the value of the labor performed. Next, I shall argue that the value of the labor performed should be determined by reference to the cost of production of that labor, taking into account not merely the worker's primary basic needs but the worker's contextual basic needs as well (I shall explain the difference between the two in a moment). Finally, I shall argue that there are no countervailing negative effects of paying such a wage, and that even if there were, this would not be a sufficient reason for failing to make the living wage the minimum.

I.

In determining what kind of wage justice requires, the first question to address is whether justice requires anything more than the wage be whatever the worker and the employer have voluntarily agreed. One might think that people should be free to work for any amount they wish. As long as their acceptance of the wage offered is voluntary, morality should have nothing left to say. But as John Rawls, probably the most influential political philosopher of the twentieth century, pointed out long ago, people will often agree to terms that are in fact unjust.[5] People have unequal bargaining power, unequal bargaining skill, unequal information, and unequal starting positions, meaning, for example, that one party may be under greater financial pressure to make a deal than the other. In these circumstances, we have no reason to expect that their agreement will be automatically just, even if these circumstances do not rise to the level that would make this agreement legally involuntary and therefore voidable. This means actual consent does not have conclusive, and in some cases any, moral force.

Rawls's approach to this problem was to replace actual consent with hypothetical consent. That is, he tried to imagine what the parties would agree to if they were both free and equal and the various inequalities in their bargaining position were eliminated. One would have to have an argument for what people would agree to in these conditions, but this approach was surprisingly fruitful for certain questions of distributive justice, such as whether people would agree to rules for society under which people of one race, gender, religion, or so on should be favored.[6] But this approach will do us no good here, for how are we to determine what wage employers would offer and workers would accept if they were otherwise free and equal in the relevant sense? The market wage does not provide a persuasive target for agreement, because we have no idea what the market wage would be if people were truly free and equal, and therefore unburdened by all sorts of differing degrees of knowledge and outside pressures. So, running the Rawlsian thought experiment here does not produce any actual suggestions, much less any determinate ones.

In *Exploitation and Economic Justice in the Liberal Capitalist State*, however, I offered an alternative approach.[7] I argued that instead of looking for either hypothetical or actual consent to determine whether a particular wage is just, we should look to the principle of reciprocity. Under that principle, an exchange is just only if each party receives something that is meaningfully equivalent in value to what they each provide. For example, a pair of shoes for a house would not meet this test; a very large number of pairs would be required to even come close. This idea goes back to Aristotle,[8] but there has been a long tradition of thought ever since that has embraced the principle of reciprocity in determining the justness of exchange transactions. The question, however, is how to measure whether what is exchanged is of roughly equivalent value. One possibility is to use the market price to do this—that is, look to the price that would be set for each party's respective contributions by a willing buyer and a willing seller under currently prevailing market conditions in the relevant geographic area. Another is to use the cost of production—that is, look to the actual, out-of-pocket cost of producing each party's respective contributions to the exchange, including the cost of any component parts and the cost of any third-party labor required to put them together as well as the cost of providing one's own labor (I will say more about how to measure this last factor in a moment).

Aristotle himself is generally thought to have measured value by reference to the market price, and others have unambiguously embraced this view. But many others have argued instead for the cost of production, and in my view, this argument is clearly more persuasive. The reason is that in a perfectly competitive market, everything—including labor—would sell for its cost of production.[9] Economists are in universal agreement on that. The only reason anything ever sells for anything else is that markets are never perfectly competitive. Indeed, even those who embrace the market price as the relevant measure of value for the principle of reciprocity note that they would make exceptions whenever there are market failures. This means that everyone is really using the cost of production as their measure; some people are merely using the market price as a ready proxy for this unless some significant market failure is expressly brought to their attention. It is the cost of production, then, that is the focus of our moral intuitions regarding when a wage is just, not the market price.

II.

The question then becomes: What is the cost of the production of labor? This may be relatively easy to determine for the production of goods, but labor is different. For the requisite labor to be produced, the laborer must exist and have a certain set of skills, knowledge, talents, and abilities. The calculations required here are complex, for unlike machines, humans are living beings whose inputs come from a huge variety of sources, many of which are difficult to measure or even fully comprehend. Of course, at the very least the cost of production includes the cost of subsistence, for only if the laborer's primary basic needs are met, including the cost of food, shelter, and clothing, is the laborer able to exist. But the cost of subsistence is merely what a slave-owning society that embraced the most minimal humanitarian concerns would require its citizens to provide their slaves, and what all politically liberal societies already require their citizens to provide to their work animals and pets. Indeed, it is difficult to see what the difference would be between a slave and a worker who is merely earning just enough to keep himself alive. Rather than bare physical subsistence, what is required in a just society is that workers be paid an amount that will enable them to be both physically and psychologically capable of working to the best of their abilities, for that is what a capitalist economy wants and needs from its workers if it is to be maximally productive. To perform at this level, in turn, each worker must not merely be able to sustain themselves, they must each feel that they are a valued part of society and be willing to endorse its fundamental precepts and obey its fundamental rules. They must not view these rules as oppressive, or feel distant and alienated from the social structure in which they live, or be contemplating revolt. And to do this, the wages generated by even the most unskilled labor must enable the worker to satisfy not only the primary basic needs that I have already identified, but their *contextual* basic needs as well.

What these are will vary, of course, according to the level of welfare in the society and even the community in which the worker lives. A television, a car, and even a personal computer may be perceived as contextual basic needs in more affluent societies. In other societies, it may be far more important to own a cellphone, a gasoline-powered generator, and a gun. The precise components of what our contextual basic needs require and therefore what constitutes the living wage in any particular community may be difficult to identify with certainty, but certainty is not required. Indeed, economists have had little trouble estimating the living wage by calculating the local cost of a basket of specified goods. A similar approach is used to estimate inflation (the cost of living), and while we might quibble over exactly what this basket should contain, even those who adopt a conservative approach commonly estimate that the living wage is at least twice what the minimum wage currently provides.[10] To the cost of this basket, however, several major expenses may need to be added. For example, a worker's contextual basic needs must include the cost of necessary medical care, if this is not already made available as part of the government's provision for every citizen's primary basic needs, and the cost of raising a family. An economy can only function smoothly when there is a steady supply of able and willing workers, and such a supply can exist only if workers are able to maintain their health and reproduce. This means the cost of childrearing and education must be included too if these services are not otherwise provided by the state. The cost of retirement must also be included if not already adequately subsidized by the government, for otherwise workers would have to save for their retirement out of wages.

Support for measuring the cost of production of labor using the contextual basic needs approach actually goes back a long way—many of the medieval Schoolmen (Catholic philosophers who among other things opined on the ethical rules governing buying and selling goods and services), David Ricardo, Robert Malthus, and even Karl Marx all argued for some version of it.[11] But the importance of ensuring that even its worst-paid workers are able to consider themselves valued members of the society is perhaps most movingly articulated by Martin Luther King Jr., in his address to striking sanitation workers in Memphis on March 18, 1968, just a few weeks before he was assassinated. In this speech, King refers several times to the idea that all socially beneficial labor must generate wages that enable the worker to satisfy his basic needs, and he expressly mentions food, clothing, shelter, and "the basic necessities of life." The failure of American society to ensure that all work does this, a failure that unfortunately continues, is outrageous and shameful. But King does not, I think, believe that this is all American society must do. The obligation to provide people with resources sufficient to allow them to satisfy their *primary* basic needs is an obligation that a nation owes to *all* its citizens, not merely those engaged in full-time labor. The latter group is owed something more than this. King argues that if we are to show the requisite "respect" for "the dignity of labor," we must ensure that the wages generated by even the most unskilled forms of labor allow the worker to participate "in the mainstream of economic life," that his wages be sufficient to provide "economic security" for him and his family, that they enable him to escape the "air-tight cage of poverty," to spend the kind of time with his children that every parent should, to send them to schools that are neither overcrowded, dilapidated, nor ill equipped, and to occasionally take his family on vacation and out to dinner as indeed more skilled workers often do.[12]

One final point: Note that our commitment to putting workers in a position to satisfy their contextual basic needs does *not* commit us to subsidizing workers who have expensive tastes and therefore require more support in order to avoid social alienation than the rest of us, a criticism that is often leveled at theories advocating the establishment of some sort of equality of welfare.[13] While we are using the *actual* cost of basic needs as the relevant measure, determining actual cost requires reference to more than any one particular individual, for the needs at issue are *contextual*. Because they are contextual, a reasonable, objective element is introduced, and this ensures that the cost of satisfying contextual basic needs does not vary from individual to individual. The worker who is perfectly happy to live alone in a tent on waste ground eating only bread and water in the midst of an otherwise modern industrialized culture is still entitled to be given the wherewithal to live like other members of society, while the worker who requires a lunch of caviar and Cabernet Sauvignon to reach the level of welfare that others reach on beer and sandwiches has no right to have these expensive tastes subsidized, for these needs are idiosyncratic, not contextual. In either case, what we are doing is ensuring that the compensation each individual receives is sufficient to make that individual feel like a full-fledged member of society, able to take advantage of the full range of benefits that social cooperation can offer, whether they do so or not, and not merely a microchip in a big machine that has no value beyond its function, to be replaced and discarded after its useful life is over. Whether a particular worker is an atypically efficient or inefficient converter of resources into welfare is of no consequence in determining whether the contextual basic needs test behind the setting of the living wage is met.

III.

The major argument against the living wage, aside from the contention that it undercuts the moral force we often (incorrectly) attach to legal voluntariness, is that regardless of whether it will help those who earn it, it will in fact cause others to lose their jobs entirely, especially among those at the bottom of the wage scale, or drop from full-time work to part-time work, for employers will necessarily have to eliminate positions and/or hours in order to fund the wage increases that the law would now require. This, in turn, would be morally wrong because it would effectively use some people (those who lost jobs or hours as a result) as a mere means to improve the lives of others, a violation of one version of the Kantian categorical imperative (a deontological argument). And it would also be wrong because regardless of the good effects of such an increase for some people, when these good effects are netted against the bad effects of increased unemployment and decreased hours, the overall effect on the common good would also be negative (a consequentialist argument).

Either of these points would supposedly justify abolishing the minimum wage, or at least resisting all efforts to increase it, but together (it is alleged) they make that argument irresistible. And there are some studies that suggest raising the minimum wage does indeed lead to a small increase in unemployment and a similarly small decrease in hours among those currently holding minimum-wage jobs.[14] On the other hand, there are also a significant number of studies that point to troubling methodological problems and biases within the datasets used by those critical of attempts to raise the minimum wage, and show that once these biases and other problems are corrected, any alleged statistically significant increase in unemployment or decrease in hours disappears.[15] In other words, the empirical claim made here about the effect of raising the minimum wage on employment is dubious at best.

Yet this argument will not go away.[16] Part of the reason, I think, is that despite the equivocal nature of the relevant empirical studies, many of those who are critical of attempts to increase the minimum wage believe that there is a conceptual argument for a causal connection between increases in the minimum wage and decreases in employment that simply cannot be refuted. Economists, they point out, tell us that except in very unusual circumstances, circumstances that do not apply here, when something becomes more expensive, people will use less of it. If this is not being confirmed by the relevant empirical studies, then something must be wrong with the way the effects of such an increase are being measured; the causal connection simply must be there.

But like so many supposed conceptual truths, what is really behind the supposedly confounding empirical results showing no decrease in employment is that there is an underlying conceptual mistake that makes the conceptual claim erroneous. A relevant consideration has been left out. And in this case, that consideration is the effect that increasing the minimum wage will have on the growth of employment in the relevant community in general. If everyone has to pay the requisite minimum wage, businesses who do cannot be undercut by businesses who do not, so there is no competitive disadvantage to doing so. If the relevant business is profitable enough, increases can be funded out of pre-increase profits and not a reduction in other costs, such as those flowing from a reduction in employees, and if the business is not profitable enough, it can raise its prices. This may cause some inefficient businesses to lose customers, but that is a good thing, not a bad thing, because these losses should be more than offset by the gains of the relevant more efficient competitors. And if everyone who employs large amounts of minimum wage labor (and remember, this is only a comparatively small number of employers) is already maximally efficient, and therefore these employers have to raise prices a little to pay for the increased cost of this labor, then there is no effect at all on profitability or employment.

Finally, and most importantly, the increased wages of those on the bottom of the income distribution mean that there is now more money being spent by them and pumped into the economy. Unlike wealthier business owners, those working for the minimum wage have the highest marginal propensity to consume—everything they earn will be spent.[17] Also, those who are now receiving a living wage will no longer need to make claims for government benefits, and taxes can go down or the public funds previously used to pay these benefits can be redirected into more productive activities. Because more money is now being spent on these productive activities, demand for goods and services is increased, and with increased demand comes increased production and therefore increased employment. In other words, any jobs or hours eliminated in response to an increase in the minimum wage should soon be replaced by new jobs at more efficient businesses enjoying an increase in demand. Of course, there are many interrelated factors at work here, and it is hard to say how these will all balance out in advance. But this is why the intuition that there is a conceptual truth somewhere in here is mistaken. While there is no guarantee that any particular individual who loses his or her job as a result of an increase in the minimum wage will get another, there is no conceptual reason why the overall low-wage employment rate should change. Indeed, it is just as likely that there will be a net increase in jobs at the higher minimum wage level, not a decrease, as indeed the more convincing studies show. There is accordingly no reason to disbelieve what the empirical results are telling us and stubbornly stick to the claim that increasing the minimum wage will necessarily decrease employment.

The other reason why the argument over the overall effects of raising the minimum wage refuses to go away is that those who argue for the living wage usually do so by arguing that it is required by our moral obligation to alleviate poverty, although they do so in a variety of different ways. Some argue directly that poverty in the midst of plenty is unnecessary and therefore an affront to justice.[18] Others, called "sufficientarians," argue indirectly from equality that we have a moral obligation to ensure not an equal distribution of resources but merely that everyone has enough to live a minimally decent life.[19] And those in the fair-trade movement advocate living wages for workers in developing countries because they see this way of addressing the extreme poverty commonly found in these countries as better than charitable giving by rich nations and grants from the United Nations and various non-governmental organizations.[20]

I do think that that raising the minimum wage to a living wage will help reduce poverty in these ways. But this is better viewed as a helpful side effect (if it happens) than a morally decisive factor. Whether raising the minimum wage will indeed have these effects cannot be determined with any degree of certainty, so if we treat this factor as critical, we simply condemn ourselves to engaging in endless ongoing arguments. More importantly, even if it were true that raising the minimum wage to a living wage would decrease employment, and thereby *increase* the number of people living in poverty, here or elsewhere, this is not a reason that weighs against the living wage. The moral force behind the argument I am making is not the alleviation of poverty in any of these ways, but the requirements of reciprocity, so the effect on employment is ultimately beside the point. Indeed, there are all sorts of wrongs that if allowed would increase employment—not ending an unjust war that is employing some part of the population; allowing companies to pollute the environment or provide unsafe working conditions or otherwise impose what economists call "externalities" (that is, costs) on others or sell goods or services for which there is demand but that we consider morally pernicious (such as dangerous drugs and sexual services); and so on. But the additional employment such activities might bring is not seen as a reason to allow these moral wrongs to be committed. If raising the minimum wage to a living wage causes losses in employment, then rather than ignore this we have a moral obligation to try to stimulate employment. And there are a great many things we can do in this regard if we want to, and we should, for employment is an important component of self-respect and we have an obligation to do our best to see that our economy produces as close to full employment as is possible.[21] But we cannot justify paying people an unjust wage by arguing that if we do not do this fewer people will be fully employed. In a just society, the solution to the problem of under- and unemployment is not employing people for less than a just wage, it is growing the economy to a sufficient extent by moral means, whatever these may be, so that all those who are willing and able to work for a just wage can find the employment they desire.

COMPREHENSION QUESTIONS

1. What's the difference between the minimum wage and a living wage?
2. If increasing the minimum wage causes some reduction in low-wage employment opportunities, should we oppose the increase?
3. Why, according to Reiff, is money in the hands of lower-income earners better for the economy than increasing profits for wealthier people?
4. What is the difference between actual basic needs and contextual basic needs? How do they compare to personal choices and expensive tastes? What analogy does Reiff use to illustrate this point?

DISCUSSION QUESTIONS

1. If increasing the minimum wage causes some reduction in low-wage employment opportunities, what might we do about this?
2. Do you think that employees who are paid a living wage are likely to be more productive than workers who aren't? Why or why not?
3. Do you think that this issue should be determined by our sense of what's morally right or by what's best for the economy? What, if any, is the difference between these two concerns?
4. Why might those who generally try to protect the interests of business owners oppose increasing the minimum wage? Why might a business owner nevertheless be in favor of increasing the minimum wage?

Case 1

Steven Horwitz claims that you can't regulate wages without regulating workers:

> Job-seekers with limited skills and productivity trying to enter the labor market for the first time have their choices limited because they cannot offer their services at a price below the minimum wage. For job-seekers whose productivity allows them to produce $10 an hour worth of value, they are not going to get hired at a $15 per hour minimum wage. The regulation doesn't just stop employers from offering low "exploitative" wages, it also stops potential employees from negotiating a wage that is acceptable to them and the firm, given the job-seeker's productivity. Minimum wage laws thereby restrict the choices of some of the most vulnerable among us, causing them to be unable to get a foothold in the labor market and acquire the skills needed to move up the income ladder.
>
> Minimum wage laws also restrict the choices of those who keep their jobs. If employers decide to retain some employees who were making less than $15, it will not be without a cost elsewhere. Wages are not the only margin on which employers offer compensation. The obvious choice here is to cut hours, but employers can also cut all kinds of non-wage benefits they provide. This could be as drastic as cutting back health benefits, but is more likely to be reducing employee discounts on food or other merchandise, no longer providing free uniforms, ending employee free access to the employer's other services or ticketed events, engaging in more micro-management to try to get more productivity out of workers, reducing the flexibility of scheduling, and so on.
>
> These are all ways that minimum wage regulates the choices of employees. There may well be a good number of employees who prefer a slightly lower monetary wage if that means more of these other benefits. A more relaxed working environment where employees get significant discounts on the good or service being sold might have enough value for some, if not many, employees to prefer a variety of lower wages to a mandated $15 without those non-wage benefits. Minimum wage laws restrict the bundles of compensation that are available to employees at the same time they restrict the bundles of compensation employers are allowed to offer. Again, regulations never affect just one side of an exchange.*

What do you make of Horowitz's points here? Do they change the way you think about Reiff's arguments? Why or why not?

———————

*https://www.libertarianism.org/columns/two-sides-every-regulated-economic-exchange

THE CYNICAL MINIMUM WAGE HOAX
JOHN F. GASKI

1. Introduction

The issue of a government-imposed minimum wage is among the most contentious of modern American economic policy disputes, maybe the most charged of all. The following mainly analytic piece first presents the conceptual terms of the issue of whether a minimum wage enforced by law is wise policy. Then, the economic theory and empirical evidence on the subject are reviewed, highlighting especially the negative, and ironic, social consequences of a mandated minimum wage. Finally, the ethical implications of such socioeconomic law are examined, with definite conclusions offered.

Of all the ways American politicians have found to insult the intelligence of their constituents, the minimum wage issue may be the crowning example. The social harm done by a government-mandated minimum wage level has been successfully obscured by the political class, while the benefits of such a law have been exaggerated, to the point of engendering and manipulating public acquiescence.

How so? What's not to like about higher wages induced by a minimum wage requirement? All workers at the low end of the wage compensation spectrum get more money as a result, do they not? Therefore, opposition to such a policy designed to help the poor would be immoral. Or so goes the conventional (non) wisdom, at least.

The most benign interpretation of this simplistic position is that some of its advocates are naïve enough to believe it. Others surely understand the non-viability of the minimum wage but argue for it disingenuously nevertheless for political reasons.

Non-viable? What problem could there be with raising low incomes by decree, with the stroke of a pen? Perhaps the most effective primer on the subject is the *reductio ad absurdum* argument often proffered by minimum wage opponents, to wit: Why raise wages to only $10 or $15 an hour? Why not $30 an hour? Why not $150? Why stop there? Why not a minimum wage of $1,500 per hour?

At that point, a lightbulb may come on with the minimum wage believer as the beginning of understanding intrudes. The nature of the illumination, of course, is the layman's crude and instinctual comprehension of the law of demand and the role of price. Force the price of labor input higher, that is, and less of it will be demanded by those who buy labor—that is, employers. What a concept! The real-world translation of this impact of higher price on the labor demand curve, unfortunately, is mass unemployment.

Yes, even the untrained layman who has been duped by minimum wage propaganda can sense that a mandated hourly wage of $1,500, $150, or even $30 could cause serious problems for employers, such as not being financially able to hire very many workers at those rates. Then, it is but a short step to the realization that the difference from those scenarios and a $10 to $15 minimum wage is only one of degree.

Substantively, the matter should now be settled. This simple logical exercise seems to be effective with rational audiences, if not with ideologues. Perhaps it has even had some impact on present readers.

The enforced minimum wage is essentially a price control—on the price of labor explicitly. As opposed to conventional price controls setting a ceiling on the price charged by sellers in the product market, a minimum wage requirement establishes a *floor* on the price paid by *buyers* in the factor (labor) market. Readers are surely aware of the disastrous history of government price controls in terms of constricting supply and causing shortages. (Recall the long lines at filling stations during the energy crisis of the 1970s.) Minimum wage laws likewise

constrict *demand* for the factor of production we know as labor, inevitably causing unemployment. Perhaps a reason for lesser visibility and notoriety of the
negative effects of the minimum wage, compared with traditional price controls,
is that instead of virtually all consumers in a jurisdiction experiencing shortages,
only a fraction of the populace, the newly unemployed fraction, directly experiences the minimum wage's damaging effects.

But if the compulsory minimum wage is so easily exposed as a charade and
pipedream, how can so many political and government leaders espouse it? Are
they economically illiterate? A few seem to be on certain issues, as many U.S.
voters would likely agree, but by and large, well-educated public officials can
hardly be so incompetent. It must be something else.

Hypothesized here instead is that many so-called public servants support
a legislated minimum wage for purely political reasons irrespective of its detrimental economic effects. In fact, they may even support the policy *because of*
those negative human effects. Although it is inadmissible to presume motives in
serious discourse except as a last resort, we may be in last-resort territory with
respect to the minimum wage issue. Regardless, supportive evidence will be produced when we return to this question later.

2. Scientific Background

On the subject of evidence, this essay's premise does demand some support.
Naturally, we are not the first to have pondered the economic consequences of
a minimum wage law. The field of economics has devoted considerable attention
to the issue—probably excessive attention given that the fundamental laws of
supply and demand hardly need more empirical verification. Nevertheless, some
of history's great economists have declaimed on the negative employment effects
of a compulsory minimum wage.

Over seventy years ago, Nobel Prize winner George Stigler foresaw that
"The higher the minimum wage, the greater . . . the number of covered workers who are discharged. . . . Whatever the number, the direct unemployment is
substantial and certain." How severe would be the unemployment effect? Even
with the minimally sized minimum wage under consideration in Stigler's time,
he estimated "possibly several hundred thousand workers" as the magnitude of
detriment, a forecast borne out in the subsequent decades.[22] The prophecy and
insight of Stigler should be enough to give pause and raise grave concern, but
there is more.

Paul Samuelson, another Nobelist, put it into poignant, human terms:
"Minimum wage rates . . . often hurt those they are designed to help. What good
does it do a Negro youth to know that an employer must pay him $1.60 per hour,
if the fact that he must be paid that amount is what keeps him from getting a
job?"[23] Although notably dated nomenclature, the disparate impact of a mandated minimum wage on the most vulnerable in society is brought into bold
relief by Samuelson's rhetorical question. (Even at this point in the presentation,
it should be clear that the minimum wage's ethical dimension can be ironic.)
And it is not as if right-wing economists are being cherry-picked for ideological

testimony here—quite the contrary, for example, as those familiar with the political slant of the late Professor Samuelson will already know. Likewise and more contemporarily, the very prominent Olivier Blanchard observes that "minimum wages . . . often make it unprofitable to hire low-skill workers. Thus, low-skill workers remain unemployed."[24]

These classic excerpts are sufficient to represent the basic theoretical foundation of how a government-imposed minimum wage causes unemployment. What of empirical examination? Studies abound, mostly establishing negative employment effects of the minimum wage.[25] A notorious exception was the Card and Krueger project of 1994, largely discredited thereafter, that purported to reveal the absence of such unemployment consequences.[26]

Of course, the *magnitude* of employment effects is a key metric in evaluating the net detriment or benefit of a minimum wage law. Most research in this area expresses the minimum wage–unemployment relation as statistical regression coefficients or elasticity exponents, but some results have been translated into absolute disemployment numbers. Apart from Stigler's prophetic but analytic rough estimate of "hundreds of thousands," some of the more prominent empirical estimates of the actual number to be disemployed at the U.S. national level by a conventional minimum wage increase comparable to the current aspiration (from $7.25 to about $10 per hour) are 128,000, 145,000, 436,000, 500,000, and 1.4 million.[27]

The present analytic commentary is a designated essay and not intended to be an academic literature review or meta-analysis, so detailed itemization and deconstruction of empirical results will not be superimposed. Fortunately, that labor has been done elsewhere more efficiently, thereby eliminating any need to "reinvent the wheel" here, and the derived information is ours for the taking. What is perhaps the leading exemplar of that type summarizes the whole field of study thusly: "A sizable majority of the studies surveyed . . . give a relatively consistent indication of negative employment effects of minimum wages. . . . [A]lmost all point to negative employment effects, both for the United States as well as for many other countries. . . . Studies that focus on the least-skilled groups provide overwhelming evidence of stronger disemployment effects."[28]

But regardless of the ultimate absolute size of unemployment effect that would eventuate from a given minimum wage law, if such an effect is generally accepted then how can there even be a question about the unethicality of the minimum wage? Is its irresponsible human damage not obvious? Again, the magnitude comes into play in grounding the prospective counter-argument: If the average positive increment in income for workers benefiting from the minimum wage increase *multiplied by* the number of workers so benefiting is greater than the aggregate loss for those suffering disemployment (i.e., their number multiplied by lost wages via job loss), then a minimum wage could possibly be justified, at least in terms of utilitarian ethics—that is, the greatest good for the greatest number. Bolstering this case, at least superficially, is the argument that the newly unemployed would receive unemployment insurance as an income buffer.

However, offsetting and possibly neutralizing this ethics defense for the minimum wage are these realities: (1) Unemployment insurance is temporary; (2) the workers most afflicted by minimum wage–caused unemployment also tend to be those who do not qualify for unemployment insurance benefits (e.g., young, short-term employees); (3) the *utility* of a modest monetary wage increment, such as the 36.7% change between $7.25 and $10 as recently proposed, is inevitably much less than the disutility of lost income associated with total job loss; and (4) the utility of each dollar gained by minimum wage beneficiaries is very likely less than the utility of each dollar lost by those who are minimum wage–disemployment victims. So when comparing aggregate income gain of minimum wage recipients with aggregate income loss of those disemployed by a minimum wage law, heavier weight should be attached to the latter category to reflect the likely higher utility of those lost dollars. Specifically, the renowned economists Kahneman and Tversky have found that the value of a dollar lost is twice that of a dollar gained.[29]

Illustrating with actual numbers, there are currently about 700,000 U.S. workers earning at the minimum wage level. Estimate about 300,000 jobs extinguished by a minimum wage increase from $7.25 to $10—the approximate mean of the reputable estimates reported previously (excepting the upside outlier, for a literal mean of 302,250). This represents $4.524 billion in annual income loss compared with a $2.288 billion gain by the 400,000 remaining employed within the minimum wage class who experience the wage rise, assuming a forty-hour workweek. If we recall the finding of double utility for money lost compared with money gained, the equivalent value of the aggregate wage loss in this example is now over $9 billion relative to the $2.288 billion in gain—and the same type of comparison applies to every individual affected as well. Case closed?

What about a "trickle-up" effect with near-minimum wages also being forced higher by a raised minimum, an effect that is sometimes alleged? Corresponding analysis prevails: more mass unemployment of that wage segment negating the lesser incremental gain of those with a wage boost. What of mitigation through governmental unemployment insurance compensation? Because limited to twenty-six weeks in most states, and assuming a typical 50% maximum formulaic share of wages replaced, the mitigation effect would reduce the loss side by about one-fourth, from approximately $9 billion of comparative utility sacrificed down to $6.75 billion on an annual basis: still a net loser when comparing with only $2.288 billion in gain by other workers. (Notably, this appraisal does not even attempt to quantify the secondary social impact of unemployment in terms of more street crime or the price inflation derived from mandated wage increases, both of which disproportionately affect the poor.)

Or might we be concerned about use of rough estimates in this analysis? Probably not, because the illustrative amounts would have to be off by an order of magnitude to alter the overall case against the minimum wage. The estimates of job losses, again, are based on empirical research by such sources as the Congressional Budget Office, Employment Policies Institute (EPI), and Federal Reserve Bank of San Francisco. *None* of the original metrics are developed by this author.

Empirical Corollary

With the referenced research reporting mostly support for a negative employ-ment effect of the minimum wage, this implies that some research, a lesser body of work, finds the contrary—if not positive effects, at least the absence of effects. What of those results? Neumark and Wascher, as cited earlier from their National Bureau of Economic Research study, offer a simple and plausible rebuttal. Most of the minimum wage enactments from the United States and other countries that serve as raw material for economic research have been relatively small in percent-age terms. For instance, the 1961 U.S. federally mandated wage increase was from $1.00 to $1.15. In 1963, the minimum went from $1.15 to $1.25 (only 8.7 percent). Therefore, it should be no surprise that many findings are non-significant statis-tically. Moreover, the abundance of other potential extraneous variables in the macro-economy that cannot be controlled for would also tend to create enough statistical "noise" to confound or suppress results.[30] More recently, though, with larger relative wage burdens enacted and under consideration, more substantial disemployment consequences can be reasonably forecast on the basis of estab-lished models.

Another Empirical Corollary: Poll Results

Should we not also consider what the entire economics profession thinks, rather than relying only on those who have studied the minimum wage issue per se, or this observer's report of that genre? So be it, and by all means. Historically, about 95% of economists, based on poll results, have agreed that a government-enforced minimum wage causes unemployment. In view of the empirical record, this should not be regarded as a news bulletin. (One must wonder about the 5% who dispute that the normal operation of supply and demand applies to the labor market.)

In more recent years, however, there has been some slippage, for whatever reason. A slightly larger minority of economists actually is willing to deny the unemployment effect of a minimum wage. In 2015, seventy-five economists signed a public letter urging an increased minimum wage—but over five hundred economists came out against it, for a ratio of 6.67 to 1.[31] (This result may con-test the caricature joke about how one cannot get economists to agree with each other, or even with themselves, on anything.) Is it conceivable that a change has occurred in the underlying law of supply and demand, or have more economists suddenly begun to construe labor market supply and demand in a novel way? A more prosaic hypothesis is hereby offered.

Contemporary survey results show that partisan Democrat academic econo-mists outnumber Republicans in their profession by about three to one. As a result, many of these Democratic scholars may find that their scientific under-standing of the minimum wage is in conflict with their ideological or policy preference—since most Democrats do favor a higher minimum wage; it is even a plank in the Democratic Party platform. (A 2015 survey by the EPI reveals that economists are indeed split along political party lines on the issue of minimum wage preference, although there is much less than one-to-one correspondence between party and preference.)[32] This cognitive dilemma causes psychological dissonance for that particular subset of economists that they can only resolve by changing either their understanding or their preference. Some will choose the former, and that may be what is showing up in the larger number, although still a minority, who profess academic allegiance to the minimum wage. Either that or perhaps they just claim to believe that the minimum wage does not induce unemployment without really believing it.

Yet the recent polling still finds an overwhelming majority of economists who recommend against a higher minimum wage on disemployment grounds— just not quite as overwhelming a spread as in the past. Per the cited 2015 EPI survey, 75% of U.S. economists oppose a minimum wage increase.

3. Conclusion

Finally, accepting the decided consensus that a government-imposed minimum wage produces substantial unemployment not likely to be balanced in the aggregate by greater utility for the still employed, or fully mitigated by unemployment insurance compensation, what can be concluded about minimum wage ethics per se?

Of the two leading ethical systems, only utilitarian teleology offers even a chance for moral support of a mandated minimum wage resembling those now in force or under consideration in the United States (*teleology* literally refers to the study of end results). That ethic, based on aggregate net benefit or "greatest good for the greatest number," still would depend on the unlikely outcome of aggregate utility gain by minimum wage employees exceeding the utility loss of the disemployed, as elaborated in the preceding. The prospect is at least dubious, so the minimum wage is a risky or reckless venture, especially from the perspective of the most economically vulnerable workers.

Based on deontological ethics, which focus on justice to, or fair treatment of, the individual, a minimum wage law appears ruled out completely due to the adverse means employed, so to speak, which essentially involve costing many workers their jobs in order to give others a raise—to put it in plain English. As acknowledged, this assessment does hinge on the validity of economic consensus. A credible basis? An alternative way of expressing it is that this particular ethical conclusion merely depends on the validity of the law of supply and demand.

Case closed. And this form of closure only serves to compound the culpability of public officials who do understand the minimum wage economics and ethics as reviewed herein but enact or advocate the job-killing policy anyway. As asked earlier, why? One possible motive is that politicians know how they benefit from the superficial attraction of a minimum wage to voters who do not comprehend the detrimental economics of the policy. So, beyond insulting public intelligence as speculated previously, it may be more a matter of exploiting widespread public ignorance. In short, opportunistic politicians get votes from the masses who think bad policy is good policy. In response, we can exhort better economic education at the secondary school level as an antidote.

What evidence is there to support such a severe hypothesis about illegitimate motivation? The best of all, first-person confirmation: As reported contemporaneously in the *Wall Street Journal*, a Clinton administration functionary admitted during that president's term that the White House hierarchy knew full well a minimum wage increase, which they supported, would cause hardship through job losses. Said the Clinton operative, "There are few of us who actually think it is good economic policy, but more than a few think it might be good politics. Those in economic circles are being told to hold their noses."[33] Furthermore, Joseph Stiglitz, President Clinton's economic council chairman and another Nobel Prize recipient, acknowledged in his own writings the negative employment effect of the minimum wage—but then attempted to deny it while in the Clinton administration![34] Minimum wage proponents appear not to have reformed much in the intervening years.

Alternatively, an even more cynical suspicion dovetails with a common partisan criticism of the political camp that favors nominally redistributive policies such as the minimum wage: They actually wish to create a larger underclass because that is their most reliable source of votes. Causing economic disadvantage via tactics such as a minimum wage contributes to that corrupt aim, obviously. Hence, the word "cynical" in this work's title. "Immoral" and "unethical" could have been added.

COMPREHENSION QUESTIONS

1. Why think that if the cost of labor goes up then the number of laborers will go down?
2. What are price controls? How does a minimum wage function as one, and what are the potential effects on employment?
3. What is double utility? How does Gaski relate this concept to unemployment and decreased economic growth?
4. What reason does Gaski give for economists changing views and supporting a minimum wage increase?

DISCUSSION QUESTIONS

1. Do you think the minimum wage conversation is about political optics or economic equity? Give support to your claim with examples from either author or from other experiences.
2. What would be a better method of ensuring just wages for workers beyond minimum wage increases?
3. How can an economy have both affordable low-skilled labor and reasonable incomes for those who work full time?

Case 2

There's ample evidence that poverty is bad for kids. Consider this, for instance:

> For the past 20 years, [Gary] Evans [of Cornell University] has followed chil-
> dren who grew up at or below the poverty line, as well as children who grew
> up at two or four times the poverty line (the income levels that the majority
> of Americans currently occupy). Through this study, Evans identified [physical
> and psychosocial risk factors for mental and cognitive developmental debilita-
> tion, including exposure to violence, household turmoil, and separation from
> a parent]. The dataset has also provided critical insight into the possible path-
> ways, such as stress, that could lead to developmental issues.
>
> For example, Evans and his colleagues were able to use neuroimaging of
> the brains of around 50 of the study's participants, half of whom grew up poor
> and the other half middle income. At this point, the participants were well past
> childhood and into their mid-20s. The brain imaging revealed that the two
> groups had different brain structure and function.
>
> "Levels of physiological stress look like they may be part of the reason,"
> says Evans. "The brains have changed—it doesn't mean that it's irrevocable
> and that you can't do anything about it, but it does mean that it's a lot harder,
> because once the trajectory is in place, it's difficult to dislodge it."
>
> Evans and his research team specifically found that the adults who were
> children of poverty had a more difficult time performing emotional regulation
> tasks. The researchers had participants look at emotional faces and neutral
> faces, and asked them to both experience the emotions and then regulate
> their emotions. Adults who grew up in low-income environments had more
> trouble regulating their emotions, which was also mirrored in different brain
> functioning in the prefrontal cortex. Moreover, these emotional regulation
> abilities may have been altered by early exposure to stress.
>
> Similarly, in Evans's longitudinal study, he found that children who grew
> up in low-income environments had a higher risk of mental health challenges
> and psychological distress. He also notes that there is not as much upward
> mobility as the "enduring American myth" suggests.
>
> "Half of low-income children, maybe more, will wind up being in the
> bottom fifth of income as adults," he says. "There is not nearly as much upward
> mobility as many Americans believe." Again, Evans points to the confluence of
> risk that these children experience early on in life.*

This study reminds us that when we talk about living wages, we aren't simply
talking about the impacts of the wage on the earner. We also need to consider the
impacts of wages on the children of earners. Does this affect how you think about
Gaski's arguments? Why or why not?

---

*https://research.cornell.edu/news-features/damaging-effects-poverty-children

REPLY TO GASKI
MARK R. REIFF

As I noted in my opening essay, those who oppose increasing the minimum wage not only claim that doing so will increase unemployment and therefore poverty among the poor, they treat this as a conceptual truth. John Gaski's essay is an excellent example of this. The claim that if you make something more expensive, people will use less of it, is presented as an irrefutable economic law. Anything that purports to show otherwise must accordingly be a "hoax," a "cynical attempt" to deceive. While no empirical evidence is needed if Gaski's conceptual claim is correct, Gaski nevertheless does cite a few empirical studies that suggest raising the minimum wage causes a small increase in unemployment among low-wage workers. For the reasons set forth in my opening essay, there are problems with each of these studies, and other, more competently performed studies have repeatedly shown no such effect. But there is some evidence to support Gaski's point, even if this alleged effect is far more modest than he suggests and is outweighed by other, more convincing evidence.[35]

The point I want to re-emphasize here, however, is that the supposed conceptual truth that is driving Gaski's outrage is not, in fact, a conceptual truth at all. But it does have a long history. In effect, it is a restatement of a very famous idea in economics: the "wages fund" theory originally advanced by J. S. Mill and certain other classical economists.[36] In brief, the theory was that there is only a certain amount of capital available to pay wages, and one can either pay this to a larger or smaller group of people—that is, keep wages where they are and therefore more people in full-time employment, or pay higher wages to some in exchange for unemployment or underemployment for others. Accordingly, neither governments, nor unions, nor anyone else has the ability to improve the real (inflation-adjusted) wages of workers. If nominal (dollar) wages go up thanks to laws setting a minimum wage, then employment will go down an offsetting amount or inflation will rise, making the nominal wage gains unreal, or some combination of both.

But the wages fund theory has long been discredited. Mill recanted his support for it in 1869.[37] Other economists followed suit, and by the early twentieth century, the theory was described as "the crowning instance of an untrue abstraction [that] has probably done more injury to the reputation of economic theory than any other generalization ever received into economics textbooks and then expunged from them."[38] What everyone realized was that the fund out of which wages are paid is neither fixed nor impossible to use for other things. This money can go instead to:

- increasing dividends to clamoring shareholders;
- repurchasing stock and thereby artificially increasing earnings per share;
- retiring debt to improve the appearance of the firm's balance sheet;
- paying excessive compensation to top management;
- funding expensive corporate acquisitions and mergers that artificially create the appearance of corporate growth;
- hoarding cash when everything else looks too risky;

- bidding up the price of assets in environments where new investment is deemed too risky; and
- a host of other unproductive places, all of which are attracting enormous amounts of money today.[39]

So, even if the wage rate were purely a distributional matter, there is no reason to believe that we can't have a higher minimum wage without causing either unemployment or inflation.[40]

But the amount available to be divided between all these functions is not purely a distributional matter.[41] The economy can also grow, increasing the "fund," as it has for many years.[42] As long as it continues to do so, higher wages can be paid with no loss in employment.[43] And if it stops, increasing the minimum wage is actually one (but only one) of the many things we can do to promote growth, as I pointed out in my opening essay. If the economy does not grow despite all our efforts, however, and certain firms do try to increase prices or lay off workers when minimum wages rise, it is both morally wrong and economically foolish for them to do so. They will be underpriced and outperformed by firms that pay for such an increase out of unproductive sources, and therefore will be punished by the market. Indeed, if this does not happen, there is some form of collusion going on and the market has competitive problems that need to be independently addressed.

Note also that while the anti-increase argument is ostensibly based on concern for the poor, this concern disappears once we move beyond this issue. No alternative approaches to helping the poor are ever mentioned. But if increasing the minimum wage were to hurt the poor,[44] there are things we can and should do to alleviate this. The need to take action on several fronts simultaneously to see that justice is done is not an excuse for doing nothing. What really seems to be driving the opposition here is the desire to protect corporate profits, for if the exploitation of workers comes down, then corporate profits, which are currently comfortably high, may come down too.[45] If this happens, however, it is a simply the result of living in a more just world. In either case, this shouldn't be of concern to anyone who believes in the free market.[46] The free market is supposed to ensure that economic resources, including labor, are allocated efficiently, because this increases productivity and creates a bigger pie and therefore potentially bigger slices for everyone. Yet even the most ardent free marketeers recognize that there are sometimes "market failures" that need to be corrected. Increasing the minimum wage is simply once such correction, for it ensures that economic resources are allocated according to the true cost of labor. Allowing employers to exploit their workers, in contrast, simply allows them to disguise their true cost of production, and the misallocation of resources that results leaves less available to be divided among the rest of us.

COMPREHENSION QUESTIONS

1. What is the "wages fund" theory? Why is it an inadequate measure of the effects of increasing the minimum wage?
2. What's the difference between a fixed distribution and an increasing fund model?

DISCUSSION QUESTIONS

1. Given the variable cost of living throughout the United States, and especially in urban centers, how should we set a single living wage at the federal level? If we can't, then what should we do?
2. Reiff suggests that lower minimum wages are motivated by the desire to protect corporate profits. Someone might say: "Look, if they were your profits, you'd want to protect them too!" Is this kind of move a helpful reminder, or does it prevent us from seeing the real issue? (Or does it do something else entirely?)

REPLY TO REIFF
JOHN F. GASKI

I have several objections to Reiff's argument for the living wage.

First, any case for a mandated wage is inescapably subjective. Reiff must rely on locutions such as "to . . . participate meaningfully in society," "contextual basic needs," and "feel that they are . . . valued," and he concedes that there is "no clear agreement on what a living wage would be" and that its grounding is "difficult to . . . comprehend." Ultimately, we would have to trust government or the ivory tower elite to determine the living wage—under this handicap of uncertainty.

Reiff tries to use labor production costs to set the bar for a living wage. Elements of the calculus are "food, shelter, and clothing," "television, a car . . . [and] personal computer," "medical care . . . and the cost of childrearing and education . . . retirement." No wonder the living wage is estimated at double the minimum wage!

Such gymnastics are unnecessary: Market-based price is not only a fair estimate of the value of a commercial offering such as labor, but it also represents the value of what is received in return. Per the *fundamental principle of exchange*, what is received by a party must be valued more than what is given up, or exchange would not occur. If Company X is willing to pay $N for John's labor, it must value the labor more than the $N surrendered. Likewise, if John supplies the labor, he must attach greater value to the $N received than to the labor expended. This illustrates why free market exchange is a positive-sum game.

Then, because labor market supply approximates pure competition, with large numbers of workers competing for jobs, the market wage will also track closely the true cost of labor, though exceeding it slightly. Hence, it is virtually inevitable that wages in a market economy already provide for a living wage, by strict interpretation. This condition renders the living wage argument largely superfluous.

* * *

Reiff downplays the moral significance of voluntary exchange, but market transactions, including the labor market, are the face of economic freedom. For an example of constrained economic choice, visit any socialist country. Therefore, it is not coherent for Rawls, as cited by Reiff, to insinuate "if" market exchange parties were free. Free market exchange indeed tends to deliver value in excess of cost for both sides of a transaction, which highlights the system's practical morality.

Apart from the misplaced "if . . . free," Rawls (via Reiff) hypothesizes "if [exchange parties] were . . . equal." This part is not disputed, although its implications are. Of course, all humans are not perfectly equal in talent, information, or effort. A liberal government endeavors to enact equality before the law, but countless sources of natural inequality are present in any society. As a result, this Rawls/Reiff hypothetical does not apply to the real world.

Moreover, real-world results show that (1) free labor markets practically ensure something even better for workers than the conception of a living wage, and (2) criticizing the U.S. economy as "shameful" on mistaken grounds of poverty is off base. How so? The official poverty rate in the United States is *always* between 12% and 15%. But if the value of all government transfer payments (e.g., food stamps) and unreported, underground income were counted, it is estimated that the poverty rate would be 5% to 6%. Then, if allowance were made for seniors who have substantial assets but low income (sometimes intentionally)—recognizing that economic status is a function of both wealth and income—the true poverty rate in the United States becomes about 2% to 3%.[47] Really. The actual level of economic distress in America is much lower than advertised. In fact, the average American in "poverty" has a higher income and living standard than the average *person* in most countries of the world as well as the average person worldwide. Truly, most poverty in the United States exists primarily because we define it as being present.

* * *

Some of Reiff's claims were addressed in my main contribution, including the living/minimum wage versus higher unemployment moral tradeoff. I'm opposed to wage intervention because of its job loss effects. Yes, there is evidence both for and against the unemployment effect of the minimum/living wage, so what can we conclude? Science cannot be done by popularity contest or opinion poll, but the economic consensus should not be ignored.

How did the economics profession arrive at the overwhelming consensus that a higher compulsory wage breeds unemployment hardship? It must have been the preponderance of empirical evidence and familiarity with the law of supply and demand. The combination of hard evidence and a scientific principle drove the conclusion that the minimum or living wage is bad medicine. This argument will not go away because it is supported by the most basic law of economics.

* * *

Reiff's analysis depends on a conjunction of questionable "ifs." "*If* the . . . business is profitable . . . increases can be funded." But with tight margins and employee costs typically 50% of expenses, layoffs have already been seen in living wage–adopting localities.

"*If* the business is not profitable enough, it can raise . . . prices." Higher prices are one possibility, but demand elasticity usually does not permit cost increases to be entirely recovered through pricing.

Finally comes the chimera about greater propensity to consume among minimum wage beneficiaries inducing greater aggregate demand and *more* jobs.

Presto! Recall, however, that those newly unemployed because of a mandated wage are also among the high-propensity-to-consume category, and my essay's arithmetic suggests that any demand gain of the first group is more than offset by job losses of the latter segment.

This is a sampling of the "ifs" that must coincide for a minimum/living wage not to produce disaster. If even one fails to materialize, the argument vaporizes.

COMPREHENSION QUESTIONS

1. What is the fundamental principle of exchange?
2. What subjective measures for calculating a living wage does Gaski reject? Why?

DISCUSSION QUESTIONS

1. If labor markets provide pure competition that provides a living wage, then what story should we tell about the development of laws and institutions (e.g., child labor laws and unions) that try to restrict labor markets?
2. What do you think of Gaski's view on poverty? If impoverished Americans still have more material wealth compared to others worldwide, does American "poverty" matter less?

FURTHER READINGS

Adams, Ronald. "Standard of Living as a Right, Not a Privilege: Is It Time to Change the Dialogue from Minimum Wage to Living Wage?" *Business and Society Review* 122 (2017): 613–639.

Baker, Peter C. "How Much Is an Hour Worth? The War over the Minimum Wage." *The Guardian*, April 13, 2018.

Cooper, David. *Raising the Minimum Wage to $15 by 2024 Would Lift Wages for 41 million American Workers*. Washington, DC: Economic Policy Institute, April 26, 2017, https://www.epi.org/files/pdf/125047.pdf.

Friedman, Milton. *Capitalism and Freedom*. Chicago: University of Chicago Press, 1962.

Gaski, John F. *Frugal Cool: How to Get Rich—Without Making Very Much Money*. Notre Dame, IN: Corby Books, 2009.

Gaski, John F. "Raising the Minimum Wage Is Unethical and Immoral." *Business and Society Review* 109, no. 2 (2004): 209–224.

Massachusetts Institute of Technology. 2018. "Living Wage Calculator," http://livingwage.mit.edu/.

Reiff, Mark R. Book talk on *Exploitation and Economic Justice in the Liberal Capitalist State* given at University Press Books, Berkeley, California, August 15, 2013. https://vimeo.com/76562180.

NOTES

1. For an early discussion of the living wage, see John A. Ryan, *A Living Wage* (New York: Macmillan, 1906); John A. Ryan, *Distributive Justice* (New York: Macmillan, 1916, rev. ed. 1927), esp. 285–390. For a more recent discussion, see Robert Pollin and Stephanie

Luce, *The Living Wage* (New York: The New Press, 1998). For a discussion of some of the roots of the movement, see Edd S. Noell, "In Pursuit of the Just Wage: A Comparison of Reformation and Counter-Reformation Economic Thought," *Journal of the History of Economic Thought* 23 (2001): 467–489; Steven A. Epstein, "The Theory and Practice of the Just Wage," *Journal of Medieval History* 17 (1991): 53–69.

2. See Lawrence Mishel, Elise Gould, and Josh Bivens, "Wage Stagnation in Nine Charts" (Economic Policy Institute, January 6, 2015), esp. fig. 8.

3. See Mark Brenner, Jeannette Wicks-Lim, and Robert Pollin, "Detecting the Effects of Minimum Wage Laws," in *A Measure of Fairness: The Economics of Living Wages and Minimum Wages in the United States*, edited by Robert Pollin et al. (Ithaca, NY: Cornell University Press, 2008), 233–253, esp. 233; Deborah M. Figart, ed., *Living Wage Movements: Global Perspectives,* (London: Routledge, 2004); Pollin and Luce, *Living Wage*, 204–214.

4. See Wider Opportunities for Women, *The Basic Economic Security Tables for the United States* (2010), http://www.wowonline.org/documents/BESTIndexforTheUnitedStates2010.pdf; Motoko Rich, "Many Low-Wage Jobs Seen as Failing to Meet Basic Needs," *New York Times*, March 31, 2011; Steven Greenhouse, "Raising the Floor on Pay," *New York Times*, April 9, 2012; Editorial, "The Case for a Higher Minimum Wage," *New York Times*, February 8, 2014; Paulina Velasco, "Down and Out in Disneyland: Study Finds Most LA Workers Can't Cover Basic Needs," *The Guardian*, March 1, 2018; Paul Butler, "What Would Jesus Do? Pay Workers a Living Wage," *The Guardian*, March 30, 2018 (the author is Bishop of Durham); Tracy Jan, "A Minimum-Wage Worker Can't Afford a 2-Bedroom Apartment Anywhere in the U.S.," *Washington Post*, June 13, 2018.

5. See John Rawls, *A Theory of Justice* (Cambridge, MA: Harvard University Press, 1971, rev. ed. 1999).

6. See Rawls, *Theory of Justice*, esp. Chapters 3, 4, and 24.

7. See Mark R. Reiff, *Exploitation and Economic Justice in the Liberal Capitalist State* (Oxford: Oxford University Press, 2013).

8. See Aristotle, *Nicomachean Ethics*, edited by Roger Crisp (Cambridge: Cambridge University Press, 2000), Bk. 5, Chapters 4 and 5, pp. 87–92, 1132a–1134a.

9. See Karl Pribram, *A History of Economic Reasoning* (Baltimore, MD: Johns Hopkins University Press, 1983), 80, 129.

10. See Edd S. Noell, "Smith and the Living Wage: Competition, Economic Compulsion, and the Scholastic Legacy," *History of Political Economy* 38 (2006): 151–174, 151; Pollin and Luce, *Living Wage*, 204–214 (listing the living wage for various localities).

11. See Bernard W. Dempsey, "Just Price in a Functional Economy," *American Economic Review* 25 (1935): 471–486, 477–482; O. F. Hamouda and B. B. Price, "The Justice of the Just Price," *European Journal of the History of Economic Thought* 4 (1997): 191–216, 200; E. A. J. Johnson, "Just Price in an Unjust World," *International Journal of Ethics* 48 (1938): 165–181, 166–171 (all describing support for this idea among the Schoolmen); David Ricardo, *The Principles of Political Economy and Taxation* (Mineola, NY: Dover, 2004), Chapter 5, pp. 54–55; T. R. Malthus, *Principles of Political Economy* (Cambridge: Cambridge University Press, variorum ed. 1989), Vol. 1, Chapter 4, Sec. 2, pp. 247–257; Karl Marx, *Capital, Volume I* (Chicago: Charles H. Kerr & Co., 1921), Chapter 6, p. 190; Karl Marx, *Value, Price, and Profit* (Moscow: Foreign Languages Publishing House, 1947), Chapter 14, p. 66; Karl Marx, "Critique of the Gotha Program," in *The Marx-Engels Reader*, edited by Robert C. Tucker (New York: W. W. Norton, 1978 [2nd ed.]), 525–541, 534–535.

12. See Martin Luther King Jr., "Address to Striking Sanitation Workers in Memphis, Tennessee," March 18, 1968.

13. See, e.g., John Rawls, "Social Unity and Primary Goods," in *Utilitarianism and Beyond*, edited by Amartya Sen and Bernard Williams (Cambridge: Cambridge University Press, 1982), 159–185, at 168–169; Ronald Dworkin, *Sovereign Virtue* (Cambridge, MA: Harvard University Press, 2000), 48–59; G. A. Cohen, "On the Currency of Egalitarian Justice," *Ethics* 99 (1989): 906–944, and "Expensive Taste Rides Again," in *Dworkin and His Critics*, edited by Justine Burley (Oxford: Blackwell, 2004), 3–29.

14. See David Neumark and William L. Wascher, *Minimum Wages* (Cambridge, MA: MIT Press, 2008), esp. 37–106; David Neumark and William Wascher, "Minimum Wages and Employment: A Review of Evidence from the New Minimum Wage Research," National Bureau of Economic Research Working Paper No. 12663 (November 2006), http://www.nber.org/papers/w12663; David Neumark and William Wascher, "Minimum Wages and Employment: A Case Study of the Fast-Food Industry in New Jersey and Pennsylvania: Comment," *American Economic Review* 90 (2000): 1362–1396.

15. See Sylvia Allegretto, Arindrajit Dube, and Michael Reich, "Do Minimum Wages Really Reduce Teen Employment? Accounting for Heterogeneity and Selectivity in State Panel Data," *Institute for Research on Labor and Employment Working Paper Series* (University of California, Berkeley, June 2008), http://repositories.cdlib.org/iir/iirwps/iirwps-166-08; Arindrajit Dube, T. William Lester, and Michael Reich, "Minimum Wage Effects Across State Border: Estimates Using Contiguous Counties," *Institute for Research on Labor and Employment Working Paper Series* (University of California, Berkeley, October 2008), http://repositories.cdlib.org/iir/iirwps/iirwps-157-07; David Card and Alan B. Krueger, "Minimum Wages and Employment: A Case Study of the Fast-Food Industry in New Jersey and Pennsylvania: Reply," *American Economic Review* 90 (2000): 1397–1420; David Card and Alan B. Kruger, *Myth and Measurement: The New Economics of the Minimum Wage* (Princeton, NJ: Princeton University Press, 1995); Christopher Ingraham, "The Effects of 137 Minimum Wage Hikes, in One Chart," *Washington Post*, February 5, 2018; Ben Zipperer and John Schmitt, "The 'High Road' Seattle Labor Market and the Effects of the Minimum Wage Increase" (Washington, DC: Economic Policy Institute, June 26, 2017).

16. See, e.g., Peter C. Baker, "How Much Is an Hour Worth? The War over the Minimum Wage," *The Guardian*, April 13, 2018.

17. See John Maynard Keynes, *The General Theory of Employment, Interest, and Money* (San Diego: Harvest/Harcourt ed., 1964).

18. See, e.g., David Neumark and Scott Adams, "Do Living Wage Ordinances Reduce Urban Poverty?" *Journal of Human Resources* 38 (2003): 490–521.

19. See, e.g., Liam Shields, *Just Enough: Sufficiency as a Demand of Justice* (Edinburgh: Edinburgh University Press, 2016); Harry Frankfurt, "Equality as a Moral Ideal," *Ethics* 98 (1987): 21–43.

20. See generally Geoff Moore, "The Fair Trade Movement: Parameters, Issues and Future Research," *Journal of Business Ethics* 53 (2004): 73–86.

21. See generally Mark R. Reiff, *On Unemployment, Volumes I: A Micro-Theory of Economic Justice* (New York: Palgrave Macmillan, 2015); Mark R. Reiff, *On Unemployment, Volume II: Achieving Economic Justice After the Great Recession* (New York: Palgrave Macmillan, 2015).

22. George J. Stigler, "The Economics of Minimum Wage Legislation," *American Economic Review* 36 (1946): 361.

23. Paul A. Samuelson, *Economics: An Introductory Analysis* (New York: McGraw-Hill, 1967 [7th ed.]), 377.

24. Olivier Blanchard, *Macroeconomics* (Upper Saddle River, NJ: Prentice-Hall, 1997), 414.
25. David Neumark and William Wascher, "Reconciling the Evidence on Employment Effects of Minimum Wages: A Review of Our Research Findings," in *The Effects of Minimum Wages on Employment*, edited by Marvin Kosters (Washington, DC: American Enterprise Institute, 1996), 55–86.
26. David Card and Alan B. Krueger, "Minimum Wages and Employment: A Case Study of the Fast-Food Industry in New Jersey and Pennsylvania," *American Economic Review* 84 (1994): 772–793; David Neumark and William Wascher, "The Effects of New Jersey's Minimum Wage Increase on Fast-Food Employment: A Re-Evaluation Using Payroll Records," NBER Working Paper No. 5224 (August 1995).
27. These estimates come from the Congressional Budget Office, EPI, Federal Reserve Bank of San Francisco, and others: Bruce Bartlett, "Minimum Wage Hikes Help Politicians, Not the Poor," *Wall Street Journal*, May 27, 1999, A26; Jeffrey Clemens and Michael Wither, "The Minimum Wage and the Great Recession: Evidence of Effects on the Employment and Income Trajectories of Low-Skilled Workers," NBER Working Paper No. 20724 (December 2014); Congressional Budget Office, *The Effects of a Minimum-Wage Increase on Employment and Family Income* (Washington, DC: CBO, 2014), www.cbo.gov/publication/44995, p. 9; John F. Gaski, "Raising the Minimum Wage Is Unethical and Immoral," *Business and Society Review* 109, no. 2 (2004): 212; Mises Institute, "Yes, Minimum Wages Still Increase Unemployment," *Mises Daily Articles* (February 9, 2015), https://mises.org/library/yes-minimum-wages-still-increase-unemployment, p. 2.
28. Neumark and Wascher, "Minimum Wages and Employment," 2.
29. Daniel Kahneman and Amos Tversky, "Prospect Theory: An Analysis of Decision Under Risk," *Econometrika* 47 (1979): 263–291.
30. Neumark and Wascher, "Minimum Wages and Employment"; William Poole, "Minimum Wage and Unemployment," *Cato at Liberty* (January 15, 2014), 2.
31. Poole, "Minimum Wage," 1; Breanna Deutsch, "Over 500 Economists Against Federal Minimum Wage Increase," *Daily Caller* (March 13, 2014), http://dailycaller.com/author/bdeutsch/; Victor R. Fuchs, Alan B. Krueger, and James M. Poterba, "Economists' Views About Parameters, Values, and Policies: Survey Results in Labor and Public Economics," *Journal of Economic Literature* 36 (1998): 1387–1425.
32. Employment Policies Institute, "Survey of U.S. Economists on a $15 Federal Minimum Wage" (November 2015), www.epionline.org/studies/survey-of-us-economists-on-a-15-federal-minimum-wage/; Daniel B. Klein and Charlotta Stern, "Economists' Policy Views and Voting," *Public Choice* 126 (2006): 331–342.
33. "Minimum Flexibility," *Wall Street Journal*, July 26, 1999, A22.
34. Joseph E. Stiglitz, "Alternative Approaches to Macroeconomics: Methodological Issues and the New Keynesian Economics," NBER Working Paper No. 3580, 1991, p. 22.
35. Note, however, that many of the statistics Gaski cites are utterly unreliable. The claim that 75% of economists oppose a minimum wage increase, for example, comes from the Employment Policies Institute, which actually has no employees of its own—it is simply one of several front groups created by Berman & Co., a Washington, DC, public affairs firm owned by Rick Berman, who lobbies for the restaurant, hotel, alcoholic beverage, and tobacco industries. See Eric Lipton, "Fight over Minimum Wage Illustrates Web of Industry Ties," *New York Times*, February 9, 2014; Lisa Graves, "Corporate America's New Scam: Industry P.R. Firm Poses as Think Tank!" *Salon*, November 13, 2013. In contrast, a University of Chicago survey found that only 34% of the economists surveyed thought that raising the minimum wage would make it harder for low-wage workers to find employment, and only 11% thought this effect was big enough to warrant treating

a minimum wage increase as bad policy. See Catherine Rampell, "What Economists Think About Raising the Minimum Wage," *New York Times*, March 4, 2013. And for a more accurate summation of the CBO findings on which Gaski also relies, see Ben Zipperer, "Low-Wage Workers Will See Huge Gains from Minimum Wage Hike, CBO Finds," Economic Policy Institute (July 9, 2019).

36. See, e.g., J. S. Mill, *Principles of Political Economy* (London: John W. Parker, 1849), Bk. 2, Chapter 11, Sec. 1.

37. J. S. Mill, "Thornton on Labour and Its Claims," *Fortnightly Review*, Part I (May 1869): 505–518, Part II (June 1869): 680–700.

38. James Bonar, *Disturbing Elements in the Study and Teaching of Political Economy* (Baltimore, MD: Johns Hopkins Press, 1911), 75. See also Scott Gordon, "The Wage-Fund Controversy: The Second Round," *History of Political Economy* 5 (1973): 14–35, 28 (noting that "by the mid-1890s, it was commonplace for one to see the wage-fund theory referred to as an archaic error").

39. For extensive discussion and examples of each of these phenomena, see Mark R. Reiff, *Exploitation and Economic Justice in the Liberal Capitalist State* (Oxford: Oxford University Press, 2013) and Mark R. Reiff, *On Unemployment, Volume I* and *Volume II* (New York: Palgrave Macmillan, 2015). For some even more recent examples, see David Leonhardt, "The Charts that Show How Big Business Is Winning," *New York Times*, June 17, 2018; Thomas Piketty, Emmanuel Saez, and Gabriel Zucman, "Distributional National Accounts: Methods and Estimates for the United States," NBER Working Paper 22945 (December 2016).

40. See my extensive discussion of this issue in Reiff, *On Unemployment, Volume II*, 41–60.

41. See A. C. Pigou, "Mill and the Wages Fund," *Economic Journal* 59 (1949): 171–180.

42. See Patricia Cohen, "Profits Swell, But Laborers See No Relief," *New York Times*, July 14, 2018.

43. See generally Reiff, *Exploitation and Economic Justice*, 216–226; Reiff, *On Unemployment, Volume II*, 41–61.

44. See David Cooper, "Raising the Minimum Wage to $15 by 2024 Would Lift Wages for 41 million American Workers," EPI (April 26, 2017).

45. See Matt Phillips, "4 Themes to Follow as Corporate America Reports a Surge in Profits," *New York Times*, July 23, 2018.

46. See Adam Smith, *The Wealth of Nations* (New York: Modern Library ed., 2000), Bk. 1, Chapter 8, pp. 77–78 (advocating a living wage as the minimum wage).

47. Douglas Besharov, "Poor America," *Wall Street Journal*, March 24, 2006, A10; W. Michael Cox and Richard Alm, "Defining Poverty Up," *Wall Street Journal*, November 2, 1999, A26; Bruce D. Meyer and James X. Sullivan, "Hardly Anyone Wants to Admit America Is Beating Poverty," *Wall Street Journal*, August 7, 2018, A15.

CHAPTER 8

Environmental Regulation

CLIMATE CHANGE AND
ENVIRONMENTAL REGULATION
SETH MAYER

1. Introduction

Despite the many reasonable disagreements about addressing climate change, discussions of the issue must start with some common ground. First, human activity is causing climate change. We have increased the atmospheric levels of greenhouse gases like carbon dioxide and methane, which trap infrared radiation and, as a result, warm the earth's climate. Second, a warming climate seriously endangers humans.[1] Sea level rise, high-intensity storms, resource scarcity, heat waves, and other environmental effects threaten human well-being, impacting our health, personal security, and economic productivity. It's impossible to predict all of climate change's consequences with complete certainty and to know exactly what level of emissions and climatic change will endanger us. What's undeniable is that ignoring greenhouse gas emissions increases the risk of very serious negative impacts on human beings.

Not only is climate change frightening, but it is difficult and complicated.[2] No single individual created climate change, but many people, spread across space and time, have accelerated greenhouse gas emissions. No individual person can fix the situation, either. An adequate response will require multiple actors to act differently and, likely, cooperate to solve the problem. The threat of climate change is global and intergenerational: It is caused by and will affect people living in different countries and different time periods. So far, the international community has failed to take on this problem.

Looking at an issue this big, some argue for extremely radical changes like moving back to pre-industrial forms of life. Others think we can't address climate change without overthrowing global capitalism and adopting an entirely different economic system. I ignore such views here. Perhaps revolutionary changes are unavoidable, but we need to consider more modest but demanding changes given how hard pursuing even incremental progress has been. We must strike a balance between developing adequate solutions before it is too late and reckoning with significant social, political, economic, and technological constraints. We must be pragmatic without being complacent and ineffective.

The changes necessary to confront this challenge will be substantial, but many strategies are available. In this essay, I'll consider technological, market-based, and regulatory approaches to climate change, arguing that technology and markets are important but insufficient; we also need increased environmental regulation.

Environmental regulations are laws that direct people and businesses to act or refrain from acting in certain ways with the goal of protecting environmental values. Such laws can promote actions that slow climate change, block actions that further its progress, and encourage actions that will enable adaptation to climate change's effects. They can create thresholds for how we can treat one another and protect individuals from the threats of climate change, along with supporting core moral and political ideals. Laws also enable us to fairly allocate the burdens of confronting shared environmental problems.

Some reject legal regulation as inefficient and overly restrictive, hoping to rely on markets and technology alone to address climate change. They believe environmental regulations unnecessarily restrict economic activity and that climate change is best addressed by more modest means. I will argue that these approaches are ultimately *too* modest given the risks that dangerous climate change presents. We should be wary that technological change and complex market policies will move too slowly, allowing too much risk of climate change's worst effects. In contrast, regulation can offer effective, sufficiently fast solutions, as well as expressing core public commitments, supporting justice and equity, and respecting human rights. Technology and markets are important, powerful tools, but for our response to climate change to be effective and morally adequate, we need environmental regulation.

2. Technological Approaches

The most starry-eyed approaches to climate change rely on technology to reduce or eliminate greenhouse gas emissions. While such innovations are necessary, they have important limitations. Technology promises lower emissions, greater efficiency, aid in adapting to climate change's effects, and, more morally problematically, the ability to manipulate the earth's climate system to avoid rising temperatures.[3] Many hope to lower emissions through things like more efficient batteries, electric grids, and transportation systems. Others float ideas like putting reflectors on satellites to deflect solar heat or altering the oceans' chemistry to increase the amount of CO_2 they absorb. An immediate worry about focusing on technology alone is that it could end up a distraction that delays real solutions. Maybe innovators will develop new technologies that fix all of our environmental challenges, but we can't just assume such efforts will succeed. Technological solutions may emerge too late, might not emerge at all, or might not emerge on a wide enough scale. Letting climate change progress while hoping technology will somehow fix everything is irresponsible.

The other issue with exclusively technological approaches to climate change is that technology does not exist in a vacuum, unaffected by politics and economics. Even when adequate technological solutions exist, they must be widely adopted, which means overcoming various social and economic barriers. People need to use technology for it to make a difference. That's more likely if it's easily available, affordable, and possible to incorporate into existing practices. Technology adoption doesn't happen automatically, though. We could make serious progress in addressing climate change just by using existing technology that hasn't yet been broadly adopted.[4] Politics, economics, and social expectations constrain even already available technological solutions.

3. Market-Based Approaches

Beyond technological fixes, many support market-based policies for handling climate change. Such policies use prices and property rights to incentivize emitters to reduce the amount of greenhouse gases they put into the atmosphere. Markets are an institutional framework where individuals and groups engage in the self-interested exchange of goods and services. A well-constructed market could help combat climate change in a few ways. Markets can encourage preserving resources and avoiding waste. If I can avoid waste while making a product, I may be able to reduce expenses and, as a result, increase profits. If I am a consumer, more efficient use of commodities may reduce my costs, too. The self-interested desire for profit can incentivize developing *and* adopting innovative technologies that use less fossil fuel. Markets can encourage thrift, which can, in turn, potentially reduce environmental harms while driving overall economic growth. If everything works ideally in a market, all sides can benefit, including the environment.

Negative Externalities and Climate Change

Actual markets don't always align with enthusiasts' hopes and dreams, however. Self-interested market actors economize only when forced to bear the costs of their activities. Sometimes they force those costs onto others, though. A polluting factory, for instance, can sell products to geographically distant consumers while imposing serious environmental costs on nearby community members. Such polluting can harm public health, damage property, or even undermine basic rights, all without affecting the factory and its consumers' expenses. The factory owners may increase profits or lower consumer costs by ignoring their environmental impact. Those directly involved in the transaction benefit, while those outside the transaction suffer. These situations involve what are called negative externalities, where unintended bad consequences from market transactions harm uninvolved parties.

The greenhouse gas emissions driving climate change are negative externalities; they create costs that emitters impose on third parties. If I produce carbon dioxide while driving a taxi or increase methane emissions by farming animals, neither I nor those to whom I offer my services bear the full cost of those emissions. Instead, those emissions harm people in the future. If I can avoid some of the costs of my activities, I have no economic incentive to try and reduce emissions while driving my cab or running my farm. At the moment, those who act in ways that increase greenhouse gas emissions are in just this situation: They can escape the full costs of their actions. The result of all of this is what is known as a "tragedy of the commons" where our climate heats up as we push our activities' costs off onto others, including people in the future.[5]

Market-Based Policies to the Rescue? Emissions Taxes and Cap-and-Trade Systems

In response to such externalities, market advocates suggest that rather than regulating pollution, we need better market incentives that price emissions at their full cost, discouraging unnecessary emissions and producing better economic results. Two common proposals are taxing emissions or instituting a cap-and-trade system for greenhouse gas emissions.[6]

Taxes on emissions, including carbon taxes, raise prices to incentivize reducing emissions below levels that would cause harmful climate change. Higher emissions costs force emitters to consider their economic choices' environmental consequences. Such a tax encourages people to economize and potentially adopt technology with lower emissions instead of imposing negative externalities on others. Carbon tax revenues could, some argue, support mitigating or adapting to climate change. For instance, tax revenue could be invested in green technology development or flood protection, among other things. A concern about carbon taxes is that emissions may not decline (or may not decline fast enough) if consumers keep emitting at high levels and just absorb some of the tax's cost.[7]

Cap-and-trade policies set an upper limit on greenhouse gas emissions, above which emissions create high risks of harmful climate change. To keep emissions below this limit, emitters get permits that allow them to emit only a certain level of greenhouse gases. If they don't use all their permitted emissions, they can sell their emission rights to someone else. The result is that emissions stay below the cap, while the ability to emit greenhouse gases is priced and traded on a market. That pricing mechanism aims to avoid the previously described tragedy of the commons. As with a carbon tax, cap-and-trade uses pricing incentives to force market actors to absorb all the costs of their choices, including negative externalities. If market actors emit, they must pay for this choice based on the price set by the emissions market. Market participants get rewarded for reduced emissions, though, benefiting either by avoiding the cost of buying permits or profiting by selling their permits to others.[8]

There are difficult questions about creating and implementing either carbon taxes or cap-and-trade, as well as disagreement about the advantages of one option over the other. What these proposals share is that they use pricing incentives to reduce greenhouse gas emissions, rather than traditional regulation's requirements, prohibitions, and standards. If every country that is a major emitter implemented either market policy aggressively enough, many hope the reduced emissions would prevent climate change's worst effects.

Just as technological fixes alone are insufficient, we can't rely only on market-based policies to address climate change.[9] Both approaches depend on the right economic and political conditions, particularly institutions structured to promote core moral and political ideals. While well-constructed markets can sometimes further justice, human rights, and democracy, fully realizing such ideals demands traditional regulations enacted by political institutions.[10]

Legal regulations can establish firm thresholds for what individuals are allowed to do and how they ought to be treated. Market policies based on pricing can't establish such constraints; they can only discourage certain activities by raising their cost.

4. Regulatory Approaches

Although market policies can help reduce emissions, legal rules and standards can accomplish goals that market systems can't, which means environmental regulations are needed to fight climate change. Regulations could require that emitters use more efficient technologies, stop using certain dangerous substances or techniques, or refrain from emitting more than a certain amount of greenhouse gases. This approach enables climate policies to reflect fundamental values like justice, equity, and respect for human rights, while making sure our response to climate change is fast and effective enough.

Public Expectation Setting

First, regulation can establish certain sorts of moral relationships between citizens while taking others off the table.[11] Prohibitions on child labor express a rejection of child exploitation, and clean air standards express that no one should be denied certain safe, unpolluted resources. Even when rules are somewhat economically inefficient, they can manifest public attitudes and commitments about which actions and interactions are acceptable.[12] Law, particularly democratically legitimate law, can represent the perspective of the public at large—deeming some actions morally acceptable and others out of bounds. It is an attempt to coordinate social action to further public purposes.

Because law can establish such purposes by instituting various rules, principles, and standards, it supports forms of collective expression that markets can't. If people view law as legitimate and as expressing public moral perspectives, it can have a more powerful effect on behavior than markets' financial incentives do.[13] Citizens care that "we the people" have marked assault as wrongful by making it illegal; we aren't only motivated by the pain and unhappiness we would experience if punished for committing assault.

In the context of climate change, regulation can establish the public expectation that everyone should receive certain threshold treatment, including not being exposed to certain environmental risks.[14] Regulation can send a message that certain values related to human life and the environment limit what sorts of economic activity are acceptable. Taxes or prices that operate in a system oriented by economic value can't express the same message. Market policies can force you to pay more for an activity, but a regulation prohibiting it can express a society's firm stance on that activity.

There is inherent value in regulation's ability to express public moral claims, as well as value in the way such expressive messages can effectively shape human action. Climate change regulations can express a commitment to refraining from emitting greenhouse gases at levels that threaten human rights and to making sure environmental burdens are shared equitably. At the same time, regulations can shape our sense of the proper public norms for interacting with the environment and each other; they don't just affect the cost of one choice versus another.

Justice and Equity

In addition, any climate policy must be just and equitable, rather than reinforcing or even exacerbating existing extreme inequalities. This concern applies at both the national and international levels. Market approaches to climate change work by raising prices on externality-producing activities. People don't just emit greenhouse gases for the fun of it, though: Common, difficult-to-avoid activities like driving or heating one's home produce emissions. While it's fair to expect consumers to bear some of their activities' costs, the burdens of such costs fall much harder on those with fewer resources. Market-based climate change policies must avoid making life unsustainable for society's most vulnerable. While unfair burdens would likely make climate policies so unpopular they would become impossible to implement, it is also unjust to burden the poor and middle class rather than shifting costs onto those with greater means. Those with wealth have, in general, already received a greater proportion of the benefits of life in a greenhouse gas–based economy. This argument for redistributive regulation is twofold: (1) Policies should avoid harming already vulnerable citizens, and (2) costs should fall more heavily on those who have benefited most from our current system. One way to avoid this problem is redistributing money collected through policies like carbon taxes as dividends to low- and middle-income households.

This point holds even more strongly internationally; wealthier countries and countries with rapid growth are most responsible for climate change.[15] Poorer countries with less responsibility for climate change will experience its worst effects, in addition to suffering more from higher emissions costs. They will be harmed by climate change, as well as particularly burdened by attempts to avoid it.[16] As many have argued, we must combat global poverty while simultaneously fighting climate change.[17] Wealthier countries must take responsibility for more of the costs of addressing climate change so that poorer societies can grow economically and pull their citizens out of poverty.[18]

Markets can't meet these redistributive demands; we will need fairness-focused legal regulations like redistributive taxation or legal frameworks that put greater restrictions on wealthier countries' emissions than poorer ones. These regulatory frameworks come from outside markets in order to constrain and shape them.

Human Rights

If addressing climate change is seen just as a matter of making markets more efficient and equitable, we'll be ignoring the strongest reason to take this problem on: the threat climate change poses to human rights. By their nature, human rights are incredibly morally significant. As a result, they create a strong demand to respond to climate change and impose constraints on any response to this problem. Regulation is an especially useful tool in supporting human rights ideals.

Allen Buchanan describes the function of the international human rights regime as follows:

> [M]ost of the rights included in the various human rights treaties can be seen as either affirming and protecting equal basic status of all individuals, or as helping to ensure that all individuals have the opportunity to lead a minimally good or decent life. There are two different kinds of threats to the opportunity to lead a minimally good or decent life against which international legal human rights provide protections: harms, including restrictions on liberties needed for autonomy, and lack of resources broadly understood (food, shelter, education, etc.). Some international legal human rights function primarily to protect against harms inflicted by the state; others contribute to well-being in a positive way by providing valuable resources.[19]

In general, the international human rights movement argues that every individual deserves a certain baseline form of treatment in recognition of their equal status. When states or other organizations undermine individuals' opportunity for the life they deserve, human rights demand a response. The human rights approach requires that political institutions respect, protect, and fulfill human rights. That is, institutions must not violate human rights, they must prevent human rights violations, and they must positively facilitate people's enjoyment of their rights.

Climate change threatens to create the conditions human rights supporters want to avoid. Simon Caney defends this conclusion, pointing to the threats climate change poses to human life, health, and subsistence, which are all supposed to be supported by rights included in the Universal Declaration of Human Rights. He notes that climate change will cause flooding and heat waves that threaten human life, increased rates of disease that impact human health, and agricultural damage that will undermine human subsistence.[20] Dangerous climate change would mean that fundamental rights intended to guarantee threshold conditions for a decent human life will be violated on a broad scale. Political institutions must avoid furthering these threats, protect individuals against them, and, when necessary, help people achieve their rights in the face of climate change. Local, national, and international institutions will all have a role to play.

Regulations that create firm restrictions and standards are necessary to guarantee individual rights—something that market incentive systems that respond to economic supply and demand can't do. The pricing incentives created by carbon taxes don't create bright lines to ensure threshold protections for rights. So long as emitters pay the tax, they can contribute to creating conditions that threaten human rights. A person can't buy permission to violate someone else's human rights, though; this aspect of such a tax is a serious problem. Insofar as cap-and-trade policies avoid this problem, it is thanks to the regulatory, non-market "cap" they include, not the pricing mechanism of "trade." Rather than offering an incentive not to pollute, a cap is a legal rule or standard; it creates a ceiling for permissible emissions that can be set up to protect human rights. The logic of rights frequently depends on such legal, non-market institutions for their protection.[21] When an activity threatens human rights significantly, legal prohibition or regulation can be superior to using market incentives to discourage it. Unacceptably risky actions can reasonably be prohibited to ensure no individual is forced to sacrifice their rights, not even to provide aggregate social benefits like the economic growth markets promise.

Effectiveness and Expediency

In addition, regulations are sometimes more effective than market mechanisms. While market price signals are important policy tools, they are not always sufficiently powerful.[22] Moreover, if monitoring is difficult or expensive, or implementation of a market policy is especially costly, top-down legal regulation can be more economically efficient than market instruments.[23] Regulation can also have a flexible structure, instituting performance standards for emitters that become more stringent or that can be otherwise adjusted over time.[24] Such flexible standards can encourage innovation, particularly when paired with subsidies for renewable technology research, development, and implementation.[25] They can even be combined with market mechanisms like permit trading in a hybrid policy.

The need to look beyond markets to address climate change is especially important given how little time we have to avert dangerous climate change. The window for avoiding climate change's most harmful effects is closing, and the risk of initiating irreversible, threatening processes is very real. We need to be careful to avoid tipping points, meaning points in the process of climate change where we pass a "critical threshold" that triggers large-scale, potentially dangerous changes in ecosystems.[26] Scientists argue that we must quickly decarbonize our economic activities, relinquishing our reliance on fossil fuel–based energy production, transportation, and so on.[27] While market mechanisms may support incremental shifts away from a carbon economy, there is good reason to worry they won't implement sufficient emissions reductions, nor do so rapidly enough.[28]

Regulations can create more immediate changes by ruling out certain activities and drawing bright lines that restrict the level of permitted emissions. There are carbon-intensive activities and technologies it makes sense to eliminate immediately. Bans or phase-outs of some uses of coal could make a serious impact, for instance.[29] Implementing performance standards or subsidies can effectively reduce emissions while spurring innovation, sometimes more than market policies will.[30] If we take protecting human rights in the face of climate change seriously, we must consider as many reasonable policies as possible, including regulations that firmly protect against threats to individuals' rights.

5. Conclusion

Ideological glorification of markets should not obscure their limitations, nor should we ignore options like legal prohibitions, regulatory standards, redistributive taxes, and other measures that may be more workable or morally desirable. As I have argued, such policies can, in some important cases, better support justice, human rights, and other important values, while sometimes functioning faster and more effectively than markets. Without rejecting markets entirely, I advocate being critical and pragmatic about relying on them—like we should be about any policy.

Market advocates often promote their policies as a way to avoid politics, but my argument brings out the impossibility of evading moral and political questions, including whether markets are always the best tool for the job. Markets, particularly the type considered here, must be constructed.[31] Setting emissions caps or carbon tax rates is a political choice, just like any choice between different policy instruments for addressing climate change. Options must be evaluated based on whether they accomplish the democratically chosen goals of the public within the constraints of justice and human rights. Efficiency and cost effectiveness aren't the only criteria for judging policies. The public should consider them when choosing policies to address climate change, but they must also consider whether markets are actually most responsive to all the relevant values and ideals. Often, policy choices involve difficult tradeoffs. We must respond to climate change on many fronts, and we must take action quickly. Any true solution will be messy and will rely on a variety of policy options.[32] Instead of an ideologically driven rejection of regulation, a pragmatic approach recognizes the goals and values that environmental regulation can promote.[33]

COMPREHENSION QUESTIONS

1. What's the common ground people need to discuss climate change?
2. What three strategies could help us address the problem of climate change?
3. Why is it irresponsible to rely on technological advancement alone to address climate change?
4. What are negative externalities? What is the "tragedy of the commons"?
5. What is the difference between a market incentive and a legal regulation? How does an emissions tax differ from a cap-and-trade program?

DISCUSSION QUESTIONS

1. Even with appropriate technological advancements to mitigate or adapt to climate change, what else is needed to ensure these advances will be effective in addressing current and future problems?
2. How can regulations express public morals? Do you think justice and equality on the global level should be considered? Do you think government regulations on any level should be used to provide environmental and social protections? Why or why not?

3. According to Mayer, legal regulations are necessary to address climate change; market incentives are not enough. Do you agree with his analysis? Why or why not?

Case 1

Consider this perspective:

> The Green Revolution began in 1954, when Norman Borlaug managed to breed "miracle wheat": a variety that produced far greater yields than conventional wheat. There were a number of other significant agricultural developments at the same time: improved fertilizers, irrigation techniques, and hybrid seeds. What's more, there was substantial state support for research on, and the dissemination of, these new technologies. The result was that total food production more than doubled between 1960 and 1985 in much of the developing world, dramatically exceeding population growth during that same period. Norman Borlaug won the Nobel Peace Prize in 1970, and said this during his acceptance speech: "to millions of these unfortunates [living in developing countries], who have long lived in despair, the green revolution seems like a miracle that has generated new hope for the future."
>
> The Green Revolution has its detractors. But the striking thing, for present purposes, is that no one could have anticipated it. We just didn't know, in 1935, that food production would skyrocket in the way it did. We couldn't anticipate the combination of new technologies, business ventures, and political alliances that generated more food than ever before, resulting in substantial declines in global hunger. And this is often the way things go. We could tell similar stories about many technological shifts in the history of humankind. Why not think, then, that things only seem so bleak because we're on this side of the next great technological breakthrough? Sure, climate change seems overwhelming now, but maybe we will look back on it as something technology and other innovations helped us easily overcome.

What should Mayer say about this sort of view? What do you think about it? What are the risks of the "techno-optimism" that this passage represents? What are the costs of *not* sharing its optimism?

SUSTAINING GROWTH
DAN C. SHAHAR

1. Introduction

According to a common narrative, our insatiable drive for economic growth has us heading toward disaster. Industrial nations have enriched themselves by wreaking havoc on the natural world—burning fossil fuels, cutting down forests, extinguishing species, and polluting the water and air. Yet, just over the horizon looms a terrible reckoning of global climate change that will reverse much of our progress. Given the stakes, the case would seem clear for aggressively reducing our impacts on the planet. But recent political experience suggests these reforms might be difficult to achieve. In the eyes of some environmentalist writers, our sluggish response to impending crisis belies a worrying addiction to growth. As Michael Renner writes in the Worldwatch Institute's *State of the World 2015*:

Endless economic growth driven by unbridled consumption is so central to modern economies and is so ingrained in the thinking of corporate and political leaders that environmental action is still often seen as in conflict with the economy, and is relegated to inferior status. We have an economic system that is the equivalent of a great white shark: it needs to keep water moving through its gills to receive oxygen, and dies if it stops moving. The challenge, therefore, is broader than merely a set of technological changes. As activist Naomi Klein has argued, saving the climate requires revisiting the central mechanisms of the world's pre-eminent economic system: capitalism.[34]

Renner's comments urge us to see the growing global economy as an ultimately self-defeating enterprise. Capitalist nations are mortgaging the planet for bigger houses and nicer cars, but these excesses will eventually have to be repaid—with interest—by future generations and the global poor. The only sensible thing to do, according to this narrative, is to kick our dependency on industrial growth and fundamentally transform our attitudes toward economic life. Rather than seeking to constantly *increase* our incomes and gross domestic products (GDPs), we should aim to *fit* our economic activities into the constraints set by nature.

Environmentalist writers have offered a variety of visions for what this might look like. At the more moderate end of the spectrum, Tim Jackson urges us to pursue policies that foster "a slower, more labour-intensive economy"[35] that emphasizes services over material goods,[36] embraces "clear resource and environmental limits,"[37] and trades rising material affluence for a more egalitarian, community-oriented way of life.[38] At the more radical end, writers like Kirkpatrick Sale push us to thoroughly decentralize our economic activities to reflect the conditions and constraints of our ecological "bioregions."[39] Spanning these wide-ranging proposals is a shared conviction that our pursuit of ever more growth is misguided and that our long-term well-being depends on arresting economic expansion.[40]

The purpose of this essay will be to challenge this commonly held view. I will argue that committing to perpetuate industrial growth is not a sign of "addiction to wealth" but rather a sensible response to the circumstances we face. According to mainstream projections, industrial capitalism is not about to implode; rather, if left to its own devices it will deliver a future that is significantly brighter than the present, especially for those around the world who currently live in poverty. Anti-growth narratives obscure the phenomenal trend of human advancement that provides the backdrop to the ecological challenges we face, and they exaggerate the extent to which problems like global climate change will threaten this trend. Putting a stop to growth for the sake of the environment would represent a cure that is worse that the disease it aims to treat.[41]

As we will see, embracing economic growth does not imply that challenges like climate change are not real or worth responding to. These problems are very real and very serious, and we ought to be doing much more than we are to protect the planet. My claim is simply that as we pursue such reforms, we should not take our eyes off the ultimate prize: the continued expansion of material prosperity around the world.

2. The Best News

Let us begin with what I consider the most important trend in human history: the unprecedented reductions in rates of poverty, death, and oppression worldwide that have accompanied industrial growth. Roughly two hundred years ago, in 1820, almost 95% of people on the earth lived in what we now consider "extreme poverty," consuming no more than the equivalent of $1.90 per day at today's price levels.[42] More than 40% of children died before reaching five years of age,[43] and (largely because of this fact) the average person born could expect to live just twenty-nine years.[44] Only about 1% of people worldwide lived in a country that could legitimately be called a "democracy," with the vast majority living under an autocratic regime or in a colony ruled by such a regime.[45] And it perhaps goes without saying that human rights abuses were commonplace. Slavery had been abolished in some parts of the world, but it continued to be practiced on a massive scale in others. Movements to recognize the rights of women were just beginning to emerge, and many groups—including homosexuals, atheists, and disabled persons— were openly abused.

Even when my grandparents were growing up, many of these horrible conditions were still in place. In 1950, more than 70% of the world's population still lived in extreme poverty,[46] more than 20% of children still died before age five,[47] and average life expectancy was still under fifty years.[48] The first steps to recognizing basic universal human rights were being taken at the international level,[49] but progress was still limited in many areas. Homosexuality, for example, was still treated as criminal behavior even in most "free" Western democracies.

Considered in light of this history, the transformations that have occurred over the last few decades are nothing short of spectacular. Today, less than 10% of the world population lives in extreme poverty.[50] Average life expectancy is over seventy years worldwide,[51] and 95% of children live to see their fifth birthday.[52] Nearly three-quarters of countries explicitly guarantee women equal treatment under their constitutions,[53] and many nations have seen a procession of groups demanding and winning recognition for their rights. We still have a long way to go, to be sure, in creating a world free from poverty, oppression, and iniquity. But for the average person—and, indeed, for the average member of a disadvantaged or marginalized group—the present day is undoubtedly the best time to be alive in the history of humanity.

We can thank economic growth for much of this progress. The unprecedented increase in material prosperity seen around the world has played a crucial role in lifting people out of poverty and extending average lifespans by decades. Economic growth has also helped to pave the way for many of our social and political advances, for it is hardly a coincidence that the loudest demands for universal rights have come from countries where people can easily meet their basic needs. Along a wide range of dimensions, then, the growth of our industrial economies has been an incredible boon to humanity.

3. The End of the Line?

Given these developments, it seems hard to imagine how anyone could think that it would be undesirable to see economic growth continue. Thus, it should be emphasized that the critics of growth have not ignored the trends I described.[54] In their view, the crucial question is not whether growth has been a good thing *so far*; rather, it is whether our historical trajectory can be sustained into the future. In their views, the "progress" I have been recounting is analogous to that of a company that delivers huge dividends to its shareholders by overtaxing its capital assets and failing to invest in their maintenance.[55] The recipients of the dividends might seem to be doing well, but such an enterprise could hardly be called a success. Along similar lines, the critics of industrial growth claim we are living high in the present at the cost of *nature's* capital, and the emerging crisis of global climate change offers a stark warning to get our books in order before it is too late. To offer another illustrative metaphor, Paul Ehrlich suggests that focusing only on what economic growth has delivered *to this point* would make us "like the guy who jumps off the Empire State Building and says how great things are going so far as he passes the 10th floor."[56]

Critics like Ehrlich suggest that humanity's rapid advancement is about to come to an end, and that trying to grow even further would only speed our demise. Yet, mainstream projections about the likely impacts of ecological hazards like climate change do not support this view. Rather, they show broad agreement that industrial growth will (and, hence, can) proceed into the twenty-first and twenty-second centuries and beyond, continuing to drive further progress for as long as people have bothered to project.

Consider, for example, *The Economics of Climate Change: The Stern Review*—a massive report prepared for the British government in 2006.[57] Of mainstream attempts to model the likely impacts of climate change, the *Stern Review* is arguably the gloomiest.[58] Its projections try to account for not only the narrowly economic effects of climate change but also a range of non-market impacts and risks of catastrophe. Moreover, it considers scenarios involving especially large amounts of climatic change, involving global temperature increases of 4.3°C above pre-industrial levels by the year 2100 and 8.6°C by 2200.[59] To capture the uncertainties surrounding the future states of the climate system, the *Stern Review* ran models with a variety of assumptions, leading to a continuum of projections depicting many possible outcomes. The average projection in its "high climate change" scenarios anticipated that people will enjoy 2.9% less consumption in the year 2100 as a result of climate change, and this figure rose to 13.8% in 2200. But these figures represent only the middle of the range of possible outcomes for these scenarios. Near the top end—the ninety-fifth percentile of estimates—the projections were graver: By the year 2200, the loss of consumption due to climate change was 35.2%.[60]

These are large figures, but it must be emphasized that they do not represent losses in consumption *relative to today*; rather, they represent losses *relative to a future in which climate change does not occur*. According to the same model used in the *Stern Review*,[61] economic growth over the next two centuries will be a powerful force. In the absence of climate change, the model estimates that the United States, the European Union, and other Organisation for Economic Co-operation and Development (OECD) countries would see their real GDPs grow to over 300% of their current levels by 2100, while less-developed countries experienced 900% increases over the same period. By 2200, real GDPs around the world would grow to between 1,800% and 13,000% of their current levels, with the highest levels of growth occurring in parts of the world that are currently the poorest.[62] (In case these numbers sound fancifully high, they are based on projected growth rates that are lower than we have observed over the last century.)

What these projections mean is that even though a world enduring high levels of climate change might see consumption drop by more than a third *relative to a world in which climate change did not occur*, the populations enduring these changes would still be many times wealthier than people today. As the *Stern Review* puts the point, "even with climate change, the world will be much richer in the future as a result of economic growth."[63] And the *Stern Review* is not alone in supporting such claims: On the contrary, recall that I have been focusing on the most unfavorable projections from the most pessimistic scenarios from this gloomiest of mainstream reports on this topic.[64] My point is that even when we look at these especially dismal projections, we do not find support for the view that continuing to try to grow our economies will be a self-defeating enterprise that ultimately leads to the reversal of recent human progress. Instead, we find virtual consensus for the claim that growth can continue long into the future, making our posterity much better off on average than the people who are living today.

4. The Case for Action

Suppose that we grant the argument that, on average, future generations will live better lives than we do today even if we allow climate change to go unabated. Presented with such a claim, one might reasonably ask: "Doesn't this prove that it is unnecessary to worry about environmental problems? Why not simply relax and enjoy our lives, knowing that the welfare of future generations will be secure no matter what we do?"

In fact, there are powerful reasons to take action on issues like climate change. For one thing, even if it is true that future generations will be well off if we take no action to address climate change, they will be even better off still if we *do* act. Relatively small investments today have the potential to yield *trillions* of dollars in benefits to our children's and grandchildren's generations.[65] Combating climate change can also help accelerate efforts to reduce poverty around the world and help prevent new pockets of poverty from emerging.[66] Thus, even if they are not required to prevent a reversal of human progress, effective climate policies still represent sound investments in the future.

Moreover, even if future people will be better off *on average* in a warmer world, this does not mean that climate change will have no victims. If mainstream projections are correct, future people will face intensified droughts, heat waves, floods, and many other hazards.[67] Rising sea levels will swallow whole communities, displacing their residents to other parts of the world.[68] Most of the people facing these difficulties will be wealthy by today's standards, but this does not eliminate the seriousness of the hardships they will face. Actions to mitigate climate change can help protect these people from severe setbacks, and it can help to soften the losses faced by those we cannot protect. Especially given our roles in contributing to the predicaments faced by these individuals, it would seem unjust to shrug off our responsibilities to them by appealing to positive *overall* trends.

We can add to these considerations even further by noting that although we have focused thus far on the interests of human beings, our actions are also generating serious impacts on the rest of the natural world. Unless we take action soon, many species will go extinct, and ecosystems and landscapes that have provided the backdrops for our civilizations will be lost or radically transformed. These consequences have significance beyond their ramifications for human interests: Our obligation not to ransack the planet goes beyond our duties to ourselves. Yet, even if we look solely at our own desires, I think we will see that we do not want to let nature's treasures fall by the wayside when we still have the opportunity to preserve them. Indeed, refusing to invest in our planet's future might seem to indicate the very kind of addiction to material wealth that this essay has been trying so hard to avoid.[69]

These brief reflections do not exhaust our reasons to take action on climate change, but I hope they suffice to show that my earlier arguments do not invalidate the case for responding to our ecological challenges. Mitigating problems like climate change can make future generations much better off and prevent the victimization of millions of individuals. Moreover, it can help protect the natural world, which is valuable for its own sake. These are powerful grounds for combating environmental problems even if failing to do so would not mean the end of the line for our progress and growth.

5. Maintaining Perspective

The foregoing arguments show that humanity's positive long-term trajectory does not invalidate the case for taking action on climate change. However, they suggest an approach that is very different from the one implied by anti-growth rhetoric. Rather than urging us to abandon industrial progress in the face of ecological challenges, the foregoing arguments push us to find a way to reconcile environmental sensitivity with a continued commitment to growth.

Over the coming decades, humanity has the opportunity to continue its progress in combating poverty, disease, and oppression. Aspirations voiced by the World Bank to "end extreme poverty by 2030" are likely too optimistic (by the World Bank's own admission),[70] but they reflect a very real expectation that we are on the path to this unprecedented outcome. When presented with such a possibility, we can see that committing to economic growth is not about being addicted to wealth. Rather, it reflects the recognition that abandoning growth in the name of environmental conscientiousness would be a cure that is worse than the disease it aims to treat.

This point becomes especially clear when we realize that, even if we take aggressive action to combat climate change, we will not be able to avert all of the dangers that lie on the horizon. Since the beginning of the Industrial Revolution, atmospheric concentrations of carbon dioxide have risen from 280 parts per million (ppm) to over 400 ppm. Concentrations of other greenhouse gases, like methane, tropospheric ozone, halocarbons, and nitrous oxide, have also increased.[71] Even if we stopped emitting these gases tomorrow, it would take a long time for natural processes to remove them from the atmosphere. Thus, a significant amount of climatic change is already "in the system"—bound to occur no matter what we do from here.

Today, the global poor are already disproportionately impacted by environmental dangers. In 2004, the UN Development Program observed that "while only 11 percent of people exposed to natural hazards [e.g., earthquakes, tropical cyclones, floods, and severe droughts] live in low human development countries, they account for more than 53 percent of total recorded deaths."[72] As the effects of climate change are felt in the coming decades, people around the world will be imperiled in a variety of ways. But given that vulnerability to climate change is so closely related to wealth, the actual consequences of climate change will depend on what people do between now and then. If nothing changes, the impacts on the least well off will be severe. But if less-developed countries succeed in growing their economies, their populations will be much better equipped to navigate ecological dangers than they are today.

This is not an impossible dream. During the twentieth century, many countries around the world experienced rapid growth and development, transforming their civilizations from poor agrarian societies into industrial powerhouses. In 1960, the average real income of a person living in the Republic of Korea (i.e., real GDP per capita, in 2010 dollars) was $944 per year. By 2010, that number had reached $22,087—more than a twenty-three-fold increase in just fifty years.[73] Consider the difference that such an increase in prosperity makes for preparing a country for the rigors of climate change. What could Korean citizens have done about a massive heat wave, drought, or flood in 1960? What can they do today? What will they be able to do in fifty more years?

It is a terrifying fact that many of the populations threatened by climate change are extremely poor, subsisting on incomes comparable to what South Koreans earned in 1960. If we really care about these people, then we will preach not the abandonment of growth but rather its wholehearted pursuit. We will find a way to combat climate change without impairing these people's abilities to transform themselves from victims-in-waiting into empowered global citizens capable of taking control of their own fates. Rather than seeing ecological challenges as a reason to give up the quest for economic growth, the predicaments faced by the poorest populations should only strengthen our resolve to continue it.

6. Why Choose?

The current state of discourse about the future of the planet can encourage the impression that industrial growth is an addiction that we would do well to cure. This essay has defended the opposite view. Although we face serious environmental challenges, the biggest story of our time is the progress we are making to eradicate poverty and injustice from the face of the planet. According to mainstream analysts, this progress will continue even in the face of climate change, and insofar as it does, this will be because we do not abandon the goal of continued economic growth. Sustaining growth is crucial because it is the best tool we have for addressing the suffering of hundreds of millions of people worldwide, and also because it is an excellent means for reducing vulnerability to environmental hazards.

What we need is not to abandon growth but rather to craft environmental policies that guide it into environmentally friendlier channels. Happily, there are many things we can do to protect our planet that do not involve shackling the global economy. Many of the policy mechanisms currently under discussion at the international level—cap-and-trade schemes, carbon taxes, and transfers of clean technologies to less-developed nations—can all fit this bill if they are designed and implemented with sensitivity. Given the importance of economic growth to the welfare of future generations, these are the opportunities we should pursue.

COMPREHENSION QUESTIONS

1. What environmentalist claim is commonly offered against capitalist development?
2. What connections does Shahar draw between trends in industrial and economic development and improved human rights and political conditions worldwide?
3. Why does Shahar think that fighting climate change should be a secondary concern to sustaining economic growth?
4. How does Shahar suggest climate change will influence the prosperity of future generations?
5. What types of environmental polices does Shahar propose that could address climate change and protect economic growth?

DISCUSSION QUESTIONS

1. According to Shahar, there is no tension between the claims that (a) future generations will be better off than people today even if we do nothing about climate change and (b) we still have good reasons to take aggressive action to combat climate change. Is he right? Or does the case for fighting climate change disappear once we recognize the positive long-term prospects for people around the world?
2. Many of Shahar's arguments revolve around projections about long-term economic trends. However, these trends are uncertain—not least because of the

potential role of climate change in shaping the future of the economy. Given the uncertainty of future climate change impacts on the world economy, are there any actions that we ought to take immediately to address climate change?

3. Shahar thinks that we should balance economic growth and climate action. But you might think that even if he's right, we shouldn't admit it. People are already *so inclined* to ignore climate change that we should just do everything we can to slow economic growth. After all, even if we push for radical climate action, we'll only get some small fraction of the changes we want. What do you think about this line of reasoning? What do you think Shahar would say about it?

Case 2

In *Reason in a Dark Time*, Dale Jamieson writes this about the *Stern Report* (which Shahar discusses):

> Imagine that the economic damages of climate change were twice or four times greater than Stern's largest estimates. This implies that future people would only be 4 times or 2 times richer than we are today. These numbers would still not seem right for expressing the losses that climate change will inflict. Suppose [more radically] that we could work the sums so that climate change was actually economically neutral over the next few centuries. Climate change would cause damages but also create opportunities that would balance them out from an economic perspective . . .
>
> I do not think that many of us would say that radically remaking the Earth's climate would be fine, so long as it were economically neutral . . . [Some would still insist on] the wrongness of perturbing the natural order in such a profound way. They might invoke God, nature, or simply the importance of precaution for support. Still others would express a sense of mourning and loss occasioned by the disruption of the human experience of nature. They might wonder what sort of people would act in such a careless way. Others would talk about the intrinsic value of animals and nature. The list of concerns could go on. What this response brings out is that for many people the problem with climate change is more than that it affects our pocketbooks.
>
> The problem with the Stern Review is not that it fails to have the right numbers but that there is more at stake than what the numbers reveal. No number seems right because the costs of climate change damages go beyond economic damages. Economic damages matter but they are not all that matters. Even if climate change were economically neutral, many people would still find something deeply wrong with humans changing the global climate.*

What could Shahar say about this? What do you think about this? How should we balance the extraordinary losses of biodiversity (for instance) against benefits to future generations?*

---

*Dale Jamieson, *Reason in a Dark Time* (New York: Oxford University Press, 2014), Section 4.6.

REPLY TO SHAHAR
SETH MAYER

1. Introduction

Despite important disagreements, Shahar's approach to climate change has significant overlap with mine. We agree about the need for a serious response to climate change, as well as economic growth's relevance for helping those in poverty. Our agreements show that the left and the right have an opportunity to work together on this issue, rather than taking a complacent, business-as-usual approach.

Nonetheless, I have concerns about Shahar's arguments. The core question is not whether growth is desirable, but when and how we should use law to shape economic activities in light of climate change. Given that, I worry that Shahar ignores some of the most plausible left-wing approaches and makes addressing climate change appear easier than it actually is. He also overstates economic growth's capabilities and understates its limitations. His narrative of progress underplays how climate change creates a need for both collective political action and the development of environmental regulations. While I don't flatly reject the policies he briefly mentions—cap-and-trade, carbon taxes, and technology transfers—he gives regulation short shrift, missing its potential to supplement or sometimes even replace such market policies.

2. Regulation, Not Rejection of Growth

First, Shahar's framing presents the options for confronting climate change in overly stark, either/or terms. The environmentalists he discusses critique growth as incompatible with addressing climate change. While such views have some influence, most philosophers studying climate change reject such strong positions, as do many on the left, generally. Shahar divides the world between those trying to grow the pie and misguided environmentalists trying to stop them. This oversimplification erases the nuance necessary to grasp our climate policy options. One needn't support abandoning modernity to think that growth—even combined with market policies and technology—isn't enough. Sometimes constraints on growth protect and promote other important values. Shahar gestures at something like this point without acknowledging how those on the left can and do accept it.

In particular, Shahar never adequately addresses regulation's proper role or the ways regulation can operate alongside market policies, because he focuses on defending growth against its critics. As a result, he doesn't discuss regulation's importance for facing up to a problem we both agree can't be ignored.

3. What Growth Is Missing

Shahar also makes translating economic growth into broad-based human flourishing sound too easy. Many benefits attributable to growth greatly depend on other factors, including aspects of the regulatory approaches I advocate, which themselves rely on political struggle.[74] To support progress, growth must exist alongside regulations and laws that protect human rights, establish environmental standards and protections, and redistribute wealth.

The story of historical change Shahar offers depicts economic growth driving most, if not all, of the progress he mentions. Although economic conditions do affect social change, progress involves much more than just growth.

Collective action and political, legal, and social circumstances are crucial, unacknowledged factors in many of Shahar's examples.[75] Progress toward racial and gender equality, LGBTQ rights, and environmental justice have all required organization, commitment, and struggle for institutional change. Strong economies don't deterministically move history forward toward justice, even if they sometimes help human beings pursue change. Instead, human effort enables democratization and the spread of human rights, often by focusing on the kinds of laws and regulations my account promotes.

Growth also benefits some much more than others—those who lose out can end up marginalized, dealing with the lion's share of growth's downsides. People exploited by or excluded from processes of economic growth, including those struggling against legacies of colonialism, have had to fight for legal protections.[76] We shouldn't simply cheer growth and credit it for what's been accomplished. It is incomplete without struggles aimed at realizing human rights and creating better institutions.

By itself, economic growth cannot address climate change or combat oppression. We must also reshape existing practices and institutions through regulations and other reforms. That means analyzing which policies are politically feasible *and* able to lower emissions to morally acceptable levels, despite political actors who have thwarted even modest climate policy. There is evidence that increased environmental regulation fits the bill.[77] In some contexts, we may *also* want market policies, but this choice depends on social and political factors Shahar doesn't consider. His historical narrative minimizes important, noneconomic causes of progress, ultimately underplaying regulation's appeal for confronting climate change.

4. Making Tradeoffs

Along with too little acknowledgment of collective action and non-economic circumstances, Shahar again makes things too simple by not exploring how potentially necessary regulation could mean sacrificing growth for other values. Without assuming regulation always means sacrificing economic growth, we may sometimes need regulation that constrains profitable, high-emissions activities.

As Shahar notes, regardless of general economic projections, some individuals and groups will be wrongfully harmed if we don't reduce emissions. Additionally, avoiding climate tipping points may require giving up some growth. Some losses that climate change threatens to cause are quite drastic and potentially irreversible.[78] Shahar seems to agree that growth's benefits don't always outweigh values like justice, human rights, democracy, and sustainability.

Nonetheless, he doesn't engage with the possibility that regulatory constraints on growth could sometimes be required.

Someone sympathetic to Shahar's position might suggest that if some people end up worse off, they might be compensated using gains made through growth.[79] Some things cannot be adequately compensated for, though, like people's lives, core human rights, and—when sea-level rise caused by climate change is swallowing up island nations—homelands. Precautionary regulation can help respect these values, even if it means giving up some economic growth. That being said, we shouldn't assume regulation and growth are always at cross-purposes, even if tradeoffs may sometimes be unavoidable.

5. Conclusion

Although left and right have common ground on climate change, there are still points of divergence. While acknowledging that overlap, I have also defended the need for collective political action and, potentially, sacrifice in taking on climate change. Our course of action, if it is to be successful, must involve environmental regulation.

COMPREHENSION QUESTIONS

1. What points do Mayer and Shahar agree on?
2. How does Mayer defend regulations that serve social justice against Shahar's arguments?

DISCUSSION QUESTIONS

1. Given Mayer's reply, how important do you think regulations are in creating a fair and just society? Is economic prosperity alone a good enough indicator of human flourishing?
2. How important do you think environmental regulations could be to protecting future generations? In what ways do you think our choices now will impact the environment and people in the future?

REPLY TO MAYER
DAN C. SHAHAR

Some bad things, like murder, are worth prohibiting. But other bad things are only bad when done too often—they would be *good* if done in moderation. Consider an overcrowded beach, for example. Overcrowding is bad, but banning people from going to the beach would be a misguided response. What is needed is a way to enable people to visit the beach without overcrowding it. Since beach-going is only bad when done in excess, and *good* in moderation, a distinctive sort of policy is warranted.

Here is one possible solution: Make a list of residents, and allow each onto the beach no more than a certain number of times per year. This might solve the overcrowding problem, but at a hefty cost. Some people *adore* the beach, and our policy will give them only as much access as people who are indifferent toward it. For beach-lovers who are restricted from the surf and sand, this policy will come with a heavy burden.

Instead of controlling each citizen's access directly, we might allocate tickets for beach entry and keep track only of those tickets. The difference with this policy is that people could transfer their tickets to others. So, if you love the beach and I don't care for it, I might be willing to trade you my tickets for, say, $20. Both of us will be better off, and as long as the number of tickets was fixed in advance, the benefit to both of us will come with no extra crowding on the beach. The policy of *capping* access to the beach and allowing people to *trade* their access rights results in the same number of people on the beach, but it delivers that result in a less burdensome way.[80]

This is the basic idea behind "market-based" approaches to environmental regulation, exemplified most notably by the concept of "cap-and-trade." Instead of requiring a specific pattern of behaviors, cap-and-trade schemes allow people to make deals with one another so that desired overall outcomes are achieved with minimal burdens. Here is how it might work in the context of responding to climate change: As a society, we set a target for total greenhouse gas emissions and allocate "permits" for the right to emit certain amounts. Then, we let individuals and firms trade among themselves so that those who place a high value on emitting may do so while those who place less value on emitting are compensated for scaling back. As long as we honor the target we set at the beginning, we ensure the overall reductions we want. But compared to a policy of demanding specific behaviors from each emitter, the cap-and-trade policy comes with much lower burdens.

Seth Mayer worries about market-based approaches like this for several reasons, some more warranted than others. To start with a worry I consider unwarranted, Mayer fears that market-based policies will not reduce emissions quickly enough. However, this seems like a much bigger problem for the approach he favors instead. If we tell every firm to reduce its emissions to a particular level (or adopt certain low-emissions technologies, or whatever), then we can expect two reactions. First, companies which already meet the requirements will do nothing, since the regulations ask nothing of them. Second, companies which do *not* already meet the requirements will fight tooth and nail to relax the standards, phase them in slowly, and "grandfather in" existing investments. So, the response under command-and-control may be slow and uneven. By contrast, a cap-and-trade scheme would incentivize our first group of companies to become even more aggressive in reducing emissions, since they could profit from selling their excess permits; it also would give our second group less reason to fight, since they would still have the option of carrying on as before, just at somewhat greater cost.

On the other hand, Mayer is right that market-based policies can be difficult to design and monitor. How will we choose the total number of permits to allocate? How will we ensure people emit only as much as they are legally allowed? On what basis will we allocate the permits? These are not easy questions.

Some reveal the potential for hidden costs: Monitoring and tracking emissions, for example, is not free. Others raise concerns about equity and justice. Under a cap-and-trade scheme, it matters greatly who is awarded permits initially and who must buy them on the market. Something will have gone seriously wrong if poor families see their energy costs skyrocket while corporate shareholders celebrate windfall profits from free permits. Mayer is right to say that a market-based approach cannot get off the ground without satisfactorily addressing these issues.

Still, problems like these are not unique to market-based approaches. "Command-and-control" schemes also have to be designed, monitored, and enforced. They may also generate hidden costs, and they may also fail to navigate the ethical quandaries they raise. And, on top of this, they have the clear disadvantage of being characteristically inflexible and undiscriminating.[81]

Command-and-control is not always the inferior option. Sometimes—as we saw in the case of murder—we want to stand firmly against immoral behavior. Sometimes there is value in applying the same rules to everyone or allowing variations only in specified circumstances. Sometimes it is simply easier to have preset requirements than to keep track of a dynamic landscape of trades and activities. But when command-and-control is the right way to go, it is usually because its inflexibility and clarity are *assets*. In the context of climate change regulation, where we face countless decisions about what activities to permit, at what levels, in what circumstances, and by which people, it is precisely the need for flexibility that recommends a market-based approach like cap-and-trade.

COMPREHENSION QUESTIONS

1. How does Shahar's analogy to controlling access to the beach relate to environmental cap-and-trade programs? Why does he think this is better than requiring a specific pattern of behavior?
2. What is the difference between "cap-and-trade" and "command-and-control" models?

DISCUSSION QUESTIONS

1. Do you think there could be a place for both "cap-and-trade" and "command-and-control" methods for environmental regulations? For example, are there some practices that ought to be completely banned while others ought to be moderated? What does Shahar think?
2. Mayer claims that market-based approaches to fighting climate change are an insufficient response to the moral impacts of destabilizing the climate system, and hence he advocates a direct regulatory approach that takes a firmer and more principled stance. What is it about direct regulations that enable them to be better communicators about morality? And is Mayer right that we should take a principled stand against contributions to climate change?

FURTHER READINGS

Broome, John. *Climate Matters: Ethics in a Warming World.* New York: Norton, 2012.
Cruz, Marcio, James Foster, Bryce Quillin, and Philip Schellekens. "Ending Extreme Poverty and Sharing Prosperity: Progress and Policies." *World Bank Group Policy Research Note* PRN/15/03. Washington, DC: World Bank, 2015.
Gardiner, Stephen. *A Perfect Moral Storm: The Ethical Tragedy of Climate Change.* Oxford: Oxford University Press, 2011.
Gardiner, Stephen, et al., eds. *Climate Ethics: Essential Readings.* Oxford: Oxford University Press, 2010.
Hope, Chris. "The Marginal Impact of CO_2 from PAGE2002: An Integrated Assessment Model Incorporating the IPCC's Five Reasons for Concern." *Integrated Assessment Journal* 6 (2006): 19–56.
Intergovernmental Panel on Climate Change. *Climate Change 2013: The Physical Science Basis.* Cambridge: Cambridge University Press, 2013.
Intergovernmental Panel on Climate Change. *Climate Change 2014: Impacts, Adaptation, and Vulnerability.* New York: Cambridge University Press, 2014, Chapter 13.
Jamieson, Dale. *Reason in a Dark Time: Why the Struggle Against Climate Change Failed— And What It Means for Our Future.* Oxford: Oxford University Press, 2014.
Roser, Max, and Esteban Ortiz-Ospina. "Global Extreme Poverty." *Our World in Data* (2017). https://ourworldindata.org/extreme-poverty.
Stern, Nicholas H. *The Economics of Climate Change: The Stern Review.* Cambridge: Cambridge University Press, 2006.
UN Women. "Infographic: Human Rights of Women." 2015. http://www.unwomen.org/en /digital-library/multimedia/2015/12/infographic-human-rights-women.

NOTES

1. Intergovernmental Panel on Climate Change (IPCC), "Summary for Policymakers," in *Climate Change 2013: The Physical Science Basis* (New York: Cambridge University Press, 2013).
2. As a result, I will not be able to address every question about climate change in the space I have here. I will not, for instance, discuss what is known in philosophy as the Non-Identity Problem. This problem is a puzzle about how our choices about how to handle phenomena like climate change, which extend far into the future, affect which people will end up coming into existence. For a description of the problem, see Derek Parfit, *Reasons and Persons* (Oxford: Oxford University Press, 1984), 351–379. For a response to the problem that fits the kind of discussion I give here, see William FitzPatrick, "Climate Change and the Rights of Future Generations: Social Justice Beyond Mutual Advantage," *Environmental Ethics* 29, no. 4 (2007): 369–388. In addition, I will not be able to delve into the important debate about discounting, which examines how to measure benefits now against benefits in the future. For a helpful introduction to this debate, see Dale Jamieson, *Reason in a Dark Time* (Oxford: Oxford University Press, 2014), 105–130.
3. There are a variety of proposals for directly manipulating the climate, often described as geoengineering. I will not address geoengineering's ethical quandaries in any detail here. For a rich ethical discussion of one such proposal, see Stephen Gardiner, *A Perfect Moral Storm: The Ethical Tragedy of Climate Change* (Oxford: Oxford University Press, 2011), 339–396. See also Benjamin Hale and Lisa Dilling, "Geoengineering, Ocean

Fertilization, and the Problem of Permissible Pollution," *Science, Technology, and Human Values* 36, no. 2 (2011): 190–212.

4. Stephen Pacala and Robert Socolow, "Stabilization Wedges: Solving the Climate Problem for the Next 50 Years with Current Technologies," *Science* 305, no. 5686 (2004): 968–972.

5. For a discussion of the intergenerational nature of climate change, see Gardiner, *Perfect Moral Storm*. Note that people alive now may end up being the "future people" harmed by climate change, insofar as the negative effects of past emissions are already starting to occur.

6. Market proponents sometimes also suggest relying on common law approaches to environmental harms. In such an approach, victims can sue polluters in order to get compensation for harms, particularly violations of property rights. For a discussion of common law approaches to the environment, see Jonathan Adler, "Is the Common Law a Free-Market Solution to Pollution?" *Critical Review* 24, no. 1 (2012): 61–85. This approach has serious limitations in the context of climate change, where emissions sources are widely dispersed and it is hard to pinpoint who it is that owes compensation to the victim. For reasons to doubt the general viability of such approaches, see Richard Lazarus, "Panel II: Public Versus Private Environmental Regulation," *Ecology Law Quarterly* 21, no. 2 (1994): 438–444.

7. John Braithwaite, "The Limits of Economism in Controlling Harmful Corporate Conduct," *Law & Society Review* 16, no. 3 (1981/1982): 493–494.

8. Because of their use of pricing incentives, cap-and-trade policies are often categorized as market-based. However, their reliance on caps means that they also include elements that are accurately characterized as regulations, a point I will discuss below. They are arguably hybrids between market policies and regulations.

9. While I offer reservations about whether market mechanisms are sufficient to address climate change, others have suggested that they are inherently impermissible, due to their commodification of polluting activity. I do not adopt such a strong stance here. For an example of the stronger claim, see Michael Sandel, *What Money Can't Buy: The Moral Limits of Markets* (New York: Farrar, Straus, and Garoux, 2012), 70–79. For a response to arguments like Sandel's, see Mark Sagoff, "Controlling Global Climate: The Debate over Pollution Trading," *Philosophy & Public Policy* 19, no. 1 (1999): 1–6.

10. For one argument that also supports the need for such regulation, see Debra Satz, *Why Some Things Should Not Be for Sale: The Moral Limits of Markets* (Oxford: Oxford University Press, 2010).

11. Mark Sagoff, "On Markets for Risk," *Maryland Law Review* 41, no. 4 (1982): 772.

12. Elizabeth Anderson and Richard Pildes, "Expressive Theories of Law: A General Restatement," *University of Pennsylvania Law Review* 148 (2000): 1503–1575.

13. Braithwaite, "Limits of Economism," 490.

14. In discussing these issues, I will focus only on moral obligations to humans, but climate change threatens non-human animals and ecosystems as well. Some argue that such creatures and systems deserve moral consideration, whether they benefit human beings or not. For examples of the vast variety of moral theories concerned with non-human animals and nature, see Peter Singer, *Animal Liberation* (New York: Harper Collins, 1975); Tom Regan, *The Case for Animal Rights* (Berkeley: University of California Press, 1983); J. B. Callicott, *In Defense of the Land Ethic: Essays in Environmental Philosophy* (Albany: State University of New York Press, 1989); Martha Nussbaum, *Frontiers of Justice: Disability, Nationality, Species Membership* (Cambridge, MA: Harvard University Press, 2006). For discussions of climate change

and non-human values, see Clare Palmer, "Does Nature Matter? The Place of the Non-human in the Ethics of Climate Change," in *The Ethics of Global Climate Change*, edited by Denis Arnold (Cambridge: Cambridge University Press, 2011), 272–291, and Darrel Moellendorf, *The Moral Challenge of Dangerous Climate Change: Values, Poverty, and Policy* (Cambridge: Cambridge University Press, 2014), 30–61. I will not consider here whether anything non-human has direct moral importance that obligates institutions to provide them or it with protection. If that were the case, it would be necessary to consider whether market policies can effectively respond to the moral value of non-human animals and nature. There is strong reason to doubt that markets can accomplish that goal, however. We should be skeptical that the amount people are willing to pay on a market to preserve and protect non-human animals and nature is equivalent to their actual moral value. If we are aiming at conservation, regulations around land use, pollution, and other human activities may, in some cases, be more effective than market approaches.

15. Lucas Chancel and Thomas Piketty, *Carbon and Inequality: From Kyoto to Paris: Trends in the Global Inequality of Carbon Emissions (1998–2013) & Prospects for an Equitable Adaptation Fund* (Paris: Paris School of Economics, 2015), http://piketty.pse.ens.fr/files/ChancelPiketty2015.pdf.

16. Robert Mendelsohn et al., "The Distributional Impact of Climate Change on Rich and Poor Countries," *Environment and Development Economics* 11 (2006): 159–178.

17. Darrel Moellendorf, *The Moral Challenge of Dangerous Climate Change: Values, Poverty, and Policy* (Cambridge: Cambridge University Press, 2014), 22.

18. In making these claims, I do not aim to wade into the debate over whether we should allocate responsibility for combating climate change based upon historical emissions rates or current emissions rates. In either case, regulation must be utilized to maintain some conception of equity. For discussions of these issues of how to justly apportion responsibility, see Simon Caney, "Human Rights, Responsibilities, and Climate Change" in *Global Basic Rights*, edited by Charles Beitz and Robert Goodin (Oxford: Oxford University Press, 2009), 227–247, and Moellendorf, *Moral Challenge*, 152–180.

19. Allen Buchanan, *The Heart of Human Rights* (Oxford, Oxford University Press, 2013), 37. Buchanan emphasizes the state in this quote, but other powerful entities, such as corporations and non-governmental organizations, must also be responsive to human rights obligations.

20. Simon Caney, "Climate Change, Human Rights, and Moral Thresholds," in *Climate Ethics: Essential Readings*, edited by Stephen Gardiner et al. (Oxford: Oxford University Press, 2010), 166–169.

21. Henry Shue, *Climate Justice: Vulnerability and Protection* (Oxford: Oxford University Press, 2014), 299.

22. Michael Hanemann, "Cap-and-Trade: A Sufficient or Necessary Condition for Emission Reduction?" *Oxford Review of Economic Policy* 26, no. 2 (2010): 247–248.

23. Daniel H. Cole and Peter Z. Grossman, "When Is Command and Control Efficient? Institutions, Technology, and the Comparative Efficiency of Alternative Regulatory Regimes for Environmental Protection," *Wisconsin Law Review* 887 (1999): 887–938.

24. Mark Jaccard et al., "Is Win-Win Possible? Can Canada's Government Achieve Its Paris Commitment . . . and Get Re-Elected?," accessed March 30, 2018, http://rem-main.rem.sfu.ca/papers/jaccard/Jaccard-Hein-Vass%20CdnClimatePol%20EMRG-REM-SFU%20Sep%2020%202016.pdf.

25. Hanemann, "Cap-and-Trade," 242.

26. For more discussion of tipping points in the context of climate change, see Timothy M. Lenton et al., "Tipping Elements in the Earth's Climate System," *Proceedings of the National Academy of Sciences* 105, no. 6 (2008): 1786–1793.

27. Johan Rockström et al., "A Roadmap for Rapid Decarbonization," *Science* 355, vol. 6331 (2017): 1269–1271.

28. Michael Mehling and Endre Tvinnereim, "Pricing Not Enough for Deep Carbon Cuts," *Nature* 552, no. 7684 (2017): 175.

29. Jamieson, *Reason in a Dark Time*, 236; Mark Jaccard, "Want an Effective Climate Policy? Heed the Evidence," *Policy Options*, February 2, 2016, http://policyoptions.irpp .org/magazines/february-2016/want-an-effective-climatepolicy-heed-the-evidence/.

30. Daniel Driesen, "Sustainable Development and Market Liberalism's Shotgun Wedding: Emissions Trading Under the Kyoto Protocol," *Indiana Law Journal* 83, no. 1 (2008): 52–57.

31. Karl Polanyi, *The Great Transformation: The Political and Economic Origins of Our Time* (Boston: Beacon Press, 1944).

32. For a discussion of this mixed approach, see Jamieson, *Reason in a Dark Time*, 201–238. To add to the menu of options, a necessary but insufficient element of addressing climate change will be local experimentation that fits into a broader system of multilevel governance. For a discussion of these issues, see Elinor Ostrom et al., "Revisiting the Commons: Local Lessons, Global Challenges," *Science* 284, no. 5412 (1999): 278–282.

33. For comments and suggestions on this essay, I am grateful to Bob Fischer, Italia Patti, Carlos Pereira Di Salvo, Julia Rockwell, Elton Skendaj, and Christer Watson.

34. Michael Renner, "The Seeds of Modern Threats," in Worldwatch Institute, *State of the World 2015: Confronting Hidden Threats to Sustainability* (Washington, DC: Island Press, 2015), 4–5.

35. Tim Jackson, *Prosperity Without Growth: Foundations for the Economy of Tomorrow* (New York: Routledge, 2017 [2nd ed.]), 203.

36. Jackson, *Prosperity Without Growth*, 141–144.

37. Jackson, *Prosperity Without Growth*, 201.

38. Jackson, *Prosperity Without Growth*, 202–205.

39. Kirkpatrick Sale, *Dwellers in the Land: The Bioregional Vision* (Philadelphia: New Society Publishers, 1985). See also Van Andruss, Christopher Plant, Judith Plant, and Eleanor Write, eds., *Home! A Bioregional Reader* (Philadelphia: New Society Publishers, 1990).

40. For other examples of anti-growth writings, see Edward Goldsmith, Robert Allen, Michael Allaby, John Davoll, and Sam Lawrence, *Blueprint for Survival* (Boston: Houghton Mifflin Co., 1972); Donella H. Meadows, Dennis L. Meadows, Jørgen Randers, and William W. Behrens III, *The Limits to Growth* (New York: Universe Books, 1972); E. F. Schumacher, *Small Is Beautiful: Economics As If People Mattered, 25 Years Later, with Commentaries* (Vancouver: Hartley & Marks, [1973] 1999); Herman E. Daly, *Beyond Growth: The Economics of Sustainable Development* (Boston: Beacon Press, 1996).

41. For recent exposition of a view similar to the one I present in this essay, see Joseph Heath, "Caring About Climate Change Implies Caring About Economic Growth" (unpublished manuscript, 2016), https://www.academia.edu/30297311/Caring_ about_climate_change_implies_caring_about_economic_growth. See, along similar (but more complacent) lines, Wilfred Beckerman, *Through Green-Colored Glasses: Environmentalism Reconsidered* (Washington, DC: Cato Institute, 1996); Julian L. Simon, *The Ultimate Resource 2* (Princeton, NJ: Princeton University Press, 1996);

Bjørn Lomborg, *The Skeptical Environmentalist: Measuring the Real State of the World* (New York: Cambridge University Press, 2001).

42. Max Roser and Esteban Ortiz-Ospina, "Global Extreme Poverty," *Our World in Data* (2017), https://ourworldindata.org/extreme-poverty.

43. Max Roser, "Child Mortality," *Our World in Data* (2018), https://ourworldindata.org /child-mortality.

44. Max Roser, "Life Expectancy," *Our World in Data* (2018), https://ourworldindata.org /life-expectancy.

45. Max Roser, "Democracy," *Our World in Data* (2018), https://ourworldindata.org /democracy.

46. Roser and Ortiz-Ospina, "Global Extreme Poverty."

47. Roser, "Child Mortality."

48. Roser, "Life Expectancy."

49. United Nations, *Universal Declaration of Human Rights* (New York: United Nations, 1948).

50. Roser and Ortiz-Ospina, "Global Extreme Poverty."

51. Roser, "Life Expectancy."

52. Roser, "Child Mortality."

53. UN Women, "Infographic: Human Rights of Women," *UN Women* (2015), http://www .unwomen.org/en/digital-library/multimedia/2015/12/infographic-human-rights -women.

54. Even the famous Club of Rome report on *The Limits to Growth* acknowledges that "it is success in overcoming limits that forms the cultural tradition of many dominant people in today's world. Over the past three hundred years, mankind has compiled an impressive record of pushing back the apparent limits to population and economic growth by a series of spectacular technological advances" (Meadows et al., *Limits to Growth*, 129).

55. Schumacher, *Small Is Beautiful*, 4–5.

56. Quoted in John Tierney, "Betting on the Planet," *New York Times Magazine* (December 2, 1990): 52–54, 74–81, at 81.

57. Nicholas H. Stern, *The Economics of Climate Change: The Stern Review* (Cambridge: Cambridge University Press, 2006).

58. For this reason, the report has been criticized by those who believe the impacts of climate change will be less severe than it anticipates. See, e.g., Bjørn Lomborg, "Stern Review," *Wall Street Journal*, November 2, 2006, A12.

59. By contrast, the studies surveyed by Richard S. J. Tol, "The Economic Effects of Climate Change," *Journal of Economic Perspectives* 23 (2009): 29–51, focus on scenarios involving 1°C to 3°C of warming by 2100.

60. Stern, *Economics of Climate Change*, 155–156.

61. Chris Hope, "The Marginal Impact of CO_2 from PAGE2002: An Integrated Assessment Model Incorporating the IPCC's Five Reasons for Concern," *Integrated Assessment Journal* 6 (2006): 19–56.

62. These figures are calculated with the GDP growth rates provided by Hope, "Marginal Impact of CO_2," 50. It worth noting that when the model claims poor countries will experience the highest levels of growth, it is not indulging in egalitarian wishful thinking; this projection simply reflects the fact that these countries are currently very poor. To see the point more clearly, suppose that I start out with $1 and you start out with $5. If someone gives us each $10, my wealth will have increased by 1,000% while yours will have increased by only 200%.

63. Stern, *Economics of Climate Change*, 160.

64. For discussion of other efforts to model the impacts of climate change, see Tol, "Economic Effects of Climate Change."

65. Stern, *Economics of Climate Change*, xvii.

66. Intergovernmental Panel on Climate Change, *Climate Change 2014: Impacts, Adaptation, and Vulnerability* (New York: Cambridge University Press, 2014), Chapter 13.

67. Intergovernmental Panel on Climate Change, *Climate Change 2013: The Physical Science Basis* (New York: Cambridge University Press, 2013), Chapter 12.

68. Intergovernmental Panel on Climate Change, *Climate Change 2013*, Chapter 13.

69. I am grateful to Bob Fischer for this last observation.

70. Marcio Cruz, James Foster, Bryce Quillin, and Philip Schellekens, "Ending Extreme Poverty and Sharing Prosperity: Progress and Policies," *World Bank Group Policy Research Note* PRN/15/03 (Washington, DC: World Bank, 2015). For skepticism regarding our prospects for meeting these goals, see Homi Kharas and Wolfgang Fengler, "Global Poverty is Declining But Not Fast Enough," *Future Development* (2017), https://www.brookings.edu/blog/future-development/2017/11/07/global-poverty-is-declining-but-not-fast-enough/.

71. Intergovernmental Panel on Climate Change, *Climate Change 2013*, Chapter 8.

72. United Nations Development Program, *Reducing Disaster Risk: A Challenge for Development* (New York: United Nations Development Program, 2004), 10.

73. World Bank, "Constant GDP per Capita for the Republic of Korea," retrieved from FRED, Federal Reserve Bank of St. Louis (2018), https://fred.stlouisfed.org/series/NYGDPPCAPKDKOR.

74. For arguments in a similar spirit, see Mark Sagoff, "Can Environmentalists Keep Two Ideas in Mind and Still Function?" *Philosophy & Public Policy Quarterly* 27, no. 1/2 (2007): 3.

75. Democratization, for instance, relies on not just economic growth, but contingent actions and events, institutional conditions, and other mechanisms. See Ronald Inglehart and Christian Welzel, "How Development Leads to Democracy: What We Know About Modernization," *Foreign Affairs* 88, no. 2 (2009): 37–39, and Daron Acemoglu et al. "Reevaluating the Modernization Hypothesis," *Journal of Monetary Economics* 56 (2009): 1043–1058. Economic growth's ability to reduce poverty is also not straightforward. Note, for instance, that America's poverty rate has remained relatively persistent in spite of growth in average GDP per capita over the last half-century or so. The relationship between economic growth and poverty reduction is complex even at the national level and depends on social, political, and legal factors that make growth inclusive. See Hilary W. Hoynes et al., "Poverty in America: Trends and Explanations," *Journal of Economic Perspectives* 20, no. 1 (2006): 47–68. For further discussion of the limits of growth for supporting human development, see Martha Nussbaum, "Women's Education: A Global Challenge," *Signs* 29, no. 2 (2004): 328–330.

76. See Hollie Nyseth Brehm and David N. Pellow, "Environmental Justice: Pollution, Poverty, and Marginalized Communities," in *Routledge Handbook of Global Environmental Politics*, edited by Paul Harris (New York: Routledge, 2014), 308–320.

77. Fergus Green and Richard Denniss, "Cutting with Both Arms of the Scissors: The Economic and Political Case for Restrictive Supply-Side Climate Policies," *Climatic Change* 150, no. 1–2 (2018), 73–87.

78. Dale Jamieson notes that—in contrast to many climate scientists' perspectives—some economistic worldviews downplay certain risks and lack a sense of urgency about climate change. See his *Reason in a Dark Time*, 136–137. My arguments are meant to align with the more precautionary approach many scientists have defended.

79. Additionally, while such compensatory policies are sometimes promised, they are often not implemented, as in the case of trade deals that harm particular groups of workers without addressing their losses. As Dani Rodrik explains, "Before a new policy—say, a trade agreement—is adopted, beneficiaries have an incentive to promise compensation. Once the policy is in place, they have little interest in following through, either because reversal is costly all around or because the underlying balance of power shifts toward them." See Dani Rodrik, "Too Late to Compensate Free Trade's Losers," *Global Policy Opinion*, June 6, 2017, https://www.globalpolicyjournal.com/blog/06/06/2017/too-late-compensate-free-trade%E2%80%99s-losers.

80. I have emphasized that cap-and-trade schemes can *equal the performance* of more direct regulations at a *lower cost*. But we can extend the same point to see that for a *given level of burden* that society is willing to bear, cap-and-trade schemes will typically be able to deliver *greater performance*.

81. Mayer says that this drawback can be mitigated by creating more flexible standards and incorporating elements from market-based policies. This is correct, but more flexibility tends to mean greater difficulties in design, monitoring, enforcement, and so on, and as more market-like elements are included, the difference between Mayer's proposal and the market-based approach blurs.

CHAPTER 9

Right to Health Care

IN DEFENSE OF A RIGHT TO HEALTH CARE
SAM FLEISCHACKER AND SHERRY GLIED

1. Introduction

Appealing to a right to health care, writes Norman Daniels, "is not an appropriate starting point for an inquiry into just health care."[1] Rights should be "harvested" from more fundamental theories of justice, he argues; alone, they are too broad and too variously defended to make clear what is being demanded and why. "The assertion of a right may . . . be the natural or only way that comes to mind to argue for just reform" of the health care system, he says, but such assertions do not make clear what is unjust about that system.

We agree that bald appeals to rights are unhelpful in moral and political argumentation. We will begin, therefore, with a sketch of what we take claiming a right to health care to achieve.

The assertion of a right to health care is a call for the government to ensure that everyone has a certain level of health care. It serves as a counter to claims that health care is a commodity like any other, which should be allocated (or not) solely by the free market. Under the assertion of a right to care, the obligation to ensure that those who need care receive it is societal, not private. The extent of government action taken to secure a right to health care might be relatively narrow, and might proceed largely via markets rather than taking the form of a bureaucratic agency, but whatever form it takes, it needs to be sufficient to ensure that everyone who needs it can get at least basic health care.

Since the assertion of a right to health care is a call for government action, it should emerge from a theory of the purposes for which governments should act. Below, we argue for a right to health care based on a theory of government action that stresses the protection of liberty—what political philosophers call a "liberal" theory of government action (a theory shared by both most "liberals" and most "conservatives" in the popular sense of those terms). We then address two potential objections to our argument, showing that a right to health care can be defined in such a way as to accommodate technological change, and that endorsing it need not entail endorsing rights to all other valuable goods and services.

2. The Significance of Freedom

On liberal theories of government—whether of the hard libertarian variety, which favors very little government action, or of a social democratic variety, which sees a significant degree of welfare programming as required by liberal ideals—the prime reason for governments to act is always the protection or enhancement of individual freedom. From Thomas Hobbes and John Locke to John Rawls and Ronald Dworkin, liberals have held that the *main* reason, if perhaps not the only reason, why free individuals agree to the coercive powers of government is to protect themselves against threats to their freedom. "Rights" are understood, in this context, to be either ways of expressing individual freedom (think here of rights of conscience) or ways of protecting individual freedom (think here of the right to due process). On this view, people have a right to health care if and only if some level of health is necessary for them to be free.

Now there are other ways of defending rights, as Daniels indicates by talking of rights as "harvested" from theories of justice. In Rawls's theory of justice, for instance, the assertion of a right may be a way of claiming a certain kind of equality. Rawls remains a liberal—he believes that governments need first and foremost to protect liberty—but he embeds his liberalism in a framework in which protecting freedom is part of a more fundamental protection of equality. And Daniels uses Rawls's framework to make a strong case that health care is essential to equal opportunity.[2] Rawls's framework is disputed by libertarians, however—the main opponents of a right to health care—since they think that governments should protect freedom alone, not equality. For this reason, we limit our argument here to one based in freedom, rather than equality.[3] If health care is a condition for the ability to make free choices, then there is a case for a right to health care that even libertarians should respect.

But the idea that there are conditions for making free choices tends to be inadequately appreciated by libertarians. Libertarians acknowledge that a person does not choose freely when someone threatens to kill or assault her or deceives her about the options among which she is to choose. They also agree that people cannot choose freely if their minds are addled by drugs or mental illness. The idea that we need to be in certain mental states in order to choose freely has wider implications, however. It may for instance require that we have enough education to understand our options,[4] or that our minds be clear enough of anxiety about grave threats to our lives or well-being that we can attend to the pros and cons of those options.

If we add some plausible further conditions for freedom, we can see how egalitarian concerns may belong under the umbrella of freedom, and further strengthen the liberal case for a right to health care. Most of the time we make choices, even on a purely personal level, within a social context: by consulting with others—friends, neighbors, co-workers—and often on the understanding that others will help us implement the choice. But we can easily be pushed around by these others unless we stand to them in relations of equality.[5] And having our basic material needs met, and having some basic level of social standing (dignity), is essential if we are to stand in egalitarian relationships. Some level of economic independence—including health care—is therefore necessary to preserving our dignity and enabling us to make truly free choices. Freedom, the keystone of liberalism, is on this line of reasoning dependent on having at least a basic level of material welfare. That level of welfare will then be, not just for egalitarians but for liberals as well, a right.

For similar reasons, civic republicanism may belong under the auspices of liberalism. Many of our choices are, after all, structured by the laws and government policies under which we live. The options I have for schooling, employment, and consumption depend heavily on what my government permits or fosters. But it follows that contributing to the shaping of those political arrangements is a further condition for my choices to be free. They are, certainly, *freer* when I can do that. This is an argument for democracy to go along with liberalism. But it is a condition on democracy that I can vote, speak my mind, and assemble with others without fear of retaliation by powerful groups in my society—that I not be *dominated* by others, as civic republicans like to say,[6] and instead be able to stand, vis-à-vis my fellow citizens, in relationships of roughly equal independence. "Roughly equal independence" is vague, of course, but it again would seem to require that my basic material needs are met—that I not risk starvation or homelessness or grave illness when I engage in political activity. Which is to say that I should be seen as having a *right* to my basic needs, including my health needs, if I am to be an equal citizen in a democracy. If my being an equal citizen is a condition for my being free, however, a right justified in this civic republican way will also be a right that liberals should accept.[7]

3. Rights to Welfare in America

All this may sound odd to American ears, given that the United States has never recognized rights to welfare. Some say that that is because rights, in America's liberal tradition, are all negative: They call on government *not* to harm or manipulate us, rather than demanding that it actively *set up* any institution for us. As it happens, this is not strictly true even of the Bill of Rights—the Sixth and Seventh Amendments require the government to institute juries, and the Second Amendment implies that states should maintain militias. And the idea that rights must be negative was wholly rejected by President Franklin Delano Roosevelt when he declared that "[f]reedom from fear is eternally linked with freedom from want" and called for a series of positive rights (including a right to health care) to supplement our negative ones.[8] In its 1970 *Goldberg v. Kelly* opinion, the U.S. Supreme Court also held that "[w]elfare, by meeting the basic demands of subsistence, can help bring within the reach of the poor the same opportunities that are available to others to participate meaningfully in the life of the community" and that the provision of welfare goods thereby serves to help fulfill the Constitution's pledge to "secure the Blessings of Liberty" to all U.S. citizens. The affinities between these claims and the various liberal, egalitarian, and civic republican arguments for a right to welfare sketched above should be obvious.[9]

But the *Goldberg* decision established only a right to due process in determining welfare eligibility, not a right to welfare itself. It was also written by a left-leaning Supreme Court that had been moving in the direction of finding welfare rights in the Constitution.[10] A few years later, in the *Rodriguez* decision that effectively ended the Court's movement toward such rights, Justice Powell denied that any American had a right to an education, even though he granted that some level of education might be "essential to the effective exercise of First Amendment freedoms and to intelligent utilization of the right to vote." The main problem with granting a right to education, in his view, was that it could not be found in the Constitution, but he also thought that a right to education could not be appropriately enforced by courts. If there is a right to education, Powell said, then there may well be rights to other kinds of welfare. "Empirical examination" may well show, he said, that "the ill-fed, ill-clothed, and ill-housed are among the most ineffective participants in the political process" and "derive the least enjoyment from the First Amendment." But supplying any of these welfare goods "presents a myriad of 'intractable economic, social, and even philosophical problems,'" which courts are not well placed to resolve. Decisions about how to provide welfare should therefore be left up to legislatures, not enshrined in a fundamental right.[11] Dissenting from this opinion, Justice Thurgood Marshall maintained that education bears a closer connection to voting and free speech rights than other welfare goods. It can be singled out as a fundamental right, he said, even if there is no fundamental right to food, clothing, and housing.[12]

4. From Welfare Rights to a Health Care Right

There is thus a respectable American tradition defending welfare rights, even if there is also a tradition opposing them. As we shall see shortly, Powell's argument against welfare rights captures the main objection to a right to health care. But first, let's consider rights to health care in the light of the line of reasoning by which Roosevelt and the pre-*Rodriguez* Supreme Court defended welfare rights. Does health care belong to the "basic demands of subsistence" that the *Goldberg* court considered necessary to liberty and citizenship? Is it similar to education, which Justice Marshall regarded as having an especially close connection with voting rights and free speech?

There is an easy answer, surely, to the first of these questions. Health care—at least to the extent necessary to avoid loss of life, loss of limbs, long-term incapacitation, and mental derangement—is surely as important to our opportunities to "participate . . . in the life of [our] community" as decent food, shelter, and clothing. It is surely a basic element of the "freedom from want" that Roosevelt linked to the "freedom from fear."

But is health as closely linked to choice as education—do we need it in order to exercise our First Amendment freedoms effectively, and to utilize our right to vote intelligently? We suggest that it is, at least in its most basic forms. Someone beset by chronic or severe illness cannot be expected to attend and speak out at political rallies, or to make clear-headed choices in a voting booth. In the first place, loss of one's limbs or bodily functions, fever, and mental derangement, to say nothing of loss of life, can quite obviously eradicate or severely obstruct one's ability to choose, let alone one's ability to be an active citizen; some minimal level of health is a condition for both personal and political freedom.[13] In the second place, severe health *insecurity*—having good reason to *worry* that one may soon lose one's bodily functions, become incapacitated, or face mental derangement or death—seems similarly to limit both personal and political freedom. How can we regard a choice as unfree if another human being threatens to kill or maim us, but *not* regard that choice as unfree if it is the only way to avoid an illness that will kill or maim us? It certainly seems absurd to say that a person who needs to devote all her resources to fending off these dangers has the same opportunity to participate in the political process as a person whose basic health needs are secure. It would seem then that health is clearly a condition for freedom.

Thus abstractly put, however, this case for a right to health care is too simple. Let's return to Justice Powell's argument against positive rights. Powell argued that presenting welfare as a right is impracticable—that there is no effective and fair way to enforce such rights. This is a reasonable concern: No one can have a right to something that cannot be supplied. But that is not the case with health care. Health care that can, with very high probability, restore a person's functioning—providing insulin to a diabetic, treating an emergent stroke with clot-busting drugs, performing a cesarean section in the event of an obstetrical emergency, or curing a case of infectious tuberculosis with appropriate antibiotics—exists and is in common use.[14] For people who need such treatments, they offer an obvious means of removing a major impediment to freedom.

Of course, something similar may be true for other goods and services that alleviate stress and improve our active capacities. And in principle we think that there may well be a liberal case for other sorts of welfare rights. But, as we discuss below, the characteristics of health care make the argument for a right to it much stronger than for other goods and services.

5. Defining the Right to Health Care

Health care has not always been efficacious. And to speak of a "right to health care" in eras in which doctors were of very dubious value—in the seventeenth or eighteenth centuries, for instance—would have been a joke.[15] Reliable medical treatments—safe surgical methods and effective drugs—are a development only of the past century or so. The question of whether people have a right to such treatment has accordingly arisen only quite recently.

Even today, not all health care has a high likelihood of restoring the fitness we need in order to make free choices. A right to health care based on freedom would not extend, for example, to active treatment of the common cold, surgical treatment of chronic pancreatitis, or removal of sebaceous cysts, all examples of care that is often provided but is unlikely to restore fitness for functioning.[16]

But these points raise a problem about the very idea of a right to health care. That some modes of health care improve, and that the line between what can and cannot be achieved by them is always changing, would appear to pose serious challenges to defining health care as a right. These features raise enormous problems of definition, and of cost, just as Justice Powell supposed. To this we respond (a) that certain welfare goods are so essential to our freedom and capacity for citizenship that governments have a responsibility to try to resolve the problems that come with recognizing a right to them, and (b) that ready solutions to those problems are available, as regards the right to health care.

In practice, distinctions between what is and what is not necessary health care have been made routinely and have not caused much more difficulty than they do with standard negative rights, the definition of which likewise changes because of technological developments (consider the question of whether wiretapping counts as a "search").[17] All very-high-income (Organisation for Economic Co-operation and Development [OECD]) countries other than the United States provide a de facto right to health care through their universal health insurance systems. Some of these also enshrine a right to medical services in their constitutions or foundational documents.[18] Jurists in these countries have successfully defined the evolution and limitations of these rights. But we need not look so far afield. Because of the prevalence of health insurance, the problem of defining what falls within the scope of health care has been addressed in the context of the U.S. private sector. Most Americans obtain health insurance through commercial contracts that define the scope of benefits covered under the umbrella term "medical necessity." Standards of medical necessity draw precisely the line that is needed to define a right, and insurers and courts have successfully implemented these standards, in both the public and private sectors, since the 1940s.[19] Finally, more transparent and formal methodologies for delineating the terms of a right to health care exist and are in use. For example, in Oregon, a review board of citizens and medical experts has prioritized condition–treatment pairs to define the scope of coverage under the state Medicaid program for over two decades.[20] While undoubtedly challenging, these three very different examples illustrate that it is abundantly possible to define and routinely update a positive right to health care.

6. A Right to Too Much?

Objections based on Justice Powell's argument against the expansiveness of welfare rights might go farther. Health is not the only social good that potentially affects freedom. Need extending a right to health care open the door to an expansive right to everything else that affects freedom? Presumably, we should be circumspect about extending rights, especially to goods and services that people can reasonably obtain for themselves.[21] Health care has three features that make it distinctive, however, and strengthen the case for health care to be a right: (1) the need for care is often urgent; (2) it is often unpredictable; and (3) it can be very costly relative to family budgets.

For many health conditions, the need for health care is urgent. In these cases, from the moment of onset of the injury, illness, or severe pain, the afflicted person is no longer able to make provision for his own care. If care is deferred over even a short period of time, the person will suffer serious and permanent consequences, as in the case of stroke, for example.[22] In this situation, a person cannot seek out or rely on voluntary assistance or make a pledge to repay the cost of care. The nearly universal acknowledgment of the desirability of making access to such urgent, life-saving care a matter of right led to the Emergency Medical Treatment and Active Labor Act (EMTALA), passed by Congress under a Republican Senate and signed by President Ronald Reagan in 1986. Under EMTALA, the emergency department of any hospital participating in the Medicare program—as virtually all general hospitals in the United States do—must medically screen all patients who seek care for a medical condition, regardless of ability to pay,[23] and, if equipped to do so, provide treatment until the condition has been resolved or stabilized.[24] While rights under EMTALA are highly circumscribed, and do not encompass the full range of treatments that would enable free choice, the law provides a first step toward a right to health care within the United States. Here, the government ensures access, but provision is entirely through the private sector. And despite Justice Powell's concerns, EMTALA has been enforced successfully for over thirty years. It is notable that no right to other material necessities of well-being—housing, food, or a job, for instance—exists in federal law.

The other two unusual features of health care—that it is unpredictable and very costly—provide a justification for extending the right to care beyond life-threatening emergencies. Because of these two features, without government intervention many people could not procure the health care that allows them to be free. The costs of health care are very unevenly distributed. Health care is most valuable to those who are seriously ill, so it is no surprise that the vast majority of medical expenditures are concentrated in a very small share of the population. About a quarter of all medical expenditures in the population in a year will be incurred in the care of just 1% of the population.[25] Improvements in medical technology over time have led to increased costs of health care, so that by about 1950, the average consumer could not plausibly save or borrow enough to pay the costs of medically necessary treatment in the event that he fell into that unlucky 1%.[26] Only a small share of these costs can be predicted in advance.[27] In consequence, the provision or purchase of insurance, which spreads the risk of an unanticipated health problem across the entire covered population, has emerged as the way costly health care is paid for in all higher-income countries.

Unregulated, voluntary markets for insurance are highly imperfect. In particular, they provide inadequate protection against the risk that a person will, at some future point, develop a chronic health condition that would predictably raise future health care costs. Although libertarian-oriented economists have speculated that complex arrangements could be made to address this risk of reclassification, even these theoretically attractive schemes, which have never been implemented in practice, could not address health risks present at birth (such as genetic risk factors) and could not accommodate changes in health care technologies.[28] These schemes also could not ensure that people who were born into lower-income families, and could not afford to buy coverage when young, would ever have the ability to avail themselves of health care that would restore their functioning should they become ill. In effect, the opportunity to be fully free citizens would be closed off to them.

Certainly, health depends on more factors than health care: adequate exercise and appropriate nutrition, for instance. But it may be less important to define access to these other factors as a right. Because they are not urgent, unpredictable, or exceptionally costly relative to incomes, all but a small minority of the population can procure some measure of these resources for themselves. Charitable organizations may be able to fill in the remaining gaps. These libertarian-preferred solutions will not work as regards health care. The unique features of health care mean that markets and charitable aid, alone, will leave many people unable to obtain the care they need to be free and to contribute meaningfully to society.

7. Conclusion

We contend, then, that a right to health care is both fully defensible in liberal terms—and in the specific liberal traditions of the United States—and far more practicable than critics of welfare rights, like Justice Powell, have maintained. This need not mean that a right to health care, or any other kind of welfare, can be derived from the U.S. Constitution, or that the Constitution need be amended to include it. But it does mean that regarding health care as a right, and not merely a commodity that some people have while others must go without, should be a guiding element of American politics. Health care is a commodity that cannot reasonably be left to the market alone without severely endangering many people's freedom.

COMPREHENSION QUESTIONS

1. What matters for defining a right to freedom? What are egalitarian concerns? Why are they important to liberal democracies?
2. What is the difference between a negative and a positive right?
3. Compared to other goods and services, why might we think that health care is more plausibly something to which people have a right?
4. How might systems of health care support positive rights?
5. In addition to health care, what else matters for ensuring well-being? What's the duty of the state in providing these needs?

DISCUSSION QUESTIONS

1. Why defend government health care programs on the ground that health care is a right, rather than offering a consequentialist case for such programs (claiming that they are good for society as a whole)? What are the costs of the rights-based approach?
2. Does granting a right to health care entail granting a right to education, public housing, and other welfare goods? Why or why not? If it does, should we endorse all these welfare rights or deny that people have a right to any kind of welfare?
3. If all other developed countries provide provisions for health care to citizens, why does the United States rely on a free-market approach? Do you think this is an effective model of administering health services? Why or why not? What would be the alternative?

Case 1

Some conservatives worry about the loss of freedom that could be associated with a single-payer health care system. Consider this passage from a recent Heritage Foundation report:

> Champions of single-payer health care always promise free care for all without exception. Your personal decisions concerning the kind of care you get or want, of course, do not count. Government officials decide what health benefits you get, when and how you get them, under what circumstances you get them, what you pay for them, and how you pay for them.
>
> For Americans who may be subject to a single-payer regime, certain key questions are unavoidable:
>
> - Where can I go if the government program does not provide what I want or what I need?
> - Is there an exit ramp from the system?
> - Can I buy an alternative health plan, a plan of my choice that will provide the coverage that I want?
> - Can I privately contract outside of the government program with a medical professional or specialist of my choice to treat my medical condition?
> - If I am permitted to do so, does the doctor or specialist who agrees to see me suffer a statutory, regulatory, or financial penalty?
> - Do private medical consultations outside of the system incur some sort of official punishment for members of the medical profession?*
>
> How might Fleischacker and Glied reply to these kinds of concerns?

———————

*https://www.heritage.org/health-care-reform/report/the-national-de

DISTRIBUTE MONEY, NOT MEDICINE
CHRISTOPHER FREIMAN

Suppose your company just wrapped up a banner year, so your boss decides to reward everyone with a bonus. She's debating whether to give out $300 top-of-the-line headphones or $300 in cash. What's the better bonus?

I say cash is better, and here's why. If an employee wants those headphones more than anything else $300 can buy, he can use the cash to buy the headphones. He's no worse off for getting the cash. On the other hand, many employees will want something other than those headphones, and they can use the cash to buy it. So giving cash rather than headphones makes none worse off and some better off.

This is a simple argument, but I find it persuasive (it remains to be seen whether my kids will agree once I start cutting them checks for their birthdays). And it applies to other cases. Take medical care. One popular policy has the state directly provide citizens with medical care or particular kinds of medical insurance. An alternative arrangement would have the state distribute cash payments directly to citizens to spend as they see fit. I will argue in favor of the proposal to distribute cash: Those who prefer the health care package that the state would have provided are free to use their cash to buy it; those who prefer something else can buy something else. It's win–win.

I'll start by sketching what a system of cash transfers would look like and explaining why a right to health care doesn't imply that the state must directly provide health care to its citizens. Next, I argue that the diversity of citizens' opinions about the appropriate quality and quantity of health care favors providing them with cash to purchase the bundle of health care that best suits their preferences. Then, I discuss two objections to a cash system: (1) It is too risky to allow citizens to purchase their own health care, and (2) it would disadvantage those in poverty and those with expensive preexisting medical conditions. I conclude that these objections are unsuccessful and that the case for cash ultimately stands.

1. Cash and the Right to Health Care

To begin, let me briefly outline the two kinds of institutional arrangements I'll be considering. The first would have the government provide health care to citizens "in kind." One example is a government health insurance program that offers a particular set of benefits. Medicaid, for instance, covers hospital and physician services, x-rays, pediatric care, prescription drugs, and so on.[29] The most extensive version of in-kind provision would be the outright nationalization of health care, whereby the government itself is fully in charge of medical resources and personnel.

An alternative to the in-kind provision of health care is a basic income. That is, the state would distribute cash payments to citizens to spend as they choose instead of directly providing them with medical care or insurance. The state could finance the basic income with the funds that would have otherwise financed the in-kind provision of health care. (For what it's worth, U.S. federal spending on health care amounts to roughly $1 trillion per year.[30])

There are different versions of a basic income. You might prefer an *unconditional* basic income, whereby the state would distribute a certain amount of cash to everyone in the country. Everyone—employed or unemployed, rich or poor—receives an income from the state. Alternatively, the state could institute a conditional basic income—for instance, citizens might need to meet work or income requirements to be eligible. I'll discuss the details of my favored basic income proposal further in Section 4, but we can set them aside for the moment since they don't matter for present purposes.

Before I make the positive case for cash, I want to note that I believe that people *do* have a right to health care; however, that people have a right to health care doesn't entail that the state itself should produce and distribute health care.[31] The right to health care implies that we have an obligation to establish institutions that give everyone access to adequate health care. But this claim leaves open the question of which *specific* institutions we ought to establish.

By analogy, people have a right to food, but this right doesn't require the state to produce and distribute the food itself. (Indeed, states that socialize food production and distribution don't have a stellar track record of feeding their citizens.) Rather, our obligation is to establish institutions that give everyone access to adequate food. The United States, for example, attempts to meet this obligation with food stamps. Instead of institutionalizing a system of state-run supermarkets, the U.S. government supplies its citizens with the means to obtain food from privately owned supermarkets.

John Stuart Mill holds a similar view about education. Mill denies "that the whole or any large part of the education of the people should be in State hands."[32] However, he is happy to give the state an indirect role in education—for instance, the state "might leave to parents to obtain the education where and how they pleased, and content itself with helping to pay the school fees of the poorer classes of children, and defraying the entire school expenses of those who have no one else to pay for them."[33] By ensuring funding for the education of all children, the state could meet its obligation to provide universal access to education without directly *supplying* education (for instance, in the form of public schools).

Just as the right to food and the right to education oblige us to establish institutional arrangements that give everyone access to those goods, the right to health care obliges us to establish institutional arrangements that give everyone access to health care. And a basic income is one such arrangement: Cash gives people access to health care just as it gives them access to toothpaste, minivans, apartments, and other goods that are bought and sold. (Of course, someone can have access to health care without actually *consuming* health care; they might choose to spend their money on something else. Hold that thought—I'll return to it in Section 3.) To be clear, I don't take this point to vindicate a basic income. At this stage, I only want to show that recognizing a right to health care doesn't require us to take a further step and insist that the state must directly provide that health care. The question of whether to prefer a basic income or in-kind provision remains open. Let's turn to that question now.

2. A Basic Income Accommodates Diverse Health Care Preferences

My first argument for cash appeals to the diversity of people's opinions about (1) the right kind of health care to consume and (2) the right amount of health care to consume.[34] A system that simply gives people the money to buy the health care they want does a better job of respecting their preferences than a system that distributes a uniform package of health care to everyone whether they want it or not.

For one, citizens disagree about *what kind* of health care to consume. Consider how different people might want to treat diabetes. The typical approach would probably be to take a pharmaceutical like metformin. "Naturopaths" might prefer not to take a prescription drug and opt for a supplement like Berberine instead. Some citizens, like certain Christian Scientists, may forgo medical intervention entirely.

A national health care or insurance plan that only covers a standard list of treatments or prescription drugs like metformin will leave the Berberine-preferring naturopath and Christian Scientists unsatisfied. They could protest that this system treats them unfairly—their interests have not been given the same consideration as (e.g.) those of the citizen who prefers the prescription drug. We might imagine Nate the naturopath objecting, "I'm a good citizen just like metformin-preferring Meg. We both pay our taxes, respect the law, and so on. So why does the state accommodate *her* health care preferences but not mine? It's not fair!"

Alternatively, the state could distribute the revenue that would otherwise have funded the system of in-kind provision directly to citizens themselves. Each of the three patients could then purchase the treatment of their choice. Everyone wins. Citizens who receive cash instead of in-kind health care may still use their cash to buy the health care the state *would have* provided. Meg, who wants to treat her diabetes with metformin, can still buy metformin. So receiving cash makes her no worse off, while it makes those with preferences that *wouldn't* be satisfied with the state's health care package better off. For instance, Nate the naturopath can now acquire the Berberine that he would not have received otherwise. A Christian Scientist who forgoes medical science receives little to no benefit from the state's in-kind provision of health care, but a basic income would provide her with re-sources that can actually contribute to her conception of the good. In short: Fewer citizens have grounds for complaint against a basic income than in-kind provision.

You might think that naturopaths and Christian Scientists are exceptional cases because of their unusual beliefs and it's unfair to criticize in-kind provi-sion for failing to include a handful of outliers. In reply, I'll first note that the naturopath is not as unusual as you might think. Roughly one-third of American adults use some form of "complementary" health care, including yoga, massage therapy, guided imagery, acupuncture, gingko biloba, ginseng, and so on.[35] That's a significant portion of the population.

What's more, consider that people who agree on the *ends* of medical care can sensibly disagree about the best *means* to those ends. Suppose Ann and Dan reject naturopathy. They both believe that the aim of medical care is to restore people to "species-typical normal functioning."[36] They both accept the efficacy of "Western medicine" and are happy to make use of it. Dan, however, buys into the adage that an ounce of prevention is worth a pound of cure, so he opts for a higher-cost, higher-quality diet to avoid getting diabetes in the first place. Ann, on the other hand, will gladly skimp on her food budget so long as she can get metformin if she becomes diabetic. With a basic income, Dan can spend more on kale and Ann can spend more on pharmaceuticals.

The point applies to preventive measures other than diet too. Stress and fa-tigue are bad for your health, so you might decide to free up more time for relax-ation and sleep by spending money "outsourcing" domestic labor (e.g., you hire someone to clean your house and subscribe to a meal delivery service). You could also spend money on personal trainers, gym memberships, dumbbells, and so on. While a system of in-kind provision could undoubtedly make some of these options available, even the most flexible system of in-kind provision is no match for the flexibility of cash.

Even people who agree about what kind of health care is best may neverthe-less disagree about *how much* health care to consume. For instance, risk-tolerant entrepreneurs might consume little in the way of medical care to save money to invest in their startup. On the other hand, people who are very risk-averse like me will prefer lots of medical care and thus happily forgo consumption of other goods to lower their health risks. (I wouldn't say I'm *neurotic*, but I do walk slowly around tables with particularly sharp corners.)

The broader point is this: What makes for a good life for you depends in part on the particulars of who you are. To borrow from Peter Railton, our good must be something that we are "cut out for."[37] Different people are cut out for different lifestyles, and different lifestyles require different levels of health care. If Picasso is debating whether to spend his surplus income on a paintbrush or marginally better health care, he may decide that the money is better spent on the paint-brush. If an aspiring Olympian is debating whether to spend her surplus income on nicer painting supplies or marginally better health care, she may decide that the money is better spent on the health care. As Mill writes, "A man cannot get a coat or a pair of boots to fit him, unless they are either made to his measure, or he has a whole warehouseful to choose from: and is it easier to fit him with a life than with a coat, or are human beings more like one another in their whole physi-cal and spiritual conformation than in the shape of their feet?"[38]

As noted, even the most flexible systems of in-kind provision will never be as flexible as cash. Suppose Dan's lifestyle requires $3,000 worth of medical care and $5,000 worth of education, whereas Ann needs $5,000 worth of medi-cal care and only $3,000 worth of education. It's hard to see how administrators working in Washington, DC, could know about the different priorities of indi-vidual citizens like Dan and Ann and tailor the system to satisfy them both. With a cash system, they don't need to: They can just give Dan and Ann $8,000 each and let them buy what they want.

Those citizens who prefer the exact quantity of health care that the state would have provided in kind are no worse off for having cash; they can simply purchase their desired quantity of health care. Crucially, though, people who want more or less health care than the state would have provided may buy more or less; thus, they're better off for having cash. Once again, we see that fewer citizens will have grounds for complaint against a basic income than a system of in-kind provision.

3. Is a Basic Income Too Risky?

Here's a worry about replacing the in-kind provision of health care with a basic income: People might put their health (or even lives) at risk by not buying enough health care.

As an initial reply, let me point out that it is perfectly reasonable to accept health risks, even serious ones, for the sake of money. You might worry about the entrepreneur who risks her health for the sake of business success by channel-ing her basic income into a startup rather than medical care. But note that she makes the same tradeoff as the entrepreneur who risks her health for the sake of business success because she works sixteen-hour days getting her startup off the ground. Although we might not find that lifestyle appealing for ourselves, we can recognize that it suits people with certain personalities and goals.

Perhaps my reply is fine as far as it goes, but there are limits. It's fine not to optimize your health at all costs, but we can't let people risk their *lives* in their pursuit of money. This view can't be right either. You could have spent thousands of dollars upgrading your used Chevy to a new, ultra-safe Volvo that reduces your chances of dying in a crash, but that's probably too expensive. A number of jobs involve choosing to risk one's life for extra income. Coal miners, commer-cial fishers, and long-haul truckers, for instance, are potentially deadly jobs that people work for the sake of a bigger paycheck. I suspect most would agree that the choice to work as a trucker need not be irrational, despite its risks.

We might also have altruistic reasons that justify the decision to trade health for cash. For example, a patient may justifiably decide to cease expensive life-saving treatment so they can leave a larger inheritance for their family. And consider that evidence suggests that a $2,500 donation to the Malaria Consortium is enough to save a person's life.[39] If anything, we'd applaud Ann for halving her $5,000 health care budget so she can spend $2,500 saving a life. But she wouldn't have this option if the state simply offered her $5,000 worth of medical care or insurance in kind.

You might be skeptical because my examples are rather grand and not representative of how most people would spend their money. Citizens are more likely to forgo health care to spare money for movie tickets or a vacation than an investment or anti-malarial drugs. And it's tempting to think that risking your health so you can afford an Alaskan cruise is irrational.

However, we trade off health for the sake of recreational value all the time and no one bats an eye. You could ruthlessly weed out every grain of sugar and white flour from your diet to optimize your health, but you don't because pie is delicious. You could hop off your couch and do pushups during commercials, but come on, let's not go nuts. Dermatologists recommend that you apply sunscreen if you're indoors but sitting near a window. You should also use it underneath your clothes if aren't wearing SPF-protective clothing. And don't forget to reapply every two hours if you're in the sun (every *hour* if you've been sweating). If you don't take these precautions, you're risking sun damage. Still, most of us don't take most of these precautions because doing so is sufficiently inconvenient. I don't think this decision is irrational.

It isn't even uncommon for people to risk *death* in the pursuit of activities that others consider to be trivial—for instance, riding a motorcycle or stock car racing. Even something as mundane as driving across the country to see the Grand Canyon puts your life at risk—you could die or suffer a serious injury in a car crash. You can die as a result of getting liposuction.[40] Climbing Mount Everest for the thrill of it can be deadly too. The point is this: At first blush, it might seem irrational for someone to buy an exciting vacation instead of more medical care. But many people make the same tradeoff between safety and recreational value in other contexts and we find it perfectly acceptable.

Note also that citizens can make risky decisions about their health care consumption even when the state provides health care in kind. Whether the state runs its own national health service or simply distributes cash, it is only making health care resources available to its citizens. In both cases, it's up to citizens themselves to take advantage of these resources. Presumably the committed naturopath who assiduously avoids pharmaceuticals and a Christian Scientist who refuses standard medical treatment won't use the options offered by (e.g.) Medicaid either. Indeed, there are probably plenty of citizens who don't take advantage of medical care simply because they find going to the doctor or taking pills inconvenient. Even if the state provides abundant health care free at the point of delivery, there will be citizens who make risky decisions about their health.

Before moving on, let me discuss one more concern. Citizens who choose not to buy health insurance may find themselves regretting their choice and wanting emergency medical care at a hospital after, for instance, suffering a serious accident.[41] I support the practice of providing such urgent care, which raises the worry that its costs will fall on taxpayers or non-profit hospitals. To address this problem, the state could mandate that citizens purchase some minimum level of health care coverage from private insurers (think of car insurance mandates). Alternatively, the state could offer a (refundable) tax credit for buying a minimum level of health insurance and place the fiscal burden of supplying emergency care for the uninsured on the shoulders of the uninsured themselves.[42] Each proposal has advantages and disadvantages; however, what's crucial for present purposes is that neither proposal puts the state in the business of providing a uniform package of health care in kind in the way that, for instance, national health insurance or national health care services do.

4. Worries About Distribution

Perhaps a basic income disadvantages the poor and those with costly preexisting medical conditions. The cash supplement that is enough to ensure that the middle-class architect can afford adequate medical care will not be enough for someone living below the poverty line. Similarly, the cash supplement that's sufficient for a generally healthy citizen may not be sufficient for a citizen with costly preexisting conditions even if they earn identical amounts. In short, distributing equal cash payments to citizens still allows for vastly unequal health outcomes.

In reply, I'll appeal to the "keyhole solutions" approach that is sometimes advocated by economists.[43] The idea here is simple: Employ policy solutions that target problems as directly as possible. If the problem is that some people won't have enough money to afford adequate medical care, then the keyhole solution is to give them more money. That is, the state can distribute different amounts of cash to different citizens depending on their income and health. This proposal solves the distribution worry while preserving the advantages of a basic income.

To address the poverty objection, the basic income can follow a simple rule: The poorer you are, the more money you receive.[44] From the perspective of distributive justice, this system would almost certainly be an improvement over existing forms of in-kind health care provision. By way of example, the U.S. government spends about $600 billion per year on Medicare.[45] Only 16% of the Medicare-receiving population is eligible due to a disability; the rest are eligible because they are at least sixty-five years old.[46] However, senior Americans are the country's *wealthiest* age group; indeed, their real household income is rising at a significantly higher rate than other groups.[47] So the U.S. government is spending hundreds of billions of dollars to buy health care for many comparatively rich Americans who can afford to simply buy it themselves. These expenditures do little to address the problem of poverty; the state would do far better to take those funds and distribute them to those who have less.

Along the same lines, if the problem is that someone doesn't have enough money to buy coverage for an expensive preexisting condition, then the keyhole solution is to give them more money. In these sorts of cases, citizens could apply for subsidies to help them pay their higher health care costs. Well-designed policies tend to allow exceptions for exceptional cases. And it's not as though allowing exceptions is a radical proposal, either—in fact, it's a component of many existing entitlement programs. For instance, while U.S. citizens are not normally eligible for unemployment benefits if they quit their jobs, exceptions can be made if they quit with good cause.[48] You can receive expedited SNAP benefits if you meet certain conditions.[49] The current U.S. health care system also allows for plenty of exemptions.[50] Thus, it's feasible that the state could design a basic income that makes extra income available to those whose health care needs call for it.

5. Conclusion

In summary, a state that provides citizens with cash instead of health care is better for some and worse for none. Those who prefer the health care package the state *would* have provided can use their additional income to buy it; those who prefer something else can buy that. A basic income respects citizens' own judgments about the quality and quantity of health care that's right for them to a greater degree than a system of in-kind provision. That citizens may choose to purchase less health care than the state would have provided is not a strike against a basic income. What's more, the state can address concerns about inequality by varying the amount of income it distributes to citizens. Thus, I conclude that the case for cash stands.[51]

COMPREHENSION QUESTIONS

1. Why is cash better than headphones in the employee bonus example?
2. What is the difference between an unconditional and a conditional basic income? Why might a government choose to employ one or the other?
3. How does a right to health care compare to a right to food or education?
4. Why would fewer citizens complain about a basic income rather than in-kind provisions?
5. Why might we not want to be governed so as to minimize risk-taking behaviors?

DISCUSSION QUESTIONS

1. If citizens have a right to health care, does the state have an obligation to provide it? Or is it sufficient to establish and support institutions that give everyone access to care?
2. Do you think cash payments can account for different preferences in individual health care choice? How does this model take unforeseen catastrophic illness and injury into account? Should a citizen be allowed to opt out of payments for life-saving treatments? Why or why not?
3. According to Freiman, cash payments provide the most flexibility in offering desired goods and services to individuals. Do you think health care is reducible to all other goods and services available for purchase? Why or why not?
4. Given the options of a national health care system that provides and administers services, or a private system with monetary compensations available from the state, which do you think would offer the most equitable approach to citizens?

Case 2

Consider this excerpt from a review of Jessica Flanigan's *Pharmaceutical Freedom*:

> Most academic philosophers live in a world of pharmaceutical paternalism: new treatments are subject to premarket approval by State regulatory agencies, and patients will only be able to access them through medical prescription. Outside academic philosophy, there has been a long tradition of pharmaceutical libertarianism, advocating for allowing patients to take their risks with experimental treatments without State or medical interference. Precisely because this tradition has had almost no philosophical echo, Jessica Flanigan's *Pharmaceutical Freedom* was a necessary book. Its broad claims and intuitions are not new. The real originality lies in the thorough examination and defence of the right to self-medicate from the standpoint of contemporary moral philosophy.
>
> Flanigan grounds her arguments on the patient's authority in knowing what will promote her overall well-being and in deciding what to do, with an original twist: she shows that supporters of informed consent should also endorse self-medication, as it is based on the same foundations. She criticizes regulatory paternalism for failing to adequately protect public health: informed self-medication could do better. Moreover, pharmaceutical regulators "wrongfully kill patients by withholding access to investigational drugs," until they are approved. Drug prescription is equally objectionable for restricting the right to die, the right to use recreational drugs, the right to self-enhancement and the right to use pharmaceuticals for non-medical reasons. Flanigan defends that patients should "develop drugs outside the formal mechanisms of the approval process, disobey pharmaceutical regulations, and protest existing policies" (p. 165), even if they do not have the support of a majority of voters ("biased against rights of self-medication"). If, at this point, you are wondering whether pharmaceutical companies do have any particular moral obligation towards patients, Flanigan defends that it is an industry like any other: there is no reason to expect that they provide affordable products. Pharmaceutical marketing (e.g., direct to consumer advertising) should be deregulated, such as any other instance of paternalistic health regulation. Tort law provides enough defence for pharmaceutical consumers to stand against any industry misdeed.*

Does Freiman's argument lend support for Flanigan's position? If so, is this a feature or a bug? (That is, if Freiman's argument *does* support Flanigan's, then is Flanigan's position plausible, such that this is a good thing, or implausible, such that we have a reason to reject Freiman's argument?)

---

*http://metapsychology.mentalhelp.net/poc/view_doc.php?type=book&id=8053

REPLY TO FREIMAN
SAM FLEISCHACKER AND SHERRY GLIED

We're pleased to see Christopher Freiman conceding that "people do have a right to health care,"[52] and that that right entails an obligation, on the part of society, "to establish institutions that give everyone access to adequate health care." In turn, we have granted that these claims "leave open the question of which *specific* institutions" ought to be established. A right to health care can be realized in many ways, and markets, rather than any direct provision of health care by the state, can be a useful instrument for the realization of that right. The point of calling health care a right is simply that it is then something that the state must make sure *is* available to its citizens, should the private sector fail, adequately, to provide it.

That said, we have grave doubts about the efficacy and fairness of Freiman's wholly market-based proposal for ensuring adequate health care for all. To begin with, we reject his analogy between a choice of headphones and a choice of health care. Headphones are a paradigm example of a discretionary good, not something the possession or lack of which could affect a person's entire capacity to lead her life. The analogy also misses a fundamental economic point: Most people today simply cannot afford the care that would benefit them if they had the misfortune to become very ill, either unexpectedly or because of a preexisting health condition (which might have been present at birth). Almost all people can afford such care only if they hold some form of public or private, explicit or implicit insurance coverage. That means that the relevant decisions in this context are not about which health care services people choose to *use*, but about which health care services an *insurance contract* should cover.

Once we move away from purchasing specific services to purchasing insurance, there are two substantial challenges in treating decisions about health care as if they were decisions about headphones. First, Freiman agrees that, regardless of their decisions, people should receive life-saving care when they need it. The promise of life-saving care at public expense, however, may lead some people, even people who can readily afford it, to forgo buying insurance coverage for services that the public will provide for free. They might also choose to forgo coverage for services that might reduce the risk or cost of requiring such free services. It's that logic that has led many libertarians to advocate for an individual mandate for health insurance that includes, at the very least, essential life-saving services.[53] A collective decision to provide life-saving care must constrain individual decisions about what coverage to purchase.

Second, insurance markets are highly interdependent. Each person's decisions about what to include in that person's insurance coverage affects the coverage available to others. For example, if people who believe that they are at very low risk for a condition choose to buy insurance that doesn't cover the cost of treating that condition, then the cost of insurance that does cover that treatment will be much higher. Insurers may not be willing to sell insurance that covers the treatment at all, anticipating that those who choose it are very likely to know that they will require it. This kind of behavior in insurance markets, known as adverse selection, can make it impossible for people who are born with or develop a condition that predictably requires costly treatment to obtain coverage for it. And if people cannot buy coverage for the treatment, they cannot obtain it, rendering arguments about free choice meaningless. So, to make health care a meaningful right, the scope of coverage that is guaranteed to everyone must include a comprehensive list of services, including services that many people may never anticipate using.

We close with an analogy to replace Freiman's headphone giveaway. Suppose your town has recently spent a lot of money investigating claims of corruption and abuse that various people have made against its officials and police. The new mayor comes up with what he thinks is a modest proposal: Any citizen who gives up the right to complain about public officials will get paid a substantial sum of money (equivalent, let us say, to half the cost, per citizen, spent on the investigations).

Would you take this offer? Some people surely would. "I live a quiet and decent life," they say to themselves, "so why do I need a right to free speech?" Or they simply value immediate and certain cash over a distant risk.

But of course if they do find themselves defrauded or beaten by a corrupt or abusive official, or accused wrongly of a crime, they are likely to regret their choice deeply and wish they had never been allowed to make it. If they are impoverished or jailed or seriously injured, they are also likely to bring harm not only on themselves but on others—their family, especially. Finally, their giving up their rights to free speech will affect the community at large. If some citizens cannot speak freely about corrupt or abusive officials, that puts everyone in greater danger of suffering at these figures' hands.

For all these reasons, the mayor's proposal would almost certainly be struck down by American courts: The right to free speech, about political wrongdoing at least, cannot be sold. In calling for health care to be treated as a right, we are arguing that something similar should hold of it. After all, your giving up health care in favor of other, less necessary goods has all the consequences of the sale of free speech rights. If you do get gravely ill, you will likely regret your choice and wish it had not been an option. You are also likely to harm other people besides yourself—your family, especially. And the fact that you decide not to pay into the pool by which health care is provided will affect the options available to everyone else in your community— making health care, indeed, unaffordable for some of your fellow citizens.

So we can leave the provision of headphones entirely up to the free choices of individuals, but we can't do that with health care. Since health is a condition *for* choice, rather than simply a result of it, leaving it up to the market alone imposes costs that can in the long run deprive many people of their ability to choose freely at all.

COMPREHENSION QUESTIONS

1. What is a discretionary good, and why do Fleischacker and Glied reject Freiman's "headphones to health care" analogy?
2. What's the difference between individuals purchasing services and what insurance contracts choose to cover?
3. Why do Fleischacker and Glied compare health care to protecting free speech?

DISCUSSION QUESTIONS

1. How does a collective decision to provide life-saving care affect the health care choices of individuals? If emergency care is guaranteed, should citizens be required to have insurance available to cover the cost of unforeseen emergency care?

2. Fleischacker and Glied argue that access to health care is like access to free speech, and general protections should be in place to keep these liberties safe. People should not be able to risk their health any more than their access to free speech. Do you think these are equivalent liberties or freedoms? If not, what's the difference?

REPLY TO FLEISCHACKER AND GLIED
CHRISTOPHER FREIMAN

As I was reading Fleischacker and Glied's terrific chapter, I began to realize we do not disagree to the extent that one might have anticipated. What matters on their view is ensuring that everyone has access to adequate health care. This means, as Fleischacker and Glied put it, "The extent of government action taken to secure a right to health care might be relatively narrow, and might proceed largely via markets rather than taking the form of a bureaucratic agency . . ."

That said, there are points of disagreement. For instance, Fleischacker and Glied argue that we can justify a right to health care by an appeal to freedom. Being sufficiently healthy is a condition for making use of one's freedom to engage in political activism, deliberate about personal choices without overwhelming stress or anxiety, and so on. A guarantee of access to health care is therefore required to ensure that citizens can live freely.

My argument, by contrast, focused on ensuring people's satisfaction with their allotment of resources. Although this is a significant philosophical difference, I won't pursue it here because we can still agree at the level of policy. A basic income is superior to in-kind provision even if you take Fleischacker and Glied's approach to justifying the right to health care: More citizens will be able to effectively exercise their freedom with a basic income than with health care provided in kind.

To see why, consider a simple case. Bill has a severe chronic illness and high health care costs. He has the spare time—but not the good health—to engage in political activism, unburdened deliberation of his options, and so on. A state that directly provides Bill with health care in kind would enable him to make effective use of his freedom. So far, so good for in-kind provision.

Now consider Jill. Jill is in terrific health and has minimal health care costs, but she has no spare time. The in-kind provision of health care does little to advance her ability to exercise her freedom. What she needs is more time, a problem that more health care doesn't solve. However, distributing cash directly to Jill *does* solve the problem. By enabling her to outsource jobs like lawn mowing, cooking, and home repair, a basic income frees up her schedule so that she can, for instance, attend a protest. In-kind provision enables Bill but not Jill to exercise her freedom, whereas a basic income enables them *both* to exercise their freedom. So even if your preferred standard is freedom rather than satisfaction, you ought to prefer a basic income.

Someone working within Fleischacker and Glied's framework might worry that distributing cash alone will allow citizens to buy too little health care.

For instance, they note that merely providing people with life-saving emergency care is not sufficient to enable them to be free. Thus, citizens with cash in hand—and perhaps constrained only by a requirement to buy *minimal* health care coverage—may not purchase as much health care as they need to live freely.

However, this concern is not a deal breaker for the basic income even on Fleischacker and Glied's terms. Remember that their aim is to provide *access* to health care, not to compel consumption of health care. Both in-kind provision and a basic income provide access to health care; neither one guarantees that citizens will make use of it. As I noted in my original piece, citizens supplied with health care in kind might nevertheless decide not to see a doctor or follow their doctor's orders. States may secure the conditions that enable people to live freely, but the choices that citizens make within those conditions are up to them.

COMPREHENSION QUESTIONS

1. Consider the Bill/Jill example. Why does Freiman think a basic income is better even if your preferred standard is freedom rather than personal satisfaction?
2. How does access to health care differ from consumption of health care?

DISCUSSION QUESTIONS

1. Even if access to health care is available, some people will choose not to use these resources. Do you think this is exercising a choice toward personal satisfaction, or potentially limiting one's future personal freedom through poor allocation of resources?
2. What is the difference between protecting people's freedoms and promoting their satisfaction? How could a basic income offer protections to personal freedom and well-being? What risk does giving cash rather than providing services pose, and how does Freiman address these concerns? Do you agree or disagree with his conclusions? Why or why not?

FURTHER READINGS

Bergthold, L. A. "Medical Necessity: Do We Need It?" *Health Affairs* 14, no. 4 (1995): 180–190.

Daniels, Norman. *Just Health Care.* Cambridge: Cambridge University Press, 1985.

Emmonds, William. "Long-Term Income and Wealth Gains Favor Older Americans." Federal Reserve Bank of St. Louis. October 5, 2017. https://www.stlouisfed.org/on-the-economy/2017/october/long-term-income-wealth-gains-favor-older-americans.

Fox, H. B., and M. A. McManus. "A National Study of Commercial Health Insurance and Medicaid Definitions of Medical Necessity: What Do They Mean for Children?" *Ambulatory Pediatrics* 1, no. 1 (2001): 16–22.

Friedman, Milton. *Capitalism and Freedom.* Chicago: University of Chicago Press, 2002.

Heymann, J., A. Cassola, A. Raub, and L. Mishra. "Constitutional Rights to Health, Public Health and Medical Care: The Status of Health Protections in 191 Countries." *Global Public Health* 8, no. 6 (2013): 639–653.

Mill, John Stuart. "On Liberty." In *The Basic Writings of John Stuart Mill*, edited by Dale Miller. New York: Random House, 2002.

National Center for Complementary and Integrative Health. "Use of Complementary Health Approaches in the U.S." https://nccih.nih.gov/research/statistics/NHIS/2012/key-findings.

Oregon Health Evidence Review Commission. *Prioritized List of Health Services*. Salem, 2018. https://www.oregon.gov/oha/HPA/CSI-HERC/PrioritizedList/4-1-2018%20Prioritized%20List%20of%20Health%20Services.pdf.

Railton, Peter. "Facts and Values" in *Facts, Values, and Norms*. New York: Cambridge University Press, 2003.

NOTES

1. Norman Daniels, *Just Health Care* (Cambridge: Cambridge University Press, 1985), 5.
2. See Daniels, *Just Health Care*, Chapter 3, and Norman Daniels, "Is There a Right to Health Care, and, If So, What Does It Encompass?" in *A Companion to Bioethics*, edited by H. Kuhse and P. Singer (Oxford: Blackwell, 2009 [2nd edition]).
3. Note that the *kind* of right to health care that can be justified under Rawls's theory may be more expansive than the kind of health care right that can be justified on grounds of freedom alone. We accept that limitation, at least for the purposes of this essay.
4. This may be one reason why Adam Smith argues for public education as a proper task of government in Part V of his *Wealth of Nations*.
5. See Elizabeth Anderson, "What Is the Point of Equality?" *Ethics* 109, no. 2 (1999): 287–337, for this relational conception of egalitarianism.
6. See Philip Petit, *Republicanism*, (Oxford: Oxford University Press, 1999), Chapters 1-2.
7. See Gareth Stedman Jones, *An End to Poverty* (London: Profile Books, 2004), for an argument to the effect that rights to welfare were originally conceived by their advocates, in the late eighteenth century, as conditions for equal citizenship. Fleischacker discusses Stedman Jones's argument, and proposes an alternative, more straightforwardly liberal reading of the late-eighteenth-century history he discusses, in his "A Right to Welfare: Historical and Philosophical Reflections," in *Distributive Justice Debates in Political and Social Thought*, edited by Camilla Boisen and Matthew Murray (New York: Routledge, 2016).
8. For a wonderful account of Roosevelt's "Second Bill of Rights" speech of 1944, and its legacy in Supreme Court decisions of the 1960s, see Cass Sunstein, *The Second Bill of Rights* (New York: Basic Books, 2004).
9. Compare Sunstein, *Second Bill of Rights*, p. 162: "[T]he Court's reference to the 'blessings of liberty,' a phrase from the preamble of the Constitution, suggested in Rooseveltian fashion that welfare benefits were central to both freedom and citizenship."
10. This is Sunstein's argument in *Second Bill of Rights*, Chapter 9.
11. Powell, majority opinion in *San Antonio School District v. Rodriguez* (1973). Internal quotation from *Dandridge v. Williams* (1970). Accessed online at findlaw.com, on August 8, 2018.
12. All fifty state constitutions mandate the creation of a public education system. In many states, this mandate is framed as a right to education. Since the 1960s, courts in many states have built on these state constitutional requirements to enforce a right to a quality education for children within the state. We are grateful to Richard Briffault for input on this issue.

13. O. Moriarty, E. B. McGuire, and D. P. Finn, "The Effect of Pain on Cognitive Function: A Review of Clinical and Preclinical Research," *Progress in Neurobiology* 93, no. 3 (2011): 385–404.
14. Oregon Health Evidence Review Commission, *Prioritized List of Health Services*, Salem, 2018, https://www.oregon.gov/oha/HPA/CSI-HERC/PrioritizedList/4-1-2018%20 Prioritized%20List%20of%20Health%20Services.pdf.
15. Oregon Health Services Commission, "Prioritization of Health Services. A Report to the Governor and the 77th Oregon Legislative Assembly" (Salem: Office for Oregon Health Policy and Research, Oregon Health Authority, 2013).
16. Oregon Health Services Commission, "Prioritization."
17. See *Katz v. US*, decided in 1967, in which the Court decided that wiretapping did constitute a Fourth Amendment violation (overturning an earlier case, *Olmstead v. U.S.*, decided in 1928, which held that wiretapping did not constitute a violation of the Fourth or Fifth Amendment). As regards the Fourth Amendment, see also *Kyllo v. U.S.* (2001), on whether the use of thermal imaging technology to detect marijuana plants counts as a "search," and *Carpenter v. U.S.* (2018), which granted Fourth Amendment protections to cellphone records. On technology and the First Amendment, see M. Ethan Katsh, "First Amendment and Technological Change: The New Media Have a Message," *George Washington Law Review* 57 (1988): 1459.
18. J. Heymann, A. Cassola, A. Raub, and L. Mishra, "Constitutional Rights to Health, Public Health and Medical Care: The Status of Health Protections in 191 Countries," *Global Public Health* 8, no. 6 (2013): 639–653.
19. L. A. Bergthold, "Medical Necessity: Do We Need It?" *Health Affairs* 14, no. 4 (1995): 180–190; H. B. Fox and M. A. McManus, "A National Study of Commercial Health Insurance and Medicaid Definitions of Medical Necessity: What Do They Mean for Children?" *Ambulatory Pediatrics* 1, no. 1 (2001), 16–22.
20. Oregon Health Services Commission, "Prioritization."
21. A related, but slightly different, potential concern is that extending rights (whether negative or positive) has spillover effects on other people and their various rights. Either your right to free speech or my right to protection of property is limited if you mean to shout your views from a rooftop using a megaphone at 3 a.m. If there is a right to at least some health care, new external effects are similarly introduced, because individual decisions about engaging in behavior that raises health risks (such as smoking, excessive drinking, or skiing) can also affect the pocketbooks of other citizens. There are several potential responses to this issue. The external effects could be ignored. The government could subsidize strategies to reduce risk (such as subsidies for smoking cessation programs). It could impose taxes on risky behavior (such as taxes on soda). Depending on system design, it could also charge higher health insurance premiums (or taxes) to those who engage in certain behaviors (as the Affordable Care Act does for smokers). From a fiscal perspective, while individual health behaviors are very important to individual health, their effects on lifetime costs are modest: Jan J. Barendregt, Luc Bonneux, and Paul J. van der Maas, "The Health Care Costs of Smoking," *New England Journal of Medicine* 337, no. 15 (1997): 1052–1057; David B. Allison, Raffaella Zannolli, and K. M. Narayan, "The Direct Health Care Costs of Obesity in the United States," *American Journal of Public Health* 89, no. 8 (1999): 1194–1199. Engaging in risky health behaviors leads to ill health, which does raise immediate medical costs, but it also leads to premature death, offsetting these costs over the life cycle. The counterbalancing effects of immediate versus lifetime costs mean that, at the population level, even universal, government-provided health insurance is not

a highly redistributive social policy: S. Glied, "Health Care Financing, Efficiency, and Equity," in *Exploring Social Insurance: Can a Dose of Europe Cure Canadian Health Care Finance?* edited by C. Flood, M. Stabile, and C. Tuohy (Montreal: McGill-Queen's University Press, 2008).

22. J. L. Saver, E. E. Smith, G. C. Fonarow, M. J. Reeves, X. Zhao, D. M. Olson, and L. H. Schwamm, "The Golden Hour and Acute Brain Ischemia: Presenting Features and Lytic Therapy in Over 30,000 Patients Arriving Within 60 Minutes of Onset." *Stroke* 41, no. 7 (2010), 1431.

23. Regardless, also, of immigration status.

24. J. M. Stieber and L. J. Spar, "EMTALA in the '90s—Enforcement Challenges." *Health Matrix* 8 (1998): 57.

25. S. B. Cohen and W. Yu, *Statistical Brief #354: The Concentration and Persistence in the Level of Health Expenditures over Time: Estimates for the US Population, 2008–2009* (Rockville, MD: Agency for Healthcare Research and Quality, 2012).

26. S. Glied, *Chronic Condition: Why Health Reform Fails* (Cambridge, MA: Harvard University Press, 1997).

27. Ian Duncan, Michael Loginov, and Michael Ludkovski, "Testing Alternative Regression Frameworks for Predictive Modeling of Health Care Costs," *North American Actuarial Journal* 20.1 (2016): 65–87; Liran Einav, Amy Finkelstein, Sendhil Mullainathan, and Ziad Obermeyer, "Predictive Modeling of US Health Care Spending in Late Life," *Science* 360, no. 6396 (2018): 1462–1465.

28. Sherry Glied and T. G. McGuire, "To Maintain Quality, Risk Adjustment Is Essential, Even in Incentive-Compatible Contracts: A Response to Cannon," 10.1377/ hblog20180124.703715; Benjamin R. Handel, Igal Hendel, and Michael D. Whinston, *The Welfare Effects of Long-Term Health Insurance Contracts*. No. w23624. National Bureau of Economic Research, 2017.

29. For more information, see "List of Medicaid Benefits," Medicaid.gov, accessed January 11, 2018, https://www.medicaid.gov/medicaid/benefits/list-of-benefits/index.html.

30. See "Health Care," Congressional Budget Office, accessed January 11, 2018, https://www.cbo.gov/topics/health-care.

31. More specifically, I believe that people have a right to the resources they need to achieve an adequate level of well-being, resources that can include health care.

32. John Stuart Mill, "On Liberty," in *The Basic Writings of John Stuart Mill*, edited by Dale Miller (New York: Random House, 2002), 110.

33. Mill, "On Liberty."

34. This section borrows arguments from an unpublished manuscript that I have co-authored with Nathan Ballantyne titled "How to Make Liberties Worth Something."

35. See National Center for Complementary and Integrative Health, "Use of Complementary Health Approaches in the U.S.," accessed January 11, 2018, https://nccih.nih.gov/research/statistics/NHIS/2012/key-findings.

36. On health care and "species-typical normal functioning," see Normal Daniels, "Health-Care Needs and Distributive Justice," *Philosophy and Public Affairs* 10, no. 2 (Spring 1981): 153.

37. See Peter Railton, "Facts and Values," in *Facts, Values, and Norms* (New York: Cambridge University Press, 2003), 64.

38. Mill, "On Liberty," 69–70.

39. "Your Dollar Goes Further Overseas," Givewell.org, accessed January 11, 2018, https://www.givewell.org/giving101/Your-dollar-goes-further-overseas.

40. For an extended discussion of this sort of case, see Jessica Flanigan, *Pharmaceutical Freedom* (New York: Oxford University Press, 2017), 9–10.

41. Thanks to Bob Fischer for pressing this concern.

42. On a tax credit as an alternative to a mandate, see John Goodman, "It's Time to Repeal Obamacare's Individual Mandate," *Forbes,* November 20, 2017, https://www.forbes.com /sites/johngoodman/2017/11/20/its-time-to-repeal-obamacares-individual-mandate /amp/.

43. On "keyhole solutions," see, e.g., Bryan Caplan and Vipul Naik, "A Radical Case for Open Borders," in *The Economics of Immigration,* edited by Benjamin Powell (New York: Oxford University Press, 2015), 202–204.

44. Milton Friedman's negative income tax is an example of this sort of policy. See Milton Friedman, *Capitalism and Freedom* (Chicago: University of Chicago Press, 2002), 191–194.

45. "HHS FY 2017 Budget in Brief—CMS—Medicare," U.S. Department of Health and Human Services, accessed January 11, 2018, https://www.hhs.gov/about/budget /fy2017/budget-in-brief/cms/medicare/index.html.

46. Juliette Cubaniski, Tricia Neuman, and Anthony Damico, "Medicare's Role for People Under Age 65 with Disabilities," The Henry J. Kaiser Family Foundation, August 12, 2016, https://www.kff.org/report-section/medicares-role-for-people-under-age-65-with -disabilities-issue-brief/#endnote_link_195198-2.

47. See William Emmonds, "Long-Term Income and Wealth Gains Favor Older Americans," Federal Reserve Bank of St. Louis, October 5, 2017, https://www.stlouisfed.org /on-the-economy/2017/october/long-term-income-wealth-gains-favor-older-americans.

48. As an example, see Virginia's policy at "FAQ's—General Unemployment Insurance," Virginia Employment Commission, accessed January 11, 2018, http://www.vec.virginia .gov/faqs/general-unemployment-insurance-questions#a124.

49. As an example, see Illinois's policy at "Emergency SNAP Benefits," Illinois Department of Human Services, accessed January 11, 2018, http://www.dhs.state.il.us/page .aspx?item=31767.

50. See "Health Coverage Exemptions, Forms and How to Apply," Healthcare.gov, accessed January 11, 2018, https://www.healthcare.gov/health-coverage-exemptions/ forms-how-to-apply/.

51. I'm grateful to Jessica Flanigan and Bob Fischer for helpful comments on a draft of this paper.

52. All quotes in this paragraph from Freiman's essay earlier in this chapter.

53. S. M. Butler, "A Tax Reform Strategy to Deal with the Uninsured," *Journal of the American Medical Association* 265, no. 19 (1991): 2541–2544; S. Coate, "Altruism, the Samaritan's Dilemma, and Government Transfer Policy," *American Economic Review* 85, no. 1 (1995): 46–57.

CHAPTER 10

Abortion

ABORTION
CHRIS TOLLEFSEN

In this essay, I argue that abortion is morally impermissible and that the state should take steps to restrict abortion by legal means. The moral argument proceeds in three steps: I argue that you and I and other readers of this essay are human beings, and thus unless we are the product of monozygotic twinning or human cloning, we began as one-celled human organisms. Second, I argue that all human beings possess fundamental rights against being attacked, damaged, or destroyed intentionally. Third, I address Judith Jarvis Thomson–style arguments that argue that the death in abortion need not be intended but only a side effect of a detaching and expulsion of the fetus. The conclusion of the argument shows that abortion, understood either as direct killing or unjust detaching, is always wrong. It also shows that, in the relevant sense, unborn human beings are persons, since persons just are those beings with rights not to be intentionally killed or treated unjustly. In conclusion, I argue that the fundamental purposes of the state include the protection of the lives of all persons within its borders from intentional or unjust killing. Thus, abortion should be considered a public, not a private, wrong, and the state has an obligation, in keeping with its fundamental purposes, to protect the lives of unborn human beings.

1. What We Are

We sometimes think and talk about ourselves as if we are souls or minds who happen to possess, for a time, a living body. We might say, for example, that were we to suffer from dementia we would "not be there anymore." In part, this way of talking reflects reasonable recognition of humans' remarkable capacity for thinking and choosing—of the mindedness that seems to distinguish humans from the other animals.

Despite its broad appeal, this form of *dualism* is misguided, and you, the reader, can see that it is so simply by paying attention to your direct experience.

340

Right now, as you read these words, you are engaged in a sensory act, making use of your eyes and your hands and oriented in space toward the physical realities of words on a page (paper or electronic), or perhaps you are listening with your ears to sound vibrations in the air as the recorded book is read to you. These are all acts of a bodily being, and specifically of the organism who is sitting, or reclining, or walking (with ear buds) here and now. But you, the reader, are also following an *argument*, a chain of thought, that makes use of abstract terms such as "organism," and "abstract" and "thought." These are all the acts of a *minded* being, a being capable of intellection. But *you* are "both" those beings, as evident by your use of the word "I": "I am seeing these words on the page, and I am understanding them." Thus, the minded being that you are is the same being as the physical, living organism that you are. It is one and the same being who reads and understands, sees and cognizes, moves and abstracts. *You* are that living organism, that human being.[1]

2. When We Began

But if that is true, then *you* came into existence whenever the living organism that is reading this book did. There was not first a living human organism and then you, as might be possible if you were a mind (or even a brain); rather, your existence began with the existence of the human animal reading or listening to this book right now.

So, when did you begin? The answer, if you aren't an identical twin or human clone, is simple: You began at fertilization, when a human sperm penetrated an oocyte and both ceased to exist, giving rise instead to a single-celled zygote. This zygote was itself a single, whole, individual member of the species *Homo sapiens*, genetically distinct from its parents, and possessed of a developmental program by which it was able to be the executive of its own growth and development to the next stage of human existence: the embryonic stage, then the fetal stage, then the infant stage, and so on.

The best evidence for this claim comes directly from the science of embryology and the authority of those who study human development and the development of other organisms, such as mice. Consider the following representative passage from K. L. Moore and T. V. N. Persaud's textbook, *The Developing Human: Clinically Oriented Embryology*:

> *Human development begins at fertilization* when a male gamete or sperm (spermatozoon) unites with a female gamete or oocyte (ovum) to produce a single cell—a zygote. This highly specialized, totipotent cell marked the beginning of each of us as a unique individual. The zygote, just visible to the unaided eye as a tiny speck, contains chromosomes and genes (units of genetic information) that are derived from the mother and father. The unicellular zygote divides many times and becomes progressively transformed into a multicellular human being through cell division, migration, growth and differentiation.[2]

There are two philosophical arguments often made against this claim that a human organism comes into existence at fertilization, but both arguments are flawed. First, some have claimed that because the early embryo is capable of twinning, it therefore can't be considered *one* individual organism. Underlying this argument must be the claim that something potentially two can't be one. But no one who has ever snapped a stick in half could believe that. Nor, in the domain of living things, are microbiologists tempted to believe that amoebae, which reproduce precisely by splitting, weren't individual organisms prior to splitting. Similarly, the phenomenon of twinning doesn't suggest that the zygote or embryo wasn't a human organism prior to twinning. Rather, it indicates that *some* human beings came to exist later than fertilization, namely, when an embryo divided, resulting in two embryos where once there was only one.

The second argument holds that the zygote (or early embryo) doesn't have sufficient unity within itself to be considered a living *whole*. This line of argument sees the early embryo as merely an aggregate (a "clump") of cells. This claim too is problematic. What could cause this mere aggregate to become *one thing*? Indeed, the transition of numerous cells into a single organism several days *later* than fertilization must be seen as a metaphysically implausible event with no explanation. Moreover, embryologists find an enormous amount of activity, much of it coordinated, among the various parts of the developing embryo, activity oriented toward ensuring the embryo's survival and growth. And this coordinated activity isn't the same in all cells. Rather, embryologists observe division of labor among the cells even of the very early embryo, and from the first cell division the roles of some cells can be distinguished from the roles of others. In consequence, biologists do not consider the embryo to be a mere heap or aggregate of undifferentiated cells.[3]

I have just defended two claims, that you and I are animal organisms, and that human organisms begin at fertilization; both concern the way things *are*. They are not yet claims about ethics, about how we ought to act in light of the way things are. Yet I have said enough to demonstrate a foundational fact: Abortions destroy the lives of actual, living, human beings.

3. Full Moral Worth and Respect

I turn now to the moral question. The question of abortion is concerned with whether it is morally permissible to kill certain human beings, namely, the unborn. Could it be that as a class the unborn are excluded from the moral protection that is owed to you, the reader, and me, the author? Might it be that such protection is owed only to a subset of human beings? Here I offer an argument in response to this question.

It is clear that the lives of the readers and author of this essay are protected by a general norm against killing: You and I are thought to be owed a form of respect that is simply incompatible with being killed for reasons such as our inconvenience, our gender, or whether we are wanted by another. But what grounds that immunity?

A reasonable answer, which certainly could be worked out in further detail, is this: You and I are beings of a profoundly special sort. We are both rational, that is, capable of reasoned reflection, and free, capable of choices not determined by anything other than the very making of the choice itself. Our possession of those two powers can be said to be the foundation for our dignity, and to entitle us to treatment always as an end in ourselves, and never merely as a disposable means, to be eliminated for the sake of another's good.

Killing a being like you or me is thus radically contrary to the dignity that we possess, as it would be in relation to any other being like us in the relevant respect: like us, that is, in possessing the powers of reason and freedom. But what kind of being is *that*?

It is, we should hold, any being that possesses *by its nature* the capacity to develop itself to the point of being able to engage in acts of reason or choice. But it would be a mistake to think that such a being must have *already* developed to the point of being able to reason and choose, or that it even be a being that *will* in fact so develop. Either view would, in fact, sanction infanticide, the former because newborns aren't *yet* able to reason and choose, the latter because a victim of infanticide would never *in fact* develop to that point. So instead, we should judge that what suffices is that it be a being whose nature it is to eventually be able to reason and choose.

Now no being comes to be able to actively exercise such powers unless it has them from the beginning of its existence—without change of nature, something not possessing these powers as *radical* potentialities simply could not develop them. And so we—you and I and all other beings like us—must have had these powers from the moment we came into existence. And accordingly, since we came into existence at conception (or slightly later if we are an identical twin), we possessed these radical powers right from the beginning of our existence.

Thus, we can judge that the norm against killing, grounded as it is on respect for a creature's dignity, protects *all human beings*, born and unborn, against attacks on their lives. Of course, that norm must be properly understood; it does not prohibit everything that *leads to death*, for that norm couldn't be followed: What would we do in a situation in which whatever we chose, a mother *or* an unborn child would die? "Ought" implies "can," so our norm governing killing must be able to be followed. So the norm must be specified: All human beings, born and unborn, are protected against *intentional* killing—that is, killing as a means or as an end. Such killing is always and everywhere morally impermissible. This is a norm we could always follow, for in the worst-case scenario, we could simply refrain from acting, thus avoiding all intentional killing.

So this argument leads to the conclusion that *no one* should ever intentionally damage or destroy the life and health of an unborn human being. Abortion, understood as the intentional killing of an unborn human being, is always and everywhere morally impermissible.

4. Abortion and Intention

I argued in the previous section that abortion, insofar as it involves intentional killing, is morally wrong. But must abortion always involve *intentional* killing? In this section, I briefly address a famous attempt by Judith Jarvis Thomson to justify abortion by arguing that it *need not* involve intentional killing. I argue that in most cases abortion does involve intentional killing, and that abortion for the sorts of reasons envisaged by Thomson would be wrongful even if the death of the unborn wasn't intended.

Thomson begins by noting that much of the debate surrounding abortion concerns whether the unborn human being is a *person*. Those who oppose abortion, she writes, typically "spend most of their time establishing that the fetus is a person, and hardly any time explaining the step from there to the impermissibility of abortion."[4] Meanwhile, "those who defend abortion rely on the premise that the fetus isn't a person, but only a bit of tissue that will become a person at birth."[5] In contrast, for the purposes of her argument, Thomson grants that the fetus is a person, and then asks whether abortion is indeed impermissible on that assumption. This is one of the great innovations of her article, and one reason it has gained such acclaim.

At this point, the reader might be struck by the fact that I didn't spend any time on the question of "personhood," but rather on the question of whether the fetus is a human being (a question elided in Thomson's contrast of "person" with "bit of tissue"). That the fetus is a human being I have shown to be a matter of settled science. Pro-choice thinkers such as Peter Singer agree with this point, conceding that it is obscurantist to deny that the fetus is a human being (what else would it be?). Unlike Singer, however, I hold that it is wrong to intend the death of any human being, whereas Singer, and many others, hold that those human beings who don't possess certain qualities—the qualities of "personhood"—may be killed justifiably.

In much bioethics, particularly that part dealing with the question of abortion, the language of "personhood" is invoked only in order to distinguish which, among all human beings, are those that don't deserve (because they aren't *persons*) the respect we generally owe to other human beings, including the respect of not killing them. But my argument, unlike those Thomson was aware of, doesn't *start* with the idea of "person" but, in a sense, *ends* with it, for the personhood of the embryo or fetus *follows* from the conclusion that embryos and fetuses are never to be intentionally killed, if we understand "person" to refer to those beings that are understood to deserve the most robust moral protections.

But, again, Thomson is interested in presenting an argument for abortion that concedes this claim—that fetuses, as human beings, should not be killed *intentionally*. To do so, she presents the reader with the following scenario: You wake up to find you have been abducted by the Society of Music Lovers, and medically attached to a famous, unconscious, and ill violinist. He needs the use of your kidneys for nine months to survive his disease; if you detach yourself from him, he will certainly die.

Thomson believes that the average reader will intuit that it would still be permissible to detach, and in the situation as described, I agree that this is a plausible analysis. Must I, by detaching, intend the death of the violinist? It seems not. Rather, I might reasonably intend to avoid the burdens of attachment. His death is thus an unintended (though foreseen) side effect of my choice to unplug.

Of course, not all side effects are permissibly accepted: Side effects must be avoided if they would be unjust burdens on others, as when a factory owner poisons—not intentionally, but as a side effect—those downstream from his factory, as part of a money-saving initiative. So is my detachment an injustice to the violinist? Not necessarily. In Thomson's scenario, the violinist has no real moral claim on me—I was abducted, after all—and so it doesn't seem unjust for me to detach, in order to avoid a nine-month involuntary confinement forced upon me by someone with no connection to me. So the death isn't intended, and there seem good reasons to accept it as a side effect, given the situation as described by Thomson.

But is elective abortion (i.e., abortion not performed to protect the life of the mother) really like this? It seems rather that the great majority of such abortions aren't like this at all. Most who seek abortion do so because they do not want, or don't feel they are ready, to be a mother. However understandable these desires are, they make clear that in such cases the woman's intention includes the death, not merely the "disconnection," of the fetus, for the fetus must die in order to prevent it from developing into a baby to which the woman is the mother. After all, if the baby lives, then even if he or she is given up for adoption, the woman will always be the biological mother of that child. It is that permanent connection that many women are trying to avoid.

Moreover, while Thomson believes that her argument only supports disconnection from (or, more realistically, expulsion of) the fetus, others have argued that the constitutional right to abortion in the United States entails a right to the *death* of the fetus, lest the right to abortion be whittled away by improvements in technology that make it possible to sustain fetuses outside the womb at earlier and earlier stages of pregnancy, or the right be forfeited in cases of botched abortions that produce live births.[6]

Suppose, however, that some abortions aren't like this. Imagine a woman who would readily permit her fetus to be removed to an external form of life support (assuming, for the moment, that this could be done without imposing disproportionate burdens on her), but who seeks detachment merely to avoid the burdens of providing the fetus further "womb room" or sustenance. In such a case, however uncommon, detaching the fetus wouldn't involve intentional killing, and the death of the unborn child would be a side effect. Could such an abortion then be morally permissible?

Not, I think, in the kinds of cases Thomson has in mind. Note first the differences in the kind of relationship the reader has to the violinist, compared with the relationship a woman who is seeking an abortion has to the fetus within her. In the former, it may make sense to talk only of "the woman" and "the violinist," but in the latter, it also makes sense to talk of "the mother" and "her child." The mother–child relationship is quite unlike the relationship between the victim and the violinist in Thomson's example, even when the mother didn't desire the relationship and even, as in the tragic case of rape, when the relationship has been forced upon her through the criminal actions of another. We are animal organisms, and mother and child share a biological relationship that is real and, because those biological beings are persons, also personal, even if it isn't desired.

This claim may strike some as extreme, even offensive, and certainly a woman who seeks abortion after suffering sexual violence may be less blameworthy than one who seeks abortion after sexual intercourse in which she freely engaged. Moreover, it is clear that when abortion is chosen to end a pregnancy that follows consensual sex, the man often bears as much responsibility (and, in some cases, more) for the abortion as does the woman.

The point here isn't to distribute blame, but to clarify that, contrary to what Thomson's hypothetical would suggest, biological relationships can *create* obligations, even if those obligations haven't been voluntarily *accepted*. Children, for example, never choose their biological parents, and yet it seems that children nevertheless have obligations to their parents that they don't have to others. Biological relations matter, morally, even though they aren't chosen. The same might be seen if Thomson's violinist scenario were changed only a little: Were you to learn that the violinist is your long-lost child, or long-lost sibling, then it is unlikely that your intuitions would be so solidly in favor of detaching; indeed, some readers might become solidly in favor of the opposite.

Those biological relationships, and the innocent dependence of the child upon the mother, suggest very strongly that it would be unjust for the mother to detach and expel the fetus in a way that it isn't unjust to detach the violinist. Ordinary duties of a mother to her child imply that the child's death can't be reasonably accepted as a side effect for anything less than a very serious reason.

So abortion, when it involves mere detachment, and no intentional killing, is also typically impermissible, because it is unjust to the child who loses his or her life in the detachment. Is this judgment about Thomson-style detachment cases as absolute as is the judgment about intentional killing? No, for it is possible to imagine situations in which detachment *is* permissible, namely, situations in which both mother or child will die if nothing is done, but the mother's life can be saved by detaching and expelling the fetus. Such a case surely involves no injustice, since the mother's life isn't being privileged over the child's. So we may conclude in this way: Abortion, understood as intentional killing of an unborn human being, is *always* morally impermissible, and abortion, understood as expulsion and detachment of an unborn human being, is *almost always* morally impermissible.

5. Abortion, Privacy, and the State

The arguments of the previous sections make clear that abortion isn't merely a *private* matter. One recourse of those who would defend abortion is to claim that arguments against it are a matter of "personal" (often religious) beliefs, not public or professional concern. Note, however, that the key premises that I have drawn upon to assess the morality of abortion—that human beings begin at fertilization, and that all human beings have the right to not be killed at will—are neither esoteric nor a matter of religious revelation. Rather, these are claims of human reason accessible to all. The first is a claim of science, the second a claim of the moral law known by reason. That moral law makes it possible for the public to recognize and defend human rights, and to evaluate particular practices, as well as explicit policies and laws, as to whether they are just or unjust.

But abortion is a public matter in a further crucial sense. What are the fundamental purposes of our most public institution, the state? Those purposes seem to include doing justice, and providing equal protection to all persons within the state's boundaries against intentional attacks upon their lives and liberty. The legitimacy of a state is founded upon its public commitment to these purposes and its success in achieving them.

Thus, when a polity excludes from the scope of its legal concern the lives of some human beings within its legal boundaries, that damages both its publicly expressed commitment to justice and equality and its success in achieving them. Widespread permission, acceptance, and practice of abortion is thus a public wrong that it erodes the core requirements for a state's legitimacy. Abortion is thus a profoundly public matter, and indeed, a profoundly public wrong, one that any just and upright state has a foundational responsibility to prevent.

COMPREHENSION QUESTIONS

1. When does a human life begin, and why is this important to Tollefsen's argument?
2. What is moral worth? What two qualifications are necessary to designate moral consideration?
3. How does Tollefsen support his claim that protection against intentional killing should begin at conception?
4. How does Tollefsen challenge Thomson's defense of abortion, specifically the violinist example?
5. Why does Tollefsen propose that abortion is a public rather than private concern?

DISCUSSION QUESTIONS

1. If society has general norms against intentionally killing human beings, do you think this norm ought to extend to the unborn—those who have the potential to develop into fully functioning human beings? Why or why not?
2. Why might someone think that familial relationships challenge the violinist example? Do you think we have special obligations to those to whom we are biologically related?
3. How should a person's intentions be factored into the abortion conversation? Is there a difference between protecting your own right to life by disconnecting from the violinist or aborting a fetus, and intentionally killing a person who requires moral consideration? Whose right to life has greater authority: an autonomous being or one who is dependent upon another?

Case 1

Consider the introduction to an article in the journal *Contraception*:

> On any given day in Cuernavaca, Cape Town, Quezon City or Calcutta, a woman with an unwanted pregnancy seeks out misoprostol to have an abortion. She does not visit a doctor or clinic but seeks a pill that she has heard can help her end her pregnancy without the risks of more dangerous self-induction methods. Women living in legally restricted settings where they do not have access to high-quality safe services or where stigma, cost or other barriers prevent them from accessing existing services are increasingly using misoprostol to self-induce abortion instead of using sticks, acid, brute force or unproven herbal remedies. In doing so, they are significantly reducing the harms caused by unsafe abortion.
>
> Harm reduction is an evidence-based public health and human rights framework that prioritizes strategies to reduce harm and preserve health in situations where policies and practices prohibit, stigmatize and drive common human activities underground. The best-known application of a harm reduction model is in the field of HIV, where needle exchange programs and safe injection centers have been shown to be highly effective in preventing HIV/sexually transmitted infection. We propose that promoting the use of misoprostol for abortion using a harm reduction approach could dramatically increase access to safer abortions. The principles of harm reduction — neutrality, humanism and pragmatism — present a conceptual framework for making misoprostol information and care available directly to women and make the case for why it is imperative that we do so.*

You may or may not share the authors' views about the importance of promoting the use of misoprostol (often called "miso"). But set that issue aside. How does the prospect of (relatively) safe medication-based abortion affect our assessment of the ethics of *banning* abortion? It seems irrelevant to the ethics of *getting* and *performing* abortions, but it might be relevant to lots of other issues, such as the costs and risks that bans impose on women, as well as the odds of effectively preventing abortions by making them illegal.

---

*Alyson Hymana, Kelly Blanchard, Francine Coeytaux, Daniel Grossman, and Alexandra Teixeira, "Misoprostol in Women's Hands: A Harm Reduction Strategy for Unsafe Abortion," *Contraception* 87 (2013): 128.

EARLY AND LATER ABORTIONS: ETHICS AND LAW
NATHAN NOBIS

Introduction

"Liberals," or people on or toward the "the Left," tend to be pro-choice about abortion. They tend to believe that, legally, women should be *at liberty* to have abortions, if they want, and so abortions should be legal. Here, I support this view.[7]

My emphasis won't be on the law, but on the ethics of abortion.[8] I argue that at least early abortions—affecting first-trimester or earlier fetuses—are not wrong. Since most abortions are early abortions, I address the ethics of most abortions. Since morally permissible behavior should not be criminalized, at least most abortions should be legal. I do argue, however, that probably all abortions should be legal, even if any later abortions are wrong.[9]

1. Defining Abortion

I propose this initial definition of abortion:

> An abortion is the intentional killing of an embryo or fetus to end a pregnancy.

Abortions are *intentional*. If a pregnancy ends because of an accident, the women did not "have an abortion." Miscarriages are called "spontaneous abortions," but these are not deliberate actions that can be morally evaluated.

Some object to the word "killing," thinking that "termination" is better. But if we think through what this "termination" is, we see that it involves taking something biologically alive and making it not alive, or killing it.

Some people are uncomfortable with this: They react that "Killing is wrong!" and so wonder if abortion should be understood as involving killing. This reasoning overlooks, however, that killing isn't always wrong: Indeed, it is often completely permissible. It's not wrong at all to kill mold, bacteria, vegetables, or tumors. These aren't even prima facie wrong to kill, meaning, *no good reason at all is needed to justify this killing*. This isn't in any way to compare human fetuses to any of these things: It just makes the point that, since killing often isn't wrong at all, defining abortion in terms of killing is not problematic.

Some understand abortion as the killing of an unborn *baby* or *child*. While people are free to use the words "baby" and "child" however they'd like, people *can* misuse words. And this seems to be a misuse of words. *Early* fetuses have none of the relevant, perhaps essential, characteristics of babies. We could ask, "What are babies like?" and use people's responses to make a list of core baby characteristics: cute, cuddly, soft, having a certain smell, can cry, can be happy, sad, or angry, needy, and so on. Early fetuses aren't like that. A visual (Figure 10.1) helps show that it is a stretch to call an embryo or early fetus a "baby" or "child."

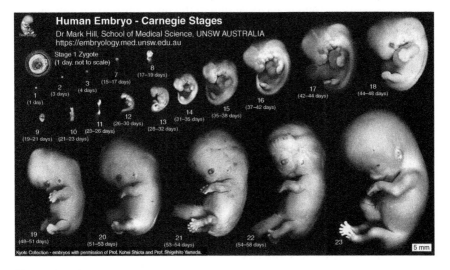

Figure 10.1

The Carnegie stages of the human embryo. Image used with kind permission of Brad Smith of the Multi-Dimensional Human Embryo Project at the University of Michigan (http://embryo.soad.umich.edu/index.html).

In sum, defining abortion as the intentional killing of an embryo or fetus to end a pregnancy is accurate, informative, and morally neutral—all that we want a definition to be.

2. Arguments, Not Circumstances

People sometimes begin discussing abortion by asking questions about abortion in particular circumstances: "*What if* it's needed to save the mother's life?" "*What if* the pregnancy is from rape?" "*What if* there are severe fetal abnormalities?" and so on. Or they begin by stating circumstances where they think abortion is wrong or not: "It's wrong if used for 'birth control'," "It's not wrong if the woman is too young to be an effective mother," and so on.

These starting points are fine, *if*—but *only if*—these statements are supported, or questions answered, with reasons. Our concern is *arguments*, the reasons given for and against specific conclusions about abortion, such as that:

Abortion is:

- (nearly) always morally wrong.
- (nearly) always morally permissible, or not wrong.
- wrong, except in these circumstances: ____.
- permissible, except in these circumstances: ____.
- sometimes morally obligatory, or wrong to not have, such as in these circumstances: ____.

People sometimes offer moral claims about abortion "in general," without being precise about which abortions they have in mind. But the details matter: Depending on the stage of fetal development and the woman's circumstances, different moral conclusions may be appropriate.

Some people also want to focus on important, but comparatively rare, abortions: for example, of pregnancies from rape (perhaps 1% of abortions) or incest.[10] Our initial focus will be on more common circumstances where for a variety of *other* reasons, a woman is pregnant but does not want to have a child (or another child, now). After this, we will discuss other important, but less common, circumstances.

We can immediately set aside circumstances, though, where the woman would die if her pregnancy continues, and so the fetus will die also, or we *must* choose between the mother and fetus. Even people who generally oppose abortion typically argue that we should save one life instead of losing two lives and prioritize the mother, not the fetus. Their view, then, is not that abortion is always wrong, but that it is wrong in *most circumstances*, or prima facie wrong.

Whether this specific conclusion, and any other, can be supported with good arguments is our concern.

3. Question-Begging Arguments

Many arguments about abortion are bad. Sometimes this is because they "beg the question," or *assume* the argument's conclusion as a premise. Question-begging arguments against abortion assume that abortion is wrong or that fetuses are wrong to kill; question-begging arguments in favor of abortion assume that abortions are not wrong or that fetuses are not wrong to kill. This is circular reasoning and must always be dismissed.

Sometimes it's obvious why an argument is question begging ("Abortion is wrong because abortion is not right"); other times reflection is needed. Here are some question-begging arguments for the permissibility of abortion:

Abortion is not wrong because:

(1) Abortion is *a personal choice.*
(2) Couples *should be able to* make that choice.
(3) Women have *a (moral) right* to have abortions.
(4) Well, if you don't *like* abortions, then don't have one!

These all seem to assume that abortion is not wrong.

About (1), we would never say that choices to commit arson or kidnapping are "personal choices." Dying your hair or quitting piano lessons, however, *are* "personal choices." "Personal choices" are *choices that are not wrong* to make. Saying that abortion is a "personal choice" *assumes* that abortion is not wrong, as does claim (2).

Regarding (3), *sometimes* when people assert that they have a "right" to do something, they are merely saying that it's not wrong to do that something. That assumption begs the question. (If they explain *why* women have such a right, the argument might not be question-begging.)

Response (4) is a slogan, not an argument, that assumes that abortion is not wrong. Imagine someone said, "Don't like *vandalism? Don't vandalize!*" "Don't like stealing? *Don't steal!*" This would be absurd because these actions are wrong. Response (4) assumes abortion is not wrong.

Here are a few question-begging arguments against abortion:

Abortion is wrong because:

(1) Abortion is *murder.*
(2) There are morally *better* options than abortion, like adoption.
(3) If a woman gets pregnant, she just *must* have the baby.
(4) Women who have abortions are *irresponsible.*
(5) A *good person* wouldn't have an abortion.
(6) Women who have abortions feel *guilty.*

These all *assume* that abortion is wrong:

(1) "Murder" means "wrongful killing," so (1) says that *killing fetuses is wrong* because *it's wrongful killing.*
(2) This assumes that abortion is a bad or undesirable option: It *may be,* but we can't just *assume* that.
(3) This asserts that women *must not* have abortions, which is to say that it's wrong.
(4) "Irresponsible" people don't do what they are *supposed to do,* so (4) assumes that abortions are wrong.

(5) This assumes that abortion is wrong and so a good person wouldn't do it.

(6) Some women feel guilty after abortions, but many do not. And just because someone feels guilty for doing something does not always mean they have done wrong: There is "false guilt." (Someone *not* feeling guilty does not show that they did not do anything wrong either!) It only shows that they *believe* they have done wrong, which doesn't mean that they really have done wrong. (6) assumes abortions are wrong.[11]

We now turn to non–question-begging arguments. If any are bad, it's for other reasons.

4. Arguments Against Abortion

A case *for* anything depends on the case *against* it being weak. Showing that there's no good reason to think that most abortions are wrong is important for showing that most abortions are permissible.

We only have space to discuss some of the most important arguments against abortion. Each claim below is given as a reason to believe that that fetuses have the right to life, or have other characteristics that make them prima facie wrong to kill, and so abortion is prima facie wrong:

- "Fetuses are human, biologically."
  Reply: Yes, but a random blob of *biologically human* cells or tissues is not prima facie wrong to kill. A malignant tumor isn't wrong to kill, and if there were somehow an independently beating human heart, it wouldn't be wrong to stop that heart.
- "We were once fetuses; there is *continuous development* from fetuses to us. Since we have rights now, we've had them at every stage of our existence."
  Reply: Our having some characteristic or right *now* does not mean we had it *then*. Most of us can walk, talk, think, feel, and make decisions but fetuses cannot, even though we developed from them. Continuous development does not, in itself, support thinking that fetuses are prima facie wrong to kill.
- "Fetuses are *human beings* or organisms."
  Reply: This claim is that fetuses are not merely biologically human, but that they are whole *beings* or *organisms*. This is true, but why would this make them wrong to kill?
  Some respond that this is obvious, since *it's just plain wrong to kill human beings*. This is not obvious, however, since embryos and beginning fetuses are human beings that are quite different from most human beings like us: They lack consciousness, cannot feel, think, perceive, or experience any of the types of things that typical born human beings can. Arguably these are important differences, since psychological or mental characteristics are what *make* us wrong to harm and kill, and early fetuses lack them.

In thinking about human beings, who likely comes to mind are human beings with whom we interact on a daily basis. We don't think about *human beings* who are born without most of their brains (anencephalic newborns, who die soon after birth) or *human beings* who have permanently lost all consciousness due to serious brain injury.

These human beings should be treated respectfully, but they can also be treated in ways that would be wrong to treat "normal" human beings: letting their bodies die and, perhaps, (actively) killing them. This is sometimes not wrong because their being alive is no value *to them* anymore: They permanently lack or have lost consciousness, awareness, and feeling.

Early fetuses are human beings but have not developed what makes life valuable: consciousness, awareness, feeling, and other features of a mental life that allow for relationships, activities, learning, and everything else that makes life worthwhile. They lack this; they are merely biologically alive; and so it is arguably prima facie permissible to kill them.

- "Fetuses are persons."

Reply: Everyone can agree that persons have the right to life, or are prima facie wrong to kill, but who or what is a person? What *makes* something, or someone, a person?

Some claim that fetuses are *persons*, from conception or soon after, and so they are prima facie wrong to kill. Others deny that fetuses are persons, especially early fetuses. These disputes sometime lead to shouting and violence, with different sides merely insisting on their definition. There are more rational ways to help determine the *essence* of personhood, however, by thinking about what *makes* us persons. Consider this:

> We are persons now. Either we will always be persons or we will cease being persons. If we will *cease* to be persons, what can end our personhood? If we will *always* be persons, how could that be?

Both options give insights into personhood. Many people think that their personhood ends at death or if they were to go into a permanent coma: Their body is (biologically) alive, but the *person* is gone.[12] And if we continue to exist after the death of our bodies, what continues to exist? The *person* (perhaps even without a body!). Both responses suggest that personhood is defined by a rough and vague set of psychological or mental, rational, and emotional characteristics: consciousness, knowledge, memories, and ways of communicating, all psychologically unified by a unique personality. A second activity supports this understanding:

> Make a list of things that are definitely not persons. Make a list of individuals who definitely are persons. Make a list of imaginary or fictional beings that, if they existed, would be persons: these beings that fit or display the concept of person, even if they don't exist. What explains the lists?

Rocks, carrots, cups, and dead gnats are clearly not persons. *We* are persons. Science fiction gives us ideas of non-human persons. Even though non-human characters from, say, *Star Wars* don't exist, they fit the concept of person: We can befriend them, work with them, and so on, and we could only do that with persons. A common idea of God is that of an immaterial person who has exceptional power, knowledge, and goodness. Are conscious and feeling animals, like chimpanzees, dolphins, cats, dogs, chickens, pigs, and cows, more relevantly like us, as persons, or are they more like rocks and cabbages, non-persons? Sentient animals seem to be closer to persons than not. So, this classificatory activity further supports a psychological understanding of personhood.[13]

Concerning abortion, early fetuses would *not* be persons on this account: They are not yet conscious or aware since their brains and nervous systems are either nonexistent or insufficiently developed. Consciousness emerges in fetuses much later in pregnancy, likely after the first trimester. This is after when most abortions occur (see below). Most abortions, then, do not involve killing a *person*, since the fetus has not developed the characteristics for personhood.

- "Fetuses are potential persons."
  Reply: If early fetuses are not persons, they are potential persons: They could, and would, become persons (and so they're not persons now). Abortion is wrong because of this, however, only if premises like these are true:

- Potential X's have the rights of actual X's, *or*
- Potential X's should be treated like actual X's.

But potential doctors, spouses, adults, judges, criminals, and so on never have the (moral or legal) rights of actual individuals of that kind, or should be treated like that. Arguments from potential are doubtful.[14]

- "Fetuses have valuable futures; they lose those valuable futures when aborted."[15]
  Reply: Don Marquis argues that in thinking about abortion, we should begin by understanding *why* it is typically wrong to kill "normal" human beings, and then attempt to apply our findings to abortion. He argues that the best explanation why it is typically wrong to kill *us* is that killing deprives us of our future good experiences, our valuable futures: If we are killed, we lose out on all the positive experiences, relationships, and accomplishments that we would have experienced. Inflicting this loss is profoundly wrong, unless done for a serious, justifying reason. Marquis thinks this explanation applies to fetuses: They have futures that they would experience, and abortion prevents them from experiencing those futures, so abortion is prima facie wrong.

While insightful, there is room for doubt. First, Marquis's explanation for the wrongfulness of killing is developed from examples where there is a *psychological connection* from the murder victim to her future: she is aware of her future and has hopes and plans for it. Fetuses don't have this *at all*. That's a potentially relevant difference, and so Marquis's explanation might not extend to fetuses.

Second, Marquis's argument might imply that contraception, even abstinence (!), is prima facie wrong. This objection begins with an abstract observation that there are single objects with multiple parts that do not touch: There is space between the parts. A dinette set is an example, but many physical items will do, since there are parts and there is some *space* between the parts, if we look closely enough. From here, we observe that there are eggs and *sperms-that-could-and-would-fertilize-those-eggs* all around us; some combinations of these are indeed *single things*, given the metaphysics above; some of these have valuable futures; and so contraception and abstinence are prima facie wrong, since they too prevent these (abstract) entities from experiencing their valuable futures. But since refraining from bringing these (abstract) individuals into actual existence is not wrong, something has gone wrong with Marquis's argument.

In sum, these are some of the most important arguments given against abortion.[16] More research and reflection is needed, but we *may* be able to reasonably reach some tentative conclusions about the case in favor of thinking that abortion is typically wrong.

5. Why Early Abortions—and So Most Abortions—Are Not Wrong

Consciousness and Ethics

If the arguments against abortion do not succeed, should we think that abortion is prima facie permissible? Almost. To fully reach that conclusion, we need some positive arguments in its favor.

Abortion debates often proceed with little factual information about fetuses or abortions. This is problematic: For any real-world ethical issue, we need to know the facts. Here is some relevant information:

- Fetal consciousness and pain:

  Most medical and scientific research finds that, at the earliest, fetuses likely become conscious and develop an ability to feel pain around the end of the second or beginning of the third trimester of pregnancy (24 weeks).[17]

- When abortions occur:

  The U.S. Centers for Disease Control and Prevention reports that "in 2014, the majority (67.0%) of abortions were performed at ≤8 weeks' gestation, and nearly all (91.5%) were performed at ≤13 weeks' gestation. Few abortions were performed between 14 and 20 weeks' gestation (7.2%) or at ≥21 weeks' gestation (1.3%)."[18]

  The Guttmacher Institute reports that two-thirds of abortions occur at eight weeks of pregnancy or earlier; 89% occur in the first 12 weeks (Figure 10.2).[19]

Figures in other countries should be investigated. But, at least in the United States, most abortions are done early in pregnancy, far before consciousness develops in the fetus.

WHEN WOMEN HAVE ABORTIONS*

Figure 10.2
When women have abortions

Two-thirds of abortions occur at eight weeks of pregnancy or earlier; 89% occur in the first 12 weeks, 2013

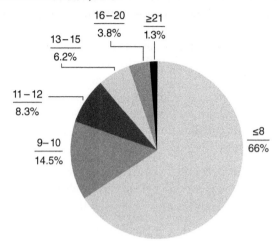

*In weeks from the last menstrual period.

This information is morally relevant because consciousness, or awareness, is the basis for all that is valuable and important for us. Death or a permanent coma is typically bad for us because our consciousness ends: *We* cease to be and nothing can go worse, or better, for us. Consider whether, when someone has permanently lost consciousness, there is any value *to that individual* in keeping his or her body alive: There is not. Pre-conscious, early fetuses are at the other end of this cycle. It's not that they haven't experienced what's of value: There is no *experiencer* of value: There is no one who is there, since a conscious individual does not yet exist.

Given these facts and quick philosophical thinking, here are three arguments in positive defense of abortion. First, a general argument from the absence of consciousness:

1. If something is not conscious and has never been conscious, then it is prima facie permissible to kill that thing.
2. Early abortions kill early fetuses that are not conscious and have never been conscious.
3. Therefore, abortions of early fetuses are prima facie permissible.

This general argument can be supported by more specific concerns. First, from concerns about *harm*:

1. To harm someone is to make them worse off, compared to how they *were*.

2. Early fetuses aren't made worse off by death: For a never-been-conscious being, nonexistence doesn't make it worse off, since it lacks a conscious perspective that can take a turn for the worse.[20]
3. So, killing does not make non-conscious beings worse off, or harm them.
4. Actions that don't harm anyone (or have a high risk of harm) are prima facie permissible.
5. So abortion is prima facie permissible.

Second, from the lack of personhood:

1. A person is a being who has at least *some* of the following: consciousness, awareness, thoughts, feelings, memories, anticipations, and so on: a mental life or mind.
2. If something is not conscious or sentient and has never been conscious or sentient, then it is definitely not a person.
3. Early fetuses are not conscious or sentient and have never been conscious or sentient.
4. So, early fetuses are definitely not persons.
5. It is prima facie permissible to kill things that are definitely not persons.
6. So, abortions of early fetuses are not wrong.

These arguments should be explained in greater detail, but the preceding discussion should help anyone understand why they might be considered sound. Let's quickly consider some questions about these consciousness-based arguments:

• "Does this mean that it's OK to kill sleeping people or comatose people?"
  Reply: No, these individuals were conscious: The sleeper will regain consciousness, and we hope the coma patient will too.
• "Does that mean 'more' conscious human beings have more rights or greater value than those with less, if that makes sense?"
  Reply: No. Why would anyone think that? We should think that *all* conscious human beings have basic rights and equal value.
• "Does that mean it'd be OK to kill someone who goes into a coma and awakens with a complete loss of all of her knowledge, memories, and personality?"
  Reply: No. If they awaken, they are conscious, and so prima facie wrong to kill. This would, however, be the start of a new person (in the same body!) if there is no psychological connection to the earlier person.

What this all suggests is that abortions, if done early in pregnancy, are prima facie permissible. This is true when abortions are sought for pregnancies resulting from rape or incest. It's also true when a woman seeks an early abortion for nearly any reason.[21] And since actions that are not wrong should not be criminalized, women should have the legal right to have abortions.[22]

The Right to Life

Some of the earlier arguments above can be seen as attempts to show that early fetuses have a right to life. They don't appear to succeed. Nevertheless, it's often assumed that if fetuses have the right to life, or are persons, abortion would be typically wrong. Judith Thomson has argued, however, that this common reasoning involves a false assumption about the right to life. Cases illustrate this:

- "You wake up in a hospital 'plugged into' a violinist, who is using your kidneys to filter his blood. You were kidnapped and put into this role. He will die without your assistance."
  Question: Does the violinist have a *right* to use your kidneys? No.
- "Your death will be prevented by the touch of your favorite celebrity on your forehead."
  Question: Do you have a *right* to that touch? No.
- "Your twin sibling will die unless *you* donate your kidney to her."
  Question: Does she have a *right* to your kidney? No.

These cases suggest that the (moral or legal) right to life is *not* a right to another person's body, even if that body is necessary to save one's life.[23] So fetuses do not have the right to their mother's bodies, even if they are persons with the right to life. So it is permissible for a pregnant woman to withhold what the fetus needs to continue living: That means that abortion, at least, does not violate rights and so may be not wrong. This insight augments the arguments above, and suggests an alternative definition of abortion:

> An abortion is the ending of a pregnancy by withholding the resources needed for the fetus to develop and be born.

Later-Term Abortions

Fortunately, abortions far later in pregnancy are rare. But when they occur, they kill conscious beings. Should later abortions be illegal?

No. According to information available on these types of abortions, they are nearly always done for very good medical reasons. Moreover, we don't want the (slow) courts interfering in these time-sensitive, complex medical decisions. So probably all abortions should be legal, even if any are morally wrong.[24]

6. Conclusion

Whatever one's politics, abortion is a momentous decision that determines, at least, whether a woman will continue a pregnancy and give birth and, usually, whether two people will be parents (or parents again). And there are, of course, the effects on the fetus. These are life-changing decisions that involve profound and intense emotions. These feelings seep into politics, but our task, as philosophical thinkers, is to examine passionate issues with a passion for thinking in calm, cool, careful, and critical manners. This passion for fact-finding, conceptual analysis, and argument evaluation should positively influence our other passions, as individuals and as a society.[25]

COMPREHENSION QUESTIONS

1. Is there a substantive difference between killing and "terminating" a fetus?
2. Why isn't killing always wrong?
3. What rare cases of abortion does Nobis set aside for this discussion? Why?
4. What are "question-begging" arguments? What's wrong with them?
5. Why does Nobis contend that early fetuses are not persons like us? What characteristics does he take to be important for personhood?
6. What distinction does Nobis make between early and late abortions? Why should all abortions be legally permissible even if some are morally wrong?

DISCUSSION QUESTIONS

1. A number of different definitions of "abortion" were offered in these readings. Which definition was best? Why? Are there other definitions that are better? Why?
2. You are a person. It's generally wrong to kill you. What is the *best* explanation of *why* you are a person or what *makes* you a person? What's the *best* explanation of why you are generally wrong to kill? Why are these explanations *best*? Do these explanations apply to any fetuses? Why or why not?
3. Judith Thomson argues that, *in general*, people do not have moral rights to other people's bodies, even if they need those bodies, or parts of those bodies, to stay alive. So, for instance, you wouldn't be violating someone's right to life if you didn't give them one of your organs that they need to stay alive. Do you agree or disagree? Why? And, more importantly, does anyone *ever* gain a moral right to someone else's body? Why? How?
4. Suppose technology will one day allow pregnant women to remove unwanted fetuses from their bodies and place them in "artificial wombs." If such technology existed, do you think that would make abortion wrong (or "more wrong," so to speak)? Or would abortions be permissible, even if this option existed?

Case 2

Here's the way the U.S. Supreme Court summarizes (part of) its decision in *Roe v. Wade*, the landmark abortion case:

> A state criminal abortion statute . . . that excepts from criminality only a life-saving procedure on behalf of the mother, without regard to pregnancy stage and without recognition of the other interests involved, is violative of the Due Process Clause of the Fourteenth Amendment.
>
> (a) For the stage prior to approximately the end of the first trimester, the abortion decision and its effectuation must be left to the medical judgment of the pregnant woman's attending physician.
>
> (b) For the stage subsequent to approximately the end of the first trimester, the State, in promoting its interest in the health of the mother, may, if it chooses, regulate the abortion procedure in ways that are reasonably related to maternal health.

Case 2 (continued)

> (c) For the stage subsequent to viability, the State in promoting its inter-
> est in the potentiality of human life may, if it chooses, regulate, and even pro-
> scribe, abortion except where it is necessary, in appropriate medical judgment,
> for the preservation of the life or health of the mother . . .
>   This holding, we feel, is consistent with the relative weights of the respec-
> tive interests involved, with the lessons and examples of medical and legal
> history, with the lenity of the common law, and with the demands of the pro-
> found problems of the present day. The decision leaves the State free to place
> increasing restrictions on abortion as the period of pregnancy lengthens, so
> long as those restrictions are tailored to the recognized state interests. The de-
> cision vindicates the right of the physician to administer medical treatment
> according to his professional judgment up to the points where important state
> interests provide compelling justifications for intervention. Up to those points,
> the abortion decision in all its aspects is inherently, and primarily, a medical
> decision, and basic responsibility for it must rest with the physician.*

Essentially, the Court thought it was important to balance the interests of those
who want abortions against a wide range of other considerations. That's why the
court didn't say that all abortions should be allowed, regardless of when they
might occur in pregnancy. Nobis doesn't tell us much about why all abortions
should be legal: He simply says that late-term abortions "are nearly always done
for very good medical reasons" and "we don't want the (slow) courts interfering
in these time-sensitive, complex medical decisions." Are these points sufficient to
show that a compromise position is mistaken (that is, a position that permits some
but not all abortions)? Why or why not? And if not, what would it take to show that
we *shouldn't* endorse a compromise position?

---

*https://supreme.justia.com/cases/federal/us/410/113/#164

REPLY TO NOBIS
CHRIS TOLLEFSEN

I'm pleased to offer a few thoughts in response to Nathan Nobis's essay defending
the moral permissibility of abortion. Let me start with something that I believe
we have in common, namely a commitment to reason in this area. Nobis says,
"Our concern is *arguments*, the reasons given for and against specific conclusions
about abortion," and I am in entire agreement.

I also agree with him about several of the arguments that he assesses and
finds wanting. I agree that many arguments on both sides are question-begging.
And some of the arguments he criticizes that are opposed to abortion also seem
problematic. For example, the claim that fetuses are biologically human is of little
relevance. Much more important is the claim that a human fetus is a human being,
and here we begin to reach the disagreements that exist between Nobis and myself.

Nobis agrees that human fetuses are human beings, and then writes, "but
why would this make them wrong to kill?" Nobis finds the reasons why it is impermissible to kill (some) human beings not in their humanity, but in the distinct
"psychological or mental characteristics" of beings like Nobis and myself. What

characteristics are those? They are *personal* characteristics; in a footnote, Nobis cites the list given by Mary Anne Warren, which includes:

"**1.** Consciousness . . . , and in particular the capacity to feel pain;
2. Reasoning . . . ;
3. Self-motivated activity . . . ;
4. The capacity to communicate . . . ;
5. The presence of self-concepts, and self-awareness . . ."

Since fetuses do not possess these traits, they are not persons; arguments that oppose abortion on the basis of fetal personhood thus are unsound.

Nobis extends this argument:

> Make a list of things that are definitely not persons. Make a list of individuals who definitely are persons. Make a list of imaginary or fictional beings that, if they existed, would be persons: these beings that fit or display the concept of person, even if they don't exist. What explains the lists?

Nobis says we will put "[r]ocks, carrots, cups, and dead gnats" on the one list, and you, me, Chewbacca, and God on the other. The classification, he believes, lends credence to the idea that personhood depends upon psychological states, and on this picture, sentient animals are closer to being persons than rocks; but fetuses are, apparently, farther away.

To me, the central question in this domain is this: Granted that you and I are persons, with moral immunities to unprovoked violence, enslavement, rape, and torture, and granted that these immunities should be extended to any beings like us in the relevant ways, what does "like us in the relevant ways" mean?

For Nobis, it means something "like us in being, right now, more or less capable of actualizing our powers of sentience, sapience, emotion," and so on. By that standard, dogs are more like us than human fetuses. But there is a way in which human fetuses are *vastly* more like us than *any* other creature of whose existence we are directly aware. Human fetuses—if they do not die, or are not otherwise impaired—will grow and develop naturally to the point of being able to exercise exactly the characteristics that impress Nobis (and me) so much. No other being of whose existence we are directly aware will *ever* do that, not even the brightest dolphin or ape.

That suggests that human fetuses and human adults are equally possessed of something that is not at all possessed by any other earthly being: a nature that is such that beings with that nature develop to the point of being able to actively display their rationality. Call that a "rational nature." That seems a radical commonality, the sort that should impress us when we are asking, "To which other beings like or unlike us in this or that way—bigger, smaller, darker, paler, younger, older—should we think that these immunities belong? Which other beings are like us in the relevant way?" Possessing a rational nature seems like the *most* important similarity to me.

Here is another reason for thinking this. Nobis raises what he thinks is a bad objection to his account: "Does that mean 'more' conscious human beings have more rights or greater value than those with less, if that makes sense?"

He answers, "No. Why would anyone think that? We should think that *all* conscious human beings have basic rights and equal value."

But here is an important feature of basic rights. Basic rights—such as the right against enslavement, torture, or rape—can be contrasted with rights such as the right to vote, or the right to drive. The former rights are held equally and, we think, inalienably by the beings who hold them. The latter rights are not so held: They can come in degrees, and they can be lost. This is not surprising: We find these rights dependent upon properties that are contingent, or variable in degree, or both: What state one is a citizen of is contingent; whether one is mature enough to drive is variable in degree. So you can have the right to vote in one place, but not another, and the right to drive a car but not a truck, or in the daytime but not in the nighttime, and so on.

We might expect, then, that "basic rights" should be dependent on properties that are *not* contingent and variable in degree. Being able to exercise rationality or being conscious, or feeling emotions, is clearly not like that, which is what leads to the objection. But being a human being, and having a rational nature, *is* a property that is necessarily held by all beings that possess it, and does not come in degrees. It is thus *the* appropriate grounding property for basic rights. And it is a property found in all human fetuses.

COMPREHENSION QUESTIONS

1. Why does Tollefsen want to begin with the fact that *we* are persons?
2. What is the difference between basic rights and contingent rights? Why is this important in understanding those rights that ought to be given to a fetus?

DISCUSSION QUESTION

1. Is it true that a fetus is vastly more like us than other fully formed or developing organisms? If so, is it true that beings who are vastly more like us than other organisms ought to receive full basic rights?

REPLY TO TOLLEFSEN
NATHAN NOBIS

I appreciate this opportunity to dialogue with Professor Tollefsen on the topic of abortion. I will note some controversies and concerns about his main argument. I hope these observations inspire further discussion of the issues.

1. Metaphysics
Tollefsen begins with some discussion concerning the *metaphysics* of "what we are" and "when we began."

What Are We?
Tollefsen argues that we are both minds *and* bodies: "The minded being that you are is *the same being* as the physical, living organism that are you . . . *You* are that living organism, that human being."

The claim isn't merely that we have minds and bodies. It's that we *are* minds and bodies *essentially*, meaning we are *identical* to both. This is a claim not just about us in the world as it actually is: It's a claim about us in every possible circumstance. And it is, at least, a claim contrary to many people's beliefs about what they are and could be.

For example, many people think that fictional stories and films involving "body swaps" (e.g., *Freaky Friday*) are, at least, *possible*: *You* could come to exist in a different body, a body formerly inhabited by another person. Many people also believe that "tele-transporters" (e.g., from *Star Trek*) are possible: *You* could come to exist in a body made of entirely new matter. And many people at least *hope*, if not confidently believe, that they will continue to exist after the death of their body in an afterlife, with a new body or even with no body at all.[26]

These examples suggest that many people believe they are not *identical* to their body. They accept mind–body "dualism": We are *related* to our bodies, but not *identical* to our bodies.

Tollefsen rejects dualism, for only briefly developed reasons. But much more is needed to really show that dualism is mistaken and that we are, in *essence*, both minds and bodies. Since refuting dualism is key to arguing that we *were* early fetuses, Tollefsen's case needs development.

When Did We Begin?

Tollefsen argues that "we" begin at conception. While our bodies begin at conception, it might not be literally true that "we" begin at conception.

To see why, we should think about when "we" *end*. Typically, this is at death of our whole bodies. "We" also end at brain death. And "we" end if we go into an irreversible coma or permanent vegetative state. Suppose Eve was in a coma for ten years, with no brain activity all that time. When did Eve end? Many would say that the person Eve *ended* ten years ago, when she fell into the coma. "*She* has been gone for 10 years," we'd say.

If "we" *end* when our consciousness permanently ends, then "we" *begin* when consciousness begins. And consciousness begins later than when the body begins. So "we" begin *not* at conception, but likely months later: mid-pregnancy or so, when the brain and nervous system are developed enough to produce consciousness.

Since Tollefsen's case depends on "us" existing at conception, these arguments also need development.

2. Ethics

Tollefsen argues that the basis of our moral rights is an *essential* or *necessary* property of all biologically human organisms or beings: a rational and free *nature* or *essence*. Since fetuses have this nature or essence, they have basic moral rights, like us, as one of us.[27]

This argument depends on some controversial metaphysics, discussed above, but there are some distinctly ethical controversies also.

Moral Explanations

Tollefsen's argument is rooted in the moral hypothesis that *we* have worth and are due respect *because* we are rational and free. This is doubtful. We are born *not* rational and free (says Tollefsen), and we often die lacking freedom or rationality. Freedom or rationality is taken from many of us by illness and injury; some people live their entire lives without either.

All these human beings, however, have worth and are due respect: They have rights. Why? A simple answer is this: They are conscious, sentient, feeling beings, and so their lives can go better and worse *for them*; in short, they can be *harmed*, and this is why they, and anyone, has rights.[28] Why do rational and free people have rights? *Because they can be harmed* is a better explanation than *because they are rational and free.*

The first step in Tollefsen's case against abortion is doubtful, since a simpler explanation is available. We should accept Tollefsen's hypothesis only if the simpler hypothesis is faulty.

Appealing to "Natures"

Why should we think that anything (or anyone) with a rational and free nature or essence has rights? Tollefsen argues this is because requiring *actual* rationality and freedom for rights implies that babies don't have rights.

Perhaps, but we can acknowledge that babies have rights on the simpler grounds they are conscious, they are feeling, and they can be harmed. Again, we should accept Tollefsen's abstract appeal to "natures" to support rights for babies only if this simpler explanation fails.[29]

Understanding the Proposal

Finally, simplified, Tollefsen proposes something like this:

> We have rights ultimately because we have a rational nature. Anything with a rational nature has rights.

But consider two similar proposals:

> We make moral decisions ultimately because we have a rational nature. *Anything with a rational nature makes moral decisions.*

> We sometimes deserve praise and blame ultimately because we have a rational nature. *Anything with a rational nature sometimes deserves praise and blame.*

Facts about fetuses show that these italicized claims are false: Fetuses only have the *potential* for decision-making and being praise- and blameworthy. So, we are due a better explanation why actual rights, not just potential rights, would result from fetuses' natures. Fetuses' natures involve many potentials and radical capacities, most of which make no difference to their current, actual properties. So, what current properties do fetuses get from their natures, and which do they not? More explanation is needed.

3. Conclusion

In sum, these are some concerns to be addressed in thinking through Tollefsen's, and similar, arguments.

COMPREHENSION QUESTIONS

1. What is mind–body dualism? Why is it relevant to discussing consciousness, and why is this important to determining when a human life begins and ends?
2. What reason does Nobis give for why rational free beings have basic rights? How does his explanation compare to Tollefsen's explanation?

DISCUSSION QUESTIONS

1. What is the difference between actual and potential rights? Do you think a non-conscious being should be afforded the same actual rights because of its potential for future development?
2. What's the moral difference between a being that's alive but lacks consciousness completely (as in early stages of fetal development) and a conscious being with severely limited cognitive capacity, such as a baby with significant cognitive impairments? What differences in treatment can this moral difference justify?

FURTHER READINGS

Boonin, David. *A Defense of Abortion*. Cambridge: Cambridge University Press, 2003.

Finnis, John. "Abortion, Natural Law, and Public Reason." In *Natural Law and Public Reason*, edited by Robert P. George and Christopher Wolfe. Washington, DC: Georgetown University Press, 2000, 75–105.

George, Robert P., and Christopher O. Tollefsen. *Embryo: A Defense of Human Life*. New York: Doubleday, 2008; 2nd ed., Witherspoon Institute, 2011.

Kaczor, Christopher. *The Ethics of Abortion: Women's Rights, Human Life, and the Question of Justice*. New York: Routledge, 2015.

Lee, Patrick, and Robert P. George. *Body-Self Dualism in Contemporary Ethics and Politics*. New York: Cambridge University Press, 2009.

Marquis, Don. "Why Abortion Is Immoral." *Journal of Philosophy* 86, no. 4 (1989): 183–202.

Nobis, Nathan. "Ethics and Abortion." In *1000-Word Philosophy: An Introductory Anthology*, 1000wordphilosophy.com/2016/03/07/the-ethics-of-abortion/.

Thomson, Judith Jarvis. "A Defense of Abortion." *Philosophy and Public Affairs* 1, no. 1 (1997): 47–66.

Warren, Mary Anne. "On the Moral and Legal Status of Abortion." *The Monist* 57 (1973): 43–61.

For factual information concerning abortion, see the Guttmacher Institute (https://www .guttmacher.org), the CDC's Abortion Surveillance System (https://www.cdc.gov /reproductivehealth/data_stats/abortion.htm), and/or any other country's national public health departments and organizations.

NOTES

1. This argument is made persuasively, and in much greater depth, by Patrick Lee and Robert P. George in *Body-Self Dualism in Contemporary Ethics and Politics* (New York: Cambridge University Press, 2009).
2. Keith L. Moore and T. V. N. Persaud, *The Developing Human* (New York: W. B. Saunders, 2003 [7th ed.]), 16.
3. For interesting evidence regarding this point, see Helen Pearson, "Your Destiny, From Day One," *Nature* 418 (2002): 14–15. The biological data are reviewed at greater length in Robert P. George and Christopher O. Tollefsen, *Embryo: A Defense of Human Life* (New York: Doubleday, 2008).
4. Judith Jarvis Thomson, "A Defense of Abortion," *Philosophy and Public Affairs* 1, no. 1 (1997): 48.
5. Thomsen, "Defense of Abortion."
6. See Jeffrey Reiman, *Critical Moral Liberalism: Theory and Practice* (Lanham, MD: Rowman and Littlefield, 1997), 190.
7. This is an introductory essay intended for readers with little or no background in ethics or philosophy. It engages a wider variety of arguments than discussions written for professional philosophers and advanced philosophy students. It does not engage every important consideration about abortion, as no short essay can.
8. To say that an action is *immoral* (or *not moral*) is to say that it is *unethical* (or *not ethical*); to say that an action is *moral* is to say that it's *ethical*. To say that an action is *morally permissible* is to say that it's *ethically permissible*; *ethically wrong* means *morally wrong* and so on. Ethics and morality are the same thing: Why there are two words to describe the same thing is unclear.
9. A not uncommon claim is that since men can't have abortions, they are not in a position to give arguments on the topic. In quick reply, this is false: Someone's sex (or gender) doesn't influence their ability to give good arguments on issues that, in many ways, mostly affect people who are importantly different from them. Women can have insights and good arguments about issues that uniquely affect men, and vice versa. Some women cannot have abortions because they don't have a uterus or cannot get pregnant: Does that mean that they just *cannot* offer reasonable views on the topic? No. And since women disagree on abortion, some women *must* give bad arguments on the topic; for instance, if one woman argues that *all abortions are wrong* and another argues that *all are not wrong*, they cannot both be correct. Women are not infallible on these topics, and neither are men. The goal for everyone is to carefully and critically evaluate any claims and arguments, whatever and whoever their source.
10. "In . . . surveys, 1% indicated that they had been victims of rape, and less than half a percent said they became pregnant as a result of incest." See Lori F. Frohwirth et al., "Reasons U.S. Women Have Abortions: Quantitative and Qualitative Perspectives," *Perspectives on Sexual and Reproductive Health* 37, no. 3 (2005): 110–118.
11. It's sometimes claimed that people who think that abortion is generally not wrong think this because of fetuses' size, level of development, location or environment, and dependency (the so-called SLED test). The suggestion is that pro-choice people think that *anything small, dependent, and undeveloped that is located in someone else's body* is permissible to kill. The objection is that this principle, and related principles, are false, so this principle fails to support thinking that abortion is permissible.

    The problem here is that no thoughtful abortion advocate accepts such a principle: Nobody should think personhood is defeated or eliminated by SLED factors. Consider a case inspired by Dr. Seuss's *Horton Hears a Who!*: If there were a baby Who, that baby would be tiny, undeveloped (at least not a developed adult and so, in a sense, undeveloped), and dependent; and we could even imagine that baby Who somehow in someone else's body (imagine the baby Who is on a speck eaten by someone, but not digested). This baby Who would be prima facie wrong to kill since that baby is a person or conscious being. The SLED factors are irrelevant to that.

The lesson here is that if a being is prima facie wrong to kill, then its size, location, dependency, and development do not matter. (This simplification ignores relevant concerns raised by Thomson, discussed below.) But if a being is *not* wrong to kill, those factors are irrelevant. Advocates of the SLED test might merely *assume*, then, that abortion is wrong, which is begging the question.

12. Some claim that permanently comatose individuals remain persons, despite the complete loss of any mental life: They are "persons with potential." (Set aside how anyone would know that a coma is permanent.) Yet they tend to think that these bodies can sometimes permissibly be let die. Since it is prima facie wrong to let *persons* die, but not wrong to let these bodies die, this suggests that these *bodies* are not persons. Personhood is a guide to how someone should be treated, so if someone can permissibly be let die, that suggests a lack of personhood. If someone replies that they *remain* persons but just have lost their consciousness, memories, abilities to communicate, and personality, we should genuinely wonder what their personhood consists in, on this view, since the concept now fails to provide guidance for action in particular cases.

13. In an important article on abortion (Mary Anne Warren, "On the Moral and Legal Status of Abortion," *The Monist* 57, no. 1 (1973): 43–61), Warren writes that "the traits which are most central to the concept of personhood . . . are, *very roughly*, the following:

    1. Consciousness . . . , and in particular the capacity to feel pain;
    2. Reasoning . . . :
    3. Self-motivated activity . . . ;
    4. The capacity to communicate . . . ;
    5. The presence of self-concepts, and self-awareness."

    Warren's definition is a plausible development of John Locke's (*Essay Concerning Human Understanding*, 1689) definition of a person as "a thinking intelligent being, that has reason and reflection, and can consider itself as itself, the same thinking thing, in different times and places." Warren's and Locke's theories explain why cabbages and rocks are *not* persons and why we *are* persons and why those other (possible) beings fit the concept of person. Both definitions arguably require *too sophisticated* levels of mental awareness, but their emphasis on psychological capacities determining personhood is what's important. This is better than understanding persons as *human beings*, since that definition doesn't allow for even the possibility of non-human persons or human beings losing their personhood.

14. Some may observe, in reply, that children should be sent to school so they can actualize their *potential*. That's true, but these children are persons, and have a psychological connection to their potential future self. And suppose we *knew*, for certain, that a child would die at, say, eighteen years old: In a sense, the child would lack the potential future that we hope all children have. But shouldn't this child still go to school? Finally, suppose someone is a *potential* brain surgeon but can realize that potential *only if* you tutor her. Are you, or is anyone, *morally obligated* to provide that tutoring, so she can realize her potential? Few would agree that this potential imposes obligations on anyone else: This insight can be applied to abortion. Judith Thomson's arguments are related (see below).

368 ETHICS, LEFT AND RIGHT

15. Don Marquis, "Why Abortion Is Immoral," *Journal of Philosophy* 86, no. 4 (1989): 183–202.
16. Here are some more arguments:

  - "The Bible (or God) says abortion is wrong."
    Reply: The Bible doesn't *clearly* discuss abortion, but *just because* the Bible (or any religious text) says an action is wrong doesn't *necessarily* mean it's wrong: for example, verses concerning slavery, violence, and, to some, loving enemies and immigrants suggest this. And, *if* God exists (and perhaps He doesn't; this is controversial!), either God would have *reasons* to oppose abortions or not, so what would those reasons be? That's our concern. Finally, religions should not determine the law.
  - "Abortions are dangerous."
    Reply: No, they are not, especially if done early in pregnancy. They are no more dangerous than many medical procedures. And pregnancy and childbirth *are* dangerous, to some degree. And dangerous actions aren't always wrong and/or should be illegal.
  - "Would you be OK it if your mother had had an abortion?"
    Reply: Would you be OK if your mother had been a nun? Or your father had a vasectomy before you were born? *Many* actions would have prevented each person's existence, but aren't wrong.

17. Research on fetal pain is easier to find than research on fetal consciousness. While it's possible to be conscious without an ability to feel pain, this might be a state where nothing can be good or bad for that individual: What this would be like for a fetus is hard to imagine, it's safe to say. For some relevant research that suggests fetal consciousness, or the capacity for pain, develops far later in pregnancy, past when most abortions occur, see, e.g., Hugo Lagercrantz, "The Emergence of Consciousness: Science and Ethics," *Seminars in Fetal and Neonatal Medicine* 19, no. 5 (2014): 300–305: "[C]onsciousness cannot emerge before 24 gestational weeks [6 months] when the thalamocortical connections from the sense organs are established. Thus the limit of legal abortion at 22–24 weeks in many countries makes sense"; Susan J. Lee, Henry J. Peter Ralston, Eleanor A. Drey, John Colin Partridge, and Mark A. Rosen, "Fetal Pain: A Systematic Multidisciplinary Review of the Evidence," *Journal of the American Medical Association* 294, no. 8 (2005): 947–954: "[T]he capacity for functional pain perception in preterm neonates probably does not exist before 29 or 30 weeks . . . the capacity for fetal pain is limited but indicates that fetal perception of pain is unlikely before the third trimester"; David Benatar and Michael Benatar, "A Pain in the Fetus: Toward Ending Confusion About Fetal Pain," *Bioethics* 15, no. 1 (2001): 57–76: "[T]he available data showing how, on balance, it tends more to support than undermine the claim that fetuses of around 28 to 30 weeks' gestation are capable of feeling pain"; among other sources.
18. Tara C. Jatlaoui, "Abortion Surveillance—United States, 2014," *MMWR Surveillance Summaries*.
19. Guttmacher Institute, "Induced Abortion in the United States," Fact Sheet, 2014.
20. Some might deny this, claiming that plants and (mechanical) machines can be harmed. While plants and machines can, of course, be *damaged*, these damages don't affect their point of view, since they don't have one: There is no way *to be* a plant or machine such that damage makes it worse *for that* plant or machine. Alternatively, the type of harm *we* would suffer if hit by a speeding truck is quite different in feel and moral significance from the type of "harm" done to a run-over plant or a typewriter, so much so that we might want to just not call those damages "harms."

21. I will observe that some people who accept this conclusion also think that abortions for, say, sex selection are morally problematic. Whether this attitude is inconsistent or not is beyond this essay.

22. This is likely consistent with thinking that nobody is morally obligated, or should be legally required, to perform abortions. But there are many people willing and able to perform medically safe abortions, so this is not a current practical concern.

23. Some respond that, in most cases of pregnancy, the woman *did something* that contributed to the fetus's existence. But doing something that contributes to someone being somewhere doesn't give them the right to be there; for example, if you *do something*, say, open a door, and someone falls into your house, that doesn't give them a right to be there. Second, to argue that "abortion is wrong because a woman did something that contributed to the fetus's existence and so it's wrong to end that pregnancy" *appears* to be question-begging: See the earlier discussion of the argument that "abortion is wrong because if a woman gets pregnant, she just *must* have the baby."

24. For important factual and legal information about later abortions, see the Guttmacher Institute's "Later Abortion" report, https://www.guttmacher.org/evidence-you-can-use/later-abortion.

25. For helpful comments on this paper, I thank Cliff Guthrie, Dan Hooley, David Morgan, Joona Räsänen, Robert Bass, Tom Metcalf, and Bob Fischer.

26. Many metaphysical issues, such as these, involve attempting to know or understand what is *possible* and using those insights to understand the nature of what is *actual*. For an introduction to some of the challenges involved in these tasks, see Bob Fischer's "Modal Epistemology: Knowledge of Possibility & Necessity" at *1000-Word Philosophy: An Introductory Anthology*, 1000wordphilosophy.com/2018/02/13/modal-epistemology/.

27. Suppose Tollefsen's metaphysics is correct and we are, in essence or nature, minds *and* bodies, and we begin at conception. Some think that this immediately shows that fetuses have basic moral rights, since we have them now and we developed from fetuses, who were once us. But just because we are some way *now* doesn't mean we've *always* been that way. "Having rights" could be a *contingent* property, one that we can gain and lose, not an *essential* or *necessary* property, one that we have, and must have, whenever we exist. Alternatively, "having rights" could be a *necessary* or *essential* property of minded, conscious beings, which we are in our essence, and our bodies only contingently related to that minded being. This is the view about what "we are," in essence that I favor.

28. This quick theory is inspired by, and supported by, philosopher Tom Regan's argument that if someone is what he calls a "subject of a life," then that someone has basic moral rights. See his *The Case For Animal Rights* (University of California Press, 1983 [2004 updated version]), 243, or his essay "The Case for Animal Rights" in *In Defense of Animals*, edited by Peter Singer (Malden, MA: Basil Blackwell, 1985), 13–26. From the essay, in response to theories that suggest that human beings without freedom or reason lack moral rights:

    [W]e are each of us the experiencing subject of a life, a conscious creature having an individual welfare that has importance to us whatever our usefulness to others. We want and prefer things, believe and feel things, recall and expect things. And all these dimensions of our life, including our pleasure and pain, our enjoyment and suffering, our satisfaction and frustration, our continued existence or our untimely death—all make a difference to the quality of our life as lived, as experienced, by us as individuals.

    Regan argues that anyone like this, anyone who is a "subject of a life," has basic rights.

29. We might also reject Tollefsen's appeal to "natures" on the grounds that, perhaps, a brain-dead individual retains a "rational and free" nature, yet lacks rights. Since rights protect against harm, and such an individual cannot be harmed, having a free and rational nature does not entail that an individual has rights. (So, any moral obligations due to that body are not because of that individual's rights; something else explains it.) If someone replies that such an individual's relevant body parts are *damaged* and so they no longer have this *nature*, then if the relevant body parts are *non-existent* since not yet developed (as in an embryo or fetus), that would seem to suggest that they lack that *nature* also.

CHAPTER 11

Political Correctness

AGAINST POLITICALLY CORRECT SPEECH
TULLY BORLAND

The word *marijuana* is now considered racist? If you say something is *lame* or *dumb* you're guilty of something called ableism? An all-women's college advocates that professors not refer to their students as *women*? What on earth is going on here? It's no wonder that, to the average person, it seems as though illegal aliens (from outer space) are taking control of the language.

In order to understand politically correct (PC) speech, we first need to understand the phenomenon of political correctness (hereafter, *PC-ness*) more generally. Once we are in a better position to understand PC speech, several different types will be distinguished, some which are worse than others. From the perspective of the political right, diagnosing PC speech is half the antidote when it comes to seeking a cure for the ailment. Finally, we shall consider some arguments for and against a particular type of politically incorrect speech, so-called hate speech.

1. An Initial Characterization of Political Correctness

As is well documented, PC-ness originated under communism, most notably in Mao Tse-Tung's Communist Party.[1] In a phrase, *PC comes from the CP*.[2] Although today PC-ness is no longer strictly associated with communism, PC-ness is a phenomenon that derives from the political left. According to *The Encyclopedia of Ethics*:

> The term "politically correct" appears to have originally been used in leftist circles either approvingly to refer to someone who correctly adheres to the party line, or more often ironically and disapprovingly to someone whose adherence to the Communist Party line was excessive, tiresome, and beyond good sense . . . "Politically correct" now carries a complex set of meanings. To describe an academic program, a bit of social behavior, or a new descriptor (*e.g.*, a "chair" rather than a "chairman") as politically *correct* is to imply that while it correctly

conforms to a liberal academic party line, it is incorrect by some other more important or more substantive measure; it is educationally unsound, unjust, an illegitimate interference with free speech, or simply unnecessary or silly.[3]

So what counts as PC is what conforms to left-wing politics, and what counts as politically incorrect is what goes against the PC. Jan Narveson argues that PC proponents have a view similar to Thrasymachus's understanding of justice in Plato's *Republic*, only inverted.[4] Thrasymachus infamously argued that justice is the will of the stronger—that is, it is whatever those with political power determine it to be, and this can change overnight. Hence, if the sovereign determines that taxation is just, then it is. Like Thrasymachus's view of justice, what counts as PC can seemingly change overnight, for instance whether it's politically correct or incorrect for someone who appears to have characteristically white features to identify as black, or whether the word *marijuana* is racist. Where it differs from Thrasymachus's view is that it has to do with the interests of the (supposedly) *weaker* or those who have been traditional minorities. Nonetheless, power is still a driving force in determining what counts as PC or PIC. People with power— politicians, university administrators, bureaucrats, diversity czars, and so on— put forward an iconoclastic orthodoxy of some sort (e.g., Marxism), declare what should or should not be done or said in the name of "justice," and then put pressure on others to conform to their dictates or face punishment. An evil or oppressive group is designated (e.g., white hetero males) to sort the good guys from the bad, and rules are then enacted to eradicate the evil (e.g., "Zero Tolerance is the watchword of the PC administrator"[5]). PC speech, then, is what the new (leftist) ruling class—either already in power or on the ascendency—deems as fit or unfit to say in an effort to maintain control of thoughts and ideas in public discourse.[6]

2. Politically Correct Speech as a Left-Wing Phenomenon

So PC speech is associated with left-wing politics. But don't simply take my word for it. Just ask yourself whether the following are politically correct or incorrect statements:

- Black males commit more crimes than white males on average.
- Men are stronger than women.
- The only thing that stops a bad guy with a gun is a good guy with a gun.
- Feminism is cancer.
- Transgenderism is a mental illness.
- Homosexual sex is immoral.
- Political correctness is a form of intolerance masquerading as a form of tolerance.
- If forced to choose between free speech versus diversity and inclusion, one should choose the former.

Of course, not everyone on the right agrees with all of those statements, but the commonality is that these statements don't adhere to the leftist party line.[7] Still, a natural objection arises. Surely it is true that people on the right sometimes engage in their own form of speech policing, but from their political point of view. At the very least, we can imagine a scenario where the political right gains control of the universities, the media, and government, imposing their version of PC speech on others. For instance, we can envision a Christian or Muslim theocracy promoting the view that not only are exclamations such as "*Goddammit!*" offensive to religious believers but also politically incorrect to say and ought to be censured. Thus, it might appear that I'm rigging the game and that we should think the scope of PC speech is broader than I'm construing it.[8]

This objection raises an important point about the political right also restricting speech, one to which I shall return again below. Still, it's a mistake to think that PC-ness is a phenomenon that occurs also on the right. *Political correctness* and *political incorrectness*, like all other words, have their meanings contingently and can change over time. Since the use of a word or phrase gives us some indication of its meaning and, as should be apparent already from what has been said above, the use today indicates speech that adheres to or diverges from the leftist party line.[9]

3. Categories of Politically Correct Speech

Among the different types of PC speech, perhaps the most important distinction is between Orwellian and non-Orwellian. The Orwellian varieties take their name from George Orwell's works, particularly *1984*. In the dystopian future of Orwell's novel, the government (under the figurehead of Big Brother) has brainwashed the public into repeating phrases such as *Ignorance Is Strength* and *Freedom Is Slavery* in order to control their thoughts and actions. The *Newspeak Dictionary*—a dictionary of PC speech—is created, and its strictures on language are rigorously enforced.

Orwellian speech, as I shall use the phrase, either distorts the truth by saying the opposite or introduces a new euphemism into the language in order to mislead or distract from the left's true ideology. A few examples of the former: In Maryland, those who are dependent on the government for food no longer get food stamps, rather they use their government issued *Independence Card*;[10] those on the political right know that when they hear university administrators talking about adding more *diversity* and *inclusion*, it indicates more uniformity of leftist thought and exclusion of heterosexual, non-disabled, white males; in reference to Obamacare, which made many insurance options illegal and financially penalized the uninsured if they didn't buy in, Nancy Pelosi said that it would lead to healthier lives while also providing the American people with "more liberty."[11]

Consider now examples of popular PC euphemisms. In the immigration debate, there is the phrase *undocumented worker*—often used to describe an immigrant who is in a country illegally and may not even work. *Undocumented immigrant* is less euphemistic but still distracts from the fact that the person has an illegal rather than legal immigrant status. Moreover, in some cases the illegal immigrant has documents, alright, *forged* and therefore *illegal documents*.[12] (Or are we now to say that such documents are *undocumented documents*?) The term *abortion* is offensive to the left since it indicates that someone has been aborted. Thus, a woman doesn't agree to have her baby aborted or killed; rather, she *terminates her pregnancy* like a boss dispassionately terminates an employee's contract. *Differently abled* replaces *disabled* because it is alleged that the latter is offensive, even though it accurately describes someone's unfortunate lack of a normal ability (e.g., someone who lacks the ability to walk). A *justice-involved youth* is the same as a *juvenile delinquent* according to Obama's former attorney general, Loretta Lynch.[13]

Non-Orwellian PC speech is hard to define, but it consists of words or phrases that help to push certain leftist narratives or agendas with less outright deception. Some examples will have to suffice: *African American* as opposed to *black*, *Native American* rather than *American Indian*, *zhe* or *zhimself* instead of *he* or *himself*, *cognitively challenged* rather than *retarded*, etc.[14] The second set of words are somehow harmful or have a suspect origin and thus are replaced and now treated as vulgarities. But unlike vulgarities that organically arise in a natural language, the PC phrases were *invented* by some on the political left and *deemed* as appropriate in opposition to their predecessors. This is why many PC terms often sound strange to ordinary people who love their native tongue; the ugly aesthetics alone are often enough for many of us not to engage in PC speech.

4. Against Politically Correct Speech

What should we think about the Orwellian variety of PC speech? The clear though unstated purpose of Orwellian speech is thought manipulation, as Orwell's *1984* memorably reveals. So if we're interested in truth and epistemic autonomy, we will avoid using Orwellian speech. Words matter because ideas matter; words have meanings and are the vehicles of ideas. But Orwellian speech obscures rather than elucidates; it seeks to put forward a particular political agenda at the expense of linguistic precision. No one concerned about the truth should be tempted to engage in using the left's semantic sophistries, nor should they engage in their own.

But social pressure makes acquiescing to the speech police tempting. No one wants to be labeled a *racist, misogynist, bigot, homophobe*, or any of the other labels leftists now use to vilify people who don't engage in the "correct" thoughts. I recall as a graduate student in the early 2000s discussing racial politics and being accosted for using *American Indian* and *black* instead of the PC terms *Native American* and *African American*. When I pointed out that, according to the U.S. Census in 1995, American Indians and blacks preferred the use of those terms to their PC counterparts, I was met with incredulity.[15] The stigma against using traditional terms can be so great that, even if one uses them *out of respect*, one will be looked upon with suspicion or worse.

Is it *ever* a good idea, from the perspective of the right, to use non-Orwellian PC terminology such as *Native American* and *African American*? Sure. For instance, if someone who is black prefers being called an *African American* and referring to such a person as *black* would cause this person unnecessary offense, then one should try to avoid referring to him as *black*. Attitudes of respect, kindness, and compassion are of paramount importance to any adequate political ideal of the right. In other contexts, attitudes such as respect might require going against another's word preferences. For example, if someone who is a white, female human identifies as a black man from another planet, compassionate respect requires using language that represents what one believes is *true*.

I said above that if we are interested in truth, we will avoid Orwellian speech. However, if our primary goal is to change the world through political action, if we see politics as war and our political opponents as enemies, then we'll be more likely to engage in Orwellian speech.[16] War is war, after all, and we'll be tempted to use whatever means necessary to achieve our ends. Yet, in a liberal democracy where core tenets are civil discourse and freedom of speech, we should strive for something better. In what follows, I shall carry on in this more optimistic task and endeavor to appeal to common ground with those who also share the ideals of a liberal democracy. In what remains, we turn our focus to another form of politically incorrect speech, namely so-called hate speech.

5. Hate Speech Codes: The Central Argument Against

Since the 1980s, speech codes have been on the rise.[17] In the Foundation for Individual Rights in Education (FIRE)'s annual survey in 2018, out of the 357 public universities and 104 major private universities, 90% had some form of speech code, and only 35 of those 461 schools received FIRE's "green light" designation for having strong free speech policies.[18] Our societies' love of free speech seems to be waning, while at the same time the general public's hatred of hate speech appears to be waxing. After all, who could not be against hate? We love being loved and hate hatred.

Yet, the very phrase *hate speech* is itself an instance of Orwellian PC speech; unbeknownst to the general public but known to those who study hate speech laws and codes, almost all hate speech restrictions have in common that they have little if anything to do with actual hatred.[19] Seldom does any restriction on hate speech mention the word *hate* at all. Rather, all have to do with left-wing identity politics. Certain groups are selected for speech protections according to categories of race, gender, sexual orientation, and the like; many codes are concerned with bias rather than hate. Yet, if we are honest, we will recognize that not all biases are bad. Biases tend to be good when based on empirical evidence (e.g., "Avoid grabbing snakes that rattle!"). But oftentimes hate speech restrictions discriminate even against reasonable biases.

And who determines the standard of whether something is biased or prejudicial? A rather striking example of what counts as prejudicial is the definition of *hate crime* by the United Kingdom's Metropolitan Police (where hate speech can count as a hate crime):

> Any criminal offence which is *perceived by the victim or any other person*, to be motivated by hostility or prejudice based on a person's race or perceived race; religion or perceived religion; sexual orientation or perceived sexual orientation; disability or perceived disability and any crime motivated by hostility or prejudice against a person who is transgender or perceived to be transgender. A Hate Incident is any incident *which the victim, or anyone else, thinks* is based on someone's prejudice towards them because of their race, religion, sexual orientation, disability or because they are transgender.[20]

Notice that in both hate crimes and incidents (a) hostility or hate need not be a factor and (b) *actual* prejudice need not be a factor either, only *perceived* prejudice. Even Orwell didn't foresee a world where *perceived thought* rather than *actual thought* would be subject for punishment by the Thought Police! Given that there is no agreed-upon definition of what counts as hate speech, arguing for or against hate speech codes *in general* might seem to be a fool's errand. Still, I think a general argument against speech codes can be offered, even if it has to be held somewhat tentatively. For clarity's sake, hereafter I shall use *hate speech codes* to refer to any dictate, be it by law or university administration, since both seek to prohibit certain forms of speech by coercion. I shall also have in mind public institutions, since we can all agree (or should!) that private institutions may more or less do as they please.

Two central ideals of a liberal democracy are respect for the autonomy of individuals and a presumption against the use of coercion. Coercion can come in many forms, from being forced at gunpoint to do a sovereign's bidding on the extreme end, to being manipulated on the less extreme end. Ideally, our aim should be to persuade each other as far as possible by offering reasons and arguments, letting the chips fall where they may and tolerating each other as far as possible.[21] In a liberal democracy, then, the burden of proof is always on those who seek to use coercion to manipulate others rather than on those who promote a free exchange of ideas.

So the primary argument against hate speech codes is as follows:

(1) In a liberal democracy, one needs sufficient reasons for coercion.
(2) Hate speech codes are essentially coercive.
(3) There are no sufficient reasons for hate speech codes.
(4) Thus, in a liberal democracy, one should be against hate speech codes.[22]

That hate speech codes are essentially coercive is straightforward. Such codes are designed to regulate behavior through the enforcement of sanctions and punishments. So, the key premise is (3). We will first look at a couple of prominent arguments that attempt to show this premise false. Finding those arguments wanting, we will end with a few more considerations in favor of premise (3).

6. Arguments for Hate Speech Codes

One initial line of critique that might seem promising is to make a rights-based argument. For instance, it might be thought that some minority group has a right not to hear offensive speech and that the relevant authorities should protect this right by force if necessary. Yet, if we believe in equality of rights, this means that we should be just as concerned with the speaker's rights as we are with the hearer's rights. For why should we prefer the one over the other? After all, the speaker might be equally offended that the hearer is offended, or equally offended that his speech is censored. Without an argument for why we should privilege the hearer's rights over the speaker's, we should prefer no coercive interference with speech.

Instead of appealing to a right not to hear offensive speech, a more promising tack is to appeal to the *right not to be harmed* by offensive speech, and then to argue that permitting certain kinds of speech increases harm sufficient to warrant restrictions on free speech rights. After all, we're all sympathetic to the fact that being called certain words is deeply offensive and can be psychologically harmful. Perhaps we should extend John Stuart Mill's *Harm Principle* to include speech as well as other actions.[23]

Several points can be made in reply. First, there is already a branch of law that deals with restitution for harms—civil law—and no one on the right or left opposes lawsuits to collect damages for being harmed. If someone says something to you that causes psychological harm, you are free to sue the person for damages. The question is whether, in addition to this legal avenue, we should have further statutes that write harms into criminal laws and university speech codes. Second, if speech codes are defended on the basis of harms, then we should also note that being told that your wife is divorcing you, that your son no longer loves you, or that you're a poor excuse for a human being can also be extraordinarily harmful. But we all agree that the right to this sort of speech shouldn't be infringed upon. Thus, the person in favor of hate speech codes needs a principled way of ruling out these sorts of cases while not ruling out offensive speech having to do with race, gender, and so forth. Third, those in favor of hate speech codes almost never recognize that being labeled a racist, misogynist, homophobe, Islamophobe, and all the other names leftists use to demonize the opposition can cause great harm. People lose their livelihoods because of false accusations of racism, yet being called a racist is never counted as hate speech. Nor should it. That's because we shouldn't have hate speech codes.

7. More Considerations Against Hate Speech Codes

The phenomenon of speech codes forces us to look at how we want to treat people and be treated. Without question there are victims of thoughtless and demeaning speech that causes harm. Yet, hate speech codes themselves can be harmful in treating minorities as infants in need of paternalistic parents by monitoring everyone's speech—what some even on the left have referred to as "the soft bigotry of low expectations."[24] But we shouldn't want to be treated as infants! The only people who are truly empowered by hate speech codes are those who enforce such codes on the rest of us. And it's not at all clear where it will end. *Healthy* is now a term of abuse because it's code for offending people who are overweight. The speech police now say that if you use it you're a *healthist* and guilty of *healthism*. There are sophomores, juniors, and seniors but no more *freshmen*, since it has the word *men* in it and is therefore sexist. What's next: *man*dible, funda*men*tal, and *man*atee? It is hard to keep up with what is allowed to be said and what is forbidden. Did you know that there are not only microaggressions, but nanoaggressions, and picoaggressions? No? Well, I don't either (I just made those up), but the fact that you didn't know this is noteworthy. Language's function is to help us communicate in a society. In well-functioning societies, everyone knows the rules. You know not to sneeze on the guy sitting next to you; he knows that saying "bless you" is no longer to invoke occult powers. But with PC speech the rules are always changing, and this favors the people in power who create the rules by making up and enforcing the use of new terminology on the rest of us.

The arbitrary nature of hate speech codes also threatens to create a new class of victims—those who are punished by law enforcement and university administrators who are either (a) ignorant of the new ruling class' hegemonic speech prohibitions, or (b) though not ignorant, courageously choose to engage in free speech knowing full well the price to be paid. Are future generations then obliged to create counter-speech policies that favor this new victim class, setting in motion a perpetual cycle of victimization and redress? Conservatives are a minority at universities; should they be the next protected class? No! We don't want to see ourselves continually as victims in need of constant paternalism from the powers that be.

If someone says something that offends you, rather than tattling on the person to some paternalistic authority, instead think of this as an opportunity to practice virtue. The ancient Stoics had a lot of sound advice about how to deal with insults. They found such occasions as opportunities to practice being magnanimous, either by ignoring the insulter or replying with humor in a self-deprecating way. Epictetus advises not even to defend yourself if someone speaks ill of you; reply instead by saying, "Ah, yes, he was plainly unaware of all my other faults, or else those wouldn't have been the only ones that he mentioned."[25]

Another reason to be against hate speech codes is that they increase the balkanization of society. When we identify ourselves as (for example) Americans, affirming fundamental principles such as life, liberty, and the pursuit of happiness, the potential for unity increases. With the introduction of a new class of codes based on one's gender, age, religion, and so forth, we are motivated to see our identity in terms of these classes so as to reap the legal rewards. As James Jacobs and Kimberly Potter remark in the context of hate crime laws, "By redefining crime as a facet of intergroup conflict, hate crime laws encourage citizens to think of themselves as members of identity groups and encourage identity groups to think of themselves as victimized and besieged, thereby hardening each group's sense of resentment."[26]

In conclusion, let us recall that language is a precious gift; through it, humans can rise above their animal natures. Though sometimes used for evil, it is also a source of good. Thus, as with other goods, we should want as few restrictions upon it as possible. Once again, Jan Narveson:

> Speech ... is a major facilitator and a highly valued component of social intercourse. It is, moreover, enormously fluid, subtle, adaptable, rich in ambiguity, unkempt, and untamed. Precisely specifying its limits is not possible, and whoever proposes to do so must be looked on with suspicion. Not allowing grown people to say things to other grown people is so fraught with peril, so threatening to the social benefits speech makes possible, that when due allowance is made, one should soberly conclude that for the generality of cases, the best speech code is none at all.[27,28]

COMPREHENSION QUESTIONS

1. What is political correctness and political incorrectness? What are the origins of these terms? Why is that supposed to matter?
2. What is Orwellian speech?
3. What is the stigma against "traditional terms"?
4. What does the expression "hate speech" mean, and why does Borland think of it as Orwellian?
5. What are two cultural ideals essential to a liberal democracy?
6. How do the notions of autonomy and coercion relate to hate speech?

DISCUSSION QUESTIONS

1. Consider Borland's argument against hate speech codes. Do you agree that such codes are coercive and manipulative? Why or why not?
2. How do you think hate speech codes function (a) in Orwellian fashion, supporting the power dynamic of those who enforce such codes, or (b) to protect individual rights?
3. In what ways are politically correct speech norms similar to and different from book burnings?
4. Do hate speech codes reinforce intergroup conflicts or provide civil liberty protections?

Case 1

Context matters when we assess speech codes: Elementary schools aren't college classrooms, college classrooms aren't workplaces, and workplaces aren't town hall meetings. Consider this context:

> [In 2019,] Facebook booted [a grab bag of users from the platform: failed white nationalist House candidate Paul Nehlen, pundit Milo Yiannopoulos, right-leaning YouTube personality Paul Joseph Watson, alt-right political activist Laura Loomer, Nation of Islam leader Louis Farrakhan, and Alex Jones and his InfoWars media outlet] . . . But the current debate over speech and social media is far bigger than Facebook. It's a product of social media companies skirting a fundamental question for more than a decade: Are they platforms—like Amazon Kindle or a cellphone network provider—or are they publishers, like Vox, InfoWars, or the *Washington Post*?
>
> For years, social media giants tried to avoid the question altogether, recognizing that under American law, digital platforms have unique protections that guard against lawsuits aimed at the content posted on those platforms. But users complained about extremism and misinformation weaponized on Facebook and elsewhere, putting Facebook, Twitter, and other tech companies under immense pressure to increase moderation and close the accounts of bad actors—the same way a publisher might reject an article or a writer.
>
> In doing so, they've gotten sucked into the political fray they wanted to avoid. Conservatives, pointing out that Facebook and Twitter are self-described platforms, are arguing that banning some users while permitting others based

Case 1 (continued)

on a "vague and malleable" rubric is infringing on free expression on sites that they view as more like a town square where all voices should be heard . . .

In a statement, Facebook said, "We've always banned individuals or organizations that promote or engage in violence and hate, regardless of ideology. The process for evaluating potential violators is extensive and it is what led us to our decision to remove these accounts today."*

How should we think about the regulation of speech on social media platforms? Are there rights at stake, given that these are all private companies (rather than government services)? What are the costs of taking a hands-off approach, letting people post whatever they want? What are the costs of regulating speech? How should we balance them?

*https://www.vox.com/technology/2019/5/6/18528250/facebook-speech-conservatives-trump-platform-publisher

IN DEFENSE OF POLITICAL CORRECTNESS AND AGAINST "POLITICAL CORRECTNESS"
MEGAN HYSKA

1. Introduction

At the first debate of the 2015 Republican primaries, moderator Megyn Kelly threw Donald Trump, then candidate for the Republican presidential nomination, a tough question:

> You've called women you don't like "fat pigs," "dogs," "slobs," and "disgusting animals" . . . Your Twitter account has several disparaging comments about women's looks. You once told a contestant on *Celebrity Apprentice* it would be a pretty picture to see her on her knees . . . How will you answer the charge . . . that you are part of the war on women?[29]

To this, Trump responded:

> I think the big problem this country has is being politically correct. I've been challenged by so many people and I don't, frankly, have time for total political correctness. And to be honest with you, this country doesn't have time, either.[30]

Judging by applause, the audience didn't think this was a cheap deflection; on the contrary, they loved it. This would not be the last time that Trump scored points by invoking political correctness. In the second presidential debate of the 2016 campaign season, then-candidate Trump observed the following:

> [Y]ou look at Orlando and you look at San Bernardino and you look at the World Trade Center. Go outside. Look at Paris . . . these are radical Islamic terrorists . . . And she [Secretary Clinton] won't even mention the word and nor will President Obama. He won't use the term "radical Islamic terrorism."[31]

The claim that Hillary Clinton and Barack Obama wouldn't use the term "radical Islamic terror" was a messy one to fact check. Obama was on the record as saying that he preferred the term "violent extremism," while Secretary Clinton tended to say "radical Islamism" or (her choice at the debate that evening) "violent jihadist terrorists."[32] While these weren't exactly the same as Trump's favored phrase, Clinton's version in particular seemed remarkably close. So why spend time noting the discrepancy? Then-candidate Trump had as much as answered these questions moments before in response to an audience member concerned about Islamophobia in America:

> Well, you're right about Islamophobia, and that's a shame. But one thing we have to do is we have to make sure that—because there is a problem. I mean, whether we like it or not, and we could be very politically correct, but whether we like it or not, there is a problem.[33]

Political correctness, goes the claim of the eventual president, was what Clinton and Obama's phrases had that his did not. Whereas opponents like Trump will say that PC-ness undermines free and productive political discourse, I hope to persuade the reader that being open to criticism of our language and culture is essential to such discourse.

In what follows, I argue that, where we endorse egalitarian ideals, we should reject aspects of our language and culture that encode non-egalitarian beliefs. I also distinguish a few varieties of opposition to PC and discuss why each fails. I close by noting that, although the phenomenon often known as PC-ness is a positive one, the *term* "political correctness" has come to be used in a way that does our democracy a profound disservice.

2. How to Have a Debate About Political Correctness

Here are a few things that have been publicly decried as politically correct in recent times: allowing transgender people to use the bathroom associated with their gender identity; asking students to refrain from dressing up as a native American or member of another ethnic group for Halloween; the establishment of "safe spaces" on university campuses; removing Confederate monuments from public sites; the #MeToo movement; and avoidance of the phrase "radical Islamic terrorism."

The first thing worth observing about the items on this list is that their being singled out as politically correct is intended as a *criticism*; today, the phrase "politically correct" is mostly used by those who think the phenomenon to which this name belongs is a negative one.

Another observation: Things that get called "politically correct" are *themselves criticisms* (explicit or implicit) of language and other practices that express and shape opinion, often accompanied by a proposed alternative to the offending language or practice. Taken together, this rejection of the old and proposal of the new amount to an (attempted) *reformation of norms*.

For our purposes here, a norm is just a standard practice in a population, though not one officially codified in law. Our daily lives are full of such norms in the form, for instance, of politeness expectations. With both norms of politeness and political correctness, the expectation that people adhere to them is backed by the threat of some kind of social stigma if they don't. This stigma comes in different forms and degrees in different contexts: If you are routinely rude to your neighbors, they may not invite you to the neighborhood block party, whereas if you are routinely quite rude to your co-workers, you may lose your job. It is in the nature of a social norm that it is enforced by some more or less nebulous threat of stigma if it is deviated from, and so while the reformed norms that opponents of political correctness take issue with are like this, they are not uniquely like this.

Finally, it is distinctive of the norm reformations that PC opponents target that they are based on a criticism of practices from a particular perspective about what a just society looks like. According to this perspective, people's entitlement to have their interests taken into consideration is the same regardless of race, sex, gender identity relative to birth assignment, sexual orientation, country of origin, disability, and so on.

So, on a value-neutral characterization, political correctness is the reformation of norms from an egalitarian perspective. The question we are really debating here is, is this sort of reformation good or bad?

3. Egalitarianism

Egalitarianism says that the needs and desires of all people in our society are equally important, regardless of their race, gender, and so on,[34] and equally deserving of reflection in our laws, policies, and social conventions. But this principle would be less worth talking about if it weren't for the fact that the United States is a country where this perspective hasn't historically been taken. We couldn't here review a full history of the injustices that have characterized U.S. history, but some familiar ones include:

- The slaughter, rape, enslavement, and displacement of Native Americans that characterized European colonization.
- The enslavement of African Americans until 1865 and the explicitly state-sanctioned violence and discrimination they faced for a further 100 years after that.
- Legal regimes that effectively treated women as the property of their husbands and male relatives, withholding their vote until 1920 and legally allowing husbands to rape their wives in some states until 1993.[35]
- The criminalization of sex between individuals of the same sex in some states until 2003.
- The coerced sterilization of over 60,000 people targeted by eugenics campaigns because they were deemed "mentally defective," or were simply poor or members of racial or ethnic minorities, continuing through the 1970s.[36]

Overcoming these injustices to the degree that we have today has taken decades, and in some cases centuries, of protest in the face of violent repression. And clearly, it's still not the case that everyone in the country is an egalitarian. First, we know that there are still explicit racists, and sexists, and homophobes in our society. There are also those who hold these views *implicitly*; these are individuals who aren't aware of some prejudice that they in fact hold or are unaware that this hidden belief is affecting their reasoning and actions. Either the explicit or the implicit opponent of egalitarianism will naturally oppose any initiative to advance egalitarian principles through cultural norm reformation, but also

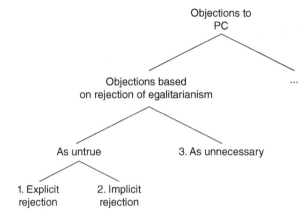

Figure 11.1
Objections to PC

through any other method. I won't engage much with this variety of objection because it becomes a debate about basic principles of equality, not about political correctness itself.

I want also to note that there are those who would probably say that they were on board with the basic principles of egalitarianism, but that U.S. society has already achieved fully satisfactory adherence to these ideals, so that further efforts to make the country more equal are unnecessary or inappropriate.

This sort of objection, that egalitarian goals may be good but that we've already met them (represented on the tree in Figure 11.1 as a type-3 objection), is one that we should engage with a bit more, but that couldn't possibly be fully rebutted here. What I will do is say something about what it would mean for equality to be achieved.

Where the opposite of equal treatment is discrimination, we can distinguish between all the discrimination that does in fact take place (de facto discrimination) and the subset of that which is explicitly encoded in law (de jure discrimination). While we've seen a move away from de jure discrimination, de facto discrimination continues, and moreover, it continues in systemic forms. Discrimination is systemic where it consists not just in occasional, one-off encounters, but in a persistent tendency to cause worse outcomes for certain people that is built into our institutions. Consider an example: According to the Federal Bureau of Investigation and Bureau of Prisons data, 31% of those killed by the police[37] and 38% of those incarcerated in U.S. prisons[38] are black, even though African Americans make up only 13% of the general population. Black Americans are dramatically overrepresented among those to whom the American justice system is most punitive: This is systemic discrimination in a central institution, and evidence that a type-3 objection, as it relates to racial equality at least, is just wrong.

But how does political correctness relate to systemic injustice? Where the problem is pervasive material harm to particular groups, who has time to be fussy about the words we use or the Halloween costumes we wear? I am sympathetic to this line of thought; I don't think that how we express ourselves is more important than changing policy to bring liberation and comfort to those who lack it. What I claim is that our history of systemic discrimination toward women, people of color, LGBT+ folks, and people with disabilities has left an imprint on our linguistic and cultural norms. The sort of norm reformation characteristic of political correctness functions to draw our attention to the ideas implicit in our conduct, and to reform our practices where this examination reveals something troubling. Moving toward justice requires such scrutiny.

4. Other Objections and Replies

We've considered a few objections to political correctness. So far, these objections have involved taking issue with egalitarianism, or with the need to work toward it. But there are other commonly aired worries about political correctness that don't require any rejection of egalitarianism. Whereas the former sort of objection had to do with substantive political disagreement, the objections to which we now turn are what we might call procedural objections; they charge that PC is troubling not because its ends are bad ones, but because it achieves them in a dishonest or harmful way (Figure 11.2).

Mind Control

In George Orwell's famous dystopian novel *1984*, a totalitarian government controls its subjects by enforcing the use of an invented vocabulary, "newspeak," which makes it next to impossible to express disapproval of the regime. The powerful suggestion in the novel is that an inability to say something makes it hard to even think that thing. Nor should anyone suppose that newspeak is entirely fictional; documenters of political culture in Nazi Germany[39] noted how reforming language was also one tool of *Gleichschaltung*, or "Nazification," the process by which the Nazi party sought to saturate every aspect of daily life.

Critics of political correctness like Jonah Goldberg, a right-wing writer who has called *Gleichschaltung* "Nazi political correctness,"[40] have argued that PC culture in the United States is basically a campaign to introduce newspeak.

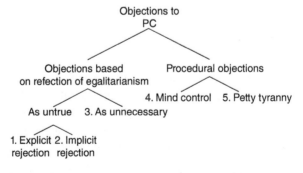

Figure 11.2
Procedural objections to PC

The newspeak objection gets traction in those cases where PC really does take the form of trying directly to modify speech, which, as I'll discuss below, is not all of them. Very few people really want to commit to the principle that campaigns of politically motivated linguistic norm change are always bad. If you think it's a good thing that uttering racial slurs is now stigmatized, then you are accepting the idea that politically motivated linguistic norm change isn't always bad, and isn't always a sign of creeping totalitarianism.

But what's the principled difference between the acceptable cases of linguistic norm change and the unacceptable ones? The advocate of PC linguistic norm reformation doesn't deny the basic premise of the mind-control objection: How we speak really does exert influence on how we think, and thus on how we behave. In fact, that's the whole reason linguistic norm reformation is sometimes worth pursuing! What the newspeak objection overlooks is that instances of so-called political correctness are not politicizing an otherwise pristinely apolitical linguistic sphere. Instead, political correctness functions to point out that our existing linguistic norms are *already* laden with political significance and that, where the political perspectives encoded are troubling ones, the norm should be changed.

Sometimes PC linguistic norm changes are motivated by a realization that, even if through confusion rather than malicious orchestration, a term we've been using implies something inaccurate or disrespectful. Consider how the language used in the mainstream to talk about transgender people has evolved in the last decade: that terms like "transsexual" and "cross-dresser" are properly acknowledged as non-synonymous with "transgender," and that using a trans person's preferred pronouns is recognized as an act of minimal decency, reflect an understanding that being trans isn't a matter of pretending to be something one isn't, or a status to which biological alteration is essential. Whereas mainstream language previously impugned the legitimacy of trans identity and so the dignity of trans people, reforming it is a natural consequence of seeing that this disrespect was a moral error.

In other cases, PC criticism aims to point out that some terms are *strategically* (if surreptitiously) used to evoke non-egalitarian sentiments. Consider the following statement made by long-time Republican strategist Lee Atwater in 1981:

> You start out in 1954 by saying "[N-word], [N-word], [N-word]." By 1968 you can't say "[N-word]"—that hurts you—backfires. So you say stuff like, uh, forced busing, states' rights, and all that stuff, and you're getting so abstract. Now you're talking about cutting taxes, and all these things you're talking about are totally economic things and a byproduct is, blacks get hurt worse than whites.[41]

This infamous statement offered an unusually candid confirmation of what antiracist activists of the time already knew: Phrases like "forced busing" (a reference to school integration), "states' rights," and "welfare" were racial *dog whistles*. Just as a literal dog whistle emits a sound too high-pitched for us to hear but audible to another audience (dogs), a political dog whistle is a phrase that carries a political message that won't be discerned by all listeners, but that those with certain (say, anti-black) attitudes, explicit or implicit, will recognize. A politician who complained about forced busing could winkingly indicate to sympathizers that they shared anti-black attitudes, even while maintaining plausible deniability. The trick is that, once a dog whistle is widely recognized as a proxy for direct expressions of racist sentiment, it loses its effectiveness; the kind of PC linguistic critique that allows us to reach that recognition is valuable because it not only stigmatizes racism and other forms of bigotry, but helps uncover these attitudes' more insidious disguises.

Some will suggest that changing language to reflect our collective ideals is fine, but that we should wait until after some widespread agreement about these ideals is reached before we do so. Otherwise, goes the worry, aren't we depriving dissidents of the raw linguistic materials needed to articulate their position, and so illegitimately cutting off debate? The answer is no, we aren't. It just isn't the case that PC linguistic changes make it impossible to articulate a position in disagreement with the egalitarian norms that they serve. A person can still express general racial animosity without the use of a slur (this, after all, is the function of the dog whistle), can still express opposition to integration or civil rights without using the phrase "forced busing," and can still dispute the proper treatment of trans people while using the phrase "transgender" rather than the aforementioned non-synonymous alternatives. While a PC overhaul of linguistic options can strip our language of advantages it once conferred on the non-egalitarian perspective and install in it certain convenient options for the expression of egalitarian sentiment, it doesn't render any particular views ineffable. Furthermore, it's not as though PC linguistic change can be imposed by fiat upon a population completely unsympathetic to it; the level of uptake that a given norm change receives is to some degree a function of the proportion of the population that sees it as judicious.

I close this discussion of the mind-control objection by noting that the category of things that now get criticized as "too PC" extends beyond efforts to revise linguistic norms. Whereas the first generation of PC critics focused mainly on things like campus speech codes, which were explicit attempts to modify speech, a recent review of the contemporary discourse around political correctness notes that critics now also target "voluntary student or faculty activities ranging from student protests, to the creation of student 'safe spaces,' to professorial uses of 'trigger warnings,'"[42] and even things like multiculturalism policies,[43] and voiced opposition to deportation of undocumented immigrants.[44]

It might be argued that what these phenomena have in common with instances of linguistic norm change is precisely a tendency to constrain speech and control thought, and that this is what unifies instances of political correctness. There is more to be said in response to this suggestion than can be offered here. However, we do have space to note that it just isn't clear how all these phenomena exert even indirect mind-controlling effects. A trigger warning, for instance, doesn't ask that anyone constrain their speech; in fact, it makes unrestricted speech compatible with the diverse and unknown sensitivities of an audience.[45]

While trigger warnings do presuppose the value of compassion for these sensitivities, they carry no other substantive political commitments; it's therefore not clear how their use could be an act of cognitive manipulation.

Petty Tyranny

Maybe the following has happened to you, or you've seen it happen to someone else: You said or did something you didn't realize was a violation of political correctness norms; you were sharply criticized and made to feel ashamed. Political correctness, you might then feel, is a menace because it threatens to let social stigma loose on perfectly well-meaning people. Jonah Goldberg articulates this worry as follows:

> Political correctness isn't literally terroristic, but it does govern through fear. No serious person can deny that the grievance politics of the American left keeps decent people in a constant state of fright—they are afraid to say the wrong word, utter the wrong thought, offend the wrong constituency.[46]

I genuinely hope that Goldberg is wrong that this state of fright is *constant*, but I am not going to deny that finding oneself on the wrong side of social stigma is, really, non-trivially distressing. Norms do not change immediately; it takes a while for the mere possibility of some practice's deserving to be phased out to percolate across a population, and then for anything approaching consensus to build around this. Paired with the fact that cultural norms work by attaching stigma to certain actions, it's not surprising that, during the process of new norms' roll-out, some well-intentioned people will find themselves on the receiving end of public rebuke.

A first response is that, for many of us, reaching political maturity requires that we discard our claims to total innocence; the mere fact that I am well intentioned doesn't mean that I haven't been participating in a harmful practice. And so, if I find myself called out for unthinkingly saying or doing something discriminatory, I hope I have the strength to receive this criticism attentively and bear up under the social disapproval that accompanies it, without descending into defensiveness. In short, if we believe in progressive reformation of norms, having the courage of this particular conviction means sticking it out through personal discomfort.

A second response, however, is that we can endorse a change in norms without saying that unlimited brutality is justified in bringing it about; we can defend egalitarianism without maintaining that no attempt at egalitarian reform has ever gone awry, even badly awry, either in misidentifying a norm that deserved to be changed or imposing punitive measures disproportionate to the crime of resisting the new norm. In changing cultural norms to make them more just, it makes sense to distinguish between the stubborn opponent of egalitarianism and someone who just hasn't had the rationale behind the new norm explained to them yet, and to be sensitive to the many gradations between these points. When we encounter someone displaying behavior that reinforces a regime of prejudice, there are lots of tough questions before us as we decide how to react. I hope that we'll be kind where we can be, and charitable about other people's intentions where this makes sense. But the fact that we sometimes mess this up, or even that it's possible for bad actors to exploit norm change as an opportunity to vent their spleen under cover of righteousness, doesn't invalidate the justice of the general project of norm change.

5. Conclusion

I've made it clear that I think the phenomenon sometimes referred to as "political correctness" is a generally positive one. Something I've hinted at, and want to close by making explicit, is that I also think that the the expression "political correctness" hurts our public discourse.

That, for instance, trigger warnings, policies of amnesty for immigration violations, and the mere expression of pro-diversity sentiment are among the phenomena now decried as politically correct suggests that the term is increasingly a derogatory term for progressive politics generally. Where this is so, to criticize something as PC is just to say that it is associated with the political left, and to suggest that the speaker is in disagreement with left-wing politics. There is something disingenuous about masking substantive political disagreement with the use of a phrase that bears a lingering association with procedural critique in this way.

Let's think back to Donald Trump's debate comments, alluded to in this essay's introduction. Would Candidate Trump not have better served the public interest by defending his choice to say degrading things about women on its merits (or else admitting his error) rather than dismissing the question with the political buzzword that "political correctness" has become? Yes. And would Trump's time spent in anti-PC polemic against President Obama and Secretary Clinton not have better informed Americans' deliberation about how to vote had it been spent offering real criticism of their policies? Clearly. If these observations have an air of naïveté about them, it is because Trump's comments were evidently not real attempts to engage in reasoned defense of his personal conduct or his policies; they were aimed at revving up a constituency for whom invocations of political correctness made salient a common animosity toward the left. While the expression "politically correct" feels like a convenient shorthand for a kind of norm change that is a disorienting aspect of contemporary life, its use is now an investment in an apparatus that mainly functions to obscure and polarize the political landscape.

COMPREHENSION QUESTIONS

1. Why is political correctness important to promoting egalitarian values within society?
2. What is a reformation of norms, and why is it associated with political correctness?
3. What is the difference between de facto discrimination and de jure discrimination?

4. What is "newspeak"? Why is it dangerous?
5. What is a political dog whistle? How does it relate to the PC conversation?

DISCUSSION QUESTIONS

1. Hyska says that "reaching political maturity requires that we discard our claims to total innocence." What does this mean? And is Hyska correct? Can we be held responsible for participating in a system that we didn't design or choose?
2. What's so bad about limiting free speech rights? Obviously, Americans care deeply about free speech. But we care about lots of things that, ultimately, aren't terribly important. (Consider, for instance, the latest Marvel movie, or most of what happens on social media.) Other countries get along fine with more restrictive speech policies. Why couldn't America do the same?
3. Recall the Megyn Kelly/Trump exchange. How was the term PC used to avoid the question at hand? How did it allow Trump to criticize the left? Was Hyska's analysis fair? Why or why not?

Case 2

Hyska responds to worries about one sort of linguistic reform, but there are other ways that people try to reform language to serve moral and political goals. Consider the way that people use the word "violence" in broader and broader ways; they don't simply use it to talk about causing physical damage, but also to talk about a wide range of other behaviors that cause negative feelings in others. Spencer Case—a contributor to this book—calls this "concept inflation." Consider his discussion of the term "gaslighting":

> One of Aesop's fables is about a shepherd boy who, out of boredom, repeatedly cries "Wolf!" when no wolf is present. As a result, the villagers lose faith in his testimony, and no one listens to his warnings when a real wolf shows up to devour his flock. The story shows why it's bad to lie and why it's in our interest to be honest. But lying is not the only manipulation of language that degrades trust. Consider a slightly different story.
>
> Suppose that instead of one shepherd boy, there are a few dozen. They are tired of the villagers dismissing their complaints about less threatening creatures like stray dogs and coyotes. One of them proposes a plan: they will start using the word "wolf" to refer to all menacing animals. They agree and the new usage catches on. For a while, the villagers are indeed more responsive to their complaints. The plan backfires, however, when a real wolf arrives and cries of "Wolf!" fail to trigger the alarm they once did.
>
> What the boys in the story do with the word "wolf," modern intellectuals do with words like "violence" [and "gaslighting"] . . . The term ["gaslighting"] originated with Patrick Hamilton's 1938 play, *Gas Light*, which was later adapted into movies in Britain and the United States, both named *Gaslight*. The plot centers around a woman who begins to lose her grip on reality because of her husband's pathological lying. According to Dictionary.com, to "gaslight" someone is "to cause (a person) to doubt his or her sanity through the use of psychological manipulation." Gaslighting is characterized by pervasive, blatant

Case 2 (continued)

lying. The perpetrator might confidently deny that the victim heard him say something that he clearly said moments ago.

Some intellectuals define "gaslighting" so loosely that it need not involve outright lying; this way, speech they dislike can be called "gaslighting." Two professors of political science at Seattle University write: "Just as the process of white supremacy does not require those who are complicit to understand the racist nature of their actions, awareness is also not determinative of whether the process of racial gaslighting is taking place." Examples of racial gaslighting, according to them, include dominant groups "tone policing" minorities who have every right to be angry about their oppression and—apparently— expressing any conservative opinion about race . . .

[This is concept inflation.] Concept inflation is a lot like lying. Immanuel Kant observed that lying couldn't be effective in a world where everybody lied, since no one would be believed. Just as lying is parasitic on a truth norm, concept inflation is parasitic on norms of usage. In Lewis Carroll's *Through the Looking Glass*, Humpty Dumpty tells Alice: "When I use a word, it means just what I choose it to mean—neither more nor less." Humpty Dumpty is wrong, however; if people could define the meanings of words as they liked, language couldn't be useful for transmitting ideas.[47]

What do you think Hyska would say about all this? Could you extend her egalitarian argument to defend a bit of "concept inflation"? Or do you think that Hyska would want to condemn revisions of words like "gaslighting"?

REPLY TO HYSKA
TULLY BORLAND

Today, giving a scientific explanation of the gender pay gap can get you fired, and tweeting against safe spaces can get you placed on medical leave.[48] Tomorrow, you could be fired or fined for owning or reading the wrong books. "Impossible!" But is it? When writing my original essay, I was given advice by some on the right and left not even to mention certain words in an essay about language and words. *Fuck* or *damn* can be mentioned, but some terms are unmentionable. Even philosophers must pretend to be children and say the *N-word* or leave out letters such as *c*nt*. Huck Finn isn't being read anymore; too controversial! Then it dawned on me: PC speech codes are like book burnings. The only way to ensure that no one is ever triggered is to make some words and ideas unmentionable and unthinkable, and the only way to do that is to get rid of them—burn them. But who decides what is committed to the flames? Today it might be you or your friends. Tomorrow it might not.

1. The Nature of PC Speech

Hyska is right that political correctness involves a reformation of norms; however, such reformation need not be tied to egalitarianism.[49] Stretching back to John Stuart Mill, there are classical liberals who consider themselves egalitarians but think that speech is sacrosanct. No matter who you are or what you think, one of the primary functions of speech is to express your deepest convictions about what you believe is *true*. Non-egalitarians suffer harm if they are forbidden to express what they think is true.

Conversely, one could be in favor of speech codes and changing norms while only paying lip service to egalitarianism. There are a number of feminists, for instance, whose main concern is to empower women, but who aren't similarly concerned to rectify the numerous adverse inequalities befalling men, such as lower lifespan, lower college enrollment, higher likelihood of committing suicide, addiction to drugs, loss of custody of children, and on and on. Thus, Hyska's depiction of PC speech is more of an abstract ideal than representative of real-life trends.[50] A better understanding of PC speech is this: whatever speech norms leftists claim should be enforced to achieve their utopian goals.

2. Just or Unjust Norm Changes?

Even if we were all egalitarians in Hyska's sense, there's room for disagreement about which norms should change. Arguments for norm changes can be based on popular, but ultimately unsubstantiated, empirical claims (e.g., trigger warnings). They can be based on popular, but extremely controversial, philosophical claims (e.g., that there are upward of 100 genders). And they can be based on popular, but ultimately speculative, estimations of the costs of allowing norms to change more slowly, while ignoring the very real costs of rapid change to the public square.

The use of so-called trigger warnings is a case in point. Everyone agrees that professors should be given the freedom to give warnings about sensitive content in a course. Yet most professors protest against one-size-fits-all policies about the content of their courses, since the professors are the real experts in their fields. Is it in the interest of the general population of students, or even those who have suffered trauma, to avoid controversial readings? A recent study found that trigger warnings *increase* one's sense of vulnerability and anxiety as well as increasing the perception that trauma victims are vulnerable.[51] It's far from obvious that codes mandating trigger warnings are in the best interest of anyone besides those who have the power to enforce them. Why not let professors decide?

Or consider the debate over codes forcing professors to use students' preferred pronouns: Is it just to force professors to learn scores of newly invented pronouns (*ze, zir, xem, pers, aer, aerself*, etc.) and memorize which apply to each student? If a professor sincerely believes that there are only two genders and not upwards of 100, should she be forced to engage in speech that she thinks perpetuates falsity? Or suppose a professor believes that gender dysphoria is the correct diagnosis of a male who feels he is a female and that therapy would be better for the person than a sex change in the long run.[52] Why should she be forced to engage in what she believes is false and harmful to the student?[53] Now, perhaps there are good reasons why the professor should give in; if so, those reasons should be given to change the professors' minds *rationally*. The alternative is that conscientious objectors to new PC policies be fired or fined, and if they can't pay the fine, *go to jail*—an extreme outcome indeed. The change in norms about racial slurs gives us guidance in how to proceed: This change occurred in the United States absent university speech codes or "hate speech" laws but instead as minds were changed in the face of arguments.[54] Why should other changes be any different?[55]

3. Democracy and Coercion

Everyone agrees that sometimes norms should change. But when? And how? If a word offends two people but changing our language offends ninety-eight, who decides? One answer: A democracy should decide. In a democracy, the majority rules even though there are provisions in place (such as a constitution) to protect basic rights of minorities. The underlying idea is simplicity itself—more people are happier when more people rule. But most people don't want to be told by the powerful PC minority that they have to speak a certain way or they'll lose their job. Nevertheless, suppose there are times when majorities shouldn't rule. In such cases, there are two means for changing the majority's norms: coercion or argumentation.[56] Coercing adults is rarely justified, so a case for coercive means (e.g., speech codes) would need to pass a high threshold. If rational persuasion is preferable, those on the left need to make the case that a norm change increases overall well-being or that there are moral rights violations so egregious that the majority should change their minds.[57,58]

COMPREHENSION QUESTIONS

1. Why do non-egalitarians suffer harm if their free speech is limited?
2. What is the difference between coercion, on the one hand, and argumentation or rational persuasion, on the other?

DISCUSSION QUESTIONS

1. Borland states, "A better understanding of PC speech is this: whatever speech norms leftists claim should be enforced to achieve their utopian goals." Do you agree or disagree with this interpretation? Why or why not?
2. How and when do you think language ought to change? What current linguistic practices do you think of as being harmful?

REPLY TO BORLAND
MEGAN HYSKA

Borland and I agree that the debate over political correctness can be conducted in two different spirits. The first is a staunchly partisan one, in which leftists think PC is good because it advances some of their substantive goals, the right disapproves of it because it detracts from theirs, and neither side is sincerely concerned with its procedural defensibility. The other is one in which parties with different substantive political commitments nonetheless try to agree to some common rules of conduct (i.e., procedural norms). Borland and I also seem to agree that this debate is only worth conducting if it can take place in this second spirit.

So in that spirit, let's examine what Borland takes to be some paradigm cases of PC to see if they display the distinctive evils he claims. His examples include the use of new, alternative language (e.g., "undocumented" instead of "illegal") as well as alleged misuses of existing language. For instance, Borland regards Nancy

Pelosi's allegation that Obamacare (i.e., the Affordable Care Act [ACA]) would produce "more liberty" as akin to the Orwellian "Freedom Is Slavery." But this analogy doesn't stick. The danger of a totalitarian government's alleging that "Freedom Is Slavery" is that it is a falsehood so outrageous (since freedom and slavery are virtual opposites) that to believe it you'd need to revise your very concept of freedom. But not all false beliefs have this concept-destroying effect. If I come to believe that it is raining when it's not, I might have accepted some bad evidence, but I probably won't have destroyed my concept of raininess. The ACA's essential tradeoff was to limit some freedoms for both consumers and insurers in order to secure a general freedom to access coverage regardless of income and preexisting conditions. Even if we conceded that this tradeoff didn't work, that it didn't produce more liberty, and that Pelosi knew it wouldn't, it's not clear that someone would have to alter their very concept of freedom in order to reach the false belief that the ACA was a liberatory policy. In any case, to concede that much would probably be to allow an interpretation too partisan to be useful in non-partisan discourse.

Borland devotes another part of his essay to arguing against hate speech codes. True university hate speech codes saw their heyday, and were subsequently subject to successful legal challenge, in the 1980s and 1990s.[59] What critics like Borland and FIRE continue to worry about is limitation on speech sneaking into general codes of conduct. Of note is that Borland's objection to hate speech codes is mediated by the rejection of a particular argument in their favor: that such codes protect an individual right not to be harmed or offended by speech. I agree with Borland's assessment that this is not a persuasive argument in favor of hate speech codes since we can't consistently defend a right against being offended. However, there are stronger arguments he doesn't consider. Our linguistic norms needn't prevent harm to individuals as such, but they should uphold justice. In part, this means preventing an individual's race or gender (among other features) from rendering him or her a target for a disproportionate share of harm.

Whereas Borland thinks that PC endangers free speech, I argue that an openness to language change is required by a commitment to freedom of speech. One thing we use speech to do, after all, is to discuss how well or poorly the language at our disposal describes the world. This sort of metalinguistic speech is as worthy of protection as any other. Borland attempts to balance a permissiveness toward language change with his anti-PC position when he says that some speech innovations (e.g., vulgarities) arise "organically" whereas PC expressions are "invented," implying that it's only the latter he takes issue with. But the invented/organic distinction is specious; all new language is invented, even as a certain amount of such change taking place over time might be called an organic feature of language communities.

Perhaps what Borland means to single out is "top-down" linguistic change, where a new phrase is invented by the powerful and disseminated via coercion. But a worry about top-down pressures on the language does not justify a presumption in favor of existing language norms; there is just as much reason to think that pre-PC linguistic norms are the consequence of powerful parties' interests having permeated the language. Consider an example: that "man" has historically been used to refer generically to human beings, reflects a belief that Simone de Beauvoir, writing in the 1940s, diagnosed as follows: "The relation of the two sexes is not that of two electrical poles: the man represents both the positive and the neuter . . . humanity is male, and man defines woman, not in herself, but in relation to himself . . . He is the Subject; he is the Absolute. She is the Other."[60] That our language represents manhood as the basic condition of humanity, and womanhood as a deviation from it, is no accident: It is the natural product of millennia of male dominance in all aspects of life. The PC suggestion that "man" not be used as though it referred to all of humanity is a rejection of the top-down effects of male dominance on the language.

For Borland, PC is "speech that adheres to . . . the leftist party line." Notably, he admits that the sort of speech-policing he takes issue with is not unique to the left; it's just that the expression "politically correct" refers only to the subset of such policing that is associated with the left. This immediately raises a question: If you dislike the policing of language not because you believe it inevitably serves leftist goals (this would in any case be simple partisanship) but because it transgresses commonly held procedural norms, why carve out leftist norm change (i.e., political correctness) as a category meriting particular attention? I suspect there is no non-partisan answer to this question; as I argued in my essay, objecting to "political correctness" is an inherently partisan exercise.

COMPREHENSION QUESTIONS

1. What two spirits can the PC conversation have?
2. What does it mean to be a partisan or non-partisan issue?

DISCUSSION QUESTIONS

1. Do you think PC-ness is more of a partisan or non-partisan concern? How ought we to handle language change in the future?
2. Hyska claims that some linguistic changes are just corrections of bias: Using "mankind" to refer to all people, for instance, just entrenches a view according to which men are dominant. What do you think about this? Can you think of other examples where this is plausibly what's going on?

FURTHER READINGS

Baldwin, James. "My Dungeon Shook—Letter to My Nephew on the One Hundredth Anniversary of Emancipation." In *The Fire Next Time*. New York: Dial Press, 1963.
Brown, Alex. *Hate Speech Law: A Philosophical Examination*. New York: Routledge, 2017.
Calhoun, Cheshire. "Political Correctness." In *Encyclopedia of Ethics*, edited by Lawrence C. Becker and Charlotte B. Better. New York: Routledge, 1992.
Free Expression on Campus: A Survey of U.S. College Students and U.S. Adults. Gallup, Knight Foundation & Newseum Institute, 2016. https://knightfoundation.org/media/uploads/publication_pdfs/FreeSpeech_campus.pdf.

Friedman, Marilyn, and Jan Narveson. *Political Correctness: For and Against.* Lanham, MD: Rowman & Littlefield, 1995.

Haney López, Ian. *Dog Whistle Politics: How Coded Racial Appeals Have Reinvented Racism and Wrecked the Middle Class.* New York: Oxford University Press, 2014.

Hughes, Geoffrey. *Political Correctness: A History of Semantics and Culture.* Malden, MA: Wiley-Blackwell, 2010.

Jacobs, James B., and Kimberly Potter. *Hate Crimes: Criminal Law & Identity Politics.* New York: Oxford University Press, 1998.

Kitrosser, Heidi. "Free Speech, Higher Education, and the PC Narrative." *Minnesota Law Review* 101 (2017): 1987–2064.

Landrieu, Jay. *In the Shadow of Statues: A White Southerner Confronts History.* New York: Viking, 2018.

NOTES

1. For a detailed account of the history of political correctness see Geoffrey Hughes, *Political Correctness: A History of Semantics and Culture* (Malden, MA: Wiley-Blackwell, 2010), especially the first two chapters.

2. This phrase was coined by William Vallicella, http://maverickphilosopher.typepad .com/maverick_philosopher_stri/2018/04/what-is-political-correctness.html (accessed June 22, 2018).

3. Cheshire Calhoun, "Political Correctness," *Encyclopedia of Ethics*, edited by Lawrence C. Becker and Charlotte B. Better (New York: Routledge, 1992), 1337–1338, http:// cw.routledge.com/ref/ethics/entries/politicalcorrectness.pdf (accessed March 25, 2018).

4. "Political Correctness Revisited," *Center for the Study of Ethics in Society Papers* 11, no. 1 (May 1998): 1–29.

5. "Political Correctness Revisited," 26.

6. Cheshire Calhoun adds, "'Politically Correct' also implies the presence of a sufficient power base to enforce compliance with whatever is politically correct, either through formal penalties or informal disapproval and shunning. That is, it implies the presence of political correctors and the threat of being corrected. As a result, political correctness is implicitly linked with authoritarianism, coercion, censorship, and the bad taste to correct others' manners." "Political Correctness," 1338.

7. As a further exercise for the reader, see how many politically incorrect statements are used in this book by authors on the right versus left.

8. This hypothetical scenario is not imaginable for some versions of right-wing politics. Anarcho-capitalists, other libertarians, and classical liberals are strongly in favor of free speech; such a scenario seems incoherent with regard to those political systems.

9. As further evidence, consider that, in the presidential campaign of 2017, almost no one objected to Hillary Clinton's use of the term *deplorables* to refer to Trump supporters *on the grounds that she was using politically incorrect speech*, even though the term was political and incorrect from the right's perspective, since the term connotes that those re-ferred to have less than human dignity. Rather, those on the right took offense; but rather than demanding that this word be listed among the annals of hate speech codes, instead they playfully appropriated the term for themselves. Consider as well that Trump was praised by many on the right because he was not afraid to use politically incorrect speech and vilified by the left for the same reason. No doubt Trump and others on the right use words and phrases in a polemical way; it's just that they don't count as PC speech.

10. http://dhr.maryland.gov/food-supplement-program/spending-food-supplement-program-benefits/ (accessed March 14, 2018).

11. https://pelosi.house.gov/issues/health-care (accessed June 22, 2018).

12. A point also made by the "Maverick Philosopher," http://maverickphilosopher.typepad.com/maverick_philosopher/2017/01/undocumented-workers-and-illegal-aliens.html (accessed March 24, 2018).

13. https://www.justice.gov/opa/pr/departments-justice-and-housing-and-urban-development-award-175-million-help-justice-involved (accessed June 22, 2018).

14. *Retarded* is a good example of the phenomenon called the "euphemism treadmill" (allegedly coined by Steven Pinker). Itself once a euphemism for such words as *moron*, *idiot*, and *imbecile*, *retarded* becomes stigmatized, and yet another euphemism is needed to replace it.

15. https://www.census.gov/prod/2/gen/96arc/ivatuck.pdf (accessed March 22, 2018).

16. We might recall Marx's protest that philosophers have only interpreted the world in various ways when the point is to change it.

17. See David Boonin, *Should Race Matter* (Cambridge: Cambridge University Press, 2011), 208.

18. https://www.thefire.org/spotlight-on-speech-codes-2018/ (accessed March 17, 2018).

19. Hate speech laws are a species of hate crime laws. For an overview of hate crime laws (including hate speech), see James B. Jacobs and Kimberly Potter, *Hate Crimes: Criminal Law & Identity Politics* (New York: Oxford University Press, 1998); Alex Brown, *Hate Speech Law: A Philosophical Examination* (New York: Routledge, 2017).

20. https://www.met.police.uk/advice-and-information/hate-crime/what-is-hate-crime/(my emphasis in the quotation; accessed March 14, 2018).

21. Where reason ends, coercion might have to be used, for instance when dealing with small children who either don't know any better or lack sufficient self-control.

22. The argument is not formally valid but could easily be made to be such.

23. John Stuart Mill's harm principle is well established in Anglo-American law. It is roughly the idea that behavior that harms others without their consent provides a non-negligible reason to regulate that behavior. For Mill, offending others does not typically count as a harm. For more on the harm principle, see the *Stanford Encyclopedia of Philosophy*'s entry at https://plato.stanford.edu/entries/mill-moral-political/#HarPri (accessed March 25, 2018).

24. For example, see Bill Maher's discussion with Charlie Rose: https://www.realclearpolitics.com/video/2014/09/10/maher_vs_charlie_rose_to_claim_islam_is_like_other_religions_is_naive_and_plain_wrong.html (accessed March 26, 2018).

25. *Discourses, Fragments, Handbook*, translated by Robin Hard (New York: Oxford University Press, 2014), 298.

26. Jacobs and Potter, *Hate Crimes: Criminal Law & Identity Politics*, 131.

27. Marilyn Friedman and Jan Narveson, *Political Correctness: For and Against* (Lanham, MD: Rowman & Littlefield, 1995), 102.

28. I thank Amy Borland, Dan Demetriou, Bob Fischer, Allan Hillman, Chad McIntosh, Jannai Shields, and William Vallicella for helpful comments on earlier drafts of this essay.

29. Megyn Kelly, "First Republican Primary Debate," Quicken Loans Arena, Cleveland, Ohio, August 6, 2015.

30. Kelly, "First Republican Debate."

31. Donald Trump, "Second Presidential Debate," Washington University in St. Louis, Missouri, October 9, 2016.

32. Amy Sherry, "Trump: Clinton Won't Use the Term 'Radical Islamic Terrorists,'" Politifact, October 9, 2016, www.politifact.com/truth-o-meter/statements/2016/oct/09 /donald-trump/trump-clinton-wont-use-term-radical-islamist-terro/.

33. Trump, "Second Presidential Debate."

34. The claim here is primarily that things like race and gender don't make a difference to the rights an individual has. I don't intend to make any commitment here about whether, say, a history of violence against others makes such a difference.

35. Jennifer A. Bennice and Patricia A. Resick, "Marital Rape: History, Research, and Practice," *Trauma, Violence, & Abuse* 4, no. 3 (2003): 228–246.

36. Alexandra Minna Stern, *Eugenic Nation: Faults and Frontiers of Better Breeding in Modern America* (Berkeley: University of California Press, 2015).

37. German Lopez, "Police Shootings and Brutality in the US: 9 Things You Should Know," Vox, last modified May 6, 2017, www.vox.com/cards/police-brutality-shootings -us/us-police-racism, cf. Jon Swaine, Oliver Laughland, and Jamiles Lartey, "Black Americans Killed by Police Twice as Likely to Be Unarmed as White People," *The Guardian*, June 1, 2015, www.theguardian.com/us-news/2015/jun/01/black-americans -killed- by-police-analysis.

38. "Inmate Race," Federal Bureau of Prisons, last modified February 24, 2018, www.bop .gov/about/statistics/statistics inmate race.jsp, cf. Michelle Alexander, *The New Jim Crow* (New York: New Press, 2010).

39. E.g., Victor Klemperer, *The Language of the Third Reich* (New York: Bloomsbury, 2013).

40. Jonah Goldberg, *Liberal Fascism: The Secret History of the American Left, From Mussolini to the Politics of Meaning* (New York: Doubleday, 2008), 300.

41. Originally printed without speaker identification in Alexander Lamis, The Two-Party South (New York: Oxford University Press, 1984); cf. Rick Perlstein, "Exclusive: Lee Atwater's Infamous 1981 Interview on the Southern Strategy," *The Nation*, November 13, 2012, www .thenation.com/article/exclusive-lee-atwaters-infamous-1981-interview-southern-strategy/.

42. Heidi Kitrosser, "Free Speech, Higher Education, and the PC Narrative," *Minnesota Law Review* 101 (2017): 1991.

43. Kitrosser, "Free Speech," 2001.

44. Kitrosser, "Free Speech," 2036.

45. For an extended description and defense of trigger warnings, see Kate Manne, "Why I Use Trigger Warnings," *New York Times*, September 19, 2015, www.nytimes.com /2015/09/20/opinion/sunday/why-i-use-trigger-warnings.html.

46. Goldberg, *Liberal Fascism*, 282–283.

47. https://quillette.com/2019/02/14/the-boy-who-inflated-the-concept-of-wolf/.

48. https://nypost.com/2016/10/30/nyu-professor-who-opposed-pc-culture-gets-booted -from-classroom/; https://pjmedia.com/lifestyle/empathy-gap-blame-james-damores -problems-google/ (a; [Accessed Septembe9/r 13, /2018).]

49. Hyska's definition of egalitarianism is also problematic: "Egalitarianism says that the needs and desires of all people in our society are equally important, regardless of their race, gender, and so on, and equally deserving of reflection in our laws, policies, and social conventions." If this is an accurate definition of egalitarianism, egalitarianism is false. It's not true that the desires of pedophiles, rapists, murders, and so forth are equally important and deserving of reflection in our laws, policies, and social conventions. Many of our desires are disordered or downright wicked. Still, if it is thought that our desires are equally important, then it's certainly the case that desiring the freedom to assert what is politically incorrect is no less important than desiring to squelch that freedom.

50. I agree with Hyska when she says that the use of *political correctness* is associated with progressive politics, but I demur when she says that "[t]here is something disingenuous about masking substantive political disagreement with the use of a phrase [*political correctness*] that bears a lingering association with procedural critique in this way." From its very inception, political correctness is a phenomenon associated with the left, and the term tracks that phenomenon. Of course, from the perspective of the left, political correctness will be seen as "positive" or good, but there is nothing disingenuous about describing political correctness as a phenomenon of the left if indeed it is. Rather, it's an unmasking.

51. https://www.sciencedirect.com/science/article/pii/S0005791618301137 (accessed September 8, 2018). See also Greg Lukianoff and Jonathan Haidt, *The Coddling of the American Mind: How Good Intentions and Bad Ideas Aare Setting Up a Generation for Failure* (New York: Penguin Press, 2018), Chapter 1.

52. Some studies suggest that upwards of 80% of children with gender dysphoria eventually come to identify with their biological sex. See https://www.transgendertrend.com/children-change-minds/; https://www.transgendertrend.com/wp-content/uploads/2017/10/Steensma-2013_desistance-rates.pdf. See the following articles discussing the success of sex-change surgeries for increasing one's happiness: http://www.thepublicdiscourse.com/2016/06/17166/; https://www.theguardian.com/society/2004/jul/30/health.mentalhealth (accessed September 14, 2018).

53. Thus, many people disagree with Hyska's assertion that using a transgendered person's preferred pronoun is an "act of minimal decency," just as many object to calling someone "black" who identifies as such but has white ancestry and to all appearances is white.

54. Hyska appears to disagree: "Some will suggest that changing language to reflect our collective ideals is fine, but that we should wait until after some widespread agreement about these ideals is reached before we do so. Otherwise, goes the worry, aren't we depriving dissidents of the raw linguistic materials needed to articulate their position, and so illegitimately cutting off debate? The answer is no, we aren't. It just isn't the case that PC linguistic changes make it impossible to articulate a position in disagreement with the egalitarian norms that they serve." But is this true? Surely not! Examples of professors silenced or fired for even entertaining arguments (whether they agree with them or not), let alone expressing politically incorrect views, abound. I invite you to ask yourself how many times in your university education you encountered *any* arguments on "the wrong side of history,"—for instance, that there are genetic explanations for IQ differences in race? Or evolutionary explanations for sex differences in STEM? Or that colonialism isn't intrinsically evil? Or in favor of patriarchy? Or against multiculturalism? Or that whites are majority victims in race-related crimes? Or that a disproportionate number of Muslims rape white women in European countries? Or that transgenderism is a mental illness? The willful lack of engagement with controversial issues is even creeping into philosophy (or "philosophy"?) where long ago *nothing* was beyond the pale of inquiry.

55. Space constraints prevent me from adequately addressing the issue of dog whistling. Two points will have to suffice.: First, it's worth noting that dog whistling is in no way confined to the right—for instance, *diversity/inclusiveness*: fewer men or whites; *working-class white*: racist knuckle-dragger; *nationalism*: white supremacy; *equality*: coercion to achieve goals of left-wing special interests; *hate speech*: right-wing speech. Second, charity compels care when condemning someone of dog whistling. For instance, not everyone on the left who says *background checks* is dog whistling about the fact that persons of minority races commit more crimes on average.

56. Hyska is not explicit about the extent to which she supports coercion in the form of speech codes and "hate speech" laws, but she seems to lean against substantive speech rights when she says, "I don't think that how we express ourselves is more important than changing policy to bring liberation and comfort to those who lack it." But how do we know when free expression should be censored to bring about "liberation"? "[W]here the political perspectives encoded are troubling ones, the norm should be changed." Troubling to whom? And to what extent should we utilize coercive means? "[W]e can endorse a change in norms without saying that unlimited brutality is justified in bringing it about." Drawing the line at "unlimited brutality" is cold comfort.

57. Hyska overlooks the coercive nature of PC norm changes when she says that "*allowing* transgender people to use the bathroom associated with their gender identity; [and] *asking* students to refrain from dressing up as a native American or member of another ethnic group for Halloween" are decried as PC (my emphases in the quotation). On the contrary, people objected to Obama's "Dear Colleague" instructions about how to interpret Title IX, not only because it confused the explicit language in Title IX of sex with gender, but also because it forced a one-size-fits-all policy on local schools that trampled on city's and state's rights. Hardly anyone objected to students being *asked* not to dress up like people from another racial or ethnic group; rather, they cringed that students were coerced not to do so.

58. Thanks to Allan Hillman and Chad McIntosh for comments on earlier drafts. If there are any mistakes, now you know who is to blame. Thanks also to Bob Fischer for the invitation to write these essays and for a number of helpful suggestions.

59. David L. Hudson Jr. and Lata Nott, "Hate Speech & Campus Speech Codes," Freedom Forum Institute, last modified March 2017, https://www.freedomforuminstitute.org /first-amendment-center/topics/freedom-of-speech-2/free-speech-on-public-college -campuses-overview/hate-speech-campus-speech-codes/.

60. Simone de Beauvoir, *The Second Sex*, translated by Constance Borde and Sheila Malovany-Chevallier (New York: Vintage, 2011).

CHAPTER 12

Religious Exemptions

RELIGIOUS BELIEF, DISCRIMINATION, AND THE LAW
JOHN CORVINO

Bob Jones University is a private non-denominational Christian school in Greenville, South Carolina. Founded in 1927, it has a history of influence in American conservative politics, having hosted major Republican presidential candidates as speakers—including Ronald Reagan, George W. Bush, and more recently, Ted Cruz.

Bob Jones University did not admit African or African American students until 1971, and then only if they were married. When in 1975 it began admitting unmarried blacks, it also expanded disciplinary rules forbidding interracial dating and marriage, as follows:

There is to be no interracial dating.

1. Students who are partners in an interracial marriage will be expelled.
2. Students who are members of or affiliated with any group or organization which holds as one of its goals or advocates interracial marriage will be expelled.
3. Students who date outside of their own race will be expelled.
4. Students who espouse, promote, or encourage others to violate the University's dating rules and regulations will be expelled.[1]

These rules remained in place until the year 2000, when they attracted renewed attention after a visit to the university by then–presidential candidate (later president) George W. Bush. Only then did the university rescind them.

Let me begin with what I take to be two uncontroversial observations. First, Bob Jones University's policy on interracial dating was *discriminatory*. Although it was worded neutrally, without reference to any particular race, it stemmed from, and contributed to, an unjust social regime. The leaders of Bob Jones University have since admitted as much.[2]

Second, this racist, discriminatory policy was based on the sincere religious beliefs of the university's leaders. Here's Bob Jones Senior, the school's founder:

> Now, we folks at Bob Jones University believe that whatever the Bible says is so; and we believe it says certain fundamental things that all Bible-believing Christians accept; but when the Bible speaks clearly about any subject, that settles it. Men do not always agree, because some are dumb—some people are spiritually dumb; but when the Bible is clear, there is not any reason why everybody should not accept it. . . .
>
> Now, notice—this is an important verse—the twenty-sixth verse of the seventeenth chapter of the Acts of the Apostles, "And hath made of one blood all nations of men for to dwell on all the face of the earth . . ." But do not stop there, ". . . and hath determined the times before appointed, and the bounds of their habitation." Now, what does that say? That God Almighty fixed the bounds of their habitations. That is as clear as anything that was ever said. . . .
>
> White folks and colored folks, you listen to me. You cannot run over God's plan and God's established order without having trouble. God never meant to have one race. It was not His purpose at all.[3]

The university reiterated this stance as recently as 1998, when a spokesperson explained: "God has separated people for his own purposes. He has erected barriers between the nations, not only land and sea barriers, but also ethnic, cultural, and language barriers. God has made people different from one another and intends those differences to remain. Bob Jones University is opposed to intermarriage of the races because it breaks down the barriers God has established."[4]

Here, then, is a stark example of religion-based discrimination—troubling, but hardly historically unique. Indeed, the university's explanation echoed wording used by the trial court judge in *Loving v. Virginia*, the case that led to the U.S. Supreme Court's striking down of anti-miscegenation laws: "Almighty God created the races white, black, yellow, malay and red, and he placed them on separate continents. And but for the interference with his arrangement there would be no cause for such marriages. The fact that he separated the races shows that he did not intend for the races to mix."[5]

Of course, other cases are more controversial today. Consider:

- Posing in front of a Confederate flag, a Florida gun retailer posts a video declaring his gun shop a "Muslim-Free Zone."[6]
- An Indiana woman is fired from her job as a Catholic school English teacher after she and her husband used in vitro fertilization (IVF) in an effort to have a second child.[7] Catholic moral teaching prohibits IVF.
- After "much prayer," a Michigan pediatrician declines to provide care for a lesbian couple's newborn baby; she sends a colleague as a substitute.[8]
- A New Jersey bridal shop refuses to sell a dress to a lesbian woman, telling her that her union would be "illegal" and "wrong." The woman had previously spent a day trying on dresses in the shop.[9]
- An Ohio baker cancels a birthday cake order after visiting a customer's Facebook page and realizing the cake was for the customer's same-sex

partner.[10] "I'm sorry," the baker wrote in a text to the customer, "I just realized your [*sic*] in a same-sex relationship and we do not do cakes for same sex weddings or parties."[11]

At the most general level, to discriminate is simply to distinguish. In that broad sense, discrimination is not necessarily a bad thing—thus, we speak of "discriminating shoppers" or "discriminating tastes." It is more common, however, to use the word in a narrower, negative sense: not merely differential treatment, but *unjust* differential treatment. In what follows, unless otherwise indicated, I will use "discrimination" and its cognates in this more common, negative sense.

The controversies arise when people differ about what justice requires. Is it discrimination to refuse to hire someone simply because of their physical unattractiveness? But what if you're hiring a model? A receptionist? Is it discrimination to refuse to place someone in a leadership position simply because she's a woman? But what if the leadership position is that of Catholic bishop? Is it discrimination to decline to provide same-sex wedding services because homosexual conduct conflicts with your religious beliefs? What about interracial weddings? Interfaith weddings?

1. Material Harm and Dignitary Harm

It is worth distinguishing two ways in which discrimination harms people. One is *material harm*: Discrimination limits people's access to goods and services. For instance, employment discrimination limits opportunities for making a living. Housing discrimination limits opportunities for a safe and comfortable home. Health care discrimination limits access to medical treatment. Public accommodations discrimination limits the ability to participate fully in the public sphere, and so on.

Some deny that these limitations constitute harms, strictly speaking: If a gun shop owner refuses to sell a gun to a Muslim, or a bridal shop owner refuses to sell a dress to a lesbian, they make these people no worse off than they were before; thus, they do not harm them.[12] For the moment, it matters less whether we categorize these examples as harms than that we recognize the different ways that discrimination affects people, one of which is by frustrating their material interests. (If you don't like "material harms," substitute the phrase "material effects.") So, for example, while there are various possible objections to Bob Jones University's interracial dating ban, one is that it *limited the educational options* of mixed-race couples.

But that's not the most important objection to the ban. After all, there were plenty of other schools willing to admit interracial couples, including other evangelical schools. Which brings us to a second and rather different type of harm: *dignitary harm*.

Although frequently mentioned in the literature, dignitary harm is seldom carefully defined. The concept sounds prima facie odd, combining a typically deontological notion (dignity) with a typically consequentialist one (harm). Dignitary harm does not merely mean offense or hurt feelings, although it often correlates with those. It is rather the harm involved in treating people as having less than equal moral standing. The "separate but equal" regime of the Jim Crow South, along with its echoes in policies like Bob Jones University's ban, provides a paradigmatic example: By treating blacks as inferior, such policies were an affront to their dignity. This would be true even if these policies had not been accompanied by widespread material harm—even if, for example, the separate facilities had been truly equal (which they were not).

Some further clarifications are in order. First, borrowing from Pablo Gilabert, we should distinguish between two different senses of dignity: dignity as a *normative status* that people possess in virtue of their humanity or rationality or autonomy or some other (possibly innate) feature, and dignity as the *social condition* of having that status acknowledged or respected.[13] Dignitary harm is concerned with the latter of these: the social condition.

Failure to distinguish the two senses can lead to odd results. Consider Justice Clarence Thomas's dissent in the same-sex marriage case *Obergefell v. Hodges*. After noting that our country has long treated human dignity as God-given and inalienable, he adds: "The corollary of that principle is that human dignity cannot be taken away by the government. Slaves did not lose their dignity (any more than they lost their humanity) because the government allowed them to be enslaved. Those held in internment camps did not lose their dignity because the government confined them. And those denied governmental benefits certainly do not lose their dignity because the government denies them those benefits. The government cannot bestow dignity, and it cannot take it away."[14]

One might just as easily (and strangely) argue that because *rights* are God-given and inalienable, we do not deprive people of their rights by enslaving them! Of course, governments cannot alter their citizens' normative status as persons. But when governments fail to recognize that status, they surely undermine dignity as a social condition.

Second, dignitary harm receives much of its force from social context. A quirky, isolated insult is less likely to threaten a person's social equality than one made in the context of systematic exclusion. My grandparents, who arrived in the United States at a time when the country was rife with anti-Catholic sentiment, experienced a greater sting from anti-Catholic slurs than I do.[15] Calling my British colleague a "limey" would not have the same effect as calling my Asian colleague a "chink" or calling me (as a gay man) a "faggot," given the different social contexts.

Finally, note how material and dignitary harm are related: The sting of dignitary harm often functions to systematically intimidate and exclude people in ways that have cumulative material effects.

2. Anti-Discrimination Law and LGBT Equality

Anti-discrimination law addresses both material and dignitary harm. It prohibits unequal treatment on the basis of traditionally targeted characteristics: generally race, sex, and religion, and in some jurisdictions others, including marital status, sexual orientation, and gender identity. Such law aims to ensure equal access in the public sphere.

It may seem paradoxical that the law seeks to promote equality by giving special attention to certain characteristics: If the goal is equality, why not treat everyone the same? But the paradox is specious. Sometimes the goal of equal treatment is best achieved by a process that gives certain factors extra scrutiny. And anti-discrimination law *does* treat all people equally with respect to those factors—after all, everyone has a race, a sex, a sexual orientation, and so on. (Not everyone has a religion, but anti-discrimination laws that enumerate "religion" generally protect agnostics and atheists too.)

Thus, in the current "culture wars" over LGBT equality, anti-discrimination law protects the conservative Christian heterosexual from unjust treatment by the gay atheist as much as it does the reverse. More so, in fact: Religion is a protected category at the federal level, whereas sexual orientation is not—indeed, fewer than half the states include it at the state level.[16]

Today, many discussions of anti-discrimination law and LGBT equality tend to focus on wedding services. Unfortunately, this focus misleadingly suggests that the biggest problem facing LGBT people is the inability to buy cakes and flowers. On the contrary: Anti-discrimination laws are mainly about access to employment, housing, and basic goods and services. LGBT people have been and continue to be the victims of unjust discrimination in these areas. Recent analyses by the Williams Institute at the University of California, Los Angeles, find that LGBT people file complaints related to employment, housing, and public-accommodations discrimination at the same rate (adjusted for population) that racial minorities and women do for race and sex discrimination.[17] The powerful phenomenon of the closet makes it likely that such discrimination goes underreported.

Consider employment discrimination. The U.S. Senate Report on the Employment Non-Discrimination Act provides some sobering statistics:[18]

- According to a 2008 report, 42% of lesbian, gay, and bisexual people have experienced at least one form of employment discrimination because of their sexual orientation.
- Twelve studies conducted in the last decade show that gay male workers are paid less on average than their heterosexual male co-workers. The wage gap identified in these studies varies between 10% and 32% of the heterosexual men's earnings.
- Lesbian couples have a poverty rate of 6.9% compared to 5.4% for different-sex married couples. Poverty rates for children of same-sex couples are twice as high as poverty rates for children of married heterosexual couples.
- A 2011 report found that 90% of transgender Americans experienced harassment, mistreatment, or discrimination at work because of their gender identity or took actions like hiding who they are to avoid it. Forty-seven percent of transgender Americans said they experienced an adverse job

outcome, such as being fired, not hired, or denied a promotion because they were transgender or gender non-conforming. Twenty-six percent of transgender Americans reported losing their jobs due to being transgender. Fifty percent of transgender Americans reported being harassed.

- Transgender respondents to a 2011 national survey were unemployed at twice the rate of the general population, and 15% reported a household income of under $10,000 a year, nearly four times the rate for the general population.

For much of this nation's history, discrimination against LGBT people was not merely tolerated but in fact legally sanctioned. The exclusion from marriage made even long-term same-sex couples legal strangers to each other, sometimes with devastating financial, legal, and personal effects. There has also been explicit governmental discrimination in employment.[19] And do not forget anti-sodomy laws, which turned most gay people into unapprehended felons, and had the further pernicious effect of limiting employment opportunities (because it's harder for felons, even presumed ones, to get jobs). Many of the loudest proponents of "liberty" today openly defended such laws, which were not struck down by the U.S. Supreme Court until *Lawrence v. Texas* in 2003.[20] Not coincidentally, these proponents defended them by appealing to religion. Here's Chief Justice Burger in *Bowers v. Hardwick* (1986), the decision that *Lawrence* overturned: "Condemnation of [homosexual conduct] is firmly rooted in Judeo-Christian moral and ethical standards. Homosexual sodomy was a capital crime under Roman law. During the English Reformation, when powers of the ecclesiastical courts were transferred to the King's Courts, the first English statute criminalizing sodomy was passed. Blackstone described 'the infamous crime against nature' as an offense of 'deeper malignity' than rape, a heinous act 'the very mention of which is a disgrace to human nature,' and 'a crime not fit to be named.'"[21]

Against this backdrop, anti-discrimination laws that enumerate sexual orientation and gender identity function to ensure that openly LGBT people, long marginalized, have a place at the table in public life. Although these laws are not mainly about wedding services, they include wedding services—which brings us to a brief discussion of the current conflicts.

3. Cake Wars

Rachel and Laurel Bowman-Cryer are a lesbian couple in Portland, Oregon, having relocated from Texas.[22] They had been together for eight years when in 2012 they decided to marry. Laurel had previously proposed numerous times, but Rachel had hesitated. She finally acquiesced in order to provide "permanency and commitment" to their two foster children, whom they hoped to adopt. The children were disabled, with "very high special needs."[23] Rachel and Laurel had taken the children into foster care after the death of their mother, who had been Laurel's best friend. The adoption was finally approved in 2013, following a bitter and emotional custody battle with the children's great-grandparents.

Once Rachel agreed to the wedding, she became excited about its planning. She and her mother attended a wedding expo where they encountered Melissa Klein of Sweet Cakes by Melissa, the bakery that had provided a cake for Rachel's mother's wedding two years prior. Eager to order from Sweet Cakes again, they made a tasting appointment for January 17, 2013.

When Rachel and her mother finally arrived for their appointment, Melissa's husband, Aaron Klein, asked for the name of the bride and groom. (Melissa was out that day.) After Rachel explained that there would be two brides, Aaron stated that Sweet Cakes did not make cakes for same-sex weddings because of his and Melissa's religious convictions. This upset Rachel, who began crying and was escorted out by her mother, who attempted to console her. Rachel felt ashamed, and was particularly concerned that she had embarrassed her mother, who not long before had disapproved of her daughter's homosexuality. When Rachel's mother returned to the shop to explain to Aaron how "she used to think like him, but her 'truth had changed,'" he quoted Leviticus 18:22: "You shall not lie with a male as one lies with a female; it is an abomination." (Leviticus makes no reference to lesbianism, but let's leave that aside.)

Wedding planning can be emotional, alternately joyous and stressful. In Rachel's case, the refusal of service hit particularly hard. Given her sensitive nature, her prior relationship experience, and her religious background—she had been raised Southern Baptist—the incident stirred up painful emotions. She cried for days, fought with Laurel, and even doubted that she was "supposed to love or be loved, have a family or go to heaven."[24]

You might think Rachel Bowman-Cryer overreacted. Indeed, a different individual, with a different emotional makeup, might have told Aaron Klein where he could stuff his cake. But not Rachel: She was hurt. Her mother was present; her children might have been as well. As Andrew Koppelman explains, by advertising their services as open to the public, the Kleins induced Rachel "to participate in the activity of her own rejection."[25] It felt like a humiliating bait-and-switch. This wasn't what she bargained for when she made the appointment with Sweet Cakes.

As a result of their refusal of service, the Kleins were eventually found to have violated Oregon's Equality Act, which prohibits discrimination in public accommodations on the basis of "race, color, religion, sex, sexual orientation, national origin, marital status or age." Sexual-orientation discrimination is the most relevant category here, although one might also make a case for sex, or even marital status.

The Kleins were fined $135,000 in damages for emotional distress. Some reports incorrectly claimed that this fine punished the Kleins for publicizing the Bowman-Cryers' address, but the labor commissioner's ruling explicitly said otherwise.[26] One could argue that the penalty was excessive, an example of the extremes of our litigious society. (I'm inclined to agree.) It's hard to deny, however, that the Kleins' refusal of service violated Oregon law.

Some deny that refusing to sell a cake for a same-sex wedding constitutes sexual-orientation discrimination: After all, the baker would equally refuse to provide a wedding cake for two heterosexual women or two heterosexual men. This objection overlooks the way in which some actions are constitutive of identity. It's like saying, "I'm not discriminating against *Catholics*, I'm just discriminating against people who attend Catholic Mass." Sexual orientation is a function of one's sex or gender and the sex or gender of those to whom one is romantically attracted; homosexual orientation is thus paradigmatically (though not solely) expressed in same-sex relationships. One reason these cases tend to arise in wedding contexts is that bakery customers' sexual orientation is generally not visible otherwise.

The Kleins are unwilling to sell cakes in precisely those instances where the cakes manifest their customers' sexual orientation. That's sexual-orientation discrimination. By analogy, it would be religious discrimination if the Kleins said that they would sell cakes to Jews, but not for bar mitzvahs, or that they would sell cakes to Catholics, but not for First Holy Communion parties.

Thus far, I've been examining this case largely from the perspective of the Bowman-Cryers, but what about the Kleins? Their interests matter too. While most discussions focus on their *religious* liberty, it may be instructive to frame the discussion in terms of liberty more generally. Consider an analogous case in which a Colorado customer, William Jack, asked an LGBT-friendly baker for a Bible-shaped cake with the words "Homosexuality is a detestable sin—Leviticus 18:22" written on it.[27] The baker, Marjorie Silva, declined, although she was willing to sell the customer a Bible-shaped cake and even provide him with an icing bag so he could decorate himself. The customer (who was clearly aiming to make a point) then filed a complaint alleging religious discrimination, but the state's human rights commission rejected it.

It is tempting to describe Marjorie Silva's Bible-cake refusal as the moral mirror image of Aaron Klein's wedding-cake refusal: Neither baker was willing to assist in conveying a message to which they were morally opposed.[28] But that's not quite right. For Silva was willing to sell the customer a Bible-shaped cake and even to provide an icing bag, knowing full well what the customer intended to write. In other words, she was willing to sell this customer the *very same items* that she would sell to any other customer. What he did with them after leaving her store was, quite literally, none of her business.

Therein lies the crucial difference between the cases: Silva's objection was about what she sold, a *design-based* objection. Klein's objection was about the customer's event, a *use-based* objection. And as I argued above, in this case *use-based* is virtually indistinguishable from *user-based*, given the close connection between same-sex weddings and the protected characteristic of sexual orientation.

Business owners generally have wide discretion over what they do and do not sell: A vegan bakery needn't sell real buttercream cakes. A kosher bakery needn't sell cakes topped with candied bacon, or in the shape of crosses. By contrast, business owners generally do not have discretion over how their products are later used: A kosher bakery may not refuse to sell bread to non-Jews, who might use it for ham-and-cheese sandwiches. A winemaker may not refuse to sell wine to priests, who might use it for celebrating the Eucharist. And so on.

Some bakers claim that they will not sell "gay wedding cakes." The problem with this response is that "gay wedding cakes" are not a thing. Same-sex couples order their cakes from the same catalogs as everyone else, with the same options for size, shape, icing, filling, and so on. Aaron Klein did not reject a particular design option, such as a topper with two brides—in which case, he might have a stronger argument. Instead, he flatly told Rachel Bowman-Cryer that he would not sell her a wedding cake *at all*.

4. Conclusion

In the context of LGBT people's history of unjust exclusion—not only from marriage but also from the freedom to live our lives openly—refusing to sell same-sex couples the very same items one sells to different-sex couples is discriminatory, humiliating, and wrong. It stems from, and contributes to, an unjust social regime, one where LGBT people are treated as second-class citizens. As in the Bob Jones case, such refusals are unjust regardless of their grounding in sincere religious beliefs, and also regardless of whether the person discriminating does so from animus, ignorance, or sheer moral carelessness. One need not equate sexual-orientation discrimination with racial discrimination to learn the lessons of history, or to recognize the ways in which people sometimes invoke religion to justify their fallible moral prejudices.

COMPREHENSION QUESTIONS

1. What's the point of the Bob Jones University example?
2. What's the difference between material harm and dignitary harm?
3. Justice Clarence Thomas said, in his dissent in *Obergefell v. Hodges*, that human dignity can't be taken away by the government. Corvino criticizes him for saying this. Why?
4. What are some of the ways in which LGBTQ people have been discriminated against?
5. What's the difference between design-based objections and use-based objections?

DISCUSSION QUESTIONS

1. Can we separate questions about *what's discriminatory* from questions about *what's right and wrong*? Go back to the Bob Jones University case. Presumably, the university changed its policy about interracial relationships because the leadership came to a new *theological* position. The leadership used to think that interracial relationships were contrary to God's will; they later came to think that such relationships *aren't* contrary to God's will. So from their old perspective, they denied that their policy was discriminatory: They thought that they

were just following God's law. It's only from their *new* perspective that they can call the old policy discriminatory. What does this mean for discussions about when people are and aren't acting in "discriminatory" ways? Do we have to say, "discriminatory *assuming that X is right (or wrong)*"?

2. The distinction between design- and use-based objections is important for Corvino's discussion of the "gay wedding cake" case (though Corvino, of course, says that there are no "gay wedding cakes"). Can you think of cases where it might be harder to draw that distinction? That is, are there cases where design and use can't be separated?

Case 1

In March 2019, the city of San Antonio denied Chick-fil-A a vendor space at its airport. The city council cited the chain's "legacy of anti-LGBTQ behavior." Presumably, the council members had the following sorts of actions in mind:

> The Chick-fil-A Foundation donated more than $1.8 million to three groups with a history of anti-LGBTQ discrimination in 2017, according to recently released tax filings analyzed by ThinkProgress. That year, Chick-fil-A's charitable arm gave $1,653,416 to the Fellowship of Christian Athletes, a religious organization that requires its employees to refrain from "homosexual acts"; $150,000 to the Salvation Army, which has been accused of anti-LGBTQ discrimination and advocacy for years and whose media relations director once claimed gay people "deserve death"; and $6,000 to the Paul Anderson Youth Home, a Christian residential home that teaches young boys that same-sex marriage is a "rage against Jesus Christ and His values."
>
> These donations were made five years after Chick-fil-A CEO Dan Cathy said the U.S. was "inviting God's judgment on our nation when we shake our fist at him and we say we know better than you as to what constitutes a marriage." Cathy's comments prompted a nationwide boycott—as well as a counter-boycott, called "Chick-fil-A Appreciation Day," created by then–Fox News host Mike Huckabee — and an eventual apology from the company, which claimed it would "leave the policy debate over same-sex marriage to the government and the political arena."*

Some Republicans introduced a bill in the Texas House to prevent cities from taking such actions in the future. The bill would have prohibited governments from denying contracts, grants, and other agreements to a person or business based on any relationship with a religious organization. However, the bill didn't pass. Rep. Matt Krause, a Fort Worth Republican who sponsored the bill, called the measure's failure "a setback." "The fact that the government can penalize someone just for who they associate with or who they donate to is something we should all be concerned about," he said. "It's very disappointing, but we'll try to find another way to have that very important conversation on the House floor."

What do Corvino's arguments imply—if anything—about cases like this? Are there any important differences between (a) the rules that ought to apply to government/business interactions and (b) the rules that ought to apply to business/private individual interactions?

---

*https://www.vox.com/the-goods/2019/3/21/18275850/chick-fil-a-anti-lgbtq-donations

PLURALISM, FAIRNESS, AND DEBATES
ABOUT DISCRIMINATION
RYAN T. ANDERSON AND SHERIF GIRGIS

In the United States, adults are free to enter or refuse almost any relationship—personal, civic, commercial, romantic—without legal interference. Freedoms of association and contract are presumed. As we explain in *Debating Religious Liberty and Discrimination*, these civil liberties are intimately related to freedoms of religion and conscience, and even the freedom of speech. Their cumulative effect is this: If the state is going to curb your freedom to associate with others on your own terms, by your own moral and religious lights, it carries the burden of proof. Government action that strains these mutually supporting freedoms must not be gratuitous. It must support a meaningful public interest, with minimal fraying of freedom.

So businesses and charities and other civic associations have ample freedom to run by their own values: to choose employees or customers or members, and standards of conduct. They're free to express and act on their own beliefs in ways that others might find compelling or trivial or deplorable. Freedoms of association and contract *just are* freedoms to "discriminate" in these ways. We tolerate such differences for the sake of creativity, initiative, vitality, and reform.

What does this presumption of liberty urge after the Supreme Court's *Obergefell* decision? This presumption of liberty favors implementing that decision with as modest a burden as necessary.[29] *Obergefell* was about state recognition and its effects: legal rules for hospital visitation and medical decisions, inheritance and taxes, and eligibility for a number of public programs and benefits. It was also meant to curb what many saw as the social harms of being denied public recognition of an enduring romantic relationship.

These material and social effects of legal recognition can be achieved without curbing private parties' freedoms. Indeed, respecting those freedoms is what flows naturally from ideals so often cited by same-sex marriage advocates: toleration for people's differences and support for their freedom to live with integrity.

So the law post-*Obergefell* should treat those who believe that marriage unites man and woman (or that sex is for marriage, or that children are owed a mother and father) as it has treated pro-life hospitals, doctors, and others since *Roe v. Wade*. These institutions and professionals are held to the same standards as others of their kind, but not to a litmus test on abortion. The state refrains from using its power to subsidize, license, and contract to coerce their consciences for being heretics on abortion. The same should go for dissenters from the state's new vision of marriage. The political settlement that has worked for four decades on abortion can work on marriage.

1. Private Adoption Agencies, Hospitals, and Charities
Adoption agencies have been casualties in battles over religious liberty for charities and are perhaps the rawest reminders of the gratuitousness of coercion in these culture wars.

In Massachusetts, Illinois, and the District of Columbia, religious adoption agencies and foster care providers have been forced to shut down rather than comply with government orders to place children with same- as well as opposite-sex couples or else lose their licenses and contracts.[30] Their closure did nothing to help a single child in need of a home, or a single couple in search of a child. (In no state do private agencies enjoy a monopoly on adoption and foster care.) Pressuring them to close only scored a political point, making vulnerable children victims of an adult culture war.

A former president of the National Council for Adoption warned that "if all faith-based agencies closed due to such laws, the adoption and child welfare field would be decimated, depriving thousands of children growing up in families."[31] Some one thousand private providers handle more than a quarter of the unrelated domestic adoptions in the United States each year.[32] Many are faith-based agencies that provide spiritual and emotional support that state bureaucracies are ill equipped to offer.

People of every persuasion can agree that having many adoption agencies is better than having fewer, and that offering some adoptive parents tailored support is better than offering none. Respecting private agencies' conscience claims serves the believers who run them, the parents who use them, and the children who might otherwise wait longer for a home. And it imposes no material harm on anyone, by anyone's score—liberal or conservative. This is one of those rare policy issues on which all the arguments seem to point in one direction.

In these cases, and in those we discuss below, the sheer fact that the entities seeking protection open their doors and services to the public should not count against them. The only question should be whether exemptions for them would impose too high a cost on others. Yes, those costs are *likelier* to occur, the more these institutions interact with the public. But once we tally such concrete third-party harms, it isn't an *extra* point against these claimants that they've stepped into the public square. To treat it that way is gratuitous—and counterproductive. The public square exists to bring a variety of voices together. It can't serve its function unless dissenters feel free to step into it. Nothing could be more at odds with that goal than counting it against dissenters' conscience claims that they choose to serve the public.

2. Educational Institutions: Creeds and Codes of Conduct
What we have said about adoption agencies applies to educational institutions. Even progressives can grant that it promises little public benefit—and does palpable harm—to deprive competent institutions of accreditation, non-profit tax status, public contracts, subsidized student loans, and other forms of support unless they violate the religious convictions of the communities they represent, in hiring, housing, or otherwise.

Here, we see the intersection of multiple civil liberties. *Pierce v. Society of Sisters* affirmed parents' authority to guide their children's education. But neither parents nor students are free to choose a religious education unless institutions are free to embrace their convictions—unless we let Notre Dame be Catholic, and Wheaton be evangelical, and Zaytuna be Muslim, and Yeshiva be Jewish. To cripple these schools for building a community around a creed—by pulling their non-profit tax status or accreditation or denying them subsidized student loans or research grants—is to rob families of the choice for a certain moral and intellectual formation in a supportive environment.

But allowing them to keep to their mission serves us all, religious or not. It gives strength and clarity to more voices in our public discussions, with intellectual benefits all around. Allowing secular as well as religious institutions to incubate their own intellectual tradition populates the wider public debate in which they all take part. Local agreement enhances global debate.[33]

Meanwhile, in a nation with thousands of institutions of every persuasion, at every level of quality, allowing some to operate by religious creeds needn't deny anyone a suitable education. So we can afford to allow religious schools to foster a milieu supportive of their values: to require teachers to share their marital or pro-life ethic, or to make rules against non-marital sexual activity (straight and gay), or to refuse to recognize groups that reject their ethical commitments. These measures empower incoming students and scholars by giving them the freedom to join a community that offers support for living by a demanding moral vision of their own choice.

And they welcome anyone who shares that vision. We haven't found a single school unwilling to employ gay or lesbian teachers who support and try to live by its message and mission. Some have dismissed teachers publicly opposed to their teachings and unwilling to try to live by them. We must acknowledge how painful and disruptive that can be for the people dismissed, and for their families, colleagues, and friends. We must do what we can to minimize those harms. But entirely eliminating these harms would curb the freedom of all—secular and religious, *including* those who leave after a change of heart—to choose institutions with a particular vision.

This isn't a conservative point. Progressives who defended Mozilla Firefox's right to oust CEO Brendan Eich over his traditional views on marriage understood the toll this would take on him, but they thought his values out of step with those that had drawn many of Mozilla's stakeholders. Concern for those parties also urges concern for students who want a school supportive of their efforts—and struggles—to live by their creeds. Leaving schools free to provide that support will serve those students while depriving no one of an institutional home. The burden of proof is on those who would brandish the law against these schools and students and families, despite the costs to everyone of a world less rich with rival intellectual traditions and supportive communities.

3. Wedding and Relationship Professionals

Wedding vendors and relationship counselors have also been targets in the religious liberty wars. Elane Photography's owners were fined more than $6,000 for declining on religious grounds to photograph a same-sex commitment ceremony. A small family bakery was fined $135,000 for refusing to bake the wedding cake for a same-sex wedding. And seventy-year-old Barronelle Stutzman was sued for declining to make floral arrangements for a same-sex wedding.[34]

Stutzman, who has employed gays and lesbians since opening her store, had for ten years designed arrangements for the couple that sued her. Her only objection was to lending her artistic talents to their wedding celebration.

Here, again, the pattern holds: Legally coercing professionals serves no serious need but works serious harms. Conservative wedding providers are few and dwindling, due to market pressures, and most important, they don't refuse to serve LGBT patrons. In case after case—with only one exception we know of, in a news climate that would thrust any exception right up to national headlines—bakers have had no problem designing cakes for gay customers for every other occasion. It's just that an exceedingly small number can't in good conscience use their talents to help celebrate same-sex weddings, by baking a cake topped with two grooms or two brides. And while coercing these cultural dissidents has vanishingly small effects on the supply of products for any given couple, it impinges seriously on particular vendors' freedoms of conscience or religion. If any harm remains in leaving these wedding professionals free, it is only the tension we all face in living with people who disagree with us on the most personal matters.

The same goes for counselors morally opposed to sexual relationships between boyfriend and girlfriend, or two men or two women. Consider Julea Ward, a graduate student dismissed from Eastern Michigan University's counseling program for asking her supervisor to assign another counselor to a gay client seeking relationship help.[35] Ward, whose religious convictions kept her from affirming same-sex sexual relationships, tried to place the client with a counselor who could. She did so ahead of time, based simply on his file. Meeting her request would have been a win–win, protecting her liberty without embarrassing him. Society should aim for these outcomes. Here, again, it isn't simply that the benefits of liberty barely outweigh the costs. It's that the benefits to people's integrity or livelihood are great, and the costs vanishingly small.

4. Anti-Discrimination Law and Dignitary Harms

There are, of course, exceptions to the rule that the law leaves people free to deal with others on their own terms, by their own lights. Anti-discrimination laws forbid private actors—individuals, businesses, and certain other associations—from treating people differently based on traits deemed irrelevant to most choices. They put the power and prestige of the law, and the threat of civil penalties, behind the ideal of social equality. That is an important goal. No one should be put to shame or marginalized for the shape of their sexual desires or their gender identity, any more than for their race or sex—or, for that matter, their height or hair color or a thousand other traits. But that isn't enough to justify a ban on anything just yet. The law isn't about siphoning evil out of every heart. It's about setting up and keeping up the conditions under which everyone can adequately pursue the basic goods of human life.

So it's too quick to glide right from the injustice of some form of discrimination to the conclusion that we should ban it. Nonetheless, presumptions can be rebutted. Liberty isn't a basic good. It's only a means. What's the best case for overcoming the presumption of freedom of contract in the cases described

above? We've already seen that there is no good reason to expect wedding professionals, adoption agencies, and educational institutions to impose material
harm—to deprive members of the LGBT community of access to goods, services,
or legal entitlements, to say nothing of social mobility or political influence or
basic needs for housing, lodging, loans, jobs, education, health care, and the like.
In short, there is no serious case for coercion in the cases above based on material
harms to LGBT people.

Most advocates of coercion in the cases above acknowledge this. They say
that coercion is needed to fight dignitary harm: cultural ideas and attitudes unfairly impugning a group's abilities, actions, character, proper social status, or
moral worth. Call these ideas and attitudes—even when the person acting on
them isn't hateful himself—"social contempt." As social contempt for a group
metastasizes, others find it harmful, dangerous, socially improper, or wrong to
deal with the group on equal terms.[36] That in turn really does impede the group's
social, political, and economic opportunities. It makes others less likely to trust
members of that group, hire them, contract with them, entrust them with the
power to vote, and so on. That's why states should take note when people are
unfairly robbed of social respect in socially debilitating ways.

When does an action contribute to social contempt of the sort the law may
target? Since the state exists to preserve the social conditions for everyone to
flourish, the question *for law* isn't what this baker secretly thinks, or how that
patron happens to react. The question is: What lesson will others draw from the
sort of interaction in question? To be a fair target of the law, a refusal must be
one that *observers would think was motivated* by demeaning ideas about a group's
abilities, character, worth, or proper place in society. That's what bestows on it
a certain *social* meaning, which can affect people's opportunities because perceived motivations are contagious. If your neighbor thinks you acted with a certain motive, she might pick it up. Actions can contribute to a culture of contempt
by sending a message that leads others to adopt demeaning attitudes or ideas.

But sometimes people *unfairly* infer that you were motivated by contempt
when there are perfectly reasonable, benign readings of your motives. If your
conduct in those cases is important for your moral or religious integrity, it would
be unfair to punish you for it—to impose a serious burden on your conscience
based on others' *unfair* readings of your actions. Of course, even if people are
wrong to draw harmful lessons from your conduct, the spread of those lessons
can still do harm to others. But then it would be fairer to contain that harm by
promoting more charitable interpretations of your actions. Fairness requires us
to exercise intellectual sympathy, to embrace more charitable available interpretations of the ideas or attitudes driving them. That is the difficult but fair path
to an equilibrium allowing everyone to thrive. And it calls on a skill—charity in
interpretation—that any pluralistic society relies on for its survival, and that *both*
sides have occasions to exercise. When Mozilla Firefox CEO Brendan Eich was
forced to resign over his views on marriage, it would've been unfair for him to
assume that all his opponents were driven by demeaning ideas about Christians'
abilities or worth, as opposed to honest beliefs about what was best for Mozilla.

And progressives must not assume that, say, Catholic Charities' placement policy stems from harmful ideas about LGBT people's abilities or worth, as opposed to honest beliefs about children's need for both male and female influences.

In sum: In deciding whether the social meaning of someone's action justifies brandishing the law against her, *at the price of her conscience*, we should ask how *reasonable* observers would interpret a refusal to offer the relevant good or service. In these scenarios, we shouldn't ban the refusal unless it could only be seen as rooted in attitudes or ideas that unfairly impugn a group's abilities, character, social status, or moral worth—the sorts of ideas that undermine people's social, political, and economic opportunities. By contrast, if a refusal's roots are simply moral convictions we find false or offensive, its social meaning alone won't justify legal coercion.

5. Same-Sex Marriage "Discrimination"

The decision of, for example, Jack Phillips—who declined to create a custom wedding cake for a same-sex marriage celebration—may convey ideas that Colorado finds offensive, but they do not perpetuate the kinds of assumptions that impede social, economic, or political mobility. Affirming Phillips's expressive freedom would not inflict the dignitary harm rightly targeted by the Civil Rights Act. The point is not simply that Phillips's decision turned on conduct (a same-sex wedding) rather than status (sexual orientation), while Jim Crow was about status (race). No, the divide between his decision and Jim Crow–era policies is different and far deeper.[37]

Jim Crow–style discrimination reflected and solidified cultural assumptions that locked a group out of markets, income brackets, social tiers, and political power. It taught that African Americans had baser interests and were variously incompetent, unreliable, and vicious.[38] Above all, Jim Crow was openly premised on the cultural assumption that it was improper for African Americans to mingle with whites on equal terms. That assumption didn't simply lead to other barriers to social mobility; it *was* such a barrier.

Again, this sort of discrimination always rests on unfair assumptions about a group's basic abilities, interests, character, or proper social role. That's why bans on it disrupted these humiliating assumptions—which reduced the impulse to discriminate and so on in an upward spiral. Put simply, anti-discrimination laws rightly promote dignity by eroding those humiliating assumptions that also debilitate a group socially, politically, and economically.

No such dignitary harms are in the offing here: In the cases described above, institutions' and professionals' convictions need not reinforce or rest on any assumptions about LGBT people's basic abilities, interests, character, or proper place in society.

How can we tell? The question isn't simply how the post-*Obergefell* refusals *are* interpreted but how it's *reasonable* to read them. Answering that requires looking at where the ideas behind these conscience claims come from and where they lead. Reasonable interpretations of particular actions will be sensitive to their intellectual history and the patterns they form.

Look first at patterns. The refusals of the bakers and photographers, charities, and universities discussed here have nothing like the sweep or shape of racist practices. They don't span every domain but focus on marriage and sex. Within that domain, they're about avoiding complicity with certain choices, not contact with groups. Barronelle Stutzman, who refused to arrange wedding flowers for her client of ten years, didn't think gay people vicious, incompetent, or unproductive; she depended on them as customers and employees. She didn't think they mattered less or deserved shunning; she employed them and served them faithfully as clients, denying them no other product. Patterns in her behavior make nonsense of these interpretations.

Indeed, her and the other refusals debated here needn't involve reasoning—or thus discriminating—based on orientation or gender identity at all. They rest on the beliefs that marriage is the one-flesh union that only man and woman can form, that sexual activity belongs in marriage, that biological sex is to be embraced, or that motherhood and fatherhood are essential.[39] Those beliefs make no reference to LGBT people one way or another. So the refusals they inspire *need* not involve orientation-based discrimination at all, invidious or not. Unless, of course, those beliefs always rest on further ideas or attitudes that *are* about LGBT people.

To answer that question, we begin by looking to history, which proves that the convictions about sexuality and marriage just mentioned weren't born of ignorance of same-sex desire or hostility to same-sex relations. They prevailed in societies spanning the spectrum of attitudes on both—including some favorable toward same-sex relations and others lacking anything like our concept of gay identity as marking a class of people. Thus, in ancient Greece and Rome, same-sex relations were common and drew no general popular scorn. And yet several ancient Greek and Roman thinkers gave arguments for the view that marriage is inherently opposite-sex—including Plato, Aristotle, Socrates, Xenophanes, Musonius Rufus, Plutarch, and others.

These thinkers could not have been motivated by animus toward a class of people of which no one even had a concept. None of these thinkers was in touch with Abrahamic religions, or ignorant of same-sex sexual relations, or biased against the latter by popular culture. They and later figures, of both East and West—from Augustine, Aquinas, Maimonides, and al-Farabi to Luther and Calvin, Locke and Kant, Gandhi and King—simply had honest, reasoned beliefs about the distinct value of male–female bonds.

This reflection on historical roots sheds light on the present. Today's moral conservatism grew out of these religious and moral traditions that taught the distinct value of male–female union; of mothers and fathers; of joining man and woman as one flesh, and generations as one family.[40] If history makes it impossible to see these intellectual streams as having their source in bigotry, it makes it unfair to assume that those they nourish are bigots. So it's wrong to coerce them just for the social meaning of their conscientious choices.

Some critics say that while it might have been possible for Aristotle or Kant or Gandhi to hold such views without animus, it isn't for us, knowing what we do now about sexuality. Not so. These traditions teach that there is distinct value in the kind of one-flesh union that only man and woman can form, and in the kinship ties that such union offers children. Those ideals don't hang on empirical assumptions (whether sound or not) about sexual orientation. Nor does the recent social trend toward a more flexible, marriage-as-simple-companionship model make these ideals irrational to keep affirming. Most conservatives also oppose this modern melting of marriage into general companionship that (they think) undermines valuable social purposes.

In short, the social meaning of—the message spread by—conduct like Phillips's is simply this: My religion teaches that marriage is inherently conjugal—a one-flesh union that only a man and woman can form. And again, history also proves that this message itself couldn't in turn have been driven by assumptions about gay people—fair or not, debilitating or neutral.

Some interactions *are* driven by demeaning beliefs about LGBT people.[41] Our point is that this isn't the only reasonable inference to draw about today's conscientious refusals. So absent material harms, it would be unfair to punish all who engage in them.

In these ways, Jim Crow could not be in sharper contrast—and not simply because the bakers' and florists' convictions are rooted in sincere faith. Being rooted in faith isn't a get-out-of-jail-free card. It doesn't matter if some under Jim Crow had sincere religious grounds for thinking that African Americans shouldn't marry whites. The point is that this idea itself—*whatever* its roots—just *is* a social norm that impedes mobility: It impedes a group's progress in every dimension, by teaching people that a particular group ought not to mix with others on equal terms. But whatever the status of views like Phillips's or Stutzman's, they don't involve—or rest on—the idea that it's improper for LGBT people to mingle on the same plane with others.

If social meaning doesn't justify coercing today's conscientious dissenters from *Obergefell*, and the material harms at issue are vanishing to non-existent—as many progressive advocates readily admit—then in these cases, freedoms of religion and expression should prevail.

COMPREHENSION QUESTIONS

1. What, exactly, does freedom of association ensure for you?
2. What's the point of drawing a parallel between same-sex marriage and abortion?
3. What do Anderson and Girgis mean when they say that "local agreement enhances global debate"?
4. What's the argument against requiring bakers to sell cakes for same-sex marriages?
5. Anderson and Girgis say that some injustice shouldn't be banned. Why?

DISCUSSION QUESTIONS

1. What *would* be a "serious need" that would justify legal sanctions against business owners? What might Anderson and Girgis say about how to draw lines here?
2. In Anderson and Girgis's view, it is unfair to assume that anyone who does not celebrate same-sex partnerships harbors animus toward LGBTQ people. Why? And how could LGBTQ advocates reply?

3. Anderson and Girgis say, of Phillips, that the message of his action is: "My religion teaches that marriage is inherently conjugal—a one-flesh union that only a man and woman can form. And again, history also proves that this message itself couldn't in turn have been driven by assumptions about gay people—fair or not, debilitating or neutral." What historical evidence do Anderson and Girgis present to support this claim? How should Corvino respond?

Case 2

Anderson and Girgis focus on legal debates, but people on both sides of these debates are also concerned about cultural trends. Consider, for instance, this op-ed by David French:

> Immanuel Christian School in Virginia [recently] landed squarely in the cultural crosshairs. Karen Pence, Vice President Mike Pence's wife, took a part-time job teaching art to elementary-school students. Karen Pence is a believing Christian. The school is a church ministry, and it upholds orthodox Christian teaching about sexuality—the belief that sex is reserved for marriage, and that marriage is defined as the union of a man and a woman.
>
> A media feeding frenzy followed, with progressive pundits across the land condemning Pence's alleged bigotry. A hashtag, #ExposeChristianSchools, popped up on Twitter, leading a *New York Times* reporter to openly call for people to come forward and discuss their Christian school experiences. And, this week, a local private academy called the Sheridan School decided to prohibit its sports teams from playing games at Immanuel. The reason? According to the text of an email from the head of school, obtained by Rod Dreher, some students felt "unsafe." No, really. Here's the key paragraph:
>
>> Since the majority of students wanted to play, we were initially planning to go to ICS with the student-athletes wearing a statement of support (such as rainbow socks or warm-up jerseys). As we talked more, we understood that some students did not feel safe entering a school that bans LGBTQ parents, students or even families that support LGBTQ rights. Forcing our children to choose between an environment in which they feel unsafe or staying home was not an option. So we decided that we would invite ICS to play all of the games at Sheridan. Since ICS declined our offer to host, we will only play our home games and will not go to ICS to play . . .
>
> Unsafe? Absurd. Just absurd. But it's worse than absurd. It's bigotry. If there have been specific incidents that make a person reasonably fear for his or her safety at Immanuel, then the head of school should identify them. Otherwise, the argument is that Immanuel's Christian environment is just too terrible to endure. It's hard to overstate how ridiculous this is . . . In my travels to public schools or to secular private schools, never once did I think that I was in a safer environment than the private Christian schools [with which I'm familiar]. If the experience at Immanuel is different from the common experience of Christian-school parents and students, we need evidence . . .
>
> [In] the fight for religious freedom, we [Christians] often focus our efforts on the less important battleground. Legal protections matter less and less when the culture drifts so far from Christianity that shunning, shaming, and exclusion become the norm.[*]

How should we think about worries of this kind?

---

[*]https://www.nationalreview.com/2019/01/this-is-what-anti-christian-bigotry-looks-like/

REPLY TO ANDERSON AND GIRGIS
JOHN CORVINO

There is much worth discussing in Anderson and Girgis's rich essay. Here, I will make some brief points about private hospitals, charities, and educational institutions before turning to a discussion of animus and the race analogy. We discuss these issues at greater length in our book together and in subsequent writings.[42]

Virtually no one wants to force doctors to provide abortions against their convictions. Conflicts arise because in some hospitals, doctors who *do* want to provide certain procedures are not permitted to do so—or even to discuss them with the patient. Religious hospitals provide nearly 20% of hospital beds.[43] They are monopoly providers in some towns, and they benefit from significant public funding and tax exemptions. Their refusals mean that, for example, women who are admitted for an emergency C-section and want a tubal ligation must schedule a second, later surgery at a separate hospital, thereby increasing their risk—regardless of their doctor's willingness. They mean that rape victims are not told about emergency contraception during the short time window in which such contraception is effective.[44] And they sometimes even mean that women are denied information about potentially life-saving treatment.[45] Religious liberty should not be a license for putting patients at risk.

The case of adoption service agencies is complicated. We all want to place as many children as possible in good homes. That goal would be best achieved if religious adoption agencies would refrain from discriminating on the basis of sexual orientation. Not only do such refusals keep children out of good homes; they also discourage good prospective parents from the adoption process. Unfortunately, several Catholic adoption agencies have closed their doors rather than comply with anti-discrimination guidelines—with the unfortunate result that fewer agencies are working to place children. Thus, as an empirical matter, it is unclear whether such guidelines make the best the enemy of the good.[46]

Finally, regarding schools: Legally, I have no objection to schools' choosing an explicitly religious character and then requiring commitment to it as a condition for admission or hiring. But there's a difference between granting that freedom and granting the significant tax benefits and other subsidies that come with 501(c)(3) status. It's fine to let "Notre Dame be Catholic, and Wheaton be evangelical, and Zaytuna be Muslim, and Yeshiva be Jewish"; it's even fine (legally) to let Bob Jones University be Bob Jones University. Whether the rest of us should continue to subsidize them when they refuse to comply with anti-discrimination law is a different matter.

Turning now to discrimination, animus, and the race analogy: Anderson and Girgis draw a sharp contrast between racial discrimination and anti-LGBT discrimination. On their telling, race discriminators are hateful people, motivated by animus, who want to avoid contact with blacks and other racial minorities, whereas sexual-orientation "discriminators" are loving people, motivated by conscience, who want merely to avoid complicity in actions that violate their beliefs.

This description is misleading twice over. Both race discriminators and sexual-orientation discriminators are a mixed bunch. As we have seen, many race discriminators have acted out of sincere moral and religious convictions. And not all sexual-orientation discriminators are gracious figures like my counterpoint authors. Quite the contrary: I have a stack of recent hate mail on my desk maligning gays as "pedophiles" and telling me that "fags" should "die of AIDS." And here's a typical recent comment on my YouTube page:

> Faggots are a hideous abomination, always were, always will be. Dress it up all you like, make it palatable as possible for this current "touchy-feely," safe-space generation; convince them all that nearby friends and relatives are all harboring gay thoughts for each other and that all of this is natural . . . then do me a solid and go read about Sodom and Gomorrah. Then go read about Jesus Christ. He said to love everyone, but never once denied that there'd be consequences for being an unnatural freak. This social acceptance of perversion will pass, and the latent backlash will be hideous.[47]

Refusals of service happen within a social context. Religious conservatives have made clear their beliefs that same-sex relationships are "unnatural" and "an abomination," that gays should remain in the closet, that we should be denied the legal right to marry, and that homosexual conduct should maybe even be recriminalized. Against this backdrop, it is not difficult to understand why same-sex couples perceive invidious discrimination when told that they cannot purchase the very same items that their heterosexual fellow citizens do.

Anderson and Girgis contend that traditional marriage norms were not born of animus. Even if correct, that contention is entirely beside the point, for at least two reasons.

First, the relevant question is not about the *origins* of these norms, but about the *maintaining* of them: One can hold (as I do) that marriage norms originally had little to do with LGBT people, but that retaining them today depends on "unfair assumptions about a group's basic abilities, interests, character, or proper social role."

Second, discriminatory acts need not be rooted in animus in order to be harmful. As we have seen, discrimination often results from sheer ignorance of the ways in which one's actions affect others.

Consider again Bob Jones University. Maybe its admissions officers hated blacks. Maybe they loved blacks but honestly believed their founder's interpretation of scripture. Maybe they had a quirky aesthetic preference for couples with consistent skin tones, much like those who argued against integrating the Rockettes on the grounds that black dancers would spoil the "look of precision."[48] The government is not really in a position to know how they reasoned, and for the purpose of applying anti-discrimination law, it doesn't need to know: The exclusionary effects are the same.

This is not to say that discriminators' reasons aren't relevant at any stage. They are relevant to how we *morally* evaluate such cases. They are also relevant contextually: The fact that such discrimination has been rooted in animus in the past makes it more likely that it will contribute to social harm in the present, whether intentionally or not. It bears repeating that the ultimate objective of anti-discrimination law is not to punish haters (not all discriminators are haters) but to ensure equal access in the public sphere.

COMPREHENSION QUESTIONS

1. What's Corvino's reply to Anderson and Girgis's claim about the social meaning of denying service?
2. What's the point that Corvino is making when he distinguishes between the origins of norms and their maintenance?
3. Why does Corvino think animus is sometimes irrelevant when it comes to discrimination?

DISCUSSION QUESTION

1. Corvino says that the purpose of anti-discrimination law "is not to punish haters . . . but to ensure equal access in the public sphere." Girgis and Anderson might accept that that's a good goal, but argue that it's one with unintended consequences: By improving access for some, you effectively marginalize others (namely, those with unpopular moral convictions). What should Corvino say to this objection?

REPLY TO CORVINO
RYAN T. ANDERSON AND SHERIF GIRGIS

We're grateful for Corvino's essays, which are—like their author—sophisticated, civil, thoughtful, and well informed. They also contain important gaps and missteps. Corvino asserts that "virtually no one" wants to force pro-lifers to perform abortions, but that consensus crumbles as we write: The prominent journal *Bioethics* just published an article by an Oxford scholar titled "Doctors Have No Right to Refuse Medical Assistance in Dying, Abortion or Contraception."[49] What would Corvino's approach commit him to holding on this issue? He doesn't say. Corvino wants Catholic adoption agencies to not "discriminat[e] on the basis of sexual orientation" but begs the question of whether preferring homes with a father and mother is orientation-based discrimination. He would allow religious schools to exist but avers that whether we "should continue to subsidize them . . . is a different matter." Yet he doesn't offer his own view of that matter. We argued that all of these institutions should be held to the same legal standards as other charities, but without a litmus test on beliefs about sex: no sexual orthodoxy. Corvino thinks that by perhaps varying which penalty is applied—loss of non-profit status or accreditation, or the levying of fines and revocation of grants—he has somehow addressed our concerns.

As for Corvino's argument that coercive laws are needed to give LGBT people access to essentials, it rests on just a few data points—on self-reported experiences of discrimination, on a straight–gay pay gap, and on a 1.5% higher poverty rate for lesbian couples. But first, these figures may already be outdated. Today, insofar as there is a gay–straight pay gap, evidence suggests it goes *the other way*. An August 2016 report from the U.S. Treasury—based on tax returns, not self-reports of discrimination—shows opposite-sex couples earning significantly less than same-sex couples. For couples with children, the gap is even more dramatic, with gay couples earning more than 2.5 times as much as opposite-sex couples.[50]

Yet even taken at face value, Corvino's bullet points alone don't justify legal coercion. It's as if, to justify coercing law-school admissions offices to admit more Republicans, we cited data showing that lawyers were disproportionately Democrats—without asking what drove the gap, whether markets and culture might close it more efficiently, what *sort* of policy could do the job if not, and at what collateral cost. Besides, when corporate giants like the NBA, the NCAA, Apple, Salesforce, Delta, and Coca-Cola threaten to boycott states over laws merely giving believers their day in court,[51] it's hard to see the case for coercing them to achieve progressives' social goals.

As for which actions to coerce: Corvino writes that even if your beliefs are rooted in sincere religious conviction, acting on them might harm others, and in ways the law should fight. We agree. We argued that your conduct could harm minorities by promoting unfair, socially debilitating attitudes or ideas about their worth, abilities, actions, or proper place in society. By this standard, bans on interracial marriage were paradigms of invidious discrimination. It doesn't matter if (as Corvino notes) some supporters had sincere religious motives for believing that blacks belonged apart and at the margins. That belief itself—about blacks' separate place in society—just *is* one of the ideas we've argued are proper targets of anti-discrimination law.

So our analysis explains why a baker refusing to bake for an interracial wedding discriminates by race. She declines based on a view about interracial marriage that in turn rests on ideas about members of a certain race: African Americans. That's race-based discrimination; what makes it invidious is that those ideas about African Americans are unfair and socially debilitating.

But while anti-gay bigotry certainly exists, we showed that it's unfair to assume that actions based on traditional sex ethics are premised on ideas harmful to gay people. Indeed, refusals to bake needn't rest on beliefs or attitudes about LGBT people, good or bad.

Corvino begs to differ: "This objection overlooks the way in which some actions are constitutive of identity. It's like saying, 'I'm not discriminating against Catholics, I'm just discriminating against people who attend Catholic Mass.'" But if Corvino were right that opposing something is always the same as opposing the identity it flows from, how could he defend his preferred policies against charges of, say, anti-Catholic discrimination? "In fining bakeries that refuse gay weddings, I'm not discriminating against Catholics, I'm just discriminating against people who have Catholic beliefs about marriage." After all, Catholic consciences flow out of Catholic identity.

The truth too subtle for our polarized culture is this: Progressives who oppose conservative views of marriage needn't be discriminating based on religion, and conservatives who oppose same-sex marriage needn't be discriminating based on orientation. In neither case does the opposition have to rest on—or cause others to adopt—demeaning ideas about a particular group.

Our nation has long recognized a parallel point about pro-lifers: Their view doesn't imply or spread misogyny. As the Supreme Court observed in 1993, "[w]hatever one thinks of abortion, it cannot be denied that there are common and respectable reasons for opposing it, other than hatred of, or condescension toward (or indeed any view at all concerning), women."[52]

Likewise, while striking down traditional (conjugal) marriage laws in *Obergefell v. Hodges*, the Court noted that the conjugal view found support in "decent and honorable premises" held "in good faith by reasonable and sincere people here and throughout the world." It didn't say that when it struck down bans on interracial marriage in 1967. It didn't because it couldn't.

After *Obergefell*, then, our policy toward conjugal marriage supporters should mirror our policy toward pro-lifers after *Roe*. We should respect their freedom of conscience.

Anti-gay bigotry should be condemned, but support for conjugal marriage isn't anti-gay. Just as we've fought sexism while respecting the consciences of pro-life doctors, we should ensure that policies needed to help LGBT people also respect the consciences of conjugal-marriage supporters. Not every disagreement is discrimination. Our law shouldn't suppose otherwise.

COMPREHENSION QUESTIONS

1. In what circumstances do Anderson and Girgis support using anti-discrimination law?
2. Why do Anderson and Girgis say that discriminating on the basis of race is different from discriminating on the basis of being a member of the LGBTQ community?
3. What is the "truth too subtle for our polarized culture?"

DISCUSSION QUESTION

1. Anderson and Girgis say that "while anti-gay bigotry certainly exists . . . it's unfair to assume that actions based on traditional sex ethics are premised on ideas harmful to gay people." Some gay people have responded: "*Any* view that rejects activities central to our identity as immoral is harmful to us." And some conservatives have answered that by this logic, one could equally say that progressive views harm conservative believers by rejecting beliefs central to *their* identity as immoral or bigoted. Who is right—one, both, or neither? Is there a general principle for telling when it is and isn't harmful to reject (as immoral) actions or ideas that others consider central to their identity? And what should follow for law and policy?

FURTHER READING

Corvino, John, Ryan T. Anderson, and Sherif Girgis. *Debating Religious Liberty and Discrimination*. New York: Oxford University Press, 2018.

NOTES

1. *Bob Jones Univ. v. United States*, 461 U.S. 574, 580–581 (1983).
2. From the university's website: "BJU's history has been chiefly characterized by striving to achieve those goals; but like any human institution, we have failures as well. For almost two centuries American Christianity, including BJU in its early stages, was characterized by the segregationist ethos of American culture. Consequently, for far too long, we allowed institutional policies regarding race to be shaped more directly by that ethos than by the principles and precepts of the Scriptures. We conformed to the culture rather than providing a clear Christian counterpoint to it. . . . In so doing, we failed to accurately represent the Lord and to fulfill the commandment to love others as ourselves. For these failures we are profoundly sorry. Though no known antagonism toward minorities or expressions of racism on a personal level have ever been tolerated on our campus, we allowed institutional policies to remain in place that were racially hurtful." "Statement about Race at BJU," Bob Jones University, http://www.bju.edu/about/what-we-believe/race-statement.php, accessed July 11, 2016.
3. Bob Jones, "Is Segregation Scriptural?" November 12, 2014, Sermons of Bob Jones: A Digital History Project, https://bobjonessermons.wordpress.com/sermons/is-segregation-scriptural/.
4. "Bob Jones University Apologizes for Its Racist Past," *Journal of Blacks in Higher Education*, http://www.jbhe.com/news_views/62_bobjones.html, accessed July 11, 2016.
5. *Loving v. Virginia*, 388 U.S. 1 (1967).
6. Kellan Howell, "Florida 'Muslim-Free' Gun Shop Owner Wins Discrimination Suit," *Washington Times*, http://www.washingtontimes.com/news/2015/nov/28/florida-muslim-free-gun-shop-owner-wins-discrimina/, accessed July 11, 2016.
7. Leigh Remizowski,"Teacher Who Was Fired After Fertility Treatments Sues Diocese," CNN, http://www.cnn.com/2012/04/26/us/indiana-in-vitro-lawsuit/index.html, accessed July 11, 2016.
8. Tresa Baldas, "Pediatrician Wouldn't Care for Baby with 2 Moms," *Detroit Free Press*, February 19, 2015, http://www.freep.com/story/news/local/michigan/macomb/2015/02/18/discrimination-birth/23640315/.
9. http://abcnews.go.com/US/nj-bridal-shop-refused-sell-wedding-dress-lesbian/story?id=14342333.
10. Amy Montgomery, "Same-Sex Couple Denied a Birthday Cake by Local Bakery," 13ABC, http://www.13abc.com/content/news/Same-sex-couple-denied-a-birthday-cake-by-local-bakery-385783221.html, accessed July 12, 2016.
11. "Ohio Bakery: No Birthday Cakes for Gay Couples" (blog entry), Joe.My.God., http://www.joemygod.com/2016/07/07/ohio-bakery-no-birthday-cakes-for-gay-couples/, accessed July 12, 2016.
12. I think this description may be somewhat misleading. If one spends a full day trying on wedding dresses and only then is told that one cannot buy one (on grounds of being a lesbian, or planning a same-sex wedding), one is certainly worse off than when one started.

13. Pablo Gilabert, "Human Rights, Human Dignity, and Power," in *Philosophical Foundations of Human Rights*, edited by Rowan Cruft, Matthew Liao, and Massimo Renzo (Oxford: Oxford University Press, 2015), 196–213.

14. *Obergefell v. Hodges*, 135 S. Ct. 2584, 2639 (2015).

15. Andrew Koppelman makes a similar point about anti-Semitic slurs. See Andrew Koppelman, "Gay Rights, Religious Accommodations, and the Purposes of Anti-discrimination Law," *Southern California Law Review* 88 (2015): 645.

16. For the current landscape, see Human Rights Campaign, "Maps of State Laws and Policies," http://www.hrc.org/state_maps, accessed September 28, 2016.

17. See Christy Mallory and Brad Sears, "Evidence of Employment Discrimination Based on Sexual Orientation and Gender Identity: An Analysis of Complaints Filed with State Enforcement Agencies," Williams Institute, October 22, 2015, http://williamsinstitute .law.ucla.edu/research/workplace/evidence-of-employment-discrimination-based-on -sexual-orientation-and-gender-identity-an-analysis-of-complaints-filed-with-state -enforcement-agencies/. See also Christy Mallory and Brad Sears, "Evidence of Housing Discrimination Based on Sexual Orientation and Gender Identity: An Analysis of Complaints Filed with State Enforcement Agencies, 2008–2014," Williams Institute, February 9, 2016, http://williamsinstitute.law.ucla.edu/research/workplace/evidence -of-housing-discrimination-based-on-sexual-orientation-and-gender-identity-an -analysis-of-complaints-filed-with-state-enforcement-agencies-2008-2014/, and Christy Mallory and Brad Sears, "Evidence of Discrimination in Public Accommodations Based on Sexual Orientation and Gender Identity: An Analysis of Complaints Filed with State Enforcement Agencies, 2008–2014," Williams Institute, February 16, 2016, http://williamsinstitute.law.ucla.edu/research/workplace/evidence-of-discrimination -in-public-accommodations-based-on-sexual-orientation-and-gender-identity-an -analysis-of-complaints-filed-with-state-enforcement-agencies-2008-2014/.

18. Thomas Harkin, "S. Rept. 113-105—The Employment Non-discrimination Act of 2013" (webpage), U.S. Senate, September 12, 2013, 15–17, https://www.congress.gov/113 /crpt/srpt105/CRPT-113srpt105.pdf.

19. For a detailed history, see Joyce Murdoch and Deb Price, *Courting Justice: Gay Men and Lesbians v. The Supreme Court* (New York: Basic Books, 2002).

20. *Lawrence v. Texas*, 539 U.S. 558 (2003).

21. *Bowers v. Hardwick*, 478 U.S. 186, 196–197 (1986).

22. The information that follows is taken from Klein, Melissa and Aaron dba Sweetcakes by Melissa, 34 BOLI 102 (2015), https://www.oregon.gov/boli/SiteAssets/pages/press /Sweet%20Cakes%20FO.pdf.

23. Klein, Melissa and Aaron dba Sweetcakes by Melissa, 34 BOLI 102, 104 (2015), https:// www.oregon.gov/boli/SiteAssets/pages/press/Sweet%20Cakes%20FO.pdf.

24. Klein, Melissa and Aaron dba Sweetcakes by Melissa, 34 BOLI 102, 105 (2015).

25. Andrew Koppelman, "A Zombie in the Supreme Court: The Elane Photography Cert Denial," *Alabama Civil Rights and Civil Liberties Law Review* 7 (2015): 77. The article is about the Elane Photography case, but the principle still applies.

26. Eugene Volokh, "No, the Oregon Bakers Weren't Fined for Publishing the Complainant's Home Address, or for Otherwise Publicizing the Complaint against Them," The Volokh Conspiracy, July 10, 2015, https://www.washingtonpost.com/news/volokh-conspiracy /wp/2015/07/10/no-the-oregon-bakers-werent-fined-for-publishing-the-complainants -home-address-or-for-otherwise-publicizing-the-complaint-against-them/.

27. Abby Ohlheiser, "This Colorado Baker Refused to Put an Anti-gay Message on Cakes. Now She Is Facing a Civil Rights Complaint," *Washington Post*, January 28, 2015,

https://www.washingtonpost.com/news/post-nation/wp/2015/01/22/this-colorado
-baker-refused-to-put-an-anti-gay-message-on-cakes-now-she-is-facing-a-civil
-rights-complaint/?utm_term=.7e8c24f6fd12. This is the customer's recollection of the
requested wording. The baker reported the request as "God hates gays."

28. I explore this comparison in "Drawing a Line in the 'Gay Wedding Cake' Case," *New York Times*, November 27, 2017, https://www.nytimes.com/2017/11/27/opinion/gay
-wedding-cake.html; accessed April 8, 2018. Portions of the next few paragraphs are taken from that piece.

29. See Ryan T. Anderson, *Truth Overruled: The Future of Marriage and Religious Freedom* (Washington, DC: Regnery, 2015).

30. See Sarah Torre and Ryan T. Anderson, "Adoption, Foster Care, and Conscience Protections," The Heritage Foundation *Backgrounder,* no. 2869, January 15, 2014, http://www.heritage.org/research/reports/2014/01/adoption-foster-care-and-conscience-protection, and Anderson, *Truth Overruled*, 88–89.

31. Thomas C. Atwood, "Foster Care: Safety Net or Trap Door?" The Heritage Foundation *Backgrounder,* no. 2535, March 25, 2011, 12, http://www.heritage.org/research/reports/2011/03/foster-care-safety- net-or-trap-door.

32. U.S. Department of Health and Human Services, Administration for Children and Families, "National Foster Care & Adoption Directory Search," Child Welfare Information Gateway, https://www.childwelfare.gov/nfcad/.

33. See Sherif Girgis, "How the Law School Can Succeed—An Invitation," *Harvard Journal of Law and Public Policy* 37, no. 1 (2014): 187–198.

34. See Anderson, *Truth Overruled*, 92–104.

35. Pew Research Center, "Tensions Between Rights of Conscience and Civil Rights," Pew Forum, June 3, 2010, http://www.pew-forum.org/2010/06/03/tensions-between-rights
-of-conscience- and-civil-rights/, accessed October 4, 2016.

36. See, e.g., Bruce Ackerman, *We the People,* vol. 3, *The Civil Rights Revolution* (Cambridge, MA: Harvard University Press, 2014), 142, 150. Portions of this and the next two paragraphs are adapted from a forthcoming piece by Sherif Girgis.

37. See Ryan T. Anderson, "Disagreement Is Not Always Discrimination: On Masterpiece Cakeshop and the Analogy to Interracial Marriage," *Georgetown Journal of Law & Public Policy* 16, no. 1 (2018). Available at SSRN: https://ssrn.com/abstract=3136750.

38. See Anderson, "Disagreement Is Not Always Discrimination."

39. For an extended philosophical and policy defense of these values, see Sherif Girgis, Ryan T. Anderson, and Robert P. George, *What Is Marriage? Man and Woman: A Defense* (New York: Encounter Books, 2012). See also Anderson, *Truth Overruled.*

40. See "Disagreement Is Not Always Discrimination," *What Is Marriage? Man and Woman: A Defense,* and *Truth Overruled: The Future of Marriage and Religious Freedom*

41. On how to properly craft public policy to protect people who identify as LGBT, see Ryan T. Anderson, "Shields, Not Swords," *National Affairs* 35 (Spring 2018). Available at SSRN: https://ssrn.com/abstract=3141908.

42. See John Corvino, Ryan T. Anderson, and Sherif Girgis, *Debating Religious Liberty and Discrimination* (New York: Oxford University Press, 2017). For my more recent views on why wedding discrimination constitutes sexual-orientation discrimination, see John Corvino, "Free Speech and Discrimination in the Cake Wars," in David Boonin, ed., *Palgrave Handbook of Philosophy and Public Policy* (London: Palgrave Macmillan, 2018), pp. 317-328; also John Corvino, "Sexual-Orientation Discrimination and the Metaphysics of Cake," *Philosophical Topics* Volume 46 Issue 2 (forthcoming).

43. Debra B. Stulberg et al., "Religious Hospitals and Primary Care Physicians: Conflicts over Policies for Patient Care," *Journal of General Internal Medicine* 25, no. 7 (2010): 725–730, doi:10.1007/s11606-010-1329-6.

44. See *Brownfield v. Daniel Freeman Marina Hosp.*, 208 Cal. App. 3d. 405, 409 (1989).

45. See *"Tamesha Means v. United States Conference of Catholic Bishops*—Complaint," American Civil Liberties Union, accessed September 26, 2016, https://www.aclu .org/legal-document/tamesha-means-v-united-states-conference-catholic-bishops -complaint. *Means v. United States Conference of Catholic Bishops*, unpublished, No. 15–1779 (6th Cir. 2016).

46. See Walter Olson, "Religious Agencies and Adoption: A Case for Pluralism" for an argument to this effect. http://www.cato.org/blog/religious-adoption-agencies-case-pluralism

47. John Corvino, *John Corvino—What's Morally Wrong with Homosexuality? (Full DVD Video)*, 2013, https://www.youtube.com/watch?v=5iXA_0MED98&lc=z12ysvwqhrmfy zv1x22ou1pynwb5wd23k.

48. As the dance troupe's director Violet Holmes put it in the early 1980s: "One or two black girls in the line would definitely distract. You would lose the whole look of precision, which is the hallmark of the Rockettes." The group was not integrated until 1987. See Bruce Lambert, "Rockettes and Race: Barrier Slips," *New York Times*, December 26, 1987, sec. N.Y./Region, http://www.nytimes.com/1987/12/26/nyregion/rockettes-and-race-barrier-slips.html.

49. Julian Savulescu and Udo Schuklenk, "Doctors Have No Right to Refuse Medical Assistance in Dying, Abortion or Contraception," *Bioethics* 31, no. 3 (2017): 162–170.

50. Opposite-sex couples earn on average $113,115, compared to $123,995 for lesbian couples and $175,590 for gay male couples. For couples with children, $104,475 for opposite-sex couples, but $130,865 for lesbian couples, and $274,855 for gay couples. See Robin Fisher, Geof Gee, and Adam Looney, "Joint Filing by Same-Sex Couples after *Windsor*: Characteristics of Married Tax Filers in 2013 and 2014," Department of the Treasury Office of Tax Analysis working paper 108, August 2016, https://www .treasury.gov/resource-center/tax-policy/tax-analysis/Documents/WP-108.pdf, accessed September 30, 2016.

51. We're referring to the backlash Indiana faced when it passed a Religious Freedom Restoration Act that closely mirrored those passed by Congress and many other states. The Act allowed private parties, including corporations, to seek exemptions from laws that burden their religious conscience (though it by no means ensured they would win every time).

52. See *Bray v. Alexandria Women's Health Clinic*, 506 U.S. 263, 267–268 (1993).

CHAPTER 13

"Bathroom Bills"

TRANS-DIRECTED INJUSTICE: THE CASE AGAINST ANTI-TRANSGENDER BATHROOM BILLS
LOREN CANNON

There have been more than two hundred pieces of legislation proposed in the last several years that have specifically targeted transgender persons in ways that severely limit our access to a flourishing life.[1] The depth and breadth of these legislative campaigns, while not wholly unprecedented, needs to be recognized as a significant attack on an already marginalized group of individuals. It is within this context that specific forms of legislation, usually referred to as "bathroom bills," have become the object of national debate. Most generally, these proposals make it a crime for certain individuals to use gendered facilities consistent with their gender identities. In this chapter, I present sufficient evidence that these kinds of bills are morally inappropriate. Anti-transgender bathroom bills (ATBBs) unjustifiably impose moral harms on transgender and gender nonconforming persons in the form of risk of physical and psychological harm, social ostracism, severe curtailment of opportunity, and lack of moral recognition.

While my intent here is to argue against these "bathroom bills" in the general case, it is important to recognize that details of these proposals can vary with regard to how the "correct" gendered facility is defined. Factors thought to be relevant include one's assigned sex at birth (the sex designated on one's birth certificate), the shape and configuration of one's genitals, or even one's chromosomal status (such a status unknown to all but a very few individuals). While these details are important, my initial focus here is on typical ATBBs that have roughly the following form: Individuals are prohibited from using gendered bathrooms (locker rooms, changing facilities, etc.) except those that correspond with their assigned sex at birth. Those assigned male at birth (AMAB) are prohibited from using facilities designated for girls or women, and those assigned female at birth (AFAB) are prohibited from using facilities designated for boys or men.[2]

To begin to understand the ramifications of these proposed policies, it is helpful to take a moment to clarify the terms used in this essay and to think about the individuals that are most affected by these proposals. In this essay, I will use the term "transgender" or "trans" in ways that have become fairly common. Generally, trans or transgender individuals experience their gendered sense of self as different than the sex assignment they were given at birth. This includes trans women, trans men, and those who identify as gender nonbinary. Legislation that is intended to target transgender individuals also negatively affect those who may not identify as transgender but who express themselves or otherwise appear different than the very narrowly defined ideal of a feminine woman (or girl) or a masculine man (or boy). In recent years, vocabulary used to describe one's gendered self has become richly diverse, nuanced, and self-affirming. However, for the purposes of this essay, I will simply use the term "gender nonconforming" (GNC) for those individuals who express or identify themselves or appear to others as residing outside narrow gender expectations and who may or may not identify as trans or transgender.

Unfortunately, few of us haven't experienced or witnessed harassment of those who are seen as transgressing traditional gender expectations. Being seen as a boyish girl (especially after a certain age) or a "sissy" boy often mean that one is poked fun at, bullied, or even at risk of assault. I wish I could say that this type of behavior is left at the playground, but statistics clearly support the claim that transgender and GNC persons are at risk for continued harassment both for how they express themselves and their gender history. According to the most extensive survey of its kind, trans persons "reported high levels of mistreatment, harassment, and violence in every aspect of life," including school bullying, harassment at work (and being fired or denied promotion due to their gender expression or identity), and being sexually assaulted, physically attacked, or verbally harassed due to being transgender.[3] Relatedly, transgender persons are statistically much more likely to be unemployed, to be homeless, to have limited health care, and consequentially to experience high levels of stress and anxiety due to living in a generally unwelcoming society.[4] Meaningful acceptance needs to begin early, and it is noteworthy that many trans individuals experience significant family rejection, making them vulnerable to a host of ills, including homelessness, hunger, and other problems.[5] This is the case even though both common wisdom and scientific research support the notion that being accepted by one's family is the start of a flourishing life and that it is the withholding of acceptance and recognition, not one's transgender identity, that is psychologically harmful.[6]

Of course, not all trans persons are white or otherwise have the same set of social privileges or burdens. It is important to note that the challenges faced by trans persons with multiple marginalized identities present even more formidable barriers. Trans persons are vulnerable to the injustices of racism, sexism, xenophobia, ableism, classism, homophobia, and other oppressions. Tellingly, trans persons of color are more than three times more likely than those of the general population to be living in poverty and have an unemployment rate four times higher than that of the general population.[7] Trans women of color are on the front lines of racism, sexism, and anti-trans bias and face exceedingly high rates of violence and assault.[8] It is against this backdrop of both social resilience and vulnerability that we can best come to recognize the unjustifiability of proposed "bathroom bills." As I will argue, these bills unjustifiably burden the already burdened and target the already targeted.

Enacted ATBBs put trans and GNC persons at risk of predictable physical and psychological harm. While so much of the rhetoric in favor of ATBBs has centered around safety of bathroom users, there is no mention of the harm that will predictably come to trans and GNC persons when/if these proposals are adopted. First, let us consider the risk of probable harm for trans women and trans feminine persons. While the common rhetoric regarding "keeping women safe" is often employed as a means to instill sufficient fear to gain support for these proposals, the concern for safety seems only applicable to cisgender (non-transgender) persons. Consider how ATBBs *require* trans women to use men's facilities, putting them at considerable risk. It is predictable that her presence in the men's restroom will be met with a variety of responses, many of which will be menacing. There are those who would regard her presence in the restroom as an invitation to verbal or physical harassment or violence. Proponents of ATBBs mistakenly argue that such measures increase safety, while they mandate that women who are trans regularly put themselves at serious risk. In the context of ATBBs, a woman in a men's bathroom will likely be thought to be there because she is trans. As such, she is at risk of harassment and violence that is sourced both in sexism and anti-trans animus. If the woman is not read as a white woman, she is yet more vulnerable to the violence inherent in racism and the deadly results of the triad of sexism, anti-trans bias, and racism. This threat of violence is not merely possible; it is predictable. The rates of violence against trans women, especially trans women of color, have regrettably only increased in the years since the passage of marriage equality.[9] While these kinds of legislative efforts cloak themselves in a concern of safety toward women, the result is, essentially, to place a target on the backs of women who are otherwise the most vulnerable to violence and harassment.[10]

Trans men are likewise put at risk for harm by requiring them (us) to use women's facilities. It is singularly ironic that, in the name of protecting women from men in restrooms, ATBBs *require* men to use women's facilities where they (we) will be seen as a dangerous threat. The negative attention that my own appearance would receive if I were to attempt to use a woman's facility is as predictable as it is unpleasant, and this is true for many trans men and trans masculine individuals. Trans masculine individuals will find that our attempt to abide by the law will result in being yelled at, harassed, assaulted, shoved or kicked out of the room, and perhaps even be reported to the police for a violation of the law. It is important to note that the threats to one's safety include more than those individuals *using* the facility at any given time. Consider the actions of guardians waiting outside a restroom for their young daughters when they believe that a dangerous man has entered the same bathroom. Given the social constructions that persist in portraying boys and men of color as violent and menacing,[11] consider again what might happen to the black trans man who enters a women's restroom in his attempt to abide by a local ATBB, and those awaiting outside have internalized these racist stereotypes. Of course, a trans man or a masculine-appearing GNC person may simply refuse to abide by the law and use men's facilities, but doing so puts them (us) at risk of civil prosecution if they (we) are found to be breaking the law. Given anti-trans sentiment generally, if the individual is thought to be AFAB or, as some mistakenly claim, "really a woman," they will be vulnerable to harassment and violence. Thus, ATBBs put trans men and trans masculine individuals at risk and produce the context that many need to choose to either be *seen* as breaking the law (and thus face potential harassment, violence, and police intervention) or *actually* break the law (which if discovered leads to prosecution, potential harassment, and violence).

The double bind just referred to, that ATBBs force individuals to choose between two unacceptable options, is a defining feature of systemic oppression and exists for all trans and GNC persons. In these cases, both abiding by the law and breaking the law put the individual at risk of violence, harassment, police intervention, and even criminal prosecution. The idea that the experience of such double binds indicate oppression was clearly articulated by feminist philosopher Marilyn Frye when she wrote, "One of the most characteristic and ubiquitous features of the world as experienced by oppressed people is the double bind— situations in which options are reduced to a very few and all of them expose one to penalty, censure or deprivation."[12] This useful idea has also been employed in the essay "Evil Deceivers and Make-Believers: On Transphobic Violence and the Politics of Illusion" by Talia Mae Bettcher. In this essay, Bettcher explains a different kind of unwinnable choice faced by trans persons, that of being seen as a *deceiver* or a *make-believer*. It is not uncommon for a trans person to be regarded as a deceiver if they (we) do not continually make our gender history public. Alternatively, if one is quite public about one's gender history, others are apt to believe that the individual is "make-believing" that they are a woman, man, gender nonbinary or gender fluid and essentially asking others to go along with the pretense.[13] Being cast as a deceiver is particularly relevant to those trans individuals who may, for the sake of their own safety and well-being, choose to use a gendered space consistent with their gender identity (as opposed to that assigned at birth) and are eventually "found out" by official or self-appointed gender police. ATBBs essentially require trans individuals to make their (our) personal histories public each time we need to use the loo, an imposition enacted only to embolden and weaponize anti-trans bias and one not imposed on cisgender persons.

It is important to recognize that while ATBBs target transgender persons, they negatively affect individuals of various gender identities and histories. Assuming that neither original birth certificates, chromosomes, hormone levels, nor physical genitalia will be officially inspected before using public restroom facilities, enforcement of ATBBs will be on the basis of appearance. In other words, whether one is in the "wrong place" or not will be determined by how a person appears and how this appearance compares to certain societal standards

of what women and men *should* look like. Given that passage of ATBBs is usually supported by fear of nefarious restroom intruders, surveillance, especially in
women's restrooms, will only be increased in order to spot such intruders as they
enter the facility. This heightened scrutiny, in the form of judging and policing
others' gender expression, will affect not just trans-identified individuals, but all
individuals who express themselves in ways that are not resolutely within strict
bigendered categories. Norms of expression, especially for women, have come
a very long way in just a few decades. It is no longer a travesty for a woman to
wear trousers, and while masculine gender norms are much less accommodating, there has at least been some recognition of a widening variety of expression.
To turn such facilities into spaces of extreme gender investigating, policing, and
enforcing is to narrow our understanding of human expression, a turn that is
both unnecessary and harmful. For GNC persons, such increased social monitoring and regulating of gender norms means that virtually no public place is free
from harassment.

As explained above, ATBBs put GNC and trans individuals at risk of verbal
harassment and physical violence. Enacting legislation that results in putting
persons at risk of predictable harm, for no demonstrable good, is wrong. But
I'm not merely offering a consequentialist argument, for the harm incurred is
not unrelated to the right of trans persons to at least a minimal level of moral
respect. Indeed, the harm of physical assault is an obvious expression that the
perpetrator does not recognize the full moral worth of another. The work of Axel
Honneth is particularly useful in that he recognizes that blows to one's body are
also blows to one's sense of self, one's autonomy, and are acts of disrespect. At the
most basic level, respecting another means to, at the very least, respect that they
have authority over their physical bodies. According to this view, "Those forms of
practical mistreatment in which a person is forcibly deprived of any opportunity
to dispose freely over his own body represent the most fundamental type of personal degradation."[14] This message of disrespect includes also the psychological
harm of being humiliated and of not even being recognized as having authority
over what happens to one's body.[15]

Even if a transgender or GNC person escapes physical violence, being harassed when simply using a bathroom is not a trivial harm and likewise represents a form of moral disrespect. To be glared at, yelled at, and/or kicked out of
a restroom facility conveys the message that the individual is unacceptable, out
of place, unwanted, and unwelcome. Repeated and/or particularly harmful cases
of such harassment have been shown to lead to post-traumatic stress disorder,
"holding it" and thus risking damage to one's urinary tract, or simply isolating
oneself from public spaces so to avoid the harassment altogether.[16] In the end,
such harassment conveys the message that an individual is unfit to participate in
public life itself. Encouraged by ATBBs, targeted individuals find that their moral
worth is suspect or explicitly denied; one is harassed or criminalized for inhabiting a condition of social impossibility,[17] as one's personhood and personal history are regarded as sufficient reason for ostracism. Whether one is denied social
participation (through a denial of relieving oneself without incurring abuse) due

to being seen as morally unacceptable as an individual, or that one belongs to a group (transgender persons) who are of less value as a collective, the result is the same: a denial of full moral status as an individual and social participant.

However we each plan our day, being any place more than a few hours requires us to acknowledge and attend to our physical being. All humans need to urinate and defecate, brush their teeth, wash their hands, and adjust their hair and clothes. Some need to deal with menstruation, and some need to take medication. To the extent that we are expected to do these activities in private and under somewhat hygienic circumstances, using bathrooms is a necessary part of social life. Given the identified ramifications of ATBBs discussed herein, GNC and trans individuals are essentially barred from public spaces subject to these laws. To deny one the ability to attend to one's physical needs is to infringe on one's opportunity to participate in society—whether that be to pursue an employment opportunity, protest one's government by picketing the state capital, or take one's child to a public zoo. Being offered a job, accommodation, or an education that denies one's basic physical needs and puts one at risk of harassment or violence is to deny that job, accommodation, or education. It is to explicitly deny any semblance of a right to equal opportunity, a notion thought to be sacrosanct by many and famously supported by philosopher John Rawls.[18] As Honneth explains, it is not just the *content* of the denial that encompasses the harm; the resulting lack of moral recognition is just as significant. He contends, "The distinguishing feature of such forms of disrespect, as typified by the denial of rights or by social ostracism, thus lies not solely in comparative restrictions on personal authority but in the combination of these restrictions with the feeling that the subject lacks the status of full-fledged partners to interaction who all possess the same moral rights."[19] Enacting legislation that puts certain members of society regularly at risk of physical harm, harassment, and social ostracism is to condemn those individuals to lives of increased marginality, isolation, and moral injury. As aptly conveyed by Richard M. Juang, "Despite its unquantifiability, recognition's importance can be measured by the consequences of its absence: an unvalued person readily becomes a target or a scapegoat for the hatred of others and begins to see himself or herself only through the lens of such hatred. An existence restricted to purely private expressions of the self, to the closet, becomes corrosive."[20]

As I have argued above, ATBBs put trans and GNC persons at risk of serious harm, and this constitutes a lack of recognition of moral worth and a denial of equal opportunity. Now, it is conceivable that one might agree with the argument presented thus far, and yet believe that ATBBs are legitimized through the need of keeping certain society members safe. Indeed, the rhetoric surrounding ATBBs predictably cites protecting (cisgender) girls and women against sexual assault, so one might question whether this is a situation in which, due to the presence of serious threats, certain civil liberties are justifiably curtailed. After all, it is not unusual to consider security and liberty as having an inverse relationship. In times that are thought to require increased security, say, in World War II when London was being regularly bombed by German forces, Londoners approved of blackout periods at which times they agreed not to use electricity. To consider an example closer to home, many can remember when airline travel did not include increased security screening in which certain liberties are curtailed and new procedures enforced. Often, arguments that support that such infringements on liberty are necessary for security have been accepted, if indeed the threat is real. Thus, it might be argued that there are times in which certain liberties need to be curtailed for the added security of all and that ATBBs are acceptable as response to a grave security threat.

The problem with this kind of argument in the case of ATBBs is that there is no security threat posed by trans or GNC persons who wish to use public facilities. In fact, there is no evidence that GNC individuals pose a threat to *anyone* using a public bathroom. As discussed before, statistically it is trans and GNC individuals who face violence and harassment at the hands of cisgender individuals, not the other way around. Thus, limiting access to gendered facilities based on one's sex assignment at birth is a solution without a problem, and a "solution" that does grave moral harm to otherwise innocent individuals. I recognize that one might argue that a cisgender man might "dress up" like a woman in order to gain access to women's facilities for the purpose of carrying out an assault, but there is little evidence supporting this fear either. As one chief records clerk of a police district without ATBBs recently asserted, there is no evidence that there is an increase in restroom sexual assaults in such locales. "We track our sex offenders, very carefully and we haven't seen any instance of sexual predators assaulting in bathrooms."[21] It has been known for decades that most sexual assaults are committed by individuals who are at least acquaintances of the victim, not by strangers in public restrooms.[22] Yet, suppose it were different. Still, this does not justify restricting bathroom access to those who are not using the restroom to perpetrate such crimes. It is as if one were banned from owning a car because someone might steal the car and use it to perpetrate a crime; from working as a physician because someone might pose as such for disreputable purposes; from traveling while having an Arabic last name because some may think only terrorists do so; from entering a woman's restroom for the purpose of assaulting another.[23] Indeed, the examples can be multiplied nearly without end. Simply put, it is unjust to non-trivially and harmfully limit someone's liberty only for the reason that there is a slight chance that another may perpetrate a crime by attempting to capitalize on that liberty. We all deserve to live lives that include safe and meaningful social participation, and taking this seriously does not include the social ostracism of trans and GNC persons.

Lastly, I recognize that the content of the argument herein may not have been what some readers expected. After all, I have not presented an argument as to why one should accept trans women as women and trans men as men. This is not because I don't accept these propositions as true and important to the full moral recognition of trans persons. I have avoided these kinds of arguments for three reasons. First, the enactment of ATBBs mean that trans and GNC individuals are denied both the right to safe and meaningful social participation and even a basic level of moral respect that should be shown to all persons. Yes, trans women are women and trans men are men, but if one does not believe this, at the very least let us attend to personal necessities in peace. Individuals of all gender identities and expressions should be recognized as embodied agents whose social participation requires the use of gendered facilities. Anything less is to deny our humanity and to weaponize personal and predictable biological function for the purpose of anti-trans bias. Second, I have not engaged in these kinds of arguments because I don't believe that there are necessary and sufficient biological conditions for being a man or a woman. Defining an individual by their genitalia (or perceived genitalia at birth), their chromosomes, their hormones, or some official designation made before they could barely open their eyes and experience this grand world is to unnecessarily reduce our human experience.[24] Furthermore, doing so disrespects the epistemic authority of trans persons to characterize our experiences and disregards the recommendations and assessments of both the American Medical Association and the American Psychological Association. Attempting to enforce such a reductionistic standard would be clearly draconian and harmful to all. Humans quite simply defy neat categorizations, and not recognizing this fact nearly always leads to moral harm. Third, such argumentation misses the fact that ATBBs negatively affect nonbinary and GNC individuals. Basic moral recognition and value need not be tied to thought-to-be-correct gender history or performance, but to human flourishing.

COMPREHENSION QUESTIONS

1. What are bathroom bills? What harms do they pose to trans and GNC people?
2. What is the double bind created by bathroom bills? Why does it affect all trans and GNC individuals?
3. What justifications are usually given to support bathroom bills?
4. Explain the common trans experience of being perceived as either a "deceiver" or a "make-believer."
5. What is the difference between material harms and harms to your moral worth? In what ways do ATBBs create the potential for material harm, and how is this related to ideas of moral respect?

DISCUSSION QUESTIONS

1. How is the "evil deceiver/make-believer" dichotomy present in the debate on transgender bathroom use? How is it related to worries regarding the social participation of trans persons generally? Are there other examples of identities that are thought of as being deceivers or as make-believers, and what are the consequences of such beliefs?
2. What kinds of harms does this author believe are relevant to this debate? What is the relationship between these kinds of harms? Can you think of other examples is U.S. history in which these same kinds of harms were present?

Case 1

"Bathroom bills" are changing. Consider, for instance, Tennessee House Bill 1274, which

> expands the attorney general and reporter's duties to include representation of [a local education agency] or certain [local education agency] employees in a court or administrative tribunal arising out of the adoption of a policy requiring students, faculty, and staff to utilize the restroom, locker room, or other facility that corresponds to that individual's biological sex.*

In other words, if this becomes law, then if a public school gets sued because it doesn't allow transgender kids to use the bathroom that they'd like to use, the state attorney general is obligated to defend that school in court. So the state wouldn't be creating bathroom-related policies, but it would be committed to defending those who create them.

Suppose we want to allow individual schools to be able to make choices about the policies they implement. If so, is there anything objectionable about having state lawyers defend those choices? (That is, *if* we say that this issue should be left up to individual schools, the state still has choices. On the one hand, the state could commit to defending schools. On the other, it could say, "It's up to you, but you have to accept any legal liability associated with the consequences.") Moreover, there's the more basic question: Is there any reason why we might want to allow local schools to make such choices for themselves?

---

*https://legiscan.com/TN/bill/HB1274/2019

A CONSERVATIVE POSITION
ON THE "BATHROOM BATTLES"
VAUGHN BRYAN BALTZLY

We are all familiar with the use of the term "liberal" to refer to those falling toward the left-hand side of the American political spectrum, but not to those on the right. But there is another sense of the term that is widely (though not universally) applicable to both left and right. Roughly, "liberalism" in this sense conveys a vision of government as secular, limited, representative, and constitutional, and a vision of citizens as free and equal. It's a political philosophy generally endorsed by those on the left ("progressives," as I shall term them) and on the right ("conservatives") alike.

But if a liberal political philosophy serves as common ground uniting left and right, liberal *social* philosophy is what distinguishes them. This is because progressives and conservatives often differ in their attitudes toward illiberal social realities—those (non-governmental) practices and institutions *not* organized according to (for example) norms of democratic governance, or the free and equal status of their members. Think, for example, of institutions and practices like marriage, the family, the church, the firm, and the military. Progressives are what we might call "compleat liberals"[25]: They wish for a society in which not only the public institutions, but also the private ones, are liberal in character. (This is the sense in which "liberal" serves as an apt label for left-leaning progressives: They are both political *and* social liberals.) Liberalizing these private institutions and practices might include, for instance, disallowing certain "traditional" ways of dividing domestic labor along gendered lines, or legally mandating that Catholics ordain and hire female priests. Conservatives, on the other hand, are often more accepting of such institutions. In fact, rather than merely *tolerating* certain il-liberal practices, they might actually go so far as to endorse or celebrate them. For example, conservatives may admire these institutions' "pedigrees"—seeing the fact that they have evolved, survived, or flourished over many generations as signs that they embody a certain internal practical logic or wisdom. To refashion them according to the progressive's demands could jeopardize much or all of their value and function. Call this the "traditionalist" strand within conservatism.

The practice of sex-segregating public restrooms and locker rooms is one fur-ther example of a putatively illiberal social custom, and it's the most recent field on which the battle between progressives and traditionalists has been waged. I am not certain which side has the stronger forces in this particular battle, but I do believe that the strength of the traditionalists' arsenal has been underestimated. Thus, in this chapter, I offer what I take to be the most powerful argument in favor of a generally traditionalist, conservative position on what has come to be known as the "bathroom battles."

This argument consists of two tactics: an "offensive maneuver" and a "defen-sive maneuver." In the former, I show how the traditionalists' standard warnings about the disruptive consequences of overturning longstanding custom (warn-ings sometimes too hastily dismissed by opponents as "mere 'slippery slope'–style reasoning") apply to matters of bathroom access. Specifically, the conservative worries that progressive intervention here will initiate a sequence of reforms with respect to other domains of sex segregation, and that the natural outcome of these reforms will be the elimination of sex segregation in athletics, college dor-mitories, beauty pageants, and a host of other areas not (currently) considered to be problematic. With the latter maneuver, I try to convince the progressive that he ought not be too dismissive of traditionalist-style reasoning, as he is likely at-tracted to traditionalist arguments in other domains. Specifically, I suggest that an appeal to traditionalism is an indispensable part of any defense of the familiar (but highly illiberal) practice of *higher education*.

Before exploring these two tactics, though, we should ensure we understand precisely what's under dispute in the so-called bathroom battles. So let's begin in Section 1 with a brief overview of the recent debate surrounding the "bathroom bills" (emphasizing a famous bill from North Carolina as a case study) before developing in Sections 2 and 3 the conservative's "offensive" and "defensive" maneuvers.

1. Bathroom Battles: What

Historically, the segregation by sex of restrooms, locker rooms, changing rooms, and other such spaces has been largely a matter of social custom.[26] However,

North Carolina's March 2016 passage of House Bill 2—the "Public Facilities Privacy and Security Act" (hereinafter "HB2")—is one prominent piece of recent legislation seeking to ratify this received social custom. HB2 directs local boards of education and public agencies in North Carolina to "require every multiple occupancy bathroom or changing facility . . . to be designated for and only used by [students/persons] based on their biological sex," where "biological sex" is defined as "[t]he physical condition of being male or female, which is stated on a person's birth certificate."[27] This has the practical effect of requiring that transgender persons[28] utilize bathrooms or changing facilities matching their sex, rather than (as they may often prefer) those matching their gender. HB2 was itself precipitated by another act of (municipal) legislation that sought to modify this same social custom: Charlotte's "Ordinance 7056."[29]

The state law did not fare well in the court of public opinion. Popular and elite sentiment seemed predominantly opposed to the bill, and corporate pressure (from organizations like PayPal, the NCAA, and the NBA) played a large role in persuading the legislature to quickly modify the measure. On March 30, 2017, North Carolina's governor signed into law House Bill 142, which among other things rescinded the portions of HB2 that concerned bathroom access. At the time, a number of other U.S. state legislatures had been considering similar bills. However, the March 2017 demise of HB2 seemed to arrest whatever momentum these bills may have had: As of spring 2018, it does not appear that any comparable bathroom bill is under serious consideration anywhere in the United States. However, it may be too hasty to conclude that the issue has been forever laid to rest. Controversial social issues sometimes take a zig-zagging path to final resolution—variously advancing onto, and receding from, societal consciousness before public opinion and policy becomes settled. (Consider, for example, the "fits-and-starts" history of the recent debate about same-sex marriage.[30])

In any event: Now that local and state governments have assumed responsibility for legislating the proper segregation of such spaces, we can appreciate the need to examine the fundamental legal and philosophical issues that arise here. One such basic issue concerns the nature of what we might term "legal-ization." Legal-ization is different than *legalization*. The latter (and more familiar) notion refers to making legal something that was formerly illegal, as when reformers advocate for the legalization of marijuana. The former, though, is the notion of using legal measures to formalize or modify a social custom that had previously been maintained principally by social convention. When should we ratify social practices by enshrining them into law? When might we use the law to alter or abolish certain social institutions? These are the questions that lie at the heart of understanding *legal-ization*.

The matter of legal-ization becomes especially important when we consider HB2's precedent-setting potential. This is because the position we ultimately adopt in response to this controversy, and the considerations we invoke to support that position, will likely bear upon many other forms of sex segregation too. Although the bathroom battles at present appear to be dormant, we may someday recognize them as having been the first in a series of challenges to other forms of sex segregation. The arguments and reasons invoked to settle the bathroom battles will doubtless prove attractive to future disputants attacking or defending sex segregation in (for example) dorm rooms or college athletics. The conservative worries that if we err in the arguments and reasons we take to have settled the bathroom issue, we may shortly find ourselves committed to other sorts of social reforms (or to existing forms of segregation) with which we are uncomfortable. It is this fear of thus carelessly setting precedent that lies at the heart of the principled conservative's reluctance to incautiously legal-ize our bathroom segregation practices. Let's turn, then, to a more detailed examination of this conservative position.[31]

2. The Conservative on Offense: *Contra* Progressivism

The conservative's "offensive" maneuver consists of three sub-tactics. First, she argues that the only consistently progressive position on the issue is a full-fledged policy of *integration* with respect to public bathrooms. Second, she alleges that the progressive case for bathroom integration generalizes: It applies likewise to all other forms of sex segregation. And lastly, the conservative performs what I shall term the "Burkean maneuver": arguing that the progressive's desire to over-turn in one fell swoop every practice of sex segregation is reckless. This is because any attempt to radically disrupt so many deeply ingrained social conventions is bound to bring about unforeseen and unintended consequences, many unwel-come. Far better, then, to refrain from legislating at all in this domain, or at least to legislate only cautiously and experimentally, in piecemeal fashion.

The Progressive Commitment to Integration

A significant amount of early trans advocacy with respect to bathroom justice pressed for the creation of gender-neutral restrooms. That is, many argued for a regime of fully *integrated* bathrooms. More recently, though, trans advocates have transitioned to calling for recognition (and enforcement) of transgender individuals' right to utilize the (segregated) restroom or locker room matching their gender identity. That is, trans advocates shifted from pursuing the cause of sex and gender bathroom *integration* to pursuing the cause of *trans-accessible segregation* of bathrooms. One reason for this shift was the recognition that a central aspect of living out one's true gender identity is the ability to access and enjoy the single-gendered spaces (both metaphorical and literal) typically re-served for one's fellow men and women. Relegating transgender individuals to "merely neutral" "third spaces" deprives them of this opportunity.

Appealing though this rationale may appear from the trans perspective, we might ask: Can a progressive, consistently with his social liberalism, endorse a regime of trans-accessible segregation? The conservative says "no": *Any* regime that preserves and enforces (via legal and/or social sanction) any variety of sex or gender segregation stands in tension with the progressive ideal of equal treatment—an ideal requiring the equal treatment of *all* citizens, in *all* spaces.

To appreciate this, let's compare two scenarios: one where we maintain trans-accessible segregated bathrooms, and another where we have integrated bathrooms. Now, let's think about individuals who are nonbinary, gender-queer, or otherwise GNC. In the trans-accessible scenario, which of the two choices—"Men's" or "Women's"—best respects their identities? It doesn't seem like either does, and what's worse, this scenario involves perpetuating the gender binary that GNC individuals find stifling, or even oppressive. Next, let's consider the case of disabled persons who have differently gendered caregivers: The situation where we have sex-segregated bathrooms deprives them the opportunity of that assistance. However, if we switch to fully integrated bathrooms, we don't disadvantage either population and instead offer a neutral solution. Granted, it isn't one that positively affirms (by enshrining into legal doctrine) any particular individual's conception of gender, but crucially, the integrated bathroom scenario serves these populations' bathroom needs.[32]

There's an analogous argument you've perhaps encountered with respect to another recent social controversy: same-sex marriage. Way back in the early 2010s, when debates on this subject were still raging, some defended a similarly neutral response to the question of expanding civil marriage to include same-sex unions along with heterosexual ones. These scholars called for the "disestablishment" of marriage.[33] On this proposal, the state—rather than taking a stand on the (then-controversial) question as to which types of life partnership properly deserve the title "marriage"—instead sidesteps this contentious issue by "getting out of the marriage business" altogether. Institutions of civil society (e.g., churches, mosques, and synagogues) could decide for themselves which domestic unions to sanctify as marriages, but it would not be an issue for legislatures or courts to decide. Such "marital disestablishmentarians" argued that their solution was most congruent with the basic liberal norm of the equal treatment of all citizens. Granted, it wouldn't positively affirm (by enshrining into legal doctrine) any particular individual's conception of marriage, but it has the virtue of neutrality—it neither affirms *nor* undermines any faction's treasured conception of the institution. Supposing disestablishmentarians are correct, then, it would seem that the progressive ought, by parity of reasoning, to favor a regime of integrated bathrooms as the proper response to controversies concerning bathroom access.

Consider finally the "overturning patriarchy" rationale, which might be seen as akin to the U.S. Supreme Court's finding in 1954's historic *Brown v. Board of Education* ruling. There, the Court ruled that a regime of "separate but equal" is incoherent—that, in virtue of declaring that facilities for black citizens had to be separate, segregated institutions were thereby declaring that black citizens were *not* equal. Likewise, a regime of segregated restrooms might express a conviction that the sexes are, in important respects, not equals. Only a regime of fully integrated restrooms and locker rooms could really express the sexes' equal status.

Of course, an opponent could point out a dis-analogy here. For while racial segregation reinforced an asymmetrical view of the two races' relative worths (specifically, the view that blacks were inferior to whites), contemporary practices of sex and gender segregation do not generally reflect a belief that one or the other is superior. In response, we might point out that—though a regime of sex-/gender-segregated bathrooms does not itself express a vision of either male or female superiority—ours is a society with a history of discriminatory, sexist norms that typically favored males. Given this heritage of patriarchy, we might regard with justifiable suspicion any remnants of sex- and gender-based separation as themselves connected to this history of male dominance.

At any rate, the *Brown*-inspired bathroom integrationist holds that *any* regime of sex segregation, including the current regime of segregated bathrooms, is tantamount to an affirmation of the "separate but equal" ideology. It should be just as shameful when applied to the sexes as when applied to races. And if restroom integration expresses a repudiation of "separate but equal"—and if furthermore it helps to ameliorate our legacy of patriarchy—then seemingly the progressive should endorse it.

To review: The conservative argues that the consistent progressive must, in accordance with his social liberalism, embrace a full-fledged commitment to bathroom integration for at least three reasons. The first is considerations of fairness to GNC individuals and those with disabilities; the second is recognition of the parallels between the case for *integration* and the (progressive) case for *marital disestablishment*; and the third is consideration of the affinity between the regime of gender-segregated bathrooms (even a comparatively more humane regime of *trans-accessible* segregation) and the now-discredited doctrine of "separate but equal" facilities for blacks and whites. However, the progressive's compleat liberalism is not completed by this endorsement of bathroom integration. Rather, much more is required—as we shall now see.

The Case for Integration Generalizes

Since each of these three reasons in support of integrationism applies with similar (if not equal) force to other domains of sex segregation, the progressive seems committed to overturning these practices too. Aren't sex-specific college dormitories discomfiting for GNC students? Don't sex-separated athletic competitions and sex-sensitive Transportation Security Administration (TSA) screenings express something like the doctrine of "separate but equal"? Doesn't it seem that hiring and admissions policies premised on distinctions between the sexes run afoul of the liberal norm of equal treatment? For the progressive, there seems to be considerable pressure to embrace a thoroughgoing policy of integration *anywhere* sex-based distinctions are found.

At this point, the progressive might deny that any of these considerations *does* generalize. He might assert that each domain of sex segregation is unique, and that what is true with respect to the prudence of bathroom and locker room integration may not apply to the cases of college dormitories and athletic competition. It's a mistake, then, to think that a progressive commitment to bathroom integration requires a commitment to integration across the board.

As with the "overturning patriarchy" rationale discussed just above, though, comparison with the past century's struggle for civil rights in the United States offers an instructive parallel. Do we think that the twentieth century's great advocates for racial integration should have reasoned as follows? "Look, we shouldn't press for *all* forms of integration, all at once! Since each domain of segregation is unique, and raises distinct concerns, let's just take these issues one at a time. They can't be meaningfully or helpfully bundled together. Perhaps we'll start with the cause of lunch-counter segregation, then move on to schools and buses ...." Doesn't this seem odd? In retrospect, we all agree that it was indeed a right and a good thing that the civil rights movement pushed for the elimination of racial segregation *across the board*. But then why would present-day progressives favor so contrary a stance with respect to today's prevailing "separate but equal" regime? (Unless they secretly believe that this *would* have been a better tactic in the fight for civil rights, and that the movement's leaders erred in lumping all forms together into a single heterogeneous category inartfully labeled "racial segregation.")

So it seems the progressive is committed to a fully generalized stance of integrationism after all. If his compleat liberalism were the complete truth of liberalism, we might consider the matter closed: Full integrationism is the only stance acceptable to anyone with any liberal leanings. However, the progressive's picture is *not* the complete truth of the matter: There is room within (political) liberalism for a principled tolerance of (social) illiberalism. This is the more nuanced liberalism of the conservative. So let us now turn to an examination of the right's (perfectly coherent, if oft-overlooked) position that, where the reach of law and public policy ends, allegedly "illiberal" values and practices need not (necessarily) yield to considerations of, say, fairness and equal treatment—norms that must prevail where the coercive arm of the state operates, but that need not prevail elsewhere or everywhere.

The Burkean Maneuver

The first thing to note here is that the liberal conservative does not tolerate or endorse illiberal practices *because* they are illiberal. Rather, it's that their illiberality is not always sufficient warrant for a "liberalizing intervention." Partly, the conservative's reluctance to forcibly liberalize results from her desire to respect the freely made choices of the parties involved in the institution or practice—including, even, the choice to live or behave in an illiberal fashion. But this reluctance also stems from a sense that such intervention is often liable to cause as much harm as good. The recognition that such liberalizing interventions often cause significant disruption and upheaval is at the heart of the conservative's "Burkean maneuver."

Invoking a strain of thought famously associated with Edmund Burke, the conservative argues that it is quite proper for liberal societies to tolerate, and sometimes even to encourage, long-established social conventions and customs.[34] This is because these institutions arose spontaneously, over repeated generations of interaction, as ways of accommodating a variety of conflicting societal and individual needs—without anyone's having explicitly designed them for that purpose. Accordingly, there is a presumption in favor of preserving these time-honored and naturally evolved traditions. (Hence the "conserving" impulse that lends conservatism its name.) Applying this Burkean insight here, the conservative holds that our received practices of maintaining various single-sex spheres embodies a certain internal practical logic that solves numerous social coordination problems—some of which we can identify and articulate, but others of which undoubtedly remain obscure to us. Obscure though this "internal practical logic" may be now, the valuable social-coordination role of sex segregation would likely become swiftly and vividly apparent to us, in retrospect, were we to incautiously rip it apart. The progressive's proposed liberalizing, legal-izing intervention on behalf of an uncompromising regime of sex integration thus risks sacrificing the social efficacy of institutions and practices that embed many generations' worth of accumulated wisdom.

3. The Conservative on Defense: In Support of Burkeanism

Progressives who think themselves disinclined to such maneuvers should check their own Burkeanism. There are likely practices and customs dear to them that are likewise vulnerable to the charge of illiberality, and institutions whose best defense likewise rests on appeal to tradition and custom. Consider the *academy*, for instance. There are few social practices less egalitarian than the admissions policies of contemporary colleges and universities in the United States. This is because our practice is to systematically deny admission to those whose cognitive and/or social misfortune has rendered them ill prepared for the rigors of college life. Our practice, in other words, is to systematically deny admission to those individuals *most in need* of a higher education—further contributing to a densely woven web of oppressive practices by which they are already disadvantaged. And focusing just on those students lucky enough to gain admission: There are few practices more cutthroat, more "socially Darwinian," than making recurring categorical distinctions among these students according to academic performance (irrespective of any relevant background conditions, and insensitive to any extenuating circumstances) and sorting them into a brutal hierarchy according to something called "GPA." And focusing now on just those students who survive this gauntlet and manage to graduate: Our society has perhaps no mechanism better suited for conferring advantage and marking privilege than the current system of rampant interinstitutional inequality *among* institutions of higher education. For those fortunate enough to earn their college degrees, postgraduation life offers ample evidence that those touting degrees from "elite" colleges and universities fare much better than those who enjoy less prestigious pedigrees. Thus, the institution of American higher education is complicit in—nay, is a central driver of—the systematic oppression of the socioeconomically disadvantaged, and the ongoing maintenance of privilege and enforcement of class distinctions.

Or so one might argue, at any rate; I happen to think such an argument would be misguided.[35] But the crucial point here is this: Anyone wishing to argue in this fashion may do so in perfect conformity with argumentative and rhetorical standards currently prevalent in certain communities of progressive critique. Anyone rejecting this critique—anyone wishing to resist (even well and progressively intentioned) efforts to remake the internal norms, standards, and practices of higher education in line with prevailing liberal principles—must come to grips with his own Burkean impulse. For the justification of these (widespread) inegalitarian and illiberal norms—norms that are centrally constitutive of current practices in higher education—may rest on no greater, or no worse, foundation than the one appealed to by our traditionalist conservative in making her Burkean maneuver.

4. Conclusion

This defense of a "right-ward" position on the bathroom battles may not be the strongest argument you've ever encountered. It certainly has its vulnerabilities. (For instance: Unless suitably refined, the Burkean rationale could seemingly likewise legitimate all sorts of unjustifiable and sexist discrimination and oppression. So it is a very powerful—perhaps *too* powerful—maneuver.) It is also modest in its aims—perhaps, for some conservative readers, disappointingly so. If valid, this argumentative strategy establishes less than certain rival conservative strategies might hope to secure. For one thing, it is merely "anti-anti-bathroom bill" rather than (say) "pro-HB2." And it is very nearly as skeptical of bills (like HB2) that seek to incautiously ratify the received practices of sex segregation as it is of those laws (like the city of Charlotte's Ordinance 7056) that seek to overturn such customs. (It merely counsels legislative prudence, in other words.) And finally, this argument no doubt leaves a number of conservative readers cold for failing to support their conviction that transgender access to bathrooms is to be blocked because the very notion of being transgender is suspect.[36] I offer no apology to such conservatives for my failure to cheer; they will have to look elsewhere (or within) for the buttressing of *that* view. All I can say in defense of this defense is that it has the virtues of being reasonable, measured, plausible, and (perhaps) original. And who knows? It might even be correct.

COMPREHENSION QUESTIONS

1. What is the difference between *being a liberal* and *liberalism*?
2. What is the difference between a liberal progressive and a liberal conservative?
3. What two approaches does the author use to support a conservative position on bathroom bills?
4. What is the *Burkean maneuver*?
5. Compare and contrast the *segregated* trans-accessible bathroom model with the *integrated* trans-accessible bathroom model.

DISCUSSION QUESTIONS

1. What are some of the benefits of being a Burkean? What are some of the (known) costs and (potential) risks?
2. There are lots of gender- and sex-related traditions that shape public life, and it's often difficult to know all their costs and benefits. Some liberals are generally suspicious of these traditions. Why might that suspicion be justified? What would be the best argument for thinking that our gender- and sex-related traditions deserve more side-eye than deference?

Case 2

Consider this story from 2015:

> Palatine, a well-off suburb of Chicago, [was] the first district in the country to be found in violation of civil rights laws on transgender issues. By forcing the transgender student—known in the media as "Student A"—to use a separate locker room, the Department of Education's Office of Civil Rights ruled that Township High School District 211 had discriminated against the student "on the basis of sex." The finding came as the result of a lengthy investigation, triggered by a lawsuit filed by Student A's parents . . . [Eventually,] the school board changed its policies to allow Student A into the girls' locker rooms, so long as the student changed behind newly installed "privacy curtains."
>
> According to the Department of Education's investigation, Student A began transitioning to a female in middle school. The student was diagnosed with gender dysphoria and currently receives an "ongoing course" of hormone therapy. But some girls at the high school say Student A has not fully transitioned, which makes some of them uncomfortable sharing a locker room. "What bothers me is the fact that this student is still anatomically a male," a 16-year-old sophomore told *The Daily Signal* on the condition of anonymity. "If the student had already undergone surgical procedures, this would be another story entirely, but as it stands I just don't feel comfortable with it."
>
> A 15-year-old told *The Daily Signal* "it just doesn't feel right." "I know Student A poses no harm to me, but it just doesn't feel right knowing someone with male anatomy is in the bathroom with me," she said, adding: "I have nothing against Student A and would be her friend if I knew her better, but when it comes down to it, I don't feel right changing in the same room as a transgender student. The locker room is already filled with so much judgment, and I barely feel OK changing in front of my naturally born girl peers."
>
> A third student, a 16-year-old sophomore, expressed frustration. "[W]e are supposed to accept this and feel like nothing really is happening, but the fact of the matter is that this did get pretty big and now we have someone with male genitals in our girls' locker room when we are changing," she said.*

What do you make of the concerns that these girls are expressing? How should school administrators respond to them? How should physical education teachers respond to them? How should school counselors respond to them?

_____

*https://www.dailysignal.com/2015/12/21/why-these-high-school-girls-dont-want-transgender-student-a-in-their-locker-room/

REPLY TO BALTZLY
LOREN CANNON

It is both a pleasure and a privilege to be able to engage in this important philosophical debate with Professor Baltzly. In this very brief response to his essay, I first identify what I take to be points of agreement between us, then present my critique of his view. I maintain that ATBBs are unjust and that this is sufficient reason for their rejection. Moreover, this rejection is independent of broad-based gender integration across the board.

Professor Baltzly and I have some points of agreement. In his argument for what he calls a "fully fledged policy of *integration*," he gives a nod toward the recognition of how the assumptions of the sex-gender binary affect nearly every aspect of society; GNC persons and even caregivers are often caught in the crosshairs of these complex navigations. I wholeheartedly agree. Second, I admit to having some Burkean tendencies myself, and I, like so many others, rely on social practices and their shared expectations daily. However, perhaps unlike Baltzly, I believe there is also reason to look at social practices with a good dose of suspicion, as I explain herein. Lastly, Baltzly does not present a case for why transgender and GNC persons should be barred from social participation, so it is not clear whether or not we have agreement on this important point.

Most generally, Baltzly's argument supports the conclusion that a conservative thinker would not accept widespread, progressive, and rapid social change. This result is quite predictable, but tells us little regarding the morality of ATBBs. Recall that Baltzly is, essentially, offering one conservative thinker's critique of the progressive thinker's argument against ATBBs. As he explains, the conservative on the offense will critique the progressive's argument against ATBBs by arguing that the logically consistent position would be to support not only fully gender-integrated bathrooms, but full gender integration across the board. Supposing the progressive thinker accepts this move toward full integration, the conservative then rejects this conclusion because "the progressive's desire to overturn in one fell swoop every practice of sex segregation is reckless." As mentioned above, the result that a conservative thinker would be against widespread and rapid social change is not surprising; that's how conservatism is often understood. But our imaginary conservative seems to believe that her progressive interlocutor has the power to singlehandedly author widespread social change "in one fell swoop." (Otherwise, there is no objection: Burkeanism gets you *slow* change, not *no* change.) However, asserting a position about the good of society is one thing; having the power to realize the content of that position in the short term, especially in a society such as ours, is another.

Furthermore, Professor Baltzly's argument is undercut by the fact that accepting or rejecting full gender integration is independent of one's acceptance of ATBBs. First, assume that one is persuaded that full gender integration is required in the long term.[37] This does not mean that an individual is being logically inconsistent if they object to ATBBs and the harm that they are apt to cause in the short term. Indeed, a prudential strategy may involve objecting to clearly unjust legislation as it is proposed and enacted, while at the same time working to improve other contexts over time. There are individuals across the country engaged in social justice issues regarding gendered bathrooms, college residence halls, and athletic competitions, and I applaud these efforts. Should we worry that such labors will "incautiously rip . . . apart" our social structures and lead to unforeseen harm? It seems highly unlikely. Indeed, there is ample evidence that it takes a dreadfully long time to recognize and dismantle the many types of structural injustices that have plagued our society from its inception. This is unfortunate, because the longer time that it takes to dismantle these oppressive structures, the more harm takes place. In any case, social change toward a just society is inhibited more by the recalcitrant attitudes of those who are unjustly privileged than any legitimate worry of social upheaval.

Second, suppose that a thoughtfully minded individual is *not* persuaded that full integration is necessary. After all, the contexts that are of concern here are distinct and may involve different factors and priorities. Still, if one is less than persuaded about full *integration*, this is not a reason to refrain from opposing ATBBs that so clearly put individuals at risk of harm and curtail social participation.

Let me conclude with my most important criticism. Professor Baltzly's argument, true to our tradition, involves the complex relationship of abstract ideas, but it lacks a discussion of the real ramifications of these proposals on targeted individuals. In my essay, I presented evidence that these proposals unjustly put trans and GNC persons at risk for harassment and violence, and curtail opportunities for them to participate in society as equal members.[38] It is *this* focus, on how certain proposals target and negatively impact marginalized persons, that I believe is the correct one. Baltzly and I agree that a Burkean tendency to accept social practices is not sufficient reason to continue those practices when they are unjust.[39] I, unlike Baltzly, believe ATBBs are and not simply a matter of preserving perhaps "illiberal" social practices that are otherwise morally neutral. Applied ethics, specifically, is a place to consider our shared human vulnerabilities, the costs of injustice, and the conditions required for all of us to enjoy meaningful and flourishing lives. In doing so, the experiences of GNC and trans persons must be taken into consideration.[40]

COMPREHENSION QUESTIONS

1. Cannon argues that being denied bathroom access is related to the right of equal opportunity and social participation. Why?
2. Why does Cannon suggest that Baltzly has an incomplete understanding of gender? What are some of the aspects of gender that, according to Cannon, Baltzly has conflated? (Check the endnotes.)

DISCUSSION QUESTIONS

1. We're perceived in lots of ways: as white, as a person of color, as a homeless person, as a GNC person, as an immigrant, as a trans person, as a disabled person, as a man, as a woman. How might these perceptions affect how we're received in a bathroom in contexts of increased bathroom surveillance? What combinations of these factors may make it more or less difficult to use public facilities with ease?
2. What are the risks to oppressed groups if we rely on a Burkean maneuver to guide policy?

REPLY TO CANNON
VAUGHN BRYAN BALTZLY

Suppose you find yourself broadly sympathetic to the position I've defended, but that someone you like and respect—a roommate, a friend, a romantic partner—inclines in the opposite direction, finding Professor Cannon's essay more persuasive. I'd like to provide here a recipe for how you might have a productive dialogue about the sometimes-conflicting, sometimes-overlapping considerations and positions raised in these two essays.[41]

For starters, it helps to establish a baseline of mutual respect and a tone of cooperative investigation. So you might begin by offering a compliment: pointing out, say, that Cannon's essay is especially admirable for grounding us in the real-life, real-world concerns (related to safety every bit as much as to identity) of real people, here and now.

In response, we might hope that your interlocutor reciprocates by acknowledging some common ground. For instance, it appears that both parties are in agreement that many bathroom bills—what Cannon characterizes as ATBBs (such as North Carolina's HB2)—are ill advised as a matter of public policy.

Next—and before directly challenging your "opponent's" view—it's good to preempt the possibility of talking past one another. For example, it might be helpful to clarify whether your friend prefers the status quo—no laws whatsoever with respect to bathroom access—or whether she prefers the passage of laws that positively affirm the legal right of transgender persons to access the segregated bathrooms (and locker rooms, etc.) matching their gender identities.[42] Cannon's essay is silent here; the position he defends is simply "*anti*-anti-transgender bathroom bill," but he doesn't tell us whether he would favor (what we might call) "*pro*-transgender bathroom bills." Whichever answer your friend provides, you might follow up by seeking guidance as to how the view extends to other positions beyond those staked out by Cannon. Would your friend be open to a regime of full-fledged integration, for instance? These sorts of clarifying, probing questions are helpful in establishing the full extent of your agreement and the precise nature of your disagreement.

Having established some common ground and a baseline for civil and productive dialogue, you're now ready to explore those places where your views diverge. It's usually good practice to invite your partner to offer the first round of criticism rather than charging onto the offensive yourself. It's similarly wise, though, to have practiced your defensive maneuvers—first by anticipating the sorts of criticisms you might hear, and second by considering some possible responses. Let's see how this might play out.

If your friend is a worthy dialogue partner, keen to assist you in spotting your position's weakest and most vulnerable flanks, she should first press you on your embrace of the Burkean maneuver. She might concede that Burkean considerations sometimes have force, while still insisting that the maneuver is invalid here. This is because the preservation of tradition is sometimes simply the preservation of injustice, and the legal-ization of traditional practices of bathroom sex segregation may simply preserve (indeed, *amplify*) current injustices suffered by trans individuals. Likewise, it may be argued that the prospective harms that would befall transgender individuals, were a bathroom bill passed,[43] perhaps outweigh the prospective harms stemming from the "social disruption" I consider in my essay.

Having anticipated this line of critique, though, you can reply that you *welcome* this opening to discuss the wider balance of benefits and harms that might result from these laws, because Cannon's essay actually seems crucially incomplete on this point: Cannon is only ever concerned with the safety of trans individuals. Nevertheless, you might press your interlocutor by insisting that she consider the question of, say, the threat to the safety of women posed by the prospect of "posers": men (let's assume only cisgendered men) who are keen to exploit, for unsavory purposes, any "newly liberalized environment" with respect to bathroom and locker room access.[44] For as emerged in the row in the United Kingdom during the summer of 2018, a considerable number of cisgendered women are increasingly emboldened to express discomfort with a contemplated change in that country's "Gender Recognition Act." (The U.K. government is considering making self-avowal the sole criterion by which public institutions could make determinations of gender—thus providing an opening, some fear, for unscrupulous parties to make disingenuous avowals for purposes of obtaining ill-gotten access to women-only spaces.[45]) Typically, trans advocates have simply dismissed such considerations out of hand (as Cannon himself does here). But it's not clear Cannon and others are correct to dismiss this concern so hastily, particularly once one begins thinking of matters in terms of straightforward proportions and probabilities.[46]

Cannon dismisses concerns about posers largely on grounds of what we might term the "non-inheritability argument"—that laws don't "inherit" the sins of those who misuse them for malevolent purposes, and are therefore not condemnable on grounds that they are (or are liable to be) abused.[47] But you might note to your interlocutor that that very point cuts right against a central argument Cannon repeatedly makes earlier in his essay—that ATBBs would foreseeably result in continued assaults against trans persons as a result of their being forced to use restrooms that don't match their gender identity. But why should ATBBs inherit the sins of those who wrongfully exploit them, while the other laws that Cannon cites don't? If the non-inheritability argument is valid, it applies to bathroom bills as well.

At this point, one of several things might happen. You may continue the discussion for a while, each of you finding the spirited but respectful exchange of contrasting ideas fruitful and stimulating. Or the conversation may begin to flag: Having identified a clear but intractable disagreement, you each may judge that you stand to gain little from continued debate. Or the conversation may slowly become a "conversion," as one party gradually persuades the other to change positions. *However* your exchange proceeds, though, I think you'll find that—by getting matters going in the manner sketched above—you've at least attained a charitable and appreciative understanding of an opponent's view. And these days, that's not nothing!

COMPREHENSION QUESTIONS

1. What recommendations does Baltzly make for having an effective dialogue between conservatives and progressives?
2. What is the non-inheritability argument, and why does Baltzly use this to critique Cannon's argument against ATBBs?

DISCUSSION QUESTIONS

1. Are there any other forms of existing sex segregation that strike you as problematic, or at least worthy of scrutiny? For example, does it seem plausible to you that the current practice of sex-segregated college athletics is condemnable as a regime of "separate but equal"? Why or why not?
2. How apt is the analogy between racial segregation and sex- or gender-based segregation? Are there reasons why we shouldn't think about the latter as being similar to the former?

FURTHER READINGS

Bettcher, Talia Mae. "Evil Deceivers and Make-Believers: On Transphobic Violence and the Politics of Illusion." *Hypatia* 22, no. 2 (Summer 2007): 43–65.
Burke, Edmund. *Reflections on the Revolution in France* (1790). https://www.earlymodern texts.com/assets/pdfs/burke1790.pdf.
Garrett, Jeremy. "History, Tradition, and the Normative Foundations of Civil Marriage." *The Monist 91*, no. 3–4 (2008): 446–474.
Henrie, Mark. "Understanding Traditionalist Conservatism." In *Varieties of Conservatism in America*, edited by Peter Berkowitz. Palo Alto, CA: Hoover Institution Press, 2004.
James, S. E., J. L. Herman, S. Rankin, M. Keisling, L. Mottet, and M. Anafi. *The Report of the 2015 U.S. Transgender Survey*. Washington, DC: National Center for Transgender Equality, December 2016.
Herman, Jody L. "Gendered Restrooms and Minority Stress: The Public Regulation of Gender and its Impact on Transgender People's Lives." *Journal of Public Management and Social Policy* 19, no. 1 (2013): 65–80.
Honneth, Axel. "Integrity and Disrespect: Principles of a Conception of Morality Based on the Theory of Recognition." *Political Theory* 20, no. 2 (1992): 187–201.
Olson, Kristina R., Lily Durwood, Madeleine DeMeules, and Katie A. McLaughlin. "Mental Health of Transgender Children Who Are Supported in Their Identities." *Pediatrics* 137, no. 3 (2016): e20153223.
Spade, Dean. *Normal Life: Administrative Violence, Critical Trans Politics, and the Limits of the Law*. Brooklyn NY: South End Press, 2011.

NOTES

1. The focus here is mostly from 2016 through mid-2018. It is relevant that in the summer of 2015, the U.S. Supreme Court's *Obergefell v. Hodges* decision was announced supporting same-sex marriage.
2. I will be attending to arguments centered on bathroom use, since it seems the most controversial, but these arguments are readily transferable to other gendered spaces with limited revision.

3. S. E. James, J. L. Herman, S. Rankin, M. Keisling, L. Mottet, and M. Anafi, *The Report of the 2015 U.S. Transgender Survey* (Washington, DC: National Center for Transgender Equality, December 2016), www.ustranssurvey.org/reports. Hereafter "USTS."

4. These claims have been supported by nearly every study on transgender persons in our country. For reference, review USTS and "A Broken Bargain for Transgender Workers, 2013" (www.lgbtmap.org/file/a-broken-bargain-for-transgender-workers.pdf). Even one of the earliest state-specific studies, "State of Transgender California," in 2008 gives the first glimpses of these problems (transgenderlawcenter.org/wp-content/uploads/2012/07/95219573-The-State-of-Transgender-California.pdf).

5. USTS, 7.

6. Kristina R. Olson, Lily Durwood, Madeleine DeMeules, and Katie A. McLaughlin, "Mental Health of Transgender Children Who Are Supported in Their Identities," *Pediatrics* 137, no. 3 (2016):e20153223, pediatrics.aappublications.org/content/early/2016/02/24/peds.2015-3223?utm_source=TrendMD&utm_medium=TrendMD&utm_campaign=Pediatrics_TrendMD_0.

7. USTS, 6.

8. Similar to note 6, this claim has been supported by several studies, including USTS, and studies by the Human Rights Campaign (HRC). See HRC's "A Time To Act: Fatal Violence Against Transgender People in America, 2017," https://assets2.hrc.org/files/assets/resources/A_Time_To_Act_2017_REV3.pdf.assets2.hrc.org/files/assets/resources/A_Time_To_Act_2017_REV3.pdf.

9. Various studies and news reports support this claim. See also Maggie Astor, "Violence Against Trans People Is on the Rise, Advocates Say," *New York Times*, November 9, 2017, and HRC, "A Time to Act."

10. Jody L. Herman, "Gendered Restrooms and Minority Stress: The Public Regulation of Gender and Its Impact on Transgender People's Lives." *Journal of Public Management and Social Policy* 19, no. 1 (2013): 65–80. The incidents of harassment or assault experienced by people of color were reported at a "much higher" rate than white respondents, as were problems experienced by those who were trans feminine rather than trans masculine (77).

11. Tommy J. Curry, "Michael Brown and the Need for a Genre Study of Black Male Death and Dying," *Theory and Event* 17, no. 3, supplement (2014), muse.jhu.edu/article/559369.

12. Marilyn Frye, *The Politics of Reality: Essays in Feminist Theory* (Trumansburg, NY: The Crossing Press, 1983), 2.

13. Talia Mae Bettcher, "Evil Deceivers and Make-Believers: On Transphobic Violence and the Politics of Illusion" *Hypatia* 22, no. 2 (Summer 2007): 43–65.

14. Axel Honneth, "Integrity and Disrespect: Principles of a Conception of Morality Based on the Theory of Recognition," *Political Theory* 20, no. 2 (1992): 190.

15. Honneth, "Integrity and Disrespect."

16. Herman, "Gendered Restrooms," 76.

17. Dean Spade. *Normal Life: Administrative Violence, Critical Trans Politics, and the Limits of the Law* (Brooklyn, NY: South End Press), 2011.

18. John Rawls, *A Theory of Justice* (Cambridge, MA: Harvard University Press), 1971.

19. Honneth, "Integrity and Disrespect," 191.

20. Richard M. Juang, "Transgendering the Politics of Recognition," in *Transgender Rights,* edited by Paisley Currah, Richard M. Juang, and Shannon Price Minter (Minneapolis: University of Minnesota Press, 2006), 242.

21. Emanuella Grinberg and Dani Stewart, "Three Myths That Shape the Transgender Bathroom Debate," CNN, March 7, 2017, www.cnn.com/2017/03/07/health/transgender-bathroom-law-facts-myths/index.html.

22. According to statistics gathered and reported by the Rape, Abuse & Incest National Network (RAINN), 8 out of 10 crimes of rape are perpetrated by one known by the victim. For crimes of sexual abuse of children, 93% of victims knew their perpetrator. (https://www.rainn.org/statistics/perpetrators-sexual-violence). According to the Department of Justice's Dru Sjoden National Sex Offender Public Website (NSOPW), only 25% of female victims are assaulted by strangers (2010) and only 10% of perpetrators are strangers when the victim is a child (www.nsopw.gov/en/Education/FactsStatistics).

23. The movie *Ocean's 8* comes to mind here. In this story, eight women pull off a diamond heist via a highly complex plan that involves posing as women attending a star-studded fashion gala. The leader of the group, played by Sandra Bullock, states she wants only women to participate in this criminal scheme since in this context, "women are invisible" and less likely to be detected. Using the arguments that some use to support ATBBs, perhaps to avoid diamond heists we should make it a crime for anyone to appear as a woman—or perhaps women should be barred from star-studded galas?

24. Many before me have made this argument. For further reading, see Jacob Hale, "Are Lesbians Women?" *Hypatia* 11, no. 2 (1996): 94–121.

25. I have borrowed this term from Mark Henrie; see pdf p. 15 of his "Understanding Traditionalist Conservatism," available at http://www.hoover.org/sites/default/files/uploads/documents/0817945725_3.pdf.

26. Though the law has not been entirely absent from this domain. The primary means by which bathroom segregation has been subject to lawful regulation is via the enforcement of *building* and *plumbing codes*—which, since the latter portions of the nineteenth century, have generally mandated the provision of separate, sex-segregated facilities. University of Utah law professor Terry Kogan has nicely documented this history in a series of publications spanning the past two decades. The "Research" page on his website offers a collection of hyperlinks to these publications (see https://faculty.utah.edu/u0028895-TERRY_STUART_KOGAN/research/index.hml); of particular interest is his May 16, 2016, article at the website "The Conversation" titled "How Did Public Bathrooms Get to Be Segregated by Sex in the First Place?" (https://theconversation.com/how-did-public-bathrooms-get-to-be-separated-by-sex-in-the-first-place-59575).

27. These quotations are assembled from Sections 1.2 and 1.3 of HB2, which mandate changes to Article 37 of Chapter 115C and to Chapter 143 of the North Carolina General Statutes, respectively. The quoted language can be found in the newly added paragraphs 115C-521.2(a)(1), 115C-521.2(b), 143-760(a)(1), and 143-760(b), found on the first two pages of the bill, which is available at http://www.ncleg.net/Sessions/2015E2/Bills/House/PDF/H2v4.pdf (accessed August 12, 2019).

28. For purposes of this discussion, I define "transgender person" in a manner congruent with the North Carolina law under discussion—namely, as anyone who identifies with a gender at odds with the one customarily associated with the biological sex recorded on his or her birth certificate. This definition, like any, raises certain complications. For example, transsexual individuals—those who have changed (at least certain central aspects of) their sex via, e.g., gender reassignment surgery and/or hormone treatments, and who have had their birth certificates updated to reflect this fact—fall outside the scope of our discussion (as they fall outside the scope of HB2). Defining "transgender person" in this fashion, then, raises worries about potential inequities: Persons with more disposable resources will be better positioned, compared to those who are poorer, to align their sex (and their birth certificates) with their gender. But as any definition seems apt to raise difficulties—and since the substance of the argument should apply

regardless of the definition—I will simply adopt the formulation that best aligns with the legislation in question.

29. This was passed on February 22, 2016. The text of this city ordinance, which prohibited discrimination in public facilities on the basis of (among other things) gender identity (having the practical effect that transgender persons could not be prohibited from using the public bathrooms and locker rooms of their choice), is available at http://charlottenc .gov/CityClerk/Ordinances/February%2022,%202016.pdf (accessed August 12, 2019).

30. This issue first entered national consciousness in 1993, after a Hawaiian court found a state law prohibiting same-sex marriage incompatible with Hawaii's constitution. But it largely retreated from view after the 1996 passage of the federal Defense of Marriage Act. State-level developments in Vermont and Massachusetts in 2003 and 2004 again brought the issue to the fore—it was a campaign issue during the 2004 presidential election—but again the matter seemed to fade from attention after George W. Bush's reelection. Sometime around 2008, then—and accelerating rapidly around 2012, until climaxing in the U.S. Supreme Court's *Obergefell* ruling in June 2015—the issue finally resurfaced in a manner that settled it seemingly once and for all.

31. Before proceeding, though, I would like to offer one final introductory note: Throughout this discussion, I will formulate matters primarily in terms of access to bathrooms. This is in keeping with the fact that, in the wider culture, these are the terms in which the controversy is most commonly expressed. However, it would be more fortunate if the controversy were to be widely understood in terms of *locker room* access— particularly since HB2 explicitly applied to locker rooms as well as bathrooms. While admittedly my evidence here is merely anecdotal, I have observed in private conversation that by far the most common "position" on this issue is actually a kind of *non*-position. That is, many people invoke some version of the following (evasive) maneuver: "Well, I don't even see what the big deal is. After all, no one can really see you in a public restroom; who *cares* about the sex or gender of the person in the adjacent stall anyway?" Formulating the issue always in terms of locker room access would preempt this (non-) response. Readers are therefore encouraged, in what follows, to keep the locker room question always at the forefront, even when the issue is expressed in terms of restrooms.

32. For the points in this paragraph, and in particular for helping me to appreciate the challenges raised by the case of opposite-gendered caretakers, I am indebted to discussants (especially Terry Kogan and Mary Ann Case) at a panel on this topic at the March 2018 meeting of the Philosophy, Politics, and Economics Society in New Orleans, LA.

33. Prominent representatives of this approach include Tamara Metz, *Untying the Knot: Marriage, the State, and the Case for Their Divorce* (Princeton, NJ: Princeton University Press, 2010) and Elizabeth Brake, *Minimizing Marriage: Marriage, Morality, and the Law* (New York: Oxford University Press, 2012). The language of "disestablishment" here is borrowed from the First Amendment to the U.S. Constitution, wherein the Congress is expressly prohibited from passing any law "respecting an establishment of religion." In other words, just as the proverbial "separation of Church and State" results in *religion's* being "disestablished" in the United States, so also do the progressive theorists discussed in the main text maintain that *marriage* ought to be similarly "disestablished."

34. This strain of thought is also famously associated with Friedrich Hayek. For a comparison of the Burkean and Hayekean versions of this argument, see Jeremy Garrett, "History, Tradition, and the Normative Foundations of Civil Marriage," *The Monist* 91, no. 3–4 (2008): 446–474. The distinctions between Burkean- and Hayekian-flavored appeals to tradition need not concern us here.

35. The reason I would not actually condemn the academy for its illiberalism is because I believe this critique rests on fundamental misunderstandings of notions like *equality*, *fairness*, *discrimination*, *oppression*, and *privilege*. But clearly, such a critique could be made—and perhaps soon *will* be commonly made—using currently widespread (mis-)understandings of these words. If and when that critique materializes, the defender of the academy could—besides mounting a defense grounded in a clarification of the proper understandings of such notions, or founded on reclaiming their proper application—also mount a defense of a broadly Burkean nature, along the lines sketched in this chapter.

36. While I do not harbor any skepticism with respect to the notion of being transgender, and while I certainly do not bear any shred of animus toward transgender individuals, I *will* confess to sharing with many conservatives a sense of befuddlement—a feeling doubtless shared too by many non-conservatives, but one whose expression appears *verboten* in certain non-conservative quarters—as to the seeming incoherence of a certain posture that I do associate with some trans advocates: "Gender isn't real; it's only a social construct—a construct, furthermore, that was created and maintained for the specific purpose of oppressing women. *Now please recognize the fact that my gender is an immutable part of my essence!!*" Granted, I do not think I have seen this posture adopted by any serious scholars. But—as with the evasive (non-)response I describe in note 31 above—it does seem to me a not-uncommon posture adopted by non-specialists in everyday conversations on this matter, both online and "in real life." (Though—again, as with the maneuver described in note 31—my evidence here is merely anecdotal.)

37. Due to the quite limited space of this rebuttal, I am not engaging in a full analysis of Baltzly's argument for full gender integration. Instead, I argue that whether or not one is so persuaded, that is independent of whether one rejects ATBBs as unacceptably unjust.

38. Baltzly is incorrect in his belief that individuals who have undergone hormone treatments and/or surgery are always able to revise their birth certificate and are consequently "outside the scope of our discussion" (endnote 4). Some states do not allow individuals to update their birth certificate under any circumstances. (He is correct in recognizing that those birth states that allow birth certificate correction often require surgical procedures that can be costly and also unwanted. This itself is a serious problem.) Second, some proposed ATBBs have attempted to limit bathroom access not according to current birth certificate (possibly revised) but original birth certificate (sex assigned at birth) or even an individual's chromosomes. So, trans individuals who have undergone physical transition and/or changed their documentation are *not* outside the scope of this discussion.

39. As Professor Baltzly states, "For instance, unless suitably refined, the Burkean rationale could seemingly likewise legitimate all sorts of unjustifiable and sexist discrimination and oppression."

40. Professor Baltzly's last footnote demonstrates a common misunderstanding about the concept of gender. He writes that he shares a sense of *befuddlement* toward a claim thought to be connected to trans activism. On his account, this claim is: "Gender isn't real; it's only a social construct—a construct, furthermore, that was created and maintained for the specific purpose of oppressing women. *Now please recognize the fact that my gender is an immutable part of my essence!!*" I believe that this confusion arises from the fact that the term "gender" is used in a variety of ways, including those that are meant to refer to gender *norms*, gender *expectations*, gender *presentation*, gender *expression*, and also gender *identity*. Recognizing this complexity allows one to similarly

recognize that one can accept that, for example, gender expression is a social construct that varies over culture and time, whereas gender identity is quite stable. An example of norms of gender expression may involve wearing a wig to express one's power and masculinity (like George Washington) or wearing a wig to express a style that seems quite feminine (like Cher). Regardless of who are wearing wigs, George Washington probably always identified as a man, Cher probably has always and will continue to identify as a woman, and Cher's son Chaz (who was very public about his gender transition) will predictably continue to identify as a man throughout his life.

41. Indeed, what follows is very much the conversation I should like to have with Professor Cannon myself, should we be fortunate enough to cross paths someday.

42. Expressed in the terms developed in my essay, you might ask whether your friend prefers a regime of legally enforced *trans-accessible segregation* to the status quo.

43. Two notes at this point: (1) I continue to use the subjunctive tense when referring to such bills, insofar as (and contrary to the impression sometimes given in Cannon's essay) no such bills have, to my knowledge, ever been passed in the United States (at least not at the state or federal level). (2) Though I will sometimes use Cannon's preferred vocabulary here, I do not endorse it: "ATBBs" seems to me an impermissibly deck-stacking maneuver. *Many* laws that proscribe and/or prescribe certain behaviors, or that establish certain customs or legal statuses, are susceptible to (frequently uncharitable) characterizations as "*anti-X*" laws. For instance, should we describe laws that preclude fifteen-year-olds from driving and seventeen-year-olds from voting and twenty-year-olds from drinking alcohol as "anti-youth age-limit laws"? Should we always preface our references to marriage law—which creates *many* legal and social benefits that are made available *only* to married dyads—with the qualifier "anti-single" or "anti-polygamist"?

44. This point becomes especially salient if, in response to your request for clarification two paragraphs above, your interlocutor professed commitment to a legal-ized regime of trans-accessible segregation.

45. For an easy-to-read official U.K. government "explainer" regarding potential changes to the Gender Recognition Act, see https://assets.publishing.service.gov.uk/government/uploads/system/uploads/attachment_data/file/721641/gra-consultation-easy-read.pdf. For an overview of the controversy that arose in this regard in the summer of 2018, see https://www.theguardian.com/world/2018/may/10/the-gender-recognition-act-is-controversial-can-a-path-to-common-ground-be-found (particularly starting with twelfth paragraph, beginning with "The story began in January 2016").

46. Here is an oversimplified demonstration of what I mean. Let us grant the reliability of the statistical sources Cannon cites regarding the degree of restroom-related harm currently experienced by trans individuals. Let us furthermore grant Cannon the claim that women would face only a very low probability of being assaulted, harassed, or voyeured by "posers" illicitly utilizing women's bathrooms. We can still ask: Just *how* low would that risk have to be, exactly, for the quantity of harm currently faced by trans individuals to still exceed the quantity of harm potentially posed by posers (a risk posed to all women, both cis and trans)? Let's do some simple number-crunching. According to p. 226 of the USTS, cited in Cannon's third and fourth endnotes, "[t]welve percent (12%) of respondents [the Report surveyed '27,715 respondents from all fifty states, the District of Columbia, American Samoa, Guam, Puerto Rico, and U.S. military bases overseas' (p. 4)] reported being verbally harassed, physically attacked, and/or sexually assaulted when accessing or while using a [public] restroom" in the preceding year. In their efforts to utilize public restrooms, that is, transgender individuals

faced (what we might term as) an "annualized violation rate" of 12%. Given that, as best we can tell, there are upwards of 1.4 million transgender individuals in the United States (two recent careful studies—cited at the end of this note—place the overall U.S. trans population at an estimated 0.6% and 0.4% of adults, respectively; we shall use the higher estimate), this works out to approximately 168,000 violations suffered by trans individuals in public restrooms per year. That's quite a lot! And of course, even one such violation is unacceptable. But now let us consider the fact that women (cis and trans alike) represent approximately 51% of the U.S. population of 326 million. Some simple algebra reveals that the relevant "annualized violation rate" for all women—the rate at which women could expect to be victimized by posers—need only clock in at a mere 0.1% before the magnitude of the harms experienced by women in general equals the magnitude of the harms currently faced by transgender individuals. And if this risk were any higher—if the annualized violation rate for all women were to *exceed* one-tenth of one percent—then the number of women annually victimized by posers in public restrooms would exceed the number of trans individuals currently victimized in public restrooms. (Note that this statistic is not limited to *physical* assaults. The annualized violation rate for all women would drop to less than 0.01%—less than 1 percent of 1 percent—to be commensurate with the USTS's reported annualized *physical* assault rate for trans individuals.) In other words, if the annualized probability of (physical or non-physical) harm to any given woman posed by posers exceeds even 0.1%, then indeed we might expect that a legal-ized regime of trans-accessible bathroom segregation would *increase* the expected net balance of bathroom-sited harms to women, *even if* it managed to utterly eliminate assault and harassment against trans individuals. Is the "poser-posed risk of violation" so obviously low—so clearly and drastically below one-tenth of one percent—that we're really warranted in dismissing it utterly out of hand? Citations: (1) for the 0.6% estimate (and concomitant estimate of 1.4 million trans individuals), Andrew R. Flores et al., *How Many Adults Identify as Transgender in the United States?* Los Angeles: The Williams Institute, June 2016, https://williamsinstitute.law.ucla.edu/wp-content/uploads/How-Many-Adults-Identify-as-Transgender-in-the-United-States.pdf; (2) for the 0.4% estimate, E. L. Meerwijk and J. M. Sevelius, "Transgender Population Size in the United States: A Meta-Regression of Population-Based Probability Samples," *American Journal of Public Health* 107, no. 2 (2017), e1–e8, http://doi.org/10.2105/AJPH.2016.303578.

47. Recall Cannon's point that we don't legally prohibit individuals from owning a car merely because "someone might steal the car and use it to perpetrate a crime."

CHAPTER 14

Privilege

PRIVILEGE: WHAT IS IT, WHO HAS IT, AND WHAT SHOULD WE DO ABOUT IT?
DAN LOWE

The popular podcast *Death, Sex & Money* featured an interview in 2017 with a woman who supported herself by regularly shoplifting.[1] While that alone would have made the episode notable, the controversy that followed focused on what "Alice" (as she asked to be called) said about what would happen if she were caught: "I'm a white female," she said, "so I feel like I would get off a lot easier than some other people would." The interviewer fell silent for a moment, and then asked her: "How does that feel to say out loud?" Alice replied: "It's . . . kind of disgusting to me, but, I mean, it's how the world is . . . "

What Alice is talking about here is *privilege*, a word that seems like it's everywhere these days. It's common to hear about "white privilege," "male privilege," or that you should "check your privilege." Yet there's little agreement on what "privilege" actually means, and as a result, such conversations tend to be heated and unproductive. This is also the case in academia, where scholars have often disagreed about the nature and definition of "privilege."[2] Here, I propose an account of privilege that aims to capture as much previous academic discussion as possible. I argue that once we have a clear understanding of what "privilege" means, many misunderstandings can be cleared up and common objections answered.

1. What Is Privilege?
Let us define *privilege* as a person's advantage due to their membership in a social group, in contexts where that membership shouldn't normally matter. If Alice's judgment is accurate, and she would be punished less harshly if she were caught shoplifting, then her example fits the definition of privilege. First, if she were caught she would have an advantage compared to others: Lenient treatment is an advantage. Second, the advantage is due to her membership in a social group: It is because she is a member of the social group *white women*. And third, in that

457

context, her membership in a social group shouldn't normally matter: The punishment should fit the crime and should not be based on the perpetrator's gender or race.

The point about context is important because sometimes a person's membership in a social group *should* matter. Members of a country club have certain perks—golfing on especially nice grass, I guess?—that non-members (like me, obviously) don't have. As long as that's the context we're talking about, those advantages aren't morally problematic. Yet if we were to find out that members of country clubs got an additional ten points automatically added to their SAT scores, that *would* be problematic, because in that context—taking the SAT—whether one is a member of the country club or not shouldn't matter. (In fact, it's natural to say that in this context and the context of shoplifting, the social group a person belongs to shouldn't *ever* matter—but as we will see later on, the qualification that membership in a given social group shouldn't *normally* matter is important.)

The definition of privilege I've proposed here is a philosophical use of the term that has been developed only recently. The original sense of the term was that a "privilege" was a special perk available to a lucky few. We still use the word in this way; if you get the chance to meet a brilliant artist, you might say, "It's a privilege to meet you." A lot of confusion about privilege comes from mixing up the new, philosophical use of the term with its original, ordinary use.

One such confusion is that if someone has privilege, they must have an easy life. In the ordinary sense of the term, a "life of privilege" would be an easy life, but in the philosophical sense of the term, one can have advantages without having an easy life. Even if Alice is correct about the advantages she would have over others, she has not had an easy life, as indicated by her stealing just to get by. Here, an analogy from the sociologist Michael Kimmel is helpful. Privilege, he says, is like walking with the breeze at your back, giving you a push in the direction you want to go.[3] While the wind at your back is helpful, it can't do your walking for you—you still have to expend energy to get where you're going. This doesn't mean that privileges are insignificant—when a number of privileges combine, the advantage can be quite significant. Nevertheless, while privilege may make some things *easier*, that's not the same as making life *easy*.

Another confusion is that privileges can never be rights. For instance, when using the ordinary sense of the term, we say, "Voting is a right, not a privilege," to draw a distinction between certain nice things in life and the basic goods to which everyone is entitled. This can make it seem like privileges are about rather trivial advantages, rather than fundamental rights.[4] But in the philosophical sense of the term, having a right could be a privilege. Consider the time in U.S. history when only men could vote. Because those men had an advantage over women, it makes sense to talk about them as privileged, even though the specific privilege we're talking about is *also* a right. Peggy McIntosh, the theorist who coined the newer use of the term "privilege," wanted to avoid this confusion; some privileges, she said, "should be the norm in a just society and should be considered as the entitlement of everyone."[5]

2. Who Has Privilege?

It's easy to talk about the existence of privilege in long-ago periods of history, where privilege was formally recognized in the law, but what about the here and now? Is Alice right when she implies that privilege exists today? It would be impractical to undertake a comprehensive account of every form of privilege that exists, but we can briefly survey a few examples of contemporary privilege:

- White privilege: Alice's story is reminiscent of a remark made by McIntosh, who notes that as a white woman, "I can go shopping alone most of the time, fairly well assured that I will not be followed or harassed by store detectives."[6]
- Male privilege: When walking home at night alone, men do not generally have to consider the risk of being sexually assaulted.
- Straight privilege: Straight people can hold the hand of their partner in public without worrying whether it is safe to do so.
- Able-bodied privilege: Able-bodied people can use the entrance of the building that is nearest to them without it being inaccessible and having to look for another entrance (if there even is one).

Not all examples of privilege are as clear-cut as these, because it is not always obvious whether certain advantages are due to one's membership in a social group, or to other factors, like one's character, upbringing, or just luck. However, even if we only focus on the clear cases, there are some patterns that help us understand how privilege works in the real world.

First, *privilege tends to be invisible to the person who has it.*[7] In each of the examples above, the privileged group does not have to deal with obstacles that the disadvantaged group must reckon with. Yet it is human nature to notice obstacles—not their absence. (And for good reason—to notice everything that is absent would be to notice an infinite number of things!) Because I am able-bodied, I couldn't tell you where the wheelchair-accessible entrance to my office building is. I'm pretty sure there is one, and I've probably even used it. But because a stairs-only entrance poses no obstacle to me, I don't notice which entrances have stairs and which do not. Yet a person in a wheelchair can't help but notice which entrances are accessible and which are not. To return to Michael Kimmel's analogy, we tend not to notice when the wind is at our backs; all we feel is our forward momentum. But if we turn around and try to walk against the wind, we notice it right away.

Second, *privilege is contextual.* Our definition already says that privilege is contextual in one way, because privilege concerns contexts where the social group one belongs to shouldn't normally matter. But privilege turns out to be contextual in yet another way: Whether membership in a social group provides one with an advantage at all depends upon the context. The examples above are taken from the context of the United States, but being white or a woman is surely different in Saudi Arabia or Zimbabwe or China.

Yet even within the United States, there are different contexts that affect who has privilege and how it functions. A few years ago, the professional basketball player Nik Stauskas said that in the NBA he was treated as if he needed to prove himself because he was white.[8] I'm not in the NBA—not *yet*, I like to tell myself—so I don't know for sure whether Stauskas is correct. But the majority of NBA players are black, and stereotypes paint whites as less athletic than blacks, so what Stauskas is saying seems plausible enough: Within the NBA, there may be a kind of black privilege. Of course, that doesn't mean that the same is true within society in general; however, it does illustrate how membership in a social group may give a person an advantage in some contexts but not in others.

Third, *privilege is intersectional.* Intersectionality acknowledges that a person is a member of multiple social groups at the same time—an individual not only has a race but also a gender, not only a sexual orientation but also a class. Accordingly, intersectionality says that a person's experiences are affected by the intersection of these identities, and thus can't be reduced to any one of them.[9] Consider, for instance, the way that lesbians are often accused of being "man-haters."[10] This is not reducible to their identity as women; heterosexual women do not in general face a stereotype of being man-haters. Nor is it reducible to their identity as homosexuals; gay men do not generally face a stereotype of being woman-haters. In other words, how lesbians are treated is due not to one aspect of their identity or another, but to the intersection of their identities as homosexual women.

Intersectionality reminds us not to reduce a whole host of privileges to one fundamental kind of privilege. It is tempting to do this with class, since it is natural to wonder whether poverty neutralizes all the advantages one might have from other aspects of one's identity. Can it really be the case that poor white people, who are sometimes callously referred to as "white trash," nevertheless have white *privilege*? The example of Alice indicates that poor whites can have privilege. The reason she steals, after all, is that she is poor, yet despite that poverty, she still has white privilege with respect to how she would be treated if caught. Of course, that doesn't mean that Alice's white privilege is the exact same as that of a rich white man—rich whites may receive advantages from their whiteness that poor whites don't get.[11] This itself is an insight of intersectionality, which reveals how privilege will change depending on the other aspects of a person's identity, including whether they are rich, poor, or somewhere in between.

Objections to the Account of Who Has Privilege

The examples considered so far seem to paint a picture of straight, white, able-bodied men as the group in America with the greatest privilege. Yet many people do not see things this way; a poll in 2017 showed that the majority of white Americans believe that whites face discrimination based on their race.[12] Indeed, it is more and more common to believe that straight white men are in fact one of the *less* privileged groups in America.

The sociologist Arlie Russell Hochschild has studied the evolution of these beliefs about contemporary American society, and what she calls "the deep story" underlying them.[13] The deep story relies on a metaphor that goes like this. Imagine that you and many others are patiently trudging up a very long hill in single file. At the top of the hill is the American Dream. You hope to reach the top, or at least, to keep moving forward, and end up further ahead than where you started. But as time goes on, you wonder whether you are actually moving forward at all, and at times you seem to be moving backwards. That is when you see people cutting in line ahead of you. And what's worse, they are doing so with the help of the very people who are supposed to be monitoring the line—the American government. If you are a white person standing in line, you see black and brown people given spots ahead of you by affirmative action. If you are a man standing in line, you see women gaining ground as their cultural achievements are celebrated in the name of diversity. If you are a straight person standing in line, you see gay people moving forward and being lauded just for coming out. Whether in terms of material benefits or cultural recognition, all these people seem to be cutting in front—and as they slide into their new place in line, they yell over their shoulder that no one is more privileged than the straight white man behind them.

According to the deep story, it is the allegedly disadvantaged groups that have more privilege than straight white men do. As I said earlier, it would be impractical to attempt a comprehensive survey of every form of privilege that exists and survey them all to see who is the most privileged. However, there are still reasons to be skeptical of what the deep story says. The deep story neglects the reason why programs like affirmative action exist in the first place—to compensate groups for some previous disadvantage. Likewise, cultural recognition of women's achievements is partly done to compensate for the fact that women's contributions were undervalued for so long. So the deep story seems to assume that these are in fact *overcompensations*, where the advantages gained by these groups are more significant than the disadvantages they faced.

We have one major reason to doubt that this is accurate: *Attempts to compensate for a group's disadvantage are almost always going to be more visible to privileged groups than the disadvantage itself.* As I noted earlier, one feature of privilege is that it tends to be invisible to those who have it. Thus, they will see little that is in need of compensation. Yet measures to compensate for a group's disadvantage are highly visible—they must be undertaken explicitly, as when companies or universities practice affirmative action as an official policy. The result is that the advantages of being a white person interviewing for a job tend to be invisible; the advantages gained by affirmative action tend to be highly visible. Or to use another example, I may not notice which entrances are wheelchair-accessible, but I see very clearly the handicapped parking spots near the front of the store that I cannot use. So although there is a great deal more to be said about this objection and the deep story than I have space for here, we can already see why the deep story lacks perspective if privilege is generally less visible than our attempts to correct it.

3. What Should We Do About Privilege?

There are a number of misunderstandings about how we should respond to privilege. Some argue that all this talk of privilege paints straight white men as the ultimate villains in contemporary America,[14] implying that one should feel guilty about privilege or be condemned for it. However, when we carefully consider the definition of privilege we've been discussing, we can see that this is irrational.

Recall that privilege is a person's advantage due to their membership in a social group (in contexts where that membership shouldn't normally matter). Yet the social groups one belongs to aren't generally the result of one's own choices, and the advantages one gets from being a member of those groups are conferred not by oneself but by society at large. These are things over which no individual has control. Accordingly, condemnation is unfair and guilt is irrational—one should not be criticized or feel ashamed for what one has no control over. And for the same reason we cannot simply choose *not* to have privilege; if it is not an individual's choice to have privilege, one cannot just choose to jettison it.

But even if the existence of our privilege isn't up to us, *how we respond to our privilege* is. You can, as a first step, try to be conscious of your own privilege. The point is not to wallow in the knowledge of your socially-conferred advantage—that self-indulgently puts the focus on yourself. Rather, the point is to empathize better with members of other social groups, to understand that they may not have the same advantages or face the same obstacles that you do. This is what it means to "check your privilege"—not to feel ashamed for having it or use it as an excuse for inaction, but to acknowledge that your experiences and perceptions of the world may be quite different from those of members of other social groups.

And most importantly, we should consider what we might use our privilege *for*. Think again about Alice. In addition to the fact that she probably shouldn't have been shoplifting, she shouldn't have been willing to benefit from using privilege in the way she did. After all, stores she shoplifted from will probably become more suspicious about shoplifters, and given the stereotypes about black criminality that linger in the background of our society, that suspicion will fall more heavily on black customers. Trevor, a listener to the podcast about Alice, called in to a subsequent episode to express his frustration about how Alice's actions contribute to the way he (as a black man) is treated when he is in a store. In Trevor's words, "I've never stolen from a store, but I'm followed around a store constantly, and it's very frustrating, because you're just like, 'I make good money, why would I be stealing from you?'"[15] All things being equal, people who have privilege should use it to change the social norms that create privilege, and not reinforce those norms.

Objections to the Account of What to Do About Privilege

An objection one might have is that we should not always try to dismantle systems of privilege, because privilege is sometimes justified. For instance, the philosopher Michael Levin has argued that it is rational to more strongly suspect black men like Trevor of being likely to commit crimes than whites, given statistics about the percentages of crimes committed by black men.[16] Accordingly, Levin argues, the police should engage in racial profiling. Since this would create a comparative advantage for whites based on their race, it would create a kind of privilege—but one that Levin thinks would ultimately be justified.

I will not weigh in on the legitimacy of racial profiling, but it's worth mentioning Levin's argument for two reasons. First, it indicates where some may disagree with the account of privilege given so far. And second, it highlights an important feature of the definition of privilege. I noted that privilege involves cases where a person's membership in a social group shouldn't *normally* matter. Accordingly, the definition allows the possibility that people's race or gender could legitimately be taken into account even in contexts like law enforcement. In other words, the definition of privilege itself doesn't settle the debate about whether practices that create privilege, like racial profiling, are legitimate. Nevertheless, whenever there is a privilege, in that context group membership shouldn't normally matter, and so people like Levin face an uphill battle in arguing that an exception should be made. In other words, according to the account here, the burden of proof is on the person who wishes to defend the creation or continuation of privilege.

Another objection one might have is that even if privilege is real, the fact that some have advantages and others have disadvantages doesn't amount to an injustice. And this is because ultimately everyone in a society like ours has the ability to overcome their disadvantages and succeed. Accordingly, we shouldn't accord privilege the attention that should normally be reserved for genuine injustices.

The problem with this objection is that it assumes that as long as it is possible to succeed despite the obstacles one faces, the obstacles themselves don't constitute injustices. This is a mistake. Suppose that a teacher, when giving a test to her students, gave all of the women fifteen minutes more to complete the exam than the men. Imagine that the men protested this unfairness, and the teacher responded: "It's still possible for you to get good grades on the exam. Yes, you may have to study more and take the test faster. But everyone in this class has the ability to succeed on this exam." This would be an unreasonable response, confusing the issue of whether the test was administered fairly with the issue of whether it is possible to succeed on the test. If we live in a society where individuals face disadvantages because of the social groups they belong to, then it's very likely that those disadvantages are unfair. Having to work twice as hard as another person for the very same thing merely because of the social group one belongs to *is itself an injustice.* If those disadvantages can be overcome, then that's good news, but that's not the point—the point is that people shouldn't have to overcome those disadvantages in the first place.

4. What's the Point of Talking About Privilege?

We are all familiar with the idea that in our society, individuals are disadvantaged because of the social groups they belong to. Talk of privilege helps us see the flip side of this pattern—that there are those whose membership in a social group is beneficial. But why think about this at all?

We have already considered some answers to this question: thinking about privilege helps us understand the nature of our society better; it can make us more empathetic people, aware of what members of other social groups go through. But I'd like to suggest a further reason that is worth contemplating: Thinking about privilege may help us understand why the disadvantages that exist in society are likely to persist over time.

If we only think about disadvantages and the ways in which society fails certain groups, it becomes somewhat puzzling why these disadvantages haven't yet been remedied. Yet when we focus on the advantages gained by dominant groups, we recognize that some groups have a vested interest in society staying the way it is. As we have seen in Hochschild's account of the deep story, groups who have a certain position in society can be profoundly defensive of their "place in line." Privileged groups will tend to resist changes to a status quo that gives them advantages. Thus, thinking about privilege not only helps us understand how the status quo is structured, but why a society with injustice may nevertheless be slow to change.[17]

COMPREHENSION QUESTIONS

1. How does Lowe define privilege? In his example, what features give Alice privilege?
2. What confusion comes from using the word "privilege" in a way that deviates from its original and ordinary use?
3. Why is context important when understanding privilege?
4. What is the "deep story," and what is the status quo?
5. Why is a reflection on the nature of privilege important to the present?

DISCUSSION QUESTIONS

1. Lowe defines privilege as "a person's advantage due to their membership in a social group, in contexts where that membership shouldn't normally matter." How can we know if a person's advantage is due to their own character, hard work, lucky breaks, or their membership in a social group?
2. Some people say that when you're accustomed to privilege, equality feels like oppression. How well does this explain why many people embrace Hochschild's "deep story" about privilege in America today?

Case 1

Consider this letter to a *New York Times* advice column:

I'm riddled with shame. White shame. This isn't helpful to me or to anyone, especially people of color. I feel like there is no "me" outside of my white/upper middle class/cisgender identity. I feel like my literal existence hurts people, like I'm always taking up space that should belong to someone else.

I consider myself an ally. I research proper etiquette, read writers of color, vote in a way that will not harm P.O.C. (and other vulnerable people). I engage in conversations about privilege with other white people. I take courses that will further educate me. I donated to Black Lives Matter. Yet I fear that nothing is enough. Part of my fear comes from the fact that privilege is invisible to itself. What if I'm doing or saying insensitive things without realizing it?

Another part of it is that I'm currently immersed in the whitest environment I've ever been in. My family has lived in the same apartment in East Harlem for four generations. Every school I attended, elementary through high school, was minority white, but I'm now attending an elite private college that is 75 percent white. I know who I am, but I realize how people perceive me and this perception feels unfair.

I don't talk about my feelings because it's hard to justify doing so while people of color are dying due to systemic racism and making this conversation

CHAPTER 14 • Privilege   465

Case 1 (continued)

> about me would be again centering whiteness. Yet bottling it up makes me
> feel an existential anger that I have a hard time channeling since I don't know
> my place. Instead of harnessing my privilege for greater good, I'm curled up in
> a ball of shame. How can I be more than my heritage?
>> Whitey*
>
> What would Lowe say about this letter? What's good about it? What's bad
> about it?

---

*https://www.nytimes.com/2018/08/14/style/white-guilt-privilege.html

WHITE PRIVILEGE: A CONSERVATIVE PERSPECTIVE
SPENCER CASE

1. Introduction

"Privilege," an ostensibly positive word, has come to refer to something profoundly negative: an all-pervasive unfairness benefiting some groups at the expense of others. White privilege seems to be a special source of concern. The White
Privilege Conference, held at various campuses throughout the U.S., attracts
more than 1,500 anti-privilege academics and activists annually.[18] Intellectuals
have created Critical Whiteness Studies, which is a discipline billed as "a growing field of scholarship whose aim is to reveal the invisible structures that produce and reproduce white supremacy and privilege."[19] Efforts to dismantle these
power structures are creating new power structures in their place. Philosopher
Andrew Pierce, who is sympathetic to this cause, writes candidly that

> [t]he conceptual framework of white privilege has been incredibly influential,
> not just on contemporary scholarship on race, but perhaps even more so on
> anti-racist activism and on the cottage industry of diversity training and educa-
> tion. For many programs (political and institutional), the acknowledgment of
> privilege serves as a kind of *therapeutic* starting point, a *confessional* precondi-
> tion akin to "admitting you have a problem" in various twelve-step enterprises.
> I do not mean this glibly.[20]

Any social movement this influential deserves scrutiny. My aim here is to expose
what I take to be the central dilemma for what Pierce refers to as "the conceptual
framework of white privilege." In short, if "white privilege" is understood in such a
way that its existence is easy to establish (i.e., whites are generally better off), then the
existence of white privilege entails nothing radical. If, on the other hand, white privilege means that whites are better off *at the unjust expense* of non-whites as I think is
often implied—so that its presence entails a need for radical political change—then
we lack grounds for saying that it currently exists. I think this criticism generalizes
to other forms of privilege (e.g., male privilege), but I won't pursue that point here.

Why is this critique worth making? Because if this conceptual framework
is confused, then the movement to eradicate white privilege might be seriously
harmful. Slogans like "love trumps hate" perpetuate the idea that the difference

between good and bad political ideas amounts to the difference between good and bad motives. What this overlooks is that crusades against genuine evils, fired by moral zeal, often produce terrible consequences. Consider alcohol prohibition in the United States. The temperance movement was not wrong in thinking that alcoholism is evil. Nonetheless, prohibition advocates, in their zeal to purify society of alcoholism, trampled on individual liberty and created conditions that allowed gangsters like Al Capone to flourish at society's expense.[21]

Anti-racist sentiment is also subject to the danger of overzealousness, and racism is perceived to be far more pervasive and insidious than alcoholism was ever thought to be. White privilege is supposed to be structural—meaning, as Shelby Steele writes, that "only structural remedies will work against it."[22] At the same time, Pierce's references to therapy, confession, and self-help programs suggest that privilege is at the same time personal, even *intimate*. It's apparently the educator's role to assist her students in the ritual purification of their souls, or at least in the mending of their psyches. Pierce, in his classroom, uses activities whose goal is "to sway the moral conscience of privileged students, convincing them that the privileges they enjoy are undeserved, and must be relinquished in the interests of justice."[23]

The movement to eradicate white privilege is thus totalistic in the sense that it rationalizes interventions ranging from the most personal level to the restructuring of society. And the mandate for intervention is open-ended. Because racism can always become more subtle, clear indicators of progress are likely to be elusive. Nor can we expect that the diversity training "cottage industry" Pierce mentions will immediately demobilize when identifiable benchmarks are reached. Inevitably, some people will develop financial interests in preserving and expanding the new power structures. Others, who derive a sense of purpose in the perpetual struggle against racism, will for that reason be reluctant to declare victory over it. We should, moreover, worry about the effects of university professors telling white students that every good thing they have is undeserved, and that future social progress will be measured in terms of their decline. If white students feel they must choose between a masochistic and an excessively proud self-conception, many will opt for the latter.[24] Such decisions may be cited as evidence that more diversity training, and more thorough pedagogical interventions, are called for. We should therefore think carefully before adopting this conceptual framework.

2. The Central Dilemma

Contemporary anti-privilege activists and academics typically trace their influence through Peggy McIntosh's 1988 paper, "White Privilege and Male Privilege: A Personal Account of Coming to See"[25] (republished in a shorter form in 1989 as "White Privilege: Unpacking the Invisible Knapsack"[26]). Although McIntosh admits that her original article constitutes "a partial record of my personal observations and not a scholarly analysis," it has been a smashing scholarly success by at least one metric: According to Google Scholar, the 1988 article has garnered

3,568 citations and the 1989 article has 4,295 as of this writing.[27] For comparison, Peter Singer's "Famine, Affluence and Morality," perhaps the most famous philosophy article in applied ethics, registers only 3,134 citations, notwithstanding a sixteen-year head start.[28] And since McIntosh's articles have influenced activists outside academia, these figures understate the impact of her ideas.

McIntosh observes that many men who recognize that women are disadvantaged are nonetheless reluctant to admit that they are overprivileged, meaning that they enjoy unearned power or dominance conferred upon them by society. (Note the implicit assumption that the existence of underprivileged groups implies that some groups have too much privilege.) She extends this observation to race, writing: "I have come to see white privilege as an invisible package of unearned assets that I can count on cashing in each day, but about which I was 'meant' to remain oblivious."[29] McIntosh unpacks her own "invisible knapsack" by enumerating some "daily effects of white privilege."[30] The list in the original article begins thus:

1. I can, if I wish, arrange to be in the company of people of my race most of the time.
2. I can avoid spending time with people whom I was trained to mistrust and who have learned to mistrust my kind or me.
3. If I should need to move, I can be pretty sure of renting or purchasing housing in an area which I can afford and in which I would want to live.
4. I can be reasonably sure that my neighbors in such a location will be neutral or pleasant to me.
5. I can go shopping alone most of the time, fairly well assured that I will not be followed or harassed by store detectives.

Some of these entries are dubious, such as: "If I want to, I can be pretty sure of finding a publisher for this piece on white privilege."[31] Are we to believe that it wouldn't have been published, or widely cited, had the author been black? Also bizarre is: "I can take a job with an affirmative action employer without having co-workers on the job suspect that I got it because of race."[32] That's because affirmative action disfavors white people, so her cohort would have no reason to suspect that she'd been rewarded because of her race. The fact that whites are almost universally disfavored in hiring and university admissions (and people know this) hardly seems like evidence of pervasive white privilege.

The biggest issue with these articles, however—and with the academic literature on white privilege that builds on McIntosh's ideas—is the ambiguity between weak and strong senses of "privilege." In the weak sense, any group that is better off than comparable groups counts as privileged. So Asians in the United States are more privileged than whites, who are more privileged than blacks, who are in turn more privileged than Native Americans. Likewise, tall people are more privileged than short people, and attractive people are more privileged than unattractive people.[33] Such comparative facts are morally relevant inasmuch as we have general duties to help less fortunate people. We should also be honest with ourselves about how much of our success is due to pure dumb luck. None of this

is revelatory. Moreover, facts about these disparities are better established by statistics than by a list of McIntosh's subjective observations.

Those who decry white privilege treat white privilege as a phenomenon especially worthy of our attention. It's hard to see how it could be if most people—all
but those in the least well-off group (and how narrowly defined can that group
be?)—enjoy some kind of privilege. At a minimum, they add that white–black
disparities either constitute, or are primarily caused by, racial injustice and that
many of the good things that whites enjoy depend upon the intentional and un-
intentional perpetuation of this injustice. That is why McIntosh laments that "My
schooling gave me no training in seeing myself as an oppressor, as an unfairly
advantaged person, or as a participant in a damaged culture."[34] To be privileged
isn't just to be better off, but to be unfairly advantaged, or even to be an *oppressor.*
This seems to imply moral culpability. Some also add that members of privileged
groups are obligated to renounce or "offset" their privilege—potentially a costly
endeavor.[35] Indeed, the focus on white privilege, as opposed to black disadvantage, suggests our obligations aren't just to uplift the downtrodden. The language
of privilege suggests justice is to be achieved in part by "leveling down," depriving the privileged of something that they don't deserve to have.

We cannot infer from the fact that whites are privileged in the weak sense
that they are privileged in the strong sense. For one thing, racism may not be
the primary cause of existing racial disparities. Black conservative Shelby Steele
observes that the role of racial injustice in explaining black woes is one of the
central bones of contention between liberals and conservatives:

> [T]he liberal looks at black difficulties—high crime rates, weak academic per-
> formance, illegitimacy rates, and so on—and presumes them to be the result
> of victimizing forces. The conservative does not deny this as a possibility but
> refuses to *presume* it. This refusal has become a contemporary mark of social
> conservatism.[36]

A modest construal of the liberal position is that many important racial disparities are primarily the products of racism. Many on the left, however, and perhaps
all who contribute to the white privilege academic literature, do seem committed
to the stronger claim that there is no serious alternative to the racism hypothesis
for any important racial disparity. Consider Shannon Sullivan's entry on white
privilege in the *Oxford Handbook of Philosophy and Race.* After adumbrating
the ways in which African Americans are worse off than whites, Sullivan writes:
"The point of it is that even though most of these disparities are the remnants of
decades of chattel slavery and centuries of legalized white supremacy, none of
them are against the law today."[37] Nothing is cited and no argument is given in
support of the claim that most racial disparities are "remnants" of the bad old
days. That claim isn't even the main clause of the sentence in which it appears.
Racial victimization is clearly the presumed explanation.

What else could explain these discrepancies? One answer is bad policy.
For example, racial preferences in university admissions are supposed to help
black applicants, but evidence exists that such preferences actually harm the

supposed beneficiaries by creating "mismatch"—that is, placing them in schools where they are less likely to succeed.[38] Another example is the "War on Drugs," which, like alcohol prohibition before it, has been a boon to organized crime. It has also led to the mass incarceration of black males.[39] Most members of the Congressional Black Caucus supported the 1986 Anti-Drug Abuse Act, which imposed harsher penalties for offenses involving crack cocaine (mostly used by blacks) than powder cocaine (mostly used by whites).[40] This policy is often showcased as a paradigmatic example of an unjust racial double standard. But these lawmakers clearly intended to help, not harm, black communities. To insist that any policy's "disparate impact" on minorities amounts to structural racism is to rule out by definition the possibility that misguided policy, rather than racism, accounts for some racial inequities.

Another explanation, defended by black conservatives like Thomas Sowell, Shelby Steele, John McWhorter, and Jason Riley, is that there is something problematic about contemporary black culture that makes it harder for blacks to succeed. McWhorter writes that although it's reasonable to draw attention to oppression where it exists, African Americans often do this "not with a view toward forging solutions, but to foster and nurture an unfocused brand of resentment and sense of alienation from the mainstream. This is Victimology."[41] One researcher found that black students in an affluent Ohio suburb performed less well than white students of the same socioeconomic background. He concluded that "[a] kind of *norm of minimum effort* appeared to exist among Black students in Shaker Heights schools" and that this apathy was at work behind the disparities in academic performance that he observed.[42] Similar claims have been made about some white communities. In his bestselling memoir about growing up in Appalachian Kentucky, *Hillbilly Elegy*, J. D. Vance writes that whites there suffer from "a culture that increasingly encourages social decay instead of counteracting it" and in particular "a lack of agency" and "a willingness to blame everyone except yourself."[43]

One early proponent of the cultural hypothesis was sociologist and later senator Daniel Patrick Moynihan. In an official document now known as the "Moynihan Report," which he wrote while serving in the U.S. Department of Labor under President Lyndon B. Johnson, Moynihan drew attention to the decline of marriage, in terms of such things as the rise of extramarital births and single-parent (female-led) households, in African American communities.[44] According to Moynihan's figures—which are debated—23.6% of African American children and 3.07% of white children were born to unmarried parents in 1963. By 2010, these figures were 73% and 29%, respectively.[45] Dozens of studies have linked fatherless households to negative outcomes, including poverty and criminality.[46] Racism and poverty both declined during this period, so they cannot be the sole causes of the trend, which also affects whites and Hispanics. The incarceration of black men already mentioned has certainly created many unwillingly absent fathers, but Moynihan identified the trend before the War on Drugs got going in earnest in the 1980s. Plausibly, we'd see fewer single-parent households among all races if the stigma against having children out of wedlock—or not marrying the other parent of your child—were as strong now as it was in earlier generations.

Critics of the cultural hypothesis often object that it amounts to "blaming the victim." But we should keep in mind that the relationship between cultural malaise and individual blameworthiness isn't straightforward. No one is responsible for the cultural environment that he's raised in. We should be cautious about morally judging people who have to negotiate life in less favorable circumstances than ourselves. At the same time, conservatives insist that to totally exempt any group of people from responsibility for their actions, including oppressed groups, is to dehumanize them. Morally judging people, especially unfortunate people, is inescapably fraught. Still, we cannot reject a hypothesis simply because it reflects poorly on struggling people, harsh as that might sound.[47]

Philosopher David Boonin objects that the cultural hypothesis isn't a genuine alternative to the view that current racial disparities are due to racism. After all, racial victimization presumably lies behind the emergence of cultural dysfunction: "[A]ppealing to the harmful effects of contemporary black culture simply pushes the question back a step: if black Americans have embraced a dysfunctional culture while other groups haven't, then why has this happened?"[48] Racism, he suggests, is the only available answer.[49] However, proponents of the cultural hypothesis, including Moynihan,[50] usually acknowledge the role of racism in creating cultural dysfunction. The issue is the *persistence*, and not the emergence, of dysfunction. Vance writes that Appalachian whites, suffering from economic decline, are "reacting to bad circumstances in the worst way possible."[51] If a bad reaction becomes habitual, then at some point it makes sense to describe the habit, and not the trauma that caused it, as the proximate cause of trouble and the issue that needs to be addressed. Conservatives can therefore consistently grant that cultural dysfunction is causally downstream from racial injustices while maintaining that it's now the primary issue that explains inequities.

It's also worth noting that not all groups respond to oppression in the same way. The Jews were the victims of one of the worst genocides in human history, the Nazi Holocaust, and centuries of marginalization before that. And yet Jews in America are doing substantially better than whites in terms of academic performance and wealth. Asian Americans, by which I mean Chinese, Korean, Japanese, and Indian people, have also been successful in the United States, though they too—and particularly the Chinese and Japanese—have been subject to unjust treatment (the former by the bluntly named 1882 Chinese Exclusion Act; the latter by internment during World War II). It's true that none of these groups was oppressed in the ways that African Americans were. The injustice hypothesis for white–black disparities in the United States would be more compelling if it also explained outcomes for other oppressed groups, particularly ethnic groups within the United States. But it doesn't seem to generalize.

Even if we could convincingly show that past and present racism is *entirely* to blame for current racial disparities—which I think is unlikely—other important claims about white privilege wouldn't follow. We wouldn't know from the truth of this causal story that whites generally benefit from black suffering now, that most of them bear significant responsibility for this arrangement, or that individual whites have an obligation to "offset" their privileges. Additional premises are needed to establish these claims, and they would be controversial. Jeremy Dunham and Holly Lawford-Smith, for example, write that in order for an advantage to count as an instance of race privilege, it must be "undeserved and systematically conferred according to race" and "entail a corresponding disadvantage."[52] That seems to mean that race privilege comes at the unjust expense of others, a stipulation common in definitions of white privilege. Even on the assumption that racism bears the lion's share of the blame for black woes, it's far from clear that whites enjoy advantages like this.

Here's a thought experiment. Suppose that poverty, crime, and other problems that cause African Americans to suffer ended overnight. Would most whites be worse off in some significant respect? True, some poor whites would face increased economic competition. There might be fewer jobs for prison guards. But on the whole whites would be *much* better off. They would live in a safer and more prosperous country, and would take more pride in their society. W. E. B. Du Bois famously wrote that whites collected "psychological wages" under Jim Crow. That is, racist policies made lower-class whites nominally part of the ruling class, providing them with a sense of superiority.[53] Although Du Bois's concept of "psychological wages" is frequently cited as an anticipation of the contemporary notion of white privilege, its current applicability is dubious. School-to-prison pipelines and other problems afflicting blacks don't make whites, or anyone, feel invested in the system. Not many whites would feel that their social status had been compromised if these problems were solved and the socioeconomic gaps between them and blacks closed for this reason.

In short, the more morally and politically significant white privilege is supposed to be, the less obvious it is that any such thing currently exists in the United States. The racial disparities that exist in the United States don't entail that the program that anti-privilege activists recommend, or any kind of radical politics, is needed. In order for white privilege to have the kind of moral and political significance that anti-privilege activists take it to have, further, highly questionable assumptions must be made. McIntosh is able to "see" that there is white privilege in this stronger sense only by looking through an ideological lens that takes these important assumptions for granted.

3. The Epistemology of Privilege

"Feminist standpoint theory" or "standpoint epistemology," a frequent companion of the white privilege conceptual framework, maintains that all knowledge is "socially situated." Members of underprivileged groups have, in virtue of their social situation, greater epistemic authority than privileged when it comes to questions that relate to the nature of their oppression.[54] Ashwini Vasanthakumar writes that "victims have what I call experiential knowledge: they are on intimate terms with oppression and have a more nuanced and visceral understanding of the harms meted out by particular injustices. Victims can tell us what it *felt* like."[55] Suppose we accept this. Can the epistemic authority of the oppressed provide independent evidence for the claim that white privilege—in the strong sense—exists?

Probably not. Although we *should* be empathetic toward people who are suffering and listen to what they have to say, we should also recognize that there are limits to how much useful information comes from being victimized. Suffering isn't knowledge. I know what it's like for my family to suffer in an economic downturn, but this painful experience gives me no special insight into the causes of recessions, nor does it tell me how to prevent future housing bubbles. Likewise a black man who suffers from poverty, or is racially profiled by police, can know what it feels like to go through these things without knowing whether his problems are manifestations of structural injustice rather than, say, the fruits of ill-conceived policies that weren't racially motivated. Nuanced answers to complicated social questions are seldom, if ever, given in "visceral" personal experience.

Even if we grant victims have an epistemic advantage in a way that makes them reliable on these issues, we should remember that they likely have some countervailing biases as well. Vasanthakumar writes that "unlike perpetrators, [victims] lack the incentive to gloss over uncomfortable details, to sanitize their complicity in wrongdoing, or to minimize the gravity of the wrongdoing." But soon after she concedes that victims may "cultivate an exaggerated sense of victimhood and the harms that it imposes, and to attribute failures or bad luck" to the system.[56] (Note this essentially describes the "victimology" that McWhorter diagnoses in contemporary African American culture.) Likewise, Pierce argues that white students are irrationally resistant to "white privilege pedagogy" because acknowledging their privilege means attributing some of their accomplishments to an external factor.[57] He doesn't pause to consider how the same self-serving bias might operate on his black students. Perhaps they are *more* receptive to white privilege pedagogy because this allows them to blame various problems their communities face on an external factor, white racism.

So it seems true that members of oppressed groups have some epistemic advantages over people who are not oppressed. These advantages, however, do not seem to be the sort that would make oppressed people especially reliable with regard to large-scale societal questions relating to their oppression. Moreover, such people are also likely to suffer from countervailing biases that would heavily qualify their supposed expertise in these matters. Finally, it's hard to see how the supposed expertise of the oppressed can be appealed to in a non–question-begging way if the very question at hand is whether a group of people is genuinely oppressed, rather than simply badly off, in the first place. We are therefore unlikely to find compelling evidence for the widespread existence of white privilege, in the strong sense, in the testimony of people who are, or consider themselves, oppressed.[58]

I conclude that the white privilege conceptual framework is a distorting lens through which to view contemporary race relations in the United States. Its widespread adoption is more likely to exacerbate than to resolve racial tensions and the problems they produce.[59]

COMPREHENSION QUESTIONS

1. Case refers to two senses of privilege: weak and strong. How are these defined? Why does Case draw an analogy between the temperance movement and Prohibition, on the one hand, and modern conversations on privilege, on the other?
2. Why is the movement to eradicate white privilege "totalistic"?
3. What is the cultural hypothesis of privilege? Why do critics think it amounts to blaming the victim?
4. What is the *white privilege framework*? How does it relate to feminist standpoint theory or standpoint epistemology? Why does Case think this position will perpetuate more harm?

DISCUSSION QUESTIONS

1. Case says that people in oppressed groups might have both "epistemic advantages" and "countervailing biases." What does he mean by this? Can you give examples of things that it might be both easier and harder to know as an oppressed person? What things might be easier and harder to know as person who *isn't* oppressed?
2. Case thinks that one central question is whether white people enjoy *unjust* privileges. Suppose they enjoy privileges, but they aren't unjust ones. Still, would white people have any moral reasons to do something about their privilege? What might that be?

Case 2

Here's a bit more from Peggy McIntosh's famous essay, "White Privilege: Unpacking the Invisible Knapsack":

> After I realized the extent to which men work from a base of unacknowledged privilege, I understood that much of their oppressiveness was unconscious. Then I remembered the frequent charges from women of color that white women whom they encounter are oppressive. I began to understand why we are justly seen as oppressive, even when we don't see ourselves that way. I began to count the ways in which I enjoy unearned skin privilege and have been conditioned into oblivion about its existence.
>
> My schooling gave me no training in seeing myself as an oppressor, as an unfairly advantaged person, or as a participant in a damaged culture. I was taught to see myself as an individual whose moral state depended on her individual moral will. My schooling followed the pattern my colleague Elizabeth Minnich has pointed out: whites are taught to think of their lives as morally neutral, nonnative, and average, and also ideal, so that when we work to benefit others, this is seen as work which will allow "them" to be more like "us."*

What is McIntosh challenging in that second paragraph? What does it mean for someone to see herself "as an individual whose moral state depended on her individual moral will"? What are some possible alternatives? Why might we want to adopt a more social conception of moral responsibility over a more individualistic one? What might some of the costs be? How might a more social conception of responsibility change the way we think about privilege, disadvantage, and injustice?

*McIntosh, Peggy. 1989. "White Privilege: Unpacking the Invisible Knapsack." Peace & Freedom Magazine, p. 10.

REPLY TO CASE
DAN LOWE

Spencer Case's central argument is founded upon a dilemma. "Privilege," he says, can be understood in either a weak or a strong sense. In the weak sense, "privilege" is merely the advantageous side of a difference in outcomes between groups. And while there clearly exist different outcomes between groups, this by itself does not entail any "need for radical political change." Accordingly, when people use "privilege," they must have a stronger sense of the term in mind. I agree with Case on all of these points. But the problem with his argument comes when he articulates what the stronger sense of privilege is supposed to amount to. Case is only able to reach his startling conclusion—that it's not clear that privilege in the strong sense even *exists*—because he sets an unreasonably high bar for the strong sense of privilege.

The strong sense of privilege, according to Case, involves several conditions:

- First, just as the weak sense entails, there must be a disparity between groups—here, he focuses on the disparities between whites and blacks invoked when discussing white privilege.
- Second, the disparity must either constitute or be caused by racial injustice. Of course, this raises the bar significantly for what can count as privilege, but the bar is even higher than it may first appear—because although Case opens the discussion by talking about racial injustice, he focuses more narrowly on racism. But to take *racial injustice* to mean *injustice caused by racism* omits the possibility that racial injustices might have other, easier to establish, causes—like the unintended collective consequences of individual actions or misguided policies.[60] One would think this is sufficient to establish a morally significant sense of "privilege," but Case does not stop here.
- Third, even in cases where a group's disadvantage *is* ultimately caused by racism, the relevant sort of disadvantage has to be *proximately* caused by racism. Case concedes that black disadvantage may be "causally downstream from racial injustices," yet he does not accept the existence of privilege because more proximate causes (what Case calls "cultural dysfunction") are "now the primary issue."[61] This raises the bar still higher, but Case is not done yet.
- Fourth, it is not enough for some group to be advantaged as the proximate result of racism—that advantage also has to come *at the expense of others.* "Advantage" can be understood in at least two ways: a comparative sense (whites are advantaged over blacks in that they are better off along various measures) and a zero-sum sense (whites are advantaged over blacks in that they are well off *because* blacks are badly off). Case argues that the strong sense of privilege must be zero sum.[62] This is the point of Case's thought experiment where the problems in the black community vanish overnight—if that would not make whites worse off, then whites are not privileged in the strong sense.

We can now fully spell out the dilemma at the foundation of Case's argument. Either privilege (*in the weak sense*) is the result of a mere disparity between groups, or privilege (*in the strong sense*) is the result of (1) a disparity (2) that is caused by racism (3) proximately (4) at the expense of another group.

For what it's worth, even if we granted Case's stronger sense as a definition of privilege, I think that (contrary to what Case argues) we would still be justified in thinking that white privilege exists. But the more immediate problem is that by raising the bar so incredibly high, Case has come up with a definition of "privilege" totally unrelated to how the term is actually used, setting up a straw person as an opponent. Note that although Case spends most of his essay on the strong sense of privilege, he cites no one who puts forward that account—or anything really close to it—as a definition of privilege. Nor is his definition necessary for privilege to be morally and politically significant. Even if just the first two conditions for the strong sense were met, privilege would still entail significant moral and political obligations. It would entail political obligations because it is generally accepted that if a political state of affairs is caused by injustice, that state of affairs is itself unjust. It would entail moral obligations because each of us has a prima facie moral obligation to work to rectify injustices.

In the real world, people's usage of "privilege" is somewhere in the middle between his weak sense and his strong sense.[66] Consider the example put forward by McIntosh of white privilege, that while black people are often profiled as potential shoplifters in stores, white people can go shopping without having to experience that indignity. Calling this white privilege involves no judgment about whether the harm experienced by black people *benefits* whites, nor about how *proximate* racism is as a cause of the behavior. This is the kind of simple, straightforward kind of thing people mean when they talk about white privilege, yet Case's account misses it entirely.

The upshot is that Case's argument is based on a false dilemma. He argues that since the weak sense of privilege isn't morally significant, and the strong sense of privilege doesn't obviously obtain in the real world, then privilege is either morally insignificant or we're unjustified in thinking it exists. But by raising the bar so very high for the strong sense of privilege, Case has created a massive gap between the weak and the strong sense of privilege, and it is in that gap that the real definition of privilege lies. The result is that Case's argument fails to address the actual concept which his essay is about.[69]

Misunderstanding the concept of privilege is perhaps not surprising in our current political context, where deep disagreements make mutual comprehension difficult. Case himself argues that the multiple uses of the term "privilege" have created confusion. Unfortunately, Case's argument ends up contributing to that confusion instead of dispelling it.

COMPREHENSION QUESTIONS

1. Why does Lowe think Case sets an unreasonably high bar for assessing whether someone is privileged?
2. What does Lowe mean when he accuses Case of introducing a straw person?

DISCUSSION QUESTION

1. Lowe contends that Case's definitions of weak and strong privilege don't match the current political conversation about privilege. Do you agree or disagree with Lowe's critique? Why or why not?

REPLY TO LOWE
SPENCER CASE

I have two main challenges to Lowe's account of privilege (and some smaller ones). First, it isn't clear why, given Lowe's definition, privilege matters so much. Second, I think Lowe underestimates the practical downsides of framing current social issues in terms of privilege.

1. Who's Privileged?

Lowe motivates the concept of privilege by drawing attention to the case of a white woman shoplifter who apparently receives lenient treatment because she is a white woman. Shortly thereafter, Lowe endorses the analogy that privilege is like a constant tailwind at the backs of certain people, those who have privilege. But if male shoplifters really receive harsher treatment because they are men, then male privilege is more like an uneven wind that sometimes blows the other way with gale force. This illustrates a tension within anti-privilege rhetoric. Privilege critics insist on the significance of rigid privilege categories (e.g., "male"). And yet privilege is simultaneously supposed to be complex, marbled, and "intersectional." Lowe, like many of these critics, seems to want to have it both ways.

Lowe defines privilege as "a person's advantage due to their membership in a social group, in contexts where that membership shouldn't normally matter." Whether an advantage counts as a privilege depends on the relevant context. How broadly should we construe it? Black affirmative action beneficiaries count as privileged if the relevant context is employment or university admissions generally. Race *normally* shouldn't matter here. (That's true even if there are exceptions that justify affirmative action.) Maybe the relevant context for assessing this kind of discrimination in light of privilege should be narrower, something like: "Affirmative action for black college applicants in a society with historical injustices against blacks." Arguably, race *is* normally relevant in this context. But if the relevant contexts for assessing privilege are always narrow, then it's not clear all forms of racial profiling are relevant to privilege. Within the context of policing an environment where there are known racial crime disparities, race could *normally* be relevant to law-enforcement practices. Moreover, it would seem, by Lowe's definition, that the people exempt from this special scrutiny because of their race aren't necessarily beneficiaries of race privilege. After all, they aren't being given an advantage in a context where race shouldn't normally matter.

There are two issues here. First, there's no way of specifying the relevant context in Lowe's definition that doesn't generate results that most privilege opponents will be unhappy with. If we construe it broadly, then affirmative action benefits, which they generally think are virtuous, count as privileges; if we construe it narrowly, then things thought to be paradigmatically relevant to race privilege turn out not to be relevant to it (e.g., profiling). Second, it's unclear why privilege is supposed to matter so much. Who cares about whether affirmative action benefits are privileges so as long as they're justified? Who cares about whether racial profiling isn't relevant to privilege if it's nonetheless wrong? For Lowe, privilege is *epistemically* important. It helps us locate injustices, but apparently generates no unique obligations (such as an obligation to offset one's privilege). We already know what the hard cases are with respect to racial justice, however. I don't think that the notion of privilege helps us investigate or address them.

2. The Costs of Privilege Rhetoric

Lowe assures us that it's a misunderstanding to think that talk of privilege vilifies white men, or implies that they should feel guilty. If so, then it's a misunderstanding encouraged by anti-privilege intellectuals and activists. Recall that Peggy McIntosh complained that her education had afforded her "no training in seeing myself as an oppressor." Clearly, anyone labeled an oppressor is being vilified. Likewise, philosopher Andrew Pierce wrote that acknowledging privilege is sometimes understood to constitute "a *confessional* precondition akin to 'admitting you have a problem' in various twelve-step enterprises." Confessing to something morally neutral makes no sense. It's true that we don't generally choose to be members of privileged groups (though the phenomenon of light-skinned non-whites choosing to "pass" as whites is an important exception). But that could mean that privilege is more like the Christian notion of original sin than ordinary sinful behavior.

Even if merely *having* privilege isn't by itself a reason to feel guilty, the moment the privileged learn that they have privilege, they can be shamed and condemned for failing to comport themselves in the ways left-wing activists want. Lowe writes that to check your privilege is "not to feel ashamed for having it or use it as an excuse for inaction, but to acknowledge that your experiences and perceptions of the world may be quite different from those of members of other social groups." Maybe checking *your own* privilege is like this, but telling someone else to check his privilege is almost certainly, and not unreasonably, going to be perceived as accusatory and condescending. Some will dismiss this as "white fragility," though it isn't fragility if the complaint is legitimate. In any event, alienating whites is more likely to spur backlash than to lead to anything constructive.

If I could give only one piece of advice to friends on the left, it would be this: Beware of tunnel vision about evil. Future tyranny may not resemble any tyranny of the past. There are many roads to hell, some of which we as a species have not yet traversed and, given all of the possible social permutations, probably some we haven't even dreamt up. Racism and sexism have been used to oppress people, but accusations of racism and sexism can also be so used. Behold the spectacle (still visible on YouTube) of Black Lives Matter protestors barging into the Dartmouth University library to shout down and curse, with racially charged language, the white students peacefully studying there. Allegedly, this was to bring attention to the problems associated with racism, but clearly, it was also a way of asserting power over other students. The invidious language of privilege feeds into this destructive tendency without doing anything to address genuine grievances.

COMPREHENSION QUESTIONS

1. How does Case criticize anti-privilege rhetoric?
2. What is the "cost of privilege" rhetoric? Why should people avoid developing tunnel vision about evil?

DISCUSSION QUESTIONS

1. Case warns that tyranny can come in new and unseen ways, and he gives a warning about watching out for the manipulation of language. Consider the Dartmouth example, from the Black Lives Matter movement. What do you think of his assessment of the situation? Are there any other factors to consider?
2. Are affirmative action policies an appropriate remedy for past injustices? Do they create a type of privilege for groups based on membership qualifications?

FURTHER READINGS

Blum, Lawrence. "White Privilege: A Mild Critique." *Theory and Research in Education* 6, no. 3 (2008): 309–321.

DuBois, W. E. B. *Black Reconstruction in America, 1860–1880* (New York: The Free Press, 1998).

Hughes, Coleman. "Black American Culture and the Racial Wealth Gap." *Quillette*, July 19, 2018. https://quillette.com/2018/07/19/black-american-culture-and-the-racial-wealth-gap/

Jessim, Lee, Thomas R. Cain, Jerrett T. Crawford, Kent Harbor, and Florette Cohen. "The Unbearable Accuracy of Stereotypes." Chapter 10 in the *Handbook of Prejudice, Stereotyping, and Discrimination*, second edition, edited by Todd D. Nelson. New York: Psychology Press, 2010, 199–227.

McIntosh, Peggy. "White Privilege: Unpacking the Invisible Knapsack." *Peace and Freedom Magazine* (July/August 1989), 10–12. https://nationalseedproject.org/white-privilege-unpacking-the-invisible-knapsack.

McWhorter, John. *Losing the Race: Self-Sabotage in Black America*. New York: Harper Perennial, 2001.

McWhorter, John. "The Privilege of Checking White Privilege." *Daily Beast*, March 15, 2015. https://www.thedailybeast.com/the-privilege-of-checking-white-privilege

Riley, Jason L. *Please Stop Helping Us: How Liberals Make It Harder for Blacks to Succeed.* New York: Encounter Books, 2014.

Sowell, Thomas. *Intellectuals and Race.* New York: Basic Books, 2013.

Zack, Naomi. *White Privilege and Black Rights: The Injustice of U.S. Police Racial Profiling and Homicide.* Lanham, MD: Rowman & Littlefield, 2015.

NOTES

1. "Why I Steal," *Death, Sex, & Money*, September 26, 2017, https://www.wnycstudios.org/story/why-i-steal-death-sex-money

2. This is complicated by the fact that many scholars do not define "privilege" generally, but instead focus on defining particular kinds of privilege, most prominently white privilege. And even in those works, "white privilege" and "male privilege" are not always defined, but are instead elucidated through examples and metaphors. For some representative definitions, see Peggy McIntosh, "White Privilege and Male Privilege: A Personal Account of Coming to See Correspondences Through Work in Women's Studies," in *Privilege: A Reader*, edited by Michael S. Kimmel and Abby L. Ferber (London: Routledge and Kegan Paul, 2016 [4th ed.]), 28–40; Alison Bailey, "Privilege: Expanding on Marilyn Frye's 'Oppression,'" *Journal of Social Philosophy* 29, no. 3 (1998), 104–119; Jeremy Dunham and Holly Lawford-Smith, "Offsetting Race Privilege," *Journal of Ethics and Social Philosophy* 11, no. 2 (2017), 1–22. Perhaps the most important precursor to contemporary scholarship on white privilege is the notion of a "psychological wage" gained by whites in America, put forward by W. E. B. DuBois, *Black Reconstruction in America, 1860–1880* (New York: The Free Press, 1998).

3. Michael S. Kimmel and Abby L. Ferber, eds., *Privilege: A Reader* (London: Routledge & Kegan Paul, 2016 [4th ed.]), 1.

4. Naomi Zack, *White Privilege and Black Rights: The Injustice of U.S. Police Racial Profiling and Homicide* (Lanham, MD: Rowman & Littlefield, 2015), 3–4.

5. McIntosh, "White Privilege and Male Privilege," 17.

6. McIntosh, "White Privilege and Male Privilege," 8.

7. McIntosh, "White Privilege and Male Privilege," 4.

8. Jason Jones, "Kings Guard Nik Stauskas Surprised by Reaction to Comments," *Sacramento Bee*, October 15, 2014, http://www.sacbee.com/sports/nba/sacramento-kings/article2667967.html.

9. Kimberlé Crenshaw, "Mapping the Margins: Intersectionality, Identity Politics, and Violence Against Women of Color," *Stanford Law Review* 43, no. 6 (1991), 1241–1299 Although Crenshaw coined the term "intersectionality," there are important precursors of the idea, most notably "A Black Feminist Statement" (1977) by the Combahee River Collective, in Susan Archer Mann and Ashly Suzanne Patterson, eds., *Reading Feminist Theory: From Modernity to Postmodernity* (Oxford: Oxford University Press, 2016), 247–252.

10. Marilyn Frye, *The Politics of Reality: Essays in Feminist Theory* (Berkeley: Crossing Press, 1983), 135.

11. Shannon Sullivan, "White Privilege," in *The Oxford Handbook of Philosophy and Race*, edited by Naomi Zack (Oxford: Oxford University Press, 2017), 336–337.

12. Don Gonyea, "Majority of White Americans Say They Believe Whites Face Discrimination," National Public Radio, October 24, 2017, https://www.npr.org/2017/10/24/559604836/majority-of-white-americans-think-theyre-discriminated-against.

13. Arlie Russell Hochschild, *Strangers in their Own Land: Anger and Mourning on the American Right* (New York: The New Press, 2016), 136–140.

14. Jonathan Haidt, "The Age of Outrage: What the Current Political Climate Is Doing to Our Countries and Universities," *National Review*, December 29, 2017, http://www.nationalreview.com/article/454964/age-outrage.

15. "Why She Steals: Your Reactions," *Death, Sex, & Money*, October 17, 2017, https://www.wnycstudios.org/story/why-she-steals-death-sex-money.

16. Michael Levin, "Responses to Race Differences In Crime," *Journal of Social Philosophy* 23, no. 1 (1992): 5–29.
17. I am grateful to Ami Cho, Barrett Emerick, Bob Fischer, Alison M. Jaggar, Katie Keller, Joseph Stenberg, and Benjamin Stine for their thoughtful comments on previous drafts of the paper. Special thanks are due to Ami Cho for her research help, Katie Keller for introducing me to the podcast episode with which I begin the article, and Spencer Case for his generosity in first suggesting I join this project.
18. https://www.whiteprivilegeconference.com/about-us.
19. Barbara Applebaum, "Critical Whiteness Studies," *Oxford Research Encyclopedia of Education*, June06, 2017, http://education.oxfordre.com/view/10.1093/acrefore/9780190264093.001.0001/acrefore-9780190264093-e-5.
20. Andrew J. Pierce, "Interest Convergence: An Alternative to White Privilege Models of Anti-Racist Pedagogy and Practice," *Teaching Philosophy* 39 (2016): 507–530.
21. Daniel Okrent, *Last Call: The Rise and Fall of Prohibition* (New York: Scribner, 2011). See also my "Moral Zealotry and the Seductive Nature of Evil," *Quillette*, March 10, 2019, https://quillette.com/2019/03/10/moral-zealotry-and-the-seductive-nature-of-evil/.
22. Shelby Steele, *A Dream Deferred: The Second Betrayal of Black Freedom in America* (New York: HarperCollins, 1998), 13.
23. Pierce, "Interest Convergence," 523.
24. That might already be happening. The Anti-Defamation League recently released a report that white supremacists are recruiting at universities at an "unprecedented" rate (https://www.adl.org/blog/white-supremacists-on-campus-unprecedented-recruitment-efforts-underway?_ga=2.265748879.1686447815.1520193949-245213182.1518552999).
25. McIntosh, "White Privilege and Male Privilege," 1.
26. Peggy McIntosh, "White Privilege: Unpacking the Invisible Knapsack," *Peace and Freedom Magazine* (July/August 1989), 10–12, https://nationalseedproject.org/white-privilege-unpacking-the-invisible-knapsack.
27. August 3, 2019.
28. Peter Singer, "Famine, Affluence, and Morality," *Philosophy and Public Affairs* 1, no. 3 (Spring 1972): 229–243.
29. McIntosh, "White Privilege and Male Privilege," 1.
30. McIntosh lists 46 in the 1988 article, 50 in the 1989 article.
31. Number 8 in the 1988 article, 9 in the 1989 article.
32. Number 35 in the 1988 article, 22 in the 1989 article.
33. On height: Shana Leibowitz, "Science Says Being Taller Could Make You Richer and More Successful—Here's Why," *Business Insider*, September 9, 2015, http://www.businessinsider.com/tall-people-are-richer-and-successful-2015-9. On attractiveness: Dina Spector, "8 Scientifically Proven Reasons Life is Better if You're Beautiful," *Business Insider*, June 12, 2013, http://www.businessinsider.com/studies-show-the-advantages-of-being-beautiful-2013-6.
34. McIntosh, "White Privilege and Male Privilege," 2.
35. For one such offsetting proposal, see Dunham and Lawford-Smith, "Offsetting Race Privilege." I criticize their proposal in an essay for *Quillette* (http://quillette.com/2017/06/24/skepticism-white-privilege).
36. Steele, *A Dream Deferred*, 13.
37. Sullivan, "White Privilege," 331.
38. See Richard Henry Sander and Stuart Taylor Jr., *Mismatch: How Affirmative Action Hurts Students It's Intended to Help, and Why Universities Won't Admit It* (New York:

Basic Books, 2012). See also Thomas Sowell, *Affirmative Action Around the World: An Empirical Study* (New Haven, CT: Yale University Press, 2004), especially Chapter 6, "Affirmative Action in the United States."

39. Michelle Alexander makes this critique in *The New Jim Crow: Mass Incarceration in the Age of Colorblindness* (New York: The New Press, 2012), especially Chapters 2 and 3. I agree with her general critique of the War on Drugs, but I disagree with the idea that this bad policy is essentially racist.

40. Riley, "Please Stop Helping Us," 72.

41. John McWhorter, *Losing the Race: Self-Sabotage in Black America* (New York: Simon and Schuster, 2001), 2.

42. John Ogbu, *Black American Students in an Affluent Suburb: A Study in Academic Disengagement* (Mahway, NJ: Lawrence Erlbaum Associates, Publishers 2003), Chapter 2, "Academic Disengagement in Shaker Heights."

43. For a further example of a cultural dysfunction hypothesis being applied to white people, this time the British underclass, see Theodore Dalrymple's *Life at the Bottom: The World View That Makes the Underclass* (Chicago: Ivan R. Dee, 2001).

44. The so-called Moynihan Report, a product of the U.S. Department of Labor Office of Policy Planning and Research, is officially titled "The Negro Family: The Case For National Action." It is available here (without, unfortunately, the helpful illustrations in the original): http://www.blackpast.org/primary/moynihan-report-1965#chapter2.

45. See the Urban Institute's 2013 report, "The Moynihan Report Revisited," https://www.urban.org/sites/default/files/publication/23696/412839-The-Moynihan-Report-Revisited.PDF.

46. David Popenoe, *Life Without Father* (New York: Simon & Schuster Inc., 1996), especially Chapter 2, "The Human Carnage of Fatherlessness." See also Barbara Defoe Whitehead, "Dan Quayle Was Right," *The Atlantic* (April 1993), https://www.theatlantic.com/magazine/archive/1993/04/dan-quayle-was-right/307015/.

47. For more evidence in favor of the culture hypothesis, see Coleman Hughes, "Black American Culture and the Racial Wealth Gap," *Quillette*, July 19, 2018, https://quillette.com/2018/07/19/black-american-culture-and-the-racial-wealth-gap/.

48. David Boonin. *Should Race Matter? Unusual Answers to the Usual Questions* (New York: Cambridge University Press, 2011), 88.

49. He also considers genetic inferiority as a possible explanation but assumes—correctly, I think—that most of his interlocutors will recoil from this hypothesis. Note that his critique of the cultural hypothesis also serves as a response to the "bad policy" hypothesis: Blacks have been uniquely victimized by bad policy because antecedent racial injustice made them especially vulnerable to being affected by it.

50. Moynihan, in the third chapter of his eponymous report, identifies slavery and Jim Crow as the causes of what he calls "the tangle of pathology" that afflicted blacks in the 1960s. In the conclusion, he writes: "What then is the problem? We feel the answer is clear enough. Three centuries of injustice have brought about deep-seated structural distortions in the life of the Negro American," 47.

51. J. D. Vance, *Hillbilly Elegy: A Memoir of a Family and Culture in Crisis* (New York: HarperCollins, 2016), 7.

52. Dunham and Lawford-Smith, "Offsetting Race Privilege," 6. There's another possible reading, which treats these advantages as being zero sum. For example, if I am the richest person in the city, that entails a corresponding disadvantage for you: that you are not the richest person in the city. But the sorts of advantages we're worried about

here involve things like educational attainment and living standards, which are not zero sum. Nor is it clear why a scheme of offsets would be needed unless we understand them to mean that racial privileges come at the unjust expense of others.

53. Du Bois, *Black Reconstruction*, 700–701.
54. Traci Bowell, "Feminist Standpoint Theory," *Internet Encyclopedia of Philosophy*, 2011, http://www.iep.utm.edu/fem-stan.
55. Ashwini Vasathakumar, "Epistemic Privilege and Victims' Duties to Resist Their Oppression," *Journal of Applied Philosophy* 35, no. 8 (2018): 470.
56. Vasanthakumar, "Epistemic Privilege," 472.
57. Pierce, "Interest Convergence," 511–512.
58. For a further development of this line of argument, see Spencer Case, "Do the Oppressed Really Know Best?" *Arc Digital*, August 15, 2018, https://arcdigital.media/do-the-oppressed-really-know-best-c13b3648ff7.
59. I would like to thank Steve Kershnar, Bob Fischer, Jonny Anomaly, and the participants of the 2018 Heterodoxy workshop in Anne Arbor, Michigan, for helpful comments on previous drafts of this essay. I would also like to thank Dan Lowe for his thoughtful and civil engagement with me on this fraught issue.
60. Case briefly discusses the possibility that even well-intentioned policies might disadvantage a racial group in an unjust way, but then sets it aside on the grounds that it does not count as racism. Of course, this simply doubles down on the assumption that racial injustice must mean "injustice caused by racism."
61. Case's writing here is a bit unclear, but his central argument must depend upon accepting this as a condition of the strong sense of privilege. As I just noted, Case explicitly concedes that conservatives can "consistently grant that cultural dysfunction is causally downstream from racial injustice." So if being caused (non-proximately) by racism was sufficient for the existence of privilege, then in making this concession Case would have just admitted that white privilege in the strong sense exists, contrary to his thesis. If this inference is supposed to be blocked by his further criterion—that privilege be at the expense of others—then the discussion of whether black disadvantage is caused by cultural dysfunction or racial injustice would be totally irrelevant to his central argument. So if this portion of his essay plays any role in supporting his central argument, it must be in establishing a necessary condition for the strong sense of privilege.
62. Case argues that white privilege being understood in this zero-sum sense is a "common" stipulation in the literature. However, Case cites only one paper, by Dunham and Lawford-Smith, "Offsetting Race Privilege," and the paper does not say this explicitly. What the authors say is that privilege must "entail a corresponding disadvantage." Case infers, "that seems to mean that race privilege comes at the unjust expense of others." However, there is no reason to make this leap: Advantages in the comparative sense *always* entail a corresponding disadvantage, since in that sense to be advantaged just is to be better off compared to someone else, and to be disadvantaged just is to be worse off compared to someone else.
66. Curiously, Case himself mentions definitions of privilege that fit right in between his weaker and stronger sense: that the privileged "enjoy unearned power or dominance conferred upon them by society" and "to be privileged is not just to be better off, but to be unfairly advantaged." One can, of course, enjoy unearned power or be unfairly advantaged in ways that fall far short of Case's four criteria for the strong sense of privilege.
69. This flaw in Case's argument also creates a problem for his argument about "the epistemology of privilege." Case considers the idea that the oppressed have special epistemic

authority about oppression, and that their testimony can thus "provide independent evidence for the claim that white privilege—in the strong sense—exists." One of Case's chief doubts about this is that suffering does not bring with it knowledge of the causes of suffering. Case argues that "a black man who suffers from poverty, or is racially profiled by police, can know what it feels like to go through these things without knowing whether his problems are manifestations of structural injustice rather than, say, the fruits of ill-conceived policies that weren't racially motivated." Here, again, Case's skepticism is only possible because he has raised the bar for the strong sense of privilege unreasonably high. By focusing on the difficulty in knowing whether certain policies are "racially motivated," Case again conflates *racial injustice* with *injustice caused by racism*. And in any event, Case overstates the proper amount of skepticism here. Although it may be difficult to know the intentions behind a person's action in any particular case, it does not follow that knowledge of intentions is difficult to know with a larger sample size. A black man pulled over by the police may not know in any particular instance that he is being racially profiled, yet if without breaking the law he is pulled over every single week, it is reasonable to infer that race plays a role in the overall pattern.

CHAPTER 15

Feminism

THE TROUBLE WITH FEMINISM
PHILIPPE LEMOINE

In this essay, I want to explain why I'm not a feminist, and why I think you shouldn't be either. If you are like the typical reader of this book, you will probably think that it doesn't make any sense. After all, isn't feminism just the belief that women should have the same rights as men, and if so how, could one disagree with that? If that's what you're thinking, then don't worry, for I agree that women should have the same rights as men. I just don't think that's what "feminism" means anymore and, if we're going to be debating the merits of feminism, it seems to me that we should first be clear about what we're talking about.

1. What's in a Word? The Meaning of "Feminism"
In the past, "feminism" was only used to describe the belief that men and women should have equality of opportunity, and while the details of this claim need to be worked out (there may be some occupations, such as gynecology, where there is a good reason to prefer men or women), I don't disagree with that. For instance, I agree that women should have the right to vote or shouldn't be barred from studying at university, but "feminism" increasingly means something a lot stronger than that.

There is plenty of evidence for this claim. In particular, several polls in both the United States and the United Kingdom found that only a minority of people identify as feminist, even though the overwhelming majority of them agree that men and women should have the same rights. For instance, a poll for Vox in 2015 found that only 18% of respondents identified as feminist, yet 85% of them said they believed in equality for women.[1] Perhaps even more striking, a British poll conducted in 2016 on 8,000 people found that only 6.7% of the population self-described as feminist, while 60.7% believed in equality for men and women but didn't self-describe as feminist. The figures for women were, respectively, 9.2% and 64.9%.[2]

I take these kinds of facts to be evidence that "feminism" is ambiguous and that it's sometimes used to talk about the belief that women should have the same rights as men and sometimes to talk about something much stronger. For instance, it's consistent to think both that women should enjoy the same rights as men *and* that they already do for the most part, but that's not what contemporary feminists typically think. Indeed, not only do feminists usually believe that women should have the same rights as men, but they also think that they don't and that they are oppressed, even in the West.

The fact that it's currently ambiguous is to the advantage of these activists, who can make very radical claims and, when they are challenged, retreat on the more innocuous meaning of "feminism" as equality of opportunity. Similarly, they can advance radical policies that most people disagree with, such as giving preferential treatment to women or requiring that quotas of them be met in hiring, by using that ambiguity to their advantage.[3]

The debate would be clearer if everyone agreed not to use "feminism" to describe the mere belief that women should have the same rights as men. Since the overwhelming majority of people agree with that, defining "feminism" in that way amounts to stipulating that feminism is correct, yet there are clearly major disagreements between people who identify as feminists and people who don't or I would never have been asked to write this essay in the first place. If the debate is to be fruitful, we must not define "feminism" in such a way that it makes the outcome of that debate a preordained conclusion.

2. A Central Claim of Feminism: Women Are Oppressed

If we do not define "feminism" in that way, however, the question naturally arises of how we should define it. This task is more difficult, because feminists hold a variety of views and often disagree with each other, yet I think it's still possible to identify a claim most of them are committed to. I think a good candidate for that is the claim that, even in contemporary Western societies, women are oppressed. Marilyn Frye, a philosopher who wrote perhaps the most influential account of oppression among feminists, calls that "a fundamental claim of feminism."[4] It seems to me that a commitment to this claim does a good job of distinguishing feminists from people who merely believe that men and women should have equality of opportunity.[5] This is not exactly a definition, but if I can show that this claim is false, I will have also shown that feminism is mistaken.

While the vast majority of feminists are committed to the claim that women are oppressed, they don't mean exactly the same thing by that, so in a sense it is not exactly the same claim to which they are committed. Feminists hold a variety of views about the nature of oppression, but I will focus on Frye's account, which as I noted above is probably the most influential. Besides, I could say very similar things against other feminist accounts of oppression, so I think I can focus on Frye's version without much loss of generality. I want to argue that feminists are confronted with a dilemma: Either women in contemporary Western societies are oppressed and in this case, on any definition of "oppression" that is not entirely ad hoc, men are also oppressed, or neither men nor women are oppressed. Before we can see why, however, we must discuss why feminists think that, even in contemporary Western societies, women are oppressed.

First, I don't think that, in the ordinary sense of the term "oppression," women in contemporary Western societies are oppressed. For instance, according to the Merriam-Webster dictionary, oppression is the "unjust or cruel exercise of authority or power." When people talk about oppression, they usually have in mind things such as the way in which black people were treated in the United States when slavery was legal, the treatment of Jews by the Nazis under the Third Reich, or indeed the severe legal and social restrictions that, even in the West, women faced up until a few decades ago. Now, whatever obstacles you think women still face in contemporary Western societies, it surely doesn't rise to that level. Even if I'm wrong about how people use the word "oppression," I think one shouldn't use the word "oppression" to describe how women are treated in contemporary Western societies, because it invites a parallel with such paradigmatic cases of oppression that is very misleading.

I think that, if they are pressed, even feminists will admit that most people would not use the word "oppression" to describe the situation of women in contemporary Western societies, although they probably think that people ought to do so. Indeed, although she never admits that she is redefining the term, Frye spends a lot of time in her influential paper anticipating objections from people who are using "oppression" in the sense this word has in ordinary language. In order to do so, she famously used the analogy of a bird cage:

> If you look very closely at just one wire in the cage, you cannot see the other wires. If your conception of what is before you is determined by this myopic focus, you could look at that one wire, up and down the length of it, and be unable to see why a bird would not just fly around the wire any time it wanted to go somewhere. . . . It is only when you step back, stop looking at the wires one by one, microscopically, and take a macroscopic view of the whole cage, that you can see why the bird does not go anywhere; and then you will see it in a moment.[6]

According to Frye, if people are denying that women in contemporary Western societies are oppressed, it is because they only attend to the obstacles they face individually, without stepping back to consider the structure they form. This is why people, including many women, don't notice that women are oppressed, even though they are.

In another paper, Frye defines oppression as "a system of interrelated barriers and forces which reduce, immobilize and mold people who belong to a certain group, and effect their subordination to another group (individually to individuals of the other group, and as a group, to that group)."[7] Women are systematically disadvantaged in a variety of ways because they are women. They are more often victims of sexual assault, have less political and economic power, are seen as mentally unstable when they exhibit anger, have to do most of the domestic work, etc.

While taken in isolation, these disadvantages may not seem to amount to *oppression*, Frye claims they reinforce each other and are part of the same structure that keep women in check, which is why together they do. Moreover, they often have the property of putting women in a bind, by leaving them with no good options as to what they should do. For instance, according to Frye, if a woman complains because a man opens the door for her, she will be seen as angry and unreasonable. But if she does not, then she is forced to consent to this ritual, which according to Frye sends the message that women are incapable. Finally, not only are these various obstacles targeting women because they are women, but they also operate to men's advantage.

3. Most Feminist Claims About Sexism Are Not Substantiated by the Evidence

The problem with Frye's definition of "oppression" is not that, according to me, it changes the ordinary meaning of the term. As long as one is clear that it is what one is doing, there is nothing wrong with that, provided that one's concept is useful and helps us better understand the world. But I don't think Frye's definition of "oppression" is particularly useful in that way, so I don't see why it should be preferred to the ordinary concept, except for political reasons.

Of course, in a sense, this is just a semantical issue. One could always stipulate that one is using "oppression" to talk about the kind of things Frye is talking about, even though it's not the same thing most people are talking about when they use that word in everyday language. But as I already noted above, semantics often matters, if only because people don't react in the same way depending on what words are used, even if they are used to say the same thing. Activists understand this, and that's why they always try to bend the meaning of words. Unless you agree with their goals, you shouldn't let them.

I don't think Frye's definition is useful because, on that definition, not just women but also men are oppressed, and this is clearly not what feminists want to say.[8] The examples Frye gives in her discussion of oppression are right out of the catalogue of injustices that, according to feminists, women continue to endure. Now I don't deny that, even in contemporary Western societies, women are systematically disadvantaged in a variety of ways and that, in many cases, it's at least partly the result of wrongful discrimination, although the precise mechanism is often not what feminists think.[9] The problem is that, in many other cases, feminists are alleging that women face disadvantages when it's not actually the case or, at least, the evidence they adduce does not show that.

For instance, as we have seen again during the last U.S. presidential election, feminists often claim that female politicians face significant gender bias. They claim that women who run for office are less likely to be seen as strong leaders, that newspapers are more likely to comment on their appearance, that people are less likely to vote for them, etc. These claims have become so ubiquitous that even people who don't identify as feminists assume they are true. Yet a recent book on that issue showed that, despite what most people think, gender bias was almost non-existent in U.S. politics.[10] Female politicians are no less likely than men to be seen as strong leaders, newspapers are no more likely to comment on their appearance, people are no less likely to vote for them, etc. Perhaps future research will invalidate some of these findings, but the important point here is that feminists constantly make these sorts of claims without offering a shred of evidence. The claim that politics is rife with gender bias is so obvious to them that it doesn't even occur to them that non-anecdotal evidence might be necessary to show it.

Feminists also claim that women are paid less than men because of wrongful discrimination, but it's really unclear to what extent this is true and, in any case, the truth is far more complicated than what feminists typically assume. It's true that, even in contemporary Western societies, women are paid less on average than men. Thus, in that sense, they are disadvantaged. But feminists often claim that it's because employers have a preference for men just because they are men. Yet the economic literature on the gender pay gap does not support that claim. It's plausible that such a preference on the part of employers explains some of the gap, but I think it's fair to say that most economists would agree that, even if it does, it can only explain a relatively small part.[11]

Indeed, once you control for number of hours worked, experience, occupation, etc., most of the gap disappears.[12] While the residual is often assumed to be the result of a preference for men just because they are men, we can't actually make this inference, because it could just reflect unmeasured difference in productivity between men and women.[13] Thus, while it's plausible that some of the residual is due to a preference for men just because they are men on the part of employers, it's not clear that a large part of it is, and it's likely that most of it isn't.

Smart feminists are aware of this, and that's why they offer a more sophisticated argument for the view that discrimination plays a large role in the gender pay gap. They correctly point out that, even if outright discrimination by employers doesn't have much to do with the gender pay gap, it doesn't follow that unfair discrimination against women is not a big part of the story. For instance, a large factor of the gender pay gap is that men work longer hours than women, but this has a lot to do with the fact that women still do most of the work at home and spend more time taking care of children. According to feminists, this is the result of discrimination against women, though not by employers. A disproportionate share of domestic tasks and childrearing still falls on women because not only men but also women themselves still hold sexist beliefs about women. Similarly, while the fact that women tend to choose different occupations than men explains a relatively large part of the gender pay gap, this fact is not innocent. Feminists claim that it's because women are socialized to prefer low-paying jobs such as nursing instead of high-paying jobs such as software development. In other words, while outright discrimination by employers doesn't explain much, more subtle discrimination in society at large does.

There is some merit to this argument. For instance, it's indisputable that a disproportionate amount of domestic tasks still fall on women, which is no doubt partly because sexist attitudes persist.[14] It's also clear that children have a major impact on the gender pay gap.[15] But despite what feminists often claim, it is really doubtful that, even if we could totally eliminate gender roles, most of the gap would not remain. For instance, both the gender pay gap and gender inequality as measured by the United Nations' Gender Inequality Index vary quite a lot in the European Union, but there is no relationship between them.[16] Indeed, the European countries that have the highest gender equality, such as Sweden and Switzerland, also have the largest gender pay gap. This is not what you would expect if, in contemporary Western societies, gender inequality were the main cause of the gender pay gap.

4. Men Are Also Disadvantaged in a Variety of Ways

I have only discussed a few examples, but hopefully it will be enough to convince you that, although there are undoubtedly ways in which women are being systematically and unfairly disadvantaged, many of the claims feminists make about that are false or at least have not been established. Thus, to the extent that, on Frye's account of oppression, women are supposed to be oppressed because of the ways in which feminists allege they are systematically and unfairly disadvantaged, their case for the claim that women are oppressed is much weaker than they think.

Moreover, even if you nevertheless think that women are sufficiently disadvantaged to count as oppressed on Frye's definition, there is a very good case to be made that not just women but also men are oppressed. Men are systematically disadvantaged in a variety of ways, and while some of it can be explained by differences between men and women (just as we have seen that some of the disadvantages faced by women could be explained in that way), the evidence is overwhelming that wrongful discrimination also plays a role. Finally, in many cases, one can also show that women are the beneficiaries. If you go back to Frye's definition of oppression, you will see that all the ingredients are present.

David Benatar carefully defended the claims I just made, so I won't try to make the case here, but I will just mention some of the ways in which men are disadvantaged.[17] They are much more likely to be victims of violence, significantly less likely to be granted custody of their children in the event of a divorce, overwhelming more likely to have a work-related accident, much more likely to be imprisoned, commit suicide at several times the rate of women, significantly less likely to attend college, etc. Moreover, when they express concern about these issues, they are often mocked, which adds insult to injury. Of course, neither I nor Benatar claim that if men are disadvantaged in those ways, it's only because of wrongful discrimination against them. But wrongful discrimination nevertheless seems to play a significant role. At any rate, the case that wrongful discrimination plays a significant role is *at least* as strong as in the case of the disadvantages faced by women and other minorities, so feminists are not really in a position to deny it unless they also want to deny that women are being unfairly discriminated against.

For instance, a recent meta-analysis found that even when controlling for a variety of legally relevant variables, men still received harsher sentences than women.[18] Another study about gender bias in federal criminal cases in the United States even found that, after controlling for a variety of legally relevant variables, men received sentences that were 63% longer than women.[19] Now, I don't claim that the whole effect is the result of unfair discrimination against men, for as should be clear by now it can be quite difficult to demonstrate the existence of that kind of discrimination. But this disparity is still more than six times as large as the anti-black bias the same author found in another article using the same methodology.[20] As far as I can tell, even other studies on gender bias in the criminal justice system, which typically find smaller effects, tend to find effect sizes that are similar to those found in the literature on racial bias in the criminal justice system.

The conclusion I want to draw from everything I have said is not that both women and men oppressed, but that *if* you want to say that women are oppressed because they are systematically and unfairly disadvantaged in various ways, then you must also say that *men* are oppressed because they are systematically and unfairly disadvantaged in other ways. Indeed, as we have seen, women are systematically and unfairly disadvantaged in some ways, but so are men, and I don't think one can make the case that overall women have it worse without ignoring the many ways in which men are disadvantaged. Of course, one could no doubt make that conclusion trivially true by putting more weight on some aspects rather than others (e.g., one could just assume that making less money is much worse than having a greater chance of being physically assaulted), but I think ultimately any justification for those assumptions would prove to be ad hoc. It's also easy to show, as Benatar does in his book, that men are being discriminated against in various ways because they are men and that often this benefits women. Thus, on Frye's definition of oppression, men are oppressed.

I take this to be a *reductio* of this account of oppression. Of course, one could bite the bullet and claim that *both* men and women are oppressed, but few people are willing to do that and certainly not feminists. Moreover, while I focused on Frye's account of oppression because it's arguably the most influential among feminists, I believe that I could say very similar things against any account of oppression on which women but not men are oppressed, even those that are critical of Frye.[21] Of course, it's always possible to define "oppression" so as to directly or indirectly stipulate that women but not men are oppressed, but I don't think any such definition would serve a useful purpose. Even if you insisted on defining "oppression" so that only women can be oppressed, it would not make the ways in which men are systematically disadvantaged any less serious than what women have to deal with. But this is precisely why we should not concede this linguistic point to feminists, because as I noted above, if "oppression" is only used to describe what women have to deal with, this is exactly what people will think.

5. Conclusion

In my view, using the word "oppression" to describe the situation of men or women in contemporary Western societies can only be misleading, as it lumps together the relatively benign ways in which men and women are currently being disadvantaged with states of affairs like the situation of black people in the United States when slavery was legal. Both men and women are disadvantaged in a variety of ways and, to the extent that it's possible, we should try to eliminate wrongful discrimination against both men and women, but we should do so in a responsible manner. We should only make claims that are supported by the evidence. Before we propose to address the injustices that we have identified, we should make sure that the policies we propose will actually help, instead of making things worse. We should refrain from stretching the ordinary meaning of words for political gain. On all these counts, I think feminists usually fall short.

COMPREHENSION QUESTIONS

1. According to Lemoine, what do most people *think* that "feminism" means?
2. According to Lemoine, how *should* we use the word "feminism"?
3. What's the point of the bird cage analogy?
4. Why is Lemoine skeptical of the gender pay gap?
5. Does Lemoine think that men are oppressed?

DISCUSSION QUESTIONS

1. What is feminism as *you* understand it? What are its aims? To what is it responding? What are its virtues and vices?
2. What does it mean to say that women are oppressed? How does Lemoine understand that idea? How else could you understand it? Are there ways of understanding it that aren't vulnerable to Lemoine's objections?
3. Suppose men *are* disadvantaged in some ways. What, exactly, does this show? Are there any differences between the *number* and *kind* of disadvantages that men face versus the number and kind of disadvantages that women face?

Case 1

Have a look at this passage from an article by Paul Benson. In it, he explores the way that women's autonomy is limited by the way that they are socialized to accept certain beauty standards:

Consider the eighteen-year-old college student who excels in her studies, is well liked by her many friends and acquaintances, leads an active, challenging life, yet who regularly feels bad about herself because she does not have "the right look." She has those familiar sorts of "imperfection" that others repeatedly have called to her attention from an early age. Her hair has never been quite curly or straight enough; her make-up is always too heavy or too light; her body is never just soft or firm enough; she has never been sure what the strong points of her appearance were, so she never has known what styles of clothing would capitalize on them. Periodically, she has tried not to care so much about all of this, but in each instance something arose to remind her that others attach significant value to a woman's appearance and that, as a woman, she would feel much happier about herself if she could sculpt her appearance more successfully. So, on top of everything else she does, she expends a great deal of time and money trying to straighten or curl her hair, to refine her cosmetic technique, to harden or soften her body, and so on, as well as trying to

Case 1 (continued)

---

keep up with all of the latest products, routines, and tricks that might help her finally to attain more success at these tasks.

As I have imagined this young woman, she is bright, sensitive, earnest, and active. But she is usually frustrated with and disapproving of herself—and sometimes disgusted by herself—because she wants her body to appear the way most other people she knows wish it to appear. She is convinced that this is a very important aim for a woman to have because nearly everything in her up-bringing and adolescent experience has affirmed its value. And her upbringing was in no way deprived, according to prevailing social standards. She received close personal attention from family and peers and found emotional and ma-terial encouragement for many of her endeavors. However, if that upbringing reliably led her gravely to misunderstand the place of feminine appearance in her value as a person, and systematically prevented her from correcting that misunderstanding, then surely the motives and judgments that occasion her persistent dissatisfaction with herself are less than fully her own. The actions she performs to "fix herself up" are not motivated autonomously.*

There is a sense in which the student's preferences regarding her appearance are hers: Plainly, she wants to look a certain way. At the same time, the environ-ment has seriously constrained her options regarding her preferences, and the preferences she has adopted are problematic: They make her life harder than it would be otherwise, and it has given her a false view of her own value. How might all this be relevant to Lemoine's discussion of women's employment preferences? How might all this affect the way we think about the gender pay gap?

---

*Paul Benson, "Autonomy and Oppressive Socialization," *Social Theory and Practice*, 17, no. 3 (Fall 1991): 387–390.

THE CASE FOR FEMINISM
REBECCA TUVEL

Do you call yourself a feminist? If so, you're in the minority. According to one poll, only 18% of Americans identify as feminist.[22] Why so few? To be sure, harsh stereotypes of feminists abound. Feminists are angry, loud-mouthed man-haters who want women to rule the world, right? If this is what it means to be a feminist, then few people will proudly claim the label. But this raises the question: What *does* it mean to be a feminist today?

It is perhaps a sign of women's progress that a growing number of people have begun to question the need for feminism.[23] Indeed, contemporary feminists would be remiss to deny the great strides women have made since the move-ment's origins in the late eighteenth century. Not that long ago, women could not vote, own property, pursue an education, file for divorce, or legally accuse their husbands of rape. It is thanks to feminism's forerunners that Western women no longer endure such formal disadvantages. Yet we would be equally remiss to deny the ongoing reality of gendered violence and oppression in Western society today. Feminism thus remains vitally important.

This chapter presents the case for Western feminism. I focus on the West not because feminism is most urgent here, but because more skepticism exists about the ongoing need for feminism in this context.[24] For this reason, I won't address global feminism's ongoing battle against women's hunger, child marriage, forced female genital cutting, female infanticide, compulsory veiling, honor killings, sex trafficking, the widespread lack of education for girls and more. I also leave unaddressed non-Western critiques of the way some Western feminists have approached these topics.[25]

1. What Is Feminism?

"I'm automatically attracted to beautiful [women]—I just start kissing them. It's like a magnet. Just kiss. I don't even wait. And when you're a star they let you do it. You can do anything . . . Grab them by the pussy. You can do anything."[26] When the recording of Presidential candidate Donald Trump's words was released, many feminists were dismayed. After all, the refusal to "even wait" to kiss or grab a woman demonstrates an overt disregard for her agency and an egregious abuse of power. That he was elected regardless suggested to many that Trump's disrespectful attitude toward women is perhaps widespread. Indeed, it is telling that Trump excused himself not by suggesting his was some idiosyncratic, one-off remark. Rather, in his defense Trump noted the prevalence of such talk, or "locker room banter" as he called it, stating that "Bill Clinton has said far worse to me on the golf course."[27]

Regardless of what Bill Clinton may or may not have said on the golf course, Trump is certainly correct that he is far from alone in regarding women as sex objects. We can say that a person is treated as a sex object if she is used as a tool for another's sexual purposes without her consent.[28] To be kissed, groped, or penetrated without one's consent is to be seriously violated; it is to be treated less like a self-ruling agent and more like a thing. Women today routinely face such violations, whether they take the form of sexual harassment, assault, or rape. The size of the recent #MeToo movement demonstrates this point vividly. In the wake of revelations of widespread sexual abuse by Hollywood producer Harvey Weinstein, millions of women across varying levels of privilege joined together online to share their experiences of sexual harassment, sexual discrimination, and sexual violence with the hashtag "me too." Individual stories range in severity, but the ubiquity of accusations points to an overwhelmingly common experience of violation at the hands of men. In addition to these harms, feminists identify other forms of violence that disproportionately target women as a group, such as marital rape (not made illegal in the United States until 1993), coercive controlling violence or "intimate terrorism,"[29] and intimate partner homicide.[30]

Such realities have led many feminists to conclude that women are oppressed. "It is a fundamental claim of feminism that women are oppressed,"[31] writes Marilyn Frye. Feminist Daniel Silvermint argues that a person is oppressed when their objective well-being is pervasively and wrongfully hindered. Objective well-being refers to those elements that make life better, such as "having self-respect, making progress in your plans and projects, being happy, experiencing connection, having and exercising autonomy, being secure, being healthy, and possessing at least some items of material value or other valuable external goods."[32] If any of these elements is pervasively and wrongfully hindered, you are oppressed on this view. For example, if a gay Muslim woman is chronically denied job opportunities on the basis of her identity as opposed to her credentials, several aspects of her objective well-being are compromised—for example, her ability to progress in her plans, to be happy, or to be secure. Her hopes and plans for her life are thwarted due to systematic barriers that block her from employment. Not only that, but the barriers are a result of discrimination and are therefore *wrong*. That the barriers are both pervasive and wrongful creates an oppressive situation. For many feminists, ongoing sexism and violence against women demonstrate that women as a group experience systematic and wrongful harm, often at the hands of men. They are thus oppressed.[33]

But what exactly does it mean to say women *as a group* are oppressed? Is the queen of England oppressed?[34] If so, does her oppression share anything in common with that of a disabled white mother on welfare? Or a Hispanic trans woman in prison? Feminists have theorized women's oppression since the dawn of the nineteenth century. But it was early black feminists who first noted the shortcomings with stand-alone treatments of sexism—and thus the need for *intersectionality*. It may be fine for the law to treat black men as victims of racism, or white women as victims of sexism. But how should the law treat black women? Since black women are not black *or* women—but rather *black women*—to treat them as victims of sexism alone (or racism alone) risks erasing their experience at the intersection. Indeed, this is precisely what happened in the 1970s when General Motors was brought up on charges of discrimination against black women employees.[35] In its defense, General Motors claimed it did not discriminate against blacks or women—it employed black men and white women. General Motors escaped discrimination charges only because black women are neither black men nor white women. In their location at the intersection, black women thus fell through the cracks.

In their battle against oppression, modern feminists pull from these insights. They maintain that an adequate feminism must acknowledge that gender is raced and race is gendered, while appreciating also how race and gender intersect with further aspects of identity—such as religion, age, class, ethnicity, and sexuality. In other words, modern feminism acknowledges that "a real-life person is not . . . a woman on Monday, a member of the working class on Tuesday, and a woman of African descent on Wednesday."[36] Today's feminists thus respond to the charge that past feminists purported to speak for *all* women while in fact speaking only for a *particular* type of woman—namely, a white, middle-class, heterosexual, and cisgender one.[37] In so doing, modern feminism cautions against simple generalizations that would lump all women together under the heading "oppressed," including the queen, the mother on welfare, and the trans woman in prison. After all, the queen's experience of her gender is inextricably bound up with her royal status. Is she oppressed, let alone in any way that resembles the experience of the mother on welfare, or the trans woman in prison? Such examples motivate intersectional feminism's rejection of sweeping claims about the oppression of any one group such as "women," since oppression is experienced differently—or not at all—by a group's different members. Rather, in the words of feminist thinker bell hooks, the multiple aspects of identity create "a diversity of experience that determines the extent to which sexism will be an oppressive force in the lives of individual women."[38] So enlarged in scope, modern feminism is thus best defined as the intersectional movement to combat oppression.[39]

2. Lived Oppression

With this background in mind, we can begin to explore some manifestations of gender-related oppression in the West. Consider first the prevalence of the *gender binary*. The gender binary says there are only two biological sexes (male and female) that correspond to only two gender expressions (masculine and feminine) and only two gender roles (man and woman). The gender binary is also *heteronormative*—it says heterosexuality is natural and normal for men and women. Consider what people sometimes say to a pregnant friend upon discovering their fetus is sexed male. The fetus kicks and a friend exclaims, "He's going to be a football player!" Together, the friends fantasize about the child's future, and the kind of woman he may one day marry. Based only on the fetus's assigned sex, a host of assumptions about the future child's gender identity, expression, and sexual orientation are made. If this sounds like a familiar narrative, it's because it reflects the gender binary—the dominant view of gender in our culture's imaginary.

Importantly for contemporary feminists, the gender binary is also *punitive*; it deems any deviation from itself abnormal or wrong, with oppressive, violent, and even fatal consequences for those who don't conform, such as lesbian, gay, bisexual, intersex,[40] transgender, and genderqueer individuals. Those who deviate in less overt ways from the gender binary are also subject to punitive consequences, such as cisgender heterosexual women and men who defy expected norms of feminine or masculine expression.[41]

For example, feminist philosopher Kate Manne argues that misogyny is best understood as the set of negative consequences visited upon women who violate norms of "good" femininity. These norms suggest that ideal women serve the dominant men in their lives with various goods such as adoration, praise, sexual services, food, comfort, and so on.[42] Good women are "men's attentive, loving subordinates."[43] These aren't the women misogyny targets. To the contrary, women who play the part of men's attentive, loving subordinates are rewarded— not punished. Some evidence for Manne's theory is found in the disparate reactions to women versus men in positions of authority. For instance, some studies have found that students give lower evaluations to instructors they believe are women as opposed to men.[44,45] Another study found that men introduce male medical speakers by their professional titles 72% of the time in contrast to 49% of the time for female medical speakers.[46] According to Manne's theory, hostility toward women in power kicks in because people implicitly expect women to play more submissive roles.

The gender binary also pressures women to adhere to expensive, time-consuming, and stringent standards of feminine appearance. Both obedience to and rejection of these standards can harm women by hindering several elements of their well-being, including their happiness, health, self-respect, self-determination, and even employment prospects. For instance, sexualized depictions of extremely thin women pervade the media and are even liable to pop up in inapt contexts, such as advertisements for food and cars. Unsurprisingly, women internalize these constant messages, often with dire consequences; ongoing media and social pressure to be thin and sexy has been linked to the prevalence of eating disorders such as anorexia and bulimia among women.[47] Or, consider feminine beauty norms such as the expectation to prettify yourself by shaving your legs, waxing your eyebrows, dyeing your hair, manicuring your nails, or wearing makeup. Across race and class lines, women devote countless hours (not to mention funds) to cultivating their appearance because the beauty industry tells them their natural bodies are inadequate. This is time and money that could be spent on more meaningful activities. Even former Presidential candidate Hillary Clinton laments the amount of time swallowed up in devotion to her appearance: "I once calculated how many hours I spent having my hair and makeup done during the campaign. It came to about six hundred hours, or twenty-five days!"[48] If women like Clinton eschew feminine appearance norms, however, they are likely to experience shame from within as well as without. Worse yet, as Manne's theory would predict, they may find themselves in a similar position to Nichola Thorp—a woman fired by her London employer because she refused to wear heels at least two inches high.[49] An investigated sparked by Thorp revealed similar experiences by hundreds of women whose employers required them to "'dye their hair blonde,' 'wear revealing outfits' or 'constantly reapply makeup.'"[50] In addition to such pressures, common practices like catcalling or ranking women on a 10-point scale of "hotness" also cause many women to feel they are undergoing a constant evaluation of their appearance.

To appreciate some especially oppressive effects of the gender binary, let's look to those who are *gender variant,* such as transgender and genderqueer people. Transgender people's gender identity differs from that typically associated with their birth-assigned sex. This is in contrast to cisgender people—the Latin "cis" meaning "on the same side as." If you were designated male at birth and identify as a woman, you are transgender. If you were designated male at birth and identify as a man, you are cisgender. Some transgender people identify as neither men nor women but beyond the traditional gender binary; these people are genderqueer. Consider now the prevalence of transphobia—prejudice against trans people. Trans people widely report experiences of harassment and discrimination from many sources such as housing facilities, employers, health care providers, police officers, or retail store owners.[51] Such harassment and discrimination negatively impact many elements of trans people's well-being such as their happiness, health, and safety. For instance, compared to the general U.S. population, trans people experience twice the rate of poverty and three times the rate of unemployment.[52] Trans people are also overrepresented in jails, prisons, and detention centers, where they may be placed in gender-inappropriate facilities and suffer physical or sexual assault.[53] They're also a staggering nine times more likely to attempt suicide.[54]

As an intersectional approach would predict, identity factors also complicate *which* trans individuals face the most oppression. For instance, trans people of color and trans people with disabilities report even higher rates of poverty and unemployment.[55] As Peter Cava explains, trans people experience varying degrees of oppression based on their "race, class, physical ability, mental ability, sexual orientation, age, religion, nationality, immigration status, body size, and other identities. It also matters whether we are transfeminine or transmasculine, whether we live as trans part-time or full-time, whether we transition hormonally, whether we transition surgically, and whether we are read as members of our self-identified genders."[56] In other words, not all trans people face similar obstacles, and the ones they do face are significantly shaped by their particular identities.

On this note—and unsurprisingly from a feminist perspective—Julia Serano notes that most anti-trans violence and sexual assault is disproportionately committed against trans women, who are victims of both misogyny and transphobia— or *transmisogyny*.[57] According to Serano, the widespread devaluation of femininity in comparison to masculinity compounds trans women's oppression. Serano contrasts the widely divergent treatment she received once treated as a woman as opposed to a man, including being subject to catcalls, sexual comments, remarks about her weight, and condescension.[58] She also laments the media's tendency to represent trans women in hyperfeminine and hypersexual ways, which she sees as part and parcel of the media's tendency to sexualize all women.[59]

Feminist analyses are more successful when they theorize oppression through an intersectional lens. The more attentive feminists are to the differences among us, the more accurate our feminism will be; drawing attention to lacunae in our theorizing about gender thus moves feminism forward. For instance, like feminists of the past, feminists today are sometimes criticized for offering theories of oppression insufficiently attentive to race and class dynamics.[60] Others have accordingly invented terms to capture further intersectional realities. For instance, Moya Bailey coined the term *misogynoir* to describe the sexism directed toward black women in particular. The term *transmisogynoir* was also invented to capture the fact that "[b]eing trans comes at a high cost, but being black and trans can cost you your life."[61] But despite their observation of such patterns, intersectional feminists remind us not to assume a shared experience for *all* black trans women or *all* white cis men—or *all* the members of any category for that matter.

Furthermore, an intersectional approach leaves room for ambiguity about the precise *cause* of wrongful treatment. For instance, some feminists have been quick to assume the centrality of transphobia in their explanation of violence against transgender prostitutes. However, others argue that activists have wrongly assumed the presence of transphobia in cases where killers were unaware the prostitutes were trans.[62] In such cases, the more accurate explanation involves prejudice against sex workers, or as one killer put it, the belief that prostitutes are "the scum of the earth."[63] Likewise, violence against trans people of color prostitutes may or may not be racially inflected.[64] In short, we can't always know the precise source of a wrong, but we don't always need to in order to know one took place. After all, when victims live at the intersection among various forms of discrimination, it's often impossible to determine the precise cause of oppression. As Kimberlé Crenshaw famously states, "If an accident happens in an intersection, it can be caused by cars traveling from any number of directions and, sometimes, from all of them . . . But it is not always easy to reconstruct an accident: Sometimes the skid marks and the injuries simply indicate that they occurred simultaneously, frustrating efforts to determine which driver caused the harm."[65]

In sum, deviations from the gender binary have discriminatory and often oppressive consequences for those who don't conform. However, whether you are a victim of oppression also depends crucially on your particular experience as shaped by the many facets of your identity. Instead of promoting blanket generalizations, an intersectional feminist approach highlights the internal diversity within groups in an effort to describe more accurately which people tend to experience the worst hindrances to their well-being.

3. Challenges for Intersectional Feminism

Intersectionality has been dubbed "the most important theoretical contribution that women's studies . . . has made so far."[66] The explosion of intersectional theory in the humanities has been remarkable. Among the many disciplines that make use of intersectionality are history, sociology, anthropology, philosophy, ethnic studies, queer studies, feminist studies, legal studies, and the humanities more broadly.[67] The major uptake of any method, however, comes with its own debates and problems. One such problem concerns the sometime tendency to reify a sad or static understanding of identity. Consider the privilege walk—an educational exercise employed on many campuses to teach intersectionality. A privilege walk begins with all students standing in a straight line. Students take one step forward or back depending on how privileged they are with respect to a particular question. Is English your first language? If yes, step forward. Can you find Band-Aids the color of your skin at the local convenience store? If no, step back. Can you walk alone at night without fear? If yes, step forward. Can you kiss your partner in public without fear of ridicule or violence? If no, step back. At the end of a privilege walk, students are in a fixed spatial arrangement that visually represents their various degrees of privilege. The benefits of such an exercise are clear; it teaches awareness of how certain aspects of your identity make life more easily lived. It also teaches students to think critically about parts of their identity previously thought unrelated to privilege.

Yet there are drawbacks to this kind of exercise as well. One drawback is the risk that a particular interpretation of your identity becomes all-significant—to be a person of color *is* to be marginalized, and nothing more. What takes center stage here is an attachment to identity framed as *injury*—as painful deviation from the norm.[68] As Wendy Brown explains, "in its emergence as a protest against marginalization or subordination, politicized identity thus becomes attached to its own exclusion. . . . [It] makes claims for itself, only by entrenching, restating, dramatizing, and inscribing its pain in politics; it can hold out no future—for itself or others—that triumphs over this pain."[69] In other words, though there's certainly a place for it, preoccupation with a wounded notion of identity can also preclude more positive ways of understanding it.

A related drawback to such an exercise is that it risks treating identities as if they are just as fixed in space as the geographic arrangement of the students. On this model, an individual is pinned down, "boxed into its site on the culture map. Gridlock."[70] Obsessed as it is with fixing one's place in the privilege–oppression matrix, the privilege walk risks blocking the potential for more fluid forms of identification.[71] What do I foreclose about who I am or could be when I proclaim I *am* "heterosexual," "cisgender," "white"? Are we all reducible to the locations on the matrix that we declare? Are the labels we proclaim merely descriptive? Or, in our repeated avowal of them, do they not also risk prescribing a model for how we *should* live and identify? As Anthony Appiah warns, "Collective identities have a tendency . . . to 'go imperial.'"[72] He continues, "What demanding respect for people *as Blacks* or *as gays* requires is that there be some scripts that go with being an African American or having same-sex desires. There will be proper ways of being black and gay: there will be expectations to be met; demands will be made. It is at this point that someone who takes autonomy seriously will want to ask whether we have not replaced one kind of tyranny with another."[73] With such scripts in place, do we not risk attachment to a stationary understanding of what our identities are and forever must be?

Intersectional feminism is a valuable orientation through which to understand power structures and overlapping axes of identity.[74] It also improves upon past versions of feminism that were insufficiently attentive to the differences among women, as well as the many manifestations of gender discrimination and oppression. But although intersectionality provides a powerful diagnostic tool, it mustn't be used to cement a melancholic or rigid understanding of identity. We must remain committed to a vision of the future that welcomes emancipatory and fluid ways of inhabiting identity.[75]

COMPREHENSION QUESTIONS

1. What is intersectionality? How is it related to feminism?
2. What is the gender binary? What's objectionable about it?
3. Suppose that misogyny is best understood as "the set of negative consequences visited upon women who violate norms of 'good' femininity." What are some examples of misogyny, so understood?
4. What does it mean to frame an identity as an injury?
5. How can an identity limit your autonomy?

DISCUSSION QUESTIONS

1. Some people think about feminism as the claim that men and women should be *treated equally*, or *have equal rights*. How is Tuvel's approach to feminism different? Lemoine thinks about feminism as the claim that women are *oppressed*. To what degree does Tuvel accept this view?
2. Can you think of any ways in which *you* are negatively affected by the gender binary?
3. Would you call yourself a feminist? Why or why not?

Case 2

Consider this report from Susan Fowler, a former Uber employee:

I joined Uber as a site reliability engineer (SRE) back in November 2015 . . . On my first official day . . . on the team, my new manager sent me a string of messages over company chat. He was in an open relationship, he said, and his girlfriend was having an easy time finding new partners but he wasn't. He was trying to stay out of trouble at work, he said, but he couldn't help getting in trouble, because he was looking for women to have sex with. It was clear that he was trying to get me to have sex with him, and it was so clearly out of line that I immediately took screenshots of these chat messages and reported him to HR.

Uber was a pretty good-sized company at that time, and I had pretty standard expectations of how they would handle situations like this. I expected that I would report him to HR, they would handle the situation appropriately, and then life would go on—unfortunately, things played out quite a bit differently. When I reported the situation, I was told by both HR and upper management that even though this was clearly sexual harassment and he was propositioning me, it was this man's first offense, and that they wouldn't feel comfortable giving him anything other than a warning and a stern talking-to. Upper management told me that he "was a high performer" (i.e. had stellar performance reviews from his superiors) and they wouldn't feel comfortable punishing him for what was probably just an innocent mistake on his part.

I was then told that I had to make a choice: (i) I could either go and find another team and then never have to interact with this man again, or (ii) I could stay on the team, but I would have to understand that he would most likely give me a poor performance review when review time came around, and there was nothing they could do about that. I remarked that this didn't seem like much of a choice, and that I wanted to stay on the team because I had significant expertise in the exact project that the team was struggling to complete (it was genuinely in the company's best interest to have me on that team), but they told me the same thing again and again. One HR rep even explicitly told me that it wouldn't be retaliation if I received a negative review later because I had been "given an option." I tried to escalate the situation but got nowhere with either HR or with my own management chain (who continued to insist that they had given him a stern talking-to and didn't want to ruin his career over his "first offense") . . .

Over the next few months, I began to meet more women engineers in the company. As I got to know them, and heard their stories, I was surprised that some of them had stories similar to my own. Some of the women even had stories about reporting the exact same manager I had reported, and had

Case 2 (continued)

> reported inappropriate interactions with him long before I had even joined the company. It became obvious that both HR and management had been lying about this being "his first offense," and it certainly wasn't his last. Within a few months, he was reported once again for inappropriate behavior, and those who reported him were told it was still his "first offense." The situation was escalated as far up the chain as it could be escalated, and still nothing was done.*
>
> How should we think about cases like this? What's the best way to describe the particular failures of HR, the manager, and the management generally? What do you think Lemoine would say about this case?
>
> _____
>
> *https://www.susanjfowler.com/blog/2017/2/19/reflecting-on-one-very-strange-year-at-uber

REPLY TO TUVEL
PHILIPPE LEMOINE

Prof. Tuvel wrote a thoughtful essay, which I think is a very good overview of the the current state of feminism in the West or, perhaps more precisely, in the Anglo-Saxon world.[76] She defines feminism as the "intersectional movement to combat oppression." What is remarkable about this definition is that, on that conception of feminism, it doesn't have anything to do *essentially* with women. Indeed, in an endnote, Prof. Tuvel herself points that out. She explains that she doesn't define feminism as the movement to combat gender oppression specifically because not all women are oppressed to the same extent or even at all because they're women. Thus, on that definition, one could be a feminist even if one doesn't believe that women are oppressed.[77]

To be clear, this conception of feminism is not peculiar to Prof. Tuvel. I believe she is accurately describing what is now the dominant form of feminism in the Anglo-Saxon world. Feminists don't want to focus on gender at the cost of ignoring other forms of injustice having to do with race, sexual preferences, etc. The problem is that many claims they make about the harms of racism, homophobia, etc. are just as poorly supported by the evidence as the claims they make about discrimination against women. Moreover, when it conflicts with the fight against what feminists perceive as racism, homophobia, etc., their commitment to the defense of women often seems to take a backseat. For instance, even after it was revealed that more than 1,500 girls and women, most of them white, had been repeatedly abused and raped for decades by gangs of mostly Pakistani men in the town of Rotherham in the United Kingdom, feminists by and large remained silent.[78] It's clear that, for most feminists, it was more important not to fuel racist stereotypes about Pakistanis than to talk about the harm that was done to more than a thousand girls.[79] One could reply that, in theory, nothing about intersectional feminism made this outcome inevitable, but in practice, this is what happened and it's not hard to see why it could happen once you define feminism in a way that makes it about oppression in general and not discrimination against women in particular.[80] It's also not surprising, when feminists are willing to sacrifice the interests of women for the sake of what they perceive as the struggle against racism, that only a small minority of women in the United Kingdom and the United States identify as feminists.

Still, despite the fact that feminists increasingly focus on other forms of discrimination rather than on discrimination against women, they remain committed to the claim that women, but not men, are oppressed even in contemporary Western societies. As Prof. Tuvel points out in her essay, even if gender sometimes interacts with other characteristics to increase, reduce, or even negate the disadvantage of being a woman, it could still be the case that, other things being equal, being a woman makes you worse off. Indeed, according to her, this is true even in contemporary Western societies, where feminists claim that women but not men are still oppressed.

To be fair, I don't think that Prof. Tuvel says that in her essay, but only that gender norms, in particular what she calls the gender binary, are oppressive of people who don't conform to them. Strictly speaking, this could include men who don't conform to traditional norms of masculinity, and indeed, feminists sometimes say that men are also victims of gender norms. But they rarely, if ever, say that men are *oppressed* and frequently criticize people who do.[81] Not, to be clear, that I agree with that claim. As I explain in my essay, I don't think that men are oppressed, only that if you want to say that women are oppressed because they are systematically disadvantaged in a variety of ways, then you also have to say that men are oppressed.

Unfortunately, as I argued in my essay, the evidence feminists adduce does not support the claim that women but not men are oppressed. Not only do I think that one can only say that by twisting the ordinary meaning of the word "oppression," but most of the examples that feminists cite in favor of this claim are either false or not supported by the evidence and, moreover, they usually ignore the ways in which men are disadvantaged.

For instance, in her essay, Prof. Tuvel cites a study that found that male medical speakers were more likely to be introduced by their title than female ones.[82] But this study is hardly conclusive. One problem with the analysis, which even the authors noted, is that it doesn't control for potential confounders such as the age of the speakers. It could be that male speakers were more often introduced by their professional titles not because they were men, but rather because they were older and more prominent in the medical field.[83] Even if the effect is real, the study is based on presentations made in just one department within the same institution, so we can hardly generalize from it.

Prof. Tuvel also claims that most anti-trans violence is committed against transgender women, which she interprets as the consequence of the widespread "devaluation of femininity." But I wasn't able to find any evidence of this claim in the work she cited and, even if it's true, another interpretation is that transgender women are often perceived as men and, as I noted in my essay, men are far more likely to be victims of violence than women.[84] Thus, even if transgender women really are more likely to be victims of violence, it could be that, instead of stemming from the devaluation of femininity, this is because people are more prone to use violence against people they perceive as men.[85] But in order to notice this alternative explanation, one has to pay attention to the ways in which men are disadvantaged, and feminists usually don't.[86]

COMPREHENSION QUESTIONS

1. Lemoine thinks that, at least in practice, there's a tension between the modern approach to feminism and the advancement of women's interests. Why?
2. Lemoine provides alternative hypotheses to explain the results of the studies that Tuvel cites. What are they?

DISCUSSION QUESTION

1. Lemoine seems to think that feminists aren't living up to their own values: They claim to care about oppression, but don't care about the oppression of men. Feminists could respond in one of two ways: They could claim that they have special reason to focus on *some* oppressed persons, or they could deny that men are oppressed. Which way should they go?

REPLY TO LEMOINE
REBECCA TUVEL

It is my pleasure to respond to Philippe Lemoine's thoughtful contribution. I offer two rejoinders to his argument. First, although many of Lemoine's points are valid, I argue that the version of feminism he tackles is dated. Second, I argue that Lemoine overlooks relevant differences between the disadvantages faced by men and women. Such differences explain why feminists generally express more concern about the disadvantageous treatment of women versus men. That being said, I agree with Lemoine that feminism is too often ill defined in today's discourse, which can unfortunately lead to confusion about the movement's aim and scope.

To my first point, Lemoine offers a compelling critique of a particular version of feminism, but one that's dated. His main target is Marilyn Frye's account of women's oppression. As Lemoine notes, Frye's account was first published in 1983. In the nearly forty years since, however, feminism has matured and improved upon narrower feminisms of the past. Instead of advocating blanket generalizations like "all women are oppressed" or "all men are privileged," today's feminists acknowledge a more nuanced reality. In line with intersectionality, contemporary feminists ask: *Which* women are oppressed? *Which* men are privileged?

It is accordingly false to state that today's feminists wish to deny men are oppressed, as Lemoine suggests. Today's feminists grant that many men *are* indeed oppressed. For instance, Lemoine notes that men are more likely than women to be imprisoned. Feminists specify, however, that not just *any* men are more likely to be imprisoned. Rather, class, race, educational background, and other factors influence which men disproportionately end up in jail. Contemporary feminists also recognize the various harmful effects of *toxic masculinity*. Toxic masculinity refers to those masculine gender norms that teach men not to display emotion or weakness, to exercise dominance over women, be the chief breadwinners, and to be aggressive. Feminists stress that toxic masculinity harms men and women alike. Indeed, toxic masculinity is likely to blame for many harms Lemoine notes men suffer, including that men are more likely to be victims of violence, lose custody battles, or experience work-related accidents. After all, toxic masculinity encourages male-on-male violence, perpetuates the idea that men should be breadwinners not caretakers, and suggests that men who fear dangerous work are "cowardly."

All this being said, although today's feminists recognize and oppose various forms of male disadvantage, Lemoine rightly notes that feminists generally resist the idea that gender norms harm men and women equally. The reason for this is twofold. First, although the dominant gender script damages men, feminists argue it teaches a far more damaging lesson to women. For instance, the dominant gender script still teaches women they are less capable than men—more suited for the kinds of tasks that require emotional rather than intellectual labor. Indeed, consider here at least one voter who expressed concern that Hillary Clinton's period could adversely affect her ability to lead the country.[87] To the degree that such beliefs about women's capabilities keep them out of the positions of power and authority that influence the very shape of society, women are subject to a major disadvantage in comparison to men—one targets their very status as moral equals.[88] The prevalence of such beliefs also explains why it's considered insulting to tell a man he's "acting like a woman." If underlying ideology suggests women are inferior to men, men will naturally take offense to the comparison. Similar to being told one acts "like a child," being told one acts "like a woman" connotes one's act is lesser—silly or unimportant. Thus, men who prefer "chick flicks," order "girly drinks," or eat "chick food" are likely objects of mockery. To the contrary, women who like watching sports, drinking beer, playing video games, or hanging out with "the guys" are often considered "Cool Girls."[89]

In a similar vein, David Benatar notes that boys who play with dolls are more likely to be mocked than girls who play with trucks. Curiously, Benatar takes such examples as proof that the feminine gender role has undergone a more successful breakdown than the masculine gender role.[90] Yet that masculine girlhood—the *tomboy*—is more accepted than feminine boyhood proves only that activities traditionally associated with girls remain *devalued*. And the reason is that what's traditionally associated with boys is still considered superior to what's traditionally associated with girls. As Amy in the novel *Gone Girl* laments, "I waited patiently—*years*—for the pendulum to swing the other way, for men to start reading Jane Austen, learn how to knit, pretend to love cosmos, organize scrapbook parties, and make out with each other while we leer. And then we'd say, *Yeah, he's a Cool Guy*. But it never happened."[91]

A second reason feminists urge us not to overstate the similarities between disadvantages suffered by men versus women pertains to *who* in general inflicts the harms in question. That is, feminists note that men disproportionately inflict many harms unevenly suffered by women, such as rape and sexual harassment. Crucially, however, women are not disproportionately responsible for harms unevenly suffered by men, such as being more likely to die in a work-related accident or to be imprisoned. Not only do women generally lack the political power to hire or imprison men, but gender norms also don't socialize women into such behaviors. Yet masculine gender norms *do* socialize many men to treat women as violable sex objects. For this reason, feminists are especially intent to challenge masculine gender norms. Although feminine gender norms are harmful, masculine gender norms sustain especially damaging—often violent—harms endured by men and women alike.

Lemoine does remind feminists that we must exercise caution when articulating our views. If today's feminism is to be truly intersectional, blanket statements about what *all* women or *all* men or *all* members of any category suffer must go out the window. Moreover, any feminism worth its salt is neither anti-male nor unconcerned with what men go through. Still, we must also respect the feminist commitment to theorize and eradicate the worst forms of gender discrimination and oppression—such as those endured by many women across the spectrum.

COMPREHENSION QUESTIONS

1. What is toxic masculinity?
2. Why think that gender scripts are, in general, worse for women than for men?

DISCUSSION QUESTION

1. Many men don't believe that the world is structured in ways that generally favor the interests of men. How should we explain this? If the world *is* structured in ways that generally favor the interests of men, why might it be difficult for men to detect this?

FURTHER READINGS

Bettcher, Talia Mae. "Intersexuality, Transgender and Transsexuality." In *The Oxford Handbook of Feminist Theory*, edited by Lisa Disch and Mary Hawkesworth. New York: Oxford University Press, 2016.

Carastathis, Anna. *Intersectionality: Origins, Contestations, Horizons*. Lincoln: University of Nebraska Press, 2016.

Hay, Carol, ed. *Philosophy: Feminism*. Farmington Hills, MI: Gale/Cengage Learning, 2017.

Manne, Kate. *Down Girl: The Logic of Misogyny*. New York: Oxford University Press, 2018.

Mikkola, Mari. *The Wrong of Injustice: Dehumanization and Its Role in Feminist Philosophy*. New York: Oxford University Press, 2018.

Silvermint, Daniel. "Feminist Perspectives on Sexism and Oppression." In *Philosophy: Feminism*, edited by Carol Hay. Farmington Hills, MI: Gale/Cengage Learning, 2017, 37–69.

NOTES

1. https://www.vox.com/2015/4/8/8372417/feminist-gender-equality-poll.
2. http://survation.com/uk-attitudes-to-gender-in-2016-survation-for-fawcett-society/.
3. Polls in the United States show that, while a majority of people support affirmative action in favor of women and minorities, the vast majority oppose preferential treatment and quotas. See http://www.aei.org/publication/public-opinion-on-affirmative-action/on that point
4. Marilyn Frye, "Oppression," in Alison Bailey and Chris Cuomo, eds., *The Feminist Philosophy Reader* (Boston: McGraw-Hill, 2007), 41. In case you think that Frye's account of oppression is idiosyncratic, it's worth noting that, according to Google Scholar, the book in which she initially published her essay has been cited 2,273 times since 1983.
5. I'm not claiming one can't find people who qualify as feminists even though they reject this claim, but given how vague the boundaries of the feminist movement are, trying to find necessary and sufficient conditions for someone to be a feminist is probably futile anyway. Nor am I saying that one couldn't find another claim that does just as good a job of setting apart feminists from people who merely believe that men and women should enjoy the same rights, only that no other claim will do a significantly better job.
6. Frye, "Oppression," 43.
7. Marilyn Frye, "Sexism," in Marilyn Frye, *The Politics of Reality: Essays in Feminist Theory* (Trumansburg, NY: The Crossing Press, 1983), 33.
8. Indeed, in her essay on oppression I already cited, Frye explicitly denies that men are oppressed. It's true that feminists will often say that even men are harmed by patriarchal social structures, which they believe still characterize even contemporary Western societies, but they also think that men benefit from the patriarchy and, if only for that reason, would reject the claim that men and women are equally harmed by it.
9. In this essay, I'm using the word "disadvantage" in a slightly technical way, which doesn't exactly correspond to the way it's used in ordinary discourse. In that sense, a person or a group of people is disadvantaged compared to other people or groups of people as soon as they are worse off in some respects, regardless of the reason. Thus, in the sense I'm using the term, the fact that someone is disadvantaged doesn't imply that he is the victim of some injustice, although he could be. For instance, people who are poor because they don't work even though they could are disadvantaged in that sense, but arguably they are not victim of any injustice.
10. Danny Hayes and Jennifer Lawless, *Women on the Run: Gender, Media, and Political Campaigns in a Polarized Era* (New York: Cambridge University Press, 2016).
11. Even Claudia Goldin, who is frequently cited by feminists for her excellent work on the gender pay gap, explicitly said that she doesn't think outright discrimination explains much if anything: http://freakonomics.com/podcast/the-true-story-of-the-gender-pay-gap-a-new-freakonomics-radio-podcast/.
12. Francine D. Blau and Lawrence M. Kahn, "The Gender Wage Gap: Extent, Trends, and Explanations," *Journal of Economic Literature* 55, no. 3 (2017): 789–865.
13. Of course, it's also possible that unmeasured productivity favors women, in which case the residual underestimates the effect of discrimination. But as far as I know, studies that attempt to measure productivity, such as Ghazala Azmat and Rosa Ferrer, "Gender Gaps in Performance: Evidence from Young Lawyers," *Journal of Political Economy* 125, no. 5 (2017): 1306–1355, always find that doing so reduces the gap, often to the point that it's no longer statistically significant, so that's very unlikely.

14. https://theconversation.com/census-2016-women-are-still-disadvantaged-by-the-amount-of-unpaid-housework-they-do-76008.
15. Henrik Kleven, Camille Landais, and Jakob Egholt Søgaard, "Children and Gender Inequality: Evidence from Denmark," NBER Working Paper 24219, 2018, and YoonKyung Chung, Barbara Downs, Danielle H. Sandler, and Robert Sienkiewicz, "The Parental Gender Earnings Gap in the United States," Working Papers 17–68, Center for Economic Studies, U.S. Census Bureau (2017).
16. I calculated the correlation and found no statistically significant relationship between them. The data I used for the gender gap come from Eurostat and can be found here: https://ec.europa.eu/info/strategy/justice-and-fundamental-rights/discrimination/gender-equality/equal-pay/gender-pay-gap-situation-eu_en. Data on the Gender Inequality Index can be found on the UN's website: http://hdr.undp.org/en/data.
17. David Benatar, *The Second Sexism* (Malden, MA: Wiley-Blackwell, 2012).
18. Stephanie Bontrager, Kelle Barrick, and Elizabeth Stupi, "Gender and Sentencing: A Meta-Analysis of Contemporary Research," *Journal of Gender, Race & Justice* 16, no. 2 (2013): 349–372.
19. Sonja B. Starr, "Estimating Gender Disparities in Federal Criminal Cases," *American Law and Economics Review* 17, no. 1 (2015): 127–159.
20. M. Marit Rehavi and Sonja B. Starr, "Racial Disparity in Federal Criminal Sentences," *Journal of Political Economy* 122, no. 6 (2014): 1320–1354.
21. Again, I'm only talking about the situation in the West, for in many other places the claim that women but not men are oppressed is a lot more plausible. But feminists claim that women are oppressed even in the West. In fact, they seem to be far less concerned about the situation of women in the rest of the world, where it would seem that feminism is far more needed.
22. Sarah Kliff, "Only 18 percent of Americans consider themselves feminists," *Vox*, April 8, 2015, https://www.vox.com/2015/4/8/8372417/feminist-gender-equality-poll.
23. According to a 2016 Washington Post survey, approximately 16 percent of women under 35 and one third of women over 35 think American feminism is "outdated." Cai, Weiyi and Scott Clement. "What Americans think about feminism today." *The Washington Post*, January 27, 2016. https://www.washingtonpost.com/graphics/national/feminism-project/poll/?noredirect=on.
24. For instance, in his critique of feminism, David Benatar takes issue not with global but Western feminism. As he writes, "It may well be the case that females are no longer systematically disempowered, subordinated or oppressed in developed countries." David Benatar, *The Second Sexism* (Malden: Wiley-Blackwell, 2012), p. 37. Post-colonial and transnational feminists have also critiqued Western feminism, albeit from a different angle.
25. See, for instance, Chandra Talpade Mohanty, "Under Western Eyes: Feminist Scholarship and Colonial Discourses," *boundary 2*, 12, no. 3 (1984); Gayatri Chakravorty Spivak, "Can the Subaltern Speak?" in *Marxism and the Interpretation of Culture,* ed. Gary Nelson and Lawrence Grossberg (London: Macmillan, 1988), 280–287; Narayan, Uma. *Dislocating Cultures: Identities, Traditions, and Third-World Feminism* (New York: Routledge, 1997).
26. Ben Mathis-Lilley, "Trump Was Recorded in 2005 Bragging About Grabbing Women 'by the Pussy,' *Slate*, October 7, 2016. http://www.slate.com/blogs/the_slatest/2016/10/07/donald_trump_2005_tape_i_grab_women_by_the_pussy.html.
27. Mathis-Lilley, "Trump."

28. On her "consent-objectification account," Patricia Marino defines wrongful instrumental use as follows: "A uses B as a genuine tool of A's purposes, really as a thing,
when A fails to consider B's decisions, when A coerces B, or deceives B or simply
forces B to do what A wants." For Marino, objectification itself is not wrong, but only
non-consensual objectification. Patricia Marino, "The Ethics of Sexual Objectification:
Autonomy and Consent," *Inquiry* 51, no. 4 (July 2008): 351.

29. The aim of intimate terrorism is control of one's partner. Michael P. Johnson,
"Langhinrichsen-Rolling's Confirmation of the Feminist Analysis of Intimate Partner
Violence: Comment on 'Controversies Involving Gender and Intimate Partner Violence
in the United States'," *Sex Roles* 62 (2010): 213.

30. Shannan Catalano, Erica Smith, Howard Snyder, and Michael Rand, "Female Victims
of Violence," *Bureau of Justice Statistics Selected Findings* (2009), https://www.bjs.gov
/index.cfm?ty=pbdetail&iid=2020.

31. Marilyn Frye, *The Politics of Reality.* (New York: The Crossing Press, 1983): 1.

32. Daniel Silvermint, "Feminist Perspectives on Sexism and Oppression," in *Philosophy:
Feminism, Macmillan Interdisciplinary Handbooks,* edited by Carol Hay. (Gale: Cengage
Learning, 2017), 37–69, 63.

33. It is worth noting that Silvermint distinguishes his account from group-based accounts
like that of Marilyn Frye, which maintain that oppression involves one group being
subordinated for the benefit of another (56). Against this, Silvermint argues that his
"effects-based" account determines whether oppression exists solely on the basis of effects on individual well-being. Unlike the group-based account, on Silvermint's view,
victims of oppression need not be "members of subordinated groups, whose subordination serves the interests of those who belong to dominant groups" (54). Silvermint,
"Feminist Perspectives," 63.

34. I borrow this example from Mari Mikkola, *The Wrong of Injustice: Dehumanization and
its Role in Feminist Philosophy* (New York: Oxford University Press, 2018).

35. Feminist legal scholar Kimberlé Crenshaw coined the term "intersectionality" in her
seminal piece "Demarginalizing the Intersection of Race and Sex: A Black Feminist
Critique of Antidiscrimination Doctrine, Feminist Theory and Antiracist Politics."
In it, she describes the case of five black women employees who lost their jobs in a
GM seniority-based layoff. The plaintiffs argued that since GM had not hired any
black women prior to 1964, GM's seniority system perpetuated discrimination
against black women employees. In response, the court stated that the plaintiffs
"failed to cite any decisions which have stated that Black women are a special class
to be protected from discrimination. . . . this lawsuit must be examined to see if
it states a cause of action for race discrimination, sex discrimination, or alternatively either, but not a combination of both." Kimberlé Crenshaw, "Demarginalizing
the Intersection of Race and Sex: A Black Feminist Critique of Antidiscrimination
Doctrine, Feminist Theory and Antiracist Politics," *University of Chicago Legal
Forum* 1 (1989): 141.

36. Kathryn Russell, "Feminist Dialectics and Marxist Theory," *Radical Philosophy Review*
10, no. 1 (2007): 33–54.

37. See below for a definition of the term "cisgender."

38. bell hooks, *Feminist Theory: From Margin to Center* (Boston: South End Press, 1984),
5. Also quoted in Silvermint, "Feminist Perspectives," 57. Such observations have led
some feminists to offer accounts more faithful to how oppression is lived on the ground
(see, for instance, the work of feminists Mari Mikkola and Daniel Silvermint).

39. I define feminism as the movement against oppression—and not gender oppression specifically—since we should not presume that gender difference always or best explains the oppression suffered by members of marginalized genders.

40. Intersex people are born with a sexual anatomy or sex characteristics that don't align neatly with typical definitions of either male or female embodiment.

41. The terms "transgender," "cisgender," and "genderqueer" are defined below.

42. Kate Manne, *Down Girl: The Logic of Misogyny* (New York: Oxford University Press, 2018), 110.

43. Manne, *Down Girl,* 49.

44. See Lillian MacNell, Adam Driscoll and Andrea N. Hunt, "What's in a Name: Exposing Gender Bias in Student Ratings of Teaching," *Journal of Collective Bargaining in the Academy* 0 (2015); Anne Boring, Kellie Ottoboni, and Philip B. Stark. "Student Evaluations of Teaching (Mostly) Do Not Measure Teaching Effectiveness." *ScienceOpen Research* (2016), https://www.scienceopen.com/document?vid=818d8ec0-5908-47d8-86b4-5dc38f04b23e.

45. Another study found that women professors are rated more highly when they conform to feminine gender expectations such as being caring and helpful. It also found that students use gender-specific derogatory language to describe women professors they dislike, such as "bitch," "bitchy," "bitch toward male students," "witch" and "feminazi." This may suggest that students are disappointed in their women professors not simply as professors but as *women.* Joey Sprague, and Kelley Massoni, "Student Evaluations and Gendered Expectations: What We Can't Count Can Hurt Us," *Sex Roles* 53, o. 11/12 (2005): 789.

46. Julia A. Files, Anita P. Mayer, Marcia G. Ko, Patricia Friedrich, Marjorie Jenkins, Michael J Bryan, Suneela Vegunta et al., "Speaker Introductions at Internal Medicine Grand Rounds: Forms of Address Reveal Gender Bias," *Journal of Women's Health* 26, no. 5 (2017).

47. Bonnie Moradi, Danielle Dirks, and Alicia V. Matteson, "Roles of Sexual Objectification Experiences and Internalization of Standards of Beauty in Eating Disorder Symptomatology: A Test and Extension of Objectification Theory," *Journal of Counseling Psychology* 52, no. 3 (2005): 420–428.

48. Hillary Rodham Clinton, *What Happened* (New York: Simon & Schuster, 2017), 87.

49. Dan Bilefsky, "Sent Home for Not Wearing Heels, She Ignited a British Rebellion," *New York Times,* January 25, 2017, https://www.nytimes.com/2017/01/25/world/europe/high-heels-british-inquiry-dress-codes-women.html.

50. Bilefsky, "Sent Home."

51. S. E. James, J. L. Herman, S. Rankin, M. Keisling, L. Mottet, and M. Anafi, *The Report of the 2015 U.S. Transgender Survey* (Washington, DC: National Center for Transgender Equality, 2016), p. 14–16, https://transequality.org/sites/default/files/docs/usts/USTS-Full-Report-Dec17.pdf

52. James et al., *The Report,* 5.

53. James et al., *The Report,* 15.

54. James et al., *The Report,* 5.

55. James et al., *The Report,* 5.

56. Peter Cava, "Activism, Politics, and Organizing," in Erickson-Schroth, *Trans Bodies, Trans Selves,* 574.

57. Julia Serano, *Excluded: Making Feminism and Queer Movements More Inclusive.* (Berkeley: Seal Press, 2013), 29.

58. Julia Serano, *Whipping Girl: A Transsexual Woman on Sexism and The Scapegoat of Femininity.* (Emeryville: Seal Press, 2007), 222.

59. Serano, *Whipping Girl*, 45.

60. Elías Cosenza Krell, "Is Transmisogyny Killing Trans Women of Color?" *Transgender Studies Quarterly* 4, no. 2 (2017): 235.

61. Angelica Ross, "Call Me Caitlyn. Sincerely, Ms. Ross," *Huffington Post*, September 4, 2015, https://www.huffingtonpost.com/angelica-ross/i-am-not-cait_b_8039492.html. Cited in Krell, "Transmisogyny," 238.

62. Vivian Namaste, "An Interview with Mirha-Soleil Ross," in *Sex Change, Social Change: Reflections on Identity, Institutions, and Imperialism* (Toronto: Women's Press, 2005) 124.

63. Namaste, "Interview," 125.

64. Vivian Namaste, "Undoing Theory: The 'Transgender' Question and the Epistemic Violence of Anglo-American Feminst Theory," *Hypatia* 24, no. 3 (2009): 20.

65. Crenshaw, "Demarginalizing the Intersection of Race and Sex," 149.

66. Leslie McCall, "The Complexity of Intersectionality," *Signs* 30, no. 3 (2005): 1771.

67. Sumi Cho, Kimberlé Williams Crenshaw, and Leslie McCall, "Toward a Field of Intersectionality Studies: Theory, Applications and Praxis," *Signs* 38, no. 4 (2013): 787.

68. Wendy Brown, *States of Injury: Power and Freedom in Late Modernity* (Princeton, NJ: Princeton University Press, 1995).

69. Brown, *States of Injury*, 73–74.

70. Brian Massumi, *Parables for the Virtual: Movement, Affect, Sensation* (Durham, NC: Duke University Press, 2002), 3. Pulling from Massumi's work, Jasbir Puar offers an influential critique of intersectionality's tendency to cement a static notion of identity in "'I Would Rather Be a Cyborg than a Goddess': Becoming-Intersectional in Assemblage Theory," *philoSOPHIA* 3, no. 1 (2012): 49–66, and *Terrorist Assemblages: Homonationalism in Queer* (Durham, NC: Duke University Press, 2007).

71. However, this isn't to endorse a rejection of identity-based politics; self-identities are deeply important to many people. Rather, it is to warn against holding our identities to inflexible scripts.

72. Anthony Appiah, "Race, Culture, and Identity: Misunderstood Connections," *The Tanner Lectures on Human Values* (1994), 134.

73. Appiah, "Race," p. 129.

74. For those who think intersectionality is decidedly not about identity but only power structures, I recommend the work of Jennifer C. Nash, "Feminist Originalism: Intersectionality and the Politics of Reading," *Feminist Theory* 17, no. 1 (12016).

75. Many thanks to Elizabeth Edenberg, Bob Fischer, Rhiannon Graybill, Alison Suen, and Chloë Taylor for thoughtful feedback on this paper.

76. In some parts of the West, such as France, intersectional feminism has not yet achieved the prominence it has in the United Kingdom and, even more so, in the United States. But intersectional feminism is growing even in those countries, and I think it won't be long before it becomes the dominant form of feminism over there.

77. Of course, that is not what Prof. Tuvel thinks, but it's worth noting that it's not ruled out by her definition of feminism.

78. See BBC News, "Rotherham Child Abuse Scandal: 1,400 Children Exploited, Report Finds," August 26, 2014, https://www.bbc.co.uk/news/uk-england-south-yorkshire -28939089, and Josh Hollyday, "Number of Child Sexual Abuse Victims in Rotherham Raised to 1,510," *The Guardian*, February 20, 2018, https://www.theguardian.com /uk-news/2018/feb/20/rotherham-sexual-abuse-victims-rises-to-1510-operation -stovewood, for more details about the scandal.

79. Thus, a search for "Rotherham" performed on September 9, 2018, on some of the most popular feminist websites returned either no results or just one article, which sometimes left out the fact that most of the perpetrators were of Pakistani heritage. Jezebel, arguably the most popular feminist website, apparently published only one article on the subject. Everyday Feminism, a prominent intersectional feminism website, did not publish a single one. Feministing, a popular feminist blog, has only a couple of lines about the scandal in a weekly roundup of news, but does not mention the ethnicity of the perpetrators, even though it's largely agreed that it played a role on both the nature of the abuse and the fact that it was allowed to go on for so long. Feminist Philosophers, which is arguably the most popular feminist philosophy website and was created by a British philosopher, published just one article about it. The F-Word, a U.K.-based feminist blog, mentions the scandal in passing in a handful of articles, but published only one article devoted to it.

80. And lest you think that the reaction, or lack thereof, of feminists to what happened in Rotherham was just an isolated episode, there are many other examples where they deliberately avoided talking about a sexual abuse scandal for similar reasons. For instance, when I did a search for "Telford," the name of another British town where more than 1,000 girls may have been abused for decades, again mostly by men of Pakistani heritage, on the same websites as before, I obtained the same results—or rather the same absence of results. See Jamie Grierson, "Up to 1,000 Children May Have Been Victims in Worst UK Abuse Ring," March 12, 2018, https://www.theguardian.com/society/2018/mar/12/1000-children-victims-worst-uk-abuse-ring-telford, for more details about what happened in Telford.

81. At least they don't say that men are oppressed *because they are men*. Of course, feminists have no problem with the view that some men are oppressed because they are gay, black, etc., but this is a completely different claim. Note also that, while as far as I can tell nothing in Prof. Tuvel's essay rules out the possibility that *men* are also oppressed, none of the alleged examples of oppression she discusses are about men.

82. Files et al., "Speaker Introductions," 413–419.

83. Indeed, according to the Association of American Medical Colleges, women made up 38% of the faculty in academic medicine but only 22% of full professors in 2015 (https://www.aamc.org/download/481182/data/2015table3.pdf), so this hypothesis is hardly implausible. Nor is this the only reason to suspect the effect might not be real. For instance, instead of comparing how often male speakers were introduced by their professional titles with how often female speakers were, the authors analyzed separately the cases where the introducers was male and those where they were female. It's only when the introducers were male that a statistically significant effect was found. Of course, it could be that it's because men but not women are biased against women in the medical profession, but it could also be that the effect is spurious and was created by splitting the sample and multiplying the comparisons. Until this result is replicated, it's impossible to know which it is.

84. Indeed, not only was I not able to find any evidence for the claim in the passage Prof. Tuvel cited, but I wasn't even able to find the claim itself.

85. It's also plausible that transgender women, who are still biologically male in many respects (especially before undergoing hormone therapy), more often engage in the kind of behavior that puts one at risk of violence.

86. I would like to thank Prof. Fischer for inviting me to contribute to this volume and providing several valuable comments, as well as Prof. Tuvel, whose thoughtful essay helped me clarify my own thoughts about feminism. I should note that, while I focused

on the points of disagreement in the interest of stimulating debate (which is the goal of this volume), there are several points on which I agree with her. In particular, I think the danger she warns about in the last section of her essay is very real, though I'm afraid most feminists will continue to ignore it.

87. Of course, this individual also failed to understand that Clinton is postmenopausal. Gina Mei, "This Letter to the Editor Argues Hillary Clinton Can't Be President Because of 'That Time of Month,'" *Cosmopolitan*, October 17, 2016, https://www.cosmopolitan .com/politics/a6447296/letter-to-the-editor-hillary-clinton-period-stigma/.

88. Kenneth Clatterbaugh, "Benatar's Alleged Second Sexism." *Social Theory and Practice* 29, no. 2 (2003): 214.

89. In her novel *Gone Girl* (New York: Crown, 2012), Gillian Flynn describes the "Cool Girl" as follows: "Being the Cool Girl means I am a hot, brilliant, funny woman who adores football, poker, dirty jokes, and burping, who plays video games, drinks cheap beer, loves threesomes and anal sex, and jams hot dogs and hamburgers into her mouth like she's hosting the world's biggest culinary gang bang while somehow maintaining a size 2, because Cool Girls are above all hot. Hot and understanding. Cool Girls never get angry; they only smile in a chagrined, loving manner and let their men do whatever they want. *Go ahead, shit on me, I don't mind, I'm the Cool Girl*" (p. 222).

90. Benatar, *Second Sexism*, 615.

91. Flynn, *Gone Girl*, 223.

٭❍

CHAPTER 16

Removing Historical Monuments

A CASE FOR REMOVING CONFEDERATE MONUMENTS
TRAVIS TIMMERMAN

1. Introduction

On August 21, 2017, white supremacist protestors marched in Charlottesville, Virginia, purportedly to protest the city's planned removal of a statue of Confederate general Robert E. Lee. On that day, white supremacist James Fields drove into a crowd of counter-protesters, severely injuring many and killing one, Heather Heyer. As of this writing, the Confederate statues in Charlottesville haven't been removed, although they were covered with tarps for about six months.[1] In the wake of the violent protests and public outcry, many other cities began removing Confederate statues from public display.[2]

This, of course, raises the philosophical question of whether Confederate monuments *ought* to be removed. I'll focus on the ethical question of whether a certain group, viz. the relevant government officials and members of the public who together can remove the Confederate monuments, are *morally obligated* to (of their own volition) remove them. I'll not be discussing the closely related question of whether it ought to be *legally obligatory* to remove Confederate monuments. Even if people are morally obligated to remove them, it doesn't follow that it should be illegal to preserve the monuments.[3] Figuring out the correct answer to related questions, however, likely necessitates first answering the moral question on which I focus.

In this essay, I argue that people have a moral obligation to remove most, if not all, public Confederate monuments because of the unavoidable harm they inflict on undeserving persons. This essay is structured as follows. In the next section, I provide some relevant historical context. I then make my harm-based argument for the removal of Confederate monuments. After that, I consider and rebut five objections.

2. A Brief History of Confederate Monuments

Without having first looked into their history, one may naturally assume that, while perhaps not created for entirely innocuous reasons, Confederate monuments at least weren't created for explicitly racist reasons. Unfortunately, that does not seem to be the case. There are a minimum of 1,728 publicly sponsored Confederate symbols in the United States.[4] Most of them were created long after the Civil War ended to, at least in part, further subjugate African Americans.[5]

Of course, plenty of Confederate monuments were created in the immediate aftermath of the Civil War. During the "Reconciliation" period between the North and the South, white Southerners used the Confederacy to promote white cultural unity.[6] Historian Fitzhugh Brundage argues that the "pursuit of white cultural unity through the Confederate commemoration went hand-in-hand with the promotion of white supremacy."[7] An immediate consequence of promoting *white* cultural unity meant excluding, "othering," non-whites.[8] Moreover, as Brundage notes, some of the early Confederate monuments were further inextricably linked to white supremacy because white supremacists were chosen to speak at their dedication.[9] So, a non-trivial number of Confederate monuments created in the immediate aftermath of the Civil War are unquestionably racist.[10]

What is particularly surprising (and depressing), however, is that the majority of Confederate monuments appear to have been created long after the Civil War for distinct, explicitly racist reasons. The majority of Confederate monuments were erected in one of two periods: the portion of the Jim Crow era between the early 1900s and 1920s and the civil rights movement in the 1950s and 1960s.[11] During the late nineteenth century and early twentieth century, Jim Crow voting laws were passed to disenfranchise African American voters. A number of advocates in Southern towns erected Confederate statues because the Confederate mythologies seemingly helped justify the Jim Crow laws.[12] Historian Jane Dailey argued that erecting public Confederate monuments near government buildings (e.g., in front of courthouses) was a "power play" aimed at intimidating African Americans.[13]

Interestingly, statues were often the monument of choice because technological innovations allowed companies to mass produce statues quite cheaply. Original bronze statues cost thousands of dollars, which was cost prohibitive for small towns with limited financial resources. Yet, mass-produced zinc statues, made by the company Monumental Bronze, sold for a mere $450. Some popular models (e.g., the "Silent Sentinel" soldier) were even sold as both Northern and Southern soldiers.[14] Many of these statues were purchased by private citizens, most notably the United Daughters of the Confederacy (UDC), to be displayed on public land and preserved with public funds.[15]

Although the majority of public Confederate monuments were created before 1950, there was a noticeable spike in Confederate memorials during the 1950s. More than forty-five Confederate monuments were dedicated or rededicated "between the U.S. Supreme Court's school desegregation decision in 1954 and the assassination of Dr. Martin Luther King Jr. in 1968."[16] These actions were examples of the same power play tactics that were used during the Jim Crow era. The rise in Confederate monuments at this time was, at least in part, the product of a backlash among segregationists.[17] So, the majority of Confederate monuments, which were created long after the Civil War had ended, are also unquestionably racist.

Even this brief overview should suffice to demonstrate that typical Confederate monuments were created by racist people with racist motivations. These facts are no secret, and this is necessary to keep in mind when considering the nature of the harm that the continued existence of public Confederate monuments causes to many.

3. A Harm-Based Argument for Removing Confederate Monuments

In this section, I'll make a straightforward harm-based argument for the removal of Confederate monuments. My harm-based argument is not exclusive to those who know the relevant history. I'll explain why Confederate monuments can also wrongfully harm those completely unaware of the racist reasons most Confederate monuments were created. In short, Confederate monuments unavoidably harm people who don't deserve to be harmed and, as such, we should remove them unless there's as strong or stronger countervailing reason to preserve them. The first part of my argument can be formalized as follows.

(1) If the existence of a monument M unavoidably harms an undeserving group, then there's strong moral reason to end the existence of M.

(2) Public Confederate monuments unavoidably harm an undeserving group, which include *at least* those who suffer[18] as a result of (I) knowing the racist motivation behind the existence of most Confederate monuments or as a result of (II) having the horrors of the Civil War and the racist history of the United States made salient when they see public Confederate monuments.

(3) Therefore, there's strong moral reason to remove public Confederate monuments.

This argument is valid, which means that if both premises (1) and (2) are true, then the conclusion (3) must also be true. Thus, if one wants to reject the conclusion, then as a matter of logic, one must also reject at least one of the premises. Notice that the conclusion only states that there's *strong moral reason* to remove the monuments, stopping short of stating that there's a *moral obligation* to remove the monuments. This is because, theoretically, there could be countervailing moral reason to preserve the monuments that's stronger than the moral reason to take them down. For instance, if an evil genius were going to destroy the entire world unless we preserve the monuments, then we would be obligated to preserve them. In the next section, I consider the most viable candidates for such countervailing reasons and argue that they don't outweigh the moral reason to remove the monuments. Before I do that, however, it's necessary to formalize the remainder of my argument.

(4) If there's strong moral reason to remove public Confederate monuments, then absent equally strong or stronger countervailing reasons to preserve them, people are morally obligated to (of their own volition) remove public Confederate monuments.

(5) There are no countervailing reasons to preserve public Confederate monuments that are equally strong or stronger than the moral reasons to remove them.

(6) Therefore, people are morally obligated to (of their own volition) remove public Confederate monuments.

Propositions (3)–(6) are also a valid argument. So, (1)–(2) entail (3) and (3)–(5) entail (6). This means that if one wishes to reject my conclusion (6), they'll have to reject premise(s) (1), (2), (4), or (5). I take (1) to be uncontroversial and obviously true. It can be derived from an exceedingly plausible moral axiom that if x unavoidably harms morally considerable beings who don't deserve to be harmed, then there's strong moral reason to prevent x.[19]

Premise (2) is also clearly true and, I believe, at least the first disjunct (I) is rather uncontroversial. People have been opposed to Confederate monuments as long as they've existed. The motivations behind the creation of Confederate monuments were transparent to those alive at the time of their creation. Countless people who lived through the civil rights era are alive today, seeing the same Confederate monuments created to further the oppression of African Americans. The millions of people who've read the relevant news stories and history texts know the history behind the Confederate monuments. Knowledge of this history factors into the manner in which people[20] suffer as a result of seeing the monuments, or even simply knowing that they are still standing.[21] One can find ample testimony from those protesting the Confederate monuments explaining how they find the continued existence of the monuments offensive and harmful.[22]

The second disjunct (II) of premise (2) should be rather uncontroversial. However, it appears to often be overlooked in the debate. Consider someone who is unaware of the racist motivations for creating (most) Confederate monuments and who has the typical cursory knowledge of the Civil War. Suppose, hypothetically, that the Confederate monument they happen to see was created for entirely innocuous reasons. Does *this* Confederate monument still unavoidably harm them? Yes; at least, it will for some people. Seeing the monument can non-voluntarily make salient America's racist past and the horrors of one of the darkest periods in American history. Having these facts made salient can clearly cause one to suffer *even if* we grant that the monument itself is not racist and was not created for racist reasons.

To further understand the nature of this harm, consider another historical example. In the mid-1970s, transgressing social norms for shock value was part of the punk ethos. Toward this end, a number of prominent punk musicians (e.g., Johnny Rotten and Sid Vicious of the Sex Pistols and Siouxsie of Siouxsie and the Banshees) wore swastika armbands or clothing on which swastikas were prominently displayed. This trend may have been started by the Sex Pistols manager Malcolm McLaren, who was himself Jewish, and who sold clothes with swastikas on them.[23] These particular punks weren't wearing swastikas because they were prejudiced, yet I contend that it was nevertheless morally wrong for them to do so. Those who saw punks donning swastikas in public (many of whom were survivors of World War II) were harmed because seeing them unavoidably made salient the horrors of anti-Semitism, World War II, and the Holocaust. This, in turn, caused them to suffer. Crucially, it could cause them to suffer *even if* they knew that the reasons behind these punks' actions weren't prejudice. The same is true in the analogous case of Confederate monuments.

As already noted, premises (1)–(2) entail (3). If one accepts (1)–(3), this leaves premises (4) or (5) for opponents to reject. Premise (4) should be as uncontroversial as (1) and can just be derived from a moral axiom that holds that if you have strong moral reason[24] to x, then absent equally strong or stronger reason to not x, you're morally obligated to x. This only leaves premise (5), which is perhaps the most contentious premise of my argument. But critics will need to identify reasons to preserve the monuments that supposedly outweigh the harm-based moral reasons to take them down. In the remaining space, I'll consider what I take to be the most popular and plausible reasons that can be used to argue against premise (5).

4. Objections

Historical Significance and Aesthetic Value

Those wishing to preserve Confederate monuments may argue that they are great works of art that have a great deal of aesthetic value. They may also claim that the monuments are historically significant and that removing them will result in a loss of historical value. If these considerations warrant rejecting premise (5), preventing the loss of the historical and aesthetic value would have to be more important than preventing the harm the Confederate monuments cause.

I deny that removing these monuments need result in the loss of any historical or aesthetic value. Plenty of philosophers have argued that works of art (including monuments) can be intrinsically valuable for historical or aesthetic reasons.[25] Yet, none would think that there's much aesthetic or historical value in the mass-produced Confederate monuments created for racist reasons. Moreover, any aesthetic value there is would be easily replaceable with other works of art.[26] This needn't be true of all Confederate monuments, of course. For instance, some may think that the Robert E. Lee statue in Charlottesville has great aesthetic and historical value. Granting this, if only for the sake of argument, I am quite confident that preserving the collective aesthetic and historical value is less important than preventing the undeserved suffering caused by the statue. To see why, consider the following. Plausibly, the *collective* amount of harm the Lee statue caused amounts to a single lifetime worth of suffering or, at least, many years' worth of suffering. Now, imagine that you find yourself in the following situation:

Steve or a Statue: A comet is falling from the sky toward an innocent person, Steve. If you do nothing, it will injure Steve so badly that he will suffer for decades before dying. If you push Steve out of the way, the comet will strike the Robert E. Lee statue and permanently destroy it.[27]

What should you do? It seems clear to me that you should save Steve instead of the statue. If this is right, then we should believe that whatever reason there is to preserve Confederate monuments for their (supposed) historical or aesthetic value, that reason is outweighed by the reasons we have to prevent the undeserved, unavoidable suffering such monuments cause.

Even if one believes there is more reason to preserve the historical or aesthetic value than there is to prevent people from suffering undeservedly, this preservationist argument fails. The reason why is that it's possible to remove the Confederate monuments without the loss of any historical or aesthetic value. This could be done, as some have argued, by placing the monuments in a museum where they can be put in the proper historical context.[28] Because monuments are reverential in nature, placing them in a museum in the proper historical context may cause them to cease to be *monuments* and, consequently, so harmful.[29] But it would not cause them to lose any of their aesthetic or historical value.

Removing Statues Erases History

A closely related response given by preservationists is that removing Confederate monuments erases history, and the consequences of erasing history can be bad. As the old saying goes, "Those who cannot remember the past are condemned to repeat it." Former Secretary of State Condoleezza Rice made this sort of argument when asked about whether Confederate statues should be preserved. She replied, "Nobody is alive today who remembers the Civil War, but by looking at [a Confederate monument] you can trigger what it meant and what it was like. You don't need to honor the purposes of people [who] were on the other side of history, but you better be able to remind people."[30]

I am extremely skeptical that Confederate monuments themselves impart much in the way of historical knowledge or lend insight into what it was like to exist during the Civil War. Any information one gains from looking at a statue or reading a plaque on a monument could be found by going on Wikipedia.[31] More importantly, however, even granting (for the sake of argument) that there would be a non-trivial loss of historical knowledge if the monuments are removed, it doesn't follow that there need be a net decrease in historical knowledge. Whatever knowledge would be lost by removing the monuments could be compensated for by the creation of additional educational resources[32] that impart the same relevant knowledge, but are not harmful in the way reverential Confederate monuments are. Finally, even if removing the monuments led to some unavoidable loss of historical knowledge, preventing the loss of that value is just less important than preventing the amount of suffering Confederate monuments cause undeserving individuals to experience.

Selective Honor

Some preservationists have argued that we can continue to preserve Confederate monuments to honor the noble accomplishments of the people they valorize without also honoring the morally heinous aspects of the people in question.[33] This claim is not obviously implausible. A statue of Thomas Jefferson, for instance, may be thought to honor him for such accomplishments as being the primary author of the Declaration of Independence without thereby, in any way, honoring him for being a vicious slaveholder.

This argument won't help the preservationist, however. Granting that it's *possible* for Confederate monuments to only honor the honorable, it does not follow that it's morally permissible to preserve them in the hopes that will happen. First, this is unlikely to be what would actually happen. As the Charlottesville protest helped demonstrate, there is a substantial number of white nationalists (a.k.a., neo-Nazis) who wish to preserve and honor morally atrocious aspects of the Confederacy. Second, would any good that comes from honoring whatever is good about the Confederacy outweigh the harm the monument inflicts on undeserving people? I think the answer is quite clearly "no" for reasons illustrated by my *Steve or a Statue* case.[34] Few would think it morally permissible to create a statue of Bill Cosby to honor him for his contribution to comedy even under the assumption that people would only be honoring Cosby for his honorable accomplishments. A good explanation for *why* this is wrong is because it's simply more important to prevent the pain that a Cosby statue would cause survivors of sexual abuse than it is to benefit people desiring to honor Cosby. The same is true with respect to Confederate monuments, and so the mere fact that it's possible to selectively honor the Confederacy does not suffice to demonstrate that premise (5) is false.

Harm-Based Reasons to Preserve Confederate Monuments

If we have strong moral reason to remove Confederate monuments because of the harm that preserving them causes, don't we also have strong moral reason to preserve the monuments because of the harm removing them would cause? After all, there's no shortage of preservationists who claim they would suffer if the monuments were removed.[35]

Much, though certainly not all, of the harm from which preservationists would suffer if Confederate monuments were removed crucially depends on them holding certain irrational beliefs or contemptible attitudes. For instance, the white nationalists chanting "Blood and Soil" in Charlottesville might lament the Robert E. Lee statue being taken down because they would view that as a hindrance to their goal of preserving the "superior" Aryan race. Were they to rid themselves of their racism, they would no longer suffer so much from the removal of the Lee statue. Assuming these white nationalists have the rational capacity to rid themselves of their irrational beliefs and contemptible attitudes, any suffering they endure that depends on them holding such attitudes and beliefs matters less than the suffering endured by people whose suffering is predicated upon rational beliefs and fitting attitudes, such as those who suffer from the preservation of Confederate monuments.[36]

Moreover, it's quite likely that the suffering that would result from the continued existence of Confederate monuments would be greater than the suffering that would result from removing them. This is largely because the continued existence of Confederate monuments would continue to cause people to suffer because of certain facts that the monuments make salient. However, were the monuments removed, their being removed would not similarly make harmful facts salient. Perhaps seeing the space where the monuments once stood would make the fact that the monuments were removed salient to some people, and having that fact made salient might cause some preservationists to suffer. But it seems highly unlikely that this would occur with much frequency. Moreover, the extent to which it would happen presumably would diminish with each generation.[37] After all, future people who grow up without having ever seen a Confederate monument wouldn't suddenly think about the absence of Confederate monuments when they're in the areas where the monuments once stood.[38] On the other hand, the continued existence of Confederate monuments would continue to make salient the horrors of the Civil War and the racist history of the United States.[39]

Slippery Slope Arguments

Finally, one may object that my argument leads to an absurd conclusion, and as such, it's reasonable to infer that there's something wrong with my argument even if one cannot identify which premise(s) is/are false. The *reductio ad absurdum* runs as follows. "If we have to remove Confederate monuments because they honor people who acted in ways that were gravely morally wrong, then wouldn't we get the absurd conclusion that we have to remove almost all monuments?" George Washington and Thomas Jefferson both owned slaves, yet few object to monuments of them. The young Mahatma Gandhi notoriously expressed racist attitudes toward black people and was an unrepentant misogynist, yet few object to monuments of him.[40] Almost every contemporary person who has been honored with a monument is someone who routinely consumed factory-farmed meat, a fact that future generations will almost certainly regard as morally monstrous. Yet no one raises this as an objection to honoring anyone with reverential monuments.

If we remove all statues of people who've committed grave moral wrongs, wouldn't we have to remove almost all statues? The answer to this question is probably "Yes." Is that absurd? Not necessarily. But, more importantly, my argument does not entail that we have to remove the statues of everyone who has committed grave moral wrongs for a few reasons. First, it's worth noting that there's a potentially morally relevant difference between people like Thomas Jefferson or Mahatma Gandhi and people like Robert E. Lee or Nathan Bedford Forrest. While all of them committed grave moral wrongs, the former group also accomplished a great deal of good and were, with respect to some issues, morally prescient. The same cannot truthfully be said of the Confederate generals.

Second, statues of people in the former camp don't cause the same amount of unavoidable harm as people in the latter camp. The motivations behind the creation of Gandhi or Jefferson monuments were not racist. They were not erected to further the oppression of anyone. Moreover, the facts that such statues make salient are generally not harmful because they concern the good that such people have done. When most people think of Gandhi, for instance, they think of his non-violent struggle for Indian independence.[41] They don't think of (or generally even know) about his racism or sexism, but they may know about his noble fight for civil rights in South Africa or his fight for the emancipation of women and public declarations of the equality of the sexes. Since these monuments are not harmful in the way, or to the degree, that Confederate monuments are, it's plausible that the moral reasons to preserve them currently outweigh the moral reason to remove them. Of course, times change and cultures continue to evolve. It's quite conceivable that, in the future, a majority of people will oppose monuments of Washington, Jefferson, Gandhi, and the like because of these people's gravely morally wrong actions. Their moral shortcomings may even become the facts that are salient when people see such monuments, and so these monuments may come to harm as many people as Confederate monuments currently do. If that time comes, and the harm-based moral reasons to remove these statues outweigh the moral reasons to keep them up, then I grant that people at that time would be morally obligated to remove them. This is not an absurd conclusion, though. On the contrary, it seems to be exactly what we should do in that situation.[42]

COMPREHENSION QUESTIONS

1. What's the takeaway from Timmerman's brief history of Confederate monuments?
2. Why think that Confederate monuments harm some people?
3. What does it mean to say that Confederate monuments have aesthetic value?
4. How does Timmerman respond to the "Don't erase history" objection?
5. What is a "slippery slope" objection in general? What's the specific slippery slope objection that Timmerman considers? How does he reply?

DISCUSSION QUESTIONS

1. Timmerman's argument is based on the claim that Confederate statues cause harm, not offense. What's the difference? Does it matter? Why or why not?
2. Imagine some distant future when people are deeply horrified by the way that we currently treat animals in factory farms. When they look at statues of our recent politicians who did nothing to end factory farming—George W. Bush, Barack Obama, Donald Trump—they are deeply upset by them. On Timmerman's view, it could work out that the statues of Bush, Obama, and Trump ought to be taken down; it would be a moral mistake to leave them up. Does this seem like the right result to you? Why or why not?

Case 1

One of the difficult questions is: What's the way forward after we recognize the divisions in a society over various monuments? Consider what one city has done:

> Vancouver, where I live, offers an unlikely example of what that approach might look like. Today the city is known for its easygoing charm and expensive real estate. 150 years ago, and for millennia before that, the area was the hunting and fishing grounds of the Musqueam, Squamish and Tsleil-Waututh peoples. Their settlements dotted the shores of the Burrard inlet and Fraser and Capilano rivers. The arrival of Europeans and founding of Vancouver precipitated their almost total erasure over the next 150 years.
>
> In 2014, Vancouver declared itself a "city of reconciliation," formally recognising its occupation of the unceded territories and embarking with local First Nations governments on a long-term plan to decolonise and indigenise the city. To begin with, some streets, parks, schools and landmarks will be renamed, including Siwash Rock, a well-known sea stack near Stanley Park whose name (derived from the French word for "savage") is seen as an offensive slur against indigenous people.
>
> The new names will be specific to the group whose territory the landmark or sign is on—for example, Sir William Macdonald elementary school, which sits on Musqueam territory, recently became Xpey' elementary school, meaning "cedar" in the local hәṅ̓q̓әmiṅ̓әṁ (Halkomelem) language. The University of British Columbia, which also sits on Musqueam territory, has replaced all of the street signs on campus with bilingual English–hәṅ̓q̓әmiṅ̓әṁ ones. The sites of historical villages will be reinscribed with signs and interpretive displays, and other artistic interventions. "The point is to make sure Musqueam, Squamish and Tsleil-Waututh are reflected and visible everywhere in Vancouver," Ginger Gosnell-Myers, the city's aboriginal relations manager, tells me.
>
> Renaming and monumentalisation are only the most obvious aspect of the process. "Colonial structures permeate every part of the city, from the place names to the architecture and the use of space, even the way city departments are organised," Gosnell-Myers says. "So for reconciliation to actually work, the plan needed to be comprehensive, too." Inspired by a similar exercise in New Zealand, the partners have together created a set of indigenous design principles that will inform the design of all future public space in Vancouver—including sightlines and building materials, the ways structures relate to the natural environment, and how they are used. There will be greater emphasis on communal, intergenerational public spaces, for example, because in the local indigenous cultures, all buildings are meant to be used by all people.*

Is this a model to follow generally? What sort of principles seem to guide the decisions that Vancouver is making? What would it look like if implemented in the United States? What are some of the limitations of this approach? Is there any reason to think that it isn't radical enough?

---

*https://www.theguardian.com/cities/2018/sep/26/statue-wars-what-should-we-do-with
-troublesome-monuments.

ASHES OF OUR FATHERS: RACIST
MONUMENTS AND THE TRIBAL RIGHT
DAN DEMETRIOU

1. Introduction

At least for now, a statue of Paul Kruger still stands in Pretoria, South Africa's Church Square, though it's surrounded by protective fencing and concrete barriers. Kruger embodied the Afrikaner experience: As a child, he was a Voortrekker who fought Zulus for control of the Transvaal; as a young man, he led Boer forces against British colonialists; later in life, he served as president of the South African Republic. Over the past few years, the Church Square monument honoring "Oom" (Uncle) Paul has been repeatedly defaced and threatened with destruction, through legal and illegal means, by black nationalists (chiefly Economic Freedom Fighters [EFF] representatives and supporters) and anti-colonialist #RhodesMustFall activists. "There is a national mandate to all the EFF branches to remove all the apartheid statues and symbols," one EFF councilman has said. "One day people are going to wake up and find the statue not being there."[43] Counter-protests, including one by an Afrikaner singer who chained herself to the monument, have made international news.[44] Plans are underway to add items to the square that celebrate the freedom struggle of non-white South Africans, but debate still rages over whether to remove Kruger's statue completely.[45]

Meanwhile, in the United States, a Charlottesville, Virginia circuit court judge has just ordered that tarps covering a monument of iconic Confederate general Robert E. Lee be removed.[46] Lee's loyalty to his people (Virginians), brilliant generalship, and quiet dignity inspire millions of devotees today, despite the fact that Lee himself wished not to be memorialized for the sake of reunification.[47] In February 2017, the Charlottesville city council voted to have the statue in Emancipation Park—until recently, Lee Park—taken down, but the process has been halted by legal challenges, as, like many places in the South, state laws protect Confederate monuments.[48] In response to the city council's vote, the 26-foot-tall equestrian statue was the scene of a "Unite the Right" rally that descended on Emancipation Park to protest the statue's removal with white nationalist and anti-Semitic chants. The right-wing protestors were met by crowds of "antifascist" counter-protesters, and state police shut down the rally. In the chaos that ensued, a right-wing activist plowed his car into a group of counter-protesters, resulting in the death of one person.[49]

These are just two of many cases of monuments jeopardized or already dismantled because of their alleged racist or (racially motivated) colonialist significance. Elsewhere, philosopher of political aesthetics Ajume Wingo and I have sought to catalogue the principal sorts of preservationist and removalist arguments one hears in the "racist monument" debate, and there are broadly leftist and rightist rationales for both positions.[50] As I cannot discuss here even all the rightist considerations relevant to this issue,[51] I'll focus only on what I see as the fundamental one, which is social cohesion, both across time and across the relevant races or ethnicities. Specifically, in this chapter I sketch a rightist approach to monumentary policy in a diverse polity beleaguered by old ethnic grievances. I begin by noting the importance of tribalism, memorialization, and social trust, and then provide policy guidance based on these concerns to the racist monument debate as it stands in the English-speaking world today.

A word on terminology: I use the phrase "racist monument" to refer to any monument seriously controversial because of its alleged racist significance. This definition entails that the above statues to Kruger, Lee, and hundreds more are indisputably "racist monuments" for the purposes of this chapter. This nomenclature is necessary shorthand because phrases such as "Confederate statues" or "colonialist monuments" are too narrow, as I want to discuss any monument thought problematic for reasons of racism, while "controversial monuments" and the like are too broad, as I wish to exclude monuments contentious because of other political or religious associations, such as the Buddhas of Bamiyan dynamited by the Taliban in 2001. I don't necessarily concede with this term that the monuments in question are "in fact" racist—indeed, there may be no sense to saying a monument is "in fact" racist beyond its seeming racist to enough people. Nor should this terminology prejudice the issue for the removalist position, for the mere fact that a monument is thought by many to be racist simply doesn't entail that it ought to be removed.

2. Tribal Assumptions

As this volume reveals, there are many conceptions of what it means to be on the political "right" or "conservative." Since the moral perspective I appeal to is older than Christianity and more properly considered "global" than "Western," some of my fellow travelers will disagree with parts of what I'm about to say.[52] Be that as it may, anyone espousing the following principles will be considered on the political right today, especially if they believe these principles apply to whites or white ethnicities as well as for other races or ethnicities.

The first principle I'll forward is that *humans are a tribal species, and political structures failing to accommodate this fact are doomed to fail.* Unlike tigers and sea turtles, humans don't go through life alone.[53] We are a highly social species that seeks the comfort and protection of clans and tribes. Tribes gobble up loners. So as long as there are significant numbers of tribalists in the world (and there always will be), even (largely hypothetical) "individualists" and "cosmopolitans" must rely on tribal loyalty for their security, property, freedoms, and dignity, since these good things are secured only by a willingness of tribemates to sacrifice for and defend the territories individualists and cosmopolitans flit between.

If you don't understand what "tribe" is, think of your family and proven friends. Think, in short, of who "has your back": who would leap to your defense if you were in trouble before even asking if you were in the wrong, who would find space for you in their homes if you had nowhere else to go, who feels an obligation to feed you if you were hungry. Tribal affiliation isn't *that* strong, usually (except in war, this level of sacrifice is typically reserved for family, clan, or gang), but nonetheless, tribemates will do these things to some degree—especially if they are thrown together in a strange land, as the behavior of expats will testify.

If you're a citizen or denizen of a high-trust Western country, you should know that the people who built that society worked hard to create institutions reliable enough for tribalism to be unnecessary below the level of the state itself. Their success at this was so spectacular that all this talk of "tribalism" may seem unsettlingly primitive. To this, all I can say here is that complacency about tribalism is as foolish as thinking that lights must turn on when you flip a switch, or that water must flow from the faucet when you turn the knob. A sense of tribal affiliation is the psychological infrastructure of any sustainable free society: If it goes, authoritarianism becomes necessary to maintain law and order.[54]

Second, *memorialization is essential to maintaining tribal identity and cohesion over time.* Humans evolved language and culture to transmit adaptive memes (units of information), and not just genes, to the next generation.[55] Populations pass on their cultures in large part by memorialization, which includes not only monuments but also *inter alia* museums (e.g., Cape Town's District 6 museum), historical sites (e.g., as the Gettysburg battlefield), temporary installations (e.g., New York City's Tribute in Light, representing the fallen Twin Towers), or one-off events (e.g., Nelson Mandela's state funeral). Memorials bend our artistic and dramatic creativity to the tasks not of making money or entertaining, but of expressing our values, remembering our tragedies, celebrating our victories, honoring our heroes, and affirming a shared identity, and thus memorialization is increasingly acknowledged as a human right.[56] If we were to use a domestic analogy, memorials wouldn't be mere decorations or microwave dinners, but family portraits, heirlooms, trophy displays, household altars, and Christmas dinners.

Is tribalism illiberal? Certainly, the liberalism committed to the primacy of the individual or hostile to borders and nationalism will be anti-tribalist. Yet liberal thinkers formerly appreciated that individual rights are secure only within a tribal shell. For instance, John Stuart Mill himself seemed concerned about tribal cohesion even for free societies (he didn't endorse liberalism for cultures still mired in "barbarism").[57] In fact, Mill was explicit in cautioning against combining various "nations" into one polity precisely because sub-state tribal loyalties either tear multicultural states apart or force their governments to become authoritarian in their struggle to maintain order: "Free institutions are next to impossible in a country made up of different nationalities. Among a people without fellow-feeling, especially if they read and speak different languages, the united public opinion, necessary to the working of representative government, cannot exist."[58]

By "nation," Mill means

> [a population] united among themselves by common sympathies which don't exist between them and any others—which make them co-operate with each other more willingly than with other people, desire to be under the same government, and desire that it should be government by themselves or a portion of themselves exclusively. . . . [Nationality is sometimes] the effect of identity of race and descent. Community of language, and community of religion, greatly contribute to it. Geographical limits are one of its causes. But the strongest of

all is identity of political antecedents; the possession of a national history, and consequent community of recollections; collective pride and humiliation, pleasure and regret, connected with the same incidents in the past.[59]

In other words, a "nation" for Mill is a "people," or a big tribe. Mill realized that a functional polity requires citizens who are more willing to sacrifice for, and cooperate with, each other than they would with mere strangers. In contemporary sociological terms, what Mill was worried about is social cohesion. And just as Mill hypothesized, sociological research suggests that diversity decreases social trust, an important element in social cohesion.[60] These declines can be counteracted only, it's hoped by researchers, if the diverse peoples constituting the polity buy into a new, overarching cultural identity—a new tribe.[61]

The conservativism of this essay, then, is a traditionalism that acknowledges tribalism as an obvious fact and sees piety toward one's ancestors, traditions, and holy places as not only a prima facie moral obligation for individuals but an important civic virtue. Tribal folkways are so typical across the world that they are better categorized as the human psychological default than an ideology.[62] For instance, these lines, written by a Victorian poet about an ancient Roman hero who fought for his people's city and holy places, are something any traditional Yoruba, Jew, Sikh, or Maori would accept as a matter of course:

Then out spake brave Horatius,
The Captain of the Gate:
To every man upon this earth
Death cometh soon or late.
And how can man die better
Than facing fearful odds,
For the ashes of his fathers,
And the temples of his gods?[63]

Noble thoughts and feelings to be sure, but also utterly *normal*. It's the contemporary Western liberal ethos that discourages tribal identification that is unusual— or, as social psychologists have recently euphemized it, "WEIRD" (Western, Educated, Industrialized, Rich, and Democratic).[64]

Rightists (and, apparently, even liberals of the past) are not opposed to tribes mapping onto religious or ethnic lines. But even if the polity in question is for whatever reason committed to diversity on these dimensions, the solution isn't to eradicate tribal sentiment, but to replace the tribe of religion or ethnicity with some form of civic or populist nationalism.

Most "tribal rightists" who think along these lines will be skeptical about the sustainability of any free yet significantly multicultural state.[65] Their skepticism is increasingly justified. At the time of this writing, moderates are converting to identitarian politics in North America and Western Europe: Rightist politics appear to be more and more popular among whites,[66] while new, ethnic/religious parties (e.g., the Turkish DENK in the Netherlands or Partij Islam in Belgium) emerge from nominally leftist parties, such as Greens.[67] Violence on campuses over "hate speech" by invited speakers has flared in recent years.[68] Canada, the United Kingdom, France, Sweden, and Germany are enforcing hate speech laws ever more rigorously in an effort to stifle rising anti-Islamic and anti-immigrant sentiment.[69] The South African government's current plans to seize white farms may prove to be the tipping point for ethnic cleansing there.[70] So there are grounds for tribal rightist skepticism about the sustainability of seriously multicultural states.

But it doesn't follow that skeptics about the feasibility of maintaining or rescuing something are a bad source of wisdom in a crisis. Indeed, skeptics may understand the dangers best, and therefore honest and well-meaning skeptics might provide valuable insight on how to avoid them. In particular, tribal rightists, not liberals, leftists, or (least of all) cosmopolitans, are likely to have the best instincts on matters of building social cohesion in ethnically divided polities.[71] That instinct tells us that forcibly destroying old tribal identities to encourage a new multiethnic tribal identity is self-defeating and unacceptably authoritarian. Widening tribal affiliation may be encouraged by the state, yes, but the process has to be far subtler than the measures called for by even many academic removalists.[72] As best I can tell, a tribal rightist committed to the long-term stability and freedom of a multicultural state with old ethnic grievances, when considering the monument controversy as it stands today in places such as the United States or South Africa, will urge an honorable compromise on monument policy that (1) gradually narrows the gap between peoples in the heritage landscape, (2) conserves all but the most offensive of the least beloved racist monuments, (3) avoids recrimination (i.e., "keeps it positive") and eschews ideological commentary in new monuments or revisions to old ones, (4) as much as politically feasible, recognizes only the offense of willing tribemates, and (5) responds to aesthetic and other "irrational" offenses more than to "objective" historical or philosophical critiques.

3. Honorable Compromises

On the assumptions above, the multicultural state isn't worth saving unless there's going to be a real sense of tribal fellow-feeling at the other end of reform. So although a tribe isn't as tightly knit as a family, it may behoove us to revisit the domestic analogy.

Imagine an interracial couple deciding how to decorate their home. In an interracial household, we would expect mementos and pictures from both sides of the family. If, for some reason, the black spouse's family didn't take many pictures or lost all their heirlooms in a fire, we would expect the white spouse to find ways to represent the black spouse's family in other ways, and to be alert to opportunities to put up new pictures of them. Likewise, although a high-trust relationship doesn't keep strict track of the numbers—we don't need to limit monuments to African Americans to exactly 13%, and we don't need exactly 10% of monuments in South Africa to be of whites—the monumentary gap between whites and blacks is impossible to ignore in the places under discussion and should gradually be closed. It would be undignified to close that gap too quickly, by erecting monuments honoring sub-par figures or unremarkable events just to even things out. But gradually, as historical research into ignored or preliterate cultures improves, and as new outstanding citizens arise, the formerly underrepresented peoples should be suitably showcased in the national household.

What about existing, or even future, racist monuments? Just as every married person knows it's possible to place on the same mantle pictures of in-laws who abused each other, we can tolerate monuments to figures who were enemies. A healthy, racially diverse citizenry will *want* their fellow citizens to feel free to honor their ancestors and draw pride in their heritage. This means that white South Africans or white Americans can appreciate that their black countrymen may not personally advocate for radical political solutions today, but still wish to honor black nationalists or separatists who struggled on behalf of their people. And black Americans or black South Africans can recognize that a white fellow citizen may not condone all that her ancestors did, but still take pride in their sacrifices or heroism. The many Native American monuments in the United States, and to a much greater degree many democratic South African monuments, demonstrate that it's perfectly possible to memorialize culture heroes for their sacrifices for their peoples, even if they were at war with the ancestors of fellow citizens and completely opposed to the creation of the modern states that now memorialize them. For example, the statues of African royal captives recently installed at their former prison, Cape Town's Castle of Good Hope, harmoniously contribute to a more complete picture of the peoples whose history shaped the Castle and South Africa itself.[73]

Nonetheless, some racist monuments, whose designs are highly ideological, leave little room for interpretation, deliberately provoke, and carry little meaning to anyone but hardened ethno-tribalists uninterested in a shared future, are good candidates for removal, *only if* they are *actually* offensive to a significant number of citizens, especially if those citizens have given costly signals of interest in a multiethnic tribal future. For example, the 2017 removal of the New Orleans' Battle of Liberty Place (BLP) monument was consistent with a tribal rightist approach.[74] But if, quite contrary to the facts, the BLP monument were not controversial, even it should have remained absent some good reason to remove it, and mere (ignored) ideological inconsistency with our legal and political aims today is not one such reason. For instance, if the people of New Orleans overwhelmingly interpreted it as a living symbol of a shameful past and/or a sort of trophy of a defeated regime, then it would be as strange to remove the BLP monument as to remove a public museum's installation about segregated drinking fountains.

For in matters of trust-building, we must remember that offense often isn't rational.[75] Insofar as we are concerned about being good tribemates, the historical context of a monument's installation or the momentousness of the historical figure or event's actual racism (e.g., that this general killed thousands for an apartheid state, that this statue was erected to bolster the Cult of the Lost Cause, etc.) is less important than the offense it actually causes fellow citizens of good will for whatever odd reason. Returning to our interracial household, a picture of a slave-owning Confederate ancestor may be perfectly acceptable, whereas a meaningless racist tchotchke, such as a minstrel show poster picked up at a garage sale, may not. The black partner knows that unlike the poster, the picture is meaningful to the white partner, and this is what matters, even though slave owning is far worse than minstrelsy. Likewise, a gracious or beloved monument to a Confederate general may be much less offensive to well-meaning black citizens than one to a figure thought to be much less racist: Washington, DC's Lincoln Park statue of Lincoln, portraying the president emancipating a kneeling black slave with arm outstretched in way thought demeaning to many, may be illustrative in this regard.[76]

That said, even conscientious tribemates shouldn't be morally concerned about everyone's offense, but only the offense of those who signal they are genuinely interested in being tribemates with the rest of us. For example, activist and commentator Angela Rye opined in one interview that "George Washington was a slaveowner. . . . [W]hether we think he was protecting freedom or not, he wasn't protecting my freedom. My ancestors weren't deemed human beings to him. So to me, I don't care if it's a George Washington statue, or a Thomas Jefferson statue, or a Robert E. Lee statue, they all need to come down."[77] Whatever Rye's reflective judgments might be, this is the language of someone uninterested in a tribal future with not only Southern whites who feel special attachment to Confederate figures, but Americans. Nor, in my view, should the conscientious tribal rightist be concerned about the offense of citizens, such as white liberals, offended on behalf of other peoples. Nor should the offense of moralistic iconoclasts, who relish scrubbing heritage landscapes and traditions, weigh upon our conscience. Tribal continuity is impossible without memorializing, and memorializing is impossible if we are constantly razing our monuments because of the moral inadequacies of our ancestors: their racism today, their sexism after that, their crimes against non-believers next, their transphobia after that. A heritage policy that dwells on historical injustices serves only to wedge apart peoples otherwise interested in a close-knit future.

Although not all offense matters morally, all offense does matter politically. And that means that the more ideological the monument, the more likely our descendants will find it morally repugnant. Here, again, it's helpful to contrast Charlottesville's Lee statue and New Orleans' BLP monument: The Lee statue was designed, and successfully so, to honor Southern valor while ignoring the question of who they fought against and what they fought for. The BLP monument, on the other hand, was explicit about the value of resisting Northern "usurpers" and called for "white supremacy." This distinction is instructive not only for monuments already around, but monuments being contemplated. Monuments can avoid being ideological without being anodyne if their message is about us, *these peoples*, not *these ideas*.[78] This means we need monuments that deftly leave unsaid who vanquished or was vanquished, who triumphed or was humiliated, whenever those facts touch upon the honor of the ancestors of those we would have as tribemates.

To sum up, heterogeneous societies interested in overcoming their divisions must adopt memorial policies that promote social cohesion and do not betray tribal trust. In the case of monuments, this principle would suggest policies, some of which I have articulated, that would say not only which future monuments should go up, but also which present monuments should come down. I argue that although some racist monuments fail this standard, many do not. Furthermore, because it is possible and usually beneficial to honor your ancestors even if they opposed the heterogeneous tribe you are part of, monuments to such figures do not *ipso facto* betray tribal trust, although they may for various—often aesthetic—reasons.

4. Conclusion

Any marriage worth having allows each spouse to maintain their family honor and their ties to the family they left behind. And as the interracial marriage case shows, people can navigate landscapes with memorials to people who were racists or fought for ethnocentric causes.[79] Granted, interracial relations in places such as the United States or South Africa are nothing like a high-trust marriage. But then again, the five policy guidelines on monuments suggested above hardly paint a rosy picture: If anything, they seem more apt for a marriage where the spouses are trying their best to avoid divorce over racial animosity, and in fact, these guidelines echo the heritage policies of Mandela-era South Africa.[80] Nonetheless, to repair or build trust, each spouse must gradually make themselves more and more vulnerable to the memorial expressions of the other, assuming each concession is reciprocated and not abused. Analogously, aggressive assaults on a people's monuments and, thus, the continuity of their ethnic tribe are bound to decrease their faith in the proposed multiethnic upgrade. Cowed peoples may be compliant, but they are not trustworthy, and they typically become so degraded as to be a burden even as subjects. Of course, alienating and intimidating the relevant populations is not a problem for those who deep down don't wish to be co-tribalists with anyone who would support maintaining a monument to Robert E. Lee or "Oom" Kruger. Casting down the monuments of your enemies is a time-honored practice of demoralization and establishing supremacy, and removalists may be gambling that the Horatiuses who rise up to defend the ashes of their fathers will be put down easily enough. They may be correct, but we should be under no illusions that the polity on the other side of such an endeavor would be both multicultural and free.[81]

COMPREHENSION QUESTIONS

1. What does Demetriou mean by "social cohesion"?
2. Why doesn't Demetriou want to talk about "Confederate monuments" specifically?
3. What follows from our being a tribal species?
4. Why is memorialization important?
5. What's the point of the marriage analogy?

DISCUSSION QUESTIONS

1. Demetriou asks us to imagine an interracial couple whose ancestors hated each other, and analogizes this to the current situation in multiracial states with a slave-holding, colonialist, or apartheid past. But isn't the actual history more akin to one family abusing the other? And since couples can divorce, does Demetriou's analogy only work if racial groups can "divorce" from each other?

2. Demetriou tests the claims against "racist" monuments against a "tribal" standard. What do you think he means by this? Do you agree that this is the right standard? More generally, do you think tribal loyalty is a civic virtue or a civic (moral?) vice?

Case 2

In 2019, a committee in the Texas House of Representatives proposed a bill according to which:

> the state, all cities in Texas and all counties in Texas would be banned from removing any monument or memorial that honors "an event or person of historic significance," if that monument or memorial was put in place more than 40 years ago. Younger monuments and memorials would be a bit more vulnerable. Changing anything on one between 20 and 40 years old would require a two-thirds vote of the House and Senate for tributes on state property, and local election to get rid of or modify any monument or memorial on municipal grounds.
>
> State Rep. James White told the *Austin American-Statesman* that it's his goal to bring order to the ongoing debate over public monuments in Texas. "I believe all Texans take their history very seriously," White said. "Just because you have the majority doesn't mean you always should do things the way you want to do it. It doesn't mean the minority voices don't have at least some ability to weigh in on the issue in a meaningful way."
>
> During debate of the watered-down version of the bill in the Senate, Houston's Borris Miles and Dallas' Royce West, the upper chamber's only black members, blasted the bill for promoting racism and hate. "The bill that you're carrying on the Senate floor today is disgraceful," Miles said. "I ask that you consider some of the pain and heartache that we have to go through—myself and some of the brothers and sisters on this floor of color—and what we've had to go through as it relates to our Texas history."*

What do you think about the bill that White supports? In what respects is it an attempt to find a compromise between different constituencies? How well does this approach fit with the way that Demetriou thinks we should approach the problem of Confederate monuments?

---

*https://www.dallasobserver.com/news/texas-religious-refusal-bill-gets-a-second-chance-11663919.

REPLY TO DEMETRIOU
TRAVIS TIMMERMAN

In his essay, Demetriou makes a novel tribalist case for the preservation of racist monuments. He and I arrived at radically different conclusions in our respective essays, and we may be further apart on this issue than most "opponents" in this textbook. For this reason, I want to first emphasize some points where our positions overlap.

First, while I find tribalism (as Demetriou conceives of it) objectionable, I don't necessarily deny that humans are a tribal species or that political structures should, in some ways, accommodate this fact. However, we no doubt disagree about how best to take these facts into account, and we may also disagree about the precise way(s) in which humans are, and are not, tribal species.

Second, Demetriou suggests a number of "honorable compromises" that the "tribal rightist" should endorse, including "narrowing the gap between peoples in the heritage landscape" by creating additional monuments for people in historically underrepresented groups. We agree this should be done.

Third, Demetriou and I agree that it can be permissible to, in certain conditions, selectively honor people who have performed grossly morally wrong acts in the past. Again, denying this would prohibit honoring pretty much anyone. Still, Demetriou and I certainly disagree about the exact conditions under which this is permissible.

Finally, Demetriou concedes that we should remove monuments "whose designs are highly ideological, leave little room for interpretation, deliberatively provoke, and carry little meaning to anyone but hardened ethno-tribalists" when such monuments are offensive to a significant number of citizens. He and I agree that these criteria apply to many monuments, including numerous Confederate monuments, and we agree that such monuments should be removed.

Demetriou rejects premises (1) and (5) of my argument. Our disagreement over (1) concerns a technical debate about the nature of reasons, one that I believe is ultimately inconsequential to the Confederate monument debate. Our fundamental disagreement concerns (5). More specifically, Demetriou believes that preserving most Confederate monuments is necessary for maintaining tribal identity and cohesion over time, which is supposedly more important than preventing the harm such monuments cause. Much of our disagreement can be traced to two points of contention:

(A) I deny that removing Confederate monuments need result in the loss of tribal identity and social cohesion.

(B) Even supposing I'm wrong about (A), I believe that it is more important to prevent the harm Confederate monuments would cause than the loss of tribal identity and social cohesion supposedly at stake.

With respect to (A), Demetriou claims that "memorialization is essential to maintaining tribal identity and cohesion over time." He also grants that memorialization can take many forms, including museums, historical sites, temporary installations, one-off events, and the like. As I explained in my chapter, it's quite possible to take down public Confederate monuments yet preserve them in private museums or historical sites. Doing so could remove the objectionable features of the monuments (e.g., their reverential nature, a lack of proper historical context, their state-funded preservation, and the racist reasons behind their current location). Yet, preserving Confederate monuments in museums or historical sites can allow for memorialization while removing these objectionable elements. So, it seems possible to grant Demetriou's claim about the importance of memorialization yet still hold that we should remove public Confederate monuments.

There's another issue in the background here. Even assuming that it would be socially disastrous if tribes were always prevented from engaging in memorialization, it doesn't follow that it would be socially disastrous to prevent certain particular instances, or types, of memorialization. This is true in the same way it would be socially disastrous to completely deny freedom of speech to all citizens, but *not* socially disastrous to prevent the Westboro Baptist Church from protesting at a fallen soldier's funeral. Generally, memorialization *may* be essential to maintaining tribal identity and cohesion over time, but preserving public Confederate monuments needn't be.

Now consider (B). Suppose, with Demetriou, that removing most Confederate monuments would result in some loss of tribal identity or social cohesion. Nevertheless, preventing the suffering such monuments cause is, all else equal, more important than preventing the suffering their removal would cause when that suffering is predicated on irrational beliefs or contemptable attitudes. Removing Confederate monuments for harm-based reasons shouldn't be construed as a threat to social cohesion. That fact that some people would (irrationally) interpret it that way doesn't preclude them from having an obligation to remove the Confederate monuments, assuming that they're part of the relevant group. Of course, the diminished social cohesion *could* be bad for everyone, including the marginalized groups that would be affected by this supposed change. But, for reasons given in my essay, I believe that removing Confederate monuments would minimize undeserved suffering.

Thus far, I have responded to the "consequentialist" component of Demetriou's argument against (5). In reply, he might fall back on the claim that people have a moral right to this sort of memorialization independent of the consequences of such memorialization. He may appeal to his marriage analogy to capture commonsense intuitions on this point. I am personally skeptical that there is a general right to memorialize. But even granting that there is one, I see no reason to believe that this right extends to cases where memorialization is harmful in the way public Confederate monuments are harmful. To motivate this claim, consider Demetriou's own marriage analogy. Even supposing that one has a right to memorialize their slave-owning ancestor, it doesn't follow that one has a right to memorialize their slave-owning ancestor *in ways that harm their partner* (e.g., by placing their picture on a mantle). This isn't to suggest that one must destroy the picture of the ancestor, only that one should find a non-harmful way to memorialize this person. Ditto for Confederate monuments.

534 ETHICS, LEFT AND RIGHT

Questions about the ethics of Confederate monuments are complex. The chapters in this text do not cover everything there is to be written on the subject. Hopefully, however, they can serve as one possible entry point into this important, difficult, debate.

COMPREHENSION QUESTIONS

1. What do Timmerman and Demetriou agree about?
2. Given the choice between (a) preventing harm from Confederate monuments and (b) sacrificing social cohesion, Timmerman goes for the former. Why?
3. Timmerman claims that there's an ethical constraint on memorializing your ancestors. What is it?

DISCUSSION QUESTION

1. Timmerman thinks that we can have our cake and eat it too: We can get memorialization without having Confederate monuments erected in prominent public places. Do you think he's right about this? Or do we have to make a choice between honoring certain historical figures and minimizing harms to current people?

REPLY TO TIMMERMAN
DAN DEMETRIOU

Travis Timmerman presents an admirably clear argument for removing Confederate monuments. In this rebuttal, I deny its first and fifth premises.

Timmerman sees his first premise,

(1) If the existence of a monument *M* unavoidably harms an undeserving group, then there's strong moral reason to end the existence of *M*,

as an application of a more general, "exceedingly plausible" principle:

If *x* unavoidably harms morally considerable beings who don't deserve to be harmed, then there's strong moral reason to prevent *x*.

Timmerman sees causing undeserved harm as a strong, although defeasible, reason not to do something. Counterexamples to this principle are abundant, however. Suppose you're basking in the glory that comes with being the starting point guard, but a young Stephen Curry transfers to your school and tries out for your team. Curry's displacing you as point guard makes your life worse, and you didn't deserve that harm, but obviously, he has no moral reason not to do so. Or imagine some classmates were distressed by your political opinions—this fact alone wouldn't give you a strong reason to abandon your views or censor yourself. In these counterexamples, the innocent parties have been harmed, but not wronged, since they had no moral claim against the harming parties not to be harmed by them in these ways.

The point holds with monuments. Surely some Chinese people feel bad when considering Mongolia's massive, recently erected monument to Genghis Khan, whose dynasty killed about half of all Chinese (60 million).[82] But hurt Chinese feelings wouldn't justify removing the Khan monument, for Chinese offense has no moral claim on Mongolia's heritage landscape. The University of Ghana recently removed a statue of (the racist?) Mahatma Gandhi, which may have insulted some Indians, but that hypothetical offense would be irrelevant to Ghana's monumentary rights, too.[83] So whether we're talking about erecting or removing monuments, a bare appeal to the harm of racial offense is insufficient.

In my essay, I supplied a "tribal rightist" standard for racist monuments generally. Unlike the Mongolian/Chinese and Ghanaian/Indian cases, black and Southern white Americans should (unless preferring a civic divorce) seriously attempt to forge a new people, analogous to how an interracial married couple from racist families should (unless they prefer to divorce) try to forge a new family. So it's not racism or racist offense as such that makes a Confederate monument problematic, but its potential faithlessness to American blacks, or at least the subset of American blacks invested in being compatriots with Southern whites.

Are Confederate monuments faithless in this way? Remove race from the equation for a moment. At least 647,000 Northerners were killed or injured in the Civil War.[84] Do, or did, Confederate monuments wrong the descendants or communities of Northern whites by betraying tribal good faith? Maybe. If the monument in question specifically gloried in Union casualties (imagine a statue of Lee sitting atop a pile of Yankee skulls), or if the monument was used only to reinvigorate the Confederacy, then the said monument would be a good candidate for Northern complaint: The aforementioned BLP monument, which referred to reconstructionist forces as "usurpers," is a plausible real-life example. Many Confederate monuments passed this test, however, and managed to honor Confederate figures and soldiers without antagonizing Northerners harmed by the war. Reciprocally, Northerners generally countenanced Confederate monuments because they were seen as beneficial for rehabilitating Southern pride, which they saw as essential to healing a divided nation.

By the same rationale, it is consistent with being a good compatriot to black Americans to preserve Confederate monuments as long as the monuments in question do not demand an anti-black interpretation (as the Battle of Libert Place monument once did, by explicitly calling for "white supremacy") and are reasonably thought to be used to venerate white Southern culture heroes. For again, monuments, like books and family portraits, can have multiple meanings or uses, some wrongly harmful and some not, and the fact that there is a mainstream anti-black interpretation or use does not morally trump other interpretations or uses.[85] (As leftists remind rightists whenever accused of being un-American for critiquing America,[86] the mere fact that a compatriot interprets an act *you* see as loyal as disloyal doesn't entail that you are betraying trust.[87])

Finally, Timmerman's premise (5),

> There are no countervailing reasons to preserve public Confederate monuments
> that are equally strong or stronger than the moral reasons to remove them,

is answered by recognizing at least two reasons to maintain monuments (assign books at public schools,[88] display art in public museums,[89] etc.) that precipitate racial offense. The first concerns cultural continuity. Monuments are an important form of memorialization, which in the civic case is like a people hanging family photos on the national walls. A multiracial state's peoples use memorials to build cohesion, inspire pride, and pass down a sense of their history, just as parents do through photos not just of their present families, but the *families they came from*. Given the facts about American itinerancy and (geographic or racial) interbreeding, in time there will be few people left who feel any attachment to Confederate monuments, at which point their removal will be unproblematic.[90] That point has not arrived. This leads us to our second reason for maintaining the Confederate monuments that pass the tribal rightist standard. The more interracial social distrust, the more likely Confederate monuments will irritate black Americans. But it's just as obvious that removalism in such a context is likely to be taken as provocative in the other direction: The more culture heroes of Southern whites are equated with Nazis, and the more their monuments are torn down in the manner done to conquered peoples, the less interest they will have in a multiracial future (which, arguably, explains the Charlottesville rally).[91] That's why Nelson Mandela's strategy of adding monuments to black culture heroes to the South African heritage landscape, rather than removing monuments to whites, seems advisable for Americans whether interracial trust is running high *or* low.

COMPREHENSION QUESTIONS

1. What's the point of the Stephen Curry example?
2. Why, according to Demetriou, did Northerners tolerate Confederate monuments after the Civil War?
3. Demetriou thinks that we'll eventually be able to take down Confederate monuments; we just aren't there yet. When will that be?

DISCUSSION QUESTIONS

1. Demetriou gives examples of cases where people "had no moral claim against the harming parties not to be harmed by them in these ways." When *would* someone have a claim against a harming party not to be harmed? Is there any reason to think that black Americans *do* have this kind of claim? Against whom?
2. Unlike Timmerman, Demetriou holds that the prospect of causing merely undeserved offense or harm does not present us with a strong reason not to do something. Do you find his counterexamples persuasive?

FURTHER READINGS

Demetriou, Dan, and Ajume Wingo. "The Ethics of Racist Monuments." In *Palgrave Handbook of Philosophy and Public Policy*, edited by David Boonin. New York: Palgrave, 2018: 341–55.

Jacobs, Michele Eileen. "Contested Monuments in a Changing Heritage Landscape," Master's Thesis, University of Kwazulu-Natal, 2014. https://researchspace.ukzn.ac.za /handle/10413/12069/.

Matthes, Erich Hatala. "Who Owns Up to the Past? Heritage and Historical Injustice." *Journal of the American Philosophical Association* 4, no. 1 (2018): 87–104.

NOTES

1. Matthew Haag, "Judge Orders Tarps Removed From Confederate Statues in Charlottesville," *New York Times*, February 27, 2018, accessed April 16, 2018, https:// www.nytimes.com/2018/02/27/us/charlottesville-confederate-monuments.html.
2. Jesse Holland, "Deadly Rally Accelerates Ongoing Removal of Confederate Statues Across U.S," *Chicago Tribune*, August 15, 2018, accessed April 16, 2018, http://www .chicagotribune.com/news/nationworld/ct-confederate-statue-removal-20170815- story.html. See also Mitch Landrieu, *In the Shadows of Statues: A White Southerner Confronts History* (New York: Penguin, 2018).
3. It's generally immoral, but shouldn't be illegal, to cheat on one's partner. Or, more closely related to this issue, most people grant that the right to free speech entails legally permitting some speech that's immoral. Alfred Brophy has surprisingly argued that preserving Confederate monuments ought to be illegal because they supposedly violate the equal protection clause of the Fourteenth Amendment ("Flying the Confederate Flag on Public Property May Violate America's 14th Amendment," Quartz, June 25, 2015, https://qz.com/437136/flying-the-confederate-flag-on-public- property-may-violate-americas-14th-amendment/).
4. A little less than half of them are public monuments, and not all of them are statues.
5. Booth Gunter and Jamie Kizzire, *Whose Heritage: Public Symbols of the Confederacy* (Southern Poverty Law Center, 2018), 8. Accessed August 16, 2018, https://www .splcenter.org/sites/default/files/whoseheritage_splc.pdf.
6. Fitzhugh Brundage, "I've Studied the History of Confederate Memorials. Here's What to Do About Them," *Vox*, August 18, 2018, https://www.vox.com/the-big -idea/2017/8/18/16165160/confederate-monuments-history-charlottesville-white -supremacy. For a more comprehensive history of this and related issues, see Fitzhugh Brundage, *The Southern Past: A Clash of Race and Memory* (New York: Harvard University Press, 2008).
7. Brundage, "I've Studied."
8. For more on "othering," see Lajos Brons, "Othering, An Analysis," *Transcience, A Journal of Global Studies* 6, no. 1 (2015): 69–90. See also Fred Dervin, "Cultural Identity, Representation and Othering," in *The Routledge Handbook of Language and Intercultural Communication*, edited by Jane Jackson (New York: Routledge, 2012).
9. Brundage, "I've Studied."
10. Or, if one wants to deny that the monuments *themselves* are racist, they were still created by racists often, at least in part, for racist reasons. Dan Demetriou and Ajume Wingo helpfully distinguish between three ways monuments can have racist significance. They

can be racist because of who they represent, because it honors someone or something racist, or because of the racist intentions of those who brought it into existence. See Dan Demetriou and Ajume Wingo. "The Ethics of Racist Monuments," in *The Palgrave Handbook of Philosophy and Public Policy*, edited by David Boonin (New York: Palgrave MacMillan, 2018).

11. Gunter and Kizzire, *Whose Heritage*. See also Miles Parks, "Confederate Statues Were Built to Further a 'White Supremacist Future'," NPR, August 20, 2017, https://www .npr.org/2017/08/20/544266880/confederate-statues-were-built-to-further-a-white-supremacist-future. Jim Crow laws refer to the set of laws in the South between the Reconstruction period (1877) and the civil rights movement (1950s) that enforced racial segregation. The civil rights movement that sought to end racial segregation gained national momentum in the mid-1950s and culminated in 1964 when the Civil Rights Act became federal law.

12. Marc Bain, "'You Can't Change History': Read Donald Trump's Defense of Confederate Statues," Quartz, August 15, 2017, https://qz.com/1054062/statues-of-confederate-soldiers-across-the-south-were-cheaply-mass-produced-in-the-north/.

13. Parks, "Confederate Statues." Considered in an ahistorical context, one may not fully appreciate how harmful these Confederate monuments are. Here Marilyn Frye's bird-cage analogy of oppression is instructive. She writes, "Consider a birdcage. If you look very closely at just one wire in the case, you cannot see the other wires. If your conception of what is before you is determined by this myopic focus, you could look at that one wire . . . and be unable to see why a bird would not just fly around the wire any time it wanted to go somewhere . . . It is only when you take a step back . . . and take a macroscopic view of the whole cage, that you can see why the bird does not go anywhere" (*The Politics of Reality: Essays in Feminist Theory* [New York: Crossing Press, 1983], 4–5). The Confederate statues, considered in isolation, are but one wire in the cage.

14. The only difference between the two models were the letters on the soldier's belt buckle. Marc Fisher, "Why Those Confederate Soldier Statues Look a Lot Like Their Union Counterparts," *Washington Post*, August 18, 2017, accessed March 5, 2018, https:// www.washingtonpost.com/politics/why-those-confederate-soldier-statues-look-a-lot-like-their-union-counterparts/2017/08/18/cefcc1bc-8394-11e7-ab27-1a21a8e006ab_ story.html?utm_term=.296cbb7938ba.

15. The UDC is still an active organization and is, as of this writing, suing cities over their attempts to remove Confederate statues the UDC funded during the Jim Crow era. See, for instance, Guillermo Contreras, "Group Sues San Antonio over Removal of Confederate Statue," *My San Antonio*, October 25, 2017, accessed November 13, 2017, https://www.mysanantonio.com/news/local/article/Group-sues-San-Antonio-over-removal-of-12306414.php, and Jeff Gauger, "UDC: We Had to Sue to Stop Illegal Removal of Caddo Confederate Monument," *Shreveport Times*, October 20, 2017, accessed November 13, 2017, https://www.shreveporttimes.com/story/news/2017/10/20/ lawsuit-filed-block-removal-caddo-confederate-monument/783966001/.

16. Gunter and Kizzire, *Whose Heritage*, 8.

17. Gunter and Kizzire, *Whose Heritage*; see, in particular, 8–10.

18. While my argument focuses on the experiential harms Confederate monuments cause people in (I) and (II), I deliberatively leave open the possibility that they may cause non-experiential harms to people outside of these groups. In fact, I think that possibility is not implausible, although I don't have space to argue for it in this short essay.

19. This is assuming, of course, that x is preventable.

20. This especially includes those people whose oppression the monuments were meant to further.
21. For an incredibly insightful analysis of *a* type of oppression that leads to this harm, see Chapter 6 (especially section 2) of Ann E. Cudd, *Analyzing Oppression* (New York: Oxford University Press, 2006).
22. Baltimore mayor Catherine Pugh raises this type of consideration when discussing her decision to remove four Confederate statues. Jake Nevins, "Baltimore Mayor on Confederate Statues: Why Should People Have to Feel That Pain Every Day," *The Guardian*, August 22, 2017, https://www.theguardian.com/us-news/2017/aug/22/baltimore-roger-b-taney-confederate-statues-catherine-pugh. In a March 19, 2018, *Daily Show* interview by Trevor Noah, Mitch Landrieu discusses how Wynton Marsalis raised this point to him, which served as a catalyst for Landrieu to change his mind about whether the statues should be removed (Mitch Landrieu, "Confronting Confederate Myths with 'In the Shadow of Statues'"). See also Marsalis's moving article, "Why New Orleans Should Take Down Robert E. Lee's Statue," in *The Times Picayune*, May 17, 2017, http://www.nola.com/politics/index.ssf/2015/12/confederate_monuments_new_orle_6.html. Multiple people raise this concern in *America Inside Out*: "Re-Righting History," directed by Cheryl McDonough, *National Geographic*, April 11, 2018. Countless more examples can be found by listening to interviews of counter-protesters who oppose preserving Confederate monuments.
23. Malcolm McLaren, "Punk? It Made My Day," *The Telegraph*, September 30, 2007, https://www.telegraph.co.uk/culture/3668263/Malcolm-McLaren-Punk-it-made-my-day.html. See also Vivien Goldman, "Never Mind the Swastikas: The Secret History of UK's 'Punky Jews," *The Guardian*, February 27, 2014, https://www.theguardian.com/music/2014/feb/27/never-mind-swastikas-secret-history-punky-jews.
24. At least, this is true of moral reasons with *requiring force*.
25. The moral value of symbolic actions and, relatedly, the moral value of symbols themselves are discussed in Chapter 6 of Jeffrey M. Blustein, *Forgiveness and Remembrance* (New York: Oxford University Press, 2014). For a good discussion of historical value in the context of historical preservation, see Erich Hatala Matthes, "The Ethics of Historic Preservation," *Philosophy Compass* 11, no. 12 (2016): 786–794.
26. Matthes convincingly argues that there's a contingent relationship between historical value and irreplaceability in "History, Value, and Irreplaceability," *Ethics* 124, no. 1 (2013): 35–64. Even if cheaply mass-produced statues have historical value, there is no reason to think that such value is entirely replaceable with harmless monuments.
27. If the reader objects to the idea that harms can be aggregated in this way, simply reimagine the thought experiment such that the comet will break into millions of tiny pieces causing non-trivial (but not life-ending) amounts of harm to millions of people unless you destroy the statue. In this case, it still seems clear to me that you should sacrifice the statue to spare millions of people harm.
28. Ta-Nehisi Coates, "Take Down the Confederate Flag—Now," *The Atlantic*, June 18, 2015, https://www.theatlantic.com/politics/archive/2015/06/take-down-the-confederate-flag-now/396290/. Holland Cotter, "We Need to Move, Not Destroy, Confederate Monuments," *New York Times*, August 20, 2017, https://www.nytimes.com/2017/8/20/arts/design/we-need-to-move-not-destroy-confederate-monuments.html?mtrref=www.google.com. Christopher Knight, "What to Do with Confederate Monuments? Put Them in Museums as Examples of Ugly History, Not Civic Pride," *Los Angeles Times*, August 18, 2017, http://www.latimes.com/entertainment/arts/la-et-cm-confederate-monuments-20170818-htmlstory.html.

29. If they're in a museum they would not be interpreted as being reverential, thereby re-moving one offensive aspect of the monuments that cause suffering. While they would still make salient the horrors of America's racist past and the Civil War, and while this would certainly still cause suffering, it wouldn't cause *unavoidable* suffering since anyone would be free to visit or not visit the museum(s) in question. Not everyone has that luxury when a monument is prominently displayed in a public space. Finally, being put in the proper historical context would make these monuments instrumental in acquiring historical knowledge, and the good gained from that (by willing museum patrons) could outweigh whatever suffering they may still cause.

30. Cameron Smith, "Condoleezza Rice Talks Religion, Confederate Monuments, and Energy Policy," YouTube video posted May 2017, https://www.youtube.com /watch?v=HoCY69iP4fk. Dan Demetriou and Ajume Wingo also cite this quote in their paper. Condoleezza Rice is not alone. Notably, a non-trivial number of black ac-tivists are arguing for preserving the Confederate monuments on these grounds. See Bradford Richardson, "Honoring Patriots or Traitors? Legacy of Confederate Statues in Eye of Beholder," *Washington Times*, August 15, 2017, https://www.washingtontimes .com/news/2017/aug/15/black-activists-want-confederate-statues-to-serve-/. See also Brian B. Foster, "Confederate Monuments Are More Than Reminders of Our Racist Past. They Are Symbols of Our Racist Present," *Washington Post*, August 24, 2017, https://www.washingtonpost.com/news/post-nation/wp/2017/08/24/confederate -monuments-are-more-than-reminders-of-our-racist-past-they-are-symbols-of-our -racist-present/?noredirect=on&utm_term=.671ff7bce840.

31. Of course, some who bother to read plaques on monuments might not bother to ac-quire that information in the absence of monuments.

32. This may include, for example, certain requirements in history classes in primary schools, funding documentaries and television series focusing on the Civil War, creat-ing a Civil War museum, as well as a plethora of other options.

33. This sort of argument is made about Confederate flags in George Shedler, *Racist Symbols and Reparations: Philosophical Reflections on Vestiges of the American Civil War* (Lanham, MD: Rowman & Littlefield, 1998), 75–90. See also George Shedler, "Are Confederate Monuments Racist?" *International Journal of Applied Philosophy* 15, no. 2 (2001): 287–308. Preservationists make this argument in the "Re-Righting History" episode of *America Inside Out*. For a devastating reply to Shedler's book, see Alter Torin, "On Racist Symbols and Reparations," *Social Theory and Practice* 26, no. 1 (2000): 153–171.

34. This is also true because that same amount and type of good in question can be gener-ated by choosing to honor someone better than any of the members of the Confederacy.

35. In fact, the most recent polls show that the majority of Americans oppose removing Confederate monuments. However, this does not necessarily mean that most of those people would suffer significantly if the statues are taken down. Chris Kahn, "A Majority of Americans Want to Preserve Confederate Monuments," *Reuters*, August 21, 2017, https://www.reuters.com/article/us-usa-protests-poll/a-majority-of-americans-want -to-preserve-confederate-monuments-reuters-ipsos-poll-idUSKCN1B12EG.

36. To be clear, I'm only claiming that much (not all) suffering that would result from remov-ing Confederate monuments is predicated on irrational beliefs and contemptable attitudes.

37. It's also worth noting, per my discussion of Jim Crow laws, that Confederate monu-ments were inexorably intertwined with other injustices. Whatever pain the removal of Confederate statues would cause isn't connected to other structural injustices. Consequently, one might think that the harm their removal would cause simply wouldn't be the same in kind or degree.

38. Unless, of course, knowledge about the past Confederate monuments was widespread and their absence is visually arresting in some way. However, this too seems highly unlikely.

39. At least they would so long as people who see the monuments know they're Confederate monuments and know about the Civil War and slavery.

40. Gandhi's racism and sexism are well documented. Concerning his racism, see Rama Lakshmi, "What Did Mahatma Gandhi Think of Black People?" *Washington Post*, September 3, 2015, https://www.washingtonpost.com/news/worldviews/wp/2015/09/03/what-did-mahatma-gandhi-think-of-black-people/?utm_term=.5d924fadc6cf. Concerning his sexism, see Michael Connellan, "Women Suffer from Gandhi's Legacy," *The Guardian*, January 27, 2010, https://www.theguardian.com/commentisfree/2010/jan/27/mohandas-gandhi-women-india.

41. There are exceptions, of course, and the current exceptions may indicate what will be the norm in the future. A statue of Gandhi was "banished" at the University of Ghana because it was viewed as racist toward black South Africans. See Jason Burke, "'Racist' Gandhi Statue Banished from Ghana University," *The Guardian*, October 6, 2016, https://www.theguardian.com/world/2016/oct/06/ghana-academics-petition-removal-mahatma-gandhi-statue-african-heroes.

42. For helpful written and verbal feedback, I am very grateful to Kurt Blankschaen, Dan Demetriou, Bob Fischer, Jens Johansson, Adam Lerner, Vicente Medina, Amanda Timmerman, and my audience at New York University, the Central APA, and the College of New Jersey.

43. Rapula Moatshe, "Oom Paul Statue Excluded from Monument; EFF Threat [sic] to Topple It," *Pretoria News*, January 29, 2018, https://www.iol.co.za/pretoria-news/oom-paul-statue-excluded-from-monument-eff-threat-to-topple-it-12988851.

44. Marianne Thamm, "Afrikaner Singer Chains Herself to Vandalised South African Statue," *The Guardian*, April 10, 2015, https://www.theguardian.com/world/2015/apr/10/afrikaner-singer-chains-herself-to-vandalised-south-african-statue.

45. Sarel van der Walt, "Paul Kruger to Get New Neighbours at Pretoria's Church Square," *Netwerk24*, May 19, 2017, https://www.news24.com/SouthAfrica/News/paul-kruger-to-get-new-neighbours-at-pretorias-church-square-20170519.

46. Haag, "Judge Orders."

47. James C. Cobb, "How Did Robert E. Lee Become an American Icon?" *Humanities: The Magazine of the National Endowment of the Humanities* 32, no. 4 (2011), https://www.neh.gov/humanities/2011/julyaugust/feature/how-did-robert-e-ee-become-american-icon.

48. Iell Kaeli Subberwal, "Several States Have Erected Laws To Protect Confederate Monuments," August 17, 2017, https://www.huffingtonpost.com/entry/states-confederate-statue-laws_us_5996312be4b0e8cc855cb2ab.

49. "Unite the Right Rally," *Wikipedia*, accessed December 15, 2017, https://en.wikipedia.org/wiki/Unite_the_Right_rally.

50. Demetriou and Wingo, "The Ethics of Racist Monuments."

51. I must ignore, for instance, the critical importance of longstanding traditions of civic honor—in which memorialization plays a key role—to combating tyranny and kleptocracy by elites, and encouraging civic sacrifice from high and low alike. Dan Demetriou, "Civic Immortality: The Problem of Civic Honor in Africa and the West," *Journal of Ethics* 19, no. 3–4 (2015): 257–276.

52. For an example of an anti-tribalist conservativism, see Jonah Goldberg, *Suicide of the West: How the Rebirth of Tribalism, Populism, Nationalism, and Identity Politics Is Destroying American Democracy* (New York: Crown Forum, 2018).

53. See among many sources Aristotle, *Politics, The Basic Works of Aristotle*, edited by Richard McKeon, translated by Benjamin Jowett (New York: Random House, 1941); Joshua Greene, *Moral Tribes: Emotion, Reason, and the Gap Between Us and Them* (New York: Penguin, 2013); Robert Sapolsky, *Behave: The Biology of Humans at Our Best and Worst* (New York: Penguin, 2017); Amy Chua, *Political Tribes: Group Instinct and the Fate of Nations* (New York: Penguin, 2018).

54. Leftists typically acknowledge this dynamic in Africa especially, where political instability is often attributed to the legacy of "artificial" colonial borders that don't reflect tribal affiliation (see, e.g., James Brook, "In Africa, Tribal Hatreds Defy the Borders of State," *New York Times*, August 28, 1988, https://www.nytimes.com/1988/08/28 /weekinreview/the-world-in-africa-tribal-hatreds-defy-the-borders-of-state.html). Rightists point out that there is a cautionary lesson here for Western nations as well.

55. Maciek Chudek, Wanying Zhao, and Joseph Henrich, "Culture–Gene Coevolution, Large-Scale Cooperation and the Shaping of Human Social Psychology," in *Signaling, Commitment, and Emotion*, edited by Richard Joyce, Kim Sterelny, and Brett Calcott (Cambridge, MA, MIT Press, 2013), 425–458.

56. "Statement by Ms. Karima Bennoune, Special Rapporteur in the field of cultural rights, at the 71st session of the General Assembly," Office of the High Commissioner, UN, October 26, 2016, http://www.ohchr.org/EN/NewsEvents/Pages/DisplayNews .aspx?NewsID=20831&LangID=E.

57. "Liberty, as a principle, has no application to any state of things anterior to the time when mankind have become capable of being improved by free and equal discussion. Until then, there is nothing for them but implicit obedience to an Akbar or a Charlemagne, if they are so fortunate as to find one." John Stuart Mill, *On Liberty*, Chapter 1, https://www.gutenberg.org/files/34901/34901-h/34901-h.htm.

58. John Stuart Mill, *Representative Government*, Chapter 16, https://ebooks.adelaide.edu .au/m/mill/john_stuart/m645r/chapter16.html.

59. Mill, *Representative Government*, Chapter 16.

60. Current research suggests that ethnic diversity either lowers social trust or lowers social trust for whites in particular, who have uniquely high social trust when they are in homogenous white areas. See especially Peter Thisted Dinesen and Kim Mannemar Sønderskov, "Ethnic Diversity and Social Trust: A Critical Review of the Literature and Suggestions for a Research Agenda," in *Oxford Handbook of Social and Political Trust*, edited by Eric Uslaner (New York: Oxford University Press, 2017), 175–204; Maria Abascal and Delia Baldassarri, "Love Thy Neighbor? Ethnoracial Diversity and Trust Reexamined," *American Journal of Sociology* 121, no. 3 (2015): 722–782.

61. Robert Putnam, "E Pluribus Unum: Diversity and Community in the Twenty-First Century," *Scandinavian Political Studies*, 30 (2007): 137–174.

62. "Tribalism, it's always worth remembering, is not one aspect of human experience. It's the default human experience," Andrew Sullivan, "America Wasn't Built for Humans," *New York Magazine*, September 19, 2017, http://nymag.com/daily /intelligencer/2017/09/can-democracy-survive-tribalism.html.

63. Thomas Babington Macaulay, *Lays of Ancient Rome*, https://www.gutenberg.org /files/847/847-h/847-h.htm.

64. Joseph Henrich, Steven Heine, and Ara Norenzayan, "The Weirdest People in the World?" *Behavioral and Brain Sciences* 33, no. 2–3 (2010): 61–82.

65. Skepticism about the sustainability of multicultural states is not warranted merely by recent history: see *inter alia* Ross Hammond and Robert Axelrod, "The Evolution of Ethnocentrism," *Journal of Conflict Resolution* 50 (2006): 926–936; Max Hartshorn,

Artem Kaznatcheev, and Thomas Shultz, "The Evolutionary Dominance of Ethnocentric Cooperation," *Journal of Artificial Societies and Social Simulation* 16, no. 3 (2013): 7.

66. Alberto Avalos, "50k 'Gen Z' Students Identify as Republican," *Hispanic Heritage Foundation*, October 27, 2016, http://hispanicheritage.org/50000-generation-z-high -school-students-identify-republican/; Perry Bacon, Jr., "Charlottesville and the Rise of White Identity Politics," *FiveThirtyEight*, August 14, 2017, https://fivethirtyeight.com /features/charlottesville-and-the-rise-of-white-identity-politics/.

67. Christ Tomlinson, "Belgian Islamic Party Announces '100 Per Cent Islamic State' as End Goal," *Breitbart*, April 7, 2018, http://www.breitbart.com/london/2018/04/07 /belgian-islamic-party-announces-islamic-state-end-goal/.

68. Sumantra Maitra, "Methods Behind the Campus Madness," *Quillette*, March 7, 2017, http://quillette.com/2017/03/07/methods-behind-the-campus-madness/.

69. See, for example, David Shimer, "Germany Raids Homes of 36 People Accused of Hateful Postings Over Social Media," *New York Times*, June 20, 2017, https://www .nytimes.com/2017/06/20/world/europe/germany-36-accused-of-hateful-postings -over-social-media.html.

70. Ahmed Areff, "'We Are Cutting the Throat of Whiteness'—Malema on Plans to Remove Trollip," *News24*, March 4, 2018, https://www.news24.com/SouthAfrica/News/we-are -cutting-the-throat-of-whiteness-malema-on-plans-to-remove-trollip-20180304.

71. Note how the institutions that Putnam, in "E Pluribus Unum," says overcome ethnic divisions are ones that have strong conservative ethics: sports, the military, the churches.

72. E.g., the short recommendations published in "Tear Down the Confederate Monuments—But What Next? 12 Art Historians and Scholars on the Way Forward," *Artnet News*, August 23, 2017, https://news.artnet.com/art-world /confederate-monuments-experts-1058411.

73. Aphiwe DeKlerk, "Statues of Royal Prisoners Unveiled at Castle of Good Hope Commemoration," *Business Day*, https://www.businesslive.co.za/bd/life/2016-12-11 -statues-of-royal-prisoners-unveiled-at-castle-of-good-hope-commemoration/.

74. "Battle of Liberty Place Monument," *Wikipedia*, accessed April 8, 2018, https://en .wikipedia.org/wiki/Battle_of_Liberty_Place_Monument.

75. On the irrationality of political symbols, see Ajume Wingo, *Veil Politics in Liberal Democratic States* (New York: Cambridge University Press, 2003).

76. Charmaine Nelson, "Racist Monuments Don't Belong in Public. But They Could in a Museum," *Huffpost*, September 28, 2017, https://www.huffingtonpost.ca /charmaine-nelson/racist-monuments-dont-belong-in-public-but-they-could-in-a -museum_a_23224080/.

77. "Rye: White Supremacist Statues Need to be Removed," *CNN*, August 18, 2017, http:// edition.cnn.com/videos/politics/2017/08/18/angela-rye-statues-washington-jefferson -lee-come-down-sot-ath.cnn.

78. If indeed monuments should dwell on telling a story about peoples rather than ideas, then mass immigration is bound to undermine any memorializing culture, and thus culture, but this point will take us too far afield.

79. In many current polls, about 30% of American blacks still oppose removal of Confederate monuments (while about 50% support it; support among whites is almost double that). See, e.g., Ariel Edwards-Levy, "Polls Find Little Support for Confederate Statue Removal—But How You Ask Matters," *HuffPost*, August 23, 2017, https://www .huffingtonpost.com/entry/confederate-statues-removal-polls_us_599de056e4b05710 aa59841c.

80. "Arts, Culture and Heritage White Paper: 'All Our Legacies, Our Common Future,'" Department of Arts and Culture, June 4, 1996, http://ocpa.irmo.hr/resources/docs /South_Africa_White_Paper_Arts_Culture-en.pdf; Annie Coombes, *History After Apartheid: Visual Culture and Public Memory in a Democratic South Africa* (Durham, NC: Duke University Press, 2003); Mcebisi Ndletyana and Denver A. Webb, "Social Divisions Carved in Stone or Cenotaphs to a New Identity? Policy for Memorials, Monuments and Statues in a Democratic South Africa," *International Journal of Heritage Studies* 23, no. 2 (2016): 97–110. It's worth bearing in mind that Mandela— who is not considered a rightist—was the son of a traditional Xhosa kingmaker, and had great instincts for building tribal unity among old enemies.
81. This research was generously supported by UC Riverside's Templeton-funded Immortality Project and the University of Minnesota's Grant-in-Aid program.
82. *Wikipedia*, "Destruction under the Mongol Empire," accessed July 2, 2018, https:// en.wikipedia.org/wiki/Destruction_under_the_Mongol_Empire.
83. Burke, "'Racist' Gandhi Statue." (Gandhi apparently said some disparaging things about blacks when he was a South African.)
84. "American Civil War," *Wikipedia*, accessed June 21, 2018, https://en.wikipedia.org /wiki/American_Civil_War.
85. Many black Americans appear to agree. The most recent major opinion polls on Confederate monuments were conducted in August 2017. According to a Huffpost/ YouGov poll, about 47% of black Americans think that Confederate monuments are more symbolic of "racism" than "Southern pride," while 17% answered the converse, and 35% answered "not sure." About half of black Americans polled approved of re-moving Charlottesville's Lee statue (this poll was taken shortly after the "Unite the Right" rally discussed in both main essays), while 11% disapproved and 40% had no opinion. See Edwards-Levy, "Polls Find Little Support." In an NPR/PBS poll conducted around the same time that asked people whether Confederate statues should "remain as historical symbols" or "be removed because they are offensive to some people," black Americans responded 44% in favor of maintaining the monuments as historical sym-bols and 40% in favor of removing them because they are offensive (http://maristpoll .marist.edu/nprpbs-newshourmarist-poll-results-on-charlottesville/).
86. For instance, many on the right felt that the National Football League players who protested police violence by "taking a knee" during the national anthem were being unpatriotic, while leftists saw the same demonstration as affirming American values; e.g., Conor Friedersdorf, "Kneeling for Life and Liberty Is Patriotic," *The Atlantic*, September 25, 2017, https://www.theatlantic.com/politics/archive/2017/09 /kneeling-for-life-and-liberty-is-patriotic/540942/.
87. I cannot delve into the question of our responsibility to accommodate irrational out-rage for the sake of civic cohesion here, but I do think we must take the psychological tolerances of peoples as realistically and nonjudgmentally as we do ecological con-straints on development.
88. E.g., the case of Mark Twain's *Huckleberry Finn*, which many people interpret as racist or at least too racially offensive to assign in schools.
89. Antwaun Sargent, "To Fight Racism Within Museums, They Need to Stop Acting Like They're Neutral," *Vice*, May 21, 2018, https://www.vice.com/en_us/article/pavpkn /to-fight-racism-within-museums-they-need-to-stop-acting-like-theyre-neutral.
90. The average American moves eleven times in his or her lifetime, so descendants of Old South stock are likely to grow up elsewhere and lose their Southern white identities.

Adam Chandler, "Why Do Americans Move So Much More Than Europeans?" *The Atlantic*, October 21, 2016, https://www.theatlantic.com/business/archive/2016/10/us-geographic-mobility/504968/.

91. Indeed, iconoclasm on these terms will serve as a cautionary example for any nation contemplating diversifying its population or its political power, for very few natives would allow in foreign populations if doing so meant losing the ability to memorialize their own ancestors and culture heroes.

CHAPTER 17

Affirmative Action

AFFIRMATIVE ACTION IS UNJUST, WRONG, AND BAD
STEPHEN KERSHNAR

1. Introduction

Affirmative action favors the applications of minorities and women to compensate for past injustice or to promote some valuable goal (e.g., equal opportunity). Depending on the program, minorities are from a relevant race, ethnicity, sexual orientation, disability, etc. Here, I defend these theses:

Thesis #1: Backward-Looking. For state institutions, backward-looking reasons do not justify affirmative action.

Thesis #2: Forward-Looking. For state institutions, forward-looking reasons do not justify affirmative action.

A backward-looking reason looks as some feature of the past as justifying a policy (e.g., unjust treatment). A forward-looking reason looks at some feature in the future as justifying a policy (e.g., increasing diversity). Affirmative action is unjust and wrong if it compensates people with state dollars who aren't owed compensation. It's bad if it's inefficient—that is, if its cost outweighs its benefit.

I focus on state institutions because a private institution may give out money or positions to whomever it wants: It owns the relevant resources. While it may be irrational, imprudent, and inefficient to compensate people not owed it, it isn't unjust because it doesn't infringe on anyone's rights. It might be bad to do so, in the sense that it reduces overall well-being, but this isn't wrong-making if there's no duty to maximize the good. If there are duties of justice, then there's no such duty.

2. The Argument for Thesis #1

Consider the standard backward-looking argument for affirmative action:[1]

(P1) If the government unjustly harms someone and both law and morality permit compensation, then, other things being equal, the government should pay compensation to the harmed party.

(P2) The U.S. government unjustly harmed current American blacks, and both law and morality permit compensation.

(C1) Hence, other things being equal, the U.S. government should pay compensation to current American blacks. [(P1), (P2)]

(P3) If, other things being equal, the U.S. government should pay compensation to current American blacks, then the U.S. government should provide and, perhaps, promote affirmative action.

(C2) Hence, the U.S. government should provide and, perhaps, promote affirmative action. [(C1), (P3)]

The "other things being equal" clause handles cases when the government doesn't have enough money, faces an emergency, or something else that would make it impossible to pay compensation or wrong to do so.

This essay focuses on affirmative action for black people in the United States, as this is the strongest case for the program and, also, the historical motivation for it. Consider the notion that distant historical injustices ground the claim to compensation. The idea is that many serious injustices—including slavery, early Jim Crow laws, racial violence, and so on—harmed black people by injuring their bodies and spirits; denying them access to capital, education, and jobs; and breaking apart their families. Moreover, these harmful effects continue to unfold into the present. Justice for the past, then, requires compensation.

Just Compensation

However, although this idea seems plausible, there are several problems with it. People have a right to be fully compensated if they are injured—for example, the right to be compensated for injuries caused by battery or drunk driving. In such a case, a victim of drunk driving has a right to be given enough money by the drunk driver so that she is "made whole"—she's no worse off than if the event hadn't happened. That is, the right amount of compensation is the amount that puts her in the same position she would be in had she not been injured. But this compensatory principle—"make the person whole"—is hard to apply in the context of affirmative action. Just compensation would make it so that current black people are just as well off in the following situations:

(a) living *with* slavery and subsequent oppression and compensation (the way things have actually gone), and

(b) living without them (the way things could have gone, but didn't).

How much compensation is that?

Unfortunately, it isn't clear that there's an answer to this question. This is for a somewhat surprising philosophical reason—namely, that it doesn't seem like you could have been born to different parents. "You" with different parents just wouldn't be you at all: It would be a completely different person, with different genes and a different history. But if slavery and various injustices had never happened, current black people simply wouldn't have existed: There is no way that things would have gone for them had slavery not happened, as they simply wouldn't exist if their ancestors had never been (unjustly) enslaved. A world in which current black people have no history of racial oppression is radically different from the actual world, and those differences make it practically impossible to determine just compensation.

We might worry that there is something squirrely about the argument in the last paragraph. However, it doesn't actually matter if that argument works. Suppose that we *can* compare how things have gone for current black people with how they would have gone give some alternative history. Then, to determine the relevant amount of compensation, we need to know how much worse (a) is than (b): that is, how much worse is it to have lived *with* slavery and subsequent oppression and compensation (the way things have actually gone) relative to having lived without them (the way things could have gone, but didn't). But for some people, (a) isn't worse than (b). Given the enormous economic differences between America and all African countries, many current black people may well be better off in America with its history of injustice than they would be if they had lived in Africa without a history of injustice. This point certainly doesn't excuse the many injustices, but it shows that we can't assume that everyone needs to be "made whole."

Moreover, even if we can make comparisons, and we can somehow tell that a particular person is worse off than she would have been, there's another issue. Compensation for past injustice has to take into account mitigating factors. For example, a person who receives a minor injury in a car accident has a duty to get medical care. If he doesn't, and then he's permanently disabled because he opted not to treat some minor injury, then he can't demand the full cost of being disabled. Mitigating factors thus reduce compensation, and in tort law, there is a duty to mitigate damages. This means that a plaintiff in a personal injury suit must take reasonable steps to treat his injuries or find alternative employment. But it's difficult to tell, with respect to any particular person to whom affirmative action might apply, whether there's been a failure to mitigate. Consider, for instance, that Americans are unlikely to be poor if they graduate from high school, live in a household in which someone has a full-time job, and have children in wedlock and after age 20.[2] Obviously, it's hard to assess whether a given person is responsible for not having tried to do some of these things. But compensation for distant historical injustice harm should be lessened to the degree that it resulted from failure to take mitigating steps. So if we can't assess whether a person is responsible for having tried to do these things, we can't assess how much compensation should be lessened.

Inheritance Theory

Let's set all these problems aside. Even if past injustices didn't directly harm current black people, they might have been harmed indirectly by being denied their inheritance.[3] If we start from this assumption, then the case for affirmative action is based on moral claims to compensation that slaves and victims of early Jim Crow held against the government, and which have since been passed down via inheritance to their descendants. Because black families were victimized by historical racism to different degrees, and because the evidence for this has likely been lost (and is, in many instances, unrecoverable), a general rule will have to be adopted regarding compensation for unpaid inheritance.[4]

The first problem with this is that inheritance was not actually given. In some cases, the relevant bequests weren't in fact made and, hence, the inheritance argument fails. As a moral matter, inheritance depends on the parents having a will or gifting their property to their children. In some cases parents might disown a child or, alternatively, simply fail to give their property away at all, whether to the child or someone else. The law might have had a default rule, but this isn't a moral claim. A moral argument can be constructed based on a parent's likely preference, but mere preferences do not create a right in another. To see this, consider Jones the animal lover. He wants to leave all his money to the Humane Society but never gets around to giving the society his property or naming the society in his will. Jones's want—that is, his mere desire, apart from the relevant legal action—doesn't result in the Humane Society having a moral right to the money.

The second problem is that even if the compensation is owed for stolen inheritance, the claim to inheritance has been diluted with each generation. To see this, consider that if a black victim of government violence has three children, each of his three children have three children, and each of their children have three children, then he has twenty-seven great-grandchildren. Thus, each great-grandchild has a right to 1/27th of the original claim. (Of course, the amount of the claim has to be further adjusted to take into account inflation and return on investment.)

The third problem is that the amount of inheritance isn't known, and our ignorance here makes it unjust to pay out a specific sum. The amount isn't known because of concern about identity of the agent (federal government, state government, or private party), degree of harm, and whether the harm came about because a party did something (doing, intending, or causing) or refrained from doing something (allowing, merely foreseeing, or not stopping). We might think that the amount can simply be the difference between whites' and blacks' income. However, that can't be right, as there are a number of other factors that might affect this difference, including cultural factors. For example, if the difference between the economic position of white and black children is in part due to the difference in the likelihood of their growing up in a single-parent family, then we have to distinguish how much of a black child's worse position is due to denied inheritance and how much of it's due to the decision of black parents to have single-parent households.

Alternately, we might think that the difference might be the commercial value of the slaves, simply because this is a test of their market value as commodities. One problem with this is that because we are talking about a theoretical measure, a better measure might be the value of their labor. This is what they would have sold were they free citizens. A second problem is that such a measure fails to include value for pain and suffering. A third problem is that infirm slaves might have had little to no commodity or labor value and yet they had a strong claim to compensation. But if we then try to use these measures, how will we quantify them?

Further epistemic problems come into play insofar as some injustices were performed by the federal government, some by state or local governments, and some by private parties. The problem of who owes compensation is made more complex because harms that occur from omission don't warrant the same amount of compensation as harms that occur via commission. To see the role of commission versus omission, consider the following. A cowardly bystander watches a woman get raped and then beaten by a motorcycle club, but doesn't call the police or take other actions to prevent or cut short the attack. He doesn't contribute to the attack. Arguably, the bystander doesn't owe the woman compensation.

Things get even murkier if the Constitution creates areas of state sovereignty involving police power and private citizen interaction over which the federal government has no authority. If this is correct, then the federal government shouldn't have to pay compensation for having refrained from preventing injustices by private citizens and state workers.

Fourth, money is more just and efficient than affirmative action as a form of compensation. This is because it more closely tracks the degree to which someone has been unjustly harmed by the past. This is just because it gives money to every black person who has been harmed rather than merely those who have been harmed and done well enough to benefit from affirmative action. Affirmative action doesn't benefit those who don't need the help or those doing so poorly they are in no position to make use of the help.

Money-based compensation is also efficient because it doesn't sacrifice efficiency by filling positions with people other than those who can best perform in a job or educational position. In addition, it's efficient because it makes clearer what tradeoffs are being made.

Consider, for example, a case when two people are competing for a spot at a medical school. The first is a better student and will be a better doctor. The second would have been better were it not for the terrible high school that he attended. The poor schooling made him a weaker student than he otherwise would be. Perhaps the second student should receive compensation and an apology, but the fact that he will likely be a worse doctor suggests that he should not be allowed to become a doctor rather than the first student. This is because he will be more likely to misdiagnose or mistreat a patient, thereby helping patients less than would his competitor. Affirmative action elevates students like the second over those like the first. In addition, it fails to benefit students from the public school who are outstanding and, thus, do not need to be given preference over more talented competitors or those that are so behind as a result of the subpar school that they are unprepared to attend college, let alone medical school. Giving victims of injustice or poor public schools money rather than positions they are less qualified for allows them to be fully compensated without making things worse for patients, clients, and customers.

In tort law, victims of injustice are compensated by being given money. This is true for class action tort suits in which many people are collectively represented. The reasons of justice and efficiency that lead to money-based compensation in those cases apply to moral claims to compensation for victims of race-based injustice. In both cases, we have many people who have been harmed through widespread injustice. Money allows many more injured people to receive compensation than does affirmative action, provides an incentive for injured parties to pursue recovery, provides a disincentive for such injustice in the future, and allows for a clear tradeoff between the resources put toward compensation as compared to those put toward other goals (e.g., education).

Table 17.1 is a summary of why distant historical injustices don't support a claim to compensation.

I should note, by way of conclusion to the argument for Thesis #1, that the case for affirmative action also doesn't succeed if we focus on recent historical injustice. If the racial injustices are recent enough, then they can be handled on an individual basis. Consider, for example, anti-discrimination suits that victims of discrimination did or could have brought. And when the injustices aren't recent, then the amount of compensation can't be reasonably estimated: There are the now-familiar concerns about the identities of the agents who harmed black

Table 17.1 Distant Historical Injustice

CLAIM	OBJECTION(S)
Direct Harm. Distant events harmed current black people.	Tricky comparisons. Relevant alternatives are non-existent or don't support affirmative action.
	Mitigation. Mitigating factors reduce compensation. Consider the reasonable steps that significantly reduce the likelihood of poverty.
	Form. As a form of compensation, money is more just and efficient than affirmative action.
Inherited Harm. The denial of inheritance harmed current black people who inherited their ancestors' claims.	Not Exist. Relevant gifts and bequests were not in fact made and hence, the inheritance argument fails.
	Dilution. The claim to inheritance has been diluted through reproduction.
	Amount. The amount of inheritance isn't known to a degree that makes paying out a specific sum unjust. The amount isn't known because of concern about identity of the agent (federal government, state government, or private party), degree of harm, and connection between the agent and harm.
	Form. As a form of compensation, money is more just and efficient than affirmative action.

people, the degree of harm, the connection between those agents and the harm, various mitigating and offsetting factors, and so on.

3. Argument for Thesis #2

Again, the second thesis I defend here is:

> Thesis #2: Forward-Looking. For state institutions, forward-looking reasons do not justify affirmative action.

Forward-looking arguments argue for affirmative action based on the net good that such programs purportedly bring about. Proponents claim that affirmative action produces benefits such as more role models, less stereotyping, improved group decision-making, less homogeneity, and other positive externalities (e.g., greater investment in intellectual capital). The problem is that such programs have a cost: They result in people who aren't the best (i.e., they're less meritorious) either having the job or taking spots in educational contexts. This is a cost because it matters who ends up in many jobs. Having someone who isn't the best person for a job often results in less work or lower-quality work. For example, if you end up with a physician who works fewer hours and whose work isn't as proficient, then you have a worse contributor to the population's health than you'd get from a physician who works longer hours and does better work. The argument against the forward-looking argument is that the cost likely outweighs the benefit.

The notion that affirmative action lessens merit-based efficiency rests on two assumptions. First, merit-based assignment is efficient, in the sense that it seems to be the most reliable way of achieving a highly desirable end—namely, ensuring that the best end up where they can do the most good. Again, there are many domains where it really matters whether the best get the job. Consider, for example, that medical admission test scores correlate strongly with medical school grades, medical board scores, and physician performance. Because medical error is one of the leading causes of death, it matters whether the most meritorious are becoming physicians. It wouldn't be surprising if the same were true when it comes to scientific research, engineering, and related technical fields, where the work often promises to improve human life (and failures can perpetuate harm in various ways).

Second, affirmative action decreases merit-based assignment. Consider, for example, test scores. On average, black law and medical students have lower standardized test scores and worse grades, and flunk their classes and boards more frequently than do their white and Asian peers. As a group, they do not outperform their scores. Nor do other methods outpredict standardized tests and grades.[5] Affirmative action favors disadvantaged minorities with lower scores, such as blacks, over other groups with higher scores, such as Asians and whites.

But how can we argue that the costs of affirmative action outweigh the benefits? This notion rests on several independent arguments. First, consider the free market. You might think that the free market in something is the most reliable indicator of the cost/benefit analysis of it. The economic free market doesn't value diversity. This is especially true for competitive fields in which contribution

Table 17.2 Forward-Looking Argument

(P1) If the cost of a program usually outweighs its benefit, then it's usually, all-things-considered, bad.

(P2) The cost of affirmative action at state institutions usually outweighs its benefit.

(C1) Hence, affirmative action is usually all-things-considered bad. [(P1), (P2)]

is measurable (e.g., National Football League, National Basketball Association, and Hollywood). Nor does the *social* free market value diversity. For example, 75% of whites have only white friends, and only 8.4% of marriages are interracial.[6] Of course, this rosy assessment of the free market is controversial. But there are other arguments available.

Second, then, consider the purported benefits of affirmative action. It's actually unclear whether the purported benefits *are* benefits. The mismatch thesis asserts that in education, affirmative action systematically mismatches affirmative action beneficiaries to their schools and this harms them. The idea is that a black student who would be a good student at California State University at Fresno might be a bad student at the University of California at Berkeley. Why? Because he's mismatched against his peers: He isn't prepared for the educational environment to which affirmative action grants him access. An analogy is that a competitive wrestler at a small Division III college might be uncompetitive in Division I. Here are some facts that illustrate the motivation for the thesis, though it's obviously true that much more evidence is needed to establish it:

> About half of black law students rank in the bottom 10% of their classes. Also, black law school graduates are four times as likely to fail bar exams as are whites; mismatch explains half of this gap.
> About half of black college students rank in the bottom 20% of their classes. Also, black college freshmen are more likely to aspire to science or engineering careers than are white freshmen, but mismatch causes black students to abandon these fields at twice the rate of whites.
> Interracial friendships are more likely to form among students with relatively similar levels of academic preparation. Thus, blacks and Hispanics are more socially integrated on campuses where they are less academically mismatched.[7]

Third, consider the best-bet argument. When a practice has a known cost and it's unclear whether a purported benefit's a benefit, let alone a weighty one, we shouldn't assume the practice passes a cost/benefit analysis. Affirmative action has a significant cost, and it's unclear whether its purported benefit's a benefit.

Table 17.2 presents an argument summary.

4. Conclusion

The upshot is this: For state institutions, backward-looking reasons don't justify affirmative action. Distant historic injustices don't justify affirmative action because the injustices didn't harm current black people. The inheritance argument also doesn't work. Forward-looking reasons don't justify affirmative action programs at state institutions because they fail a cost/benefit analysis. We shouldn't support affirmative action.

COMPREHENSION QUESTIONS

1. What's the difference between forward- and backward-looking reasons?
2. Why is it hard to apply the "make the person whole" principle in the case of affirmative action?
3. What are some of the "mitigating factors" that affect how much compensation a person deserves?
4. What is inheritance theory, and why shouldn't we think that it supports affirmative action?
5. What is "merit-based efficiency," why should we want it, and why doesn't it favor having affirmative action policies?

DISCUSSION QUESTIONS

1. Kershnar wants us to consider how current African Americans would be doing if historical injustices such as slavery and Jim Crow laws had not occurred. Is this the right question to be asking?
2. If current African Americans should be compensated for past injustices such as slavery and Jim Crow laws, why shouldn't this be done via money?
3. Do the benefits of affirmative action outweigh its costs?
4. Are people likely to be harmed if physicians, teachers, and engineers who have lower test scores and grades than their competitors are chosen for jobs and educational spots?

Case 1

In *Grutter v. Bollinger*, a 2003 U.S. Supreme Court case, the Justices ruled that the Equal Protection Clause doesn't prohibit a law school from using race in admissions decisions for the sake of providing certain educational benefits—namely, the ones associated with having a diverse student body. Here's what the Court said:

> We have long recognized that, given the important purpose of public education and the expansive freedoms of speech and thought associated with the university environment, universities occupy a special niche in our constitutional tradition . . . In announcing the principle of student body diversity as a compelling state interest, Justice Powell invoked our cases recognizing a constitutional dimension, grounded in the First Amendment, of educational autonomy: "The freedom of a university to make its own judgments as to education includes the selection of its student body." . . . From this premise, Justice Powell reasoned that by claiming "the right to select those students who will contribute the most to the 'robust exchange of ideas,'" a university "seek[s] to achieve a goal that is of paramount importance in the fulfillment of its mission." . . .
>
> As part of its goal of "assembling a class that is both exceptionally academically qualified and broadly diverse," the Law School seeks to "enroll a 'critical mass' of minority students." . . . The Law School's interest is not simply "to assure within its student body some specified percentage of a particular group merely because of its race or ethnic origin." . . . That would amount to outright racial balancing, which is patently unconstitutional . . . Rather, the Law School's

Case 1 (continued)

concept of critical mass is defined by reference to the educational benefits that diversity is designed to produce.

These benefits are substantial. As the District Court emphasized, the Law School's admissions policy promotes "cross-racial understanding," helps to break down racial stereotypes, and "enables [students] to better understand persons of different races." . . . These benefits are "important and laudable," because "classroom discussion is livelier, more spirited, and simply more enlightening and interesting" when the students have "the greatest possible variety of backgrounds." . . . [N]umerous studies show that student body diversity promotes learning outcomes, and "better prepares students for an increasingly diverse workforce and society, and better prepares them as professionals." . . . These benefits are not theoretical but real, as major American businesses have made clear that the skills needed in today's increasingly global marketplace can only be developed through exposure to widely diverse people, cultures, ideas, and viewpoints.*

What do you think of these arguments for a diverse student body? What do you think Kershnar would say about them? Which dimensions of diversity strike you as most important for educational reasons? Why?

_____

*https://supreme.justia.com/cases/federal/us/539/306/#tab-opinion-1961291

AFFIRMATIVE ACTION IS NOT MORALLY WRONG
KRISTINA MESHELSKI

The Civil Rights Act of 1964 established that discrimination based on race, gender, religion, or national origin was illegal in the United States. The term "affirmative action" first appeared around this time to describe any policy or law that the U.S. government might impose upon federal contractors in order to ensure their compliance with the Civil Rights Act. Under President John F. Kennedy, federal contractors were encouraged to actively recruit black employees. Later, under President Lyndon B. Johnson, affirmative action was expanded so that construction firms, public hospitals, and universities were required to establish goals for hiring women and racial minorities, as well as timetables to meet those goals. In 1978, the Supreme Court outlawed the use of racial quotas in college admissions, though universities may still consider an applicant's race in their admissions decisions, as long as this is the only way the campus can achieve racial diversity, and as long as the consideration does not amount to a quota system. However, in some states, race-based affirmative action is banned entirely; these are California, Washington, Michigan, Nebraska, Arizona, Oklahoma, and Florida. Among the universities that are allowed to consider the race of applicants as one factor among many in their admissions decisions, very few actually do, and these tend to be the most elite institutions.

Given this history, we must note that accepting a non-white applicant to a college only because of their race, the most talked-about and controversial kind of affirmative action, was legal for an extremely brief period in the United States and may have never actually been practiced. Meanwhile, rejecting non-white applicants only because of their race has a long history.

Nevertheless, I will argue that if we had used a strict racial or gender quota system in our college admissions that would be morally permissible. I will say it is prima facie morally permissible, to indicate that it is permissible on its own, considered apart from other countervailing factors about the particular circumstances that may make some instances impermissible (e.g., where the quota system may have the effect of increasing, rather than decreasing, racial disparities).

There are many moral arguments one can make on behalf of affirmative action. Philosophers have argued for the permissibility of affirmative action as a method of achieving racial diversity,[8] as a proxy for achieving other kinds of diversity, as a form of reparations for past injustices,[9] as a way to mitigate against other forms of disadvantage that people of color face,[10] as a means of achieving racial integration,[11] or as a means of achieving equality of opportunity.[12]

I will not make this kind of positive argument for affirmative action; rather, I will claim that the arguments against affirmative action rest on a false premise that is so pervasive it has even many supporters convinced. This is the idea that procedures for awarding jobs and college placements have an independent value and we should avoid rigging them to achieve particular outcomes. This is why many believe that instituting a quota system for college admissions should be avoided, because it unfairly tampers with the admissions procedures that ideally should be left alone. I argue to the contrary that this idea is a conceptual mistake. The outcomes of these procedures are not something we should judge separately from the procedures themselves. College admissions or job search processes cannot be considered fair unless their outcomes are also fair. Exposing this conceptual mistake reveals that affirmative action is by itself morally innocuous.

First, I'll walk through the argument that there is something morally wrong with affirmative action. I can't address all possible arguments against affirmative action, but I believe this one is extremely common. Essentially, it is the argument that it would be unfair to allow someone's race or gender to determine that they would be awarded a job or college placement, or that someone else would not be awarded those things. I think the core of the argument for this is a mistaken idea of procedural justice, but first, I will have to tease apart a few related ideas that may contribute to confusion.

1. Job Qualifications and Meritocracy as an Ideal

One might think that it is unfair to elevate an unqualified candidate over a qualified candidate only because of their race. Even if this were true, it is irrelevant to the discussion. It is irrelevant because there is no one that seriously wants to hire someone who is unable to do the job they are being hired for. Affirmative action, when it is used, merely elevates some qualified candidates over other qualified candidates. In the case of college admissions, there is always some minimum threshold of qualification, and more than enough applicants meeting that threshold. In a job situation, if we were to for some reason purposely hire someone unqualified, this wouldn't be unfair to the qualified person who is passed over so much as it would be unfair to the people who might be relying on that unqualified person's work.

Now, putting aside the spurious case of the completely unqualified candidate, one might think that it would be unfair not to elevate the most qualified candidates above the less qualified candidates. I'm not sure why this would be true unless one is committed to a thoroughgoing meritocratic worldview, in which coveted jobs or college placements, and therefore one's chances in life generally, should be awarded as prizes to only the most deserving. This, to me, is a horrifying ideal. Some particular competitions surely should be decided mostly by merit, but to the extent that jobs and college placements are extremely valuable and also scarce, a fully meritocratic society would also be one in which those who were not found sufficiently meritorious would not have a chance. This is especially bad to the extent that the jobs that exist are the ones that happen to be profitable for someone with capital and are not determined by social need. Think, for example, what kind of life and social status a disabled person would have in such a society.

This is all to say that I do not see the desirability of a society that is capitalist, experiences at least moderate scarcity, and is purely meritocratic. This would mean that your life chances are highly dependent on what kind of college and what kind of job you have, and yet there is not enough of either of those things for everyone. So some people would be seriously deprived, and the others face the anxiety that they might be deprived if they do not measure up. Equal opportunity, sometimes thought to be obviously good, is of course only valuable in this type of already bad situation. If resources were already available to most people, we would not be so concerned with our opportunity to get them.

But even if we do not independently value meritocracy, or equal opportunity, there remain ethical questions about how things should be done in the non-ideal situation in which we currently find ourselves. In this situation, given that there are scarce resources that are awarded on the basis of competition among many qualified applicants, what would it take for these procedures to be fair? I will refer to this as a question about *procedural justice*. We are now back to considering the original question of whether awarding these resources on the basis of race or gender would be fair. In order to answer this question, I must say something about procedural justice in general.

2. Procedural Justice

Procedural justice, I maintain, has different referents in different contexts. One context, probably the most familiar one, is in the legal system. In this context, procedural justice refers to the fairness of the process itself, as opposed to the fairness of the outcome. So, for example, this allows us to say that the defendant had a fair trial, even when they were wrongly convicted. There are certain contexts in which we want to consider the fairness of the process entirely apart from the fairness of the outcome of the process. We can, following the philosopher John Rawls, call this *imperfect procedural justice*.[13] It is so called because a just procedure in this case does not reliably lead to a just outcome. The trial procedures aim to convict all and only guilty people, but they are an imperfect means to this end.

Sometimes we are lucky enough to find procedures that are perfectly designed to achieve particular outcomes, as, for example, when two greedy people are splitting a dessert. The perfect procedure dictates that the one who cuts the dessert in half should not be the same one who chooses the piece. This Rawls calls *perfect procedural justice*, but it has of course a limited application, and I offer it here as an example of another way that procedure may relate to outcome.

The third and final type of procedural justice was what Rawls called *pure procedural justice*. In this type of procedural justice, we don't have a truly independent way to evaluate what outcome is fair. When splitting the dessert, we know before we begin that equal pieces would be fair. In the criminal trial, we know before we begin that convicting guilty people and acquitting innocent people would be the fair outcome. However, in pure procedural justice, we don't know what a fair outcome of the procedure would be because these are cases in which the substance of the procedure is determining the fairness of the outcome.

For example, imagine two cooperatively owned factories. In factory A, the workers agree that anyone who works over forty hours a week will receive a bonus paycheck that amounts to their equal share of the extra profits made. By instituting this pay rule, the factory increases its production and its profits. In factory B, the workers decide to prohibit working more or less than forty hours a week and agree to all equally share in the profits they make. Workers in factory B may receive lower paychecks than workers in factory A because they may make less profit overall. But we cannot really say whether it is unfair that workers in B get less money than workers in A, or that workers in A work more hours than workers in B. Each factory chose its own procedure for dividing up the profits, and in each factory, what counts as a fair outcome is determined by the pay rule—that is, which procedure—the workers chose to institute.

This type of pure procedural justice is not to be confused with the case of imperfect procedural justice, in which the procedure itself is given independent value. Nor is it like the case of perfect procedural justice, in which the procedure of one person cutting the dessert and the other person choosing their piece has no importance at all, outside of the fact that it leads to the fair outcome. Rather, in pure procedural justice, the procedure itself produces the outcome and thus cannot be evaluated independently from the outcome it produces.

Our intuitions about the two factories should track this. If workers in factory A started to feel worn out by the implicit pressure to work overtime, or perhaps found that competition for higher bonus pay was making their workplace atmosphere uncomfortable, they might see that the procedure they had previously voted for is leading to an outcome they no longer find fair, and call for a new vote on overtime and bonus pay to make their procedures more like factory B. Conversely, if workers in factory B found that their profits could not keep up to meet their needs without some workers working overtime, they might call for a change in procedure to make themselves more like factory A. Both are instances of people seeing that a procedure leads to an outcome that they don't like and changing their procedures so that they can achieve different outcomes. There seems to be nothing particularly unfair about factory A voluntarily becoming more like factory B, or factory B becoming more like factory A. We can even take this intuition one step further and say that in cases of pure procedural justice like this, we are required to continually evaluate both outcomes and procedures to ensure their fairness.

This is the sense of procedural justice we should apply to instances of affirmative action. The first thing we must acknowledge is that disparities in wealth between whites and every other racial group are disturbingly high, as is the continued existence of a pay gap between men and women. It is my view that explicit and significant discrimination is still very common, but even someone who doubts this must see that we are a highly unequal society and that this inequality is correlated with race and gender. We are also a society that does not attempt to secure employment for everyone, so we have a large labor surplus, and we use our higher education system as a gatekeeping mechanism for many of the most desirable jobs. Since racial and gender inequality is so bad, we can confidently say that this is not the outcome that we want. Any instinct that such inequality might not be unfair must be based on the idea that women or people of color either do not want or do not deserve anything close to parity.

If we take it as a given that current outcomes are not fair, then I submit that pure procedural justice allows us to design procedures to achieve the outcomes we do want, including using racial and gender quotas when hiring for desirable jobs or admitting to colleges. This is in contrast to the commonly held view that though current disparities are bad, we are somehow doing something wrong by trying to fix them directly. This can only be based on a mistaken idea of procedural justice, one that believes the hiring or admissions procedures to be independently fair. One reason someone might think this is that they might value meritocracy for its own sake, but as I've previously suggested, this is in fact an extreme view. In order to believe that any deviance from meritocracy is unfair, one would have to believe both that it is possible to ascertain which college and job applicants are more meritorious than others at a fairly fine-grained level, and also that fairness requires that we always order ourselves that way.

Another reason someone might believe this is that they might be inappropriately applying the notion of imperfect procedural justice to these instances that I have argued are best understood as pure procedural justice. How can we tell when a procedure should be judged by an independent notion of fairness (as in the criminal trial) versus judged in part by the procedure's outcome? In fact, very few procedures can be evaluated according to independent notions of fairness that do not involve their outcomes. The criminal trial may be unique in this respect. Further, when the procedures are so central to determining one's economic prospects, it is especially important to realize that their outcomes are at least partly determinant of their fairness.

Returning to the factory example, we cannot say that it is unfair that a worker earns more money in factory A than a worker in factory B. Nor can we say that the system that forbids overtime is less fair than the system that incentivizes it.

Since these procedures are evaluated along with their outcomes, we cannot judge either the outcomes or the procedures against each other in isolation. Since the paychecks were different because of different procedures, and those procedures were adopted knowing they would yield different levels of profits, the procedures are tied up with the outcomes.

While we can know that current levels of racial and gender disparities in wealth and income are not fair, we can't say exactly who should have what amount of money or exactly who should have which job. These things will be determined by procedures that we must consider when we are evaluating the fairness of each outcome. But current procedures for determining these things are not special in the way that the procedures of a criminal trial are. They do not deserve to be protected from interference and given a status above their outcomes. Being admitted to college or given a job is not a prize that distinguishes the person who is best at something; rather, these are valuable resources that determine one's economic standing, and often the economic standing of one's children. So to the extent that we agree that the current racial and gender disparities in economic success are not desirable outcomes, there is nothing wrong with awarding desirable jobs and college places according to a quota system for those applicants who meet qualifications.

3. Affirmative Action Is Not Morally Wrong

Perhaps you now agree that these procedures do not have a value independent of their outcomes. Still, you might object that this particular type of interference amounts to racial or gender discrimination, which is a bad thing. I don't think this is right, for two reasons. One is that discrimination of this type is not harmful. Those who benefit from affirmative action are obviously not harmed, and those who do not benefit are merely experiencing what must be experienced by someone. The sense in which the losers of this process are harmed is that the resources they want are not offered to everyone. This, I agree, is a harm, but if someone was going to be denied access, then with or without affirmative action that harm would take place. The use of one's race or gender to determine who has access does not do any further harm. The second reason that the use of affirmative action does not amount to racial discrimination is that it does not express an attitude of disdain toward the groups that do not benefit from it. It would not be motivated by a desire to dominate them, nor would it contribute to their groups being systematically cut off from resources and so cause widespread disparities. If it did do the latter, it would no longer be affirmative action by definition.

In a decision supporting the use of affirmative action, Justice Blackmun called it an "ugly but necessary" policy,[14] and in a decision arguing against the use of affirmative action, Justice Roberts called it "discriminating on the basis of race."[15] It is a commonly held view that affirmative action is in itself morally wrong, though supporters will hold that it is a good and necessary antidote to our current situation, and one that we can hope to someday no longer need. My view is that this confuses the ideals of imperfect procedural justice, in which our procedures are independently valuable, with the ideals of pure procedural justice, in which our procedures and the distribution of goods and resources that result from these procedures must be evaluated as one whole. Affirmative action is not to be considered an illegitimate interference in hiring or admissions procedures, as these procedures themselves are not sacrosanct. If these procedures do not lead to the results that we want, we may employ affirmative action in order to ensure better results.

The view I am arguing against would hold that economic procedures must be kept free from interference that tries to direct more resources to certain racial and gender groups. The burden of proof should be on this view to show why these procedures are so special. For example, in the criminal trial, there are good reasons why we would not want to allow police unrestricted rights to search and seize property, even if such rights would allow them to convict more guilty people. We believe citizens need a measure of privacy, and that this has value apart from whether it furthers or hinders the goals of criminal conviction. The legal rights against search and seizure, and the rules the state must follow in prosecution, are developed in order to guard these rights and not to simply lead to any particular outcome. (It should be noted that here I'm discussing the U.S. legal system in an idealized sense, because I'm attempting to draw out some common intuitions about the value of this idealized system. The truth is that the idealized system that we value doesn't in fact exist, and many people are denied these rights in practice. Still, I think our intuitions about the value of the idealized version of this system serve a useful contrastive purpose here.)

So, while the rights one should enjoy against criminal prosecution are laid out in procedures that serve to respect these rights, on the other hand our economy is just the means by which we agree to divide up the resources that we jointly produce. Some would say that resources should be divided according to desert, so that those who produce the most value should receive the most reward. Some would prioritize equality over desert. And, further, there may be quite a lot of disagreement over the proper theory of value we employ when evaluating who or what has contributed the most to the resources that have been produced. My argument here does not depend on a particular view of how to answer these questions, but only on the claim that economic procedures are not analogous to legal procedures when we evaluate the fairness of each. (And I should note that my arguments against a pure meritocracy are not meant to rule out economic procedures that reward desert in any fashion, just those that exclusively reward merit.)

Some might think that economic procedures should be thought of as rights protecting (like the criminal trial) rather than just distribution mechanisms. On this view, one might argue that a college applicant has a right to be considered for only their achievements and not their race or gender. I am willing to say that this right might exist if college admissions were not one of the primary means by which our society distributes economic resources. I'm also suggesting that college admissions should not be used in this way. However, given that they are, I do not believe there are any rights to be considered on the basis of merit alone.

A corollary to my argument is that we could replace certain antidiscrimination laws with either race-conscious or randomized mechanisms and still not violate any rights. For example, when considering applicants to a desirable job for which there are more qualified applicants than positions available, choose among them by hiring only the people of color. Or put the résumés in a hat and pick the winners. Better yet, we could distribute jobs and resources more evenly, so that the stakes of every job and college application are lowered, and everyone can be assured a minimal income and a degree of dignity.

COMPREHENSION QUESTIONS

1. Meshelski says that we shouldn't want a fully meritocratic society. Why?
2. What is procedural justice? What is imperfect procedural justice? Perfect procedural justice? Pure procedural justice?
3. Why is it morally OK to rig our admissions policies to improve racial equality?
4. Meshelski says that if you don't benefit from an affirmative action policy, you aren't harmed. Why not?
5. Meshelski disagrees with Justice Blackmun, who called affirmative action an "ugly but necessary" policy. Why?

DISCUSSION QUESTIONS

1. Imagine someone who says that he was harmed by an affirmative action policy. You might think he's right: Someone is harmed if something makes him worse off than he would otherwise be, and (let's say) he would have gotten the job if there hadn't been an affirmative action policy. So, he's worse off (jobless) than he would otherwise be (employed) due to the policy. What should Meshelski say to this?
2. Meshelski says that "our economy is just the means by which we agree to divide up the resources that we jointly produce." How else might we think about our economy? What are the costs and benefits of this way of thinking about it?

Case 2

Consider this op-ed by Berlin Fang, a Chinese educational writer:

[Affirmative action, or AA,] is hitting Asian Americans especially hard. Many Asian American families focus on using schooling to achieve social mobility, but when Asian American students have high test scores, some admissions officers paint them as nerds who do not have leadership skills and do not care about community service. Getting a good grade, which in many cases reflects self-discipline, hard work, and a culture of growth, sometimes instead defines Asian students as less capable of anything else, which is not true.

AA is also misguided, as it could favor a rich black doctor's kids at the expense of a poor Asian kid. It could push back a kid from a struggling white family to give way to a Latino banker's kid. No, universities would argue, we do not only look at race. Admission preferences are "holistic." Unfortunately, holistic admission can be easily used as an excuse to justify stricter criteria for Asian Americans, and the term carries the hidden bias that Asians are less holistic as human beings. Nothing reinforces stereotypes more than AA policies in this day and age.

Case 2 (continued)

> Supporters of AA policy may have the good intention of providing remedies for past wrongs and injustices such as slavery. However, I do not see why we should ignore other wrongs different people groups have suffered. Japanese Americans may have grandfathers and grandmothers thrown into concentration camps in World War II. Vietnamese Americans may come from families whose homes were burned to the ground from air-dropped bombs. Then there are descendants of Chinese railroad workers, and those who were denied employment due to the Chinese Exclusion Act. The political weaponization of history cherry picks which historical injustices to care about, instead of supporting equality and justice for all. It's time to stop such condescending "favors." Focus instead on creating a fair environment for each racial or ethnic group to thrive.*
>
> What do you think about Fang's argument here? Is there a way to address his concerns while still preserving affirmative action for members of other groups? What would Meshelski say about Fang's reasoning here?

---

*https://thefederalist.com/2019/05/02/affirmative-action-racist-un-american/

REPLY TO MESHELSKI
STEPHEN KERSHNAR

Professor Meshelski gives a new and powerful argument for affirmative action. She begins by asserting that when it comes to assigning educational positions and jobs, we are in a situation of pure procedural justice. In this type of procedural justice, there is no independent way to evaluate what outcome is fair. She claims that few procedures can be evaluated according to independent notions of fairness that do not involve their outcomes. She further claims that in the United States, racial and gender disparities in wealth and income are unfair. However, she notes, we can't say exactly who should have what amount of money or which job.

Meshelski further argues that this affirmative action does not amount to racial or gender discrimination for two reasons. First, those whom affirmative action favors are not harmed, and those it disfavors are merely experiencing what must be experienced by someone. Second, affirmative action does not amount to racial discrimination because it does not express disdain toward favored groups.

Here is her argument:

(P1) If the assignment of resources (e.g., contracts, educational opportunities, and jobs) is a case of pure procedural justice and one procedure eliminates an unfair outcome, then, other things being equal, it is permissible.

(P2) In the United States, the assignment of resources is a case of pure procedural justice and affirmative action eliminates an unfair outcome.

(C1) Hence, other things being equal, in the United States affirmative action is permissible. [(P1), (P2)]

Consider the second premise. There is reason to doubt that the assignment of resources is an instance of pure procedural justice. Consider, for example, a state that reserves 90% of its business, law, and medical school spots for white males.

Intuitively, this procedure is unfair regardless of whether this produces a desirable outcome. There is thus reason to believe that some procedures that distribute resources are unfair independent of their outcome. Meshelski might respond that the above procedures are unfair in part due to the outcomes they produce. I do not share this intuition. Perhaps I am wrong.

It is also unclear whether affirmative action eliminates an unfair outcome. First, there is some reason to believe that affirmative action hurts the groups it is trying to help. The mismatch thesis asserts that in education, affirmative action mismatches affirmative action beneficiaries to their peers, resulting in their doing worse at school (e.g., dropping out more and getting worse grades).

Second, it is unclear that differences in education, income, and wealth are unfair. Americans are unlikely to be poor if they graduate from high school, live in a household in which someone has a full-time job, and have children in wedlock and after age 20. Some of the disparity in resources is due to group differences along these lines. Consider that 70% of black births and 53% of Hispanic births are out of wedlock.[16]

Some of the differences between groups are due to other differences in habits, family structure, and values. For example, Asian American households make on average 40% more than the average American household ($80,720 vs. $57,617).[17] Asian Indian households make $95,000 per household (2012 number).[18] This difference is likely not due to people preferring them.

There are also differences in preferences. For example, in the United Kingdom, female physicians are six times more likely not to work full-time than men (42% vs. 7%). In the United States, 25% of female physicians don't work full-time.[19] This pattern will produce a difference in the income and wealth of male and female physicians, but choice rather than discrimination or other unfairness explains the difference.

Even if Meshelski's argument is sound, it still does not follow that the outcomes favor affirmative action all things considered. This is because the price of admitting or hiring people who are less meritorious may be quite high. This is one reason why competitive markets do not put much, if any, value on diversity. Consider, for example, professional sports leagues. In general, markets are better than other methods we have for weighing costs and benefits.

Let us consider medicine as a way to see the problem with deemphasizing merit. Many deaths are due to medical errors. The problem is made worse because thousands of doctors continue to practice despite misconduct.[20] If the diversity-related cost (less merit per doctor) outweighs the diversity-related benefit (e.g., less unfairness and more role models), then it fails a cost/benefit analysis. Of course, it is difficult to determine whether the diversity-related cost (less merit per doctor) outweighs the diversity-related benefit (e.g., less unfairness and more role models). It would be helpful to know, for example, how many additional deaths and injuries from physician error are outweighed by a 1% increase in medical school diversity (if, in fact, favoring diversity over merit would lead to such harms). Consider one of the people who was chosen over Alan Bakke.[21] Bakke famously sued over affirmative action at a state medical school. Bakke was a NASA engineer and Marine Corps captain and likely had much higher board scores than affirmative action beneficiaries, such as Patrick Chavis. Chavis was a disaster. A judge found him grossly negligent when one of his patients died and two barely survived his botched liposuction operations, and his medical license was suspended. Obviously, Chavis is an exceptional case, and most affirmative action beneficiaries are not nearly as bad. Still, this case indicates that there is a cost to affirmative action. Across a population, it may be significant.

In summary, it is unclear whether affirmative action is a matter of pure procedural justice. Even if it is a matter of pure procedural injustice, it is unclear whether it lessens unfairness. Even if it is a matter of pure procedural injustice and lessens unfairness, this still doesn't show that affirmative action is justified all things considered.

COMPREHENSION QUESTIONS

1. Kershnar gives an argument against thinking that "the assignment of resources is an instance of pure procedural justice." What is it?
2. Kershnar says that competitive markets don't tend to value diversity. What does this mean?

DISCUSSION QUESTIONS

1. Kershnar suggests that there are "differences in preferences" between men and women, black people and white people, and so on. What does he mean? How should we think about these "preferences"? Insofar as they're real, might such preferences themselves be the result of discrimination or unfairness?
2. Consider Kershnar's discussion of Bakke and Chavis. What is he trying to show? Does this argument succeed?

REPLY TO KERSHNAR
KRISTINA MESHELSKI

In Kershnar's argument against backward-looking affirmative action, he focuses on the problem of determining who deserves to be compensated for injustices in the past. His claims that we cannot assess how much compensation is warranted to people today for wrongs done to their ancestors are based on applying standards used in tort law. However, standards that apply to compensating people for harms inflicted on them personally are inappropriate in the context of distant and continuing harms inflicted on an entire group of people. There are many black people today who have been victims of racial discrimination, ranging from physical assault to being denied employment opportunities. These people deserve direct compensation, and in these cases, it would make sense to use the typical tort law standards of "making them whole"—assuming they took mitigating steps to help themselves. We would not offer a living crime victim affirmative action as compensation, so the analogy to torts is not apt.[22]

If we are considering affirmative action as compensation for harm, then it is important to consider both the harm and the benefit that accrued to those doing the harm. The people who captured and sold slaves, as well as the people who forced slaves to work for them, made large profits. Many people alive today still benefit from the generational wealth that was built by slave labor. Redlining (the practice of permitting black people to buy homes only in certain neighborhoods and denying them mortgages) raised the home values of many white homeowners, and many of these homes remain a source of value today and have been passed down to the original owner's descendants. Similarly, many white people today had parents, grandparents, or great-grandparents who benefited from legal employment discrimination, and studies suggest that racial discrimination is still prevalent in hiring decisions, despite being illegal in the United States since 1964.[23] Because the white people who benefited from these institutions in the past were doing only what was legal and condoned by the government, it makes sense for the government to make some sort of symbolic restitution by preferring to hire a black candidate when presented with equally qualified candidates. This is similar to the way that we expect the British Museum to return artifacts it plundered from the former U.K. colonies, or the way we expect Swiss banks to return profits they made from selling artwork stolen by the Nazis to the heirs of the people stolen from. Though we cannot measure how these losses affected current people descended from the wronged parties, we can reasonably expect that something be done to atone for what we now recognize as a grave injustice.

In my own view, affirmative action is not the best remedy for these harms: Direct reparations would be better.[24] However, though money would be better, using affirmative action to compensate for the harms at issue would not be unjust, because affirmative action for no reason at all is not unjust. There is no moral principle that affirmative action violates, as I argued in my main essay.

Kershnar also claims that affirmative action is problematic for forward-looking reasons. For instance, he fears that affirmative action will elevate unqualified students over qualified students, and suggests that this could lead to medical schools promoting unqualified doctors. It is worth addressing this directly. In public schools, affirmative action can only be used to elevate a black candidate over a white candidate when the other measures of their worth are roughly equal (because the candidate's race can only be one factor among many for their admission). So, if we believe that test scores are an adequate predictor of physician quality, then most actual cases of affirmative action are denying admission to an equally or only slightly less qualified white candidate in favor of a black candidate.[25] But furthermore, even if we admitted less qualified applicants over qualified ones, we should still note that doctors must pass licensing exams. Test scores prior to medical school are used as a proxy for determining who might become a good doctor, but there is a reason we don't just pick the students with the best MCAT scores and hand them a license to practice medicine. It's because we cannot accurately predict who will be a better doctor simply based on those scores. The task of protecting the public from unqualified or dangerous physicians must be handled primarily by state licensing boards, hospital supervisors, and others who monitor physician performance, not by medical school admissions offices.

Additionally, there are serious reasons to doubt the "mismatch thesis" on which Kershnar places undue weight. The mismatch thesis claims that black students who receive affirmative action may be harmed by attending more prestigious schools than they would otherwise have attended. It's based on comparisons of graduation and bar passage rates for black law students in various schools, and its advocates believe that black students in more selective schools are more likely to fail the bar and/or fail to graduate than black students at less selective schools. However, this finding is influenced by the fact that graduation rates for black students are much higher at historically black law schools than they are anywhere else. So, the comparison sets an artificially high standard if these schools are counted among the less selective schools, and the finding wouldn't hold if we were to include those schools among the more selective ones. Also, another study of black and Latino students found that they enjoyed large advantages on the labor market by enrolling in selective colleges.[26] "Mismatch" is far from accepted science and not something on which to base our assessment of affirmative action in general.

To summarize, Kershnar and I agree that there are more effective ways to compensate for past wrongs than affirmative action. Furthermore, I don't disagree that cost/benefit analysis should be a factor when considering whether to implement any given program of affirmative action. However, here I consider his claims about some specific types of higher education to be based on faulty information. And I reiterate my claim that it isn't unjust to hire or promote someone other than the most meritorious candidate. In a larger sense, his worries that affirmative action will help undeserving people and put the public at risk are held up by racist assumptions that aren't borne out by the facts.

COMPREHENSION QUESTIONS

1. What's wrong with using the standards that apply in tort law to determine who should be compensated for past injustices?
2. How has the law helped to create inequality?
3. What's wrong with the "mismatch thesis"?

DISCUSSION QUESTION

1. Meshelski concludes by saying that Kershnar's objections to affirmative action "are held up by racist assumptions that aren't borne out by the facts." Why not simply say that his assumptions are *false*? What is it about these assumptions that makes them *racist*? (I'm not saying they *aren't* racist: I'm asking you to offer a definition of the word "racist" that implies that Kershnar's assumptions count as racist.)

FURTHER READINGS

Anderson, Elizabeth. *The Imperative of Integration.* Princeton, NJ: Princeton University Press, 2010.

Appiah, Anthony, and Amy Gutmann. *Color Conscious: The Political Morality of Race.* Princeton, NJ: Princeton University Press, 1996.

Arneson, Richard. "Against Rawlsian Equality of Opportunity" *Philosophical Studies* 93 (1999): 77–112.

Bell, Derrick. "Diversity's Distractions" *Columbia Law Review* Vol. 103, No. 6 (Oct. 2003).

Boonin, David. *Should Race Matter? Unusual Answers to the Usual Questions.* New York: Cambridge University Press, 2011.

Boxill, Bernard. *Blacks and Social Justice.* Lanham, MD: Rowman & Littlefield, 1992 (2nd ed.).

Katznelson, Ira. *When Affirmative Action was White: An Untold History of Racial Inequality in Twentieth-Century America.* New York: Norton, 2005.

Kershnar, Stephen. "The Inheritance-Based Claim to Reparations." *Legal Theory* 8, no. 2 (2002): 243–267.

Regents of the University of California v. Bakke. 1978. 438 U.S. 265.

Sander, Richard, and Stuart Taylor Jr. *Mismatch: How Affirmative Action Hurts Students It's Intended to Help, and Why Universities Won't Admit It.* New York: Basic Books, 2012.

NOTES

1. See Judith Jarvis Thomson, "Preferential Hiring," *Philosophy and Public Affairs* 2, no. 4 (1973): 364–384.
2. See Isabel V. Sawhill and Ron Haskins, "Five Myths About Our Land of Opportunity," *Brookings Institute,* November 1, 2009.
3. See Stephen Kershnar, "The Inheritance-Based Claim to Reparations," *Legal Theory* 8 (2002): 243–267.
4. Alternatively, compensation might be owed to past black people. On this account, it can be paid off by giving the money or opportunities to their descendants. On this account, current black people are never owed compensation, but are merely the beneficiaries of the people to whom it's owed. The idea here is that we want to compensate people who in the first half of the 1800s were injured. They are gone, so we can't directly compensate them. We compensate them by giving the money to their likely beneficiaries or, more likely, the beneficiaries of their beneficiaries. On this account, the money is never owed to the beneficiaries. Rather, the beneficiaries are merely the recipients of the money owed to the deceased slaves and other victims of distant historical injustice.
5. See, for example, Association of American Medical Colleges, Table A-24: MCAT and GPA Grid for Applicants and Acceptees by Selected Race and Ethnicity, 2013–2014 through 2015–2016 (Aggregated), July 10, 2016, https://www.aamc.org/data/facts/applicantmatriculant/157998/factstablea24.html and D. Andriole and D. Jeffe, "A National Cohort Study of U.S. Medical School Students Who Initially Failed Step 1 of the United States Medical Licensing Examination," *Academic Medicine* 87, no. 4 (2012): 529–536, esp. note 7.
6. See Emily Swanson, "Do Most White Americans Really Only Have White Friends? Let's Take a Closer Look," *Huffington Post,* September 3, 2014, http://www.huffingtonpost.com/2014/09/03/black-white-friends-poll_n_5759464.html. Only 0.4% of whites have a black spouse; see Roland G. Fryer Jr., "Guess Who's Been Coming to Dinner? Trends in Interracial Marriage over the 20th Century," *Journal of Economic Perspectives* 21, no. 2 (2007): 71–90.

7. See Richard Sander and Stuart Taylor Jr., "The Painful Truth About Affirmative Action," *The Atlantic*, October 2, 2012, http://www.theatlantic.com/national/archive/2012/10/the-painful-truth-about-affirmative-action/263122/, and Richard Sander and Stuart Taylor Jr., *Mismatch: How Affirmative Action Hurts Students It's Intended to Help, and Why Universities Won't Admit It* (New York: Basic Books, 2012).

8. Anthony Appiah and Amy Gutmann, *Color Conscious: The Political Morality of Race* (Princeton, NJ: Princeton University Press, 1996).

9. Thomson, "Preferential Hiring."

10. Thomas Nagel, "Equal Treatment and Compensatory Discrimination," *Philosophy and Public Affairs* 2 (1973): 348–363.

11. Elizabeth Anderson, *The Imperative of Integration* (Princeton, NJ: Princeton University Press, 2010).

12. Lesley Jacobs, *Pursuing Equal Opportunities: The Theory and Practice of Egalitarian Justice* (Cambridge: Cambridge University Press, 2004).

13. John Rawls, *A Theory of Justice* (Cambridge: Harvard University Press, 1999). My discussion of Rawls's three types of procedural justice that follows is taken from pp. 73–78. I develop the Rawlsian argument for affirmative action in more detail in "Procedural Justice and Affirmative Action," *Ethical Theory and Moral Practice* 19, no. 2 (2016): 425–443.

14. *Regents of the University of California v. Bakke* 438 U.S. 265 (1978).

15. *Parents Involved in Community Schools v. Seattle School District No. 1*, 551 U.S. 701 (2007).

16. See Table 9 in Centers for Disease Control and Prevention, *National Vital Statistics Reports*, U.S. Department of Health and Human Services, 2018, https://www.cdc.gov/nchs/data/nvsr/nvsr67/nvsr67_01.pdf.

17. Centers for Disease Control and Prevention, *National Vital Statistics Report*.

18. See Karthick Ramakrishnan and Farah Ahmad, "Income and Poverty: Part of the "State of Asian Americans," *Center for American Progress,* July 21, 2014 accessed August 4, 2019, https://cdn.americanprogress.org/wp-content/uploads/2014/08/AAPI-Income Poverty .pdf.

19. For the idea that having many female physicians is leading to a problem in the United Kingdom, see Max Pemberton, "Part-Time Women Doctors are Creating a Timebomb," *The Telegraph*, March 24, 2013, http://www.telegraph.co.uk/women/womens-health/9950248/Part-time-women-doctors-are-creating-a-timebomb.html. For the notion that female veterinarians are more likely to work part-time and work fewer hours, see Ryan Gates, "Commentary: Why Women are Leaving the Veterinary Profession," *dvm360*, October 1, 2014, http://veterinarybusiness.dvm360.com/commentary-why-women-are-leaving-veterinary-profession, and Katie Burns and Malinda Larkin, "The Gender Gap: Why Do Female Veterinarians Earn Less than Male Veterinarians," *Journal of the American Veterinary Medical Association*, April 1, 2013, https://www.avma.org/news/javmanews/pages/130401e.aspx.

20. Thousands of doctors continue to practice despite serious misconduct. See Peter Eisler and Barbara Hansen, "Thousands of Doctors Continue Practicing Despite Errors, Misconduct," *USA Today*, August 20, 2013, https://www.usatoday.com/story/news/nation/2013/08/20/doctors-licenses-medical-boards/2655513/.

21. See Douglas Martin, "Patrick Chavis, 50, Affirmative Action Figure," *The New York Times*, August 15, 2002, http://www.nytimes.com/2002/08/15/us/patrick-chavis-50-affirmative-action-figure.html and Timothy O'Neill, *Bakke and the Politics of Equality: Friends and Foes in the Classroom of Litigation* (Middletown, CT: Wesleyan University Press, 1985).

22. Though I reject his line of argument here, I want to note that in his discussion of mitigating factors, he assumes that a poor person without a college degree who has a child out of wedlock is poor because of those things, when evidence equally supports the hypothesis that they have done these things because they are poor. Either way, it is also a leap to assume these things are fully within our own control and thus we could be blameworthy for not choosing to do them.

23. The studies I am referring to are conducted by asking employers to evaluate how likely they are to hire a potential candidate by looking at their résumé. The study authors use identical résumés, but they change the names to indicate the applicant's race. Since the résumés are identical, the fact that the "black" candidates are less likely to be hired than the "white" candidates can only be due to the applicant's perceived race. See LincolnQuillian, Devah Pager, Ole Hexel, and Arnfinn H. Midtbøen, "Meta-analysis of Field Experiments Shows No Change in Racial Discrimination in Hiring Over Time," *Proceedings of the National Academy of Sciences* 114, no. 41 (2017): 10870–10875. for example.

24. As it happens, Kershnar agrees that "money is more just and efficient than affirmative action as a form of compensation," though I doubt he agrees that any compensation at all is warranted.

25. Kershnar is mistaken in his assertion that MCAT scores correlate with physician performance. There is no widely accepted measurement of "physician performance." MCAT scores do correlate with medical school grades and board exams, though there are certainly individual cases in which people's scores on one thing did not predict their scores on the others. This indicates that we need the board exams (what I refer to as the licensing exams) to serve as a gatekeeper and weed out anyone who should not be given a medical license. We have to protect the public from unqualified doctors whether they were students with good MCAT scores or students with bad MCAT scores.

26. Dale and Krueger 2011. This study and others critical of mismatch are discussed by William Kidder, "A High Target for 'Mismatch': Bogus Arguments About Affirmative Action," *Los Angeles Review of Books*, February 7, 2013, https://lareviewofbooks.org/article/a-high-target-for-mismatch-bogus-arguments-about-affirmative-action/. Not discussed is the additional factor that the research for mismatch is based on law students, and there are very few black law students at elite law schools to base these findings on.

◆◌

CHAPTER 18

Racial Profiling

AGAINST RACIAL PROFILING
ANNABELLE LEVER

Philosophical approaches to racial profiling (RP) tend to operate at some remove from actual police practice. The reason is fairly straightforward: You don't need philosophical analysis to protest police brutality and racism. Most philosophers suppose that RP can only be justified if it is consistent with respect for the bodily integrity, the dignity, and the freedom and equality of racial majorities and minorities. They are therefore only interested philosophically in its justification (or lack thereof), on the assumption that it is a practice that is not intrinsically brutal, demeaning, humiliating, and of no particular use in combating crime. Nonetheless, most philosophers are clearly aware of, and concerned by, racial injustice in our societies. They explicitly assume that RP as currently practiced is not consistent with justice. What they want to know, however—and what they hope philosophical analysis will reveal—is whether the fact that existing practices of RP are unjust means that *all* forms of RP must be unjust. They are particularly interested in the question whether the mere fact that a society has a racist past, whose consequences are still manifest in racial inequalities and injustices in the present, is *sufficient* to render all forms of RP unjust. Thus, even when the philosophical debate on profiling abstracts from police brutality and from the deliberate humiliation and mistreatment of minorities by the police, it assumes that we are interested in RP within societies much like contemporary democracies, in which despite public commitments to treat people as equals, our relations are marked by very substantial forms of racial inequality and injustice.

"Racial profiling is a crime prevention and detection method, used by police officers, which takes racial identity into account to select and investigate suspects,"[1] although police are generally not concerned with people's personal "identity," but rather with their "race" as conventionally defined. So, let's define RP as "any police-initiated action that relies on the race, ethnicity, or national origin and not just on the behavior of an individual."[2] And let's concentrate on *preventive/preemptive profiling,* rather than *post-crime profiling.* The latter is concerned to narrow down the range of suspects necessary to identify the perpetrator of a known crime; the former is an effort to identify those who are about to commit a crime, such as drug or weapons smuggling, whether or not they have already engaged in illegal acts, such as buying an illegal weapon, in order to do so.

Preemptive RP is controversial both because it is preemptive—no known illegal act has yet been committed—and because of the racial component in the decision to intervene. As no known crime has been committed, preemptive police tactics, such as "stop and search" or "stop and frisk," raise the natural concern that unless the acts to be prevented are limited in number and carefully described, police efforts to prevent crime will undermine the principle that people should be able to get on with their lives without explaining themselves to political authorities, if they are not evidently a threat to the rights and liberties of others. The racial dimension of RP makes those concerns more acute, and it is therefore the twin factors of preemption plus race that lie behind much of the political and philosophical controversy concerning RP.

So, let's limit our discussion to cases that (a) involve the use of *behavior,* not just skin color and morphology, in the determination of suspicion, and that (b) include profiles of "whiteness" as well as "blackness," where whiteness is an appropriate element in the statistical profile of the person likely to commit a particular type of criminal act.[3] (c) Let us also abstract, for the moment, from issues of police brutality and what relationship, if any, police brutality might have to the practice of profiling people as likely criminals—although, as Randall Kennedy, Naomi Zack, and I explain, there are good reasons to think that police brutality is endogenous to preventive profiling, and not merely a matter of a few bad cops, or an institutionally racist police culture.[4] The reasons to make these abstractions for philosophical purposes are fairly clear: If race, however defined, is sufficient to justify police stopping and searching people, independent of what they are doing, it would have little probative value in preventing crime, as most people, whatever their skin color or morphology, do not commit crimes. More specifically, if RP meant simply stopping black people, regardless of their behavior, it would be a case of racial discrimination pure and simple, and would be seriously unjust. It would be seriously unjust even if police stops and searches involved no brutality, rudeness, or fear whatsoever, because being stopped and searched by the police is, in itself, an unpleasant experience that requires an instrumentally rational justification, and because racial discrimination by the police, whose job is to protect us, is an exceptionally grave injustice. Indeed, the fact that discrimination by the police, and by officers of the state more generally, is so morally serious makes it impossible to see how it could ever be justified.

So, on the understanding that we are concerned with the philosophical justification of RP as something that might be useful in the prevention of crime, and on the understanding that we are abstracting from problematic features of current practice, such as police brutality and discrimination, what would be wrong with RP? After all, if RP is better than other methods at preventing crime, and is used fairly such that it targets appropriately more favored social groups as well as those that are less favored, what could be wrong with it? We all have interests in life, liberty, property, and feelings of security. So if RP significantly contributes to these good things, how could we object?

Well, let's briefly describe some objections before looking at them more closely and then considering how far they tell decisively against RP. And let's divide those worries into three groups. The first is a worry about the effectiveness of RP as a crime prevention tool when most people, whatever the ascriptive or voluntary group to which they belong, do not engage in crime, let alone violent crime.[5] Second, let's consider the objections to RP based on the burdens it places on racialized minorities, and the likelihood that it will exacerbate forms of injustice that we already find hard to deal with and have urgent duties to remedy. And finally, let's consider the problems that RP poses for the police, as compared to forms of crime prevention. Although this latter factor is rarely discussed in the literature, it is, I believe, of considerable importance in the reasons to prefer alternative forms of crime prevention, such as random stops or universal searches to RP.

1. RP Is Unlikely to Be Effective

We do not know the size of the total criminal population, nor of that part of the criminal population for which racial profiles are standardly used.[6] Hence, a real worry with RP is that it can quickly take on the quality of a self-fulfilling prophecy. If police stop sufficiently more black people than white people (on the assumption that the former are more likely to be engaged in crime than the latter), they are likely to find more black people who are breaking the law than white people *even if* police stops of black people are less good at identifying crime than police stops of white people, as is, apparently the case.[7]

Because crime is rare, the overwhelming majority of the people who fit a police profile will never commit the particular crime for which the profile has been drawn up, and will be unlikely to engage in criminal activities at all.[8] For example, Steve Holbert and Lisa Rose claim that only 2% of black people are arrested for committing any crime in a given year.[9] This figure seems to be in line with other findings. Thus, in their studies of violence in 180 Chicago neighborhoods from 1995 to 2002, Sampson et al. found that "although 3,431 violent offenses were reported, personal violence is still relatively rare overall, with the prevalence of robbery (0.3%), purse snatching (0.3%), arson (0.4%), attacking with a weapon (2.3%), and gang fighting (3.9%) all less than 5% averaged across the 3 waves of data collection. Even the most common item, hitting someone (18.7%) is reported by fewer than 20% of subjects. Carrying a hidden weapon (7.6%) and throwing objects at another person (8.2%) are in the middle. These prevalence estimates comport with national norms."[10]

Predictive police stops on the basis of statistical profiles alone are therefore unlikely to catch criminals, so their instrumental justification depends on their *relative virtues* compared to other ways of detecting and preventing crime, not on their *absolute* advantages. However, it is difficult to estimate those comparative advantages when the size of the criminal population is a matter of speculation, when prejudice and unequal legal resources may affect arrest rates, and when rates of legal convictions may also reflect legal and extra-legal incentives to plead guilty even if one is innocent—a particularly serious problem in the United States given practices of plea bargaining.[11] Thus, it is difficult to show that preventive profiling is an effective police tool, or more effective than the alternatives, and these problems are particularly acute, because the best way to prevent crime may not be a matter of *policing* at all, but of changes in social policy more generally.[12]

2. RP and Racial Injustice

We have seen that it is hard to show that RP is effective—whether in absolute or in comparative terms. And this matters, because RP has moral and political disadvantages that are extremely serious. Indeed, given the difficulties of RP that we are about to examine, mere effectiveness would be insufficient to justify its use. As we will see, RP is likely to exacerbate longstanding problems of racial injustices; to lead to the death and serious injury of innocent members of racialized minorities; and to increase distrust, hostility, and fear of the police by those who they are sworn to protect. It will only be possible to justify RP, then, in rare, and exceptional, circumstances.

Preemptive RP is, unfortunately, likely to reinforce racist beliefs about groups, by fostering misplaced claims about the causal importance of race in criminal behavior and by fostering a misplaced essentialism about race, be it biological or cultural.[13] Indeed, it seems likely to cement prejudice about the frequency, severity, and distribution of criminal behavior in society, because profiling draws public attention *to* differential rates in the propensity to break the law, and *away from* evidence that most people do not engage in crime, whatever the ascriptive or voluntary groups to which they belong.[14] Respect for our fellow citizens is inconsistent with the use of police tactics that will predictably make it harder to combat racial disadvantages and injustices that we already have a duty to alleviate.[15] Hence, given what we may call "background injustice," or the continued effects in the present of racial injustices inherited from the past, RP is unlikely to be justified as an ordinary police practice.

For example, even if black people are the main victims of black criminals, it is hard to see how the RP of black people would advantage black people.[16] Given residential and occupational segregation, "black on black" crime mainly occurs in neighborhoods and workplaces where most people are black, just as "white on white" crime mainly occurs in neighborhoods and workplaces where most people are white. While any racial or ethnic group will benefit from police success in catching or preventing attacks against them, it is doubtful that racial or ethnic profiles will be particularly useful in the process. Just as you are unlikely to distinguish one academic from another by looking for a middle-aged white man among the professors on most European or American campuses, so looking for a "young black male" in an area where young black males are common is unlikely to help you deter crime. Rather, it seems that the main beneficiaries of the RP of black people will be white people, because white people make up the majority of the population who will be safeguarded, and will be able to benefit from any advantages that RP brings without suffering the main burdens of RP.[17] On the other hand, young black men, and those who love and depend upon them, will bear the overwhelming share of the costs of RP, whether or not they share in the benefits. This division of the costs and benefits of security cannot be justified as an ordinary part of policing, once we take background injustice into account, for that would be to compound the burdens on some of the most vulnerable groups in our societies, and to exacerbate injustices that we have a duty to repair. Hence, as Randall Kennedy has argued,[18] RP may perhaps be justified in very exceptional circumstances, as long as special forms of approval, supervision, accountability, and compensation are in place. However, RP is nearly always unjustified given its intrinsic properties and its likely consequences, even if we abstract from the shame and horror of police violence, brutality, and prejudice.

3. RP and Harms to the Police

RP creates risks and dangers for the police that are not true of alternative ways of trying to prevent crime, such as random searches or universal searches. Random and universal searches treat racial majorities and minorities the same, so there is no particular reason why they should stigmatize and unfairly burden the innocent, or unfairly treat some guilty people worse than others. However—and this is often overlooked—because these forms of preemptive search mean that the police do not need to decide whom to search, they *protect the police* from stigma and hostility, and give them the evidence with which to confront and correct their own prejudices, without unfairly implying that they are *more prejudiced or racist* that the general population. Put simply, RP is likely to exacerbate patterns of distrust and hostility among young black men and older white police, and to tar all members of the latter, as well as the former, because of the bad behavior of their worst members.

RP, unfortunately, is also likely to foster police violence against unarmed civilians who are black, even when the police are not particularly racist.[19] RP tells the police that they have more to fear from black people than other people, since the rationale for profiling is that being black makes one more likely to engage in illegal behavior in general, and violent crime in particular. Not surprisingly, then, police are more likely to fear and anticipate violence from black people than from white people, and to react violently to behavior that they mistakenly see as threatening.[20] Conversely, black people have reason to hate and fear the police and to anticipate violent reactions from them because they are black, no matter how innocent they are.[21] In short, RP is more likely than alternative police tactics to make ordinary police work difficult, dangerous, and dispiriting, and to create the avoidable risk that nervous police officers will behave in ways that are both immoral and illegal.

There are, then, at least three compelling reasons to reject RP. As we have seen, the burden of proof in arguments over police searches is on those who would justify, rather than those who would oppose, RP—and that burden of proof is unlikely to be met.[22]

COMPREHENSION QUESTIONS

1. Why is the history of our country important for the ethics of RP?
2. How does Lever define RP?
3. Why doubt that RP is effective?
4. What burdens does RP impose on racialized communities?
5. Why is RP bad for the police?

DISCUSSION QUESTIONS

1. Why does Lever set aside issues like police discrimination and brutality? Why aren't they part of the conversation? Should they be?
2. Suppose that Lever is wrong and RP is *highly* effective. Would her second and third arguments still work? Would they still show that it would be unjust and unwise for the police to engage in profiling? Or do those arguments depend on the first one about efficacy?

Case 1

"Predictive policing" is a powerful new tool in law enforcement. Essentially, police departments feed crime-related data into an algorithm that spits out predictions about the times and locations of future crimes. This turns out to be surprisingly reliable, and it helps departments allocate scarce resources to the spots where crime is most likely to occur. It has actually reduced crime in some areas. However, there are worries:

> The first issue with predictive policing is that the algorithms really re-create police practices from the past rather than predict crime in the future. The data behind these algorithms can overestimate crime in minority neighborhoods and underestimate it in white neighborhoods. Even if a predictive policing algorithm is not hard coded to consider race or income, it can still lead police to be dispatched predominantly to low-income and minority neighborhoods. In Los Angeles, one of the first cities to adopt predictive policing, community members in low-income and minority neighborhoods report seeing the police "all the time," while residents in affluent neighborhoods see the police "rarely," according to the Stop LAPD Spying Coalition, an activist group.
>
> [Second, these] algorithms are often deployed in secret, making it impossible for the public to scrutinize them. Police in New Orleans quietly used predictive policing algorithms for several years without ever announcing they were doing so; even members of the City Council were left in the dark. In Chicago, the police department has resisted countless calls to disclose the details of how its algorithm predicts which people are most likely to be involved in gun violence. Several years ago, for example, police showed up unannounced to Robert McDaniel's home on the west side of the city and warned him not to commit any more crimes. McDaniel, who had multiple arrests on suspicion of minor offenses but only one misdemeanor conviction, learned that he had made the department's "heat list," meaning he was considered among those most prone to violence—either as a perpetrator or victim—according to the *Chicago Tribune.*[*]

What do you think about this technology? What do you think Lever would say about it?

---

[*]https://www2.bostonglobe.com/magazine/2019/04/17/can-predictive-policing-help
-stamp-out-racial-profiling/7GNaJrScBYu0a5lUr0RaKP/story.html

IN DEFENSE OF CRIMINAL PROFILING
AND ITS RACIAL COMPONENT
T. ALLAN HILLMAN

1. Introduction

The term "racial profiling" has entered the national lexicon to such an extent that there is little hope in its being replaced by a more accurate label. It bears noticing that, strictly speaking, there is no such practice. A *profile* (noun) is no more and no less than a list of characteristics meant to capture a particular kind of person or thing, and so we may correctly speak of a personal profile (e.g., short, heavy, Caucasian male with less-than-average intelligence and a boisterous personality) or a geographical profile (e.g., low, grassy terrain with few trees and the occasional stream). In order *to profile* (verb) a person or thing, I must assess whether and to what extent that person or thing falls under the previously established list of characteristics.

Of course, our concern here is a criminal profile, a list of characteristics that tends to satisfy the kind of person who commits a crime of a particular sort. Such a profile may be built by paying due attention to (a) arrests or convictions within a certain region, (b) psychological or criminological studies involving persons who have engaged in specific criminal activities, and even (c) data accumulated by way of first-person experience by a player in the justice system (e.g., a police officer). The profile itself typically includes information such as physical characteristics (including race or ethnicity), offender background, habits and beliefs, and the like.

When combined with witness statements and evidence collection, a profile may enable an investigator to narrow down the field of possible suspects. For instance, after a complete analysis of a murder scene, the investigator may determine that the suspect is likely a white male in his early to mid-thirties with anger control issues, a loner with few acquaintances, a poor relationship with his family, and minimal education. This type of profiling is what we might call retroactive profiling, the practice of determining from a specific crime scene the likelihood of the suspect's possessing characteristics x, y, or z.[23]

The more controversial type of profiling is predictive profiling: Here, a profile is used in order to prevent a crime that has not yet occurred or is (possibly) in the process of occurring. For example, suppose that a motorist with characteristics x, y, and z is pulled over for violating traffic laws. Why, we might ask, does the officer pull over *this particular* driver rather than some other? Among his reasons for the traffic stop may be some combination of those very characteristics—perhaps drivers with *those* features are more likely to be smuggling illegal drugs than drivers without those characteristics. The practice of predictive profiling is thought to be particularly controversial because a suspect's race/ethnicity plays some role as one of the determining characteristics in the decision of a legal official to act. Accordingly, the suspected drug smuggler may be pulled over under the pretense of a traffic violation at least in part because he is of a particular race/ethnicity. Predictive profiling of this sort has been given the label *racial profiling*, or *RP*.

Regardless of whether the term is accurate,[24] let's define RP for the purposes of what follows: the use of race/ethnicity by a law enforcement official as *at least one factor* within the overall criminal profile that determines whether to investigate a person for criminal activity.[25] At least two practical concerns have been voiced by those who oppose the practice. First, RP is not a particularly effective or productive tool, certainly neither effective nor productive enough to warrant it as a policy to be adopted by law enforcement agencies. As such, the practice is irrational in the instrumental sense—that is, it's a bad way to achieve a goal, whatever that goal happens to be. Second, RP involves a base variety of stereotyping that is morally problematic, particularly as it concerns the race or ethnicity of the individual who, at least on the surface, satisfies the criminal profile. Our interest in what follows will be to demonstrate that the apparent difficulties underlying these two worries are just that: merely apparent.

2. RP as Instrumentally Rational

Instrumental rationality is the sort of rationality that an agent uses who wishes to achieve the most efficient or cost-effective means in order to achieve some end. Suppose that my goal is to lose two pounds. In order to achieve this goal, I may (a) go to the gym and exercise while maintaining a balanced diet, or (b) go to my primary care doctor and request that surgery be performed whereby exactly two pounds is removed from my physique. Now, both (a) and (b) would result in my achieving my desired goal. Yet, clearly, (a) represents a more effective balance of time, financial expenditure, and common sense in light of my modest goal. In short, instrumental rationality in this circumstance dictates that I choose option (a) over (b).

Institutional entities such as police departments can be understood to utilize instrumental rationality in a similar way: What is the most cost-effective and efficient means to achieving the desired result of criminal apprehension and prosecution? One may imagine that law enforcement agencies have determined that, in order to secure the public good, RP is a policy procedure that promises to aid in bringing about the desired results. That is, along with witness testimony, evidence collection, and forensic science, RP is an investigative tool that enhances rather than diminishes law enforcement effectiveness. Why think this is so?

According to empirical data, certain racial demographics are overrepresented in particular areas of the criminal justice system as compared to their population numbers. As of 2010, for instance, black Americans composed just over 13.5% of the U.S. population and yet accounted for 38% of violent arrests nationally; they were also 6.5 times more likely than white Americans to be identified by victims as suspects in robberies.[26] With these data in hand, law enforcement officials may reason as follows: (1) Members of some racial/ethnic groups in the United States are more likely, on average, to commit certain kinds of criminal offenses than are members of other groups; (2) it's instrumentally rational for law enforcement officials to adopt those policies that will enable them to apprehend larger numbers of offenders; and (3) RP is a policy that enables law enforcement officials to apprehend larger numbers of offenders. Therefore, (4) law enforcement officials ought to adopt the policy of RP.[27]

Whether (1) is true, of course, will depend upon available empirical data. At least in a large range of cases, it certainly does appear that the correlations between racial group and criminal tendency stand up to scrutiny. As for (2), this simply seems to follow straightforwardly from the very function of law enforcement within U.S. society. One might wonder what the proper function of a police department *is* if it is not (at least) to deter crime and to apprehend lawbreakers. Since (4) follows from (1)–(3), that leaves us with (3). *Does* RP enable law enforcement officials to detect and apprehend larger numbers of offenders than they would be able to detect and apprehend absent such a policy?

It seems so. After all, it stands to reason that if a certain demographic disproportionately commits a certain type of crime, then police officers aiming to curb that type of crime would selectively target that particular demographic in order to effectively do so. Suppose that illegal drugs in a certain city are transported more often than not by black individuals. In order to capture, arrest, and convict more criminal offenders, police officers would reasonably adopt a policy of targeting—disproportionately to other racial/ethnic demographics—black persons with other representative characteristics (e.g., appropriate age group, male, particular type of vehicle). Such a policy would be expected, on average, to result in bringing more offenders to justice and reducing crime.

Consider an example from the work of Randall Kennedy, who describes "the fact pattern presented in a federal lawsuit of the early '90s, *United States v. Weaver*":

> An officer from the Drug Enforcement Administration stops and questions a young man who has just stepped off a flight . . . The officer has focused on this man for several reasons. Intelligence reports indicate that black gangs in Los Angeles are flooding the Kansas City area with illegal drugs, and the man in question was on a flight originating in Los Angeles. Young, toughly dressed, and appearing very nervous, he paid for his ticket in cash, checked no luggage, brought two carry-on bags, and made a beeline for a taxi upon deplaning . . . [T]he officer also took into account the fact that the young man was black. When asked to explain himself, the officer declares that *he considered the individual's race, along with other factors, because doing so helps him efficiently allocate the limited time and other resources at his disposal.*[28]

The officer makes an excellent point. Law enforcement agencies must constantly deal with limited resources, whether budget constraints, outdated equipment and technology, or personnel shortages. Officers of the law cannot investigate *everyone*, and so many choices about who should be investigated must be made, of necessity, with limited time to carefully reflect (i.e., in "the heat of the moment") and in the absence of complete information.[29] As such, law enforcement officials *should* utilize all of the information that they do have, including empirical facts about race/ethnicity as it relates to crime, and the (fallible) probabilistic judgments that such facts may entail.[30] RP worked out beneficially in this case, enabling a law enforcement official to thwart criminal activity. Far from being an irrational course of action, the practice of RP is both eminently reasonable and an invaluable investigative tool.[31]

3. RP as Morally Permissible

Of course, that a practice is rationally defensible in the instrumental sense does not imply that it is morally appropriate. For example, perhaps it is determined by a series of empirical studies that the most efficient and cost-effective way to curb littering in national parks is to execute those who break anti-littering laws. While this course of action may be rational in the instrumental sense, it is undoubtedly problematic from a moral perspective. So, even if RP is a rational practice, it may be morally wrong nonetheless. On the contrary, I shall argue that it is morally permissible.

Objectors to the moral permissibility of RP typically argue in one of two ways: (1) if we are to gauge the costs of RP against its benefits, we will recognize that the balance of harm caused far outweighs its advantages, or (2) irrespective of whether RP does or does not result in beneficial consequences, it is a morally inappropriate practice insofar as it violates the moral and/or legal rights of individuals on whom it is practiced. Let's consider each of these in order.

As an investigative tool, the purported benefits of RP are less crime, more secure communities, and a more efficient police force. The more interesting question, however, is this: What kinds of harms or drawbacks might be intimately associated with RP? At first blush, there appear to be harms of two kinds: physical harm and mental, emotional, or otherwise psychological harm. We can, it seems to me, immediately rule out physical harm as an intrinsic consequence of RP. This is so because there is nothing about the practice of RP that, by its very nature, raises the probability that it will result in physical harm to the person profiled.[32]

No, if RP can be reasonably suggested to result in harms, those harms will be in some way psychological in nature. Such harms may impact individuals taken singly, or communities altogether. According to critics of RP, among the harmful results of the practice may be feelings of resentment and indignation by minorities against both law enforcement officials and society at large, loss of faith in the good will and honest intentions of police officers, and an overall lack of motivation to aid police officers in their quest to keep communities secure and free of crime. These potential drawbacks to RP are serious and deserve to be addressed.

Unfortunately, it is unclear that these psychological harms are in fact results of RP per se rather than some other and unrelated social phenomenon (e.g., the consequences of decades of perceived racial animus directed at minorities). Let's consider a hypothetical case. Bob Smith is a black motorist who has been pulled over for speeding. While he is warned to keep his speed to the posted limit, officers observe the contents of his car for signs of drug paraphernalia and the like. The officers request to search his car; they receive permission and uncover a large quantity of heroin, whereupon Bob Smith is arrested. Question: Was Bob Smith caught on the basis of RP? Given the information provided, we simply do not know. Nor, importantly, does Bob Smith know. Police officers are not in the habit of informing suspects of a crime as to the strategies used in order to investigate them. While Bob Smith may suspect that RP played some role in his being initially pulled over, he quite simply has no evidence that this is the case. It may be a result of RP, but it equally as well may not be. As David Boonin puts it, "If a cop engages in racial profiling but no one is aware of this fact, after all, then none of the negative consequences that the objection appeals to [i.e., the psychological harms discussed above] will occur."[33] And so, the objection from psychological harms seems to depend on the assumption that suspects are explicitly aware that they have been racially profiled, an assumption that is questionable at best in any given individual case.[34]

But suppose then that the psychological outrage generated by RP is not based on individual cases per se, but is instead a communal reaction. Black Americans (say) are aware of the practice as an investigative technique used by police officers, and so indignation arises from the recognition that their group *qua* group is being selectively targeted for these particular kinds of crimes (while other groups are not). They are (say) resentful because it is their group that is disproportionately affected by the practice, and this is so independently of any individual case.

Here, as David Boonin has argued, the opponent of RP faces a dilemma:[35] Either the resentment purportedly due to RP is independently justified, or it is not. If we suppose that it is independently justified, then there is something about the practice that is wrong, and it is this wrongness that leads to the resentment. But what is it about RP that is wrong? This must be identified independently of the resentment that it allegedly causes. Merely pointing out the resentment does not do enough to show that RP is itself morally objectionable.

Now suppose that the resentment purportedly due to RP is not independently justified. That is, RP is wrong *because* it causes some variety of resentment or outrage in a certain segment of the population. Consequently, the question arises: Is this enough by itself to show that RP is morally inappropriate? It seems not. Many people are resentful of—indeed, furious about—the fact that hundreds or even thousands of abortions are performed daily in the United States. Many people are resentful of—and, again, furious about—the fact that same-sex marriage has been legalized by the U.S. Supreme Court. But do psychological facts about a group of persons—such as feelings of resentment or outrage—really determine the morality or immorality of a certain practice? In a word, no.

Let's now turn to the second primary sort of objection lodged against RP: It violates the rights of those on whom it is practiced. Some have alleged that RP violates constitutional protections enshrined in the U.S. Constitution, such as the right against unreasonable searches and seizures (the Fourth Amendment) or the right to equal protection under the law (the equal protection clause of the Fourteenth Amendment). While we do not have the space here to enter into complex constitutional arguments, perhaps we can generalize these legal rights under one overarching moral right, say, *the right to be treated fairly and reasonably by those in authority*. Suppose that a traffic stop by a law enforcement official depends upon a preexisting criminal profile, one in which the racial component occurs. While the police officer pulls over the suspect on the basis of some traffic violation, the officer uses the stop as a pretext to search the suspect's vehicle for (say) illegal drugs or weapons. This, say opponents of RP, violates the moral right of the accused in virtue of the fact that the suspect is treated unreasonably and unfairly on the basis of his race.

If the primary concern underlying the alleged violations of a suspect's rights involves his being treated unreasonably or unfairly on the basis of his race or ethnicity, perhaps we might here reflect on the extent to which government officials may *ever* take race into consideration when dealing with citizens. So, let's compare a case of RP—in particular, a traffic stop occurring on the basis of a pre-existing criminal profile—with other instances in which law enforcement officials may utilize racial/ethnic characteristics during the course of an investigation. Such a comparison may shed light on the moral permissibility of RP.[36]

Consider a scenario wherein a murder has occurred, and a witness reports to police officers that the offender is a black male who drove away in an unidentified vehicle. Undoubtedly, in such a situation, it is morally appropriate for law enforcement officials to utilize roadblocks in the hopes of catching the killer. Furthermore, we would expect the officers manning the roadblocks to pay extra attention to black males. Now, why is this significant? It is significant because any interpretation of the relevant moral principle—*persons have the right to be treated reasonably and fairly by those in authority*—that would make RP a morally illegitimate practice would also make an officer's scrupulous attention to black males in the above-mentioned scenario morally problematic.

To see why, notice that *if* the objector to RP is correct in the view that RP does violate the right to reasonable and fair treatment by those in authority, then it does so because the person being profiled is singled out on the basis of his race. It is this fact that is allegedly unreasonable and unfair, and so RP is on this basis immoral. Yet, in our scenario, it seems clear that none of the police officers at the aforementioned roadblocks believe that *every single black male* who passes the roadblock is guilty of the crime. Instead, the fact that the witness described the suspect as black simply raises the probability that any individual black driver is more likely to be the culprit than any individual white driver. Similarly, in cases of traffic stops that occur at least partially on the basis of RP, it is the fact that the subject's race is probabilistically relevant that drives the officer's actions. Thus, if the moral right is to be consistently applied in the way that the opponent of RP suggests, then the police officers in this scenario cannot legitimately use the fact that a particular male is black as a test case for more scrutiny. Yet, surely, this is absurd.[37]

4. Objections and Replies

Here, I will treat two possible objections to my account that may arise from opponents of the practice of RP.

The Objection from Police Brutality

The popular media and the public at large are often guilty of conflating RP on the one hand, *police brutality or abuse* on the other. It is undoubtedly the case that police brutality or abuse in any form is morally unacceptable, and all available means ought to be utilized in order to eliminate its occurrence. However, RP is occasionally tarred with the same brush, a sort of guilt by association, and this is unfortunate. After all, *any* police action or policy directed toward persons of any race or ethnicity would be morally objectionable if it was practiced in a cruel and abusive way, including the interrogation of witnesses, the issuing of speeding tickets, or the arrest of suspected criminals. We object to such practices only when they are occasioned by undue violence and ruthlessness. So, while the problem of police brutality or abuse may be in need of further attention and rectification, it is an issue altogether different from the practice of RP.[38]

The Objection from Identity Characteristics

Perhaps it is always wrong for officials to treat a person differently from others simply on the basis of a feature that constitutes part of the person's very identity, a feature that is beyond the control of the individual. So, it is wrong to treat any particular black driver differently from any particular white driver if the basis for the differential treatment is due at least in part to the subject's race. Yet, this sort of objection cannot be sustained, it seems.

First, it may be responded that there are features of suspected criminals, whether beyond one's control or not, which are probabilistically relevant to a police investigation. Race/ethnicity certainly seems to be one of them. Consider an analogy: We would certainly expect medical professionals to take a race-based approach to medicine in certain contexts (e.g., perhaps blacks as a group are more prone to a particular illness or condition than are other groups). In these instances, physicians would be focusing on the prior probability of a fact about the racial group taken as a whole in order to better do their job. Similarly, as Neven Sesardić argues, since black Americans at present have a higher incidence of certain criminal offenses than other groups, "shouldn't the police be allowed to keep this in mind and act on that true belief in some situations . . . ?"[39] Like the physician, the police officer is simply taking into consideration the prior probabilities of group behavior in order to better do her job.

Second, suppose that it is granted that while the characteristic *is* probabilistically relevant, it should still be ignored because it is a feature of one's identity that is "beyond one's control." Here, too, the objector faces a difficulty. In many other analogous instances, our moral scruples are not threatened by treating people differently on the basis of such unique and identifying characteristics. Men are more prone to violent offense than are women; young men are charged higher insurance premiums than are young women. Yet, one rarely (ever?) hears of a man complaining of being treated differently on the basis of a characteristic beyond his control. So, if the objection is to succeed, there must be some additional argument forthcoming that explains why or how the objection from identifying characteristics works in the case of (say) black individuals but not in the case of men generally.[40]

5. Conclusion

The motivation for RP policies in law enforcement is driven by the urge to more successfully apprehend criminals. According to empirical studies, the fact is that certain demographic groups are more apt than others to commit certain crimes. This fact is reasonably accounted for by those who develop criminal profiles. While the racial component does not exhaust such a profile, it is an integral part of it. As I hope to have shown, racial profiling—as it is unfortunately known—is a reasonable, effective, and morally permissible investigative tool utilized by some law enforcement agencies as an adopted policy and by certain individual officers as a tactical strategy.

COMPREHENSION QUESTIONS

1. What is a profile? Why does Hillman talk about profiles?
2. What is predictive policing?
3. What makes something "instrumentally rational"? Why does Hillman think that RP is instrumentally rational?
4. Why does Hillman think that the benefits of RP outweigh any costs?
5. Why does Hillman think that RP doesn't violate anyone's rights?

DISCUSSION QUESTIONS

1. Even if it is—in principle—OK for the police to *consider* race when they are deciding whom to pursue, we might worry that they often give race *too much weight* in their deliberations. And since it's hard not to make that mistake, we might think that the police should ignore race just to avoid that error. What do you think of this line of reasoning? What should Hillman say by way of reply?
2. Hillman says that you can't be psychologically harmed by RP if you don't know that you were racially profiled. But you can *suspect* that you were profiled, and be harmed on that basis. Is there anything Hillman can say to this objection?

Case 2

Consider this case from Houston, Texas:

> In the Facebook video shared [in May 2019] by Clarence Evans, a white deputy says he has an arrest warrant from Louisiana . . . [The] law enforcement officer grabs Evans in front of his Houston home and calls him "Quentin," the name of the fugitive. Evans repeatedly asks the Harris County Precinct 4 constable deputy to show him a picture of the fugitive while refusing to show his ID . . . "You don't know my name, so how can you tell me I have a warrant in Louisiana?" Evans asks the deputy in the video.
>
> If Texas law enforcement stops and asks someone who is not driving for identification, that person is not legally required to do so . . . A person who is not driving only has to identify themselves if they are arrested.
>
> As the confrontation continues, another deputy arrives, bringing a phone with a picture of the suspect. After the first deputy shows the photo, Evans shouts, "What are you trying to say? I look like him because I got dreads and I'm black?" The second deputy glances at the photo, then separates the first deputy and Evans, who can be heard saying he wants to file a report on the incident. "I get it, I get it," the second deputy says as he tries to calm Evans.

Case 2 (continued)

> The video ends with Evans asking the woman recording the video to get the fugitive's photo. According to Evans' post, the photo showed a black man in his 50s with dreadlocks. The suspect is at least 20 years older . . .*
>
> The worry, of course, is that the deputy was engaging in RP. Does that seem like the best explanation? If not, then what is? If so, what should we infer from cases like this? Does it show that RP is generally unreliable? If not, what *does* it show?
>
> _____
>
> *https://www.usatoday.com/story/news/nation/2019/05/15/clarence-evans-alleged-racial
> -profiling-video-mistaken-identity/3687516002/

REPLY TO HILLMAN
ANNABELLE LEVER

RP as actually practiced in police departments is unlikely to be morally justified—especially in the United States, where it is, in any case, illegal. It is unlikely to be justified because the statistics that purport to show the rationality of RP depend on conceptions of "race" that may well be inconsistent, based on illegal stops, searches, intimidation, and also based on convictions obtained illegally, or on practices of plea bargaining that, while legal, will strike many as shockingly coercive, arbitrary, and indifferent to both truth and justice. It is therefore important that whatever justification for RP we offer avoids naïveté about the nature, extent, and consequences of racialized injustice in our societies; takes seriously the ways that racial injustice intersects with other forms of structural injustice in our societies; and does not write off as deluded or confused the objections to RP of those who are its main victims.

Unfortunately, Hillman's arguments for RP appear to suffer from these difficulties. For example, "race" as is used in crime statistics—or in their interpretation—is hardly a stable technical term, whose meaning is self-evident. Racial disparities in criminal statistics, therefore, will not pick out anything useful if the people who are included in the different racial groups are not stable or, at least, mutually consistent. For example, a sociological study of disparities in crime rates in Chicago for 1995–2002 showed that Mexican Americans had lower rates of violence than both white and black Americans, and this "was explained by a combination of married parents, living in a neighborhood with a high concentration of immigrants and individual immigrant status" itself.[41] Were crime figures for Mexican Americans to be assimilated to those of white Chicagoans, therefore, we would get a seriously misleading picture of the distribution of crime and of its correlates.

Or consider some other figures offered by Sampson and his collaborators. "In Atlanta one in six residents were dislocated by urban renewal; the great majority of these were poor blacks. Nationwide, fully 20 percent of all central-city housing units occupied by blacks were lost in the period 1960–70 alone . . . [T]his displacement does not even include that brought about by more routine market forces (evictions, rent increases, commercial development)." Moreover, "the negative consequences of deliberate policy decisions to concentrate minorities and the poor in public housing" have led to "massive, segregated housing projects that have become ghettos for the minorities and disadvantaged . . . *[P]ublic housing is a federally funded, physically permanent institution for the isolation of black families by race and class.*"[42] Thus, while one of every five poor blacks lived in ghettos or areas of extreme poverty in 1970, by 1980 nearly two out of every five did so.[43] So policies that may appear on their face to have nothing to do with the racial characteristics of crime—such as urban renewal or government support for home ownership—turn out to explain why some social groups, rather than others, face crime and violence as an everyday part of their lives, and may find themselves tempted to engage in it as a rational strategy for improving their lot in life, or drawn into it through friendship, loneliness, anger, depression, or despair. Once one recognizes the extent of racial injustice in our societies, in other words, it seems clear that combining RP with affirmative action is wholly inadequate as a response to the insecurity and violence that bedevil our societies, or as a remedy for the deep and pervasive injustices that scar so many lives in our societies, as well as our relations to those not of them.

But let's turn, for a moment, from young racialized men and women—the primary victims of RP in criminal matters—to the problems that RP poses for the police. After all, the police, like racialized minorities, have collective as well as individual interests in protection from arbitrary and prejudiced judgments about their sentiments, beliefs, and behavior. And, like other people, they have reasons to value ways of carrying out their work that enable them, individually and collectively, to test the adequacy of their intuitions and judgments against relevant evidence. Random or universal searches are, to policing, what anonymized exams or auditions are to teachers, employers, and orchestras. If their justification is to protect those who are likely to suffer from prejudice and discrimination, a non-negligible advantage of such methods is that teachers and employers can come to learn from their mistaken attributions of quality and causality, while minimizing the harmful consequences of those mistakes for others, or of their recognition and correction for themselves. Of course, we don't always take the chances offered us to correct our errors, nor do we always see those chances when they appear. But if one disadvantage of RP as a crime-prevention strategy is its likelihood of perpetuating unjustified views about people's propensities to crime, it is likely also to perpetuate unjustified prejudice against the police themselves.

In short, there are good reasons to be skeptical of the conceptual, empirical, and normative assumptions that make RP appear an effective and attractive crime-prevention tool. Resources are, of course, scarce, relative to the demands upon them. That is a reason to take seriously the ideas of those, like Jonathan Wolff and Avner de-Shalit, who highlight the importance of ways to decouple one form of social disadvantage from another, even when we are unable adequately to eliminate them.[44] It is an additional reason to take seriously the views of those who are most likely to be victims of violent crime, and who also suffer from forms of insecurity that most proponents of profiling do not. They have little enough voice in the academy, as in our societies at large. All the more reason to attend to what they say and to the consequences of their absence from philosophical and political debates.

COMPREHENSION QUESTIONS

1. What's Lever's point about the study of crime in Chicago?
2. What does housing policy have to do with RP?
3. Why, exactly, is it bad *for the police* for them to engage in RP?

DISCUSSION QUESTION

1. You can imagine Hillman saying: "Lever herself admits that there is more crime in certain racialized communities than others. Why isn't that an argument *for* RP rather than an argument against it?" What should Lever say in reply?

REPLY TO LEVER
T. ALLAN HILLMAN

In Annabelle Lever's thoughtful and articulate piece in opposition to RP, she lodges three objections in particular against the practice. First, she alleges that it is an ineffective tool for combating crime; second, it places an undue burden on minorities, a burden that is likely to have among its consequences further injustices to an already overburdened social group; and finally, the practice is at least indirectly harmful to the police, stigmatizing them as prejudiced against minority populations. Since in my own essay I attempted to overcome the second type of objection more so than the others, I will focus here on objections one and three.

Why, according to Lever, is RP unlikely to be effective? One reason is that its continual practice creates something like a "self-fulfilling prophecy": The more often minority citizens are targeted by police officers, the more likely it is that such citizens are found to be guilty of some sort of criminal behavior. Counterfactually, *had* the police instead targeted (say) a majority group, the same sorts of offenses would have been discovered in the same statistical distribution. So, suppose that RP is abandoned entirely by all police officers in the United States; the result, it is argued, would be that criminal categories would not be distinguishable so readily by race.

Perhaps it's true that those who are targeted by police are more likely than those who are not targeted to be arrested for some crime or other. It seems reasonable to think that *if* police officers looked elsewhere for criminal activity, they would be likely to find it. However, this does not by itself discredit the (at least apparent) empirical fact that members of certain races—at least within the United States—are more likely than other racial demographics to commit certain types of criminal offense. In particular, the fear that RP is little more than "self-fulfilling prophecy" can be seen to be misguided if we pay close attention to criminal reports made by victims of violent crime (e.g., assault, rape, armed robbery). What a recent survey has shown is that nearly 25% of such offenders, as identified by victims, are black, even though blacks constitute somewhere around 13% of the population as a whole. So, as David Boonin has argued, "the rate at which black people are identified by victims as the perpetrator of a crime . . . is roughly twice what it would be if black Americans committed such crimes at the same rate as the population as a whole," and these statistics are "very close to the results of studying arrest reports."[45] While this is only one data point, of course, it appears to me to be an especially telling one, particularly against the claim that appeals to statistics concerning profiled individuals are circular.

Lever's final objection to the practice of profiling concerns the putative harms to police officers themselves. The idea seems to be this: If police officers search randomly—and, as a consequence, treat all races the same—then "police do not decide whom to search" and such behavior will "*protect the police* from stigma and hostility, and give them evidence with which to confront and correct their own prejudices." I admit to being unsure precisely what to make of this as an *objection* to RP. After all, it seems to me that we as a democratic citizenry might *want* for police officers to make decisions, albeit reasonable ones, about whom to search and, ultimately, arrest for criminal behavior. Of course, it is debatable, I suppose, as to just how instrumentally rational RP is in fact—even though I have argued that, statistically speaking, it is perfectly rational in this sense. But until it is conclusively demonstrated that the practice is irrational, this line of objection appears to beg the very question at issue. It amounts to little more than the blanket recommendation, "If police officers cease to utilize the practice of RP, then they will be liked and trusted more by a certain component of the citizenry." For my own part, I am certainly far from convinced that this is true, even apart from its (in)efficacy as an objection to RP.

Still, for the sake of argument, let's consider this line of thinking in more detail, viz., RP may lead to distrust and suspicion directed toward police officers by a minority demographic. Either this distrust and suspicion is earned by the behavior of police officers or it is not. If it is not earned by the actions or attitudes of police officers, then the distrust and suspicion is unwarranted; in this case, we should educate the particular groups in question about the fact that their animosity toward police officers is unjustified.[46] On the other hand, if the distrust and suspicion *is* earned by the behavior of police officers, then there must be something about RP that is immoral independently of the distrust and suspicion that it causes (i.e., we are assuming that the members of the targeted demographic are *rightly* distrustful and suspicious). But what might this be? We are not told. And so, this objection "doesn't provide a reason to think that people would be justified in being [distrustful or suspicious] by RP. Rather, it argues from the assumption that people will, in fact, be" distrustful and suspicious because of it.[47]

Finally, this objection appears to assume without argument that police officers *are* prejudicial in an offensive sense, so much so that a universal, random search procedure would enable them to "confront and correct their own prejudices." Yet, might it be the case that, rather than prejudice or racial animus, police officers (like most rational agents) operate with certain prior probabilities in mind? If it is the case that prior probabilities, or base rates, do track differences in criminal behavior—particularly violent criminal behavior—between certain demographics, then police officers are doing precisely what it is they are supposed to do—apprehend criminals by the most reasonable, efficient, and morally permissible method.

COMPREHENSION QUESTIONS

1. Why does Hillman think that we should reject the "self-fulfilling prophecy" view of RP?
2. Hillman handles the "RP is bad for the police" objection in two ways. What are they?

DISCUSSION QUESTION

1. Suppose that 25% of violent criminals are black. What can you infer about the probability that a particular black person is a violent criminal? Compare: As of 2019, roughly 17% of Americans are Hispanic. What can you infer about the probability that a particular Hispanic person is an American? (Remember: Most Hispanic people are neither in America nor Americans. The question isn't: What's the probability that a particular Hispanic person *in America* is American?)

FURTHER READINGS

Boonin, David. *Should Race Matter? Unusual Answers to the Usual Questions.* Cambridge: Cambridge University Press, 2011.

Engel, Robin, and Kristin Swartz. "Race, Crime, and Policing." In *Oxford Handbook of Ethnicity, Crime, and Immigration*, edited by Sandra Bucerius and Michael Tonry. Oxford: Oxford University Press, 2013, 135–165.

Harris, David A. *Profiles in Injustice: Why Racial Profiling Cannot Work.* New York: New Press, 2003.

Holbert, Steve, and Lisa Rose. *The Color of Guilt and Innocence: Racial Profiling and Police Practices in America.* San Ramon, CA: Page Marque Press, 2004

Kennedy, Randall. *Race, Crime, and the Law* (New York: Vintage Books, 1998 [1st Vintage Books ed.]), 153.

Lever, Annabelle. "Racial Profiling and the Political Philosophy of Race." In *Oxford Handbook of Philosophy of Race*, edited by Naomi Zack. New York: Oxford University Press, 2017, 425–435.

MacDonald, Heather. *The War on Cops.* New York: Encounter Books, 2016.

Risse, Matthias. "Racial Profiling: A Reply to Two Critics." *Criminal Justice Ethics* 26, no. 1 (2007): 4–19.

Sampson, Robert J., Jeffery D. Morenoff, and Stephen Raudenbush. "Social Anatomy of Racial and Ethnic Disparities in Violence." *American Journal of Public Health* 95, no. 2 (2005): 224–232.

NOTES

1. Naomi Zack, *White Privilege and Black Rights: The Injustice of U.S. Police Racial Profiling and Homicide* (New York: Rowman and Littlefield, 2015), 47.
2. Mathias Risse and Richard Zeckhauser, "Racial Profiling," *Philosophy & Public Affairs* 32, no. 2 (Spring 2004): 131–170, 136.
3. Some arguments for racial profiling appear to assume that we can distinguish people into biological races with heritable characteristics of character and intelligence; see, for

example, Michael Levin, "Comments on Risse and Lever," *Criminal Justice Ethics* 26, no. 1 (2007): 29–35. However, most philosophers of race deny that "race" is biologically real. Instead, they see it as a social construct, so that "races" are just social classes based on hierarchies of color and morphology, rather than, say, occupation and wealth. See, for example, Sally Haslanger, *Resisting Reality: Social Construction and Social Critique* (Oxford: Oxford University Press, 2012), 221–247, or Lionel K. McPherson and Tommie Shelby, "Blackness and Blood: Interpreting African American Identity," *Philosophy & Public Affairs* 32, no. 2 (Spring 2004): 171–192.

4. Randall Kennedy, *Race, Crime, and the Law* (New York: Vintage Books, 1998 [1st Vintage Books ed.]), 153; Annabelle Lever, "Why Racial Profiling Is Hard to Justify: A Response to Risse and Zeckhauser," *Philosophy & Public Affairs* 33, no. 1 (2005): 94–110.

5. Steve Holbert and Lisa Rose, *The Color of Guilt and Innocence: Racial Profiling and Police Practices in America* (San Ramon, CA: Page Marque Press, 2004); Robert J. Sampson and William Julius Wilson, "Toward a Theory of Race, Crime and Urban Inequality," in *Crime and Inequality*, edited by John Hagan and Ruth D. Peterson (Palo Alto, CA: Stanford University Press, 1995), 37–54; Robert J. Sampson, Jeffery D. Morenoff, and Stephen Raudenbush, "Social Anatomy of Racial and Ethnic Disparities in Violence," *American Journal of Public Health* 95, no. 2 (February 2005): 224–232.

6. Arthur Isak Applbaum, "Bayesian Inference and Contractualist Justification on Interstate 95," in *Contemporary Debates in Applied Ethics* (Chichester, U.K.: John Wiley and Sons, 2014 [2nd ed.]), 219–232.

7. David A. Harris, *Profiles in Injustice: Why Racial Profiling Cannot Work* (New York: New Press, 2003); Bernard Harcourt, "The Shaping of Chance: Actuarial Models and Criminal Profiling at the Turn of the Twenty-First Century," *University of Chicago Law Review* 70, no. 1 (Winter 2003): 105–128, esp. 121–125.

8. This feature of profiling raises worries about arbitrariness and prejudice about who actually is stopped by police, even if we are not concerned with the profiling of disadvantaged racial minorities. For a discussion of these problems, see Annabelle Lever, "Race and Racial Profiling," in *The Oxford Handbook of the Philosophy of Race*, edited by Naomi Zack (Oxford: Oxford University Press, 2016), 425–435.

9. Holbert and Rose, *Color of Guilt and Innocence*, 126.

10. Sampson et al., "Social Anatomy," 227–228.

11. Jed S. Rakoff, "Why Innocent People Plead Guilty," *New York Review of Books*, November 20, 2014, http://www.nybooks.com/articles/archives/2014/nov/20/why-innocent-people-plead-guilty/; Nancy Gertner et al., "Why Innocent People Plead Guilty: An Exchange," *New York Review of Books*, January 8, 2015, http://www.nybooks.com/articles/archives/2015/jan/08/why-innocent-plead-guilty-exchange/.

12. Sampson et al., "Social Anatomy"; Jonathan Wolff, *Ethics and Public Policy: A Philosophical Inquiry* (London: Routledge, 2011).

13. Lever, "Race and Racial Profiling."

14. Zack, *White Privilege and Black Rights*; Holbert and Rose, *The Color of Guilt*; Sampson and Wilson, "Toward a Theory of Race"; Sampson et al., "Social Anatomy."

15. Annabelle Lever, "What's Wrong with Racial Profiling? Another Look at the Problem," *Criminal Justice Ethics* 26, no. 1 (2007): 20–28; Jeffrey Reiman, "Is Racial Profiling Just? Making Criminal Justice Policy in the Original Position," *Journal of Ethics* 15, no. 3 (2011): 3–19.

16. This assumption figures in Risse and Zeckhauser, "Racial Profiling," as well as in Kasper Lippert-Rasmussen, *Born Free and Equal?: A Philosophical Inquiry into the Nature of Discrimination* (Oxford: Oxford University Press, 2014).

17. In particular, white people make up the majority of consumers for illegal drugs such as cocaine, as well as prostitution, which is illegal in many countries. Black people and other racially disadvantaged groups are disproportionately likely to be part of the production and distribution chain of these illegal activities, even if they are not among their prime beneficiaries or directors of these activities. So, racial profiling at best makes it safer for white consumers and non-consumers to go about their lives, while making life more difficult and dangerous for all minorities, whether or not they are involved in illegal activities.

18. Kennedy, *Race, Crime, and the Law*, Chapter 4.

19. That is why it is a mistake to treat all police violence as "external" to RP, rather than the predictable result of RP itself.

20. Lever, "Why Racial Profiling."

21. See Kennedy, *Race, Crime, and the Law*, 152–153, for fear as an example of the "powerful feelings of racial grievance against law enforcement authorities" (151). Kennedy quotes from Don Wycliff, a journalist, that he feels "ambivalence tilting towards antipathy" for the police, and ascribes this to the way that "a dangerous, humiliating and sometimes fatal encounter with the police is almost a rite of passage for a black man in the United States." Indeed, Kennedy stresses that even a hypothetical "Office Friendly" is not exempt from the downward spiral of misunderstandings, exaggerated fear of blacks, and recriminations that "lead to the sort of conflicts which have often vexed relations between police departments and black communities" (154 and later 157). It is important to remember that what is at issue, either in profiling by the police or by citizens, is a supposition of *criminality* (although, unfortunately, racial stereotyping is not limited to that, but typically includes assumptions about the defective intelligence, beauty, and manners of minority groups). Hence, the rage racial profiling generates is particularly acute. And because it is criminality, not intelligence, beauty, or good manners, behind racial profiling by the police, there are obvious reasons why violence and police abuse cannot be divorced from the harms of profiling in the way that they probably could be divorced from other forms of racial stereotyping.

22. Kennedy, *Race, Crime, and the Law*, 136–167; Lever, "Race and Racial Profiling," 425–435; Lever, "Why Racial Profiling," 94–110; Reiman, "Is Racial Profiling Just," 3–19.

23. As a tool used by law enforcement agencies, retroactive criminal profiling is a relatively recent phenomenon that has its roots in forensic psychology and applied criminology; its practice burgeoned in the 1970s through the efforts of the Federal Bureau of Investigation (FBI)'s Behavioral Science Unit, and has been thoroughly embedded in the popular culture by film and television. For a history of behavioral science as utilized by the FBI, see Don DeNevi, John Cambell, Stephen Band, and John Otto, *Into the Minds of Madmen: How the FBI's Behavioral Science Unit Revolutionized Crime Investigation* (New York: Prometheus, 2003). For a less academic and more personal (and riveting) account, one that demonstrates how the forensic psychologist constructs criminal profiles for serial killers and serial rapists, see John Douglas and Mark Olshaker, *Mindhunter: Inside the FBI's Elite Serial Crime Unit* (New York: Simon & Schuster, 1995).

24. I do not in fact think that the term is accurate. It makes little sense to think that, in general and by habit, police officers are investigating individuals based *solely* upon their race. The reasons that a police officer has to (say) pull over a motorist may certainly involve the motorist's race, but typically other reasons will be present as well (e.g., the age of the motorist, the sex of the motorist, the kind of vehicle). Philosopher

William Vallicella has argued that "*racial* profiling," strictly speaking, is both theoretically and practically incoherent. As he concisely puts it, "A profile cannot consist of just one characteristic." See his "Is There Such a Thing as *Racial* Profiling?" at http://maverickphilosopher.typepad.com/maverick_philosopher/2014/12/is-there-such-a-thing-as-racial-profiling.html.

25. For a similar definition, see David Boonin, *Should Race Matter? Unusual Answers to the Usual Questions* (Cambridge: Cambridge University Press, 2011), 302. The "at least one factor" qualifier is crucial since "[r]acial profiling involves targeting by race, but it need not involve targeting exclusively by race" (302).

26. For these and other relevant data, see Robin Engel and Kristin Swartz, "Race, Crime, and Policing," in *Oxford Handbook of Ethnicity, Crime, and Immigration*, edited by Sandra Bucerius and Michael Tonry (Oxford: Oxford University Press, 2013), 135–165. Hard empirical data concerning the results of racial profiling by police departments are difficult to obtain for, among other reasons, police officers (and departments themselves) are hesitant to admit to sanctioning a practice that is so controversial in the public eye. As a result, most "data" utilized by defenders and opponents of racial profiling tend to be (at best) only inferentially linked to the practice (e.g., figures related to police brutality, statistics concerning the race/ethnicity of those pulled over by traffic police) rather than direct empirical evidence.

27. David Boonin develops and defends a version of this argument, what he calls "The Rationality Argument," in Chapter 10 of his *Should Race Matter?* For another defense of the rationality of racial profiling based on probability and decision theory, see Neven Sesardić, "Is Racial Profiling a Legitimate Strategy in the Fight Against Violent Crime?" *Philosophia* 46, no. 4 (2018): 981–999.

28. Randall Kennedy, "Suspect Policy: Racial Profiling Usually Isn't Racist. It Can Help Stop Crime. And It Should Be Abolished," *New Republic* (September 13 & 20, 1999), https://newrepublic.com/article/63137/suspect-policy.

29. This point—that legal officials must make probabilistic judgments on the basis of (necessarily) incomplete information—is dealt with in admirable detail by Boonin in his *Should Race Matter?*, especially 310–312.

30. Kennedy goes on to reveal that the U.S. Court of Appeals agreed that the officer's conduct was, in fact, constitutional.

31. A separate, though significant, question arises in conjunction with the points just raised: Someone may rightly ask to what extent, if at all, the racial component of a criminal profile carries disproportionate weight by law enforcement officials (as compared to other elements of the profile). For further details (and pointers to other relevant literature), see Risse and Zeckhauser, "Racial Profiling," especially 140–142.

32. One may object that thinking about racial profiling in isolation from other social and political realities present in our day and age—as arguably I appear to do here—is problematic. That is, given the implicit (and explicit) biases that are allegedly dominant in our society, it stands to reason that a practice like racial profiling may in fact perpetuate racial inequalities of various kinds. If so, such harms must enter into calculations of the possible negative consequences of racial profiling. While this objection deserves consideration, I lack the space to deal with the issue in any depth here. For further consideration, see Lever, "Why Racial Profiling"; Matthias Risse, "Racial Profiling: A Reply to Two Critics," *Criminal Justice Ethics* 26, no. 1 (2007): 4–19; Lever, "What's Wrong." For a related objection to racial profiling from the possibility of its resulting in physical harm, see section 4 in this essay.

33. Boonin, *Should Race Matter?*, 338.

34. One may object that one's first-person knowledge in this situation is irrelevant. Consider: Many white job candidates who fail to secure jobs believe that they have been victims of reverse discrimination. This is so even if the potential employer did not take race into consideration at all when making the hire. Still, there appears to be some psychological harm in believing that one has been passed over for employment in virtue of a factor beyond one's control. Similarly, there may be psychological harm experienced by a black person who wonders whether he has been pulled over by a police officer simply in virtue of a factor beyond his control and one that is irrelevant to whether he committed a specific crime. Perhaps there is something to the analogy here such that the lack of awareness on the part of the motorist is irrelevant to the psychological harm involved. Yet even if this is so, we may argue that such harms as these are part of the price for reducing the risk of criminals not being apprehended by the police. For example, consider minority members who live in dangerous communities. Would they accept the tradeoff between (a) more security from robbery and assault and (b) the psychological costs of knowing that racial profiling is taking place (and may even impact them personally)? It seems reasonable to think that such a tradeoff would be acceptable to most people. Thanks to Bob Fischer for pointing out this issue.

35. The entirety of the following argument can be found in more detail in Boonin, *Should Race Matter?*, 340–341.

36. The following criticism of rights-based objections to racial profiling is due to David Boonin. See his *Should Race Matter?*, 336–337. While my argument here is general, it bears mentioning that he also discusses different ways in which we might interpret specific constitutional laws like the Fourth Amendment and the equal protection clause. He finds that under no interpretations of these laws, so long as the laws are consistently applied, can racial profiling be deemed morally impermissible. See all of his Chapter 11. For other interesting defenses of racial profiling from a moral point of view, see Sesardić, "Is Racial Profiling."

37. It would be absurd for many reasons, not the least of which is this: All citizens—of any race or ethnicity—would correctly complain that it was *their* right to fair and reasonable treatment that was being violated by police officers who ignore the racial component of such a profile in this situation. That is, any citizen would rightly complain of the time and energy wasted by police who searched *everyone* while a murderer is on the loose in their midst.

38. As Risse and Zeckhauser ("Racial Profiling," 139) note, even if police abuse were eliminated entirely, the practice of racial profiling could still serve as an effective investigative tool. Conversely, the immediate elimination of racial profiling as a police tactic would not result in the consequent end to police abuse. So, even if we were to agree that *both* racial profiling and police brutality were problems, they would require separate treatment.

39. The medical analogy is his. See Sesardić, "Is Racial Profiling."

40. I am thankful to Neven Sesardić (private correspondence) for this line of response.

41. Robert J. Sampson, Jeffrey D. Morenoff, and Stephen Raudenbush, "Social Anatomy of Racial and Ethnic Disparities in Violence," *American Journal of Public Health* 95, no. 2 (February 2005): 224–232, 231.

42. My italics. Sampson and Wilson, "Toward a Theory of Race," 43.

43. Sampson and Wilson, "Toward a Theory of Race," 42.

44. Jonathan Wolff and Avner de-Shalit, *Disadvantage* (New York: Oxford University Press, 2007), 133–154, and on the "concentration" effects of disadvantage that make it

all but impossible to compare the social circumstances of poor white and poor black Americans, see Sampson and Wilson, "Toward a Theory of Race," esp. 39, 41–43, 53.

45. Boonin, *Should Race Matter?*, 313–314 (footnote omitted). The data here cited are due to Fred Pampel, *Racial Profiling* (New York: Facts on File, 2004), 26.

46. As Sesardić has argued in "Is Racial Profiling," "Isn't the best way to deal with people's *wrong* beliefs to talk to them and convince them to adopt *true* beliefs? Isn't this better than keeping them in the state of ignorance and adopting a condescending attitude toward them?"

47. Boonin, *Should Race Matter?*, 341.

CHAPTER 19

Guns

POLICE VIOLENCE: A RIGHTS-BASED ARGUMENT *FOR* GUN CONTROL
LUKE MARING

The best arguments against gun control invoke moral rights—it might be good if there were fewer guns in circulation, but there is a moral right to own firearms.[1] Rather than emphasizing the potential benefits of gun control, this essay meets the best arguments on their home turf. I argue that there simply is no moral right to keep guns on one's person or in one's residence. In fact, our moral rights support the mutual disarmament of citizens and police.

1. No Right to Carry; No Right to Keep at Home

Gun advocates have developed two rights-based arguments. One cites recreation; the other invokes self-defense.

The recreation argument holds that citizens are entitled to use guns for "target shooting, various sorts of shooting competitions, and hunting."[2] Fortunately, gun control needn't rule out any of these activities. Consider a variation on China's gun laws: Citizens may neither carry firearms nor keep firearms in their residences. If they wish to shoot, citizens may use and store certain kinds of guns at certified ranges. If they wish to hunt, citizens can apply for a temporary permit to check out hunting rifles or single-shot shotguns—though these permits will be granted only to those who pass a gun safety exam and whose background is free of certain red flags (e.g., domestic abuse, mental illness, or assault charges).[3] Recreation is a common foundation for rights-based arguments against gun control.[4] All such arguments fail: Recreation is compatible with robust gun control.

What about self-defense? The right to self-defense, as sensible gun advocates agree, does not entail the right to keep weapons we cannot use safely and reliably—that is why there is no right to keep bombs or nerve gas.[5] The problem is that there is little reason to believe that ordinary citizens can safely and reliably defend themselves with guns.

Gun advocates write as though firearms make self-defense easy—even the physically frail can simply pull the trigger and the ne'er-do-well goes down.[6] Some of our surest evidence tells a different story. Trained professionals *routinely* hit the wrong things, particularly in high-pressure situations. One study found that in gunfights between 1998 and 2006, officers in the New York Police Department missed 82% of their shots.[7] Outside gunfights their accuracy was better, but they still missed 70% of the time. A second study examined the accuracy of five different police departments over ten years and found that police miss 70% to 85% of the shots they take.[8] Several further studies reach virtually identical conclusions, estimating that "bullet hit rates"—the percentage of bullets fired by police that *hit* their intended targets—hover between 14% and 30%.[9] Still another study references the "well-documented inaccuracy of police officers,"[10] and yet another concludes (a bit scathingly) that "it is difficult to reconcile demonstrated police handgun accuracy with the commonly held notion that the police are competent with their handguns by way of their participation in mandated . . . training."[11]

I don't make these observations to criticize police. The point is that professionals with significantly more training and experience than ordinary citizens regularly hit the wrong things. The point is that ordinary citizens will almost certainly be worse.

Compare: If taking free throws on weekends is your only practice, you should not expect to become a competent basketball player. Good coaches schedule scrimmages so that players can practice split-second decision-making and hone their technique under pressure. Even then, players find that mere scrimmage is not enough. They need regular, real-game experience to prepare for the pace and tension of actual play. Performing under pressure is a skill that needs to be practiced.

Wielding a gun against a mortal threat is, to put it mildly, performing under pressure. As one military veteran puts it, "Fight or flight. Adrenaline floods your body. Time doesn't exist. Your heart beats outside your chest. Fine motor skills stop working. People urinate and defecate themselves. Good luck holding steady aim at a moving target."[12] That is a description of highly trained military personnel facing gunfire. It is absurd to think that ordinary citizens—whose training and experience consists mostly of "free throws" taken under the controlled conditions of the range—will outperform cops. These points should be obvious, but they need to be said: Free throws won't make us basketball stars, trips to the firing range won't make us better than police at confronting armed threats, and average citizens are not action heroes in waiting.

Critics will probably counter by pointing to high estimates of defensive gun use—ordinary people can use guns just fine; we have studies that prove it. But those studies are problematic for two reasons.

First, they might not be accurate. In *More Guns, Less Crime*, John Lott argues that guns deter crime and that more guns deter crime better. But as several experts have already pointed out in peer-reviewed journals, Lott explains a decrease in crime by citing right-to-carry laws when the shift is more plausibly explained by the end of the crack epidemic.[13] No longer employed by a college or university, Lott has continued to do research in the Crime Prevention Research Center, a conspicuously pro-gun non-profit. Much of its leadership has ties to the National Rifle Association (NRA).[14] Its website advertises Lott's discredited *More Guns, Less Crime* alongside more obviously partisan works—such as Lott's *The War on Guns: Arming Yourself Against Gun Control Lies*.[15]

No one—including me, of course—is wholly free of bias. But Lott and the Crime Prevention Research Center are particularly concerning. Compare: Big soda companies have sponsored studies suggesting that high consumption of sugar has few, if any, bad effects on health. Their obvious bias combined with their history of standing behind discredited research means that we should be *highly* skeptical about the next study sponsored by Big Soda. Lott's and the Crime Prevention Research Center's obvious bias, combined with their history of standing behind discredited research, should together inspire a similar skepticism.

Gary Kleck and Marc Gertz famously conducted a telephone survey asking the heads of 5,000 households whether they had used a gun in self-defense.[16] On that basis, they estimated that Americans successfully use guns in self-defense roughly 2.5 million times per year. Asking people about their experience using guns seems like a perfectly reasonable thing to do. But as David Hemenway points out, it invites social desirability bias.[17] People often shade the truth when their doctor asks how much they drink. By the same token, people are likely to exaggerate when a social scientist asks about their feats of self-defense. This is not a criticism of the people Kleck and Gertz interviewed. It is a well-documented psychological tendency that researchers have to account for.

Kleck responds to Hemenway's critique.[18] But the response does not appear in a standard academic journal. It appears in the *Journal on Firearms and Public Policy*—a publication funded by the Second Amendment Foundation, whose self-described mission is "education in support of gun rights,"[19] and whose financial sponsors include gun manufacturers.[20] Moreover, Kleck's response is odd. He complains that Hemenway focused on design flaws (e.g., social desirability bias) that would lead to overestimation while ignoring design flaws that would lead to underestimation. But if one (a) knows that there are design flaws, (b) doesn't know how much some of those flaws will raise the overall estimate, and (c) doesn't know how much others will lower it, skepticism is the rational conclusion.

There are other high estimates of defensive gun use, but they stand opposed to a formidable volume of peer-reviewed research. In less than an hour, I found more than twenty peer-reviewed studies in reputable journals that (a) criticize high estimates of defensive gun use, (b) conclude that guns are highly correlated with increased homicide rates, (c) find that gun control decreases homicide rates, or (d) report that guns are not, on average, useful for self-defense.[21] And I barely scratched the surface.

Furthermore, scientific consensus is not favorable to gun advocates. Between 2011 and 2014, social scientists published 468 articles on firearms. Surveys suggest that 71% of the authors believe that "strong gun laws help reduce homicide."[22] Only 5% believe that guns make a household safer, and only 12% believe that carrying a gun outside the home reduces one's chance of being killed. Admittedly, my training is in moral theory, not data collection or linear regression. I cannot be absolutely certain that the scientific consensus is correct. But one thing is perfectly clear. Anyone who focuses on the handful of studies suggesting high rates of defensive gun use is ignoring a *mountain* of contrary evidence.

The second problem with high estimates of defensive gun use is that *even if* scientific consensus is wrong to doubt them, they often measure the wrong thing. They need to show that ordinary citizens reliably hit their target—and only their target—when they are terrified and fighting for their lives. Instead, such studies often aim to show that people who use guns to "resist" crime are better able to protect themselves. But "resistance" is a broad category—it includes, for example, brandishing a gun one can't reliably use and scaring off would-be criminals by incompetently spraying bullets about.[23] Compare: If ordinary people can't safely and reliably deploy nerve gas, they shouldn't have it, even if a handful of studies concludes that nerve gas is useful for scaring off would-be criminals.

Can't ordinary people train and become competent with firearms? Possibly. But police departments across the country are full of trained professionals who routinely hit the wrong things. We should not expect ordinary citizens to do better. Perhaps you have used a gun in self-defense. Unfortunately, even that might not be solid evidence. There are an enormous number of guns in circulation, and sheer luck guarantees that ordinary citizens will win a few firefights. Given that trained professionals miss so often, the rational conclusion is probably that you got lucky.

So: There is no moral right to keep a gun on one's person or in one's residence. The recreation argument is compatible with robust gun control, and the self-defense argument fails. There is no reason to believe that average citizens—even those who visit the firing range to take "free throws"—are action heroes who will reliably outperform cops.

2. An Armed Police Force Violates Our Moral Rights

A 1979 study on police violence reports that the United States "simply does not know how many of its own citizens it kills each year under the authority of the state."[24] Thirty-nine years later, there is still no official tally of citizens shot dead by police, but a few organizations have recently begun counting online news reports. In each of 2015, 2016, and 2017, estimates suggest that U.S. police shot and killed roughly one thousand citizens.[25]

In many of these cases, the officer involved was responding to an armed threat. But in 2015 alone, reports indicate that the police shot an estimated 235 unarmed people.[26] In other cases, victims were mentally ill, obeying the law while armed, or breaking the law without posing the sort of threat that warrants lethal force. How many have U.S. police wrongfully killed since they began carrying guns in the mid-1800s? Each wrongful death is a straightforward violation of a citizen's right to life.

If data on police killings are scant, data on injuries are almost non-existent. But it strains credibility—well past its breaking point—to suppose that an organization shooting often enough to kill a thousand in a single year isn't also hurting quite a few. Non-fatal injuries can seriously compromise people's lives, causing debilitating pain and major cognitive deficits. Not all of these injuries are wrongful—in some cases the officer had good reasons to pull the trigger—but it would be naïve to think all injurious shootings are justified. Wrongful injuries are a second straightforward violation of citizens' rights.

And there is a third: In addition to causing death and injury, police sometimes use their firearms to wrongfully intimidate citizens. We have probably all, by now, seen footage of police drawing their guns on harmless, unarmed people. In one case, the victims were children, simply playing basketball at the time.[27] In some cases of intimidation, officers pointed their firearms at citizens. But guns can contribute to wrongful intimidation without being drawn. Some gun advocates argue that firearms deter at least some would-be criminals; the inevitable flip side of the coin, however, is that firearms make wrongful intimidation all the more terrifying.

How common is wrongful intimidation? There is, once again, no even remotely comprehensive database. But there are many communities—such as Ferguson, Missouri—that have largely adversarial relationships with police. The Truth Telling Project has given black citizens in Ferguson and elsewhere a platform to explain their experience. According to their testimony, bullying and intimidation by police is a wholly expected, routine fact of life.[28] Ferguson is far from the only community in America with an adversarial relationship to the police, so it would be *exceptionally* naïve to think that wrongful intimidation is a small-scale problem.

One might object: "Lots of public services cause casualties—ambulances inevitably cause the odd accident and buses inevitably hit a pedestrian now and again. There should be nothing surprising or troubling about the fact that the practice of law enforcement has a human cost. The only question is whether law enforcement does more good than harm."

The objection fails because while the casualties caused by ambulances and buses are tragic, they are accidental. The drivers are not out looking for people to run down, nor has the state issued them tools whose main purpose is to kill. By contrast, police in the United States are given guns and ordered to use their near-monopoly on lethal force. Some officers deliberately kill, injure, or intimidate citizens who ought not be killed, injured, or intimidated.

Political conservatives sometimes criticize liberals for trusting the state—and while my sympathies mostly run to the progressive left, the conservatives are on this score exactly correct. The great insight of conservatism is that governments are not grand impartial arbiters dispassionately pursuing the common good. Rather, as Mill observes in his critique of Hobbes, governments are social machines that "must be worked by men, and even by ordinary men."[29] Ordinary people are capable of great good. But in our worst moments, we are vindictive and violent, petty and power-hungry, or frightened and unreliable. Wrongful deaths, injuries, and intimidation are the predictable result of giving ordinary people guns, badges, and the discretion to use lethal force—at least in the United States.[30]

Nothing thus far should be controversial—no one can seriously think that citizens have no right against wrongful death, injury, and intimidation. One might, however, be tempted to minimize the moral problem: Relative to the size of the U.S. population, arming police does not lead to all that many rights violations.

A quick word of caution: What was true in 1979 is still true. We simply do not know how many the police wrongfully kill, injure, or intimidate. Current estimates are probably low. But there is a deeper issue. The moral problem resides not just in the sheer *number* of rights violations, but also in their *nature*.

Three factors combine to make these rights violations an urgent matter of justice. First, an armed police force costs money, and the government coercively extracts the necessary resources from citizens. Our government, that is, forces victims to finance the violation of their own rights.

Second, police officers have a special obligation to protect citizens' well-being. Compare: It is terrible for anyone to assault children, but it is especially terrible when parents assault their own children. Children have a moral right to their parents' protection, and that raises the moral stakes. The moral bonds between parents and children are thicker than the bonds between state and citizen, but the point remains: Police have a special obligation to protect citizens' well-being. Wrongful death, injury, and intimidation are terrible in their own right, but they are especially terrible when police victimize the citizens they are sworn to protect.

Third, whereas public transportation—by its very nature—requires buses or other high-capacity vehicles, law enforcement does not require firearms. Americans often regard unarmed police as a bizarrely impractical idea, but officers without guns are the reality in much of the United Kingdom, New Zealand, Iceland, and elsewhere. In fact, the British Metropolitan Police chose not to carry guns precisely because of their dedication to police work. They saw order achieved through armed coercion as the task of an occupying military, and sought to create a "civil police [that] could not win the compliance of the civil population by fear and coercion."[31]

Of course, countries with unarmed police don't typically have high rates of gun ownership, but that doesn't compromise the point. The nature of police work doesn't require guns in the same way that the nature of mass transit requires high-capacity vehicles. So we have a choice: We can (a) disarm both citizens and police, or (b) allow citizens to keep their guns and also arm the police. The choice between (a) and (b) is a question of values, and I am making a values-based (specifically a rights-based) argument that we should choose (a).

Put these three factors together and the deep moral problem comes into view. The state forces citizens to pay for officers' guns—lethal tools not required by the nature of law enforcement. The predictable result is that people with a right to protection are instead wrongfully killed, injured, and intimidated. Imagine a parent who took money from her child's piggybank to finance disciplinary schemes that, in addition to being unnecessary, were likely to cause death, injury, or terror. Such a parent would be a criminal—even if she treated her child well on other occasions. The special obligations between parent and child are, again, stronger than those between state and citizen. But the difference between these cases is one of degree, not one of kind. From a moral perspective, we cannot condemn the parent's conduct without reaching a similar conclusion about governments that arm police.

My argument, so far, is guilty of a major omission. Police disproportionately violate the rights of minorities, especially black and Native Americans.[32] Police violence and race is topic enough for a book, and I am not the person to write it. But one thing should be obvious. As wrong as it is to make people finance the needless violation of their own rights, it is even worse when the victims tend to be minorities who face discrimination on many other fronts too. Arming the police predictably leads to *urgent* violations of citizens' rights.

3. What Should We Do?

What should we do? The moral ideal is clear. Arming police predictably leads to serious, widespread violations of our rights. Realistically, we cannot disarm the police without first disarming ourselves. But since there is no moral right to keep guns on one's person or in one's home—recreation is compatible with gun control; the self-defense argument fails—there is no rights-based argument against doing that. The morally ideal response is mutual disarmament of citizens and police.

Mutual disarmament could help police and citizens see each other in a less threatening light. Too often, an officer mistakes a harmless object for a gun, pulls his own weapon, and shoots a citizen wielding only a sandwich, an umbrella, a cellphone, an apron, or a Bible.[33] Some of these are clear examples of officer incompetence, but I do not think all of them are. Imagine: You are an officer. You know that there are more than 300 million guns in the United States, and you know of fellow officers killed on the job. Then, you go on patrol looking precisely for armed and dangerous people. These conditions are *perfect* for making normal people see threats and guns where neither exists. Our lack of meaningful gun control can put well-intentioned police in an impossible situation.

Is mutual disarmament unrealistic? A knee-jerk affirmative answer is common, but there is little argument behind it. Australia got rid of its most dangerous guns by making it illegal to possess a wide range of firearms, and then launching a buyback program to compensate gun owners for the weapons that were newly illegal. In the United States, that strategy would require repealing or modifying the Second Amendment, which could prove difficult. But there are alternatives. We could impose substantial taxes on ammunition and then offer to buy back the guns that people can no longer afford to shoot. It would be the Australian plan with economic persuasion instead of legal coercion: Rather than selling their guns to the government to avoid legal prosecution, citizens could sell their guns to recoup money on an investment they can no longer afford to use. Or we could do something more radical. We could require that bullets sold in the United States have a non-standard diameter, so that new bullets couldn't be fired by any of the guns currently in circulation. The guns in circulation would eventually run out of bullets to shoot.[34] A buyback program would then give citizens the chance to recoup money from firearms they could no longer find ammunition for. The fact that guns are useless without ammunition is a foothold: We might be able to begin mutual disarmament without undertaking the long legal struggle of repealing or revising the Second Amendment.

And we needn't stop there. The solution to America's gun problem could be multipronged. We could, in addition to the above, impose strict liability on gun manufacturers: Manufacturers could be held legally responsible for harms perpetrated with certain classes of firearms. The idea is that gun manufacturers would be less cavalier about what they sell, and to whom, if they had "skin in the game." We could impose strict liability on gun owners, so that owners could be held legally accountable for any harm caused by their weapons. We could require universal background checks, make it illegal to sell to people with a history of domestic abuse or other violent crime, make it illegal to carry guns outside gun ranges or hunting trips, and more. Again, as Section 1 of my essay shows, there is no rights-based objection to any of these measures.

I hope that some combination of these strategies could, in time, make America a mostly gun-free society. Our gun problem is daunting, and it may take decades to solve, but the field is *wide open*. We haven't tried anything. So I want this last section of my essay to serve as an invitation. Perhaps you have ideas about how gun control could work, about how to minimize negative consequences, or if mutual disarmament is unrealistic after all, about how close we can get.

My thesis is that we respect *everyone's* moral rights. By allowing gun owners to use and store certain weapons at certified ranges, and by allowing qualified citizens to temporarily check out hunting rifles or single-shot shotguns, we can respect the right to recreation. By not allowing citizens to carry guns on their person or keep guns in their homes, perhaps we can disarm police and respect citizens' moral right against wrongful death, injury, and intimidation. The violation of these rights is not only shockingly common, but egregious: Officers violate the rights of those they are sworn to protect, and citizens are forced to finance it. That is not something we can accept in the name of being "realistic"—particularly not before we have even tried to fix it.

COMPREHENSION QUESTIONS

1. What are the two rights-based arguments against gun control that Maring addresses?
2. According to Maring, under what conditions do people have the right to use weapons in self-defense?
3. What is the point of Maring's basketball analogy?
4. What are Maring's criticisms of John Lott's argument in *More Guns, Less Crime*?
5. What are Maring's criticisms of Gary Kleck's and Marc Gertz's arguments?
6. How does Maring respond to the claim that people have a right to use guns in self-defense if they are well trained and competent in using them?
7. In Maring's view, why are wrongful killing, injury, and intimidation by police particularly morally problematic?

DISCUSSION QUESTIONS

1. Maring's argument that ordinary citizens do not have the right to own guns to use in self-defense focuses on shooting accuracy. Should it? Why or why not?
2. Are there any moral rights that are *protected* by the existence of armed police forces? What are they? And is it possible for unarmed police forces to protect them?
3. Maring suggests that if police weren't armed with guns, there would be fewer incidents of wrongful killings, injuries, and intimidation carried out by police. Is disarming police the only or best way to accomplish this goal? Why or why not?
4. What moral problems, if any, might arise if the government were to use "economic persuasion" to limit gun ownership?

Case 1

Maring's argument, as he notes, doesn't address the topic of police violence and race. Neither does it address the more general links between gun violence and racism in the United States. In a 2015 *New York Times* opinion piece, philosopher Gary Gutting suggests that the government's failure to act to prevent gun violence violates duties to protect citizens against racism:

> [F]ew [opponents of gun violence] actually see guns as existential threats to fundamental American values. In this, however, we are mistaken. Our permissive gun laws are a manifestation of racism, an evil that, in other contexts, most gun-control advocates see as a fundamental threat to American society.
>
> We've heard a lot recently about how blacks still don't feel safe in this country. You can argue about how seriously to take complaints from black students at elite universities or even whether outrageous cases of unjustified police shootings are just isolated occurrences. But there's no argument that black people in the "bad parts" of our cities have to live with utterly unacceptable levels of gun violence. In 2010, blacks, who make up only 13 percent of the population, were 55 percent of gun homicide victims. It's no surprise that blacks favor stricter gun controls considerably more than whites do.
>
> How does racism enter into this picture? Let me put it in personal terms. I spend a fair amount of time in Chicago, where the newspapers regularly offer front-page reports of shootings from the previous night. Checking *The Tribune* on a recent morning, I learned that two people were killed and a dozen wounded. You might think that a steady stream of such reports (this year, Chicago will have over 2,700 shootings, with over 400 people killed) would induce high levels of fear, especially since many shootings occur on the streets. In fact, I'm not particularly afraid, since—like most Chicagoans—I'm hardly ever where the violence occurs. There's something to worry about only if you live in certain overwhelmingly black communities on the West and South sides of town. (The papers publish helpful maps showing how the killings are distributed.) These are where almost all the shootings occur, and the large majority of victims (and perpetrators) are black. The patterns are similar in other large American cities, so that those who live with gun violence as an imminent, personal threat are mostly black.*

What do you make of this argument? How important is it to consider racism as a factor in moral arguments about gun control? Where would you rank it relative to other concerns?

*https://opinionator.blogs.nytimes.com/2015/12/28/guns-and-racism/

THE MORAL CASE FOR GUN OWNERSHIP
TIM HSIAO

1. Introduction

I'll argue in this essay that individuals should be allowed to own firearms. In making the case for this position, I'll defend the following two claims:

1. The best research does not show that gun ownership results in more harms than benefits. This fact, in addition to the substantial self-defense benefits that guns offer and the value of personal liberty, supports a presumption in favor of gun ownership.
2. Even if the overall harms of gun ownership were to outweigh its overall benefits, there is still a presumption in favor of reasonably permissive gun ownership.

Since this essay gives a *moral* case for gun ownership, I won't consider any appeals to the constitutional right to keep and bear arms. While I do believe that the Constitution does support an individual right to keep and bear arms (a claim affirmed by the U.S. Supreme Court in *District of Columbia v. Heller* and *McDonald v. Chicago*), the arguments in this paper imply that if the Second Amendment had never existed, the state should still allow the private ownership of firearms for purely moral reasons.[35]

2. The Consequences of Gun Ownership

Most debates over gun ownership revolve around the effects that guns have on society, both good and bad. Both sides claim that the evidence favors their side. Let us therefore begin with a brief analysis of the empirical literature on gun ownership.

Gun ownership may affect society in three ways. First, guns may have a net benefit (e.g., reducing crime). Second, guns may have a net negative (e.g., increasing crime and suicides). Third, gun ownership may have no net effect either way (e.g., the benefits and harms cancel out). Many who oppose gun ownership ground their opposition in the belief that guns increase social harms, especially crime. The best research, however, does not support this position.

In a comprehensive review of the literature, criminologist Gary Kleck examined the findings of forty-one studies that assessed the impact of gun ownership on homicide and overall crime rates.[36] These included studies that examined gun ownership both within the United States and in other countries. These studies were evaluated on the basis of whether they took into account three important methodological considerations: (1) whether they used a valid measure of gun ownership, (2) whether the authors attempted to control for a just a handful of confounders, and (3) whether they took steps to control for reverse causation—that is, increased gun ownership being a response to high crime rates rather than the cause. Stronger studies took into account these considerations. Weaker studies did not.

Of the initial ninety findings that were generated by these studies, only twenty-six (29%) supported the claim that guns cause an increase in overall crime rates, while the remaining sixty-four (71%) found no significant positive association. Once Kleck further evaluated these findings on the basis of the three methodological criteria listed above, he found that the methodologically stronger studies were less likely to support the claim that guns cause an increase in both overall crime and homicide rates.

Overall, most of the studies on both sides were of poor quality. Of the forty-one studies evaluated, fourteen did not control for a *single* confounder, while only six controlled for more than five. All six of these studies found no evidence that gun ownership increases overall crime rates. Out of the twenty-eight findings that used a valid measure of gun ownership, twenty-three found no positive effect on overall crime rates. Finally, only six out of ninety total findings adequately controlled for reverse causation; all six found that gun ownership had no positive effect on overall crime rates. Taking all of these methodological criteria into account, Kleck found that *none* of the studies that took into account all three considerations supported the claim that guns had a positive effect on crime rates. In other words, *the methodologically strongest studies all support the conclusion that gun ownership does not increase homicide rates or overall crime.*[37]

Many proponents of increased gun control argue that cross-country comparisons between the United States and other developed countries show that increased gun availability leads to more violence.[38] This is based on the observation that many countries with more restrictive gun control have less crime. But inferences of this kind are misleading.[39] Historically, many Western countries have had homicide rates lower than the United States long before restrictive gun control was enacted.[40] While it is true that decreased gun availability is sometimes associated with less crime, the effect of gun availability does not operate uniformly across all countries.[41] Rather, the effects of gun ownership in a particular country are heavily shaped by existing cultural and sociological factors.[42] Gun availability in Latin American countries, for example, is associated with increased violence, and research suggests this is due to the presence of a machismo culture, which encourages harsh interpersonal violence. Since aggressors in these countries are more willing to inflict great harm or death, they naturally select weapons that mirror their intentions. By contrast, gun availability in Eastern European countries is negatively associated with both gun violence and overall homicide. Here, gun ownership decreases crime because guns provide a "deterrent against potential aggression in an era characterized by weakened collective security."[43] Hence, gun ownership in these countries tends to be motivated by a desire for peace rather than aggression.

In sum, since the effect of gun availability operates differently in each country, it would seem reasonable to conclude that gun availability in itself (without regard for sociological, historical, and cultural factors) has no net effect on crime rates, a finding that is supported by Kleck's review.

What about other potential social harms of gun ownership, such as increases in overall rate of suicides and accidents? Here, there are at least three points to consider.

First, we should note that the majority of the social harms of guns are crimes. In 2011, there were over 414,000 crimes involving firearms (11,100 of which were homicides, compared to 19,990 suicides, 14,675 non-fatal accidents, and 590 fatal accidents).[44] If gun ownership does not increase the overall crime rate—which the best evidence suggests—then this fact by itself significantly weakens the anti-gun position. At the very least, this should count against many gun control measures that are aimed specifically at crime control.

Second, the evidence is not at all clear that gun ownership leads to higher rates of suicide. As with homicide, the effects of gun availability on suicide are not uniform across countries. Again, cultural and structural factors play a heavy role in determining how guns affect suicide. This is confirmed by sociologist Mark Konty and criminologist Brian Schaefer, who used data from the global Small Arms Survey and World Health Organization to analyze the effects of gun availability in 168 nations.[45] They found that "structural factors, like deprivation, explain a large portion of the cross-national variation in homicide and suicide" and that "the accessibility of firearms does not produce more homicide or suicide when other known factors are controlled for."[46] Likewise, Don Kates and Gary Mauser, reviewing data from several countries, found no evidence that gun ownership increases overall suicide rates.[47] They note that countries with lower rates of gun ownership do not fare better than countries with higher rates of gun ownership when it comes to the rate of overall suicide. Indeed, many countries with lower gun ownership rates have rates of overall suicide that are higher than those of neighboring countries in which gun ownership is more prevalent.[48]

Among public health studies claiming to find a positive relationship between guns and suicide, Kleck points out that most fail to control for even a few confounders that likely affect suicide risk.[49] These studies tend to be among the most methodologically primitive. Stronger studies do not tend to support the thesis that gun ownership increases the total suicide rate.[50] And while it is true by definition that there cannot be gun accidents without gun ownership, this is true of ownership of any kind of item. Moreover, fatal gun accidents (which are very low when compared to suicides and homicides) have been continually decreasing even while gun ownership has not.[51] The likely explanation for this is not the passage of "safe storage" gun control laws, but increased gun safety awareness.[52]

A third point worth noting when considering social harms is that the defensive benefits of guns, combined with their extremely frequent use in self-defense, simply *outweighs* the (at most) modest harms they may be associated with. Here, there is a very strong consensus in the literature that guns (a) are very effective at self-protection and (b) are frequently used for this purpose. Consider the following findings:

- Out of eight different forms of robbery resistance, "victim gun use was the resistance strategy most strongly and consistently associated with successful outcomes for robbery victims."[53]
- "Victim gun use is associated with lower rates of assault or robbery victim injury and lower rates of robbery completion than any other defensive

action or doing nothing to resist. Serious predatory criminals perceive a risk from victim gun use that is roughly comparable to that of criminal justice system actions."[54]

- "The most effective form of self-protection is use of a gun," and "there does not appear to be any increase in injury risk due to defensive gun use."[55] Victims who resisted robberies and burglaries with guns were less likely to lose property than those who resisted with other means.
- Men and women who resisted with a gun were less likely to be injured or lose property than those who resisted using some other means or who did not resist at all. In the case of women, "having a gun really does result in equalizing a woman with a man."[56]
- Out of sixteen different forms of victim self-protection, "a variety of mostly forceful tactics, including resistance with a gun, appeared to have the strongest effects in reducing the risk of injury."[57]
- Defensive gun use "is most often effective at helping the victim rather than hurting them."[58]
- Resistance with a gun decreased the odds of robbery and rape completion by 93% and 91%, respectively.[59]

Taking stock of these points, the Institute of Medicine and National Research Council concluded in a 2013 review of the literature that "studies that directly assessed the effect of actual defensive uses of guns (i.e., incidents in which a gun was 'used' by the crime victim in the sense of attacking or threatening an offender) have found consistently lower injury rates among gun-using crime victims compared with victims who used other self-protective strategies."[60]

When it comes to the number of defensive gun uses, the findings of at least *nineteen* different surveys show that guns are used very frequently in self-defense.[61] While these surveys differ in their exact findings, all confirm the thesis that defensive gun uses are very common, or at least more common than criminal uses.[62] Estimates range from around 760,000 to 3 million defensive uses of guns each year, compared to around 414,000 criminal uses of guns in 2011. The methodologically strongest survey, conducted by Kleck and Marc Gertz, found that guns are used in self-defense upwards of 2.5 million times each year.[63] A later survey, conducted by the Police Foundation and sponsored by the Department of Justice, confirmed these findings.[64] Additionally, Kleck and Gertz found that "as many as 400,000 people a year use guns in situations where the defenders claim that they 'almost certainly' saved a life by doing so."[65] They point out that even if only 10% of this figure were correct, it would still exceed the number of lives lost each year from gun deaths (which number around 33,000). These considerations strongly suggest that the defensive benefits of gun ownership vastly outweigh whatever social harms that it is associated with.

Critics of Kleck and Gertz sometimes argue that these numbers are inconsistent with the findings of the National Crime Victimization Survey (NCVS), which suggests only around 70,000 defensive gun uses each year. However, the NCVS was never designed to measure defensive gun use to begin with. Respondents to the NCVS are not asked about defensive gun use at all; they merely are provided with the option to volunteer this information if they indicated that they were the victim of a crime.[66] Among surveys that *are* designed to measure defensive gun use, there is unanimity that defensive gun uses are very frequent.

There is also the question of the number of crimes that are *deterred* by gun ownership. Unlike crimes that are disrupted by defensive gun use, these are crimes that never actually occurred due to fear of encountering an armed citizen. Using several techniques of measuring crime deterrence, Lawrence Southwick found that *at least* 400,000 crimes each year are deterred by handgun ownership, with the actual number probably being around 800,000 to 2 million.[67] If we include defensive uses, there are in total around 2 to 4 million fewer crimes completed each year because of civilian handgun ownership.

If these claims are even close to being true, then gun ownership carries with it significant benefits that arguably outweigh the risks.

3. The Argument from Liberty

What conclusions can we draw from the empirical data? Consider now the *argument from liberty*: Individuals have an undefeated presumption to own X if owning X is not intrinsically immoral and there are no overriding contingent reasons to prohibit owning X.[68] This is just saying that if there are no good reasons to prohibit someone from owning something, then they should be allowed to own it.

It does not seem as if owning a gun is intrinsically wrong, for we can surely imagine *some* cases in which it is permissible to own a gun. Anyone who insists that gun ownership is intrinsically wrong is claiming that there is *no possible situation* in which gun ownership can be justified, and surely this claim is too strong.

What about the second criterion? Are there any overriding contingent reasons to prohibit gun ownership? Given the facts considered earlier, this is doubtful.

Since there do not seem to be any good reasons to prohibit gun ownership, we can conclude that individuals should be allowed to own guns. At the very least, this establishes a prima facie (i.e., "at face value") right to own guns.

It is important to note that the argument from liberty does *not* appeal to any benefits that guns might offer. The claim is simply that there is a presumption in favor of liberty, and that there are no good reasons to override this presumption when it comes to gun ownership. Hence, the defender of the argument from liberty does not have to show that guns are beneficial per se.

4. Arguments from Self-Defense

Many people who acquire guns do so because they perceive them to be effective at self-protection. This point is easy to understand: The simplicity and ease of operating a gun makes them seemingly ideal tools for use in self-defense.

Guns provide defensive advantages that other common weapons cannot easily match. Unlike most other weapons, guns require only a modicum of physical ability, can be deployed from a considerable distance, and can be quickly used multiple times. This fact allows guns to equalize physical disparities that are commonly exploited in violent crimes. As we saw earlier, the evidence is very clear that guns (a) do in fact benefit the user when used in self-defense and (b) are frequently used in self-defense. We can conclude, therefore, that individuals have a strong prima facie interest in owning firearms for self-protection against criminal assault.[69] These points also extend to gun carrying, for the act of carrying one's gun is simply one way of exercising ownership.[70]

The need for individuals to effectively resist criminal assault encompasses perhaps the most common and well-known formulation of the self-defense argument for gun ownership. However, there is another equally important but somewhat neglected version of this argument: self-defense from rogue governments.[71] On this point, political scientist R. J. Rummel has estimated that as many as 262 million people were murdered by their own government during the twentieth century.[72] Even by conservative estimates, this means that any given human being who was unjustly killed during the twentieth century was more likely killed by his own government than by an individual criminal.

While Western democracies have been relatively stable, there is no reasonable assurance that this will continue indefinitely. The right to bear arms against one's government is the right to renegotiate the terms of the social contract or to effect regime change when one's government becomes tyrannical. If, as most people think, government exists for the sake of the governed, then this recognition of right is absolutely essential for the protection of all other rights. If this right were to be relinquished through disarmament, its relinquishment would very likely be *permanent* and *irreversible*. This is too high a price to pay, even if it appears unlikely that one's government will become tyrannical in the near future. Political forecasting is fraught with difficulties, and long-term forecasting is all but practically impossible.[73]

Even the record of a government as stable as the United States has been marred by significant violations of the rights of minorities, so it is not very much of a stretch to imagine that this could happen again in the near future, and on a much larger scale. The track record of state-sanctioned citizen slaughter from the nineteenth century shows that when governments do go bad, they tend to go *extremely* bad. We should think of an armed citizenry as providing a *deterrent* or *insurance* against government abuse. The costs of armed resistance make it less likely for a government to go bad, much like seat belts reduce the chances of being injured in an accident.[74] Of course, gun ownership does itself come with costs, but these costs are outweighed by the risk of an out-of-control government.

5. But What If the Harms Outweighed the Benefits?

Although I believe that the empirical evidence shows that guns do not increase social harms, this point is not necessary to make the case for gun ownership.

Accordingly, I shall now defend the second claim of this paper: *Even if the overall harms of gun ownership outweigh its overall benefits, there is still a presumption in favor of reasonably permissive gun ownership.*[75]

Many critics of gun ownership assume that if the overall balance of evidence is in their favor, that this is sufficient to justify either a total ban on gun ownership or extremely restrictive regulations. Thus, Nicholas Dixon calls for a complete ban on handgun ownership on purely utilitarian grounds.[76] David DeGrazia, while taking a less restrictive position (which he calls "moderate" gun control), has argued that prospective gun owners must demonstrate a special need that goes beyond mere self-defense.[77] However, neither of these proposals follows from the claim that guns tend to be more harmful than they are beneficial.[78]

Against Prohibitionism

Even if it turned out that guns produce more harms than benefits, there are still benefits. The fact that these benefits may be *outweighed* does not mean that they are *erased* (indeed, the very idea of outweighing presupposes that there is something to be said for the side that is being outweighed). Not even the most ardent defender of gun control would deny that gun ownership is beneficial for at least *some* people. So given that guns do have benefits, this is something that we should want to promote. Reducing the harms of gun ownership is compatible with simultaneously trying to maximize whatever benefits guns do have. From a utilitarian point of view, then, we should attempt to *maximize the overall benefits of guns while minimizing their overall harms.* This can be done, at least in principle, without banning gun ownership for *everyone.* By resorting to a blanket prohibition without first attempting to enact less restrictive measures so as to maximize the very real benefits of guns, Dixon's utilitarian argument for handgun prohibition actually violates utilitarian reasoning. It does not follow that because handgun ownership in general tends to be more harmful than beneficial, every instance of handgun ownership is harmful. The default utilitarian position would be to find a less restrictive way of regulating handgun ownership that attempts to yield the best ratio of costs and benefits. A total prohibition would be justified only as a *last resort* after less restrictive methods have been shown to fail.

Against Restrictive Licensing

In light of these points, we should attempt to promote *responsible* gun ownership. This means that we need some kind of test by which we can reliably determine who is and who isn't qualified to own a gun. DeGrazia, who argues that handgun ownership is on average self-defeating, nevertheless recognizes that some people should be allowed to own handguns. Accordingly, he argues for a policy under which prospective gun owners must satisfy two criteria.[79] Those wanting to own a gun must (a) demonstrate a special need to own a gun, one that goes beyond mere self-defense, and (b) pass a rigorous course in handgun safety.

But even though DeGrazia takes seriously the fact that gun ownership is not counterproductive for everyone, his "moderate" proposal is still far too restrictive. Even if we grant his claim that handgun ownership is on average self-defeating, this does not tell us anything about the specific individuals for whom it is self-defeating. By putting the burden of proof on *all* prospective gun owners to justify their need to own a gun, the state is assuming that *everyone* falls within the average. This assumption is clearly unjustified. Since individuals have at least a prima facie right to own a gun, the burden of proof is on the government or licensing authority to show that it is defeated when it comes to a particular individual seeking a license. The mere fact that this right may be defeated for the majority won't suffice, since this fact doesn't tell us whether a particular individual falls within the majority. Indeed, since the whole point of a licensing system is to *determine* who is qualified and who isn't, it cannot work by assuming in advance that all applicants are unqualified until proven otherwise.

Thus, it is incumbent upon the *state or licensing authority* to provide a reason to override the prima facie gun rights of individuals. By putting the burden of proof on all prospective gun owners to justify their need to own a gun, it is assumed that their prima facie right to own a gun is either non-existent or already overridden. DeGrazia's "moderate gun control" actually ends up violating the rights of those for whom gun ownership is not counterproductive. He may very well be correct that gun ownership is on average self-defeating, but his solution to this problem is unjust to those who do not fall within the average.

The fair and equitable thing to do would be to allow anyone who satisfies an objective list of rigorous criteria the ability to purchase and own guns instead of demanding that every applicant justify their need. In other words, gun licensing should be *non-discretionary* or "shall-issue." This is not to say that licensing standards cannot be rigorous, only that a just licensing system for handgun ownership must put the burden of proof on the licensing authority, not the applicant.

It is not wrong to impose a test or some other standard in order to prevent certain ineligible individuals from partaking in a risky activity, so long as the test does not work by treating everyone's right to partake in that activity as defeated until proven otherwise. While background checks and safety courses meet this requirement, a special need-based test does not.[80]

6. Conclusion

The best research does not show that gun ownership results in more harms than benefits. But even if it did, there would still be a presumption in favor of reasonably permissive gun ownership. We are left, then, with a broad but powerful case for private gun ownership.[81]

COMPREHENSION QUESTIONS

1. What are the significant benefits of gun ownership Hsiao identifies?
2. In Hsiao's view, what makes a study methodologically strong?

3. According to Hsiao, citizens need firearms to defend themselves against criminal assault and . . . ?
4. Why does Hsiao believe that a rigorous licensure process (where you have to demonstrate a special need to own a gun and take a course in handgun safety) is too restrictive? What does he propose instead?
5. What reasons does Hsiao offer in support of his claim that people should be allowed to own guns even if gun ownership does more harm than good?

DISCUSSION QUESTIONS

1. What do you make of the disparities between Hsiao's and Maring's presentations of the available evidence related to gun violence and gun control? Whom do you trust to offer well-founded empirical evidence on this issue (perhaps Hsiao, Maring, someone else, or no one)?
2. Does what you know about government procedures for issuing driver's licenses inform your assessment of Hsiao's argument against DeGrazia's proposed licensure procedures for gun ownership? If so, how so? If not, why isn't the comparison useful?

Case 2

Katarzyna Celinska considers the hypothesis that gun ownership and attitudes about gun control reflect competing individualistic and collectivistic cultural traditions in the United States. She writes:

> The importance of individualism is evident in the historical tradition of gun ownership in the United States, the enduring profile of typical gun owners, and the subcultural behavior and values of some gun owners. On the other hand, the tendencies to control widespread gun ownership and to rely on government to provide security can be viewed as expressions of collectivistic values . . .
>
> The results [of this investigation] demonstrate that, in fact, these cultural values do explain some gun ownership and predict attitudes toward gun permits. Specifically, the index of individualism and collectivism was a significant predictor of household and respondent gun ownership in the enlarged sample. Even more importantly, individualism appears to be one of the main predictors of attitudes against gun permits. Having individualistic values is a consistent predictor in all logistic models, regardless of the sample size and the type of gun ownership (whether individual or household). Consistently, being more individualistic than collectivistic increases the odds of opposing gun permits.*

Do you agree that cultural values like individualism and collectivism inform beliefs about gun ownership and policy? Is one value more important or better than the other? With regard to the issue of gun control, can these differing values be reconciled? How *should* they be reconciled?

---

*Katarzyna Celinska, "Individualism and Collectivism in America: The Case of Gun Ownership and Attitudes Toward Gun Control," *Sociological Perspectives* 50, no. 2 (2007): 232, 244.

REPLY TO HSIAO
LUKE MARING

Official-looking—yet unreliable—information is more accessible now than ever before. We need to ask three questions about the sources we encounter.

Q1: Is the source peer-reviewed?
An article passes peer review when experts think it merits publication. Researchers send their work to a journal; the journal finds experts to review it; and if the experts think the research has sufficient merit, the journal publishes it.

Hsiao leans on non–peer-reviewed sources—sources not vetted by experts. Examples include studies published by John Lott's Crime Prevention Research Center (CPRC), which is not an academic journal but a conspicuously pro-gun non-profit organization. Hsiao also cites "Would Banning Firearms Reduce Murder and Suicide," an article published in the official-looking *Harvard Journal of Law and Public Policy*. But as an independent fact-checking organization reports, the "paper in question was not peer-reviewed, it didn't constitute a study, and it misrepresented separate research to draw shaky, unsupported conclusions."[82]

Q2: Does the source come from an organization or researcher with a narrow and extreme ideological bent?
We all have biases, but Lott and the CPRC stand out. They have ties to the NRA,[83] and some of those ties are especially damning.

Ted Nugent was a long-time fixture on the CPRC Board of Directors and is famous for outbursts like this: "Obama, he's a piece a shit. I told him to suck on my machine gun."[84] David A. Clarke currently remains on the CPRC Board. His twitter feed reads: "Visit MY website . . . for UNFILTERED, UNAPOLOGETIC . . . CONSERVATIVE COMMENTARY . . . Libs must be accompanied by an ADULT who must bring a change of diapers for the crybullies."[85]

Organizations so strongly affiliated with the worst partisan pundits deserve skepticism. Yet Hsiao cites Lott and the CPRC as authorities.[86]

Q3: Is there a consensus opinion among experts, and, if so, does the source contradict it?
Even peer-reviewed studies by experts make mistakes. So rather than relying on a handful of articles, we need to read widely. The problem is that Hsiao's citations are both narrow and one-sided.

Hsiao cites Kleck's and Gertz's infamous estimate that there are 2.5 million cases of defensive gun use in America each year.[87] He more or less ignores widely accepted criticisms—their study invites social desirability bias and probably overestimates by a large margin.[88] Hsiao cites a literature review by Kleck suggesting that gun prevalence has no significant effect on crime rates. He ignores a different, and similarly robust, literature review suggesting the opposite conclusion.[89]

So here's the score: Along with non–peer-reviewed works by questionable sources, Hsiao cites a handful of articles by Kleck and his associates. Kleck and associates say that gun prevalence is nothing to worry about, but scientific consensus tells the opposite story. Only an estimated 5% of experts believe that guns make a household safer, only 12% believe that carrying a gun outside the home reduces one's chance of being killed, and 71% believe that strong gun laws help reduce homicide. A staggering 84% believe that the proliferation of guns in the United States has created a serious public health problem.[90]

Might Kleck be correct, despite swimming against such a substantial tide? He accuses his critics—in a non–peer-reviewed journal financed by gun manufacturers—of distorting the evidence to fit their "political intentions."[91] But if we trust scientific consensus about the causes of global warming and the safety of vaccines, we should probably trust it here too.

Moreover, even if we stifle worries about the reliability of Hsiao's sources, many of the studies he cites can't prove what he needs them to prove. High estimates of defensive gun use generally count it a success when armed people resist assailants by, say, merely brandishing guns they can't reliably use, or scaring off assailants by incompetently spraying bullets about. The studies Hsiao cites, in other words, are not designed to show that ordinary citizens reliably hit their target—and only their target—when they are terrified and fighting for their lives.

If scientific consensus changes, I will change my mind. If study after peer-reviewed study were to confirm that ordinary citizens are accurate when the pressure is highest, I will concede that there is a right to use guns for self-defense.[92] But I don't expect that to happen. Trained professionals with experience—the police—hit the wrong thing between 70% and 85% of the time.[93] Ordinary citizens will almost certainly be worse.

Nonetheless, Hsiao and I share important common ground: wariness of armed state forces. But we draw different conclusions. Hsiao thinks we should arm ourselves; I do not. Mutual armament of citizens and police in the United States has been a disaster. The worst police deliberately violate citizens' right against being wrongfully killed, injured, or intimidated; well-meaning officers make costly mistakes because they are legitimately concerned about the gun-carrying public; and the costs of this whole arrangement fall disproportionately on black and Native American citizens. Further arming ourselves so we are even more threatening to police is not the key to defusing this situation. We need de-escalation.

So here, in closing, is the policy that respects our right to recreation, our liberty to own guns, *and* our right against being wrongfully killed, injured, or intimidated by the forces sworn to protect us. Citizens may own, store, and use guns at certified ranges. If they pass screening, citizens may temporarily check out hunting rifles or single-shot shotguns for hunting. But no one—ordinary citizens or police—may carry guns on their person or keep guns in their homes.

I don't know how to enact this policy. If the open-minded study America has thus far resisted shows that the costs of mutual disarmament would be too high, I don't know the second-best option. But Hsiao's sources notwithstanding, *those* are the issues we should be debating.

COMPREHENSION QUESTIONS

1. In Maring's view, what are the three questions we need to ask about the sources of information that shape our beliefs?
2. What evidence would Maring need to change his mind about the right to use guns for self-defense?

DISCUSSION QUESTIONS

1. Do you think Maring's criteria for information sources are sound? Would you change or add any criteria?
2. How might Hsiao respond to the criticism that his citations are "narrow and one-sided"?

REPLY TO MARING
TIM HSIAO

I'm grateful to Luke Maring for advancing the debate with his tightly argued contribution. Due to space considerations, I will only discuss problems with his central arguments.

1. Can Civilians Safely and Reliably Defend Themselves?

There are at least four problems with Maring's argument that there is no right to own or carry guns because civilians aren't capable of safely and reliably defending themselves with them.

First, Maring thinks that the inaccuracy of police marksmanship casts doubt on the claim that civilians can "safely and reliably win actual firefights."[94] This doesn't follow. One doesn't need to be an expert marksman to win a firefight. "Winning" in the context of resisting a criminal action simply means getting the assailant to break off his attack. It need not end in his injury or death. Hence, one can win a firefight even if he misses most of his shots. Indeed, criminals tend to pick "easy" targets, and so they will tend to break off an attack when a victim resists.[95] This is why forceful resistance in general is associated with lower rates of injury.[96]

Maring might object that missing one's shots does not count as a safe use of a firearm. However, he incorrectly assumes that the safe discharge of a firearm requires accurate shot placement. This is not true. Inaccurate shooting is only unsafe when it puts others at great risk of harm (i.e., when one does not fire towards a "safe direction"). A shooter who misses his shots can still be using his gun safely if he fires at a clear backstop.[97]

Second, someone who uses a gun in self-defense uses it for the purpose of *warding off an attack*. Since this can be done without firing a shot, the actual discharge of a firearm is not required in order for an action to count as a safe and reliable use of a gun. Rather, all that's required for a successful defensive gun use (DGU) is that a gun be *introduced* to stop or prevent an attack. Whether this involves firing a shot, threatening force, or brandishing is irrelevant.[98]

Third, even if civilians are not good shooters, the vast majority of studies on the effectiveness of DGUs nevertheless indicate that guns are very effective at ensuring safe outcomes.[99] The Institute of Medicine and National Research Council concluded in a 2013 literature review that "studies that directly assessed the effect of actual defensive uses of guns (i.e., incidents in which a gun was '*used*' [emphasis mine] by the crime victim in the sense of attacking or threatening an offender) have found consistently lower injury rates among gun-using crime victims compared with victims who used other self-protective strategies."[100] Subpar accuracy may not be *ideal*, but it appears to be *adequate* for successful self-defense.[101]

Maring's response is that these studies do not truly measure the effectiveness of guns, since they may include cases in which guns were not safely and reliably used. But "using" a gun consists of more than just firing it. Although firing a shot is perhaps the best way to stop a criminal, brandishing and threatening force also involve using a gun.[102] Putting all these uses together, the findings are clear: DGUs are very effective at self-defense.[103] Not only that, since the vast majority of DGUs do not involve firing a gun, they are also *safe* for both the victim and the assailant.

Fourth, even granting Maring's argument, his conclusion is too strong. Suppose that the majority of civilians are not qualified to own guns. This wouldn't show that there is *no* right to own guns full stop. The problem with appealing to averages is that it leaves out people who do not fall within the average. What about civilians who *are* qualified to use their guns (there are *plenty* of them)?[104] Do they not have at least a prima facie right to own a gun? If so, then we can fall back to the thesis I defend in the second part of my article: Given that guns are beneficial for *some* people (to the point of saving their lives), we should devise some sort of test to distinguish the qualified from the unqualified.

2. Does an Armed Police Force Violate Our Moral Rights?

Maring's second argument is that each wrongful death from an armed police force is a "straightforward violation of a citizen's right to life." Hence, the police ought to be disarmed. I have two responses to this argument.

First, one might invoke the doctrine of double effect.[105] We might say that in allowing police officers to wield firearms, the government doesn't *intend* any subsequent rights-violations that may occur. It may intend the use of force, but it doesn't intend rights-violations as such. Moreover, although rights-violations are a reasonably foreseen side effect of an armed police force, this bad side effect is simply outweighed by the good that firearms bring to police—namely, their ability to equip police officers with the means to defend themselves. Given that 57,180 police officers were assaulted in the line of duty in 2016 (2,377 with a firearm, 1,096 with a knife, and 9,122 with other dangerous weapons),[106] there is a strong interest in favor of an armed police force. The government may *allow* rights-violations as "collateral damage" or "acceptable losses" provided that (a) it does not *positively will* that they occur and (b) there is a commensurate good.

Second, Maring's argument proves too much. If every government rights-violation by means of some tool, service, or resource is sufficient to justify a presumption in favor of removing that tool, service, or resource, then government itself would be rendered powerless to do anything. After all, one might argue that revenue services, social services, regulatory bodies, the military, and other government agencies should be stripped of their powers because they routinely use the powers, services, and resources at their disposal to violate the rights of individuals.

Now, Maring may respond by saying that these rights-violations are *incidental* to the agencies in question, whereas some police officers "deliberately kill, injure, or intimidate citizens who ought not to be killed, injured, or intimidated." However, this is equally true of these other agencies as well. Both conservatives and liberals routinely complain about how certain government policies are by design unjust or discriminatory. Since corrupt government officials do and often act intentionally in ways that violate rights, Maring's argument would imply that the government itself should be stripped of its power. This would arguably render his argument self-defeating, since the government would be stripped of its legislative power to ban firearms.

In conclusion, Maring has not established his case for civilian and police disarmament.

COMPREHENSION QUESTIONS

1. Hsiao identifies four problems with Maring's argument that people don't have a right to use guns in self-defense. What are they?
2. Hsiao grants that violations of citizens' rights are a "reasonably foreseen side effect of an armed police force." Why does he think police should carry firearms?

DISCUSSION QUESTIONS

1. Recall the comparison Maring draws between guns and illegal weapons (i.e., bombs and nerve gas). How well does Hsiao respond to this part of Maring's argument?
2. Do you think police officers' right to defend themselves outweighs the violations to citizens' rights that Hsiao and Maring identify?

FURTHER READINGS

Baker, Deane-Peter. *Citizen Killings: Liberalism, State Policy, and Moral Risk.* New York: Bloomsbury, 2016.

Bernstein, C'Zar, Timothy Hsiao, and Matt Palumbo. "The Moral Right to Keep and Bear Firearms." *Public Affairs Quarterly* 29, no. 4 (2015): 345–363.

DeGrazia, David, and Lester Hunt. *Debating Gun Control.* New York: Oxford University Press, 2016.

Dixon, Nicholas. "Handguns, Philosophers, and the Right to Self-Defense." *International Journal of Applied Philosophy* 25, no. 2 (2011): 151–170.

Dixon, Nicholas. "Handguns, Violent Crime, and Self-Defense." *International Journal of Applied Philosophy* 13, no. 2 (1999): 239–260.

Halbrook, Stephen. *That Every Man Be Armed: The Evolution of a Constitutional Right*. Albuquerque: University of New Mexico Press, 2013.

Hemenway, D., and E. P. Nolan. "The Scientific Agreement on Firearm Issues." *Injury Prevention* 23, no. 4 (August 2014): 221–225.

Hsiao, Timothy. "Against Gun Bans and Restrictive Licensing." *Essays in Philosophy* 16, no. 2 (2015): 180–203.

Hsiao, Timothy. "The Ethics of 'Gun-Free Zones.'" *Philosophia* 45, no. 2 (2017): 659–676.

Hsiao, Timothy, and C'Zar Bernstein. "Against Moderate Gun Control." *Libertarian Papers* 8, no. 2 (2016): 308–325.

Huemer, Michael. "Is There a Right to Own a Gun?" *Social Theory and Practice* 29, no. 2 (2003): 297–324.

Kleck, Gary. *Targeting Guns: Firearms and Their Control*. New Brunswick, NJ: Transaction, 1997.

Kleck, Gary, and Don B. Kates. *Armed: New Perspectives on Gun Control*. Amherst, NY: Prometheus, 2001.

Lott, John. *More Guns, Less Crime*. Chicago: University of Chicago Press, 2010 (3rd ed.).

Lott, John. *The War on Guns: Arming Yourself Against Gun Control Lies*. Washington, DC: Regnery, 2016.

Testimony of Black Citizens in Ferguson, Missouri, and Elsewhere: http://thetruthtellingproject.org/.

Wheeler, Samuel C. "Arms as Insurance." *Public Affairs Quarterly* 13, no. 2 (1999): 111–129.

Wheeler, Samuel C. "Self-Defense: Rights and Coerced Risk-Acceptance." *Public Affairs Quarterly* 11, no. 4 (1997): 431–443.

NOTES

1. Bernstein, Hsiao, and Palumbo build their argument on the "right of self-defense" (C'zar Bernstein, Timothy Hsiao, and Michael Palumbo, "The Moral Right to Keep and Bear Firearms," *Public Affairs Quarterly* 29, no. 4 [October 2015]: 346). Michael Huemer argues that "individuals have a right to own firearms . . . that is not overridden by utilitarian considerations" (Michael Huemer, "Is There a Right to Own a Gun?" *Social Theory and Practice* 29, no. 2 [April 2003]: 297). And according to Lance Stell, our fundamental rights condemn gun control (Lance K. Stell, "Gun Control and the Regulation of Fundamental Rights," *Criminal Justice Ethics* 20, no. 1 [2001]: 28–33).

2. Huemer, "Is There A Right," 301–306.

3. For a comparison of different countries' gun laws, see: "How to Buy a Gun in 15 Countries," *New York Times*, accessed March 13, 2018, https://www.nytimes.com/interactive/2018/03/02/world/international-gun-laws.html?action=click&module=Top+Stories&pgtype=Homepage.

4. Huemer, "Is There a Right," 304–306.

5. Huemer, "Is There a Right," 323. Deane-Peter Baker, "Gun Bans, Risk, and Self-Defense," *International Journal of Applied Philosophy* 28, no. 2, (2014): see abstract. Bernstein, Hsiao, and Palumbo, "Moral Right," 323.

6. Huemer never even mentions the difficulty of wielding a gun in self-defense (Huemer, "Is There a Right"). Bernstein, Hsiao, and Palumbo go even further, writing that "firearms are relatively easy to use" (Bernstein, Hsiao, and Palumbo, "Moral Right," 348). Deanne-Peter Baker is to my knowledge the *only* philosophical defense of gun ownership that recognizes the need for training (Baker, "Gun Bans," footnote 28). But Baker

relegates the point to a footnote, and his article does not leave the impression that the relevant training will be all that difficult.

7. Bernard D. Rostker, Lawrence M. Hanser, William M. Hix, Carl Jensen, Andrew R. Morral, Greg Ridgeway, and Terry L. Schell, *Evaluation of the New York City Police Department Firearm Training and Firearm-Discharge Review Process* (Rand Center on Quality Policing, 2008), 14, http://www.nyc.gov/html/nypd/downloads/pdf/public _information/RAND_FirearmEvaluation.pdf.

8. Bryan J. Vila and Gregory B. Morrison, "Biological Limits to Police Combat Handgun Shooting Accuracy," *American Journal of Police* 13, no. 1 (1994): 1–30.

9. For a survey of these results, see Gregory B. Morrison and Bryan J. Vila, "Police Handgun Qualification: Practical Measure or Aimless Activity," *Policing: International Journal of Police Strategies and Management* 21, no. 3 (1993): 526–527.

10. Michael D. White, "Hitting the Target (or Not): Comparing Characteristics of Fatal, Injurious, and Noninjurious Police Shootings," *Police Quarterly* 9, no. 3 (September 2006): 303–330, see abstract.

11. Morrison and Vila, "Police Handgun Qualification," 529.

12. "I've Been Shot in Combat. And as a Veteran, I'm Telling You: Allowing Teachers to Be Armed Is an Asinine Idea," *Charlotte Five*, accessed March 13, 2018, https://www .charlottefive.com/arming-teachers/.

13. David Hemenway, "Review of 'More Guns, Less Crime: Understanding Crime and Gun Control Laws/Making a Killing: The Business of Guns in America,' by Lott, J.," *New England Journal of Medicine* 339, no. 27 (1998): 2029–2030. John Donohue, "The Final Bullet in the Body of the More Guns, Less Crime Hypothesis," *Criminology and Public Policy* 2, no. 3 (2003): 397–410.

14. Ted Nugent is a former rock star and a fixture on the board of directors for the NRA. Brad Thor is a controversial novelist and a "lifetime member of the NRA" (https://www .facebook.com/BradThorOfficial/posts/10202509209910132). David Clarke Jr. is an embattled former sheriff who has received substantial gifts from the NRA ("Bice: As Sheriff Clarke's Profile Soars, Gifts Roll In," *Journal Sentinel,* accessed March 31, 2018, https://www.jsonline.com/story/news/investigations/daniel-bice/2016/09/18/bice -sheriff-clarkes-profile-soars-gifts-roll/90429910/). And Joyce Lee Malcolm is the Patrick Henry Professor of Constitutional Law and the Second Amendment at George Mason's Law School, a position funded by the NRA.

15. "Crime Prevention Research Center," accessed March 13, 2018, http://crimeresearch .org/cprc-research/.

16. Gary Kleck and Marc Gertz, "Armed Resistance to Crime: The Prevalence and Nature of Self-Defense with a Gun," *Journal of Criminal Law and Criminology* 86, no. 1 (1995): 150–187.

17. David Hemenway, "Survey Research and Self-Defense," *Journal of Criminal Law and Criminology* 87, no. 4 (1997): 1430–1445.

18. Gary Kleck, "Degrading Scientific Standards to Get the Defensive Gun Use Estimate Down," *Journal on Firearms and Public Policy* 77 (1999): 77–137.

19. "Return of Organization Exempt from Income Tax," accessed March 15, 2018, https:// www.saf.org/wp-content/uploads/2017/12/SAF-990-2016.pdf.

20. "Sponsors," accessed March 15, 2018, https://www.saf.org/sponsors/.

21. See, e.g., Andrew Anglemyer, Tara Horvath, and George Rutherford, "The Accessibility of Firearms and Risk for Suicide and Homicide Victimization Among Household Members: A Systematic Review and Meta-analysis," *Annals of Internal Medicine* 160, no. 2 (2014): 101–110; Donohue, "The Final Bullet"; Eric W. Fleegler, Lois K. Lee,

Michael C. Monuteaux, et al., "Firearm Legislation and Firearm-Related Fatalities in the United States," *JAMA Internal Medicine* 173, no. 9 (2013): 732–740; Hemenway, "Review of More Guns, Less Crime"; Hemenway, "Survey Research and Self-Defense"; David Hemenway, T. Shinoda-Tagaway, and Matthew Miller, "Firearm Availability and Female Homicide Victimization," *Journal of the American Medical Women's Association* 57 (2002): 100–104; David Hemenway and Sara J. Solnick, "The Epidemiology of Self-Defense Gun Use: Evidence from the National Crime Victimization Surveys 2007–2011," *Preventative Medicine* 79 (October 2015): 22–27; David Hemenway and Matthew Miller, "Firearm Availability and Homicide Rates Across 26 High-Income Countries," *Journal of Trauma and Acute Care Surgery* 49, no. 6 (December 2000): 985–988; David Hemenway and Matthew Miller, "State-Level Homicide Victimization Rates in the U.S. In Relation to Survey Measures of Household Firearm Ownership, 2001–2003," *Social Science & Medicine* 64, no. 3 (February 2007): 656–664; Lisa M. Hepburd and David Hemenway, "Firearm Availability and Homicide: A Review of the Literature," *Aggression and Violent Behavior* 9, no. 4 (2004): 417–440; Leo Kahane, "The Effectiveness of Gun Control Laws: A Comment on the Work by Kwon, Scott, Safranski and Bae and Their Debate with Kovandzic," *American Journal of Economics and Sociology* 58, no. 3 (July 1999): 523–528; B. Kaleson, M. E. Mobily, O. Keiser, J. A. Fagan, and S. Galea, "Firearm Legislation and Firearm Mortality in the USA: A Cross-Sectional, State-Level Study," *Lancet* 387 (April 2016): 1847–1855; Arthur L. Kellermann, Frederick P. Rivara, Norman B. Rushforth, et al., "Gun Ownership as a Risk Factor for Homicide in the Home," *New England Journal of Medicine* 329 (1993): 1084–1091; Martin Killias, "Gun Ownership and Violent Crime: The Swiss Experience in International Perspective," *Security Journal* 1, no. 3 (1991): 169–174; Martin Killias and Henriette Hans, "The Role of Weapons in Violent Acts: Some Results of a Swiss National Cohort Study," *Journal of Interpersonal Violence* 17, no. 1 (January 2002): 14–32; Ik-Whan G. Kwon and Daniel W. Baack, "The Effectiveness of Legislation Controlling Gun Usage," *American Journal of Economics and Sociology* 64, no. 2 (April 2005): 533–547; L. K. Lee, E. W. Fleegler, C. Farrell, E. Avakame, S. Srinivasan, D. Hemenway, and M. C. Monuteaux, "Firearm Laws and Firearm Homicides: A Systematic Review," *JAMA Internal Medicine* 177, no. 1 (January 2017): 106–119; Frederic Lemieux, "Effect of Gun Culture and Firearm Laws on Gun Violence and Mass Shootings in the United States: A Multi-Level Quantitative Analysis," *International Journal of Criminal Justice Sciences* 9, no. 1 (June 2014): 74–93; M. Siegel, C. S. Ross, and C. King, "The Relationship Between Gun Ownership and Firearm Homicide Rates in the United States, 1981–2010," *American Journal of Public Health* 103, no. 11 (2013): 2098–2105; M. Siegel, C. S. Ross, and C. King, "Examining the Relationship Between the Prevalence of Guns and Homicide Rates in the USA Using a New and Improved State-Level Gun Ownership Proxy," *Injury Prevention* 20, no. 6 (December 2014): 424–426; Wolfgang Stroebe, "Firearm Availability and Violent Death: The Need for a Culture Change in Attitudes Toward Guns," *Analyses of Social Issues and Public Policy* 16, no. 1 (2016): 7–35.

22. "Firearm Researcher Surveys," accessed March 14, 2018, https://www.hsph.harvard.edu/hicrc/firearm-researcher-surveys/. These survey results were the foundation for a peer-reviewed journal article: D. Hemenway and E. P. Nolan, "The Scientific Agreement on Firearm Issues," *Injury Prevention* 23, no. 4 (August 2014): 221–225.

23. One study, for example, found that victims reduce their chance of injury when they use guns to resist their assailants. But part of the reported reduction comes by way of making threats rather than actually firing a gun (Gary Kleck and Miriam A. Delone,

"Victim Resistance and Offender Weapon Effects in Robbery," *Journal of Quantitative Criminology* 9, no. 1 [1993]: 55–81).

24. L. W. Sherman and R. H. Langworthy, "Measuring Homicide by Police Officers," *Journal of Criminal Law & Criminology* 70, no. 4 (1979): 553.

25. For 2015, see https://www.washingtonpost.com/graphics/national/police-shootings/ For 2016, see https://www.washingtonpost.com/graphics/national/police-shootings-2016/. For 2017, see https://www.washingtonpost.com/investigations/nationwide-police-shot-and-killed-nearly-1000-people-in-2017/2018/01/04/4eed5f34-e4e9-11e7-ab50-621fe0588340_story.html?utm_term=.ac9e52ada509. The true number of citizens shot dead by police will include those whose stories did not make the news, and those whose cases were inaccurately reported.

26. "The Counted: People Killed by Police in the US," *The Guardian*, accessed March 31, 2018, https://www.theguardian.com/us-news/ng-interactive/2015/jun/01/the-counted-police-killings-us-database.

27. "'Don't Shoot Me': Video Shows Police Stop 5 Black Youths at Gunpoint," *M Live*, accessed March 31, 2018, http://www.mlive.com/news/grand-rapids/index.ssf/2017/04/police_release_video_of_five_b.html.

28. Many testimonies and media clips can be found through http://thetruthtellingproject.org/.

29. John Stuart Mill, *Considerations on Representative Government* (Project Gutenberg, 2013), Chapter 1, https://www.gutenberg.org/files/5669/5669-h/5669-h.htm.

30. Japanese police carry guns but rarely use them. But that does not mean that rights violations are not the predictable result of arming American police. First, lots of things are very different in Japan, including extremely strict gun control. Unlike their American counterparts, Japanese police don't worry about being shot by citizens. Second, there are not, so far as I know, data on how often Japanese police wrongfully intimidate citizens. Though they rarely shoot, Japanese police might still be violating citizens' rights.

31. P. A. J. Waddington, "Armed and Unarmed Policing," in *Policing Across the World: Issues for the Twenty-First Century*, edited by R. I. Mawby (Taylor & Francis Group, 1999), 155.

32. "The Forgotten Minority in Police Shootings," *CNN*, accessed March 31, 2018, https://www.cnn.com/2017/11/10/us/native-lives-matter/index.html.

33. "8 Harmless Objects That the Police Have Mistaken for Guns," *The Grio*, accessed March 31, 2018, http://thegrio.com/2014/10/10/8-harmless-objects-mistaken-for-gun/.

34. I first heard this idea in a conversation with Mark Lance.

35. For an excellent analysis of the historical and constitutional basis of the right to bear arms, see Stephen Halbrook, *That Every Man Be Armed: The Evolution of a Constitutional Right* (Albuquerque: University of New Mexico Press, 2013).

36. Gary Kleck, "The Impact of Gun Ownership Rates on Crime Rates: A Methodological Review of the Evidence," *Journal of Criminal Justice* 43, no. 1 (2015): 40–48.

37. See also a recent study by Kleck and colleagues that concluded that "the evidence fails to support the hypothesis that gun control laws reduce violent crime." Gary Kleck, Tomislav Kovandzic, and Jon Bellows, "Does Gun Control Reduce Violent Crime?" *Criminal Justice Review* 41, no. 4 (2016): 1–26.

38. See, for example, Martin Killias, "International Correlations Between Gun Ownership and Rates of Homicide," *Canadian Medical Association Journal* 148 (1993): 1721–1725; David Hemenway and Matthew Miller, "Firearm Availability and Homicide Rates Across 26 High-Income Countries," *Journal of Trauma* 49 (2000): 985–988. It is worth noting that in Kleck's meta-analysis, these two studies were among the methodologically worst.

39. One common example is Australia, which implemented a gun buyback program in 1996. Although touted as a success, there is no evidence that the buyback program was effective in reducing gun violence. Both firearm homicides and suicides were already on a downward trend for more than a decade prior to the buyback. The gun buyback did not seem to accelerate these trends. See the discussion in John Lott, *The War on Guns* (Washington, DC: Regnery, 2016), 109–116. See also Gary Kleck, "Did Australia's Ban on Semiauto Firearms Really Reduce Violence? A Critique of the Chapman et al. (2016) Study," SSRN Working Paper (December 2017), https://papers.ssrn.com/sol3/papers.cfm?abstract_id=3086324.

40. Jan Luiten van Zanden, Joerg Baten, Marco Mira d'Ercole, Auke Rijpma, Conal Smith, and Marcel Timmer, eds., *How Was Life? Global Well-Being Since 1820: Global Well-Being Since 1820* (Paris: Organization for Economic Co-operation and Development, 2014): 147, Figure 8.1. One might also consult the interactive chart at https://ourworldindata.org/homicides and plug in the relevant countries.

41. Another point to note is that the findings of many cross-cultural studies depend heavily on the inclusion of the United States within the samples. Critics have pointed out that once the United States is excluded from the samples, the effect of gun availability on homicide becomes insignificant. This seems to suggest that factors aside from gun availability play a crucial role in explaining the disparities between the United States and other nations.

42. Irshad Altheimer and Matthew Boswell, "Reassessing the Association Between Gun Availability and Homicide at the Cross-National Level." *American Journal of Criminal Justice* 37 (2012): 682–704; Mark Konty and Brian Schaefer, "Small Arms Mortality: Access to Firearms and Lethal Violence," *Sociological Spectrum* 32, no. 6 (2012): 475–490.

43. Altheimer and Boswell, "Gun Availability and Homicide," 696.

44. Michael Planty and Jennifer L. Truman, "Special Report: Firearm Violence, 1993–2011," *Bureau of Justice Statistics*, May 2013, http://www.bjs.gov/content/pub/pdf/fv9311.pdf; Centers for Disease Control, "Leading Causes of Nonfatal Injury Reports, 2001–2013," http://webappa.cdc.gov/sasweb/ncipc/nfilead2001.html; Kenneth D. Kochanek, Sherry L. Murphy, and Jiaquan Xu, "Deaths: Final Data for 2011," *National Vital Statistics Reports* 63, no. 3 (2015), http://www.cdc.gov/nchs/data/nvsr/nvsr63/nvsr63_03.pdf.

45. Konty and Schaefer, "Small Arms Mortality." See 476–478 for criticisms of existing studies.

46. Konty and Schaefer, "Small Arms Mortality," 475.

47. Don B. Kates and Gary Mauser, "Would Banning Firearms Reduce Murder and Suicide?" *Harvard Journal of Law and Public Policy* 30, no. 2 (2007): 649–694.

48. Kates and Mauser, "Would Banning Firearms," 691. "Sweden, with over twice as much gun ownership as neighboring Germany and a third more gun suicide, nevertheless has the lower overall suicide rate. Greece has nearly three times more gun ownership than the Czech Republic and somewhat more gun suicide, yet the overall Czech suicide rate is over 175% higher than the Greek rate. Spain has over 12 times more gun ownership than Poland, yet the latter's overall suicide rate is more than double the former's. Tragically, Finland has over 14 times more gun ownership than neighboring Estonia, and a great deal more gun-related suicide. Estonia, however, turns out to have a much higher suicide rate than Finland overall."

49. Gary Kleck, "Macro-Level Research on the Effect of Firearms Prevalence on Suicide Rates: A Systematic Review and New Evidence," *Social Science Quarterly* 100, no. 3 (2019): 936–950; Gary Kleck, "The Effect of Firearms on Suicide," in Jennifer Carlson,

Kristin Goss, and Harel Shapira, eds., *Gun Studies: Interdisciplinary Approaches to Politics, Policy, and Practice* (New York, NY: Routledge, 2018).

50. Kleck, "Macro-Level Research," and Kleck, "The Effect of Firearms on Suicide"; also see Kleck, *Targeting Guns: Firearms and Their Control* (New Brunswick, NJ: Transaction, 1997), 265–289.

51. National Shooting Sports Foundation, "Firearms-Related Injury Statistics," 2015 ed., *Industry Intelligence Reports*, http://www.nssf.org/pdf/research/iir_injurystatistics2015.pdf.

52. National Shooting Sports Foundation, "Firearms-Related Injury Statistics." On the effects of safe-storage laws, John Lott and John Whitley found that "safe-storage laws have no impact on accidental gun deaths or total suicide rates." See Lott and Whitley, "Safe-Storage Gun Laws: Accidental Deaths, Suicides, and Crime," *Journal of Law and Economics* XLIV (2001): 659–689. Elsewhere, Lott found that there is "no positive statistically significant relationship between gun ownership rates and either accidental gun deaths or suicide for all ages." See Lott, *The Bias Against Guns: Why Almost Everything You've Heard About Gun Control Is Wrong* (Washington, DC: Regnery, 2003), 179.

53. Gary Kleck and Miriam Delone, "Victim Resistance and Offender Weapon Effects in Robbery," *Journal of Quantitative Criminology* 9, no. 1 (1993): 55–81.

54. Kleck, *Targeting Guns*, 184.

55. Gary Kleck and Don B. Kates, *Armed: New Perspectives on Gun Control.* (Amherst, NY: Prometheus, 2001), 288–293.

56. Lawrence Southwick Jr., "Self-Defense with Guns: The Consequences." *Journal of Criminal Justice* 28 (2000): 351–370.

57. Jongyeon Tark and Gary Kleck, "Resisting Crime: The Effect of Victim Action on the Outcomes of Crimes," *Criminology* 42, no. 4 (2004): 861–909. It is worth noting that the Tark and Kleck study is the most authoritative of all extant studies on this topic.

58. Timothy Hart and Terance Miethe, "Self-Defensive Gun Use by Crime Victims: A Conjunctive Analysis of Its Situational Contexts," *Journal of Contemporary Criminal Justice* 25, no. 1 (2009): 6–19.

59. Rob Guerette and Shannon Santana, "Explaining Victim Self-Protective Behavior Effects on Crime Incident Outcomes: A Test of Opportunity Theory," *Crime and Delinquency* 56 (2010): 198–226.

60. Alan I. Leshner, Bruce M. Altevogt, Arlene F. Lee, Margaret A. McCoy, and Patrick W. Kelley (eds.), *Priorities for Research to Reduce the Threat of Firearm-Related Violence* (Washington, DC: National Academies Press, 2013), 16.

61. See the discussion in Kleck and Kates, *Armed*. Also see Kleck, *Targeting Guns*, 147–159.

62. Leshner et al., *Priorities for Research*, 15.

63. Kleck and Gertz, "Armed Resistance to Crime."

64. Philip Cook and Jens Ludwig, "Guns in America: National Survey on Private Ownership and Use of Firearms," *National Institute of Justice Research Brief* (May 1997). Also see Cook and Ludwig, "Defensive Gun Uses: New Evidence from a National Survey," *Journal of Quantitative Criminology* 14, no. 2 (1998): 111–131. See Kleck and Kates, *Armed*, 213–283, for a discussion of their results.

65. Kleck and Gertz, "Armed Resistance to Crime," 180.

66. There are a host of other problems with using the NCVS to estimate defensive gun uses. See the discussion in Kleck and Kates, *Armed*, 229–235.

67. Lawrence Southwick Jr., "Guns and Justifiable Homicide: Deterrence and Defense," *St. Louis University Public Law Review* 18 (1999): 217–246.

68. I borrow this formulation from C'Zar Bernstein, "Gun Violence Agnosticism," *Essays in Philosophy* 16, no. 2 (2015): 232–246.

69. This argument is developed in detail in Michael Huemer, "Is There a Right to Own a Gun?" *Social Theory and Practice* 29, no. 2 (2003): 297–324; and Bernstein, Hsiao, and Palumbo, "Moral Right," 345–363.

70. Moreover, from the perspective of self-defense, one's interest in a reasonable means of self-protection clearly extends outside of the home. This fact is made all the more evident when we consider that in 2008, 82% of violent crimes (65% of rapes, 84% of robberies, and 82% of assaults) occurred away from the home. U.S. Bureau of Justice Statistics, *Criminal Victimization in the United States, 2008 Statistical Tables*, 2011, Table 65, http://www.bjs.gov/content/pub/pdf/cvus08.pdf. See also Timothy Hsiao, "The Ethics of 'Gun-Free Zones,' " *Philosophia* 45, no. 2 (2017): 659–676.

71. This point is developed in Samuel C. Wheeler III, "Arms as Insurance," *Public Affairs Quarterly* 13, no. 2 (1999): 111–129. See also Halbrook, *That Every Man Be Armed*, 1–30, for the historical basis of this argument.

72. R. J. Rummel, *Statistics of Democide: Genocide and Mass Murder Since 1900* (Berlin: LIT Verlag, 1998). Rummel originally estimated the number to be around 178 million but has since adjusted it upwards to 262 million in light of new information.

73. Thus, as Wheeler points out, "[g]iven that disarmament is so hard to unilaterally reverse, it is difficult to imagine sufficient assurance that one's government for the next two hundred years will keep its relatively clean record of government observance of rights." See Wheeler, "Arms as Insurance," 123.

74. One might wonder whether the idea of civilians taking up arms against a modern government is even feasible given modern military power. To see what is wrong with this argument, one only needs to look at the activities of the Viet Cong in Vietnam, the mujahedeen in Afghanistan, and insurgents in Iraq. Moreover, revolutions do in fact occur in governments with relatively advanced military assets (and many times, popular support causes elements of the military to defect), so this idea is not at all far-fetched. Finally, and most importantly, this objection misses the point. The claim is not that an armed citizenry will be able to overthrow government with ease, but that an armed citizenry reduces the probability of a government going bad by raising the costs of tyranny. Wearing a seat belt might not completely mitigate the chance of a fatal injury, but it does reduce the risk of one occurring.

75. For another response, see Timothy Hsiao, "Natural Rights, Self-Defense, and the Right to Own Firearms," *Public Discourse*, http://thefederalist.com/2018/02/27 /americans-right-guns-even-makes-us-less-safe.https://www.thepublicdiscourse .com/2018/10/42765/; Timothy Hsiao, "How to Think About the Gun Control Debate," *Think: Philosophy for Everyone* 18, no. 52 (2019): 21–29.

76. Nicholas Dixon, "Why We Should Ban Handguns in the United States," *St. Louis University Public Law Review* 12, no. 2 (1993): 243–283; Nicholas Dixon, "Handguns, Philosophers, and the Right to Self-Defense," *International Journal of Applied Philosophy* 25, no. 2 (2011): 151–170.

77. David DeGrazia, "The Case for Moderate Gun Control," *Kennedy Institute of Ethics Journal* 24, no. 1 (2014): 1–25; David DeGrazia, "Handguns, Moral Rights, and Physical Security," *Journal of Moral Philosophy* 11 (2014): 1–21.

78. The following arguments are developed in more detail in Timothy Hsiao, "Against Gun Bans and Restrictive Licensing," *Essays in Philosophy* 16, no. 2 (2015): 180–203.

79. DeGrazia, "Handguns, Moral Rights," 17. "[F]or some individuals, gun ownership is not self-defeating. Arguably, their prerogative to own guns for the purpose of self-defense should not be curtailed just because gun ownership is self-defeating for the majority."

80. One might wonder whether there can be a non-discretionary licensing system that is able to reliably exclude those who are unqualified. As it turns out, similar systems have already been adopted by many states for gun carrying licenses. Using concealed carry license revocation data from Florida and Texas (two of the leading states in terms of active licensees), the CPRC found that individuals licensed to carry concealed weapons are, as a class, extremely law-abiding. In Florida, where more than 2.6 million licenses have been issued since 1987, the annual firearms-related license revocation rate (i.e., revocations stemming from the misuse of a firearm) is 0.003%, while the revocation rate for all violations is 0.012%. In Texas, where there are over 584,000 permit holders, the revocation rate in 2012 was 0.021%. To put these numbers in perspective, "the annual rate of such violations by police was at least 0.007 percent. That is about twice the 0.003 percent rate for permit holders in Florida." Additionally, the "rate of all crimes committed by police is 0.124 percent—a number about 6 times higher than the rate for in Texas and about 10 times higher than for Florida." See John Lott, John Whitley, and Rebekah C. Riley, "Concealed Carry Revocation Rates by Age," *Report from the Crime Prevention Research Center*, August 4, 2014, http://crimeresearch.org/wp-content /uploads/2014/08/Concealed-Carry-Revocation-rates-by-age.pdf.

81. Thanks to Spencer Case, Dan Demetriou, and Bob Fischer for comments on an earlier version of this paper.

82. https://www.snopes.com/fact-check/harvard-flaw-review/.

83. Ted Nugent is a former rock star and a fixture on the board of directors for the NRA. Brad Thor is a controversial novelist and a "lifetime member of the NRA" (https:// www.facebook.com/BradThorOfficial/posts/10202509209910132). David Clarke Jr. is an embattled former sheriff who has received substantial gifts from the NRA ("Bice: As Sheriff Clarke's Profile Soars, Gifts Roll In," *Journal Sentinel,* accessed March 31, 2018, https://www.jsonline.com/story/news/investigations/daniel-bice/2016/09/18 /bice-sheriff-clarkes-profile-soars-gifts-roll/90429910/). And Joyce Lee Malcolm is the Patrick Henry Professor of Constitutional Law and the Second Amendment at George Mason's Law School, a position funded by the NRA.

84. https://www.rollingstone.com/music/music-news/ted-nugent-threatens-to-kill -barack-obama-and-hillary-clinton-during-vicious-onstage-rant-94687/.

85. https://twitter.com/SheriffClarke?ref_src=twsrc%5Egoogle%7Ctwcamp%5Eserp%7Ct wgr%5Eauthor. Emphasis in original.

86. Lott's books loom large in Hsiao's article. Hsiao cites *More Guns, Less Crime; The Bias Against Guns: Why Almost Everything You've Heard About Gun Control Is Wrong*; and *The War on Guns: Arming Yourself Against Gun Control Lies.*

87. Kleck and Gertz, "Armed Resistance to Crime."

88. Hemenway, "Survey Research and Self-Defense."

89. Anglemyer, Horvath, and Rutherford, "Accessibility of Firearms," 101–113.

90. Hemenway and Nolan, "Scientific Agreement." This study also asks experts how strongly the evidence supports their answers. The survey asked fifteen different questions, and the answers cited above are, in the experts' view, some of those most strongly supported by the available evidence. My point is not that this article is unassailable; the point is that expert consensus is our best guide to the truth, and that expert consensus does not appear friendly to Hsiao's position.

91. Kleck, "Degrading Scientific Standards," 93.

92. The right to keep a gun for self-defense would still have to be balanced against our right to an unarmed police force. But I admit that the gun control debate becomes much more complicated if ordinary citizens can reliably hit their target when the pressure is highest.

93. I provide citations in my essay. See endnotes 7–11.

94. Maring assumes that civilians are less accurate and proficient than police, but this can be questioned: Research has found that "officers had no advantage over intermediate shooters and a small advantage over novices." See William J. Lewinski et al., "The Real Risks During Police Deadly Shootouts: Accuracy of the Naive Shooter," *International Journal of Police Science & Management* 17, no. 2 (2015): 117–127.

95. In James Rossi and Peter Wright's famous survey of prison inmates, a majority of respondents answered that they would avoid a victim whom they knew was armed and would provide resistance. See James Rossi and Peter Wright, "The Armed Criminal in America: A Survey of Incarcerated Felons," U.S. Department of Justice, National Institute of Justice, https://www.ncjrs.gov/pdffiles1/Photocopy/97099NCJRS.pdf.

96. Tark and Kleck, "Resisting Crime," 861–909.

97. This is something that shooters are routinely taught to do in basic handgun and concealed carry courses (in fact, it is one of the cardinal rules of gun safety).

98. Indeed, the majority of DGUs involve cases in which victims merely threaten the use of force.

99. Indeed, as Kleck points out: "Evidence pertaining to police use of firearms also indicates that civilians who use guns for self-protection are actually less likely to shoot innocent parties than police officers. To be fair, though, crime victims usually have the advantage of knowing who the offender in the crime is, while police officers often enter crime situations where they cannot distinguish offenders from victims or bystanders." Gary Kleck, "The Nature and Effectiveness of Owning, Carrying, and Using Guns for Self-Protection," in Gary Kleck and Don B. Kates, *Armed: New Perspectives on Gun Control* (Amherst, NY: Prometheus, 2001), 287.

100. Leshner et al., *Priorities for Research*, 16. To my knowledge, there is only one study showing that DGU is ineffective at self-defense (Hemenway and Solnick, "Epidemiology of Self-Defense Gun Use"), which suffers from a number of problems. For example, the Hemenway and Solnick study controlled for only six confounders, while the superior Tark and Kleck study controlled for thirty-six. Indeed, Hemenway and Solnick failed to control for at least 10 variables that were statistically related to injury and property loss, variables which Tark and Kleck controlled for.

101. Additionally, Maring's claim about inaccurate police marksmanship needs to be qualified. Officers are more likely to miss their shots when firing from *longer distances* (over 20 feet) and when the officer is *struggling* with the suspect (presumably while attempting to apprehend the suspect, something which civilian self-defenders are not required to do). See Michael D. White, "Hitting the Target (or Not): Comparing Characteristics of Fatal, Injurious, and Non-Injurious Police Shootings" *Police Quarterly* 9, no. 3 (2006): 317. However, most gunfights happen at *shorter distances*. A study of shootings in Memphis, Seattle, and Galveston found that most occured at a distance of under ten feet. See Kleck, *Targeting Guns*, 221. Additionally, 92% of FBI shooting incidents from 1989 to 1994 occurred at a distance of under ten feet. See Tom Givens, "Finding Relevant Training," in *Straight Talk on Armed Defense*, edited by Masaad Ayoob (Iola, WI: F+W Media, 2017), 133. Finally, according to available Federal Bureau of Investigation data on the distances of the gunshot killings of 421 police officers from 2005 to 2014, 50% were killed at a distance of five feet or less, while 68% were killed at a distance of ten feet or less. Federal Bureau of Investigation, *Law Enforcement Officers Killed & Assaulted* (2014), Table 38, https://ucr.fbi.gov /leoka/2014/tables/table_38_leos_fk_with_firearms_distance_between_victim _officer_and_offender_2005-2014.xls. All this is crucial because, as White points out,

"the distance between the officer and suspect is clearly related to shooting accuracy. For fatal shootings, 10 ft or less appears to be the threshold distance; for non-injurious shootings, accuracy drops off considerably beyond 20 ft." White, "Hitting the Target (or Not)."

102. They are "uses" in the sense that a gun played the causal role of stopping an attack.

103. Additionally, guns are very used frequently in self-defense, up to 2.5 million times each year. In his article, Maring points toward some criticisms of this number. For a response, see Kleck, "Nature and Effectiveness," and Kleck, "Response Errors in Surveys of Defensive Gun Use: A National Internet Survey Experiment," *Crime and Delinquency* 64, no. 9 (2018): 1119–1142.

104. Successful accounts are not hard to find. The "Active Self Protection" YouTube channel has compiled and analyzed hundreds of successful civilian DGUs caught on camera. Yet for individuals who were able to use guns successfully in self-defense, Maring's response is that they simply "got lucky." This strikes me as rather flippant. We should surely give credit where it is due and affirm that there are some individuals who can in fact use guns competently instead of attributing successful DGUs to "luck."

105. For an explanation of the doctrine of double effect, see David S. Oderberg, "The Doctrine of Double Effect," in *A Companion to the Philosophy of Action*, edited by T. O'Connor and C. Sandis (Oxford: Wiley-Blackwell, 2010), 324–330.

106. Federal Bureau of Investigation, *Law Enforcement Officers Killed & Assaulted* (2016), Table 75, https://ucr.fbi.gov/leoka/2016/tables/table-75.xls.

CHAPTER 20

Military Spending

WE HAVE THE BEST MILITARY BUDGET
MARK ZELCER

1. Introduction
This chapter explains and justifies high levels of American military spending. The argument is based on the many benefits, and few drawbacks, that heavy and comparatively heavy spending provides. In our non-ideal world, military spending should be encouraged if it increases global safety; promotes economic, diplomatic, social, and technological benefits; promotes the U.S. view of the greater good; and ensures that the United States has the robust and risk-averse defense infrastructure that democratic citizens demand. Current spending levels serve these ends, and they couldn't be achieved if the United States spends substantially less. So, current levels of spending are appropriate.

2. Preliminaries
Two preliminaries. First, this essay assumes that the reader does not particularly dislike the United States, wants it to succeed, and wishes its interests advanced. If you want the United States to fail, stop reading. The United States needs a military that enables it to flourish and promote its interests over those of other nations. If you don't share that aim, you won't be impressed by what follows. Relatedly, many smart, well-educated people dislike the military and, by extension, significant military spending. But their education isn't necessarily a reason to agree with them. To the contrary, intelligence makes one especially susceptible to a documented cognitive bias against the military,[1] which may make their arguments against military spending perhaps somewhat disingenuous. So even if you do want the United States to flourish, you may be inclined to downplay the costs of reducing military spending, especially in the imperfect world in which we live. We need to think carefully and critically about the benefits of the status quo, and the price we pay for changing it.

Second, we realize that, ideally, international conflict is not resolved using military might. However, military spending is not utopian. Our case is grounded in sidestepping an ideal conception of justice designed for a world where international conflicts are resolved non-violently. Countries are indeed going to resort to violence when it suits their purposes, and so our goal should be to set conditions for as much cooperation and pacifist interaction as possible, between as many peoples as feasible, given the liberties we value.

Ideal theories are most useful when it is possible to implement any utopian scheme we might want. We would have nations adopt principles of conflict resolution that they would choose in a Rawlsian "original position," where no one knows the condition of her country. But such an approach is completely insensitive to the political facts of the actual world and cannot justify any realistic recommendations that can guide our actions. We choose a more pragmatic approach here.

We need our non-utopian approach because most governments can be viewed as rational actors. Their behavior can be interpreted as what Plato might call "Thrasymachian"—nations act as if justice is doing what is in their best interest to the extent they can get away with it. If this is so, an ethical proposal cannot assume a standpoint in which some nation acts in the interest of advancing a universal ethical agenda. At the current stage of the development of the community of nations, a state with aspirations to a superior conception of transnational justice still cannot opt out of everyone else's scheme of justice by, say, dismantling their military when no one else does. They will be taken advantage of for doing so. Democratic citizens would never let their government be so taken advantage of. The United States must do the same, and people of goodwill must strive to enhance, refine, and promote a view of the greater good with the ultimate goal of non-violent conflict resolution between nations. Thus, our present interest is not in justice per se, but in promoting *conditions necessary for various conceptions of justice* such as peace among nations, domestic stability, security, and order that expand outward toward allies, neighbors, and then others. A robust American military brings us closer to these goals.

Finally, we believe that even in an ideal world, adhering to principles of international justice does not mean eliminating militaries, but rather minimizing them to allow for basic defense against potential harm. One who thinks that military spending can be completely eliminated presumes either that there will be no desire to cause norm violations or that it is unproblematic that nations are harmed. We believe the former stance is hopelessly naïve and the latter pernicious. In the actual non-ideal world, any case regarding military spending must instead regard the appropriate *amount* of military spending: Should the United States aspire to remain the global military hegemon, or should it spend just enough for basic defense?

We argue that the benefits of life, liberty, safety, and prosperity increase around the world if the United States remains the global military leader and decrease without any global leadership, with the leadership of another of today's major powers, or by replacing the United States with a coalition of nations. These benefits are necessary to promote realistic, ethical goals.

3. Protection

A country that fears for its own safety is hardly in a position to keep others safe. If the United States aspires to promote conditions of peace and order beyond its borders, it must begin by protecting itself. Usually, the more a country spends on defense, the better protected it is and the more threats and kinds of threats it is protected from. The more military capability it has, the greater deterrent it projects. Protection is the basic reason militaries exist, and all countries want as much as they can get. Basic protection entails defense against current and anticipated threats against the United States and its allies. This is not cheap.

Current known threats are incredibly diverse and include conventional attacks involving troops; armor-, air-, and water-based weapons; supersonic intercontinental missiles with a variety of unimaginably horrific payloads; crippling attacks against vital infrastructure like water and electric grids; cyberattacks; economy-crippling cyberespionage; and information warfare. (The technology to defend against much of this does not yet exist.) The United States must be protected against attacks on its soil and its interests abroad, against its way of life, and against a dynamic and evolving set of state-sponsored terror networks, lone radicals, and paramilitary forces, each with its own motives, opportunities, and resources.

These threats are difficult to stay on top of, and it is even more difficult to anticipate the next enemy and its next move. Unfriendly nations and political entities are well funded and have proven to be imaginative and adaptive in the ways they cause harm. Sophisticated intelligence partnerships and espionage networks are vital to understanding who our enemies are and what they are planning. A large research and development infrastructure is important to discover and exploit the potential in new technology before adversaries can. Again, not cheap.

Since technological limitations preclude stopping every attack, much of a country's deterrence strategy is in advertising its ability to retaliate, hence the importance of offensive capability for deterrence. Offensive warfare requires sophisticated modern weapons, trained and talented individuals, and a space-based communication system. And you have no idea what it costs to keep a nuclear arsenal up to date. Some of the U.S. arsenal is coming up on a half-century old and is at the point of having to be modernized or dismantled. All this just to maintain the disincentive to attack the United States.

Setting the conditions for international cooperation also requires attending to and protecting allies. The United States is pledged to protect and aid a variety of territories, nations, and strategic allies with whom it has diverse relationships. Why? In part because it can, and it strikes many Americans as the right thing to do. More pragmatically, there are some nations for whom the United States is their only defense against invasion, colonial aggression, and the forced imposition of foreign values (e.g., Poland, Taiwan, and what is left of the Ukraine). As a former colony itself, the United States ought to have particular sympathy for countries facing these prospects. China, Russia, and a changing cast of dictators have expansionist ambitions and capabilities. If your country borders one of them and you are not a U.S. ally, you are either pretty close to being a vassal or you are worried you might soon become one. For decades, only U.S. military support assuaged South Korean fear of being overrun by a North Korea intent on subsuming its citizens under its communist dictatorship. Without U.S. military intervention, terrorist armies would return to Iraq, Iranian proxy militias would go unchecked in Lebanon and Yemen, and terror groups like Boko Haram and al-Shabab would flourish throughout Africa. New forms of genocide and colonialism would almost inevitably arise.

Putting aside mere sympathy for the plight of smaller nations, there are also selfish reasons to spend significant amounts of money to protect allies. First, it is in any country's interest to maintain as much of a monopoly on power as it can. Having offensive and defensive capabilities, where others do not, increases the prospect of long-term self-preservation. Protecting allies allows the United States to retain such a monopoly and be able to pursue its long-term strategic and ethical goals.

Just as importantly, it is in the interest of global stability if fewer nations feel compelled to develop their own massive military complexes. There are already too many nations with large arms industries, substantial militaries, and nuclear capabilities, and it is in everyone's interest not to increase their number. By credibly pledging to protect a nation (like Japan) or group of nations (like most of Europe), the United States gives those nations incentives to allocate their resources away from indigenous military development and toward their own stability and vision of the good life. (It is cheaper to buy weapons than create an arms industry.) The less a country militarizes, the less of a threat it is to the United States and everyone else.[2] There is therefore adequate reason to protect as many countries as possible who want to be under the U.S. defense umbrella. The more nations that are militarily self-reliant, the less safe all nations are.

Second, economic advantages accrue to the country at the forefront of military technology and arms manufacturing. Weapons sales is big business. The more money spent, the more research and development there is, the more the United States can sell to allies. If the United States does not sell weapons, someone else will, and the U.S. economy and military lose out in absolute and relative terms. Countries less liberal, less democratic, and less peaceful gain capital and incentive to develop their arms industries.

Also, the more spent on weapons development, the more weapons and military assurances can be offered to other countries as part of diplomatic barters. Much foreign aid is given in the form of military assistance and interoperability that buys diplomatic goodwill (soft power) and affords the aided country a greater sense of security. Some countries get advanced weapons (e.g., Israel), and others get Special Forces assistance as part of cooperative agreements (over 70% of countries worldwide!). This strengthens the U.S. ability to dole out "carrots" and makes the United States a more effective peacemaker and ally. Moreover, the stability that comes with such a powerful military makes the United States an attractive partner in matters of military, economic, cultural, and social cooperation. If the United States loses its military might, it loses an important part of what makes it so stable, and such an attractive partner and peace broker.

U.S. stability is shared with countries in its sphere of influence. Besides providing resources for internal and external defense, U.S. stability includes protecting global shipping lanes for everyone who cares to use them. It also uses the same resources to interdict piracy around Africa and reduce human trafficking and illicit drugs and weapons smuggling globally. The United States can do this because its military can project power. It can exercise military might far beyond its borders, from nearby regions, to far-away Japan or the Middle East. Projecting power requires space-based weapons, foreign bases, special operations personnel, intelligence-gathering operations, and aircraft carrier groups. But these power projection platforms add up and, as they say, a billion here, a billion there, and pretty soon you're talking real money.

Of course, the United States cannot protect everyone from everything. At a certain point, we encounter a decreasing marginal utility, whereby each dollar spent defends against a more remote, less severe, and less vital threat. But technology is not even at the point where all known kinds of major attack can be defeated. That is the nature of an arms race, and it is one that the United States cannot safely opt out of. There is a constant stream of new and emerging technologies that U.S. adversaries are always looking to perfect and exploit. Russia, for example, has intimated that it developed hypersonic ballistic weapons with nuclear capabilities. Those are simply too fast to be defeated with existing technology. National banks face ransomware attacks and electronic theft. Your ballot boxes are hackable.

It would be nice to live in a world where all this is someone else's problem and someone else paid for it, but like it or not, the United States plays a unique and expensive role in the international order, one it cannot abdicate without severe planetary repercussions. If you worry about American safety and global stability, be prepared to spend money. Thankfully, however all this spending nets far more than protection.

4. Economic Benefits

If the United States did not otherwise *need* a large military, military spending is not the *most efficient* way for a government to stimulate an economy. But it is *a* way. Military spending stimulates the economy by buying products and creating jobs, many of which are in the rapidly diminishing blue-collar sector.

The labor pool is enriched because the U.S. military is an organization relatively free of prejudice that supports highly skilled jobs as well as many positions open to people with minimal education and no "connections." It provides training that is often transferable to the broader work sector after service. The training often captures those less suited to traditional civilian educational environments. Although not all service members transfer their military skills to the civilian world, they are valuable to employers for their discipline, leadership experience, and appreciation of teamwork.

Additional economic advantages accrue from the innumerable benefits that military research has spawned. Each innovation is a story unto itself, but some examples stand out: the internet, virtual reality, GPS, atomic energy, radar, duct tape, digital photography, jet engines, sanitary napkins, and the modern t-shirt all have military roots. Some of these, especially the expensive ones, are the direct result of the U.S. military's deep pockets; some are the result of happenstance, necessity, and clever innovation. But without the spending, humanity would have little of this. Private corporations might have developed some of these, but between the financial risks and the perceived-to-be-limited civilian market, companies generally balk at such big projects. Anyway, the United States and the world are likely better off since the internet was not invented, owned, and controlled by a private corporation like Microsoft and GPS satellites are not in Google's hands. A world in which private companies owned such crucial infrastructure would be one in which cellphones would be too expensive and would be available to far fewer people than they are now. A world where the U.S. military did not invest in the Manhattan Project would be a world where there is no atomic energy. Almost no civilian company has the resources for such a large speculative gamble. The military budget is an important avenue to pursue sophisticated large-scale research projects that may have revolutionary societal benefits that would otherwise go unfunded.

5. Whose View of the Common Good?

It is a perhaps sad but true fact of the world that she who enforces treaties shapes their rules. She who shapes the rules shapes them after her own image and according to her particular view of the greater good. Without the United States as the main power player in global treaties like those governing trade, anti-smuggling efforts, anti-piracy initiatives, copyright infringement, law of warfare, the environment, etc., someone else would step in. There is no global default, except perhaps an anarchic system in which everyone is worse off. In the power vacuum that would ensue if the United States decreased its global military commitments, someone else would take charge, and whoever takes charge would likely be worse than the United States, certainly worse *for* the United States and liberal democracies. The world would be subordinated to another's view of the greater good—most likely China's or Russia's, whose lack of respect for the environment, human rights and dignity, and diplomacy is notorious and who have kept out of significant conflict only to avoid the prospect of facing off against the United States.

We could hope that the United Nations or a similar organization would take charge, keep the peace, secure shipping lanes, deter pirates, and guard the global commons and digital commons with rules and protocols fair to all. But in reality, the UN is a microcosm of the world, dominated by those nations, good or evil, who make disproportionate financial and military contributions. When the responsibility for financing the UN is spread out, each country pays as little as it can get away with. And even if the UN takes from and gives to each nation equitably, there is no reason to believe it would resolve conflicts any better than it does now.

6. Risk Aversion

As an aside, there is a problem that few democracies can ignore. Militaries in liberal democracies are under pressure from all sides of the political spectrum to become more risk averse with the lives of their service members. In a memorable 2004 press conference, a soldier headed for Iraq, in the early days of the war, confronted the U.S. Secretary of Defense and asked why he was being sent to war without the latest up-armor on his Humvee. A national discussion ensued. Why does the military not ensure that each deploying soldier is outfitted with the highest-tech gear? Who would go to war with a less-than-perfect military? The Secretary of Defense was embarrassed because the United States had not spent enough in advance. This is merely one anecdote, but the moral we draw is that democratic citizens generally are demanding that even war come with minimal risk. You can put a price on risk aversion, and it's hefty. The more we spend, the fewer people die.

7. Alternatives?

Plato, 2,300 years ago, had a scheme to eliminate military spending: He proposed creating a state that nobody wants. The original "minimal state" in the *Republic* is so Spartan (literally) that there is virtually nothing worth protecting. But although Plato initially seems to view this as ideal, the *Republic* immediately points out that this is not a place anyone would want to live. It is so simple it has no "luxuries" like furniture, good food, or doctors. It also cannot help anyone else. The United States has no easy route to making itself so unappealing a target that no one would want to harm it or take its resources. But are there better ways to avoid spending heavily on a military that still promotes global stability?

If the United States were only worried about a land invasion, it could create a massive Swiss-style militia where every adult male is conscripted and most citizens act as part of a ubiquitous defense force. (Given the number of weapons in private hands in the United States, it effectively has such a militia everywhere outside big cities.) But invasion is hardly a serious concern in the nuclear and cyber age. Perhaps the United States can free-ride. It can disarm and hope a sympathetic nation would protect it should the need arise: Only one nation in a coalition needs to counter each threat; the rest can use its technology. But all nations cannot free-ride off one another: Some nation must make the investment.

If the United States does not invest, there is no liberal democracy with the resources, space, manpower, infrastructure, money, and creativity to effectively take its place. It is possible that a scheme for nations of goodwill to chip in equally would work, but the evidence of the North Atlantic Treaty Organization (NATO) suggests that it still requires a central nation to provide most of the resources. Such an alliance also puts the United States at the mercy of other nations' bureaucracies to develop the military capabilities that the United States happens to need.

One might think that the requisite military and its relevant technologies could be developed as the need arises, the way the United States mobilized for World Wars I and II. A response might be best expressed by citing a "truth" that the U.S. Special Operations community takes for granted: "Competent Special Operations forces cannot be created after emergencies occur." What holds true for Special Operations holds true for a broad swath of military threats. In today's rapidly evolving technological environment, a country must invest preemptively to stay in front of emerging threats. Defending against novel threats—cyber, land, terror, space, information, biological, drone, nano, whatever—is not something one can do without planning. Crises emerge much quicker than they ever have, and countries need actionable plans in place. Countries support basic research because they do not know what will pay off. A strong, adaptive military must support a broad spectrum of defense technology because a wide variety of threats would be exploited as soon as it stops paying attention. The enemies of the United States are adaptable and exploit every technological avenue they can.

8. What Is Saved?

A final comment. If the United States drastically decreases military spending, the financial repercussions would be complex and not entirely clear. What is clear, however, is that decreased military spending does not mean that money has just been freed up for spending elsewhere. If the Navy is denied funding for a new aircraft carrier, there is no reason to think that there is suddenly $11 billion (or so) freed up for a new hospital, school, prison, or social program. There is also no reason to think taxes will decrease; the U.S. budget simply does not work that way. The United States might end up borrowing a bit less against the future, spend down the deficit a bit, and, in the long run, have less to pay back, but the military's loss will not be your public school's gain, certainly not anytime soon. While it is rhetorically powerful to say that x can be funded if we don't spend on y, the reality is not that simple. *Both* x and y depend on what the country wants. If it wants that new homeless shelter, Congress can appropriate funds for it more or less independently of other expenditures. Congress does not spend its money on the military and then check to see what remains in the government's bank account for other projects.

9. Conclusion

It sounds ironic, but setting the conditions for a better world, at least now, requires that the countries that most desire peace maintain the best ability to wage war. It requires big isolated bases, many in other countries; it means confronting bad guys far away; it means maintaining a massive web of diplomatic ties; it means spending ungodly sums of money on research to develop new weapons and countermeasures to keep America safe and deny its enemies environments in which to thrive. Most of all, it means employing armies of people to work far behind the scenes, away from an already worried populace, to hold the world as we know it together. It would be nice to spend all that money caring for the world's most vulnerable, but without the minimum global stability that the U.S. military provides, far fewer people would have any chance at all.

COMPREHENSION QUESTIONS

1. What makes Zelcer's approach "non-ideal" or "non-utopian"?
2. Why does Zelcer say we should we protect allies?
3. What are the economic benefits of the military?

4. Zelcer says that "[it] is a perhaps sad but true fact of the world that she who enforces treaties shapes their rules." What does this mean, and what's supposed to follow from it?
5. Zelcer doesn't think we have any good alternatives to spending a lot of money on the military. Why not?

DISCUSSION QUESTIONS

1. Zelcer writes that the "United States needs a military that enables it to flourish and promote its interests over those of other nations." Lots of countries don't have militaries that allow them to promote their interests over those of other nations. Do they lack something they need? Or is the United States special in needing this? And why would the United States need it?
2. Zelcer says that "[if] the Navy is denied funding for a new aircraft carrier, there is no reason to think that there is suddenly $11 billion (or so) freed up for a new hospital, school, prison, or social program." Why does he say this? Isn't it true that if we could borrow the money to pay for an $11 billion aircraft carrier, we could borrow it to build schools? If not, why not? And if so, what does this show about the choices we face?

Case 1

According to its website,

> [t]he Institute for Spending Reform is a nonprofit, nonpartisan organization dedicated to finding solutions to our country's escalating national debt, the challenge of our generation. Credible research and impartial information are crucial aspects of fiscal responsibility, so we engage in and promote rigorous academic research on federal spending and budgeting. We have conducted original research on fiscal rules and the debt limit, the US budgeting system, and a range of issues. With this site, we hope to provide a clear set of options, not a binding policy prescription, for addressing the nation's largest department.*

This Institute is not some wildly liberal think tank, as shown by the fact that the Charles Koch Foundation recommends its proposed solutions.† Here, for instance, are three of their main proposals, each of which comes along with several specific action items:

> **Acquisitions.** Inefficient acquisitions are one of the most obvious opportunities for improvement within the Pentagon budget. Between 2001 and 2011, more than $46 billion went toward weapons systems that never entered production—and appropriators have a duty to ensure that such costs occur only as part of unavoidable trial and error, not circling the wagons for political reasons.

> **Pentagon Restructuring.** In 2018, as the Pentagon prepares to undergo its first-ever audit, identifying overlap, inefficiencies, and waste within

---

*https://strongamericaguide.org/who/
†https://www.charleskochinstitute.org/issue-areas/foreign-policy/the-military-spending-debate/

Case 1 (continued)

the department is more important than ever. While much of the responsibility with certain tasks rests on the executive branch, there are ample opportunities for Congressional leaders to pressure the Administration and Pentagon leadership to take these important actions—both to save money in the immediate term and avoid future waste and duplication.

VA Services & Retirement. It is impossible to forget the scandal that rocked the Veterans Administration just a few short years ago. Americans were rightly outraged as veterans who had served the country honorably were subject to deplorable conditions and lack of care. While several key steps have since been taken to protect whistleblowers and ensure more accountability, more opportunities for reform exist. The following summarizes some options for lawmakers to save money and better care for veterans in the future.[†]

Have a look at the website and glance through some of the specific action items. Presumably, Zelcer would be sympathetic to at least some of them. If that's right, however, then what does that reveal about his essay? What is he really trying to show? What sort of criticisms of the military budget is he most concerned to answer? And how are those criticisms tied to larger disagreements about the place of the United States on the global stage?

[†]https://strongamericaguide.org/wp-content/uploads/2018/02/Guide-for-a-Strong
-America-February-2018.pdf

THE U.S. MILITARY NEEDS TO BUDGET: DECREASING MILITARY SPENDING IN THE TWENTY-FIRST CENTURY
JENNIFER KLING

Current U.S. military spending makes up roughly 54% of federal discretionary spending. In 2015, the U.S. federal discretionary spending budget was about $1.11 trillion, $598.5 billion of which went to the military.[3] For fiscal year 2016, Congress boosted the amount spent on the military up to $611.2 billion, roughly a 5% increase from 2015 levels of federal military spending.[4] (This boost strongly outpaces inflation; the U.S. dollar experiences an average inflation rate of 1.67% per year.[5]) In addition, the United States alone accounts for one-third of all military spending globally, and spends more on its military, in absolute terms, than the next eight countries combined.[6] In short, considered in either absolute or comparative terms, the United States spends an extraordinarily large amount of money on the military.

Of course, while this data is interesting, alone it doesn't tell us whether U.S. military spending is too low, too high, or just right. To reach any of those conclusions, a normative argument is needed, and in what follows, I argue that the United States ought to reduce its military spending. I first address consequentialist political arguments regarding military spending that are focused on safety and security, and the economy. I then address a justice-oriented argument regarding military spending that is focused on domestic and international opportunity costs. Ultimately, whether the concern is about the consequences of decreasing military spending, or the justice of decreasing military spending, I conclude that we ought to decrease U.S. military spending.

1. Safety and Security

The usual argument for increasing, or at the very least maintaining, U.S. military spending is that it keeps us (Americans) safe. More precisely, the argument goes as follows: It is important to keep us (Americans) safe from the threat of terrorism, warfare, and military conflict. Spending more money is a good—although of course not the only—way to ensure that the U.S. military is the best and the biggest in the world, and having the best and the biggest military in the world is the best way to increase our (American) safety and security. Furthermore, this argument can be expanded to include other friendly national groups and countries as well: The best way to increase our allies' safety and security is by ensuring that no one dares to challenge American military supremacy. And a good—although of course not the only—way to ensure that, you might think, is to spend more on the American military, so that it is the best and the biggest in the world.

This consequences-oriented view is initially plausible; spending more money often improves and strengthens institutions, and the threat of force can sometimes deter those who are considering aggressive action. However, this argument is ultimately mistaken, because it equates increasing American military prowess with increasing national and global safety and security. Secure international relations, as many theorists have argued, are dependent on the existence of a relatively stable balance of power within the international community.[7] This complex balance of power between multiple countries does not have to be equal; different countries can have more or less military, economic, political, and soft power, so long as no one country is in a "position of preponderance"—that is, so long as no one country has enough power to fully dictate others' actions.[8] When such a balance of power exists, no one country can act unilaterally without the threat of reprisal, and so they are in general less likely to act aggressively. Thus, a balance of power allows for, and encourages, a more or less secure international order. As Hedley Bull puts it, "the existence of a general balance of power throughout the international system as a whole has served to prevent the system from being transformed by conquest into a universal empire . . . to protect the independence of states . . . [and has] provided the conditions in which other institutions on which international order depends . . . have been able to operate."[9] Put simply, a balance of power secures international order.

While this is somewhat counterintuitive, it can be made clearer by thinking through which of the following scenarios is the most stable, from a safety and security standpoint:

> **Scenario A:** One country is overwhelmingly powerful, and has the capacity to take over the world, or at least most of it, at any time. All of the other countries live in fear.

> **Scenario B:** Two countries are overwhelmingly powerful, and know and/or believe that a fight between them would end in global annihilation. So, they

fight proxy wars using various other countries, each trying to destroy the other through attrition and various underhanded means.

Scenario C: A number of countries have the capacity both to attack enemy states and to defend themselves from sudden attacks. Not wanting to endanger their members, they have made public, multilateral treaties with various other countries in order to deter attacks from rogue states.

Scenario A is only safe for the members of the overwhelmingly powerful country, and even then, it is only so safe, because, as we learn from Thomas Hobbes, people tend to band together to attack that which makes them deeply afraid and insecure.[10] Thus, it is not stable. Scenario B is only safe for the members of the two powerful countries; it is highly insecure for everyone who happens to be a member of some other country, where a proxy (hot or cold) war could break out at any time. Because of the propensity for proxy wars, Scenario B too is not very stable. Scenario C is safe for the members of all of the countries that are involved in the multilateral treaties; it is only unsafe for members of rogue states. Any rogue state could attack, but is held in check by the knowledge that, if it were to attack, it would face immediate, and severe, reprisals. So, while Scenario C is not perfectly secure, it is more stable than the other two scenarios, because any country that would upset the balance is held in check by various controls. But Scenario C just describes an international balance of power. So, while a balance of power is not perfectly safe, we can see, by thinking through various alternative possibilities, that it does secure international order.

On this understanding of international relations, when the balance of power suddenly shifts, conflicts of various kinds erupt. So, in order to maintain national and global safety and security, it is necessary to work to maintain the current balance of power. But recall what the goal of increased U.S. military spending is, for those concerned about security: It is precisely to shift the balance of power toward the United States, to make the United States, if not a preponderant power, then certainly one that no one else dares to aggress against militarily. In other words, the goal is to move toward Scenario A. As Senator Marco Rubio puts it, when arguing for increased military spending, "the world is a safer place when America is the strongest military power in the world."[11] The problem is that this move deliberately works to undermine both the current balance of power and the very idea of a balance of power, which is essential to stable international relations. If the aim is global safety and security, then, increased U.S. military spending actually works against this aim by undercutting one of the key bases of global stability.

In addition to balance-of-power concerns, it is worth considering whether the existence of an outsize American military weakens the commitment of the United States to finding peaceful, non-militaristic solutions to international and regional conflicts. In general, it is better to avoid war than to go to war: War is hell, and the world is safer, and more secure, when alternative, non-militaristic solutions are sought.[12] But when a country has a strong military, it is at least somewhat likely to use it; this is part of why Japan was required to get rid of its military after World War II. The current Japanese constitution, written under the auspices of occupying American forces in 1947, forbids Japan from maintaining a military or from using force internationally. As historian John W. Dower argues, the Japanese, upon accepting the constitution, embraced—by necessity—the notion of influencing the international community by "finance, not force."[13] The lack of a Japanese military, and thus of Japanese military spending, has required the Japanese government to seek alternative, non-militaristic solutions to regional and international conflicts.[14] Of course, it may be that Japan has been able to seek non-militaristic solutions because it is widely known that they have the ability to call upon their allies, who do have militaries, if need be. So, this is not an argument against having any military at all; rather, it is an argument to the effect that increasing military spending, and thereby creating an outsize military, decreases the incentive to seek non-militaristic solutions, which in turn makes the world less safe and secure. There is some truth to the old adage that, when what you have is a hammer, everything looks like a nail. So, if the goal is to promote global safety and security, we ought to decrease U.S. military spending, in order to make the U.S. military a less useful and available hammer.

In addition to global safety and security concerns surrounding U.S. military spending, there are also domestic safety and security concerns. The U.S. military employs primarily Americans; famously, the U.S. military is an all-volunteer fighting force.[15] Including active-duty personnel, the National Guard, and reserve forces, the U.S. military has roughly 2.3 million troops.[16] This is just under 1% of the American population, which, as of 2018, is 327 million.[17] In part because of the nature of the American military, service men and women often have their families on or near their assigned duty base. Such family members, although they remain civilians, primarily use "their" base's facilities for their social, cultural, political, educational, and everyday needs, and make up their own subculture, one dedicated to the American military and the military lifestyle.[18] Once American military members complete their term of service (on average, terms range from two to ten years), they, with their families, reintegrate into the civilian population.

But military veterans, and their families, often struggle to reintegrate into the American civilian population, in part because many veterans suffer from post-traumatic stress disorder (PTSD) and other mental and physical health issues that are not easily identifiable.[19] In addition, many veterans have difficulty succeeding as civilians because they have been trained to respond to both interpersonal and political conflicts with the threat, and subsequent use, of physical force.[20] The ability and willingness to injure and kill is a necessary quality in an American combatant, and one that basic training strives to instill, but it is difficult to reconcile with those qualities required by American civil life, which include, at a minimum, a willingness to agree to disagree, a reliance on law enforcement, and a general unwillingness to use violence. Military families also find the so-called lax discipline of civilian life difficult, in part because they are used to their behavior being scrutinized in the fishbowl environment of a duty base, and in part because corporal punishment for minor infractions is common within active-duty military families but increasingly uncommon within the U.S. civilian population.[21]

This is not to say that American military members and veterans are inherently violent or predisposed to use violence in their private lives; it is simply to say that military culture and civilian culture pull apart in certain basic areas, especially regarding the use of physical force. Because of this, it is not clear that having a large military—which is one of the results of increased U.S. military spending—improves domestic safety and security. In fact, it might be said to degrade domestic safety and security; after all, the more people in a population who are conditioned to use violence, the more violent that society will tend to be. And furthermore, such violence statistically tends to be aimed at the most vulnerable members of the American population, such as women and children. In one study of husband-to-wife spousal aggression, "reports of severe aggression were significantly higher in the standardized Army sample than in the comparable civilian sample (adjusted rates of 2.5% vs. 0.7%, respectively)."[22] Regarding child abuse, researchers found that, while overall rates of child abuse are similar between military and civilian populations, physical abuse is much more common in the military, while neglect is more common in the civilian population.[23] Although more studies are needed, researchers have posited that military service adds some increased risk for family violence.[24]

Ultimately, decreasing U.S. military spending would likely lead to a smaller, more efficient military, which would result in fewer American citizens being trained and conditioned to respond to conflicts with the threat, and subsequent use, of physical force. Crucially, such violence affects not only military families and veterans, but also other vulnerable groups. Although just 6% of the U.S. population are veterans, 19% of police officers are veterans, because police department hiring practices favor applicants with military experience.[25] These veterans-turned-police-officers are overwhelmingly white, and are more likely than their civilian counterparts to use excessive physical and lethal force in the course of executing their official duties.[26] And, because of their military background, they are more likely to be assigned to beats with disproportionate amounts of crime and violence; that is, to beats that are disproportionately populated by black and brown Americans.[27] Although precise data about police brutality is difficult to obtain, the problem is severe enough that in 2009, the Justice Department issued a guide for police departments that specifically warned that veterans may "mistakenly blur the lines between military combat situations and civilian crime situations, resulting in inappropriate decisions and actions—particularly in the use of less lethal or lethal force."[28]

Police brutality is not a national or global security issue; rather, like family violence, it is a domestic security issue. And increasingly, the concern is that police brutality is exacerbated by the addition of military culture—after all, one-fifth of police are veterans—to police culture. Because police brutality is linked to militarism in this way, simply decreasing the number of veterans in police departments may well decrease instances of police brutality. This is not to conclude that veterans are solely, or even primarily, responsible for police brutality, but it is to say that veterans are programmatically trained in the military to use escalating levels of force, and that training does not disappear when they reenter the civilian workforce as police officers. So, while decreasing the size of the U.S. military, through decreasing U.S. military spending, will not end either family violence or police brutality, it could help lessen their prevalence, and thus actually improve domestic safety and security.

This is not an argument against having a military; the U.S. military plays a number of important social and political roles, not the least of which is deterring military attacks against the United States and its allies. However, if the goal is to improve domestic safety and security, we might do better to decrease U.S. military spending, in order to create a situation where fewer members of society are trained and conditioned to use escalating levels of force in response to interpersonal, social, and political conflicts. The overall security benefits of having a military outweigh the overall security costs of having one, but the overall security benefits of having an outsize military (which is one result of increased military spending) may not outweigh the associated domestic costs.

2. Military Economics

So far, I have argued that increased U.S. military spending actually undermines global and domestic safety and security by (a) shifting the balance of power that is essential to stable international relations, (b) weakening the commitment of the United States to finding peaceful solutions to international and regional conflicts, and (c) creating a subculture of American citizens who are trained to respond to conflicts with the threat, and subsequent use, of physical force. However, consequentialist arguments for increased military spending do not focus solely on safety and security; they often consider economics as well. The U.S. military, so the argument goes, is a primary driver of both domestic and international economic growth. In 2015, the Department of Defense (DoD) spent $408 billion on payroll and contracts within the United States, providing secure employment for millions and making up 2.3% of the U.S. gross domestic product (GDP) for that year.[29] Internationally, U.S. military installations pump billions into the relevant local economies, which the DoD argues provides jobs and foreign economic stability.[30] To put it simply, the argument is that increased U.S. military spending results in "long-term economic gains."[31]

The U.S. military does employ large numbers of Americans and citizens of other countries, purchase tons of both material and non-material goods, and pay for the research and development of new technologies. Following Keynesian economics, in times of inadequate purchasing power (e.g., during a recession or depression), increased U.S. military spending is an effective means of job creation and economic stimulation, and hence of economic growth. This is because, in a stagnant economy, the private sector is wary of expanding, and so increased military spending (which is a government investment) could fill in the gap, so to speak, and spark the desired economic effects. But it is essential to realize that this is only true during recessions, depressions, severe stagnations, etc.; Keynes argues for little government spending when employment is high and there is sufficient demand to stimulate the private sector.[32] Military Keynesianists ignore this crucial point and argue for increased U.S. military spending on economic grounds—although they notably do not argue for increased government spending in other areas—regardless of the state of the U.S. and other economies.

The main problem with regarding increased U.S. military spending as a primary driver of economic growth is that the U.S. military is functionally a monopoly. First, military jobs are prevented by military hiring and promotion practices from being market-sensitive. Thus, military personnel are essentially prevented from competing for jobs in an open market, and so military wages can be (and are) kept artificially low.[33] This straightforwardly prevents some economic growth in a capitalist system, which partially depends on wages being sensitive to market demand for those jobs. In addition, and more seriously, the DoD is famous for mismanaging, wasting, and in some cases losing altogether, taxpayer dollars on various armament and other military expenditures.[34] This is because the U.S. military is screened off from many of the economic pressures of capitalism: It is not subject to competition and need not demonstrate to a controlling board of directors that it is operating in the most economically efficient way possible.[35] This enables the U.S. military, unlike a private corporation, to throw good money after bad and to operate deeply in the red for years at a time.[36] This is not to say that the U.S. military should be privatized; the military is an essential public good, and should remain one. But the U.S. military does have all of the economic problems that monopolies typically have, and so should not be relied on as a steady, efficient engine of economic growth in a capitalist economy.

Because the U.S. military has a clear "monopolistic or oligopolistic structure," it is highly economically inefficient; thus, throwing more federal funding at the U.S. military is a highly inefficient way to stimulate the economy.[37] So, while increased U.S. military spending can boost a stagnant or depressed economy, it is in fact a hindrance, rather than a help, to healthy national and global capitalist economies. That money would be better spent, in terms of economic growth, on direct private-sector funding and on public works, such as education, job training, and infrastructure projects, designed to create more points of entry into local, regional, national, and international private markets. Decreasing U.S. military spending would—as well as providing the DoD with some incentive to pay closer attention to its budgeting—free up U.S. government funding for other, more economically fruitful projects. So, if the goal is the maintenance of a healthy, robust economy, then we ought to decrease military spending.

3. Opportunity Costs

So far, I have focused on some key consequentialist arguments around military spending; in what follows, I turn to a key justice-oriented argument, popularized by Dwight D. Eisenhower, that increased U.S. military spending involves serious opportunity costs. For every resource spent in some particular way, it could provide other benefits if used differently. Thus, every decision about resource use has an associated opportunity cost. As Eisenhower put it in his 1953 Chance for Peace speech, regarding the opportunity costs of increased military spending,

"Every gun that is made, every warship launched, every rocket fired signifies, in the final sense, a theft from those who hunger and are not fed, those who are cold and are not clothed. This world in arms is not spending money alone. It is spending the sweat of its laborers, the genius of its scientists, the hopes of its children."[38] Importantly, Eisenhower was not arguing for the abolition of the military; rather, he was arguing that it is necessary to weigh the opportunity costs of increased military spending, because the potential civilian uses of those resources, if they were redirected, could be enormously beneficial.

Of course, it is difficult to know how monetary resources, if they were funneled away from the military and toward other public works projects, would be used; we cannot assume that other public institutions are any less inefficient than the military. However, estimates have shown that reallocating even as little as $1 billion from the U.S. military toward clean energy, health care, and education would create substantially more domestic job growth than if that money were to remain allocated to the military. In particular, such a reallocation would create many more stable midrange and high-paying jobs in those industries than would be created by the U.S. military with the same amount of funds.[39] This would seriously reduce economic inequality, and, if paired with robust education and diversity initiatives, could greatly reduce racial inequalities as well.

Furthermore, in addition to job creation and growth, and the associated reduction of various domestic inequalities, if roughly 10% of U.S. military spending (about $59.8 billion, as of 2015) were reallocated toward global sustainable development, that would be enough to make major progress toward achieving several of the UN's 2015 Sustainable Development Goals.[40] Such justice-oriented goals include eradicating extreme poverty and hunger, providing universal primary and early secondary education, and providing access to clean water and sanitation.[41] While such goals are not aimed primarily at achieving justice for U.S. citizens, their achievement would benefit U.S. citizens, not only because many U.S. citizens are subject to extreme poverty and hunger, etc., but also because it is a truism that the world is safer when it is more just, when more people have the basic necessities required to live and thrive.

This is not an argument for decreasing military spending down to nothing; at some point, the opportunity costs of reallocating U.S. government funding away from the U.S. military will start to outweigh the civilian benefits of doing so. However, unless it can be demonstrated that the U.S. military needs—and uses efficiently—the federal funding that it currently receives, there is no reason to think that decreasing U.S. military spending, and redirecting some of those freed-up funds toward other public works projects, will harm the military more than it will benefit both U.S. civilians and the world. So, we would do better to redirect some, if not much, of the federal funding that currently goes to the U.S. military into other areas, such as clean energy, education, health care, infrastructure, and regional stabilization, which more reliably contribute to overall economic growth, domestic and global security and development, and the attainment of justice. Although U.S. military spending should not disappear from the U.S. federal budget, it should, in the final analysis, decrease.

COMPREHENSION QUESTIONS

1. Kling says we shouldn't think that increasing American military prowess is equivalent to increasing national and global safety and security. Why not?
2. Why is a balance of power important?
3. Kling thinks that a large military incentivizes the wrong kinds of solutions. What does she mean, and why does a large military have this effect?
4. What are some of the costs of military life on combatants and their families?
5. What does the military have to do with the police?
6. Why does Kling think that the military is economically inefficient?

DISCUSSION QUESTIONS

1. Both Kling and Zelcer focus at least partially on how military spending impacts the U.S. (and the global) economy. If they focused instead on how military spending impacts the environment, would that change the debate?
2. The U.S. military, in some arenas, has been a progressive social force (e.g., the U.S. military integrated well before public schools and is much more economically egalitarian than the average private corporation). Should these facts about the progressive role of the military be factored into discussions about military spending?

Case 2

Consider this:

> Global military spending last year rose to $1.8trn . . . the highest level in real terms since reliable records began in 1988, during the cold war, and 76% higher than in 1998, when the world was enjoying its "peace dividend" . . . The spending boom is driven, above all, by the contest between America and China for primacy in Asia. Start with America. In 2018 it raised its already-gargantuan defense budget for the first time in seven years, ending an era of belt-tightening imposed by Congress. The boost reflected the Trump administration's embrace of what it calls "great power competition" with Russia and China—requiring fancier, pricier weapons—in place of the inconclusive guerilla wars it had fought since 2001.
>
> America's military heft has no equal . . . China is far behind. It spends somewhere between a quarter and two-fifths of what America does (the precise amount is unclear, say experts, because Chinese spending is so opaque). Nor is its military expenditure growing at a 10% clip, as it did on average in the years between 2000 and 2016. But it has risen relentlessly for a quarter-century, completely changing the balance of power in Asia.
>
> Between 2009 and 2018, America's defence spending fell by 17% in real terms whereas China's grew by 83%—accelerating under President Xi Jinping and outpacing every other big power. "No one has ever presided over anywhere close to this level of Chinese military development in Chinese history before Xi," notes Andrew Erickson, a professor at the US Naval War College. Its navy has been a particular beneficiary. Between 2014 and 2018, China launched naval vessels with a total tonnage exceeding that of the entire Indian

Case 2 (continued)

> or French navies, notes IISS, another think-tank. Even so, the country's defence spending is still smaller as a proportion of GDP than that of any other top-five country: 1.9% to America's 3.2%. That means it has room to grow, should the geopolitical mood darken.*
>
> Here's a pessimistic reading of these facts: We are, essentially, entering a new Cold War with China. Does this pessimistic reading seem plausible to you? Why or why not? And if it does seem plausible to you, how—if at all—would that affect the way you think about Kling's arguments?
>
> _____
>
> *https://www.economist.com/international/2019/04/28/military-spending-around-the -world-is-booming

REPLY TO KLING
MARK ZELCER

While Kling and I disagree about the route to take, we have a common goal in securing a safer world.[42] I argued that a powerful American military is needed, while she would prefer a weaker one. It is possible that I am just more risk-averse with respect to American security. Regardless, the problem of global stability is complex, and it behooves us to be cautious.

Kling's argument involves outlining possible configurations of international power and encouraging us to think through these scenarios to discover which is most secure. However, this is an approach where data and sophisticated mathematical analysis should trump thought experiments with problematic empirical assumptions. Contrary to her analysis, nations are not the only relevant actors in power politics; we must consider terror networks, multinational corporations, and other entities that shape global politics and economics. We must also consider all the main causes of war. Is great power politics largely responsible, or is it religion, competition for resources, domestic concerns, or some combination of these or other factors?

This complex debate about hegemonic stability versus balance-of-power politics, central to Cold War–era international relations theory, was not resolved in favor of Kling's Scenario C, in which maximum stability is achieved by balancing global power. It was not resolved at all. It is now a less prominent question, and modern political theorists are still deeply divided. We cannot accept this particular theory merely because it sounds fair and we like what it says about military spending.

Less controversially, Kling also suggests that nations with strong militaries are more likely to use force than diplomacy. This is another instance where we need to be careful. Kling's claim sounds plausible, but so does the claim that countries with weak militaries are more likely to have force used against them than they are to be diplomatically courted. In any case, even if it is true that nations with powerful militaries resort to war before diplomacy, it does not follow that the United States should have a weak military. We are interested in whether a preponderant power is *more likely* to resort to war than whatever kind of power the United States would be with a more limited military. This is a different kind of claim requiring a different kind of evidence than Kling provided.

It could be reasonably argued that liberal democracies like the United States with strong militaries make war *less* common, not more. A nation can use a powerful military to threaten and coerce, but threats neither kill people nor topple governments; war does. When U.S. diplomats negotiate from a position of strength, it obviates the need to actually deploy troops, as it decreases the likelihood that it will face military challenges.

It is also worth clarifying something we both considered: reallocating the military budget and spending the money better elsewhere. Talking about reallocation makes sense if the U.S. government is treated intuitively as an ordinary citizen, which we cannot do. Simplifying somewhat, the government expects a certain amount of tax revenue, which, unlike for individuals, is adjustable according to its needs. It has programs that must be funded by law and programs the president recommends funding. Again, unlike citizens, if the amount that the president and Congress ultimately agree to spend is higher than the anticipated tax revenue, Congress authorizes the government to borrow. In 2016, the United States ran a $587 billion deficit[43] and spent $611.2 billion on the military. So, cutting the military budget by just over 96%, leaving a remaining military budget similar to Australia's, should allow the United States to break even without borrowing. In the extreme case, if we eliminated the military entirely we would run a measly $24.2 billion surplus.

But taxes are no more fixed than expenditures, and one would think that less spending would make the electorate want lower taxes. Spending more on some favored project is a choice we can technically make now anyway—just borrow more—but we lack the national will. Imagining what we could do with money we save overlooks the fact that spending less here and more there are two entirely separate legislative issues, not the single matter of shuffling money from one account to another. A budget surplus might incentivize some spending elsewhere, but it is just as likely to incentivize tax cuts or paying down debt. We should worry that eliminating tax-paying jobs and defense contracts will reduce tax revenue to the point that we would anyway have to borrow to cover existing expenditures.

In the spirit of compromise, it may be worth seriously considering how to reallocate money within the military budget to remove some of the problems associated with a large military while preserving the U.S. defense posture and its special role in international affairs. I think most people, including myself, agree with Kling that where possible, the military should not waste taxpayers' money. If we can do the same job more cheaply, it is worth exploring. Investing in people over technology might be a good way to start strengthening the military without overtaxing its budget. The U.S. military has good people. It is unproductive and offensive to implicate them in every social ill from child abuse to racial intolerance. Invoking stereotypes of violence-prone veterans, PTSD, and mental illness should not persuade anyone that a smaller military will make for a better country. But if the military could be more selective and invest more in education, training, medicine, resilience, and veteran care, it would eliminate domestic problems neither of us wants. If the military developed personnel with better technical, cyber, information operations, diplomatic, and interpersonal skills, it would have a force that appears tactically less threatening while maintaining or increasing current strategic security goals. Such an investment in American people, our greatest asset, is something we should all be able to agree upon.

COMPREHENSION QUESTIONS

1. Zelcer says that Kling is ignoring important actors on the global stage. Whom does she leave out?
2. Why does it matter whether other countries are interested in "diplomatically courting" the United States?
3. Zelcer says that we lack the national will to . . . ?
4. Where do Zelcer and Kling agree?

DISCUSSION QUESTIONS

1. Kling claims that some political scientists argue that a smaller U.S. military will make the world safer. Zelcer claims that this is a matter of ongoing debate. How might political scientists or politicians start to figure out who is correct?
2. How might Zelcer respond to the charge that no other country feels the need to spend exorbitantly on the military, so why does the United States? Why is maintaining the global order the responsibility of the United States?
3. Do governments with stronger militaries really use force more often than governments with weaker militaries? Does having a stronger military cause a government to look for opportunities to use it?

REPLY TO ZELCER
JENNIFER KLING

Mark Zelcer argues that current levels of U.S. military spending are justified because they promote the conditions necessary for various conceptions of justice to flourish. In particular, high levels of U.S. military spending enable the United States to provide a minimum level of global stability, without which far fewer people would have any chance of surviving and living minimally decent lives. In what follows, I note some areas of agreement between our two positions, as well as some remaining points of contention.

1. An Oversimplification of the Debate

I agree with Zelcer that having a strong, prepared, robust U.S. military is essential. In contrast to Zelcer's picture of the debate about military spending, though, I maintain that there is a third—and a fourth, and a fifth!—option, *between* current outsize levels of spending and spending just enough for basic defense, that allows the United States to maintain a robust and prepared military that has the capacity to promote minimum global stability. Those options, as I argued in my initial essay, are to reduce the military budget by different amounts, and then use various other mechanisms, such as those of capitalism and democracy, to increase military efficiency and domestic and international security.

Zelcer has argued that military spending is essential; I agree. That is not the debate. The debate is about current levels of military spending, and Zelcer has not shown that *any* reduction in spending will inevitably lead to a serious, harmful reduction in the minimum global stability that is so important to U.S. interests, and that the U.S. military currently provides. Zelcer seems to see only two possibilities in this debate, where there are in fact many. There is a difference between spending less and then working to boost efficiency, and wholly abdicating responsibility for one's role in the international order.

2. A (Somewhat) Myopic View of Threat Response and Reduction

Throughout his essay, Zelcer considers the nature of the threats that the United States has to deal with, and rightly points out that those threats are both serious and ever-mutating. But it is not clear that all of those threats can be deterred or dealt with via military might; after all, they have not been so far! Increased military might, and by implication increased military spending, is not a panacea to all of the threats that the United States faces. As the old story goes, if you want to build the best iron lung for polio victims, create and fund a government institution dedicated to the task. But if you want to cure polio, provide funding to a myriad of private corporations, university labs, and governmental task forces.

American military interventionism has not wholly succeeded in making the world safer; despite U.S. interventions worldwide—indeed, perhaps partially because of them—terrorism, genocide, and new forms of colonialism all currently exist. Zelcer's somewhat sanguine view of American military interventionism ignores its costs, and so must be tempered with the knowledge that there is no silver bullet for global stability. To defend the status quo of current military spending on this basis ignores past experience that the way to solve complex problems is to avoid putting all your eggs in one basket. To truly give the greatest number of people a chance for survival and a minimally decent life, we should decrease U.S. military funding—at least somewhat—and increase U.S. funding to other peace-building and global stabilization projects.

3. Budgeting and American Interests

Both Zelcer and I conceive of the state as a rational actor, one concerned to do whatever is in its best interests that it can get away with. However, we differ in that Zelcer conceives of those best interests quite narrowly (safety, security, and economy), while I conceive of them as being potentially more broad (not only safety, security, and economy, but also justice, peace, and well-being). My understanding of American interests as being rather more complex than Zelcer allows is informed by a point that Zelcer himself makes, which is that, in a democracy, the interests of the state are set by its citizens. So, if U.S. citizens are concerned with justice, peace, and well-being, as well as safety, security, and the economy, then so too is the United States itself. As Zelcer puts it, international and domestic geopolitical interests, and the allocation of the funding necessary to instantiate those interests, "depend[s] on what the country wants."

So, if "the country"—that is, the majority of U.S. citizens—decides to agitate for a partial reallocation of the military budget to domestic public works projects such as schools and hospitals, then that is what will occur, budget-wise (absent certain sorts of common non-democratic interference). And importantly, on this view of budgeting and American interests, what the country wants can *change*; citizens can be persuaded to take up different, and complex, positions on a variety of issues. So, while current public sentiment may favor extraordinarily high levels of military spending—perhaps because of a misunderstanding about the tangled relationship between spending and "bestness"—that sentiment could (and, I argue, should) evolve.

4. Argument by *Ad Hominem*?

Finally, it is worth noting that Zelcer starts off his essay with something of an *ad hominem*, suggesting that academics who argue against increased levels of military spending should not be trusted (at least in relation to such arguments) because "intelligence makes one especially susceptible to a documented cognitive bias against the military." Of course, I am biased; it is a trivial point that everyone is biased in different ways. However, accusations of bias are not helpful to rationally evaluating the arguments for and against a position, especially in the absence of any explanation as to *how* the supposed bias operates in the arguments in question.[44] So, I have here focused on a rational evaluation of the arguments for and against decreasing U.S. military spending, rather than on any (surely futile) effort to demonstrate that I either am, or could be, a wholly impartial, objective observer.

COMPREHENSION QUESTIONS

1. Kling says that Zelcer is oversimplifying the debate. How?
2. Kling says that the military "is not a panacea." What does this mean, and why does she think it's true?
3. Kling accuses Zelcer of beginning with an "*ad hominem*." What's an *ad hominem*? What did Zelcer say that counts as one? Why is it objectionable?

DISCUSSION QUESTIONS

1. Kling says that "in a democracy, the interests of the state are set by its citizens." Does that seem true in the United States? Do you feel as though U.S. citizens are driving the agenda of the United States?
2. Kling says that "Zelcer conceives of [U.S. interests] quite narrowly (safety, security, and economy), while I conceive of them as being potentially more broad (not only safety, security, and economy, but also justice, peace, and well-being)." Would Zelcer agree? Why or why not?

FURTHER READINGS

Bull, Hedley. *The Anarchical Society: A Study of Order in World Politics*. New York: Palgrave Macmillan, 2012 (4th ed.).

Gay, William. "The Military-Industrial Complex." In *The Routledge Handbook of Pacifism and Nonviolence*, edited by Andrew Fiala. New York: Routledge, 2018, 255–267.

Hossein-Zadeh, Ismael. *The Political Economy of U.S. Militarism*. New York: Palgrave Macmillan, 2006.

Walzer, Michael. *Just and Unjust Wars*. New York: Basic Books, 1977 (4th ed.).

Wertsch, Mary Edwards. *Military Brats: Legacies of Childhood Inside the Fortress*. New York: Harmony Books, 1991.

NOTES

1. Mark J. Brandt and Jarret T. Crawford, "Answering Unresolved Questions About the Relationship Between Cognitive Ability and Prejudice," *Social Psychological and Personality Science* 7, no. 8 (2016): 887.

2. Reihan Salam. "The United States Doesn't Spend Enough on Its Military." http://www.slate.com/articles/news_and_politics/politics/2015/11/military_spending_the_case_for_spending_more_not_less.html.

3. Adam Taylor and Laris Karklis, "This Remarkable Chart Shows How U.S. Defense Spending Dwarfs the Rest of the World," *Washington Post*, February 9, 2016, https://www.washingtonpost.com/news/worldviews/wp/2016/02/09/this-remarkable-chart-shows-how-u-s-defense-spending-dwarfs-the-rest-of-the-world/?utm_term=.78b4a62e42a7.

4. Kate Blanchfield, Nan Tian, and Pieter D. Wezeman, "World Military Spending Was $1.69 Trillion in 2016," Stockholm International Peace Research Institute, accessed January 15, 2018, SIPRI.org.

5. "CPI Inflation Calculator," Bureau of Labor Statistics, accessed January 17, 2018, BLS.gov.

6. Blanchfield, Tian, and Wezeman, "World Military Spending."

7. Hedley Bull, *The Anarchical Society: A Study of Order in World Politics* (New York: Palgrave Macmillan, 2012 [4th ed.]), esp. 97–121. See also Martin Wight, "The Balance of Power and International Order," in *The Bases of International Order: Essays in Honour of C. A. W. Manning*, edited by Alan James (London: Oxford University Press, 1973), 85–115.

8. Bull, *Anarchical Society*, 98.

9. Bull, *Anarchical Society*, 106–107.

10. Thomas Hobbes, *Leviathan*, edited by Richard Tuck (Cambridge: Cambridge University Press, 1991), esp. Chapter 13.

11. Quoted in Reihan Salam, "The United States Doesn't Spend Enough on Its Military," *Slate*, November 12, 2015, http://www.slate.com/articles/news_and_politics/politics/2015/11/military_spending_the_case_for_spending_more_not_less.html.

12. Michael Walzer, *Just and Unjust Wars* (New York: Basic Books, 1977 [4th ed.]), 22–32.

13. John W. Dower, *Embracing Defeat: Japan in the Wake of World War II* (New York: W. W. Norton & Company, 1999), 73.

14. J. A. A. Stockwin, "Does Japan Have a Special Attitude Towards Peace? [1987]," *Japanese Foreign Policy and Understanding Japanese Politics: The Writings of J. A. A. Stockwin* (The Netherlands: Brill, 2012), 111–124.

15. Louis G. Yuengert, "America's All Volunteer Force: A Success?," *Parameters* 45 (2016): 53–64. Of course, whether current American service men and women are *really*

volunteers is an entirely separate question, one that I cannot engage with here. The answer depends in part on what counts as volunteering, and in part on what counts as coercion. Nevertheless, it is true that there is no draft or requirement of military service in the United States, and so current American military troops are, at least formally, volunteers.

16. "Department of Defense (DoD) Releases Fiscal Year 2017 President's Budget Proposal," U.S. Department of Defense, Release No. NR-046-16, February 9, 2016, https://www.defense.gov/News/News-Releases/News-Release-View/Article/652687/department-of-defense-dod-releases-fiscal-year-2017-presidents-budget-proposal/.

17. "U.S. and World Population Clock," U.S. Census Bureau, accessed March 30, 2018, https://www.census.gov/popclock/.

18. Mary Edwards Wertsch, *Military Brats: Legacies of Childhood Inside the Fortress* (New York: Harmony Books, 1991), esp. 33–35.

19. Gregory G. Garske, "Military-Related PTSD: A Focus on the Symptomatology and Treatment Approaches," *Journal of Rehabilitation* 77, no. 4 (October–December 2011): 31–36.

20. Josefin Sundin, Nicola Townsend Fear, Amy C. Iversen, Roberto J. Rona, and Simon C. Wessely, "PTSD After Deployment to Iraq: Conflicting Rates, Conflicting Claims," *Psychological Medicine* 40, no. 3 (March 2010): 367–382.

21. Mary R. Truscott, *BRATS: Children of the American Military Speak Out* (New York: E. P. Dutton, 1989), 106–107.

22. Richard E. Heyman and Peter H. Neidig, "A Comparison of Spousal Aggression Prevalence Rates in U.S. Army and Civilian Representative Samples," *Journal of Consulting and Clinical Psychology* 67, no. 3 (April 1999): 239, 239–242.

23. James E. McCarroll, Robert J. Ursano, Zizhong Fan, and John H. Newby, "Classification of the Severity of U.S. Army and Civilian Reports of Child Maltreatment," *Military Medicine* 169, no. 6 (June 2004): 461–464; H. Chamberlain, V. Stander, and L. L. Merrill, "Research on Child Abuse in the U.S. Armed Forces," *Military Medicine* 168, no. 3 (April 2003): 257–260.

24. E. D. Rentz, S. L. Martin, D. A. Gibbs, M. Clinton-Sherrod, J. Hardison, and S. W. Marshall, "Family Violence in the Military: A Review of the Literature," *Trauma Violence Abuse* 7, no. 2 (April 2006): 93–108.

25. Simone Weichselbaum and Beth Schwartzapfel, "When Warriors Put on the Badge," The Marshall Project, March 30, 2017, https://www.themarshallproject.org/2017/03/30/when-warriors-put-on-the-badge.

26. Weichselbaum and Schwartzapfel, "When Warriors Put on the Badge."

27. The reasons for why those areas with more crime and violence are disproportionately populated by black and brown Americans are complicated, and have to do with a long history of institutional racism, redlining and ghettoization, disenfranchisement, and economic suppression, among other things. For a good discussion of these issues, see Michelle Alexander, *The New Jim Crow* (New York: The New Press, 2010).

28. "Employing Returning Combat Veterans as Law Enforcement Officers," International Association of Chiefs of Police (IACP) and Bureau of Justice Assistance, U.S. Department of Justice (Washington, DC: IACP, 2009), 14.

29. "Military's Impact on State Economies," National Conference of State Legislatures, February 21, 2017, NCSL.org.

30. Jean Dreze, "Militarism, Development and Democracy," *Economic and Political Weekly* 35, no. 14 (April 2000): 1171–1183.

31. Ismael Hossein-Zadeh, *The Political Economy of U.S. Militarism* (New York: Palgrave Macmillan, 2006), 45.

32. Peter Custers, "Military Keynesianism Today: An Innovative Discourse," *Race & Class* 51, no. 4 (2010): 79–94.

33. John Bellamy Foster, Hannah Holleman, and Robert W. McChesney, "The U.S. Imperial Triangle and Military Spending," *Monthly Review* 60, no. 5 (October 2008), https://monthlyreview.org/2008/10/01/the-u-s-imperial-triangle-and-military-spending/.

34. Hossein-Zadeh, *Political Economy*, 181–186.

35. Of course, the DoD does answer to Congress and, more broadly, to the American people. However, Congress is notoriously hesitant to hold the DoD responsible, in any serious way, for any financial mismanagement and/or financial misdeeds that come to light, in part because of political pressures and in part because the DoD is considered to be "too big to fail." See William Gay, "The Military-Industrial Complex," in *The Routledge Handbook of Pacifism and Nonviolence*, edited by Andrew Fiala (New York: Routledge, 2018), 255–267.

36. Hossein-Zadeh, *Political Economy*, 186–192; Foster, Holleman, and McChesney, "U.S. Imperial Triangle."

37. Hossein-Zadeh, *Political Economy*, 186.

38. Dwight D. Eisenhower, "The Chance for Peace," delivered before the American Society of Newspaper Editors, April 16, 1953, Eisenhower Presidential Library, Museum & Boyhood Home, eisenhower.archives.gov.

39. Robert Pollin and Heidi Garrett-Peltier, "The U.S. Employment Effects of Military and Domestic Spending Priorities: 2011 Update," Political Economy Research Institute (PERI), University of Massachusetts, Amherst (December 2011), 1–11.

40. Sam Perlo-Freeman, "The Opportunity Cost of World Military Spending," Stockholm International Peace Research Institute, April 5, 2016, SIPRI.org.

41. "Sustainable Development Goals," United Nations Department of Economic and Social Affairs, accessed March 25, 2018, https://sustainabledevelopment.un.org/sdgs.

42. Thanks to Bob Fischer for helpful comments.

43. https://www.cbo.gov/publication/52152.

44. Contrast this with a position that maintains that women shouldn't hold public office. If one of the premises offered in support of this position is that women can't handle making difficult decisions, then we could credibly accuse the person arguing for that position of bias, because we could show that her biases are supporting a false premise. But without such an interrogation of the argument, it is impossible to know what, if any, role bias is playing in her argument, and so accusing her of bias is simply name-calling, not critical analysis.

CHAPTER 21

✤⟶

Voting Ethics

VOTING FOR THE LESSER EVIL
MICHAEL LABOSSIERE

Given the general attitude toward politicians, it is no wonder voters often see elections as a choice between evils. While the 2016 contest between Clinton and Trump is a paradigm case of such a choice, it has confronted American voters across the decades. In 1972, Democrats debated whether to vote for Democratic senator George McGovern, and the result was the election of Nixon. In the controversial election of 2000, Democrats debated about voting for Al Gore—which resulted in Bush's victory. In 2017, Republican voters in Alabama helped elect Doug Jones over the controversial Roy Moore.

While there is a guiding truism about choosing between evils, that one should choose the lesser, voters are often averse to voting for a candidate they dislike, even when they are the lesser evil. This leads to the moral question of whether a voter should vote for a lesser evil rather than not voting at all. I contend that this is exactly what voters should do.

While there are many moral theories, the two best fits for this matter are consequentialist ethics and deontological ethics. While consequentialist ethics vary, they share the principle that the right action maximizes positive value for the morally relevant beings. John Stuart Mill and Thomas Hobbes are both paradigm examples of consequentialists. As might already be suspected, the consequentialist approach can provide an effective way to argue that one should vote for the lesser evil.

One of the primary competitors to consequentialist ethics is deontological ethics, as exemplified by Immanuel Kant. According to these theories, actions are inherently wrong or right, and a choice for even a lesser evil could thus be regarded as wrong. On such a view, voting for a third party or even not voting might seem to be the right action. Fortunately, it can be shown that even deontology can be used to morally justify voting for the lesser evil. I now turn to the consequentialist approach.

1. The Consequentialist Approach

While there are many forms of consequentialist theories of ethics, they all share the basic principle that the action that should be taken is the one that maximizes positive value for the beings that are morally relevant. As such, a consequentialist must specify the measure of value as well as determine who counts, thus defining the scope of morality.

The consequentialist approach has considerable appeal: If something has positive value (like cake), then having more of it is preferable to having less. Likewise, if something has negative value (like mosquito bites), then having less is preferable to having more. People also accept that entities vary in their value. For example, we tend to value our fellow humans, especially those who might share cake, more than we value mosquitoes.[1]

Perhaps the best-known form of consequentialist ethics is utilitarianism of the sort professed by John Stuart Mill. According to Mill, "actions are right in proportion as they tend to promote happiness; wrong as they tend to produce the reverse of happiness."[2] For Mill, happiness is pleasure and the absence of pain while unhappiness is pain and the absence of pleasure. Mill is rather generous in terms of who counts—happiness should be brought to "all mankind and so far as the nature of things admits, to the whole sentient creation."[3]

A consequentialist approach makes it easy to craft a moral argument in support of voting for the lesser evil. Voting for the lesser would make it more likely that the least harm would be done to those who matter morally. As such, voting for the lesser evil would seem to be the least bad choice. However, there might be a better option, and this necessitates considering alternatives.

Since utilitarians aim at maximizing utility, they would also need to consider the consequences of not voting. While not voting would microscopically increase the chance of the greater evil winning, utilitarians could use the resources they would spend voting to engage in other activities (such as working for a charitable cause or rescuing puppies) that would create positive value outweighing the moral value of the alternative. Hence, one should not vote for the lesser evil but instead engage in another activity that would maximize value.

Addressing this matter requires drawing a distinction between act and rule utilitarianism. The act utilitarian assesses the ethics of each action on an individual basis. In contrast, a rule utilitarian assesses an action based on its conformity to a correct moral rule. The correctness of a moral rule is determined by the utility it would yield by its inclusion into the set of moral rules that everyone follows.

There are two problems with the act utilitarian argument against voting for the lesser evil. The first is that the same sort of reasoning applies to voting in general: There will (almost) always be something other than voting that will create more positive value. As such, this view would seem to entail that people should, in general, never vote. While appealing to anarchists, this view would be rather problematic for maintaining a democracy.

The second is that even if the argument only applied to voting for the lesser evil (and, of course, the greater evil), the broad adoption of this act utilitarian view by ethical people could have terrible consequences. To be specific, the ethical people would not vote in an election between evils, and this would leave the election to be decided by the unethical voters—who might, being unethical, vote for the greater evil. As such, while each individual act of not voting and doing something better would seem to be the right thing to do, the collective act of not voting and doing something "better" could easily result in the greater evil winning, which is likely to be far worse than the collective good done by those not voting. Under rule utilitarianism, the rule of not voting for the lesser evil would thus be a bad rule. As such, ethical people should vote, even if the best option is the lesser evil.

While voters who decide to vote based on consequences would have selected their moral approach, they still need to decide on a measure of value, make an estimate of which candidate would do the least evil, and sort out the scope of morality. As such, two consequentialist voters could make radically different assessments about the best (or least evil) vote. As an example, a voter who places the most value on maximizing the success of businesses would assess the consequences of voting for a candidate differently from a voter who favors an equitable distribution of wealth.

One way to address this problem is to take the view of an ideal utilitarian citizen: As a citizen, each person has a responsibility to the other citizens, because it is not just them and their values that matter, but everybody. Each citizen must consider how their vote will impact other citizens and, perhaps, people across the world. As such, voters who want to be good citizens should hold their nose and vote for the lesser evil. This would decrease the chance of the greater evil being inflicted on the society, thus making it the least bad thing to do.

One counter to this ideal utilitarian approach is ethical egoism. On this consequentialist view, each person limits the scope of morality to themselves. Ayn Rand, a favorite of the Tea Party, is a paradigm of an ethical egoist. As she saw it, each person should act from selfishness and do what is in their best interest. She even wrote a book entitled *The Virtue of Selfishness*.[4] On this view, people should always take the action that maximizes their self-interest. Roughly put, for ethical egoists, they are the only ones with moral value. The opposing moral view is altruism, the view that other people count morally. While there are degrees of altruism, egoism is absolute: If you are an ethical egoist, then only you count morally.

While it might seem somewhat odd, the right choice for ethical egoists would still be to vote for the lesser evil. This would, of course, be the lesser evil defined in terms of their own interests rather than in terms of everyone.

It could be contended that it is a viable option to vote for a non-viable third candidate who is seen as non-evil by the potential voter. This could be a third-party candidate already on the ballot or a write-in candidate. One reasonable concern about voting for the lesser of two evils rather than going with a (non-evil) third party candidate who cannot win is that it perpetuates the two-party lockdown of the American political system. In the context of consequentialism, the argument for voting for the non-viable third party would be based on the hope of long-term consequences rather than the short-term consequences. The hope is that the lockdown on politics by Democrats and Republicans could eventually be broken by a viable third party. This would be done by the process of building a movement, signaling to candidates and other voters that they are willing to vote for third parties, and so on. If the third party is likely to be better than the Democrats or Republicans, then the good consequences might outweigh all the evil of not voting for the lesser evils.

It could also be argued that having a non-evil third party that gets some votes is good for the population by pushing the lesser and greater evils toward non-evil positions to win votes. The deciding factor would be whether the positive consequences of eventually getting a viable or at least influential third party would be worth the cost of getting there. On the face of it, this hope seems to be quite a gamble—especially since the third party might just add another evil to the mix. As such, voting for the lesser evil is still the right thing to do.

2. Deontological Ethics

While the consequentialist approach is intuitively appealing, there is also considerable weight to the view that certain actions are just wrong (or right), regardless of the consequences. For example, there are strong intuitions against mass roundups of people with infectious diseases even if such an approach could save lives. Those who accept deontological ethics hold, as Kant claimed in the *Fundamental Principles of the Metaphysics of Morals*, that "the moral worth of an action does not lie in the effect expected from it, nor in any principle of action which requires to borrow its motive from this expected effect."[5] Put roughly, the action itself is good or bad. So, if a person chooses an action that is good, "this is a good which is already present in the person who acts accordingly, and we have not to wait for it to appear first in the result."[6] Likewise, bad actions are already bad and are not bad because of harmful consequences they might produce. One illustration of this, albeit in a fictional context, are video games that track a character's ethical progress (or decline). The points are gained (or lost) as soon as the player makes the choice rather than after the consequences are sorted out in the game.[7] In terms of deciding what to do, Kant put forth his categorical imperative. The gist of this principle is that an action is morally acceptable if the person who wants to take that action can will, without contradiction, that everyone can take that sort of action as well. If a person cannot, rationally, will this, then the action would be wrong. For example, Kant would say that cheating at a game would be wrong because the cheater wants to cheat to gain an advantage and hence cannot will that everyone be allowed to cheat—this would take away their advantage.

Intuitively, voting in favor of a candidate one regards as evil would be a morally wrong act, albeit a minor form of wrongness.[8] This, of course, assumes that supporting evil is itself an evil. This seems reasonable, and an analogy can be drawn to the legal notion of aiding and abetting a criminal. To voluntarily and knowingly assist a criminal in their crimes, even in a small way, would make one a part of the crime. Likewise, voting for an evil candidate would be to aid them in their misdeeds. Voting for the lesser evil would be less evil than supporting the greater evil but would still be an evil action. To use the crime analogy again, voting for the lesser evil would be like aiding a lesser criminal instead of aiding a greater criminal. While this is less bad, it is still criminal. Likewise, voting for the lesser evil would be less bad than voting for the greater evil, but would still be wrong. As such, moral voters would seem to need an option that allows them to avoid doing *any* evil.

One obvious option would be to not vote at all. This is analogous to refusing to aid any criminal, be they greater or lesser. So, if a person regards the only viable candidates as evil, then the right thing to do would be to not vote for any of them—thus avoiding the risk of committing an evil action by supporting, in however miniscule a degree, an evil person. To illustrate, consider a ploy beloved by fictional villains: The villain offers the hero a choice between killing one person or "making" the villain kill many people. While a consequentialist approach would generally favor killing the one to save the many, choosing the lesser evil would still appear to be an evil action. After all, the hero would still be murdering an innocent person even if it is to save the many. Likewise, voting for the lesser evil would still be evil, albeit less evil.

If the hero refuses the villain's "generous" offer, the hero is not to blame for the villain killing the many—that is all on the villain. Likewise, if a voter decides to not vote for any evil and the greater evil is elected, the responsibility lies on the candidate for being evil and those who supported the greater evil. Going back to the crime analogy, this would be like refusing the villain's offer. The murder would be on the villain, not on the person who refuses to aid the villain. The kidnapping would also be on the kidnapper, should that criminal prove successful. Thus, the ethical voter should not vote if the candidates only come in degrees of evil. Even if the greater evil wins because of this, ethical voters would seem to remain pure in their ethics—they have not supported evil with their vote.

While this view is appealing, a moral problem is that not voting is still a choice that could allow the greater evil to win and is thus still an evil action. Going back to the villain example, deciding against killing the one person was wrong not because the hero killed the many, but because the hero's choice resulted in the death of many rather than one. While the hero seems to retain their moral purity, their choice doomed the many. As such, either they are no longer morally pure, or their moral purity came at the price of the deaths of the many. It is, of course, true that the deaths are on the villain—but the hero could have saved the many and that responsibility falls on them. On the face of it, choosing to allow many to die rather than staining one's hands seems to be an evil choice. Likewise, choosing to remain morally pure in an election and potentially allowing the greater evil to win would thus appear to be the wrong choice because it forces others to bear the burden of one's effort to remain morally pure.

A deontologist who still favors not voting could try to make use of another beloved philosophical conundrum, the trolley problem. In the stock trolley problem, there is a runaway trolley heading down a track. While you cannot stop the trolley, you can choose to let it run over five people tied to the track or divert it so it runs over one person tied to another track. As a non-trolley example, a superhero might have to choose between catching a single falling person or catching a falling bus packed with people. In this case, the right thing to do would be to catch the bus. In this example, the hero lets one person die so that they can save the many. This seems to be the right choice be it assessed by consequentialist or deontological ethics. This choice does not make the hero evil; they were forced into making the choice and had no other viable options. The same logic applies to voting: The voter who votes for the lesser evil is analogous to the hero who elects to kill the one to save the many. This voter is taking an active role in the evil, albeit to try to avoid a greater evil. Pulling the lever is analogous to pulling the trigger. The voter who does not vote is like the hero who lets the one die. They are not taking an active role in the death of the person and thus have no responsibility for this evil. While this is an appealing narrative, there is a better interpretation.

The person who does not vote is not like the hero who catches the falling bus rather than the falling person. Rather, they are like a "hero" who lets both the bus and the person fall, leaving it to others to sort out the carnage. This is because voters who do not vote take no action when they could have done so—just like a "hero" who refuses to try to rescue anyone because they do not wish to be responsible for the outcome. But, by not acting, they become responsible for the outcome—at least in a very small degree. This responsibility provides the path toward arguing that even under deontological ethics a person should still vote for the lesser evil.

Voting for a person one regards as evil would be an evil action, as argued above. However, in the case of politics one must think of more than oneself and one's moral choice—one must also consider the responsibility one has to other citizens and society. As such, a person should be willing to bear the tiny burden of voting while holding their nose to try to protect others from what they regard as a greater evil. To go back to the hero analogy, it is better for the hero to accept the guilt of not saving the one person so that they can save the bus full of people than it is to do nothing and let everyone die.

So, while it is wrong to vote for even the lesser evil, it is even worse not to vote at all. So, someone who regards two candidates as evil should vote for the one they think is the lesser evil.

A deontologist who still insists that not voting is the right choice could point to the fact that it makes virtually no difference whether an individual voter votes. After all, in a large election a single vote has only a microscopic impact on the outcome. As such, it could be argued that a voter has no obligation to intervene when the odds of making a difference are miniscule, especially when doing so would make them a party to evil. Going back to the villain example, it would be as if the villain told the hero that if they killed the person, the villain would offer a one-in-a-million chance of sparing the many. In the falling bus example, it would be as if a normal person were trying to find a way to save the people on the bus before it hit the ground—not impossible, but not worth calculating the odds.

Interestingly, the anarchist Henry David Thoreau advanced this sort of argument in support of his rejection of voting.[9] As such, if the deontologist were right about not voting for the lesser evil because of the odds, then this would seem to apply to not voting in general. While Thoreau would approve, this would be problematic for democracy. There is also the fact that this view would entail that people should not even bother to try when the odds are terrible. While this might be a very practical view, it does not seem morally commendable. Also, as Kant noted, it is not the outcome that matters—it is the action. So, even if the odds of success were absurdly low, the right action would still be the right action. And voting for the lesser evil is the right action.

A last point of consideration is the implications of Kant's categorical imperative in this situation. As noted above, Kant contended that an action is, roughly put, acceptable for one person to do if they are willing to allow everyone to do that same sort of action. Now, imagine if a person wanted to not vote simply because there were only evil candidates. On Kant's view, they would have to be willing to allow everyone to not vote. But the evil candidates and evil people would presumably vote—thus the election could very well go to the greater evil. But a good person cannot will the triumph of the greater evil, so a deontologist must accept that voting for the lesser evil is the right action. All that remains is the matter of whether to vote for a third-party candidate.

If there is a non-evil third-party candidate running, then deontological ethics would seem to guide a person to vote for them. After all, the vote for the non-evil candidate would avoid supporting evil while seeming to avoid the evil of not voting. If the non-evil third-party candidate were viable, then this would clearly be the right choice—there are no reasons to settle for a lesser evil if one can get a non-evil. But the push to vote for a lesser evil only arises when there is both a greater evil and a lack of a viable non-evil option. In that case, voting for a non-evil third party instead of voting for the lesser evil would increase the chance of the greater evil winning, and assisting a greater evil is worse than assisting a lesser evil—as argued above. As such, voting for a non-viable, non-evil third-party candidate would be morally equivalent to not voting. Thus, deontological ethics would also guide the ethical voter toward voting for the lesser evil.

COMPREHENSION QUESTIONS

1. Why, on rule utilitarian grounds, is abstaining from voting for the lesser of two evils morally objectionable?
2. What kinds of concerns does the "ideal utilitarian citizen" take into consideration when making voting decisions?
3. At first glance, it looks like a deontological approach to voting between two evils would require abstaining from voting. Why?
4. What, in LaBossiere's assessment, does deontology ultimately require of someone who is faced with voting between two evil candidates?

DISCUSSION QUESTIONS

1. In his discussion of the deontological perspective, LaBossiere likens (1) voting for the lesser evil to (2) diverting a trolley so that it runs over only one person instead of five and (3) choosing to catch a falling bus full of people rather than a single falling person. What, if any, are the morally relevant differences between these three cases?
2. LaBossiere believes that voting for a non-evil third party (rather than voting for the lesser of two evils) is morally right, but only if the third-party candidate is viable. What makes such a candidate viable? How would you know whether they were viable?

Case 1

Writing for the *Washington Post*, Travis Rieder suggests that two kinds of moral principle influence our thinking about voting for the lesser of two evils: minimizing harm and maintaining personal integrity.

> The angry rejection of the idea that one ought to vote for someone she finds objectionable is not only understandable, but I think tied to something deeply important. Voters are being told that they ought to vote so as to minimize harm, which sounds like a moral commandment. But these voters also have a conflicting moral belief—that they ought not endorse a candidate they take to be corrupt. They are being put in the position of choosing an external moral principle over an internal one. . . .
>
> When the consequences of one's action or inaction get bad enough, following through for the sake of keeping one's hands clean starts to seem self-indulgent. Indeed . . . you may sometimes be required to violate your principles for the greater good.
>
> [F]ocusing on our integrity is the most justifiable when the action that we are being asked to take deeply violates our most central life commitments, and the cost of not acting is relatively low.*

What do you think of this argument? What does it have in common with LaBossiere's view, and where does it diverge?

---

*https://www.washingtonpost.com/posteverything/wp/2016/08/13/is-the-lesser-of-two-evils-an-ethical-choice-for-voters/

AGAINST VOTING OBLIGATIONS
PATRICK TAYLOR SMITH

1. The Ethics of Voting Badly

People have been complaining about the incompetence, irrationality, and ignorance of voters for as long as there has been democracy. Whether it is property restrictions, literacy tests, colonial trusteeship, or educational requirements, there's a long and inglorious history of elites trying to restrain the potentially immoral excesses of the "mob" by restricting the franchise of those who are supposedly not ready to govern themselves.[10] Historically, the attempt to limit voting rights has been a conservative affair, a defense of the traditional rights and privileges of the political class combined with a fear that an enfranchised working class would seek property redistribution or, worse, outright revolution. Currently, the Republican Party—in the name of preventing voter fraud—seeks to limit the franchise of voters who are likely to vote for their political opponents,[11] and many argue that felons, including those who have fully paid their debt to society, are simply too vicious to be allowed to vote again.[12] It is important to keep this history in mind as we explore arguments about whether some people are too ignorant or immoral to participate in their own governance.

Yet, whether a state may restrict voting rights is a different issue from the individual ethics of voting. There are many actions that I have a right to do—where the state would be acting unjustly if it stopped me—that are nonetheless wrong. For example, I may have the right to make utterances that are racially offensive but it is still true that I shouldn't. Similarly, some have argued that voters ought to refrain from voting if they are sufficiently ignorant, irrational, or immoral.[13] These arguments can cross the political spectrum, with some on the right saying that people with mostly liberal views should not vote because they are ignorant of economics while some on the left argue that those with mostly conservative views should not vote because they have sexist views about women in the workplace. The basic idea, then, is that voting can have effects on other people and that we should wield that power responsibly. If we vote in ways that are ignorant, irrational, or immoral, then we act negligently and risk harming others. So, you have a duty to vote well or to not vote at all.

I, however, want to reject these arguments.[14] Instead, I will defend the idea that voting is in the realm of the ethically discretionary: You can vote for whomever you want, however you want, without wronging anyone else. Thus, you can vote for the lesser of two evils or for the person who most represents your values. The reason, on my view, is that in a functioning democracy, your vote sends a useful signal about what you believe and value. This signal can be politically productive even if it is uninformed or wrong-headed, and so your vote is up to you. In other words, no one has a right that you vote a particular way or can demand that you must refrain from voting or else you disrespect them. It is important to be clear about this claim. I remain neutral but am sympathetic to the idea that ignorant or vicious voters can be criticized for their behavior in some ways. These voters might very well be frivolous, cruel, or imprudent. My view, however, is that bad voting does *not* violate any obligations of *justice*, and so a bad voter's fellow citizens—either collectively, individually, or in particular groups—lack a right against bad voting. In order to show this, my argument will be in two steps. First, I will show that bad voting violates no person's rights in a legitimate state that possesses a robust democracy and constitutional protections of basic interests. Then, I will show that voting is irrelevant to our obligations to resist tyranny in states that are deeply unjust or illegitimate.

2. Institutionalism

The argument for an obligation to vote well looks straightforward. Voting is an exercise of power, representing an attempt to direct the machinery of the state in one direction rather than another. One should not act in ways that risk violating the rights of others, and that is precisely what one does when one votes with insufficient information, votes irrationally, or votes with deeply problematic biases and prejudices. Some have likened bad voting to pollution;[15] a tiny bit of pollution may be innocuous, but your action is still wrongful because it risks combining with other acts of pollution to cause serious harm. Thus, even if we accept that your vote usually does not make a difference, you are still obligated to do it well. Otherwise, the state may harm your fellow citizens and you will share in the responsibility for the bad consequences of your choices. Of course, there is much disagreement about what constitutes good voting, so let's only describe voting as bad if it violates some very obvious and widely shared norms or principles. So, even if I hold very strongly to some specific ideology—such as socialism, liberalism, or libertarianism—and thereby think everyone else is immoral, we will not call something bad voting *merely* because it is bad in the ideological sense. Instead, we will call voting bad if it satisfies at least one of three conditions. First, voting is bad if it is based in ignorance; that is, a bad voter does not understand basic facts about the political system or the likely effect of their policies. Second, voting is bad if it is irrational such that a bad voter chooses policies that fairly straightforwardly contradict the satisfaction of their own preferences. So, if a voter wants higher economic growth and then votes for policies that clearly and demonstrably hamper economic growth, the voter is being irrational. Finally, voting is bad if it can very clearly be shown to be motivated by deeply and obviously immoral beliefs such as inveterate racism, sexism, or anti-Semitism. Each one of these requirements should be understood as being fairly minimal. Voters need not be perfectly rational, informed, or moral; rather, they must be not grossly and obviously uninformed, irrational, and immoral. If they fail these conditions, then they are bad voters. I concede that there are and will be such bad voters in almost any political system except those that are almost impossibly utopian. The question is whether bad voters violate the rights of their fellow citizens or fail to fulfill their obligations of justice with their votes.

We need to know what our obligations of justice are in order to determine whether bad voters fail to fulfil them. The view I defend is called *institutionalism*, originating with John Rawls.[16] Institutionalism is the idea that there is a moral division of labor between institutions and individuals. The principles of justice—those that, for example, say that every person should enjoy equal voting rights—are the purview of the basic institutions of society, including and especially the legal system and the government. These institutions are created and maintained by sets of rules, offices, and norms that distribute goods, privileges, powers, and rights. They are judged to be just insofar as they are regulated by the correct principles. Individuals, by contrast, need not directly bring about just distributions but should support the institutions, reform them if necessary, and follow their just rules. So, institutions set the rules while individuals engage in whatever goals or actions they see fit as long as they follow their rules and support the institutions. This preserves a wide area of discretion and autonomy for individuals.[17]

A useful, if controversial, example of institutionalism involves Rawls's discussion of the labor market. Rawls argues that if we have created fair institutions, then people are permitted to use their labor power in the following way.[18] Suppose that society would benefit if a doctor lived in rural Alabama in order to treat deeply impoverished people, but that doctor preferred to live in San

Francisco. Rawls suggests that because the doctor has discretion over which job she takes and where, our society might need to incentivize the doctor to move to Alabama by offering higher salaries to those who work in underprivileged areas. *Individualists*[19] argue that the doctor may have an obligation to work in Alabama without the raise. After all, if she chose to work in Alabama, the government could spend that money making other poor people better off. Thus, the doctor should try to directly bring about a world where the principles of justice are better satisfied. *Institutionalists*[20] argue that the doctor may justly bargain for better pay because she is only indirectly responsible for the principles of justice: She need only support the institutions and follow their rules. Something similar is true of voting: If you follow the rules and support the system, your voting behavior is discretionary.

Institutionalism is most plausible when two conditions obtain. First, institutionalism is necessary when the "background conditions" need to be fair for our choices to be voluntary. Consider the idea that I "consent" to paint a fence for my neighbor. In order for that consent to be meaningful, I cannot be forced to accept the contract due to starvation or other dire need. Yet, neither myself nor my neighbor can guarantee that I will not be in dire need. For that, we will need to coordinate the actions of many people using various institutions. We have a division of labor: We act voluntarily "in the foreground" while institutions maintain the background justice. Second, if bad institutions make it too difficult—in terms of judgment or the need for information—for individuals to act justly, then we should focus on institutions rather than individual behavior. Institutionalism works as a view when good institutions are needed for stable, long-term good outcomes and can compensate for bad behavior, while bad institutions make it excessively difficult or costly to engage in good individual behavior.

3. Good Institutions, Bad Behavior, and Social Epistemology

Let's imagine a well-functioning—or "well-ordered"—democracy. Basic liberties, such as freedom of speech, the press, and assembly, are effectively protected by a powerful set of constitutional rules and norms. People enjoy the fair value of political liberty where each person can participate in and influence political decisions on a roughly equal footing. There's an independent judiciary and a robust party system offering clear positions concerning the future of the polity. Finally, this well-ordered system has regular, free, and fair elections with some portion of the electorate being bad voters. I argue that, in a well-ordered system, these bad voters are harmless or even beneficial.

Two elements of this argument are essential. First, we have the results of social epistemology.[21] Beginning with Aristotle,[22] democracy has long been justified via its ability to *aggregate* information from a diverse citizenry. From the Condorcet voter theorem[23] to the superiority of polling the audience in *Who Wants to Be a Millionaire*, epistemologists, scientists, and political theorists have discovered that a group of non-experts can outperform an expert.[24] However, groups only outperform experts under certain conditions. You need to have a diverse group of people and to avoid groupthink where everyone only says what they think the group wants to hear. Second, our votes only lead to policy outcomes in tandem with political institutions. These institutions represent a *filtering* mechanism, such that if they work well, they can take up good or useful information and discard the bad. To continue with the pollution metaphor, the other political institutions of society—from an independent judiciary to constitutional protections of basic rights to a robust civil society—can act as scrubbers to keep the pollution from hurting others while still enjoying the benefits of whatever the factory happens to be producing.

Furthermore, well-ordered institutions not only filter out bad information, they can actually put irrational or uninformed actors to good use in order to help the process generate even better outputs. Philip Kitcher uses the Nobel Prize to show how this works in the sciences:

> The very factors that are frequently thought of as interfering with the rational pursuit of science—the thirst for fame and fortune, for example—might actually play a constructive role in our community's epistemic projects, enabling us, as a group, to do far better than we would have done had we behaved like independent epistemically rational individuals.[25]

Kitcher's idea is that we need to incentivize people to do the epistemically *irrational* strategy—pursue a scientific project that is less likely to work—because if everyone did the same experiment or pursued the same theory, we would fail to fully explore the less likely but still live scientific possibilities. We need people to avoid groupthink and be willing to be the odd person out. Thus, we create an incentive structure whereby if someone does go with the rarer, less likely possibility and it pans out, they get a prize. In other words, if everybody dispassionately and rationally pursues the best scientific theory, the community as a whole will suffer. We need people to selfishly pursue fame and fortune in order to get the best scientific outcomes.

This community will do even better if we create smaller institutional structures that amplify and direct those incentives in productive ways. So, whether this "harnessing irrationality" strategy succeeds depends not only on incentives, but on power and influence. Kitcher writes:

> [A] single deserter from method I cannot contribute enough effort to method II to make that method profitable. What is needed is for several people to jump ship together. Imagine, then, that the community is divided into fiefdoms (laboratories) and that, when the local chief (the lab director) decides to switch, the local peasantry (the graduate students) move, too. . . A certain amount of local autocracy—lab directors who can control the allegiances of a number of workers—can enable the community to be more flexible than it would be otherwise.[26]

A carefully calibrated distribution of power can make it such that scientifically *irrational* behavior creates real diversity and helps the community avoid groupthink. Thus, good systems can usefully direct "bad" behavior in order to make the entire system work better.

These insights apply to voting. Bad voters have information that would be useful for policymakers to have. However, that information might be fragmentary, discombobulated, confused, and shot through with vicious or ignorant attitudes. Since we know that bad voters possess an admixture of good information and bad, we need institutions that will filter out the bad information and incentivize policymakers to take up and act upon the good. The latter can be accomplished pretty straightforwardly by ensuring widespread voting rights and making it easy for everyone to vote in order to avoid limiting available perspectives by restricting the ability of people to participate in the process, especially on arbitrary bases like race, class, or gender. That will limit the information pool to those who are likely to agree with each other, and this means that the information-aggregation benefits of democracy will be lost.

Our political system also needs to prevent bad information or bad outcomes from happening, and a well-ordered polity can do this in several ways. Political parties, for example, can play a mediating role like that of lab groups, influencing voter beliefs and testing voter beliefs against expert opinion in productive ways. In other words, most people mediate their voting through a party structure, and parties can play a role in "laundering" the information provided by voters in order to make it more coherent, informed, and rational. Furthermore, there are many mechanisms in place to ensure that political outcomes do not become unacceptably bad if they are functioning properly. These myriad institutions can block the negative risks of a bad vote. A constitution provides counter-majoritarian veto points, such as the Bill of Rights, in order to protect fundamental interests, setting limits to state action. Independent judiciaries are insulated from voter behavior and apply a different set of norms for reasoning about legal rights. Legislative veto points constrain the rate at which voter behavior influences policy, and independent agencies—such as the Federal Reserve—are given objectives, such as maintaining full employment, that are not immediately or easily subject to specific legislative accountability. If things go well and institutions are well ordered, then bad voters can participate, providing useful information, while avoiding the risk of creating truly bad outcomes.

4. Bad Institutions, Good Behavior, and Resistance to Oppression

Things, however, do not always go well. Institutions can fail, and political systems can be tyrannical or despotic. If you know your regime is likely *not* going to respect basic rights and that the various institutions designed to ensure that bad outcomes do not occur have been corrupted, bypassed, or eliminated, then it seems like you should vote for the best possible option. In other words, if it is reasonably clear that there are no well-ordered institutions to make sure your bad votes will be useful, then you are obligated to resist this illegitimate state by either voting for the best possible option or not voting at all. So, according to this argument, institutionalism is false and you have a direct obligation to vote well when the state is badly ordered. Otherwise, you are complicit in the injustice. I want to respond in three steps.

First, unjust institutions tend to sever the *causal link* between voter behavior and political outcomes. One problem with deeply unjust institutions is that voters have little control over political outcomes. In authoritarian and quasi-authoritarian states that lack basic rights protection, the connection between even an informed and well-intentioned voter's actions and how the state behaves is irregular and unreliable. Parties and politicians in illegitimate or deeply unjust states are frequently deceptive about their preferred policies and about the actual effects of state action. What's more, even if one votes in a well-meaning reform candidate, that candidate will be hemmed in by unjust social, economic, and political structures that will produce unpredictable consequences. Unjust institutions have a strong tendency to sever the causal link and predictability that allow us to be good voters. So, if being a good voter requires that we have reasonable beliefs about the consequences of our actions and that we refrain from taking excessive risks, then dysfunctional and unjust institutions tend to make bad voters of us all. Thus, what seem to be fairly uncontroversial and minimal requirements for voters will—when combined with poor institutions—become exceedingly difficult for anyone to satisfy.

Second, unjust institutions sever the link of *moral responsibility* between votes and political outcomes. That is, even if we grant that bad voting behavior plays some causal role in bad outcomes, it might be unfair to hold voters accountable for those outcomes. Suppose we can find cases where the state is deeply unjust and yet sufficiently transparent about its policies and their effects that we can distinguish between good and bad voters. Yet, even in those cases, bad votes are translated into action by vicious political actors. And unlike in a well-ordered and just constitutional order where there might be some kind of effective and legitimate legal requirement that political power inhere in the people through elections, unjust political orders are composed of actors who are not compelled to accept the results of elections or follow the will of the voters. That is part of what makes them unjust. Perhaps we should hold voters morally accountable for the outcomes of a just system because part of what makes that system just is its self-governing nature; the people rule themselves. Yet, since the unjust political order—which has its own influence upon the political outcomes—operates between the voter and the result, and the actions of the politicians, bureaucrats, and magistrates are unjust, it would be unfair to hold voters morally responsible for the actions of vicious politicians. For example, consider the relationship between a prosecutor appointed by the dominant party in a quasi-authoritarian state that oppresses political opposition and a bad voter who did, in fact, vote for the dominant party. This state prosecutor then abuses their authority and imprisons an enemy of the state, unconstrained by the rule of law. The unjust actions of the dominant party and the prosecutor are necessary to translate the bad vote into bad policy. So, in other words, having an unjust human agent intervene between your action and its consequences mitigates your personal responsibility for what the unjust agent does.[27]

Third, even if we have obligations to resist tyranny,[28] refraining from voting is neither necessary nor sufficient to satisfy them. Let's imagine a state that is reliably responsive to voters despite being unconcerned for and routinely undermining their basic rights. Now consider two citizens who are interested in resisting the state. Citizen A refrains from voting but does little else, wanting to avoid complicity in the regime. Citizen B, however, continues to the vote for the dominant party because she is deeply ignorant of the political system. Yet, when she sees individuals being mistreated by the state, she takes on great personal risk in order to resist state action and protect people suffering from its predations.

I want to suggest two things about the comparison between A and B. First, A's refusal to vote is not an adequate response to the injustice of the state; he is, at least, obligated to do more than that, in part, because the individual causal influence of a single vote is quite small. So, refraining from voting is certainly not *sufficient* for satisfying one's political obligation to resist oppression; A is not doing enough. Citizen B, on the other hand, does seem to be doing enough. She is risking herself to protect people from being harmed and is actively working to foil the unjust policies of the state. Unfortunately, she might be sufficiently ignorant or irrational that she still believes that the dominant party is acting in good faith and that these attacks are the result of a "few bad apples." But this belief is practically irrelevant to her resistance; she still acts to prevent these attacks and wants them to stop. The fact that she continues to vote for the dominant party has an exceedingly minor causal influence, if it has any influence at all, when compared to her protection of the victims of state tyranny. On net, she has done all that could be reasonably asked of her. The reason for this asymmetry between voting and other kinds of resistance is that while voting can be useful—in terms of information aggregation—without being causally effective, meeting one's obligation to resist tyranny requires that resistance have some reasonable prospects for stopping the injustice. So, one can be a bad voter and still be a good resister, while refraining from voting does not make one a good resister. So, refraining from voting is neither necessary nor sufficient for meeting one's political obligations in the face of tyranny.

To be an institutionalist is not to argue that we have no political obligations at all. Quite the contrary, our political obligations are quite robust: Follow and support institutions when they are just; resist and reform institutions when they are not. Bad voting does not violate our obligations—and non-voting does not fulfill them—in either case. If we live in a just society, then bad voting can be productively directed and filtered by our various social and political institutions. If we live in an unjust society, then non-voting is neither necessary nor sufficient for fulfilling our obligations to resist tyranny. In some ways, we should find all of this unsurprising. Rather than focus our attention and our moral opprobrium on bad voters—who usually become bad voters because of bad institutions—we should expend our energy and direct our actions toward changing the deeper social structures that shape our lives.

COMPREHENSION QUESTIONS

1. Smith argues that bad voting doesn't violate obligations of justice. For him, what counts as a bad vote?
2. From an institutionalist perspective, what general duties do individuals have regarding justice?
3. What are some of the institutions that help mitigate the risks of bad voting, and how do they do it?
4. Under what conditions is institutionalism most plausible?
5. Smith rejects the claim that there is an obligation to vote well in order to resist unjust institutions. What reasons does he offer for rejecting it?

DISCUSSION QUESTIONS

1. Smith argues that bad voting is permissible in part because it sends politically productive signals. What useful signal, if any, might a vote motivated by "inveterate racism" send?
2. Is voting the only or best means through which citizens can send signals or provide information to policymakers? Why or why not?
3. Imagine a society in which the majority of voters are uninformed, irrational, or deeply prejudiced. Does this change your evaluation of Smith's argument? Why or why not?
4. Smith asks us to take our attention away from bad voters and place our efforts on changing unjust institutions. How might he respond to the objection that voting well is a primary means of changing unjust institutions?

Case 2

Dal Bó, Dal Bó, and Eyster (2018) offer empirical evidence that most people will choose policies that offer direct, short-term benefits to themselves over policies that benefit themselves and others in the long run through indirect means. In their view, institutions don't correct for this tendency to make bad long-term decisions and may even reinforce it.

> Of course, identifying a demand for bad policy . . . in the laboratory does not necessarily mean that outside of the lab such demand will dominate forces promoting good policies. One could hope that public discourse and political competition would result in voters learning about the total effect of policies, thus bridging the gap between public opinion and reliable evidence. However . . . a vast literature in economics and political science—both theoretical and empirical—has considered politicians as reflecting, more than shaping, the positions of voters. To the extent that public opinion and voter preferences matter for the selection of policies, understanding how people think about policies appears relevant for our knowledge of how societies choose to regulate themselves.*

What should we do in light of this information? If voters' demands are highly influential on institutional decision-making, does that mean that you have an obligation to vote rationally? Why or why not? How might Smith respond?

*Ernesto Dal Bó & Pedro Dal Bó & Erik Eyster. (2018). "The Demand for Bad Policy when Voters Underappreciate Equilibrium Effects," Review of Economic Studies 85(2), pages 991–992

REPLY TO SMITH
MICHAEL LABOSSIERE

Smith makes an often-overlooked point: Some actions are wrong to do *and* wrong for the state to restrict. In addressing his main points, I will operate within this sensible assumption and claim that while bad voters should not vote, they should not be denied the right.

Key to Smith's argument is the claim that bad voting is acceptable in "well-ordered systems" because it is either harmless or beneficial. In support of this view, he draws an analogy to how the Nobel Prize supposedly uses irrationality to get good results.[29]

One problem here is that bad voters do not seem analogous to Nobel seekers. Seekers are not bad scientists doing science badly—they are competent scientists motivated by fame. Bad voters are not offered an irrational incentive to vote; they are bad at voting. A more apt analogy would require claiming that bad scientists would be more beneficial than harmful to science, but this claim is implausible. Further, comparing voting to doing science would seem to tell against tolerating bad voters.

Smith contends bad voters are beneficial because they have useful information and are thus not obligated to vote well (or not at all). Using a science analogy, this is like claiming scientists are not obligated to do good science because bad scientists would somehow be beneficial to science. This seems contrary to fact. Just as scientists should do good science, voters should vote well. But perhaps bad voters are, unlike bad scientists, beneficial because they add a useful diversity of badness to the population.

While there are good arguments for having a diverse voter pool, the sort of diversity bad voters offer would not seem to be beneficial. To use an analogy, while it can be beneficial to have a diverse team working on a business problem, this does not entail that including people terrible at the task would be beneficial. Their badness would most likely offset any advantages gained by the diversity they contribute. Smith disagrees with this, and it is to this I now turn.

In arguing bad voters are harmless, Smith relies heavily on his claim that a healthy system would prevent them from doing harm. He does note that they could do harm, so systems are needed to protect against bad information and bad outcomes. Smith's position here is quite reasonable. A few bad voters in a healthy political body could be like a few allergens or pathogens in a healthy human body: They are harmless and can be beneficial to the immune system. However, the pathogen analogy indicates a problem with his view.

Bad voters who vote for candidates/policies who could damage the systems needed to protect against bad information and outcomes are analogous to pathogens that seriously threaten the immune system of even healthy bodies. To illustrate, if bad voters help elect officials who undermine the press, roll back the protection of civil rights, attack the judiciary, and damage government agencies protecting people, then they would damage the systems Smith claims keep their badness in check. As such, if bad voters are virulent or numerous enough, they would be like a disease that overwhelms the body and would then be harmful.

So, by Smith's own argument, bad voters should not vote if they are virulent or numerous enough to damage the systems he relies on to argue they are harmless. They should also not vote if the systems are not adequate to prevent their inflicting meaningful harm.

Smith seems to be creating a bit of a false dilemma by considering only ideal healthy systems and tyrannical systems, while leaving out the range of possibilities in between. He is right that when bad voters are in ideal systems (and thus harmless) there is no moral reason they should not vote. But it is easy enough to imagine scenarios involving less-than-ideal systems in which they can do harm—cases in which they can overwhelm the systems. In those situations, Smith's reasoning would seem to entail that it would be wrong of bad voters to vote and they should not do so. The current United States seems to be a scenario of this type. For example, the systems that are supposed to protect minorities and the working poor are not adequately robust to defend these citizens from the consequences of bad voting, and there are numerous other examples where bad voters have done and could do serious damage to their fellow citizens. In addition to considering bad voters in ideal systems, Smith also considers voting in tyrannical systems.

In addressing voting in an oppressive state, Smith effectively argues that not voting is neither necessary nor sufficient for fulfilling the obligation to oppose oppression. He is right that a person who votes in ignorance yet actively opposes oppression is better than someone who does not vote but does nothing else. Bad voters can be good resisters, and non-voters can be bad resisters. However, I agree with Henry David Thoreau about the importance of not lending support, in however small a way, to an unjust state.[30] Voting in a repressive state also helps give the state the appearance of legitimacy, which is one reason that opposition groups that have no chance of winning often boycott such elections. As such, good voters should not vote in very bad states, bad voters should not vote in okay states, and bad voters can vote in very good states.

COMPREHENSION QUESTIONS

1. What's problematic about the analogy Smith draws between Nobel seekers and bad voters?
2. When does LaBossiere think that bad voters should refrain from voting?
3. How might bad voters adversely affect institutions?
4. According to LaBossiere, what kind of political system is in place in the United States? How are institutions in the United States affected by bad voting?

DISCUSSION QUESTIONS

1. LaBossiere agrees with Smith that "when bad voters are in ideal systems (and thus harmless) there is no moral reason they should not vote." Do you agree with them? Why or why not?

2. How might Smith respond to the objection that even his own reasoning seems to entail that bad voters shouldn't vote in less-than-ideal political systems in which bad votes can do harm?
3. It's unlikely that the voters Smith and LaBossiere identify as bad voters see themselves as such. If this is true, and if the state should not deny them the right to vote, then what are the practical implications of LaBossiere's conclusions (e.g., "bad voters should not vote in okay states")?
4. What do you think would help more voters to be good voters?

REPLY TO LABOSSIERE
PATRICK TAYLOR SMITH

In response to Michael LaBossiere's excellent essay on the ethics of voting, I would like to make three points. Since the ethics of voting tends to be "non-partisan," in the sense that many of the arguments cross-cut political parties and ideologies, it is unsurprising that our disagreements and agreements do not clearly match up to right and left, liberal and conservative, and Democrat and Republican.

My first point is that while LaBossiere is interested in how you should vote, I am interested in whether you *owe it to other people* to vote a certain way. Voters likely have good moral reasons to take steps to avoid political catastrophes by voting for the lesser evil. However, it does not follow that simply because voters *should* do something, others have a *claim* on you to vote a certain way. In order to understand this distinction, it might be useful to point to Mill's discussion of perfect and imperfect duties in Chapter Five of *Utilitarianism*.[31] Perfect duties are those that are owed to a *specific person*, while imperfect duties are those duties that you simply have to do *enough*. So, if I promise my student that I will be available for office hours and I fail to show up out of laziness, I have wronged that student. Yet, if I fail to give some spare change to a homeless person on the street, I have not necessarily wronged him even if I have acted badly or selfishly. This is because the duty to keep my promises is perfect, owed to particular people who now have a right or claim that I do what I promised. On the other hand, the duty of beneficence—to help those in need—is a moral requirement that I do enough to help people, but it is not a requirement to specifically help each person in need. One way to understand the difference between LaBossiere and myself is that I am interested in the question of whether the duty to vote well is a perfect duty of sufficient strength that voting badly amounts to a violation of some person's *rights*, while LaBossiere asks the question of whether failing to vote for the lesser evil is a morally negligent failure of an imperfect duty. It is perfectly consistent to answer "No" to the first question while answering "Yes" to the second. This distinction is nonetheless important because it is usually—though perhaps not always—true that a variety of social responses are justified only when you fail in your perfect duties. So, if you are interested in whether you should resent or shun your bad-voting friends or whether the government can incentivize or force you to vote a certain way, then it might matter whether good voting is a perfect or imperfect duty.[32]

Second, consider the scope of LaBossiere's rule utilitarian argument. He argues that we need to develop a rule that people vote for the lesser evil because, in part, if people who are motivated by act utilitarianism refrain from voting, then only unethical people will vote. Yet, one important element of strategic bargaining is *precommitment*.[33] That is, if you announce in advance you are willing to compromise, then the opposing parties will offer an extreme deal, knowing that you'll give in. Politicians in your own party and voters in the other party might continually offer more and more extreme solutions opposing your preferences because that will lead to a compromise closer to their actual preferences than yours. One way to combat this is to commit yourself to positions ahead of time where you can credibly threaten to walk away if they are violated. By demonstrating a willingness to be unreasonable, you can get a better deal from your opponents. This is often what activists do: They stake out positions on which they are unwilling to compromise in order to drive politicians toward a compromise equilibrium closer to their preferences. Thus, there is value in being unreasonable. Yet, this strategy can lead to disaster if your opponents reject you entirely and your preferences do not influence the outcome at all. So, perhaps we need to be more specific about *how evil* the "greater evil" will be. If we have a well-functioning constitutional order where the greater evil is not all that bad, then perhaps it can be acceptable to hold the line on one's commitments, depending on whether there are better ways to influence politicians. It would also fail to apply when the gulf between the greater and lesser evil is of a sufficient size: The risk of severe harm would be too great in that case. So, perhaps we should amend LaBossiere's view to something like this: You have an obligation to vote for the lesser evil *unless* the greater evil is not that bad, and refraining from voting for the lesser evil will (likely) have long-term strategic benefits that outweigh the risks.

Lastly, I want to focus on difference between voting and advocacy. Most of LaBossiere's arguments depend on the effects of one's vote. Yet, it seems like these arguments apply to a much greater extent to those who advocate for or run as third-party candidates than the voters themselves. Susan Sarandon[34] and Ralph Nader[35] have done much more than any individual voter to bring political catastrophe upon the United States. Perhaps one thing we need to be clear about is the context of our ethical judgments. If the ethics of voting is about what *I* should do when everyone *else* is unchanged, then my vote probably doesn't matter. If the ethics of voting is about what I should do if everyone *will* vote like me, then I should vote for the best candidate. But if the ethics of voting is what I should do *as a representative member of a potential swing group*—where that group's votes can change, and they vote as you do—then we have an interesting, ethical question and LaBossiere helps us answer it.

COMPREHENSION QUESTIONS

1. How does Smith apply Mill's distinction between perfect and imperfect duties to the question of voting?
2. According to Smith, what is the central difference between his argument and LaBossiere's?

3. What is Smith's position on whether we owe it to others to vote in a certain way? LaBossiere's? What reasons, if any, are offered by each?
4. How does Smith bring his institutionalism into his response to LaBossiere?

DISCUSSION QUESTIONS

1. How important is it to consider the quality of others' lives when making a decision about voting? What about their rights?
2. At the end of his response, Smith offers a few points on which the ethics of voting may turn. Which do you think is most important, and why?

FURTHER READINGS

Anderson, Elizabeth. "An Epistemic Defense of Democracy: David Estlund's *Democratic Authority*." *Episteme* 5, no. 1 (2008): 1291–139.
Aristotle. *Politics*, Book III, Chapter 11, "The Authority of the Multitude," trans. by C. D. C. Reeve (Cambridge: Hackett Publishing, 1998).
Brennan, Jason. *The Ethics of Voting*. Princeton, NJ: Princeton University Press, 2011.
Kant, Immanuel. *Fundamental Principles of the Metaphysics of Morals*, trans. Thomas Kingsmill Abbott. New York: Cosimo, 2008.
Landemore, Hélène. *Democratic Reason: Politics, Collective Intelligence, and the Rule of the Many*. Princeton, NJ: Princeton University Press, 2013.
Mill, John Stuart. *Utilitarianism*. London: Parker, Son, and Bourn, 1863.
Müller, Jan-Werner. *What Is Populism?* Philadelphia: University of Pennsylvania Press, 2016.
Rawls, John. *Justice as Fairness: A Restatement*. Cambridge, MA: Belknap Press of Harvard University Press, 2001.
Thoreau, Henry David. *Walden and "Civil Disobedience."* New York: Signet Classics, 1980.
Vance, J. D. *Hillbilly Elegy: A Memoir of a Family and Culture in Crisis*. New York: HarperCollins, 2016.

NOTES

1. Mosquitoes rarely, if ever, share cake.
2. John Stuart Mill, *Utilitarianism* (London: Parker, Son, and Bourn, 1863), 9–10.
3. Mill, *Utilitarianism*, 17.
4. Ayn Rand, *The Virtue of Selfishness* (New York: New American Library, 1964).
5. Immanuel Kant, *Fundamental Principles of the Metaphysics of Morals*, trans. Thomas Kingsmill Abbott (New York: Cosimo, Inc., 2008), 17.
6. Kant, *Fundamental Principles*, 17.
7. Bioware's games (www.bioware.com) often feature such systems, especially the *Dungeons & Dragons*–based games that have an explicit alignment system.
8. Minor because voting for an evil makes a very small contribution to that evil. To use an analogy, stealing a penny from a person is wrong, but a very small evil. But, if many people individually steal a penny each so that the person has no money left and cannot afford to live, then a serious collective evil would have been committed. Voting works the same way: A single vote for an evil candidate in a large election contributes very

little to their chance of victory, but the total of votes for that evil candidate decides whether they win or lose.

9. Henry David Thoreau, *Walden and "Civil Disobedience"* (New York: Signet Classics, 1980).

10. Alexander Keyssar, *The Right to Vote: The Contested History of Democracy in the United States* (New York: Basic Books, 2001).

11. Zoltan Hajnal, Nazita Lajevardi, and Lindsay Nielson, "Voter Identification Laws and the Suppression of Minority Votes," *Journal of Politics* 79, no. 2 (2017): 363–379.

12. Melanie M. Bowers and Robert R. Preuhs, "Collateral Consequences of a Collateral Penalty: The Negative Effect of Felon Disenfranchisement Laws on the Political Participation of Non-felons," *Social Science Quarterly* 90, no. 3 (2009): 722–743.

13. Jason Brennan, *The Ethics of Voting* (Princeton, NJ: Princeton University Press, 2011).

14. Patrick Taylor Smith, "Why Bad Votes May Be Cast and Why Bad Voters May Cast Them" in *Ethics in Politics: The Rights and Obligations of Individual Political Agents*, edited by Emily Crookston, David Killoren, and Jonathan Trerise (New York: Routledge Press, 2016), 219–238.

15. Jason Brennan, "Polluting the Polls: When Citizens Should Not Vote," *Australasian Journal of Philosophy* 87 (2009): 535–549.

16. John Rawls, *Justice as Fairness: A Restatement* (Cambridge, MA: Belknap Press of Harvard University Press, 2001), 52–56.

17. A useful way to think about institutionalism would be the rules of sports and the obligations of the players. The rules of a game, such as baseball, may be designed in order to be entertaining for fans. Yet, a player is under no obligation to choose less effective but more entertaining strategies over more boring, successful ones. The player can simply try to win and need not aim directly at entertaining fans. Of course, the player cannot *cheat*, but the objective of the system of rules and the objective of the player can be separate.

18. Rawls, *Theory of Justice*, 67–69.

19. Liam B. Murphy, "Institutions and the Demands of Justice," *Philosophy and Public Affairs* 27 (1998): 251–291.

20. Joshua Cohen, "Taking People as They Are?" *Philosophy and Public Affairs* 30 (2001): 363–386.

21. The idea that democracy produces better results than experts has played a key role in justifications for democracy. See Elizabeth Anderson, "An Epistemic Defense of Democracy," *Episteme* 5 , no. 1 (2012): 129–139, and Hélène Landermore, "Yes We Can (Make It Up on Volume): Answers to Critics," *Critical Review* 26, no. 1–2 (2014): 184–237.

22. Aristotle, *Politics*, translated by C. D. C. Reeve (Cambridge: Hackett Publishing, 1998), Book III, Chapter 11, "The Authority of the Multitude."

23. The Condorcet jury theory says that as long as people are somewhat more likely than not to get the answer correct, adding more people increases the likelihood the majority will be correct.

24. James Suroweicki, *The Wisdom of Crowds* (New York: Doubleday, 2004).

25. Philip Kitcher, "The Division of Cognitive Labor," *Journal of Philosophy* 87 (1990): 14–16.

26. Kitcher, "Division of Cognitive Labor," 17.

27. This is analogous to the doctrine of "intervening causation" with regards to legal liability. If you act negligently but another person's wrongful action mediates between that negligence and its bad effects, your responsibility for the bad effects has been lessened. H. L. A. Hart and Tony Honoré, *Causation in the Law* (Oxford: Clarendon, 1985, 2nd ed.).

28. Carol Hay, *Kantianism, Liberalism, and Feminism: Resisting Oppression* (London: Palgrave Macmillan, 2013).

29. As a general point, there is also the paradox of irrationality arguments like this: If being "irrational" yields good results, then that is not being irrational. In the case of Nobel seekers, it does not seem irrational to explore potentially fruitful but more risky areas—as Pascal noted, taking risks to achieve rewards does not offend reason. Blaise Pascal, *Pensees*, trans. John Warrington (London: Everyman's Library No. 874, 1932).

30. Thoreau, *Walden and "Civil Disobedience."*

31. Alan Ryan, ed., *John Stuart Mill and Jeremy Bentham: Utilitarianism and Other Essays* (New York: Penguin Books, 1987).

32. Generally, we might think you can exercise social sanctions against someone—by punishing, shunning, or resenting them in ways that inflict costs or harms upon them—when they have failed a duty in a way that *wrongs* someone. There might be exceptions to this rule—a sufficiently selfish person might deserve shunning or indignation—but showing that someone has transgressed a perfect duty goes a long way toward justifying negative responses of all kinds.

33. The *locus classicus* on precommitment strategies is *Arms and Influence* by Thomas Schelling (New Haven, CT: Yale University Press, 1966).

34. Susan Sarandon is a well-regarded film actress who received considerable criticism for arguing—especially, but not only, on Twitter—that there was little difference between Hillary Clinton and Donald Trump and that people should vote for the Green Party candidate Jill Stein instead.

35. Ralph Nader is a consumer advocate, focusing on automobile safety. In 2000, he accepted the Green Party nomination for president and played a spoiler role, deliberately campaigning in swing states such as Florida. Al Gore lost Florida by fewer than 600 votes, while the Green Party received over 90,000.

Index

Note: Tables, figures and notes are indicated by *t*, *f*, or *n* respectively.